Child and Adolescent Development

SECOND EDITION

Child and Adolescent Development

Kelvin L. Seifert *The University of Manitoba*

Robert J. Hoffnung *University of New Haven*

HOUGHTON MIFFLIN COMPANY   BOSTON
Dallas   Geneva, Illinois   Palo Alto   Princeton, New Jersey

*For the Fullers—Barbara Anne, Barbara Irene, and
Russell   K. L. S.*

To Shoshana and Zvi Etkin   R. J. H.

Cover photograph by James Scherer

Anatomical and biological illustrations by Nancy Kaplan on pages 77, 78, 79, 109, 111, 112, 131, 155, 157 (bottom), 281, 416, and 518

Graphs and charts by Networkgraphics on pages 63, 154, 273, 387, 479, 510, 511, 532, and 593

Illustrations by Patrice Rossi on pages 51, 157 (top), 312, 422, 470, and 548

Illustrations by Elizabeth Seifert on page 297

All other credits appear on page A-1, which constitutes an extension of the copyright page.

Printed in the U.S.A.

Library of Congress Catalog Card Number: 90-83005

ISBN: 0-395-43236-7

CDEFGHIJ-VH-998765432

BRIEF CONTENTS

CONTENTS

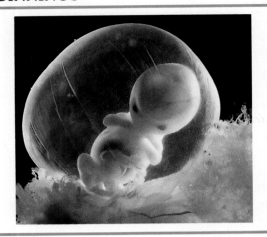

Jennifer

Laura

Brian

MULTICULTURAL VIEWS

PERSPECTIVES

PREFACE

The longer each of us has worked in the field of developmental psychology, the more we have wanted to share our knowledge of child and adolescent development with others. This desire became even stronger after each of us became parents and as we watched our children grow up. Both our professional and personal experiences impressed on us not only the tremendous complexity of human development, but also the practical importance of studying development to all of society. We felt in addition that acquiring a genuine understanding of how a person unfolds and develops into a unique human being was one of the most fascinating of undertakings, and we wanted to help others share in this exciting intellectual challenge.

Audience

Child and Adolescent Development, Second Edition, is a broad-based and comprehensive introduction to developmental psychology from birth through adolescence. The text is appropriate for all undergraduates taking a first course in child development or child and adolescent development, regardless of the department in which the course is taught.

Purpose and Goals of the Second Edition

This book has been designed to help students clearly understand the complex, dynamic process of development in children and adolescents. We have sought to communicate to students the freshness and vitality of real, fully dimensional children and to convey the idea that development, above all, is a *human* process.

We have also sought to convey to students that the developmental psychologist's understanding of children and adolescents is based on information derived *scientifically.* Throughout the book, we communicate this fact by discussing various research methods and the care that must be taken in interpreting research data.

Although our book is thoroughly grounded in research, we have written it for the introductory student. Accordingly, we have tried to keep our writing clear, low-key, and nontechnical. We have also woven countless concrete details about children into the text. These serve to enliven, illuminate, and make more meaningful our discussion of developmental theory, concepts, and research.

Increasingly, the real world in which children are growing up today is a multicultural one. Hence, another key goal of this edition is to help students understand how ethnicity affects the development of children, both in North America and around the world, and to better appreciate the role that context plays in development. We touch on this theme throughout the text and give it special attention in a new feature called *A Multicultural View.*

Although for convenience and comprehensibility, this book has divided human change into discrete topics and stages of development, we believe readers need to be reminded that real children and adolescents do not come divided. They not only grow, think, and feel; they do all of these things at once, and in a pattern that makes each person truly unique. To emphasize this important point, we have introduced a feature called *Bridges,* which we describe more fully later on in this Preface.

Content of the Second Edition

Child and Adolescent Development, Second Edition, provides broad and salient coverage of development from birth through adolescence. It offers a balanced and eclectic selection of topics, a foundation of both classic and recent research, and an examination of timely (and even controversial) issues such as child abuse, genetic engineering, and homeless and runaway adolescents.

As in the preceding edition, the text consists of sixteen chapters divided into six parts. Part One, "Studying Development," introduces students to the field of developmental psychology and describes the theories and methods that guide our understanding of child and adolescent development. Part Two, "Beginnings," examines the role genetics plays in shaping whom a child becomes and traces the events of the very earliest period of development: from conception through birth. Each of the remaining four parts concentrates on a specific age-range of child development — the first two years, the preschool years, the middle years, and adolescence — and is composed of a trio of chapters on physical, cognitive, and psychosocial development. We believe that this combination of a topical organization within a generally chronological framework offers instructors a maximally flexible sequence that can be used with a variety of different course structures. Moreover, it reflects one of the key themes of this book, the interrelationship of all aspects of development.

Every chapter has been thoroughly updated, and much of the content has undergone substantial revision. New coverage to this edition includes the ecology of development (Chapter 1); information-processing theory (Chapter 2); and fragile-X syndrome, Tourette's syndrome, chorionic villus sampling, and genetic engineering (Chapter 3). Chapter 4 contains the latest research on the effects of maternal age, cocaine, AIDS, alcohol, and cigarettes on the developing fetus, as well as new coverage of the effects of medications during delivery. Among the many other additions to this revision are sections on failure to thrive (Chapter 5), emotional development in infancy (Chapter 7), reactive attachment disorder (Chapter 8), Vygotsky's zone of proximal development (Chapter 9), Gilligan's theory of moral development (Chapter 12), prejudice in school-age children (Chapter 13), the psychological influences of school (Chapter 13), hormonal influences on social and emotional development (Chapter 14), as well as greatly expanded coverages of sexually transmitted diseases and adolescent pregnancy and parenthood (Chapters 14 and 16). In addition, new coverage of multicultural and cross-cultural research and issues appears in every chapter.

Special Features

The Second Edition of *Child and Adolescent Development* includes two major new features designed to enhance student's understanding of developmental psychology.

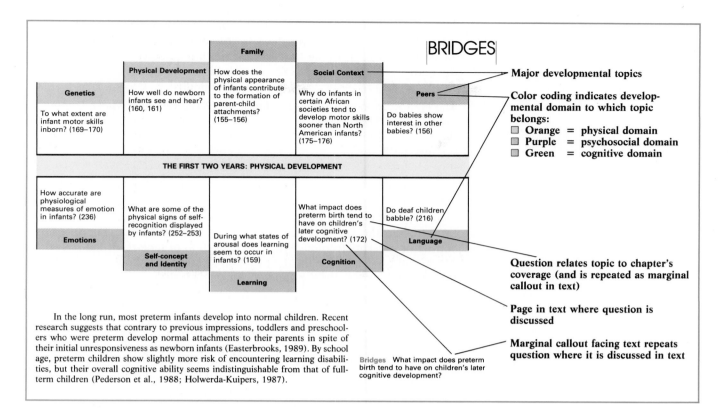

In the long run, most preterm infants develop into normal children. Recent research suggests that contrary to previous impressions, toddlers and preschoolers who were preterm develop normal attachments to their parents in spite of their initial unresponsiveness as newborn infants (Easterbrooks, 1989). By school age, preterm children show slightly more risk of encountering learning disabilities, but their overall cognitive ability seems indistinguishable from that of full-term children (Pederson et al., 1988; Holwerda-Kuipers, 1987).

Bridges What impact does preterm birth tend to have on children's later cognitive development?

■   *A Multicultural View* is a series of boxed inserts that focus on selected multicultural or cross-cultural topics related to child and adolescent development. Appearing in each chapter, they cover such topics as "the development of ethnic awareness in the preschool years," "cross-cultural variations in attachment," and "children's conceptions of illness in different cultures." (For a complete list of Multicultural Views, see page xv.) We hope these boxes will increase reader's awareness of the importance of context and ethnicity in the development of children and adolescents.

■   *Bridges,* a diagram that appears in the opening pages of each of the chapters in Parts Three through Six, graphically illustrates interconnections among key developmental topics and domains. (A reduced-sized version of Chapter 5's *Bridges* diagram appears above.)

1. Each *Bridges* diagram links the coverage of that particular chapter to ten major topics in developmental psychology: genetics, physical development, family, peers, social context, emotions, self-concept and identity, learning, cognition, and language.

2. For each of these topics, the *Bridges* diagram presents a provocative question that relates the topic to coverage in that chapter and also provides in parentheses the pages in the text where the reader can find a discussion of the question.

3. Each of the ten topics is color-coded to indicate the specific domain to which it belongs: orange for the physical domain, purple for the psychosocial domain, and green for the cognitive domain.

4. Finally, the exact place in the text where each question is discussed is marked with a marginal callout and a repetition of the question. Typically, 80 percent of the questions in a chapter's *Bridges* diagram are discussed in that chapter and the rest are discussed in the other two chapters of that part. Asterisks precede callouts in multicolumn text.

Our goal in devising this new feature is not only to pique curiosity and evoke reader interest but also to help students see the interactive nature of all development, a theme that we articulate in Chapter 1 and throughout the text.

The First Edition of *Child and Adolescent Development* contained a number of special features that instructors and students told us were particularly helpful, and as a result, we have retained them in the new edition. Included among these features are the following:

- *Interviews* with children and adolescents of various ages, as well as with parents and professionals whose comments illuminate aspects of development, are interspersed throughout the text. These interviews reinforce and bring to life the text's coverage of concepts and theories. The interviews consist of excerpts from an extensive collection of tape-recorded interviews conducted especially for this text by Bob Hoffnung. Follow-up questions at the end of each interview provide further reinforcement.
- *Case-study photo essays* at the beginning of each age-level part trace the development of four different children over a period of years. There are studies of a low birthweight infant, a preschooler who must adjust to the birth of a baby brother, a school-age girl, and an adolescent son of divorced parents. Striking photos and relevant documents and facsimiles are blended with the text's sensitive narrative and explanatory comments. These original case-study photo essays can help students directly appreciate that all aspects of development are interconnected and that development is a human process that affects real people living in a real world.
- *Boxed inserts,* titled "Perspectives," are incorporated throughout the text. These extend the text discussion by highlighting significant research or digging deeper into important contemporary issues. (A complete list appears on pages xvii–xviii.)

In addition, the Second Edition of *Child and Adolescent Development* incorporates a number of carefully designed pedagogical features that not only help students learn the text material but also make it easier for both instructors and students to use the book. All of these have been enhanced in the Second Edition by the use of full color throughout the text. Included are the following features:

- *A chapter outline and focusing questions* at the beginning of each chapter serve as advance organizers and help students prepare for the material to be covered in each chapter.
- *Marginal glosses* printed in bold reinforce key points throughout the text.
- *An extensive photo and line art illustration program* provides further reinforcement to the text's discussion of concepts and theories.
- *End-of-chapter summaries* list the important topics covered in the chapter, grouped by heading.
- *Key terms* are highlighted in boldface type in the text and a list of key terms (with cross-references to the page numbers on which the terms are defined) appears at the end of each chapter.
- *End-of-chapter questions* — entitled "What Do You Think?" — are included to stimulate further thought about text material and call on the student to relate personal values and experiences to the issues discussed.
- *Annotated lists of selected readings* that provide further insight into the chapter's topics and may be of special interest to students appear at the end of each chapter.

- *A glossary* of more than four hundred key terms and concepts appears at the end of the text.
- *Bibliographical references* for all in-text citations appear at the end of the text.

Ancillaries

The Second Edition of *Child and Adolescent Development* is accompanied by an extensive package of instructor and student aids.

Student Handbook   The Student Handbook has been extensively revised and expanded. It contains for each chapter a set of learning objectives, a chapter outline, a brief overview of material covered in the chapter followed by a series of contextual fill-in-the-blank statements, a list of key terms to be defined, short-answer study questions, multiple-choice questions with a special answer feedback section that explains why each option is either right or wrong, and a set of student activities.

Instructor's Resource Manual   This manual has been revised and expanded. It includes for each chapter a set of learning objectives, a detailed lecture outline (a new feature of this edition), a chapter overview, suggested supplementary lecture topics, suggested discussion and demonstration topics, annotated additional references, and a set of media resources.

Test Bank   The thoroughly revised version of the Test Bank consists of more than thirteen hundred multiple-choice items in alternate forms and sixty essay questions, along with learning objectives for each chapter. To provide instructors with maximal flexibility in constructing examinations, answers to the multiple-choice items are listed both in a special section at the end of the book and next to each item. For the instructor's convenience, alongside each item is also information on the topic covered by the test item, the pages in the textbook where the answer can be found, and whether the test item calls for factual or applied knowledge.

Computerized Test Bank   This is an interactive computerized version of the Test Bank, available in IBM, Macintosh, and Apple II formats.

Transparencies   A set of eighty overhead transparencies, most in full color, is available free upon adoption of the text. It consists of the figures and *Bridges* from the text and a variety of charts and definitions, as well as four generic *Bridges* with space left for instructors to insert their own questions.

Audiotape Program: *Voices: An Interview Resource*   This set of four half-hour audiocassettes consists of excerpts from an extensive series of interviews with children and adolescents conducted by Bob Hoffnung, along with explanatory comments. It is available free upon adoption of the text.

Listening Guide   Accompanying the audiotapes is a printed guide that includes all transcripts, additional commentary, exercises, and activities.

Acknowledgments

This book would not have been possible without the help of many individuals. We especially wish to thank David Hunter and Julian Ferholt whose friendship and colleagueship were invaluable and Aaron Hoffnung for his encouragement and support. We are particularly grateful to The University of Manitoba, which provided time for this project from its beginning, and to the University of New Haven and Joseph Chepaitis, its Dean of Arts and Sciences, for their support.

A number of reviewers made constructive suggestions and provided thoughtful reactions at various stages in the development of the manuscript, and we are very appreciative of the help we received from them. In particular, we would like to thank:

M. K. Alderman, *University of Akron*

Elva Allie, *Tarrant County Junior College*

Cathie Atkins, *San Diego State University*

Judith Blomberg, *San Francisco State University*

Linda Carson, *Des Moines Area Community College*

Winona Cochran, *Bloomsburg University of Pennsylvania*

Carol Lynn Davis, *University of Southern Maine, Gorham*

David J. Dixon, *Southwest Missouri State University, Springfield*

David H. Dodd, *University of Utah, Salt Lake City*

Jim Duffy, *Memorial University of Newfoundland*

Thomas Fitzpatrick, *Rockland Community College*

Jose Gonzalez, *Edinboro University*

Lillian Grayson, *Simmons College*

David J. Hansen, *West Virginia University*

Gregory F. Harper, *State University of New York, Fredonia*

Algea Harrison, *Oakland University*

Karen N. Hayes, *University of New Mexico, Albuquerque*

Bert Hayslip, Jr., *University of North Texas*

George W. Holden, *University of Texas, Austin*

Rosanne R. Holliday, *Southwestern College*

Deborah Jacobvitz, *University of Texas, Austin*

LaVerne K. Jordan, *Olivet Nazarene University*

Barbara Kane, *Indiana State University, Terre Haute*

Mary Lou Kelley, *Louisiana State University, Baton Rouge*

Kit Lowder, *Illinois Central College, Peoria*

Mary Ann McLaughlin, *Clarion University of Pennsylvania*

Nancy E. Meck, *University of Kansas, Kansas City*

Gerald J. Mikosz, *Moraine Valley Community College*

Richard E. Miller, *Navarro College*

Philip Mohan, *University of Idaho, Moscow*

Cheryl Newburg, *Kutztown University of Pennsylvania*

Earl N. Newman, *Central State University, Edmund*

Barbara J. Nicoll, *California State University, Los Angeles*

Ligaya Paguio, *University of Georgia, Athens*

B. Kay Pasley, *Colorado State University, Fort Collins*

Jean S. Phinney, *California State University, Los Angeles*

Beverly Shumer, *University of Michigan, Ann Arbor*

Thomas A. Skurky, *Fort Lewis College*

Sue Sommers, *Butler County Community College*

Alan S. Waterman, *Trenton State University*

Sue C. Whisler, *Mansfield University*

Sara J. Willoughby-Herb, *Shippensburg University of Pennsylvania*

Donald H. Wykoff, *Slippery Rock University of Pennsylvania*

We would especially like to thank the following individuals for their assistance in developing the four case-study photo essays that appear in this book: Susan Buckler, Alan Carey, Helen Cohen, Johanna Granoff, and Sara Richlin. We are also very grateful to all of the people who participated in the interviews that appear in this book and on tape and who were so willing to share with us their thoughts and perceptions about development.

Special, warm thanks should go to our editors at Houghton Mifflin, who worked especially long and hard to help this book reach its full potential.

Finally, we would like to thank our families, who rearranged much of their lives so that we could have time to write this book and who provided us with numerous examples of child and adolescent development.

Kelvin L. Seifert   *Robert J. Hoffnung*

Introduction

Child and Adolescent Development

PART ONE

Studying Development

s infants grow into children, and children grow into teen-agers, they experience a great many changes. Some of these changes are small and fleeting; many, however, are relatively permanent and long-lasting. It is these developmental changes that are the subject of this book and of the field of study known as developmental psychology.

The study of development offers much insight into human nature — why we are what we are and how we became that way. Yet describing development is a complex task, so this book begins with two chapters that orient you to what lies ahead. They explain just what development is and describe some of the most important tools of developmental psychology — namely, the theories and methods that guide our understanding of child and adolescent development. With these two chapters in mind, you will be ready to begin looking at the focus of developmental psychology, the children themselves.

CHAPTER 1

Introduction: Studying Development

Focusing Questions

- What in general is human development?
- Why is it important to know about development?
- How did the formal study of children and adolescents emerge during the last several centuries?
- What general themes or issues are currently important in developmental psychology?
- How do developmental psychologists go about studying children and adolescents?
- What ethical considerations should guide the study of children?

 ou are probably a lot different now from when you were a child. When you were two, you probably could not tie a shoelace, button your coat, or turn a doorknob reliably. When you were six, you probably struggled to read even one line of print. When you were twelve, you may have wondered whether you would ever be truly liked and respected by your friends.

Changes like these — and many others, too — mark every human life. Some are obvious, such as the transformation of a speechless infant into a talkative preschooler or the revisions that children make in how they handle academic tasks as they get older. Other changes are subtle and may go unnoticed: alterations in hormones circulating in the blood as children approach adolescence, for example, or gradual increases in the importance of peers from one year to the next. But obvious or subtle, changes make us human, and many of them alter our lives profoundly.

THE NATURE OF DEVELOPMENTAL CHANGE

This is a book about change. In particular, it is about change that is **developmental** in nature, meaning that it contributes to a person's long-term growth, feelings, and patterns of thinking. Some developmental changes may be relatively specific, as when an infant takes her first unassisted step. Others may be rather general, as when a schoolchild becomes increasingly able to cooperate with peers in work projects or in play. But on the whole, developmental changes tend to unfold gradually, even though once they appear, they sometimes seem quite unlike any behaviors a child showed previously. A ten-year-old boy, for example, may not believe that the chances are high that he will go on a date with a girl sometime during the next five years; indeed, his own parents may find this hard to believe!

Differences between development and other kinds of change

Not every change is truly developmental, however. Cold weather in the winter causes changes in behavior, such as putting on warmer clothing and selecting indoor activities more frequently. But when the weather warms up again, these behavioral changes tend to disappear. Such changes *could* result in human development (for example, when a preschooler is able to put on his winter coat and boots without any help from anyone else), but most of the time they do not. On the other hand, not every human development involves change; some developments are characterized primarily by continuity. Once a child's basic sense of self develops, it remains rather constant as the child grows older.

Three Domains of Development

As these examples suggest, human development can take many forms. For convenience, this book distinguishes among three major types, or **domains**, of development: physical, cognitive, and psychosocial. The first of these has to do with **physical development** or biological growth. It includes changes in the body (in the brain, sense organs, muscles, bones, and so forth) and in the ways a person uses his or her body (motor skills and sexual development, for example). It also **Physical** includes the effects of aging, such as changes in eyesight or in muscular strength. But it does not usually include physical changes when they result from accident, illness, or other special events. Like other forms of development, physical growth or maturation often spans very long periods.

Cognitive development has to do with changes in reasoning and thinking, with language acquisition, and with how individuals gain and store knowledge **Cognitive** of their environments. It includes what we commonly call learning, but more as well. Learning refers to comparatively important changes in thinking, feeling, and behavior, but it tends to be limited to changes that result from relatively specific experiences or events. Often, too, learned changes occur over a short time — sometimes even just hours or minutes — but as later chapters show, some important cognitive developments take much longer than this to occur.

Psychosocial development concerns changes in feelings or emotions as well as changes in how individuals relate to other people. It includes relationships with family, peers, and teachers as well as an individual's personal identity or **Psychosocial** sense of self. Because identity and social relationships tend to evolve together, we discuss them together throughout this book. But both developments also depend on other kinds of change. How a person looks physically can affect how she feels about herself and can affect her relationships with her friends. And her powers of reasoning can influence her ability to understand the needs of others and in this way affect the quality of her relationships with others. Each form of development, it seems, affects all of the others.

The three domains in fact connect in many ways. Physical growth makes the cognitive process of language acquisition possible; but language also makes early social relationships more possible. In turn, social relationships provide settings for further cognitive learning and for nurturing further physical growth. And so on. Later chapters try to point out connections like these wherever appropriate. They also highlight the connections with graphic diagrams, called *Bridges*, that link the main themes of each chapter with other developmental topics.

An Example of Development: Aaron

To understand these ideas, consider a young child named Aaron. At age four, Aaron attended a day-care center that gave him a lot of choice in play activities. Aaron gravitated toward the toy vehicles, sending them on make-believe trips along the numerous roads that he built with blocks. But Aaron was not satisfied with the commercially made toy vehicles at the day-care center; soon he began building his own cars and trucks out of interlocking plastic blocks.

At this age his assemblies were simple and relatively small; he had not developed enough physically or cognitively to build anything complex. To the dismay of his teachers, he sometimes got frustrated because he could not make

Changes happen in all domains — physical, cognitive, and psychosocial. As this baby refines her motor and thinking skills and develops a capacity for empathy and caring, she (hopefully) will grab the cat less and pet it more. In time, she may display toward it the same degree of affection and loyalty shown by this school-age boy toward his horse.

certain blocks stick together properly or because he could not remember how to repair a vehicle if it happened to fall apart. Yet he persisted with his building projects, and gradually his efforts paid off.

During his elementary school years, Aaron became something of a classroom expert on building all kinds of structures with interlocking plastic blocks. His dexterity had improved enough so that he could complete very large, intricate constructions without "messing up," as he put it. His memory for past work was definitely better, too: when a large plastic-block castle partially fell apart, Aaron could pretty easily remember how it was supposed to go together again.

No doubt some of his success stemmed from all the building he had done since his early days at the day-care center. As his first-grade teacher noted, he approached block-building problems like an expert. In building a large project, Aaron focused attention on larger subprojects and on how these subprojects fit together. He seemed to let the detailed steps take care of themselves. "How do you go about building a train with all these blocks?" his teacher asked one day. "Simple," said Aaron. "Make a caboose and an engine; do the cars last 'cause you might not know how many you can make." In answering the same question, his less experienced classmates focused more on the physical steps than on the overall design: "You fasten the two blocks like this and then just keep doing that for a long time."

But Aaron's expertise occasionally got him into trouble. To do his large projects, he needed the lion's share of the plastic blocks, and hoarding them sometimes made him unpopular with classmates. Sometimes, too, Aaron lacked patience when he saw the simplicity of some of the other students' projects. "That's boring," he said of a classmate's small car, much to the annoyance of the classmate. On other occasions, in efforts to be helpful, he would intervene with his friends' building in order to show them a better, more architecturally sound way. But the other students did not always consider Aaron's efforts helpful, like the time he told a classmate, "That block tower's going to topple in two seconds," after which he commandeered the tower for himself and began rebuilding it.

After a number of unpleasant encounters like this, Aaron began to suspect that most other first-grade students did not think about building with plastic blocks the same way that he did. He began watching his peers more closely as they built, and he devoted less exclusive attention to what *he* could do with the blocks. Aaron's teacher reinforced this change when she noticed it by conversing briefly with Aaron about whatever he was observing ("Look at what Shannon is making, Aaron; neat, eh?").

Gradually it dawned on Aaron that other students were not viewing the activity in the same way that he had been. "They're just learning," he said, "so they need to think a lot when they work." Aaron began giving fewer suggestions, but the ones he gave seemed better timed to when students truly needed them. By the end of the school year, he had earned a minor reputation as someone to consult about construction problems with the plastic blocks. This reputation made it easier for Aaron to ask his classmates for help with matters, such as spelling hard words, that he found troublesome.

Aaron's experiences illustrate changes in each domain of human development. As a young preschooler at the day-care center, Aaron's talent for plastic blocks suffered from, among other things, limitations in his physical growth. During the first few months there, Aaron could barely fit two simple blocks together because his fingers were not developed enough to do so. His parents responded by buying him a small set of oversized plastic blocks for building; "Big Blocks for Little Fingers," it said on the package. Aaron used these for awhile but soon lost interest because the blocks, although oversized, were not numerous enough to interest him.

By grade school, Aaron's physical limitations had diminished considerably, thanks to the physical growth in his hands and more months of practice at using the plastic blocks. By the end of second grade, in fact, he could handle the blocks with a dexterity that amazed his teachers and parents. At the same time, cognitive developments had also affected Aaron's talents: as an older child, he could remember all kinds of information more easily than before and use the information in his building projects. Aaron had seen pictures of several big bridges in a magazine article, for example, and remembered how they looked well enough to build a replica of one of them.

Aaron's block-building talent also affected his psychosocial development. At first the effect was negative: his interest in building blinded him to the feelings and reactions of his less experienced classmates. But these negative encounters also stimulated positive social developments. Aaron used his mishaps with classmates to begin focusing on the classmates' own perspectives about building with blocks. Eventually Aaron's focus on others led to better relationships with them. Aaron's reasons for building then began to shift: instead of using block building only as a motor and cognitive challenge to solve by himself, Aaron increasingly used building projects as a way to make and keep friends. "Let's build something together," he would suggest.

After early elementary school, Aaron stopped playing regularly with plastic blocks, but his talent for them remained. As a young teenager, he found that he could thrill his younger brother and sister by occasionally building them an extremely complex structure. In junior high school, one of his favorite classes was drafting, where he could draw pictures of complicated machinery using realistic perspective.

As he got older, Aaron's talent for spatial relations developed further: Aaron gravitated toward science classes in high school and toward engineering in college. These choices were encouraged by social expectations: friends, family, and teachers often implied to Aaron that science and engineering were good fields "for a boy." But he genuinely liked scientific and technical work, especially laboratory sessions, where he could effectively assemble and use equipment.

Interrelationship of developmental changes

Aaron's story shows the importance of each major domain of development in the lives of actual individuals. More importantly, however, his story also shows how closely each domain intertwines with the others. Both for Aaron and for all the rest of us, development evolves as a pattern rather than as discrete units or pieces. This book identifies and describes many separate threads of development. But in learning about these, return to Aaron from time to time to remind yourself that in real life the threads create a tapestry.

WHY STUDY DEVELOPMENT?

Knowledge of normal development

Knowing about human development can help you in four major ways. First, it can give you realistic expectations for children and adolescents. Developmental psychology tells you, for example, when infants usually begin talking, and it suggests when schoolchildren tend to begin reasoning abstractly. Admittedly, it generally tells you only averages for children; it tells only when most children, or a "typical" child, acquire a particular skill, behavior, or emotion. But knowledge of these averages can nonetheless help you know what to expect from specific, individual children.

Guidance in responding to actual behavior

Second, knowledge of developmental psychology can help you respond appropriately to children's actual behavior. If a preschool boy says that he wants to marry his mother, should she ignore his remark? Or should she make a point of correcting his misconception? If a third-grade child seems more interested in her friends than in her schoolwork, should her teacher discourage contact with friends? Or should the teacher try to figure out ways of using friends to support the child's school studies? Developmental psychology can help to answer questions such as these by indicating the sources and significance of many of the thoughts, feelings, and behavior patterns of children.

Recognition of unusual development

Third, knowledge of development can help you recognize when departures from normal are truly significant. If a child does not talk very much even by age two, for example, should her parents and doctors become concerned? What if she still does not talk much by age three or four? Or if a teenager admits to having had sexual intercourse "once or twice" by age fifteen, should his parents worry that he is becoming promiscuous? How about if he is only thirteen, or eleven? We can answer these questions more easily if we know what *usually* happens to children and adolescents. And knowing what usually happens (being

Among other things, developmental psychology can help to give you appropriate expectations about children and adolescents. It can also help you to understand behaviors that might otherwise cause worry or concern.

aware of the universal trends, that is) makes up a great deal of the content of developmental psychology.

Finally, studying development can help you understand yourself. Developmental psychology makes the processes of psychological growth explicit, processes that each of us may overlook in our personal, everyday lives. Even more important, it can help you make sense out of experiences you have had — such as whether it really mattered that you reached puberty earlier (or later) than your friends.

Self-understanding

THE HISTORY OF DEVELOPMENTAL STUDY

For as long as people have been having children, parents and other care-givers have relied on practical or intuitive knowledge about child-rearing. But during most of human history, this knowledge remained rather informal: child-rearing advice was passed down the generations by demonstration ("Look how I feed her") and by word of mouth ("I always try strawberry tea for that illness"). Rarely, if ever, did anyone attempt to formulate existing knowledge into systematic, conscious theories about growth and development.

Childhood and Adolescence as Concepts

In fact, until just a few hundred years ago, children in Western society were not really perceived as full members of society or even as genuine human beings (Ariès, 1962; Hareven, 1986). During medieval times, infants tended to be regarded rather like talented pets: at best interesting, and even able to talk, but not creatures worth caring about deeply. Children graduated to adult status early in life — around age seven or eight — by taking on major adultlike tasks for the community. Children who today would be attending second or third grade might then have been caring for younger siblings or working in the fields. Or they

Early adult status

might have been apprenticed to another family to learn a specialized trade, such as carpentry or tailoring. In any case they would have missed out on most of what we now consider "childhood" — a time protected from the pressures and risks of adult living and devoted to activities specially designed for children, such as school.

Because children took on adult responsibilities so soon, the period we call "adolescence" was absolutely unknown. Until the twentieth century, there was little awareness of the adolescent years as a unique period in a person's life, one distinct from both childhood and adulthood. Teenagers assumed adult roles. Although these roles often included marriage and child-rearing, most people in their teens lived with their original families, helping with household work and with caring for others' children until well into their twenties (Laslett, 1975; Lasch, 1975–1976; Good, 1975).

Adolescence unknown before twentieth century

All this may seem harsh by modern, middle-class standards, but it may have been simply realistic. Relatively large proportions of children died early in life, especially in infancy. Some historians suggest that this made it unrealistic for parents and others to care too deeply about children when they were first born (Ariès, 1962; Laslett & Wall, 1975). Parents were likely to be devastated by a child's death if they deeply loved him or her from birth. Children instead had to "prove" their ability to survive, so to speak. Once they did so, however, their efforts were needed immediately by family and community, which more often than not were functioning at subsistence levels. Hence, early recruitment to adult work became commonplace, along with early adult status. These circumstances left little time for play and fun. But adult-style work did give children a more important economic place in their communities than most modern children enjoy.

Early mortality as a factor

In spite of these historical changes, though, many children living in the 1990s do not experience "childhood" in the idealistic way described above. Children of migrant farm workers, urban children who see homeless people and drug users on their way to school (or who are themselves homeless or involved in selling drugs), and children living in areas affected by war and violence hardly lead lives protected from adult pressures. One research study, for example, found that two thirds of all teenagers at an inner-city walk-in clinic had witnessed a shooting, and that nearly one quarter of them had witnessed a murder (Zinsmeister, 1990). Even middle-class children are subject to social stresses that are becoming increasingly prevalent, ranging from divorce, child abuse and family violence, to pressures to grow up too quickly.

Early Precursors to Developmental Study

At the end of the seventeenth century, certain philosophers began arguing that childhood was a special period of life with special needs that differed from the needs of adulthood. They discussed these needs in their works, even though they were a long way from agreeing about what children's special needs actually were. John Locke (1693/1699) proposed that the newborn's mind is a *tabula rasa* ("blank slate") and thus that the child must acquire all ideas from experience. Locke's notion implied that the least experienced individuals — children — differed importantly from the most experienced individuals — adults. Children, it seemed, "needed" adults to teach them things — an idea that took another two hundred years to become commonplace in society as a whole.

Locke's and Rousseau's ideas

Another philosopher, Jean-Jacques Rousseau (1763/1911), proposed methods for educating children based largely on the assumption that young people can be "perfected" through careful observation of and respect for their emerging needs. These philosophical attitudes come close to assumptions underlying much of modern developmental study. But respect for children's special needs was still far from widespread in society as a whole.

The concept of childhood as a distinct period in a person's life is a relatively modern invention, at least judged by the ways children have been portrayed in paintings over the centuries. Until the nineteenth century, painters generally depicted children as miniature adults, with adultlike clothing, facial expressions, and bodily proportions. By the nineteenth century, though, childhood had come to be seen — and valued — as a unique time, one that was quite different from adulthood. Children were expected to wear special types of clothing and hairstyles and engage in their own kind of activities and pastimes.

It took changes in economic and social conditions to create awareness of childhood in the public at large. Society was becoming less rural and more industrialized. During the eighteenth century, factory towns began attracting large numbers of workers, who often brought their children with them. "Atrocity stories" became increasingly common: reports, for example, of young children in England becoming caught and disabled in factory machinery (Shaftesbury, 1868) or of children essentially abandoned to the streets during their parents' long working hours. In retrospect, it is not clear how common these situations really were (Lasch, 1975–1976), but they were common enough to arouse considerable concern about the special needs of children and youths.

Awareness of children's needs

Partly because of these changes, many people became more conscious of childhood and adolescence as unique periods of life, ones that influenced later development. At the same time, they became concerned with arranging appropriate, helpful experiences for children. A French physician, Jean Itard (1806/ 1962), achieved considerable fame by partially rehabilitating a "wild boy" — a youngster found living alone in the woods in France in 1799. The attention given to his work reflected the new belief that children needed nurturing environments — chiefly family and schools — in order to grow up properly, or "develop." A few hundred years earlier, Itard's work might have received little, if any, notice.

The Emergence of Modern Developmental Study

During the nineteenth and twentieth centuries, the growing recognition of childhood led to new ways of studying children's behavior. Some of these methods relied on careful, detailed observation of children under natural circumstances.

A Multicultural View

Growing Up in India

In many parts of the world today, childhood is understood differently than in the West. Although in these countries conceptions of childhood resemble Western conceptions from earlier historical times, there are also crucial differences from earlier Western ideas. It is misleading to view non-Western societies as earlier versions of our own.

Childhood in India is a good case in point. In the traditional Hindu parts of this society, infants and young children receive a good deal more protection and intimate nurturance than their counterparts in Western families do (E. Erikson, 1969; Kakar, 1982). Typically, infants are breast fed well into toddlerhood — much older than is usual in the West. During the first four or five years of life, children are rarely separated from their mothers; children come on virtually all errands and visits, even when the excursions do not concern them. During this period, mothers take their child-nurturing work very seriously and are expected to do so by Hindu society. Guidance, discipline, and spoiling — major concerns among Western parents — are not serious issues for traditional Hindu mothers, who see their primary task as helping children develop a deeply trustful attitude about the world.

But eventually the protection and nurturance come to an end. For a boy, the end comes suddenly at about age five, when parents and other relatives expect the boy to begin conforming to adult standards of behavior, to give up playing with younger children, and to spend most of his time in the company of other boys and men. As part of these changes, the boy even has to give up eating meals with his mother and other females and take his meals instead with males.

For a girl, protection and nurturance persist a few years longer than for a boy. But she, too, faces a drastic change: sometime between age eleven and age thirteen she gets married, not to someone she chooses but to a young man selected by her parents and the man's parents. At this point she is likely to leave home permanently in order to live with her husband's family. Many of her in-laws will be virtual strangers to her — sometimes including her new husband.

Because the changes happen so suddenly for each sex, they often create stress for young Hindus, as well as sadness and nostalgia for times past. Yet in most cases the changes are manageable, thanks to the emotional and practical supports provided by Hindu families. A majority of these are **extended families,** meaning that households consist of adult relatives living together (usually adult brothers) who have brought their spouses to live with them after they marry (Mandelbaum, 1970). This circumstance helps reduce the loneliness that children feel after they leave the intense, early care of their mothers (Kakar, 1982). A Hindu boy may miss his mother when he stops eating meals with her, but his new companions — his father and other males — have had similar experiences and respond to his feelings tactfully, although with reserve. A Hindu girl may also miss her mother when she marries, but she may become a mother by her late teens. In the context of an extended family, her pregnancy is not considered the burden that a teenage pregnancy seems to be in the West. On the contrary, early pregnancy confers status on the mother; and in any case, the girl's extended family is likely to contain other, more experienced women to assist the young mother with child care.

Others were based on scientific experiments designed to test particular ideas under carefully defined conditions. Both observation and scientific experimentation have continued to the present day as methods of studying children.

Early observational studies

Modern observational studies of children emerged in the nineteenth century from **baby biographies**, detailed diaries of particular children, usually the authors' own. In English, one of the most famous biographies was written and published by Charles Darwin (1877) and contained lengthy accounts of his son Doddy's activities and accomplishments.

Later psychologists drew on the rich detail of this method but at the same time gave it both more focus and more generality. Arnold Gesell observed children at precise ages doing specific things, such as building with blocks, jumping, and hopping (Gesell, 1926). After studying more than five hundred children, Gesell generalized standards of normal development, or **norms** — that is, behaviors typical of children at certain ages. Although the norms applied primarily to the white, middle-class children Gesell tested and to the specific situations and abilities he observed, they still gave a more wide-ranging picture of child development than was possible from baby biographies alone.

Gesell's and Piaget's research

The method of focused observation still persists in child development

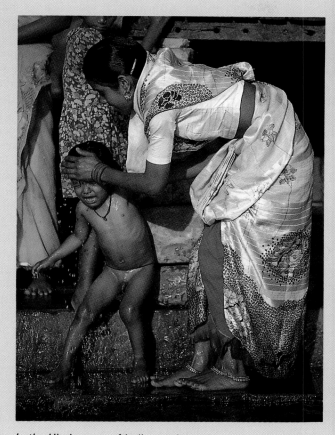

In the Hindu parts of India, mothers give their young children a good deal more physical care and emotional nurturance than commonly occurs in North America.

Viewed one way, then, Hindu childhood resembles childhood in earlier periods of Western history. Hindu boys and girls acquire adult roles and status relatively early, even getting married and bearing children as adolescents. And they tend to live their entire lives in complex households of relatives, as did youths earlier in Western history.

But Hindu childhood differs importantly from typical childhood experiences in the West, either ancient or modern. In particular, Hindu children experience much more intimate care and nurturance than have been typical in Western families, and they experience it for longer periods of childhood. Western children, by contrast, have encountered more mixed responses from their families (Somerville, 1984). To some extent, Westerners have regarded children as a beautiful blessing, creatures to be admired and loved for their intrinsically childlike qualities. At the same time, however, Westerners have regarded children as deficient — as creatures lacking discipline, a sense of right and wrong, and willpower. This attitude has translated into chronic concerns among Western parents about appropriate methods for guiding, disciplining, and setting limits with young children. It has also created concerns about how to stimulate independence and self-reliance as early in childhood as possible (Elkind, 1987). These are reasonable concerns, given the unique conditions of Western family life. Here, unlike in traditional Indian society, parents can expect relatively little help from others in caring for their children, and they can expect teachers and other representatives of society to favor children who can indeed work independently yet reliably.

research. One of the most influential observers in this century was Jean Piaget, who described many details of his three children's behavior as infants (Piaget, 1963). He did not observe all possible behaviors of his children, however, but focused instead on behaviors that illustrated their growing cognitive skills, or ability to think. Piaget has influenced modern developmental psychology to such an extent that we discuss his work at length later in this book.

CURRENT ISSUES IN DEVELOPMENTAL STUDY

As child development has evolved as a discipline, several issues about the nature of human development have emerged and endured: nature and nurture, continuity and discontinuity, and context and universality in development. Because these issues pervade the entire field of developmental psychology as it currently exists, we discuss them in several places later in this book, as well as here.

Nature and Nurture

Importance of heredity and environment

Theorists have long argued, and still do, about the relative importance of inborn qualities of persons (their **nature**) compared to skills and qualities they acquire through their experiences and environment (their **nurture**). A few qualities may be totally inborn — eye color, for example. But psychologists agree that nearly all human qualities result from *both* nature and nurture. Your height depends on how tall your parents were (nature), but it also depends on the nutrition and exercise that you get as you grow up (nurture). Cognitive development shows the dual effects of nature and nurture, too. Infants seem biologically programmed to learn language (nature), even though they learn only the language that they hear spoken to them (nurture).

In practice, determining the exact contributions of nature and nurture can be very difficult. The same quality or behavior can result from different mixtures of genetic and environmental circumstances. Valerie and Wendy may both be active, restless individuals. Yet Valerie may behave this way largely because she was born with an active temperament. Wendy may behave this way primarily because her parents value a child who is physically active and on-the-go and have praised and supported these qualities since Wendy's birth.

In spite of such ambiguity, it is often important to find out the relative contributions of heredity and environment. If Joe is very overweight, the weight problem probably stems partly from a genetic tendency to weigh more and partly from habits formed about nutrition and exercise. But how much has genetics contributed, and how much has learning added? And in exactly what ways? The answers to these questions will influence how parents and professionals may

Perspectives

The Nature and Nurture of "Wolf" Children

Tragically, some children grow up in extreme isolation from human contact; some even grow up in the wilderness or among wild animals. Children who miss out on all human contact in these ways are called feral, or "wolf," children. About fifty documented reports of wolf children have been published in the past three hundred years, and their cases have provided important, naturally occurring studies of the relative impact of nature and nurture on human development (Malson, 1972). The qualities that wolf children acquire in their isolation may suggest what constitutes true, inborn human nature. Qualities that they acquire later, after they have been discovered, trained, and educated, may suggest the limits of human nurture — the limits of what learning and experience can provide.

One of the most widely discussed feral children was the Wild Boy of Aveyron, discovered living in the woods of southern France about 1800 (Lane, 1976). Victor, as he came to be called, looked about ten or eleven years old at the time he was found. He could not speak or understand any language, he preferred to trot on all fours rather than walk, and he did not pay sustained attention to anything for very long. At first Victor also seemed afraid of humans and lacked all social graces; he would eat a pile of garbage as readily as a plate of well-prepared food.

Victor received education and physical care for five years from a physician, Jean Itard, who later published reports of

Victor's progress in considerable detail (Itard, 1806/1962). During that time, the boy made substantial gains in several areas, although he never became a fully functioning, normal young adult. Victor gradually learned to comprehend the names of many people and objects as well as simple verbal requests and other sentences. Eventually he even learned to read a few words. Victor also learned to show affection for his teacher and governesses (giving hugs, smiling). His behavior showed increasing signs of moral development, as when he put a forbidden toy or food back in the cupboard, looking sheepish or ashamed as he did so.

But Victor never learned to produce more than a few isolated words, even though he could understand considerably more language than this. He also never learned enough social skills to live without supervision, and in later years, he seemed puzzled by sexuality. Itard (and others) reported that Victor responded to young women with a mixture of interest, confusion, and fear. In their company, Victor would sit silently next to one of them, proceed to pinch her hands, arms, and lower legs, and then suddenly push the woman away.

Observations such as these persuaded some commentators of the time that considerable amounts of social and intellectual behavior could *not* be trained and were therefore innate. Others argued that Victor must have been brain damaged or mentally retarded at birth, so that his progress

assist Joe with his weight problem. To the extent that it comes from learned habits, they should concentrate on modifying those habits. To the extent that it comes from genetic inheritance, they should set realistic goals for Joe's weight and help Joe (and the other persons close to Joe) to accept those goals.

Continuity and Discontinuity

Psychologists also differ a great deal about whether human development is a gradual, continual process or whether it consists of relatively sudden leaps or transitions from one distinctly different stage to another. At one extreme are those who picture development as continual, meaning that it is the gradual accumulation of more of the same behaviors and personal qualities acquired earlier. In this view, an older child is like a younger child who knows more facts, has engaged in behaviors longer, and has therefore refined them more fully. In general, fifteen-year-olds know the meanings of more words than do five-year-olds; they can write more legibly; they can describe their feelings in more detail. In general, too, a fifteen-year-old who was outgoing as a five-year-old is probably still sociable as a teenager; only the *ways* of showing sociability have changed. All of these differences make older individuals seem as if they have acquired more of what they had already acquired earlier in life.

Development viewed as continual process

But other psychologists have pointed out developmental changes that seem discontinuous and sudden. In this view development is discontinuous and qualitative, meaning that it proceeds by relatively sudden changes in behavior from one distinct stage to another. Qualitative development is like the change of a

or lack thereof showed little about the essence of human nature or about the limits of human training and nurture. Because Itard knew nothing of Victor's birth or early childhood, neither he nor anyone else could rule out these possibilities.

Whatever the case, Victor's story shows two significant principles of development. One is the importance of timing, or **critical periods,** for learning and development. Acquiring full language ability, for example, may require not only language training, as Itard provided for Victor, but also exposure to language at the proper time — in this case during the first few years of life, before Victor was discovered. The other principle is the cumulative effect of development: before learning new, civilized behaviors, Victor had to overcome or set aside behaviors learned previously in the wild. Learning to eat with conventional knives, forks, and spoons required first *un*learning prior habits of eating with the hands, thus slowing down Victor's progress.

Like the Wild Boy of Aveyron, other wolf children have shown improvement after their discovery and training begin. The exact kind of progress varies with the child and his or her circumstances, but it is almost never complete. In a recent, shocking case in Los Angeles, for example, a girl named Genie was released from a closet where she had lived for the first thirteen years of her life (Curtiss, 1977). Genie had no language when first discovered, but she eventually

acquired much more extensive vocabulary and grammatical skills than Victor had ever been able to do. But Genie's language always remained below average for a child her age, and her accent, or pronunciation, was always flawed — much as when a person learns a foreign language late in life.

All things considered, then, what can wolf children teach us about the relationship of nature and nurture? Primarily, they suggest that human contact in infancy and early childhood is crucial to normal human development. Human contact presumably allows teaching, learning, and other forms of experience to have their humanizing impact. But the study of wolf children does not yield the exact details of inborn human nature — if indeed these details can ever be identified (Shattuck, 1980). Ambiguity about human *na*ture remains because the wolf children do not really fail to learn because of their isolation. What they learn is the result of a radically different *nur*ture that involves chronic deprivation, malnutrition, and (in some cases) mistreatment. The later education of wolf children must always overcome these highly unusual experiences. This fact means we must be cautious about generalizing from wolf children to others who have had more normal amounts of human contact.

Development viewed as series of distinct stages

caterpillar into a butterfly or a tadpole into a frog: the moment of transformation happens relatively quickly (even though the processes leading to this moment were slow and steady), and afterward dramatically new behaviors occur. After many experiences handling and releasing a ball, for example, an older infant may one day begin searching for the ball even when it rolls out of sight and demanding it when he cannot find it. This action marks a distinctly qualitative alteration in the child's beliefs about the ball and in his understanding of the concept of permanence: now the ball seems to exist all the time, not just when the child can hold it and look at it. These psychologists say that a child experiencing a number of such qualitative changes is entering a new stage, meaning that a set of new psychological skills are emerging more or less together and that the skills differ fundamentally from those that led up to them.

Universal and Context-specific Development

Changes that every child undergoes

Traditionally, psychologists have concentrated on human development that is universal, or independent of specific circumstances. They have identified a number of behaviors and skills that develop in virtually all normal children. At about four months of age, virtually all infants smile at a human face, and at about ten to twelve months, most speak their first words. As children get older, truly universal developments become harder to identify, largely because individual experiences have more time to create individual differences among children. Nonetheless, a number of universal changes may occur. Certain kinds of logical reasoning about concrete objects and relations may develop between the ages of five to seven (Sternberg, 1984a); other, more abstract reasoning may happen only later.

Often, however, the culture in which a child grows up makes a difference in when and how children develop particular qualities and behaviors (LeVine, 1989). In learning about numbers, for example, young Japanese children have an advantage over English-speaking children because the Japanese language uses "place value" in naming all numbers (Harkness & Super, 1987). Literally translated from the Japanese, the number *17* is "ten-seven," rather than a word that bears only indirect relation to place value, such as the English word *seventeen*. As a result, Japanese teachers may not have to work as hard as English teachers to convey an understanding of place value to first-grade students (Miura & Okamoto, 1989). Thanks to a feature of Japanese culture (its language), Japanese elementary students may therefore develop this specific mathematical skill sooner than English-speaking students of similar age (Stevenson et al., 1986).

Cultural circumstances affect social skills and attitudes as well as cognitive skills. For example, notions of morality or ethics vary widely among societies, particularly as children grow into adolescence and adulthood. In India, children do *not* gradually develop the belief common to North American culture that autonomy and independence are necessarily "good" (Schweder et al., 1987). As a result, Indian children adopt certain behaviors — such as calling their father only by his last name — that may seem quaint to Americans but that actually show respect for the community when viewed from within the culture.

Influence of culture and context

These complications have made some developmental psychologists focus increasingly on the **context**, or circumstances, surrounding children's development (Bronfenbrenner, 1979a, 1979b). Contexts vary widely in scope and nature. A child's immediate family provides one of the most specific and influential contexts for development: the personalities and relationships of family members affect the unique skills, behaviors, and attitudes acquired by a child. Other contexts may be broader and may be shared by many individuals. The neighborhood in which a child grows up is a context that may influence her perceptions

The social context can have a considerable impact on children and adolescents, influencing, for example, their choice of role models — whether they be cowhands or rock stars. Developmental psychology tends to emphasize processes that transcend such differences, but an understanding of development is often enhanced by taking the social context into account.

of society and opportunities to acquire various skills. Still other contexts may be shared by an entire society. Often these amount to the overall patterns of values, beliefs, and customs that make one society distinctive from another. In the United States, a belief in individual responsibility is one such context. This belief helps to justify relatively free economic practices, but it also leads society to give fewer government-sponsored services to assist care-givers in raising children than is typical of most modern societies (Zigler, 1986).

TABLE 1.1   Basic Issues in Developmental Psychology

Issue	Crucial Question
Nature and nurture	How much are qualities, behaviors, and skills inborn, and how much are they acquired through experience?
Continuity and discontinuity	How much does development simply continue earlier acquisitions, and how much does it lead to qualitatively new behaviors and skills?
Universal and context: specific development	How much can developmental psychology identify developmental processes and milestones that happen to everyone throughout the world, and how much should it take specific human and cultural contexts into account?

METHODS OF STUDYING CHILDREN AND ADOLESCENTS

The Scientific Method

Research studies of human development all follow certain general procedures called the **scientific method**. It is these procedures that make developmental psychology a science. (Scarr, 1985). In general, being scientific in psychology means doing *all* of the following:

1. *Formulating research questions* Research begins with questions. Sometimes they refer to previous studies, as when a developmental psychologist asks, "Do Piaget's studies of thinking work with children from Third World countries?" Other times, research questions refer to issues important to society, such as "Does preschool education make children more socially skilled later in childhood?"

2. *Stating questions as hypotheses* A **hypothesis** is a statement that expresses a research question precisely. In making a hypothesis out of the preschool education question above, a psychologist needs to be more specific about "preschool education," "socially skilled," and "later in childhood." Each term contains ambiguities that the hypothesis must clarify before it can be studied scientifically. Does "preschool education" mean a nursery emphasizing free play or one oriented to cognitive skills? Does "socially skilled" refer to a child who initiates activities and leads other children into them? Or does it refer only to one who smiles frequently and responds to friendly overtures? Does "later in childhood" mean one year after the end of preschool or five years?

3. *Testing the hypothesis* Having phrased a research question as a hypothesis, researchers can conduct an actual study about it. As described further in the next section, however, they can do this in a number of ways. The choice of method usually depends on a mixture of convenience, ethics, and scientific appropriateness. Under ideal conditions, researchers may use more than one method to study a particular hypothesis. Such multiple studies usually lead to more valid and clear conclusions, but because they also take more time and effort, they are not very often done.

4. *Interpreting and publicizing the results* After conducting the study itself, psychologists have a responsibility to report their results to others by pres-

Perspectives

The Ecology of Development

One of the most outspoken advocates of the contextual point of view has been Urie Bronfenbrenner (1979a). His approach to development emphasizes two points: environmental contexts are important influences on a child's development; and the child is an active participant in initiating and responding to the development process. Bronfenbrenner sees this process as influenced by four overlapping *ecological contexts* — that is, the naturally occurring circumstances surrounding living beings. He calls these contexts the microsystem, the mesosystem, the exosystem, and the macrosystem (Bronfenbrenner, 1979b; Bronfenbrenner & Crouter, 1983).

1. *The microsystem* This context is the immediate setting in which a child or young person lives and the relationships among the people in this setting. For preschoolers, the microsystem is made up of members of the immediate family. For older children and teenagers, there are usually several microsystems, which include friends and (eventually) workmates. Because of differences in people and relationships, microsystems vary widely and therefore cause development to vary among individual children.

2. *The mesosystem* This context is the array of settings and relationships among settings that a person experiences as he or she grows up. A mesosystem is a set of microsystems. As preschoolers get older the mesosystem expands to include the classroom and the neighborhood, as well as the home. These settings have differing relationships to each other, depending on how and where a child happens to grow up. In a low-income inner-city neighborhood, for example, home and school may seem worlds apart; the opposite may be true for children in high-income suburban neighborhoods. These differences affect human development.

3. *The exosystem* This context is the array of settings that affect a child's development even though the child may not directly experience these settings. A parent's workplace, for example, may remain invisible to a developing child. Yet the workplace influences child development indirectly by affecting the parent's economic success, feelings of exhaustion or of pride, and social connectedness to the community. These factors can influence a parent's success as parent and therefore either enhance or hamper a child's development.

4. *The macrosystem* This context is made up of the ideas, customs, and institutions of a society that influence child development. A belief in "individual effort," for example, is an idea shared widely in the macrosystem that constitutes North American society. This belief affects important child-rearing practices and institutions related to children. It may help to justify giving children responsibility for household chores (Sutton-Smith, 1986), and it is used to justify schools that emphasize individual academic effort (Holloway, 1988).

These contexts of development — Bronfenbrenner's "systems" — affect whom children get to know and what they get to do as they grow up. Directly or indirectly, developmental contexts reward children for some behaviors more than for others and therefore affect how development unfolds. Later chapters draw attention to some of these contexts and point out how they modify universal processes of development.

---

enting them at conferences, publishing them in journal articles, or both. Their reports should include reasonable interpretations or conclusions based on the results. Ideally, the reports on research should include enough detail to allow other psychologists to repeat (or replicate) a study themselves in order to test the conclusions. In practice, the limits of time (at a conference presentation) or space (in a journal) sometimes compromise this ideal.

There are a wide range of ways to carry out the steps listed above. Understanding these ways, at least in general outline, helps you in making sense out of research studies you read about.

Ways that Research Studies Vary

Each of the ways that developmental psychologists use to study children has particular strengths and limitations. Some research questions lend themselves better to one method than to another. Unfortunately, however, some research questions prove relatively hard to answer by *any* method.

Viewed broadly, research studies vary along four major dimensions: (a) how much to emphasize quantitative (or numerical) measurement, (b) how much to purposely intervene in children's behavior and lives, (c) the kind of time frame to use, and (d) the number of children (or "subjects") to observe or study at a time. Studies combine these dimensions in various ways, depending on the questions they are investigating. Developmental research therefore does not always fall neatly into categories or types. The classifications below purposely simplify the full diversity of the field to help in explaining it.

Quantitative Versus Qualitative Studies

Emphasis on measurement

Quantitative Studies   Studies that seek to *measure* behavior, to attach numerical values or quantities to observations of how children act, are called **quantitative studies.** Measurement is both appropriate and easy to understand for many features of development. Consider a toddler who is just learning to talk. A quantitative study can measure certain features of his language development: it can average the number of words the child speaks in his earliest sentences (called the MLU, or mean length of utterance). Or it can tally the size of the child's vocabulary. Or it can count the number of grammatical forms that he seems to understand.

In some studies, however, quantitative measurement proves difficult and inappropriate. How can a psychologist compare an emotion shown by an infant with an equivalent emotion shown by a schoolchild? If an infant shows anger by crying ferociously and a schoolchild shows it by making a sarcastic remark, are the two individuals showing the same "amount" of anger or different amounts? Sarcasm and angry crying are hard to compare, partly because they look so different and partly because they are hard to measure. There is no obvious unit of amount, equivalent to the MLU in language development, on which to base meaningful measurement of these behaviors.

Measuring emotions has proved especially challenging to psychologists. How can we compare the unhappiness felt by this infant with the unhappiness felt by this adolescent girl? Do they really experience the same emotion?

Qualitative Studies   In situations such as these, qualitative methods prove especially helpful. **Qualitative studies** observe or record features, aspects, or qualities of children's behavior without primarily attaching amounts or quantities to them. Measurement may sometimes occur in qualitative studies, but it is not a primary focus of them. One qualitative research study, described in the book *GNYS AT WRK* (Bissex, 1980), documented how one five-year-old taught himself to read and write. The bulk of this work consists of observations of incidents that revealed how this child gradually developed an understanding of written language. (The title, in fact, is an observation of an early, self-invented spelling by the child: GNYS AT WRK stands for "genius at work.")

Emphasis on observation

Another qualitative research study investigated the daily lives of adolescents (Csikszentimihalyi & Larson, 1984). In this study, investigators arranged for teenagers to telephone a central tape recording machine periodically and simply describe their current activities and feelings in everyday language. In both the *GNYS AT WRK* and the adolescent study, quantitative tabulations of the qualitative information abounded, but they did not take the place of qualitative information.

Naturalistic Versus Experimental Studies

Developmental studies also differ in how much they control, change, or intervene in the events they observe.

Naturalistic Studies   At one extreme, **naturalistic research** purposely observes behavior as it normally occurs in natural settings, such as at home, on a playground, or in a classroom. Suppose that you wondered whether young children show sex-typed preferences and behaviors more in the presence of the opposite sex than in the presence of the same sex? How could you investigate this hypothesis using a naturalistic method?

A naturalistic study might locate preexisting groups with different combinations of the sexes. A nursery school classroom might contain such groups, so you could try observing children's daily free play in these rooms. In doing so, you could compare children's behaviors in same-sex groups with their behaviors in cross-sex groups. For this study, you would concentrate only on behaviors that seemed sex-typed, such as aggressive and boisterous behavior among boys and shy behavior among girls. Does playing in a mixed-sex group exaggerate these behaviors, reduce them, or have no consistent effect? In trying to answer this question, you would confine your attention to situations and behaviors that normally occur.

A naturalistic study like this one can provide considerable information about children, but it also faces special complexities in interpreting results. Suppose that the same-sex play groups turned out to show *more* stereotyped behaviors. Unfortunately, you still might not feel sure how to interpret this difference: did same-sex children reinforce each other's stereotyped behaviors? Or did children with a general tendency toward stereotyped behaviors gravitate toward same-sex groups? Or did same-sex groups tend inevitably to choose relatively stereotyped activities (trucks for boys and dolls for girls), and did these activities in turn stimulate relatively stereotyped behaviors? You can sometimes sort out rival possibilities like these by conducting further naturalistic studies, but sometimes, too, the questions require experimental studies.

Difficulties in interpretation

Experimental Studies   Compared to naturalistic studies, **experimental studies** try to arrange circumstances so that just one or two factors or influences vary at a time. In using experimental research in your study of the effects of gender

In naturalistic research, psychologists observe children's behavior as it normally occurs in a pre-existing setting or context.

Decisions about what and whom to observe

on sex-typed behaviors, you would not observe naturally occurring play groups. Instead, you would set up or organize groups with very specific characteristics: only so many children in each group, only certain specific toys available to them, and only certain amounts of time to interact. You would, in fact, hold constant any factor that might influence sex typing in children's play, *except* for the one you are studying. In your study, the one factor you would vary would be the sex composition of the play groups; you would arrange for some groups to contain both sexes but others to contain only one sex. Sex composition would therefore be the **independent variable**. The amount of sex typing in the children's play behavior would *depend* on your manipulation of the groups' sex composition and would thus be the **dependent variable**.

Controlling variables in this way also requires making decisions about the **population**, or group to which the study refers. The relevant population in your study might consist only of middle-class, white, preschool children. Any interpretations of the results would apply only to this group and not to other ethnic groups or age groups in our society. To make sure that the experiment does indeed refer just to this population, you would have to take a **random sample** of the population to which this study refers. In this case that would mean selecting white, middle-class preschoolers by chance. In later studies, of course, you could sample other populations, such as other ethnic groups or other age groups. If you did so, however, you would be able to generalize your results only to these other groups or populations.

Experimental studies have a number of precautions to ensure that their findings have **validity**, meaning that they measure or observe what they intend to measure. One way to improve validity is by observing not one but two sample groups, one called an experimental, or treatment, group and the other called a control group. The **experimental group** receives the treatment or intervention related to the purposes of the experiment. The **control group** experiences conditions that are as similar as possible to the conditions of the experimental group but without experiencing the crucial experimental treatment. Comparing the results for the two groups helps to explicitly establish the effects of the experimental treatment.

Consider how you might design an experimental study of whether war toys (guns, tanks, missiles) affect children's aggressiveness. The experimental and control groups might both be given time to play with toys in specially organized playrooms. The playrooms would be identical except for the selection of toys: the room for the experimental group would include various war toys, but the room for the control group would not. Researchers could then observe the children's play in each room, looking for signs of aggressiveness. Any aggression that occurs is likely to result from the war toys because the children, the rooms, and the play opportunities are similar in every other important way.

Note that *both* groups — experimental and control — are needed to explicitly test the experimental question. Without including a control group, researchers could not know whether increases in aggression actually resulted from the war toys or from factors *other* than the selection of toys. Perhaps just visiting a strange playroom excites children, and that excitement leads to more aggression. The control group helps to rule out alternative possibilities like this one.

Another way to ensure validity in experimental research is to use **blind administration** or treatments, which means concealing the true purposes of the experiment from the children, from the person administering the experiment (called **single blind** experiments), or from both (a **double blind** experiment). Without blind administration, experimenters may unknowingly do or say things that bias their observations or that bias children's responses to support the experimenters' preconceptions.

Potential biases in experimental research

Consider how such biases might occur in an actual research study. Suppose that the study wanted to know whether boys or girls talk more in mixed-sex social groups. And suppose that the researcher already suspected, but did not really know for sure, that boys talk more in these groups. To study this research question with*out* blind administration, the researcher might set up some "discussion groups" after school, tell the groups his purposes, and observe their conversations.

Without blind administration, two biases might happen. First, the researcher might accidentally hint to students about his preconceptions — "I'm not sure, but I suspect you boys will talk more than you girls." Noticing these hints, the children might try to oblige the researcher by allowing the boys to talk more, so as not to "spoil" the research. Second, in making actual observations of conversations, the researcher might rely on his preconceptions to judge ambiguous interactions: if the sexes talk about equally, the researcher's preconceptions might still make him "see" the boys talking more.

This second bias can be reduced by getting someone other than the researcher to make the actual observations — someone without as much concern or stake in how the study turns out. The first bias — of self-fulfilling research results — can be reduced, too, by having the researcher temporarily conceal the true purposes of the study from the children. Instead of saying, "I am observing which sex talks more," he can say, "I want to learn what children know about . . ." and give them a topic to discuss. By taking the children's minds off of gender differences, this strategy of temporary deception can produce more natural conversations and therefore allow more usable observations. But because it does deceive, the strategy obliges the researcher to fully discuss the true purposes of the study with the children afterward. In the study described here, the emotional and interpersonal "cost" of deception may be fairly small; but from time to time psychological studies occur in which the ethical costs have been significantly larger. We discuss the ethics of research more fully at the end of this chapter.

Clear results versus artificiality

Because of its logical organization, the experimental method often gives clearer results than naturalistic studies do. But people sometimes do not behave naturally in experimental situations, so one criticism of the experimental method is that it runs the risk of artificiality. Naturalistic research does not face this particular problem, but it does run a greater risk of ambiguity in its results.

Compromise Methods and Mixtures   Sometimes psychologists resolve these dilemmas by designing studies that have elements of both experimental and naturalistic methods. Such compromises are often called **quasi-experimental** ("partially experimental") **research**. As an example, consider again your study of sex typing in children's play. How could you investigate this problem without either using existing nursery classrooms (the naturalistic method) or setting up contrived groups (the experimental method)? Perhaps you could find situations that include some of the real-life normality of nursery schools as well as some of the systematic control of experimental groups.

Advantages of mixed designs

Perhaps, for example, you could persuade an existing nursery school to modify its daily routines to intentionally create same-sex and cross-sex groupings. At certain times or on certain days teachers would encourage, or even require, same-sex play groupings; at other times they would encourage or require cross-sex groupings. Such groupings would have more naturalness to them than experimentally contrived groups would. But their composition would also be more predictable than in most normal nursery classrooms. The procedure would therefore contain elements both of an experiment and of naturalistic observation.

Time Frames for Studying Development

Because human development by nature occurs gradually over a long period, developmental psychologists have essentially two choices: either allow a long time to observe it or else compare people of different ages at the same point in time. The first approach is called **longitudinal study**, and the second is called **cross-sectional study**. Each method has its own advantages and problems.

Subjects of different ages at same point in time

Cross-sectional Study   The cross-sectional approach compares groups of children or adolescents who are similar in every way except their age. Suppose a psychologist wonders about the ability to solve jigsaw puzzles — an important sign of small motor coordination and other spatially related skills. How does this skill grow or change during childhood and adolescence? In a cross-sectional study, a psychologist would observe children of different ages attempting to solve one of these puzzles — perhaps some six-year-olds, some twelve-year-olds, and some eighteen-year-olds. If the groups came from comparable backgrounds, then comparing their performances and styles of solving the puzzle would suggest something about how this skill develops.

Cross-sectional studies have proved very popular in studying development because they can be done rather quickly and easily. The puzzle-solving study might be completed in just a few months, or even less. Unfortunately, the method can often gloss over the processes that actually contribute to long-run development. How, or by what steps, does puzzle performance improve over the years? What specific events or subskills combine to enhance performance as time goes by? By itself, a cross-sectional study often cannot answer these questions because it really compares only age groups rather than development within individuals.

The most serious limitation of cross-sectional studies, however, is their inability to distinguish among **cohorts**, or groups of individuals who happen to be born at the same time and who therefore have similar developmental experiences. A cohort of children born in 1930 shared experiences of less education and less comprehensive health care than a cohort born in 1960. As a result of this difference, comparing their abilities and health cross-sectionally in 1990 may make the older cohort appear to be less intellectually able and less healthy. The cross-sectional method may create the impression that the differences in ability and health reflect true developmental change, instead of the effects of being born earlier in the century. Cross-sectional methods always contain this ambiguity, and only a longitudinal study can begin to resolve it.

Limitations of cross-sectional studies

Cross-sectional methods also obscure changes in relative abilities and performance styles. As teachers sometimes note, a child who shows outstanding skill at one age will not necessarily remain outstanding throughout her life. Someone who excels at puzzles at age six may not still do so at age twelve or eighteen; conversely, a child who shows only middling ability early in childhood may become more outstanding later on — not only compared to her own earlier skill but even in her relative rank among peers. What events or processes cause shifts like these to occur? Cross-sectional studies cannot really answer this question as well as longitudinal ones can.

Longitudinal Study   The longitudinal approach observes the same subjects periodically over a relatively long period, often years. By nature, therefore, it can monitor the changes within individuals as well as between them, and it can offer more clues about what may cause the changes to occur. A longitudinal study of jigsaw puzzle ability would locate the same children at several different ages and each time observe them attempting to solve a puzzle. Over the long run, the study could identify which children improved and when. And it could identify which stayed the same or even worsened in performance. Combining these observations with other information about the subjects might suggest ideas about what makes puzzle-solving ability develop and what the "typical" developmental path for this ability is.

Same subjects at different points in time

Although longitudinal study may therefore be more truly "developmental" than cross-sectional study is, it, too, has its problems. By definition, longitudinal study takes many months or even years to complete — and this does not even count the time a psychologist needs just to get organized. This much time can cause a researcher many headaches. For one thing, children in longitudinal studies sometimes become overly familiar with the testing and observation procedures. They may improve their puzzle skills simply because they face the same puzzles time after time over the course of months and years.

Limitations of longitudinal studies

Longitudinal studies also pose certain practical problems. Some of the original children may move away; or the investigator may become hopelessly tied up with other work and fail to complete the original study; or the field of developmental psychology may lose interest in the research question. In general, too, longitudinal studies are far more costly than cross-sectional ones — research assistants must be hired for years, not months. Given these obstacles, psychologists have tended to emphasize cross-sectional rather than longitudinal studies. There are prominent exceptions to this rule, however; we discuss some of them later in this book.

Sequential Study   Sometimes the dilemmas of the time frame are solved by combining elements of cross-sectional and longitudinal study. In the case of puzzle-solving ability, children of different ages can be compared at one point

Combining cross-sectional and longitudinal studies

Longitudinal studies are especially well suited to studying long-term constancy and change in particular individuals or groups. These brothers keep the same smiles from childhood to adolescence, but a longitudinal study might also reveal other continuities — and some significant changes as well.

in time (cross-sectional) and then followed for a few years before testing again (longitudinal). Six-year-olds and nine-year-olds can be compared initially and then can be observed again three years later. Like a cross-sectional study, a sequential study produces relatively immediate results; and like a longitudinal one, it traces individuals' actual development. As a compromise, therefore, sequential studies have much to recommend them.

Sampling Strategies

In addition to all the variations described so far, developmental studies vary in how many persons they observe or collect information about.

Surveys   At one extreme are large-scale **surveys,** which may sample hundreds or even thousands of individuals about particular facts or opinions. Examples of these are the familiar Gallup Polls published in magazines and the newspapers; but many psychological studies have also used this method. Surveys are especially useful for identifying the frequency of specific behaviors or attitudes, such as the percentage of parents who believe in spanking their children or the average age at which teenagers first experience sexual intercourse. Because surveys sample relatively large numbers of people, they run less risk of producing results that are misleading because of random variations among individuals' responses.
    But surveys do have limitations. Survey results can vary significantly depend-

TABLE 1.2 *Cross-sectional, Longitudinal, and Sequential Research Studies*
Cross-sectional studies are more convenient to do, but longitudinal ones show developmental trends more explicitly. Sequential studies offer a compromise between these positive qualities of the other two types.

Goal:
To observe and compare the behavior of children aged five, ten, and fifteen.

Cross-sectional:
Example: Three different age groups observed during the same year
Length of study: 1 year

	Group 1	Group 2	Group 3
Age at time of observation	5 years	10 years	15 years
Time when observations made	Year 1	Year 1	Year 1

Longitudinal:
Example: One group observed at three intervals over a ten-year period
Length of study: 10 years

	Group 1	Group 1	Group 1
Age at time of observation	5 years	10 years	15 years
Time when observations made	Year 1	Year 6	Year 10

Sequential:
Example: Two different groups, each observed at two intervals over a five-year period
Length of study: 5 years

	Group 1	Group 2
Age at time of first observation	5 years	10 years
. . . and of second observation	10 years	15 years
Time of first observation	Year 1	Year 1
. . . and of second observation	Year 6	Year 6

ing on the exact wording of questions; consider the difference between "Does your child have a tantrum at least once a week?" and "Does your child have a tantrum several times a month?" Questions such as "How often do you have sexual relations?" may also produce untrustworthy results because they delve into private matters that people may not be completely truthful about. And questionnaires require subjects who can articulate their thoughts well and sometimes even put in writing. This limitation leaves out certain people of interest to developmental psychology, such as preschoolers and infants.

Interviews   If a research study seeks complex or in-depth information, it often uses **interviews,** which are face-to-face directed conversations. Because these take time, interview studies usually focus on a smaller number of individuals than a survey does — perhaps just several dozen individuals or so. Often interviews can explore a person's thinking more thoroughly than can written questionnaires: the interviewer can explain the research purposes more clearly, clarify questions as needed, and follow up on individuals' responses if they are unclear.

But interviews are also prone to certain biases. One bias is sampling: if investigators are going to interview relatively few individuals, how can they make sure those individuals truly represent the broader population? If fifty teenagers describe what leads to popularity, how can a researcher be sure that their opinions reflect all teenagers' views?

Interviews can also suffer from personal biases within interviewers and interviewees. Some combinations of the two experience better rapport than others and therefore produce more useful interview results. Research *about* interview studies (versus research *using* interviews) shows that it helps for interviewers to have training and experience and that similarity in gender, age, and social status is important for many topics, especially relatively personal ones (F. Fowler, 1988).

Case Studies   Useful developmental research can also be done on just a few individuals or even on just one. A study of a single individual or of a few individuals considered as a unit is called a **case study.** In general, case studies try to pull together a wide variety of information about the individual case and then present the information as a unified whole. Case studies emphasize the relationships among specific behaviors, thoughts, and attitudes in the life of the individual being studied.

A case study of a child might combine direct observations, interviews with

TABLE 1.3   Differences Among Research Methods in Developmental Psychology

Method	Strengths	Limitations
Quantitative studies	Provides relatively precise measurement of behaviors or variables being studied	Measurements may only appear to be precise; studying relationships among behaviors may require relatively complex statistical procedures
Qualitative studies	Provides information about relationships among variables that cannot be measured quantitatively	Can be misleading about the extent or strength among variables
Naturalistic studies	Shows behavior in normal settings; shows relations among behaviors	Obscures cause and effect; unusual but important behaviors may not happen to occur
Experimental studies	Eliminates or reduces irrelevant events and influences	Experimental setting may be artificial; not all research questions lend themselves to experimentation
Cross-sectional studies	Suggests developmental trends by comparing ages; relatively fast and convenient form of study	Can obscure cohort and historical changes
Longitudinal studies	Documents developmental changes within particular groups of subjects over relatively long period	Subjects may drop out over time; requires sustained commitment by investigators
Sequential studies	Compromises between cross-sectional and longitudinal studies; gains some of the unique strengths of each	Loses some of the unique strengths of cross-sectional and longitudinal studies
Surveys	Samples can be more representative because of larger sample sizes; less prone to personal biases of researcher	Subjects must be able to read and write; questions can be more ambiguous than expected
Interviews	Allows clarification and exploration of questions; helps to see subject's own viewpoint	Responses affected by personal qualities of interviewer and of subject
Case studies	Shows individual as a whole; good for exploring possible new relationships among behaviors and traits	Selection of case(s) may be quite biased; difficult to distinguish important behaviors from trivial ones; generalization can be difficult

the child or with her family, questionnaires if appropriate, and even preexisting documents such as doctors' or teachers' records if these were relevant to the study. By drawing on a wide range of information, such a case study could serve two different research purposes. First, it could explore an aspect of child development, looking for new or unexpected connections among the child's behaviors, needs, and social relationships. This is the most common use of case studies. Second, it could confirm whether connections previously found in experimental studies actually occur in everyday, nonexperimental situations, even when conditions are not carefully controlled. The second of these two uses resembles the naturalistic studies described earlier in this section, except that by definition, the case study focuses attention on only a very limited number of children as subjects.

But case studies do gain these advantages at some cost. There is no guarantee that the few subjects used in a case study actually represent the population of children being investigated. A case study of how children make friends may happen to choose a rather aggressive individual as a case and may therefore produce rather misleading results. Or even if typical individuals are indeed chosen as cases, their behavior may show a bewildering variety that interferes with the formation of firm conclusions. Or the children studied may show two dozen friendly behaviors, only some of which are truly important in the forming of friendships. But which ones? Other research strategies may be needed to answer this question.

ETHICAL CONSTRAINTS ON STUDYING DEVELOPMENT

Sometimes ethical concerns influence the methods that can be used to study a particular question about development. Take the question of punishment: what kinds of punishment work best with children, and for what reasons? For ethical reasons, we may not be able to study certain aspects of this problem directly. Observing parents actually scolding and reprimanding their children would require delicacy at best. At worst, if the punishment became severe or physical, ethics might require our active intervention simply to protect a child from abuse.

For ethically sensitive questions, we may instead have to satisfy ourselves with less direct but more acceptable methods of study. We can interview a variety of parents about the methods of punishment that they do in fact use, or we can ask experts who work directly with families what methods they think that parents typically use. A few courageous families might allow us to observe their daily activities, with the understanding that we are interested in observing how they punish their children. But by being volunteers these few families may not represent other families very well.

Considered in general, research about human beings must face at least three ethical issues: confidentiality, full disclosure of purposes, and respect for the individual's freedom to participate (American Psychological Association, 1981). In developmental psychology, all of these issues are complicated by the youthfulness of the subjects, and by the responsibilities their parents have for them.

1. *Confidentiality* If researchers collect information that might damage individuals' reputations or self-esteem, they should take care to protect the identity of the participants. Observing parents' methods of punishment might require this sort of confidentiality. Mothers and fathers may not want just anyone knowing how much and how often they experience conflicts with their children. Chances are, children would not want this information made public either. In

Ethical principles governing developmental study

such cases investigators should not divulge the identities of participating families without their consent, either during the conduct of the study or afterward when the results are published.

2. *Full disclosure of purposes* Parents (and their children) are entitled to know the true purposes of any research study in which they participate. Most of the time, investigators understand and follow this principle carefully. But misleading of participants can be tempting at times. In studying parents' punishment techniques, researchers might suspect that stating this purpose honestly may cause certain families to avoid participation — especially the ones with the most discipline problems. Or investigators might suspect that telling families the truth about the study would make families distort their behavior — perhaps making them self-consciously hide their worst conflicts. According to this argument, therefore, intentional misleading of parents would produce more complete observations of conflicts and parental punishment techniques. In this sense dishonesty might make the research more "scientific." But investigators would purchase this benefit at the cost of their long-run reputation with the participants. Purposeful deception may sometimes be permissible, but only when no other method is possible and when participants are fully informed after the study of the deception and its reasons.

3. *Respect for individual's freedom to participate* As much as possible, research studies should avoid pressuring parents or children to participate. This may not be so simple as it first appears. Because psychologists have a relatively high status in society, some parents may feel reluctant to decline an invitation from them to participate in "scientific research." Investigators may therefore have to bend over backward to assure parents that participation is indeed voluntary. They cannot simply assume that parents or children will automatically feel free to decline if approached. After all, what parent wants to interfere with the progress of science?

No particular research method is immune from ethical constraints. Whether a research project is a survey or a naturalistic case study, an investigator may have the opportunity to violate confidentiality but should not do so. Likewise, manipulation and deception are options in the design of any type of study — even naturalistic studies, where investigators may deceive by purposely misleading children about their true research purposes or about whether the children are being observed for research purposes at all.

When all three principles are well met, they allow for what psychologists call **informed consent:** the person or group being studied understands the nature of the research, feels that her (or their) rights are protected, and feels free either to volunteer or to refuse to participate. Informed consent therefore forms a standard or ideal for research to aim for and one that most studies do in fact approximate. As the discussion above indicates, however, a completely informed consent may prove difficult to achieve in some cases.

Special ethical problems related to the study of children

This is especially so for research about children, who tend to be dependent on the goodwill and wisdom of parents and of other adults, including researchers (Katz, 1984). In studying people of this age, investigators may sometimes wonder whether their participants can fully understand the purposes of a study, even when its purposes are explained. How well can children really understand why investigators might want to observe conflicts between them and their parents? Even if a goal like this makes sense to children, can they really feel free to participate or not? Or will children usually feel that they must cooperate with whatever adult investigators ask? If the children are very young, perhaps parents can decide on their behalf, but when do children become mature enough to be consulted directly?

Ultimately, the right to decide about whether to participate in a research study rests with the child, provided that the child can understand the nature of the study and feels truly free to decline participation. When these conditions hold only partially, as with young children, parents then share the ultimate right to decide with the child. When the conditions do not hold at all, as with infants, parents essentially take over the right to decide about participation.

These guidelines do not, however, relieve research investigators of responsibility for the child's decision to participate, particularly when the child is young. The investigators must still follow a principle called **in loco parentis,** a Latin phrase meaning "in place of parents." The principle of in loco parentis requires investigators to act at all times in the best interests of the children being studied, much as the children's parents do in everyday affairs (Steininger et al., 1984). This means not only respecting parents' and children's decisions about participating but also looking after the children's welfare once a study is under way. If a study of children's games led (accidentally) to aggression or hurt feelings, in loco parentis would require the investigator to do whatever the parents might do to remedy the problem, which could include stopping the research observations of the games.

THE STRENGTHS AND LIMITATIONS OF DEVELOPMENTAL KNOWLEDGE

As this chapter demonstrates, human development has to be studied in particular ways and with particular limitations in mind. Because time is a major dimension of development, the impact of time must be approached thoughtfully. Yet the very nature of time poses real problems for studying at least some major questions: sometimes people "take too long" to develop compared to the time available to study them. And because developmental psychologists deal with people, they must treat their objects of study with respect and live by usual standards of decency and consideration for human needs. Finally, because they deal with especially young people, developmental psychologists must sometimes take extra care to determine the true best interests of their subjects, even when those subjects do not know what they are being asked to do or do not feel free to refuse even when they do know.

Lest these limitations sound overly discouraging, be assured that in spite of them, developmental psychologists have in fact accumulated considerable knowledge of children and adolescents in recent decades and are continuing to do so. The succeeding chapters in this book should make that point amply clear. Developmental psychology does not have definite answers for some important questions about human nature — but it *does* have the answers for a good many others.

SUMMARY OF MAJOR IDEAS

The Nature of Developmental Change

1. Developmental psychology concerns how thoughts, feelings, personality, social relationships, and motor skills evolve as individuals get older.

2. Development occurs in three major domains: physical, cognitive, and psychosocial.

3. The domains of development influence each other in many ways, and individuals always develop as whole persons rather than in separate pieces.

Why Study Development?

4. Studying development can help give you appropriate expectations about the behavior of children and adolescents.

5. A knowledge of development can help you to respond appropriately to the actual behavior of children.

6. A knowledge of development can help you to recognize when unusual behaviors are cause for concern.

7. Studying development can give you self-knowledge and understanding of your past.

The History of Developmental Study

8. Until just a few hundred years ago, childhood and adolescence were not regarded as distinct periods of life.

9. At the end of the seventeenth century, philosophers began arguing that childhood was a special period of life; economic conditions lent support to their arguments.

10. In the nineteenth and early twentieth centuries, some of the studies of child development consisted of baby biographies, of structured observations of children at specific ages, and of standardized tests of ability.

Current Issues in Developmental Study

11. Currently, developmental psychology focuses on at least three major themes or issues: the impact of nature and nurture, the extent of continuity and discontinuity in development, and how much development is universal and how much is specific to the child's context.

Methods of Studying Children and Adolescents

12. Research about developmental psychology tries to follow the scientific method: formulating research questions, stating them as hypotheses, testing the hypotheses, and interpeting and publicizing the results.

13. Studies vary according to whether they use measurement techniques, if and how much they intervene, what time frame they use, and how many children they investigate.

14. Studies of children and adolescents sometimes use naturalistic methods in which preexisting conditions or contexts are preserved as much as possible.

15. Other studies use experimental methods that try to control or hold constant most conditions while varying only one or two specified variables.

16. Still other studies combine naturalistic and experimental methods in various ways.

17. Many developmental studies use a cross-sectional organization that compares individuals of differing ages at one point in time.

18. Other studies follow developmental change directly by using a longitudinal organization.

19. Sometimes cross-sectional and longitudinal designs can be combined to get the advantages of each.

20. Depending on how many people are to be observed, research projects may use survey, interviews, or case studies to collect information.

Ethical Constraints on Studying Development

21. Ethical considerations guide how development can be studied and sometimes rule out certain studies altogether.

22. Generally, developmental studies should be guided by the principles of confidentiality, full disclosure of purposes, and respect for the individual's freedom to participate.

23. Research about children should strive for informed consent from children and their parents.

24. Even after a study has begun, researchers should act according to the best interests of the child, a principle called in loco parentis.

KEY TERMS

developmental (4)	population (22)
domain (5)	random sample (22)
physical development (5)	validity (22)
cognitive development (5)	experimental group (23)
psychosocial	control group (23)
development (5)	blind administration (23)
nature (14)	quasi-experimental
nurture (14)	research (24)
context (16)	longitudinal study (24)
scientific method (18)	cross-sectional study (24)
hypothesis (18)	cohort (25)
quantitative study (20)	survey (26)
qualitative study (21)	interview (27)
naturalistic research (21)	case study (28)
experimental study (21)	informed consent (30)
independent variable (22)	in loco parentis (31)
dependent variable (22)	

WHAT DO YOU THINK?

1. How do people's experiences as children affect their interest in learning about developmental psychology? Does it make them more interested or less?

2. On balance, do you think children were happier five hundred years ago? Or did they feel the same? Explain.

3. What position would you take on each of the issues outlined on pages (13–17)? Take note of your opinions, and see whether they remain the same after reading most of this book.

FOR FURTHER READING

Ariès, P. *Centuries of Childhood: A Social History of Family Life*, trans. Robert Baldick. New York: Vintage Books, 1962.

This book traces the development of family life and of the modern idea of childhood and adolescence. It has become a classic in the field of family studies, although more recent research now makes some of it seem overstated. Medieval parents, for example, probably did care about their children more than Ariès gives them credit for, and many modern familes do treat their children as economic assets under certain conditions.

Bronfenbrenner, U. *The Ecology of Human Development: Experiments by Nature and by Design.* Cambridge, Mass.: Harvard University Press, 1979.

This book presents one of the most clear and thorough arguments for the importance of social context in human development. The author describes many psychological studies that can make sense only if the circumstances surrounding the studies are taken fully into account. He also argues that psychological research can progress only if it uses *both* naturalistic and experimental methods.

Elkind, D. *The Hurried Child: Growing Up Too Fast Too Soon.* Reading, MA: Addison-Wesley, 1981.

Elkind, D. *All Grown Up and No Place to Go.* Reading, MA: Addison-Wesley, 1984.

Elkind, D. *Miseducation: Preschoolers at risk.* New York: Knopf, 1987.

These books, as well as others by David Elkind, summarize the important current issues about the welfare of children in today's society. The first book listed above focuses on school-age children, the second on teen-agers, and the third on preschoolers. Along with identifying issues, Elkind suggests how parents and professionals can use knowledge about developmental psychology to look after the interests of children and youths.

Kagan, J. *The Nature of the Child.* New York: Basic Books, 1984.

The author of this volume discusses the major issues current in developmental psychology today and challenges many of the field's most widely held assumptions. He proposes, for example, that early life experiences are not necessarily more influential on human development than later life experiences are. He also proposes that families do *not* exert as much influence on children as is commonly supposed. Whether you agree with the author's ideas or not, the book is thought provoking.

Kessel, F., and Siegel, A. (eds.). *The Child and Other Cultural Inventions.* New York: Praeger, 1983.

This book describes many of the ways that child development is affected by history and culture. A number of developmental psychologists present this viewpoint, each in a separate chapter. After each chapter, some of the other authors informally comment on the ideas of the chapter.

Steininger, M., Newell, J. D., and Garcia, L. *Ethical Issues in Psychology.* Homewood, IL: Dorsey Press, 1984.

This is a comprehensive discussion of the issues that come up in psychological research with human beings. It applies well to developmental research on children. As the book shows, the ethical issues are much broader than presented in this chapter: in addition to protecting children from (psychological) abuse, researchers also have obligations to protect children's reputations and privacy, among other things.

CHAPTER 2

Theories of Development

Focusing Questions

■ What are developmental theories, and why should we spend our time learning about them?

■ How have Freud's ideas about unconscious conflict and Erikson's theories about psychosocial crises influenced thinking about development?

■ How do developmental theories based on learning principles contribute to our understanding of developmental change?

■ What does Piaget's theory of cognitive development reveal about how our ability to think changes from childhood through adolescence?

■ How does information-processing theory help us understand how a child solves problems?

■ What are the advantages and disadvantages of using developmental theories, and how do you decide which one is best?

hen Elizabeth, age three, began nursery school, she cried and screamed every day when her mother left her. "Home!" and "Mama!" were the only words she seemed able to produce in between her sobs, which continued for much of each morning. Her teachers were concerned and met to discuss what to do about Elizabeth.

"It's best to ignore the crying," said one teacher. "If you give her lots of special attention because of it, you will reinforce the crying, and she'll just keep going longer."

"But we can't just ignore a crying child," said another. "This is a new and strange situation, and her crying shows that she is feeling insecure and abandoned. Look at her! She needs comfort and emotional support, so that she can feel safer and more secure. At least give her a hug!"

"I think that she is unsure whether her mother really will come back for her," said a third teacher. "Perhaps we can find ways to help her understand and remember our daily routine here."

What actually happened? Whose advice did the teachers follow? They agreed to try not to make too much of a fuss over Elizabeth's tears and to give her lots of comfort and support when she was not crying. They also helped Elizabeth draw a picture chart of the daily schedule and tape it to her cubbyhole. Last, they talked with her mother about what they had observed and the solutions they were trying.

How well did it work? Elizabeth did stop crying — more quickly, in fact, than any of the teachers had expected. Although all three teachers agreed that Elizabeth was clearly happier and more at ease, no one was sure exactly how or why the change had come about.

THE NATURE OF DEVELOPMENTAL THEORIES

Each of the teachers' approaches reflects a different set of ideas and beliefs about children and their development. Whether they know it or not, most people —

teachers, parents, students, and even children themselves — are guided by "informal theories" of human development. In reading about Elizabeth, did you find yourself agreeing in particular with one of the teacher's comments? If so, it is probably because you share that teacher's informal theoretical orientation.

What Is a Developmental Theory?

The purpose of any theory is to help us understand the world and guide our future actions. A good theory does four things. First, it systematically *organizes* what is already known about a subject, including facts that may be conflicting or confusing. Second, it tries to *explain* what is going on in terms of helpful principles, mechanisms, and processes. For example, theories of social and emotional development help us to understand better how children feel and act and how and why their feelings and actions change with age and experience. Likewise, theories of cognitive development help us to understand how children learn to think and solve problems and what we can and cannot expect of them at certain ages or stages. Third, a good theory is *generative* — it suggests and generates new ideas and research activity. Fourth, a good theory is *testable*, which means that developmental researchers can systematically evaluate the accuracy of the theory's claims.

How theories aid understanding

Human development, as we point out in Chapter 1, refers to long-term changes and the patterns of these changes during a person's lifetime. Developmental theories try to describe and understand these changes by discovering the principles that underlie *the process of change.*

Many motor skills, such as riding a bicycle or making a chewing gum bubble, develop in predictable sequences or stages.

Stage Theories of Development

Many developmental theories focus on the concept of developmental stages, and for that reason they are known as **stage theories.**

Common Characteristics of Stage Theories All stage theories of development agree that stages have certain distinguishing features:

1. All intact organisms follow the same order or sequence of stages in their development. (For example, all physically normal infants go through the same three stages of sitting, walking, and running during their development.)

2. Each stage is qualitatively (or structurally) unique and different from all other stages. (Walking is qualitatively different from sitting, and running is qualitatively different from walking.)

3. The stages represent a logical progression in development, with later stages achieving greater complexity and integrating the accomplishments of earlier stages. (The ability to walk depends on the earlier achievement of the ability to sit, and development of the complex skills involved in running depend on the prior accomplishment of walking.)

Children experience similar changes in other areas of their development. For example, as a child learns to write, he integrates his previously acquired skills at drawing and manipulating things with newly developing skills in using language and reading. Likewise, his development of intimacy with female friends during adolescence calls on his earlier experiences of friendship but also reflects a much higher level of sophistication and complexity. Thus, all stage theories agree that human development, like that of other living organisms, follows a logical progression that can be identified and studied.

Differences Among Developmental Theories

Theories differ in how they explain the processes and mechanisms of developmental change. Some, such as Piaget's theory of cognitive development, see change as the result of built-in, biologically determined tendencies known as maturation. Others, such as behavioral and social learning theories of development, consider learning and experience as the primary sources of developmental change. Theories also differ in their assessment of how actively individuals participate in their own development and how aware they are of the changes that are taking place. Finally, theories differ in which aspects of developmental change they seek to explain.

Maturation versus learning

To what degree are changes in an individual's development mainly dependent upon *learning*, and to what degree do they depend on *maturation*? Some changes, such as growth in size and muscle coordination, clearly seem maturational, whereas others, such as skill in playing baseball or tennis, clearly seem learned. But for many developmental changes, the relative contributions of learning and maturation are less clear. Talking is a good example. One developmental issue is determining to what degree all children learn to talk, regardless of what they are taught, and to what extent their talking depends on particular learning experiences.

Activity versus passivity

Theorists differ in their view of how active or passive individuals are in their own development. For instance, behavioral learning theorists believe that developmental change is caused by events in the environment that stimulate individuals to respond, whereas theorists such as Piaget and Erikson see change as a more active process in which the individual tries to solve the conflicts and problems of everyday life successfully.

Conscious versus unconscious development

There is also disagreement about how conscious or aware people are of their own thoughts and actions. At one extreme are many behavioral learning theorists, who believe that awareness is the rule; at the other extreme are psychodynamic theorists such as Freud, who believe that people are consciously aware of only a small fraction of their thoughts and feelings. Interpretations of the degree of consciousness can be very important to a parent who is trying to understand why his child has "forgotten" to do her homework or to two friends who are trying to understand why they are fighting.

Breadth versus depth

Another difference concerns what theorists try to explain. Some theories focus on broad changes in people's development, whereas others try to explain more specific issues. For example, Erikson's theory attempts to explain the development of personality during the course of a life, whereas social learning theories limit themselves to explaining specific issues such as the development of sex roles and aggression. A third type of theory limits itself to a particular developmental process. The behavioral learning theories of Skinner and Pavlov, for example, attempt to explain all developmental change in terms of stimuli and responses.

Now that we have briefly discussed several of the ways in which theories of development differ, let us take a closer look at the theories that have been most influential and useful in the field of child and adolescent development.

PSYCHODYNAMIC THEORIES OF DEVELOPMENT

Psychodynamic theorists believe that development is an active, dynamic process that is most strongly influenced by the individual's social and emotional experiences. A child's development is thought to occur in a series of stages. At each stage, the child experiences conflicts that he must to some degree resolve in order to go on to the next stage. The psychodynamic theories that have been most influential in developmental psychology are those of Sigmund Freud and Erik Erikson.

Freudian Theory

Sigmund Freud (1856–1939) was the father of psychodynamic theory. His ideas have influenced almost all views of development, including many of the informal theories that we all hold. As you study Freud's theory, you will realize that popularly held notions about hidden or unconscious conflict, the Oedipus complex, and the importance of early childhood originated with Freud.

Freud was born in 1856 and lived in Vienna, Austria, for most of his life. An intense and brilliant student, he first became a physician and then a neurological researcher. His interest in children's development grew out of the discovery that the physical symptoms of certain adult patients were not really caused by physical illness at all. Rather, these symptoms, which included paralysis of the hands, arms, and legs, loss of speech, and even blindness, seemed to be caused by emotional factors.

First through the use of hypnosis and then by means of his own newly developed method of encouraging patients to talk freely, which he called **psychoanalysis,** Freud discovered that if his patients could remember certain hidden or unconscious emotional experiences, their symptoms would eventually disappear. Many of these forgotten experiences had occurred during early childhood; often, they involved emotionally upsetting sexual and aggressive conflicts. After discovering the power of these emotions, Freud devoted the rest of his career to developing his psychosexual theory of development and to helping people by using psychoanalysis. As we shall see, Freud's theory strongly emphasizes developmental stages, which are biologically determined but also influenced by experience, and unconscious processes. Although Freud's theory goes into a great deal of depth and is fairly complicated (his complete works run to more than twenty volumes), the main ideas are not hard to understand.

Many of Sigmund Freud's ideas about motivation, sexuality, and the unconscious have become so pervasive in contemporary society that we often do not realize that they originated with Freud.

The Three-Part Structure of Personality   Freud found it useful to think of each individual's personality as consisting of three parts, or functions: the id, the ego, and the superego. The **id,** which is present at birth, contains a basic, unprocessed sexual or life energy called **libido.** Libido refers to all of the ways in which human beings seek to increase pleasure and avoid discomfort by fulfilling their physical and emotional needs, a process known as the **pleasure principle.** The id tries to satisfy a person's biological needs and desires by motivating behavior that impulsively seeks to maximize pleasure and avoid discomfort without any regard to the realities involved. The newborn infant is all id, crying for food and comfort but with no realistic idea of how to get them.   **Id**

The **ego** — the rational, reality-oriented, problem-solving part of the personality — develops during early infancy as the infant encounters frustration in having her needs met. The ego functions according to the **reality principle,** a process by which the infant learns to delay her id-driven impulses for instant gratification and to find more realistic and appropriate ways of satisfying her needs.   **Ego**

The **superego** — the moral and ethical part of the personality — develops at the end of early childhood and includes the child's emerging sense of *conscience*, or right and wrong, as well as the *ego-ideal*, an idealized sense of how he should behave. The superego acts like an all-knowing, internalized parent, punishing the child with guilt for unacceptable sexual or aggressive thoughts, feelings, and actions and setting standards that he must live up to. Even though   **Superego** the superego can sometimes be overly moralistic and unreasonable, it does provide a person with the standards by which to regulate his moral conduct and take pride in his accomplishments.

Stages of Psychosexual Development   Freud believed that development occurs through a series of psychosexual stages, each focusing on a different area of the body. At each stage, developmental changes are caused by the conflicts a child or adolescent experiences in trying to satisfy her libido. According to Freud, overindulgence, deprivation, or unresolved conflicts among the id, ego, and superego could lead to a *fixation*, or blockage in development at that stage. In this view, an individual's personality traits reflect the patterns typical of the stage at which a fixation occurred. Freud's psychosexual stages are outlined in Table 2.1.

During the **oral stage,** from birth to about one year, an infant seeks physical and emotional pleasure through his mouth: through nursing a breast or bottle, chewing, biting, spitting, licking, and tasting the world. At first, the id and its pleasure principle are dominant. The infant is an impulsive, self-centered, and unrealistic being who is unable to delay pleasure or to distinguish between the wish to be fed or comforted and the reality of actually having these needs met. Although the infant desires instant satisfaction of his needs, even the most caring parent cannot always meet a baby's demands instantly, and sometimes the infant simply has to wait to be fed or changed. As he matures, a baby learns to tolerate such frustrating delays and to distinguish between the fantasy of being fed and the reality of getting food. If he receives adequate care, he will also learn to recognize and communicate his needs in a way that helps ensure that they are met. If he does not, however, and is overindulged or deprived during the oral stage, he might later develop an *oral-dependent* personality, finding it difficult to make decisions for himself and excessively relying on oral activities such as eating and smoking for a feeling of security and well-being.

By toddlerhood (age one to three), the infant has entered the **anal stage** of psychosexual development. According to Freud, the physical center of sexual pleasure shifts to the anus and to activities related to elimination. The toddler

Unresolved conflicts can lead to fixation

Oral stage

Anal stage

TABLE 2.1 *Freud's Psychosexual Stages and Developmental Processes*

Psychosexual Stage	Approximate Age	Description
Oral	Birth–1 year	The mouth is the focus of stimulation and interaction; feeding and weaning are central.
Anal	1–3 years	The anus is the focus of stimulation and interaction; elimination and toilet training are central.
Phallic	3–6 years	The genitals (penis, clitoris, and vagina) are the focus of stimulation; resolution of the Oedipus or Electra conflict, sex role, and moral development are central.
Latency	6–12 years	A period of suspended sexual activity follows Oedipus conflict resolution; energies shift to physical and intellectual activities.
Genital	12–adulthood	The genitals are the focus of stimulation with the onset of puberty; mature sexual relationships develop.

Developmental Processes

Development occurs through a series of psychosexual stages. In each stage the child focuses on a different area of her body, and how she invests her libido (sexual energy) in relationships with people and things reflects the concerns of the stage she is in. New areas of unconscious conflict among the id, ego, and superego, the three structures of personality, also occur. Conflicting pressures from the id to impulsively achieve pleasure, from the ego to act realistically by delaying gratification, and from the superego to fulfill moralistic obligations and to achieve idealistic standards, threaten the ego. The ego protects itself by means of unconscious defense mechanisms, which keep these conflicts from awareness by distorting reality.

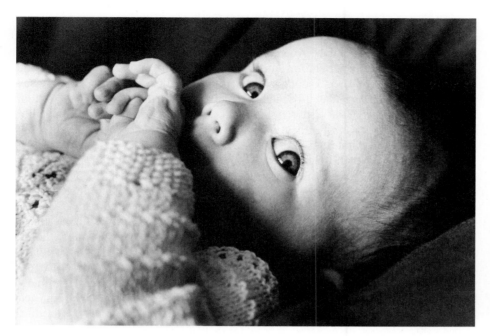

Psychodynamic theories focus on the inner life of the child. Freudian theory in particular emphasizes the importance of very early emotional experiences. Babies certainly show emotion, but because they cannot speak for themselves, critics say it is hard to assess whether early experiences matter as much as Freud claimed.

finds both pleasure and worry in her bowel movements. Pleasure derives both from the physical feeling of elimination and from the sense of accomplishment in these "productive" efforts. But she may worry that in giving up her body product she is losing a permanent part of herself. A second source of concern is the issue of control: who determines when, where, and in what conditions elimination occurs. According to Freud, a child who is treated too strictly or overindulged during this stage may develop an *anal-retentive* personality style, being overly strict and stingy in her feelings about herself and relationships with others, or an *anal-explosive* personality, having difficulty in controlling angry and aggressive feelings and impulses.

Gradually, a child's libidinal interest shifts to his genitals, and by age three or so he enters the **phallic stage** of development, when he is increasingly interested in gaining pleasure from touching or fondling his genitals, sometimes to the displeasure of his parents. During this stage, according to Freud, a child develops an intense sexual interest in the parent of the opposite sex. Even though children are largely unaware or unconscious of these feelings, their actions often reveal their intense desire to have this parent exclusively to themselves, and they are jealous or angry when their desires are not fulfilled. For example, children of this age frequently want to sleep in their parents' bed, and the snuggling that was once so comforting can now feel a little disturbing as the children act in ways that are openly seductive. They also ask disturbing questions, such as "Daddy, do you love me as much as Mommy?" and "Mommy, when I grow up, will you come and sleep with me in my bed and marry me like Daddy?"

The child's discovery of the intensity of his sexual feelings for one parent and feelings of jealousy and anger toward the other leads to a conflict: he does not want to give up the sexual desire, but he fears that if he does not do so, he will be punished by the same-sex parent for his angry wish to get rid of that parent. Freud named the desire for the opposite-sex parent and the disappointment that follows the realization that the same-sex parent will always win the sexual competition the **Oedipus conflict** when it occurs in boys and the **Electra conflict** when it occurs in girls.

One way these conflicts are resolved is through **identification**, the process by which the child becomes like the parent she fears (the mother for a girl and

Phallic stage

Sexual feelings for opposite-sex parent

Oedipus and Electra conflicts

the father for a boy). Over time, the child unconsciously takes into her own personality, or *internalizes* many of the important qualities of the same-sex parent. Being like his father protects a boy both from his own anger and from his fear of his father's retaliation, and at the same time allows him to continue to be close to his mother. Freud believed that identification with the same-sex parent is the basis for a child's development of a permanent sense of sexual identity. Identification is also the basis for superego development; the child internalizes the moral and ethical values of her parents and society and in the process develops a personal sense of right and wrong.

Freud's theory of how girls resolve the phallic stage is different from his theory for boys and also more confusing and controversial. He believed that a girl experiences feelings of envy and inferiority because she does not have a penis and feels contempt for all females once she discovers that they, too, lack penises. Imagining that her mother is responsible for this loss, a girl shifts her desire to her father, fantasizing that this will allow her to possess what she has lost. Later, according to Freud, she substitutes the wish to have a baby for the wish to have a penis (S. Freud, 1938, 1965). Because Freud believed that girls do not experience the fear of retaliation from their mothers that boys fear from their fathers, he theorized that girls never totally give up their libidinal interest in their fathers and never develop as strong a superego or sense of morality and ethics as boys do.

Latency period

Following the phallic stage, the child enters the **latency period.** During this period, psychosexual development is largely suspended or put "on hold," and a child's energies shift to physical and intellectual activities, although work to resolve the Oedipus or Electra conflict continues at a low-keyed and unconscious level.

Note that Freud's theory of how girls resolve the Oedipal conflict is not supported by research observations and thus has gained little support. His prejudicial attitudes toward women have been widely criticized, as we shall see.

Genital stage

The latency period ends when the child enters the **genital stage,** which emerges with the onset of puberty and continues throughout life. Freud believed that as boys and girls undergo the major physical changes associated with sexual maturity, their latent libidinal energy resurfaces with an intensity that can be disturbing. The center of sexual excitement is again the genitals, and the psychosexual task is to learn mature, adult patterns of heterosexual activity.

Defense Mechanisms In Freud's view, the ego has the job of managing the conflicts that arise among the three functions of personality. It accomplishes this through the use of **defense mechanisms,** or unconscious ways of reducing anxiety by distorting reality. Because both the id and the superego are essential to life (what would life be without impulse and passion or without conscience and ideals to strive for?), the ego cannot easily resolve the conflicts between them. The next best solution is to remove the conflict from awareness by burying it or making it unconscious.

During the phallic stage, for example, the ego is threatened by the irrational and unrealistic desires of the id for sexual gratification and by the equally irrational and unrealistic demands of the superego for responsible behavior. One of the ego's compromise solutions is the defense mechanism of identification. ("If you can't lick them, join them.") A second is **repression,** which means that a person forces upsetting thoughts and feelings out of consciousness, for example, by forgetting a significant experience. A third is **sublimation,** in which sexual and aggressive energies are channeled into safer outlets for passion, such as schoolwork, sports, hobbies, and friendships.

Regression is among the ego's other defense mechanisms. When faced with a situation that is so frustrating that it threatens to overwhelm the ego with

A Multicultural View

A Cross-cultural Test of Freudian Theory

Freud's developmental theory suggests that (a) children everywhere go through the same stages of psychosexual development, and (b) at each stage, excessive satisfaction (overindulgence) or excessive frustration (deprivation) may lead to a *fixation,* or partial failure in development, that makes progression to the next stage difficult. To test the validity of these two hypotheses across cultures, John Whiting and Irvin Child (1953) conducted cross-cultural research on socialization and child-rearing practices using data collected from seventy-five pre-industrial cultures.

Whiting and Child labeled fixations resulting from a high degree of indulgence *positive fixations* and those resulting from excessive frustration or deprivation *negative fixations.* During the oral stage, for example, if a child's demands for food are always indulged and too great an emphasis is placed on nursing and feeding, a positive fixation may occur. As a result, the child remains overly dependent on oral activities such as eating, drinking, and thumbsucking as sources of satisfaction or reward, at times to the exclusion of other activities. Negative fixation during the oral stage may result from a parent's excessive strictness about feeding, including strict limitations on how long a child can nurse and how much he can eat, and from a generally negative atmosphere where eating is experienced as upsetting rather than as pleasurable or satisfying. A negative oral fixation may be reflected in conflict and discomfort with eating, kissing, and other oral activities. Similar patterns of fixation may result from overindulgence or overly strict socialization regarding elimination and toilet training during the anal stage or regarding sexual interest and exploration during the genital stage.

Whiting and Child proposed that because illness was a major source of anxiety in pre-industrial cultures, the explanations they gave for the causes of illness would closely reflect the patterns for dealing with anxiety that members learned during the socialization process at each stage of psychosexual development. To test the hypothesized relationship between strict socialization and negative fixation, each of the seventy-five cultures was rated on how strict and anxiety producing its socialization was. Each culture was also categorized as to whether it used oral, anal, and/or sexual explanations of illness. For example, oral explanations blamed illness on certain foods or poisons or on verbal spells/incantations performed by other people. Anal explanations blamed illness on bodily products such as feces, urine, nail and hair clippings, and saliva; on the use of charms, curses, spells, incantations, rituals, and other compulsive behaviors; or on the failure to perform required rituals. The study also looked for dependence explanations (soul loss or spirit possession) and aggression explanations (disobedience to spirits or magical weapons).

The results of the study found strong support for a relationship between strict, depriving socialization and oral, anal, and sexual explanations of illness (which were thought to reflect socialization experiences during the oral, anal, and genital stages). Strong support was also found for aggression explanations but not for dependence explanations. When a similar procedure was used to test the relationship between socialization and positive fixation, however, no significant relationships were found.

Such cross-cultural evidence in support of "Freudian" concepts still remain tentative until additional studies with larger samples are conducted. Moreover, there is little evidence to date that cross-cultural differences in child-rearing result in differences in social competence during adulthood (Whiting, 1981).

anxiety, a person may *regress*, or return to an earlier and less mature way of handling problems. For example, a very tense and frightened five-year-old may not be able to tolerate the upset of being left at school for the first time and may regress by wetting her pants like a two-year-old in the anal stage. Adults can also regress. A classic example is the hard-driving workaholic executive who has just suffered a heart attack and is so overwhelmed with anxiety and dread by the conflict between his helplessness and his need to be strong and invulnerable that he acts like an irrational, demanding child, throwing tantrums and refusing to cooperate with those who are caring for him.

When present in moderation, such defense mechanisms (there are others) are extremely useful for healthy development. But if a person relies on them too heavily, the resulting distortion of reality often creates psychological problems.

Strengths and Weaknesses of Freud's Theory   One limitation of Freud's theory is that it is vague in defining key concepts and does not provide rules for systematically relating concepts to each other. For example, how do we really understand the concept of libido or id?

Weaknesses

Another weakness is that it is difficult or impossible to test many of Freud's conclusions. For one thing, Freud often did not make clear how he collected his data and on which observations he based specific conclusions. For another, the concepts of the theory are not scientifically testable because it is possible to predict contradictory outcomes. For example, will children who are frustrated in the anal stage develop habits of orderliness, cleanliness, and obedience, or will they be rebellious and messy? Why should a girl who fears her father not seek to be like her mother?

The theory is also culture-bound, meaning that it may not be true for development in other cultures. For example, the Oedipus complex is not likely to be observed in societies where children are raised by aunts or uncles or by other members of their community. And how can we explain the normal development of gender identity and morality among children raised by single parents?

Freud's theory has also been criticized on the grounds that it reflects his era's prejudices against women, and that it inaccurately portrays the realities of women's social, sexual, and moral development. For example, there is no evidence to support Freud's claim that women's moral development is less adequate than men's or that to achieve mature sexuality women must shift from clitoral to vaginal satisfaction (Gilligan, 1982; Mitchell, 1974).

A last major criticism is that Freud's conclusions are not based on direct observations of children but rather on the memories and fantasies of adults he treated for psychological problems. Not surprisingly, many of his findings are not supported by direct observations of children. For example, the development of the ego and basic trust seems to be more strongly related to physical closeness and responsive interaction between care-giver and infant than to the parent's fulfillment of the child's need for food, and the development of morality and sexual identity seems more closely tied to the child's desire for parental approval and to changes in her cognitive ability than to her fear of punishment.

Strengths

Among the strengths of Freud's theory are its breadth, the richness of its concepts and clinical observations, and its unwillingness to sacrifice complexity for easy understanding. Its concept of psychosexual stages attempts to explain personality development in a very comprehensive way.

Another strength of the theory is its appreciation of conflict, both within the developing personality and between the individual and society. Rather than overlooking the irrational, hidden, and contradictory aspects of developmental change, the theory uses such concepts as unconscious conflict and defense mechanisms to further our understanding. For example, some critics suggest that Freud's theory does accurately describe the mental representation and beliefs of men and women who live in a society that to a large extent continues to be male dominated and to discriminate against women in many ways. Rather than taking Freud's theory literally, they think that his theory is better viewed as a tool for understanding the myths that make it difficult for people to change unjust social realities (Mitchell, 1974).

Freud's influence

Freud's appreciation of the importance of the inner, emotional lives of children and their parents has led developmental experts and parents to look more carefully at how the qualitative aspects of early childhood experiences, and the parent-child relationship in particular, influence development. As a result, psychoanalytic theory has generated considerable research in these areas. Although difficult to scientifically test, Freud's rich observations and concepts have had a great impact on our thinking about children and their development.

In the next section, we discuss the theory of Erik Erikson, a theory that is very much an extension and elaboration of the work of Freud.

Erikson's Psychosocial Theory

Erik Erikson (1902–   ) grew up in Europe. He studied psychoanalysis with Freud's daughter, Anna, who strongly influenced his ideas about personality development. A fuller description of Erikson's life and work is presented in the accompanying Perspectives. In Erikson's view, personality development is a life-long process through which a person tries to resolve the conflicts created by biological maturation and the psychological, and social challenges that he encounters.

Psychosocial Stages of Development   Stages play a central role in Erikson's theory as they do in Freud's, but Erikson's stages of development differ from Freud's in some major ways. The first and most obvious difference is that Erikson believed that development did not end at adolescence but continued throughout a person's lifetime.

A second difference is that Erikson's stages are based on a series of social, rather than sexual, conflicts, which all individuals must successfully master in order to achieve adulthood. (These stages are summarized in Table 2.2.) For example, all school-age children in our contemporary society are expected to attend school in order to master certain basic academic and social skills. Doing so requires that they successfully resolve the crisis of industry and inferiority. The precise nature of this crisis may differ at different points in history and for different cultures (E. Erikson, 1982).

Erikson's theory also differs from Freud's in that it places much greater emphasis on social experience than on maturation; on rational, conscious, ego processes than on irrational and unconscious ones; and on the child as an active rather than a passive participant in the process of developmental change.

Erikson's first stage corresponds to Freud's oral stage and involves the psychosocial crisis of **trust versus mistrust**. Because infants are extremely helpless and dependent on their care-givers, during this period they develop a basic trust in their parents (and others) to care for them adequately; or, if they do not, they

Using Freud's theory as a starting point, Erik Erikson expanded it to cover the life span and modified the stages to place more emphasis on social encounters.

Trust versus mistrust

TABLE 2.2   Erikson's Psychosocial Stages and Developmental Processes

Psychosocial Stage	Approximate Age	Description
Trust versus mistrust	Birth–1 year	Focus on oral-sensory activity; development of trusting relationships with care-givers and self-trust
Autonomy versus shame and doubt	1–3 years	Focus on muscular-anal activity; development of control over bodily functions and activities
Initiative versus guilt	3–6 years	Focus on locomotor-genital activity; testing limits of self-assertion and purposefulness
Industry versus inferiority	6–12 years (latency period)	Focus on mastery, competence, and productivity
Identity versus role confusion	12–19 years (adolescence)	Focus on formation of identity and coherent self-concept
Intimacy versus isolation	19–25 years (early adulthood)	Focus on achievement of an intimate relationship and career direction
Generativity versus stagnation	25–50 years (adulthood)	Focus on fulfillment through creative, productive activity that contributes to future generations
Ego integrity versus despair	50 and older	Focus on belief in integrity of life, including successes and failures

Developmental Processes

Development of the ego or sense of identity occurs through a series of stages, each building on the preceding ones and each focused on successfully resolving a new psychosocial crisis between two opposing ego qualities. No stage is fully resolved, and more favorable resolution at an earlier stage facilitates achievement of later stages.

Autonomy versus shame and doubt

remain mistrustful of people, living in fear that they will be abandoned. According to Erikson, development of basic trust is fundamental to later stages of development because failure to do so may seriously interfere with a child's courage and ability to meet further challenges.

Having learned to trust others, the child must go on to resolve the crisis of **autonomy versus shame and doubt,** which corresponds with Freud's anal stage. Here he must learn to what degree he can take pride in his own body and in his ability to decide how to use it and to what degree he will experience shame and doubt about his choices. For example, it is inevitable that any child will make errors of both control and judgment during toilet training. A child who is treated respectfully for his failures as well as for his successes will eventually achieve autonomy (independence and self-direction) in this area, but one who is consistently shamed and humiliated may develop an inadequate, doubting sense of autonomy.

Initiative versus guilt

During Erikson's third stage, the child focuses on her genitals as a source of pleasure and on achieving greater independence of movement or locomotion and overall activity. Both contribute to the psychosocial crisis of **initiative versus guilt.** (Initiative refers to beginning new activities and exploring new ideas.) This crisis involves all conflicts that occur when a child takes on more than she can handle, including the Oedipus conflict. It is easy to underestimate how strong and frightening a child's feelings and impulses can be at this age. If a child's loving and hating feelings and her conflicting impulses to be independent and dependent are ignored, belittled, or ridiculed, her resulting negative feelings can

Perspectives

Erik Erikson's Identity Crisis: An Autobiographical Perspective

How do theorists' own life experiences influence their theories of development? In one of his many books, Erik Erikson writes about his own identity crises and how they influenced his developmental theory. Later in this chapter we consider how the personal experiences of two other theorists, B. F. Skinner and Jean Piaget, influenced their theoretical work. When you have finished reading this chapter, it might be interesting to consider how well each of their theories explains their developmental experiences.

Erik Erikson was born in 1902 and grew up in southern Germany with his mother, who was Danish, and her husband, a German pediatrician. Erikson recalls that "all through my earlier childhood, they kept secret from me the fact that my mother had been married previously; and that I was the son of a Dane who had abandoned her before my birth. . . . As children will do . . . I more or less forgot the period before the age of three, when mother and I had lived alone" (E. Erikson, 1975, p. 27).

As he entered adolescence, reports Erikson,

identity problems sharpen[ed] with the turn of puberty when images of future roles [became] inescapable. My stepfather was the only professional man in an intensely Jewish small bourgeois family, while I . . . was blond and blue-eyed, and grew flagrantly tall. Before long, then, I was referred to as a "goy" [outsider] in my stepfather's temple, while to my schoolmates was a "Jew." . . . Although during World War I, I tried des-

perately to be a good German chauvinist, [I] soon became a "Dane" when Denmark remained neutral. (pp. 27, 28)

During this period, Erikson decided that he would be an artist and a writer — a rejection of the more middle-class values of his family. He spent most of his time traveling, painting, and writing, and he occasionally taught art.

In the Europe of my youth, the choice of occupational identity of "artist" meant, for many, a way of life rather than a specific occupation — or, indeed, a way of making a living — and, as today, it could mean primarily an anti-establishment way of life. . . . At the time, like other youths with artistic or literary aspirations, I became intensely alienated from everything my bourgeois family stood for. At that point, I *set out* to be different. [After graduation from high school] I went to art school, but always again took to wandering. I now consider those years an important part of my training. (pp. 25, 28)

Erikson recalls that his search for a professional identity also involved crisis. "To return briefly to the stepson theme: one might suspect that later on I had to succeed in making a professional lifestyle out of my early existence on what Paul Tillich has described as a life on boundaries, for throughout my career I worked in institutional contexts for which I did not have the usual credentials — except, of course, for my psychoanalytic training proper" (p. 30). Before he studied psychoanalysis, he was an artist: "Psy-

be very destructive. Also, a child's tendency to try new things that are beyond her level of skill and experience may lead to guilt about not fulfilling parental expectations.

Erikson interprets the next stage, which runs roughly from age six to twelve and corresponds with Freud's latency stage, as one when children must resolve feelings of **industry versus inferiority.** As children leave the protection of their family and enter the world of school, they must successfully master a new set of challenges. They must develop a belief in their ability to learn the basic intellectual and social skills required for full membership in our modern industrial society and a sense of being able to start and complete tasks successfully. Thus, failure to be "productive" can lead to a belief in their own inferiority. The child who consistently fails in school is in danger of feeling alienated from society or of thoughtlessly conforming in order to gain a sense of belonging.

Industry versus inferiority

The physical changes of puberty, which include sexual maturation, occur during the next stage, when adolescents must resolve the crisis of **identity versus role confusion.** Teenagers undergo reevaluation of who they are in many areas of development, including the physical, sexual, intellectual, and social. Frequently, conflicts from earlier stages resurface. As we see in Chapter 16, modern industrial society does not make it particularly easy for teenagers to establish identities that meet both their needs for independence and individuality and society's expectations for interdependence and conformity. Premature choice of identity, prolonged confusion about one's role, or choice of a permanently "negative" identity are three potentially destructive outcomes of role confusion.

Identity versus role confusion

chology as such did not attract me [and] I must concede that the first course in psychology I ever took was also the first (and the last) I flunked" (pp. 22, 23).

It was not until Erikson was almost thirty and moved to Austria at the invitation of a close friend that his career as a psychoanalyst and developmental theorist really began. "My own training in psychoanalysis was conducted by Anna Freud, who accepted me as a fellowship candidate on the basis of the fact that she and her friends had witnessed my work with children as a private tutor and as a teacher in a small private school" (p. 24). After studying and practicing psychoanalysis in Vienna, Erikson was forced to leave Austria by the rise of Hitler. Erikson emigrated to the United States, where he has lived and worked ever since.

Erikson's career has been exceptional, both because of the creative work he has produced and the fame he has achieved and because he has done this without the benefit of even a college degree, much less any other professional credentials. In the 1930s, Erikson worked as a psychoanalyst with children and debated whether to return to school for a professional degree. Instead, he accepted a research appointment at Yale Medical School. He then joined the Yale Institute of Human Relations, where he worked with an interdisciplinary team of psychologists, psychiatrists, and anthropologists, and conducted field studies of the Sioux Indians in South Dakota.

In the 1940s, he moved to California to study the life histories of children living in Berkeley and then the lives of the Yurok Indians. He joined the faculty of the University of California at Berkeley in the early 1950s but was soon fired because he refused to sign a "loyalty oath," part of the fanatical anti-Communist crusade of Senator Joe McCarthy. Erikson says of this experience, "I was fired before the first year was up, and after being reinstated as politically dependable, I resigned because of the firing of others who were not so judged. As I think back on that controversy now, it was a test of our American identity; for when the papers told us foreign-born among the nonsigners to 'go back where we came from,' we suddenly felt quite certain that our apparent disloyalty to the soldiers in Korea was, in fact, quite in line with what they were said to be fighting for. The United States Supreme Court has since confirmed our point of view" (pp. 42–43).

> It would seem almost self-evident now [says Erikson] how the concepts of "identity" and "identity crisis" emerged from my personal, clinical, and anthropological observations in the thirties and forties. I do not remember when I started to use these terms; they seemed naturally grounded in the experience of emigration, immigration, and Americanization. . . . I will not describe the pathological side of my identity confusion, which included disturbances for which psychoanalysis seemed, indeed, the treatment of choice. . . . No doubt, my best friends will insist that I needed to name this crisis and to see it in everybody else in order to really come to terms with it in myself. (pp. 43, 26)

According to Erikson, the formation of identity presents a major crisis during adolescence.

Postadolescent stages

Erikson's final three stages occur after adolescence. The first is **intimacy versus isolation**: the young adult must develop the capacity to develop close and committed relationships with others while tolerating the fears of fusion and loss of identity that such intense intimacy raises. In adulthood and midlife, a person faces the crisis of **generativity versus stagnation.** Generativity is the feeling that one's work, family, and other activities are both personally satisfying and socially meaningful in ways that contribute to future generations: stagnation results when life no longer seems purposeful. Finally, during later adulthood and old age, people must confront the psychosocial crisis of **ego integrity versus despair.** Ego integrity refers to the capacity to look back upon the strengths and weaknesses of one's life with a sense of dignity, optimism, and wisdom. It is in conflict with the despair resulting from physical problems, economic difficulties, social isolation, and lack of meaningful work experienced by many elderly in our society.

Three developmental forces

According to Erikson, throughout these eight stages an individual's personality development will be influenced by three interrelated developmental forces: his biological and physical strengths and limitations; his unique life circumstances and developmental history, including early family experiences and how well he has resolved the previous developmental crises; and the particular social, cultural, and historical forces at work during his lifetime — for example, racial prejudice, rapid technological change, or war.

Conflicts are never fully resolved

According to Erikson, people never fully resolve any of their psychosocial conflicts. Rather, they achieve more or less favorable ratios of trust to mistrust, industry to inferiority, ego integrity to despair, and so on. For example, if the early adulthood crisis of intimacy versus isolation is resolved strongly in favor of intimacy, the person is thought to be better equipped for future developmental challenges; a less strong leaning toward intimacy may make things more difficult. Crises are also not necessarily resolved at certain points in life; unresolved conflicts may resurface and achieve fuller resolution later in life.

Strengths and Weaknesses of Erikson's Theory Erikson's theory shares some of the major limitations of Freud's psychodynamic theory. Erikson's concepts are difficult to define in a way that allows them to be scientifically tested, and because his evidence is based mainly on personal observations, it is hard to replicate. For example, until recently, researchers studying how adolescents resolve the crisis of identity versus role confusion (see Chapter 16) have found it difficult to determine just which of the many aspects of personal identity are most important or how their presence can be reliably measured.

Weaknesses

Although Erikson makes it clear that development may be influenced by specific social, cultural, and historical differences, his stages are strongly biased toward Western European and North American experiences and thus may not be valid for much of the rest of the world's population.

Two important strengths of Erikson's theory are its understandability and its ability to stimulate new ideas. Because its concepts are simpler and more straightforward than Freud's, they help make psychodynamic theory accessible to a wider audience. Erikson's extension of developmental stages through the life cycle has significantly contributed to the growing interest in adult development during the middle and later years (Levinson, 1978, 1986); and his systematic linking of each stage to the social, cultural, and historical challenges or crises of normal development that we can readily recognize in our own lives makes it an attractive theory to both experts and newcomers to developmental psychology. Erikson's theory is also more hopeful than Freud's: by learning which social conditions help or hinder development, we may create greater possibilities for fostering development and preventing developmental difficulties.

Strengths

Erikson's insights about the overall process of identity formation and, more specifically, about identity conflicts during adolescence and young adulthood have been very useful to parents, teachers, and developmental experts as well as to youngsters themselves.

BEHAVIORAL AND SOCIAL LEARNING THEORIES OF DEVELOPMENT

Learning is generally defined as relatively permanent changes in observable behavior as a result of experience. Compared with psychodynamic theories, learning theories are fairly straightforward and rely on a few basic concepts to explain development. This tendency to reduce development to simple learning, coupled with the fact that learning theorists have little to say about developmental stages or processes, leads some developmentalists to think of these theories more as approaches than as full-fledged theories of development. Nevertheless, because they do share with other developmental theories the goal of creating a systematic framework for describing and understanding developmental change, we have chosen to describe them as theories rather than approaches. These theories clearly emphasize learning rather than maturation and conscious rather than unconscious developments. They also are narrow in their focus compared to Freud's and Erikson's theories.

Behavioral Theory

Behavioral theorists believe that the learning experiences that occur during the course of a person's life are the sources of developmental change. Thus, by modifying existing learning opportunities or by creating new ones, the course of an individual's development can be changed.

Ivan Pavlov, a Russian scientist who lived from 1849 to 1936, and B. F. Skinner, an American born in 1904, are separated by history, geography, and culture, and their theories emphasize different models of learning. Nevertheless, most learning theorists rely on the work of both in describing and understanding development. As behaviorists, both theorists claim that only observable behavior is useful in understanding learning and development and that in time all developmental activity, no matter how complex, will be explained by one basic set of laws of learning.

Pavlov: Classical Conditioning Pavlov began developing his behavioral theory while studying digestion in dogs, work for which he won the Nobel prize. While measuring how much saliva the dogs produced in response to food, he discovered that the dogs began to salivate even before they could smell or see the food. Stimuli that were connected or associated with the food, such as the sound of the footsteps of the feeder, seemed to have the power to elicit salivation.

In his well-known experiments, Pavlov rang a bell just before feeding a dog. Eventually, the dog salivated whenever it heard the bell, even if it did not then receive any food. Pavlov called the process by which the dog learned to respond in this way **classical conditioning.**

When the experiments began, the sound of the bell was a neutral stimulus because it really did not affect the dog's response to food. But once its sound had been paired with the food a number of times, it lost its neutrality; in Pavlov's terms, it became a learned, or **conditioned, stimulus** because it now had the power to bring about salivation. The salivation itself was called the **conditioned response.** Pavlov named the food stimulus the **unconditioned stimulus** and the dog's responding salivation the **unconditioned response** because the connection between the two was an inborn, **unconditioned reflex** — that is, an involuntary reaction, similar to the eyeblink.

Through the process of classical conditioning, reflexes that are present at birth may help infants to learn about and participate in the world around them. For example, classical conditioning of the sucking reflex, which allows newborn infants to suck reflexively in response to a touch to the lips, has been reported using a tone as the conditioned stimulus (Lipsitt & Kaye, 1964). Other stimuli — such as the sight of the bottle and the mother's face, smile, and voice — may also become conditioned stimuli for sucking and may elicit sucking responses even before the bottle touches the baby's lips. (See Figure 2.1.) Because attempts to classically condition a variety of other infant reflexes have met with mixed success, the developmental role of classical conditioning may be limited, at least during infancy (Sameroff & Cavanaugh, 1979).

Nevertheless, numerous examples of classical conditioning not directly tied to reflex responses occur throughout development. For example, a college student who has had a very negative experience in a particular math course may develop "math anxiety" in response to anything mathematical, even balancing her own checkbook. On a more positive note, a child who loves cuddling his mother or father may come to love bedtime stories, not necessarily because of the stories themselves, but because of their association with bedtime cuddling.

Skinner: Operant Conditioning Like Pavlov's theory, B. F. Skinner's learning theory, known as **operant conditioning,** is based largely on research with animals, in this case rats and pigeons. Both classical and operant conditioning maintain that *all* learning and developmental change, in both humans and lower order animals, can eventually be explained by one set of basic scientific laws of behavior.

An important difference between operant and classical conditioning should be noted. The starting point in classical conditioning is a small number of inborn,

Conditioning in infancy

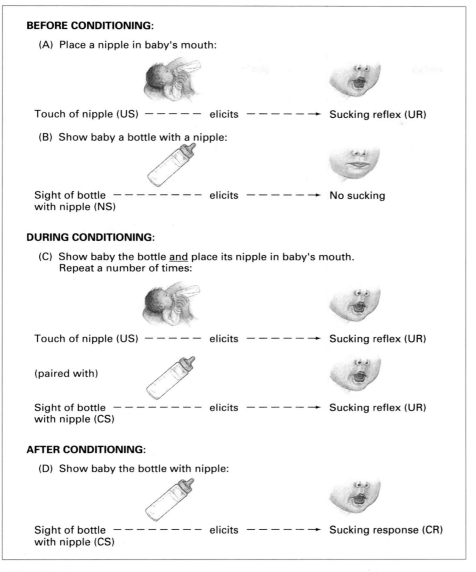

BEFORE CONDITIONING:

(A) Place a nipple in baby's mouth:

Touch of nipple (US) — — — — elicits — — — — → Sucking reflex (UR)

(B) Show baby a bottle with a nipple:

Sight of bottle — — — — — — elicits — — — — → No sucking
with nipple (NS)

DURING CONDITIONING:

(C) Show baby the bottle <u>and</u> place its nipple in baby's mouth. Repeat a number of times:

Touch of nipple (US) — — — — elicits — — — — → Sucking reflex (UR)

(paired with)

Sight of bottle — — — — — — elicits — — — — → Sucking reflex (UR)
with nipple (CS)

AFTER CONDITIONING:

(D) Show baby the bottle with nipple:

Sight of bottle — — — — — — elicits — — — — → Sucking response (CR)
with nipple (CS)

FIGURE 2.1
Illustration of Classical Conditioning
In the above example, the nipple in the baby's mouth is an unconditioned stimulus (US), which without any prior conditioning brings about, or "elicits," the sucking reflex, an unconditioned response (UR). (A) The nipple in mouth elicits a sucking reflex; (B) the sight of a bottle is a neutral stimulus (NS) and has no effect; (C) once the sight of the bottle (neutral stimulus) is repeatedly paired with the nipple in the mouth (UCS), the sight of the bottle becomes a conditioned (learned) stimulus (CS), which now elicits sucking, the conditioned response (CR).

unconditioned reflexes such as the sucking and eyeblink reflexes, none of which is under an individual's voluntary control. These are also called *respondent behaviors*. In contrast, the starting point in operant conditioning can be any response that an individual makes as she *voluntarily* reacts to stimuli in the environment. These are called *operant behaviors* and include crying, smiling, head turning, and even sucking (if controlled by the individual). Because we have more operant behaviors than respondent behaviors, operant conditioning has been much more widely applied in understanding and influencing child and adolescent development.

Classical conditioning involves involuntary behaviors

Operant conditioning involves voluntary behaviors

B. F. Skinner has developed one of the most popular forms of behaviorism — operant conditioning. Its success may stem from its many practical applications.

Punishment versus negative reinforcement

Skinner's idea of operant conditioning is based on a simple concept called reinforcement. **Reinforcement** is defined as the process in which the likelihood of a particular response occurring again is strengthened or increased as a consequence of having been followed by a certain type of stimulus. There are two types of reinforcement. **Positive reinforcement** occurs when following a particular response (a baby's saying, "da-da," for example), a rewarding stimulus (such as his father smiling and saying "good boy!") is added that strengthens the response and increases the likelihood that the response ("da-da") will occur again under similar circumstances. **Negative reinforcement** occurs when following a particular response an undesirable or unpleasant stimulus is removed, thereby strengthening the response and its likelihood of recurrence. For instance, Sarah, a four-year-old, misbehaves at the dinner table. When she does so, her parents give her their attention, which she negatively reinforces by ending her crying and misbehaving.

Punishment is often confused with negative reinforcement, but they really are quite different. Whereas negative reinforcement strengthens behavior, **punishment** weakens a behavioral response by either adding an unpleasant stimulus or by removing a pleasurable one following the response's occurrence. Punishment stops or suppresses behavior, and it may include physical (e.g., spanking) or verbal (e.g., yelling) stimuli or the removal of privileges. In Sarah's case, talking to her angrily or threatening her with no dessert might serve to suppress her misbehavior at the dinner table. Contrary to what many believe, however, punishment rarely, if ever, eliminates the unwanted behavior. (A fuller discussion of punishment is presented in Chapter 10.)

How consistently must reinforcement follow a particular response in order for learning to take place? Surprisingly, people often learn more effectively in response to **partial reinforcement** (when a response is reinforced only some of the time) than to total reinforcement. The compulsive quality of gambling may

Perspectives

Skinner's "Dark Year"

In an article with the above title, psychologist Alan Elms (1981) proposes that a theorist's own life history and personality characteristics are likely to influence the choice of a theoretical model. Using information gathered from Skinner's own scientific and autobiographical writings and from what others have written about him, the article describes Skinner's "Dark Year," a period during his youth when he failed as a creative writer and seemed to experience a major identity crisis that ultimately influenced his theoretical work. Elms also reports that Skinner experienced a second developmental crisis during "mid-life," which significantly influenced his writing of the novel Walden Two. *In the discussion that follows, however, we limit ourselves to discussing Skinner's first identity crisis and how it may have influenced his developmental theory.*

In his autobiography (1976), B. F. Skinner jokingly mentions an identity crisis, reporting that when he woke up one morning, he found part of himself — his left arm — missing. Following a frantic search, he found it "twisted sharply under his neck, with the circulation cut off" (Elms, 1981, p. 472). During his last term at college, Skinner felt that he

had to choose an occupation; he decided to become a writer. He had quite a bit of experience writing for college publications, and Robert Frost had sent him a letter encouraging his writing. Skinner decided to spend a year writing. Although his father was skeptical, he agreed to support his son at home for the year — as long as he would agree to "go to work" at the end of that year if his writing career was not well under way.

According to psychologist Alan Elms, who wrote an article about Skinner's identity crisis, Skinner was already conceding failure within three months, saying that "the results were disastrous. I frittered away my time" (Skinner, 1967, p. 394). "The truth was," he wrote later, "I had no reason to write anything. I had nothing to say, and nothing about my life was making any change in that condition" (Skinner, 1976, pp. 264–265). He thought his parents were at fault for "unwittingly forcing" him into this situation; he also claimed that they ridiculed him for having "effeminate" interests (Skinner, 1976, pp. 264–265). Further, he blamed his hometown, Scranton, for being "ready to quench any ideas of my own I may have. . . . I am too sensitive to my surroundings to stand it." Nevertheless, he felt bound by the agreement with his father to give writing a try for a year: "I

Reinforcement takes many forms. For this child the sight and sound of pulling a tissue out of a box are positive reinforcers that encourage him to continue his tissue-pulling behavior.

found myself committed, with no hope of reprieve, to what I came to call the Dark Year" (Skinner, 1976, p. 265).

Elms believes that Skinner found the Dark Year so unhappy for several reasons. "Not only did Skinner discover that he was unable to write anything important, but he was often the object (or fancied himself to be the object) of jibes and innuendos from people who would have considered even a successful writing career as inappropriate for a healthy young man" (Elms, 1981, p. 472). "I was desperately hungry for intellectual stimulation," Skinner wrote, "but there was no one with whom I could talk or even correspond seriously. I was confined to the autistic, not to say auto-erotic, satisfactions to be found in a notebook" (Skinner, 1976, pp. 271, 279–280). Lonely and isolated, Skinner began to spend long hours sitting in the family library. He wrote,

> Cleverness lost its glamour for me. . . . Nothing is worth doing. . . . The world considers me lazy because I do not earn bread. The world expects of me that I should measure up to its standard of strength, which means that if I "got a job" for eight hours of office work . . . I should be a man. . . . I see clearly now that

the only thing left for me to do in life is to justify myself for doing nothing. (Skinner, 1976, pp. 282–283)

Skinner began to see his way out of his Dark Year when he discovered the writings of Watson and Pavlov. Their ideas about behavioral learning "gave focus to his previously scattered reading in psychology" (Elms, 1981, p. 473) and, soon, to a clearer vocational purpose and sense of personal identity. Skinner came to think of himself as a behaviorist, and he was accepted to Harvard's graduate program in psychology. In a letter to his parents at the end of his first year at Harvard, he wrote, "I am looked upon as the leader of a certain school of psychological theories. . . . The behaviorists, whom I represent, have acquired a good deal of strength this year. . . . Many of the new men, coming here this year, will come over to our 'party,' giving us moral and physical support." Convinced that his position was correct and others' theories wrong, he began to develop a group of followers. Soon his identity as a behaviorist was firmly in place. His identity crisis was resolved, at least for the moment, by his wholehearted acceptance of the ideology of radical behaviorism.

be due, in part, to the very slim and unpredictable number of payoffs, or reinforcements available, which causes the gambler to repeat his response over and over. Similarly, the negative behavior of a "problem child" may be especially reinforced by the inconsistency of her parents' attention.

Extinction occurs when the removal of a reinforcer leads to the disappearance of the response it was maintaining. Generally, responses that are no longer reinforced tend to be extinguished. Responses that have been partially reinforced, however, are more resistant to extinction because the pattern of reinforcement is variable and unpredictable. Our gambler, for instance, has no way of knowing for sure whether bad luck or bad card dealing is keeping him from getting his payoff, so he keeps trying. Likewise, a child who receives occasional but unpredictable attention from her parents for obnoxious behavior may continue to act that way long after the reinforcements have stopped.

Strengths and Weaknesses of Behavioral Theories   The main strengths of behavioral theories are the simplicity of the basic ideas and the ease with which behavioral techniques can be applied successfully in various situations. Teachers, psychologists, and parents find the concepts relatively easy to learn and to apply. In the classroom, teachers use behavioral learning techniques to manage difficult children and to help children control their behavior more effectively. Psychologists use these methods to help parents reduce their children's bedwetting and temper tantrums and work out better relationships with their teenagers. Behavioral learning techniques have also been used to help children with retardation or behavioral disorders increase their socially desirable behaviors and extinguish those that are undesirable.

Nonetheless, the simplicity of behavioral theories and the ease with which they can be applied can be drawbacks. Many critics believe that the behavioral learning approach loses sight of the humanity of children by reducing their activity to simple patterns of stimuli, responses, and reinforcers. These critics claim that a child's unwillingness to take out the garbage, achievements in school, social relationships, and feelings about himself cannot really be understood in terms of reinforcement theory.

One practical problem concerns choosing appropriate reinforcers. Although we may think that food, money, and praise are effective reinforcers, all depend on the conditions and the subjective judgment of the person whose behavior is to be influenced. For example, if a child feels that she is being manipulated or taken advantage of, none of the typical rewards at an adult's disposal will get her to do better at school. A second problem is the choice of the behavior to be reinforced. Even a promise of a trip to Disney World as a reward for a report card with all A's is likely to fail if the child lacks the academic background or study skills needed to make that goal a realistic possibility.

Cognitive behavioral approaches that use reinforcers to modify thoughts as well as actions have increasingly challenged the traditional view that behaviors must be directly observable to be modified (Meichenbaum, 1977). Because children's thoughts, feelings, and expectations about themselves and others often influence their actions in important ways, modification of children's thinking by means of reinforcement can be an effective way of influencing their actions. For example, impulsive children have been successfully trained to talk to themselves in ways that enhance their development of self-control (Meichenbaum & Goodman, 1971).

Another important weakness of behaviorism involves the issues of power and control. The reinforcement situation is based on an inequality of power. People who control a greater number of the reinforcers (teachers, parents, other adults) can use this power to influence those who control less of the reinforcers and who are therefore less powerful (children). Use of behavioral learning tech-

Margin notes:

Strengths

Weaknesses

Cognitive behavioral approaches

Risk of ignoring children's feelings

niques to change children's behaviors may be harmful, say its critics, because behavioral theory provides little or no insight about human beings and their developmental needs.

Behaviorists respond to this criticism by claiming that because operant conditioning can be found in almost every aspect of our everyday life, it is better to use its techniques in constructive than destructive ways. But this response sidesteps the issue. A more effective response is to note that behavioral learning should be viewed *solely* as a technique and used only when guided by a clear set of understandings and values. For example, the use of the "time-out" technique for controlling the disruptive behavior of an emotionally disturbed child may be a helpful and constructive part of a broader treatment approach that seeks to understand the sources of upset. It is sensitive to what the child is thinking and feeling about things, including the "time-outs," and it is committed to discovering solutions that are developmentally best for the child.

Time-out technique

Social Learning Theory

Operant conditioning helps to explain why people engage in some behaviors more (or less) frequently. But it does not really explain how more complex behaviors develop, how children learn certain behaviors without ever actually performing them or being reinforced for them, or what the importance of various learned behaviors is for human development. Why does a preschooler suddenly begin to talk sternly to his stuffed animals when he puts them to bed? Why does a thirteen-year-old suddenly adopt a punk look? Social learning theorists attempt to answer such questions.

Even though social learning theorists accept the importance of classical and operant conditioning, their approach focuses on the important ways in which social influences and a child's cognitive activity (including her beliefs and expectations) influence learning and development. They argue that sudden changes in behavior are not learned through either classical or operant conditioning but rather through observation of others (Bandura, 1977). The preschooler observes his parents' child-rearing behaviors and imitates them while playing with his animals, and the teenager sees others dressing in punk clothes and imitates what she sees. Although what the child learns may not precisely duplicate what he observes, it is close enough for us to recognize the model on which it is based.

Some theorists believe that observational learning involves more than mere imitation of the behaviors of other people. They suggest that through observing and trying out what they have seen, children actually internalize important qualities of the models they observe. Called **modeling**, this process is very similar to the psychodynamic concept of identification.

Learning by observing models

Although social learning theorists emphasize observable behavior and reinforcement, many also believe that there is more to social learning than meets the eye. To put it simply, a child who learns by observation must be able to pay *attention* to the model, must *remember* what she has learned until there is an opportunity to try it out, and must possess enough physical or *motor skill* actually to try out what she has learned. Observational learning occurs even among infants, but it becomes increasingly important as children get older and become better able to pay attention to models and to remember and later try out what they have observed.

Current formulations of social learning theory emphasize the importance of **reciprocal determinism** in learning and the development of personality. According to this view, change is a result of the mutual interaction of a person and his stimulus environment; people actively participate in determining and changing situations and are not merely passively influenced by them. Their attitudes,

Mutual interaction of individual and stimulus environment

expectations, and feelings about themselves and others must also be considered if their development is to be more fully understood (Bandura, 1986; Mischel, 1984).

Strengths and Weaknesses of Social Learning Theory   In comparison with the behavioral theories, the social learning theory provides greater flexibility in defining the basic unit of what is learned because it does not limit its scope solely to observable behaviors. As a result, teachers, parents, and other people involved with children find social learning concerns very useful for understanding complicated changes such as learning to ride a bike and the development of sexual identity and morality.

But this approach, like the other learning theories, lacks an overall theoretical explanation for development, and underestimates the importance of children's unobservable thoughts and feelings. If we want to understand how children develop the ability to think and solve problems, and how these abilities influence other aspects of development, we need to consider Piaget's theory of cognitive development, which focuses on these issues.

COGNITIVE THEORIES
OF DEVELOPMENT

The two theories of cognitive development discussed in this section — Piaget's cognitive theory and information processing theory — share a strong interest in how children's thinking and problem solving develop and how such cognitive activities contribute to the overall process of child and adolescent development.

Piaget's Theory

Jean Piaget (1896–1980) was one of the most influential figures in developmental psychology. Just as Freud's ideas have radically changed our thinking about human emotional development, Piaget's ideas have changed our understanding of the development of human thinking, or **cognition**.

Born in 1896 in Switzerland, Piaget became interested in scientific research as a young child and published his first scientific article at the age of ten. A naturalist, philosopher, and mathematician, he devoted his early research to observing the development of his own children, and much of his later work was an effort to expand on the theories he devised as a father.

Piaget's theory of cognitive development views thinking as a conscious process and places major emphasis on developmental stages that are closely tied to maturation. Although the theory focuses on the single issue of cognitive change, it does so in great depth.

Key Principles of Piaget's Theory   Piaget believed that children's thinking develops in a series of increasingly complex stages, or periods, each of which incorporates and revises those that precede it. For example, Piaget believed that preschool children are highly egocentric in their thinking. Piaget did not mean that children are selfish: rather, they are self-centered and not yet able to observe situations from a perspective other than their own (Piaget, 1959). For example, a preschool child might say to his mother, who is in the next room, "I'm putting this here," totally unaware that she cannot possibly see where her son is pointing or to what object he is referring. A four-year-old girl who replied, "a little red wagon," when asked what her father would like for his birthday was not revealing

Jean Piaget's ideas did not become popular in North America until the 1960s — relatively late in his career. Since that time they have stimulated much research and have found wide support among educators.

Perspectives

Piaget's *Méthode Clinique*

Piaget's unique *méthode clinique* (clinical method) for studying the growth of thought in children diverges significantly from the more systematic and controlled psychological experiments that have been the hallmark of modern developmental psychology. It combines careful naturalistic observation, individual case study, and a flexible approach to forming and testing a series of changing hypotheses that emerge from the researcher's interactions with the child being studied. (See Chapter 1 for a review of research methods in developmental psychology.)

In using the method himself, Piaget often began with careful naturalistic observation of the child's behaviors and interactions with her surroundings; he then developed hypotheses concerning the structure and rules that underlie the behaviors and interactions. Next, he tested these hypotheses by slightly changing the surroundings, either by rearranging the materials, by posing the problem in a different way, or by suggesting to the subject a different response than the one predicted from the theory.

In the following example, Piaget reports his observations of his own infant, Laurent, who at the age of nine months is in the process of discovering object permanence:

> Laurent is placed on a sofa between a coverlet (A) on the right and a wool garment (B) on the left. I place my watch under A; he gently raises the coverlet, perceives part of the object, uncovers it, and grasps it. The same thing happens a second and a third time. . . . I then place the watch under B; Laurent watches this maneuver attentively, but at the moment the watch has disapppeared under B, he turns back toward A and searches for the object under that screen. I again place the watch under B; he again searches for it under A. (cited in J. Phillips, 1969, p. 28)

The Piagetian method of investigating children's thinking is exceptional in that it seeks to understand the reasons and rules that underlie their beliefs, opinions, and approaches to solving problems. Central to this method are conversations with each child about the responses that he has given; the goal is to assess the quality of thinking involved, regardless of whether an answer is "right" or "wrong" (Beard, 1969, p. xiv).

The following example, which Piaget designed to better understand the child's conception of number, clearly illustrates the highly interactive nature of the *méthode clinique.* The child was first presented with a number of coins and a large number of flowers and then asked how many flowers could be purchased with the coins if the price of each flower were one coin. The following is a transcript of one such interaction:

> Gui *(four years, four months)* puts 5 flowers opposite 6 pennies, then made a one-for-one exchange of 6 pennies for 6 flowers *(taking the extra flower from the reserve supply).* The pennies were in a row and the flowers bunched together: "What have we done? — We've exchanged them. — Then is there the same number of flowers and pennies? — No. — Are there more on one side? — Yes. — Where? — There *(pennies). The exchange was again made, but this time the pennies were put in a pile and the flowers in a row.)* Is there the same number of flowers and pennies? — No. — Where are there more? — Here *(flowers).* — And here *(pennies)*? — Less. (Piaget & Szeminska, 1952)

Critics have pointed out that shifting experimental procedure to fit the responses of a particular subject makes it difficult for other researchers to repeat or replicate the procedure and makes it more likely that the child may be influenced by the experimenter's expectations about how she should answer. Defenders of the procedure emphasize that efforts are made to deliberately provide the child opportunities for responses that do not fit the theory and that Piaget believed that because the structure of knowledge is expressed through action, the investigator must continually adjust his own responses if he is to follow the child's actions and discover their underlying structure (Phillips, 1969). What both defenders and critics do agree on is that Piaget's work has revolutionized our thinking about cognitive development and has generated an enormous amount of productive work in this area.

---

selfishness. More likely, she was unable to distinguish her own perspective about what would make a pleasing gift from her father's perspective. As children enter their school years and have more and more contact with other children, they become increasingly able to see the world from another person's perspective.

Egocentrism

What precisely makes a child develop from one state to the next? Piaget answered this question in several ways. First, there are the methods by which a child responds to new experiences. He may interpret new ideas or experiences on the basis of the concepts he already knows (Piaget referred to these organized patterns of thought and actions as **schemes**). This process is called **assimilation**. For example, a preschooler may see a truck but call it a car because the concept "car" is already well established in her thinking, or an adolescent may joke or act tough on his first date because these behaviors are familiar to him from past social situations with his male friends. On the other hand, the same preschooler may correctly use the concept "bird" to refer to several very different winged creatures, say a chicken, a pigeon and a parakeet; our teenager may act very courteously toward any very old person because of the scheme he has previously developed in his experiences with his own grandparents. In all four cases, the children are responding to the present in terms of the past, which is the essence of assimilation.

In **accommodation,** a child modifies existing schemes to better fit new ideas or experiences. Instead of calling a truck by the wrong name, the preschooler searches for a new name and begins to realize that some four-wheeled objects are not cars. Similarly, instead of acting like a ruffian, the boy on his first date begins to modify his concept of appropriate behavior and tries to behave in a more gentlemanly way. In these cases, the individuals respond to new experiences more on their own terms, even if they do not do so perfectly.

According to Piaget, development occurs because of the interplay between assimilation and accommodation, a process he called **adaptation.** Concepts are deepened or broadened by assimilation and stretched or modified by accommodation.

Piaget's second explanation for developmental change involves the circumstances in which a child finds herself. That is, adaptations result from a combination of circumstances. Obviously *experience* matters; if she does not see a truck, a preschooler can neither assimilate that object to the concept of "car" nor accommodate her thinking to this new category of vehicle. But some experiences can occur only through **social transmission,** the process through which we are influenced by, and to some extent adopt, the information and ideas in the culture and society in which we live. This process is similar to the social learning theorists' idea of observational learning through imitation and modeling. For example, the teenager's actions on his first date involve both assimilation and accommodation, and both his roughhousing and his gentlemanly behavior are conventional, although each is learned from a different group of people. A third explanation for developmental change is physical maturation: a child has to reach a certain minimal level of biological development to name an object.

Together, these processes create a state of cognitive equilibrium, in which an individual's thinking becomes increasingly stable, general, and harmoniously adjusted to the environment. The preschooler who is learning about trucks adapts her thinking to more varied types of vehicles. The adolescent learns how to adjust his behavior to the specific situation — when to goof around and when to behave more maturely.

All individuals experience temporary cognitive *disequilibrium* when they encounter new experiences that challenge their existing schemes for understanding the world. According to Piaget, a central goal of intellectual activity is to establish an harmonious balance, or *equilibrium,* between one's thought processes and experiences with the environment. The process by which this is achieved is called **equilibration.** If an earlier way of thinking or acting does not work in a new situation, cognitive change is stimulated. Inevitably, says Piaget, such changes increase the sophistication and maturity of a child's thinking, and so she moves into a new phase of development — a new cognitive stage.

Piaget's Cognitive Stages   Let us now take a closer look at Piaget's cognitive stages, which are simplified in Table 2.3.

1. *The sensorimotor stage (birth to two years)* Piaget believed that in the **sensorimotor stage,** an infant's understanding of the world is based on simple unlearned reflexes such as sucking, grasping, and looking. Piaget referred to the patterns of these reflexes as *innate schemes.* These schemes rapidly change,

Interplay between assimilation and accommodation

Cognitive disequilibrium spurs development

TABLE 2.3 Piaget's Cognitive Stages and Developmental Processes

Cognitive Stage	Approximate Age	Description
Sensorimotor	Birth–2 years	Coordination of sensory and motor activity; achievement of object permanence
Preoperational	2–7 years	Use of language and symbolic representation; egocentric view of the world
Concrete operational	7–11 years	Solution of concrete problems through logical operations
Formal operational	11–adulthood	Systematic solution of actual and hypothetical problems using abstract symbols

Developmental Processes

The earliest and most primitive patterns, or schemes, of thinking, problem solving, and constructing reality are inborn. As a result of both maturation and experience, thinking develops through a series of increasingly sophisticated stages, each incorporating the preceding ones. These changes occur through the processes of assimilation, in which new problems are solved using existing schemes; accommodation, in which existing schemes are altered or adapted to meet new challenges; and equilibration, in which separate schemes become organized into new and more sophisticated patterns of thought and action.

however, as the infant adapts them to fit new experiences. For example, a two-month-old baby has a sucking scheme. He soon learns that the nipple of a bottle requires a slightly different sucking scheme from the nipple of a breast; later, sucking his thumb involves further changes. It is through this process that cognitive development occurs.

At first the "thoughts" and "ideas" of an infant are based completely on experience of the world through her five senses (sensory experience) and through direct physical activity with objects (motor experience). For instance, an infant has no idea of a ball apart from her direct experience with actual balls. This is because she does not yet have verbal or visual symbols (words or mental pictures) for such round playthings. For the baby, thinking is still limited to sensing and manipulating, and what is out of sight is literally out of mind.

Even though it may be hard to see how sensing and manipulating are really "thinking," Piaget in fact showed that sensorimotor intelligence gradually becomes organized in ways that are very similar to the more complex and abstract thinking that older children and adults are capable of. The details of this process are described in Chapter 6. Essentially, as the infant becomes more familiar with balls, she develops an idea of "ballness" that covers all of her specific experiences with such round objects. According to Piaget, this mental image of "ball" represents a scheme. In fact, the gradual development of schemes that represent all of the ideas and events in a child's experience is the basis for the development of thinking. The first schemes refer to specific physical actions and sensory observations, such as "the time that I pushed, licked, tasted, and drooled on the bright red ball that Daddy placed in my crib." The more sophisticated schemes of older children grow out of these earlier ones; a school-aged child's general idea (or scheme) of "roundness" might be constructed from earlier schemes like *baseball, balloon, orange,* and *beachball.* By the end of the sensorimotor stage around age two, the young child's schemes will have greatly increased in number and complexity.

Schemes provide a framework for thinking

Between the ages of eight and twelve months, the child will also have achieved **object permanence,** the understanding that people and things continue to exist even when he cannot see, hear, touch, smell, or taste them directly. This skill makes play much more interesting, but it can also make life more difficult for parents.

Continuity of existence

For example, when Linda, the babysitter, found Jill (seven months) and her friend Carey (eight months) fighting over a stuffed dog, she easily settled their dispute by simply giving each infant a different toy. Once the original toy was out of sight, it was also "out of mind" and quickly forgotten. A few months later, however, when she tried the same tactic to settle a similar dispute, both children loudly protested, indicating that they wanted the toy back and would not accept a substitute. In this case, Linda's "failure" was due to the children's "success" in achieving an understanding of object permanence.

2. *The preoperational stage (two to seven years)* During this stage, which lasts from about age two to age seven or so, there is a major shift from the action-oriented schemes of the sensorimotor period to schemes based on the use of language and other forms of symbolic representation. Something that is operational is guided by specific rules, During the **preoperational stage,** a child's thinking begins to follow certain predictable rules, but the child has not fully mastered them. He also begins to develop the ability to figure things out and solve problems with words as well as actions. For example, if one of two doors into the kitchen is closed, the child can mentally "eliminate" the closed door without actually having to try it, and he will go through the other door.

Use of language and other symbols

Preoperational children experiment with using symbols to represent the world in several ways. One is **deferred imitation,** which is much like the kind of imitation social learning theorists describe. Suppose that Rosa, who is three, hears her pet dog Morris barking one morning. She may not respond to it then, but later in the afternoon she wrinkles her face and says, "Woof-woof, woof-woof!" This is a case of deferred imitation.

Symbolic thinking during this stage is also obvious in children's **dramatic play,** in which they try out the roles and behavior of their parents and other important people. A good example of "playing house," in which children pretend to be various family members and act out domestic scenes with which they are familiar. Although children's dramatic play is not always well organized by adult standards, it may at times confront us with performances that are all too accurate and true to life. In fact, careful observation of children's dramatic play can yield important insights into what they may be thinking and feeling.

Perhaps the most widespread sign of children's increasing symbolic skill comes from the development of language. During the preoperational years, children progress from using single words as whole sentences to constructing mature grammatical sentences. The content of what they say changes, too: early speech, such as "See dog," tends to refer mainly to current, "here and now" experiences, but later speech increasingly refers to the past or the future ("Remember when we saw that falling star?").

3. *The concrete operational stage (seven to eleven years)* After children become skillful at making representations, they begin learning how to coordinate them logically. As they do so, they enter the **concrete operational stage.** According to Piaget, *operations* are logical relationships among concepts or schemes. During this stage, which lasts until age eleven or so, children become able to use logical relationships for the first time, although this new ability is largely limited to objects and events that are real, tangible, and concrete.

Relating ideas logically

The changes in thinking associated with the concrete operational stage are illustrated in the following Piagetian experiment. A child is shown two equal balls of clay and then watches as one of the balls is rolled into a long, thick snake. A preoperational child will think that the two balls now have different amounts of clay, but a child who has mastered concrete operations will know that despite the change in shape, both pieces still contain the same amount of clay.

Belief in constancy in spite of changed appearance

Developmental psychologists have found these changes in many other similar tasks. The belief that the quantity or number of something stays constant in spite of changes in its appearance is called **conservation.** Note that conservation requires a belief in constancy, not a perception of it. A child (or an adult, for that matter) cannot really see whether the amounts of liquid are equal in two containers of different shapes; she can only know that they are. Success at this task, then, depends partly on knowledge of the containers' past as well as on beliefs about the general behavior of liquids.

Concrete operational skills help a child to explore and solve problems, but as we noted, the child is still limited to thinking about real or concrete things rather than abstract ideas. Consider Nguyen, an eight-year-old who enjoys collecting bugs and butterflies and knows a great deal about their behavior. Ask him anything about how they look, their feeding patterns, or their scientific names and classifications, and he will probably be able to answer. But ask him about more abstract things, such as why different species have developed differences in size, shape, and coloring, and he will probably not know what to say. Later in the concrete operational period, of course, Nguyen can answer such a question increasingly well, but by then he may already be entering Piaget's fourth major cognitive stage.

4. *The formal operational stage (eleven through adulthood)* Sometime during adolescence, children learn to think logically, abstractly, and scientifically, at which point they enter the **formal operational stage.** Here are two problems that require formal operational thinking for their solution:

- *Problem 1*   Suppose all *wugs* were *fets* and all *fets* were *tuts*. If you saw a *fet,* would it more likely be a *wug* or a *tut?*

- *Problem 2*   What makes a pendulum swing faster or slower — its length, the amount of weight on the end, or the angle from which you release it?

The first of these problems requires logical reasoning, of course; more important, it requires reasoning in the abstract, in the absence of any real, tangible objects. Formal operational thinking allows people to solve problems by using only abstract symbols, in this case *wugs, fets,* and *tuts.* A child who has

Abstract thinking

According to Piaget, children think in qualitatively different ways as they develop. Very young children usually think about objects and experience by looking and touching. Many adolescents, on the other hand, can plan and reason abstractly.

reached the concrete operational period could solve this problem if real objects were involved. Test this idea for yourself, if you like, by recasting Problem 1 in real terms: replace *wugs* with *fathers, fets* with *men,* and *tuts* with *people.* Does it make the problem easier? Yes, says Piaget — in fact, easy enough for a concrete operational child to solve.

The second problem requires the person answering it to test the influence of each of the three factors, or variables (length, weight, and angle), on the speed of the pendulum's swing. What is called for is an experiment in which each factor is systematically tested while the other two are held constant. The formal operational child or adult might try different lengths of cord while using only one weight and while being careful to release the pendulum from the same angle for each test. After noting the influence of the cord's length in this way, she would shift her attention to trying different weights systematically while keeping the length of the cord and angle of release constant. Finally, she would try varying the angle of release while keeping the cord length and pendulum weight constant.

A child who had not yet achieved formal operational thinking would not be able to conceive of all the hypothetical possibilities and then systematically vary each factor until the problem was solved. It is the ability to conceive of a model that exhausts all the logical possibilities and to systematically carry it to its conclusion that distinguishes both formal operational and scientific thinking from earlier stages. When a child has mastered this kind of thinking, he is an adult, at least in Piagetian terms.

Strengths and Weaknesses of Piaget's Theory   Piaget's states of cognitive development provide a clear and thorough framework for looking in detail at the process by which children develop. As such, his theory has been extremely useful for educators and other professionals working with children. In fact, it has come to be the guiding force in planning curricula and in educating parents about reasonable expectations for their children.

Another strength of Piaget's theory is that it integrates a wide range of information about cognitive change and serves as an important tool for stimulating new research. In doing so, it has led researchers to become much more aware of children's intellectual capabilities and of the content of their thinking.

A third strength of the theory has been its implications for other areas of developmental psychology. It has provided a basis for stage theories of moral development, social cognition, sex-role determination, play, racial awareness, and the development of identity, just to name a few.

In spite of the wide implications of Piaget's theory, however, its narrow focus on intellectual change, almost to the exclusion of social and emotional influences, is problematical. If we were to depend solely on Piaget's work, we might think that intellectual development occurs independently of the major social and emotional changes described by Freud, Erikson, and the social learning theorists. Similarly, the assumption that cognitive stages are universal — that they hold for all people in all places at all times — is a weakness that Piaget shares with all stage theorists to some degree. There are indications that some of the changes that Piaget attributes to built-in stages are due to the particular methods that he and his followers have used to study children's thinking.

In summary, Piaget's theory has had an enormous impact on our thinking about cognitive development. It has integrated a wide and diverse range of information in a systematic way and stimulated a great deal of new research. The cognitive developmental approach has also proven to be extremely useful in explaining various aspects of socialization, including sex-role development (Kohlberg, 1964), sex typing (Bem, 1981), moral judgment (Kohlberg, 1966), and the development of racial attitudes (P. Katz, 1976).

Strengths

Weaknesses

Impact of Piaget's theory

Information-Processing Theory

In recent years an alternaitve to Piaget's cognitive theory has gained attention and support. The alternative is **information-processing theory,** which focuses on the precise, detailed features or steps involved in mental activities (Newell & Simon, 1972). The steps are modeled on the workings of a computer, and computers are often used to test specific hypotheses made by the theory. Originally, the information-processing viewpoint referred primarily to adult thought processes, but gradually it has proved useful in explaining cognition in childhood and even in infancy.

Key Principles of Information-Processing Theory   Figure 2.2 shows one information-processing model of human thinking. According to the model, when a person tries to solve a problem, she first takes in information from her environment through her senses. In more everyday terms, she looks at a page of print or listens to the words spoken by another person. The information gained in this way is kept briefly in the **sensory register,** the first memory store. The sensory register records information exactly as it originally receives it, in much the way that a camera might take a snapshot of a scene. Unlike a photograph, however, information is the sensory register fades or disappears within a fraction of a second unless the person processes it further.

Information that a person pays special attention to is transferred to **short-term memory** (STM), the second memory store. The short-term memory corresponds roughly to "momentary awareness," or whatever the person is thinking about a particular instant. The short-term memory can hold only limited amounts of information — in fact, only about seven pieces of it any one time. After about twenty seconds, information in short-term memory either is forgotten or is processed further so that it moves into **long-term memory** (LTM), the third memory store.

Information can be saved permanently in long-term memory. Doing so requires various cognitive strategies, such as rehearsing information repeatedly or organizing it into familiar categories. You can remember the main ideas of a

Sensory register

STM: Temporary storage

FIGURE 2.2
An Information-Processing Model of Learning

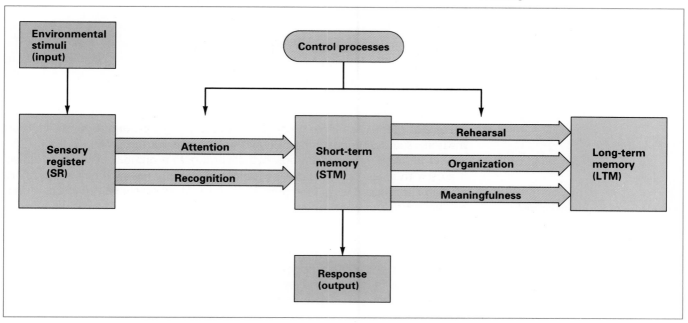

LTM: Permanent storage

textbook chapter longer, for example, if you go over the chapter more than once and group its ideas logically while you do so. Ironically, the organizing process also works better if you already have a lot of knowledge about the information you are trying to remember. Prior knowledge probably helps by giving you a richer network of categories and ideas for organizing your new knowledge.

Unlike short-term memory, long-term memory probably has unlimited capacity for storage of new information. The problem comes in retrieving information. As odd as it sounds, a person cannot always remember how to recall something. Most of us experience this problem when an old acquaintance's name is on the tip of our tongue or when we remember only that the friend's name "begins with the letter *w*, I think." But most of us can remember certain events that happened long ago better than many events that happened much more recently.

The information-processing model provides a useful way of understanding thinking. As the following discussion shows, certain processing functions change as children grow older.

Developmental Changes in Information Processing   As children grow older, they experience several cognitive changes that allow them to process information more efficiently and comprehensively. Changes occur in cognitive control processes, in metacognition (or knowledge about knowledge), and in the amount of knowledge itself.

Ways to organize and direct learning

Control Processes   The most important developmental change in information processing is the acquisition of **control processes,** which direct an individual's attention toward particular input from the sensory register and guide the response to new information once it enters short-term memory. Usually control processes organize information in short-term memory, as when a student reads an arithmetic problem, ponders it in its head, and immediately announces the answer. Sometimes control processes also relate information in STM to previously learned knowledge from LTM, as when a youth hears a song on the radio and notes its similarity to another song heard previously. And sometimes control processes consist of strategies about how to learn information effectively — strategies, for instance, about how to remember a person's telephone number.

Control processes are like very well remembered long-term memories — so well remembered, in fact, that they operate automatically. An adult reading a book does not think, "I am remembering how to read now"; the person simply begins the relevant control processes automatically, without conscious thought. For a first-grade student, however, controlling the process of reading may be quite conscious: the child must attend deliberately to every act of reading, in addition to attending to the content or meaning of the reading material itself. Partly because she divides her attention in this way, a young, less experienced reader often comprehends less when reading a difficult passage.

Knowledge of how thinking and learning work

Increases with age

Metacognition   As children grow older, they develop **metacognition,** which is an awareness and understanding of how thinking and learning work (Forrest-Pressley et al., 1985). Metacognition helps learning in a number of ways. It allows a person to assess how difficult a problem or learning task will be and therefore to plan appropriate ways of approaching them. More specifically, metacognition, or "knowledge of how cognition works," involves knowledge of self, knowledge of task variables, and knowledge of which information-processing strategies are effective in which situations. For example, although most preschool age children have little awareness of themselves as learners and of the limitations in how much they can remember, because older school children are much more aware of limitations in how much they can remember, they are able to more realistically approach memory tasks. Similarly, because knowledge of how the characteristics of a learning task affect its difficulty increases with age, older children can tell

The chess-playing abilities of these youngsters are closely tied to increases in their knowledge of chess and in their awareness and understanding of their own thought processes and problem-solving strategies.

that it is easier to demonstrate that they have learned something by recognizing it on a list than by having to recall the same material without any assistance. Finally, as knowledge of learning strategies increases with age, older children are better able to use such techniques as rehearsal and mnemonics (helpful associations) to maximize their learning and memory.

Knowledge Base As children grow older, they acquire not only more metacognitive knowledge but knowledge of many other kinds as well. Gradually some children become comparative experts in particular areas, whether in math, sports, or knowledge of how to get along with peers. Their initial knowledge and skill in an area make learning further knowledge and skill in the same area easier because new information can be related more meaningfully to prior information.

Development of expertise

According to many information-processing theorists, changes in the knowledge base are not general, stagelike transformations such as those proposed by Piaget (Chi et al., 1988). Instead they are specialized developments of expertise based on the gradual accumulation of specific information and skills about a field, including information and skills about *how* knowledge in the field is organized and learned efficiently. A very good chess player is an expert in chess, but she is not necessarily advanced at other activities or in other realms of knowledge. The talent probably reflects long hours of one major activity, playing chess games, during each of which she learns a little more than during the last one. Eventually, the chess player accumulates a large knowledge base about chess: memories of board patterns, moves, and game strategies that worked in the past.

Strengths and Weaknesses of Information-Processing Theory   By identifying many specific elements of thinking, information-processing theory conveys much of the complexity and intricacy of human cognition as it occurs during specific tasks. This quality is a real advantage compared to the major alternative theory of cognition — Piaget's — which tends to sweep over the specifics of cognitive performance in order to highlight long-term changes in cognitive competence. Compared to Piaget, information-processing theory is more fully a theory of

Strengths

performance — how people actually *do* think on a given occasion rather than how they *could* think at each stage, when at their best.

This strength has been useful to educators who have used the theory to find better ways to teach conventional school subjects such as mathematics and reading (Hall, 1989; Resnick, 1989). Professionals have also used information-processing models to better understand how children think when they have learning disabilities (Henker & Whalen, 1989).

Another important strength of information-processing theory is that it attempts to define its terms and concepts with clarity and precision, and there is a high level of logical consistency among the various parts of the model. Because its concepts can thus be turned into testable scientific hypotheses, this approach has been generative in stimulating considerable research.

Weaknesses

Information-processing theory also has a number of weaknesses. One important weakness is its failure to explain the processes involved in cognitive development or how cognitive development is related to the social and emotional contexts in which learning occurs (Greeno, 1989). There is also a tendency in some versions of the theory to assume that human beings behave like computers, ignoring the fact that unlike computers, thoughts, feelings, and motivations play a major role in how people learn. Some newer versions of information-processing theory have addressed these limitations by focusing more explicitly on how motivations and attitudes influence learning (L. Anderson, 1989a, 1989b; Belmont, 1989).

DEVELOPMENTAL THEORIES COMPARED: IMPLICATIONS FOR THE STUDENT

We have now come to the end of our review of several of the most important theories in developmental psychology, having explored in some detail the suggested stages and processes involved in children's psychosexual, emotional, social, and cognitive development. What conclusions might we draw? And in what way are these theories useful as we investigate children's development in the rest of this book?

One conclusion is that no single theory adequately describes or explains all of development. Each theory has a somewhat different focus, a different set of assumptions, and a different set of concepts. Nevertheless, although they differ considerably, they do seem to reflect some degree of basic agreement about children. For instance, most theorists agree that children go through perceptible stages of growth (see Table 2.4). Freud, Erikson, and Piaget agree that adolescence, to take one example, is marked by achievement of adult or near-adult levels of adjustment. For Freud, that adjustment is psychosexual in nature; for Erikson, it involves identity formation and social functioning; and for Piaget, it involves the ability to think and solve problems in a formal operational way.

Agreement among the theories

The same holds true for infancy. Freud's emphasis on oral activity and the development of the ability to distinguish between what is real and what is not is consistent with Erikson's belief that this stage involves the senses and the developmental crisis of trust versus mistrust. Piaget's idea of a sensorimotor period defines an infant whose approach to thinking and problem solving would be recognized by Freud and Erikson, and that infant's level of cognitive development is fairly consistent with the psychosexual and psychosocial achievements that Freud and Erikson describe.

Table 2.4 Developmental Theories Compared

	Psychodynamic		Cognitive		Behavioral Learning	Social Learning
	Freud	*Erikson*	*Piaget*	*Information Processing*	*Pavlov; Skinner*	*Bandura*
Main Focus	Personality (social, emotional)	Personality (social, behavior, identity)	Cognitive (thinking, problem solving)	Cognitive; steps and processes involved in problem solving and other mental activity	Learning specific observable responses	Learning behavior, cognitive response patterns, social roles
Key Concepts	Id, ego, superego; psychosexual conflict; defense mechanisms	Life span development; psychosocial crisis	Schemes, assimilation, accommodation, equilibrium	Sensory register, short-term memory (STM), long-term memory (LTM), metacognition, knowledge base, control processes	Classical and operant conditioning, extinction, reinforcement, punishment	Imitation, social learning, modeling, cognitive learning, reciprocal determinism
Characteristics						
Stages	Yes	Yes	Yes	No	No	No
Role of maturation	Moderate	Weak	Strong	Strong	Weak	Weak
Role of experience	Strong	Strong	Moderate	Moderate	Strong	Strong
Role of unconscious	Strong	Weak/moderate	None	None	None	None
Role of conscious	Moderate	Strong	Strong	Strong	Strong	Strong
Breadth of focus	Wide	Wide	Moderate	Narrow	Narrow	Moderate
Generativity	Strong	Moderate	Strong	Moderate	Weak	Moderate
Testability	Weak/none	Weak/moderate	Moderate	Strong	Strong	Strong

Even though each of the theories has contributed significantly to expanding our knowledge in its particular area of focus, none should be viewed as providing a complete explanation of development. Taken together, the theories are complementary and can be used in conjunction with one another to provide a fairly comprehensive view of child and adolescent development.

The theories complement each other

As we suggested at the beginning of this chapter, theories are useful because they help us to systematically organize and make sense of large amounts of information about children's development. Theories also stimulate new thinking and research and guide parents and professionals in their day-to-day work with children. For example, knowledge of cognitive theory is helpful in providing guidelines for teachers and parents who want to design educational programs appropriate to particular children's competencies. Similarly, Erikson's psychosocial theory alerts us to the predictable developmental crises of childhood and adolescence, enabling us to be more appropriately responsive to our children's needs.

Advantages of using theories

On the other hand, because they guide and direct our perceptions of and thinking about children, reliance on theories may predispose us to focus on certain aspects of development, to make certain assumptions, and to draw conclusions about development that are consistent with the theory but not necessarily accurate. For example, overreliance on the cognitive approach may lead a

Disadvantages of using theories

Even though developmental theories sometimes seem to contradict each other, they are often looking at different aspects of the same behavior. If proponents of Freud, Piaget, Erikson, and Skinner looked at this scene, what would each of them see?

Theories help deepen understanding

teacher to underestimate the contribution of social and emotional factors to a child's academic difficulties. Similarly, a parent who is predisposed to interpret his child's irresponsible behavior in terms of psychological conflict may overlook the fact that this same behavior is frequently modeled and reinforced by the child's older brother.

Even though the usefulness of developmental theory to experts may be easy to appreciate, how do we judge its importance to students and other nonprofessionals? Clearly, we are all indirectly influenced by the work of developmental researchers and professionals, but an understanding of developmental theories can be directly useful to students and other nonprofessionals in some very important ways. Theories help individuals to organize more easily and effectively what they already know about child and adolescent development based on their personal experiences. Theories can also help people to broaden and deepen their *understanding* of the principles, processes, and stages of developmental change and to sharpen their own informal ideas and theories about development.

As you read the chapters that follow, notice that the theories are applied selectively, depending on the ages and developmental issues that we are discussing. We encourage you to refer back to this chapter whenever you have questions about the material, and to make your own judgments about which theory (or theories) fit best. Last, keep an eye on how your own theory of development changes as you read the book and talk with your teacher and classmates. By the end of the course, if not sooner, you are likely to have a much clearer idea of your theoretical orientation as well as a much clearer idea of what development is all about.

SUMMARY OF MAJOR IDEAS

The Nature of Developmental Theories

1. Theories are useful in organizing and explaining the process of development and in stimulating and guiding developmental research, theory, and practice.

2. According to the stage theories, development proceeds in a series of stages, each of which is more complex and qualitatively different from those that precede it.

3. Developmental theories differ in the degree to which they emphasize stages, maturation versus learning, conscious versus unconscious processes, breadth versus depth of focus, and active versus passive participation of the child.

Psychodynamic Theories of Development

4. The theories of Freud and Erikson see development as a dynamic process that occurs in a series of stages, each involving psychological conflicts that the developing person must resolve.

5. According to Freud, personality development is energized by three conflicting processes: the unconscious, irrational, pleasure-seeking id; the largely conscious, rational, realistic ego; and the superego, which is the voice of conscience and morality.

6. The Freudian approach describes five stages of psychosexual development: oral, anal, phallic, latency, and genital.

7. During the oral and anal stages, the mouth and then the anus are the focus of children's social and emotional experience — both pleasurable and unpleasurable — and of the conflicts they encounter in having their needs fulfilled.

8. During the phallic stage, the genitals are the focus of sexual and emotional activity; resolution of the Oedipus or Electra conflict results in the establishment of gender identity and the development of the superego.

9. Latency, a period of little psychosexual activity, anticipates the physical changes of puberty and the genital stage, which is the final stage of psychosexual development.

10. Erikson's theory, a revision of Freud's, outlines eight developmental stages encompassing the life span, each defined by a unique psychological crisis that is never completely resolved.

11. Erikson's work has contributed to our understanding of the overall process of identity development, particularly the crisis of identity versus role confusion, which occurs during adolescence.

12. Although imprecise and difficult to test scientifically, psychodynamic theories have been very influential in stimulating and guiding developmental research and work with both normal and disturbed children.

Behavioral and Social Learning Theories of Development

13. Pavlov's theory of classical conditioning has helped to explain the process by which developmental changes occur.

14. Skinner's operant conditioning theory emphasizes the influence of reinforcement, punishment, and extinction in developmental change.

15. Operant conditioning approaches have been particularly helpful in helping children who have difficulty acquiring basic social skills and regulating and controlling their own behavior.

16. Social learning theories emphasize the contributions of observational learning, modeling, cognitive processes, and reciprocal determinism in developmental change.

Cognitive Theories of Development

17. Piaget's theory explains the underlying structures and processes involved in the development of children's thinking and problem solving.

18. According to Piaget, thinking develops in a series of increasingly complex and sophisticated stages, or periods, each of which incorporates the achievements of those preceding it.

19. New ways of thinking and problem solving are achieved through the joint processes of assimilation (fitting a new scheme of thinking or action into an existing one) and accommodation (changing an existing scheme to meet the challenges of a new situation).

20. During the first, sensorimotor period, the infant's thoughts and ideas are based completely upon the sensory experiences and direct physical activity with objects: he achieves an understanding that objects exist independent of his sensory awareness.

21. During the preoperational period, ages two to seven, the child's thinking begins to follow predictable rules and relies increasingly on his ability to use language and other symbols.

22. The concrete operational period, ages seven to eleven, witnesses an increasing ability to think logically and the achievement of conservation, the belief that the quantity of things remain constant in spite of changes in their appearance.

23. Cognitive development reaches completion during the formal operational period, when the child becomes able to rely exclusively on abstract symbols to conceptualize and systematically solve real and hypothetical problems.

24. Piaget's cognitive theory has had an enormous impact on research, theory, and application, particularly in the field of education.

25. Cognitive theories have also been used to explain the development of sex roles, sex typing, moral judgment, and racial attitudes.

26. Information-processing theory focuses on the steps involved in thought processes. According to this theory, information is first kept in the sensory register, then in short-term memory, and finally in long-term memory.

27. As children grow older, they experience cognitive changes in control processes, metacognition, and their knowledge base.

Developmental Theories Compared: Implications for the Student

28. Although developmental theories differ in both their focus and in their explanatory concepts, together they provide a fairly comprehensive view of the process of developmental change.

29. Theories may at times seem too complicated and abstract to be immediately useful and may at times interfere with efforts to observe and think about children in ways that are not anticipated by the theory involved.

30. By systematically organizing what is already known about development and by proposing explanations that can be tested through formal and informal observations, developmental theories are so useful a tool for experts and nonexperts alike that they are well worth the effort required to understand them.

KEY TERMS

developmental stages (37)
stage theory (37)
psychoanalysis (39)
id (39)
libido (39)
pleasure principle (39)
ego (39)
reality principle (39)
superego (39)
oral stage (40)
anal stage (40)
phallic stage (41)
Oedipal conflict (41)
Electra conflict (41)
identification (41)
internalization (42)
latency period (42)
genital stage (42)
defense mechanism (42)
repression (42)
sublimation (42)
regression (42)
trust versus mistrust (45)
autonomy versus shame and doubt (46)
initiative versus guilt (46)
industry versus inferiority (47)
identity versus role confusion (47)
intimacy versus isolation (48)
generativity versus stagnation (48)
ego integrity versus despair (48)
classical conditioning (50)
conditioned stimulus (50)

conditioned response (50)
unconditioned stimulus (50)
unconditioned response (50)
unconditioned reflex (50)
operant conditioning (50)
reinforcement (52)
positive reinforcement (52)
negative reinforcement (52)
punishment (52)
partial reinforcement (52)
extinction (54)
modeling (55)
cognition (56)
scheme (57)
assimilation (57)
accommodation (58)
adaptation (58)
social transmission (58)
equilibration (58)
sensorimotor stage (58)
object permanence (59)
preoperational stage (60)
deferred imitation (60)
dramatic play (60)
concrete operational stage (60)
conservation (60)
formal operational stage (61)
information-processing theory (63)
sensory register (63)
short-term memory (STM) (63)
long-term memory (LTM) (63)
control processes (64)
metacognition (64)

WHAT DO YOU THINK?

1. When you began this chapter, what negative and positive views did you have about developmental theories? In what ways have your views changed? Why?

2. Does Freud's description of the Oedipus conflict and its resolution explain what actually happens? Based on your own observations, what evidence seems to support his ideas? What evidence contradicts them?

3. Erikson proposes that adolescence involves the crisis of identity versus role confusion, and young adulthood, the crisis of intimacy versus isolation. Based on your own observations, how accurate is Erikson about what happens during these two stages of development?

4. Earlier in this chapter, two examples were used to illustrate the qualities of abstract thinking during Piaget's formal operational period: "wugs, fets, and tuts" and the "pendulum problem." Do you think that being able to think in this way is better than thinking more concretely? Why or why not?

5. Which of the theories do you find the most interesting? For what reasons?

6. Which of the theories do you think is most useful in understanding human development? Why?

FOR FURTHER READING

Crain, W. *Theories of Development: Concepts and Applications,* 2nd ed. Englewood Cliffs, NJ: Prentice-Hall, 1985.

This thorough and readable review of the major developmental theories compares them and discusses their practical implications.

Eagle, M. *Recent Developments in Psychoanalysis: A Critical Evaluation.* New York: McGraw-Hill, 1984.

This book provides a high level of coverage of the most recent developments in psychoanalysis and critically examines the underlying assumptions, theoretical arguments, and conclusions of each.

Erikson, E. *Identity, Youth and Crisis.* New York: Norton, 1968.

Erikson presents his developmental theory with an emphasis on identity development during adolescence and young adulthood. Chapter 3, "The Life Cycle: Epigenesis of Identity," is most relevant for the student who wants to sample Erikson's work first hand.

Freud, S. *New Introductory Lectures on Psychoanalysis,* ed. and trans. J. Strachey. New York: Norton, 1965.

This basic introduction to Freud's ideas is based on his lectures to an audience that included nonexperts unfamiliar with his work. It is recommended for the student who wants to read something Freud actually wrote. Even though his ideas are complex, his writing style is surprisingly clear and interesting.

Hall, C., and Lindzey, G. *Theories of Personality,* 3rd ed. New York: Wiley, 1978.

This classic, systematic, and straightforward review of the

major theories of personality from the standpoint of traditional psychology is a useful reference source.

Mitchell, J. *Psychoanalysis and Feminism.* New York: Pantheon, 1974.

In this high-level critique of the psychoanalytic theory of traditional and nontraditional Freudian theory from a feminist perspective, the author is willing neither to accept Freud's prejudices nor to dismiss his insights and contributions. She provides a challenging corrective to those who are willing to do so (difficult reading, for the highly motivated student).

Phillips, J. *The Origins of Intellect: Piaget's Theory.* San Francisco: Freeman, 1969.

This is a clear and concise review of Piaget's cognitive theory.

Skinner, B. F. *Walden Two.* New York: Macmillan, 1948.

This novel describes a fictional utopian community that is guided by the assumptions of behavioral learning theory and the principles of operant conditioning.

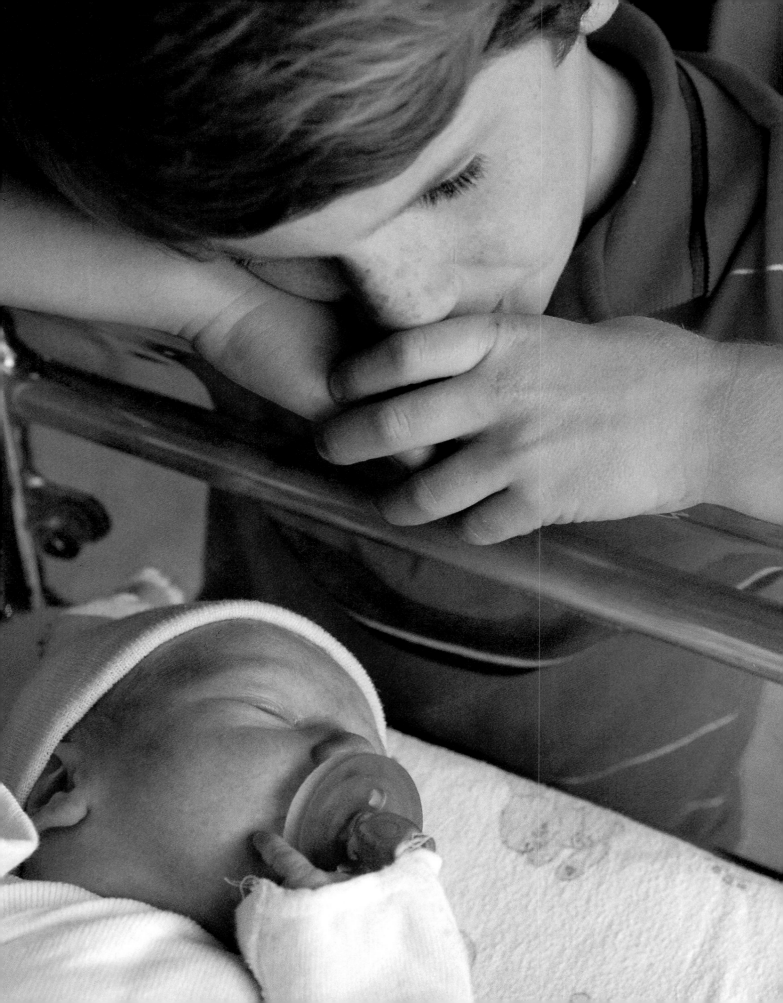

PART TWO

Beginnings

lthough you might think of human development as starting in infancy, it actually begins at the moment of conception. We become individuals partly because of our genetic endowments, which are determined the moment sperm meets egg, and partly because of events that happen to us while still in our mothers' wombs.

The next two chapters look at these influences. They show some of the ways in which heredity affects whom a child becomes, not only physically but cognitively and socially as well. And they describe what actually happens during the thirty-eight weeks or so before birth, as well as the events surrounding birth itself.

By childbirth — a time of wonder, anxiety, and joy — the baby has already undergone many changes. But there is plenty of room to learn from experience — and the child will undergo many more changes throughout his or her life.

Genetics

Focusing Questions

- How are genetic differences usually transmitted from one generation to the next?
- How do genes work to make a person a distinct individual?
- What are the most common sorts of genetic abnormalities, and what are their causes?
- What can experts in genetics do to help parents diagnose and respond to genetic problems?
- How do heredity and environment each contribute to the development of individual children?

 vast number of human qualities are inherited, from the shape of our earlobes to the sound of our voices. Even complex personal behaviors such as how much we mull over problems may be at least partially inherited. What makes these things "run in families"? Stated more formally, how is genetic information conveyed from one generation to the next?

This chapter explores answers to this question. To do so, we first describe the basic biological processes involved in human reproduction, then explain how genetic information from two individuals is combined and conveyed from parents to children. Genetic abnormalities receive special attention, not because these outnumber normal genetic processes but because they shed considerable light on those processes. The chapter then addresses an issue that psychologists have found especially important: the relationship between heredity and environment. All psychologists agree that both factors influence human development, but the exact nature of these influences is often complex and ambiguous. Finally, we end by describing ways of using knowledge of these relationships to benefit parents.

MECHANISMS OF GENETIC TRANSMISSION

Although we still lack many details about how genetic information is combined and transmitted, we do know that it begins with the reproductive cells, or **gametes,** of a child's parents. In the father, the gametes are produced in the testicles, and each is called a **sperm** cell; in the mother, they develop in the ovaries, and each is called an **ovum,** or egg cell. The sperm and egg cells contain genetic information in molecular structures called **genes,** which form threads called **chromosomes.** Any human sperm or egg cell contains only twenty-three chromosomes, but each chromosome contains thousands of genes.

The Role of DNA

The genes themselves are made of **deoxyribonucleic acid,** or **DNA.** All DNA molecules have a particular chemical structure — a double helix, or spiral — that allows them to divide easily and create new, duplicate DNA molecules reliably (see Figure 3.1).

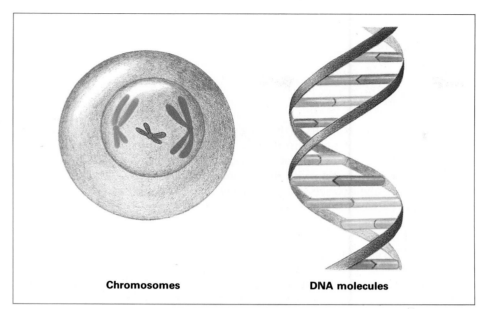

Chromosomes   **DNA molecules**

FIGURE 3.1
Genetic Structures
Forty-six chromosomes are located in pairs on the DNA molecules.

The DNA in the genes contributes in two ways to genetic reproduction. First, it contains the code of genetic information that the individual needs as she develops; and second, it can share this information widely through its ability to divide and reproduce. The first of these features helps account for the numerous genetic differences among individuals, and the second accounts for the overall consistency and regularity of much individual development.

But DNA can make these contributions only under the right conditions. In particular, the ovum and sperm cells must unite to form a single new cell, called a **zygote.** This happens when one sperm attaches itself to the surface of the egg. The attachment triggers a biochemical reaction on the surface of the ovum that prevents any further sperm from attaching and that allows the one remaining sperm to gradually penetrate into the ovum. Within a few hours, the walls of the sperm and the nucleus both begin to disintegrate, releasing the chromosomes of each former gamete into the new zygote. After a few more hours, a new wall forms around the newly combined set of chromosomes — all twenty-three pairs — and conception is complete. (See Figure 3.2.) At this point the zygote is still

Fertilization

FIGURE 3.2
Gametes and Zygote
At fertilization, the twenty-three single chromosomes in the father's sperm combine with the twenty-three in the mother's ovum (egg), producing a zygote with a complete set of twenty-three chromosome pairs.

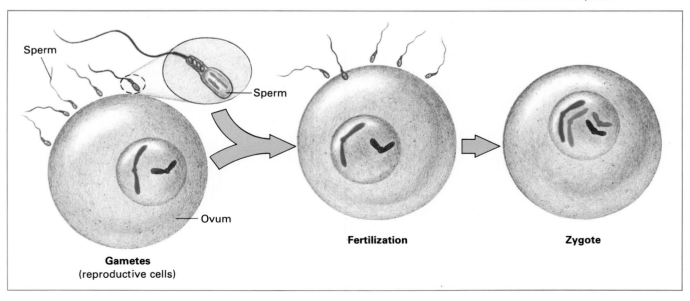

Sperm

Sperm

Ovum

Gametes
(reproductive cells)

Fertilization

Zygote

so small that hundreds of them could fit on the head of a pin, yet it contains sufficient genetic information in its DNA molecules to eventually develop into a unique human being.

Mitosis and Meiosis

Two kinds of cell division

The human being develops from this single cell through a process of cell division. There are two kinds of cell division: one kind for reproductive cells and one for all other cells. The cell division of most cells is a relatively simple process called **mitosis.** The process begins with the chromosomes, which duplicate themselves and divide; then the two sets of chromosomes move to opposite sides of the cell. A wall forms between the two sets, and eventually two cells form from the one that existed before. (See Figure 3.3.) This process goes on continually in all tissues of all human beings, from conception until death.

The cell division of reproductive cells (gametes) is a more complex process called **meiosis.** This process involves several steps: first the chromosomes duplicate, then they exchange segments with each other, then the cell divides, and then the two resulting cells divide again. The first division resembles mitosis, but in the second division the chromosomes do *not* duplicate, they only divide evenly between the two new cells. As a result, gametes end up with only *one-half* the usual number of chromosomes carried by all other cells — just twenty-three chromosomes instead of the forty-six contained everywhere else in the body. (See Figure 3.4.)

Combining genes from both parents

The single cell formed by conception contains the normal, larger number of chromosomes because it combines the chromosomes from the sperm and from the ovum. Once the zygote forms, it and all its descendants divide by mitosis. Each cell of a developing child therefore acquires copies of the same forty-six chromosomes, and each cell thus contains the same set of genes, the same DNA molecules, and the same code, or genetic instructions, to guide its development. But even before birth, some cells "decide" to become legs and others to become

FIGURE 3.3
Mitosis

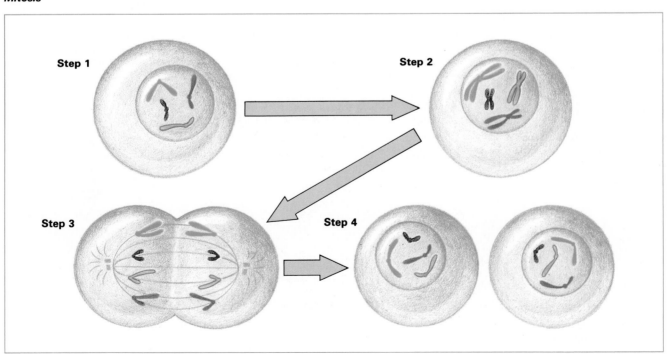

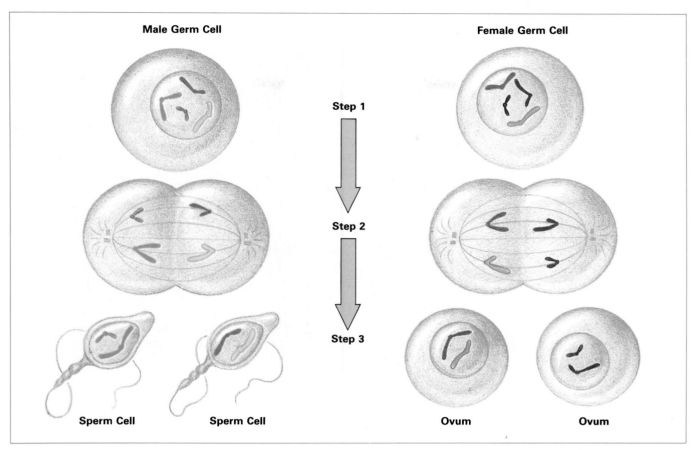

Male Germ Cell

Female Germ Cell

Step 1

Step 2

Step 3

Sperm Cell   Sperm Cell   Ovum   Ovum

FIGURE 3.4
Meiosis

eyeballs, for reasons we do not completely understand. Apparently each cell uses its genetic information differently, depending on its physical and chemical relationships to other, neighboring cells.

INDIVIDUAL GENETIC EXPRESSION

As you may have guessed, genetic information does not usually translate directly into a particular trait. In fact, sometimes genetic traits may be expressed only to a limited extent or not at all! This happens for a number of reasons. In the following section some of the mechanisms that account for the various ways in which genetic information is (and sometimes is not) translated into developmental change are explored.

Genotype and Phenotype

Biologists distinguish between the **genotype,** the set of genetic traits an individual inherits and the **phenotype,** the set of traits the person actually displays during his life. The genotype refers to a child's *potential*: to his inborn capacity to grow especially tall, to gain excess weight, or to pass blue eyes on to his children. The phenotype refers to the child's *actual* appearance and behavior; to how tall the child becomes, how much weight he gains over the years and whether he himself has blue eyes.

Genetic transmission accounts for many of the similarities — physical and even behavioral — among relatives. But as with this family, it also accounts for some of the differences.

Influences on phenotype

The phenotype is really a combination of the genotype's potential and the life experiences that modify that potential. As a result, the phenotype often does not coincide with genotype. For example, two newborn infants can have identical genotypic potential for weight, but one may end up heavier and the other may end up thinner because one family feeds its baby more and the other family encourages more exercise. On the other hand, children may look alike (have the same phenotype) even though they differ in potential (have different genotypes). Although two eight-year-olds weigh the same, one may have gotten that way by dieting and the other simply by eating whatever she wanted. In this case, genetic potential differs, but outward appearances are the same. There are also other genetic processes at work that determine who a child becomes.

Dominant and Recessive Genes

Genes are inherited in pairs, one from each parent. However, the influence of each gene on the characteristics that the child ends up with is not always equal. One of the processes affecting the child's characteristics is whether a gene has more or less influence in determining a particular trait. Genes that have greater influence are called **dominant genes.** Genes whose influence is less powerful because they are controlled or blocked by the dominant gene whenever they are paired with it are called **recessive genes.** Table 3.1 lists a number of common dominant and recessive traits.

For a recessive gene to gain in influence it has to be paired with another recessive gene. Eye color provides a good example. Let us pretend that human eyes only come in two colors: blue and brown. Most Caucasian children are born with blue eyes, but from about six months of age, a child's eyes remain blue only under certain conditions. Because blue eyes are a recessive trait and brown eyes are a dominant one, a child's eyes will remain blue only if he has received the appropriate blue-producing gene from both parents. If he receives

TABLE 3.1   Some Common Dominant and Recessive Traits

Dominant Trait	Recessive Trait	Dominant Trait	Recessive Trait
Brown eyes	Gray, green, hazel, or blue eyes	Short fingers	Fingers of normal length
Hazel or green eyes	Blue eyes	Double-fingers	Normally jointed fingers
Normal vision	Nearsightedness	Double-jointedness	Normal joints
Farsightedness	Normal vision	Type A blood	Type O blood
Normal color vision	Red-green color blindness	Type B blood	Type O blood
Brown or black hair	Blond hair	Rh positive blood	Rh negative blood
Nonred hair	Red hair	Normal blood clotting	Hemophilia
Curly or wavy hair	Straight hair	Normal red blood cells	Sickle-cell anemia
Full head of hair	Bald-headedness	Normal protein metabolism	Phenylketonuria (PKU)
Normal hearing	Some forms of congenital deafness	Normal physiology	Tay-Sachs disease
Normally pigmented skin	Albino (completely white) skin	Huntington's chorea	Normal central nervous system functioning in adulthood
Facial dimples	No dimples	Immunity to poison ivy	Susceptibility to poison ivy
Thick lips	Thin lips		

Note: Many common traits show dominant or recessive patterns. Sometimes, too, a trait may be dominant with respect to one trait but recessive with respect to another.

it only from one parent or from neither, he will end up with brown eyes. From a genetic standpoint, there are three times as many ways to have brown eyes as to have blue ones. Table 3.2 illustrates this example.

Even for simple traits such as eye color, however, the dominant-recessive distinction does not explain phenotype fully. Very few physical traits have a completely either-or quality. Not even eye color really does, for that matter — look carefully at all your friends, and you will see that a few probably have hazel or greenish eyes and some have darker brown eyes than do others. How can we account for variations such as these?

Transmission of Multiple Variations

The genes responsible for eye color, or for any other trait for that matter, often take on a variety of different forms called **alleles.** Earlier we assumed that the gene responsible for eye color can take only two such forms, or alleles — blue and brown. In reality, the gene for eye color can occasionally take on a third allele, which often leads to hazel eyes.

Because all human beings inherit two sets of chromosomes, one from each parent, and because the genes responsible for any specific characteristic are inherited in pairs, when a person inherits two identical alleles for a particular

TABLE 3.2   Eye Color: An Example of Genetic Transmission

Child's Genotype	Possible Outcomes			
	BB	Bb	bB	bb
Child's Phenotype	Brown eyes	Brown eyes	Brown eyes	Blue eyes
	Homozygous	Heterozygous	Heterozygous	Homozygous

Note: B = gene for brown eyes, which is dominant for eye color; b = gene for blue eyes, which is recessive for eye color.

Most physical traits result from the combined influence of gene pairs inherited from both parents. The degree of resemblance between a child and a given parent depends upon the particular pattern of gene variations involved.

Matched pairs of genes versus mixed pairs

trait, the person is said to be **homozygous** for that trait. When a person inherits two different alleles for the trait, the person is said to be **heterozygous** for that trait. In the case of eye color, heterozygous persons show the phenotype of the dominant allele and therefore have brown eyes. Only homozygous persons can show the phenotype of one of the recessive alleles and have blue or hazel eyes. (See Table 3.2.) But not all examples of genetic transmission work this simply. Sometimes heterozygosity can lead to a phenotype that differs from any of those produced in purely homozygous individuals; such as "dirty blond" hair or fingers that are neither short nor normal in length.

Multiple forms of genes

Many genes have more than two alleles, and when they do, the traits they govern can vary in more complex ways. The four major human blood types, for example, are based on three alleles of the same gene. Two of these are dominant forms, and one is recessive. The three alleles can combine in six possible ways to produce the four blood types. Each type has a unique chemistry that allows it to mix only with certain other blood types, so determining blood genotype matters quite a lot for medical patients who receive blood transfusions.

Not all alleles occur with equal frequency. One of the three alleles of blood type does not occur nearly so often as the other two do, and different parts of the population inherit the blood-typing alleles with different frequencies. Black people differ significantly from white people, for example, in the comparative frequencies of each of the major blood types.

Polygenic Transmission

Unlike eye color and blood type which can vary only in a limited number of qualitatively distinct ways, many other traits seem to vary along a continuum of varying degrees. Height shows this quality: very tall parents usually have tall children and very short parents usually have short children, but a tall and a short parent most often have children of medium height. This is because height differs from eye color in the way it is genetically transmitted. A person does not usually have "all" height or "none" of it, as she might have totally blue or totally brown eyes. Instead she has some amount — more or less of it.

Traits such as height seem to result from the combined influence of many genes, each of which contributes a small part to the trait (Mather & Jinks, 1977). Because of their multiple sources, these traits are often called **polygenic,** meaning "coming from many genes." Many — perhaps most — physical traits are polygenic. In addition to height, skin color has this quality; so does hair color and body weight. In all these cases, children show a marked tendency to have a phenotype that is intermediate between those of their parents. For example, the child of an American of German descent and an American of Chinese descent will tend to have a skin color between the shades of his parents. But notice that this is only a tendency. A few children of very dark parents may look rather light-skinned, and vice versa, just as a few children of very short parents may tower above them, or vice versa. Such inconsistencies occur because parents at one extreme sometimes carry recessive genes for the other extreme. If the recessive genes combine during conception, the child can look markedly different from his parents in that particular trait.

Although psychologists disagree about how much genetics can determine psychological development, most agree that some genetic influence does occur and that this influence is almost always polygenic. The potential to develop skill at taking intelligence tests, for instance, depends partly on genetic endowment. But the skill varies in amount among individuals; we each have more or less of it, not all or none of it, in spite of jokes to the contrary. And continuous variation occurs in behavioral styles or in what psychologists call temperament (A. Thomas & Chess, 1977). We all have greater or lesser tendencies to fidget when we are made to sit still for a long time; only a few people at one extreme can sit completely still for hours, and only a few at the other extreme are immediately climbing the walls.

Because polygenic phenotypes vary by small degrees, environment can influence them in relatively important ways. A light-skinned person can get darker by spending time in the sun; an overweight person can embark on a diet; and a fidgety person can teach herself to sit still for a longer time. Such experiences matter less to traits that are simply transmitted by a single gene; there is no way to change eye color, even though you can cover your irises with tinted contact lenses.

The Determination of Sex

One pair of chromosomes among the usual twenty-three pairs determines whether a child develops as a male or a female. In women this pair looks pretty much like any other pair of matched chromosomes. In men one member of the pair is noticeably shorter than the other. The longer sex chromosome in either sex is called X, and the shorter one in men is called Y. Genetically normal men therefore always have a mixed combination, XY, whereas normal women always have an XX combination.

Whether a child becomes male or female depends on events at conception. All ova, or egg cells, contain a single X chromosome, whereas a sperm cell may contain either an X or a Y. If a Y-bearing sperm happens to fertilize the egg, then a male zygote develops, and if the sperm happens to be X-bearing, then a female zygote develops.

During the first several weeks following conception the developing male or female embryos possess a set of bisexual gonadal, or sex, tissues, which can develop into either male or female sex structures. Between the fourth and eighth weeks of the embryo's development, if the Y chromosome is present, it triggers the gonadal tissue to develop as testes. If the Y chromosome is absent, as in a normal female embryo, gonadal tissue develops as ovaries.

Oddly enough, more Y sperm than X sperm succeed at fertilizing the ovum, even though they have no advantage in numbers. The Y success rate produces perhaps as much as 30 percent more male zygotes (Mittwoch, 1973). The advantage decreases during prenatal development; by birth, boy babies outnumber girl babies by only about 6 percent, although the ratio varies among different societies and racial groups. Later in life, the tables are turned; by about age thirty-five, women begin to outnumber men.

Genetic vulnerabilities of males

The trend suggests that males may be more vulnerable than females, at least genetically. Much of this vulnerability probably stems from the nature of the Y chromosome carried by all males. The Y chromosome is much shorter than its matching X chromosome and may therefore lack many of the gene locations of its matching X chromosome. In males, therefore, any genetic abnormalities on the single complete X chromosome may translate relatively often into phenotypic abnormalities. Most of these abnormalities are either fatal to the male fetus or put it at serious medical risk. Female fetuses and infants possess a second X chromosome, and because it tends usually to be both normal and genetically dominant, women are protected from many of the genetic abnormalities common among men.

Note, however, that beyond childhood men may also die sooner than women for environmental reasons; they more often hold stressful or physically dangerous jobs, and gender roles more often discourage them from attending to their medical needs when illnesses first develop. In recent decades, as more women have taken on traditionally male habits (such as smoking) and entered traditionally male jobs, they have begun narrowing the gender gap in health and longevity.

Genetic influence on longevity

Even so, the sex difference in longevity is probably partly genetic. This conclusion is supported by the rather large number of genetic abnormalities linked to genes on the X chromosome (Tobach & Rosoff, 1978). Table 3.3 lists a few of these, which are often called **sex-linked recessive traits.** One of these is **hemophilia,** an inability of the blood to clot and therefore to stop itself from bleeding. Hemophilia occurred widely in various royal families of Europe, where princes and kings frequently died because of it. Men were more affected than women because hemophilia apparently derives from particular defective recessive genes on the X chromosome. Because women by definition always have two X chromosomes, they had to inherit two of the recessive, problem-causing genes before they actually suffered from hemophilia. Men only needed to inherit one of the recessive genes, so they were more vulnerable.

TABLE 3.3   *Sex-Linked Recessive Traits*

Condition	Description
Color blindness	Inability to distinguish certain colors — usually reds and greens
Hemophilia	Deficiency in substances that allow the blood to clot; also known as "bleeder's disease"
Muscular dystrophy (Duchenne's form)	Weakening and wasting away of muscles, beginning in childhood
Diabetes (two forms)	Inability to metabolize sugars properly because the body does not produce enough insulin
Anhidrotic ectodermal dysplasia	Lack of sweat glands and teeth
Night blindness (certain forms)	Inability to see in dark or very dim conditions
Deafness (certain forms)	Impaired hearing or total hearing loss
Atrophy of optic nerve	Gradual deterioration of vision and eventual blindness

Note: All of the above traits are carried by the X chromosome, and all are recessive. As a result, they occur more rarely in females than in males.

GENETIC ABNORMALITIES

Once in a while, genetic reproduction goes wrong. Sometimes too many or too few chromosomes transfer to a newly forming zygote. Or sometimes the chromosomes transfer properly but carry particular defective genes that affect a child physically, mentally, or both. The changes almost always create significant handicaps for the child, if indeed they do not prove fatal.

Variations in the Number of Chromosomes

Most of the time, inheriting one too many or one too few chromosomes proves fatal. One extra, after all, forces several thousand "wrong" genes on the developing fetus, and it certainly cannot cope easily with so much genetic misinformation. In a few cases, however, children with an extra or a missing chromosome survive past birth and even live fairly normal lives. Three such cases are mentioned here; as it happens, each is named after the doctor who first published a description of it.

Down Syndrome   People with **Down syndrome** have almond-shaped eyes, round heads, and stubby hands and feet. More important, they show some degree of mental retardation, although usually not enough to keep them from learning to manage a good deal of their own lives or from holding routine jobs; nor does it prevent them from having agreeable dispositions. Unfortunately, people with Down syndrome also show greater-than-usual vulnerability to a number of serious diseases; for instance, they have twenty times the usual chances of contracting leukemia, a cancer that affects bone marrow tissue.

Down syndrome occurs in about one baby in every six or seven hundred in the human population as a whole. Probably it happens much more frequently than this at the time of conception, but significant numbers of affected fetuses do not survive until birth. The condition occurs much more often in babies of older mothers (more than thirty-five years) and very young ones (less than eighteen). Recent genetic studies show that the age of the father may matter as well — older fathers confer more risk — but the effect is not as obvious as in the case of mothers (Arehart-Treichel, 1981). Older fathers may produce larger numbers of defective sperm because they have had longer exposure to environmental hazards. Older mothers experience longer exposure to hazards as well and in addition face another problem: by the time mothers reach their late thirties their ova, which were formed before birth, have been waiting several decades to be released by their ovaries, and many may have begun to deteriorate.

Older mothers produce more Down syndrome babies

In fact, there appear to be two types of Down syndrome. In the **nondisjunction type,** which is most common, chromosomes assign unevenly to the gamete cells; as a result, gametes have an extra twenty-first chromosome or are missing one entirely. Although the extra chromosome can be contributed by either parent at any age, if the couple is older, the likelihood is that the chromosome came from the mother.

In the **balanced translocation type,** which accounts for about 4 percent of Down births, a child has a normal number of chromosomes, but chromosomal damage is present because a segment of one chromosome has shifted to another chromosome. This type of Down syndrome comes from a genetic abnormality passed on by either parent; it is not caused by the age of the parents (Feinbloom & Forman, 1987). Table 3.4 summarizes the risk of having a Down syndrome baby for women of different ages.

Because of their greater susceptibility to infectious diseases, many Down syndrome children die early in childhood. Those that survive have an almost normal life expectancy. Down children achieve many of the same developmental

TABLE 3.4 Maternal Age and the Risk of Having a Down Syndrome Baby

Age of Mother	At Any Pregnancy	After a Previous Down Baby
29 or below	1 in 1,000	1 in 100
30–34	1 in 600	1 in 100
35–39	1 in 200	1 in 100
40–44	1 in 65	1 in 25
45–49	1 in 25	1 in 15

Source: Pueschel & Goldstein (1983).

Children with Down syndrome, like these two girls, learn academic material only very slowly. But with special educational help and proper social support, they can lead very satisfying lives.

milestones as normal children do, but at a much slower pace. Nevertheless, Down children never achieve the level of intellectual and psychosocial development needed to lead independent, self-supporting lives as adults and therefore throughout their lives require extensive support from family and service programs or from institutions.

A single X chromosome

Turner's Syndrome   A person with **Turner's syndrome,** which affects only women, has a single X in the sex chromosome instead of the normal XX. The single X results in a female who is short — around four or five feet tall. Her neck tends to be short as well, and extra folds of skin give it a webbed appearance. A woman with Turner's syndrome has ears that are set lower than usual. When she reaches puberty, she tends not to develop secondary sexual characteristics such as breasts and pubic hair. She does show basically normal intelligence as defined by conventional IQ tests, but: she may have serious difficulties at solving problems that require spatial visualization, such as finding her way through a maze.

In the population as a whole, this condition is much less frequent than Down syndrome; only about one in thirty-five hundred adult women has Turner's syndrome. As with other genetic abnormalities, though, the numbers are higher if we measure from conception instead of from birth or among adults; abnormal pregnancies account for much more than their share of spontaneous abortions.

An extra X chromosome

Klinefelter's Syndrome   Instead of missing a sex chromosome, a person with **Klinefelter's syndrome** has at least one extra, most commonly an extra X, to create an XXY pattern. Such a person is phenotypically male, but he tends to have small testes even after puberty and to remain sterile throughout life. In contrast to the short, squat build of a Turner's syndrome woman, the Klinefelter's syndrome man tends to be long-legged, and he often develops small breasts. Overall, Klinefelter's syndrome affects about one in five hundred newborn males.

Abnormal Genes

Even when a zygote has the proper number of chromosomes, it may inherit specific genes that can create serious medical problems for the child after birth.

In many cases these prove lethal. But this is not always the case: here are three that are at least manageable, if not fully curable.

Rh Disease   Rh disease (or *erythroblastosis*) is a condition in which the mother's blood develops antibodies that attack the red corpuscles of a fetus's blood, thereby weakening or even killing the fetus before it is born. The problem is caused by a substance in the blood called the **Rh factor** (named after *rh*esus monkeys, in whom it was first discovered). The dominant form of this factor is called *Rh positive*, which is the form that most individuals inherit. The recessive (and less common) form is called *Rh negative*.

Rh disease occurs when a man who is Rh positive conceives with a woman who is Rh negative. In most of these conceptions, the child inherits the dominant, positive form of the Rh factor, and a small amount of the children's blood crosses the placenta into the mother's own bloodstream. This causes no problem for the first baby, but this pregnancy stimulates the mother to form antibodies to Rh positive blood, as if the positive blood were actually a harmful foreign substance. This process resembles what happens when a person's blood forms antibodies to fight off viral illnesses, but in this case the mother's immune system has mistakenly identified the fetus's blood as harmful.

How Rh disease occurs

Later pregnancies suffer from the antibodies formed during the first pregnancy: the mother's antibodies attack the red blood cells of later fetuses. The severity of the attack varies, depending on the amount of Rh positive blood which crosses the placenta in both the first and second pregnancies, and on the general health of the mother. Until the early 1960s, Rh disease used to kill about ten thousand infants each year and caused various birth defects in at least twice this number (Butnarescu & Tillotson, 1983).

Since the 1960s, however, new medical techniques have made Rh disease very rare. Infants at risk can now be given blood transfusions before they are born, even through the walls of the mother's uterus. And the mothers themselves can be inoculated shortly after the birth of their first infant with Rh negative blood that already contains antibodies (called **Rhogam blood**). This treatment seems to prevent Rh negative mothers from forming any further antibodies that might jeopardize future pregnancies. When Rhogam blood is given to the mother, any antibodies that she has already formed usually disappear within a month or two after birth.

Managing Rh disease

Fragile-X Syndrome   In a condition known as **fragile-X syndrome,** which affects about one individual in one thousand, a chromosome is compressed or separated in two or more places. Most fragile-X males exhibit some degree of mental retardation ranging from mild to severe. Fragile-X females generally are intellectually normal, although a minority display mild retardation. Fragile-X may also be associated with infantile autism, a serious early childhood disorder involving delayed or absent language and communication and bizarre self-stimulating behavior (Nussbaum & Ledbetter, 1986; W. Brown et al., 1982; Carpenter et al., 1982).

Compressed or separated chromosomes

Tourette's Syndrome   A condition known as **Tourette's syndrome** appears to be related to a single abnormal allele. The onset of Tourette's generally occurs between two and twenty-five years of age. Its symptoms include recurrent, involuntary, repetitive, rapid, purposeless motor movements affecting multiple muscle groups (such as eye blinking and jumping); multiple vocal ticks including throat clearing, grunting, barking, and sniffing; and various obsessive concerns and compulsive behaviors such as the use of obscene language (Pauls & Leckman, 1986; Pittman et al., 1987).

One abnormal allele

PKU   Phenylketonuria (PKU) is a disorder that severely diminishes a child's ability to utilize an amino acid called phenylalanine that is found in milk and milk products and is essential to normal nutrition and growth. The disorder is caused by a single recessive allele carried by a relatively small fraction of people; but because PKU is recessive, many people are carriers without realizing it. Left untreated, PKU causes phenylalanine to build up to dangerous levels in the child's blood and spinal fluid, which can eventually lead to brain damage and mental retardation.

Prevention of PKU through diet

A carefully planned diet during infancy and childhood can prevent these problems if PKU is diagnosed early in infancy (Ambrus & Horvath, 1978). In recent years, therefore, many hospitals and states have routinely tested all newborns for this condition and have had dramatic success at preventing the effects of it. This strategy has helped individual children and their families, but of course it has not removed the gene that causes the problem in the first place.

PKU shows clearly the difference between genotypes and phenotypes. Infants with one particular genotype — the PKU deficiency — can grow either into a healthy phenotype or get sick enough to die, depending on the nutrition they receive. Infants who differ in PKU sensitivity can end up with similar phenotypes: both normal and sensitive babies can be healthy when conditions are right.

Sickle-Cell Anemia   By now you may be wondering why nature tolerates so many harmful genetic abnormalities or why they do not disappear as the generations go by simply because people with abnormalities have such serious health problems. Even in societies with modern medical services, genetically different people have a harder time than most in simply surviving.

Sickle-cell anemia suggests one possible answer to this question: sometimes a genetic condition may benefit people in general even though it hurts individuals in particular. **Sickle-cell anemia** is a condition in which a person's red blood cells intermittently acquire a curved, sickle shape instead of having the usual circular shape. The condition is not harmful if only a small proportion of blood cells become sickle-shaped, but a large proportion can clog circulation in the small blood vessels because the cells literally cannot squeeze through the tiny channels.

Explanations for sickle-cell anemia

Sickle-cell anemia is caused by a single recessive allele of a gene that is especially common in people living in tropical climates, such as Africa and the Middle East. But therein lies a clue to its real "purpose." The gene that causes the anemia also confers increased resistance to malaria, an especially troublesome disease in tropical areas. The gene confers this resistance, however, only among people with a particular genotype: those who carry just one unmatched sickle-cell allele along with one dominant, non-sickle-cell allele.

In the case of this condition, heterozygous individuals have a few signs of sickle-cell anemia but strong immunity to malaria, which is probably a large benefit to their health at a relatively small physical cost. Homozygous people either avoid anemia completely by having two dominant genes or suffer badly from it because they have two recessive genes. Either way, they contract malaria at very high rates. As it turns out, very large proportions of individuals in tropical areas are heterozygous. The troublesome allele seems to have been "invented" for their benefit — and at the expense of people who contract anemia.

Huntington's Chorea   A **chorea** is a gradual deterioration of the nervous system that leads to increasingly jerky, involuntary movements. **Huntington's chorea** appears only after about thirty-five years of age, and it always proves fatal. Before that age, a person usually has no way of knowing whether he will get the disease.

Disease carried by dominant gene

Unlike most genetic diseases, Huntington's chorea is carried by a dominant gene rather than a recessive one. By their nature, diseases carried by dominant genes usually disappear after a number of generations because they usually cause the carriers to die before reaching child-bearing age. But because Huntington's

Perspectives

Genetic Screening and Counseling for All Couples?

The risks of genetic disorders, and the advantages that sometimes result from knowledge about them, make some professionals propose that all couples should receive screening and counseling, regardless of their personal history or particular situation. In fact, mass screening has occasionally been tried for selected genetic problems in the United States. In 1976, for example, Congress passed a law requiring all citizens to be tested for vulnerability to sickle-cell anemia, and several states even began to implement this law (Nyhan, 1976).

But this screening program and others like it have created considerable ethical debate. Critics argue that mass screening constitutes an invasion of privacy because it requires disclosure of personal medical information to public agencies. According to this viewpoint, individuals and couples should be free to choose whether or not to participate in any particular screening program. If a couple is at risk for sickle-cell anemia, Tay-Sachs disease, or any other genetic disorder, then no one but that couple should decide whether to make the fact public.

But advocates of mass screening also have ethical reasons for their position. The suffering caused by genetic disorders, they point out, affects many people besides the child. Parents and relatives also suffer, psychologically and often economically, in their efforts to care for a permanently disabled child. And the medical profession and society as a whole use up valuable resources in treating and caring for a child with special needs — resources that are scarce and could be used in other ways for the greater good of society. Because genetic disorders affect so many people for such long periods, some argue that society has a right to demand mass screening.

Those favoring mass screening also argue that an effective screening program pays for itself by reducing human misery and increasing health and overall productivity. They also point to widespread ignorance about genetic risks. Surprisingly large numbers of couples apparently do not know of or understand even the most common genetic problems, such as Rh disease and the risk of Down syndrome for older mothers (Massarik & Kaback, 1981). Given that many couples are at risk without knowing it, a universal screening program might help these individuals and produce a healthier society in the process.

Unfortunately, given the number of known genetic disorders, truly universal screening may not be practical, even if it were considered ethical. Many couples would be tested unnecessarily; those who missed a particular test would have to be tracked down; and taxpayers would have to pay for all this activity. A more practical approach might be to screen only specific groups known to be at high risk. Amniocentesis, for example, currently tends to be used only for the very oldest mothers. Only blacks might be tested for sickle-cell anemia, and only Jews might be tested for Tay-Sachs disease.

This strategy might work for some genetic disorders, but focused screening can create unnecessary, negative stereotypes about the groups targeted for screening (Falek, 1975). Testing Jews for Tay-Sachs disease could create the impression that most Jewish people have this disease, when in fact only a small minority do. Routine testing for sickle-cell anemia in fact eventually ended for a similar reason. Black leaders argued that the program made black people seem more universally afflicted by sickle-cell anemia than they really are: in doing so, the program amounted to a subtle form of genocide because black couples were indirectly being discouraged from conceiving children, even when they were free to do so.

Genetic counseling also has its share of ethical problems. Rightly or wrongly, some couples feel that their medical and genetic backgrounds are their own business, and no assurances of confidentiality by counselors can make them feel otherwise (Money, 1975). Other couples oppose counseling for religious reasons; even if they know that they are genetically at risk, they are unwilling in principle to abort a pregnancy. At best, counseling simply wastes their time; at worst, it coerces them. Counselors can avoid these problems, of course, by working only with volunteers. But then counselors fail to reach some couples who might actually welcome counseling, if only they knew how and where to get it. Apparently, no strategy of screening and counseling, whether universal or voluntary, works perfectly.

---

chorea appears late in life, individuals have been able to confer the unwelcome gene on their offspring before they know that they have the disease, so this particular dominant genetic disorder has persisted.

Tay-Sachs Disease   **Tay-Sachs disease** is a disorder of the nervous system that occurs with highest frequency among people of German or Eastern European (Ashkenazi) Jewish origin; Tay-Sachs affects one baby out of every twenty-five hundred. It also affects people of Spanish or North African (Sephardic) Jewish origin as well as Amish, Italian Catholics, and French-Canadians. In the United States, about one Jewish person in thirty carries the gene for this disorder, but because the gene is recessive, only about one Jewish infant in nine hundred

Imbalance in nerve cells

develops the disease. Nevertheless, this still constitutes a serious genetic concern (B. Muir, 1983).

Tay-Sachs disease disturbs the chemical balance in an infant's nerve cells. At birth the baby may seem fairly normal, but by about six months of age she may show poor tolerance for sudden loud noises and may seem weak and slow to develop. Motor skills that she initially acquires may later be "forgotten" or lost, and the baby becomes progressively more apathetic and irritable. Eventually, deterioration of the nervous system may cause convulsive seizures and lead to deafness and blindness. Most Tay-Sachs babies die by their third birthday. Ironically, they may actually die from a much more common illness, such as pneumonia, simply because their condition has robbed them of their bodily resistance to illness.

GENETIC COUNSELING

Some genetic problems can be reduced or avoided by sensitive counseling for couples who may carry genetic disorders. Couples in need of such counseling may know of relatives who have suffered from genetic diseases, or they may belong to an ethnic group at risk for a particular disorder, as black Americans are at risk for sickle-cell anemia. More immediate signs of genetic risk include the birth of an infant with some genetic disorder or the spontaneous abortion of earlier pregnancies.

Difficulties in estimating risk

Genetic counselors should be thoroughly trained in genetics and in working with other professionals because the counselor must have complete access to potential parents' medical and genetic history in order to help them estimate their chances of having a healthy baby. Making such estimates may be harder than it first appears because couples (and their doctors) do not always know all the genetically relevant information, such as what diseases various relatives experienced in past generations. Of course, estimates of risk may be even harder for couples to live with than for counselors to make because the parents must face considerable uncertainty about the fate of their future child. Nonetheless, it is probably better to decide whether to risk conception on a basis of knowledge rather than of ignorance.

Once the actual genetic risk is clarified, counselors can recommend alternatives from which a couple can choose. The two most obvious alternatives, of course, are to avoid conception completely or to take the chance of conceiving a healthy baby. Modern medical techniques sometimes offer two further options: (a) prenatal diagnosis and possible abortion and (b) medical treatments early in infancy. The usefulness of these techniques, however, depends on the specific genetic problem, and all four alternatives have certain drawbacks.

Prenatal Diagnosis

Sometimes genetic disorders can be detected after conception but before birth using various diagnostic techniques. (See Table 3.5.) Blood tests of a couple, for example, can determine an infant's risk for Rh disease or Tay-Sachs disease. Blood samples can even be drawn from the fetus itself, through the mother's womb, to aid in this diagnosis.

Diagnostic Techniques   Amniocentesis is another diagnostic method that can detect abnormalities in the fetus's chromosomes well before birth. Amniocentesis can be performed between the fourteenth and sixteenth weeks of pregnancy. The

TABLE 3.5   What Conditions Can Prenatal Diagnosis Detect?

Procedure	Conditions Detected
Ultrasound	Pregnancy; fetal growth; whether fetus has aborted; presence of a tubal (ectopic) pregnancy; multiple pregnancies; atypical fetal position (e.g., breech presentation); fetal abnormalities (e.g., limb defects).
Amniocentesis	More than seventy-five genetic disorders including Tay-Sachs disease; Down syndrome; sickle-cell anemia; cystic fibrosis, the most common forms of muscular dystrophy, and hemophilia; maturity of fetal lungs when preterm delivery is under consideration; prenatal medical treatment in some cases.
CVS	Can detect many of the chromosomal abnormalities and conditions detected by amniocentesis but is not as sensitive to more subtle abnormalities.

Source: Feinbloom & Forman (1987).

method involves drawing out of the uterus a tiny amount of the amniotic fluid in which the infant floats during pregnancy and analyzing it. This fluid contains cells that have the fetus's genetic makeup rather than the mother's, so it can be used to determine whether the fetus has abnormal chromosomes, as children with Down syndrome or neurological disorders do.

Fluid contains genetic information

Minor complications such as uterine cramping, vaginal bleeding from the uterus, and leaking of amniotic fluid through the vagina occur in about one out of one hundred procedures. In one out of four hundred procedures there is miscarriage, maternal bleeding at birth, or injury to the fetus associated with this procedure, although recent studies suggest that there is no increased risk for loss of the fetus as a result of amniocentesis (Feinbloom & Forman, 1987).

Chorionic villus sampling (CVS) is a fairly new procedure, which is performed between the eighth and tenth weeks of pregnancy to test for most of the same genetic disorders as amniocentesis does. It involves collecting and analyzing tissue by inserting a thin hollow tube (catheter) through the vagina into the uterus between the uterine lining and the chorion. The *chorion* is a tissue layer that surrounds the embryo for the first two months of its development and that later develops into the placenta. A syringe attached to the tube sucks up several of the *chorionic villi*, projections of tissue that transfer oxygen, food, and waste between the mother's circulation and that of the embryo and that are genetically identical with the embryo (Feinbloom & Forman, 1987).

This technique allows parents to know in the very early weeks of pregnancy if the fetus has inherited a serious defect. This gives them time to decide whether to have a therapeutic abortion. The advantages of CVS over amniocentesis is that it can be performed much earlier in the pregnancy (when it is safer to have a therapeutic abortion if the fetus has inherited a serious defect and the parents so choose), and it eliminates the small risk of miscarriage that is present with amniocentesis. Because CVS cannot detect more subtle chromosomal abnormalities, amniocentesis is sometimes used to check for these or to confirm unclear findings from CVS. A second limitation is that CVS is currently available only in a small number of major teaching hospitals. The major risk of CVS is abortion, which at present occurs in about 0.2 percent of the cases studied (Begley et al., 1984; Schaeffer, 1987; Feinbloom & Forman, 1987).

CVS can be performed early in pregnancy

Ultrasound is another useful diagnostic technique. It allows medical personnel and parents to actually view the fetus. In this procedure, high-frequency sound waves are projected through the mother's womb. When they bounce off the fetus, medical equipment uses the echoes to create a television image of the child in much the way that sonar works. The resulting image often helps to determine whether the fetus is oriented properly for birth with its head down;

Use of television imaging

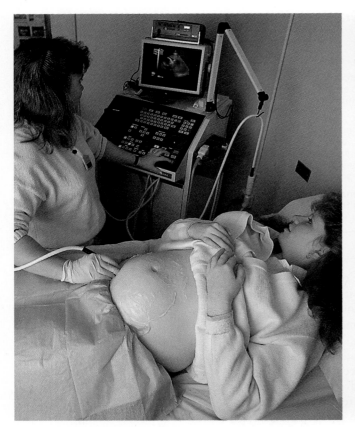 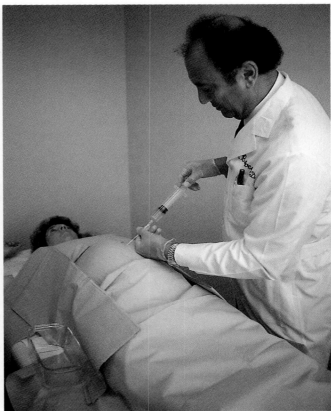

In the photo above, ultrasound helps a mother to "see" her unborn child on a television screen. In the photo at right, amniocentesis is under way; it will indicate whether the fetus's chromosomes are normal.

Limitations of prenatal diagnosis

but the image can also help determine whether the child has approximately normal limbs and external and internal organs. Although there is no reported evidence of fetal abnormalities as a result of ultrasound, there is some concern that its use may affect the ovaries of the mother and female fetus.

Medical personnel can combine these techniques with information about a couple's genetic background to make more precise predictions about whether a particular pregnancy will end with a normal, healthy baby. Note, however, that prenatal diagnosis may not detect certain kinds of problems. Huntington's chorea, for example, is carried by a single gene and therefore escapes all current methods of prenatal diagnosis, and fetuses destined to get this disease look quite normal not only before birth but for a long time thereafter. Note, too, that even a clear diagnosis of a genetic disorder presents couples with an agonizing decision about abortion (Schowalter et al., 1983). If they continue the pregnancy, they know they will encounter a lifetime of special responsibilities as parents; if they abort, they may regret losing the baby or feel that they have abandoned their responsibilities. Or they may believe that they have acted responsibly in protecting their child from a painful or abnormal life and in protecting society from the burden of special care.

Early Medical Treatments

If a couple does decide to continue an abnormal pregnancy to term, medical treatments can sometimes alleviate or even eliminate certain genetic disorders. As we have already discussed, the effects of PKU can be avoided by careful planning of an infant's diet so as to avoid the particular amino acids that PKU

Perspectives

The Potential and Ethical Problems of Genetic Engineering

During the 1980s, significant advances in genetic technology demonstrated that foreign DNA could be directly introduced into the cells and chromosomes of complex mammals. These advances have raised the possibility that at some point we may be able to intervene directly to correct genetic errors underlying a number of human hereditary diseases.

Several possible strategies for **gene therapy**, the medical replacement or repair of defective genes in living human cells, have been outlined by David Suzuki and Peter Knudtson (1989):

1. *Gene insertion* This involves the insertion of one or more copies of the normal version of a gene into the chromosomes of a diseased cell, with the hope that these normal genes can produce sufficient quantities of a missing enzyme or protein, for example, to overcome the inherited deficit.

2. *Gene modification* This technique involves the chemical modification of the defective DNA sequence within the living cell with the goal of recording its genetic message to match that of the normal allele for that gene. In theory, this technique would be less likely to disrupt the extremely complex arrangement of genes on chromosomes and would therefore reduce the possibility of side effects.

3. *Gene surgery* This would involve the precise removal of a faulty gene from a chromosome, perhaps with a highly accurate laser device, followed by its replacement with a cloned substitute. The goal of synthesizing DNA sequences to replace defective ones is at present far beyond the reach of genetic technology.

Even the most optimistic proponents of gene therapy are aware of its limitations. For one, only a small fraction of human diseases are traceable to defects in one or more genes or chromosomes. Fewer than three thousand diseases, most of which are extremely rare, appear to be traceable to the activity of a single gene. Examples of these are albinism, cystic fibrosis, and galactosemia (D. Suzuki & Knudtson, 1989; McKie, 1988; Weatherall, 1985).

In addition, Suzuki and Knudtson (1989) suggest that there are a number of significant potential medical risks associated with gene therapy. One problem is that geneticists cannot yet control the precise chromosomal destination of genes sent into a target cell and cannot even be certain of the quantity of cloned copies that will be delivered. The haphazard addition of genes could disrupt the body's finely tuned genetic self-regulation and distort the intricate chemical interactions of healthy genes.

A second problem is genetic damage, which may occur if a randomly inserted gene or multiple copies of that gene land in the middle of an existing gene, disrupting the normal gene's DNA sequence. Genetic damage can also occur if the intrusion of a randomly inserted gene stimulates a normal gene to transform itself into a cancer-causing gene, or **oncogene**. Until gene therapy strategies can ensure absolute accuracy, they run the risk of accidentally causing cancers in treated cells. A third problem is that even if the germ (reproductive) cells of someone suffering from a hereditary disease could be genetically repaired, the five to ten hidden defective recessive alleles that the average individual carries would continue to be transmitted.

Gene therapy also raises important ethical issues. Perhaps the most serious issue concerns attempts to alter the genotype of the human species. Suzuki and Knudtson (1989) suggest that there is a "moral difference" between altering the body cells of an individual and altering the germ cells that regulate human genotype. Although the life of a body cell is finite and is limited to the life span of the individual, changes in genes are potentially immortal: they can affect future generations and the course of human development itself. Do we have the ethical right to make decisions that may irreversibly change the genotype of the human species?

If we are willing to consider such risks, who should have the power to make such choices and by what process? The disastrous attempts of the Nazis to use genetic engineering to create a "super race" and to eliminate unwanted ethnic groups attests to the most serious dangers of genetic engineering. Even in a democratic society such as our own, there is a danger that those with the economic and political power to control genetic technology will make decisions that are destructive to human beings. There is ample evidence of this danger in the decisions currently being made about the natural environment in general and endangered species in particular.

Even if the goals of genetic engineering are limited to, for example, the redesign or elimination of the genes responsible for specific hereditary disorders or unwanted traits, there are other potential problems. Because as a species we depend on genetic variability to help us adapt and survive, successful attempts to control this variability, some of which produces genetic disease, may hurt us all in the long run. Also, because most human characteristics are influenced by complex combinations of genes, the alteration or removal of a gene responsible for one undesirable trait may interfere with the development of other desirable traits whose genetic causes are not yet understood. In what cases, then, do the medical and psychological risks of genetic alteration to the human species outweigh the gains to the individual — and vice versa?

The answer to this and other important questions about genetic engineering will depend both on future advances in technology and on social policy decisions based on political, economic, and, above all, ethical considerations.

babies cannot utilize. And Rh disease can be treated even after it affects a pregnancy through blood transfusions to the fetus or to the newborn infant.

More often than not, however, genetic disorders cannot be cured or controlled this well. Couples at genetic risk need to face this fact and decide what they want to do about it (Lebel, 1978). Genetic counselors cannot make these choices for couples. Instead, they must lay out the facts and alternatives and offer support for whatever choices the couples end up making.

As we have seen, genetic inheritance has a profound impact on an individual's development. But the environment in which a person grows up also plays an important role. In our next section, we examine how genetics and environment interact to influence the course of developmental change.

Treat or not?

RELATIVE INFLUENCE OF HEREDITY AND ENVIRONMENT

Since the beginning of the 1980s there has been an increasing acceptance of the importance of hereditary (genetic) influences on individual differences in development. But the very same data from behavior-genetic research that support the importance of heredity also provide the best available evidence for the importance of environmental influence. This is because the complex behaviors that are of interest to psychologists and society (for example, temperament, intelligence, personality) are influenced at least as much as much by environmental factors as by genetic ones (Plomin, 1989).

Key Concepts of Behavioral Genetics

Untangling the effects of heredity from the effects of environment has become the special focus of **behavior genetics,** the scientific study of how genetic inheritance (genotype) and environmental experience *jointly influence* behavioral development (phenotype).

Behavioral geneticists have relied upon two concepts to shed light on how genes influence development: canalization and range of reaction. **Canalization** refers to how strongly genes are able to direct and limit development in the face of environmental influences. The stronger a genetic predisposition is, the more resistant it will be to environmental influence (Waddington, 1966). For example, the stages of a normal infant's perceptual-motor development (sucking, turning over, sitting up, crawling, and walking) are strongly (or deeply) canalized and will predictably occur under a wide range of environments and experiences. On the other hand, many other important developmental characteristics, such as personality, temperament, and intellectual functioning, appear to be less canalized and are much more susceptible to environmental influences, including family and schooling.

Some traits resistant to environment

Range of reaction, the second concept, refers to the limits a genotype can set on the range of phenotypes that a person may exhibit in response to different environments (Gottesman, 1963). For example, if three infants start life with different genetic endowments (genotypes) for intelligence — one low, one middle, and one high — the different levels of intelligence they actually develop (phenotypes), as measured by IQ tests, will depend on how each child's intelligence is nurtured as she grows up. Thus, in a supportive environment the child with low endowment may achieve an IQ that is actually equal to (or even higher than) that of the child with a middle range endowment who grows up in a restricted or below average environment. Nevertheless, the first child can not be expected

How much of the resemblance between these three generations is due to heredity, and how much due to environment? Note the similarities in their facial features and perhaps even in their smiles and temperaments.

to achieve an IQ score equal to that of children with high genetic endowment because this is beyond the upper limit of her range of reaction.

A child's genetic endowment may sometimes actually influence the kind of environment to which he is exposed. In some instances, an *active relationship* exists between genes and environment in which the child actively chooses or helps create an environment that supports and extends his genetic predisposition. Thus, a child with an active, outgoing temperament may seek out and create stimulating situations, thus increasing this trait, whereas a child with a more passive, less outgoing temperament child may seek out and elicit experiences that reinforce passivity (Scarr & McCartney, 1983). Likewise, a *passive relationship* can exist between genetic and environmental influences over which the infant or young child who is affected has little or no control. For example, parents who are genotypically highly emotional will probably expose their children to an emotionally charged environment in addition to passing on to them the same genetic endowment.

Relationships between genes and environment

To further untangle heredity from environment, behavioral geneticists have devised a number of ways to assess **heritability,** the contribution heredity makes to characteristics such as intelligence and personality (Plomin, 1989). These methods include observations of specieswide behavior, studies of animal breeding, and studies of twins and adopted children.

Observations of Specieswide Behavior

Many behaviors seem to come naturally — without learning — to every member of a particular species. Young goslings, for example, will follow almost any moving object as soon as they are able to move, a behavior that biologists have called **imprinting** (Lorenz, 1960). The moving object does not have to be an adult goose; a mother chicken, or even a motorized robot, will attract them just as well. For several reasons, imprinting seems to be hereditary. First, all goslings can be imprinted as newborns, before they have had any experiences to teach them the behavior. Second, imprinting occurs only during a rather short, well-defined period after birth — what biologists and psychologists call a **critical period.** And third, once imprinting occurs, it is irreversible; goslings get stuck, so to speak, on the first large moving object that they happen to see.

Significance of specieswide behavior

A broad range of animals, including humans, exhibit specieswide behaviors — that is, behaviors common to all members of the species. Some psychologists believe, for example, that smiling may be genetically programmed, because even deaf and blind infants smile. And some think that a capacity to acquire language may be genetically programmed because nearly all children learn their first language easily without any explicit effort by their parents to teach them.

But note that the animal or human requires certain experiences for even the most universal behaviors to develop properly. Goslings may be genetically ready to imprint on any moving object, but only experience can provide them with that object. If by chance their environment contains nothing moving during the first few days of their lives, the goslings will never learn to follow anything. All children may be predisposed to smile, but some eventually learn to smile much more broadly and more often than others do. And all infants may be genetically ready to acquire language, as shown by the universal tendency to babble, but a few infants — notably those who are deaf — never actually hear spoken language, so their speech becomes impaired.

Lessons from Animal Breeding

Studies of animal breeding consistently suggest the combined effects of heredity and environment. In one classic study, for example, psychologists began with a group of fairly average laboratory rats, which they tested for skill at learning a maze; to do so the psychologists counted the errors each rat made as it repeatedly navigated the runways of the maze. Eventually every rat learned the maze perfectly, but some took much longer than others to learn it. Over several generations, the "bright," fast-learning rats were allowed to breed only with one another, and the "dull" rats were allowed to breed only with other slow ones. Eventually, the two groups diverged widely in the maze-learning skill; even the dullest of the bright rats outperformed the brightest of the dull ones (Tryon, 1940; Lindzey & Thiessen, 1970).

All hope was not lost, however, for the dull rats. Later research showed that the rats differed only in the way that they had been bred to differ — that is, in their ability to learn a particular sort of maze (Searle, 1949). If the rats had to press a lever to get food, both groups learned at about the same rate. The breeding experiments, then, apparently did not show that a generalized skill — a sort of animal IQ — follows the same genetic rules as physical characteristics or simple inherited behaviors. Current research shows similar patterns for a whole barnyard of animal species, including ducks, chickens, mice, cats, and cattle (Simmel & Bagwell, 1983).

Related experiments on animals have suggested that the proper environment can make animals more "competent." Laboratory rats and mice, for example, seem to benefit from being kept in a cage enriched with extra objects to handle and chew, interesting nooks and crannies to explore, and the like (Krech et al., 1962, 1966). Such animals learn mazes more quickly as a result of their "better upbringing," regardless of their original level of skill. As with humans, however, the animals show wide individual differences in spite of their equally improved environments.

For psychologists, studies of the genetics of animal behavior have both advantages and problems. They have the obvious advantage of speed: animals, especially rats and mice, can create new generations in weeks instead of years. And psychologists do not need to concern themselves deeply with the ethics of their matchmaking; presumably a rat does not really care which rat it mates with. But studying animals carries the risk of **anthropomorphism,** the tendency to imagine that animals think, feel, and behave in the same ways that humans do. Fast-learning rats may at first seem to show "intelligence" in the human sense of the term, but closer observation suggests other interpretations. Perhaps the "maze-bright" rats were just more impulsive physically and therefore less apt to sniff their way around a maze in a way that an observer might interpret as "taking wrong turns."

Nevertheless, the essential conclusions of these studies have been supported widely by current research on several species of animals (Simmel & Bagwell, 1983). For animals, learning a particular skill depends on both inheritance and the proper opportunities. As the following section shows, this idea applies to people, too.

Studies of Twins and Adopted Children

Identical twins (those who develop from one fertilized egg) provide one sort of natural experiment for comparing the effects of heredity and environment. By developing from one egg, they offer two individuals with the same genetic endowment. Any differences between them therefore probably reflect the influence of environment. The catch is to find twins who grow up in different environments. Usually parents and society offer twins similar experiences, thus compounding their preexisting genetic similarity. Nevertheless, some twins do grow up with very different life experiences, particularly if they grow up in separate families because of the death of their parents.

"Natural" experiments on heredity and environment

Unrelated children adopted into a family provide another sort of natural experiment for comparing the effects of heredity and environment. These children share environments with their adopted siblings and parents, even though they have completely unrelated genotypes. Differences between adopted children and their adopted relatives should therefore tell something about the influence of their genetic differences. But such comparisons are far from precise because family members never live in exactly the same environment; one sibling may be encouraged to wash dishes, whereas another may be urged to study especially hard.

In spite of these limitations, studies of twins reared apart and of adopted children have shed a great deal of light on the relative contributions of heredity and environment to human development. The major research methods for studying these children are the **twin design** and the **adoption design.** In the twin

Because these twins are identical, they share entirely the same genotype, and differences between them reflect differences in their environments.

design, the degree of similarity between identical twins is compared with the similarity between fraternal twins (those who develop from two eggs); in the adoption design, genetically related individuals reared apart and genetically unrelated individuals reared together are compared.

Bridges   How influential is genetics in determining intelligence?

Intelligence   General intelligence as measured by standardized IQ tests, for example, shows both hereditary and environmental components. Close relatives tend to have more similar IQ scores than distant relatives do, and relatives of any type have more similar scores if they live together than if they live apart (Nichols, 1978; Bouchard & McGue, 1981; Pederson et al., 1985). Adopted children score more closely to their biological parents than to their adopted parents (Skodak & Skeels, 1949; Honzik, 1957). In addition, two major ongoing longitudinal studies of cognitive development (the Louisville Twin Study and the Colorado Adoption Project) are finding that genetic influence on IQ increases substantially during childhood and that these differences continue into adulthood (Wilson, 1983; Ploman et al., 1988; DeFries et al., 1987).

Personal Traits   Comparisons of twins reared apart do suggest that a wide variety of personal behaviors and traits are at least partially hereditary. Many twins who grew up separately report liking the same sorts of foods and the same sorts of clothing. Often they independently adopt similar hairstyles, use their free time for similar recreations, and laugh at the same sorts of jokes. What makes these similarities surprising is that twins do not need to live together to acquire them (Bouchard, 1981).

Differences in temperament at birth

Temperament   Temperament refers to an individual's consistent style of responding to the broad range of environmental events and situations that she encounters. Although there are differences in how researchers define temperament, a variety of studies find that infants display differences in such temperamental patterns as activity level, irritability, emotional responsiveness, and sociability at birth. Because these differences are present well before the babies have had much time to learn unique behavioral styles, they are probably due to genetic influence (Buss & Plomin, 1984; Goldsmith et al., 1987).

Consider the tendency to smile. Some infants smile more quickly and frequently than others do or for longer periods of time. Young identical twins, it seems, are rather similar in their smiling styles; they tend to smile at the same sorts of stimulation and at similar frequencies, even within the first few months of life. Compared to fraternal twins, in fact, identical twins are significantly more alike in smiling behavior (Freedman, 1976). And identical twins show similar responses to strangers; they both become about equally anxious or equally curious (Plomin & Rowe, 1979). Again, fraternal twins differ more markedly from each other than do identical twins.

Parents certainly report differences in their infants' temperaments even when the babies are newborn. One major study of parents' reports identified nine ways in which parents said that their babies differed (A. Thomas & Chess, 1977, 1981):

1. *Activity level* How much does the baby move around?
2. *Rhythmicity* How much does the baby's need for food, sleep, and elimination follow a regular, clockwork schedule?
3. *Approach-withdrawal* How much does the baby seem drawn by or withdrawn from novel stimuli and new situations?
4. *Adaptability* How easily does the baby adjust to new situations and new people?
5. *Intensity of reaction* How expressive or strong are the baby's emotional reactions — does she laugh instead of smile or whimper instead of howl?

6. *Threshold of responsiveness* How sensitive is the baby to stimulation — does she require a lot before she responds?

7. *Quality of mood* How much of the time does the baby seem happy versus fussy?

8. *Distractibility* How well does the baby pay attention to an ongoing activity in spite of other stimulation going on around her?

9. *Attention span* How much does the baby stay with one activity of her own accord instead of shifting repeatedly from one to another?

By studying these dimensions, Thomas and Chess found three general patterns of temperament. They called the first of these "easy" babies because they showed mostly positive moods, regular body functions, and good adaptation to new situations. The second group, the "difficult" babies, showed the opposite; negative moods, irregularity, and high stress in new situations. The third group, the "slow to warm up" babies, resembled the difficult ones but were less extreme; they were moody and relatively unadaptable but did not react violently to new stimuli. As we might expect, many babies did not fall neatly into any of these groups.

Three patterns of temperament

Because these differences emerge immediately after birth, some psychologists believe they result at least partly from differences in genotypes. The original classification of temperaments, however, depended partly on a biased source of information: parents' reports about their newborn children. More recent studies have reduced the problem of parental bias in reporting by using two additional measures of temperament — behavior ratings by pediatricians, nurses, teachers, and other individuals familiar with the child and direct observation of the child. These studies have confirmed earlier findings of temperamental differences at birth (Plomin, 1989).

To what degree do early differences in temperament persist through childhood, adolescence, and adulthood? Studies have found that broad temperament patterns such as emotionality, activity level, sociability, shyness, and irritability are pretty stable throughout life and have concluded that such patterns are largely genetic (Buss & Plomin, 1984; Plomin, 1986). They also find, however, that early temperamental patterns can be modified by environmental factors, includ-

Although infants vary widely in temperament, most adopt a relatively "easy" style of responding, which allows parents to meet their needs more reliably and completely.

A Multicultural View

Ethnic Differences in Temperament

A growing body of research indicates that the culture a child grows up in may significantly shape various temperamental characteristics. In one culture, a given temperamental characteristic may meet one kind of response and have one meaning; in another culture, the same characteristic may mean something else entirely.

In order to separate out cultural influences on temperament from biological influences, Margot Prior, Michael Kyrios, and Frank Oberklaid compared parent ratings of temperament in infants from four to eight months across four cultural groups: American, Chinese, Australian, and Greek-Australian (Prior et al., 1987). The Infant Temperament Questionnaire (ITQ) described on pages 98–99 was used to rate the infants on nine temperamental dimensions (see Table 3.6).

These results of this study were intriguing. American and Australian infants were rated as more approaching, more adaptable, more positive in mood, and more distractible (easier to soothe) than were the Chinese or Greek-Australian infants. American and Australian infants were also much more regular in their eating, elimination, and sleeping than Greek and Chinese infants. The Chinese infants were rated as more intense and showed a greater sensitivity (lower threshold of response) to stimulation than the American and Australian infants did.

Greek infants were rated as significantly less persistent than either American or Chinese infants. They also showed a predominantly negative temperamental profile (negative mood, low approach, low distractibility, low adaptability). Greek and Chinese infants exhibited significantly more negative mood than Australian and American infants did.

Prior and her researchers did not explain all of these

TABLE 3.6 Comparison of Infant Temperament in Selected Cultural Groups

Dimension	Cultural Group			
	American	Australian	Greek	Chinese
Activity level	H	H	L	L
Rhymicity	H	H	L	L
Approach-withdrawal	H	H	L	L
Adaptability	H	H	L	L
Intensity of reaction	L	L	H	H
Threshold of responsiveness	L	L	H	H
Quality of mood	H	H	L	L
Distractibility	H	H	L	L
Attention span	H	H	L	H

Note: H = high level of temperamental dimension. L = low level of temperamental dimension.

differences as the result of culture. They reported that the high intensity and low reactivity of the Chinese infants were consistent with what other researchers had found and might have reflected an inherited, physiologically based pattern of arousability and responsivity. Likewise, the high intensity, low distractibility, and low level of adaptability reported for the Greek infants might also have reflected an inherited temperamental difference. A similar conclusion was reported by Daniel Freedman, who found that Caucasian babies were more irritable and

Temperament patterns are stable

ing patterns of child-rearing and relationships with family members and friends. As noted earlier in the chapter, temperamental patterns tend to remain most stable where there is a passive relationship between heredity and environment and most subject to change when an active relationship between heredity and environment exists. Thus, an infant who is irritable at birth will be more likely to continue to exhibit that trait if his parents reinforce it and less likely to do so if they do not.

Personality Not only infant temperament but also certain features of personality show genetic influence. When judged by written personality tests, for example, identical twins resemble each other more closely than fraternal twins do. Identicals are more closely matched in their levels of **extroversion,** which is the tendency to be outgoing and interested in things and people other than yourself (Eaves & Eysenck, 1976). And identicals are more closely matched in levels of anxiety and fearfulness.

harder to comfort than Chinese-American infants were, even though the mothers in both groups had received the same prenatal preparation and care (Freedman, 1976, 1979).

But, according to Prior, all these differences could have reflected cultural differences in child-rearing practices. For example, the temperament pattern reported for the American and Australian infants (but not for the Chinese and Greek infants) might have been related to the high levels of sociability and extroversion, and to positive and relaxed attitudes that characterize American and Australian cultures. Similarly, the temperament pattern reported for the Chinese and Greek infants might

have been related to the fact that Chinese and Greek infants are kept in close proximity to their primary caregiver, are not encouraged to interact with other people, and are therefore more restricted in the amount of stimulation and interaction available to them.

In addition, the higher activity levels reported for the American infants might have reflected the high level of energy and activity in American middle-class society and the tendency for American mothers to actively arouse and stimulate their infants. In contrast, the lower energy and activity levels reported for the Chinese and Greek infants might have reflected the fact that because they are generally "wrapped up" (swaddled) in the first year, their energy and activity levels are low.

The authors also suggested that differences in regularity of biological functions (rhythmicity) might have been as much a product of the mother's behavior as the infant's. For Chinese and Greek infants, who received low ratings on that dimension, feeding and sleeping times may be more "child-centered," with more emphasis on immediate gratification of the infant's needs. American mothers, on the other hand, are more likely to set meal and sleep times according to their own schedules. Thus, Greek and Chinese infants may not learn to adapt as early as Australian and American infants do to the varying demands of the social environment and may be less easily distracted from their attempts at self-gratification. Similarly, Greek infants may have less need to persist in their expressions of hunger or dissatisfaction, a tendency that may account for their lower scores on this dimension. Prior and her colleagues concluded by calling for additional research to disentangle the role of particular cultural expectations and influences, maternal interaction styles, and actual infant temperament characteristics.

Ethnic and cultural differences may significantly influence a child's temperament.

Heredity may create these similarities directly, as it seems to do with infant temperament. Or it may contribute indirectly by creating unique environments for children with unique genotypes. Consider two pairs of twins. Claire and Yvette are fraternal twins, and perhaps because of this they score more differently on standardized tests of school achievement than Carl and Nicholas, who are identical twins, do. Over a period of time, these children's differences in school performance lead their parents and teachers to offer them different educational opportunities. Claire, who seems brighter, gets more special attention during class than Yvette. In first grade, Claire is placed in the top reading group in her class, while Yvette ends up in the bottom group. Because Carl and Nicholas seem more similar to begin with, however, they are put in the same reading group — the middle one. By the end of the year, Claire has not only learned to read significantly better than Yvette has but seems more confident as well. Carl and Nicholas, in contrast, continue to seem rather similar in achievement and in self-confidence.

Indirect influences on personality

Genetic differences may have affected the original levels of academic performance of these children. But as time went on, experiences increased these differences through **a self-fulfilling prophecy:** teachers and parents responded to beliefs about each child's capacities and arranged experiences for each in response to these beliefs. In this indirect way, genotype influenced phenotype, even over a rather long period.

Mental Illnesses and Disturbances   Serious mental illnesses reveal genetic influences. One such illness is **manic-depression.** A manic-depressive person experiences extreme alternations of mood, sometimes feeling very elated and excited, then shifting suddenly to a period of deep depression or despair. Manic-depressive conditions run in families in ways that are somewhat independent of the personal relationships among family members (Claridge & Margan, 1983). Family members do not share the condition just because they share the same conglomeration of family conflicts and tensions. But this does not mean that family conflicts and tensions play no role in mental illness; it only means that they are not the only cause.

Relatives' tendencies to experience similar illnesses

How do we know? One reason is a phenomenon called **concordance,** or the tendency for pairs of close relatives to become mentally ill. Identical twins show much stronger concordance than fraternal twins do. If one twin becomes manic-depressive, the chances of his sibling also becoming manic-depressive are substantially higher if that sibling is an identical twin rather than a fraternal one. This fact suggests that genetic endowment may somehow affect an individual's tendency to become manic-depressive. But it does not prove that the influence is direct. As we have seen, at least some genetic influences are rather indirect.

Hereditary patterns also occur in **schizophrenia,** a severe mental disorder with a number of symptoms (American Psychiatric Association, 1986; Diederen, 1983). The thinking of schizophrenics often seems fragmented or incoherent; in conversation, they may shift topics suddenly and unaccountably and with no apparent awareness that a shift has occurred. Schizophrenics may suffer from delusions of persecutions ("Everyone is out to get me!"), and they may experience hallucinations, such as voices that seem to be speaking to them. When the disorder is at its worst, it may also involve a blunting or flattening of feelings. The person's face and voice may convey little expression of any kind, although sometimes inappropriate feelings burst out at unexpected moments. For example, a schizophrenic person may laugh loudly about a painful early memory.

Strong concordance among schizophrenic relatives

Concordance among schizophrenic relatives is strong, and it is particularly strong among especially close relatives. If one member of a pair of identical twins becomes schizophrenic, her twin sibling has thirty times the usual chances of becoming schizophrenic herself (Gottesman, 1978). The condition traces through biological families more consistently than through adopted families; children placed for adoption show high concordances with their biological siblings and parents, not with their adopted families.

Accounting for such trends has stimulated much research but has led to few definite answers. Current professional opinion tends to believe that future schizophrenics may differ metabolically and therefore genetically from normal populations in ways that make them more likely to become ill. But the illness itself may occur only under unusual, rather stressful circumstances. No single gene or chromosome has been found to mark schizophrenics or their metabolism clearly, but certain differences in bodily chemistry do occur and are suspected of playing a role in predisposing individuals toward schizophrenia. In this way mental illness differs from Down syndrome, which is clearly associated with a particular, observable chromosomal error. With schizophrenia, analysis of genes remains ambiguous, and we cannot know for sure who will become ill.

Cautions and Conclusions About the Influence of Heredity and Environment

As we have seen, there is much evidence to suggest that heredity plays a very significant role in determining key aspects of our intelligence, temperament, and personality. But we need to remind ourselves of the limits of hereditary influence. Although the genetic influence on individual differences in behavioral development is usually significant and often substantial, nongenetic factors contribute more than one-half to the development of most complex behaviors. In the case of schizophrenia, for example, identical twins show concordance of less than 40 percent, which means that in almost one-half of the cases of schizophrenia, environmental factors play a significant role in the development of the disorder (Plomin, 1989). Rather than ruling out the role of heredity, these findings suggest that heredity contributes a tendency or predisposition to develop schizophrenia given certain environmental conditions.

For another, when environmental factors are influential, they tend to operate on an individual-by-individual basis rather than on a family-by-family basis. In other words, they tend to make children in the same family different from one another rather than to make an entire family different from other families. Thus, environmental factors are especially useful in accounting for differences among family members. Siblings (brothers and sisters) in the same family appear to experience considerably different environments in terms of parental treatment and their interaction with one another and their peers (Plomin, 1989).

Environmental factors work on individual basis

We should view cautiously the strong current trend to minimize environmental contributions in favor of an overly simplistic (and perhaps optimistic) belief that most or even all developmental behaviors are primarily genetic in their origin. However tempting the hope that complex behavioral problems (e.g., intellectual performance, schizophrenia, alcohol abuse) can be understood and perhaps solved by reducing them to genetic causes, behavioral genetic research leaves little doubt that *both* nature and nurture are important in human development.

GENETICS AND DEVELOPMENTAL PSYCHOLOGY

In spite of its limitations, knowledge of human genetics contributes to human welfare in two ways. First, it clarifies the origins of many behaviors (Kaplan, 1976). According to conventional wisdom, behaviors are either "learned" or "inborn"; human genetics suggests instead that many of them are actually both. Second, knowledge of genetics can suggest realistic limits to how much to expect from many ordinary life experiences. How much can education really make people "more intelligent"? How much can parents expect a child with an active temperament to learn to be quieter? After learning the complex answers that genetics usually gives to questions like these, professionals can, and should, shift attention to individuals: how can we know whether *this* child will develop normally or whether *that* one will experience a chronic disorder? For these more personal questions, we need more knowledge of individual development, such as that offered by genetic counseling. Such an orientation is also provided by other branches of developmental psychology, which we describe in the following chapters.

SUMMARY OF MAJOR IDEAS

Mechanisms of Genetic Transmission

1. Genetic information is contained in a complex molecule called deoxyribonucleic acid (DNA).

2. Most bodily cells produce tissue by simple division of their genes, chromosomes, and other cellular parts by means of a process called mitosis.

3. Reproductive cells, or gametes, divide by a process called meiosis, and recombine into a zygote at conception.

4. The process of meiosis gives each gamete half of its normal number of chromosomes; conception brings the number of chromosomes up to normal again and gives the new zygote equal numbers of chromosomes from each parent.

Individual Genetic Expression

5. A person's phenotype is the pattern of traits that the person actually shows during his or her life.

6. A person's genotype is the set of inherited genetic traits; it depends on the pattern of chromosomes and genes inherited at conception.

7. Although most genes exist in duplicate, some — called dominant genes — may actually influence the phenotype if only one member of the pair occurs.

8. Recessive genes do not influence the phenotype unless both members of the pair occur in a particular form.

9. Many genetic traits are transmitted by the combined action of many genes.

10. Sex is determined by one particular pair of chromosomes, called the X and Y chromosomes.

Genetic Abnormalities

11. Some genetic abnormalities occur when an individual inherits too many or too few chromosomes.

12. The most common abnormalities of this type are Down syndrome, Turner's syndrome, and Klinefelter's syndrome.

13. Other genetic abnormalities occur because particular genes are defective or not normal, even though their chromosomes are normal; examples are Rh disease, PKU, sickle-cell anemia, Huntington's chorea, and Tay-Sach's disease.

Genetic Counseling

14. Experts on genetics can provide parents with information about how genetics influences the development of children and about the risks of transmitting genetic abnormalities from one generation to the next.

15. Several methods now exist for diagnosing genetic problems before a baby is born, such as amniocentesis, CVS, ultrasound, and various blood tests.

16. After a child is born, some genetic abnormalities are treatable with current medical techniques.

17. Given the permanence and importance of genetic problems when they occur, genetic counselors should help couples to reach informed decisions about their pregnancies that take personal circumstances into account as well as scientific information.

Relative Influence of Heredity and Environment

18. Behavior geneticists study how genotype and environment together influence phenotype. They use the concepts of canalization and range of reaction to determine the strength of genetic predisposition.

19. Whether the relationship between genes and environment is active or passive can determine how genetic predisposition influences a child's life.

20. Studies of animal breeding show that heredity and environment operate jointly to affect problem-solving skills in animals.

21. Studies of identical twins and of adopted children suggest the joint operation of heredity and environment.

22. Observations of infant temperament suggest that babies may be born with somewhat individual styles of emotional reaction.

23. Certain personality traits such as extroversion and certain mental illnesses such as schizophrenia may be inherited to a certain extent, but they are also substantially influenced by environmental experiences.

24. When environmental factors are significant, they operate on an individual, rather than a family, basis.

KEY TERMS

gametes *(76)*	Down syndrome *(85)*
sperm *(76)*	Turner's syndrome *(86)*
ovum *(76)*	Klinefelter's syndrome *(86)*
genes *(76)*	Rh disease *(87)*
chromosomes *(76)*	fragile-X syndrome *(87)*
deoxyribonucleic acid	Tourette's syndrome *(87)*
(DNA) *(76)*	phenylketonuria
zygote *(77)*	(PKU) *(87)*
mitosis *(78)*	sickle-cell anemia *(88)*
meiosis *(78)*	Huntington's chorea *(88)*
genotype *(79)*	Tay-Sachs disease *(89)*
phenotype *(79)*	gene therapy *(90)*
recessive genes *(80)*	amniocentesis *(90)*
dominant genes *(80)*	chorionic villus sampling
alleles *(81)*	(CVS) *(91)*
homozygous *(82)*	ultrasound *(91)*
heterozygous *(82)*	behavior genetics *(94)*
polygenic traits *(83)*	imprinting *(95)*
sex-linked recessive	critical period *(95)*
traits *(84)*	concordance *(102)*
hemophilia *(84)*	

WHAT DO YOU THINK?

1. Does our society overrate or underrate the impact of genetics on human development? Does genetics affect our lives more than we care to admit or less than most of us realize? Explain your opinion.

2. How would you feel if you had a child with Down syndrome? What do you think would be your first reactions?

(If possible, you might also discuss this question with some parents who really did give birth to such a child.)

3. Are modern medical techniques unwittingly maintaining many hereditary disorders by keeping many abnormal children alive now who in the past might have died? If so, does this pose an ethical problem?

FOR FURTHER READING

Anderson J. K. *Genetic Engineering.* Grand Rapids, Mich.: Zondervan, 1982.

Walters, W., and Singer, P. *Test-Tube Babies.* New York: Oxford University Press, 1982.

Both books discuss current and future methods of artificial reproduction and the many practical and ethical issues surrounding them. The first book concludes that artificial methods of genetic control should be used only sparingly, if at all; the second conveys more hopeful optimism.

Blatt, R. J. R. *Prenatal Tests: What They Are, Their Benefits and Risks, and How to Decide Whether to Have Them or Not.* New York: Vintage Books, 1988.

This book describes in nontechnical language the current range of prenatal tests, their advantages and disadvantages, the nature of the results, and implications for the family.

Feinbloom, R. I., and Forman, B. Y. *Pregnancy, Birth and the Early Months: A Complete Guide* (rev.) Reading, MA: Addison-Wesley, 1987.

This comprehensive and well-grounded discussion looks at many of the major issues facing parents during pregnancy, birth, and infancy. This book is particularly strong on prenatal development and birth.

McKie, R. *The Genetic Jigsaw: The Study of the New Genetics.* New York: Oxford University Press, 1988.

This book covers recent developments in genetics and genetic engineering in an informative and interesting way and is a good introduction to the topic.

Suzuki, D., and Knudtson, P. *Genethics: The Clash Between the New Genetics and Human Values.* Cambridge, MA: Harvard University Press, 1989.

This book offers a well-organized coverage in nontechnical language of state-of-the-art developments in genetics. It provides a balanced presentation of the ethical questions involved in such issues as genetic screening in the workplace, gene therapy, biogenetic weapons, and the patenting of genetic material.

Wenegrat, B. *Sociobiology and Mental Disorder.* Reading, MA: Addison-Wesley, 1984.

The author describes the sociobiological viewpoint: how principles of evolution can be used to explain various important human behaviors. He then suggests how many mental disorders can be understood as specific deviations from biological and evolutionary norms.

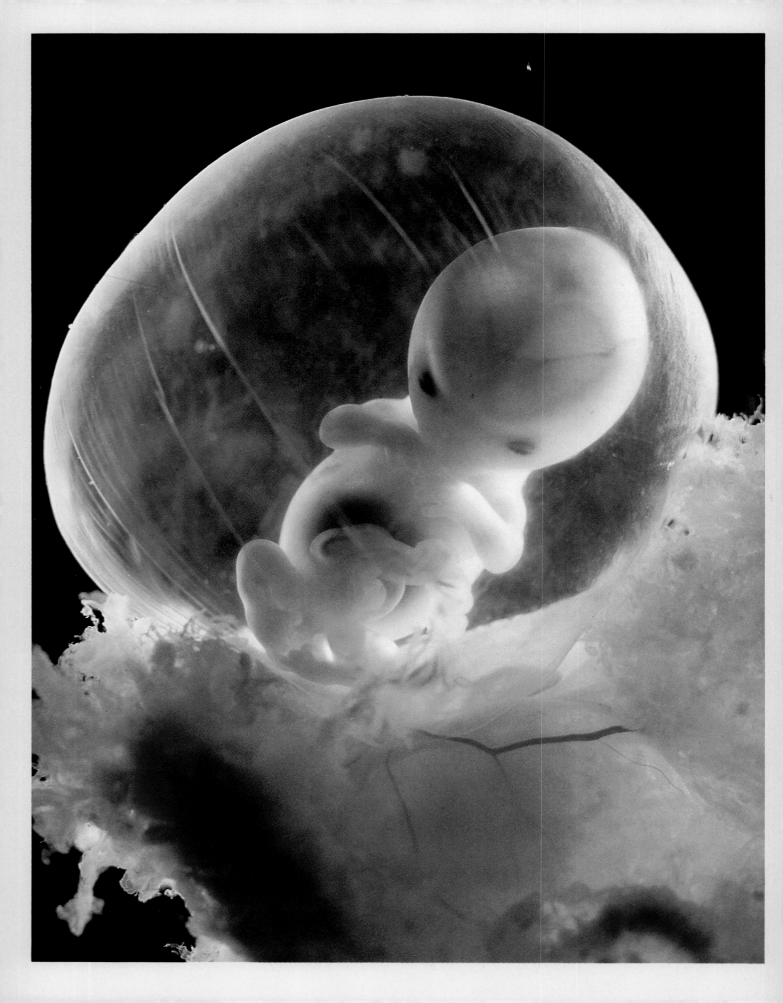

CHAPTER 4

Prenatal Development and Birth

Focusing Questions

■ What conditions must be met for conception to occur, and what happens to the developing embryo during the three stages of development that occur between conception and birth?

■ What prenatal risks may the developing baby be exposed to during a typical pregnancy?

■ What changes occur to an expectant mother during the course of her pregnancy?

■ How long do each of the three stages of the birth process take, and what happens during each?

From the moment of conception, a child becomes a biological possibility, even if the one-celled zygote's status as a human being is ambiguous. Early during its nine months inside the womb, a fetus acquires all the essential human physical features and some rudimentary human behaviors as well. It is influenced by changes in its environment, by its own rapid physical growth, and by the well-being of its mother and the stresses and supports that affect her. Altogether, these internal and external influences create a truly unique person.

How do microscopic cells become people? In this chapter we describe the events and processes of development before birth, pointing out how these developments affect the child after birth. We also look at some of the risks and problems of prenatal development and of birth and at their long-term impact on the child.

PRENATAL STAGES OF DEVELOPMENT

In the section that follows, we see that prenatal development begins with conception and then continues through discrete periods, or stages. The first is the **germinal stage,** or period of the ovum, which occurs during the first two weeks of pregnancy; the **embryonic stage** lasts from the third week to the eighth week; and the **fetal stage** lasts from the eighth week until birth.

Conception

Egg cells develop in the ovaries

Let us look first at the microscopic actors of prenatal development, the gametes that we described in Chapter 3. One of them is the **ovum,** or egg cell. The egg cells develop in two small, almond-shaped organs, the ovaries, which normally release one egg cell during each menstrual cycle. The egg travels down one of the fallopian tubes toward the uterus, where the baby will develop. The opening of the uterus, the cervix, connects to the woman's vagina, which receives the male's penis during intercourse and, upon ejaculation, the male's reproductive cells. (See Figure 4.1.)

Eggs cells begin to develop well before a girl begins having menstrual cycles or is otherwise ready for intercourse. At birth, in fact, a girl's ovaries contain several hundred thousand ova, which are already partially developed. Many of

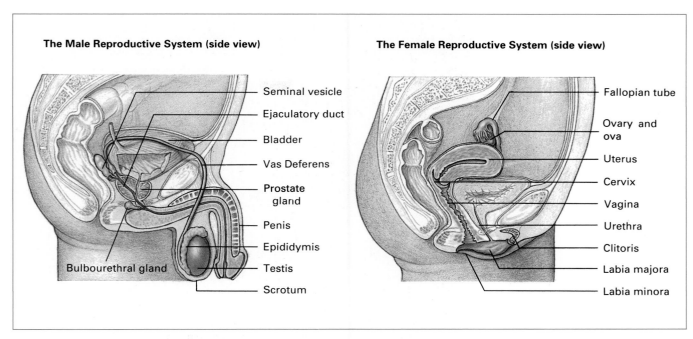

The Male Reproductive System (side view)

- Seminal vesicle
- Ejaculatory duct
- Bladder
- Vas Deferens
- Prostate gland
- Penis
- Epididymis
- Bulbourethral gland
- Testis
- Scrotum

The Female Reproductive System (side view)

- Fallopian tube
- Ovary and ova
- Uterus
- Cervix
- Vagina
- Urethra
- Clitoris
- Labia majora
- Labia minora

FIGURE 4.1
Male and Female Reproductive Systems

these degenerate or die, however, during the dozen or so years before the girl begins menstruating, and many more fail to mature fully after that. So a woman ends up with a relatively small, fixed supply of potential ova (Butnarescu & Tillotson, 1983). In this respect she differs markedly from a man.

Male reproductive cells are called **spermatozoa,** or sperm cells. They develop in the testes, which are located in the bag of skin called the scrotum, that is underneath and behind the penis. (See Figure 4.1.) The sperm get a late start compared to ova; the testes do not begin producing sperm in quantity until puberty, or about twelve to fourteen years after birth. They soon make up for lost time, however, by producing millions of sperm, and production continues relatively undiminished well into a man's old age. Each sperm cell has a head and a long tail, rather like a tadpole, that helps it swim through the female reproductive organ.

Sperm cells develop in the testes

To create a **zygote** — a fertilized egg cell — at least one sperm cell from the man has to find and penetrate one egg cell from the woman. That moment marks **conception.** Even though potential parents may consider conception all too easy to accomplish, from the gametes' point of view the job is extremely challenging. For a couple to conceive successfully, every one of the following conditions must be met:

1. The ovaries must release one healthy egg cell.
2. The egg cell must migrate most of the way down the fallopian tube.
3. A large supply of sperm cells must be deposited as far as possible up the vagina, preferably at or near the cervix.
4. At least some of the sperm must swim the right way instead of the wrong way — that is, up through the uterus to the fallopian tubes.
5. At least some of these sperm must survive the journey, even though the woman's uterus is slightly acidic and therefore toxic to sperm.
6. A few sperm must reach the ovum.
7. One sperm must penetrate the ovum to form a zygote.

Conditions necessary for conception.

Timing is crucial in this process. The ovum normally lives only about twenty-four hours after it is released and the sperm only about forty-eight hours (Harris,

Timing is critical

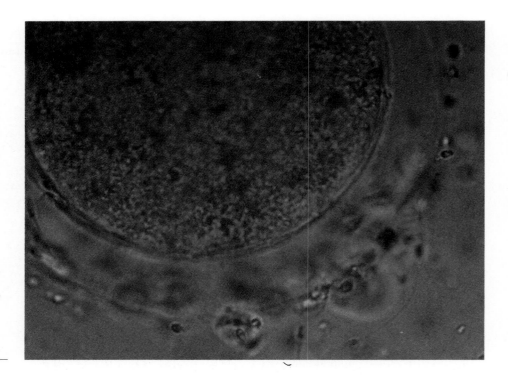

Conception occurs when a sperm cell penetrates an ovum, or egg cell. Almost immediately the wall of the new zygote changes so that no other sperm can enter.

1983). These limits give a couple about three days, or seventy-two hours, each month when intercourse is likely to result in conception and pregnancy. The period lasts from about two days before the egg is released (the sperm can survive that long) until about one day afterward (when the egg dies). This fertile period usually occurs about halfway through a woman's menstrual cycle, but it may happen at some other time.

Other, less direct factors also affect whether conception occurs. For example, some men produce much denser concentrations of sperm than others do, although even a relatively low concentration usually contains more than enough gametes to ensure conception if the sperm can just get to the ovum (Silber, 1980). The numbers of sperm are also reduced considerably if intercourse has already occurred recently — say, within the previous twenty-four hours. And conception becomes less likely if either partner is relatively old, meaning more than about forty years (Silber, 1980). Age apparently diminishes the man's concentration of sperm somewhat; more importantly, it may lead to an increased number of defective gametes in either the man or the woman. Stress can also reduce the chances of conception. This can happen in the obvious way by discouraging lovemaking in the first place or more mysteriously and indirectly by somehow preventing ovulation or implantation of the zygote.

All these influences can amount to either obstacles or protections, of course, depending on whether a woman wants to become pregnant. Either way, they can be frustrating because of the indirectness with which they operate. And either way, getting pregnant can prove as difficult for some couples as it is easy for others.

The Germinal Stage (The First Two Weeks)

Once a sperm and ovum join successfully, the resulting zygote begins to divide and redivide. The original cells form a tiny sphere called a **blastocyst,** which looks something like a miniature mulberry or raspberry. After about three days, the blastocyst contains about sixty cells; but these become smaller at the same time as they become more numerous, so the blastocyst is still scarcely larger than the original zygote. While these divisions occur, the blastocyst floats down the remainder of the fallopian tube, helped in part by gentle squeezing motions similar to the digestive motions of the intestines.

The blastocyst, which is filled with fluid, rapidly undergoes a number of important changes. The cells along one of its sides thicken to form the embryonic disk, out of which the baby will eventually develop. The blastocyst also differentiates into three different layers; an upper layer, or **ectoderm,** which later develops into the epidermis (outer layer of skin), nails, teeth, and hair, as well as sensory organs and nervous system; the **endoderm,** or lower layer, which becomes the digestive system, liver, pancreas, salivary glands, and respiratory system; and, somewhat later, the **mesoderm,** which becomes the dermis (inner layer of skin), muscles, skeleton, and circulatory and excretory systems. In a short time, the placenta, the umbilical cord, and the amniotic sac (to be discussed shortly) will also form from blastocyst cells.

After a few more days — about one week after conception — the blastocyst adheres to the wall of the uterus. The attachment is called **implantation** because the blastocyst buries itself like a seed in the wall of the uterus. (See Figure 4.2.) The fully implanted blastocyst is now referred to as the **embryo.** Implantation takes about another week to occur fully, so it is complete at about the time that the woman might expect another menstrual period. It also signifies the end of the germinal stage and the beginning of the next phase of prenatal growth during which the developing child begins to grow differentiated cells.

The Embryonic Stage (Third Through Eighth Weeks)

Growth during the embryonic stage (and the fetal stage that follows) occurs in two patterns: a **cephalocaudal** (head to tail) pattern and a **proximodistal** (near to far, from the center of the body outward) pattern. Thus, the head, blood vessels, and heart — the most vital body parts and organs — begin to develop earlier than the arms, legs, hands, and feet. Figure 4.3 illustrates some of these changes in slightly simplified form. Already the heart is beating; inside, the

FIGURE 4.2
The Germinal Stage of Prenatal Development

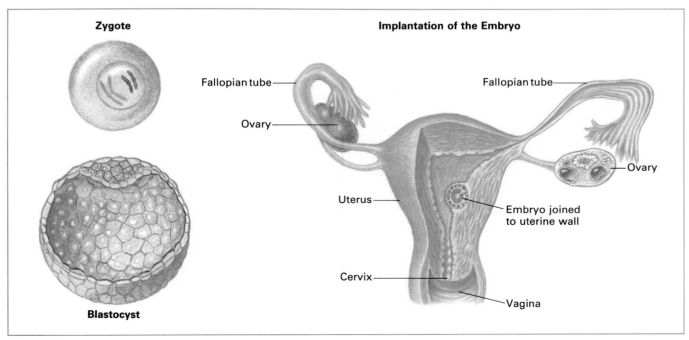

Zygote

Implantation of the Embryo

Fallopian tube

Ovary

Fallopian tube

Ovary

Uterus

Embryo joined to uterine wall

Cervix

Vagina

Blastocyst

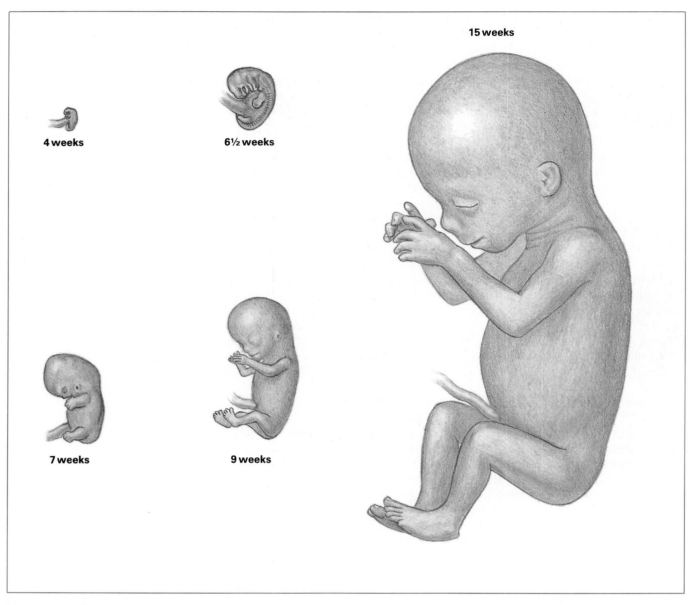

15 weeks

4 weeks

6½ weeks

7 weeks

9 weeks

FIGURE 4.3
Development During the Embryonic and Fetal Stages

Structures supporting the embryo

embryo already has a small digestive system and a nervous system. Because it measures only about one inch long, the embryo's parts do not have fully adult shape, but they are nonetheless unmistakable (P. Harris, 1983).

While these developments are taking place, a **placenta** forms between the mother and embryo. This is an area on the uterine wall through which the mother can supply oxygen and nutrients to the child and the child can return waste products from her bloodstream. In the placenta, thousands of tiny blood vessels from the two circulatory systems intermingle; although only minute quantities of blood can cross the separating membranes, nutrients pass easily from one bloodstream to the other. Some of them are pushed actively from one to the other as if by a sort of pump, and others float freely through the vessel walls by a process called **osmosis.** Although many toxic chemicals and drugs in the mother do not spread easily by osmosis, others do, and, as we discuss later, seemingly harmless chemicals can sometimes prove devastating to the child.

The embryo is connected to the placenta by the **umbilical cord,** which consists of three large blood vessels, one to provide nutrients and two to carry

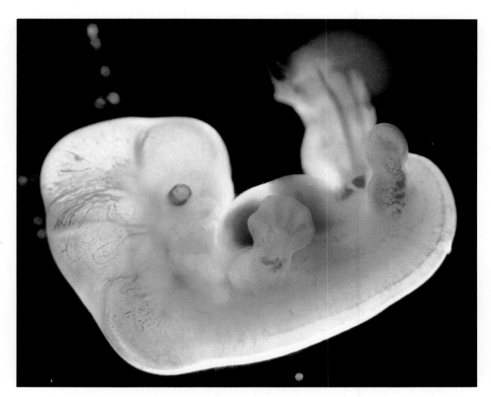

The environment and anatomy of an embryo change dramatically during the first two months of pregnancy. By the end of the third week, the embryo is surrounded by a thin sac of fluid, which cushions it from bumps and provides a more uniform temperature. The embryo shown here is at the end of the fifth week after conception. Note its leg buds and eyes.

waste products into the mother's body. The cord enters the embryo at a place that becomes its belly button, or navel, after the cord is cut following birth. The cord contains no nerves, so cutting it hurts neither the mother nor the child. For the same reason, no neural signals or messages can pass through the cord between mother and child before birth, even though they certainly communicate in other ways.

By the end of the eighth week, an **amniotic sac** has developed. The sac is a tough, spongy bag filled with salty fluid that completely surrounds the embryo and serves to protect the future baby from sudden jolts and to maintain a fairly stable temperature. The baby floats gently in this environment until birth, protected even if its mother goes jogging, sits down suddenly, or takes a walk in a snowstorm.

The Fetal Stage (Ninth Week to Birth)

After about eight weeks of gestation, the embryo develops its first bone cells, which marks the end of differentiation into the major structures. At this point the embryo acquires a new name, **fetus,** and begins the long process of developing relatively small features, such as fingers and fingernails and eyelids and eyebrows. Their smallness, however, does not make them unimportant; for example, the eyes experience their major growth during this stage of development. The fetus's newly developing eyelids fuse shut at about ten weeks and do not reopen again until the eyes themselves are essentially complete, at around twenty-six weeks.

Not only the eyes but most physical features become more adult-looking during this period and more truly human in proportion (P. Harris, 1983.) The head becomes smaller compared to the rest of the fetus's body (even though it remains large by adult standards) partly because the fetus's long bones — the ones supporting its limbs — begin growing significantly, so its arms and legs look increasingly substantial.

Landmarks of fetal development

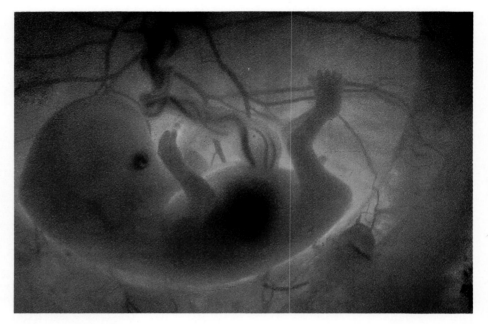

By the twelfth week, arms, hands, fingers, toes, and feet are clearly visible. The fetus begins exercising its limbs almost as soon as they develop, but it is not until sometime around the fourth or fifth month that the mother begins feeling these movements. The umbilical cord connecting the fetus to the placenta remains taut — and therefore untangled — because it is constantly filled with blood. Vessels and arteries proliferate throughout the fetus's body and are easily visible because the skin is still rather transparent.

By the third month the fetus is able to spontaneously move its head, legs, and feet. If its palm is touched, it exhibits a grasp reflex by closing its fist; if the sole of its foot is touched, its toes will spread (Babinski reflex); and if its lips are touched, it will respond with a sucking reflex. In addition the fetal heartbeat can now be heard through the wall of the uterus. As muscles develop more fully, the reflexes that first appeared during the third month become stronger.

By the fourth and fifth month, the mother may feel **quickening** of the fetus, or movement inside her womb. These are generally simple and reflexive actions

During the middle trimester of pregnancy, the fetus grows rapidly, as you can see by comparing this sixteen-week-old fetus with the eleven-week-old fetus in the previous photograph. By sixteen weeks, the fetus looks quite human, but it still cannot survive outside the womb.

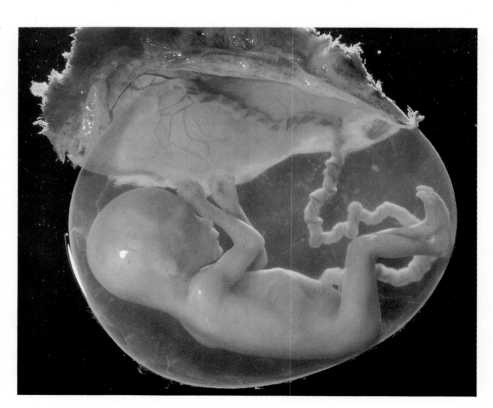

— hiccups, a wave of an arm, or a kick. These movements have in reality been going on for many weeks by the time most mothers notice them, but as the womb becomes more crowded, the fetus inevitably hits its walls more often.

Although the fetus increases in weight throughout pregnancy, large gains do not occur until near the end of pregnancy. By twenty weeks, or about halfway to birth, the fetus typically measures about 50 percent of its final prenatal length but only about 10 percent of its final weight (Hamilton, 1984). That makes the fetus about twelve inches long and only about ten ounces in weight; it is still a very tiny baby. But this slow weight gain only seems slow in comparison with the development lying ahead; compared with what has already happened, it has gained impressively. At four weeks, for example, it measured only about one-eighth of an inch long and weighed only about one one-hundredth of an ounce!

By the beginning of the seventh month, the fetus is about sixteen inches long and weighs approximately three to five pounds. It is able to cry, breathe, swallow, digest, excrete, move about, and suck its thumb. The reflexes mentioned earlier are fully developed. By the eighth month it weighs five to seven pounds and has begun to develop a layer of body fat that will help it to regulate its body temperature after its birth.

PRENATAL INFLUENCES ON THE CHILD

In spite of the individuality sometimes attributed to unborn children, biologically they develop in ways that are far more alike than different. As we have noted, physical structures develop in a particular sequence and at fairly precise times. Psychologists and biologists sometimes call such regularity **canalization,** which refers to the complex, seemingly inevitable unfolding of growth or developmental processes (Scarr-Salapatek, 1976; McCall, 1981). In normal conditions, specific events or influences have little long-term effect on highly canalized maturation, even if they affect development temporarily. Whether a pregnant mother drinks four glasses of milk every day or never drinks milk may not change the course of her pregnancy noticeably, as long as she does include calcium in her diet and her fetus does get enough nutrients. By nature, ordinary differences like this make no difference to maturation, as long as they *are* "ordinary."

Typically, prenatal development is a highly reliable process so that prospective parents generally worry much more than they should about whether their baby will be all right. In fact, 97.5 percent of human infants are perfect at birth, and of the 2.5 percent who are not, half have only minor defects such as hammer toes, extra fingers or toes, and birthmarks (Guttmacher & Kaiser, 1984).

But certain conditions can interfere with even the highly canalized processes of fetal development. These conditions are sometimes called **risk factors** because they increase the chance that the future baby will have medical problems but do not guarantee that these problems will actually appear. Risk factors vary widely in nature and scope, but all have in common the capacity to influence embryonic and fetal development negatively (Stechler & Halton, 1983). Some of these risks are related to the mother's biological characteristics, including characteristics that are influenced by psychological and social stress. A second set of risks involves exposure to disease, especially to viruses. Exposure to drugs and other chemicals constitutes a third set of risk factors.

As the complex sequence of prenatal development proceeds, the timing of the development of each new organ or part of the body is particularly important. There is a limited, "one-time-only" period during which each particular change can occur. This **critical period** is strictly determined by the complex genetic codes in each cell and by the particular set of prenatal conditions that must be

Perspectives

Alternatives to Normal Conception

Approximately 10 million women of child-bearing age have difficulty conceiving (L. Lord et al., 1987). In 1982, an 11 percent infertility rate was reported for women between the ages of twenty and twenty-four and a 25 percent rate for women between thirty-five and forty-five. A problem in any part of the complex process of conception can make a couple infertile. If the problem is in the male's reproductive system, it is usually related to the quantity or strength of the sperm produced. If the problem is due to the female's reproductive system, it is the result of structural abnormalities in the fallopian tubes or uterus or failure to ovulate and release mature eggs from the ovaries. An estimated 1 million American women a year develop pelvic inflammatory disease when sexually transmitted infections such as chlamydia spread into the uterus and fallopian tubes, and one in four women with the disease loses her ability to conceive. Indeed, sexually transmitted diseases account for one-fifth of all cases of infertility.

Earlier in this century, the only alternative for such couples was to adopt a child. But now medical techniques offer at least three additional options (Staurovsky, 1983). These vary in practicality and popularity, but from a strictly medical standpoint, they all work fairly reliably.

The most common alternative is **artificial insemination.** This method involves inserting sperm into the woman's vagina, either on or near the cervix, and holding the sperm in place for a few hours. The male donor is usually *not* the husband of the woman because studies have shown that inserting the husband's sperm in this way is in most cases no more effective than normal intercourse (Silber, 1980).

Instead, the donor remains anonymous. In practice, donors are often male medical students or interns who are easily accessible to doctors and who are physically and mentally fit. Usually they are paid for providing their sperm, but they never learn who receives it.

Artificial insemination is safe and easy to carry out. Most importantly, it induces pregnancy just as effectively as normal intercourse among fertile couples does; about 20 percent of couples get pregnant in any one month, whichever method of insemination they use. But artificial insemination has one major limitation: it requires a fertile, healthy female. Stated differently, it can help couples only when the male alone lacks fertility. It can do nothing for women whose ova are not healthy, whose reproductive tracts (the fallopian tubes) have been damaged, or who lack a normal, healthy uterus.

For some of these women, **in vitro fertilization** can help. In this technique, one or more ova are removed from the mother surgically and are mixed in a test tube with sperm from the father (hence the popular name "test-tube baby"). If conception takes place, the zygote is allowed to grow in the test tube briefly and then is reinserted surgically into the mother's womb. If all goes well, the embryo implants itself in the wall of the womb and proceeds to develop normally. The surgery uses small, needle-like instruments inserted through the mother's abdomen; because she is anesthetized, she feels no pain.

Even so, the procedure demands a lot, both of medical technology and of the embryo itself. And it can help only certain women, such as those with defective fallopian tubes;

in place for each change to occur. If the critical period is impeded or blocked, the changes that were scheduled to occur may be disrupted or prevented from occurring at all.

The nine months of pregnancy are generally divided into three **trimesters,** each lasting three months. Development is most vulnerable during the first trimester, so disruption during this period may lead to spontaneous abortion or to serious birth defects. For example, disruption during the third week, when the basic structures of the heart and central nervous system are just beginning to form, is likely to threaten further development. Similarly, interference in the fourth and fifth weeks, which are within the critical period for the first stage of arm and leg development, may lead to underdeveloped and malformed limbs. Because the critical periods for embryonic and fetal development are in the first trimester, disruptions in the second and third trimesters are in general less likely to have severe consequences.

Biological Risks

The age of the mother can sometimes increase the biological risks associated with child-bearing. Until recently, all pregnant women older than thirty-five were

a woman must still have a usable, healthy womb and produce usable, healthy ova. As a result, in vitro fertilization does not occur very often. In 1985, for example, only four hundred babies were conceived by this method in the entire United States, compared with more than ten thousand who were conceived by artificial insemination (Harper's Index, 1986). Most of these test-tube babies, however, developed normally after they were reimplanted in their mothers' wombs.

Perhaps a better parallel to artificial insemination is a controversial variation called **surrogate mothering.** This alternative uses artificial insemination, but instead of inserting sperm from a substitute father into the real mother, the sperm from the real father is inserted into a substitute mother. Like any other case of artificial insemination, the procedure works well at creating a new baby. Some potential parents and medical staff therefore argue that surrogate mothering offers an important service to couples who learn that their infertility results from the woman instead of from the man.

But many potential parents feel less comfortable with a substitute mother than with a substitute father (Menning, 1980). What if the surrogate mother (as in the case of Baby M) changes her mind and wants to keep the baby? What if the child is born with a disability?

In any case, surrogate mothers usually expect to be paid several thousand dollars for their services — quite a bit more than sperm donors — in order to compensate for the months of time and effort in gestating a baby. The cost naturally restricts their services to relatively well-to-do cou-

ples. It probably also contributes to negative opinions about surrogate mothering because cultural stereotypes dictate that women should love babies for their own sake and not deal with them as economic commodities.

Alternatives to normal conception raise a variety of ethical and legal issues (Otten, 1984). To whom should such procedures be available? Should single women who want to raise children by themselves be given artificial insemination? Should a woman who feels pregnancy would damage her career, or a woman who is afraid of the pains of childbirth, be allowed to contract a surrogate mother? Should these procedures be limited to those who can afford to pay the many thousands of dollars involved, or should they be available to those with less resources?

Who is/are the legal parent(s) — the woman who donated the egg, the man who donated the sperm, the woman who carried the embryo after in vitro fertilization, the couple who arranged for these procedures?

And what are the rights of the child? Should the child be told how he was conceived, and, if so, at what age? What are the legal rights and responsibilities of the donor to the child? What is the impact of alternative conception on the developing child and his family?

These and similar questions may result in greater caution in the use and selection of alternative methods of conception, but as long as the technology exists, individuals unable to have their own children and desperate to be parents will continue to seek it out.

believed to have a slightly higher risk of complications and even death during pregnancy or delivery. More recent research has led to a somewhat different conclusion (Buehler et al., 1986). Complications of pregnancy and prenatal development are only somewhat more likely for women who are older than thirty-five and having a first child. They are more likely than women in their twenties to be ill during pregnancy, to have longer and more difficult labors, and to deliver infants who are small, premature, or stillborn or who have congenital defects such as Down syndrome (see Chapter 3 for more information on Down syndrome) (Browne & Dixon, 1978). But when pregnant women older than thirty-five with major medical problems are eliminated from study, the rest do not show a greater incidence than younger women of any of these complications (with the exception of Down syndrome) (Grimes & Gross, 1981; Stein, 1983). Thus, healthy pregnant women older than thirty-five are not at significantly greater risk than younger women are.

On the other hand, young mothers, especially those in their early teens, are at greater risk of having low birth-weight infants, stillbirths, or problems during delivery (Monkus & Bancalari, 1981). This is due in part to the fact that because teenage mothers have not completed their own growth, their bodies are not able to meet the additional nutritional demands of a developing fetus. Additional factors that contribute to the higher risk of teenage pregnancies are the fact that teenage mothers are more likely to be poor and less likely to get adequate prenatal care or to have the maturity of judgment to adapt their life-styles to the demands of pregnancy (Furstenberg et al., 1989).

Several other physical characteristics of the mother during pregnancy can lead to increased chances of spontaneous abortion, or miscarriage (McKenzie, 1983):

1. Having had several previous pregnancies (at least four or five), especially if some of these involved medical problems
2. Being very overweight or underweight — that is, more than about 25 percent different from the average weight for the mother's height and frame (being only a little overweight does not create risk)
3. Being very short in stature (under five feet tall, to be specific) and small in size of frame

But, keep in mind that many women who live with risks like these have no problems at all with their pregnancies. This qualification is especially true of women who have only one risk factor, but it is even true of women with more than one. To be "at risk" means only that there is a higher than usual chance of problems; it does *not* mean a certainty. The distinction is important for all risks to pregnancy, including the ones we discuss in the next sections.

Illnesses

Rubella   Until recently, the disease that most commonly created problems during pregnancy was German measles, or rubella, which is caused by a virus that apparently can infect the embryo or fetus by passing through the placenta into the fetal bloodstream if the mother contracts the illness. If the virus invades during the first two months of pregnancy, it is likely to cause blindness, deafness, heart defects, damage to the central nervous system, and mental and emotional retardation. Should it occur during the second trimester, after the fetus is fully formed, its effects are less severe but may include hearing, vision, and language problems.

Effects of rubella

The chances of abnormalities in an infant born to a mother who has been exposed to rubella depend largely on the timing of the exposure. Approximately 47 percent of babies born to mothers who had rubella during the first month of pregnancy displayed abnormalities; 22 percent of newborns whose mothers had the disease during the second month and 7 percent of those who contracted it in the third month were seriously affected (Michaels & Mellin, 1960). Because of the successful public health efforts during the past decade to inoculate schoolchildren and women at risk, the current incidence of rubella in the United States is now extremely low, perhaps affecting only one out of every one thousand deliveries.

Certain other viruses can also infect the fetus, in spite of the protection offered by the placenta: typhoid, diphtheria, syphilis, gonorrhea, genital herpes, and acquired immunodeficiency syndrome (AIDS).

Effects of syphilis and gonorrhea

Syphilis and gonorrhea   If a pregnant woman is in the first years of a syphilis infection, the fetus is likely to die if the mother is untreated. Later in the course of the infection, syphilitic women may give birth to healthy children. The newborn's symptoms include lesions, rashes, and anemia; if the syphilis is untreated, the child may develop dental deformities, hearing problems, and many of the problems associated with adult syphilis discussed in Chapter 14 (Beeson & McDermott, 1971). Fetuses that contract gonorrhea in the birth canal may later develop eye infections or become blind. It is now standard practice to put drops of silver nitrate or penicillin in newborns' eyes to protect against this because gonorrhea may be present in the mother without obvious symptoms.

Genital Herpes   There are two types of herpes virus. Type one (oral herpes) produces the cold sores commonly encountered on the mouth and lips and does not appear to affect the fetus. Type two (also called herpes simplex or genital herpes) causes blisters on the genitalia of men and women and has become a common sexually transmitted disease for which there is no cure. It is most frequently transmitted to the baby at birth as the newborn comes in contact with herpes lesions on the mother's genitals (Hanshaw, Dudgeon, & Marshall, 1985; Feinbloom & Forman, 1987). About 33 percent of all infected newborns die, and another 25 to 35 percent suffer such disabilities as blindness, permanent brain damage, and other serious neurological disorders. Transmission of herpes by mothers with active herpes infections can be prevented by Caesarean delivery, a procedure in which the baby is surgically delivered through the mother's abdomen.

Caesarean delivery prevents transmission

AIDS   In 1988 pediatric cases of acquired immunodeficiency syndrome accounted for almost 2 percent of the total reported cases of AIDS in the United States. It is estimated that by the end of 1991, 10,000 additional children will be infected with the human immunodeficiency virus (HIV) but will not yet have developed the symptoms of AIDS. This will reflect a 1,000 percent increase between 1986 and 1991 (Task Force on Pediatric AIDS, 1989). A disproportionate number of affected children are from minority groups, blacks constitute 53 percent of the pediatric cases of AIDS, and Hispanics constitute 23 percent.

Seventy-eight percent of AIDS cases in children involve perinatal (at the time of birth) transmission from an infected mother to her child, either through the placenta or through contact with HIV-contaminated blood at the time of delivery. In the majority of these cases, the mother's infection can be linked to her own intravenous (IV) drug use or the IV drug use of her sexual partner. Because AIDS has an incubation period of up to five years in adults, pregnant women may be unaware that they have the virus or that it can be transmitted to their offspring. Most children infected perinatally show symptoms before age one.

Aids may also cause serious malformations in the developing embryo and fetus. Prenatal AIDS infection can lead to an abnormally small skull and facial deformities that include a prominent boxlike forehead, eyes that are widely spaced and off centered, and thickened lips. These abnormalities are more severe and appear in the first year of life when the virus was transferred to the fetus early in its development (Task Force on Pediatric AIDS, 1989; Minkoff et al., 1987).

Treatment of HIV-infected children with antiviral drugs is still in its early trial stages. Treatment of the secondary infections that result from the immune deficiency has improved, but it is unlikely that a cure will be found for this terminal illness in the near future. Although children with AIDS appear to survive longer than adults with AIDS, the typical life expectancy of a child born with AIDS is not yet known. The medical aspects as well as the psychological consequences of AIDS/HIV are devastating. A multidisciplinary team approach that works with the medical, psychological, social, and economic problems and stresses involved with AIDS has been found the most effective in caring for afflicted infants and children (Task Force on Pediatric AIDS, 1989).

Caring for children with AIDS

Toxoplasmosis   About 25 percent of the U.S. population contracts toxoplasmosis, a disease caused by a parasite that is present in uncooked meat and in the feces of infected cats. Although the mother may show no signs of illness, this disease can lead to fetal brain damage, blindness, or even death.

Hypertension   Hypertension (high blood pressure) is more likely to occur in the third trimester and is frequently associated with **eclampsia,** a disease that in its early ("pre-eclampsia") stages involves a buildup in the mother's bloodstream of waste materials from the fetus that are normally eliminated by the mother's kidneys. Because of the resultant water retention, the mother gains weight and her hands, feet, and ankles swell. Generally the fetus is not at risk, and these pre-eclampsia symptoms can be treated with a restricted salt diet, diuretics (which help to eliminate excess body fluids), and bed rest. If the condition persists, the mother's health may be endangered and the fetus may be delivered prematurely (Beeson & McDermott, 1971).

All of these diseases are risky partly because the extent of illness in the mother does not reliably match the extent of its effect on the fetus; a mother with a mild case of rubella can carry what turns out to be a badly deformed child. The uncertainty makes prevention of illnesses the best strategy and curative treatments only a distant second best.

Teratogens

During the early weeks of its life, the embryo is especially vulnerable to various unusual or unnatural substances taken by the mother. Because many of these substances can permanently damage an embryo's growth, they are sometimes called **teratogens,** after ancient Greek words meaning "monster creating." Teratogens include substances that most people consider harmful, such as alcohol and cigarette smoke, but they also include medications — substances intended simply to help.

Drugs   A drug called thalidomide illustrates dramatically how this can happen. Thalidomide is a seemingly harmless sedative, prescribed for calming the nerves, promoting sleep, and reducing morning sickness and other forms of nausea. But if a woman uses it during the first two months of pregnancy, the embryo's arms and legs become badly deformed. Thalidomide was prescribed widely in the early 1960s, and soon after the affected children began to be born, medical researchers began to suspect that a drug was responsible.

Unfortunately, the damage done by toxic drugs or chemicals does not always show itself as obviously or as soon as thalidomide did. For about twenty-five years following World War II, another drug, diethylstilbestrol (DES), was prescribed frequently to pregnant women because of its ability to prevent miscarriages. The drug was especially useful during the early months, when miscarriages happen most often. At birth the babies of women who took DES seemed perfectly normal, and they remained so throughout childhood. As they became young adults, however, many of the daughters of DES mothers developed cancers in the vagina or cervix. The sons of these mothers did not develop cancer, but they did have abnormalities in the structure of their reproductive organs (Johnson et al., 1979; Bibbo et al., 1977). Even the daughters who did not get cancer had significantly more problems than usual with their own pregnancies; they had more spontaneous abortions and stillbirths as well as more minor problems, and they had these whether or not their families had had histories of difficult births (Barnes et al., 1980).

All of these effects only emerged years after DES had achieved wide use. While the unfortunate first generation of DES children was growing up, doctors continued to prescribe the drug and thereby created still more children with problems.

Not surprisingly, heavy narcotics such as heroin also affect the fetus. At birth, the child of a woman who uses heroin immediately begins to have withdrawal symptoms, including vomiting, trembling, and irritability (Zelson, 1973).

Unfortunately for the baby, the symptoms may not become serious until several days after birth, when she has left the hospital. Even when the infant has recovered from withdrawal, she often develops slowly during the first year. (M. Strauss et al., 1976), and she is at risk for dying suddenly and unaccountably during this time as well (Chavez et al., 1979).

Cocaine is also a powerful teratogen. Mothers who use cocaine and cocaine derivatives such as crack regularly have a greater than normal risk of miscarriage or premature delivery. Their babies are more likely to be lower birth weight than normal, more irritable, and more susceptible to serious respiratory problems (Bartol, 1986; MacGregor et al., 1987; R. Weiss & Mirin, 1987). Cocaine use by a pregnant woman is also related to high blood pressure in the mother and her fetus, and there are reported cases in which the unborn fetuses of mothers who use cocaine have died of strokes (Thomas, 1986). The babies of cocaine-addicted mothers may be born already addicted (M. Strauss et al., 1975; Briggs et al., 1986).

Effects of cocaine

Almost all drugs may affect the developing embryo or fetus, depending on their particular characteristics, dosage, frequency, timing of use, and so on. This has led many doctors to stress to pregnant women the dangers of drugs and to prescribe medication only in extreme cases. It is wise for pregnant women to take no drugs (including nonprescription ones) without their doctor's permission.

Alcohol   Even in biblical times, people suspected that alcohol harmed an unborn child: "Behold, thou shalt conceive and bear a son; and now drink no wine nor strong drink, neither eat any unclean thing" (*Judges 13:7*). Both then and now, babies born to mothers who consume too much alcohol have **fetal alcohol syndrome** (FAS), such babies do not arouse easily and tend to behave sluggishly in general (Clarren & Smith, 1978). In addition, babies of heavy drinkers have more than twice the usual chances of showing minor physical abnormalities, such as a thin upper lip or a short nose. Particularly if their mothers drink during the last trimester, babies may also suffer from heart defects, small heads, and distortions of the joints and may show mental retardation and slowed motor development (Palmer et al., 1974; Streissguth et al., 1978).

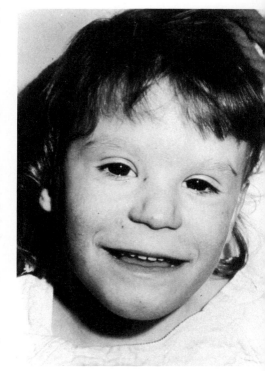

This child has the short nose and thin upper lip characteristic of fetal alcohol syndrome. She, like other children with the syndrome, is at risk for a variety of motor and neurological impairments.

Even moderate drinking and occasional binges can put the fetus at risk. In one study, pregnant women drank ginger ale mixed with one ounce of vodka — about as much alcohol as a typical mixed drink at a restaurant or bar contains. The researchers observed the fetuses in the second trimester both before and during the drinking and found that their breathing became seriously disturbed within a few minutes of the mothers' beginning to drink (Fox et al., 1978). Most fetuses slowed down or even stopped breathing for many minutes at a time. They did not die, of course, because they did not yet really need their lungs to obtain oxygen, but their behavior suggested serious physical depression caused by a modest amount of alcohol.

More recent studies have found that moderate daily drinking during pregnancy (two ounces of hard liquor, nine ounces of wine, or two beers) is related to lower birth weight, lack of responsiveness and arousability, and an increase in the occurrence of heart rate and respiratory abnormalities in infants. These infants achieve lower mental development scores at eight months and at four years and have higher rates of learning disabilities (Briggs et al., 1986; Streissguth et al., 1984).

Apparently alcohol depresses not only brain functioning but the very growth of the brain. Several pieces of evidence support this idea. Brain nerve cells of "alcoholic" fetuses may fail to develop properly — that is, they may not connect widely with numerous other brain cells (Clarren & Smith, 1978). This effect occurs most strongly during the last three months of pregnancy, when the fetal brain is growing the fastest, and least strongly during the first few months of pregnancy (Matsunaga & Shiota, 1980).

Even moderate drinking can be dangerous

No completely proven safe dosage of alcohol for a pregnant woman has been determined. It has been estimated that the chances of an FAS-affected fetus being born to a woman who consumes more than four drinks daily is about 33 percent and about 10 percent for a woman who consumes between two and four drinks per day (Feinbloom & Forman, 1987).

Programs to help pregnant mothers curb their drinking have had best results for the children when they emphasize the importance of abstention even during the last few months of gestation; mothers who cut back throughout pregnancy give birth more often to healthy, alert babies, compared with mothers who only cut back early and resume drinking later in their pregnancy (Rosett et al., 1980).

Smoking interferes with the fetal oxygen supply

Cigarettes Smoking, too, can harm the fetus, but the effects are more general than is true for alcohol. Observations of mothers suggest that two key elements of cigarette smoke, nicotine and carbon monoxide, interfere with the supply of oxygen to the fetus. Because of the reduced amount to oxygen entering the fetus's bloodstream, the baby's heart must beat much faster than usual, so that by the time the mother has finished a five-minute cigarette, the fetus's heart is beating 20 percent faster than it normally does, and it will continue doing so for ten or fifteen minutes (Quigley et al., 1979). By reducing the supply of oxygen, smoking slows the baby's metabolism and growth generally. Even exposure to smoke from others (passive smoking) can also adversely affect pregnant women and their fetuses.

Smoking during pregnancy has been found to result in reduced birth weight and increased risk of premature delivery and higher infant mortality (Werler et al., 1985). Women who smoked a pack a day or more compared to women who did not smoke were found to have a 20 percent greater chance of delivering their baby at thirty-seven weeks or earlier and a 60 percent greater chance of delivering at thirty-three weeks or earlier (Shiono et al., 1986).

Some studies suggest that infants of smoking mothers have other problems as well. They have more chance of being born with minor physical deformities such as cleft lip or palate, and more chance of becoming jittery or excessively active during early childhood (Evans et al., 1979).

Diet and Nutrition

Importance of the mother's current diet

Studies of animals show clearly that undernourishment during pregnancy hurts the offspring in various ways (Hurley, 1977, 1980). As a rule deprivation early in the gestation leads to specific physical deformities, and later deprivation leads to overall low birth weight. These and other facts imply that most nutrition for the fetus comes from the mother's current diet, not from her reserves of fat. At least among animals, a poor diet for the mother harms both the mother and the offspring; the fetus is not isolated nutritionally by virtue of living in the uterus.

Although the principle seems to apply to human mothers and children as well, ethical considerations prevent testing it because we certainly cannot starve pregnant mothers on purpose just to clarify our knowledge about diet during pregnancy. A number of indirect trends do however, suggest that undernutrition can hurt unborn children seriously.

First, children born during World War II in combat areas tended to be smaller than usual, and there were more than the usual number of stillbirths (Stein et al., 1975). The families of these children generally experienced severe famine during the war, but they also experienced other serious stresses that probably contributed to problems during pregnancy.

Second, children who die in the womb or immediately after birth sometimes show features that resemble malnutrition in animals; they lack normal amounts of fat tissue, and certain internal organs are sometimes relatively underdeveloped

(Naeye et al., 1973; Naeye, 1979). But not all stillborn and aborted children show such signs, even when their mothers seem undernourished.

Third, very slender or underweight mothers experience birth complications more often than other women do, including more premature births and more babies who are quite small (L. Edwards et al., 1979). Not all small babies develop in underweight mothers, however, and sometimes mothers are naturally slender rather than malnourished.

Taken together, these trends suggest that poor nutrition may affect human fetal development just as it affects animals. But the evidence applies primarily to very severe restrictions of diet — those that are severe enough to endanger the mother's health as well as her child's. In more moderate cases, the evidence remains unclear. Human mothers are not as nutritionally vulnerable as small laboratory animals are: human beings are comparatively large as animals go and therefore may not be harmed until deprivation of food is serious and sustained. Also, pregnancy takes a proportionally smaller diversion of a human mother's nutrition than of a small animal's nutrition; a rat almost doubles its weight during pregnancy, but if a human mother did the same, she would gain more than one hundred pounds in nine months!

Because of these factors, moderate failures of nutrition may make comparatively little difference to humans — as long as they are only moderate. To a certain extent, human mothers can get away with eating too many candy bars during pregnancy as long as that is their only nutritional mistake. Even so, no medical expert would ever condone such mistakes because even moderately poor nutrition can cut down on a mother's reserves of health and energy.

For the majority of well-nourished mothers, nutrition specialists make surprisingly few precise recommendations about foods and nutrients that help fetal development, and some of their suggestions are hedged with qualifications (Vermeersch, 1981). Nutritionists do agree, however, on one major modification of diet; pregnant women should eat more than usual, though not necessarily "for two," as the saying goes. How much more? Estimates range from 200 to 1,000 calories per day more than the woman ate before pregnancy as long as the extra calories consist mainly of carbohydrates and protein. The extra calories help to promote weight gain, which in turn helps to ensure a healthy baby at birth (Naeye, 1979b; Cater, 1980). Contrary to the advice given just a generation ago, nutritionists and doctors now encourage women to gain about twenty-five or thirty pounds during pregnancy. And contrary to common belief, most of this gain does not go to making the baby bigger; it simply contributes to the health of both mother and baby. In addition, nutritionists recommend that pregnant women get extra calcium (usually by drinking milk) because they must provide for the growing bones of the fetus and sometimes for breast feeding. Multiple vitamin/mineral supplements are recommended as well.

Eating a healthy and well-balanced diet during pregnancy is a way for a mother to help insure adequate nutrition and healthy development for her baby.

Pregnant women should eat more than usual

Stress

Stress refers to chronic feelings of worry and anxiety. Most mothers and fathers feel significant stress just about having a baby, which is something of a crisis even in the most positive families. Parents often feel surprised and shocked at the news of pregnancy, even if they have planned to have a child. Later they may worry about whether the baby will be all right, about whether they can really afford to have it, and about whether they are really ready psychologically to be parents. These feelings are all stressful, but when they are kept within reasonable bounds, they are quite inevitable and normal. They cause no long-run damage to the baby.

Women who experience severe and prolonged anxiety just before or during pregnancy, however, are more likely to have medical complications and to give

TABLE 4.1   Factors that May Affect the Fetus

Maternal diseases: Rubella, chicken pox, mumps, herpes simplex, syphilis, gonorrhea, AIDS, tuberculosis, malaria, toxoplasmosis
Maternal drug use: Thalidomide, DES, heroine, cocaine, crack, alcohol, tobacco
Maternal diet: Inadequate nutrition
Maternal stress: Chronic and at high levels, especially toward the end of pregnancy
Environmental hazards: Radiation, toxic chemicals, pollution

birth to infants with abnormalities than women who do not. Emotional stress has been associated with greater incidence of spontaneous abortion, difficulty in labor, premature and low weight birth, newborn respiratory difficulties, and physical deformities (Norbeck & Tilden, 1983). Although maternal stress and anxiety during late pregnancy have been associated with newborns who are hyperactive, irritable, and irregular in their feeding, sleeping and elimination, that is probably largely due to continuing anxiety in the mothers after childbirth (Sameroff & Chandler, 1975; Vaughn et al., 1987).

Environmental Hazards

Radiation

A broad range of environmental hazards can be destructive to prenatal development. These include exposure to radiation from nuclear explosions, nuclear plant accidents, industrial materials, and medical X-rays; to industrial chemical pollutants such as carbon monoxide, the cigarette smoke of others, lead, mercury, and PCBs in the air or water; to fertilizers, herbicides, and pesticides in the food chain; to food additives; and even to excessive heat and humidity. (See Table 4.1.) Although the careful parent may take steps to avoid some of these hazards, many are beyond the range of individual control and require efforts on a national or even international scale.

PARENTAL REACTIONS TO PREGNANCY

Pregnancy is a beginning, and expectant mothers and fathers get ready for the birth of their baby and parenthood by creating, often in an unconscious manner, a set of images of what parenthood will be like (Galinsky, 1987). These images of parenthood are based, in part, on memories. First-time expectant parents develop images based on their own childhood experiences and on how they would have liked their own parents to treat them — for example, with more closeness, more caring and intimacy, greater acceptance, less criticalness. For parents who already have children, a review of their own experiences in parenthood and wishes for the future are also involved.

Reasons for Having a Child

Images are also influenced by life circumstances, one of the most important of which are the reasons for wanting (or not wanting) the child. When researchers asked prospective parents, "Why do you want to have a child?" the following reasons were most frequently given:

1. The validation of adult status and social identity in the community and social network in which they live

2. The expansion of self, including ties to the future and a sense of immortality

3. The achievement of moral values in the sense that one is doing something good by having and raising a child

4. The creation of a family that is larger than just husband and wife

5. Stimulation, novelty, and fun

6. Achievement, competence, and creativity (people take pride in producing a baby)

7. Power and influence through directing and controlling the life of the baby

8. Social comparison and competition with others

9. Economic utility, based on the expectation that the baby will grow up to be someone who will help support the family economically and emotionally (Hoffman & Hoffman, 1973).

For parents who already have a child, the desire to provide a sibling for the first is a major reason for having a second child. Another common reason for wanting a child, particularly for teenagers, is to have someone to love and be loved by. A parent's reasons for wanting a child and whether a pregnancy is planned or unplanned can influence their feelings about pregnancy, too. For example, women who planned their pregnancies and who wanted children for self-growth reasons have been found to be more positive about having children than women who did not. They see parenthood as an opportunity to expand their sense of self and to intensify and enrich their marriages. Women who are more negative about becoming a parent either have unplanned pregnancies, see having a child as a way to escape their current life circumstance, or consider a child a source of status or security (Leifer, 1977).

Effects of Pregnancy on the Mother

Naturally, the developmental changes in the fetus have a profound effect on its mother. During the germinal stage (the first two weeks of the first trimester), the mother may not detect any signs of pregnancy; in fact, she may lose the microscopic "baby" at any time without ever knowing that it existed. After implantation, however, the future infant makes its presence felt rather quickly by its impact on the mother's metabolism, or body chemistry. Implantation initiates changes in about thirty different bodily chemicals, or **hormones,** that regulate the pregnancy (Vermeersch, 1981). For some women, nausea or morning sickness often marks early pregnancy, others experience no symptoms at all.

By the start of the second trimester, or fourth month of pregnancy, most women have recovered from morning sickness and fatigue. Changes in estrogen levels, among other things, may promote water retention during pregnancy, which increases the volume of the mother's blood substantially. It also causes edema, or generally swollen tissues, which gives some mothers puffy skin and swollen ankles. Increased progesterone promotes new fat deposits all over the woman's body. These may have served as nutritional insurance in prehistoric days, when food supplies were less predictable, but now they can be frustrating to a woman who wants to be slender. Progesterone also causes muscles to relax. This apparently helps the uterus to stretch, which is essential during pregnancy. But at the same time, the muscles of the intestines can become lazy or too relaxed to digest properly. Constipation sometimes results, especially in later pregnancy.

Effects of hormonal changes

The quickening that the mother usually first experiences during the fourth or fifth month is often good news for the mother: feeling the fetus's movements

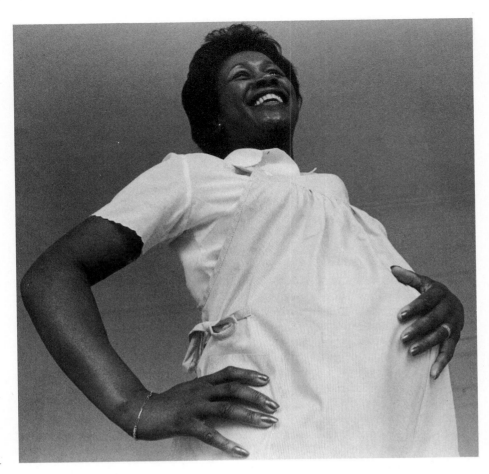

In about the fourth or fifth month of pregnancy, a woman begins feeling the fetus move. The timing varies: some babies are more "gymnastic" than others, and many women notice movement more in later pregnancies.

Discomfort in later pregnancy

is proof that the baby exists and is alive. As the pregnancy progresses, the mother may find that she needs to urinate more frequently because as the baby grows it exerts pressure on her bladder. It also grows upward and presses on the diaphragm, making it hard for the mother to breathe. By the middle and latter part of the third trimester, she may find it uncomfortable to sit for long periods of time or walk with the usual ease. This is because her pelvic joints have become more flexible in preparation for the baby's passage through the birth canal and because of the increased weight that she is carrying — usually between twenty and thirty pounds, depending upon her size.

Women also experience psychological changes with pregnancy. By the third trimester, the various discomforts and the many months of waiting can begin to seem endless. Even though they know the changes in their bodies are not permanent, many women feel that they are becoming less and less attractive and have concerns that they will not be able to get back into shape once the baby is born. First-time parents in particular have many concerns about the responsibilities of caring for a new baby and about the changes it will make in their lives; the complex metabolic and physiological changes the mother undergoes can contribute to mood swings and feelings of upset and anxiety.

Women vary widely in the amount of discomfort they experience. Nevertheless, despite some discomfort and anxiety, women welcome many of the physical and psychological changes. Particularly for the first-time mothers, these changes confront the pregnant woman with a new sense of herself as a person who is on the threshold of parenthood and the many special rewards and satisfactions that it brings. Many women take great pleasure in their changing sense of their bodies

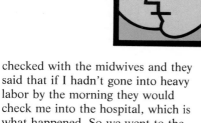

A Talk with New Parents

The Childbirth Experience

Paul and Alice Ascari were interviewed in the dining room of their home. Robert, aged six months, rested contentedly in Paul's lap for most of the interview.

Interviewer: What was the experience of having a baby like?

Paul: Well, I'm sure it was different for each of us, but it was thrilling for me. We had some misconceptions about what it would be like. We'd taken our cassette recorder . . . and sort of thought that it was going to be kind of a home birth setting [at a birthing center]. Unfortunately, Alice's water broke, and they ended up using drugs and fetal monitors so that we were a little bit disheartened at the outset.

Anyway, after we got all hooked up and we changed our mindset about what it was going to be like, we really got into the routine of pushing and counting and breathing and my being the coach and massaging. I was really right there and it really felt spectacular. When the little guy finally came out, it seemed like the ultimate triumph. Like reproduction itself.

Interviewer: How did you decide to use a birthing center?

Paul: I don't like hospital settings and white stuff. And I tend to think of birth as a natural process, not as an illness. And, you know, for thousands of years, billions of people have been born in places other than hospitals, so that it is clearly possible to do so. So we wanted, as much as possible, to have a natural birthing experience. We were extremely fortunate in having a birthing center near us with really top-notch medical facilities — while it is still a fairly relaxed environment — and very professional, competent midwives. As it ended up, we had the midwives, but not the birthing center.

Interviewer: What reservations did you have about using a birthing center?

Alice: People gave us examples of situations where there really had been emergencies and where not being in a hospital really made a difference. And I would say that I don't share Paul's aversion to medical facilities. I thought being in a hospital was fine. So I wasn't crushed when we couldn't do it in the birthing center. I was, in fact, relieved to learn that we couldn't have gone there anyway because of my water breaking so early.

Interviewer: What kind of preparation did the two of you have for the birth?

Paul: We took a standard four-week birthing class at our health plan and practiced the breathing patterns. We also did some reading.

Alice: We spent a lot of time wishing that we were preparing more, but our lives were so busy that we just didn't have a chance to do it, and I went in feeling very unprepared and afraid.

Interviewer: What fears did you have?

Alice: I had fears about what the pain would be like and just not knowing what it took to give birth and how hard it would be. While it was happening I remember saying. "Oh, now I know why people don't do this very often; it's painful." And I was fine. And the experience was not horrible. Afterwards, I kept on repeating to people who asked me how it was, "If I knew this person was coming out, I would have been rushing to the hospital hours early because it was such a wonderful thing to have this baby."

Interviewer: How did you know that labor had begun?

Alice: It was around six in the evening. We had had a big potluck supper here, and I was coming down the stairs just after people had left when my water broke. So I had a flood on the staircase. I called and

checked with the midwives and they said that if I hadn't gone into heavy labor by the morning they would check me into the hospital, which is what happened. So we went to the hospital to be checked but then were sent home. My contractions had started during the night, so that I had begun, officially, having my birth in the early hours of the morning. At eleven o'clock the next morning we checked into the hospital.

Interviewer: How did you first know that labor was beginning?

Alice: Everyone had said this and it's true — it's unmistakable. Once you're really having contractions, you can't confuse them with anything else. But they are impossible to describe; at least I found that other people's attempts to describe them to me in advance were not helpful.

Interviewer: Paul, what did she say to you?

Paul: Well, I was supposedly timing them and yet we were asleep, so she would wake me up and say, "I'm having another one." I had my little stopwatch and the contractions seemed about twenty minutes apart, and she said they were too painful to sleep but not intolerable. It was kind of deceptive because they never advanced beyond what were first-phase contractions, so they were painful but she wasn't dying.

Interviewer: About how long did it take from the time your contractions started until the baby's head showed?

Paul: About four or five hours.

Alice: The other thing that I think surprised us was that I didn't physically go through the stages of birthing that all the books and all the classes tell you about. I used one slow breathing pattern through all *(continued)*

A Talk with New Parents (continued)

of it. The contractions didn't change, but I didn't feel physically different so that everybody, including myself, was really shocked when we did finally check and learn that the baby was almost there. But I kept saying, "But I didn't experience much change and what happened to transition? And all the phases. . . ."

Interviewer: What was it like to first see your baby?

Alice: We were pushing and pushing and they had a mirror, which I wasn't really looking at because I was intensely concentrating on pushing, and everyone went, "Oh!" And I didn't know what was wrong, and they could see his dark hair coming out so I knew that he was on his way. So that was just such a wonderful, exciting moment. And then I barely felt like I was part of the process. And, in a way, you

don't know when you're having contractions because you know that if you're doing everything successfully, you're just letting your body do its own work. So, pushing was really an exciting thing, and each time I felt Paul and the midwives were really being helpful in letting me know how far the baby's head was coming out. It was just so wonderful!

Interviewer: You both have big smiles on your faces!

Alice: It was just really super. And he's so wonderful. There is something so unique and wonderful about having an infant that I think if women who are frightened the way I was before the delivery only knew in a concrete sense that they would be guaranteed this wonderful, exhilarating, challenging experience rather than just hearing someone else say it, that fear would really disappear.

Follow-up Questions

1. What were the Ascaris' reasons for choosing a birthing center? In your opinion, how appropriate were their concerns?

2. Based on Alice's description of her labor and delivery and your reading of this chapter, in what ways did her childbirth experience follow a typical pattern, and in what ways was it atypical?

3. Did the Ascaris' classes and other preparation for childbirth prove helpful?

4. In what ways did the attitudes of Alice and Paul toward childbirth change as a result of their own experiences with it?

BIRTH

When the baby is ready

After thirty-eight weeks in the womb, the fetus is considered "full term," or ready for birth. By this point it will weigh around seven and one-half pounds, but it can weigh as little as five or as much as ten pounds and still be physically normal. The fetus measures about twenty inches or so at this stage — almost one-third of its final height as an adult.

During the last weeks, the womb becomes so crowded that the fetus assumes one position more or less permanently. This orientation is sometimes called the fetus's presentation, and it refers to the body part closest to the mother's cervix. The most common orientation, and the most desirable medically, is a **cephalic presentation,** which means that the head is pointing downward. But two other presentations also occur; feet and rump first (**breech presentation**) or shoulders first (**transverse presentation**). These orientations used to jeopardize an infant's survival, but modern obstetric techniques have reduced their risk greatly.

Although parents and doctors often dearly wish that they could predict the exact moment of the onset of labor, so far no one has been able to do so. Several theories have been suggested, however, to explain why labor begins when it does. It may be that the uterus becomes stretched beyond some natural limit, and as a result it evacuates itself, rather like an overfull intestine does. Or perhaps certain hormones in the fetus combine with hormones in the mother to initiate the process; the combination may reach some crucial concentration or balance. If so, then to some extent the fetus tells the mother when it is ready.

Most fetuses develop normally for the usual thirty-eight to forty weeks and face their birth relatively well prepared. When the labor process begins, it, too, usually proceeds normally. The uterus contracts rhythmically and automatically so as to force the baby downward through the vaginal canal. The contractions occur in a relatively predictable sequence of stages, and as long as the baby and mother are healthy and the mother's pelvis is large enough, the baby is usually out within a matter of hours.

Stages of Labor

It is not uncommon for the mother to experience "false labor," or Braxton-Hicks contractions, in the last weeks of pregnancy, as the uterus "practices" contracting and relaxing in preparation for actual labor. The **first stage of labor** usually begins with relatively mild and irregular contractions of the uterus. (See Figure 4.4.) As contractions become stronger and more regular, the cervix (opening of the uterus) widens, or dilates, enough for the baby's head to fit through. Toward

FIGURE 4.4
The Process of Delivery
(A) before labor begins; (B) labor; (C) crowning; (D) emergence of the head

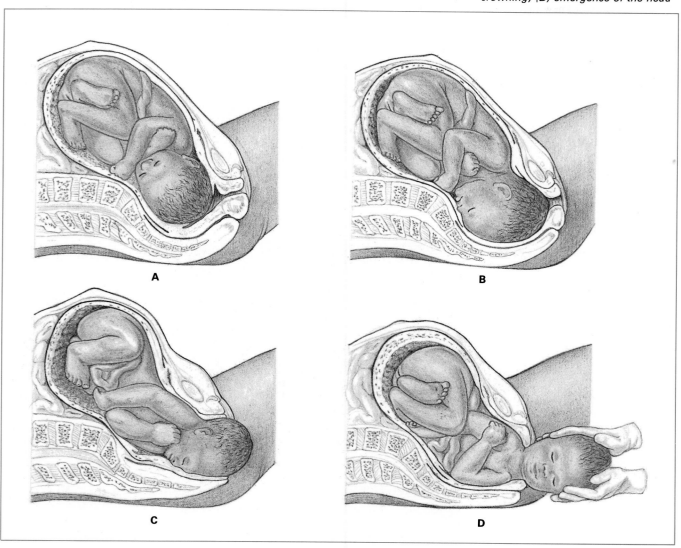

A

B

C

D

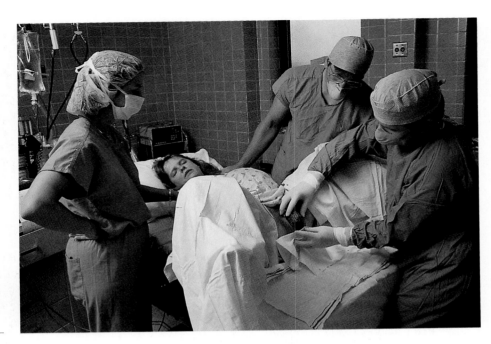

Crowning — when the baby's head can first be seen at the opening of the vagina — marks the beginning of the second stage of labor.

Dilation

the end of this stage, which may take from eight to twenty-four hours for a first-time mother, a period of **transition** begins. The cervix nears full dilation, contractions become more rapid, and the baby's head begins to move into the birth canal. Although this period generally lasts for only a few minutes, it can be extremely painful because of the increasing pressure of the contractions.

The **second stage of labor** is from complete dilation of the cervix to birth. It usually lasts between one and one and one-half hours. During the **third stage of labor,** which lasts only a few minutes, the afterbirth (consisting of placenta and umbilical cord) is expelled.

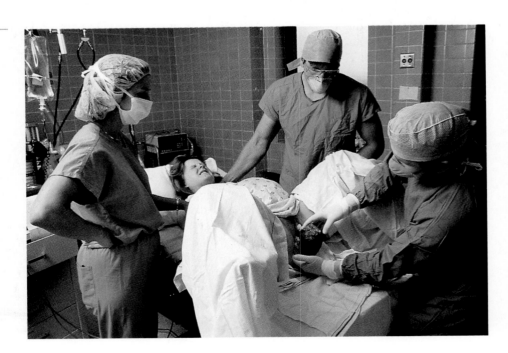

After a few additional pushes by the mother, the head emerges, followed shortly thereafter by the newborn's shoulders, chest, legs, and feet.

Managing Discomfort in Childbirth

Women vary widely in how much pain and discomfort they experience during labor. Some babies fit the birth canal more easily than others do and are therefore easier to expel. In addition, women vary in their tolerance for pain, partly because of basic physiological differences — perhaps even genetic differences — and partly because of the stresses of modern childbirth techniques. Until recently, a typical hospital birth called for a sterilized, clinical delivery room full of bright lights and imposing equipment and attended mostly by comparative strangers — the doctors and nurses. The surroundings may have made some women anxious and therefore more vulnerable to pain.

Women vary in tolerance for pain

Nonmedicinal Methods   To counteract this possibility, various methods of **prepared childbirth** have been devised to help parents rehearse or simulate the actual sensations of labor well before the actual delivery date. Although the various prepared childbirth programs that are now available in most hospitals and communities differ from one another in certain details, all generally emphasize educational, physical, and emotional preparation for the birth process and active involvement of the mother and father (or other partner). Typically, such programs encourage the mother to find a coach (often her spouse or a relative) to give her personal support during labor (Lamaze, 1976).

Rehearsing for labor

One well-known preparation program, the Lamaze method, strongly advocates participation of both *the mother and father* during the weeks preceding delivery and during the delivery itself. Women are taught techniques for managing the discomfort of labor that include relaxation techniques and breathing methods for each stage of labor. Labor either without drugs or with minimal drugs is encouraged, and the importance of birth as a shared emotional experience is stressed. Women giving birth using Lamaze techniques report less discomfort, more positive attitudes regarding the birth process, and less reliance on medication to manage the discomfort (Cogan, 1980).

The Lamaze method

Not only the mother benefits from the Lamaze or similar methods. A father's involvement in preparing for delivery and in the delivery process itself has been found to positively influence his experience of birth, his behavior toward the mother and baby during delivery, and his attachment relationship to his new infant (Peterson et al., 1979).

What about the experience of the infant? Frederick Leboyer, a French obstetrician, believed that conventional hospital deliveries in which the infant is suddenly forced to leave the warm, dark, quiet, and protective environment of the mother's womb and is thrust into the bright, noisy, cold, and overstimulating world of the delivery room are disruptive and upsetting to the newborn (Leboyer, 1975). He developed a "gentle birth" experience in which both parents actively participate. The delivery room is warmed, quiet, and dimly lit. Immediately after birth, the infant is placed on the mother's abdomen where the infant remains for several minutes before the umbilical cord is cut. The baby is then placed in a warm bath by the father where she is gently bathed and massaged by both parents (Leboyer, 1975).

"Gentle birth"

Are Leboyer's claims of lasting benefits for children born using his method supported by research? One study compared deliveries using the Leboyer method with deliveries in which standard methods were used. In the standard delivery group, lighting was not dimmed, the cord was cut within sixty seconds, and no bath was given. In both birthing situations, the postnatal care was gentle, mothers and fathers actively participated in the birth, they gently handled their infants, and they interacted with their newborns. According to the results, there were no significant advantages found for the Leboyer infants (Nelson et al., 1980). A second study that reported similar birth experiences failed to discover differences

A Multicultural View

Cultural Differences in Perceptions of Pain During Childbirth

An important issue in modern childbirth involves decisions about if and when medication should be used to manage the discomfort and pain that can be associated with the birth process. Professionals who assist women in deliveries find it difficult to determine how much discomfort or distress a laboring woman is in and how to respond appropriately. Cultural differences in how pain or discomfort is experienced and expressed also complicate such assessments.

Janice Morse and Caroline Park studied differences in perceptions of pain of childbirth among four different cultural groups living in western Canada: English-speaking Canadians, Ukrainians, Hutterites, and East Indians (Morse & Park, 1988). Parents who were about to have hospital deliveries were asked to compare the pain of childbirth with eight other painful events: heart attack, kidney stone, severe burn, toothache, gallstones, eye injury, broken bone, and migraine.

The Canadian sample had the highest mean rating for childbirth pain of 11.15 (12.9 for females and 10.55 for males). The views surrounding birth for this group were similar to those of most middle-class Americans. They expected it to be painful and used a variety of methods to prepare for it, but they also knew that if labor became too uncomfortable, they would be offered or given medications to relieve the pain.

The next highest average rating was 9.52 for the East Indian sample (10.68 for women and 9.16 for men). The emphasis on purity and innocence in East Indian culture means that females are not taught directly about the process of birth. During labor East Indian women expressed discomfort by vocalizing (crying, yelling, or complaining) continually.

The Hutterite sample had an average rating of 7.92 (9.93 for women and 5.88 for men). The Hutterites are a collection of religious, agricultural communities that reject technology and maintain strict traditional and patriarchal customs and values that rigidly restrict a woman to the maternal role. Contraception is not allowed unless maternal health is threatened, and family size averages 10.4 children. During pregnancy there is no change in women's work role or diet, and the discomfort of childbirth is viewed as God's will (Morse & Park, 1988).

The Ukrainians reported the lowest overall ratings of discomfort of childbirth (2.14), with ratings of 2.11 for females and 2.4 for males. They are also agricultural and have strong religious values but are more flexible regarding the use of contraception and the roles of women. Deliveries for both the Hutterites and the Ukrainians were relatively calm and unemotional, with the women dealing with their discomfort in a quiet and uncomplaining manner.

Morse and Park note that the two cultures that rate childbirth discomfort the highest (the Canadians and the East Indians) do not consider childbirth to be a natural event, as reflected in the medicalization of childbirth in Canadian culture and the withholding of information about birth in East Indian culture. On the other hand, the Hutterite and Ukrainian cultures consider childbirth to be more of a natural event that does not have to be extensively managed or purposefully ignored. Whatever the reasons, the amount of discomfort attributed to childbirth varies markedly among cultures. Although the study measured how painful childbirth was *thought to be* rather than how painful childbirth *actually* was, the findings imply that the expectant mother's cultural beliefs about delivery may affect the amount of distress she experiences during labor and delivery.

---

between gentle birth and conventional birth babies in either behavioral dispositions or developmental milestones during the first year of life (Maziade et al., 1986).

The failure to find advantages for the Leboyer infants in these studies is probably due to the fact that the non-Leboyer infants also experienced gentle and responsive delivery and postnatal care and a high degree of parent participation. Although Leboyer's specific techniques have not gained wide acceptance, an increasing number of deliveries are conducted in a calm and gentle atmosphere in which parents who so desire can actively participate. Deliveries involving heavy medication, rough treatment of the baby, and little or no parent participation are becoming less the norm.

Medicinal Methods   In spite of good psychological preparation, however, most mothers do feel some pain during labor contractions. In good conditions, many mothers can endure this pain until the baby is delivered. But conditions are not always good: sometimes labor takes an unusually long time, and sometimes a mother finds herself less well prepared than she thought she was. In such cases, pain-reducing drugs such as narcotics or other sedatives can make the experience bearable. But they must be used cautiously. Most pain relievers cross the placenta and can therefore depress the fetus seriously if they are given at the wrong time or in improper amounts.

Pain relief

During the final stages of delivery, two other forms of pain relief are available. Doctors may inject a sedative into the base of the woman's spine; the two most common of these procedures are called an *epidural* and a *spinal.* They allow the mother to remain awake and alert during the final stages of labor, but they also prevent her from controlling her contractions, which can be quite helpful when the baby is finally expelled. Nitrous oxide, which is commonly used by dentists, has also been used to take the edge off the pain of the peak contractions of labor while allowing the mother to remain conscious.

Giving a mother either a general or local anesthetic before surgery removes all pain, of course, but both mother and child may take a long time to recover from it. Mothers who receive general anesthetics for delivery stay in the hospital for more days after delivery, on the average, than do mothers who receive other kinds of medication, at least partly because it takes several days for them to recover from the medication (Hamilton, 1984). In addition, the bonding between mother and child is delayed while the mother and child are recovering from the effect of anesthesia. The major types of medications used during labor and delivery, their administration, and their effects are presented in Table 4.2 (Feinbloom & Forman, 1987).

A more drastic approach is to give the mother a general anesthetic and remove the baby surgically, a procedure called **Caesarean section** (from the Latin meaning "to cut"). Techniques for this surgery have improved substantially over the past decades; the operation now takes only about half an hour, most of which is devoted to sewing the mother up again after getting the baby out. The incision is also smaller than it used to be (just a few inches), generally oriented horizontally, and located rather low on the mother's abdomen. Partly because of these improvements, hospitals now deliver increasing numbers of babies by C-section — up to 25 percent of all the births in some hospitals.

This last fact has worried some medical experts and parent advocates in spite of the safety of the practice (Hausknecht & Heilman, 1978; Kliot & Silverstein, 1980). They agree that Caesareans save lives, but they wonder whether surgical delivery of babies has actually become too easy to choose. If it has, then some doctors may actually turn the natural process of childbirth into an unnecessarily complex medical emergency.

Too many Caesareans?

Good reasons for selecting a Caesarean delivery include situations in which vaginal birth places the health of the fetus or mother at significant risk, such as in the case of *fetal distress* or of *pre-eclampsia-eclampsia* that cannot be controlled. Although selection of a Caesarean delivery purely for the convenience of the physician is no longer accepted as valid, there are many "gray" areas in which the number of Caesarean births can be decreased without increasing the risk to the mother or baby. These situations, which include *dystocia* (failure to progress in labor), *breech presentation,* certain instances involving *fetal distress,* and a previous Caesarean delivery, are now the focus of ongoing study by a panel of the National Institutes of Health, which has published guidelines to help professionals and parents make choices that reduce the inappropriate use of Caesarean deliveries (Feinbloom & Forman, 1987).

Problems During Labor and Delivery

Problems can interfere with labor and delivery in three ways: through faulty power in the uterus, through a faulty passageway (the birth canal), or through

TABLE 4.2   Effects of Medications Sometimes Used During Delivery

Type	Administration	Positive Effects	Negative Effects
Analgesics	By injection (in controlled doses) during the first stage of labor to reduce pain.	Reduces pain, causes some drowsiness and euphoria (sense of well-being and tranquility); women participate in labor and delivery.	Passes through the placenta to the fetus. Can depress respiratory centers in the baby's brain if the baby must breathe on its own. Can sedate babies and therefore cause drowsiness and decreased responsiveness for first few hours after birth or longer. Naloxone hydrochloride (Narcon) can be used to reverse the respiratory depression effects of analgesics.
Local Anesthesia Spinal	By injection into the spinal canal in controlled doses when the cervix is fully dilated (beginning of second stage of labor); numbs sensory and motor nerves so that the mother's pelvic area and legs cannot be moved voluntarily.	Mother can remain awake and aware during labor and delivery, can be used for either vaginal or Caesarean birth, is highly effective in eliminating pain.	Loss of voluntary muscle control prevents mother from bearing down and decreases force of uterine contraction, resulting in need for forceps and episiotomy. Risk of drop in mother's blood pressure, some risk of postspinal headache, slight risk of total body paralysis if excessive dose of anesthetic is given. Small amounts of drug may pass through the placenta to the baby.
Epidural	By injection during the active phase of the first stage of labor to numb the sensory nerves after their exit from the spinal canal.	Pain and sensations are generally eliminated. Mother is awake. Some voluntary movement is preserved, although it is less effective because a women's sense of position and tension is blocked by the medication.	Only partially effective in 12 percent of the cases and not effective in 3 percent. Can produce decreased blood pressure. Associated with decreased uterine contraction, slowing of labor, inability to push effectively during the second stage (necessitating an episiotomy), use of forceps, and a highly medical-type birth. Accidental administration of too high a level of anesthesia can cause widespread temporary paralysis and respiratory and blood pressure problems. "Spinal headache" sometimes occurs.
General Anesthesia	A mixture of nitrous oxide and oxygen is inhaled; is less commonly used than blocking agents.	Easily administered, rapid onset of effect. Anesthetic of choice in emergencies in which time is critical and baby must be delivered quickly.	Drug passes directly to the fetus. Mother is nearly asleep and not an active participant in the birth. Possibility that woman may vomit and breathe stomach contents into lungs, producing a chemical pneumonia. Babies and mothers are less alert and responsive following birth, and recovery time for mother is longer.

a faulty passenger (the baby itself). These problems actually interconnect in various ways, but it is convenient to distinguish among them (Buckley & Kulb, 1983).

Faulty Power   Sometimes the uterus does not contract strongly enough to make labor progress to an actual delivery. The problem can occur at the beginning of labor, or it can develop midway through a labor that begins quite normally, especially if the mother becomes worn out and discouraged after hours of powerful contractions. In many cases, doctors can make the contractions stronger by giving the mother an injection of the hormone oxytocin. But the resulting artificial contractions have to be watched carefully because they often do not match the needs of the baby or the mother as well as natural contractions do. Such **induced labor** can damage the baby and mother by forcing the baby through the canal before the canal is ready or by wasting the mother's scarce energy just when she needs it the most.

In about one delivery in two thousand, the uterus itself may rupture because

Oxytocin-induced contractions

of the power of its contractions (Hamilton, 1984). The condition is quite serious; the mother may bleed to death in just a few moments if she is unattended, and in the process the baby almost always dies. Because uterine rupture happens somewhat more often among mothers who have previously delivered babies surgically, hospitals used to require such mothers to plan on delivering all later babies by Caesarean section. Recent improvements in surgical techniques, however, have left these mothers with stronger uterine walls, and as a result, many doctors now permit them to attempt natural labor as long as the hospital staff watches carefully for any signs of rupture. If problems do develop, then a Caesarean section can still be organized and performed quickly and safely.

Faulty Passageway   Problems can also occur with the placenta. Sometimes it develops too close to the cervix, so that it blocks the baby from moving down the birth canal during labor. This condition is called *placenta previa,* from Latin words meaning "placenta in front of the passageway." Placenta previa usually makes itself known by causing bleeding from the vagina late in pregnancy, but because this bleeding is painless, mothers (and doctors) have a tendency to underestimate its significance. If left untreated, placenta previa can leave the fetus somewhat undernourished because it prevents enough blood from reaching the fetus, and it sometimes blocks a normal delivery entirely so that the baby must be delivered by Caesarean section.

Placenta blocking the baby

Even if the placenta implants far enough away from the cervix, it may occasionally partly separate from its base against the wall of the womb, a condition called *abruptio placenta.* This condition also causes vaginal bleeding, but unlike placenta previa, the bleeding can be quite painful. Partly as a result, doctors are more likely to detect the problem relatively soon after it occurs. No sure remedy exists, except for the mother to live sensibly and relatively quietly. Sometimes doctors advise absolute bed rest if they believe that substantial portions of the placenta have separated, but this much enforced inactivity can cause mothers almost as much worry as the condition itself (Hamilton, 1984).

Faulty Passenger   Usually a baby enters the birth canal head first, but occasionally one may turn in the wrong direction during contractions. A breech presentation, with the bottom leading, is risky for the baby, whose spine can be broken if a contraction presses it too hard against the mother's pelvis. Or the baby may not get enough oxygen because it cannot begin its own breathing until after its nose comes out. In many cases, a skilled midwife or doctor can deliver a breech baby with no problem, but if the baby gets stuck part way out of the vagina, medical staff may use **forceps** to pull it the rest of the way out of the birth canal. Used with care, forceps, which resemble scissors with long, blunt ends, need not hurt the baby.

Problems with the baby's position or size

A small but significant proportion of babies are simply too big to pass through the mother's pelvis and vaginal canal, a problem sometimes called *cephalopelvic disproportion* (literally, a disproportion of the head and pelvis). Extra hours of labor do not help to push such babies through; their heads are simply too big to fit, although often by only a fraction of an inch. Unfortunately, the problem does not usually reveal itself until well into labor. Such a mismatch of size can result from genetic influence, but, ironically, it also results from an especially healthy, well-nourished pregnancy, which creates an especially large baby. In any case, if the mismatch is too severe, it can threaten the life of the mother or the child, so doctors may interrupt the labor and deliver the baby surgically.

Fetal Monitoring   In most hospitals, electronic fetal monitoring is used to record uterine contractions and the fetal heart rate. Uterine contractions are externally measured by a pressure gauge strapped to the mother's abdomen that electronically represents changes in the shape of the uterus on graph paper. Fetal heart rate can be picked up by an *external* ultrasound monitor placed on the abdomen over the uterus or *internally* by a wire — leading through the vagina and screwed into the scalp of the fetus — that more sensitively records electrical changes in the fetus's heart.

Although *internal fetal monitoring* is extremely helpful in high risk and emergency situations, experts have questioned its routine use for low-risk deliveries. Because the amniotic membranes must be ruptured to permit attachment of the electrode to the baby's scalp, the very procedure designed to identify the fetus at risk of distress may itself contribute to fetal distress. In addition, the mother must lie in bed for as long as the wires are attached (Feinbloom & Forman, 1987). Experts have also noted that "high-tech" birth imposes psychological burdens as well by shifting the center of focus from the experience of the mother and baby to readouts from the equipment. This makes birth a less human experience (Davis-Floyd, 1988).

Premature Birth

Occasionally, of course, a baby is born prematurely: approximately 10 to 15 percent of the live births in the United States occur before the full term of pregnancy is reached (Feinbloom & Forman, 1987). An infant is general considered **premature** (or **preterm**) if he has a prenatal age of less than thirty-seven weeks. The bigger and more mature the infant at birth, the greater are his chances for survival. With the best neonatal intensive care, survival rates of 45 percent or more have been reported for babies weighing less than 2.2 pounds (1,000 grams), and more than 80 percent of babies weighing 3.3 pounds (1,500 grams) or more survive (Feinbloom & Forman, 1987). Intensive-care nurseries use computerized equipment to continuously monitor the vital signs (blood pressure, heart rate, temperature, and blood chemistry) of premature newborns so that immediate steps can be taken if problems arise. Pages 144–147 describe the experience of one premature child named David who was born at thirty-one weeks and weighed 3.65 pounds at birth.

Breathing problems of preterm infants

Respiratory distress syndrome (RDS) is a leading cause of death among preterm infants. One cause of RDS is a lack of *surfactant,* a substance that develops in the amniotic fluid at about the thirty-fifth week and that helps lubricate the air sacs and prevent the lungs from sticking together. This problem may be reduced by providing surfactant to babies who lack it. In fact, even full-term babies with normal surfactant development are more likely to have trouble with breathing than with any other single physical process (Root, 1983).

Compared with full-term babies, preterm infants experience a higher incidence of abnormalities in physical growth, motor behavior, neurological functioning, and intellectual development (Taub et al., 1977; Kopp & Parmalle, 1979). Paradoxically, the high-level equipment and intensive medical care that have helped to save the lives of preterm infants may also contribute to the development difficulties they are more likely to experience. Incubators, monitoring equipment, and intensive treatment may restrict the important physical and emotional contact and interaction between infant and parent that are essential

Interference with bonding

to the formation of early emotional bonds (Cornell & Gottfried, 1976; Gottfried et al., 1981).

Also, preterm babies account for between 23 and 40 percent of all battered children even though they make up less than 10 percent of all babies; this may be due to the fact that prolonged separation such as that imposed by intensive care units has been found to be associated with increased incidence of child abuse during infancy and early childhood (Kennell et al., 1979). As a result, parents with infants in intensive-care units are now encouraged to spend as much time as they want with their infants and to assume as much of their routine care as is possible in order to facilitate physical and emotional contact and more normal development of early parent-infant relationships. This is discussed at greater length in Chapter 5.

FROM BIOLOGICAL TO PSYCHOLOGICAL DEVELOPMENT

The process of prenatal development presents a contradictory picture. On the one hand, it seems highly predictable and insensitive to the influences that might change its course. Starting from a single cell, the process rapidly unfolds and develops in an increasingly complex sequence of interrelated patterns of change, all of which have become highly canalized over the thousands of years of human evolution. It is as if from the moment of conception, the emergence of the newborn baby nine months later is never in doubt. Although deviations from these normal developmental pathways do occur, they are not really genuine alternatives to normal prenatal development; rather, they seem to emphasize further the predictability of most embryos and fetuses.

On the other hand, although birth marks the end of prenatal development, it is only the beginning of the incredible range of developmental changes that are to follow: changes that are much less canalized or predictable. The knowledge that biology seems to lose its hold on the child once she emerges from the womb and that the environment and experience take over may be overwhelming to a new parent. Indeed, the range of problems that can occur between conception and birth is quite limited when compared to what a child will experience between birth and adulthood. Nevertheless, as we discover in the chapters that follow, biology and experience continue to stay too closely intertwined to be sharply distinguished from one another. The path a child's development takes will be only partially determined by her experiences, including the efforts of her parents.

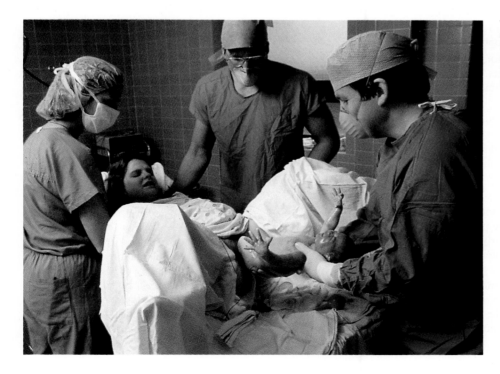

After all the hard work of labor, a baby! No matter how exhausted she may feel, a mother usually is glad to see her new child, especially once reassured that it is healthy.

SUMMARY OF MAJOR IDEAS

Prenatal Stages of Development

1. Prenatal development begins with conception, in which a zygote is created by the union of a sperm cell from the father and an egg cell, or ovum, from the mother.

2. Prenatal development divides into discrete periods, or stages.

3. The germinal stage occurs during the first two weeks following conception; the zygote forms a blastocyst, which differentiates into three different cell layers and then implants itself in the uterus wall to form the embryo.

4. During the embryonic stage, which lasts from the third through the eighth weeks of pregnancy, the placenta and umbilical cord form and the basic organs and biological systems begin to develop.

5. During the fetal stage, which spans from the ninth week until the end of pregnancy, all physical features complete their development.

6. Embryonic and fetal development follow a cephalocaudal (head to tail) and a proximodistal (near to far) pattern of development.

Prenatal Influences on the Child

7. Pregnancy is generally divided into three phases or trimesters, each lasting three months.

8. Particularly during the early part of the first trimester, there are critical periods when embryonic development is highly vulnerable or at risk to disruption.

9. Certain biological risks to prenatal development are associated with the physical and biological characteristics of the mother, including her age, physical size, and state of health.

10. Illnesses such as rubella, syphilis, genital herpes, and AIDS can irreversibly harm the embryo or fetus, particularly during its critical period of development.

11. Teratogens, which include alcohol, smoking, and drugs such as thalidomide, DES, cocaine, and heroin, can cause physical malformations, developmental retardation, or death.

12. Inadequate diet and nutrition and stress can adversely influence prenatal development.

13. Environmental hazards such as radiation or industrial pollution can harm the developing embryo or fetus.

Parental Reactions to Pregnancy

14. Pregnancy causes many complex hormonal and biological changes in the mother that can be physically and psychologically uncomfortable, particularly at the beginning of the first and end of the last trimester.

15. An expectant mother may not only feel physically uncomfortable but also feel impatient, and concerned about her baby's well-being; in addition, she may experience excitement, wonder, and elation about the special experiences of pregnancy, childbirth, and motherhood.

16. Whereas an expectant father shares many of the mother's concerns and upsets and may even feel threatened by the loss of his wife's attention and support, he also experiences great pleasure and excitement about the events.

17. The presence of adequate social and emotional support from friends, family, and neighbors can contribute significantly to reducing the stress of pregnancy and to making it a positive experience.

Birth

18. Toward the end of the third trimester, the mother may experience "false labor," including contractions of the uterus; she also may have a bloody vaginal discharge shortly before true labor begins.

19. Labor occurs in three distinct but overlapping stages.

20. During the first stage of labor, which may last from eight to twenty-four hours for a first-time mother, uterine contractions increase in strength and regularity, and the cervix dilates sufficiently to accommodate the baby's head.

21. The second stage of labor lasts from the complete dilation of the cervix until birth and takes one or one and one-half hours.

22. During the third stage of labor, which lasts only a few minutes, the afterbirth is expelled.

23. Prepared childbirth and pain-reducing drugs such as narcotics, sedatives, and nitrous oxide can make the experience of childbirth more comfortable.

24. In recent years drugs have been used more cautiously in childbirth because of their potentially adverse effects on the recovery of both infant and mother.

25. One of the problems that may arise during labor and delivery is insufficient uterine contractions, or faulty power.

26. A faulty passageway caused by blockage of the birth canal by the placenta (placenta previa) is another problem that may occur.

27. A third type of problem — faulty passenger — may occur if the baby's physical position or large head size prevents completion of the journey through the birth canal.

28. Most hospitals use electronic fetal monitors to keep track of fetal heart rate and uterine contractions.

29. Preterm babies may experience significant complications after birth; however, the bigger and more mature they are at birth, the greater are their chances for survival.

KEY TERMS

germinal stage *(108)*
embryonic stage *(108)*
fetal stage *(108)*
ovum *(108)*
spermatozoa *(109)*
zygote *(109)*
conception *(109)*
blastocyst *(110)*
embryonic disk *(111)*

ectoderm *(111)*
endoderm *(111)*
mesoderm *(111)*
implantation *(111)*
embryo *(111)*
cephalocaudal development *(111)*
proximodistal development *(111)*

placenta *(112)*
osmosis *(112)*
umbilical cord *(112)*
amniotic sac *(113)*
fetus *(113)*
quickening *(114)*
artificial insemination *(116)*
in vitro fertilization *(116)*
surrogate mothering *(117)*
canalization *(115)*
risk factor *(115)*
critical period *(115)*
trimester *(116)*
teratogen *(120)*
fetal alcohol syndrome *(121)*
eclampsia *(120)*
hormone *(125)*
cephalic presentation *(130)*
breech presentation *(130)*

transverse
  presentation *(130)*
first stage of labor *(131)*
transition *(132)*
second stage of labor *(132)*
third stage of labor *(132)*
prepared childbirth *(133)*
Caesarean section *(135)*
induced labor *(136)*
forceps *(137)*
premature *(138)*
preterm *(138)*
respiratory distress syndrome
  (RDS) *(138)*

WHAT DO YOU THINK?

1. How has reading this chapter influenced your views about pregnancy?
2. Based on your reading, what advice might you give to prospective parents concerning changes in their lifestyle to minimize prenatal risks?
3. How might you reassure expectant parents about their concerns regarding whether their baby will be all right?
4. What do you know about your own parents' reactions to their pregnancy with you?
5. What was the process of your own birth like? What problems or complications may have been involved in it?

FOR FURTHER READING

The Boston Women's Health Collective. *The New Our Bodies, Ourselves: A Book by and for Women.* New York: Simon and Schuster, 1984.

This revised and updated version discusses many aspects of women's bodies, health care, and well-being from the personal perspectives of women themselves. Its section on pregnancy is an excellent source of information about what the events and experiences are really like.

Hees-Stauthamer, J. *The First Pregnancy: An Integrated Principle in Female Psychology.* Ann Arbor, Mich.: UMI Research Press, 1985.

This book presents an in-depth study of the subjective, emotional experiences of four women, each older than thirty and pregnant for the first time.

Jones, C. *Sharing Birth: A Father's Guide to Giving Support During Labor.* New York: Quill, 1985.

This guide helps fathers prepare for an active role in the process of childbirth.

Kitzinger, S. *The Complete Book of Pregnancy and Childbirth.* New York: Knopf, 1980.

This is a clear, easy-to-follow explanation of the various physical and psychological changes during pregnancy and the first week of infancy.

Leboyer, F. *Birth Without Violence.* New York: Knopf, 1975.

The originator of the "gentle birth" method describes its procedures. The book includes striking photographs.

Michaelson, K. L. *Childbirth in America: Anthropological Perspectives.* South Hadley, MA: Bergin & Garvey, 1988.

This collection of eighteen articles emphasizes the role of culture in childbirth. Major topic areas included are decisions in pregnancy, birth and birth style, babies in crisis, and becoming a parent.

PART THREE

The First Two Years

As parents and other proud relatives keep discovering, infants grow and change more rapidly than the rest of us. Parents who take snapshots of their children find that they must do so every few months — or even weeks — in order to keep up with these changes. In a matter of months, infants become able to smile, sit, and babble. In just a few more months, they acquire language and the first symbolic skills and take their first tentative steps. And throughout all these events, they acquire definite attachments to particular care-givers.

These changes are crucial in many ways: they make infants seem much more "human" than they were as newborns. And they lay important foundations for all future development. The next three chapters describe these critical changes.

David's Case

David was born nine weeks preterm. Before his birth, his mother had looked forward to seeing her baby in the delivery room. Instead, her first contact came in the intensive care unit of the hospital, where nurses had already attached David to a respirator to help him breathe. Like many preterm infants, David's biggest problem was his lungs; he had respiratory distress syndrome and experienced many episodes of apnea. He was fragile for many weeks after he was born, and this fact affected his parents deeply for a long time. They worried about whether David would survive and about whether he would develop normally.

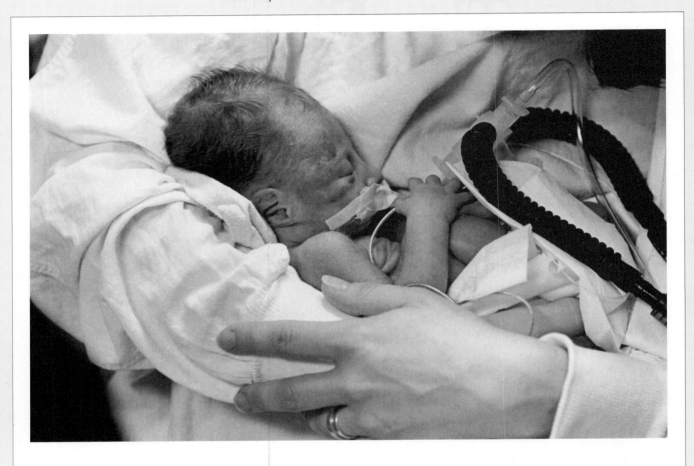

This hospital report shows just how immature David was. He was born weighing less than 4 lbs. — enough to have good chances of survival but only given intensive hospital care. His Apgar scores were lower than normal primarily because of his breathing problems and his general lack of responsiveness.

Patient's Name: Baby boy Bernhard   **DOB:** 6–25–84
AMCH #: 819290   **Adm:** 6–25–84 **Disch:** 7–21–84

HISTORY AND PHYSICAL:

Baby boy Bernhard was born in our DR and admitted to the NICU with RDS and prematurity. He was born to a 29 year old 0 + G3P0020 female. EDC and dates by temperature chart suggested approximately 31 weeks, and the ultrasound indicated a 1300 gram baby. The delivery was by low oulet forceps and the child weighed 1650 grams with apgars of 4/8. The baby needed bagging in the DR and GFR began immediately. Subsequent chest x–rays were consistent with RDS.

DISCHARGE SUMMARY:

In summary, this is a baby who was born 31 weeks of gestation, mildly SGA for size, who had moderate respiratory distress syndrome and needed the respirator for 3 days. The lungs resolved and the remainder of the hospital course was uncomplicated. During the hospitalization, the parents were greatly involved in the child's therapy and showed a very sophisticated level of parenting. At the time of discharge, the physical exam was quite normal and the followup routine was set up with the baby and the private pediatrician.

JEFFREY GREENE, M.D.
NEONATOLOGIST

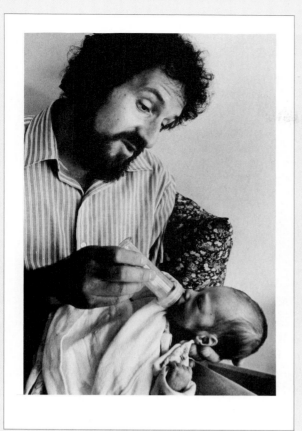

During David's hospital stay, the medical staff encouraged his parents to visit with him often. These visits seemed to help ease their worries. Because his sucking reflex was not well developed, David was fed his mother's milk from bottles. Before long, his reflexes strengthened and he was able to drink well.

David went home from the hospital after one month. During his early months his mother worried about him a lot. At first he seemed limp and floppy and often not very alert. She read avidly in books about infant care, looking to see whether David was developing "on schedule."

In time David's parents became less concerned about their baby's sheer physical survival. But they still worried. David seemed a bit quieter than they thought a baby should be, and by five months of age he still had not rolled over. But David did seem to hear sounds — like the family cat whenever it meowed — so his pediatrician urged them to be patient.

By the time David was six months old, his doctor said that he was indeed developing well, although he was definitely behind full-term infants in most motor skills. By now, for example, he still could not sit up reliably without a pillow or hand behind his back. But he watched his parents avidly whenever they came in the room and often smiled at them when they talked to him.

A real change occurred in David's mother one day when David was ten months old. A neighbor who was visiting commented, "He's so observant and so interested and careful in the things he handles!" That was the first time that David's mother began thinking that her son might be truly talented in some ways rather than simply slow to develop in general. The doctor had already stated this idea to her, but it had not sunk in until now.

When David was about thirteen months old, sometimes he even became too active. Now he could stand up in his crib during nap times, pound on the wall, and talk loudly in a mixture of babbling and occasional real, single words. Both his parents enjoyed his new accomplishments and only now and then thought about the fact that some of them were still "behind schedule" compared to other babies.

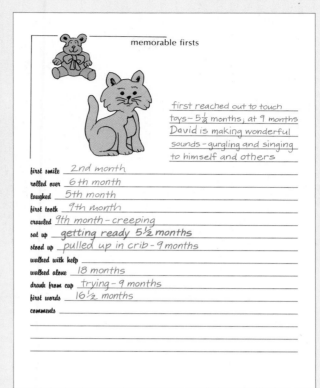

As David neared his second birthday, his parents' concerns were generally typical of parents of toddlers. They tried to support his efforts to gain greater autonomy and self-control. David became interested in using the toilet, for example, although not often at the right time. His mother was patient with his erratic bladder and bowels, believing that time would eventually cure this particular problem.

By the time he was two, friends and neighbors could not guess that David had been preterm unless his parents told them. He was just as big and tall as other children his age. And even though he had a somewhat quiet temperament, he loved playing outdoors just like other children. He even adopted a favorite tree stump, which he turned into a "horse" that he rode often. David's mother found herself willing (and even relieved) to let him play on his own for brief periods — a far cry from her attitude when David had been younger.

CHAPTER 5

The First Two Years: Physical Development

Focusing Questions

- What do newborn infants look like, and how do they act?
- How do infants' sleep patterns change as they get older?
- How do infants' senses operate at birth?
- How do motor skills evolve during infancy? What influences the course of their development?
- What are the effects of low birth weight on infant development?
- What do infants need nutritionally during the first two years, and what dietary deficiencies are common in their diets, both in North America and around the world?
- What are the relative advantages of breast feeding and bottle feeding?

nne was looking at the journal she had kept about her daughter since Michelle was seven months old.

- February 7: This week Michelle began pushing herself backwards on her stomach to get around — not very efficient, but it works!

- April 9: For two weeks she has been *creeping,* not crawling. She raises up her tummy, pushes her body forward (like a seal!), and plops down. Jim and I can't help laughing — she looks so ridiculous.

- June 10: Crawling all over the place — mostly after the dog. Gets mad when King walks away; then she cries and "forgets" how to locomote.

- August 10: Michelle's really working at walking. 3–5 steps at a time, mostly when one of us is encouraging her. She really looks different — especially now that she's vertical.

Now Michelle was almost two, and Anne read about Michelle's changes with awe and wonder. Anne could not believe how fast Michelle had grown during infancy — nor how few of Michelle's infant accomplishments she had actually had time to record in her journal.

As Anne can attest, during the first months of life, a baby's behaviors evolve rapidly. By her second birthday — considered the end of infancy — she seems much more mature or human — more able to think for herself and to express interest in people and more able to choose how to use her energies and attentions — than she did at birth. She is still "just a baby," of course, but at twenty-four months she is a very competent one.

This chapter traces some of these physical developments through the first two years of life. It begins by discussing very young infants: what they look like and how they act immediately after birth. It then investigates babies' nervous systems, including the growth of their brains and how they are affected by sleep patterns, before going on to discuss the development of the senses. Then the chapter shifts attention to how infants develop motor skills, beginning with their early, inborn reflexes and ending with the first major voluntary skills, such as walking and grasping at objects. For normal infants these skills develop at much the same time and in much the same sequence. But the skills also vary significantly according to the circumstances that individual children encounter, and the chapter describes several circumstances that can cause variation. Finally, the chapter discusses infants' nutritional needs: what food they need immediately at birth, how these needs change as they get older, and how diet can affect infants' physical development and even (in extreme cases) whether they survive infancy at all.

APPEARANCE OF THE YOUNG INFANT

As the last chapter showed, birth continues rather than begins physical development. Most organs have already been working for several weeks, or even months, prior to this event. The baby's heart has been beating regularly; his muscles have been contracting sporadically; and his liver has been making its major product, bile, which is necessary for normal digestion after birth. Two physical functions, however, do begin at birth: breathing and ingestion (the taking in of foods). Even some behaviors, such as sucking and arm stretching, have already developed, although generally these have not advanced as far as the baby's physical functions.

The First Few Hours

When first delivered, the newborn baby, or **neonate,** definitely does *not* resemble most people's stereotypes of a beautiful baby. No matter what her race, her skin may look rather red — redder than parents usually expect, especially if they have never paid close attention to newborn babies before. She may be covered with various substances, such as fluid from the amniotic sac, blood from the placenta, and bits of brownish fluid from her own bowels. Many babies, especially if born a bit early, also have a white waxy substance called **vernix** on their skin, and their bodies may be covered with fine, downy hair called **lanugo.** If an infant is delivered vaginally rather than by surgery, her head may be somewhat elongated or have a noticeable point on it; the shape comes from the pressure of the birth canal, which squeezes the bones of her skull together for several hours during labor. Within a few days or weeks the baby's head fills out again to a more normal shape, leaving gaps in the bones. These are sometimes called **fontanelles,**

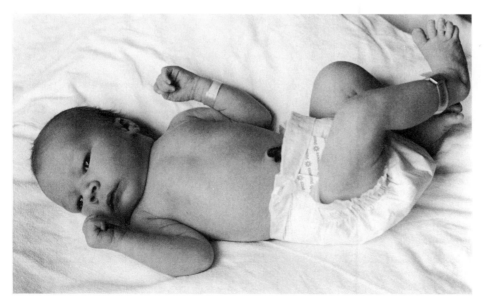

In the first few minutes after birth, healthy newborn babies are quite alert and responsive to sights and sounds. Soon, though, they begin spending most of their time asleep.

or "soft spots," although they are actually covered by a tough membrane that can withstand normal contact and pressure. The gaps do not all grow over with bone until about eighteen months.

Early bonding

Typically, newborns react vigorously to their surroundings during the first fifteen or thirty minutes of life. They may cry, look around, or suck, generally using their inborn reflexes (described later in this chapter). Before long, however, they fall asleep (labor can wear them out, too!), and usually they do not revive again for a few hours. Some psychologists therefore consider the earliest minutes and hours of life especially important for getting parents and children interested in each other — for "parent-infant bonding," as it is sometimes called (Klaus & Kennell, 1976).

Unfortunately, not every delivery goes smoothly enough to allow immediate or leisurely contact following birth. Some babies and mothers will only survive the aftermath of a difficult labor and delivery if they receive instant medical attention that requires their separation. Are such parents and babies jeopardized in their relationships with each other? Are they less able to become attached to each other over the long run? Not necessarily, as long as other forces exist to encourage a good relationship as the baby gets a little older (Lamb & Hwang, 1982).

Is the Baby All Right?

The Apgar Scale   Because hospitals cannot always afford to have a pediatrician attend every birth, doctors and nurses need a way of deciding quickly which newborns need immediate attention from a pediatrician and which are healthy enough to wait a bit longer. The Apgar Scale (named after its originator, Dr. Virginia Apgar) helps to meet this need (Apgar, 1953). The Apgar Scale does not give a lot of detail about a baby's condition, but it does help identify those infants who may need special medical help right away.

The **Apgar Scale** consists of ratings that are simple enough for nonspecialists to make, even during the distractions surrounding the moment of delivery. To use it, someone at the delivery calculates the baby's heart rate, breathing, muscle tone, color, and reflex irritability and assigns a score from 0 to 2 to each of these five characteristics. Babies are rated one minute after they emerge from the womb and again at five minutes. Each time they can earn a maximum score of 10, as shown in Table 5.1. Most babies in fact earn nine or ten points, at least

TABLE 5.1   The Apgar Scale

Characteristic	Score		
	0	1	2
Heart rate	Absent	Less than 100 beats per minute	More than 100 beats per minute
Efforts to breathe	Absent	Slow, irregular	Good; baby is crying
Muscle tone	Flaccid, limp	Weak, inactive	Strong, active motion
Skin color	Body pale or blue	Body pink, extremities blue	Body and extremities pink
Reflex irritability	No response	Frown, grimace	Vigorous crying, coughing, sneezing

Source: Apgar (1953).

Family

How does the physical appearance of infants contribute to the formation of parent-child attachments? (155–156)

Physical Development

How well do newborn infants see and hear? (160, 161)

Social Context

Why do infants in certain African societies tend to develop motor skills sooner than North American infants? (175–176)

Genetics

To what extent are infant motor skills inborn? (169–170)

Peers

Do babies show interest in other babies? (156)

THE FIRST TWO YEARS: PHYSICAL DEVELOPMENT

How accurate are physiological measures of emotion in infants? (236)

Emotions

What are some of the physical signs of self-recognition displayed by infants? (252–253)

Self-concept and Identity

During what states of arousal does learning seem to occur in infants? (159)

Learning

What impact does preterm birth tend to have on children's later cognitive development? (172)

Cognition

Do deaf children babble? (216)

Language

---

by five minutes after delivery. If a baby scores between four and seven points at one minute, he is given immediate special medical attention (Apgar & Beck, 1973), which almost always includes examination by a pediatrician, and is then carefully observed during the next few hours and days for problems that may develop. David, the preterm infant described on pages 144–147, received this sort of special care; he scored 4 at one minute and 8 at five minutes, primarily because of breathing problems.

Babies who score less than 4 on the Apgar Scale face serious medical risk. Their heart rate is slow, their breathing is irregular and difficult, and their muscle tone is rather weak. Instead of the healthy pink color that results from an ample supply of oxygen in their blood, babies with low Apgar ratings may look blue in their extremities, or even all over their bodies. And they do not respond strongly when stimulated; a sudden noise, for example, produces no startle reaction. Such babies need intensive care immediately if they are to survive. Their most immediate problem usually concerns breathing: often they require oxygen and special apparatus to make breathing less difficult. With intensive medical care, however, most of these babies do survive.

Signs of risk

The Brazelton Neonatal Behavioral Assessment Scale   Although Apgar scores reflect a baby's condition in the moments after birth, other observations are needed to assess health and behavior later in infancy. One such method is the **Brazelton Neonatal Behavioral Assessment Scale** (Brazelton, 1973, 1979), a neurological and behavioral test that is usually given on the third day of life and often repeated again a few days later. It is intended to determine how well infants can regulate their responses to various stimuli.

To give the test, a skilled observer purposely arouses the infant from deep sleep and moves her through alert wakefulness to distressed crying, then back through the quieter states and eventually to sleep again. To accomplish all these changes, the observer presents the baby with a rattle, ball, bell, and other stimuli, including the examiner's face and voice. Altogether, the examiner notes twenty

Assessing responsiveness

different neurological reflexes during the test as well as responses to twenty-six different stimuli. At each step the observer notices not only how well and how quickly the infant responds but also how quickly she quiets herself afterward. Having the ability both to respond and to quiet shows good neurological health. As babies develop further during infancy, they continually need both abilities; they cannot afford to ignore the interesting sights and sounds around them, but they also cannot afford to let those sights and sounds overwhelm them (Sameroff, 1979).

Newborn Weight

As adults we are used to having a fairly fixed bodily size, with only minor changes in our waistlines, perhaps, as the years go by. Not so for young infants: changes in size, weight, and bodily proportions are a constant occurrence in their lives. Viewed by casual adult observers, a young infant seems first to be small and second to be growing rapidly. Viewed by adults who know the infant well, however, the baby seems primarily to grow and change weight and only secondarily to be small (Eichorn, 1979).

At birth a typical baby weighs about seven and one-half pounds, or 3,400 grams — about as much as a large cat or a small dog. Because they are so small, neonates have a rather large surface area compared to their weight. As a result they lose heat more easily than adults do, and they have to consume more calories just to keep warm. But neonates also need to gain weight during the earliest

FIGURE 5.1
Height and Weight Growth During the First Two Years

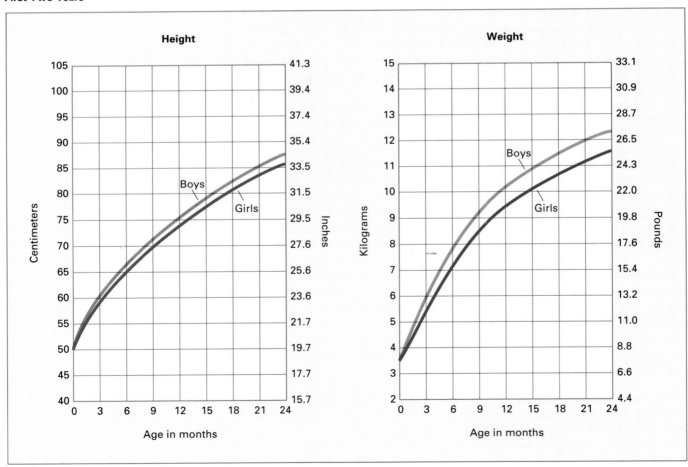

months; by four months of age they have typically doubled their birth weight (see Figure 5.1). How, then, can they keep themselves warm and gain quite a lot of weight at the same time?

The answer is, they eat. Because the baby still has no teeth, he has to drink all his calories. A newborn will usually consume about one quart of breast milk or infant formula in twenty-four hours. Considered as a proportion of his body weight, this is the same as if an adult drank ten to twenty quarts per day. And of course the baby must excrete after capturing the valuable nutrients from these huge amounts. No wonder, then, that diapers and feedings form the center of a newborn's life.

Need for calories

Size and Bodily Proportions

Lying down, a new baby measures about twenty inches, or fifty centimeters. Her length matches her adult size more closely than her weight does: her twenty inches represent more than one-quarter of her final height, whereas her seven and one-half pounds represent only a small percentage of her adult weight.

Even though this fact suggests that newborns should look skinny, they usually look chubby or overweight instead. Babies' heads take up almost one-quarter of their length, and their limbs are disproportionately short (see Figure 5.2). Their chests seem small compared to their stomachs, which often stick out like a middle-aged person's pot belly. Bones contribute much less to overall weight than they do for adults: they are small and thin in proportion to the baby's size. For all these reasons, babies tend to look rather fat and cute.

Babies' proportions and general physical appearance may have psychological consequences by fostering attachments, or bonds, between infants and the people who care for them, which promotes feelings of security. The cuteness of infants' faces in particular seems to help; most babies have unusually large foreheads, features that are concentrated in the lower part of the face, eyes that are large and round, and cheeks that are high and prominent. Dolls and cartoon characters have these facial features, too, although often in exaggerated form, and so do a variety of animal species. The pattern of babyish features occurs so widely among animals, in fact, that biologists who study animal behavior suspect that it has universal and genetically based power to attract parental or nurturing responses among adult animals (Lorenz, 1970). Mothers in some species of ducks, for example, take care of baby ducks even when the babies are not their own.

Bridges How does the physical appearance of infants contribute to the formation of parent-child attachments?

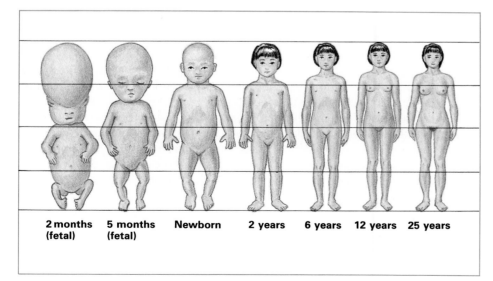

FIGURE 5.2
Body Proportions, Fetal Period Through Adulthood

2 months (fetal) 5 months (fetal) Newborn 2 years 6 years 12 years 25 years

The normal facial features of infants — large forehead and eyes, high cheekbones, small mouth — help stimulate attachment in adults.

Cuteness apparently affects humans in comparable ways, although not as automatically as among other animals. The mere sight of a babyish face creates interest in a wide variety of human beings and in a wide variety of situations. Interest occurs both consciously and unconsciously. Not only do people say that they find babies attractive; their bodies respond to babies with enlarged pupils and faster heartbeat. Unlike many other animal species, humans are interested even if they are not mothers or other adults; babies, for example, seem at least as interested in fellow babies as many adults are (McCall & Kennedy, 1980; Berman, 1980).

Bridges Do babies show interest in other babies?

DEVELOPMENT OF THE NERVOUS SYSTEM

The **central nervous system** consists of the brain and nerve cells of the spinal cord. Together, they coordinate and control the perception of stimuli as well as motor responses of all kinds. The more complex parts of this work are accomplished by the brain, which develops rapidly from just before birth until well beyond a child's second birthday. At seven months past conception the brain weighs about 10 percent of its final adult weight, but by birth it has more than doubled, to about 25 percent of final adult weight. By the child's second birthday it has tripled and is about 75 percent of final adult weight (Tanner, 1978b).

Reasons for increase in brain size

Most of the increase results not from increasing numbers of nerve cells, or **neurons**, but from the development of a denser or more fully packed brain. This happens in two ways. First, the neurons put out many new fibers that connect them with one another; and second, certain brain cells called **glial cells** put out fatty sheathing, or **myelin**, that gradually encases the neurons and their fibers. Because impulses can travel relatively easily through myelin sheaths, myelin allows nerve fibers to transmit impulses much faster (more than ten times!) as

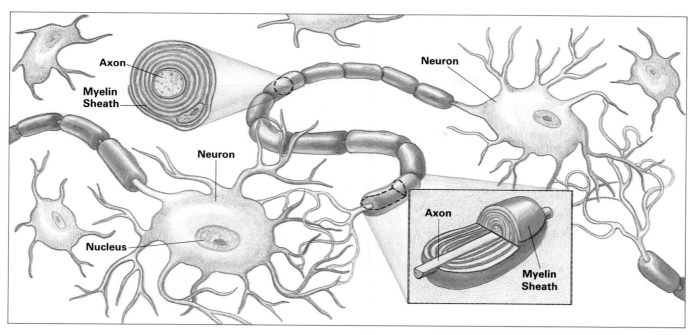

FIGURE 5.3
The Process of Myelinization

well as more reliably. Figure 5.3 illustrates these anatomical parts. The myelin acts like the insulation on an electric cord: it keeps impulses from short-circuiting on other fibers and ensures that they discharge only at designated places along the nerve fibers.

Myelinization begins before birth, proceeds rapidly during the first four years of life, and finally finishes in adolescence. Myelinization may account for certain improvements in motor and perceptual skills during infancy and childhood, although certainly not all of them (Brierley, 1987). The first neurons to be fully myelinated, for example, are those associated with the sense organs; and partly for this reason infants' senses work nearly as well as adults' within just a few months of birth (Brierley, 1976).

Growth of the Brain

At birth and for about the first six months, neural activity is dominated by the relatively primitive, or "lower," areas of the brain called the **brain stem** and the **midbrain**, which regulate relatively automatic functions such as breathing, digestion, and general alertness or consciousness. Figure 5.4 shows where these parts are located in the brain. As babies approach their first birthday, however, the "higher" part of the brain, called the **cerebral cortex**, becomes more active. Although even newborns respond to sights and sounds, it is not until age one that their responses seem conscious and that they can perform at will simple motor actions such as reaching and wiggling their fingers.

By the end of infancy the overall anatomical features of the brain are reasonably well established, but its various parts continue to develop specialized functions. The left hemisphere, for example, appears to specialize in language. As a result, most three-year-olds understand language more accurately and easily if it is fed into the left hemisphere (or half) of their brain with special earphones (Hiscock & Kinsbourne, 1980). In spite of such specialization, however, other facts suggest that children's brains retain flexibility for many years. Children whose normal brain language centers are damaged, for example, can usually recover most of their language ability as long as the damage occurs before adolescence. Apparently they recover because the brain finds new areas of the **cerebrum** to devote to language processing.

Basic brain anatomy

FIGURE 5.4
The Brain

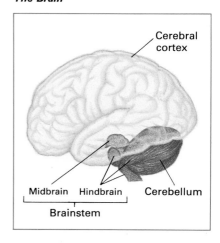

Effects of sensory stimulation

To a large extent, brain specialization appears to be driven or stimulated by sensory experiences. For instance, animals who are blindfolded or physically restrained become handicapped for life in ways related to their deprivation (Parmalee & Sigman, 1983). Dogs who are prevented from experiencing pain can burn themselves badly simply by sniffing at an ordinary candle flame too closely. Such dogs apparently do not develop normal sensitivity to pain. Partly as a result of this neural deficit, they have trouble learning to protect themselves from ordinarily painful stimuli such as heat from a candle. The nerve fibers that register pain, either in their nose or in their brain, simply do not grow properly.

States of Sleep and Wakefulness

One important function of the brain is to control infants' states of sleep and wakefulness. It thus regulates how much stimulation infants experience, both externally and internally. Periodic sleep helps infants to shut out external stimulation and thereby allows them to obtain general physical rest. But as pointed out below, certain kinds of sleep may also increase internal stimulation and thereby encourage healthy brain development.

Sleep   Very young infants vary from deep sleep to wakefulness, with much more of the former than of the latter. In the days immediately after birth newborns sleep an average of sixteen hours per day, although some may sleep as little as eleven hours a day and others as much as twenty-one (Berg & Berg, 1979). For most infants the amount of sleep decreases steadily with each passing month. By the age of six months, babies average just thirteen or fourteen hours per day and by twenty-four months just eleven or twelve. But these hours still represent considerably more sleeping time than is typical for adults.

REM sleep

Newborns divide their sleeping time about equally between relatively active and quiet periods of sleep. The more active kind is named **REM sleep**, after the "*r*apid *e*ye *m*ovements" or twitchings that usually accompany it. REM sleep generally seems restless: sometimes infants' limbs or facial muscles twitch, and their breathing seems faster and more irregular. In the quieter kind of sleep (**non-REM sleep**), infants breathe regularly and more slowly, and their muscles become much limper.

Infants spend more time sleeping than doing anything else. Even by the age of two, most babies still need to sleep twelve hours a day.

TABLE 5.2 States of Arousal in Infants

State	Behavior of Infant
Non-REM sleep	Complete rest; muscles relaxed; eyes closed and still; breathing regular and relatively slow
REM sleep	Occasional twitches, jerks, facial grimaces; irregular and intermittent eye movements; breathing irregular and relatively rapid
Drowsiness	Occasional movements, but less than in REM sleep; eyes open and close; glazed look; breathing regular, but faster than in non-REM sleep
Alert inactivity	Eyes open and scanning; body relatively still; rate of breathing similar to drowsiness, but more irregular
Alert activity	Eyes open, but not attending or scanning; frequent, diffuse bodily movements; vocalizations; irregular breathing; skin flushed
Distress	Whimpering or crying; vigorous or agitated movements; facial grimaces pronounced; skin very flushed

Source: Wolff (1966).

During the night infants experience cycles of REM and non-REM sleep; for young infants, these begin with REM sleep, and each cycle lasts about one hour. Adults experience similar cycles of sleep, but they usually begin with non-REM sleep, and each cycle lasts at least two hours. Furthermore, adults usually report dreaming during REM sleep. Although infants may also dream during REM sleep, the unique cycles of their sleep suggest that REM sleep may serve other purposes. One possibility is that periods of REM sleep stimulate babies' brains in general and in doing so foster healthy growth of nerve fibers and glial cells. This possibility is supported by studies that show that neonates engage in shorter and fewer REM sleep periods if they receive a lot of sensory stimulation when they are awake (Boismier, 1977).

Unfortunately for parents, a baby's extra sleep does not usually include long, uninterrupted rest periods, even at night. It is more common in the first few months for the baby to wake frequently — often every two or three hours — but sometimes unpredictably. Studies of brain development suggest that much of the unpredictability may result from the physical immaturity of the baby's nervous system: his brain may have frequent, accidental "storms" of impulses because it is not yet fully formed (Parmelee & Stern, 1972; Emde & Robinson, 1979).

States of Arousal   Although infants show various states of arousal from the day they are born, as they get older their patterns of arousal begin to resemble those of older children (Berg & Berg, 1979). Table 5.2 summarizes the various states. The largest share of time, even among older infants, goes to the most completely relaxed and deepest form of sleep.

Variations in arousal make a practical difference to parents, other caregivers, and to babies themselves. During the alert times a baby is most likely to look at her surroundings and begin forming initial impressions of them. She begins noticing human faces a few months after birth but increasingly so throughout the first year. Sometime before her six-month birthday, she begins showing special preference for the faces that care for her the most, and she begins noticing that various sounds and sights usually occur together — that a mouth opening and shutting, for example, usually occurs when a human voice comes her way. These experiences constitute the earliest perceptions and may stimulate the earliest attachments.

On the other hand, a fully alert state may not be the only condition in which young babies learn. Infants fail to habituate, or get used to, sounds and other

Sleep dominates

Bridges   During what states of arousal does learning seem to occur in infants?

Perspectives

Sudden Infant Death Syndrome

Every year about two out of every thousand young infants die in their sleep for no apparent reason. Doctors call this **sudden infant death syndrome**, or SIDS. The problem is most frequent among infants between the ages of two months and four months, although SIDS, also called crib death, can happen to babies as young as one month and as old as one year. It is the leading cause of death among infants who survive the first few weeks after delivery.

SIDS is disturbing because it is so mysterious. Typically, parents put a seemingly healthy baby down to sleep as usual, but when they come in to get her up again, they discover that she is dead. A few cases have even occurred when parents are actually holding their sleeping infant (Franciosi, 1983). Sadly, because of the absence of obvious health problems, parents often blame themselves for the death, suspecting that somehow they have neglected their child or hurt her in some way (Mandell, 1988). Even more unfortunately, friends and relatives often concur in blaming the parents, simply because they can think of no other way to explain SIDS. Other obvious causes simply do not occur; the baby does not choke, vomit, or suffocate. She seems just to stop breathing.

One proposed theory about SIDS emphasizes abnormal breathing patterns among infants who may be at risk. Most infants (and children, too) experience occasional **sleep apnea**, or temporary stoppages of breathing during sleep. But some experts argue that SIDS infants experience apnea more frequently than usual or that they experience it for longer periods at a time (Guillemault, 1988). Another theory suggests that SIDS happens primarily at a special developmental transition: just when inborn reflex control of breathing begins to fade in importance but before infants have firmly established breathing under voluntary control (Lipsitt, 1982). For most infants this transition happens at about two to four months of age — just when SIDS happens most often. Perhaps at this time infants cannot respond effectively to *any* blockage of their nasal passages.

Since 1985, some researchers have argued that SIDS infants suffer from heart problems: their nervous systems do not prompt regular, strong heartbeats and in essence cause the baby to suffer a heart attack (P. Schwartz, 1988; P. Schwartz et al., 1988). In this view, the heart problems contribute to irregular breathing, rather than the other way around. Unfortunately, it is hard to determine which gives out first — heart or lungs — because babies who experience SIDS are usually not discovered until after they have died.

stimulation that occur during more active REM sleep. Heart rates speed up in reaction to such stimulation, suggesting the possibility that infants do some sort of mental processing of the stimulation even while asleep (Johnson et al., 1975; Weinberger et al., 1984). The processing may constitute a sign of learning about the environment, but at present this is not certain.

SENSORY DEVELOPMENT

All of the human senses operate at birth. This conclusion follows from a variety of observations and experiments with neonates. Sometimes, for example, newborn infants prefer slight changes in brightness, as shown by their staring longer at a light that changes slightly in intensity than at one that does not. And sometimes newborns' heart rates change when a sensation changes; a slightly louder or higher sound can have this effect. Under certain conditions, too, newborn babies respond overtly to a sensation; they sometimes turn toward a sound, for example, or away from a bad odor. Behaviors and responses like these show that newborns have a full complement of senses. But observations also reveal that they have certain sensory limitations as well.

Visual Acuity

Bridges How well do newborn infants see and hear?

Infants can see at birth but without the clarity of focus or acuity (keenness) characteristic of adults with good vision. They can track a bright light even before they leave the hospital delivery room, as long as the light lies near their

If medical researchers could in fact identify a basic cause, it would help future infants at risk for SIDS; those babies could wear monitors that indicated interruptions in breathing (if lungs were the problem) or heart rate (if that was it) and that prompted parents or medical personnel to give the baby immediate, appropriate help (Kelly & Shannon, 1988). But so far the use of monitors has not been practical on a widespread scale because the monitors can be cumbersome, often cause a lot of unnecessary alarm, and occasionally do not function properly.

Medical research has identified several factors that make a particular family or infant more likely to experience SIDS. Very young mothers and fathers (less than twenty years) stand more chance of having a SIDS infant; so do mothers who smoke cigarettes or who have serious illnesses during pregnancy. Mothers who are poorly nourished during pregnancy also carry more risk than mothers who keep reasonably well nourished. But certain babies also have more risk of SIDS, independent of their parents' qualities; boys die of SIDS more often than girls, for example, and infants born small (less than seven pounds) die more often than bigger infants. These relations do not mean, however, that being a boy or being small actually *causes* SIDS. They only mean that for reasons still not understood, SIDS seems to happen more frequently to boys and small infants.

Even taken together, however, factors such as these do not predict SIDS very accurately. The vast majority of high-risk infants never die, whereas some infants with few risk factors do die of SIDS anyway (Peterson, 1988). This fact creates problems in translating the studies of risk factors into concrete recommendations for medical personnel and parents because following the risk indications too literally can arouse fears among many parents unnecessarily. The most useful recommendations are ones that are good for all families, whether or not they are at risk for SIDS. For example, it is a good idea to recommend that parents should not smoke and that an infant's room should be humidified if possible whenever she catches a cold. This is sound medical advice for everyone, but unfortunately it is not a guarantee against SIDS. For parents whose babies died of SIDS, many hospitals and communities have created support groups, where couples can share their grief and come to terms with it.

line of vision and moves fairly slowly. When looking at single lines, however, newborns reveal their poor acuity. To be noticed by newborns, such lines must be about ten times as wide as necessary for adults, and if the lines lie off to one side of the infants' line of vision, they must be even wider (Cohen et al., 1979). These facts imply that infants have distance vision of about 20/200 or worse, which means that they can see at twenty feet what an adult with good vision can see at two hundred feet. Newborns see more clearly at short distances, and especially at about eight to ten inches, but even their near vision may not become well established until about one month of age (Banks, 1983).

Limitations of early vision

Visual acuity improves a lot during infancy, but it still does not reach adult levels until the end of the preschool years (Acredolo & Hake, 1982). An older infant (one- or two-years-old) often has 20/30 or 20/40 vision, meaning he can see fine details at twenty feet that adults can seé at thirty or forty feet. This quality of vision is quite satisfactory for everyday, familiar activities; in fact, many adults have visual acuity no better than this, without even realizing it. But this level of visual acuity does interfere with seeing distant objects and may even be one reason (among several) that preschool children often do not profit from large-group, classroom-style teaching, which usually requires good distance vision.

Infant vision is nearsighted

Auditory Acuity

Auditory acuity refers to sensitivity to sounds. Infants can hear at birth but not as well as adults. Any sudden loud noise, such as the sound caused by dropping a large book on the floor, demonstrates that they can hear. The sound produces a dramatic startle reaction, called a Moro reflex: the neonate withdraws her limbs suddenly, sometimes shakes all over, and sometimes also cries (Bench,

Bridges How well do newborn infants see and hear?

1978). But not all noises produce this reaction. Pure tones, like the sound of a flute, cause relatively little response. Complex noises containing many different sounds usually produce more: a bag of nails spilling on the floor, for example, tends to startle infants reliably (Bench et al., 1976).

Even when they do not startle overtly, however, newborn infants do respond internally to sounds. Electrodes attached to their heads register small electrical responses to most ordinary noises that are moderately loud (Schulman-Galambos & Galambos, 1979). Soft sounds or noises, however, do not produce electrical responses, even when they are loud enough to do so in adults. Judged in this way, infants seem just a bit hard of hearing compared to adults, although of course they are far from deaf. These differences persist through much of the second year of infancy. Children begin sensing very soft sounds sometime toward the end of infancy, judging both by the electrical brain waves described above and by their increasingly overt responses to sounds, language, and music, as observed by parents.

Taste and Smell

Even at birth infants clearly prefer sweet tastes; they suck faster when an artificial nipple delivers sugar water than when it delivers plain water. Other taste preferences, however, seem much less clear-cut than they are among children and adults. Newborn infants will suck *less* for saltwater, for example, but only if the saltwater is delivered automatically between bursts of sucking. If saltwater comes as a result of each suck, they show no significant decrease from their normal rates of sucking (Crook, 1978). Other tastes (bitterness and sourness) have even less effect on newborns' sucking behavior. This fact does not prove that neonates do not experience these tastes; it only shows that they do not respond to the tastes by modifying one of their most powerful reflexes, sucking.

Newborns react to a variety of smells, both good and bad. A faint odor of ammonia or vinegar, for example, makes one-week-old infants grimace and avert or turn away their heads (Rieser et al., 1976). They can even locate the general direction of the bad odor. If it is presented repeatedly but from different directions each time, newborns usually turn away from the odor and rarely toward it. Presumably they respond to differences in the amount of stimulation to each nostril; the one closer to the odor probably receives a stronger dose and perhaps also receives it sooner. This difference apparently gives infants the information they need to turn in the most effective direction, which is away.

Breast-feeding newborns can also recognize the odor of their mothers' breasts. One study demonstrated this sensory ability by hanging two breast pads in front of one-month-old infants, one pad on each side of the head (MacFarlane, 1977). One breast pad had previously been worn by the infant's mother, but the other had not. The used pad therefore carried the mother's aroma, unlike the alternate pad. When confronted with this choice, infants spent more time facing or looking at their mothers' breast pads. They did so even when the experimenters substituted a pad from another breast-feeding mother for the clean pad. Apparently the newborns discriminated among various mothers' odors and preferred the aroma of their own mother.

Touch

Newborn infants have many reflexes that show sensitivity to touch. A light stroke on the cheek, for example, normally causes a baby to turn his head in the direction of the stroke; placing a finger on the baby's lips normally causes him to begin sucking motions; and touching the bottoms of his feet normally causes him to fan his toes outward. Parents in many cultures have discovered that wrapping a newborn infant in a cloth or blanket, or even just holding her firmly, tends to reduce crying and fussing; in part such quieting implies sensitivity to touch, although it may also result from the interesting sights and sounds involved in being swaddled or held (Hirschman et al., 1982).

In newborns, in fact, touch may help development in many ways. A lot of the benefit occurs by way of the central nervous system. The closeness brought on by touching, holding, and carrying relaxes both the baby *and* the care-giver (Hofer, 1987; C. Brown, 1984). So tactual behaviors encourage healthy physical development in the baby, on the one hand, and make the care-giver more able to be alert and attentive to the baby, on the other.

Furthermore, certain innate responses to touch can facilitate visual development (Bushnell, 1981). Stroking a baby's cheek, for example, causes a response called the rooting reflex: the baby automatically turns his head in the direction of the stroking and begins to suck. The response sets the stage for a new cognitive achievement — learning that certain tactual and visual sensations are equivalent. In this case the baby both sees and feels something at the same time — whether it is a finger, the mother's breast, or whatever else that happened to brush his cheek.

At birth one particular kind of touch — pain — seems less well developed than it is among slightly older infants or children. It is possible to evoke a painful or negative response to a pinprick, such as a baby might receive for a blood test, in one-day-old infants. But most infants this young seem somewhat less sensitive to painful stimulation than they do even a few days later (Lipsitt & Levy, 1959; Anders & Chalemian, 1974). The insensitivity may actually help newborn infants to endure one particularly stressful experience: birth itself.

Changes in sensitivity to pain

MOTOR DEVELOPMENT

The infant's very first movements or motions appear to be inborn and automatic; they are called **reflexes**. During the first months of life, most reflexes disappear or become incorporated into relatively purposeful or voluntary movements. When they have these qualities, they are called **skills**. Both reflexes and skills are also called **motor abilities**; the term *motor* refers to movement or motion.

Early Reflexes

Pediatricians have identified more than two dozen inborn reflexes. A few of these, such as sucking, clearly help the baby to adapt to her new postuterine environment. Others look more like evolutionary vestiges of behaviors that may have helped earlier versions of *Homo sapiens* to cope — by clinging to their mothers, for example, at the sound of danger. Although a few reflexes, such as blinking, breathing, and swallowing, persist throughout a person's life, most reflexes disappear from the infant's repertoire of skills during the first few months. Their disappearance, in fact, helps doctors to judge whether a baby is developing normally. Persistent newborn reflexes may suggest damage to the nervous system or generally retarded development.

Nature of reflexes

Rooting and Sucking If you gently stroke the cheek of a newborn he will turn his head to the side that is being stroked. His searching behavior is called **rooting**. Under normal circumstances it helps the baby to locate his mother's breast because he will nose around for it if it happens to brush the side of his face just prior to nursing.

Mouthing is one of the first reflexes shown by infants. As they get older, they begin mouthing objects voluntarily in order to literally "get the feel" of new objects.

If the baby then finds the nipple, he will begin **sucking** powerfully and rhythmically — and without being taught. Actually, any object will cause sucking if it intrudes far enough into his mouth; a finger, for example, makes a good pacifier. Later in the infant's first year, the sucking reflex comes under more voluntary control and broadens to become **mouthing**, a mixture of gnawing and chewing. The infant begins using his mouth as a major way to learn about new objects; for a time, it seems, he puts practically everything into his mouth. His preference for mouthing and chewing is not surprising given his earlier reflexes of rooting and sucking.

Moro Reflex   A newborn will startle dramatically in response to sudden loss of support, even if the loss does not really threaten to hurt her. The startle response is called the **Moro reflex**. A common way of testing for it begins with the baby lying flat on her back. The tester first lifts the baby's arms gently so that her shoulders no longer touch the table, although the rest of her body still safely contacts it; then the tester releases the baby's arms. Normally the infant will spread her arms, shake, make horrible faces, and possibly cry. Gradually she will bring her arms together again, as if to grab at something. The response looks much like the startle of children and adults and may in fact be a precursor to it. At some time earlier in human evolution, the Moro reflex may have helped infants who were being carried to grab more tightly when they experienced sudden loss of support. At present, however, it is significant mostly because it helps doctors to diagnose normal development of the nervous system. Healthy infants show the response when they are born but lose much of it as they approach their sixth month.

Some, although not all, sudden, loud sounds also cause infants to startle. This inconsistency may make some parents wonder whether their newborn can actually hear, but careful observation shows that the nature of the stimulation matters to young babies. Their state of alertness affects whether or not they startle to a particular sound; sometimes the same noise will simply produce attention rather than startle behaviors (Leavitt et al., 1976). Well before their second birthday, however, their reactions resemble those of normal adults: they startle less and less often, and their response no longer shows the reflex pattern described above.

Grasping   Place something — say a finger — into a newborn's palm firmly, and he will grasp it. Like the stepping reflex, his early grasping may facilitate later, more intentional grasping behaviors such as the ones that a child needs to explore toys and to balance himself. But unlike the case with the stepping reflex, opportunities for grasping normally continue throughout infancy. Once past the first few weeks of life, infants are generally left free to use their hands for large parts of the day or even all the time. The opportunity gives extra practice and may explain why most babies become skillful with their hands sooner than they become skillful with their feet.

Survival reflexes versus primitive reflexes

Table 5.3 summarizes these and other significant reflexes that babies have immediately after birth. Some, such as breathing, serve obvious physical needs; in Table 5.3 these are called **survival reflexes**. Others, such as the tonic neck reflex, serve no obvious physical purpose, although they may be vestiges of important reflex behaviors at earlier stages of human evolution. Such reflexes are called **primitive reflexes** in Table 5.3. Among both survival and primitive reflexes, some may set the stage for developing more refined versions of the same behaviors later in childhood. The grasping reflex may function this way. Such precursors help babies to begin life already prepared to acquire certain skills more easily than others. At the same time, however, infants must have certain experiences, such as the chance to actually grasp objects, for later skills to develop.

TABLE 5.3 Major Reflexes in Newborn Infants

Reflex	Description	Development	Significance
Survival Reflexes			
Breathing reflex	Repetitive inhalation and expiration	Permanent, although becomes partly voluntary	Provides oxygen and expels carbon dioxide
Rooting reflex	Turning of cheek in direction of touch	Weakens and disappears by six months	Orients child to breast or bottle
Sucking reflex	Strong sucking motions with throat, mouth, and tongue	Gradually comes under voluntary control	Allows child to drink
Swallowing reflex	Swallowing motions in throat	Permanent, although becomes partly voluntary	Allows child to take in food and to avoid choking
Eyeblink reflex	Closing eyes for an instant ("blinking")	Permanent, although gradually becomes voluntary	Protects eyes from objects and bright light
Pupillary reflex	Changing size of pupils: smaller in bright light and bigger in dim light	Permanent	Protects against bright light and allows better vision in dim light
Primitive Reflexes			
Moro reflex	In response to a loud noise, child throws arms outward, arches back, then brings arms together as if to hold something	Arm movements and arching disappear by six months, but startle reaction persists for life	Indicates normal development of nervous system
Grasping reflex	Curling fingers around any small object put in the child's palm	Disappears by three months; voluntary grasping appears by about six months	Indicates normal development of nervous system
Tonic neck reflex	When laid on back, head turns to side, arm and leg extend to same side, limbs on opposite side flex	Disappears by two or three months	Indicates normal development of nervous system
Babinski reflex	When bottom of foot stroked, toes fan and then curl	Disappears eight to twelve months	Indicates normal development of nervous system
Stepping reflex	If held upright, infant lifts leg as if to step	Disappears by eight weeks, but later if practiced	Indicates normal development of nervous system
Swimming	If put in water, infant moves arms and legs and holds breath	Disappears by four to six months	Indicates normal development of nervous system

The First Motor Skills

Motor skills are voluntary movements of the body or of parts of the body. They can be grouped conveniently according to the size of the muscles and body parts involved. **Gross motor skills** involve the large muscles of the arms, legs, and torso. **Fine motor skills** involve the small muscles located throughout the body. Walking and jumping are examples of gross motor skills, and reaching and grasping are examples of fine motor skills.

On the whole, the sequence in which skills develop follows two trends, or principles, that guide development in general. The **cephalocaudal principle** (literally, "head to tail") refers to the fact that upper parts of the body become usable and skillful before lower parts do. Babies learn to turn their heads before learning to move their feet intentionally, and they learn to move their arms before they learn to move their legs. The **proximodistal principle** (literally, "near to far") refers to the fact that central parts of the body become skillful before peripheral or outlying parts. Babies learn to wave their whole arms before wiggling their wrists and fingers. The former movement occurs at the shoulder joint, near the center of the body, but the latter occurs at the periphery. Stated differently, the shoulder movement is relatively proximal, whereas the finger movement is relatively distal.

Principles of motor-skill development

Large Motor Development in the First Year   Almost from birth, and before reflex behaviors disappear, babies begin doing some things on purpose. By the age of four weeks or so, most babies can lift their heads up when they are lying on their stomachs. What makes this achievement remarkable is its purposefulness: babies seem to practice the action repeatedly when they get the chance and are not preoccupied with hunger or other discomfort (Ames et al., 1979). Unlike, say, the sucking reflex, head lifting is not inevitably provoked by any particular stimulus or event. Babies are apparently rewarded simply by getting a new view of the world and a better feel for how their muscles work.

Early voluntary movements

After a few months, voluntary movements become much more common than the reflexes with which babies are born. By two or three months, one-half of all babies can roll over in bed; but it takes until the age of five or six months for one-half of all babies to sit without props or supports (Frankenburg & Dodds, 1967). At six or seven months, many babies have become quite adept at using their limbs; they can stick their feet up in the air and "bicycle" with them while a parent tries valiantly to fit a diaper on this moving target. At ten months the average baby can stand erect, but only if an adult helps. By their first birthday (twelve months), one-half of all babies can dispense with this assistance and stand by themselves without toppling over immediately.

By the age of seven months, on the average, babies become able to locomote, or move around, on their own. At first their methods are crude and slow; a baby might simply pivot on her stomach, for example, in order to get a better view of something interesting. Consistent movement in one direction develops soon after this time — although the movement does not always occur in the direction that the baby intends!

Locomotion

Techniques for getting around vary a lot among infants. The most common first method is *crawling*, in which the infant uses his arms to drag himself across the floor. Many babies also figure out the more efficient method of *creeping*, or walking on hands and knees with the body suspended above the ground. Still others learn to *hitch* themselves, alternately folding and unfolding themselves

Infants are highly motivated to move around. One of the first ways is by rolling over, an action that rewards the baby with a whole new perspective on his or her surroundings.

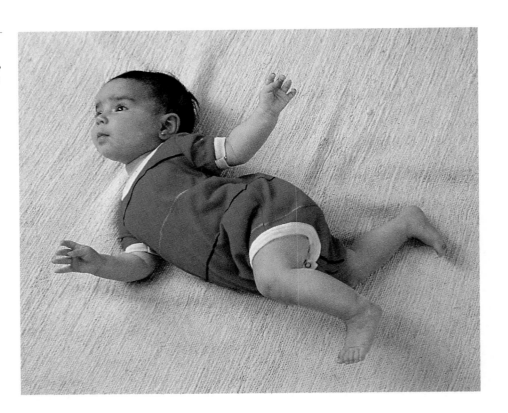

Before learning to walk, infants use a variety of methods for moving about; creeping is just one of them.

like a caterpillar. And by the age of nine or ten months, most babies learn to *cruise*, or move about the room upright by holding onto furniture for support. But these techniques do not develop in a reliable sequence. Most infants do not learn them all, and a few never learn any of them but go straight from sitting to walking.

Crawling, creeping, and cruising offer new opportunities to children and make new demands on parents. On the one hand, locomotion means that babies can entertain themselves better than before. They can relieve their own boredom simply by traveling to new locations and getting new toys for themselves. On the other hand, babies who move can get into everything, including poisons under the kitchen sink or heavy tools stacked in the basement. As locomotion develops, parents find that they must continually scrutinize their living quarters for safety, a process some parents call childproofing.

Reaching and Grasping   As pointed out earlier in this chapter, even newborn infants will reach for and grasp objects that they can see immediately in front of themselves. As you might expect, they often fail to grasp objects successfully; they often make contact with the object but fail to enclose it in their fingers. This early, crude reaching disappears fairly soon after birth, only to reappear at about four or five months of age as two separate skills, reaching and grasping. These soon serve infants in many ways. By their second birthday, for example, most babies can turn the pages in large picture books one at a time, at least if the paper is relatively indestructible.

How do early and later reaching differ from each other? Careful, filmed observations of both kinds have given some answers to this question. The earlier reaching and grasping seem fused in a single act: the baby's hand closes on the object at the same instant that it arrives at the object. Older babies separate the two actions: first they reach, and then they grasp at the object a split second later. The delay makes them much more successful at actually grabbing things.

Changes in reaching and grasping

In addition, early reaching and grasping seem to be guided by sight rather than by touch. A very young baby will try to grasp an optical illusion — an object projected by mirrors, for example, or by a camera (Bower, 1981). Older babies, around five months of age, will not close their hands around an optical illusion; they must first touch the object before trying to grab it. Moving their hands *to* an object, however, now seems under skillful visual control.

These changes in reaching and grasping probably constitute refinements from constant practice, but how so? The earliest reach-and-grasp action may

With time and practice, infants improve and modify their early grasping reflex to fit a variety of objects and circumstances.

change simply because it succeeds so rarely. The reaching part of the action may remain, however, because it often rewards the baby with interesting results. Grasping, meanwhile, is generally not reinforced unless an object is actually touched. In the long run, then, grasping comes under tactual (that is, touching-related) as well as visual control. The different ways in which reaching and grasping are rewarded may therefore account for their evolution in which the early, fused reflex gives way to two independently rewarded and more precise skills. The differentiation occurs with little conscious encouragement by adults.

Walking   A reasonably predictable series of events leads up to true walking in most children; Table 5.4 describes some of these. By the age of about twelve to thirteen months, most children take their first independent steps. Well before two years, they can often walk not only forward but backward or even sideways. Some two-year-olds can walk upstairs on two feet instead of on all fours (Bayley, 1969). Usually they use the wall or a railing to do so. Usually, too, coming downstairs proves more difficult than going up; one solution is to creep down backward, using all four limbs.

Learning to walk

How do these changes develop? To some extent, the earlier skills may stimulate and give practice for the later ones. Sitting, for example, may give practice in balance, which helps in standing next to furniture; standing by furniture in turn improves balance and muscle development so that standing alone becomes possible; and so on. Each step in such a sequence rewards the child simply by giving her new opportunities to explore her body and to see her world from new perspectives. Her parents may motivate her by praising her occasionally, but their comments may actually matter relatively little. The practice itself may be its own reward.

As reasonable as this explanation sounds, it has certain flaws. Not all children do learn movement skills according to a predictable sequence; some,

TABLE 5.4   Milestones of Motor Development (in months)

Motor Skill	When 25% of All Infants Can Do This	When 50% of All Infants Can Do This	When 75% of All Infants Can Do This
Lift head up 45 degrees	Birth	1.2	2.0
Roll from stomach to back	2.0	2.8	3.7
Push chest up with arms	2.0	3.0	3.1
Pull up with assistance	3.2	4.0	5.0
Sit without assistance once up	4.8	5.5	6.5
Stand holding onto furniture	4.9	5.8	8.6
Pull self up to stand	5.9	7.1	9.0
Sit self up without assistance	6.1	7.1	9.2
Walk holding onto furniture	7.2	9.2	10.2
Stand well alone	9.7	11.5	13.1
Walk well alone	11.1	12.1	13.4
Walk backward	12.2	14.2	15.5

Source: *Denver Developmental Screening Test* (Frankenburg and Dodds, 1967).

for example, creep only after they have mastered walking. And individual children, normal in all respects, learn motor skills at rather different ages: full-fledged walking, for example, may happen as early as nine months or as late as eighteen months. Yet these children presumably all have access to the crucial learning tool, namely, their own legs and feet. Do some infants therefore practice harder or just have an inborn ability to learn faster?

Nature and Nurture in Skill Development   These questions about walking illustrate an important issue that pervades developmental psychology: the relative contributions of genetic endowment (nature) and of experience (nurture) to children's overall growth. Most developmental trends obviously depend on both genetics and experience, but the *way* in which each factor contributes is often unclear. Consider the ambiguities of the following examples:

Bridges   To what extent are infant motor skills inborn?

■ Heavier children (and adults) are significantly less active than lighter-weight ones (Rodin, 1977). If this difference exists for infants as well, it might cause heavier infants to practice motor skills less. Here genetics might be guiding the original weight differences, but learning would account for the later differences in physical skills. At the same time, however, experience may contribute to differences in weight; in particular, some children gradually become heavier because their family diet is unusually high in calories.

■ Identical twins are especially likely to acquire motor skills, including walking, at very nearly the same age (R. Wilson, 1972). This fact suggests that genetics influences how fast infants learn to walk. But it does not really prove it because identical twins also tend to have environments that are similar. Twins therefore end up with unusually similar learning opportunities as well as identical physiology. In principle, studying identical twins reared apart might solve this particular ambiguity; but in practice, separated twins are often not very representative of children as a whole because only highly unusual circumstances can cause twins to be separated.

Confusion between nature and nurture seems inevitable, even in experiments that try explicitly to vary only one of these factors without varying the other. The problem is illustrated by two studies — one a classic and the other more

At first, walking takes concentration, and it often seems to be its own reward. Note the wide stance that characterizes this beginning walker.

recent — that tried to "teach" older infants specific motor skills. In the classic study (Gesell & Thompson, 1929), one member of a pair of identical twins was taught to climb stairs, beginning at the age of forty-six weeks. Her training began with assistance from an adult at moving from one step to the next, often at first simply by being lifted. Her twin received no training and in fact was prohibited from all encounters with stairs until she was fifty-three weeks old. At this point the trained twin could climb stairs much better than her inexperienced sister. Yet even on her very first attempt, at fifty-three weeks, the untrained sister managed to climb the stairs. After just three weeks more, both girls performed equally well, in spite of the prior differences in training.

Although this study seems to suggest that maturation (or effects due to the aging process) matters more than learning (acquired knowledge and skill), it may really show only the many different ways in which a child may learn a motor skill. In this case the untrained twin indeed encountered no stairs during her waiting period, but she was free to crawl every day and free to practice any motor techniques that she might choose. Such crawling may have given her as much preparation for stair climbing as her sister got. If so, then learning or experience in addition to maturation may account for the results.

A second, more recent study also suggests that maturation and learning both play a role in learning to walk (Zelazo et al., 1972). In this study someone held newborn infants upright so that their feet lightly touched a table, stimulating them to "walk." These infants did learn true walking earlier than the average, even though their reflex walking had long since disappeared. Evidently the experience of early practice did somehow influence their walking, although the precise connection between their early, inborn reflex and their later walking remains unclear. In this case learning built on a genetically given base, and the final product, walking, was a mixture of the two influences.

VARIATIONS IN GROWTH AND MOTOR DEVELOPMENT

Infants vary, of course, in how they grow and develop. Some grow faster than others, and not all acquire motor skills in the same order. Two otherwise similar children may learn to walk at different times: one when he is only ten months old and the other when he is nearly sixteen months old. Yet both may fall within the normal range of motor development. Several factors contribute to differences like these. The most important is the weight of the infant at birth, but gender and ethnic or cultural background seem to make some difference as well. Consider, for example, these three children:

- Pilar was born two months before her due date and is now almost two years old. She has begun speaking in two-word sentences only recently, saying "Daddy home," for example, and "Truck loud." Her slow language development is not a serious problem, at least so far. But her parents feel sure that she is taking longer to acquire language than other children of her age.

- Jonelle and Leon are fraternal twins. Like a lot of twins, they have spent considerable time playing together. Now that they are eighteen months old, both of them can walk without assistance. But Leon practices this skill much more than Jonelle does. Often he runs (or stumbles) down the hall, apparently just for the fun of it. Sometimes Jonelle will do this, too, but not as often. More typically she sits in one place, using her hands for some purpose, such as pulling clothes out of her parents' dresser drawers.

■ Tom has been cruising (walking by holding onto furniture) since he was only seven months old — some sort of record, his parents feel sure. Perhaps as a result he has developed an early taste for exploring the entire house where he lives and for investigating the cupboards, boxes, and wastebaskets that it contains. His parents worry about accidents that may result from his curiosity, but they also feel proud of his motor ability and enjoy encouraging him in order to see what he will do next. Now, at two years, he can walk to the grocery store faster than his two older brothers did at the same age. His mother finds that she no longer needs to take the baby stroller for this errand.

Each of these children raises important questions about what makes growth and motor development vary. Is Pilar's somewhat slow language development somehow the result of her unusually early birth? Have the twins, Jonelle and Leon, acquired different activity levels by subtle learning processes, or was some of this conferred on them genetically? And how much can Tom's parents really influence Tom's precocious motor development? The next sections discuss such questions as these.

Low Birth-Weight Infants

For medical purposes, newborns are considered **low birth-weight** infants if they weigh less than 2,500 grams, which is about five and one-half pounds. Such low weight can happen for either of two reasons. First, some babies do not develop as quickly as normal, even though they are carried for about the usual term of forty weeks. They are called **small-for-date** infants. Second, some babies develop at about normal rates but end their gestation significantly earlier than usual. If they are born sooner than about thirty-seven weeks from conception, they are called **preterm**, or short-gestation, infants. Until recently, medical research did not distinguish clearly between small-for-date and preterm infants; both were simply regarded as "premature infants" (Kopp & Parmalee, 1979).

Preterm infants face many more medical risks than do small-for-date infants. The extent of the risks depends on the infant's physical maturity. Physically immature infants look different from normal full-term infants: they tend to be redder and darker than normal, whatever their race, and their skin is often transparent enough to see blood vessels through it (Nelms & Mullins, 1982). Often they are covered with lanugo and have a thicker coating than usual of the white, waxy vernix. And, of course, immature newborns are smaller than usual; a normally developing infant will weigh only about two pounds, for example, if born two months early, compared to the average of seven and one-half pounds for normally developed full-term infants.

Appearance of physically immature infants

Causes of Low Birth Weight Low birth weight, either preterm or small for date, can result from several factors. As we saw in Chapter 4, one of the most common is malnourishment of the mother during pregnancy; mothers who do not eat well during pregnancy tend to have small-for-date babies. But other harmful practices — smoking cigarettes, drinking alcohol, or taking drugs — can also depress birth weight. Mothers from certain segments of the population, such as teenagers and the very poor, are especially likely to give birth to preterm babies, most likely because of their own poor nourishment or because of their lack of access to good prenatal care. Even among mothers who are well nourished and well cared for, however, some infants are born smaller than is medically desirable. Multiple births (twins, triplets) usually result in small-for-date babies; so can some illnesses or mishaps, such as a serious traffic accident that causes damage to the placenta.

Consequences of Preterm Birth   In spite of recent advances in helping preterm infants survive and develop, their neurological abilities are affected by early birth (Kitchen et al., 1986). In general, the reflexes of preterm infants tend to be sluggish, weak, and poorly organized. Preterm infants do not startle as reliably or grasp as automatically and strongly at objects. Their muscles often seem flabby or overly relaxed, which is a sign not only of immature muscle development but also of insufficient nerve impulses to stimulate good muscle tone. Preterm infants tend to lie fully extended instead of with their arms and legs slightly flexed or bent, and if someone pulls gently on their arms to extend them, their arms do not recoil as completely or smoothly as those of a full-term infant. Jerky, random movements dominate instead, and sometimes there is no recoiling movement at all. At comparable points in their gestation, full-term infants presumably have these limitations, too; but they are still inside their mothers' wombs at the time.

Outside that protected environment, preterm infants must cope with many tasks for which they are not well prepared. These include the obvious vital processes, such as breathing and digesting food. But they also include some less obvious ones. Once outside the womb, preterm infants must suddenly regulate the amount of sensory stimulation they receive. Just like full-term babies, they need to see things and hear things in order to stimulate the development of their senses. But they also need to avoid overloading their senses with too many sights and sounds. One way to avoid overstimulation is to sleep periodically and deeply; yet even though preterm infants sleep more than full-term infants do, they have more trouble keeping their sleep peaceful and smooth. For example, they have more sleep apnea — or times when breathing stops for perhaps fifteen or twenty seconds.

Neurological limitations persist in some preterm infants for the first two or three years of life (Kitchen et al., 1987; Mazar et al., 1988), which causes the babies to develop specific motor skills a bit later than full-term infants. Some of the delay is more apparent than real. A four-month-old born two months preterm, for example, in many ways resembles a two-month-old born at full term; both infants have lived eleven months from conception. Other delays may reflect stresses associated with preterm birth (like parents' being overprotective) rather than the physical effects of early birth as such.

In the long run, most preterm infants develop into normal children. Recent research suggests that contrary to previous impressions, toddlers and preschoolers who were preterm develop normal attachments to their parents in spite of their initial unresponsiveness as newborn infants (Easterbrooks, 1989). By school age, preterm children show slightly more risk of encountering learning disabilities, but their overall cognitive ability seems indistinguishable from that of full-term children (Pederson et al., 1988; Holwerda-Kuipers, 1987).

Whether a particular preterm infant develops later problems depends a lot on the support she receives from parents and from her environment as she grows up. Children from stable and relatively well-off homes tend to develop better, perhaps because they have more opportunity and encouragement for developing their skills and abilities at their own pace. By the time they begin school, they show good relationships with their family and no or few signs of learning impairment (Breslau et al., 1988). Children from families under economic or social stress, however, are more likely to continue showing social and cognitive deficiencies (J. Cohen & Parmalee, 1983).

Helping Low Birth-Weight Infants   Because conventional hospital routines often do not help preterm infants to regulate their sensory needs, health care providers have begun experimenting with ways to do so. Some doctors and nurses have provided such babies with miniature waterbeds, for example, which rock gently and slowly at about the same speed as a mother's normal breathing

(Korner, 1981; Barnard, 1981). In theory, at least, the arrangement simulates a normal experience in the womb. Other programs have tried stimulating preterm infants with extra handling in spite of their initial unresponsiveness (Helders et al., 1988). Both approaches have shown very encouraging results. With waterbeds, after several months the infants are healthier and physically larger than preterm infants raised in conventional stationary hospital cribs. With extra handling, the infants are more responsive to sounds and display more normal motor behaviors. All in all, these techniques seem promising and helpful.

Low birth-weight infants and their parents face special challenges in becoming attached to each other. Hospitals have recently tried to facilitate these attachments by encouraging parents to handle their low birth-weight infants even during the first days after birth, when the babies are still receiving intensive care in the hospital. This is essentially what happened to David, the case study discussed on pages 144–147; his parents visited him frequently at the hospital and even gave him little bottles of breast milk. Whether practices like these really affected David very much, they at least encouraged his parents' confidence and increased their faith in his capacity to develop normally eventually.

Bridges What are the effects of low birth-weight on the development of parent-infant attachments?

After low birth-weight babies go home, however, their parents may continue to worry about their health and face challenges in forming good relationships with them. Low birth-weight infants tend to respond to their parents less than normal babies do, at least at first. In David's case, for example, his parents noted that he seemed "floppy and limp" at first, although not after a month or two. Perhaps to compensate, parents of such babies (although not necessarily David's parents) sometimes initiate more contacts — poking, talking, offering a pacifier, and the like — than parents of full-term babies do (Crnic et al., 1983). From the perspective of a preterm infant, therefore, parents may sometimes "try too hard" to interact; and from the perspective of the parents, the infant may sometimes seem unresponsive.

Attachment in low birth-weight infants

Parents and their tiny babies also smile at each other less than usual (Field, 1980). Under good conditions these initial differences need not become lasting problems, and the parents and children eventually develop relationships that are healthy and gratifying. But if the parents face other stresses (such as poverty), they may lack the time or energy to overcome the initial difficulties in making contact with their baby. To avoid forming a permanently poor relationship, such parents may need help from a social worker or a nurse in understanding their infant's development, so that they can enjoy that development as it unfolds. Luckily, extra stresses and needs were not a problem for David's parents.

Gender Differences

During the first two years the genders do not differ in competence and only sometimes in performance. That is, what babies *can* do under good conditions has relatively little to do with their gender, at least during the first year or so of infancy. Boys and girls sit upright at about the same age and stand and walk at about the same time. All the major milestones, in fact, develop at about the same rate.

How infants use their time, however, is another matter. Almost as soon as they can move, boys show more activity. Even before birth, late in pregnancy, they move about in their mothers' wombs more than girls do. The trend continues after birth: one-year-old boys engage in more gross motor activity than one-year-old girls do (Teitelbaum, 1976). Boys move around more, using whatever locomotor skills they have developed thus far, whereas girls spend more time quietly using fine motor skills to investigate the contents of the kitchen wastebasket, for instance. Presumably these gender differences stem at least partly from different encouragement by parents and perhaps also from the children's own desires to

Early difference in level and kind of activity

A Multicultural View

Cultural Differences in Motor Stimulation

Around the world, societies vary greatly in how they stimulate infants and toddlers physically. In some societies babies go through the day swaddled tightly in cloth slings carried by their mothers. Babies in these cultures get little chance for the kind of sensorimotor exploration described by Piaget. In other societies, including our own, babies spend a lot of the day in cribs, on the floor, or on the ground. The physical openness of this arrangement gives them comparatively more chances to explore the world.

These differences in stimulation often have effects on both motor and social development. Certain African cultures give their infants unusually frequent chances to sit upright and to practice "walking" when held at a standing position by adults and older children (Munroe et al., 1981). These opportunities appear to stimulate toddlers in these societies to learn to walk early and well, compared to North American toddlers. Early walking in turn may prove especially valuable in these societies, which do not yet rely heavily on cars, bicycles, and the other vehicles so commonplace in North American society.

Tight swaddling of infants also affects both motor and social development. Consider Navaho Indian infants, who spend nearly all of their first year of life bound and swaddled to a flat board, so that their arms and legs extend straight down along their bodies (J. Whiting, 1981). Apparently as a result, Navaho toddlers acquire certain motor skills, such as walking, a little more slowly than Anglo-American children do. But the delays do not apply to many other skills, such as reaching and grasping, and the deficit disappears entirely by the end of early childhood; six-year-old Navahos do not differ signifi-

Swaddling infants, a practice in many cultures, tends to slow children's motor development temporarily, but not permanently.

model "correct" sex-role behavior. But given the very young age of the children, some of the difference may be genetically based.

By age two — and onward throughout early childhood — boys and girls tend to show different motor abilities, even in optimal, testlike situations. In general, girls excel more often at fine motor skills; for example, they can usually build a tower of blocks sooner, taller, and with fewer mistakes than boys can (Ames et al., 1979). Girls also excel more often at skills involving balance and rhythm, such as the dancing sometimes done in nursery school classrooms. Boys excel more often wherever speed or strength is required: they usually run faster outdoors and pound the play dough harder at nursery school (Malina, 1982).

But the underlying reasons for such differences remain ambiguous. The differences could stem partly from differences in practice during infancy, partly from children's self-consciousness about excelling at the "wrong" skills and partly from slight but undeniable biological differences between the sexes. In spite of these trends, boys and girls are more alike than different during their early years. Many boys have good balance, and many girls pound the play dough very hard indeed.

cantly from cradle- or crib-raised children in overall motor ability (Kagan, 1973, 1984).

The Navahos' swaddling may have social effects that are more lasting, however. In particular, Navahos may develop different feelings about their mothers from those of cradle-raised children. In a sling, a baby communicates with his mother through **kinesthetics**, or subtle movements and changes of balance. With a small wiggle, for example, a baby can inform her mother that she is uncomfortable or that she wants to nurse. Crying and vocalizing are seldom needed, and mothers can satisfy most discomforts almost immediately. Infants therefore lead a comparatively contented life but only until they must leave the sling; then they experience an unusually abrupt reduction in their contact with their mother.

The cradles and cribs of Anglo-Saxon infants offer a rather different experience. Such babies must summon their mothers by crying or fussing, and very often mothers are too far away to come immediately. Vocalizing and capturing adults' attention therefore take on special importance for such babies (B. Whiting, 1978). Unlike the sling-raised infants, cradle babies experience no sudden reduction in contact with their mothers: in this sense, their weaning is more gradual and gentle.

These circumstances may help explain a number of observations by anthropologists about the social development of children (Munroe et al., 1981). Children from sling cultures, it seems, tend to express more mixed feelings about their mothers as they grow older. Such children, and especially boys, find relations with the opposite sex especially problem filled because their first intimate relationship was both extremely gratifying and unac-

countably betrayed. Sling cultures help deal with these feelings by encouraging strong separation of the sexes during childhood and youth.

Children from cradle cultures may express more worries about dependency because their first intimate relationship took real effort to maintain. For cradle children, independence is therefore both valuable and difficult to achieve. Such children are supposed to get along with a constantly changing set of classmates, baby-sitters, and neighbors, for example, even though these people are comparative strangers and may have alien interests and temperaments. Cradle societies try to deal with this challenge by giving young children extra training in human relations through nursery schools and books that help parents raise happier children.

Cultural and Racial Differences

Physical growth and motor development also vary among racial and cultural groups around the world. At birth, for example, Swedish infants weigh about 3.8 kilograms, 40 percent more than Hindu infants (2.3 kilograms) born in India do. Black American children weigh about 10 percent less at birth (3.0 kg) than white American children (3.3 kg) do. These differences apparently do not result from simple malnutrition or from other obvious health problems among the smaller children. The differences, and others like them, exist even among well-off groups in all countries (Meredith, 1981).

As infants grow, they show further differences according to the culture or society in which they live. In general, infants in a number of African societies develop motor skills sooner than North American infants, even when the families live in similar economic circumstances (Super, 1981). The difference is especially marked in sitting and walking: African infants can do both actions almost two months earlier than white American infants can. The reasons for this precocity in motor development remain unclear, but at least some of the difference may

Bridges Why do infants in certain African societies tend to develop motor skills sooner than North American infants?

result from cultural practices. Anthropologists have reported efforts in several African societies to actively teach children both to walk and to sit. Sitting is taught by placing infants in a small depression and propping them up with blankets or clothes (Super, 1982); walking is taught by holding infants upright when they are still rather young and encouraging them to exercise their inborn stepping reflex. As discussed earlier in this chapter, this method does indeed promote earlier and more skillful walking (Zelazo et al., 1972). In underdeveloped Third World communities, acquiring sitting and walking skills may in fact assist children and their families; life in an African village may require more walking than life in a North American town. Over time, therefore, early motor development may become a general cultural value, even among well-off members of underdeveloped societies.

NUTRITION DURING THE FIRST TWO YEARS

The physical developments described in this chapter depend, of course, on good nutrition during the first two years. Like older people, babies need diets with appropriate amounts of protein, calories, and specific vitamins and minerals. For various reasons, however, infants do not always get all the nutrients they need. Often poverty accounts for malnutrition: parents with good intentions may nevertheless be unable to afford the right foods. In other cases conventional eating practices interfere: in spite of relatively expensive eating habits — like going to fast-food restaurants — some families may not provide their children with a balanced diet.

Special Nutritional Needs of Infants

Compared with other children, infants eat less in overall or absolute amount. A well-nourished young baby in North America might drink somewhat less than one liter (about .95 quart) of liquid nourishment per day. This amount definitely would not keep an older child or young adult well nourished, although it might prevent starving.

In proportion to their body weight, however, infants need to consume much more than children or adults. Every day, for example, a three-month-old baby should ideally take in more than two ounces of liquid per pound (or about 150 ml of liquid per kilogram) of body weight. An eighteen-year-old needs only about one-third of this amount (NAS/NRC, 1980). Similar differences occur in the need for calories (or energy), for protein (or chemical building blocks), and for most vitamins and minerals. The changes are due to more efficient nutritional processing and less vigorous growth.

The Breast Versus the Bottle

Someone (usually parents) must somehow provide for an infant's comparatively large appetite. Whenever breast feeding is possible, health experts generally recommend human milk as the sole source of nutrition for at least the first six months or so of most infants' lives and as a major source for at least the next six months. In some cases, of course, this recommendation proves difficult or impractical to follow. Babies who need intensive medical care immediately after birth cannot be breast fed without special arrangements; and for one reason or another, some women may choose not to breast feed, and certain babies and mothers may not succeed well in this activity, even after trying it. For these infants, formulas can be prepared and fed in bottles.

Why do pediatricians recommend breast feeding? Studies of infants and mothers suggest four major reasons. First, human milk seems to give young infants more protection from diseases and other ailments: breast-fed infants catch fewer colds and viruses of all types, experience fewer allergies, and experience fewer serious illnesses. The ways human milk confer this benefit are not completely understood. One reason is that human milk is always sterile, even at comfortable lukewarm temperatures at which bottle milk might begin to grow bacteria. Another reason is that a protein in human milk, called **secretory IgA**, binds or attaches to viruses and bacteria in the infant's intestine. By acting like a sort of intestinal paint, this protein prevents the viruses and bacteria from creating gastrointestinal disorders (Goldman & Goldblum, 1982). This sort of benefit is so important that many hospitals now try to offer human milk in bottles to infants needing intensive care.

Builds immunity

The second reason for preferring human milk concerns its nutritional composition. Overall, such milk matches the nutritional needs of human infants more closely than formula preparations. Human milk contains more iron (an important nutrient for infants) but less casein (a protein prominent in cow's milk that many infants have trouble digesting). Human milk also contains helpful amounts of cholesterol, a form of fat that contributes to heart problems in later life but that seems to protect against this possibility when digested in early infancy.

Closely matches infant's nutritional needs

A third reason for preferring human milk is physical. Breast feeding develops the infant's jaw and mouth muscles because it requires stronger sucking motions than does bottle feeding. For much the same reason, the breast also tends to satisfy infants' intrinsic needs for sucking better than a bottle does. This fact makes pacifiers less necessary, and it makes excessive sucking — and therefore overeating — less likely to occur.

Satisfies infant's sucking needs

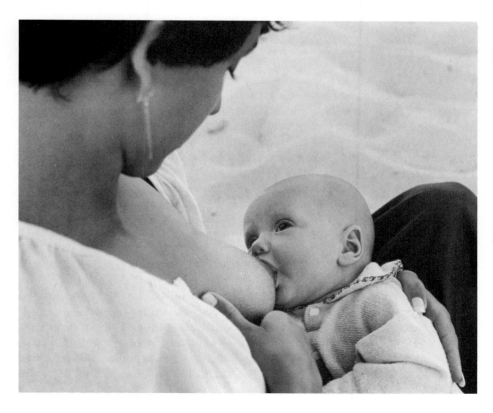

In recent decades, increasing numbers of mothers have chosen to breast feed their babies, as recommended by most pediatricians.

Fosters attachment

A fourth reason for preferring human milk has to do with its effects on mother-infant relationships. Infants who breast feed spend more time snuggling close to their mothers, and vice versa. A breast-feeding mother and child seem to spend more time gazing into each other's eyes, like two people in love, and the mother appears to offer feeding sessions in closer response to the infant's true hunger. Apparently these behaviors may promote strong, secure attachments between mother and child, which help infants' social and cognitive development later in childhood (La Leche League, 1988).

Why should breast feeders engage in more attachment behaviors? In part, the practice may feel more intrinsically gratifying than bottle feeding. Partly, too, the benefit may stem from the kind of mothers who choose breast feeding; maybe they are people who already have extra time to spend with their infants, no matter what feeding practice they happen to adopt (Pollitt et al., 1984). Or maybe, as Freud suggested, breast feeding is satisfying sensually, if not sexually, to mother and child. If so, they may become more attached to each other than if they shared only a bottle.

These considerations have probably contributed to a rise in the popularity of breast feeding during the past two decades. In 1971, for example, the proportion of North American mothers who breast fed immediately after the birth of their child was about one in four, but by 1981 this proportion had risen to one in two. Even more dramatic increases have occurred in women's persistence at breast feeding. In 1971 only one woman in twenty was still breast feeding when her infant was six months old, but by 1981 this proportion had risen to one woman in four (Martinez & Nalezienski, 1981). Increases occurred in all parts of society, but they were largest among women who were relatively well educated and well informed about experts' advice on child-rearing.

Whether they feed by breast or by bottle, parents must decide when and how often to offer their infant milk. At one extreme, babies can be fed at regular intervals, such as every three or four hours, whether they become fussy in the meanwhile or not. At the other extreme, babies can be fed *on demand*, no matter how recently they may have had a previous meal. A fixed schedule creates a certain predictability in the lives of new parents because they can know relatively precisely when to take time out for feedings. Whether it also creates predictability in the minds of young infants, however, is more questionable because many infants can protest long and hard if they do not get to eat when they feel hungry. Demand feeding relieves the stress of waiting out such protests until the designated meal time. It creates more interruptions, however, which can be especially bothersome for parents of bottle-fed infants, who must keep preparing formula. Sometimes parents worry that feeding on demand will make their infants overweight or obese. If formula is prepared properly, infants cannot become overweight on it; and breast milk is inherently incapable of giving an infant excessive calories (Spock, 1989).

Parents should introduce solid foods slowly, to insure that their infants have developed enough to digest the food comfortably. Sensory experience of food remains a primary motive for eating throughout infancy — and often even throughout life.

Nutrition in Later Infancy

After about six months infants can be introduced gradually to solid foods, such as strained cereals and strained fruits. As babies become tolerant of these new foods, parents can introduce others, which sometimes require a more mature digestive system: strained meats and cooked eggs, for example. Overall, the shift to solid foods often takes many months to complete. As it occurs, parents must begin paying more attention to their baby's nutritonal needs. Many solid foods do not contain the broad range of nutrients that breast milk and formula so conveniently do.

A Talk with a Pediatrician

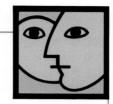

Eating and Sleeping Schedules in Infancy

Dr. Ellen Ross is a pediatrician who treats newborn infants through adolescents. She also is on the faculty of the medical school in her city, where she teaches nurses and pediatricians in training. At the start of the interview, which was conducted at her office, Dr. Ross mentioned that her own experiences as the mother of two children have helped her better appreciate the feelings and needs of her patients and their families.

Interviewer: What are the typical questions and problems that a family faces in caring for their newborn infant?

Dr. Ross: For really young babies, under a month old, the fact that nobody gets a decent night's sleep drives everybody crazy. That's the big one. The schedule, the schedule! How can I get my baby on schedule? I know when I was being brought up, they were very rigid about feeding. You had to feed a baby every four hours, and if you varied from that schedule, you were going to spoil and ruin [the baby] for life. Now we have a very strong feeling that demand feeding — that is, feeding the baby when he or she is hungry — is right. However, it's often hard to know when a baby is hungry.

Interviewer: How do babies and their parents get their sleep schedules straight?

Dr. Ross: In the beginning, they don't have them straight, and sleep schedules can be a big source of frustration. Then gradually, by the end of the second to fourth week, the baby will usually sleep a longer stretch at night, perhaps four to five hours, and that's a great relief. Being awakened night after night by a baby can be a great source of stress

to a family who are already exhausted by the responsibilities of adjusting to the care of a new baby. Some babies need more help in trying to stretch that out, and I sometimes say don't let the baby sleep for more than four hours in the day so that the baby will sleep longer at night.

Very often the best medicine is for somebody else to put the baby to sleep, rock the baby, and change the baby after the mother has breast fed, so that the mother has only actually been up for fifteen minutes or so and can let somebody else do the rest. During the day the mother should get some rest and is possible have help from somebody else in caring for other children, housework, and chores so that she can concentrate on nursing the baby.

Interviewer: A little earlier, you said that it is often hard to know when the baby is hungry. How do parents learn to tell?

Dr. Ross: As a baby gets older you get to know the different cries. In the beginning, though, you don't really know. And so a baby who is asleep wakes up and may need to be changed or held and may not calm down, may be rooting around and sucking on his fist and everything he can get his hands on. He is relieved when he gets either the breast or the bottle, so you say, aha, hungry. However, babies will suck on anything. They have a sucking reflex. So that sucking is not necessarily connected to hunger.

Interviewer: So he could be sucking just because he enjoys it rather than for food?

Dr. Ross: Exactly. So some people will pop a bottle in the baby's mouth every time he cranks or cries. Or the breast. So the bottle or breast becomes a human pacifier, and the mother is resentful and tied to the baby and it feels horrible. I tell people that although I do

believe in demand feeding, if the baby has had a decent feeding and it's under two hours, it's very, very unlikely that your baby is truly hungry. And you should try other alternatives. Maybe a pacifier. Maybe holding the baby and letting him suck on your finger. If you have to, you can feed the baby, but as a regular pattern it should not be less than two hours between feedings.

Interviewer: What other concerns do parents have about feeding?

Dr. Ross: Is my baby getting enough? Sometimes parents are upset about breast feeding because you can't measure the quantity of milk. They say, how will I know the baby's had enough? So I say if the baby is urinating well, and having regular bowel movements, and is comforted and falls asleep and at least is calm and satisfied after feeding, and is showing some weight gain between visits to the pediatrician, you know the baby has had enough.

Follow-up Questions

1. If you were a new parent, how might you feel about Dr. Ross's way of talking with parents?

2. What are some of the advantages and disadvantages of breast feeding mentioned in this interview? What do you think are Dr. Ross's views concerning the issue of breast feeding versus bottle feeding?

3. The infant's rooting and sucking behaviors that Dr. Ross describes are discussed in this chapter. Where do they come from? What functions do they serve?

A Multicultural View

The Effects of Serious Malnutrition

In certain developing nations, large numbers of infants grow up seriously undernourished. Their nutritional deficiencies do not concern specific vitamins or minerals, as is more often true of malnourished infants in North America. Instead they consist of basic insufficiencies of either or both of the major nutritional building blocks, protein and calories. When both of these are deficient for prolonged periods, an infant or child develops a disease called **marasmus** (from a Latin word meaning "to waste away"). Babies with marasmus become increasingly emaciated, weak, and listless as their condition worsens. They also suffer significant delays in motor development and perform significantly lower than healthy children do on standardized tests of intelligence (Cravioto & Delicardie, 1982). If marasmus has gone far enough, the motor and cognitive delays persist even if the child's nutrition eventually improves.

Serious malnutrition can also take the form of **kwashiorkor**, if the child receives enough calories but little or no protein. Children suffering from kwashiorkor are noticeable because they develop enlarged or bloated abdomens; but they also tend to lose their hair and to develop lesions (cuts or breaks) in their skin that do not heal. Children with either kwashiorkor or marasmus have lowered resistance to disease and often die from a virus or infection from which a well-nourished child might recover.

Although both forms of malnutrition can affect infants or children at any age, each form has a "preferred" age group. Marasmus tends to afflict infants relatively often. This happens because the mother may also be severely undernourished, so that she cannot produce enough breast milk or enough milk of sufficient nutritional quality. It also happens because many Third World mothers have attempted to feed their infants from bottles under conditions that can actually harm their babies rather than nourish them. Many such mothers cannot read the instructions on the containers of formula; and in any case, conditions of poverty make sterilizing bottles and water difficult, if not impossible. Probably for these reasons, bottle-fed infants suffer from marasmus much more often in impoverished areas of the Third World than they do in well-off areas of those same countries or of North America (Grant, 1982). In essence, the infants reject the wrongly prepared formula or become too sick to digest it.

Kwashiorkor tends to affect toddlers and young children rather than infants. This happens because in many Third World societies, mother's milk is the only high-quality source of nutrition. Infants who are breast feeding

Malnutrition in North America   Often North American diets do fail to provide enough of three specific nutrients: vitamin A, vitamin C, and iron. Prolonged deficiencies of vitamins A and C seem to create deficits in motor ability (Pollitt et al., 1984), and deficiency of iron seems to create deficits in cognitive performance (Pollitt, 1987). For about 4 to 5 percent of all infants, these nutritional deficiencies are serious and deserve immediate remedy. For another percentage that is probably about the same size, the nutritional deficiencies are less severe but still a cause for concern.

Even when undernourished infants appear healthy and "bright," however, they may be at risk for later problems in development because poorly nourished families often experience other serious deprivations, such as poor sanitation, poor health care, and lack of educational opportunity. Under these conditions, it might not take much to turn mild undernourishment into severe malnutrition and thus reduce adequate cognitive and motor performance to below satisfactory levels.

Obesity and Overnutrition   In calorie-rich societies such as our own, eating too much can pose a serious problem for some individuals. The most obvious result of eating too much is to become extremely overweight, or **obese**. The nature and extent of this effect depend partly on just how much an infant overeats and when during development the overeating occurs.

In the short run, what infants eat affects how much they weigh. Big, heavy infants tend to have diets that are high in calories. They tend to drink more milk

Effects of moderate excess

therefore remain relatively healthy. When they are weaned, however, they must start eating other foods, and if these lack enough protein, they may develop kwashiorkor.

These ideas suggest three ways of responding to severe malnutrition. First, mothers in Third World countries should be encouraged to breast feed rather than bottle feed. Persuading them to make this change may be possible, although it is not simple: many mothers (in North America as well) regard bottle feeding as better because it is more "modern." Second, the prevalence of kwashiorkor among toddlers suggests that nutritional programs should pay special attention to children's transition from breast or bottle feeding to solid foods. Are mothers finding easily digestible foods for children, to initiate this phase of nutrition? Do local conditions provide easily digested alternatives to mother's milk?

Third, and perhaps most important for developmental psychologists, the facts about severe malnutrition suggest that even poorly nourished parents need more than food (McKay et al., 1978): they need information about health — about the significance of sterilization, for example — and they need basic general education, too, so that they can read the labels on jars when they are trying to feed their children.

This fact creates ambiguities in assessing the effects of undernutrition in North America. Infants from poorly nourished families typically also experience other serious deprivations, such as poor sanitation, poor health care, and lack of educational opportunity. Because their parents may also suffer from poor health and a general lack of resources, the parents may not offer much stimulation for their babies' development or a very secure base from which to explore and learn about life. These conditions may contribute to the retarded motor and cognitive development mentioned above.

Overall, preventing malnutrition holds much more promise than correcting it once it occurs (Lozoff, 1989). Prevention can happen most effectively through programs aimed at educating parents about the nutritional needs of infants, including their needs even *before* they are born. In many communities, hospitals and other community agencies have organized such programs, with good results. At the same time, however, doctors and nurses continue to find malnourished infants and so must offer to parents whatever information and support are necessary to minimize the long-term negative effects *after* they have appeared.

than usual, and they tend to be started early on solid foods, which are often relatively high in calories (Dubois et al., 1979). Contrary to what some parents fear, however, weight in infancy correlates little with weight in childhood and even less with weight in adulthood (Poskitt & Cole, 1977). Heavy babies stand only a slightly greater chance than lighter ones of becoming heavy children and then only if they are very heavy indeed to begin with.

This fact stems from the way in which fat cells store energy during most of infancy. For most children, extra calories are stored as extra fat. Under normal circumstances most of this fat is deposited within existing fat cells. As a baby grows and becomes more active, much of this fat is burned off; the fat cells shrink in size, and the child looks more slender or less chubby as he approaches his second birthday (Knittle et al., 1979). The shrunken fat cells remain ready, however, to enlarge later in life whenever the child eats more calories than he really needs.

Infants seem to develop somewhat differently, however, if they are extremely overweight (say, more than 30 percent above average). In addition to developing enlarged fat cells, these infants also grow completely new fat cells. Once formed, these new fat cells do not disappear; they remain as extra storage places for any extra calories in the future. Extremely overweight infants therefore may live with some added risk of remaining overweight throughout childhood and adulthood. Nevertheless, the risk does not guarantee obesity later on. As long as such children follow a moderately healthy diet and get reasonable amounts of exercise, they tend to develop quite normally.

Effects of extreme excess

Similarities to malnutrition

Multiple causes

Failure to Thrive   When an infant or preschool child fails to grow at normal rates for no apparent medical reason, she is suffering from a condition called **failure to thrive**. About 6 percent of children show this condition in North America at one time or another, although not necessarily continuously (Drotar, 1985). In some ways the condition resembles malnutrition, especially as it occurs in developing nations: failure-to-thrive and malnourished children both develop motor and cognitive skills more slowly than usual; both experience higher rates of school failure and learning disabilities; both are more likely to live in disadvantaged circumstances and to have parents living under physical or emotional stress.

At one time professionals tended to attribute failure to thrive to lack of nurturance and love between parent and child. More recent research, however, suggests a more complex picture (Russo & Kedesdy, 1988): failure to thrive now seems to have many sources, both physical and psychological, and both in the child and in his environment. Consider this pattern. An infant has a genetically quiet, slow-to-respond temperament, making it more difficult for her mother to establish emotional contact. If the mother also happens to experience a number of other stresses (low income, illness, or disapproval from others for the new baby), the relationship between mother and infant is put at risk. A vicious cycle may develop of poorly timed feedings and clumsy efforts to nurture the infant, who persistently resists the mother's love — and even her food. Yet the cycle has *not* developed because the mother did not care about her infant or because the infant did not want food or affection. Parents and children can eventually get out of unpleasant relationships like this, especially if professionals help the parents understand how the situation developed.

TABLE 5.5   Infant Mortality in Selected Nations

Nation	Infant Mortality (per 1,000 Live Births)
Finland	5.5
Japan	6.3
Sweden	6.7
Switzerland	6.9
Hong Kong	7.5
Canada	7.9
Denmark	7.9
Netherlands	7.9
France	8.0
Norway	8.5
Fed. Rep. Germany	8.9
Ireland	8.9
Singapore	9.3
United Kingdom	9.3
Belgium	9.4
German Dem. Rep.	9.6
Australia	10.0
Spain	10.5
United States	10.6
New Zealand	10.8
Italy	10.9
Austria	11.0
Israel	12.3
Greece	14.0
Czechoslovakia	14.0

Source: U.S. Department of Health and Human Services (1988). Figures refer to mortalities during 1985.

Infant Mortality   In the past several decades, health care systems in North America and around the world have substantially improved their ability to keep infants alive. The **infant mortality rate** is the proportion of babies who die during the first year of life, and this number has decreased steadily during this century. In 1950, about twenty-nine out of every one thousand infants died; by 1986, this number was less than eleven out of every one thousand infants (Kessel, 1988). The averages conceal wide differences within society, however. Families with very low incomes are about twice as likely to lose an infant as are families with middle-level incomes (about eighteen babies per one thousand versus nine per one thousand). Likewise, black families are twice as likely as white families to lose an infant — perhaps because of the historic correlation of race with income level in American society (Klienman, 1988).

Infant mortality in the United States and Canada is two or three times lower than in many Third World countries (Cochrane & Mehra, 1983). Surprisingly, however, mortality in the United States is actually *higher* (that is, more babies die) than nineteen other developed nations, including Canada, Japan, Sweden, France, and Great Britain. Table 5.5 shows these differences. The higher mortality comes as a surprise because the United States is more generally affluent than many of these other nations and because the American medical system actually originated many of the life-saving techniques that have allowed infant mortality to decline around the world.

Cross-cultural investigations of infant mortality rates in European countries have given clues about the reasons for the relatively poor American rate and have implied ways to improve it (Wagner, 1988). The research overwhelmingly indicates that parents need social supports as much as they need access to basic medical techniques and knowledge. In Europe this support takes several forms. Most European countries provide pregnant mothers with free prenatal care. Frequently, this care is provided by medically trained (and usually female) midwives, who are more able to give the time needed to establish a supportive relationship with pregnant women.

Most European countries also protect working mothers legally: pregnant women get special, generous sick leave; get at least four months of maternity leave with pay; and are protected from doing dangerous or exhausting work (like night shifts). Every European country also begins a regular cash payment to parents when their child is born, the amount and duration depending on the condition of the child and the number of children already in the family. Altogether, these policies and practices communicate emotional support to pregnant mothers and their spouses in ways not currently available in the United States.

INFANCY: THE REAL END OF BIRTH

During the first two years of infants' lives, several changes make them seem much more like individuals or real people than they did on the day they were born. As children approach their second birthday, for example, many of their basic physical needs and skills have stabilized. Now they can swallow and even chew a variety of foods, even if they still lack a lot of teeth and make a mess out of eating. And now, too, they can (sometimes!) sleep through the night.

Complementing this new stabililty are new behaviors. Two-year-olds can move around, even if they are sometimes still clumsy. Most importantly, a lot of their movement is voluntary; a toddler may wander away in a department store, for example, because *he wants to*. Such movements are facilitated by infants' physical growth during the first two years. By their second birthday, they can use their hands and feet to help them implement choices, however crudely at first. As the next chapters show, the first two years also make infants seem more human in two other major ways: by preparing them to think in symbols and by helping them to form definite attachments to parents and peers.

SUMMARY OF MAJOR IDEAS

Appearance of the Young Infant

1. The newborn infant has several distinctive physical characteristics: he is covered with lanugo and vernix and has several "soft spots," or fontanelles, on his head, which will eventually grow over with bone.

2. For most mothers, the first few hours are an important time for establishing a positive relationship with their new baby.

3. The health of most newborns is assessed quickly after delivery with the Apgar Scale. For infants who may need it, a more complete assessment can be done a few days later with the Brazelton Neonatal Behavioral Assessment Scale.

4. The average newborn infant born at full term weighs about seven and one-half pounds. Her bodily proportions, such as having a large head, make her look cute. These proportions may foster the formation of attachments with adult care-givers.

Development of the Nervous System

5. A child's brain grows rapidly during infancy, especially in the cerebrum, and at the same time parts of it begin to develop special functions.

6. Infants sleep almost twice as much as adults do, but the amount gradually decreases as they get older. They also experience various states of arousal.

Sensory Development

7. At birth infants can already see and hear but without as much accuracy or acuity as adults have.

8. Newborn infants show a definite preference for sweet liquids, a definite aversion to foul odors, and less sensitivity to pain than older infants do.

9. All of the senses develop rapidly and reach adult levels of acuity and sensitivity by the end of infancy.

Motor Development

10. Infants are born with a number of physically useful reflexes, such as rooting and sucking.

11. Infants also are born with several reflexes, such as the Moro reflex, whose primary significance is to indicate normal development of the nervous system.

12. Motor skills appear during the first year of infancy and include reaching, crawling and its variations, and walking.

13. Learning opportunities contribute to the development of motor skills, but so do infants' inborn reflexes and growth processes.

Variations in Growth and Motor Development

14. One of the most important influences on early motor development is low birth weight, caused by either slow prenatal development or short gestation.

15. Preterm infants often show many abnormalities: they may have trouble breathing and digesting, and their reflexes may not be well developed.

16. Gender differences in motor behavior appear even during infancy, when boys are generally more active than girls.

17. Infants from different cultural and racial groups vary significantly in size and in the time when they develop certain motor skills, such as walking.

Nutrition During the First Two Years

18. Infants need more protein and calories per pound of body weight than children do.

19. Compared with bottle feeding, breast feeding has several advantages: it conveys immunity to illnesses, breast milk is more nutritionally complete, breast feeding helps develop an infant's jaw and mouth muscles, and breast feeding may promote a positive relationship between mother and child.

20. After weaning from breast or bottle, infants need a diet rich in protein and calories. Most North American families can provide these requirements, although many fail to provide specific nutrients that children need, which in extreme cases can lead to deficits in cognitive development.

21. A common problem with North American diets is overnutrition, which can make infants seriously overweight or obese. Mild amounts of extra fat in an infant, however, do not usually influence how much the infant weighs as a child or adult.

22. Sometimes, for a complex of reasons, infants fail to thrive normally.

23. Infant mortality has decreased in the recent past; but in the United States it is still not as low as it should be.

KEY TERMS

neonate (151)
vernix (151)
lanugo (151)
fontanelle (151)
Apgar Scale (152)
Brazelton Neonatal
    Behavioral Assessment
    Scale (153)
attachment (156)
central nervous system (156)
neuron (156)
glial cell (156)
myelin (156)
brain stem (157)
midbrain (157)
cerebral cortex (157)
cerebrum (157)
REM sleep (158)
sudden infant death
    syndrome (SIDS) (160)
sleep apnea (160)
reflex (163)
skill (163)
motor ability (163)
rooting reflex (163)
sucking reflex (164)
mouthing reflex (164)
Moro reflex (164)
survival reflex (164)
primitive reflex (164)
motor skill (165)
gross motor skill (165)
fine motor skill (165)
cephalocaudal
    principle (165)
proximodistal
    principle (165)
low birth weight (171)
small for date (171)
preterm (171)
kinesthetics (175)
secretory IgA (177)
marasmus (180)
kwashiorkor (180)
failure to thrive (182)
infant mortality rate (182)

WHAT DO YOU THINK?

1. Do you think you are attracted to babies because they look cute? How do you think you would feel about cuddling an infant who did not look cute but who was physically deformed with, say, a cleft palate?

2. If walking develops at least partly through learning, why not simply teach infants to walk as soon as possible? What do you think would be the short- and long-term effects of doing so, both on the infant and on you?

3. If you were to become a parent, would you breast feed or bottle feed? If you are a parent, which did you choose? Explain why.

4. How, specifically, can you keep an older infant from becoming seriously overweight? What keeps some parents (and infants) from implementing these suggestions?

FOR FURTHER READING

Brazelton, T. B. *What Every Baby Knows*. New York: Ballantine Books, 1988.

This author has a gift for colorful and readable descriptions of infants, children, and their families and the everyday problems and challenges they encounter. This book, like others by Brazelton, intersperses concrete descriptions and interviews with family members with commentary that helps put the concrete accounts into perspective. Because the children and families are all "real life," the book does not confine itself to physical developments; it also includes cognitive and social developments as well.

Godwin, A., and Schrag, L. (eds.). *Setting Up for Infant Care: Guidelines for Centers and Family Day Care Homes*. Washington, DC: National Association for the Education of Young Children, 1988.

If you are interested either in learning about or in actually providing infant care, this book is a good starting place. It discusses a wide range of issues about infant care, from the psychological development of infants to "how-to" advice for starting an actual infant center or family-care home for infants.

La Leche League International. *The Womanly Art of Breastfeeding*, 4th ed. New York: Plume Books, 1988.

Fildes, V. *Breasts, Bottles, and Babies: History of Infant Feeding*. Edinburgh: Edinburgh University Press, 1986.

Here are books on the merits of breast feeding. The second is among the most widely read on the subject, supports the practice unabashedly and enthusiastically, and has relatively little tolerance for bottle feeding. The first one takes a more balanced perspective because it traces the rise and fall of breast feeding as a cultural practice.

Ornstein, R., and Thompson, R. *The Amazing Brain*. Boston: Houghton Mifflin, 1984.

Restak, R. *The Brain*. New York: Bantam Books, 1984.

These books describe the basic anatomy and functioning of the human brain. Both are very readable. Ornstein and Thompson rely on interesting, creative diagrams by a talented illustrator, David Macaulay. Restak's book mainly uses photographs (many in color) made for a recent television series about the brain.

Spock, B., and Rothenberg, M. *Baby and Child Care*, 5th ed. New York: Pocket Books, 1985.

This is the classic, best-selling "Dr. Spock" book meant to assist in raising children (although the newest edition has a co-author). It attempts to cover a wide span of years and a wide range of issues, but its real strength lies with its treatment of physical development, especially during infancy.

CHAPTER 6

The First Two Years: Cognitive Development

Focusing Questions

■ What clues do infants give about their cognitive processes? How can we learn about infants' thinking?

■ Do infants see and hear in the same way that adults do?

■ What does "thinking," or cognition, consist of at different periods of infancy?

■ What are the three types of learning, and how do infants demonstrate them?

■ What steps do infants and toddlers go through in acquiring language, and how do adults affect this language acquisition?

rom birth, infants begin acquiring knowledge about their environment. Consider, for example, William and Greta:

■ William, nine months old, laughs when his father puts on a Halloween mask. But two days later, when a family friend tries on the same mask, William cries in distress. Six months later he laughs when the friend tries on the mask again, but he shies away from trying it on himself. The same mask seems to have changed meaning more than once.

■ Greta, eighteen months old, discovers her mother's box of postage stamps. For a time she forgets all else in favor of staring at the stamps and making little piles of them according to color. She is so engrossed that she cannot hear her mother calling her for dinner while she is doing this.

These examples illustrate two psychological processes, perception and cognition. The first of these, **perception,** refers to the brain's immediate or direct organization and interpretation of sensations. Perceptual processes occur when an infant notices that a toy car is the same car no matter which way he orients it. As the infant turns the car upside down in his hands, his visual image of it changes, yet he still perceives the changing patterns as one unchanging car. He is not fooled into thinking that the car has acquired a different identity when he turns it upside down. Perception has an automatic, involuntary quality as well: Greta cannot help staring at the postage stamps and comparing one with another, and William cannot help noticing that different people wearing the same mask look similar but also just a bit different.

Cognition is a more general term for all the processes by which humans acquire knowledge. It includes perception, reasoning, and language skills, all of which make up thinking and learning. Greta uses cognitive skills when she groups the stamps by color. William, on the other hand, is so young that we cannot be sure whether he really reacts cognitively to the mask he sees. But older children or adults would almost surely do more than perceive the mask if faced with the same situations that William experienced; they might consciously wonder who was behind the mask each time, why the person had put it on, and the like. As these examples show, cognition not only draws on perception but influences it as well. Greta's thoughts keep her from perceiving her mother's voice calling her to dinner.

Most activities include both perception and cognition. When you hear a university professor lecture, you may perceive the sounds that he makes as language, but you probably also apply cognitive skills to make sense of them. Otherwise the lecture is only so much linguistic noise.

This chapter looks at how infants develop cognitive and perceptual abilities and therefore at how thinking in infancy can be studied. How can we learn anything psychological about a person who cannot talk and who may not even be able to gesture or move very well? The answer to this question makes possible many other answers about infant perception and cognition. A number of these are presented throughout the chapter. The discussion then focuses on the most human of all cognitive qualities — language — and incidentally suggests how children behave and think when they are on the verge of leaving infancy and entering childhood.

WAYS OF STUDYING PERCEPTION AND COGNITION IN INFANTS

How can we know whether a very young infant, who mostly just sleeps, is actually noticing an interesting sight or sound, much less thinking about it? Consider Elizabeth, who is only two months old:

> For two hours Elizabeth had slept. Now she lay in her mother's arms with eyes barely open, while her mother talked affectionately to her. The mother nodded her head while she talked, exaggerated her voice to sound singsong, and even dangled a key chain in front of Elizabeth's eyes for a moment. Elizabeth stared more or less in the direction of all these events; she did not respond in an obvious way, although she did not avert her eyes from it all or go back to sleep.

Maybe Elizabeth noticed her mother's efforts, but then again, maybe she did not. Either way, we could not find out by simple observation; a more complex investigation would be required. Infant psychologists have developed several interrelated techniques for inferring the perceptions and "thoughts" of babies. One measures changes in infants' states of arousal; another, how they respond to especially familiar sights and sounds; and still another, their readiness to habitually perform those behaviors that they find rewarding.

Arousal and Infants' Heart Rates

One way to understand an infant's cognition is to measure his heart rate (HR) with a small electronic stethoscope attached to his chest. The changes in HR are taken to signify variations in the baby's arousal, alertness, and general contentment.

Infant psychologists make this assumption because among adults, HR varies reliably with attention and arousal (Lacey & Lacey, 1978). Typically HR slows down, or decelerates, when adults notice or attend to something interesting but not overly exciting: when they read the newspaper, for example. If adults attend to something *very* stimulating, their HRs speed up, or accelerate. Watching a lab technician draw blood from your own arm, for example, often causes a faster HR. On the whole, novel or attractive stimulations produce curiosity and a slower HR; potentially dangerous or aversive stimulations produce defensiveness, discomfort, and a faster HR — at least among adults.

Very young infants — from one day to a few months old — show similar changes, but we need to take several precautions when we study their HRs. For one thing, young infants should be observed when they are truly alert, and as we have already pointed out, newborn babies often spend a lot of time drowsy or asleep. For another thing, newborn or very young infants require relatively gentle and persistent stimuli, such as a quiet, continuous sound or a soft light

Heart rate studies

Qualities of infants' attention

that moves slowly or blinks repeatedly (Berg & Berg, 1979; Hirschman et al., 1982). Many stimuli that seem harmless to adults or to older children apparently overstimulate very young infants and consequently accelerate their HRs instead of decelerating them. Many one-month-olds show a faster HR at the mere sight of their mothers, even though the infants may look as if they are just studying their mothers' faces calmly (Field, 1979). In spite of these problems, however, studies of HR have provided a useful way of measuring infants' attention, perception, and memory.

Recognition, Memory, and Infant Habituation

Even though infants cannot describe what they remember, they do often indicate recognition of particular objects, people, and activities. Familiar people, such as mothers, bring forth a special response in one-year-olds, who may coo suddenly at the sight of them, stretch out their arms to them, and even crawl or walk to them if they know how. Less familiar people, such as neighbors or the family doctor, tend not to produce responses like these and in fact may even produce active distress.

Habituation studies

Babies' responses to the familiar and the unfamiliar provide infant psychologists with a second way of understanding infant perception and cognition. Psychologists study infants' tendency to get used to and therefore to ignore stimuli as they experience them repeatedly; this tendency is called **habituation** (Bornstein, 1985). One habituation strategy offers a baby a standard, or "study," stimulus — a simple picture to look at or a simple melody to hear. Like most adults, the baby attends to the study stimulus carefully at first but gradually pays less attention to it. In other words, she habituates to it. After the baby has studied the stimulus for a suitable period of time, the investigators present the original study stimulus along with a few other stimuli. If the baby really recognizes the original, she will probably respond to the others as comparatively novel. She will look longer and harder at the new stimuli, and her HR will slow down as well.

Babies often show preferences for novel stimuli. By sucking on a special nipple, the baby in the experiment pictured here brings a visual pattern into or out of focus. Typically, a new pattern prompts intense and rapid sucking at first, but as the baby habituates or gets used to the pattern, he sucks less frequently and strongly.

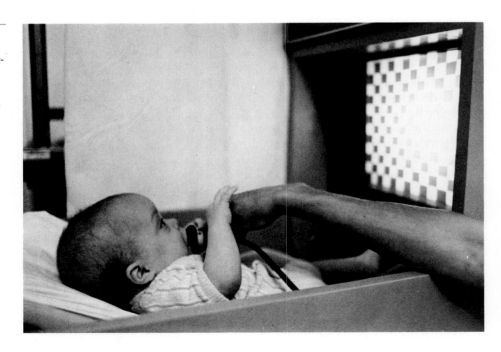

Physical Development	Genetics	Peers	Social Context	Family
How does hearing impairment in infants affect their language development? (223)	What sights and sounds do newborn infants seem genetically predisposed to notice and respond to? (192, 197)	What effect does interaction with peers in a day-care setting seem to have on infants' developing cognitive and linguistic abilities? (233)	Why do North American babies fuss more and make more verbal demands than do babies in Kenya or Mexico? (221)	In what ways do parents influence infants' language acquisition? (219–222)

THE FIRST TWO YEARS: COGNITIVE DEVELOPMENT

Emotions	Self-concept and Identity	Learning	Cognition	Language
How is separation anxiety related to cognitive development during infancy? (244)	What cognitive abilities are necessary for an infant to develop a self-concept? (204)	When do infants begin to imitate? (212)	What is the cognitive significance for infants of the game peek-a-boo? (201)	What words do children use first? (218)

This method has shown that young babies recognize quite a lot of past experiences. One classic habituation study found that four-month-old girls recognized a familiar visual pattern among three others that differed from the original (McCall & Kagan, 1967). Another showed that HR slowed down when five-month-olds heard a familiar melody replayed in a different rhythmic pattern (Chang & Trehub, 1977). Still another found habituation even in newborns: they "noticed" when a light brush on their cheek changed location, as revealed by changes in their HR (Kisilevsky & Muir, 1984). Sometimes, too, recognition persists for very long periods. Six-month-olds, it seems, can still recognize an original study picture two weeks after they first encounter it — a performance that matches adults' recognition memory in some situations (Fagan, 1973).

Long-term memory in infancy

Results of habituation studies may help explain why parents rapidly become convinced that their babies know them as special people. Elizabeth may already have been recognizing her mother or responding to her differently from other interesting sights and sounds, and her mother may have sensed this. Overall, monitoring infants' HR has given psychologists a useful method for learning something about what infants attend to and perceive in their environment, especially when the infants are too young to respond in other ways.

INFANT PERCEPTION

As mentioned earlier, *perception* refers to how the brain organizes and interprets sensations. Perception operates relatively automatically; when your best friend walks up to you, your brain almost instantly converts an oval-shaped pattern of colors and lines from an unorganized batch of sensations into an organized whole called your friend's face. This automatic quality has made some psychologists wonder whether children are born already possessing perceptual skills. Others believe that many such skills originate during infancy through some sort of learning that happens naturally to most normal infants. As it turns out, research on these possibilities suggests a bit of truth in both of them.

Children acquire a number of perceptual skills during infancy. Each corresponds to one or another of the five human senses: vision, hearing, touch, taste, and smell. The first of these, vision, has been studied more than any of the others; and the first two, vision and hearing, account for the large majority of research about infants' perception. This emphasis reflects society's widespread (but probably unjustified) belief that touch, taste, and smell are "minor" senses, ones that we can live without more easily than vision and hearing.

Visual Perception

Early visual preference

Given that children can see at least to some extent during infancy, what do they perceive? Some of the earliest research on this question excited a lot of interest because it seemed to show that infants — even newborns just two days old — could discriminate between human faces and abstract patterns and that they looked at faces longer than at either patterned disks or plain, unpatterned disks (Fantz, 1963). The researchers presented infants with various combinations of these stimuli side by side and carefully observed which of them the babies spent the most time looking at. At all ages studied (birth to six months), infants showed a clear preference: they stared at a picture of a human face almost twice as long as at any other stimulus picture. Young infants, it seemed, were inherently interested in people.

Bridges   What sights and sounds do newborn infants seem genetically predisposed to notice and respond to?

More recent studies of visual preferences, however, have qualified this conclusion substantially (Haith, 1979; Banks, 1983). It is not the humanness of faces that infants enjoy looking at, but their interesting contours, complexity, and curvature. Newborns are particularly attracted to contours, or the edges of areas of light and dark. But such edges can be provided either by the hairline of a parent's head or by a properly constructed abstract drawing. When infants get to the age of two or three months, their perceptual interest shifts to complexity and curvature. At this age an infant prefers looking at a pattern of many small squares rather than at one of just a few large squares. And he prefers looking at curved lines to looking at straight ones. These qualities, too, are provided by human faces, but not by faces alone.

Object Constancy   **Object constancy** refers to the perception that an object remains the same in some way in spite of constant changes in the sensations that it sends to the eye. A baby's favorite toy duck never casts exactly the same image on her retina from one second to the next. The image continually varies depending on its distance and on its orientation or angle of viewing. Somehow the baby must learn that this kaleidoscope of images really refers to only one constant duck — that the duck always *is* the same but keeps *looking* different. Several studies show that infants begin acquiring this knowledge very early indeed.

Size constancy: same object at different distances

Consider the development of **size constancy,** the perception that an object stays the same size even when viewed at different distances. In one early study, newborn babies were conditioned to suck at the sight of a cube that measured precisely twelve centimeters across (seven inches) and was placed exactly one meter (thirty-nine inches) away (Bower, 1966). Later the babies were shown several cubes of different sizes and at different distances. These included one that cast an image exactly the size of the original but that was in fact larger and farther away. The babies were not fooled by this apparent identity of retinal images. They preferred to look at the original cube regardless of its distance — that is, they sucked on their pacifiers more while looking at the original cube than at any substitute one. Apparently they knew when an object really was the same size and when it only looked the same size.

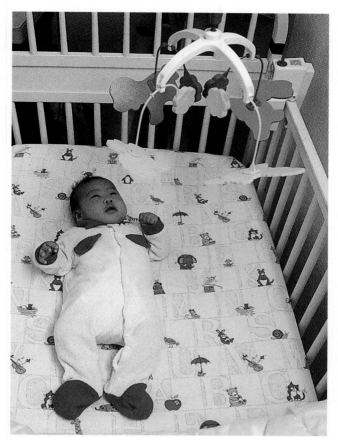

Young infants concentrate longer on certain shapes and contours, even when these are not part of a human face. Newborns are especially attracted to contours and to patches of light and dark. A few months later, they prefer complex patterns over simpler ones, and curved lines over straight ones. Such changes may sometimes explain why a baby's interest in a mobile like this one waxes and wanes.

This conclusion is clouded, however, by infants' preference for objects at certain distances (McKenzie & Day, 1987). In particular, they prefer near objects — things at about one meter or less — to objects that are farther away. Anything that babies see at this relatively close distance promotes attentiveness, whether or not they have seen it before. Visual life occurs literally within an arm's reach for infants, especially when they are young; and it is hard to know for sure what they think about sights that are beyond this range.

Do babies perceive an object as being the same even when its shape changes because the angle from which babies view it changes? This particular perception is sometimes called **shape constancy.** The perception depends on the ability to recognize apparent but unreal changes of shape. A rubber doll held upright casts a different image on the eye from the same doll lying down. But this change in shape is only apparent; compare it with the real change caused by squeezing the rubber doll hard with both hands.

In general, research on this skill suggests that infants acquire shape constancy gradually, beginning at around three months of age. Typically they demonstrate this skill, like many others, by habituating — in this case to shapes viewed at various angles or orientations. In one study young infants looked at a two-dimensional square presented at various sidelong or oblique angles (Caron et al., 1979). When the square was later presented "flat on," along with another, novel shape, the infants paid more attention to the novel shape and tended to ignore the familiar one. Because the infants had never seen the familiar square at a flat-on angle before, they must have somehow made mental allowances for its various changes in orientation during the experiment. Somehow, that is, the infants abstracted its true squareness from several not-so-square viewings of the shape.

Shape constancy: same object at different angles

Generally, young infants — about three months — show constancy only for simple shapes. Older infants — around eight months — can also recognize complex forms such as faces or abstract drawings even when they are presented at sidelong or tilted angles (L. Cohen & Strauss, 1979; Ruff, 1980). For the most difficult figures, gentle movement or rotation seems to help infants to identify shapes. In these cases the older infants react somewhat like adults who are viewing a piece of sculpture: they must see all sides of it in order to take it in or perceive its full identity.

Variability of constancies

All of these qualifications make it hard to say when exactly babies acquire either shape or size constancy. A young infant's daily expression of various object constancies is likely to seem tentative and ambiguous to a parent or other adult. One day the child responds as if an object is the "same" at different distances or orientations, yet the next day the child conveys ignorance of constancy. The variability happens for two main reasons: because object constancy depends partly on a child's attentiveness and because it depends partly on prior memories of the object, both of which are somewhat fragile in early infancy.

Functions of constancies

Whatever the timing of their appearance, shape and size constancies serve important functions in babies' long-term development. These constancies help infants to distinguish familiar objects from novel ones and to begin seeing the world as predictable and secure. Gradually, mother is mother and father is father whether viewed from the side or from the front and whether viewed from ten feet or two feet. Shape and size constancies also help infants learn about new, inanimate objects more efficiently. Familiar objects are recognized more often and more quickly as familiar, allowing a baby to concentrate attention on newer, unexplored objects.

Depth and Space Perception   Even if the infant perceives the size and shape of objects fairly accurately, he must still navigate successfully from one place to another. Consider a baby named Joel, who has recently learned to crawl around his house. Joel must realize that the rooms in his house stay put when he crawls or walks, even though they look like they move. And he must notice that stairs are different from floors: one of them makes him fall, if he is not careful, but the other feels secure. Realizations like these require Joel to orient his actions to the world or space outside his own body and to understand its layout accurately. In other words, he must perceive depth and spatial orientation accurately. Each of these perceptions appears and then changes during the course of infancy.

Depth perception refers to a sense of how far away objects are or appear to be. Infants begin having this kind of perceptual skill about as soon as they can focus on objects at different distances, at around two or three months of age. This conclusion is demonstrated by the now classic experiment with the **visual cliff** (E. Gibson & Walk, 1960). In its basic form, this consists of a table covered with strong glass, under which is a surface textured with colored squares, such as shown in the photograph on this page. Part of the textured surface contacts the glass directly, but another part is separated from it by several feet. Visually, then, the setup resembles the edge of a table, but the glass provides ample support for an infant even in the dropped-off area. A baby who crawls onto it will seem to float in midair.

The visual cliff

On this apparatus, even very young babies, just two months old, discriminate between the two sides of the visual cliff. They find the deep side more interesting, as suggested by the extra time they take to study it. Young babies show little fear of the deep side, judging either by their overt behavior or by their heart rates, which tend to decrease during their investigations of the cliff. This finding implies that they are primarily curious about the cliff rather than fearful of it.

Babies old enough to crawl, however, show significant fear of the visual cliff, their heart rates increase markedly, and they will not crawl onto the deep side in spite of coaxing from a parent and in spite of the solid support they feel

Infants' behavior on a visual cliff reflects both their knowledge and their feelings about depth. Even babies too young to crawl or creep find the deep side of the cliff more interesting than the shallow side. But only babies who have begun crawling or creeping show fear or wariness of the deep side, comparable to an adult's fear of heights.

from the glass (Rader et al., 1981; Campos et al., 1978). Why the change? Perhaps infants' crawling skills allow them to perceive distances more accurately than before, or perhaps once they can crawl they know from experience that falling can be painful, so they become more cautious about heights.

Infants also show depth perception in their responses to looming motions, in what is sometimes called a "loom-zoom" procedure. Here the infant watches a screen on which a shape seems to approach rapidly (loom) and then retreats again (zoom). Children and adolescents typically respond by wincing or by raising their arms to protect themselves from what looks like a sure collision. If infants perceive depth in the way adults do, presumably they, too, should respond defensively.

Sensitivity to looming

Do they? Some experiments have reported defensive reactions in infants as young as three months (Bower, 1977; Slater et al., 1985); in these, the babies raise their arms, widen their eyes, and act distressed. But other studies of looming have reported no defensive reactions at all (Yonas, 1979; Yonas & Pettersen, 1979). Skeptics therefore suggest that occasional defensive reactions may really show something else — perhaps poor muscle coordination when the baby is tracking a looming shape. Often the contour of such a shape rises substantially as it looms; the baby must therefore look up to keep watching it, even if she is not actually afraid of it. If she looks too high, she will have trouble keeping her arms and face from suddenly flipping backward: hence her "fearful" response.

This possibility does not mean, however, that genuine depth perception is impossible in younger babies. A baby may know that something is looming at him but not be afraid of it. Or he may simply be too poorly coordinated to show fear, even if he feels it. As with the visual cliff studies, fear and perception may be two different developments.

Later on in infancy, children use their perceptions of depth to orient themselves in three-dimensional space. Eighteen-month-olds come to believe that their spatial environment remains still or fixed even when they themselves move. As adults we take this orientation for granted. Walking from one room to another, for example, does not make the rooms move; it only makes them look as if they do.

Spatial orientation

One psychologist studied the development of spatial orientation by placing infants in a room with two windows, one to their left and the other to their right (Acredolo & Evans, 1980). The babies were taught to expect the experimenter to appear at one of the windows whenever a buzzer sounded. They easily learned to do so and before long turned to the proper window whenever the buzzer sounded but before the face appeared. At this point the babies were moved to the other side of the room, so that finding the face now meant turning in the opposite direction from before. As it turned out, only relatively old infants — nearly eighteen months old — corrected the direction in which they turned to see the face. Younger infants responded much more egocentrically — that is, with reference only to their own bodies. If they originally learned to turn right, they apparently assumed that turning right remained correct even though they had moved.

Sensitivity to spatial orientation

But even young babies did not ignore their surroundings completely. Some six-month-olds switched their directions appropriately, and many more did so when the two windows in the experiment were distinguished clearly with unique and obvious star decorations. In another, related experiment, younger infants proved less self-centered if tested in their own homes rather than in a comparatively barren laboratory room (Acredolo, 1979). Perhaps knowing the layout of their homes made them more aware of the reality and permanence of space outside their own bodies. Or perhaps the younger babies felt more relaxed at home and therefore performed better. Or perhaps both.

Auditory Perception

Infants respond to sounds even as newborns; but what do they perceive from sounds? What kind of sense do they make from the sounds that they hear? These questions are important because infants' ability to discriminate sounds makes a crucial difference in their acquisition of language, as discussed later in this chapter.

But gaining skill at discriminating sounds takes many months. Consider LaVonne and Daniel:

■ At about five o'clock each day LaVonne, two months old, cries unaccountably. Her father finds that running the vacuum cleaner quiets her down immediately. He also finds that it keeps her quiet more or less indefinitely or at least until he cannot stand the sound of the vacuum anymore.

■ Daniel, fourteen months old, sometimes gets fussy. His mother finds that playing music quiets him down rapidly. Popular vocal singing seems to keep him quiet the longest, although every kind of music works for at least a little while.

Most adults would guess that Daniel is perceiving some sort of meaning from what he is hearing, such as the melodic structure of the songs or some of the words being sung. But LaVonne cannot be getting meaning from what she hears; more likely she is quiet because she is tuning out or "averting her ears" from the noise.

Research confirms these informal impressions. Under certain conditions infants can indeed organize the sounds they hear, and in this sense they can hear as well as perceive what they hear. For example, infants just two days old can locate sounds, as shown by the way they orient their heads toward the noise of a rattle (Clifton et al., 1981a). But they often take much longer than children or adults before responding. Instead of needing just a fraction of a second, as adults do, full-term infants require an average of two to three seconds before orienting (or looking at) a sound that occurs off to one side. Infants born one month preterm require even more time — an average of twelve seconds — to respond (Field et al., 1980). These delays may explain why pediatricians and others used to believe that newborn infants could not hear: the sounds that they offered to the babies, such as a single hand clap, may not have lasted long enough for the infants to respond.

Although infants can locate sounds, their skill at doing so has certain limitations. They are better at locating relatively high-pitched sounds, such as those made by a flute or a small bird, than low-pitched sounds, such as that made by a foghorn (Morrongiello et al., 1982). This fact has sometimes led some experts to suggest that infants have a "natural" preference for female — that is, high-pitched — human voices. Studies of voice preferences, however, have not confirmed this possibility (Aslin et al., 1983), probably because newborns' range of special sensitivity lies well above the pitch of even female voices and because male and female voices are usually more similar in overall quality than gender stereotypes suggest.

For the first few months of life, infants locate sounds only by the differences in loudness of the sounds when they reach each ear (Clifton et al., 1981b). This allows only fairly crude judgments about the direction of a sound (during the newborn period, of course, a baby may not need very precise judgments). By about the fourth month of life, however, infants begin using an additional source of information that increases their accuracy considerably — namely, the slight differences in *when* a sound arrives at each ear. A sound originating off to the left arrives at the left ear a few thousandths of a second sooner than it arrives at the right ear. The difference in timing in fact reflects the direction of the sound fairly precisely. Toward the middle of their first year, infants show signs of noticing these split-second differences when they are created artificially through stereophonic loudspeakers. Much more often than would occur by chance, they turn toward the direction of these artificial sounds.

Locating the direction of sound

Bridges What sights and sounds do newborn infants seem genetically predisposed to notice and respond to?

Refinements in sound localization

INFANT COGNITION

As perceptual skills develop, children begin to put them to cognitive uses. A one-month-old infant may notice the dark eyes painted on the face of a doll and stare a long time at them out of interest. But an eighteen-month-old can do more than that: she can talk to the doll in babbles that resemble language or cuddle the doll briefly as if it were a real person. All in all, the older infant combines perception with other skills she is developing. In doing so, she shows the first signs of cognition, or methods for thinking or gaining knowledge about the world.

At first infant cognition has little to do with the symbolic forms that develop in most children and adults. Instead it emphasizes active experimentation with and manipulation of materials. Only by the end of infancy does truly symbolic thought emerge. Even then it is still scattered among large amounts of concrete doing, seeing, and hearing; but its mere existence marks a significant new development for the child.

During their first year, infants explore objects with their senses, often through biting and chewing. Gradually they shift their attention from these sensorimotor actions to the objects on which they perform the actions — a crucial step in developing mental representations of objects.

Piaget's Theory of Sensorimotor Intelligence

Piaget's theory of cognitive development, described in Chapter 2, provides one of the most complete outlines of infant intelligence (Piaget, 1963). According to this viewpoint, infants think by way of *sensory* perceptions and *motor* actions: by doing things to and with the objects that they see. Piaget called this activity **sensorimotor intelligence.** He identified six stages during infancy that mark significant developments in sensorimotor intelligence; these are summarized in Table 6.1.

In general, these stages show three trends as infants grow older. First, infants' thinking becomes less **egocentric,** which means that they become increasingly able to take others' viewpoints into account. Being less egocentric in this sense does not necessarily make infants less selfish in everyday behavior — less apt to grab others' toys, for example — but it does make them more aware of any differences between their own needs or opinions and those of others.

More symbolic thinking

Second, infants show a trend toward abstract or symbolic thinking. Instead of needing to handle a toy car in order to understand it, infants become increasingly able to form an idea of a car without touching and seeing one tangibly. This ability becomes very strong by the end of the first two years of life; for Piaget, it helps to mark the end of infancy.

Development of schemes

Third, as infants' motor skills become more complex, they form structures that Piaget called **schemes.** In relation to infants, schemes are organized patterns of actions or thoughts that help the baby make sense out of the environment and adapt to its requirements. A baby's grasping motions form a scheme, for example, as do a baby's sucking motions. Eventually, as described below, internal, or mental, concepts and ideas develop out of such patterns of behavior. These are sometimes also called schemes (or sometimes *schemas* or *schemata*); but Piaget himself more often called later cognitive structures and patterns by other names such as *operations* or *systems,* depending on their exact nature (Miller, 1988, p. 41).

As we discuss more fully in Chapter 2, Piaget argued that sensorimotor intelligence develops by means of two complementary processes, assimilation and accommodation. **Assimilation** consists of interpreting new experiences in terms of already existing schemes. A baby who is used to sucking on a breast or

Less egocentrism

bottle may use this same action on whatever new, unfamiliar objects he encounters, such as rubber balls or his own fist. **Accommodation** consists of modifying existing schemes to fit new experiences. After sucking on a number of new objects, an infant may modify this action to fit the nature of each new object; she may chew on some new objects (her sweater) but not on others (a plastic cup).

The interplay of assimilation and accommodation leads to new schemes and eventually to the infant's ability to symbolize objects and activities. Let us look at how Piaget believed this transition occurs.

Stage 1 — Early Reflexes: Using What You're Born With (birth to one month)

According to Piaget, cognitive development begins with reflexes, those simple, inborn behaviors that all normal babies can produce at birth. As it happens, a majority of such reflexes remain just that — reflexes — for the individual's entire life; sneezing patterns and blinking responses, for example, look nearly the same in adults as in infants. But a few are notable for their flexibility — chiefly sucking, grasping, and looking. These behaviors resemble reflexes at birth, but they quickly begin to be modified in response to the experiences that the newborn encounters. They give infants a repertoire from which to develop more complex skills, and their susceptibility to influence makes them especially important to cognitive development during infancy.

Take sucking. Mothers who have breast fed know that the first feeding or two can be awkward: the infant noses around inefficiently for the nipple and may fail to connect with it even when the nipple is right under her nose, so to speak. But within just a week or two she is noticeably faster at finding it, usually to the relief of her mother. In that same period, too, she has probably begun sucking on other objects as well: her own fist, the corners of her blanket, or her daddy's little finger. Sometimes she simply sucks on air. All these sucking motions differ slightly from one another in style or form, and each evolves into a *scheme*, in the Piagetian sense.

Modifications of reflexes

TABLE 6.1   Some Features of Infant Cognition According to Piaget

Stage	Age in Months	Characteristics
1: Early reflexes	Prenatal–1	Reliance on inborn reflexes to "know" the environment; assimilation of all experiences to reflexes
2: Primary circular reactions	1–4	Accommodation (or modification) of reflexes to fit new objects and experiences; repeated actions focusing on infant's own body
3: Secondary circular reactions	4–8	Repeated actions focusing on objects; actions used as means toward ends, but haphazardly; early signs of object permanence
4: Combined secondary circular reactions	8–12	Deliberate combinations of previously acquired actions (or schemes); AnotB error; early signs of sense of time
5: Tertiary circular reactions	12–18	Systematic application of previously acquired actions (or schemes); well-organized investigations of novel objects, but always overt
6: The first symbols	18–24	First symbolic representations of objects; true object permanence; deferred imitation

Source: Piaget (1936).

Repeated actions involving the body

Stage 2 — Primary Circular Reactions: Modifying What You're Born With (one to four months)

Soon after the baby begins modifying his early reflexes, he begins building and differentiating action schemes quite rapidly. Within a month or so, in fact, he sometimes repeats them endlessly for no apparent reason. Because of its repetitive quality, Piaget calls this behavior a **circular reaction.** The baby seems to be stimulated by the outcome of his own behavior, so he responds for the mere joy of feeling himself act. At this point the circular reactions are called **primary circular reactions** because they still focus on the baby's own body and movements. Waving an arm repeatedly constitutes a primary circular reaction; so does kicking again and again.

During this period, the young infant practices her developing schemes widely. She grasps everything in sight, or sucks on it, or looks at it, or listens to it. These behaviors rapidly become less reflexive. By now the baby may literally shape her mouth differently for sucking her fist and for sucking her blanket. In this sense she can begin to recognize the objects all around her, and she implicitly also begins to remember previous experiences with each type of object. But this memory has an automatic or compulsive quality, unlike the relatively conscious memories that children have later in life.

Commonly occurring schemes

During this stage babies begin to vary in their preferred schemes. Some emphasize looking; others, grasping; still others, vocalizing. The variations may foreshadow later differences in temperament and personality, at least if "later" means simply later in infancy or early childhood. Nevertheless, nearly all babies develop and exercise certain schemes in common. For example, nearly all suck their thumbs at least occasionally — a scheme that evolves from early grasping and sucking reflexes. Nearly all do a good deal of active looking around; doing so helps give them the wide eyes that can make infants so appealing. And nearly all begin to vocalize (just openmouthed cooing at first) during this period, apparently for the sheer joy of hearing their own voices. The schemes for visual inspection may help make possible the perceptual developments that were described earlier in this chapter, and the vocalizations may contribute to early sensitivity to language, as described at the end of this chapter (Molfese et al., 1982).

Stage 3 — Secondary Circular Reactions: Making Interesting Sights Last (four to eight months)

As they practice their first schemes, young infants broaden their interests substantially. Before long, in fact, they move their attention beyond their own bodily actions to include objects and events immediately around them. Shaking his arm, for example, no longer captivates a baby's attention for its own sake; he has become too skilled at arm shaking for it to do so. Now a behavior like this becomes useful rather than interesting. A baby at this stage may accidentally discover that shaking his arm will make a mobile spin over his head in a crib, or create an interesting noise in a toy he happens to be holding, or make parents smile with joy. In all these cases, shaking an arm becomes a means to other ends. At best it is primitive means, however, because the usefulness of the behavior originally occurs to the baby by chance.

New focus on objects

Once primitive means are discovered, a baby at this stage will repeat a useful procedure endlessly in order to maintain and study the interesting results. The repetition is a circular reaction like the ones in the previous stage, but with an important difference: now the circular reactions orient to external objects and events rather than to the baby's own body and actions. Now results matter. If arm shaking fails to keep the mobile spinning, the baby will soon stop her effort; if she finally figures out the nature of the mobile, she will also stop. Either way, the repetition is not governed by her earlier motivation simply to move — her squirming scheme, so to speak. To differentiate this new orientation from the earlier one, Piaget called such repetitions **secondary circular reactions:** repetitions motivated by external objects and events.

Secondary circular reactions create two parallel changes in the child's motor schemes. On the one hand, he uses existing schemes ever more widely than before. He tries to suck on more and more of the toys that come his way. On the other hand, he begins to discover that schemes can be combined to produce interesting results. An infant may happen to reach toward an object (one scheme) and discover that doing so makes it possible to grasp the object (another scheme). At first the combination happens accidentally; but once it does happen, a baby at this stage can produce the new combination of schemes deliberately on future occasions.

Secondary circular reactions also implicitly show that the infant is now acquiring at least a hazy notion of **object permanence,** a belief that objects have existence separate from her own actions and continue to exist even when she cannot see them. In the first two stages of infant cognition, objects often seem to disappear from the baby's mind as soon as she loses sight of them or as soon as she no longer touches them. She may stare at or grasp a toy duck, but a parent or an older sibling can sometimes take it from her without causing distress; at most the baby will simply keep staring blankly where the duck used to be and then turn to other activities. In a phrase that Piaget might have invented (but did not), out of sight is out of mind in early infancy.

Early signs of object permanence

This is not so, however, as babies enter the second half of their first year. By Stage 3 they will look for an object briefly if they have been watching it carefully or manipulating it just beforehand. Naturally their first searching skills leave something to be desired, so it helps if the hidden object is actually partially visible and within easy reach — the toy duck's tail should stick out from under a blanket if that is where it is hidden. But the first signs of symbolic thought are there because infants must have some sort of idea of the toy duck if they are going to bother searching for it.

Stage 4 — Combined Secondary Circular Reactions: Deliberate Combinations of Means and Ends (eight to twelve months)

At this stage, instead of just happening on connections among schemes, the infant purposely uses her knowledge of the connections gained in the prior stage. In Stages 1 and 2, she may have developed separate schemes for opening her mouth and for chewing food. In Stage 3 she may have accidentally discovered that the first scheme is a means

Schemes used more widely

Playing peek-a-boo becomes popular with babies when they acquire the secondary circular reactions that Piaget described for Stage 3 of infant cognition. Even though the mother disappears temporarily, an infant at this stage knows that she must still exist behind that blanket. The baby is delighted to have this belief confirmed when she reappears.

Bridges   What is the cognitive significance for infants of the game peek-a-boo?

toward the other: mouth opening is means toward eating. Now, in Stage 4, the baby starts using this means-end connection widely. Like a young bird in a nest, the baby opens her mouth in order to "produce" food to chew on. Of course, she may eventually discover that the connection does not always work: sitting with a mouth wide open may sometimes produce no food at all or occasionally produce bad-tasting medicine instead of good-tasting food.

At this stage the infant still lacks alternatives to the single-purpose, fragmented schemes he has developed so far. As he encounters the limitations of these schemes, he gradually modifies and expands (or accommodates, as Piaget would say) his initial schemes that connected means with ends. In the example above, he may learn to open his mouth at the sight of some foods but not others. He may also add other behaviors to the mouth-opening scheme, such as pointing to favorite foods, thereby turning the original scheme into a more general food-requesting scheme. As these accommodations occur, the infant moves into the next stage of cognition.

The AnotB error

The relatively fixed, stereotyped quality of schemes at this stage may derive from the infant's heavy reliance on motor action as a method for understanding objects. One of the most dramatic illustrations of this possibility is the **AnotB error** (read "A, not B, error") illustrated by the following sequence. Hide a toy under a blanket while the infant carefully watches. Normally she can retrieve the toy easily at this stage. But then make the problem more complicated: hide the toy under blanket A and then transfer it to blanket B. Do this in full view of the infant. Where does the child first look for it? Not under the correct blanket, B, but under blanket A, where she previously retrieved the toy successfully.

The infant makes this mistake, Piaget argues, because her knowledge of the toy really amounts to memory of the actions she has taken with it — especially of successful actions. Other studies of the AnotB error support this interpretation. In one study, for example, babies were moved from one side of a table to the other after watching the toy being moved from blanket A to blanket B (Bremner & Bryant, 1977). Under these conditions the babies tended to reach for blanket B, which now required the same motor action that blanket A had originally required. The babies' relatively fixed motor response therefore still governed their actions, even after they had been moved. The behavior resembled the egocentric head-turning experiments described earlier in this chapter.

Early awareness of time

Even though a baby's schemes are still fragmented, he is now developing an intentional quality that allows him for the first time to anticipate events in the near future. For parents, the new sense of time can be both good news and bad. The baby may open his mouth wide for bananas but clamp it shut for medicine. He may wave his arms in delight at the sound of his bathwater being drawn, but he may fuss and protest at being carried anywhere in the vicinity of his diaper-changing table. In each case he anticipates the results of actions or schemes. More precisely, he anticipates accurately as long as the consequences are fairly immediate; "far time" — just a few hours or even several minutes away — still has little meaning to him.

Stage 5 — Tertiary Circular Reactions: Active Experimentation with Objects (twelve to eighteen months)   At Stage 5 the infant deliberately varies the schemes for producing interesting results or ends. Previously, at Stage 4, she could combine schemes, but only one pair at a time and only if an appropriate situation for using the combination happened to occur. Now, in dealing with a new object, the baby can run through a repertoire of schemes in a trial-and-error effort to learn about the object's properties. Piaget called the variations **tertiary circular reactions** (meaning third-level circular reactions) to distinguish them from the simpler forms of repetition that dominate the earlier stages.

Consider bathtime again. Now, at Stage 5, the infant purposely varies how he splashes: first gently with one hand, then harder, then gently again but with two hands, and so on. These actions resemble secondary circular reactions in focusing on the results of actions rather than on the actions themselves. But they go beyond earlier forms of repetition by their deliberate variation. The baby now acts as if he is comparing the variations among themselves, and the comparisons in fact seem to occupy more attention than the individual results do. In the bath, the baby does not care so much about the individual splashes as about their differences and similarities.

These purposeful variations in behavior, however, are still organized largely by trial and error, not by systematic plans. Given a rubber ball, for example, some babies may try dropping it from different heights and onto different objects. But no matter how delighted these infants are with the results of these variations, they will not think to vary the dropping conditions carefully or experimentally. They will not try slight changes in altitude each time or assemble objects with slightly differing bounciness for landing platforms. These more systematic efforts require mental representations of the ball and of the bouncing activity and must therefore wait until the next and final stage of sensorimotor development.

Meanwhile, babies still cannot solve problems by insight — that is, by mentally forming or running through solutions prior to overt action. Their belief in object permanence at Stage 5 shows this limitation. They no longer make the AnotB error, but they can still be fooled if the search problem is made a little harder. A ball shifted from blanket A to blanket B can still baffle infants if they do not actually get to see it moved; they may not think to look under blanket B if they did not actually see the ball put there. Instead, they simply stare at the situation, looking surprised, perhaps, and confused. Babies respond this way even though a moment earlier they may have successfully solved a classic AnotB problem in which they did in fact see the ball get moved. Taken together, these behaviors suggest two things: first, that infants are not tied as much as before to particular successful actions for help in solving problems and, second, that they still fail to imagine the solutions to problems.

Stage 6 — The First Symbols: Representing Objects and Actions (eighteen to twenty-four months)   At this stage, the motor schemes that the child previously explored and practiced overtly begin to occur symbolically. For the first time he can begin to imagine or envision actions and their results without actually having to try them out beforehand.

Consider a Stage 6 child who wants a favorite toy that is just barely out of reach on a high shelf. Near the shelf, as it happens, sits a small stool that she has played with numerous times. How to get the toy? Earlier in infancy the baby might simply have stared and fussed and eventually either have given up or have cried. At this late stage, things are different. The baby surveys the situation, observes the stool, pauses briefly. Then, with a purposeful air, she places the stool under the toy, climbs up, and retrieves the toy. What is important here is the lack of false starts or, conversely, the presence of only a single, correct attempt. The infant may succeed even though she may never before have used the stool to reach high objects. According to Piaget, trial and error is no longer the method of choice; now the infant tries out solutions mentally to envision their results. Only when she determines a workable action in her mind does she carry it out.

Skill with mental representations makes true object permanence possible. A child at the end of infancy will search for a toy even after it has been hidden in the fully adult sense. If a ball disappears behind some shelves, he will go around to the other side to look for it. He will search appropriately, even though he cannot know in advance exactly where behind the shelves the ball will turn up. In the ball-and-blanket situation described above, the child can now play more complex games of hide-and-seek. She usually looks first under the blanket where the toy disappeared; but if she fails to find it there, she will search under any and all other blankets and sometimes even under the table and in the experimenter's pockets. Relatively extensive search is made possible in part by the child's new conviction that toys and other objects do in fact have a permanent existence independent of her own activities with them. They do not, in other words, just disappear.

Deferred imitation

Mental representations also make possible **deferred imitation,** a behavior that will figure importantly in play and learning later in childhood. In deferred imitation, the child copies or duplicates a behavior, or at least aspects of a behavior, at a significantly later time than when he first experienced it — sometimes days or even weeks later. Having seen her father brush his teeth, the Stage 6 child does so, too; but she may do so twelve hours later, when her father is not even around. Or having heard his older sibling exclaim "Yum! Good!" at one night's dinner menu, a child may do so as well. But he makes his exclamation at dinner two days later, even if none of the other family members happens to feel quite so ecstatic about the food.

These behaviors all depend on the child's ability to form and maintain representations (thoughts or memories) of the relevant experiences, which later become available for expression again. As we shall see, representational skill proves crucial in early childhood. It contributes to children's play because much play involves reenactment of previous experiences and roles. It makes possible much language development because the child must learn to use words and expressions when they are appropriate and not just at the time she hears them uttered. And it makes possible the first real self-concept because sooner or later the child realizes that he, too, has a (relatively) permanent existence akin to the permanence of all the things and people in his life, whether toys, pet dogs, or parents.

Bridges What cognitive abilities are necessary for an infant to develop a self-concept?

Baby Jill's Intelligence: An Example

The relationships among the six stages of sensorimotor intelligence become clearer if we look at how an infant might use the same object differently at different ages. Baby Jill acquired a ball when she was born and used it for the next several years. During that time, of course, her ways of using the ball changed dramatically, as shown in the following descriptions (comments are in italics). The ball was about four inches in diameter and was made out of rubber but had a cloth covering. Mostly it was red, but it had a large black spot on each side, so that it looked rather like an eyeball when viewed from the proper angle.

1. *Stage 1: Early reflexes* When Jill first came home from the hospital, her mother suspended the ball over Jill's diaper-changing table so that the black spot looked down at Jill directly. Day after day Jill stared hard at the ball and its black spot and followed it whenever her mother made it swing gently.

Here Jill used one of her earliest reflexes, in this case visual tracking of objects.

2. *Stage 2: Primary circular reactions* At two months, Jill sucked on the ball a lot and grabbed at it whenever one of her parents put it directly into her hands. The ball was just soft enough for Jill to do these things. She still liked to look at the ball swinging above her changing table, but she was starting to find her parents' faces more interesting.

Jill was modifying or accommodating her reflexes — sucking, grasping, tracking — to fit new experiences that were occurring to her. Her interest still lay primarily with her own actions rather than with the objects she was encountering.

3. *Stage 3: Secondary circular reactions* At six months, Jill discovered that *she* could make the ball swing above her changing table simply by waving her hands and feet. Every once in a while one of her limbs would accidentally catch the ball and send it spinning and swinging wildly.

By now her attention had shifted away from her own body (primary circular reactions) to an object outside herself and to what it could do (secondary circular reactions).

4. *Stage 4: Combining secondary circular reactions* When Jill was ten months old, her father took the ball down one day during a diaper change but happened to put it behind a bottle of talcum powder. Jill looked hard at the partially hidden ball, then firmly knocked over the bottle of powder and got hold of the ball. Her father was dismayed at how hard she hit the talcum powder but was also somewhat impressed. He did not remember her acting so purposefully before just to get something else.

Jill had become interested in combining schemes or actions. Her exploration of the effects of these schemes, however, was still guided primarily by chance discoveries.

5. *Stage 5: Tertiary circular reactions* At fifteen months, Jill preferred to have the ball down on the floor where she could get at it. One day she gathered together all the balls in the house — about five, to be exact. She tried bouncing each one down the stairs in turn; some seemed to bounce higher than others. Another time she tried floating the balls in the toilet. They all floated well except for her original red-and-black ball, which got its cloth covering waterlogged. (For some reason her parents did not enjoy her putting the balls in the toilet.)

Her investigations of the ball now had become rather systematic as if she were purposely trying out a conscious repertoire of actions to see what effect each would have on the ball.

6. *Stage 6: Symbolic representation* Just before her second birthday, Jill lost her red ball. She looked in her usual storage spots: her bottom dresser drawer and her (now little used) changing table. Where was it, anyway? When she could not find it, she asked her parents for help because she knew it had to be around somewhere.

In searching for the lost ball, Jill showed object permanence — a belief that the ball continued to exist even when out of sight. To hold this belief, she must have formed some sort of symbolic representation of the ball in her mind.

By this point, both Jill and the ball had gone through a lot together. At the end of her infancy, Jill had considerable skill at motor manipulation of objects as well as some beginnings of mental representation of objects. She no longer needed to have an object such as the red ball literally in hand. The ball had assisted in this development, as had countless other toys, of course, and countless sensory and manipulative experiences with them.

Assessment of Piaget's Theory of Infant Cognition

Piaget's theory has stimulated considerable study of infant cognition. A lot of this research has confirmed the main features of the theory (Harris, 1983b), whereas other parts have called attention to additional aspects of infancy that at least complicate Piaget's original presentation, even if they do not contradict it outright. Here is a sampling of both the confirmations and the complications.

The Integration of Schemes   Do infants begin life with fundamentally separate sensorimotor schemes, as Piaget argued, and only gradually learn to combine or integrate them? Some such combining must surely happen, but there is also evidence for the opposite trend: some important schemes may begin as integrated wholes and only later become differentiated into parts. As pointed out in Chapter 5, newborn infants will reach for and grasp a small object placed in front of them at the proper distance. They will do so even if the object is created only by a projected image (Bower, 1981, 1989). Such behavior implies that young babies tend to regard sight and touch as connected rather than separate or, in Piagetian terms, that they have a single early scheme for seeing and reaching, not one scheme for seeing and another, separate one for reaching.

Vision and hearing may also have inborn integrated schemes. Infants just a few days old will turn to look at the source of a sound as long as the direction lies within their physical capacity to turn (Muir & Field, 1979). In addition, they show signs of connecting their parents' faces and voices within two or three weeks: they will look more at a photograph of their mothers, for example, if a recording of their voices is playing. And infants just a few months old prefer looking at a film that matches a soundtrack to one that does not match (Spelke, 1983). This conclusion was suggested by a study in which young infants looked at two films side by side, one with a kangaroo bouncing up and down and the other with a toy donkey doing the same thing but at a different speed. When a soundtrack of bouncing rhythms was made to coincide with one film but not the other, the infants spent more time watching the coordinated picture.

Such evidence complicates Piaget's assertion that schemes primarily begin as separate, discrete reflexes and do not start integrating until midway through infancy. At the same time, however, the evidence does not really contradict Piaget. Given the complexity of human organisms, it is perfectly possible for both trends to occur at once. Some schemes may begin as integrated wholes and develop that way in at least certain situations, and others may begin as relatively specific reflexes and later combine.

Motor Limitations Versus Cognitive Limitations   Some infant psychologists question Piaget's six stages because they feel that the stages confuse the child's motor abilities with his cognitive or thinking abilities (Bower, 1981). Object permanence, for example, implicitly depends on a child's capacity to conduct a search: to walk around the room, to lift and inspect objects, and the like. Perhaps younger infants "lack" classic object permanence, this argument goes, simply because they lack motor skills or at best use them only clumsily.

To test this possibility, psychologists have redesigned the usual object permanence test so that it requires very little motor coordination from the infant. In one variation (Bower & Paterson, 1973) the baby simply watches an object disappear behind a screen. A moment later the object either does or does not reappear at the other edge of the screen. Under these conditions, even twenty-week-old infants show what looks like surprise if the object does not reappear: they stare more intently and widen their eyes. The behavior suggests a belief in object permanence; after all, why else would they show surprise? Unfortunately, their behavior can also be interpreted in other ways; it resembles attention to an interesting and changing visual display — a scheme that Piaget predicts to be well within the abilities of even young infants (Von Hofsten & Fazel-Zandy, 1984).

The Effects of Memory   Piaget explains most infant thinking in terms of motor schemes: repeated, familiar actions that allow infants to know their environment.

Connections among early schemes

"Looking" at sounds

Object permanence in early infancy

Perspectives

Support and Education for Parents of Infants

Given the unremitting demands of caring for an infant, it is not surprising that programs have emerged to help parents with this job. These programs take several forms, such as actual care for infants in child-care centers and discussion groups organized by parents. Most often, however, programs to enrich infants' development consist of home visits to individual parents by trained educators.

A good example is the Florida Parent Education Infant and Toddler Program (or PEP, for Parent Education Program). This program consists of a series of intervention projects for infants between the ages of three months and three years; it began in 1966 and continues in revised forms into the present (Jester & Guinagh, 1983). Altogether the projects have involved more than five hundred parents and infants as well as about fifty parent educators. The parents all come from poverty-level communities, as do the educators, who receive five weeks of special training by the PEP project before beginning their work. By using members of the parents' own communities, the project leaders hope to create better rapport between the parents and the parent educators.

After their training, the parent educators visit each family once a week for about thirty to sixty minutes per visit. During each visit they demonstrate at least one new activity that is appropriate for that infant's level of development. At the same time they discuss the activity with the parent (usually the mother) and often discuss any other concerns that she may have about her child as well. Project leaders devise activities from a variety of sources ranging from Piaget's cognitive tasks to standardized observations of infant development (Bayley, 1969; Gesell, 1943) and to informal opinions and personal experiences of the staff with infants. With a three-month-old, for example, one activity is simply to reach repeatedly for a toy animal. With a twelve-month-old, one activity is hiding a toy under a blanket (the AnotB problem).

The visits have created considerable warmth and support between the educators and many of the parents. But problems have occurred. For one thing, the adults are sometimes tempted to "test" the babies rather than simply encourage them to play and practice the new activities; once a child

has succeeded at an activity, both the parent and the educator tend to move on rapidly to the next activity in the sequence. Another problem has been balancing the educator's attention between the parent and the infant: some educators prefer to interact with the child and leave the parent feeling ignored. Still another problem concerns older siblings in the family: often they want special attention from the visitor, to the point where some mothers feel obliged to arrange baby-sitting for the siblings just to achieve enough quiet for a successful home visit.

In many ways the PEP project is typical of home-based programs to assist parents of infants. How successful are such programs, all things considered? In the short run, home visits produce important gains in infants' cognitive skills, as measured by standardized tests of infant IQ (Bayley, 1969). Home visits also make parents' interactions with their infants more positive and improve their self-esteem as parents (Slaughter, 1983). The long-run effects are not nearly as obvious, but longitudinal studies of parent education programs nonetheless suggest that there are several positive ones. Children from the PEP project have been much less likely than children from similar socioeconomic backgrounds to require special education classes or services when they enter elementary school.

In general, the exact curriculum selected for home-visit activities does not affect the success of the programs as much as do the warmth and enthusiasm of the parent educators who implement the activities (D. Powell, 1986). This finding does not mean, however, that curriculum is not important or that any curriculum will work with any child or parent. Instead it means that curriculum activities are probably construed or interpreted very differently by individual parents and children, depending on their individual needs and levels of development. In general, therefore, the curriculum may simply act to encourage parents to observe their infants more closely, to enjoy what they see in their infants, and to share their concerns and questions with another interested adult, the parent educator.

The AnotB error in particular supposedly reflects the child's dependence on overt actions or motor schemes of this type. But does it really? Maybe the error really shows the infant's poor memory, which has not yet developed very far. In the AnotB task, after all, the baby does at least have to remember, first, that the toy has been moved recently and, second, that it began by lying under the first blanket. As obvious as these ideas may seem to adults, a young infant may have trouble remembering them.

Memory effects

Considerable evidence suggests that memory does in fact affect infants' performance in the AnotB task. One study found that imposing slight delays on the infant's search interfered with performance much more for younger infants performance than for older ones (Kagan, 1979). Seven-month-olds who correctly

Effects of delays on performance

solved the problem without any delay could generally also tolerate a three-second delay before searching for the toy, but they failed if they had to wait seven seconds. Ten-month-olds could manage even seven seconds without difficulty.

These trends imply that infants find it demanding simply to remember the relevant facts in the task: where things are and are not located and when and whether they were in fact moved. Their memory problems, however, do not so much contradict Piaget's emphasis on motor development as supplement it. The most complete explanation of the AnotB error therefore seems to use both ideas: infants probably use memory when they can but supplement it with Piagetian motor schemes whenever necessary. If an infant cannot recall where the toy is hidden, at least she can reenact the means she used for finding it in the past (Butterworth, 1977). This multiple strategy actually resembles the way adults sometimes search for a lost object: if you cannot recall where you left it, you may retrace your steps up to the time you remember seeing it last — using, in essence, an action scheme.

The Effects of Motivation   Piaget's account of infancy implies that infants are motivated somewhat automatically if presented with moderate challenge or difficulty. They will perform "middling" tasks without much coaxing and within a reasonable time period if given a chance. This happens, according to Piaget, because of equilibration, which is the interplay of assimilation and accommodation; practicing a partially developed action scheme is its own reward. So adults should have a relatively easy time seeing an infant perform partially learned schemes, which are usually tasks of moderate difficulty.

All this may have been true for Piaget, who observed his own infant children in natural play in his own home. In many situations, however, motivation cannot be taken for granted, as research on infants frequently suggests. There are times, as every parent knows, when a baby is just too tired to look, or too indifferent to bother shaking a rattle, or too hungry to search for a hidden object. And there are times when he is just too content to do much of anything active. Often these conditions impair an infant's performance and make him seem more immature than he really is.

Often, too, such conditions simply create confusion about an infant's preferences. If a baby looks equally at two pictures, is it because she sees no differences between them, because she just likes the pictures equally well, or because she is patiently waiting for the experiment to finish? This kind of ambiguity seems to be inherent in any study that identifies human preferences simply by overt behavior.

Even adults sometimes lack object permanence: they may give up the search for a missing object without ever finding it and then forget that they even tried to search for it. Such behavior strongly resembles Stage 3 infant behavior. It happens particularly when adults do not really care whether they find the object or not. By the same token, babies asked to search for toys under blankets may not care whether they find the toys; from their point of view, the search may amount to just an arbitrary task. If so and if they fail to pursue the search, do they lack object permanence or merely lack interest in the task?

Performance Versus Competence   These questions about motivation illustrate a more general problem with Piagetian theory, as applied to both children and infants: by emphasizing the nature of competence, it tends to neglect the immediate causes of performance. An infant — or anyone, for that matter — may be *able* to do something without necessarily *choosing* to do it. Even if an infant does show his highest competence in one situation, he may fail, for various reasons, to do so in a situation that differs from the first one only slightly. As mentioned above, even a few seconds' delay can change some infants' success

A Talk with Melissa and Her Parents

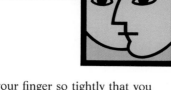

Infant Cognition and Communication

The interview and observations that follow are based on a visit with eight-month-old Melissa Diaz and her parents, Maria and Andrew, in their home.

Interviewer: How does Melissa let you know what she wants?

Maria: She makes little clicking sounds that are something like this. (She demonstrates.) And she also shakes her head. I think that she learned that from her older brother. He taught her that.

Interviewer: What is she trying to communicate with her head shaking?

Maria: I'm not sure. In the last couple of days she stopped doing that. A week ago she spent large portions of the day shaking her head "no."

Interviewer: Was it at times that she didn't want to do something, or was she just practicing?

Maria: No, no, I think that she just wanted to do something. To show us something.

Andrew: She's an understandable child.

Interviewer: How else does she communicate?

Maria: Of course, she cries when she is unhappy. And she is a very good smiler.

Interviewer: She seems to have noticed me again. She stopped for a minute to look at me and give a big smile.

Andrew: She is a wonderful smiler. She does use it to get attention. She also makes various baby-type sounds. She usually doesn't get upset, but when she does she has a good, loud cry.

Maria: She was always an easy baby to read. She whimpered or cried when she was unhappy and cooed and smiled when she was content, which was most of the time. If she was gassy after a feeding, she scrunched up her face in a funny way and you knew that you had to burp her.

Interviewer: She's looking at us. What do you think she is thinking? When you have a young baby, do you make guesses about what is going on inside her head?

Maria: We did that a lot with our first baby. We used to make up all this stuff about what he was doing. We were always trying to guess what he was thinking.

Andrew: The reason we would try to figure out what he was thinking and doing is that there was no doubt that you were dealing with another human being who had thoughts and clear motives and stuff, even when he was very young.

Interviewer: Even when he was two or three months old?

Andrew: Even that early. Certainly by the time he was Melissa's age. I mean, he almost demanded that style and level of interaction. You know, he wouldn't be happy until he had that level. Which is still true now.

Maria: Melissa is less outwardly directed. She will be happy by herself . . . finding things for herself to do for longer periods of time. As you can see, she's just going to play with her foot for a while. Check out her fingers. Hold her hand up in the air, looking at it just to see it.

Andrew: In a way, she is just as easy to communicate with, but just doesn't demand as much communication as her brother did when he was an infant.

Interviewer: What changes have you observed in Melissa's way of thinking and solving the problems she encounters?

Maria: Well, for the first month or so she probably didn't do too much thinking. She certainly was alert. She spent most of her time looking around at things and listening. She had a strong grip and would grab onto your finger so tightly that you could pick her up that way. And, of course, she was a good eater and spent a lot of time sucking.

Interviewer: How about when she was two or three months old?

Maria: Well, she was very quick to learn how to suck the nipple of a bottle and her pacifier, and by the time she was three months old she was able to grab her bottle and sort of hold it while she sucked, if you propped it up a little.

Andrew: I also noticed that she learned to look for you when you came into the room and turn her head when you talked to her. She also became very interested in playing with her fingers and seemed to be much better coordinated in general.

Interviewer: What about more recent developments, say, in the last two or three months?

Maria: Well, she certainly has learned to make noise. When she was six months old her grandmother gave her one of those little rubber froggies that squeak when you squeeze it. At first she was only able to make a sound with it by accident, but soon she learned to squeeze it again and again. She also has learned to make sounds in response to your talking to her, almost like carrying on a conversation.

Follow-up Questions

1. How closely does Melissa's development follow the stages described by Piaget?

2. Which of Piaget's cognitive stages do you think Melissa is currently beginning? Why?

3. Do you think that Melissa will be an early, average, or late talker? Why?

rates on the AnotB task, creating very different impressions about their abilities in the two conditions. Problems with distinguishing competence from performance crop up throughout psychology and throughout developmental psychology in particular. As it turns out, identifying the immediate causes of performance may be done more easily outside the Piagetian framework than inside it.

BEHAVIORAL LEARNING IN INFANCY

Three kinds of learned behavior

One framework for studying the specific performance of infants has come from **behaviorism,** or what psychologists sometimes also call **learning theory.** As described in Chapter 2, learning theory focuses on changes in specific behaviors (sometimes called responses) and on the specific, observable causes and consequences (stimuli and reinforcements) of these behaviors. Typically, learning theorists identify three kinds of behavioral learning: classical conditioning, operant conditioning, and imitation.

Infants show signs of all three types of learning, at least by the age of about three months. Infant psychologists have not concentrated equally on each type of learning, however. Instead, the large majority of studies of infant learning concern operant conditioning (Olson & Sherman, 1983). This fact makes conclusions about operant conditioning in infants more definite than those about the other types.

Classical Conditioning

Nature of UCS and CS

As described in Chapter 2, this form of conditioning consists of transferring control of a reflex response by pairing two stimuli together. One of the stimuli (the unconditional stimulus, or US) is chosen from among ones that automatically produce a particular unconditioned response (UR), and the other (the conditional stimulus, or CS), is chosen from among those that do not. Here is a simple example of how classical conditioning might occur for an infant:

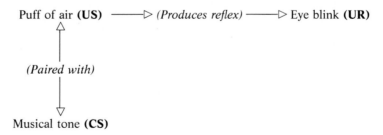

Although it may not matter much whether an infant blinks to music, certain other classically conditioned behaviors may well matter significantly to an infant's long-term development. One of these is the conditioning associated with a parent's face, a stimulus that initially is relatively neutral. Looking at a parent usually occurs together with a variety of emotional and physiological responses. Hunger pangs and hunger satisfaction often *both* occur in the presence of the parent's face because parents usually approach the baby when she is hungry and stay with her until after she finishes feeding. As diagrammed, the process looks like this:

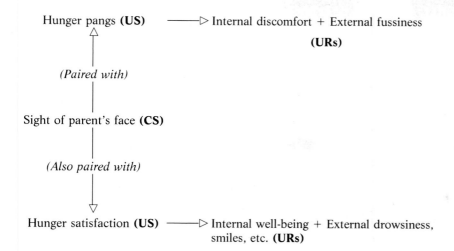

Eventually, therefore, the mere sight of the parent can trigger both positive and negative responses in the child. The multiple conditioning may foreshadow the emotional complexity of parent-child relationships that develops later in life and suggest one way that one person might develop "mixed feelings" about another person.

Classical conditioning occurs reliably and clearly from about the age of six months onward. Before that age, however, efforts to demonstrate this kind of conditioning have produced conflicting results. Some infant reflexes prove conditionable to some neutral stimuli, but not all combinations of stimuli and responses can be conditioned. The musical tone can in fact be conditioned to an eye-blink response even in three-month-old infants (Sameroff & Cavanaugh, 1979), but it cannot be conditioned successfully to a reflex change in infants' pupil size. A change in the lighting can reliably make infants' pupils get smaller, but pairing a tone with the change in lighting does not condition this reflex, no matter how many pairings occur.

Mixed results with infants

These irregularities imply that young infants may be genetically prepared to learn certain sorts of connections from their environment and genetically constrained from or limited in learning others. It is as if they notice some connections in their world, such as a tone and a puff of air, but not others, such as a tone and a change in brightness. Because such constraints have long been recognized in studies of conditioning among animals, it seems reasonable to expect analogous limitations among human beings (Hinde & Stevenson-Hinde, 1973). As infants become toddlers, they presumably overcome some of these limitations in classical conditioning, thanks in large part to their growing abilities to think and reason about connections among stimuli. Unfortunately, developmental psychologists have done little research to test this possibility among older infants and toddlers. Instead they have given the bulk of their attention to another form of behavioral learning: operant conditioning.

Genetic predispositions to some associations

Operant Conditioning

In this form of learning, infants get a reward or reinforcement if they perform some simple action or set of actions. By turning their heads, for example, they may get to see an interesting toy or picture; in this case the reinforcement is viewing the interesting toy, and head turning becomes the learned or conditioned behavior. Such actions tend to be performed more often than actions that are not reinforced.

Nature of operant conditioning

Many studies have found infants quite capable of learning through operant conditioning. Newborns will learn to suck on a pacifier more rapidly if doing so yields a tiny amount of sugar water; or they will learn to blink their eyes more often if doing so causes a pleasant voice to speak or a melody to play (Olson & Sherman, 1983). One reason that infants seem to learn to breast feed so easily is the strong reinforcement the behavior brings in the form of mother's milk and motherly comfort.

Operant learning versus reflex responses

As with classical conditioning, infants are predisposed to learn these particular behaviors. All examples of operant conditioning in infants rely on those few behaviors that young babies can already do, which are mainly their inborn reflexes. By nature, reflexes occur easily — in fact, almost *too* easily. As parents often discover, for example, any slight provocation — such as a touch on the baby's cheek — can stimulate sucking movements in young babies. Such readiness to respond creates confusion about when infant responses really constitute learning rather than general excitement. For example, when do sucking movements show true operant learning: a specific behavior performed more often because a specific reinforcement results from it? And when do sucking movements simply amount to a reflex that is itching to occur, so to speak, and that would happen in response to almost any stimulus?

The confusion between learning and excitement diminishes as babies grow older because they acquire behaviors that are more truly voluntary. Even as babies get older, however, they acquire many behaviors, both desirable and regrettable, through what appears to be operant conditioning. A six- or nine-month-old will babble longer and more frequently if parents smile and express praise when he does so. A twelve-month-old will learn to wave good-bye sooner and more frequently if reinforced with praise or encouragement. And a two-year-old may learn to scream at her older sibling when she wants a toy that the older child has because her screaming has been inadvertently reinforced: it causes the older child simply to abandon the toy, or it summons a parent who assumes (not always accurately) that the older child somehow caused the screaming.

Imitation

Bridges   When do infants begin to imitate?

As make-believe play demonstrates, children obviously learn to imitate at some point in development; but exactly how early, and by what processes? Early research on these questions generally found that infants could engage in different kinds of imitation at different points during infancy. In general, they imitated actions that they could see themselves perform sooner than they imitated actions that they could observe only in a model. Imitating a hand gesture such as waving, for example, proved easier than imitating an unusual face made by an adult (Uzgiris & Hunt, 1975). And deferred imitation proved hardest of all: only children nearing their second birthday could save their imitations until the day after they saw a model perform them (McCall et al., 1977). All of these findings are consistent with Piaget's theory of infant cognition.

But these studies do not tell the whole story about imitation in infancy. Other research has found what seems to be imitation performed even by newborn infants (Meltzoff, 1988). One-week-old babies tend to stick out their tongues in imitation of adults and wiggle their fingers after seeing adults model this behavior. Distinguishing voluntary imitation from general, automatic excitement, however, remains a problem, as it does with other studies of very young babies. One research study highlighted this ambiguity especially well: it showed babies pictures of human faces depicting various emotions (Kaitz et al., 1988). Although the babies responded with emotional facial expressions of their own, the expressions of the babies did not match those in the pictures. In fact the emotions on

Imitation provides a rich source of learning for most infants and toddlers, as it apparently has done for this young telephone conversationalist. To occur, though, imitation depends both on symbolic thought and on motor skills, both of which improve rapidly as children move into the preschool years.

the babies' faces were hard to classify at all; they just looked "wrought up" at the sight of expressive human faces. At present, therefore, we still have more to learn about the origins of imitation during the newborn period.

LANGUAGE ACQUISITION

When Michael, the son of one of the authors, was an infant, he went through several phases in using language.

■ At twelve weeks of age, Michael made openmouthed cooing noises when he was feeling content. Sometimes these sounds were vaguely similar to ordinary vowel sounds, but they seemed to vary unpredictably. Michael cooed a lot in the morning when he first woke up, which pleased his father and mother. His sister said that his cooing sounded rather like the heavy breathing of an obscene telephone call, but his parents disagreed (and wondered how on earth his sister knew what obscene calls sounded like).

■ By six months of age, Michael had added consonant sounds to his vocalizations to produce complicated babbling noises. His most productive time for this activity continued to be the morning, although he "said" quite a lot whenever he was feeling generally content. Certain sounds seemed to be favorites: "da" and "gn." Sometimes Michael repeated these and other sounds — "da, da, da, da." His father thought Michael repeated sounds when he was feeling especially happy.

■   At fifteen months, Michael could produce about six words, but he did not pronounce them as adults would. The family cat was "dat"; his favorite food, yogurt, sounded like "yugun"; and airplanes were simply "der!" (as in "Look there"?). He seemed to understand dozens of words and sentences, although it was hard to be sure because he probably picked up clues about meaning from the behavior of his parents. When Michael was tired one day, he came immediately when his mother said, "Come sit here" in a sympathetic tone of voice. But when she said the same thing in a cross tone of voice the next day, he looked at her with an impish smile and went the other way.

■   At about his second birthday, Michael sat "reading" a children's book to himself. Occasionally real phrases could be heard ("bug ate leaf"), but mostly Michael sounded as if he were mumbling or as if he were talking in the next room. When he finished, he walked to the kitchen and phrased a three-word question: "What's for lunch?"

As these examples show, a great deal of language develops during infancy; indeed, language is one of the most clearly human of all developments of this age period and perhaps of the entire life span.

Language has several aspects, and infants must acquire them all to become verbally competent. First, they must learn the sounds of the language — its **phonology.** Second, they must begin learning something of its purposes and meanings — its **semantics.** And third, they must piece together its organization — its **syntax.** Infants must learn to use all three aspects of language in two ways: both to talk meaningfully and to listen with comprehension.

Phonology and semantics develop rapidly during infancy and are therefore the focus of this chapter. Syntax, however, begins developing late in infancy, when children begin combining words together into phrases and sentences. Because syntactic development finishes well after infancy — around age four or even later — it is discussed with other aspects of early childhood cognition in Chapter 9.

Three aspects of language

Theories of Language Acquisition

How can infants make such major cognitive strides in a matter of just months? Linguists and psychologists have proposed several theories to answer this question. Learning theories of language suggest several processes that may affect language acquisition. Originally one of these processes was thought to be reinforcement: parents praise or respond to their babies' vocalization and in so doing stimulate more mature forms of language (Skinner, 1957). This idea makes some sense for parents of infants who have not yet learned to speak; just looking at babies often makes them coo and babble more (Harris, 1983). It is not true, however, for parents of toddlers and preschoolers. Research shows conclusively that parents of these children respond just as positively to ungrammatical utterances as to grammatical ones (P. DeVilliers & DeVilliers, 1978), so reinforcement cannot be shaping or modifying children's language toward more mature forms.

More likely learning processes are mutual imitation and accommodation. Infants and parents engage in games of mutual imitation even before the infants can speak (Stern, 1977). One of them utters a noise or a coo; then the delighted partner responds with the same noise or coo, which is followed by another imitation, and so on. In games like these, infants not only practice the phonology or sounds of their native language but also practice taking conversational turns.

Learning theories of language

Limits of reinforcement

Imitation of language

As a child begins to acquire a usable vocabulary and syntax, her parents may also simplify and rephrase their utterances to make them more accessible to her. These efforts seem to model language more effectively for toddlers by giving them samples of language to study as they converse.

For some linguists, even imitation and accommodation do not go far enough in explaining the ease and speed with which infants acquire language. They propose a nativist theory instead; all human beings, they argue, are genetically predisposed to acquire language (Chomsky, 1976). The inborn skills that accomplish this task are sometimes called the **language acquisition device (LAD).** Evidence for LAD comes from three facts: (a) that all healthy infants acquire language without explicit training, (b) that no other species of animal acquires language to nearly the same extent as the human species does, and (c) that certain areas of the brain become clearly specialized for language functions during childhood.

LAD and inborn language predisposition

The debate between learning theories of language and nativist theories of language is far from over — if indeed it ever will be. Because of its importance and complexity, we return to these issues in more detail in Chapter 9, which discusses language development in preschool children. First, however, let us look at the steps that infants actually go through as they acquire their native language.

Phonology

Every language uses a finite number of sounds, or **phonemes,** which combine to make the words of the language. English has about forty-one of these, which are illustrated in Table 6.2. Particular phonemes result from particular physical arrangements of the vocal apparatus: the tongue, mouth, nose, throat, and vocal cords. Often very small physical changes in the apparatus can create distinctively different phonemes. The sounds /th/ and /t/, for example, differ primarily in

Nature of phonemes

TABLE 6.2 The Phonemes of English

Vowel	As in:	Consonant	As in:
a	can, carrot	b	bet, nib
ā	late, day	d	dog, bid
ä	father, mama	f	fog, cuff
		g	gas, big
e	men, ferry	h	hot, ahead
ē	be, honey	j	job, fudge
		k	kiss, sick
i	bit, mist	l	list, mellow
ī	pie, nice	m	mother, slim
		n	nut, can
ō	open, hoe	p	pod, cup
ô	claw, for	r	rug, sort, clear
oo	cool, flew	s	sit, hiss
oo	cook, bull	t	tar, bit
yoo	use, dew	v	vast, cave
yoo	union, sure	w	wish, sweet
oi	foil, boy	y	yes, opinion
ou	out, loud	z	zoo, ooze
u	but, color	ch	check, catch
ur	curse, infer	sh	shoe, fashion
		th	thin, bath
ə	around, item, circus	th	this, bathe
		zh	measure, seizure
ər	larder, persuade		
		ng	sing, ringer

Note: The examples given for each phoneme often sound slightly different from each other but are grouped together because they are commonly perceived as the "same" sound.

how tightly the tongue is held against the upper teeth. Holding it loosely causes air to leak out and creates the sound /th/, as in *there*; holding it tightly leads to an explosion of air and creates the sound /t/, as in *tear*. In typical speech we often produce sounds partway between /th/ and /t/, but these inaccurate phonemes are almost always perceived as if they belong squarely to one category or the other. We hear the badly spoken examples as either a true /th/ or a true /t/.

Perceiving Phonemes   In acquiring language, infants must learn to notice phonemes and to ignore any meaningless variations. Although the task may seem demanding, it actually proves surprisingly easy, even for a baby. It proves so easy, in fact, that some language specialists suspect that human beings are genetically and physiologically disposed toward noticing phonemic differences (Eimas & Miller, 1980).

A variety of evidence supports this possibility. As mentioned earlier in this chapter, infants just one month old can distinguish between vocalizations and nonhuman sounds. They tend to turn toward the source of the vocalizing and to show other physical signs of attending to human voices even in the midst of nonhuman noise (R. Eisenberg, 1976). At the very least, such attention should make learning phonemic distinctions possible, although not inevitable.

Categorical perception of sounds

Infants also seem disposed to hear certain phonemes categorically, which means that they perceive sounds as belonging completely to one phoneme or another, never as partway in between (Eimas & Miller, 1980, 1981). Such categorical perception should make language acquisition inherently easier. It is not, however, a uniquely human ability. Similar perceptual abilities exist in rhesus monkeys (Morse & Snowdon, 1975) and even in chinchillas (Kuhl, 1976); yet monkeys and chinchillas do not learn to talk! Presumably they lack other crucial skills, anatomy, and experiences that human infants normally have. So perception of phonemes must be necessary to language acquisition but not sufficient for it.

Intrinsic motivation to babble

Babbling   Although skill at producing phonemes takes longer to develop, it, too, seems biologically influenced. Sometime between four to eight months of age, infants begin babbling in increasingly complex and random ways. They apparently do so for the sole reward of hearing themselves vocalize — an example of a Piagetian primary circular reaction.

What suggests that babbling is motivated intrinsically? For one thing, the sounds made during babbling go far beyond the phonemes uttered by a child's parents, so babies apparently do not learn to babble by directly imitating the language they hear. For another thing, even deaf children babble in normal ways, except that they stop somewhat abruptly around their first birthday, presumably because they lack the reward of hearing themselves speak (Lenneberg, 1967).

Bridges   Do deaf children babble?

Immunity to teaching

Babbling persists well into the second year and overlaps with the appearance of the child's first meaningful words. Unlike the development of words and verbal utterances, however, it never proves susceptible to teaching. Parents can increase a baby's overall amount of babbling by reinforcing it with smiles and praise, but they cannot influence the selection of particular babbling sounds (Dodd, 1972). When infants finally do begin using the sounds of their own language, they apparently do so partly by their own choice and in the context of producing their first real words. At that point, which happens around the first birthday, parents' language also starts influencing infants' language more directly, as is explained later in this chapter. Overall, therefore, infants who babble convey the impression of being predisposed to acquire language, but they also convey an impression of not yet being quite ready for full-fledged dialogue.

Learning the melody of language

Late in infancy, some babbling may sound rather like true language because it becomes quite complex and because it acquires the normal **intonation,** or rise and fall in vocal pitch, of the child's native language (Bernstein-Ratner, 1987).

Mostly, however, babbling seems simply to reflect the baby's pleasure at hearing himself speak. Given its playful quality, adults usually enjoy hearing him "speak" as well.

Semantics and First Words

The semantics (or meanings) of a language are never mastered fully, even by adults. To test this idea on yourself, scan any page of a large unabridged dictionary and see how far you must go before you encounter an unfamiliar word. Most people, it seems, never learn even a majority of the words or terms in their native language. This happens partly because words get much of their meaning from the real world rather than from each other. Most of us simply do not live long enough to learn all of these relationships with the real world.

Learning semantics, therefore, is something that children begin in infancy but do not nearly complete (see Table 6.3). Somewhere around their first birthday, most infants will use their first words or at least make sounds that parents take to be words. By their second birthday, they may be using as many as fifty words appropriately. Nevertheless, at this age, some children may still be acquiring their first words, and most still have only a shaky, limited command of many words. From ages two to three, vocabulary increases rapidly, thanks partly to the child's newly emerging skill with longer sentences. An average three-year-old may know several hundred words; an average five- or six-year-old can use a few thousand words, or about one-half the vocabulary she will ever command, even as an adult (L. Dunn & Dunn, 1981). Note this, however: the averages hide large differences among individual children, both in the overall size of their vocabularies and, as explained below, in the types of words that they select to learn.

These figures refer only to children's **expressive language,** which is their ability actually to use a word appropriately in conversation. Expressive language is complemented by **receptive language,** which is the ability to understand or comprehend language used by others. Generally, receptive language develops

TABLE 6.3   Milestones in Language Acquisition During Infancy

Approximate Age	Vocal Accomplishment
4 weeks	Cries of displeasure
12 weeks	Contented cooing, squealing, gurgling; occasional vowel sounds.
20 weeks	First signs of babbling; most vowel sounds, but only occasional consonants
6 months	Babbling well established: full range of vowel sounds and many consonants
12 months	Babbling includes the melody or intonation of the language; utterances signal emotions; first words are produced; the child understands several words and simple commands
18 months	Expressive vocabulary between three and fifty words; intricate babbling interspersed with real words; occasional two- and three-word sentences
24 months	Expressive vocabulary between fifty and three hundred words, although not all used accurately; babbling gone; many two-word sentences or even longer; nonadult grammar; the child understands most simple language intended for him

Source: P. DeVilliers and DeVilliers (1978).

Siblings serve as important models of behavior and language for younger infants as they grow and develop.

sooner than expressive language; put in plainer terms, babies can understand more than they can say. The difference in receptive and expressive capacities shows up in many exchanges between parents and their infants. For example, if a father asks his ten-month-old, "Can I have a bite of your cookie?" the baby may offer him one. The same infant may not use any of those words himself for several more months or combine them into a sentence for another year or more.

One-word utterances

Functions of First Words   The first words of a child are sometimes called **holophrases** — literally, "whole phrases" — because the child often uses one word to express a complete thought. Like the longer utterances of adults, holophrases serve a variety of purposes, depending on the situation or context. Sometimes infants utter a word in order to get or deal with an object, saying "Hankie!" to mean "I'm now going to reach for the handkerchief." Or they may use a word to guide or regulate the actions of people; the same "Hankie!" may then mean "Please play peek-a-boo with me using the handkerchief." Or they may simply use a word to comment on a situation, as a sort of infant version of idle conversation; in that case, "Hankie!" may just mean "Look at that interesting handkerchief right there with the pretty colors on it."

Interpreting holophrases

Knowing which function the child intends depends on knowing the situation in which she is speaking as well as something about her growing interests and previous experiences. Responding to one-word utterances therefore involves guesswork, even for the best of parents. Interpreting them is made easier, however, by the fact that children learn to communicate even before they acquire verbal holophrases to attach to their nonverbal messages (Nelson & Lucareillo, 1985). Gestures, facial expressions, and the like can and do accomplish a wide range of communicative functions. Because the nonlinguistic cues continue after a child begins speaking first words, they sometimes provide a way of "translating" the first words into more elaborate, adult language.

Bridges   What words do children use first?

Individual Differences in First Words   What words do children use first? On the whole, they seem to prefer objects that stand out from their surroundings in some way: ones that move, or make noise, or go away and come back (Greenfield, 1982). The child's own mother or father may fulfill these criteria but often not as well as some other people and things around the house do. *Dog* may appear as an early word more than *sun* or *diaper* does, even though the latter two objects are probably experienced more frequently and universally by children than dogs are (Nelson, 1985). Proud parents notwithstanding, words for family members — including *mama* and *daddy* — may appear early but not necessarily at the very beginning.

In spite of some overlap, children continue to differ as they expand their vocabularies. Researchers found that one- and two-year-olds learned nonsense words more easily if those words were constructed from the phonemes already in their very first words. They learned *bex* faster if its sounds — /b/, /e/, and /x/ — were already occurring in words of their existing vocabularies (R. Schwartz & Leonard, 1982). This trend suggests that infants may pick and choose new vocabulary, at least at first; perhaps they bias their selection in favor of words that they already find easy to pronounce.

Impact of phonemes

Other research finds that children vary in how much they emphasize different language functions in their first utterances (Nelson, 1981). Some use their first language to refer to objects and objective events — *car* and *book* and so on — whereas others use it more to express feelings and relationships — *hello* and *goody*! Presumably these differences are encouraged partly by differing family environments. Some families, after all, may speak of objects more than of feelings, or vice versa. But to some extent word preferences may also represent a learning strategy adopted by the child; just as he may find a word easier if he already knows the phonemes in it, so he may also find an utterance easier if he has already used similar ones on previous occasions.

Object words versus feeling words

Parental Influences on Language Acquisition   Even though many of these comments may make language acquisition seem beyond human influence, parents do in fact affect this process. When infants are very young, parents will often talk with them as if they were full-fledged adult partners in a conversation. Consider this mother speaking to her three-month-old child:

Bridges In what ways do parents influence infants' language acquisition?

MOTHER: How is Kristi today? (pause) How are you? (pause) Good, you say? (pause) Are you feeling good? (pause) I'm glad for that. (pause) Yes, I am. (pause) What would you like now? (pause) Your soother? (pause) Um? (pause) Is that what you want? (pause) Okay, here it is.

By asking questions in this "conversation," the mother implies that Kristi is capable of responding, even though her infant is really much too young to do so. Furthermore, the mother leaves pauses for her baby's hypothetical responses. Observations of these kinds of pauses show that they last just about as long as in conversations between adults (Roth, 1987); it is as if the mother is giving her baby a turn to speak before taking another turn herself. When her child remains silent, the mother even replies on her behalf. In all these behaviors, the mother teaches something of turn taking in conversations, and she expresses her faith that the infant will eventually learn these conventions herself.

Turn-taking exchanges

When infants finally do begin speaking, parents continue this strategy. At the same time, however, they also simplify their language significantly. Sentences become shorter, although not as short as the child's, and vocabulary becomes simpler, although not as restricted as the child's (Garvey, 1984). These extra strategies help teach a new lesson — namely, that words and sentences do in fact communicate and that language is more than interesting noises and babbling. By keeping just ahead of the infant's own linguistic skills, parents can stimulate the further development of language.

Parents' response to early language

This style is sometimes called **motherese,** meaning a dialect or version of language characteristic of mothers talking with young children (Gelman & Shatz, 1977). In addition to shorter sentences and simpler vocabulary, speech in motherese has several unique features. It tends to unfold more slowly than speech

The dialect of parenting

A Multicultural View

Cognitive Effects of Verbal Interaction

Around the world, societies show wide differences in when and how much mothers speak with their infants, and some of the differences have important effects on children's eventual cognitive development. One study documented mothers' differences in five societies: a town in rural Kenya, an Indian (not Hispanic) village in southern Mexico, a small town in Italy, a large city in Sweden, and suburban Boston (Richman et al., 1988). On the whole, the interactions of American and European mothers emphasized looking at and talking with their infants: mothers more often engaged in extended one-way "conversations," even with three-month-olds, while looking directly at the babies. In these societies, on average, such dialogues increased in frequency and duration as a child neared her first birthday; at the same time holding and cuddling decreased in frequency. Kenyan and Mexican mothers, in contrast, spent more time in physical contact with their babies, no matter what their babies' age. In fact, these mothers carried or fastened the infants to their backs almost constantly each day, interrupting this contact only to nurse or feed them. Verbal interaction and extended, direct gazing at the infants happened relatively infrequently.

Such differences apparently stem from a mixture of living conditions and cultural beliefs about children's cognitive competence. In many societies (including the Kenyan and Mexican Indian ones), mothers have considerable housework to get done and relatively little adult help in doing it. Frequently, they recruit older children as assistant housekeepers and child-minders, but even this strategy still leaves them with more demanding duties of housework than in more technologically advanced soci-

Constant close contact between mother and infant, as in Kenya, may encourage more nonverbal communication and result in infants who fuss less than is customary in North American society.

between adults and to use a higher and more variable or singsong pitch; it generally contains unusually strong emphasis on key words ("Give me your *cup*"). Parents speaking motherese also tend to repeat or paraphrase themselves more than usual ("Give me the cup. The cup. Find the cup, and give it."). Presumably the repeated attempts are needed just for parents to make themselves understood, although they probably also give the infant practice in comprehending the relationships among sentences and in responding appropriately.

Language exposure and competence

Research shows clearly that parents' conversations with infants are extremely important to the infants' development. The Harvard Preschool Project, a longitudinal study conducted at Harvard University, observed the contacts (both social and nonsocial) between parents and their infants that occurred naturally in the families' own homes (B. White et al., 1979; B. White, 1985). At various intervals the infants were assessed both for their intelligence and for their social skills. When the assessments were correlated with the results of the home observations, one result stood out clearly: the most competent infants, intellectually and socially, had parents who directed large amounts of language at them. The most competent received about twice as much language as the least competent infants in this study did. But the most competent infants also stimu-

eties (B. Whiting & Edwards, 1988). Under these conditions, mothers often have little time left for verbal interactions with infants.

Yet lack of verbal interaction also reflects beliefs about children's competence. Among natives of the Solomon Islands (in the southern Pacific Ocean), parents generally believe that infants can understand a lot of language long before they can produce any (Watson-Gegeo & Gegeo, 1986). The islanders also value verbal skills highly. In spite of relatively heavy work loads, therefore, mothers speak to infants a lot, beginning well before the infants' first birthday, with the intention of accelerating specific verbal skills.

How does being talked to affect infants' development? Within North American society, maternal talk during infancy correlates significantly with babies' competence several years later, when they have become preschoolers. Children who have verbally interactive mothers during infancy show better language comprehension as four-year-olds and show higher competence at solving simple problems involving both verbal and nonverbal reasoning (Bornstein & Tamis-Lemonda, 1989).

But the reasons for the benefits of maternal talk are not really clear. Maternal talk probably is much too complex for a three-month-old or a six-month-old infant to learn directly. Perhaps instead of providing language models directly, mothers' talk during early infancy simply reflects a lasting personal quality that becomes helpful later: parents who enjoy talking when their babies are very young are likely to still enjoy talking several years later, when their babies have become toddlers and preschoolers capable of more efficient verbal learning.

Another benefit of early maternal talk may lie with its responsiveness, especially when a baby is *not* in distress. A child's grunts, gestures, and smiles often communicate meaning long before the child can use words or sentences. A parent's prompt, verbal response to these sounds may help build an infant's confidence that he is an effective communicator and in this indirect way encourage the child to learn and use verbal communication later in childhood.

So far, however, these benefits of maternal talk have been demonstrated primarily for mainstream North American society, where verbal skills and verbal reasoning are valued highly. When this sort of language is not valued as much, a lot of North American–style maternal talk may *not* benefit an infant; it may instead make the baby too talkative for the community and leave the baby out of place.

*Some North American language skills, furthermore, can be unpleasant, even by North American standards. Cross-cultural studies consistently show, in particular, that babies fuss more in North American society than in others and make more verbal demands for attention, using whatever language or vocabulary they currently have at their command (LeVine, 1988). These behaviors seem to result at least partially from the verbal emphasis that North American mothers foster. As a rule, societies that emphasize close physical contact between mother and infant, such as in Kenya or southern Mexico, have infants who fuss less and who in this way seem more content.

Bridges Why do North American babies fuss more and make more verbal demands than do babies in Kenya or Mexico?

lated interactions with their parents, primarily by procuring various simple kinds of help, for instance, in pouring a glass of juice or placing the final block on a tower. These "services" probably benefited the infants by offering many opportunities for parents to talk with them ("Shall I put the block on top?").

More recent research shows that certain types of conversation can encourage children's language development (Snow et al., 1987). One helpful kind is *contingent dialogue,* which is conversation that responds sensitively, specifically, and immediately to children's verbalizations. When an infant says "Teddy?" to his parent, for example, the parent does not ignore the comment but replies or extends it meaningfully — perhaps by saying "I'm not sure where Teddy is; I haven't seen him this morning" or "Would you like Teddy now?"

Responsive conversations

Another valuable kind of conversation is "scripted" or *textual dialogue,* which is routine or ritualized language embedded in a highly familiar situation. The setting itself is so familiar that it assists in interpreting the language. Many everyday routines promote this kind of language: bathing and diapering, for example, encourage the same predictable remarks time after time ("Are you wet?" "First let's take your shirt off" and so on). So do children's songs and nursery rhymes. In spite of their repetitiveness — in fact, precisely because

Routine conversations

When talking with infants, adults and even older children tend to speak "motherese," a simplified form of talking that helps infants and toddlers acquire language.

of it — textual dialogues allow children to place language in a larger, more meaningful context.

Paradoxically, however, a bit of parental *in*sensitivity or conversational *in*competence may also help infants to develop their language skills. Moderate ignorance about an infant's intended meanings can challenge the infant to speak more fully and explicitly. This sort of "beneficial ignorance" seems to account for how fathers and siblings help the development of infant language (Mannle & Tomasello, 1987). Because fathers and siblings tend to know an infant less well than mothers do (in spite of changing family roles), they speak relatively explicitly and elaborately with one- and two-year-olds. And they prompt relatively explicit language from the infants in return.

Given the number of ways that parents and other people can stimulate language acquisition, it is not really surprising that nearly all children acquire high verbal competence in just a few years (Genishi & Dyson, 1984). Universal success at learning to talk does not mean that adults have no influence on this important cognitive skill. It means instead that language acquisition is "overdetermined": society supports language learning in so many ways that if a child fails to experience that support in one way, she is still likely to experience it in some other way.

THE END OF INFANCY

The word *infant* comes from a Latin term meaning "not speaking." By this standard, a child approaching his second birthday is no longer an infant. He is talking now and is often using more than one word at a time.

Almost from birth he communicates nonverbally: he smiles and frowns,

Perspectives

The Effects of Hearing Loss on Language Development

The sense of hearing contributes a great deal to the normal development of language. *Infants with significant hearing loss cannot distinguish the usual phonemes or sounds of their language, and words and phrases seem indistinct. As a result, cracking the code of language does not come as easily to such children as it does to most others. And they cannot be sure that their own speech reproduces their native language accurately.

Because of these difficulties, children with hearing impairments tend to lag behind most children in verbal skills. Children with hearing loss tend to test relatively poorly on standardized intelligence tests (Furth, 1973), which rely heavily on language in all of its forms. In taking such a test, children must listen to spoken instructions, read problems or statements, and state things clearly to an examiner. All of these activities pose more of a challenge to those with hearing impairment, especially if their hearing loss is very great.

Part of the problem lies with their lack of opportunity for verbal give-and-take. Infants (and children) profit from chances to engage in conversation actively: to respond to others' comments using whatever language skills they command at the moment. This fact was illustrated dramatically by one hearing child whose parents were profoundly deaf (Bard & Sachs, 1977). The parents were anxious that their child's language should not be impaired by their own linguistic limitations, so they encouraged their child to watch as much television as possible in order to give him lots of "good" language models to imitate.

Unfortunately, however, simply listening to others talk on television did not help the child's language at all. By the time he was three and one-half he still could not speak normally. He could lip-read somewhat, however, and communicate with his deaf parents by using standard sign language. He could also use a few words (like *Kool-Aid*) that he had picked up from watching television, but he could not combine them into strings that made meaningful phrases or sentences. Fortunately, speech therapy helped this boy to acquire oral skills relatively quickly. In his case, therapy consisted of lots of chances to converse.

As it happens, this case also shows the ease with which infants and children learn languagelike systems of communication, even if the system happens not to rely on the usual verbal skills. The lip-reading that this boy apparently learned naturally derived its structure and sense from the same grammar and semantics that hearing children learn, and so did the sign language that the boy learned. Making signs and lip-reading were just as complicated as oral speaking and listening, yet just as easy for him to learn. These facts give strong support to the idea that human infants are predisposed to learn language in one or another of its many forms and to use it conversationally (Garvey, 1984; Geschwind, 1985).

*Bridges How does hearing impairment in infants affect their language development?

gestures and babbles. He uses these skills to both develop and demonstrate his cognitive abilities, but he also uses them to develop social relationships, as described in the next chapter. Both by thinking and by communicating, the two-year-old learns who he is as well as who his parents and siblings are. At the same time, when all goes well, he becomes attached to these people as individuals, and his early, vague emotions turn into feelings with more focus. Pleasure becomes love, rage becomes anger, and anxiety becomes fearfulness. As the next chapter shows, these are not mere changes in labels; they signify real emotional and social growth.

SUMMARY OF MAJOR IDEAS

1. Perception is the immediate organization and interpretation of sensation, whereas cognition refers to all the processes (including perception) by which humans acquire knowledge.

Ways of Studying Perception and Cognition in Infants

2. Infants' arousal is reflected by changes in their heart rates (HRs), as long as the stimuli that caused arousal are relatively gentle and persistent.

3. Infants' recognition of the familiar is reflected by their habituation to stimuli — the tendency to attend to novel stimuli and to ignore familiar ones.

Infant Perception

4. Studies of visual perception show that infants under six months of age perceive, or at least respond to, a variety of lines and patterns, such as those usually found on a human face.

5. Young infants, including newborns, show size and shape constancy in visual perception, which means that they respond to objects somewhat independently of their distance and orientation.

6. Infants also show sensitivity to depth, as in the visual cliff experiments, as well as to objects that loom at them.

7. Infants do not orient themselves in space reliably and accurately until they are nearly eighteen months old.

8. Newborns can already localize sounds to some extent, but babies do not do this accurately until about six months of age.

Infant Cognition

9. Piaget has proposed six stages of infant cognitive development during which infants' schemes become less egocentric and increasingly symbolic and organized.

10. The most important achievement of these six stages is the use of symbolic representation, as shown by infants' increasingly firm belief in object permanence.

11. Research on Piaget's six stages generally confirms his original observations, but it also raises questions about the integration of early schemes and about the effects of motor skills, memory, and motivation on infants' cognitive performance.

Behavioral Learning in Infancy

12. Learning theory offers a framework for understanding immediate, specific changes in infant behavior.

13. Like children and adults, infants typically experience three kinds of behavioral learning: classical conditioning, operant conditioning, and imitation.

14. Behavioral learning tends to be ambiguous among infants less than three months old because it is difficult to distinguish learning from general, automatic excitement.

Language Acquisition

15. To become verbally competent, babies must learn the phonology (sound), semantics (meaning), and syntax (organization) of language.

16. Babbling begins around six months of age and becomes increasingly complex until it disappears from use sometime before the infant's second birthday.

17. Around their first birthday, infants begin using single words, or holophrases, to serve a variety of language functions.

18. Infants show important individual differences in their selection of first words, but generally they use words for objects in their environment that are distinctive in some way.

19. Parents probably influence language acquisition mainly through modeling simplified utterances, recasting their infant's own utterances, and directing considerable language at the infant as she grows.

KEY TERMS

perception (188)
cognition (188)
habituation (190)
object constancy (192)
size constancy (192)
shape constancy (193)
depth perception (194)
visual cliff (194)
sensorimotor intelligence (198)
egocentric (198)
scheme (198)
assimilation (198)
accommodation (199)
circular reaction (200)
primary circular reaction (200)
secondary circular reaction (200)
object permanence (201)
AnotB error (202)
tertiary circular reaction (202)
deferred imitation (204)
behaviorism (210)
learning theory (210)
phonology (214)
semantics (214)
syntax (214)
language acquisition device (LAD) (215)
phoneme (215)
intonation (216)
expressive language (217)
receptive language (217)
holophrase (218)
motherese (219)

WHAT DO YOU THINK?

1. Given the research described at the beginning of this chapter, what would you tell an enthusiastic new mother who is convinced that her four-week-old infant recognizes and responds to her more than to any other person?

2. If infants perceive constancies of size, shape, and depth even during the first few months of life, does this fact imply that they really acquire object permanence well before Piaget's theory says that they do?

3. Between about eight and twelve months of age, some babies show distress at separations from their primary caregiver (usually the mother). How might Piaget's theory of infant cognition explain why this distress occurs?

4. Think about how you might get through a day using only one-word utterances or at most two-word utterances. How would you keep from being misunderstood, and how would you satisfy your various needs?

FOR FURTHER READING

Bower, T. G. R. *The Rational Infant: Learning in Infancy.* New York: W. H. Freeman, 1989.

Lamb, M., and Campos, J. *Development in Infancy: An Introduction.* New York: Random House, 1982.

A number of texts about infant development are available, but these two are especially good at conveying a feel for *how* research is done on infants — how one study evolves out of another and why this field of research can be especially intriguing. Bower presents persuasive evidence that infants can "think" more fully than most people (including Piaget) expect, although his interpretations are not shared by all psychologists.

DeVilliers, P., and DeVilliers, J. *Early Language.* Cambridge, MA: Harvard University Press, 1979.

Genishi, C., and Dyson, A. *Language Assessment in the Early Years.* Norwood, NJ: Ablex Press, 1984.

These are two very readable accounts of language acquisition, beginning at birth and extending through the preschool years. The DeVilliers book is intended to stimulate interest but not to be especially thorough. Genishi and Dyson serves a similar purpose but is more comprehensive (see their chapters on language in school settings).

Dittman, L. (ed.). *The Infants We Care For.* Washington, DC: National Association for the Education of Young Children, 1986.

Bredekamp, S. (ed.). *Developmentally Appropriate Practice in Early Childhood Education Programs Serving Children from Birth Through Age 8,* expanded ed. Washington, DC: National Association for the Education of Young Children, 1987.

The first book (Dittman's) describes what you need to know in order to set up and run a child-care center for infants. The second book covers similar material but also includes information about preschool centers. In the eyes of many early childhood educators, the second book (Bredekamp's) comes close to "the" authoritative statement of the "right" way to work with infants and preschoolers.

Gleason, J. (ed.). *The Development of Language.* Columbus, OH: Merrill, 1985.

This is a still more comprehensive introduction, written by a half-dozen different authors. Like the two shorter language books above, this one takes a functional, or "language-use," perspective, which is the most dominant current perspective in language study.

Sutton-Smith, B. *Toys and Culture.* New York: Gardner Press, 1986.

Sutton-Smith is partly anthropologist (someone who studies cultures) as well as psychologist (someone who studies individuals). He brings both perspectives to this book, showing what toys *mean* to children and to adults. He argues that toys are not trivial; they reflect and shape deep values about family, education, modern technology, and economics. This is an interesting, sometimes disturbing book.

White, B. *The First Three Years of Life,* rev. ed. Englewood Cliffs, NJ: Prentice-Hall, 1985.

This book discusses the cognitive development of infants and toddlers, primarily from the point of view of parents. It offers suggestions for fostering optimal cognitive development based partly on the results of the Harvard Preschool Project discussed at the end of this chapter.

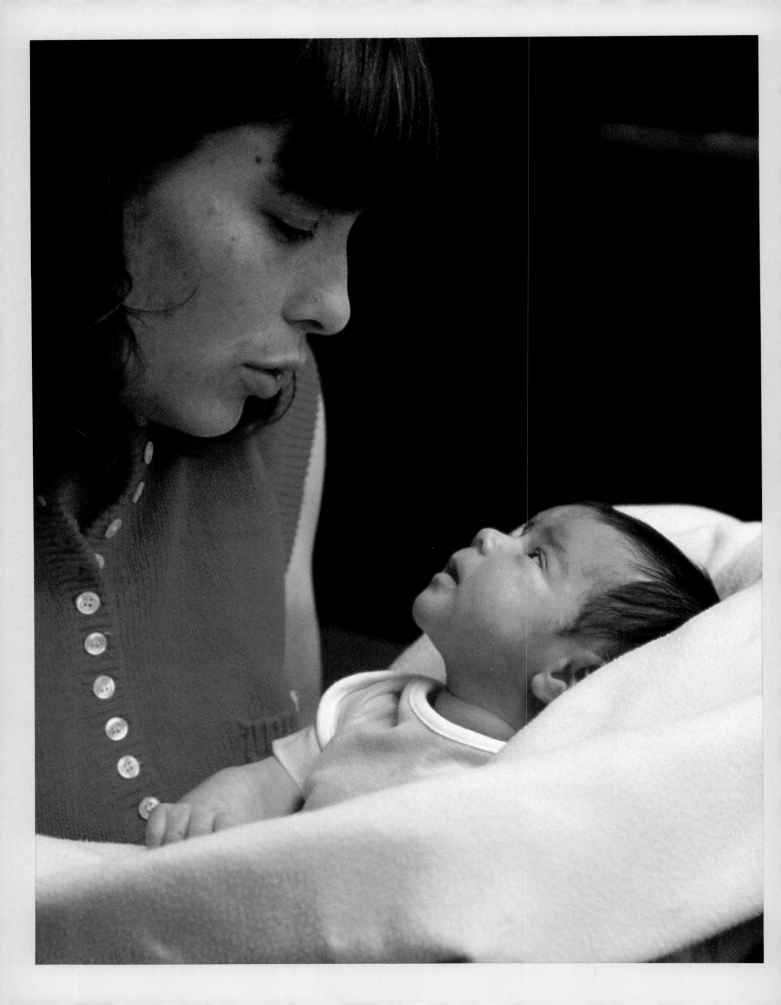

CHAPTER 7

The First Two Years: Psychosocial Development

Focusing Questions

- What are the social capabilities of a newborn infant and how are they facilitated by parent-infant synchrony?
- How do an infant's interactions with father, siblings, and peers differ from those with her mother?
- What are an infant's emotional capabilities, and how do differences in infants' temperament affect social development?
- What experiences enable an infant to develop secure attachments, and what are the consequences if such attachments fail to develop?
- What are the causes of child abuse and neglect?
- Why is autonomy so central to development during toddlerhood?

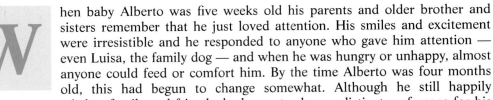

hen baby Alberto was five weeks old his parents and older brother and sisters remember that he just loved attention. His smiles and excitement were irresistible and he responded to anyone who gave him attention — even Luisa, the family dog — and when he was hungry or unhappy, almost anyone could feed or comfort him. By the time Alberto was four months old, this had begun to change somewhat. Although he still happily responded to family and friends, he began to show a distinct preference for his mother and his oldest sister, Lydia, who helped their mother care for him. When he saw or heard either of them, he became especially happy, active, and noisy. As you might expect, this caused some jealousy among the rest of the family.

Somewhere between the age of nine and eleven months, Alberto's preferences for specific people became much stronger and more obvious. He clearly preferred his mother to any other adult and responded to his sister Lydia more than to any of the other children. Now able to crawl, he tried to follow his mother wherever she went, and he cried when she left the room. During this period he also began to do something he had never done before: he sometimes became upset when unfamiliar people visited, even if they were friendly.

By the time he was two, Alberto was walking and talking well. Although he still demanded a good deal of attention from his mother and still preferred to play with Lydia, he rarely got upset when other family members cared for him, and he seemed quite happy to socialize with almost all friendly visitors, even those he had never met before.

These changes in Alberto are typical of some of the important psychosocial changes that occur during infancy. As we describe in the preceding chapters, infancy is the time when children learn to walk and think and talk and, in a very broad sense, become more fully "human." Although infants are highly dependent upon their care-givers for meeting their needs, they are anything but passive. Almost from the moment of birth, infants become increasingly active and sophisticated participants in their own psychosocial development observing and interacting with the people around them.

As an infant grows older, she comes to form close and enduring emotional attachments with the important people in her life and sometimes shows her concerns about them very dramatically. She wails when a strange nurse approaches her in the doctor's office, and she greets her mother or father warmly when one of them "rescues" her from the nurse. At other times the baby may participate in relationships in more subtle ways, such as attending closely to older brothers and sisters while they play — more closely, in fact, than her siblings attend to her. At still other times she may express her needs or feelings in ways that are downright confusing to the people around her; for example, she may refuse particular foods when a parent offers them but take them happily from a baby-sitter.

These behaviors convey two of the major themes of psychosocial development in infancy: trust and autonomy. Infants are learning whom they can count on and to what extent. If, thinks the baby, my mother and father leave me with a stranger, can I count on them to return? What if they leave me with a new baby-sitter for the whole evening? Infants are also learning when and how to make choices for themselves. When, thinks the baby, can *I* decide what strangers to investigate? And when can *I* decide which foods I will eat? Infants' concerns for autonomy and for intimate trust intertwine closely during their first two years although many observers of children believe trust develops earlier than autonomy does (Maccoby, 1984; Stern, 1985).

In this chapter we explore the essential role that early social interactions and attachments play in the development of trust and in the achievement of autonomy. We also look at theories of personality development during infancy, the ways in which attachments are formed, the emergence of self-knowledge and self-awareness during later infancy, and the problem of child abuse.

EARLY SOCIAL RELATIONSHIPS

Infants seem to have a natural tendency to be social participants. Immediately after birth, they are capable of many social responses. For example, a newborn will turn his head toward the sound of a human voice and actively search for its source; attend to and show preference for a voice with a female pitch; pause regularly in his sucking pattern for human voices but not for similar nonhuman tones; and look at and visually follow a picture of a complete human face but not a picture of a scrambled one. He will even prefer the smell and taste of human milk over formula, water, or sugar water (Brazelton, 1976).

Parent-Infant Synchrony

Frequently the social interactions between parent and infant involve a pattern of close coordination and teamwork in which each waits for the other to finish before beginning to respond. This pattern of closely coordinated interaction is called **parent-infant synchrony.** For example, infants only a few weeks old are able to maintain and break eye contact with their mothers at regular intervals and to take turns in making sounds and body movements (Stern, 1977, 1985; Tronick, 1989). Studies using videotapes reveal that a mother and her baby actually have "conversations" that resemble adult dialogues in many ways, except for the child's lack of words.

Early "conversations"

How do such exchanges occur? A mother may gaze steadily at her baby, waiting patiently for her to vocalize, move, or at least look. When the action eventually happens, the mother may respond by imitating the infant's gesture or by smiling or saying something. She will time her responses to allow the baby a turn in this game, just as if the child were a fully competent person in a social exchange (Stern, 1977, 1985). As the interaction continues, the baby typically shows increasing tensions: her movements and sounds become not only more frequent but more sudden and jerky as well. At some point the infant releases or breaks the tension by looking away from her mother and spends the next few moments looking at or touching objects instead of people. This provides a break from sociability, although social exchanges may of course serve equally well as rest periods from nonsocial interactions. In any case, after a suitable interval the mother and infant catch each other's attention again, and the cycle of turn taking begins all over.

Until an infant is several months old, responsibility for coordinating this activity rests with the parent. But after a few months the baby becomes capable of initiating social interchanges and of influencing the content and style of his parent's behavior. Not surprisingly, babies who are especially sociable early in infancy are likely to have mothers who form especially strong emotional attachments or connectedness with them later in infancy (Clarke-Stewart, 1973; Waters, 1978). Some of this continuity is caused by the baby, not the mother. The smiles, gazes, and vocalizing of a friendly baby prove hard for his mother to resist, and after several months of experience with such a baby, the mother becomes especially responsive to his communications. Presumably the mother's increased responsiveness in turn reinforces her infant's social nature.

Of course babies who are older influence their mothers in other ways. For example, in a study of mothers' efforts to teach infants less than a year old to reach for a hidden object, researchers found that a mother's teaching style depended a lot on how her baby acted during the orientation period that preceded the experiment. Mothers adjusted their teaching approach to the skill level of the child. If the baby already showed some skill at reaching for objects, the

The infant's contribution

Parents and their infants often show a striking synchrony in their movements and gestures. In these exchanges, it is often hard to tell who is leading whom.

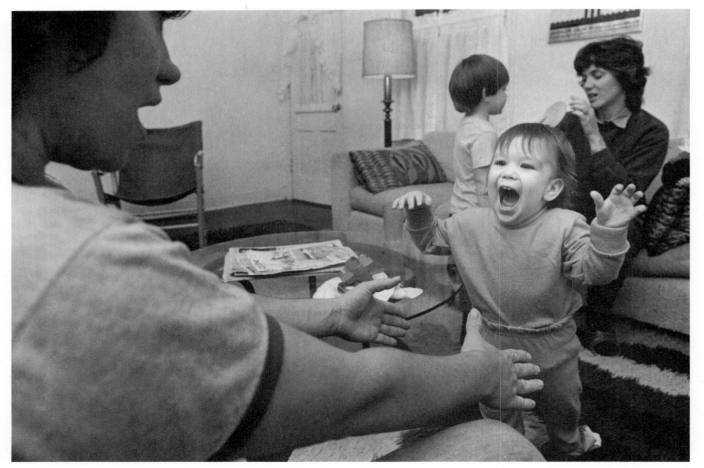

		Family		
	Genetics	How do parents contribute to the development of competence in toddlers? (255)	**Social Context**	
Physical Development	How do innate temperamental differences in infants influence their relationships with their parents? (238)		How do American cultural values and beliefs contribute to the existence of child abuse in the United States? (258)	**Peers**
What are the effects of low birth-weight on the development of parent-infant attachments? (173)				What conditions foster the development of peer friendships among infants and toddlers? (235)

THE FIRST TWO YEARS: PSYCHOSOCIAL DEVELOPMENT

What are some of the important milestones in the emotional development of infants? (236)	In what ways is an infant's growing self-awareness expressed in everyday situations? (253–254)		How does an infant's cognitive development contribute to the development of attachment and basic trust during the first two years? (244)	How does language development reflect a toddler's growing self-awareness? (254)
Emotions		Why do infants and toddlers learn to exert self-control over their own behavior? (250–252)		**Language**
	Self-concept and Identity		**Cognition**	
		Learning		

mother tended simply to demonstrate or model the task; if not, she was more likely to work up to the task through many steps, first placing the object visibly within easy reach, then hiding it partially, and then hiding it still more (Kaye, 1976; Cohn & Tronick, 1987; Dowd & Tronick, 1986, 1989).

Social Interactions with Fathers, Siblings, and Peers

Even though infants may interact more with their mothers than with anyone else, they actually live in a network of social relationships in which a number of other people make at least minor contributions to their social life — and sometimes major ones (Hodapp & Mueller, 1982). Fathers often belong to this network and so do siblings and peers. How do contacts with these people compare with a baby's contacts with her mother?

Father-Infant Interactions   For a long time developmental psychologists largely ignored the fathers of infants, in part because of a belief that fathers had little direct contact with young babies. For example, one early study suggested that fathers talked with their three-month-old infants only about one minute per day (Rebelsky & Hanks, 1971). Later studies reported much higher rates of involvement — in the neighborhood of two or three hours per day for fathers, as compared with nine hours for mothers (Parke, 1981; Belsky et al., 1984). Even with this much involvement fathers are not generally the primary care-givers, but they definitely play a significant role in their infants' experiences.

Infants' social episodes with fathers follow the same cycle of buildup and withdrawal that characterizes infants' interactions with their mothers (Yogman et al., 1977). Nevertheless, although mothers and fathers play many of the same games, their styles differ. Play episodes with fathers tend to have sharper peaks and valleys — higher states of excitement and more sudden and complete withdrawals by the baby. Compared to mothers, fathers tend to jostle more and talk

More active interchanges

less, and they roughhouse more and play ritual games like peek-a-boo less. Fathers also devote a higher proportion of their time with the baby to play than mothers do (40 percent versus 25 percent) (Kotelchuck, 1976).

How do we explain these differences? Past experience with infants, the amount of time routinely spent with them, and the usual ratio of care-giving to play that parents assume may influence parents' style regardless of their sex. For example, when fathers who served as primary, full-time care-givers were compared with fathers who took the more traditional secondary care-giver role, researchers found differences in how the two groups played with their infants. Primary care-giver fathers acted very much like mothers, smiling more and imitating their babies' facial expressions and vocalizations more than secondary care-giver fathers did. Nevertheless, primary care-giver fathers were just as physical as secondary care-giver fathers (Field, 1978).

Paternal competence

Do stylistic differences mean that fathers are less competent than mothers with their infants? Most studies suggest not. In one, fathers played with their newborn infants in virtually the same ways that mothers did (Parke & O'Leary, 1976; Lamb, 1981), cooing and smiling at them and talking to them. In another, fathers were found to feed their babies just as successfully as mothers; they intervened appropriately when the baby spit up and fed comparable amounts of formula (Parke & Sawin, 1976).

Although their styles may be somewhat different, both mothers and fathers are capable of interacting with their young infants in responsive and appropriate ways; this is particularly true of whichever one is the primary or full-time care-giver. But whether or not a particular father or mother will be a responsive care-giver depends on his or her personal qualities, past experiences, and motivation, as well as on the care-giving situation and the particular infant.

Interactions with Siblings   Approximately 80 percent of children in the United States and Europe grow up with siblings, and the time they spend together in their early years is frequently greater than the time they spend with their mothers or fathers. In many cultures children are cared for by siblings; from the age of one or two they are nursed, fed, disciplined, and played with by a sister or brother who may be only three or four years older (Weisner & Gallimore, 1977; Dunn, 1985). Firstborn children are likely to monitor very closely the interactions of their mother with a new baby and try to become directly involved themselves. Observational studies found that children as young as eighteen months old tried to join in bathing, feeding, and dressing their sibling; of course, they also tried to tip over the baby's bath, tune the television, spill things, and reorganize the kitchen when their mothers cuddled and cared for the new baby (J. Dunn, 1985; Stewart et al., 1987).

In talking to their younger siblings, children make many of the same adjustments as their mothers do, using much shorter sentences, repeating comments, and using lots of action-getting features (baby talk or motherese). In turn, infants tend to respond to their siblings in much the same way as they do to their parents. But they also quickly learn the ways in which siblings are different from parents, particularly if the sibling is young. Because younger children lack their parents' maturity and experience, they are less able to focus consistently on meeting the baby's needs rather than their own. For example, a four-year-old who is playing with his eight-month-old sister may not notice that she is becoming overstimulated and tired and needs to stop; or on another occasion, he may become jealous of the attention that she is getting and "accidentally" fall on her while giving her a hug. If parents keep in mind the needs and capabilities of each of their children and provide appropriate supervision, interactions with siblings are likely to make an important positive contribution to an infant's development.

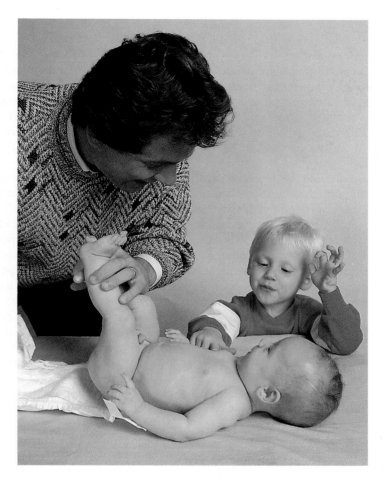

Each member of a family has a unique style of interacting with a new infant.

Interactions with Other Care-givers

Infants also interact with other nonparent care-givers including day-care teachers, other relatives, and family friends. A growing number of studies have explored the interactions of infants and their day-care providers and how these compare with parent-infant interactions (Clarke-Stewart, 1989; Belsky, 1988). For example, comparisons of a group of eighteen-month-old infants enrolled in day-care centers and of a matched group of infants cared for at home revealed more adult-infant play, touching, and reciprocal smiling in the day-care group and more verbal responsiveness to their mothers' talking, more crying, and more encounters with maternal restrictiveness in the at-home group. Play with toys was at a higher developmental level for the day-care infants than for the home care group, which was due in part to their greater opportunity to interact with infant peers (Rubenstein & Howes, 1979, 1983; Rubenstein, Howes, & Boyle, 1981).

Follow-up studies indicated that children who had been in day care as infants did as well or better than children who had not on measures of sociability, social competence, language persistence, achievement, self-confidence, and problem solving. Children who had been in day care as infants or at a later age were far more demanding, independent, and assertive and less willing to comply with adult demands than were children without day-care experience. This may reflect the greater ability of the day-care children to think for themselves and persist in getting their own way (Clarke-Stewart, 1989).

Bridges What effect does interaction with peers in a day-care setting seem to have on infants' developing cognitive and linguistic abilities?

Impact of day care

Role of grandparents

Living in an extended or three-generation family can also contribute to the quality of infant social development, particularly for infants in single-parent families and for infants who are at risk (Tinsley & Parke, 1984). For example, maternal grandparents have been found to buffer the infant against the negative effects of insensitive parents or siblings, and infants who were judged to be anxiously attached at two months were more likely to change to securely attached at eighteen months if they were living in households composed of their mothers, their maternal grandmothers, and their mothers' siblings than if they were not (M. Wilson & Tolson, 1986).

Interactions with Peers   Until very recently there were few studies of infant-infant interactions, perhaps because in most families, infants do not have regular, long-term relationships with peers (Mueller & Vandell, 1978). It was generally believed that interactions with peers do not develop as quickly as those with parents (Bridges, 1933). According to this view, infants do not get along very well: they grab each other's toys and hair and treat each other as mere objects or toys, especially if no real toys are available. True cooperation, it was thought, does not emerge until well beyond age two, after such skills have been learned through earlier interactions with parents.

Interest in other infants

Recent observations of infants, however, have found that even young babies show considerable interest in other babies and in much the same ways that they show interest in their parents — by gazing, smiling, and cooing. Sociability of this kind develops with peers at the same time and at the same rate as it does with parents (Field & Roopnarine, 1982; Vandell, 1980).

As might be expected, babies become more social with experience. In one study, for example, eleven infants and eleven toddlers were observed over time

In their first contacts with peers, infants often treat each other like interesting objects and show little awareness of each other's thoughts and feelings.

in a nursery school class. All of the children became friendlier with each other during the four-month semester of the nursery, vocalizing, smiling, and exchanging toys more frequently. Interestingly, although the infants were fifteen months younger, they came close to equaling the toddlers in both types and amounts of social behavior (Roopnarine & Field, 1982; Hartup, 1989).

When given the choice, infants often prefer playing with their peers to playing with their mothers. In one study, infants aged ten to twenty-four months were each placed in a room with both their mother and another infant. The ten-month-olds looked at and followed their peers more often than their mothers; toddlers (aged twelve to twenty-four months) talked with, imitated, and exchanged toys with their peers more frequently than with their mothers (Rubenstein and Howes, 1976).

Toddlers in day care spend about 25 percent of their time interacting positively with other toddlers. They are more likely to express positive feelings and play competently with peers than with adults or when by themselves. Repeated contact with a peer in a familiar setting with a familiar care-giver and minimal adult interference appears to facilitate the development of peer friendship. Peers also support the autonomy of toddler from mother and offer the toddler an alternative source of stimulation and comfort (Rubenstein & Howes, 1979, 1983; Hartup, 1989). But so far, there is no evidence of a difference in relating between toddlers who have attended day care and children who have had equal access to peer experience in their homes.

In conclusion, although an infant's social interactions with his mother and father are generally the most important of his early social experiences, interactions with siblings and peers also contribute to his social development. The quality and developmental impact of experiences with siblings and peers will reflect to some extent the degree to which parental supervision of such contacts is responsive to the needs of the baby and of the other children as well. Both under- and over-protectiveness may have negative consequences. For example, a parent who does not allow an older brother or sister to play with the baby is depriving both siblings of an important social experience. But allowing siblings to play without adequate supervision or delegating too much child-care responsibility to an older brother or sister is likely to have negative effects. Taken together, these early social interactions provide the basis for the emotional and personality development that follow.

Playmates of choice

Bridges What conditions foster the development of peer friendships among infants and toddlers?

EMOTIONS, TEMPERAMENT, AND PERSONALITY DEVELOPMENT IN INFANCY

As in adult relationships, emotions play an important role in the social relationships of infancy. In the following sections we discuss the role of emotions and **temperament** — the infant's typical or characteristic way of feeling and responding. Following that we discuss theories of personality development during the first two years.

Emotions in Infancy

Researchers have long recognized changes in infant crying, smiling, frustrations, and fear of strangers and of novel or unusual stimuli, but they have only recently appreciated the range and complexity of infant emotion (L. Yarrow, 1979). One

Perspectives

Milestones in Emotional Development

Stages in infant emotional development have been extensively studied and described by some researchers. Stanley and Nancy Greenspan (1985) have written about what they call "milestones" of emotional development — the typical changes that children exhibit as they achieve greater sophistication, mastery, and competence in their affective understanding and behavior.*

Milestone I, regulation and interest in the world, occurs from birth to three months. During this period, the infant learns to self-regulate. She learns how to feel calm, relaxed, and not too overwhelmed by her new environment while at the same time maintaining an active and attentive interest in the world that she experiences through her senses. With the help of her parents, a baby learns to communicate when she has had too little, too much, or just the right amount of stimulation. An infant that does not learn to self-regulate will find it difficult to handle the challenges of the milestones that follow.

In achieving *Milestone II, falling in love* (two to seven months), the calm and self-regulated infant now finds the human world the most enticing, pleasurable, and exciting of all experiences. He eagerly explores his parent's face, responds to his parent's rhythms with smiles and joyfulness, and in general, becomes more responsive to social interactions.

During *Milestone III, developing intentional communication* (three to ten months), the infant now begins to participate in dialogues with her parent. She begins to learn about cause-and-effect: her smile will produce a smile in her parent, and her "goos" and "gahs" will produce parental "oohs" and "aahs."

Milestone IV, the emergence of an organized sense of self, occurs between nine and eighteen months. The baby now learns to connect small units of feeling and social behavior developed earlier into larger, more complicated, and well-organized patterns. Toward the middle of this stage, he is able to express complex patterns of thoughts and feelings that contain his wishes (for instance, for food or comfort), his intentions (taking mother to the refrigerator or bringing daddy a favorite picture book), and even his sense of satisfaction (he eats some cheese with great pleasure).

Milestone V, creating emotional ideas, occurs between eighteen and thirty-six months. The infant is increasingly able to express her emotions through ideas and to create them in her imagination. She now is capable of fantasy play, which expresses a wide range of emotions including dependency, pleasure, curiosity, assertiveness, protest and anger, and setting of self-limits (expressed by punishing a doll or stuffed toy for being naughty or by saying "no more cookies"). She now is also able to imagine that there are monsters in her closet.

Milestone VI, emotional thinking: the basis for fantasy, reality, and self-esteem, is achieved between thirty and forty-eight months. The child learns to further organize and manipulate his emotional understanding. For example, the emotional elements of his pretend play become more complex and true to real-life situations. He also eventually learns to separate make-believe from reality and to work with ideas in a planful way. For example, he can now say "Last night I dreamed there were monsters in my closet. Tonight I'm going to dream about kittens."

A limitation of the Greenspans' approach is that their stages overlap considerably in when they occur, making it difficult to scientifically test them. However, their rich and detailed description of the general pattern of changes in children's emotional development is a useful guide to parents and others who wish to better understand this important aspect of development.

---

*Bridges   What are some of the important milestones in the emotional development of infants?

Bridges   How accurate are physiological measures of emotion in infants?

reason for the delay is the difficulty in studying the feelings of infants, who are not fully aware of or able to communicate the subtleties of what they are feeling. Take the case of an infant's fear responses: whereas earlier it was thought that an infant's fear could be fully explained in terms of fear-producing stimuli such as noise or loss of support, current research has taught us that the baby's expectations and understandings play an important role. Loud sounds or incongruous stimuli such as a mother's face covered with a mask will in some situations lead to fear responses but in other circumstances to smiling and laughter (Scarr & Salapatek, 1970; Sroufe & Wunsch, 1972).

The physiological aspects of emotion, such as changes in heart rate, can be reliably measured, but their relationship to specific emotions still remains unclear. Happiness, sadness, fear, and anger can be reliably identified from facial expressions, but more subtle variations in emotion are more difficult to pinpoint (L. Yarrow, 1979). In the long run, reports and ratings of children's behavior by their parents and others who know them well probably hold the most potential for learning about what they are feeling; in fact, parents' reliable judgments about their infants' feelings play an essential role in parent-infant synchrony.

It is generally recognized that infants show joy and laughter by three to four months, fear by five to eight months, and other more complex emotions such as shame sometime in the second year of life. Some researchers believe that even younger infants are sensitive to the positive and negative feelings of their care-givers and are quite capable of responding to adult fears and anxieties. It is likely that they respond to cues similar to those used by adults, such as slight variations in voice quality, smell, and touch, as well as variations in facial expression and body language (L. Yarrow, 1979; Sroufe, 1979; Izard, 1982; Tronick, 1989). (See Table 7.1.)

Temperament

Even at birth, infants differ in their patterns of physical and emotional activity and responsiveness. These characteristic patterns are called temperament. In the now classic New York Longitudinal Study, more than one hundred thirty infants were studied from birth through their elementary school years (A. Thomas & Chess, 1977) and rated on nine aspects of temperament. Three main patterns emerged, and each was found to have a different effect upon the individual child's social interactions.

- Average or easy children tended to be very regular and adaptable. They were happy babies who generally responded positively to new experiences, were easy to comfort, and developed secure relationships readily. They also were less likely to have behavioral problems.

- Slow-to-warm-up children were relatively inactive and slow to adapt to new experiences. They rarely showed strongly negative (or positive) moods and reacted moderately to new situations. Somewhat shy and standoffish at first, these babies tended to do fine once they warmed up.

- Difficult children were irregular in their patterns of eating, sleeping, and general activity. They were moody, reacted intensely to new or stressful situations, and were more likely than other children to stimulate criticism and negative reactions from their care-givers. As you may guess, formation of secure relationships was most difficult for these children and their parents.

Classifying babies in this way has been helpful in predicting problems for the minority of children who are difficult or slow to warm up. For example, newborn infants whose biological rhythms are irregular, who experience discomfort during feeding and elimination, and who do not communicate their needs very clearly are often difficult for their parents and are more likely to experience problems in developing good relationships with them. This is particularly true when mothers have little or no help and emotional support from relatives and friends in caring for their difficult babies (parenting can improve when emotional support from friends or relatives is made available) (Waters et al., 1980; Crockenberg, 1981; Crockenberg & McClusky, 1986). Nevertheless, few successful predictions have been made regarding the "easy" group, which includes most children. Therefore, predictions of infant emotions and personality based on temperament may be of limited use when globally applied; a more interactive approach that also considers the characteristics of their parents and their family situations may prove more useful. Brazelton, for example, who has categorized babies as *quiet, average,* and *active,* has found that the developmental outcomes for each group depend largely on the expectations and temperaments of the particular care-givers involved (1983). Thus, an active baby may be a pleasure for one parent and a serious problem for another.

How stable or enduring are specific temperamental differences over time? Researchers report moderate stability for sociability, shyness, activity level, and irritability during infancy and through the childhood years (Kagan, Reznick, &

TABLE 7.1 Development of Infant Emotions

Approximate Age (in months)	Emotion
0–1	Social smile
3	Pleasure smile
3–4	Wariness
4–7	Joy, anger
4	Surprise
5–9	Fear
18	Shame

Source: Izard (1982) and Sroufe (1979).

The New York Longitudinal Study

Infants vary in temperament, from easy-going to difficult; these variations may affect their long-run development significantly.

Bridges   How do innate temperamental differences in infants influence their relationships with their parents?

Snidman, 1987; Buss & Plomin, 1984; Goldsmith et al., 1987; Riese, 1987). Nevertheless, temperament never exists in a vacuum; environmental influences play a major role in supporting or modifying temperament throughout the course of development. The temperamental characteristics of many children change significantly over time. This suggests that the degree to which temperamental style contributes to personality development is strongly influenced by the reactions a child evokes from parents and other care-givers and by the "goodness of fit" between a child's temperamental style and parental attitudes, expectations, and responses (A. Thomas & Chess, 1977).

Because a newborn infant's temperament can strongly influence her parents' earliest feelings and responses to her, it can have a significant impact on the infant-parent relationship. For example, babies who are described as "cuddlers" appear to receive more warmth and affection from their parents than "non-cuddlers" do (Schaffer & Emerson, 1964). Similarly, if parents early on find their baby difficult (or easy), they may then label and consistently treat her as such.

Within-family differences in how parents perceive and react to their children's personalities can emphasize or deemphasize a child's unique temperamental qualities; children may act in ways that are more or less consistent with their own temperamental tendencies and with the expectations and reactions of their parents (Plomin, 1989; Plomin, Schachter, & Stone, 1985). For example, parents of a shy child may reinforce that tendency by labeling him as shy and by directly and indirectly supporting and reinforcing that trait; or they may deemphasize it by not labeling him and by treating him as a child with average sociability. Similarly, at any point in his development, a shy child may decide to reject that view of himself and become a more outgoing person.

Additional factors that may influence parents' interactions with the infant's temperamental qualities include birth order, the sex of the baby, the presence of other siblings, and the parents' expectations regarding their child's temperament. For example, parents are likely to respond more positively and comfortably to their new baby when there is a good fit between their expectations and the new baby's actual temperament than when the fit is poor (Korner, 1974; Sprunger et al., 1985).

A Talk with Jennifer and Her Parents

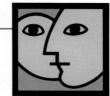

Infant Temperament

The following is part of an interview that was conducted with the Granoff family in the living room of their apartment. Members of the family are Jennifer, age eight months; her brother, Thomas, age three; her sister, Loretta, age fifteen; and her parents, Joyce and Michael.

Interviewer: You mentioned earlier that Jennifer has been an easy baby from the time she was born. Please tell me more about that.

Michael: She has always had a very even disposition. The only time she is ever cranky is when she needs to sleep or when she's hungry, but we usually feed her often enough so that doesn't happen too much.

Joyce: She is an extremely regular baby. She goes to bed every night at about the same time and sleeps all night long. When she wakes up she is cheerful and waits patiently in her crib until we get there. Sometimes we don't even know that she's awake. Some babies are grumpy. They wake up screaming and crying. Her brother is sometimes that way. People I used to work with have a little girl who's a little younger than Jennifer, and a completely different baby — wiry, squirmy, and difficult to hold and to comfort.

Interviewer: Is it harder or easier to have that kind of baby?

Joyce: I don't know. I think that her parents find her more difficult. She seems to need to interact with her parents all of the time and constantly demands attention. Jennifer is remarkably independent. And although she'll fuss a little if she realizes that you have left her by herself in her room for more than a couple of minutes, once you come back, then she'll be all right. Her brother, Thomas, was very different. It was always a struggle to put him to sleep and he was much more difficult to comfort.

Interviewer: What calms Jennifer when she's unhappy?

Michael: Singing, food, walking with her, rocking her, sitting with her on the couch.

Interviewer: Is it different for different children?

Michael: I think that many of the same things work, but there are also differences. One of the things that works for her brother is patting him on the back, which she doesn't like. It has never worked for her. She could care less. I keep trying to do it and it's never worked.

Joyce: The astonishing thing about having more than one kid is how unique they are.

Interviewer: How early can you tell that?

Joyce: From the first day.

Michael: I probably can't say the first day, though I'm sure that Joyce can. I would say I definitely noticed it in the first week, though.

Interviewer: Your husband mentioned earlier that Thomas was much more active and communicative from the start.

Joyce: Oh, he was. It was clear very early that he was tuned into exactly what we were doing. His doctor called him a very visual kid. He was always looking, looking, looking at everything. You could always see that he was intensely interested in things around him. Jennifer is also interested and curious. Her brother was more focused. She'll get interested and curious, but without that intensity. She'll get interested in things that come her way, or play by herself. He reaches out. He'll look out at things, for example, when he is riding in a car.

Interviewer: You seem to have a strong feeling that temperamental differences are important.

Joyce: Yes, I do. Often I feel that kids turn out to be the way they are. You really can't do much about it. Their temperaments seem to come with them. You can mold and shape other things, but temperament seems to be pretty much set.

Interviewer: Is that something that you discovered early on?

Joyce: No. It took me fifteen years to learn. (She laughs.) I think I was surprised at the level at which this temperament is almost, if anything, innate. Their activity level, their cheerfulness, curiosity, and all that stuff. I think that in the first week you can tell what your baby's going to be like on those levels. It doesn't mean that you can tell how your baby is going to turn out. Environment also plays an important part.

But the temperament sets them up for everything else. If you've got an easy-to-get-along-with baby, a baby that sleeps a lot, you don't get angry at the baby, you don't get frustrated, you're not uptight all the time, you're more relaxed. So you're easier on the baby.

Follow-up Questions

1. Can you explain Jennifer's qualities that her parents describe without referring to the concept of temperament?

2. How closely does Joyce and Michael's understanding of temperament fit with what is presented in this chapter? In what ways is it different?

3. If you could talk with them, what additional questions would you like to ask the Granoff family?

Personality Development During the First Two Years

Even in the first weeks and months of life, an infant's temperament and the reactions she elicits from her care-givers may provide the initial basis for the development of her **personality** — the unique pattern of physical, emotional, social, and intellectual characteristics that will distinguish her from all other individuals. At the same time, changes resulting from physical and cognitive maturation and the increasingly complex social and emotional interactions that emerge between the infant and her care-givers come to play an increasingly important role. Thus, the differences in personality that emerge are significantly influenced by the child's experiences, particularly her interactions with others.

In this section we briefly discuss three main views of personality development during infancy: Freud's oral and anal stages of psychosexual development, Erikson's psychosocial crises of basic trust versus mistrust and of autonomy versus shame and doubt, and Mahler's mother-child symbiosis and individuation.

The Freudian View   According to Freud's psychosexual theory, which is discussed in Chapter 2, the **oral stage** of development occurs during the first year of infancy. Feeding and other oral activities provide the infant with his earliest encounters with the outside world and with his first basis for distinguishing between fantasy and reality. Conflicts between the infant's desire for immediate gratification and the care-giver's ability and willingness to be responsive contribute to the beginnings of a separate and differentiated sense of self (Freud, 1983).

An infant who fails to receive good enough care during this stage may become overly dependent as an adult or unable to depend upon others at all. More serious disturbances in this early infant-care-giver relationship may lead to basic insecurity and serious disturbances in the individual's ability to form interpersonal relationships and a coherent and integrated sense of self.

At approximately age one, infants enter the **anal stage** of psychosexual development. The focus of personality development shifts to the pleasurable (and unpleasurable) experiences related to elimination and the control of bodily functions. Again, the quality of parental responses to the child's successful and unsuccessful attempts at self-control will affect personality development. If parents are overly harsh and negative in their responses, or if they provide too little support and guidance, the child may later experience problems in controlling her impulses. Anal-compulsive personality styles and obsessive-compulsive neuroses later in life are thought to be related to disturbances during the anal stage (Freud, 1983). Although these predictions have not received much empirical support, Freud's theoretical views have helped focus the attention of researchers on the importance of early parent-child interactions.

Erikson's Crises   As you probably recall from Chapter 2, Erikson believed that infants explore and experience not only with their sense of taste but with their other senses as well. During an infant's first year, which Erikson (1963) called the oral-sensory period of development, he must successfully resolve the psychosocial **crisis of trust versus mistrust** that he will be adequately cared for by his parents. Care-giving that is consistently and sensitively responsive to the infant's needs forms the basis of trust and provides a foundation upon which he develops his social and emotional relationships with others and his personality. Inconsistent, inappropriate, or neglectful care-giving is likely to interfere with or undermine the development of such trust during infancy and throughout a person's development.

Between the ages of one and three, children encounter the muscular-anal period and must successfully resolve the psychosocial **crisis of autonomy versus shame and doubt** (Erikson, 1963). Much as in Freud's anal stage, the conflicts here involve the child's struggles to control her own thoughts, feelings, and actions. According to Erikson's theory, insensitive, unresponsive parenting that is overly controlling or that fails to provide the supervision and guidance that ensure the child's physical and emotional safety may contribute to an individual having problems with autonomy in the future (Erikson, 1963).

Mahler's Theory of Symbiosis and Individuation   Margaret Mahler and her colleagues have proposed that following the first few weeks of infancy, during which an infant is in a state of "normal autism" and largely unaware of the world around him, infancy is characterized by a **symbiotic mother-child relationship**. In this symbiosis, which goes on for about a year, the mother psychologically experiences the child as an extension of herself rather than as an independent person, and the infant experiences himself as part of his mother (Mahler, 1974; Mahler et al., 1975). During this period the infant must develop a secure base from which to explore the world later. Clinical observations of mothers and their infants indicate that there are differences in the degree to which such symbiosis occurs, depending in part on the extent to which a particular parent derives pleasure and enjoyment from such intense closeness and upon how receptive the infant is to his mother.

Beginning about halfway through the infant's first year and continuing through her second, the process of **separation-individuation** occurs. Separation means that the infant achieves increasingly greater autonomy and independence from the care-giver to whom she has been so closely connected. Individuation reflects the child's development of an identity distinct and separate from that of her parent.

Perspectives

The Development of Smiles

Parents are not imagining things when they see their newborn infants smile from time to time. The first smiles happen mostly when infants are asleep. "She is dreaming," some parents may suggest; others may say, "She has tummy gas." Most likely, however, neither of these explanations is correct. Infant psychologists suspect that the first smiles show responses to moderate but sudden stimulation during sleep. Early smiles, they point out, occur only during REM sleep, when bursts of mental impulses often occur in young babies (Emde et al., 1976; Sroufe & Waters, 1976).

After a few weeks, external stimulation will also make an infant smile, but only if it is presented carefully. Rousing an infant gently from a deep sleep to a lighter, drowsy sleep often works; ringing a bell or making some other soft noise usually elicits a smile. Moderate jostling or jiggling can produce a smile even when the baby is awake and alert. Still later, around three months of age, the stimulation no longer has to involve the infant's body at all. Now even an interesting picture will make him smile if it is presented repeatedly. So will a game of peek-a-boo, at least if someone familiar is playing it. These more mature pleasures apparently draw on infants' developing ability to remember or recognize earlier experiences; in peek-a-boo, for example, babies recognize earlier encounters with the familiar face (Emde et al., 1976; Sroufe & Waters, 1976).

At all of these stages, smiles actually *follow* the stimulation rather than accompany it. Even the sleep smiles of newborn babies happen only after bursts of nerve impulses, as electrodes attached to infants' skulls demonstrate (Sroufe, 1979). The consistent, notable delay suggests what adults often report about their own smiles of pleasure — namely, that they signify relaxation from mild excitement and not the excitement itself. You smile *after* the punch line to a joke, not during it.

In both infants and adults, the key to pleasurable smiling consists of temporary tension or excitement. Other patterns of stimulation create other emotions. Too much excitement, for example, or sustained and unending excitement, creates distress and prolonged tension and prevents smiling; certain feature films may emphasize excitement so much that some adults feel upset rather than satisfied by them. Likewise, some infants may feel distressed by a peek-a-boo game that goes on too long or that is managed too aggressively. On the other hand, too little stimulation creates boredom. Then infants (and adults) tend to go looking for interesting sights and activities; perhaps this is one origin of mischief making among babies (and some adults).

Similarities in the three theories

These three theories of personality development during infancy are remarkably similar. To a large extent, this is due to their common roots in Freud's psychoanalytic theory. Each emphasizes the importance of an intense, responsive, and secure relationship between infant and care-giver during the early months of infancy, and each suggests that the security of such a relationship naturally leads to the next development: the infant's individuation as a distinct and separate person through the assertion of autonomy, independence, and self-control. Finally, each theorist believed that a relatively successful resolution of the conflicts or crises involved in this process prepares the infant to take on the new challenges of childhood.

In the following section, we discuss more fully how a secure and responsive bond, or attachment, develops between an infant and his care-giver.

ATTACHMENT FORMATION

The concept of attachment

Attachment refers to the intimate and enduring emotional relationship between infant and care-giver during the infant's first year of life — a relationship that is characterized by reciprocal affection and a shared desire to maintain physical closeness (Ainsworth, 1973). Because attachment cannot be observed directly, it must be inferred or deduced from a number of commonly observed infant behaviors that serve to establish and maintain physical closeness with care-givers (Bowlby, 1969, 1973, 1980). Three of these — crying, cooing, and babbling — are **signaling behaviors;** four others — smiling, clinging, non-nutritional sucking, and following — are **approach behaviors.** Although researchers do not agree as to whether these *specific* attachment behaviors are biologically inherited, the tendency to seek proximity is thought to be biologically determined and essential to infant survival in much the same way that food is.

Harlow's studies of monkeys

One important source of support for attachment theory has come from a well-known series of studies of infant rhesus monkeys by Harry Harlow (Harlow 1959; Harlow & Harlow, 1962). Infant monkeys who were taken away from their mothers at birth and raised with artificial wire and terrycloth substitute mothers displayed many of the attachment behaviors mentioned above. Of particular interest was the finding that if these infant monkeys were forced to make a choice, they preferred physical contact with a warm, soft, terrycloth substitute mother that did not provide food to contact with a cold, hard, wire mother that provided milk from a bottle but that was not soft and huggable. Harlow also found that infant monkeys who were deprived of physical closeness but who were otherwise well cared for exhibited extreme fear and withdrawal, an inability to establish social and sexual relations with peers, and much higher rates of illness and death.

Although we must be cautious about drawing conclusions about human infants from studies of monkeys, these findings suggest that **contact comfort**, a key attachment behavior, may be a primary need during infancy, much like the need for food. They also suggest that severe deprivation of physical closeness with a care-giver may have major negative consequences for subsequent development.

Current views

Currently, most developmental psychologists believe that attachment relationships develop over time. They also believe that attachment involves a highly mutual and interactive partnership between parent and child, who both have strong, although unequal, needs to achieve physical and emotional closeness with each other. This view is influenced by recent discoveries about the interactive nature of social relations between infants and their care-givers.

Attachment — the tendency of young infants and their care-givers to seek physical and emotional closeness — provides an important basis for achieving secure and trusting relationships during early childhood.

Phases of Attachment Formation

Attachments are thought to develop in a series of phases, which are partly determined by cognitive changes (described in the previous chapter) and partly by interactions that appear to develop quite naturally between infants and their care-givers (Bowlby, 1969).

Phase I: Indiscriminate Sociability (birth through two months)   As we mentioned earlier, infants just a few weeks old are able to respond actively to and promote contact and attraction with other people. Their cries, smiles, coos, and gazes are hard to resist or ignore — just try listening to the prolonged crying of a baby or looking into an infant's smiling face, and see if you can resist responding!

In this phase an infant uses her limited attachment behaviors less selectively than she will as she grows older. If she is crying, for example, a variety of people will probably be able to comfort her, and she will not be too particular about which faces she smiles at and who receives her coos and gazes. Not all adults will be equally effective at comforting an infant, but the point is that most very young babies are not highly choosy.

Phase II: Attachments in the Making (two through seven months)   Almost as soon as an infant begins smiling and socializing with everyone, he begins to show an increasing preference for the individuals with whom he is most familiar and who are most responsive to his needs. A baby's preferences in turn reinforce his parents' affection. During this phase, most babies still generally accept certain

Preferences for specific persons

forms of attention and care from comparative strangers as well and also tolerate temporary separations from their parents with little upset.

Phase III: Specific, Clear-cut Attachments (seven through twenty-four months)
In this phase the infant's preferences for specific people become much stronger. In part this is due to the infant's ability to represent persons mentally, a skill achieved in Piaget's fourth stage of sensorimotor development (see Chapter 6). In addition, the greater mobility that comes with crawling and walking contributes to the development of specific, clear-cut attachments. At this phase, toddlers can seek proximity to their care-givers and use their mothers or fathers as a safe base from which to explore the world. Toward the end of the second year, most toddlers are developing significant verbal skills, which allow them to increase their involvement with their parents and others.

Both **separation anxiety** — an infant's upset at being separated from her care-giver — and **stranger anxiety** — a wariness and avoidance of strangers — appear near the beginning of this phase. The achievement of object permanence — the understanding that objects, including people, continue to exist even when they cannot be directly seen, heard, touched, tasted, or smelled — is thought to be an important basis for separation anxiety and attachment development. The source of stranger anxiety is still unclear because it sometimes occurs even when the care-giver is present.

Phase IV: Goal-Coordinated Partnerships (twenty-four months onward)
By the age of two the infant is becoming skilled at mentally representing and remembering both objects and events; he is moving beyond the sensorimotor thinking described by Piaget. He also is better able to understand the feelings and points of view of his parents and to adjust his own accordingly. For example, he is now better able to tolerate delays and interruptions in his desire for his parents' undivided attention, whether it is the competing need for attention of an older brother or sister, a telephone call, or a household chore that intervenes. The baby can also increasingly tolerate short parental absences, safe in the belief that his parents will in fact return. This ability is related not only to past experience but, more important, to attachment relationships grounded in a sense of basic trust.

Assessing Attachment: The "Strange Situation"

The most widely used method for evaluating attachment is called the **"strange situation."** Originally developed by Mary Ainsworth for infants who are old enough to crawl or walk, the procedure consists of eight brief social episodes with different combinations of the infant, her mother, and a strange adult (Ainsworth et al., 1978). It confronts the infant with a cumulative series of stressful experiences: being in an unfamiliar place, meeting a stranger, and being separated from her parent.

The first episode lasts for one-half minute and the remaining seven for three minutes each. First the parent and infant enter the room; the baby is allowed to explore the room while her mother is present. Then a stranger enters the room, talks to the mother, and moves toward the baby; the parent leaves the infant alone with the stranger. After a while the mother returns to her baby and the stranger leaves; then the baby is left alone in the room. The stranger again enters the room and is alone with the infant. Finally, the mother again returns to the room and the stranger leaves.

Based upon the infants' patterns of behavior in the strange situation, three main groups were identified: Types A, B, and C. Type B infants, consisting of about 70 percent of all infants studied, show the following **secure attachment**

Bridges   How is separation anxiety related to cognitive development during infancy?

Bridges   How does an infant's cognitive development contribute to the development of attachments and basic trust during the first two years?

Episodes in the "strange situation"

pattern of responses to the "strange situation." When first alone with their mother, they typically play happily. When the stranger enters, they are somewhat wary but continue to play without becoming upset. But when they are left alone with the stranger, they typically stop playing and search for or crawl after their mother; in some cases they cry. When the mother returns, they are clearly pleased to see her and are likely to stay closer to her and to cuddle more than before. When left alone with the stranger again, the infants are easily comforted, although signs of distress may be stronger, and they quickly recover from the upset by actively seeking contact comfort with the mother on her return. Type A infants (20 percent) display an **anxious-avoidant attachment** pattern. They rarely cry when separated from their mother and when reunited show a pattern of mixing proximity-seeking and avoidant behaviors or a pattern of ignoring their mother altogether. Finally, Type C infants (10 percent) display an **anxious-resistant attachment** pattern. They show some signs of anxiety even in the periods preceding separation. They are intensely upset by separation and when reunited with their mother actively seek close contact with her while resisting her efforts to comfort them (Ainsworth, 1979).

As we shall see, these three patterns appear to be related to parental child-rearing styles as well as to children's future personalities.

Consequences of Different Attachment Patterns

Secure attachment early in infancy benefits babies in several ways during their second year of life. For one thing, Type B toddlers tend to cooperate better with their parents at twenty-two months than other babies do (Londerville & Main, 1981). They comply better with rules such as, "Don't run in the living room!" and they are also more willing to learn new skills and try new activities that their parents show them (as when a parent says, "Sit with me for a minute and see how I do this"). In the face of problems that are too difficult for them to solve, toddlers who are securely attached are more likely than others to seek and accept help from their parents. At age five, these children are found to be better able than other children to adapt to changes in preschool situations (Matas et al., 1978; Arend et al., 1979; Slade, 1987).

Less securely attached infants may not learn as well from their parents. Anxious-resistant (Type C) infants often respond with anger and resistance to their parents' attempts to help or teach them. Such babies may at times invest so much time and energy in conflicts that they are unable to benefit from their parents' experience and to explore their environment. Given a roomful of toys and a mother who has recently returned from an absence, for example, a Type C child may use up a lot of time alternating between being angry at and snuggling with his mother, instead of getting on with his play. Anxious-avoidant (Type A) infants do not have this particular problem, but because of their passivity, they also miss out on parental efforts to teach or help them and ultimately may discourage parents from even trying to be helpful.

Such differences persist even into the preschool years. One study found that children rated as securely attached at age one seemed more likely to seek attention in positive ways in nursery school at age four (Sroufe et al., 1983). When they needed help because of sickness or a hurt, or just wanted to be friendly, they found it easy to secure attention by approaching their teachers fairly directly, and they seemed to enjoy the attention when they received it. Less securely attached infants, whether Type A or Type C, tended to grow into relatively dependent preschool children. They sought more help more frequently but seemed less satisfied with what they got. Their methods of seeking attention differed, too: anxious-resistant children showed signs of chronic complaining or whining, whereas anxious-avoidant children tended to approach the teacher very

A Multicultural View

Cross-cultural Variations in Attachment

Even though almost all infants become attached to their parents somehow, the patterns by which they do so vary around the world. Results from the "strange situation" suggest this clearly. Among infants from northern Germany, for example, Type A responses occur nearly twice as frequently as among infants from North America (Bretherton & Waters, 1985). Among infants from Japan, on the other hand, Type C responses occur much more frequently than among infants from North America.

These differences result partly from differences in cultural values around the world and from the child-rearing practices that these values foster. In northern Germany people value personal independence especially strongly (Grossman et al., 1985) and believe that children should obey parents more consistently than is usually expected in North America. As a result, infants need to learn not to make excessive demands on parents; they must minimize crying and fussing and do without extra bodily contact. During early infancy, mothers encourage these qualities by remaining relatively unresponsive to their infants' moment-by-moment behavior, so in northern Germany, unresponsiveness may signify not personal rejection of the child so much as an ordinary desire to raise a good citizen. The results show up in the "strange situation" as Type A attachment: a larger than usual number of young children seem not to care when reunited with their mothers.

Child-rearing practices probably also influence the responses of Japanese children to the "strange situation." Separations between Japanese infants and their mothers are quite rare by North American standards. One study of attachment patterns reported that one-year-old Japanese infants were left alone or with another adult only two or three times per month on the average (Mikaye et al., 1985), and when they were left with another adult, that adult was usually someone already intimate with the child, such as the father or a grandparent. In Japan, therefore, babies frequently have almost no experience with strangers. Probably as a result, the "strange situation" proves especially traumatic for them. Their extreme protests resemble Type C resistance: crying, anger, fear, and clinging when the mother returns. As with the German infants, these behaviors do not necessarily represent failures in child-rearing; they more likely represent the fulfillment of typical cultural practices.

But cultural values and practices cannot explain all the differences. Even in northern Germany many babies become securely attached, Type B individuals. In fact, many do so even though observations show that their mothers follow culturally approved practices of aloofness. In Japan some infants become Type C infants even though they have had considerable experience with strangers as baby-sitters and even though their mothers follow essentially Western child-rearing styles. Observations of these babies in their homes suggest that they were born with somewhat irritable or fussy temperaments, which may predispose them to becoming Type C in spite of their mothers' practices.

On balance, attachment seems to result from the combination of several influences: cultural values, inborn temperament, and the child-rearing practices of a particular family. The meaning of these attachment relationships, however, may not always be revealed by the "strange situation"; what looks like an attachment failure for one child may in fact be a success, given that child's circumstances.

indirectly, literally taking a zigzagging path to reach her. Having done so, they then tended to wait passively for the teacher to notice them.

Note, however, that these findings do not necessarily imply that secure attachments are set early in infancy once and for all. Instead, attachment is likely to be an extended process, one that in fact takes years to unfold fully (Main et al., 1985). The parental factors that contribute to a baby's insecure relationships at age one are still likely to be operating at age four, and the child's attachment style will continue to reflect the quality of her experiences with her parents. On the other hand, changes in family circumstances and in parent-child relationships can to some degree alter the quality of earlier attachments, for better or worse. (Thompson et al., 1982; Feiring et al., 1987).

Although we have emphasized the major role of the parents in parent-child interactions and in the development of the attachment relationship, it is by no means a one-sided process. From birth onward, the infant plays an active role in initiating and responding to interactions with his care-givers. How strongly his temperamental predispositions influence this process depends to a large degree upon how well they fit and interact with the temperaments, expectations, and capabilities of his parents. Therefore, it would be incorrect to give parents too much credit for raising a happy and well-adjusted child and unfair to place too much blame on parents whose child has encountered developmental problems.

Influences on Attachment Formation

Although children are most likely to form strong attachment relationships with their mothers — who most often are their primary care-givers — they may form equally strong attachments with their fathers as well. And because a growing proportion of families with young children have two working parents or are headed by a single mother who works, maternal employment and day care have come to play an increasing role in the development of attachment. The following section explores the roles of mothers and fathers as well as the contribution of maternal employment and nonmaternal child care to the development of attachments in infancy.

The Role of the Mother   A major determinant of individual differences in attachment is the quality of the infant-mother relationship during the first year of life. A mother's capacity to respond sensitively and appropriately to her infant and to feel positively about her baby and the baby's strengths and limitations appears to be more important than the sheer amount of contact or care-giving. Mothers of securely attached infants are more responsive to crying, more careful and tender in holding their baby, and more responsive to their infant's particular needs and feelings during both feeding and nonfeeding interactions than are mothers of less securely attached infants (Crockenberg, 1981; Ainsworth et al., 1978).

Quality vs. quantity of care

How much maternal stimulation an infant receives also makes a difference. In a study of mother-infant interactions at home when the babies were one, three, and nine months old, babies who were judged to be securely attached at one year received a moderate degree of maternal stimulation at each of the three ages. Anxious-avoidant children received overly high levels of stimulation, and anxious-resistant children received the lowest level of reciprocal interaction (Belsky et al., 1984). Recent longitudinal studies suggest that the style of the mother's care-giving, including how responsive she is to her baby's signals, may be most important (Goldberg et al., 1986; Crockenberg & McCluskey, 1986).

Appropriate stimulation

The Role of the Father   Most studies have found no differences in most babies' preferred attachment figure during their first two years. Infants appear to be equally attached to both mother and father, even though the mother is typically the primary care-giver (Lamb, 1977a. c.; Belsky et al., 1984). As we pointed out earlier in the chapter, however, there are differences in how fathers and mothers interact with their infants; fathers are generally more vigorous and physical, and mothers are quieter and more verbal in their interactions.

The Effects of Maternal Employment   Fifty-three percent of married mothers with children age one and younger are in the labor force, which is more than double the 1970 rate of 24 percent (U.S. Bureau of Labor Statistics, 1987). Maternal employment is a social phenomenon that affects *both* working and nonworking mothers and one that has contributed to recent changes in child-rearing patterns, such as decreased sex typing of children and increased participation of fathers, even in families where mothers are not working (L. Hoffman, 1989).

The effects of maternal employment on the infant or young child are rarely direct and are almost always influenced by a variety of intervening conditions,

Good quality day care can play an important role in the lives of working mothers and their children.

Long-term effects

such as economic and cultural differences between families, the mother's "morale," the father's satisfaction with his wife's employment, the husband-wife relationship, the father's role in the family, the type of work and number of hours it demands, and the availability and quality of nonmaternal care (L. Hoffman, 1989). Thus, the consequences of whether a mother works or not for the child's development may be less important than the factors just mentioned. It is therefore not surprising that although studies find that working mothers exhibit higher levels of interaction and verbal stimulation when they are with their infants, no clear differences were found in how working and nonworking mothers interact with and care for their infants when only employment status is considered (L. Hoffman, 1989).

Although mothers employed more than twenty hours per week spend less with their infants and preschool children, they compensate for this by spending more weekend and other nonwork time and by increasing the amount of direct interacting and talking with their child (Easterbrooks & Goldberg, 1985; L. Hoffman, 1984, 1989). Employed mothers place greater emphasis on independence training than do full-time homemakers, who may see the child's movement toward independence as a threat to their major role and source of self-esteem. One interesting consequence of this is that in a recent study of toddlers, in dual-wage families, securely attached eighteen-month-olds showed less dependency behavior, whereas in single-wage families, they showed more (L. Hoffman, 1989; Weinraub et al., 1988).

With few exceptions, research comparing dual-wage and single-wage families reveal few consistent differences in the characteristics of the infant or young child. One area in which differences have been reported are studies of parent-infant attachment using the strange situation. Although no differences are generally found between single- and dual-wage families, full-time employed mothers appear to be more likely than part-time employed and nonemployed mothers to have insecurely attached infants (L. Hoffman, 1989; Belsky, 1988; Clarke-Stewart, 1989).

This finding should be interpreted with caution, however, because the strange situation may not be a valid means of evaluating attachment in children of working mothers. This is because they may be more comfortable in situations in which they are temporarily separated from their mother or are with other adults (L. Hoffman, 1989).

Longer-range effects of maternal employment must be interpreted with equal caution. The children of working mothers tend to show better social and emotional adjustment as reflected in a higher sense of self-esteem and better family and peer relations; they also tend to be less sex stereotyped in their beliefs and attitudes. There is some indication that the young child whose mother is employed is less compliant and more peer oriented, although this appears to depend on the nature of the nonmaternal care available. When compared with full-time mothers, working mothers seem willing to grant their children greater independence when they are ready for it and to interact more effectively with their youngsters when at home (Cherry & Eaton, 1977; D. Gold & Andres, 1987a, b; Weinraub, Jaeger, & Hoffman, 1988).

The Effects of Day Care   The growing number of dual-wage and single-parent families and changing views about child-rearing and family life have led to increased interest in nonmaternal child care to supplement the care given within families.

It is estimated that 16.3 percent of all children two years and younger with working mothers and 33.9 percent of children three to four years old whose mothers work receive a significant portion of their regular daytime care in organized day-care centers. An additional 2.2 percent of children two and younger and 22.7 percent of three-to-four-year-olds are cared for by nonrelatives, largely in homes other than their own (U.S. Bureau of the Census, 1987).

In general, participation in out-of-home care that is stable, well staffed, and responsive to each child's needs does not appear to interfere with the emotional attachments between an infant and her parents. Day-care experiences during infancy appear to promote greater peer orientation and peer-related social skills, but they also appear to promote lower levels of cooperation with adults and conformity to adult expectations, although these findings may be more a function of the particular educational and child-rearing philosophies of the adults rather than of day care in general (J. Schwartz et al., 1974; Clarke-Stewart, 1989).

Effects on social skills

Nevertheless, infants who are disadvantaged or otherwise at risk are more likely to develop anxious-avoidant infant-mother attachments in day-care situations that lack stability and are inadequately responsive to children's needs (Belsky and Steinberg, 1978; Vaughn et al., 1980; Belsky, 1988).

In conclusion, several points should be noted. First, the great majority of infants exhibit a strong and persistent tendency to form intense attachment relationships with their important care-givers, who are usually (but not necessarily) their mother and father. Second, the secureness of an infant's attachments are closely related to the overall responsiveness and consistency of the relationship between infant and care-giver. Third, the development of secure attachments is closely tied to successful resolutions of the crisis of trust versus mistrust in early infancy and the crisis of autonomy versus shame and doubt during toddlerhood (Erikson, 1963).

Day care, even for infants and toddlers, has few negative effects on children, as long as the care is of high quality and parents feel satisfied with it.

THE EMERGENCE OF AUTONOMY

By the second year of life, the relatively secure base of attachment that most infants have achieved with their parents and other family members allows them to begin to shift their attention outward to the physical and social world. In spite of remaining anxieties about separations, the achievement of a sense of basic trust in their relationships with their care-givers enables toddlers to show increasing interest in new people, places, and experiences. For example, an eighteen-month old may no longer bother to smile at his mother while he plays near her, and he does not need to return to her for reassurance as often as he used to.

Parents may welcome this behavior as a move toward greater independence and at the same time experience a loss of intimacy for which they may not be quite ready. But for various reasons this shift is both inevitable and developmentally important. For one thing, an older infant can move about rather easily and therefore find much to explore without help from others, and these newfound abilities to crawl, climb, and walk make her more interesting as a playmate for other children and thus less dependent upon her parents for her social life. For another, her rapidly developing thinking and communication skills contribute to her increasing autonomy.

Effects of mobility and communication

These competencies create new challenges for both the toddler and his family as they reach a new developmental crisis: autonomy versus shame and doubt. **Autonomy** is the ability to govern and regulate one's own thoughts, feelings, and actions freely and responsibly while at the same time overcoming feelings of shame and doubt. Toddlers must somehow practice making choices — an essential feature of autonomy — in ways that cause no serious harm to themselves or others.

Effects of parental support

Parents must learn to support their child's efforts to be autonomous but must do so without overestimating or underestimating her capabilities or the external dangers and internal fears that she faces. If they are unable to provide such support, and show their disapproval of failures by shaming their child, a pattern of self-blame and self-doubt may develop. In such cases a child is more likely to be painfully shy and unsure of herself or overly demanding and self-critical and relatively unable to undertake new activities and experiences freely.

A good example of such parental support can be found in "David's Case" (pp. 144–147). Although his parents were somewhat worried in David's early months about his prematurity and about his being "behind schedule" in some areas of development, at age thirteen months they took pleasure in his alertness and ability to stand and manipulate his toys, patiently supported his efforts to become toilet trained at nineteen months, and allowed him to play in the yard on his own (for brief periods of time) when he was two.

Parents must help their infants to master this crisis of autonomy by continually devising situations in which their relatively mature baby can play independently and without undue fear of interference — by putting the pots and pans where they can be reached, for instance, but hiding the knives. And children need social as well as physical safety. Chewing on a sister's drawing or dumping the dirt out of the flowerpots can have negative social consequences even when it does not have dangerous physical ones, so parents must help their infants learn how to avoid social perils by being selective about their activities.

Sources of Autonomy

Bridges   Why do infants and toddlers learn to exert self-control over their own behavior?

Why should infants and toddlers voluntarily begin to exert self-control over their own behavior? Developmental psychologists have suggested several possible answers to this question, based on the various theories outlined in Chapter 2. Each has some plausibility, although none may be complete in itself.

After their first birthday, infants begin to show increasing autonomy in their play and other activities, which sometimes leads them into unsafe situations. This autonomy is fostered by their improving motor skills and cognitive development.

Identification   According to psychoanalytic theory, **identification** is the process by which children wish to become like their parents and other important attachment figures in their lives. The intensity of a young child's emotional dependence upon her parents creates an intense desire to be like them, so as to please them and guarantee their love; this dependence also creates anger because of the helplessness and fear of abandonment that the infant inevitably experiences during even brief periods of separation. Because it is so upsetting to be angry at the very person upon whom one is so dependent for love and care, identification can also be motivated, as is the later Oedipal situation, by the unconscious desire to protect oneself from the upset by being like the person who is the object of that anger. Both mechanisms, of course, may operate at once; and either may occur without the child's knowledge.

Children's wish to be like parents

Operant Conditioning   **Operant conditioning** stresses the importance of reinforcement for desirable behaviors, including behaviors that reflect self-control. If a two-year-old gives his infant brother a gentle hug, for example, his parents are more likely to praise him than if he squeezes his brother so hard that he cries. According to the principles of operant conditioning, the reinforced behavior should eventually occur more frequently and the unreinforced ones should happen less often. Over time, reinforcement should therefore lead to an increasingly responsible child — or, more accurately, to a child who behaves in increasingly responsible ways.

According to this view, adults will tend to reinforce a child for more grown-up behaviors, such as independent exploration ("What did you find?") and self-restraint ("I'm glad you didn't wet your pants"). Operant conditioning resembles identification in assuming that parents can motivate children, but it also assumes

Reinforcement of grown-up behaviors

their influence occurs in piecemeal ways; that is, the child acquires specific behaviors rather than whole personality patterns, and the behaviors eventually add up to autonomy and self-restraint.

Observation and imitation of parents

Observational Learning   According to the theory of **observational learning,** the key to acquiring autonomy and self-control lies in the child's inherent tendency to observe and imitate parents and other nurturant individuals. If parents act gently with the child's baby sister, for example, the child will come to do so, too (although her interpretation of what "gently" is may, on occasion, be influenced by feelings of sibling rivalry). Similarly, if young children observe their mother taking pots and pans from the kitchen cabinet, it is a fair bet that they will attempt to do the same. In fact, much of the "child proofing" of a house is necessitated by a young child's skill at observational learning. The process of observational learning implies that autonomy and self-control are acquired in units or behavioral chunks that are bigger than those described by operant conditioning but smaller than those of psychoanalytic identification.

Social-referencing: A Common Denominator   All three explanations of developing autonomy have something in common: they involve **social referencing,** the child's sensitive awareness of how his parents and other adults are feeling and his ability to use these emotional cues as a basis for guiding his own emotional responses and actions (Campos & Stenberg, 1981). For example, infants and toddlers reveal social referencing when they visit a strange place. Should they be afraid of the new objects and people or not? How safe is it to be friendly and to explore? In the absence of past experiences of their own, they evaluate such situations on the basis of their parents' responses: if their parents are relaxed and happy, they are likely to feel that way, too; if their parents are made tense or anxious by the situation, the children will be more likely to feel that way also. By one year, infants will approach and play with unfamiliar toys if a nearby stranger is smiling and avoid them if he looks fearful (Klinnert et al., 1986).

Referring feelings to important adults requires skills that only an older infant possesses. She must know how to interpret her parents' bodily gestures and facial expressions as well as understand their verbal comments. And she must do so while at the same time monitoring or paying attention to the people and events around her. Because younger infants cannot divide their attention in these ways, their reactions tend to be less sensitive to subtle changes in parents' moods.

Development of Self-knowledge and Self-awareness

The sense of self that develops late in infancy shows up in everyday situations as well as in situations involving self-restraint. One very interesting series of studies explored the development of self-knowledge in infants who were nine to twenty-four months old by testing their ability to recognize images of themselves in mirrors and on television (Lewis & Brooks-Gunn, 1979a).

Mirror recognition

Because most of the infants could not verbally indicate whether or not they recognized themselves, the researchers devised an ingenious method for assessing self-recognition: they secretly marked each infant's nose with red rouge while pretending to wipe it. Then they observed the infants as they examined the mirrors. Infant responses included smiling at the mirror, touching the mirror, touching their bodies, pointing at the mirror, acting silly, and touching the red mark on their noses.

Nose touching was interpreted as a clear-cut sign of self-recognition. Infants of all the ages studied directed more behavior toward themselves when their

Bridges   What are some of the physical signs of self-recognition displayed by infants?

noses were marked than when they were not. But only infants fifteen months old and older were able to focus specifically on what was different — their red noses — an ability that increased with age.

In the TV experiments, infants were tested under three conditions. In the live condition, they watched images of themselves live on TV; in the prerecorded condition, they watched videos of themselves that had been recorded a week earlier; and in the other-baby condition, they watched TV recordings of another baby. In each of the three conditions a stranger was shown sneaking up on the infant at the end of the experiment. The researchers recorded the infants' attempts to imitate and to play with the TV images, their facial and vocal expressions, their movements toward and away from the screen, and their reactions to the stranger. A key question was whether the infants would turn toward the stranger they had seen in the live condition and whether they would do so in the prerecorded and other baby conditions as well.

TV recognition

The researchers found that infants as young as nine months old responded to the live images of themselves by playing more, by acting more positively, and by turning more often to the approaching stranger than in the other two conditions. This early self-recognition appeared to be based on *contingency* — that is, on the connection between their own movements and the movements of the image they were viewing. By the time infants had moved into their second year of life (approximately fifteen months), they had become increasingly able to distinguish themselves from other infants by using noncontingent cues such as facial and other physical features.

Aspects of Self-awareness   Recent studies have outlined several dimensions or themes in the development of self-awareness late in infancy (Kagan, 1981). As shown below, often a child expresses self-awareness in very ordinary situations, but this fact does not diminish the importance of the expression to the child. In fact, the very commonness of such situations means that they are influential in the lives of infants and toddlers.

Bridges In what ways is an infant's self-awareness expressed in everyday situations?

As infants approach their second birthday, they begin showing signs of awareness of themselves as individuals.

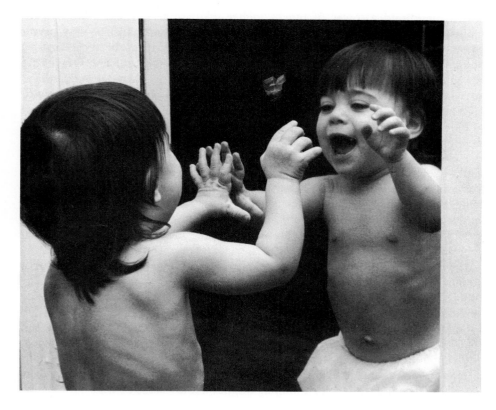

Knowledge of standards

By the end of their second year, most children show an increasing appreciation of the standards and expectations of others regarding how they should behave toward both people and things. For example, a broken toy can be troubling, even if the child did not break it; he may show it to an adult and verbally express concern and a need for help (like "Broken!" or "Daddy fix?"). A crack in the kitchen linoleum may now receive close scrutiny, even though several months earlier it went unnoticed and several months later it may go unnoticed again. Language that implies knowledge of standards — evaluative vocabulary such as *bad, good, dirty, nice,* — appears as well (Bretherton et al., 1981). Such knowledge combines with other behaviors to suggest that the child is beginning to sense an identity for herself.

Distress at modeled behaviors

The modeling or performance of simple behaviors by an unfamiliar adult can prove distressing for older infants and toddlers. One study showed this by having an adult perform some simple act, such as making a doll talk on the telephone, which was well within the children's current abilities. Even though each child's mother was present, and even though the children had previously seemed happy and content, seeing the action carried out by a strange adult made many two-year-olds fret, cry, or cling tightly to their mothers (Kagan, 1981). Most children at least looked worried, and most interrupted their play for significant periods of time to watch — reactions that went beyond ordinary "stranger reactions" to the adult.

Comparisons of performance

Why should such overtly modeled behavior upset a child? For one thing, seeing a stranger perform an activity usually reserved for family members may be disturbing. But more importantly, the child probably senses that his own performance may differ from the adult's and in particular may fall short of it. The child's reactions imply that he now considers himself a separate entity or person; why else might his performance differ from someone else's? This interpretation seems especially plausible in light of the child's growing awareness of standards in general.

Smiles of accomplishment

By the age of two, children show satisfaction in purposely initiating challenging activities or behaviors for themselves, and they often smile at the results. A girl may build a tower of blocks higher than usual and smile broadly the moment she completes it; another may make a strange noise — say, a cat meowing — and then smile; still another may put her teddy bear carefully to bed under a blanket and then giggle. In each case the child confronts a task that is somewhat difficult by her current standards, but she purposely attempts it anyway. Her behavior suggests an awareness of what competent performance amounts to and of her own ability to be successful. This knowledge reflects part of her sense of self and contributes to its further development. (We discuss the development of competence more fully later in this chapter.)

Giving directions to adults

Whether or not he can talk much yet, a two-year-old sometimes directs adults' behavior. He may invite an adult to play, handing a pretend teacup to the adult, or he may request help, looking imploringly at a nearby adult after struggling unsuccessfully to open a small box. These behaviors may include language, but they do not need to; a gesture or well-timed glance can often accomplish the same result. Whether verbal or not, however, the child apparently believes that he can influence adult behavior. In essence, he implies that he is now a person living among other people, even if he still lacks many of the skills he may see in older children and adults.

Self-descriptive utterances

By their second birthday, most children have made a good start at using language (see Chapter 6). They have gone beyond using single words and are combining two or three words into rudimentary sentences: "Me go," "Big cat," "See truck!" and the like. Frequently they express personal needs and wants, implying an awareness of themselves as individuals. Also scattered among their utterances are indications of knowledge about their social roles; saying "my sister" or "That's Daddy," for example, implies a knowledge of who plays which

Bridges How does language development reflect a toddler's growing self-awareness?

roles within the child's family. At this point, of course, the knowledge may be far from accurate or complete, but evidence for it has at least begun to emerge.

Development of Competence and Self-esteem

From the beginning of infancy through the end of toddlerhood, children achieve a growing sense of basic trust, autonomy, competence, and, ultimately, self-esteem. In fact these developments go hand in hand. Autonomy, as we have discussed, is made possible by a child's secure and basically trustworthy relationships with her primary care-givers. **Competence** (skill and capability) develops as a result of the child's natural curiosity and desire to explore the world and the pleasure that she experiences in successfully mastering and controlling that world (B. White, 1959, 1975a, b). Much like the infant's need for proximity and attachment to her care-givers, her motivation to explore and master the world is thought to be relatively autonomous and independent of basic physiological needs for food, water, sleep, and freedom from pain.

In a series of studies of toddlers and their mothers, researchers found that although mothers of highly competent children did not spend more time interacting with them than mothers of children who were not as competent, there were important differences in the *quality* of their interactions and the stimulation that they provided. These mothers supported and encouraged their infants' curiosity and their desire to explore the world around them by providing a rich variety of interesting toys and experiences that were both safe and appropriate to the children's level of competence. They played with their toddlers in ways that were responsive to the children's interests and needs and used language that their infants could clearly understand.

Bridges How do parents contribute to the development of competence in toddlers?

These parents were also more likely than others to encourage their children to accomplish the tasks they had initiated themselves by actively guiding them and praising them for accomplishments, rather than actually performing the tasks for them (White, 1975a). As you might have guessed, this approach requires considerable patience, the ability to tolerate the child's frustration when things do not work out the first few times, and a firm belief in the child's need and potential to be an autonomous and competent person. Perhaps the most important quality of these parents was their ability to interact sensitively and appropriately with their children and to experience pleasure and delight (at least most of the time) in these interactions. This same quality appears to be most important in the development of secure attachment relationships and continues to be important throughout childhood.

A natural outcome of such parenting is the early emergence of a strong sense of **self-esteem:** a child's feeling that he is an important, competent, powerful, and worthwhile person who is valued and appreciated by those around him. As we shall see, the childhood experiences that follow infancy continue to make major contributions to this important aspect of identity.

Not all parent-child relationships are consistently supportive of a child's developing sense of competence and self-esteem. And in some extreme instances, a parent's treatment of his or her child may be characterized by abuse or neglect.

CHILD ABUSE AND NEGLECT

In a small but significant number of cases, infants and children experience serious maltreatment at the hands of their parents or other care-givers. Most often, maltreatment results from a complex set of factors, which we will discuss shortly.

Maltreatment can take several forms. Sometimes the child may be injured physically: she may turn up at a doctor's office with an odd or disturbing combination of cuts, burns, bruises, or broken bones. Her parents or guardians may report that she "had an accident," even though no typical accident could cause the injuries that the child actually has. In other cases, maltreatment may consist of emotional neglect: the mother may simply ignore her child, feel indifferent to him, and chronically fail to respond to his bids for attention or to his other needs. The most tangible evidence of neglect is the **failure-to-thrive syndrome,** in which the infant seems seriously delayed in his physical growth and is noticeably apathetic in his behavior. In still other cases of maltreatment, the child may not be neglected so much as abused emotionally: one or both parents may continually ridicule or belittle her, for example. Physical problems in such cases may be minor or even absent, although the child's self-confidence may be seriously undermined.

Historical roots

The abuse and neglect of children have historical roots in biblical, ancient Greek, and Roman times, when parents' had absolute power and authority over their young children. During much of European history, infanticide (the killing of infants) was widely used to limit population growth and rid society of infants with birth defects and diseases; and until child labor and compulsory education laws were passed to protect young children, they were exploited and abused in factories, farms, and other workplaces (Langer, 1972). Not until 1962 was the concept of child abuse brought to public attention by Henry Kempe, a pediatrician (Kempe et al., 1962). In 1974 Congress passed the Child Abuse Prevention and Treatment Act, and by then all fifty states had passed legislation requiring those in the helping professions to report cases of abuse and neglect (Bybee, 1979).

Legislation to protect children

Defining Abuse

The definition of any problem significantly influences any attempts to solve it. Kempe originally defined abuse exclusively in terms of its physical effects on the child. Currently five types of maltreatment are included in legal and professional definitions of abuse: (a) physical abuse, which includes assaults on children that produce pain and physical injury including cuts, bruises, and broken bones; (b) sexual abuse, which includes sexual molestation, intercourse, and sexual exploitation; (c) physical neglect, which includes exposure of children to conditions where they receive insufficient food, clothing, shelter, medical care, and so on; (d) emotional neglect, in which parents or other care-givers fail to provide children with the basic nurturance and emotional support required for normal development; and (e) psychological abuse, which involves actions that damage a child's emotional, social, or intellectual functioning. The frequency and intensity of the abusive behavior and the degree to which it is intentional should all be considered in evaluating a potentially abusive situation (Gelles, 1982; Rosenberg, 1989).

Types of maltreatment

Incidence of Abuse

Differences in how abuse is defined, in methods used to study it, and in the proportion of cases that are actually reported make it difficult to estimate accurately how much abuse there is. A national survey of family violence against children in 1975 estimated that fourteen out of every hundred parents of children aged three through seventeen treated their children violently enough to be abusive (Gelles, 1978). This adds up to approximately 46 million children per year. Violent acts included kicking, biting, punching, hitting with an object, beating up, and threatening or hurting with a knife or gun (Belsky et al., 1984). Because infants are even more vulnerable to physical and emotional abuse and neglect, the rate of abuse among them is likely to be even higher. In 1987 more than 1.1 million cases of child abuse were reported, and according to the National Committee for Prevention of Child Abuse, more than eleven hundred children died of abuse in that year (*U.S. News & World Report*, 1988).

Causes of Abuse

Abuse is caused by many factors, which vary in how directly or indirectly they affect the individuals involved. Together, they form a multilevel **causal environment**, or context. Each level of influence is embedded, or "nested," in a broader level, and each has the potential to affect all others. As Belsky (1980) points out, each of the four levels (described below) is significant to some degree in families where abuse occurs.

Ontogenic Level: Developmental History of the Individual Parent   *Ontogenic level* refers to the unique background and personal history of the abusing parents. A parent's own childhood history can contribute to child abuse. Parents who were abused, neglected, or rejected as children are more likely than others to neglect and abuse their own children. Parents who were not directly abused themselves but who observed family aggression and violence are also at greater risk of abusing. Ignorance about children's development because of lack of knowledge about and experience with the parenting role may also contribute to maltreatment, as may a parent's untreated emotional or drug-related problems.

The Microsystem: Family Interactions   **Microsystem** refers to a person's everyday life situations and environment. The microsystem is most directly responsible for child abuse. For young children, the microsystem is the family. The family can be viewed as an interactive system in which every member, including each child, is a potential contributor to the quality of life and to abuse. Infants who are premature, passive, and socially unresponsive and children who are hyperactive, colicky, and difficult to comfort are more likely than others to be abused.

Role of the infant

    Whether or not the behaviors of such "difficult" infants contribute to abuse depends on how their parents respond and on the patterns of parent-child interactions that develop. For example, studies comparing abusive and neglectful families with those that were not abusive found that mothers from maltreating families had 40 percent less positive interactions (affection, support) and 60 percent more negative interactions (threat, punishment) with their children than mothers from nonabusive families did. In addition, children from abusive families displayed almost 50 percent more negative behavior than children from normal families did (Burgess & Conger, 1978). In a study of thirteen- to thirty-five-month-old toddlers in day care, children who had been abused were found to display more physical aggression toward peers and care-givers than those who had not been abused did (George & Main, 1979).

    Families in which physical and verbal violence occurs between parents suffer from a higher than usual likelihood of parent-child abuse (Steinmetz, 1977). Parents who are having problems in their own relationship and who may have unhappy childhood histories may unconsciously participate in a **role reversal,** expecting their children to act like parents and to fulfill the emotional needs that neither their own parents nor their spouses can adequately meet (Belsky, 1980).

Violence between parents

The Ecosystem: Work and Neighborhood   **Ecosystem** refers to the somewhat broader influences outside of the family that indirectly contribute to the quality of life and patterns of abuse within it. Two very important ecosystem influences

Stress of unemployment

Social isolation

Bridges How do American cultural values and beliefs contribute to the existence of child abuse in the United States?

Wide acceptance of physical discipline

are work and neighborhood. One major way in which the world of work influences the family is by its absence: unemployment has been found to be highly related to family violence, against both women and children. Financial stress, personal powerlessness, and lack of self-esteem as well as the conflicts that are created by the increased presence of an unemployed father in the home all serve to trigger abuse (Belsky, 1980). As we noted earlier in this chapter, the quality of parents' work experiences, their level of satisfaction (or dissatisfaction) with work, and the level of conflict between work and family life are all likely to influence patterns of child-rearing.

The neighborhood in which a family lives and the quality of community life that it offers also contribute to abuse. For example, in a study of high-risk and low-risk neighborhoods, families' ratings of the quality of life were predictive of the likelihood of abuse, even when neighborhoods were comparable in terms of the incomes and backgrounds of the families that lived there. Thus, two neighborhoods could be economically and culturally very similar but very different in their risk of abuse. Life in high-risk neighborhoods involved greater social isolation and "social impoverishment" — a pervasive lack of informal and formal social support for child-rearing from neighbors, schools, and community services. Socially isolated and without support, abusive families were unlikely to be observed by anyone else, and they were often unable to turn to others for advice or help. Families in high-risk neighborhoods were also found to make little or no use of preventive services and to seek help primarily in times of crisis, as compared with families in low-risk neighborhoods, who sought help as a part of everyday life (Garbarino & Sherman, 1980).

The Macrosystem: Culture and Society   A society's **macrosystem** — its social and economic conditions, its social and political policies, and its values and beliefs (especially with regard to children, families, and violence) — also plays a very significant role in the existence of child abuse. The willingness of contemporary U.S. society to accept violence on an international scale (war and the arms race) and on the domestic scale (violence on TV) creates a context in which family violence is acceptable. Observation of violent models outside the family is likely to increase violence within it.

In addition, the widely held belief that physical punishment is an acceptable means of controlling children provides a context in which physical abuse is more likely. In one survey, two out of three educators, police officers, and clerics who were questioned condoned physical discipline (such as spanking with the hand), and more than 10 percent believed that hitting children with belts, straps, and brushes was acceptable for maintaining control (Belsky, 1980). In 1973 the Supreme Court ruled that schools have the right to use corporal (physical) punishment for disobedient children — a decision based on the assumption that unlike adults who have been convicted of criminal behavior, children who have been disobedient do not have the right of protection under the Eighth Amendment from cruel and unusual punishment (Belsky, 1980). The difficulty in eliminating child abuse as long as such microsystem influences exist is emphasized by research findings that child abuse is rare in countries where physical punishment is infrequently used (e.g., Sidell, 1972).

Treatment and Prevention

There are two major approaches to solving the problem of child abuse: treatment and prevention. Treatment involves working directly with the parents and child after abuse (or the danger of abuse) has been discovered, and its goals are to reduce or eliminate instances of further abuse and to provide rehabilitative treatment for the physical and psychological injuries suffered by the child, for the abusing parent or parents, and for other family members.

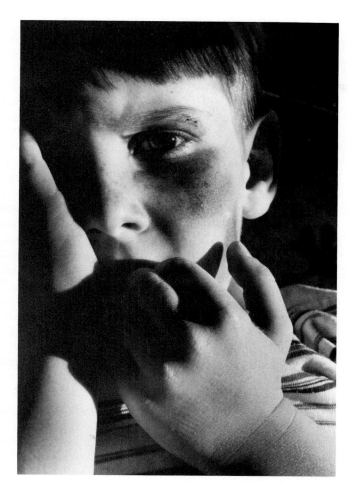

The scars left by child abuse are psychological as well as physical. Abused children can develop pervasive mistrust of adults and stand more risk of becoming abusive parents themselves.

Casework and intensive individual and family counseling and psychotherapy are often used to help the parents and their child understand the causes, consequences, and personal meanings of their destructive feelings and behaviors and to make changes that will allow them to live together in less destructive ways. Self-help groups such as Parents Anonymous, parent aides who assist abusive and neglectful families in their homes, crisis nurseries, foster care for the abused child, and short-term residential treatment for family members or for the entire family unit are among the treatment alternatives that have been employed with some success (Starr, 1979). A fairly recent study that evaluated the effectiveness of eleven different model treatment programs involving more than twelve hundred families found a reduction in abuse and neglect in 42 percent of the treated families but a recurrence of abuse or neglect in 30 percent. Parent aides and/or Parents Anonymous in conjunction with casework proved to be most effective, with a 53 percent reduction in abuse or neglect, but researchers also found a greater likelihood that abuse would recur (Starr, 1979).

Types of treatment

Although treatment is an important aspect of dealing with abuse, it has several important limitations. It is very costly, and the number of families in need far exceed the helping resources available. It is a reactive approach, offering help only after considerable damage has often already occurred. And it holds little promise of successfully challenging the factors that contribute to maltreatment or of preventing new cases from occurring.

Whereas treatment of abuse focuses on limiting the negative consequences to abusive families through rehabilitation, prevention attempts to protect families from factors that cause abuse and to reduce or eliminate those factors when possible. There are two levels of prevention, secondary and primary. *Secondary*

Goals of secondary prevention

prevention attempts to reduce the likelihood of abuse by (a) strengthening and supporting families who are at risk for abuse; (b) helping high-risk families to avoid situations that might make abuse likely; and (c) taking steps to help families when the first warning signs occur.

The major strength of secondary prevention is obvious: families can be helped *before* rather than after most of the damage occurs. It also has major weaknesses, however. First, because it is extremely difficult to identify high-risk families reliably, many families are wrongly labeled, resulting in unnecessary upset, misuse of helping resources, and potential violation of individual rights. High short-term cost is a second weakness of secondary prevention, although if this strategy actually prevents abuse among high-risk families, its long-term costs may in fact be very small.

Secondary prevention programs include early and extended contact between parents and their newborn infants to improve the early parent-child relationship, home visitors and parent aids to assist parents with young children, and home safety, money management, job finding, health maintenance and nutrition, leisure time counseling programs designed to identify and address problem areas of abusive (and potentially abusive) parents (Rosenberg & Reppucci, 1985).

Primary prevention: eliminating the causes

Primary prevention has the goal of reducing or eliminating the factors that contribute to or cause abuse on a populationwide basis. Rather than helping particular families that are abusing or are at risk of doing so, primary prevention attempts to alter the general conditions that affect *all* children and families. Primary preventive approaches include education for parenthood, elimination of corporal punishment, the development of a bill of rights for children, and various social policy supports for parents and their children, including more and better jobs, funding for preschools and day-care centers, inexpensive health care, and so forth.

For example, education-for-parenthood programs exist in quite a number of junior and senior high schools and allow adolescents to learn firsthand about children and parenthood. Day-care centers and preschool programs that involve parents also appear to contribute to the prevention of abuse (Hoffnung, 1983). The limitations of primary prevention include its high initial cost and the difficulties involved in evaluating its effectiveness.

Increasing competency and skills

Live theater and television have also been used to increase the competencies, personal resources, and coping skills of parents thought to underlie the development of positive parent-child relationships. Elementary school-based programs have helped provide groups of parents with information and skill training in child-rearing (Rosenberg & Reppucci, 1985). Another type of program has focused on preventing the onset of abusive behavior through media campaigns, information, crisis and referral services, and efforts at the neighborhood and community levels to increase the ability of existing social networks to provide support and feedback to families.

Education

THE COMPETENT INFANT

In just a matter of months a baby has often tripled in weight and doubled in height; he has learned to move about freely and independently; he has formed important relationships with particular people and places. The mature toddler is starting to know that he is a unique and separate individual, like everyone else. As we have seen in Chapter 6, he has also made a good start in developing his capacities to think, listen, and talk. It generally becomes clear somewhere around his second birthday that he is definitely not a baby anymore.

But what, then, has he become? For convenience, the next several chapters simply call him a preschooler — a child who is too young to begin elementary school. It should be noted, however, that a considerable number of children who are not yet school age attend day-care centers, family day care, or nursery school on a regular basis. Although a preschool child may be too young for elementary school, she is definitely ready and eager to learn more about the physical and social worlds outside her immediate family. If all has gone reasonably well up to now, she can use her family as a secure base to explore these larger worlds, which include the children next door, the department store downtown, and the children and teachers at a nursery school or day-care setting.

From the two-year-old's point of view, home is still a very important place, but it is no longer the world in its entirety. From his parents' point of view, the daily burden of child care has declined markedly, although it has certainly not disappeared yet. A toddler may not need to have her diapers changed for much longer, but she will still need prepared meals for years to come. He may no longer seek attention several times per hour, but he will still seek it many times a day. The child still has a lot of growing and learning to do in the preschool years.

SUMMARY OF MAJOR IDEAS

Early Social Relationships

1. A newborn infant has a natural tendency to participate socially in her world.

2. An infant's social interactions are closely coordinated or synchronized with those of his mother.

3. The similarities in the type and quality of an infant's interactions with both her mother and her father are much greater than the differences.

4. According to a number of studies, day care helps infants develop social competence and responsiveness.

5. Recent studies indicate that when given the opportunity to do so, infants engage in active social interactions with their siblings and peers and often prefer them to their parents as playmates.

Emotions, Temperament, and Personality Development in Infancy

6. Infants appear to be capable of a complex range of emotional responses and are quite sensitive to the feelings of their care-givers. It is likely that they use cues similar to those used by adults, such as variations in voice quality, smell, touch, facial expression, and body language.

7. Even at birth, infants exhibit differences in their patterns of physical and emotional responsiveness and activity level, called *temperament;* these differences both influence and are influenced by the feelings and responses of their care-givers.

8. Freud, Erikson, and Mahler each emphasized the importance of developing an intense infant-parent relationship that is emotionally responsive to the baby's needs and that allows a basic sense of trust in others to develop.

9. Freud, Erikson, and Mahler emphasized the infant's own need to individuate from his parent during the second year of life and to become a separate, autonomous person who can successfully regulate his own feelings, thoughts, and actions without undue anxiety.

10. Failures to achieve a reasonably intense and trusting relationship during early infancy or to gain autonomy and self-control during toddlerhood may interfere with a child's future development.

Attachment Formation

11. Attachment — the tendency of young infants and their care-givers to seek physical and emotional closeness with each other — is thought to provide an important basis for achieving secure and trusting relationships during early infancy.

12. Attachment develops in a series of phases from indiscriminate sociability at birth to goal-coordinated partnerships at two years old.

13. The "strange situation," which confronts the infant with the stress of being in an unfamiliar place, meeting a stranger, and being separated from her parent, has been used to study the development of attachment.

14. Secure attachment is most likely when the care-giver is able to respond sensitively and appropriately to the infant.

15. Infants are equally capable of forming secure attachments to their mother and their father, even though the mother is typically the primary care-giver.

16. The effects of both maternal employment and day care on attachment depend largely on how the mother feels about herself and her role as a parent and on the ways in which the situation helps or hinders her ability to care for and enjoy her baby. The quality of her experience and the quality and consistency of the day care are also important.

17. Insecurely attached infants tend to be less able than securely attached infants to get help from parents and teachers when they need it or to accept it when it is offered.

The Emergence of Autonomy

18. Sources of the growing autonomy that characterizes the second year of infancy include identification, operant and observational learning, and social referencing.

19. During toddlerhood there are also significant increases in self-knowledge and self-awareness. These changes are reflected in the growth in the toddler's awareness of adult standards, distress at behaviors modeled by unknown adults, and the tendencies to smile following an accomplishment, to give directions to adults, and to speak self-descriptively.

20. Toddlers are strongly motivated to achieve greater competence through successfully mastering and controlling the physical and social worlds around them. Competence is fostered by parents who encourage their infant's curiosity by providing opportunities that are challenging, safe, and appropriate to the child's capabilities.

21. Increasing self-esteem in the infant is the natural outcome of supportive parenting.

Child Abuse and Neglect

22. Child abuse and neglect can take emotional as well as physical forms.

23. Legal and professional definitions of abuse specify five types of maltreatment: physical abuse, sexual abuse, physical neglect, emotional neglect, and psychological abuse.

24. Child abuse is thought to affect 46 million children per year; causes occur at the level of the individual parent, the family, the neighborhood, and the culture.

25. Responses to abuse frequently focus on treating the victims and their family. Attempts at prevention occur on two levels: primary (reduction of factors that cause abuse on a societal level) and secondary (reduction of factors at the family level).

KEY TERMS

parent-infant synchrony *(229)*	"strange situation" *(244)*
temperament *(235)*	secure attachment *(244)*
personality *(240)*	anxious-avoidant attachment *(245)*
oral stage *(240)*	anxious-resistant attachment *(245)*
anal stage *(240)*	autonomy *(250)*
trust versus mistrust *(240)*	identification *(251)*
autonomy versus shame and doubt *(240)*	social referencing *(252)*
symbiotic mother-child relationship *(241)*	competence *(255)*
separation-individuation *(241)*	self-esteem *(255)*
attachment *(242)*	failure-to-thrive syndrome *(256)*
signaling behaviors *(242)*	causal environment *(257)*
approach behaviors *(242)*	ontogenic level *(257)*
contact comfort *(242)*	microsystem *(257)*
separation anxiety *(244)*	role reversal *(257)*
stranger anxiety *(244)*	ecosystem *(257)*
	macrosystem *(258)*

WHAT DO YOU THINK?

1. What advice would you give new parents about establishing social relationships with young infants? In what ways would your advice to fathers differ from your advice to mothers? What would you advise them about their baby's interactions with siblings and peers?

2. When you were an infant, did you have a quiet, average, or active temperament? How did your temperament suit your parents and other family members. To what degree do you think your current temperament is consistent with your temperament as an infant?

3. What have been your own family experiences with maternal employment and child-care alternatives? What are your reactions to the discussions of these topics in the chapter? How do you think you will deal with these issues should you become a parent?

4. In your opinion, what needs and behaviors of young infants and toddlers cause the most difficulties for the typical parent? Which of these might be hardest for you?

5. If you were asked your opinions about how state and federal funds should be used to deal with the problem of child abuse, what would you recommend?

FOR FURTHER READING

Belsky, J., Lerner, R., and Spanier, G. *The Child in the Family.* Reading, MA: Addison-Wesley, 1984.

This book explores how the contexts of family, work, neighborhood, culture, and society jointly and interactively influence the social and emotional development of children and their care-givers. Its discussions of such complex and timely issues as divorce, maltreatment, and the dual-worker family are particularly interesting.

Brazelton, T. B. *Infants and Mothers: Differences in Development,* (rev. ed.) New York: Delacorte, 1983.

The author provides a very lively and readable description of infants and their families during their first year together. Using many delightful examples of everyday activities, he helps the reader to compare the developmental changes in Louis, an "average" baby, Laura, a "quiet" baby, and Daniel, an "active" baby, on a month-by-month basis. His clear, nontechnical writing style conveys an appreciation of what life is really like for infants and their families.

Greenspan, S., and Greenspan, N. T. *First Feelings: Milestones in the Emotional Development of Your Baby and Child.* New York: Penguin Books, 1985.

This unique book clearly and concretely helps parents to recognize and encourage their children's emotional growth and to better appreciate and understand their own emotional experiences as parents.

Leach, P. *Babyhood,* 2nd. ed. New York: Knopf, 1987.

This is a straightforward, well-documented, nontechnical, highly informative discussion of the physical, intellectual, and emotional development of infants, with an emphasis on helping parents.

Parke, R. *Fathers.* Cambridge, MA: Harvard University Press, 1981.

This book thoughtfully discusses the important role of fathers as care-givers and parents during infancy and childhood. It includes coverage of divorce, father absence, and stepfatherhood, issues that present difficult challenges to fathers and their families.

Stern, D. N. *The Interpersonal World of the Infant: A View from Psychoanalysis and Developmental Psychology.* New York: Basic Books, 1985.

This creative and highly readable synthesis of current psychoanalytic theory and the latest development research helps in understanding the inner life and interpersonal world of infants.

Stern, D. N. *The First Relationship*, 4th ed. Cambridge, MA: Harvard University Press, 1985.

This is an updated version of Stern's readable account of the development of infant-parent communication.

White, B. *The First Three Years of Life.* Rev. ed. New York: Prentice-Hall, 1987.

This book, which is based on a TV series by the same name, is written as a guide for parents (and future parents) during the first three years of their baby's life. A particularly useful feature is its specific recommendations for how parents can actively support the physical, emotional, and intellectual development of their child.

PART FOUR

The Preschool Years

Although most of us remember relatively little of our preschool years, parents often believe these years are among the most gratifying for their children. Perhaps this is because children begin participating more fully in their families during this time. Now they talk and play with parents and siblings much more — and, of course, they sometimes infuriate everyone more, too. In all these senses they "belong" more fully than ever.

Preschoolers become more social during this period partly because of the more complex motor skills they acquire — riding a trike or climbing a jungle gym can impress parents as well as friends. In addition, with their new cognitive skills, preschool children can engage in extended conversations and try out new social roles in play. The preschooler's world is a rapidly expanding one, and for parents as well as children, the preschool years are both exhausting and exhilarating.

Jennifer's Case

Jennifer was a relatively easygoing first child. She did her share of fussing, of course, but overall her moods were mostly happy — and her bad moments were at least predictable. Jennifer's frequent smiles and affectionate nature seemed to make all her parents' efforts worthwhile.

By the time she was three, Jennifer was no baby any more. She had conversations with her parents on all sorts of topics; went eagerly on walks outdoors, even on the coldest days; dressed herself (mostly); and used the toilet when she needed to. For the time being, things seemed comfortable around the house.

One month after Jennifer's third birthday, her mother became pregnant. Her parents told Jennifer about the expected baby almost as soon as the pregnancy was confirmed. "You'll have a brother or sister," her parents said, "but we don't know which it will be. Someone to play with." Jennifer seemed to like the idea and was curious about how the baby was growing inside her mother. But she also started to waken in the middle of the night and began to suck her thumb more, and her parents wondered if these changes were related to the new baby.

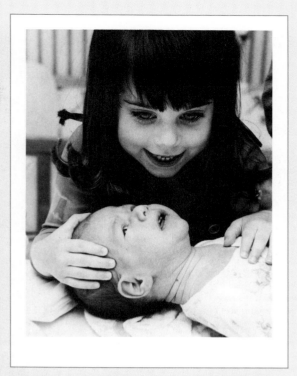

"It" eventually turned out to be a baby boy, Joey. But Joey himself was something of a disappointment, in spite of all the talk and preparation for him beforehand. "He doesn't do much, does he?" commented Jennifer one day. Joey just slept, and sometimes Jennifer liked to cuddle with him then.

Disappointment soon turned to frustration. To her dismay, Jennifer found that she had to touch and hold Joey in the "right" ways and be really gentle. It seemed, too, as if her parents were always fussing over Joey more than he deserved. Jennifer tried to fuss over him, too, but it didn't seem to work for her.

But having Joey around was not all bad. After a few months he began smiling at his mom and dad and sometimes even at Jennifer! Gradually Jennifer figured out how to hold Joey's attention for several minutes by showing him toys at just the right distance and by doing it very quietly. Her parents encouraged these times by praising Jennifer's successes with Joey. They also encouraged her to "help" with Joey's bath — mainly by looking on. And her mother made a baby carrier for her so that Jennifer could carry her own "baby" on errands, "just like mama."

May 21

Dear Mom,

    I think things are going OK these days with Jennifer. I feel bad because lately I just haven't had the kind of time for her that I used to have — I realized yesterday that I had not sat down with her alone for 3 days. Maybe it would help if I got a babysitter sometimes so Jennifer and I could do special things together.

    She really does have some good times with Joey, especially now that he's begun babbling. You should see them! She tries to imitate his sounds; then they have a "conversation"; and then they both giggle.

    Hope that one of these days you can come visit us. I know that Jennifer would love to see you — and so would I!

              Love, as always,
              Diane

Even so, life was not the same after Joey arrived. Jennifer spent more time by herself, partly because her parents were often busy with Joey, but partly also because she was sorting out what had happened to her life since becoming a big sister. Sometimes she wondered how anyone as incompetent as Joey could ever deserve so much attention!

As Joey developed new skills, Jennifer began finding him more interesting. Often, when Joey woke up early in the morning, he would wake Jennifer and she would climb into his crib — much to his delight — and the two of them would "talk" and play together. Jennifer's mother was glad to see the two children getting on so.

After Jennifer entered kindergarten, she had less time for feeling jealous of Joey. She made new friends at school and found herself relying less on Joey for companionship. "He's not as smart as my friends," she told her parents. But when a friend came, she always introduced Joey. "That's my brother," she said with pride and emphasis.

By the time Jennifer was six and Joey was two, she had stopped thinking of him as a baby. Joey still infuriated her sometimes, like the time he stuck clay inside her shoes. But other times it was nice to have him around. With two children to suggest buying ice cream, for example, her parents found it harder to resist than before. And Jennifer had to admit that with Joey for a brother, she felt a bit more like she belonged to a whole "family," not just to a pair of parents.

CHAPTER 8

The Preschool Years: Physical Development

Normal Physical Development

Rate of Growth in the Preschool Years
Influences on Growth
Understanding Physical Growth

Brain Development

Organization of the Brain
Hemispheric Lateralization
Lateralized Behaviors

Other Bodily Changes

Preschool Sensory Development
Childhood Diseases
Bladder and Bowel Control

Motor Skill Development

Fundamental Motor Skills
Can Fundamental Motor Skills Be Taught?
Fine Motor Coordination: The Case of Drawing
  Skills

Gender Differences in Physical Development

Effects of Children's Physical Growth

Effects on Adults
Effects on the Child

Focusing Questions

■ What influences how fast preschool children grow, and why do they develop different bodily proportions?

■ How does the brain become organized during early childhood?

■ What does illness teach young children about their bodies and the world?

■ What motor skills do children acquire during the preschool years, and what refinements do they make in them?

■ What differences in physical development, if any, exist between the sexes during early childhood?

■ How does children's physical and motor development affect their relationships with their parents?

C hildren grow more slowly during the preschool years — from two to six — than they do during infancy, but growth nonetheless has a major impact on their lives as a whole. Not only does physical growth make new motor skills possible; it affects children's social, emotional, and cognitive development. To understand something of these relationships, consider two children — Maria and Kimberly learning to swim. Each enrolls in the same swimming class, but before long Maria is swimming better than Kimberly. Why does this happen?

Most of the time such a difference stems from a mixture of physical, social, emotional, and cognitive factors. Maria is larger than Kimberly; even at the beginning of the swimming class, she was able to hold her breath longer and paddle more powerfully. She also gets more social support from home for learning to swim; her parents are devoted swimmers and take her to the pool in between lessons. Because of differences like these, she has developed a concept of herself as a good swimmer, one who is strong, holds her breath well, and can count on help at swimming when she needs it.

This chapter looks closely at such factors, investigating how physical growth and motor skills influence each other and psychological processes during early childhood. To do so, the chapter describes the overall nature and extent of physical growth and then looks at some motor skills typically acquired during early childhood. Some of these, such as learning to walk, are relatively universal among all children. Other skills, such as ice-skating, are rather unique to particular groups of children. Woven into our descriptions are implicit notions of what constitutes typical or normal physical development. As we point out repeatedly, however, such norms do not in and of themselves constitute prescriptions for how children *should* develop physically. Evaluating growth is also important, but it is different from describing growth. The chapter tries to respect this separation.

TABLE 8.1 Average Height and Weight, Early Childhood

Age (Years)	Height (Inches)	Weight (Pounds)
2	34.5	27.0
3	37.8	31.5
4	40.9	36.0
5	43.6	40.5

Source: Hamill et al. (1979).

NORMAL PHYSICAL DEVELOPMENT

Physical growth in the preschool years is relatively easy to measure and gives a clear idea of how children normally develop during this period. Table 8.1 shows the two most familiar measurements of growth, standing height and weight. At

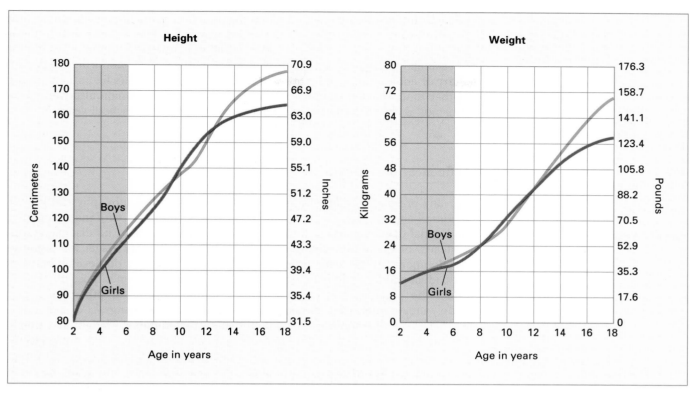

FIGURE 8.1
*Growth in Height and Weight from
Two to Eighteen Years*

age two, an imaginary average child in North America measures about thirty-three or thirty-four inches tall, or about two feet and ten inches. Three years later, at age five, he measures approximately forty-four inches, or about one-third more than before. The typical child weighs about twenty-seven pounds on his second birthday but about forty-one pounds by his fifth. (See also Figure 8.1.) Meanwhile, other measurements change in less obvious ways. His head grows about one inch in circumference during these years, and his body fat decreases as a proportion of his total bodily tissue.

Rate of Growth in Preschool Years

The **velocity** of growth is the rate or speed by which children change size over a period of time. Table 8.2 shows velocities for height and weight during early childhood. As the table shows, increases in height slow down during this period, even though height itself continues to increase. In other words, a young child puts on inches most quickly during the early part of the preschool period. Sitting height — measured from the buttocks upward — grows more slowly than standing height during early childhood, and it slows in proportion to overall standing height throughout the period (Johnston, 1979.) Weight, in contrast, increases by fairly equal increments each year: by about four or five pounds, to be exact.

These velocities and their relationships to each other lead to steady changes in bodily proportions and cause preschool children to look less and less like babies. Children's legs become longer as a proportion of their total length. Their build becomes less chunky because each addition of weight represents a smaller proportion of their previous weight and because skinfolds of fat become relatively thinner over time.

Velocities of growth vary among children and among the major parts of children's bodies, and these differences help to accentuate the unique appearance

TABLE 8.2   Velocities of Growth for Height and Weight, Early Childhood

Age (Years)	Height Increase per Year (Inches) from Previous Year	Weight Increase per Year (Pounds) from Previous Year
2	5.0	5.2
3	3.3	4.5
4	3.1	4.5
5	2.7	4.5

Source: Hamill et al. (1979).

of each child as she gets older. During the preschool years some children become relatively long-legged, although not necessarily tall; others develop relatively big shoulders or especially small feet. And facial dimensions change in ways unique to each child. Often these specific changes reshuffle somewhat during the growth spurt of adolescence, and to a certain extent the child looks like a new person at that time. But the essential proportions and patterns remain afterward. Like it or not, a child's looks begin taking shape during the preschool years.

Influences on Growth

For any preschool child who is reasonably healthy and happy, physical growth is remarkably smooth and predictable, especially compared with many cognitive and social developments. All in all, physical growth contains no discrete stages, plateaus, or qualitative changes like the ones described by Piaget for cognitive development. At the same time, however, large differences do develop between individual children and between groups of children. Sometimes these differences affect the psychological development of young children; at other times they simply create interesting physical variety among human beings.

Growth is usually smooth

The overall smoothness of growth means that childhood height and weight can predict adult height and weight to a significant extent, although not perfectly. A four-year-old who is above average in height tends to end up above average as an adult. Nevertheless, correlation between childhood and adult height is imperfect because of individual differences in nutrition and health and, most of all, in the timing of puberty. Apparently, children who experience puberty later than average tend to grow taller than children who experience it early. Variations in the timing of puberty can therefore alter a child's relative size as an adult.

Genetic Background   Most dimensions of growth are influenced substantially by heredity. Tall parents tend to have tall children, and short parents have short children. Weight shows similar patterns, even though it can be influenced strongly by habits of exercise and diet; a tendency to be heavy or thin is inherited to a significant extent. Contrary to popular belief, both parents contribute equally to these tendencies (Brennan, 1985). Sons do not necessarily resemble their fathers' growth patterns more than their mothers', nor do daughters resemble their mothers' more than their fathers'. A child with one tall parent and one short parent therefore stands equal chances of being either tall or short. On the average, in fact, such children are middling in height, although they vary widely as individuals.

Ethnic differences in growth

Races and ethnic groups around the world also differ in growth patterns (Eveleth, 1979). Children from Asiatic groups, such as Chinese and Japanese, tend to be shorter than European and North American children. The latter in turn are shorter than children from African societies. Shape differs among these groups as well, although the differences do not always become obvious until adolescence. Asiatic children develop comparatively short legs and arms relative to their torsos and relatively broad hips. African children do just the opposite: they develop relatively long limbs and narrow hips. Olympic athletes reflect these differences; records consistently show Asiatics performing better in events requiring upper-body strength, such as wrestling, gymnastics, and weight-lifting, whereas Africans tend to excel in events requiring a long stride, such as running (Tanner, 1978b; Greene & Johnston, 1980).

Such trends do not result from differences in nutrition or health care. Well-off children from these societies show the same relative differences, even though their diets are comparable in overall quality. And with a minor exception noted below, the same differences exist whether children are living in their native

BRIDGES

Family — How may family attitudes affect how often a preschool child gets sick? (284–285)

Physical Growth — Why are preschool children in industrialized countries taller and heavier today than preschool children were one hundred years ago? (275)

Peers — What effect does mastering specialized motor skills have on preschool peer relations? (294)

Genetics — Is left- and right-handedness inherited or learned behavior? (282)

Social Context — To what extent do preschool children's drawings vary from culture to culture? (296)

THE PRESCHOOL YEARS: PHYSICAL DEVELOPMENT

Self-concept and Identity — How do children's growing motor skills affect how they think about themselves? (302)

Emotions — Why do poor emotional relationships with parents sometimes prevent preschool children from growing normally? (278)

Learning — Can fundamental motor skills be taught? (293)

Cognition — In what ways are a preschooler's physical growth and cognitive development interconnected? (300)

Language — How does the organization of the brain affect the way that children process language? (280)

country or have emigrated to another, more affluent one, where medical care might tend to be better. Apparently nutrition and health care do affect growth, but they do not override genetic and cultural factors.

Nutrition and the Secular Trend During the last one hundred years or so, children in industrialized countries have been getting larger and heavier (Van Wieringen, 1978). The development is often called the **secular trend.** Each decade since 1900, five-year-olds have been taller than in the previous decade by about one or two centimeters, or about one-half inch. Recently the trend has extended to certain non-Western countries; in Japan, for example, five-year-olds have been getting taller by as much as three centimeters per decade since 1950.

Of greater significance than the secular trend in height and weight is the fact that present-day children reach maturity more rapidly. Girls now have their first menstruation about thirty or forty months (or three years) earlier than they did one hundred years ago (Tanner, 1973).

The facts also suggest that the trend may reflect general improvements in nutrition during infancy and early childhood as well as decreases in serious or "classic" childhood diseases. Growth changes in Japanese children illustrate this possibility. In 1950 young children growing up in Japan were significantly shorter than children of Japanese ancestry growing up in the United States, and the Japanese-Americans were in turn shorter than Anglo-American children. These children had all been born near the end of World War II, when food and medical services in Japan did not match those found in the United States. By the 1970s, however, Japanese children in Japan had become just as tall and heavy as children of Japanese descent growing up in the United States, although they were still not as tall as Anglo-American children. During the intervening decades, diet and medical services had come to resemble or even surpass those found in the United States.

Some of the secular trend may also result from **hybrid vigor:** the tendency of genetically dissimilar individuals to produce comparatively larger and more vigorous offspring (Van Wieringen, 1979). The notion of hybrid vigor is borrowed from the study of plants; fruit trees, for example, produce larger and

Historical changes in size

Faster maturity

Bridges Why are preschool children in industrialized countries taller and heavier today than preschool children were one hundred years ago?

Physical benefits of hybridization

As a result of improvements in nutrition and health care, children in industrialized nations have grown larger over the last century. Nevertheless, certain specific nutritional problems remain — in particular, the consumption of excess sugar and fat.

healthier fruit if they cross-pollinate with differing strains of trees rather than with highly similar or identical strains. In like manner, according to this view, human beings may bear stronger and healthier children if they come from genetically dissimilar lineages. Some population specialists have argued that over time people tend to marry and reproduce with dissimilar individuals, so that over time they also tend to produce children who are more vigorous and generally larger. The process may have accelerated in recent decades because modernization of society has encouraged emigration. Now more than ever, people move from the country to the city to the suburbs, or from one city to another, or even from one nation to another, which enables them to meet and marry people from dissimilar genetic backgrounds.

The end of the secular trend

In spite of these facts, new evidence shows that the secular trend may be coming to a conclusion. The most recent surveys of growth show smaller increases among children than earlier ones did (Lohman & Roche, 1984; Roche, 1979). Apparently the benefits of diet and medicine may have reached their natural limit. If so, this suggests that future differences in growth patterns among individuals and groups may reflect genetic differences to a comparatively greater extent than in the past.

Disease   Although serious illnesses do interfere with growth, it can often be hard to judge exactly how much. The trouble is that children with serious illnesses often have other conditions that retard growth; they may have been small-for-date, or they may have suffered from chronically poor nutrition during infancy. These conditions can lead not only to slow growth but also to various sicknesses, which in turn may contribute to the problem.

Differential effects of diseases

To hold back growth, an illness must be fairly major. Preschool-age children in certain impoverished rural parts of Central America tend to be shorter and lighter in weight if they have suffered continually from diarrhea during infancy (Condon-Paolini et al., 1977), but similar children are not shorter and lighter if their illnesses have mainly consisted of upper-respiratory-tract infections (colds).

Children from affluent parts of these same societies do not usually get sick enough to impair their growth. Nor do children from societies that are generally well-off; a middle-class American child is just as likely to grow large (or small) if he catches colds frequently as if he does not (Johnston, 1979).

Certain specific diseases and conditions do retard growth, in many cases by reducing the normal absorption of nutrients over a long period of time. Childhood diabetes can retard growth, at least partly by interfering with the normal use of sugars in the body. So can any chronic infection of the intestine, such as amoebic dysentery or worms, by preventing the normal digestions of foods. Nutritional deficits can also develop because of chronic intolerance to certain foods, such as to the gluten in wheat products or to the lactose in milk products. Children with these conditions suffer in various ways, but to a large extent they simply become malnourished, and like other malnourished children, they do not grow as rapidly as usual (Merck Laboratories, 1985).

Effects of disease on nutrition

Not all diseases that influence growth do so by affecting nutrition. About one preschool child in ten thousand develops a deficiency in her **endocrine glands,** which produce growth hormones (Tanner, 1978b). As a result, growth simply slows down considerably; by age five, for example, an afflicted child may measure only about two and one-half feet tall (or eighty-five centimeters), which is about nine inches (or fifteen centimeters) shorter than average. Occasionally doctors can trace such growth deficiencies to an anatomical disorder (such as a tumor) of the glands that control growth. More often, however, they can find no obvious cause. In either case, the condition can usually be treated by injections of whatever hormones the child appears to be missing.

Effects of hormone deficiencies

Injections of hormones are a useful strategy, however, only for children who have a diagnosed hormone deficiency and do not deviate far from normal height or weight. Because growth hormones are powerful medicines full of unknown side effects, doctors tend to prescribe them only in situations where their benefits are certain and their risks are small. Hormones do not make a desirable treatment for children who are merely shorter than average but want to become taller or whose parents want them to become taller.

Once the causes of slow growth are diagnosed correctly and treated, children can often recover by growing much faster than usual until they have reached the normal range of size for their age. At that point growth slows down again to relatively normal rates and becomes relatively immune to short-term and minor changes in the children's health and nutrition. This process is often called **catch-up growth,** and it suggests that genetics may influence the rate of physical growth significantly as long as children receive basically good nutrition and physical care.

Catch-up growth

Given how much children normally vary in height, how can doctors tell if a child is abnormally short? One way is to observe how children's bones are hardening. Bone hardening is called **ossification** and it is a normal growth process that continues until adolescence. Ossification reveals itself in X-rays of children's joints, such as their hands or feet: as initial soft bone (called "cartilage") converts to mature, hard bone, it shows up more visibly in the X-rays. By comparing a child's skeletal growth with X-rays of normally developing children, experts can estimate *bone age* for a particular child. In general, bone age should correspond to a child's physical height: tall children should have an "old" bone age, and short children should have a "young" bone age. In most cases this correspondence does indeed occur; but when it does not, a child has a true growth problem.

Bone age shows maturity

Even for children without growth problems, growth varies depending on the time of the year. Children grow almost three times faster in the spring (April through June) than in the fall (October through December) (Marshall & Swan, 1971). The difference is large enough to be perceptible, making a child seem much faster growing in one season than in another. The reasons for the cycle are not clear. Obviously it does *not* depend on photosynthesis (as tree growth does), but the growth spurt does seem to depend somehow on how much light the child experiences. Blind children do not show seasonal cycles of growth: nor do children living near the equator, where sunlight remains relatively constant throughout the year.

Emotional Factors   Although most variations in growth stem from genetic, health, or physical causes, differences can occasionally also result from emotional factors. Sometimes too much stress in a family can keep children from growing normally, a condition called **deprivation dwarfism** (Gardner, 1972) or **failure to thrive** (Drotar, 1985). Children with this condition seem apathetic and weak, and their relationships with parents tend to involve conflict and impaired rapport. Partly because of this social impairment, psychologists have lately called deprivation dwarfism by the name **reactive attachment disorder (RAD)** (American Psychological Association, 1980). Psychologically, young preschoolers with RAD do not respond strongly or normally to their parents, as if they do not feel attached to them.

Bridges   Why do poor emotional relationships with parents sometimes prevent preschool children from growing normally?

The condition apparently results from situations that interfere with normal positive relationships between parent and child, especially during infancy or the early preschool period. For example, parents suffering from the stresses of unemployment, chronic conflicts, or other painful circumstances may make a scapegoat of a child who needs more attention than other children in the family. The result is a bad relationship that may lead the child to eat poorly or be plagued by constant anxiety. This nervousness can interfere with sleep or the production of growth hormones.

Impact of stress and conflict

Even in situations such as these, however, the causes of failure to thrive are not well established. Mothers of children who fail to thrive usually show no dramatic qualities that might account for the children's growth problems. One study observed such mothers with their preschool-age children once a week for many months and interviewed the mothers about their children as well (Pollitt et al., 1975). As a group, the mothers expressed reasonably normal beliefs about and goals for their children. In practice they did impose fairly strict discipline, spank their children more than usual, and seem a bit less affectionate than mothers of normal children. But the observers could not tell whether the mothers caused these problems or whether the children had temperaments that created barriers between them and other members of the family.

The most recent research suggests that RAD results from a lack of *synchrony,* or "mesh," between parents' expectations and the child's inherent styles of responding (Drotar et al., 1985). The lack of synchrony is the result of many factors operating together for quite some time. Conflicts between parents and grandparents can contribute to stress between parents and child; so can unemployment or other economic hardship. A child whose natural response style is slow can also make RAD a bit more likely; so can a serious, prolonged illness in the child. In these cases the child tends not to respond as parents expect, and if the parents take the child's unresponsiveness personally, their relationship with the child can eventually deteriorate. But note that no *one* circumstance "causes" RAD; it grows out of a pattern or sequence of circumstances.

Importance of nonverbal communication

Overcoming attachment disorders

If reactive attachment disorder has not persisted for too long, it can usually be reversed in the short run through special nutritional and medical intervention to help the child regain her strength and begin growing normally again. This strategy does not solve any long-term problems in the relationships between parents and RAD children, of course. Such problems require relieving parents of some of their stress through counseling for parents or training workshops in the skills of parenting. Long-term solutions also require psychological help for the child in learning new, less passive responses to people. And they require practical help, too, such as jobs for the unemployed or high-quality child care for those who need it.

Understanding Physical Growth

Because physical growth can be measured simply and objectively, it has proved relatively easy to study in large populations or societies. But for several reasons, trends in growth among populations can be misleading. First, as you may already suspect, group trends hide important individual differences. Even though Asiatics may average a shorter height than Africans, certain Asian children are nonetheless taller than certain African ones. Facts like these must be brought to bear whenever physical stereotypes may influence a child's opportunities in life. It is not fair to assume that a child will have health or learning problems just because he happened to have a very low birth weight; the success of such children depends on too many other factors to support that conclusion (Miesels, 1984; Brazelton, 1980). Low birth weight may create risk, but it does not imply certainty of failure. Likewise, we cannot assume that every tall preschooler will make a good basketball player or that every overweight child will turn out to be clumsy.

Individual variations

Second, population differences in growth can create the impression that heredity and environment affect all aspects of growth to the same extent, when in fact they do not. Some features of growth change noticeably because of experiences; a child may become more overweight or underweight depending on what she eats and on how much exercise she gets. Other features seem to depend almost completely on genetic endowment; at what age a child acquires permanent teeth seems to depend entirely on genetics and not at all on nutrition or illness (Demirjian, 1978). And as we have already discussed, some features of growth, such as the secular trend, may be guided by both genetics and experience.

Variations in relative importance of heredity

The third caution about growth trends concerns the value of physical size. Because low birth-weight children experience more risks, are bigger children therefore likely to be healthier? In North American society, for the vast middle range of sizes, the answer to this question seems to be no; normal variations make little difference to children's later health. But sheer size has a different significance in less affluent societies. In non-Western rural communities, being large actually reduces a child's chances for good health and long life (Stini, 1972), and small mothers in such societies actually give birth successfully more often than large mothers do (Frisancho et al., 1977). The reasons for this are not clear. Perhaps being small reduces the amount of food a person needs, and in a society where food may be scarce, needing less may be an advantage.

Relationship of size and health

BRAIN DEVELOPMENT

Taken as a whole, the brain does most of its growing quite early in life. By the time an infant reaches the age of two, her brain averages about 75 percent of its final adult weight and by the age of five, about 90 percent of final adult weight. Only a few other organs (such as the eyes) are so well developed at such an early age (Yeterian & Pandya, 1988).

Brain growth during early childhood happens in two ways. First, as we note in Chapter 5, a lot of growth comes from the development of *myelin sheaths*, the insulating covers that surround mature nerve fibers and allow the fibers to conduct impulses reliably and efficiently. Myelinization among fibers that connect the "higher" cerebral cortex with the somewhat "lower" cerebellum does not finish until about the age of four. These particular fibers assist children in achieving fine motor skills, such as writing and drawing. To some extent, therefore, such school-related skills depend partly on brain development as well as on muscular development, social encouragement, and opportunities to practice.

Improved conduction

Increasing brain complexity

In addition to myelinization, some nerve cells continue to extend fibers between and among themselves, and capillaries continue to grow near these fibers to provide them with the nutrients that they need. As a result, a young child's brain looks increasingly dense and complex when viewed under a microscope (Lynch & Gall, 1979).

Organization of the Brain

Generalized brain activity

Given this density and complexity, how does the brain sort out and perform the diverse functions of being human? Contrary to a widespread belief, it does *not* work like a telephone switchboard; individual stimuli or thoughts do not confine themselves to select nerve fibers, as if the fibers acted like wires. Instead a stimulus generates neural activity over wide areas of the brain and sometimes even in the entire brain. Some of this response shows itself when electrodes are placed on an individual's head. But the locations of brain activity can be mapped even more accurately by injecting tiny, harmless amounts of radioactive substances into the blood and measuring which parts of the brain then accumulate especially large amounts of the substances (Lassen et al., 1978). Active brain cells and fibers, which require larger amounts of blood, therefore give off more radiation, and can be "photographed" by this technique.

Specialized brain areas

In spite of responding widely to most stimuli, the brain also shows relationships between the kind of stimulation it receives and the area that responds most strongly. A visual image, like the sight of a cat, produces the strongest activity in an area called the **visual cortex** located near the back of the head in the cerebral cortex. The sounds of speech produce their primary response in the **auditory cortex** and specifically in a place called **Wernicke's area** located near the left side of the cerebral cortex.

Bridges How does the organization of the brain affect the way that children process language?

By the end of the preschool years, similar relationships between brain activity and many overt behaviors exist. Simple voluntary movements, such as lifting an arm, produce their largest neural activity in the **motor cortex** located just forward of the top of the head, and the child's own speech usually produces its primary activity in a place called **Broca's area** located on the left side of the cerebral cortex and somewhat to the front. These and other areas of specialized activity are illustrated in Figure 8.2.

Hemispheric Lateralization

During the preschool years, children begin showing definite **hemispheric lateralization,** which is the tendency for the left and right halves of the brain to perform separate functions. In general, the left hemisphere deals increasingly with information on an item-by-item or linear basis, and the right hemisphere identifies relationships or patterns among the items (Bensen & Zaidel, 1985; Gazzaniga, 1988).

The difference in function is quite noticeable in a task called **dichotic listening.** In this task, a child wears headphones that feed sounds or information to each ear separately. Because of the layout of the nerve cells in the brain, the experimental sounds are conducted to particular hemispheres for processing. As it happens, the sounds initially go to the hemisphere *opposite* the ear that receives each sound. Under these conditions, if the information given to each ear is relatively linear or sequential, such as a string of digits, the ear connected to the left hemisphere tends to hear its sounds relatively earlier and with fewer errors. But if the information emphasizes patterns, such as melodies, the right hemisphere functions better.

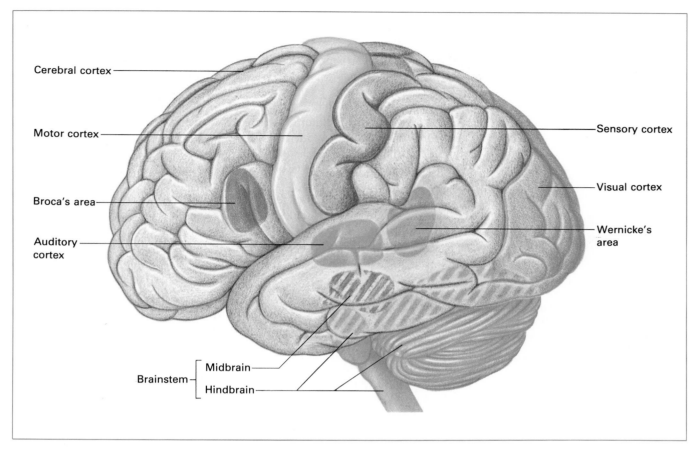

Cerebral cortex

Motor cortex

Broca's area

Auditory cortex

Sensory cortex

Visual cortex

Wernicke's area

Brainstem — Midbrain / Hindbrain

FIGURE 8.2
Regions of the Brain

Similar trends happen with the other senses, including touch and vision (Cummings, 1985). Consider these two tasks:

Examples of brain lateralization

- *Touch* Give preschool children a simple three-dimensional shape, such as a wooden cube, inside a bag or box. Ask them to feel it without seeing it. On the average, children figure out its overall shape more easily by feeling with their left hands, but they can count the corners of the shape more easily with their right hands.

- *Vision* Show a drawing of a simple shape to preschoolers. If you ask them to copy it line by line (a linear task), they will tend to do this faster and more accurately if they view the drawing in their right visual field. But if you ask them to match the drawing with other identical ones (a patterning task), they will perform better if both shapes lie to the left side of their visual field. The drawing can be confined to just one-half of the child's visual field by asking the child to look steadily at a point straight ahead and then flashing the drawing to one side or the other of the point for just an instant. In an instantaneous exposure, the child does not have time enough to redirect gaze, which could accidentally cause the drawing to span both halves of the visual field.

Experiments like these imply that the hemispheres specialize in function even among young children. Note, however, that most everyday tasks probably obscure hemispheric specialization simply because they usually require the activity of both halves of the brain. A child in nursery school, for example, might discover that a shape is a cube, but most likely he will handle it with both hands, look at its overall shape, and count the corners — all at once.

Lateralized Behaviors

In contrast to hemispheric lateralization, lateralized behaviors are quite evident in everyday life, even among preschool-age children. **Lateralized behaviors** are actions that individuals prefer to perform with one side of their body more than with the other. The best example is handedness: offer a toy to a five-year-old, and most likely she will take it with her right hand rather than her left. But persons of all ages show lateral preferences (usually right-sided) for a variety of behaviors. Most of us have a favorite eye for looking through a telescope or keyhole, a preferred ear for listening on the telephone, and a preferred foot for squashing a bug on the floor (Coren et al., 1981).

Lateral preferences emerge during the preschool years and become stable about the time children begin school. There is a low correlation between lateral preferences; right-handed children stand slightly greater chances than left-handed children of being right-eyed, but sometimes they turn out left-eyed instead. A few children (and adults) become truly equal in their lateral preferences or at any rate become very selective about their preferences. They may learn to write equally well with both hands, or they may learn to write with one hand but throw a ball with the other.

Bridges   Is left- and right-handedness inherited or learned behavior?

Lateralized behavior must have at least partly biological or genetic origins. It is hard to see what experiences might cause a majority of three-year-olds to choose to use their right ears for listening to a seashell. Hand preference runs in families: siblings and twins are much more likely than usual to prefer the same hand, as are parents and their children. Boys are left-handed slightly more often than girls, and children with genetically caused mental retardation are much more likely than usual to be left-handed (Springer & Deutsch, 1989). All of these facts imply genetic influences on lateralized behaviors.

But learning probably does affect lateral preferences somewhat. A right bias is strongest among preschool children for behaviors that are taught explicitly, such as eating with a spoon; the bias is weakest for behaviors that children

Perspectives

Hand Preference and the Right-Shift Theory

Although there is little doubt that genetics contributes to hand preference somehow, explaining just *how* it contributes has proved elusive and challenging. One puzzle is the inheritance pattern of left-handedness. Children with two left-handed parents are not all left-handed; as it turns out, only about one-half of them are. But because this proportion is still much higher than in society at large, genetics obviously does matter in some subtle or complex way. But what is that way?

One intriguing explanation is the **right-shift theory**, proposed by Marian Annett (1985). According to the right-shift theory, individuals inherit either a right-handed bias in fine motor skills (called the "right-shift factor") or else *no* lateral preference at all. A child who inherits the right-shift factor is predisposed to become fully right-handed. One who does not inherit the factor will eventually acquire a hand preference anyway but do so by learning from others. Society will encourage these "impartial" children toward right-handedness; but many will adopt left-handedness anyway as a result of chance experiences.

This combination of genetics and learning accounts very closely for the proportions of left- and right-handed individuals observed in society (Corballis, 1983). Theoretically, children of two left-handed parents actually inherit *no* preference rather than a left-hand preference; so these children eventually adopt each hand in about equal proportions, as indeed happens. Children of two right-handed parents present a more complicated genetic picture. That is because right-handed parents really consist of two groups: a majority who are genetically biased by the right-shift factor and a minority who are genetically impartial but became right-handed anyway through learning. Some children of this latter group may therefore also lack the right-shift factor and end up left-handed in spite of their right-handed parents. This outcome also in fact happens; about 2 percent of children with two right-handed parents are nonetheless left-handed.

Why should a genetic right-hand bias have evolved at all? One possibility is efficiency. Even in prehistoric times, a bias favoring one particular hand may have improved fine

By the preschool years, children show definite preferences for using one hand more than the other. They also have less noticeable preferences for a particular foot, eye, and ear.

usually learn spontaneously, such as digging in a sandbox. And right-hand bias increases during the life span. About 85 percent of children during the preschool years favor their right hand, but more than 95 percent of adults during old age do so.

This shift may not seem like much, but it is too large to happen by chance. It suggests that learning affects hand preference in either of two ways. Perhaps society encourages left-handers to switch hands throughout the life span, and eventually some left-handers do in fact switch. Or perhaps older persons reflect

Social influences on handedness

motor coordination, as when using tools or eating small pieces of fruit. One hand could specialize in these tasks and therefore become better at them. But why would genetics favor the shift to the right but not also provide a "left-shift factor" in equal proportions?

One explanation (still speculative) is that the right-shift factor exists primarily to assist another, more important psychological activity, which is language (Springer & Deutsch, 1989). Right-handedness is just an accidental by-product of this more important function. According to this line of reasoning, the underlying right-shift factor assists by causing the fine motor skills of speech production to be processed in the left half of the brain, the same half where the perceptual skills of speech comprehension occur. Placing these two activities close to each other may help them to cooperate, so to speak, and stimulate better language ability overall. By the same token, lacking a right-shift factor would put a child at greater risk for language and learning disabilities. Survey research does indeed confirm this last prediction: left-handed individuals (who lack the right shift)

experience language and learning problems more frequently than do right-handed individuals, although still only a small minority of the time.

Considered as a whole, the right-shift theory is persuasive, but it leaves important questions unanswered. For one thing, it does not explain why most left-handed persons have good overall language skill in spite of supposedly inefficient brain organization. And it does not explain why children with accidental damage to the left part of the brain sometimes learn to process language satisfactorily in the right half of the brain. So more pieces remain in the puzzle, even though some of them are starting to fall into place.

the influence of school practices earlier in this century, when teachers often worked to get left-handers to write with their right hands. Either way, learning causes the change, not genetics (Curtiss, 1985). Society's influence may begin early, as in nursery school classrooms that do not contain enough left-handed scissors.

OTHER BODILY CHANGES

Preschool Sensory Development

Visual acuity, or sharpness of vision, improves during the preschool years. As a toddler, acuity for distant stationary objects or shapes — such as the letters on a traditional eye-examination chart — is only about 20/60, meaning that a two-year-old recognizes shapes at twenty feet that an adult can recognize at sixty. Paradoxically, their near vision is often imperfect as well: many preschoolers have trouble focusing on shapes that are less than about two feet away. By about age five, the distant vision improves substantially for most preschoolers, but near vision remains a problem for some individuals during the early school years. About one child in ten needs glasses by the age of seven, even after vision has matured (D. Vaughan et al., 1986).

Imperfect visual tracking

Vision for moving objects remains difficult for much longer. Tracking a pattern of moving dots, for example, proves very confusing, even for a five-year-old (VanOeffelen & Vos, 1984). Some children have trouble coordinating the gaze of each eye with the other (this ability is called *binocular vision*). In some cases, problems with tracking and coordination may persist into kindergarten and first grade and account for a child's initial difficulties in scanning a line of print when first learning to read (Harley & Lawrence, 1984).

For most children, *auditory acuity,* or sharpness of hearing, is more fully developed by the preschool years than is visual acuity. But hearing a specific tone in the midst of other tones can be confusing. Inability to isolate sounds may account for some children's apparent distractibility when they first enter school (Moores, 1987). In a classroom, even accidental rustling noises can compete strongly with the teacher's voice for the child's attention, although there may be other reasons for distraction as well.

Childhood Diseases

Colds and Other Minor Viruses   During the preschool years, children catch numerous viral illnesses, but the number declines as they get older. Two-year-olds generally get more than eight respiratory ailments (mostly colds) each year, whereas five-year-olds catch only about six or seven (Denny & Clyde, 1983), although the number sometimes rises temporarily when children first enter nursery school or kindergarten. Because these illnesses tend to occur mostly during the winter months, some preschool children may seem sick almost continuously at that season, and families with more than one young child may constantly have someone sick with a viral illness.

Many minor illnesses

Some differences in rates of illness reflect developing psychological differences among children and their families in how they conceive of illness and in which ailments they believe deserve complaining about (S. Wilkinson, 1988). In some families a runny nose is commonly regarded as a "cold," whereas in others it may also require a fever, coughing, and fatigue before it even seems worth

Bridges   How may family attitudes affect how often a preschool child gets sick?

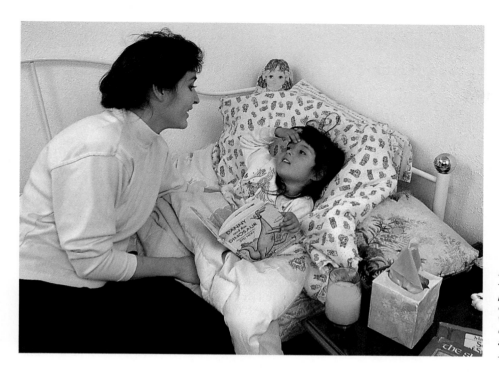

Minor illnesses — mainly colds and flu — are far more common during the preschool years than later during childhood and adolescence. In families with more than one young child, it often seems as though someone is sick almost all of the time.

considering as a "sickness." The difference in definition affects how many "colds" a child (or his parents) reports having each year and how much discomfort the child attributes to illness.

Although these illnesses definitely cause inconvenience to parents and create crankiness in young children, they do have cognitive and social benefits (Parmalee, 1986). Minor illnesses teach young children about the nature of disease — that it originates both with germs and with unhealthful behaviors and that it can sometimes be contagious. Minor illnesses may also develop children's sensitivity to their own and others' feelings. For example, they learn that physical discomfort differs from personal unhappiness: one requires comfort and love, and the other requires rest and perhaps medicine as well. Making this distinction probably helps preschool children to understand the nature of feelings more clearly.

Psychological benefits of minor illness

Serious Illnesses During Early Childhood   Serious illnesses are ones that incapacitate children for many days or weeks, that require close medical supervision, and that can even end in death if left untreated. Until recent decades, such illnesses included most of the classic childhood diseases such as measles, mumps, and diphtheria.

Improved living conditions, better medical care, and immunization programs have decreased the incidence of these diseases and have made fatalities from them much less common. In 1930 five or six preschool children (ages two to four) out of every one thousand died of one of the major infectious childhood diseases or of complications of the disease. In recent years, in contrast, less than one child in every one thousand died in this way (Klienman, 1988). In the meanwhile, one serious, new illness has appeared: AIDS, which has occurred even among infants and children. So far, AIDS has remained extremely rare among preschool children, although there is no guarantee it will remain rare in the decades ahead (Osborn, 1988).

Ironically, the very infrequency of serious illness creates medical dangers. Parents may become too casual about immunizing their children in the belief that the major diseases have been eliminated and that "children don't get really

Perspectives

Relationships Between Poverty and Health

By a number of measures, young children from low-income families are less healthy than those from middle- and high-income families. The number of short-term illnesses, such as colds and ear infections, is one way to judge, Preschool children from low-income families get these about 25–50 percent more frequently than do preschoolers as a whole (Wadsworth, 1986). And children from low-income families are much more likely to be undernourished — meaning they chronically lack essential vitamins, iron, or protein. They are two or three times as likely to be extremely thin and to be much shorter than average. During the 1980s, about 11 million preschool children were malnourished in the United States alone, and the large majority came from low-income families (L. Brown & Allen, 1988).

Viewed broadly, there are two main reasons for inequalities in children's health. The first is the connection between poverty and nutrition. Contrary to a common stereotype, poverty does *not* lead to malnourishment because the poor misspend limited food budgets on frivolous or unnutritious items. Surveys instead show that they actually buy a more well-rounded diet than do the more affluent (U.S. Department of Agriculture, Food and Nutrition Service, 1987). But poverty does limit the ability to buy sufficient quantities of the right foods: families living below the poverty line generally spend more than one-third of their overall income on food, which is more than twice the proportion spent by middle-income families. For this reason, among others, health experts estimate that somewhere between 20 and 25 million Americans (about 10 percent of the population) experience chronic hunger on an essentially permanent basis (Physicians' Task Force on Hunger, 1985).

More than one-half of these chronically hungry people are infants and young children, and their hunger puts their health at risk. In general they have less resistance to diseases, both minor (such as colds) and major (such as influenza). They also show delays in social, emotional, and cognitive development that are apparently the result of an overall lack of energy (Barrett et al., 1982). In looks and appearance, they may show signs of *failure to thrive*: a thin and frail appearance, slow physical growth, and a tendency toward apathy (Drotar, 1985). Yet the importance of these signs may be missed by an untrained eye; the child may just look skinny and seem "lazy."

The second reason for inequalities in health is that the health care system provides less help to the poor and to their children than to the more well-off. The gap begins before birth: low-income mothers are less likely to receive medical attention during pregnancy, causing health problems in themselves or their fetuses to be overlooked. And the gap continues after birth: infants of low-income mothers are less likely to receive check-ups from a doctor and less likely to be seen by a doctor if they get sick (Blendon, 1986a).

In the United States, medical services for the poor are paid through MEDICAID, a federally sponsored insurance program created in the 1960s. But despite Medicaid, much inequality in health services persists. In the 1980s, in an effort to limit the costs of medical services, many states made the standards for eligibility stricter than they originally were (Rowland et al., 1988). Therefore, a person or family had to be "poorer" than before — in some states even living at only *one-half* the income level of the official federal poverty line. Some states also set limits on services, such as the number of days a person could stay in a hospital or the number of visits to a doctor per year. Still others required preauthorization from state health authorities for services that exceeded a certain cost ($500, for instance).

What can society and concerned individuals do to reduce these economically induced inequalities in health and health care? One public response to hunger has been community food banks and food kitchens, in which service agencies collect donations of food from individuals, farmers, or commercial food stores and make these available to needy individuals free of charge. Unfortunately, demand for this service far exceeds the supply of it (U.S. Conference on Mayors, 1984; Food Research and Action Center, 1987). Much of the staff for food banks consists of volunteers, and volunteers are not always available where the need happens to be the greatest. Nor do donations always consist of the most nutritional or most needed foods.

Some communities have responded to the gap in health care by establishing community health clinics in areas with high levels of poverty (B. Pless & Haggerty, 1985). These clinics work explicitly to build rapport with the community. They recruit community members to serve on the board of directors, and they charge low fees based on families' abilities to pay. Unlike many publicly insured health services, furthermore, clinics place no restrictions on what health problems a person chooses to bring to the clinic or on which doctor in the clinic a patient chooses to see. Because clinics tailor services to locally expressed needs, communities (it is hoped) receive better health care than they otherwise would. As a side benefit, the existence of clinics can sometimes enable hospitals serving low-income communities to concentrate more fully on treating truly difficult medical cases and less on relatively minor ailments. Why? Because many low-income people, lacking money for a doctor of their own, use the hospital emergency room as a substitute because the emergency room is frequently an insured medical service. Community clinics make this strategy less necessary.

sick anymore." This idea is indeed true, but only because of the thoroughness of immunization programs and because of the continued vigilance of medical personnel in identifying cases of serious illness, however rare.

The apparent good health of preschool children also hides wide differences in health among individuals and groups of children. Rural and low-income children in particular are about twice as likely to die of an infectious disease as urban and middle-income children are, probably because of their lack of access to medical care. And throughout society, boys are twice as likely to die from a disease as girls are (Butler et al., 1984).

Variations in incidence of fatalities

Differences in illness rates reflect a combination of factors. Some families have less access to health care than do others. In the United States, this is especially true for low-income families compared to middle- and high-income families; but to some extent it is also true of rural families compared to urban ones. Some children have more "hardy" genetic endowments than do other children, which keep them from getting sick as often or as severely. This appears to be why girls get sick less often than boys. From birth to death, females are actually the medically "stronger" sex, contrary to gender stereotypes.

Bladder and Bowel Control

Sometime during the preschool years, most children acquire control of their bladder and bowels. As parents will testify, the process includes many false starts and accidents. Most commonly, daytime control comes before nighttime control — sometime before a child's third birthday, although individuals vary widely and somewhat unpredictably. Typically, too, daytime control of the bladder and

In the long run, successful bladder control depends on both physical growth and the child's own motivation.

A Multicultural View

Toilet Training in Uganda and Northern India

All over the world, young children have to learn acceptable ways to control their bladder and bowels. Every society has times, places, and methods for these necessary functions. How a society conveys this knowledge to children, however, varies from indirect modeling by others to rigorous, explicit teaching. Strictly speaking, "toilet training" happens only in those societies (including the United States) that expect parents and children to make a conscious effort to achieve this training; often "toilet learning" might make a better term (B. Whiting & Edwards, 1988).

To understand the variation, consider the Gandan people, who are the dominant ethnic group of the nation of Uganda, located in central Africa. Gandans live mostly in rural villages and in a climate that is warm and tropical, although not excessively hot. Studies of Gandan child-rearing suggest that parents worry about children learning bladder and bowel control much less than do parents in Western society (Ainsworth, 1975).

Yet Gandan mothers begin toilet training when babies are only two or three months of age — before they can even sit up — and far earlier than most Western experts recommend to Western parents. Training consists of *okusimba*, a word meaning "to plant," in which the mother holds the young baby outdoors over a spot of ground with feet dangling and waits briefly for urine or feces to appear. Among two-month-olds, mothers choose arbitrary but likely times, such as just after waking or after a meal. If the baby produces nothing, the mother tries again later, although always at a time that the mother suspects is likely to produce urination or defecation. As

babies get older, they begin giving signs of needing to empty bladder or bowels, such as by grunting or squirming somehow. Mothers respond to these signs in older infants immediately with *okusimba*, no matter what the mothers are doing at the time.

Even though Western experts usually caution against training as early as do the Gandans, Gandan infants show few signs of resistance or resentment about *okusimba*. Virtually all children, furthermore, acquire full bowel and bladder control by age four. Why is such an early start workable in Uganda, even though it may not be in the West? One key seems to be the Gandan mothers' constant attentiveness and constant proximity to their infants. In Gandan society, mother and baby are rarely separated during the baby's first two years of life: they even sleep together, and the mother always carries the baby with her while doing daily tasks. The constant proximity may help mothers to learn their infants' body language, including their elimination "language," so to speak. *Okusimba* may therefore be a response to the baby's intrinsic toileting needs rather than an imposed schedule that babies must learn.

The ease of toilet learning may also stem indirectly from the tropical and rural conditions of Gandan life. Unlike Western toddlers, Gandan toddlers have to learn only a few key places where *not* to urinate or defecate (for example, not on mother's bed), rather than where they *must* do these things. This form of toileting may be inherently easier to understand and perform than its Western equivalent, which requires a specific location (the toilet) in a specific room (the bathroom). By the time

---

Daytime control

of the bowels occurs at very nearly the same time. Some pediatricians believe that this fact implies that children decide when they wish to begin exercising control, perhaps in order to begin feeling more grown up (Brazelton, 1980). If so, reminders and enforced visits to the toilet may make rather little difference to most toddlers. Too many reminders, in fact, may actually slow their progress down by making them anxious or defiant about bladder or bowel control.

Nighttime control

Nighttime bladder control often takes much longer to achieve than daytime control. About one-half of all three-year-olds still wet their beds at least some of the time, and as many as one in five six-year-olds do the same (Spock, 1976). The timing of nighttime control depends on several factors, such as how deeply children sleep and how large their bladders happen to be. It also depends on anxiety; worried children do tend to wet their beds more often than relaxed children. Unfortunately, parents may sometimes contribute to young children's anxieties by becoming overly frustrated about changing wet sheets night after night.

Achieving control over bladder and bowels reflects the large advances children make during these years in controlling their bodies in general. As infants, they could not always be sure of reaching successfully even for an object that was nearby, and their first efforts to crawl and to walk often ended in falls or in

Gandan children can move around on their own, they seem willing and able to save their urine and feces for the one acceptable place, the relatively warm and hospitable out-of-doors.

But such easygoing practices do not occur everywhere in the world. Middle-class urban families of northern India, for example, present a more troubled picture. In northern India toilet training does not begin until after a child's second birthday, about the age recommended by Western experts on child-rearing. Yet it seems to achieve *less* success, on average, by the time Indian children are five years old (Sharma, 1981).

A pattern of conditions accounts for the incomplete success. Indian mothers and care-givers tend to indulge one- and two-year-old infants in all areas of living. This includes urinating and defecating. Indian infants do wear diapers, but wetting or soiling on furniture or floor sometimes happens anyway and is tolerated with little chastising or criticism. Mothers simply clean up the mess, with at most only mild criticism of the child at this age (Khalakdina, 1979).

Sometime after the child's second birthday, however, mothers change their style abruptly, take the child to the toilet purposefully, and admonish him strongly to urinate and defecate there, rather than in diapers or on the floor. The new style of training continues unabated for the next two or three years until (it is hoped) the child learns to eliminate all urine and feces in the toilet.

Observational studies of this practice suggest that it succeeds in training bladder control but not bowel control: by age five, almost one-half of middle-class Indian children still have soiling accidents (Sharma, 1981). At this same age, the large majority of Western children have already achieved both forms of control.

Why are so many Indian children delayed in achieving bowel control? Several factors in Hindu society make it hard for either parents or children to take an easygoing attitude about bowel training, such as is typically recommended by Western child-rearing experts (Spock & Rothenberg, 1985). For one thing, except in a small number of larger cities, a majority of homes do not have toilets with running water. Even in middle-class homes, toilets resemble what Westerners would call "outhouses," but ones built into the home in a way that allows them to be emptied of sewage periodically from the outside (Deshpande, 1979). Because they are apt to be small, dark, and smelly, toilets do not lend themselves to casual activity or to halfhearted attempts at defecating.

For another, bowel control may be problematic because Indian families live in unusually crowded conditions when judged by world standards. Cross-cultural studies of child-rearing tend to find that crowding encourages mothers and care-givers to exercise more control over the details of children's behavior compared to mothers and care-givers in less crowded societies (B. Whiting & Edwards, 1988). In crowded living quarters, even simple activities such as sleeping or quiet play can affect other family members' own choice of activities significantly. In the case of bowel training, crowding may therefore encourage a harsher attitude about using the toilet.

moves in the wrong direction. During the preschool years, those problems no longer occur. Instead of concentrating on whether they can simply get their bodies to move, children of this age can begin concentrating on what they actually want to do with their bodies.

MOTOR SKILL DEVELOPMENT

As a young child grows, she becomes more skilled at basic physical actions. Often a two-year-old can walk only with considerable effort — hence the name *toddler*. But a five-year-old can walk comfortably in a variety of ways: forward and backward, quickly and slowly, skipping and galloping. A five-year-old can do other vigorous things, too, that were impossible a few years earlier. She can run and jump and climb, all with increasing smoothness and variety. She can carry out certain actions that require accuracy, such as balancing on one foot, or catching a ball reliably, or drawing a picture.

Influences on motor development

This section describes in more detail how milestones like these are reached under naturally occurring conditions. Because natural conditions vary a great deal in real life, we must take for granted a certain range of conditions. In particular, we assume that children have no significant fears of being active; that they have a reasonably daring attitude, but not an excessively daring one, toward trying out new motor skills; that they are in good health; and that their physical growth has evolved more or less normally. For some children, unfortunately, these conditions are not at all natural (Malina, 1982). For them, therefore, the following descriptions may need to be modified.

After describing motor development, we look at the effects of altering such conditions. Can very young children be taught motor skills? Can they become skillful sooner or more fully by receiving training from adults? Will such training affect physical skill development later on in childhood and adolescence? As you will see, the answers to these questions are not definite, but they do have interesting implications for people who care for young children.

Fundamental Motor Skills

Preschool children have obviously moved well beyond the confines of reflex action, which constituted the first motor skills of infancy. From age two to about age five, they experiment with the simple voluntary actions that adults use extensively for their normal activities — actions such as walking, running, and jumping (see Table 8.3). For older individuals, these actions are usually the means to other ends. For very young children, however, they lie very much in the foreground and are frequently goals in themselves.

Even early in the preschool period, some motor skills are acquired through purposeful teaching. But most — such as running — develop through children's own informal activities.

Walking and Its Variations   From a child's point of view, walking may seem absurd at first: it requires purposely losing balance, then regaining balance fast enough to keep from falling. As older infants, children must still pay attention to these facts, even after a full year or so of practice. Each step is an effort unto itself. Children watch each foot in turn as it launches (or lurches) forward; they may pause after each step before attempting the next. Typically, too, infants are top-heavy, and this requires them to keep their feet far apart, as if straddling a horse, to keep from falling down. In spite of these precautions, spills are plentiful in infancy, and walking is often rather slow.

But after a year or so of experience children can usually walk without looking at their feet. Around their second or third birthday, their gait becomes more regular and their feet get closer together. Stride — the distance between feet in a typical step — still remains considerably shorter than that of a normal adult. This makes short distances easy to walk but long distances hard for a few more years.

Running appears early in the preschool years, shortly after walking begins to smooth out. At first it looks more like a hurried walk than a true run, and the child may have trouble stopping himself once he has begun. At first, too, the run may not really involve one of its defining features — namely, a brief instant of complete separation from the ground (Fortney, 1983). Not until the end of the preschool period, around age five, are these problems corrected. By then the child is probably swinging her arms as she strides in order to counterbalance the large twisting motions of her legs. These arm motions also help the child to stop. Without their counterbalancing effect, children go into a sort of uncontrolled spin at the end of the run.

Jumping and Its Variations   At first a jump is more like a fast stretch: the child reaches for the sky rapidly, but his feet fail to leave the ground. Sometime around his second birthday, one foot may finally leave the ground — or even both feet

TABLE 8.3 Milestones in Preschool Motor Development

Approximate Age	Gross Motor Skill	Fine Motor Skill
2.5–3.5 years	Walks well; runs in straight line; jumps in air with both feet	Copies a circle; scribbles; can use eating utensils; stacks a few small blocks
3.5–4.5 years	Walking stride 80 percent of adult; runs at one-third adult speed; throws and catches large ball, but stiff-armed	Buttons with large buttons; copies simple shapes; makes simple representational drawings
4.5–5.5 years	Balances on one foot; runs far without falling; can "swim" in water for short distance	Uses scissors; draws people; copies simple letters and numbers; builds complex structures with blocks

Note: The ages given above are approximate, and skills vary with the life experiences available to individual children and with the situations in which the skills are displayed.
Source: Roberton and Halverson (1984).

may. Such early successes may be delayed, however, because the child may put his arms backward to help himself take off, as if he were trying to push himself off the floor. Later, perhaps around age three, he shifts to a more efficient arm movement — reaching forward and up as he jumps — which creates a useful upward momentum.

Early jumping

Success in these actions depends partly on what type of jump the child is attempting. Jumping down a step is easier than jumping across a flat distance, and a flat or broad jump is easier than a jump up a step. By age five or so, most children can broad jump across a few feet, although variations among individuals are substantial (Clark & Phillips, 1985).

A more complex variation of jumping is hopping. Because hopping uses one foot instead of two, children must have more strength in their jumping leg and especially good balance in it as well. Not surprisingly, hopping appears later than jumping — usually sometime between the third and fourth birthdays. Even then children may succeed only at a few hops at a time and only if they do not need to propel themselves to any particular place. As children's strength and balance improve, they can of course hop longer and begin going places while hopping; a five-year-old can cover a distance of fifty feet or so in a matter of just seconds. As they perfect skills like these, many five-year-olds also become able to jump rope, a skill that requires precise timing of hops for a sustained period. Most children do not become truly accomplished at jumping rope until well into the school years, and many boys never do because this skill often becomes stereotyped as "girls' play."

Hopping

Climbing As parents often note, a child may learn to climb stairs even before she learns to walk. At first she simply uses her crawling skills to go up the steps. Soon after she does learn to walk, she applies her new form of locomotion to steps. She walks up in a lockstep or mark-time style, placing one foot up, then bringing the other foot up to the same level before attempting the next level with the original foot. A railing or adult hand to hold helps a child in trying these actions; not until well into the school years can children manage stairs completely without holding on to anything. By age three or four, with these qualifications, most children can go up stairs fairly smoothly. By then, in fact, many can use their feet alternately, just as adults do.

Going down stairs presents a more difficult challenge than going up because the child has to look at the large depth into which he is descending and because he must also lean into the chasm a little each time he takes a step. These facts may account for delays in learning this particular kind of climbing. Often children

Difficulties of descending

Because not all children have access to playgrounds, the skills developed in this setting vary more among individuals than running or walking, for which nearly all children possess the required "equipment."

revert to earlier, more infantile methods when they begin trying to descend stairs, such as sitting down, moving in the mark-time style, or crawling down backward. Even by about age five, some children still dislike descending stairs and will do so only with encouragement from adults. This fact illustrates a common feature of most fundamental motor skills: they often depend on children's motivation, courage, and confidence, not simply on physical maturation.

Early throwing

Throwing and Catching   For infants or toddlers, first throws may happen by accident. The child may just be waving an object and happen to release it suddenly: away it goes. Once intentional throwing begins, however, children actually adopt more stereotyped methods at first than they do later in childhood (DuRandt, 1985). At first, they launch all balls in much the same way — usually with a general forward lurch — regardless of the balls' size or weight. As skill develops, children vary their movements according to the balls' characteristics; they give more wrist movement to small balls and more arm movement to large ones. At the same time, children begin to vary among themselves even in how they throw the same type of ball; some develop a persistent wrist twist over and above the twist needed for particular balls, whereas others develop a special torso turn all their own (Roberton & Halverson, 1984).

Styles of early catching

Catching proceeds through similar phases. Early in the preschool period, children may extend their arms passively to receive an oncoming ball. This method naturally works only if the thrower aims the ball perfectly. By around age four, children introduce flexibility to their methods by moving their hands in last-minute response to the oncoming ball and so forth. By school age, some children have become very skillful at catching: their arms and hands remain flexible until the ball actually arrives and can therefore compensate for unexpected angles and speeds as the ball approaches. Not surprisingly, this technique puts far less demand on a thrower to be accurate.

Can Fundamental Motor Skills Be Taught?

Such skills as jumping, throwing, and catching seem to improve as children practice them, which implies that motor skills can be taught just as other skills are. To find out whether this is true, we must distinguish between *fundamental* motor skills and relatively *specialized* motor skills. Fundamental skills are ones that nearly every child learns eventually simply by participating in human society. Walking, for example, is a fundamental motor skill; so are reaching and grasping. Specialized motor skills are ones that not everyone learns and that require special training, such as ballet dancing, swimming, and ice-skating. Among physically normal children, specialized skills are much more teachable than are fundamental skills (Schmidt, 1988). The reverse may sometimes be true among children with particular physical handicaps; for them, a normally fundamental skill such as walking may amount to a specially learned achievement.

Because most activities during early childhood emphasize fundamental motor skills rather than specialized ones, some researchers have concluded that it is harder to train young children in motor development than it is to train somewhat older ones (Kleinman, 1985). According to this viewpoint, children pick up most of their training from naturally occurring, universal events in life. Skillful running, for example, depends on the growth of particular, rather sizable physical muscles and bones. It also depends indirectly on such "unrelated" skills as keeping balance and judging distances accurately, neither of which is fully developed in a young child.

Often, therefore, specialized training in fundamental skills does not teach the skills as effectively as a "curriculum" of naturally occurring experiences does. Normally, a preschool child may learn best to run by running — and also by

Fundamental versus specialized skills

Bridges Can fundamental motor skills be taught?

Learning motor skills from experience

The development of some motor skills, such as swimming, requires the special efforts of teachers, parents, and the children themselves.

standing, walking, tumbling, jumping, and the like — all of her own accord. Providing general opportunities and encouragement may therefore help, but focused instruction may overlook the true breadth of a young child's physical educational needs.

Nonetheless, even preschool children acquire some skills that are specialized. Certain young children learn to swim, and others learn to skate. Neither of these skills happens without special efforts by the children and their teachers. Preschool children respond to specialized training to the extent that the training respects their current stage of growth and takes advantage of their growing abilities to plan and coordinate fundamental motor actions. The result is unusually early learning of specialized skills, although the learning is not usually as rapid as can occur later in childhood or in adolescence.

As children leave the preschool period and enter the school years, specialized skills may also acquire social qualities because mastering a unique skill usually confers status and respect on a child and helps to win friends. A good baseball player is usually in demand, and children who know how to swim are more likely to be invited to swimming parties.

Fine Motor Coordination: The Case of Drawing Skills

Not all motor activities of young children involve the strength, agility, and balance of their whole bodies. Many require the coordination of small movements but not strength. Tying shoelaces calls for this **fine motor coordination;** so do washing hands, buttoning and zipping clothing, eating with a spoon, and turning a doorknob.

One especially widespread fine motor skill among young children is drawing; in North American culture, at least, virtually every young child tries using pens or pencils at some time, and often tries other artistic media as well. The scribbles or drawings that result probably serve a number of purposes. At times they may be used mainly for sensory exploration: a child may want to get the feel of paintbrushes or felt-tip pens. At other times, drawings may express thoughts or feelings; a child may suggest this possibility by commenting, "It's a horse, and it's angry." Children's drawings also probably reflect their knowledge of the world, even though they may not yet have the fine motor skills necessary to convey their knowledge fully. In other words, children's drawings reveal not only fine motor coordination but their self-concept, emotional and social attitudes, and cognitive development.

Drawing shows two overlapping phases of development during the preschool period. From the ages of about two and one-half to four, children focus on developing nonrepresentational skills, such as scribbling and the purposeful drawing of simple shapes and designs. Sometime around age four, they begin attempting to represent objects (Kellogg, 1969). Yet even though representational drawings usually follow nonrepresentational ones, the two types also stimulate each other simultaneously. Children often describe their early scribbles as if they referred to real things, and their practice at portraying real objects helps to develop their nonrepresentational skills further.

Prerepresentational Drawing   Around the end of infancy, children begin to scribble. A two-year-old experiments with whatever pen or pencil is available to him, almost no matter what its color or type. In doing so, he behaves like an infant and like a child. As with an infant, his efforts primarily focus on the activity itself — on the motions and sensations of handling a pen or pencil. But like an older child, a two-year-old often cares about the outcome of these activities: "That's a Mommy," he says, whether it looks much like one or not.

Bridges   What effect does the mastering of specialized motor skills have on preschool peer relations?

Importance of drawing skills

Representational and nonrepresentational drawings

Preschool children make major strides in fine motor coordination, as often shown by their steadily improving drawings. Eventually, though, children use this coordination primarily for other purposes, such as writing or tying shoelaces.

Contrary to a popular view of children's art, even very young children are concerned not only with the process of drawing but with the product as well (J. Gibson & Yonas, 1968).

A child's interest in the results of her drawing show up in the patterns she imposes on even her earliest scribbles. Sometimes she will fill up particular parts of the page quite intentionally — the whole left side, say, or the complete middle third. And she often emphasizes particular categories of strokes — lots of straight diagonals or lots of counterclockwise loops (Golomb, 1981). Different children select different types of motions for emphasis, so the motions are less like universal stages than like elements of a personal style. Even after a child learns to combine simpler strokes and motions, her combinations remain unique. Some children begin combining circles, crosses, and lines in various combinations (Goodnow, 1977; Kellogg, 1969).

Patterns in early drawings

In general, the scribbling of very young children resembles their early babbling. All infants vocalize, and most infants produce the same overall range of sounds. But the particular phonemes selected by one child escape prediction; at any point in time, the choices often seem to come out of nowhere. Likewise, given the opportunity, all children scribble, at least in North American society; and most children produce a similar range of lines and curves. But any one child selects a unique set. Predicting his selection proves almost impossible (Gardner, 1980; Goodnow, 1977), but the very uncertainty constitutes one of the delights of working with young children.

Representational Drawing   While preschool children improve their scribbling skills, they also develop an interest in representing people, objects, and events in their drawings. This interest often far precedes their ability to do so. A three-year-old may assign meanings to scribbles or blobs in her drawing: one blob

Attributing the "real" to drawings

may be "Mama," and another may be "our house." Events may happen to these blobs, too: Mama may be "going to the store" or "looking for me."

During the preschool years, and for a long time thereafter, the child's visual representations are limited by his comparatively rudimentary fine motor skills. Apparently he knows more, visually speaking, than his hands can portray with pens or brushes. Prefabricated materials suggest this possibility. Given an outline of a person and some cutouts of body parts (nose, mouth, eyes, and so on), a young preschooler can assemble a human being quite skillfully, putting most of the parts where they ought to go. But given a pencil and paper, a young preschooler may still produce only a rudimentary drawing of a person: a circle with dots for eyes, perhaps, and sticks for legs (Fucigna & Wolf, 1981). Figure 8.3 shows this tendency for one particular child. Only as the child reaches school-age, do her drawings of persons become relatively realistic.

Those early representations do not show poor observation by children of the visual realities around them. More likely these drawings show the good but approximate representations that are possible with the graphic skills available to the child. If a child has practiced a particular set of loops and curves a lot, she uses these to portray objects and events; she cannot in fact do otherwise. She may furthermore assign meanings to her loops and curves that often go well beyond their visual content. A tadpole person may represent both a head and a torso, even though it looks only like a head (Freeman, 1980). Often, too, a child describes her drawing by mentioning many more body parts than actually can be seen in the picture. And sometimes she can draw a much more sophisticated human being if simply asked to do so; the simpler version, in other words, functions as a visual shorthand in the child's spontaneous drawings.

Cross-cultural Differences in Picture Perception   Of course, the child's rendering of a person may also be a culturally conventional shorthand. From society, children probably learn particular ways of depicting human beings and other objects in much the way they learn particular children's games or particular linguistic expressions. If so, children around the world should vary a lot in the content and style of what they draw as well as in what they see in others' drawings. Do children from Africa and Asia make their first human beings look like tadpoles? And whether they do or not, would they recognize North American drawings as representations of people?

The answers are mixed. What children draw does depend, not surprisingly, on what they see in the world around them. If their world contains cars and tall buildings, these objects are relatively likely to turn up in their drawings. If their world contains oxen and grass houses, they will more often appear in representations (Winner, 1982). Children who are encouraged to draw flowers in school tend to draw more flowers, and those who are encouraged to draw airplanes draw airplanes. To this extent, culture makes a difference in learning to draw.

But not all aspects of children's drawings show variation among cultures. One example is the perception of depth in pictures. Bantu children and adults from South Africa have no exposure to drawings of any kind in their normal lives. Yet when shown ordinary line drawings of outdoor scenes, they have no trouble discerning the depth intended by such pictures; they know, that is, which objects are supposed to be near the front of the picture and which ones are in the background (Hagan & Jones, 1978).

Neither do the fine motor skills for drawing show much cultural variation. Tibetan children easily learn to make complex drawings with Western-style crayons. Like the Bantus, they lack exposure to pictorial drawings, yet one study found that they needed only a few hours to catch up to the skill levels of North American children of equivalent ages (Gardner, 1980). After this much practice, the school-age children made rather realistic drawings of trees and houses, although of course these objects looked like the ones that Tibetan children knew rather than like the North American versions.

Effects of motor skill level

Bridges   To what extent do preschool children's drawings vary from culture to culture?

Variations in picture content

Constancy in depth perception

3 years, 2 months

3 years, 7 months

4 years, 0 months

4 years, 0 months

4 years, 2 months

4 years, 9 months

5 years, 1 month

FIGURE 8.3
Samples of Elizabeth's Drawings from Ages Three to Five Years

GENDER DIFFERENCES IN PHYSICAL DEVELOPMENT

In spite of wide individual differences, preschool boys and girls develop at almost exactly the same average rates (Pissanos et al., 1983). This applies to practically any motor skill of which young children are capable, and it applies to both gross motor skills and fine motor skills. Any nursery classroom is therefore likely to contain children of both sexes who can run very well and children of both sexes who can paint well or tie their shoelaces without help. This is especially true among younger preschool children, those aged three or four.

By the time children begin kindergarten at age five, slight gender differences in physical development and motor skills appear, with boys tending (slightly) to be bigger, stronger, and faster. Yet these differences are noticeable only as averages and only by basing the averages on very large numbers of children (Tanner, 1978b). In spite of the slight differences, therefore, more than 95% of actual children find themselves more skillful and bigger than some members of *both* sexes and less skillful and smaller than certain others of both sexes. The small difference in the gender average makes no practical difference in the everyday lives of most children or in the lives of the teachers and parents who sometimes plan physical activities for them.

Nonetheless, the fact remains that by the time children start school, a few children in any large city or community are bigger, stronger, and faster than *any* other children; most of these few children are boys. These few individuals may

Gender differences are small

But individual differences are large

On the average, boys and girls develop motor skills at almost the same rate during the preschool years.

A Talk with Jimmy's Mother

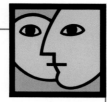

Physical Development in the Preschool Years

This interview was conducted over coffee in Carol Levin's kitchen. Her three-year-old son, Jimmy, was taking a nap in his room.

Interviewer: What types of active play does Jimmy do?

Carol: He likes building. He's in a building phase. He builds with big blocks a lot. He also loves to play with [plastic blocks that snap together]. He builds all kinds of great structures with those. . . . We have also been doing some hammering and nailing in the garage with scrap lumber.

Interviewer: Can Jimmy hammer a nail if you start it for him?

Carol: Yes. He hammers and saws. . . . He also loves digging dirt.

Interviewer: When he digs, is it for the joy of digging? Or is he planning on making something with it?

Carol: He seems to have something going on. He digs with earth-moving equipment and shovels and pails. He likes the sandbox, but likes to dig just in the dirt out in the yard if we let him.

Interviewer: What else does he do?

Carol: There is a little bike that he rides. It's a two-wheeler with training wheels, but he has trouble with it because it doesn't work very well. He climbs more than he ever did. At the playground he'll climb up "climbs." He climbs trees at home.

Interviewer: Does he sometimes get so high that he can't get down?

Carol: No, he always gets down. He brings ladders over to the apple tree and he puts that against the tree and climbs up and hangs out there and swings off the lower branches.

Interviewer: Does he run a lot?

Carol: Yes. In the house especially. He runs everywhere. He runs more than he walks.

Interviewer: What about things like throwing a ball?

Carol: He has a good arm. He always has. Even when he was younger he could throw. He throws straight. He plays once in a while when we play baseball and he'll bat the ball.

Interviewer: Can he hit it?

Carol: Yes, he has hit it. He doesn't hit it consistently, but he tries. His new interest is croquet. I have no idea where he picked this up, but he

takes a rock and a stick and says he is playing croquet.

Interviewer: How about his play with smaller things like puzzles or drawing?

Carol: He's never been a puzzle kid. He never likes to do puzzles. He draws more now. He makes his letter J and he scribbles on paper and comes up with fantastic stories about what they are. He doesn't draw things yet, but after he scribbles he'll look at it and tell you something about it. What's on his mind.

Follow-up Questions

1. What *fundamental* and *fine* motor skills does Jimmy display? How typical are they of a child his age?

2. What challenges might Jimmy's physical development create for his parents?

3. How might Carol's role as a parent affect her observations and evaluations of Jimmy's motor development?

get much more than their share of attention, furthermore, because of their physical excellence. This contributes to the (mistaken) impression that boys are larger and more skillful than girls *in general*. In this way (among many others), stereotypes are born.

But the mistaken impression of gender differences in children's growth and motor development probably also comes from differences in how preschool children spend their time. Compared with girls, preschool boys do spend more time in active and rough-and-tumble play, and girls spend more time doing quiet activities such as drawing or playing with stuffed animals (Fagot & Kronsberg, 1982). These differences may give the impression that boys are incapable, or at least less capable, of fine motor skills and that girls are physically weaker.

Perhaps such differences do develop for some children by the end of the school years simply as a result of differences in practice that accumulate over a period of years. Perhaps, too, boys choose active play partly for genetic or hormonal reasons. But in any event, five-year-olds have only begun to accumulate these differences in motor experience and to make appropriately gender-typed choices in their play. Taken as groups, preschool boys and girls do not really differ very much.

EFFECTS OF CHILDREN'S PHYSICAL GROWTH

Effects on Adults

Bridges   What are the effects of preschoolers' physical growth on their parents and other care-givers?

The physical and motor developments that affect a child during the preschool years also affect the adults in the child's life — most notably, his parents or other care-givers. The changes in the child create, or at least encourage, major changes in how these people deal with him (Maccoby, 1984).

Consider the changes in size that preschool children experience. A two-year-old is often still small enough to be handled. When necessary, her parents can pick her up and move her from one place to another, physically remove her from danger, and carry her (at least partway!) if a distance is too far for her to walk.

By age five, a child has often outgrown these physical interactions, not only figuratively but literally. His parents or other adults may still lift and cuddle him sometimes in play or in an emergency, but they are probably beginning to avoid doing so on a regular basis. To a significant extent, the child may now simply be too bulky and tall. More and more rarely can parents save a child from danger by picking him up suddenly or speed him along a long hallway by carrying him piggyback. They must somehow get the child to do these things for himself.

Usually, of course, parents succeed at this task. By age five, a child can think and talk about her own actions much more than before, and her improvements help guide her own actions. The handling that used to be literal now becomes mostly figurative; now *handling* means negotiating and discussing with the child, not lifting her up or carting her around.

Bridges   In what ways are a preschooler's physical growth and cognitive development interconnected?

More than sheer physical growth brings about these changes. By age five or so, a child has also improved various motor skills quite a lot. Walking poses much less of a problem than it did just a few years before, which is fortunate for the child's parents because they find themselves expecting much more walking from the child anyway. It is fortunate for the child, too, because he now finds it easier to comply with these raised expectations.

Increasing physical competence

Improvements in motor skills also change the agenda for a child's daily activities. A two-year-old may spend a good part of her day experimenting with fundamental skills: walking from one room to another, or tearing toilet paper to shreds, or taking pots and pans out of a cupboard. These activities are often embedded in an active social and cognitive life: the child may smile (or frown) at her parents while she works, and she may "talk" about what she is doing as well. But the motor aspects of her activities absorb a significant part of her attention throughout the day. The child may return repeatedly to a staircase, for instance, as if compelled to get the hang of climbing it; no reward needs to lie at the top step, except the satisfaction of a job well done.

A two-year-old's parents must therefore spend significant time making sure that the child comes to no physical grief in his motor explorations. They must make sure that the child does not fall down the stairs, or splash into the toilet bowl, or discover a sharp knife among the pots. Their role as safety experts can dominate their contacts with the child, particularly if the child is active.

Less parental surveillance

By the end of the preschool period, minute-to-minute physical surveillance recedes in importance. A concern with safety remains, of course (see Table 8.4 for common accidents and their remedies), but it is more abstract than before; rules about dangers make their appearance ("Don't climb on that fence; it's rickety"), along with the hope that a five-year-old can remember and follow the rules at least some of the time. The shift toward rules also results from increasing confidence in the child's motor skills. Now parents are apt to believe that their child can go up and down stairs without stumbling very often.

The new motor skills that preschoolers develop bring with them new risks and create new safety concerns for their parents and other caregivers. What hazards may be waiting for these three-year-olds?

The child's motor development has contributed to this belief and to the increasingly indirect methods of surveillance that go with it. Overworked parents may sometimes think to themselves, "She's five now and ought to be able to handle the stairs by herself." But to a large extent they also think, "I have seen her handle the stairs pretty well, so now I do not have to watch her every time." To this extent the child herself has created a new, more mature child-rearing practice in her parents.

During the preschool period, many parents discover a special need for patience in their dealings with their children. Simple actions such as tying shoelaces or putting on socks may take longer than before simply because children now insist on doing many of these things themselves. For similar reasons, walking to the store may now take longer; a three -or four-year-old may prefer to push the stroller rather than ride in it, thus slowing everyone down. And preschoolers may have their own agenda on a walk, such as noticing little rocks on the sidewalk or airplanes in the sky, which differs from parents' goals. On good days these behaviors offer some of the joys of raising children, but on bad days even well-meaning parents often lose their tempers over them.

Increased parental patience

Physical development changes recreation and play, too. At age two, a child probably cannot play baseball. By age five, he may make something of a start at it. At age two, he may enjoy looking at pictures in a book and drawing a few lines of his own; by age five, he may spend long periods making elaborate pictures himself. At age two, he may listen and bounce to music in a general way; by age five, he may swing to it with more refined movements.

New recreations

These new skills often have teachable elements to them, and that fact creates a new sort of contact with parents and with others who care for the child. Now adults can begin showing and encouraging the practice of new skills in a more active, sustained, and focused way than before; depending on their personal interests and values, in fact, they may even feel obliged to do so. Both adult and child may find such teaching and learning easier because they no longer have to monitor every fundamental physical action of the child. A few years before, one false step might have made a young child fall. But now these terms have meta-

TABLE 8.4 *Common Accidents, Remedies, and Preventions Among Preschoolers*

Accidents	What to Do	How to Prevent
Drowning	Unless you are trained in water safety, extend a stick or other device. Use heart massage and mouth-to-mouth breathing when and as long as needed.	Teach children to swim as early in life as possible; supervise children's swim sessions closely; stay in shallow water.
Choking on small objects	If child is still breathing, do not attempt to remove object; see a doctor instead. If breathing stops, firmly strike child twice on small of back. If this does not help, grab child from behind, put your fist just under her ribs, and pull upward sharply several times.	Do not allow children to put small objects in mouth; teach them to eat slowly, taking small bites; forbid vigorous play with objects or food in mouth.
Cuts with serious bleeding	Raise cut above level of heart; apply pressure with cloth or bandage; if necessary, apply pressure to main arteries of limbs.	Remove sharp objects from play areas; insist on shoes wherever ground or floor may contain sharp objects; supervise children's use of knives.
Fractures	Keep injured limb immobile; see a doctor.	Discourage climbing and exploring in dangerous places, such as trees and construction sites; allow bicycles only in safe areas.
Burns	Pour cold water over burned area; keep it clean; then cover with *sterile* bandage. See a doctor if burn is extensive.	Keep matches out of reach of children; keep children well away from fires and hot stoves.
Poisons	On skin or eye, flush with plenty of water; if in stomach, phone poison control center doctor for instructions; induce vomiting only for selected substances.	Keep dangerous substances out of reach of children; throw away poisons when no longer needed. Keep syrup of ipecac in home to induce vomiting, but use *only* if advised by doctor.
Animal bites	Clean and cover with bandage; see a doctor.	Train children when and how to approach family pets; teach them caution in approaching unfamiliar animals.
Insect bites	Remove stinger, if possible; cover with paste of bicarbonate of soda (for bees) or a few drops of vinegar (for wasps and hornets).	Encourage children to recognize and avoid insects that sting, as well as their nests; encourage children to keep calm in presence of stinging insects.
Poisonous plants (e.g., poison ivy)	Remove affected clothing; wash affected skin with strong alkali soap as soon as possible.	Teach children to recognize toxic plants; avoid areas where poisonous plants are growing.

Source: Brody (1982).

phorical meanings. False steps for a five-year-old usually mean mistakes, not actual physical stumbling; and while a fall may still mean a physical tumble, it is also beginning to refer to a failure.

Effects on the Child

Bridges How do children's growing motor skills affect how they think of themselves?

As the preceeding discussion implies, physical growth gives preschool children many opportunities for increased self-esteem. Now they can walk, skip, and run reliably, whereas before they could only "toddle." Now they can reach for specific objects without fear of breaking, dropping, or crushing them. Now they can write their own name, whereas before they could at most only say it. All these developments, as well as others, give a young child reason to feel proud.

By age five, children are firm believers in the value of physical growth. Parents admonish preschoolers to "act like a big boy/girl." Peers emulate older children by showing off their best motor skills to each other — their best ball throws, or their best tricks on a swing set at the park, or their best chalk drawings on the sidewalk. "Growing up" becomes a goal, one that more children approach with optimism because the hassles, worries, and limitations of adulthood still seem invisible, incomprehensible, or at least far away. For a number of years longer, many young children concentrate on consolidating their cognitive and social talents because their physical development, for now at least, seems to be both reliable and vigorous.

As children's physical skills improve, they can take on new responsibilities, such as doing dishes. Both they and their parents may therefore start viewing them as more capable and grown up.

SUMMARY OF MAJOR IDEAS

Normal Physical Development

1. Between ages two and five, growth slows down and children take on more adult bodily proportions.
2. Usually growth is rather smooth during the preschool period. Genetic and ethnic background affect its overall rate, as does the quality of nutrition and children's experiences of illness.
3. During the past hundred years, children in industrialized countries have tended to grow larger and faster, although the trend may now be slowing.
4. If children fall behind in growth because of poor nutrition or hormonal deficiencies, they can often achieve catch-up growth if slow growth has not been too severe or prolonged.

Brain Development

5. Between ages two and five, the brain completes its overall growth by developing new fibers and myelin sheaths.
6. Although the brain continues to function as a whole, certain areas develop special importance for particular mental and motor functions.
7. During the preschool period, children first begin showing hemispheric lateralization in certain mental and motor functions.

Other Bodily Changes

8. Visual acuity and auditory acuity increase during this period.
9. Minor viral illnesses occur repeatedly during these years, although young children rarely get seriously ill.

10. Differences in illness rates among children reflect environmental factors, such as reduced access to health care by low-income families, and genetic predisposition.

11. Children tend to achieve daytime bladder and bowel control early in the preschool period and nighttime bladder control late in this period.

Motor Skill Development

12. Preschoolers acquire and refine many fundamental motor skills, including walking, running, jumping, hopping, climbing, throwing, and catching.

13. Adults can teach some motor skills, but many seem to develop simply through natural daily experiences of young children.

14. Fine motor skills such as drawing also emerge during the preschool years.

15. Children's drawings begin with scribbles or prerepresentational drawings and later include representational drawings as well.

16. The content of drawings varies widely with children's cultural and personal experiences, but their perception of depth and motor skills may develop fairly universally around the world.

Gender Differences in Physical Development

17. Boys and girls differ only slightly in growth and motor performance during the preschool period; individual differences are far greater than gender differences.

18. The slight differences in performance and somewhat larger differences in daily motor behavior may contribute to gender stereotypes about motor ability.

Effects of Children's Physical Growth

19. Between ages two and five, children's increasing physical competence causes parents to monitor their safety in new ways and to make up and revise rules for their children to follow.

20. Preschoolers' increasing physical independence can challenge parents' patience in a variety of situations.

21. In general, children's growth and motor development help them to learn about their world and help parents to teach their children as well.

22. Preschoolers' physical accomplishments are a source of pride and self-esteem.

23. Because their physical development now seems assured, five-year-olds can begin turning their attention on consolidating cognitive and social talents.

KEY TERMS

velocity *(273)*
secular trend *(275)*
hybrid vigor *(275)*
endocrine gland *(277)*
catch-up growth *(277)*
ossification *(277)*
deprivation dwarfism *(278)*
failure to thrive *(278)*
reactive attachment disorder (RAD) *(278)*
visual cortex *(280)*
auditory cortex *(280)*
Wernicke's area *(280)*
motor cortex *(280)*
Broca's area *(280)*
hemispheric lateralization *(280)*
dichotic listening *(280)*
lateralized behavior *(282)*
fine motor coordination *(294)*

WHAT DO YOU THINK?

1. If a child is relatively tall at age four or five, do you think that she will still be relatively tall later in childhood? What about in adulthood? Explain.

2. Why do you suppose that human beings tend to have a preferred hand? Speculate about why this quality may have evolved.

3. How (if at all) should parents and care-givers try to train toddlers to use the toilet? Give some reasons for your recommendations.

4. What ways do you think would work best in fostering the development of motor skills in preschool children? Do you consider these methods to be genuine teaching or not?

5. As stated in the chapter, young children clearly affect the behavior of parents. Do you think that these effects cause permanent psychological changes in parents? Or do they disappear when the children get older?

FOR FURTHER READING

Gazzaniga, M. *Mind Matters: How the Mind and Brain Interact to Create Our Conscious Lives.* Boston: Houghton Mifflin, 1988.

Brierley, J. *Give Me a Child Until He Is Seven: Brain Studies and Early Childhood Education.* London: Falmer Press, 1987.

Both of these books speculate about how the developing anatomy of the brain affects major psychological activities, such as learning, memory, and feelings. The second one focuses on young children; the first one tends to be adult oriented. Both go somewhat beyond what brain research definitely proves, but they make interesting reading.

Paley, V. *Mollie Is Three.* Chicago: University of Chicago Press, 1986.

The author describes her experiences as a preschool teacher, focusing on how one child, Mollie, used her time across one entire school year. Among other things, the descriptions document the many ways that a child of this age grows in a short period of time — not only physically but also cognitively and socially — and how development in one area often stimulates developments in other areas.

Payne, V., and Isaacs, L. *Human Motor Development: A Lifespan Approach.* Mountain View, CA: Mayfield, 1987.

This book is a wide-ranging, readable account of children's motor abilities, including the development of those abilities during the preschool years. It describes ways of determining children's motor skills and is sensitive to how children's attitude about physical activity gradually colors their physical performance and their willingness to participate in sports.

Wilkinson, S. *The Child's World of Illness: The Development of Health and Illness ·Behavior.* Cambridge: Cambridge University Press, 1988.

Although the title may imply it, this book is not about children's actual illnesses. It is about how children understand or conceive of illness and how they express their understandings. It shows that much "illness behavior," such as displayed during a genuine illness, is actually a role that children learn during a number of years. The book does not say that being sick is just playacting; it merely points out vividly that being sick has more psychological elements than we often realize.

Winner, E. *Invented Worlds: The Psychology of the Arts.* Cambridge, MA: Harvard University Press, 1982.

The author describes the development of artistic performance in three major realms: literature, music, and visual art. The latter topic elaborates on the discussion of children's drawings that occurs in this chapter. Winner explains competing theories of how children acquire artistic sensitivity and the motor skills needed for drawing; she evaluates evidence for stages in the development of drawing skill; and she discusses cross-cultural comparisons of the children's art.

CHAPTER 9

The Preschool Years: Cognitive Development

- What are the special strengths and limitations of preschoolers' thinking?
- How do preschool children process visual and auditory information?
- How does the syntax used by preschool children differ from that used by older children and adults?
- What processes probably account for language acquisition, and how can adults assist those processes?
- What is the nature of the relationship between language and thought?

W hile a child is growing physically, another miracle begins: when he is just about two years old, he begins representing the world to himself and others. For one thing, he can talk and understand much of others' speech. "Kitty run!" the boy says, pointing to the local cat. "Yes," replies his father. "She's chasing a bird." The young boy nods and says, "Bird gone now. Bad kitty?" and he looks to his father for confirmation. "It's okay this time," the father says. "The bird flew away soon enough." Unlike an infant, this child does not really need to handle or manipulate the objects he is thinking about. He can comment on the cat even after it disappears.

For another thing, a young preschool child can reenact experiences in new and creative ways through **make-believe,** a form of pretend play in which he simulates people, objects, animals, and activities in his efforts to understand them. This child may "become" the cat — crouching down, ready to pounce — the next day. If asked about what he is doing, he will probably know that it is "just pretend." He is not likely to think that he has actually become a cat, no matter how convincing his performance. In make-believe, he is beginning to create symbols and to understand them.

Even though his symbolic or representational skills still leave much to be desired, they mark a major achievement. This chapter and the next look at several kinds of symbolic skills and at how young children make use of them. This chapter concentrates on thinking, or problem solving, and on early language acquisition. Chapter 10 concentrates on more social activities, such as play, family relationships, and early relationships outside the family. As we shall see, these topics do not divide as easily in real life as they do in textbooks.

THINKING IN PRESCHOOLERS

Preschoolers' thinking has a mixed, in-between quality: in some ways it is still like that of an infant, but in others it is like a schoolchild's thinking. This quality occurs in nearly every aspect of cognition, but here we look at just a few, especially egocentrism, animism, classification skills, and reversibility. Other major aspects of cognitive development (for example, memory and attention) change importantly during the preschool years, too, but for convenience we save major discussion of them for Chapter 12. The aspects of cognition considered here stem from the observations and theorizing of Jean Piaget. As pointed out below, however, recent studies of children's thinking have significantly modified his ideas about these aspects.

Piaget's Preoperational Stage

At about the age of two, according to Piaget, children enter a new stage in their cognitive development (Piaget, 1963). Infancy has left them with several important accomplishments, such as the belief that objects have permanent existence and the capacity to set and follow simple goals, as when they purposely remove all the clothes from every drawer in their house or apartment. Infancy has also left them with the knowledge that their senses all register the same world — now children know that hearing their mother in the next room means that they can probably see her soon and that seeing her probably also means that they will hear from her.

The preoperational stage — roughly ages two through seven — extends and transforms these skills. During this stage, children become increasingly proficient at using **symbols,** which are words or actions that stand for something else. During this stage, too, children extend their belief in object permanence to include **identities,** or constancies, of many types: a candle remains the same even as it grows shorter from burning, and a flower growing out of the sidewalk remains the same flower even though its growth changes its appearance from day to day.

Achievements of the preoperational stage

Preoperational children also sense many **functional relationships,** or variations in their environments that normally occur together. Preschool children usually know that the hungrier they are, the more they will want to eat; and that the bigger they are, the stronger they tend to be; and that the faster they walk, the sooner they will arrive somewhere. Of course they still do not know the precise functions or relationships in these examples — exactly how *much* faster they will arrive if they walk a particular amount faster. But they do know that a relationship exists.

These are all cognitive strengths of preschool children, and they mark cognitive advances over infancy. But as the *pre-* in the term *preoperational* implies, Piaget's original theorizing actually focused on the limitations of children's thinking during early childhood. He pointed out that from age two to seven, children often confuse their own points of view with those of other people, that they cannot classify objects and events logically, and that they are often misled by single features of their experiences. Taken together, these limitations distinguish preschool children from school-age children. They are important enough to deserve discussion, but before we get to them, let us look in more detail at the most significant achievement of the preoperational period: the child's use of symbols.

Limitations of the preoperational stage

Symbolic Thought

As we just noted, *symbols* are words, objects, or behaviors that stand for something else. They take this role not because of their intrinsic properties but because of the intentions of the people who use them. A drinking straw is just a hollow tube and does not become a symbol until a preschooler places it in the middle of a mound of sand and declares it a birthday candle. Likewise, the sound /bahks/ lacks symbolic meaning unless we all agree that it refers to a hollow object with corners: *box.*

Nature of symbols

Probably the most significant cognitive achievement of the preoperational period is the emergence of **symbolic thought,** the ability to think by making one

Bridges   What is probably the most important cognitive achievement of preschool children?

object or action stand for another. Throughout their day, two-year-olds use language symbolically, as when they say "Milk!" to procure a white, drinkable substance from the refrigerator. They also use symbolic thought in make-believe play by pretending to be people or creatures other than themselves. By about the age of four, children's symbolic play often includes actions (getting down on all fours), objects (a table napkin for a saddle), and words (saying "Neigh!" in a loud voice).

Significance of symbolic thought

Symbolic thinking helps preschool children in three ways. First, it gives them convenient ways of remembering objects and experiences. If a young child can recall the word *swing,* she can more easily recall the pleasant experience she had sitting on a board suspended from two chains. Second, symbols help young children to think and solve problems about their experiences. Suppose a child sees two four-footed, furry pets outdoors and wonders how they are different. She can probably solve this problem easily if she knows a few relevant symbols, such as the words *dog, cat, large,* and *small.*

Third, symbols help children to communicate what they know, even after they have had an experience. Having gone to the store, they can convey this experience to others either in words ("I went shopping") or through pretend play ("Let's play store, and I'll be the clerk."). By its nature, communication fosters social relationships among children; but it also fosters cognitive development by allowing individual children to learn from the experiences of others. More precisely, communication allows individuals to learn from the symbolic representations of others' experiences. Not surprisingly, these benefits do not occur all at once. Preschool children need time and practice to develop symbolic skills to high levels of proficiency.

Preschoolers' play often relies on their growing abilities to represent objects and events symbolically. A mound in the sand may become a castle and a ridge may become a wall.

		Family		
	Physical Development	How can parent-child interactions encourage language development? (333–334)	Social Context	
Genetics	In what ways does the cognitive development of preschoolers affect what they see and hear? (319–320)		What is the significance of socioeconomic differences in tests of language development? (334–335)	Peers
Are children innately predisposed to acquire language? (331–332)				How does cognitive egocentrism affect friendship formation during the preschool years? (313)

THE PRESCHOOL YEARS: COGNITIVE DEVELOPMENT

In what way does cognitive development affect the development of empathy? (362)	How does a preschool child's developing ability to think symbolically affect the child's developing sense of self? (343)	Do bilingual pre-schoolers begin with a single language system that gradually becomes two separate languages or do they keep their two languages separate from the start? (328)	What is probably the most important cognitive achievement of preschool children? (309–310)	What kind of education programs benefit preschoolers the most? (319)
Emotions				Learning
	Self-concept and Identity		Cognition	
		Language		

Egocentrism in Young Children

Egocentrism refers to the inability of a person to distinguish between his own point of view and that of another person. It is literally a centering on the self in thinking. As used here, the term does *not* mean a motivation to be selfish at the expense of others; such an attitude presupposes a knowledge of differences among individuals that young children usually do not have. Instead, egocentrism stems more from **perceptual dominance,** or **centration** — the tendency (common among preschoolers) to focus on only one aspect of an object or situation and to ignore other aspects. Perceptual dominance, or centration, occurs when a child thinks that the volume of a glass of milk depends entirely on how tall the glass is and forgets to notice how wide it is.

Young children think egocentrically sometimes but not always. Piaget illustrated this variation by asking children sitting at a table on which models of three mountains had been constructed how a doll would see the three mountains if the doll sat at various positions around the table (see Figure 9.1). A three-year-old — one of Piaget's preoperational children — commonly believed that the doll saw the layout no differently from the way he did himself; given several drawings of mountains from which to pick the doll's view, the child tended to choose the one that simply reproduced his own viewpoint rather than some other perspective (Piaget & Inhelder, 1967).

Nevertheless, with some modifications even young children adopt others' perspectives on a task like this. In one variation, four-year-olds were shown a table with two partitions that formed a cross, as shown in Figure 9.2 (Cohen, 1983). At the table, too, were two dolls, one dressed as a policeman and the other dressed as a boy. The policeman was put in various positions around the table, and the child was asked to place the boy doll behind the partitions where the policeman could not see it. According to the experimenter, the policeman was trying to chase and catch the boy. The preschool child thus had to imagine the perspective of the policeman — much the same challenge as in Piaget's mountain experiment.

Preschoolers' perspective

Modifications that improve perspective

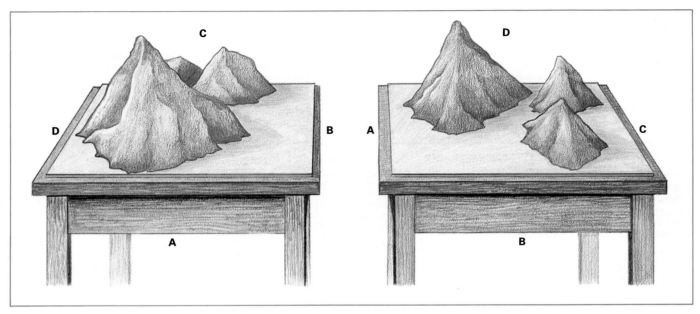

FIGURE 9.1
Piaget's Three Mountains Experiment

Preschool children in this experiment proved quite skillful at taking the policeman's perspective, even when the task was made more complicated by having two police dolls search for the boy doll at the same time. This required the children to coordinate *three* perspectives at once. Why the difference in performance on this task and on Piaget's? The policeman situation may have seemed more familiar, perhaps, and therefore easier to solve. Few children literally have been chased by a policeman, but most have been chased by their friends in play. To this extent, the children may have practiced the policeman task in their own lives. At the same time, they may have felt more motivated to solve the police-chase version because it may have seemed less arbitrary than Piaget's version.

FIGURE 9.2
Variation on Three Mountains Experiment

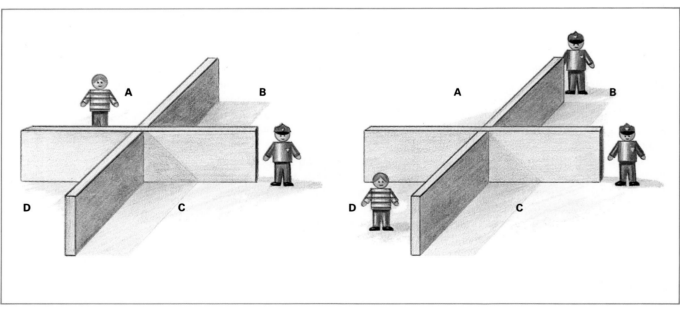

In situations requiring communication, too, young children show definite, but incomplete, signs of egocentrism. A variety of studies — along with much common observation — show that preschoolers often explain tasks and events rather poorly (Flavell et al., 1986). In describing a drawing to someone, they may leave out crucial terms or relationships. They may leave out so much, in fact, that copying a simple diagram according to their instructions is virtually impossible, no matter how sensitive the listener may be. Near the end of the interview with Audrey, for example, Audrey assumed that the interviewer knew someone named Sammy.

On the other hand, preschool children do sometimes show awareness of confusion and ignorance when it is expressed by others. One study found that preschool children explained a drawing better to a person who was blindfolded than to someone who was actually looking at the drawing while the child was explaining it (Cohen, 1983). The blindfold apparently signaled or emphasized the gap in perspective between the child's knowledge and the listener's and encouraged the child to consider the other's needs more carefully when talking.

Taken together, these studies suggest that egocentrism exists in early childhood but is not always in evidence. Preschool children do recognize the existence of different perspectives and sometimes make allowances for that fact. They judge other people's comprehension separately from their own comprehension and separately from the intrinsic qualities of utterances. But they do often fail to realize just how badly people can misunderstand each other even in simple, ordinary communication — as when one of these four-year-olds tries to teach a friend how to tie shoelaces:

JILL: You want to learn to tie laces?
KATE: Okay. (*She stares in another direction.*)
JILL: First you make a . . . make a . . . do this. (*She makes a loop.*) Do you see?
KATE: (*still staring elsewhere*): Uh-huh.
JILL: Okay, so then you stick it through. I think that's called a knot. (*She fumbles a bit.*) Actually I'm not so good at this part. Oh, now it'll work. (*She succeeds.*)
KATE: Yep.
JILL: You ready to try it now? (*She unties the laces again.*)
KATE: Sure, now I know what to do. (*There is a long pause; then she walks off to play, leaving her laces untied.*)

Like a lot of preschool conversations, this one fails for a mixture of reasons. First, the children do not agree on how to gain each other's attention reliably; Kate is looking away and possibly daydreaming when Jill thinks Kate is paying attention. Second, Jill (and probably also Kate) lacks facility and accuracy in calling attention to and labeling her actions; is she making a knot, a bow, or something else? Third, Kate does not understand how to signal real understanding to Jill; apparently she thinks that simply being agreeable is enough.

Animism and Artificialism

In the preschool years, a child often expresses **animism,** a belief that nonliving objects are in fact alive and human. One child showed animism by discussing his shoe like this: "Hey! This shoe won't fit. Get on there, shoe! There; that's more like it. . . . Shoe, are you tired of squeezing my foot?" Here the shoe is treated as a person or at least as something human enough to take on the role of listener in this conversation.

Poor communication skills

Bridges How does cognitive egocentrism affect friendship formation during the preschool years?

Examples of animism

Even without being actual participants in a conversation, however, objects and events can take on living qualities:

PARENT: Why do the clouds move?
CHILD: Because the wind blows them. It goes *poof!* at them.
PARENT: Is that the only reason?
CHILD: Well . . . um . . . sometimes the wind gets tired, so it stops to rest for a while.

As these examples suggest, animism generates a lot of the cute remarks that adults enjoy in young children.

Artificialism refers to a belief that all objects, whether living or not, are made in the same way, usually by human beings. A child may believe that the sky is blue because someone painted it blue with a paintbrush or that rain is caused by someone using a large sprinkling can.

Causes of animism and artificialism

To a certain extent, animism and artificialism are both special forms of egocentrism. In animism, children assume that various objects and events have the same qualities that they themselves have, namely, human and living ones. In artificialism, they assume that their immature, incomplete knowledge of the world is in fact complete, and they therefore overgeneralize from it.

But egocentrism may not be the whole cause for these errors; imitation of adults may also contribute. An adult might easily say, "My car doesn't like me today" because the car will not start; in so doing, she implies that the car has feelings like a person or at least like some sort of intelligent being. Even though the adult may excuse her comment as "just a figure of speech," a young child who happens to be listening may not dismiss the expression so lightly: for him, it may model animistic thinking.

As with egocentrism, children express animism more in some situations than in others. As a rule of thumb, they are more likely to attribute human qualities to objects with which they are relatively unfamiliar (Laurendeau & Pinard, 1972). They may persist with animism longer in describing an airplane than in describing a toy truck that they play with every day. But by school age, children usually figure out which objects are genuinely alive, even by adult standards, and which are not.

Classification Skills

Classification refers to the placement of objects in groups or categories according to some sort of standards or criteria. Young preschool children can reliably classify objects that differ in just one dimension or feature, especially if that dimension presents fairly obvious contrasts. Given a collection of pennies and nickels, a pre-schooler can usually sort them by color, which is their most obvious dimension of difference. Given a boxful of silverware, a young child might sort it by type: knives, forks, and spoons. Or she might group dishes by how they are used in real life, putting each cup with one saucer rather than separating all cups from all saucers (Sugarman, 1983). These simple groupings represent cognitive advances over infancy.

Groupings made by preschoolers

Preschoolers can sometimes also manage more complex classification tasks but not as reliably. One prime example of their mixed success is **class inclusion:** the ability to compare a subset of objects with some larger, more inclusive set of objects to which it belongs. Red flowers and white flowers both belong to the larger, more inclusive (or general) class of flowers, and white cows and black cows both belong to the larger class cows.

The class-inclusion task

How well can preschool children handle inclusive relationships? Piaget found that young children can easily compare subsets with each other but cannot

Most preschool children can classify objects according to simple, obvious dimensions such as color and size. They have trouble, though, in classifying according to more than one dimension at the same time or when categories are based on abstract properties.

easily compare one subset with the group as a whole (Piaget & Inhelder, 1969). Suppose a preschooler is asked, "Are there more red flowers or more white flowers?" and then "Are there more red flowers or more flowers?" He typically can answer the first question correctly but often fails at the second, which he tends to answer as if he is comparing the red and white groups in spite of being asked to compare the red group with the whole group. He will say, for example, that a collection of four red flowers and two whites has more red flowers than flowers (incorrect); but he will also say that the collection has more red flowers than white flowers (correct).

So sometimes the child seems to answer a different question from the one asked. Why? Piaget suggested that the preschooler cannot decenter her thinking, meaning that she cannot broaden her focus to take account of more than one dimension at the same time. In class-inclusion tasks, the child must pay attention to the dimensions of color (is it white or red?) *and* of "flowerness" (is it a flower or something else?). In practice, however, a preschooler can sustain attention to only one of these at a time — usually the most concrete, noticeable dimension, which in this case is color. So any question that refers to two dimensions at once may cause trouble.

Reasons for inclusion errors

Piaget believed that young children's difficulties with class inclusion happen in most situations and types of problems. More recent studies, however, have shown convincingly what many observers of children have sensed all along: that in some conditions, young children can solve surprisingly complex problems, including class-inclusion problems. One study modified the inclusion task by changing the wording and materials slightly. It used white and black cows but

Successful class-inclusion tasks

laid them all on their sides — "because they are sleeping," the experimenter explained. Then children were asked one of two questions: "Are there more black cows than cows?" (Piaget's version of the question), and "Are there more black cows than sleeping cows?" (new version). The addition of the word *sleeping* to the question caused twice as many young children to succeed at this task (McGarrigle et al., 1978). In another variation in the same study, even the first question produced more success if the last word — *cows* — was spoken with heavy emphasis.

These changes suggest that communication problems may influence children's success as much as their thinking abilities do (Flavell et al., 1986). Evidently children can compare a subset (black cows) with its inclusive set (sleeping cows) if the question and the materials make clear the need for that kind of comparison. Piaget's form of the problem, some argue, does not do so. As a result, a young child may simply answer questions that she considers likely to be asked. In effect, when faced with an unusual or unexpected question, she does what many older children and adults do: she gives the interviewer the benefit of the doubt and responds to what she thinks the interviewer must have meant to ask (D. Olson & Torrance, 1983). In the inclusion task in particular, this means giving simple, one-dimensional comparisons, not comparisons between specific classes and general ones.

Developmental differences in problem solving

Thus, a preschool child may understand more than Piaget originally gave him credit for. Note, however, that this still does not make him the cognitive equal of an older child. As we see in Chapter 12, a school-age child handles cognitive problems in ways distinctively different from those of a preschool child. The older child is less apt to find Piagetian questions as ambiguous as the younger child does, and she knows more ways to clarify surprising or vaguely phrased questions when they do occur. The preschooler can seem relatively skillful when someone else arranges the conditions properly, but the school-age child can take a larger role in arranging the proper conditions herself.

Reversibility and Conservation

Many problems require **reversibility** in thinking, which is the ability to undo a problem mentally and go back to its beginning. If you lose a pair of glasses, reversible thinking can help to find them: you retrace your recent actions in your mind until you encounter or visualize the glasses again. Reversibility, it turns out, contributes to a major cognitive achievement of middle childhood, **conservation,** which is the ability to perceive that certain properties of an object remain the same or constant in spite of changes in the object's appearance. Children usually do not begin to achieve conservation until about age six.

Limitations of preschoolers' reversibility

Often preschool children either cannot or do not use reversible thinking, even when the situation calls for it; and this fact can sometimes make their thinking disjointed or fragmented and in turn make them solve some problems incorrectly. As with other symbolic skills in this age period, however, a lot depends on how the task is presented. Typically, Piaget's classic tests for reversibility in thinking make children seem less capable or mature than more recent revisions do.

Consider the following Piagetian test of reversibility. First you show a preschool child two tall glasses of water with exactly the same amount in each. Then the child watches you pour the water from one of the tall glasses into a third, wide glass. Naturally, the water line in the wide one will not be as high as it was in the tall one. Finally, you ask the child, "Is there more water in the wide glass than in the [remaining] tall glass, or less, or just as much?"

How will a young child respond to this problem? According to Piaget, his nonreversible thinking may make him forget the identity of water levels that he saw only a moment earlier; after all, as a nonreversible thinker, he cannot easily imagine pouring the water back again in order to convince himself of the tall glasses' equality. Instead he is forced to solve the problem on the basis of the current appearance of the water — by comparing the looks of the tall and the wide glasses. More often than not, the big difference in their appearance leads him to say that the amount of water has changed as a result of its being poured. In Piagetian terms, he fails to conserve, or believe in the constancy of the amount of liquid in spite of its visible changes (Inhelder & Piaget, 1958).

Conservation of liquid

Note that the preschool child's lack of reversibility does not handicap him in all types of problem solving. Questions involving nonreversible phenomena do not prove as difficult as those involving reversible phenomena (Piaget et al., 1968). Consider these questions:

Identity problems

■ (*After a candle burns to a short stub*): "Is it still the same candle as before?"

■ (*After a seedling grows taller*): "Is it still the same plant as before?"

■ "Could you ever be a boy/girl?" (*whichever the child is not*)

All three questions prove confusing for a very young preschooler (age three or so) but are answered confidently and correctly by most children by about age five — about two years earlier than children typically can answer conservation-related questions (Flavell et al., 1986, Seifert, 1973). The difference may stem from several factors, among which is the nonreversible nature of the truth in these cases; because the crucial object or feature in fact remains visibly fixed over time, reference to the past proves unnecessary or even distracting. In other words, even if the candle becomes short, it still looks like a candle, and even if the seedling becomes tall, it still looks like a plant. Because of these constancies, even preoperational children can be relatively skillful in problems involving nonreversible phenomena.

But problems that do require reversibility are affected a great deal by how they are presented or described to the child. Consider the water conservation task. One study found that asking children the question not only after but also before pouring the water caused them to conserve *less often* than asking them only afterward (Rose & Blank, 1974). Why the difference? Perhaps repeating the question makes some children believe that the experimenter wants them to change their response; after all, why else would she repeat herself? Because most children begin the conservation task by agreeing that the glasses hold equal amounts, obliging children may feel compelled to give nonconserving responses against their own better judgment.

Procedures that increase conservation responses

Another study further confirmed the importance of the experimenter's intentions by arranging for reversibility experiments to occur "by accident" (McGarrigle & Donaldson, 1974). The study used "Naughty Teddy," a teddy bear who occasionally swooped over the interview table and disarranged everything on it. Sometimes the bear "accidentally" caused the tall glass of water to spill into a wide tray; in these conditions, young children conserved far more frequently than when an experimenter poured the water on purpose. This result suggests that the classic version of the experiment may underestimate young children's ability to reason. Rather than being handicapped by nonreversible thinking, some children may do what adults often do: respond to the expectations of the situation and of the people in it (E. Langer, 1985). Apparently children, like everyone else, edit their responses.

How Cognitive Development Occurs

Inconsistencies in cognitive performance, like the ones just described, may happen because preschool children depend on the social context or circumstances in order to develop new cognitive skills. Children do not simply learn fundamental thinking skills alone; they do not just interact with and "cogitate" about

A lot of cognitive development occurs because of the support and structure provided by adults — in what Vygotsky calls the "zone of proximal development."

objects and experiences. Instead, either directly or indirectly, they learn in conjunction with adults or with older, more experienced peers (Grotevant, 1989; Wertsch, 1989). The older individuals provide models of how problems should be solved, and they offer hints and information about how to approach or think about a problem. The help may sometimes be deliberate (as in school) or accidental (as more often at home), but either way it allows a child to handle problems that are just a bit beyond the ones she can deal with alone.

The gap in difficulty between independent thinking and socially supported thinking is called the **zone of proximal development,** the area in which problems are too difficult to solve alone but are not too hard to solve with support from adults or from more competent peers. The concept originated with Soviet psychologist Lev Vygotsky (1978; Wertsh 1985) and has created a lot of interest among developmental psychologists because it suggests how stages and skills may emerge and evolve. In learning about number, everyday conversations between parent and child play a significant role (Saxe et al., 1984):

PARENT: Here are four books for you and the same for your brother.
CHILD: The same? (He investigates his brother's pile of books.) No, he has more (spoken with annoyance).
PARENT: No really, they're the same. Take another look.
CHILD: He does have more.
PARENT: Try laying his out in a row. Then lay yours out, too. Then compare.
CHILD (does as suggested, then counts each row): One, two, three, four. One, two, three, four. The same! (He looks satisfied.)

In this example, the parent provides a framework that the child cannot provide for himself and that allows the child to solve the problem for himself. First, the parent states the problem in a helpful way ("They're the same"); then she gives hints about how to solve it. But the final solution remains with the child. The help occurs in the child's personal zone of proximal development. Without it, the child might not have solved the problem, at least at this point in his cognitive development.

How Skillful Is Preschool Symbolic Thinking?

As the studies described so far suggest, preschool symbolic thinking often has a "now you see it, now you don't" quality. In many ways — through language and dramatic play — young children can represent experiences reliably. In other ways, however, they cannot give adultlike responses to many tasks that require symbolic thought; the classic Piagetian experiments illustrate this limitation. And in still other ways, young children prove more capable of symbolic thought than Piaget gave them credit for, at least in his original theorizing (Carey, 1985).

Such variations make sense in children who are just beginning to represent experiences symbolically. After all, they still have a lot of developing to do before they can consolidate their thinking skills fully. The experiments that qualify or limit Piaget's findings do not, however, really disprove the basic usefulness of Piaget's stage theory of development. Instead they suggest a number of complexities about cognitive development in early childhood.

Variability

Impact of social developments

In particular, research on early cognition suggests that children often combine their social motivations and intuitions with their cognitive ones; perhaps only adults try to separate them for convenience in studying children. And the research suggests that language affects cognitive performance significantly and possibly affects cognitive capacity as well. Somehow words and sentences guide a child in solving problems, and they do so more significantly than Piaget believed, at least originally. This idea is important enough to deserve further attention and explanation in the next part of this chapter.

Perspectives

What Kind of Education Is Best for Preschoolers?

During the 1970s and 1980s a number of states began funding classrooms for four-year-old children, especially children at risk for educational failure because of poverty or special learning needs (Marx & Seligson, 1988). The change has focused new attention on what amount and kind of education are appropriate for preschoolers.

Those favoring extensive education for four-year-olds point out that the percentage of mothers of preschoolers who work has increased enormously in the past decade and that this circumstance increases demand for early childhood education of all types (Grubb, 1989). Others point to early education as a way of promoting excellence in education and of simultaneously minimizing dropouts and illiteracy (National Governors' Association, 1986).

Unfortunately, these two bases of support do not necessarily lead to similar proposals for early childhood programs. Proposals motivated by the needs of working mothers tend to favor programs with long hours and full years so as to accommodate mothers' needs for child care. Proposals motivated by the need to prevent academic failure give priority to enriched, focused educational experiences, even though teachers often find these easier to provide in relatively short-term programs that last only part of the year or part of each day.

In theory, these two goals could be combined in a single program: one with long hours *and* an enriched educational environment. In practice, many early childhood programs have not succeeded in making the combination simply because of the costs involved. Running a program for long hours and creating a highly educational environment both cost money. Salaries are higher for full-day programs than for half-day programs; but they are also higher if a program has to recruit teachers or curriculum consultants with special skills in making the program educational or developmentally appropriate. Most early childhood educators want to combine long hours of service with high-quality programming, but often they do not have the resources, either financial or professional, to do so. (Mitchell, 1988; Mitchell et al., 1989; Mitchell & Modigliani, 1989).

Partly in response to these dilemmas, government and educational agencies have encouraged the development of model programs, so that other, local programs could simply adapt a model to local circumstances rather than design a program completely from scratch. Some models have constructed curricula based heavily on Piaget's ideas about cognitive development (Kamii & DeVries, 1977; Weikart, 1986). In these, children spend a lot of time in sensorimotor activities, such as sand and water play, or in preoperational activities, such as make-believe play. Other models may organize activities around structured materials, which children are guided to use in particular ways. Programs inspired by the work of Maria Montessori (1964), for example, give children sets of cylinders graded by size and designed to fit snugly into a set of size-graded holes in a board. A child experiments with the cylinders and holes in order to discover the best way to fit them.

In spite of the diversity among model programs (and hence among *all* programs for young children), evaluations suggest that a wide range of approaches are about equally effective in promoting overall cognitive growth (Consortium for Longitudinal Studies, 1983), although programs do seem to develop different *patterns* of skills, depending on their program's goals (L. Miller & Bizzell, 1983). Two factors seem to underlie successful early childhood programs. First, teachers in such programs regard themselves as competent observers of children's educational needs and as capable of making important decisions in tailoring a curriculum to particular children (Bredekamp, 1986). Second, the vast majority of successful programs and teachers view an early childhood curriculum as an integrated whole rather than as something made up of independent subject areas or skills (Seefeldt, 1987, 1990). Singing a song, for example, is not just "music"; it can also foster language development, motor skills (if children dance along), arithmetic (through counting and rhythm), and social studies (if the song is about members of the wider community).*

*Bridges   What kind of education programs benefit preschoolers the most?

PERCEPTUAL DEVELOPMENT IN PRESCHOOL CHILDREN

Sometimes preschool children can perceive visual and auditory stimuli as well as adults, but other times they cannot. The differences in performance reflect their growing, but still incomplete, capacities for information processing. As a rule, preschoolers can make simple perceptual judgments (like the difference in the size of two circles) just as competently as adults can, as long as the judgments involve relatively little memory or cognitive reorganization. But judgments that require more complex thinking (like comparing the area of a rectangle with one

Bridges   In what ways does the cognitive development of preschoolers affect what they see and hear?

seen the day before) often lead to many errors in what preschoolers "see" and "hear," apparently because their attention is diverted away from actual stimuli, and toward the processing of those stimuli.

Visual Perception

Farsightedness

During the preschool years, vision becomes increasingly important as a source of information; yet preschoolers still cannot see as well as older children. They are usually farsighted; that is, they can see distant objects almost perfectly but have trouble focusing on nearby objects, such as a line of ordinary print in a book (Cratty, 1986). For some children, farsightedness probably causes certain practical problems, such as discomfort in drawing for long periods or in doing other work that takes close visual concentration. As preschoolers get older, however, their near vision tends to improve, a fact that helps children cope with the major tasks of elementary school, such as reading and writing.

Not only does visual acuity improve during early childhood; visual perception also improves in several ways. First, children learn to *discriminate,* or notice visual differences among objects, better. Second, they *integrate* what they see increasingly well, which means that they coordinate one sight better with another sight as well as with specific motor actions. And third, children improve their *visual memory,* or ability to recognize and recall specific visual stimuli. The three processes overlap a lot in daily life, but it is helpful to consider examples of each process separately.

During the preschool years, children improve in their ability to track small moving objects, like these ants. Many preschoolers are still a bit farsighted, though, until they are about five or six years old.

Visual Discrimination   **Visual discrimination** refers to the ability to distinguish or discern differences in what is seen. Preschool children can make visual discriminations as long as they involve relatively simple or obvious distinctions. A four-year-old can usually tell you which of two stuffed animals looks brighter, or whether two pencils look exactly the same in length, or whether two toy cars have exactly the same shape (Frostig et al., 1966).

Simple distinctions possible

But when visual discriminations require noticing underlying dimensions of objects, preschool children do not perform as well. Researchers demonstrated this limitation by showing preschool children slides of objects in groups of three (Farnham-Diggory & Gregg, 1975), then asking them to match two of the objects in some way. One slide showed a red truck, a red apple, and a brown book; for this slide, children were asked, "Which objects are most alike in color?" On this test, even older preschoolers (five-year-olds) did not perform very well: only about 12 percent could match the objects reliably by color. In fairness to the children, however, note that adult subjects in this study did not perform well either: only about 50 percent of adults matched the pictures by color reliably. In spite of the simplicity of the task, both adults and children made numerous discrimination errors.

Abstract groupings more difficult

The difficulty of discriminations like these depends a great deal on the particular dimension or distraction in question. In general, children find identity discriminations the easiest; these are ones in which the child must simply decide whether or not two objects are exactly alike. Harder than these are discriminations about color, and still harder are ones about shape. Most of the time, adults' discriminations reflect this same sequence — identity, color, and shape — although at more sophisticated levels (Williams et al., 1978, 1979). The sequence has implications for the design of educational toys: if a puzzle is supposed to teach differences in shape, painting each piece a different color can distract from this goal because the colors constitute easier clues in sorting the pieces.

Variations in difficulty of discriminations

Visual Integration   **Visual integration** refers to the ability to coordinate particular sights with each other as well as with appropriate physical actions. Throwing and catching a ball require visual integration: a child must watch the ball carefully from one instant to the next and move her hands appropriately to make the catch. The fact that children generally improve at catching balls shows that they are acquiring visual integration during the preschool years. A variety of other motor skills from drawing pictures and tying shoelaces to jumping rope and playing tag with another child suggest the same idea. All of these activities require children to coordinate what they see and to coordinate these sights with what they do. And children improve at all such tasks between the ages of two and five.

Coordinating sights and actions

But there are limits to these improvements. Preschool children often have particular trouble in coordinating actions and sights in the presence of distracting stimuli. Many four-year-olds are quite capable of dressing themselves, but they fail badly at this task if they are listening to a favorite record at the same time. Others can draw skillful pictures, but only as long as they do not talk; to comment on their drawings, they must temporarily interrupt their work.

Problems with distractions

Some problems in visual integration occur because children try to take account of increasingly large numbers of stimuli. In some ways, therefore, older preschoolers set themselves harder perceptual problems than younger preschoolers do. Suppose that children must sort a stack of cards by shape; but suppose also that the cards differ not only by shape but sometimes also by color. How well do the children do? When the cards are all the same color and differ only in shape, older children sort the cards better than younger children do (H. Williams et al., 1979). Eight-year-olds make fewer errors than five-year-olds; they demonstrate a better discrimination of basic shapes, such as triangles, squares, rectangles, and circles. But when the cards differ in both dimensions at

Coordinating the feel of this container and the sight of the juice with the sight of these cups is one form of visual integration, a skill that children achieve early in the preschool period.

once — in both shape and color — older children perform no better than younger children. Apparently the older children cannot purposely disregard color, even though they know it is irrelevant to this particular task; in everyday terms, they get mixed up. Younger children, however, do just as well in the presence of the distracting dimension. Apparently, therefore, they are not so much confused by the irrelevant dimension as oblivious to it.

Visual tracking

Coordinating visual perception with physical actions can also prove challenging. When very young children track a moving object, such as a ball suspended from a string, they often have trouble separating their eye movements from their head movements. Three-year-olds cannot separate them at all; they inevitably move their heads to follow an object (Bizzi, 1974). Four- and five-year-olds can separate these actions a bit, but more for vertical movements (a falling or rising ball) than for horizontal ones (a moving train). Not until school age can children track objects consistently in all directions, including diagonal ones (H. Williams et al., 1979).

Improvement in visual recognition and recall

Visual Memory Visual memory refers to the ability to recall or recognize simple sights, such as a familiar face or the color of a friend's clothes. During the preschool years, children become better at this sort of task, at least when they have to remember only for fairly short periods of time (H. Williams, 1983). Flashing shapes onto a screen for a few seconds demonstrates the nature of these changes. When the number of shapes is fairly small — say, three or four — even rather young children can remember what they have seen quite well. In this case, they remember almost as well as adults do. Preschool children reach their limits when remembering larger numbers of shapes (say, six or eight).

Whether this difference results completely from perceptual skills is not clear. Older children and adults have many cognitive or thinking skills that help them to perceive more clearly (E. Gibson, 1969). They can draw on a larger vocabulary of accurate descriptive labels; they are more likely to know terms such as *ellipse, diamond,* and *parallelogram* in addition to *circle, square,* and *triangle.* They also tend to use labels for parts of shapes, such as *corner, angle,* and *curve.* These labels may relieve older individuals from actually having to visualize certain shapes in order to remember them. Some of the time, instead, they may simply recall the labels and their meanings and thus piece together a mental picture of the shape.

Language as an aid to visual memory

Auditory Perception

In some ways, hearing develops more quickly than vision. By the age of two or three, most children have very good **auditory acuity,** meaning that they can notice small or soft sounds as well as young adults can. They can also discriminate speech sounds quite well. These sounds are the *phonemes* of language, like the /b/ and /d/ sounds in the word *bad.*

Good acuity of hearing

But producing these sounds still poses problems for many children (DiSimoni, 1975). Their errors are the source of many endearing remarks heard by parents and nursery school teachers. "See that fuwwy teddy beah," says a three-year-old, meaning "See that furry teddy bear." Another says, "I'm shaning my cothes; then I'll have some zhuice," meaning "I'm changing my clothes; then I'll have some juice." Most of the time, preschool children can perceive (or hear) phonemic differences long before they can produce them (Birch, 1976), as in this conversation at the dinner table:

Common errors in producing phonemes

CHILD: Daddy, please give me a pomato.
DADDY: Do you mean a tomato or a potato?
CHILD: A POMATO!
DADDY: A tomato?
CHILD: No.
DADDY: A potato?
CHILD: Yes!

Most children (although not all) eventually grow out of such mistakes, probably by a combination of perceiving more accurately how adults speak and of practicing the sounds themselves. Their improvements smooth the way for other major developments in language ability, which are described in the next section.

LANGUAGE ACQUISITION IN THE PRESCHOOL YEARS

For most children, language expands rapidly after infancy. Dramatic development occurs in *syntax,* or the way the child organizes utterances. But significant changes also happen in semantics and in communicative competence. As we mentioned in Chapter 6, *semantics* refers to what the child means by his utterances; **communicative competence** is how the child adjusts his utterances to the needs and expectations of different situations and speakers.

Aspects of language development

Because of the comparative importance of syntactic development during the preschool years, we emphasize this particular topic here, leaving major discussion of semantics and communication for Chapter 12. Making this division does not imply, however, that these three aspects of language develop in isolation from one another. Quite the contrary: as the discussion of syntax emphasizes, how a child organizes an utterance (her syntax) depends in part on what she wants to say and the meaning of her words (her semantics) and in part on when she wants to say it and to whom (her communicative competence). Conversely, her meanings and intentions sometimes stimulate her to learn new ways of organizing utterances and stimulate the adults in her life to model them as well (Whitehurst, 1982). Some of these relationships are illustrated in the examples that follow.

The Nature of Syntax

The *syntax* of a language is a group of rules for ordering and relating its elements. Linguists call the elements of language morphemes. **Morphemes** are the smallest meaningful units of language; they include words as well as a number of prefixes and suffixes that carry meaning (for example, the /s/ in *houses* or the /re/ in *redo* and verb-tense modifiers (for example, the /ing/ in *going*).

Syntactic rules operate on morphemes in several ways. Sometimes they mark important relationships between large classes or groups of words. Consider these two pairs of sentences:

1a. John kissed Barbara.	*and*	2a. Frank kisses Joan.
1b. Barbara kissed John.		2b. Frank kissed Joan.

Significance of syntax for language

These sentences differ in meaning because of syntactic rules. In the first pair, a rule about the order or sequence of words tells us who is giving the kiss and who is receiving it: the name occurring before the verb is the agent (the kisser), and the name after the verb is the recipient (the kissee?). In the second pair of sentences, the morphemes /es/ and /ed/ tell something about when the event occurred; adding /es/ to the end of the word signifies that it is happening now, but adding /ed/ means that it happened in the past. These rules, and many others like them, are understood and used by all competent speakers of the language. Unlike textbook authors, however, the speakers may never state them and may be only barely aware of them.

Kinds of syntactic rules

Syntactic rules vary in how regular or general they are. Some apply to large, open-ended groupings or classes of words; this quality makes them **generative** — that is, speakers can create or generate brand-new sentences almost infinitely by applying the rule to brand-new morphemes. The examples above are generative in this sense. Replacing *John* with *fish*, for example, and *Barbara* with *water* creates the strange sentence "Fish kissed water." This sentence may sound odd, but it nevertheless conveys some idea of who was doing the kissing and who was receiving it. Even nonsense words can fit into the same syntactic framework: "Gokems kissed splibs." We may have no idea of what (or who) *gokems* and *splibs* are, but the syntax of the sentence still tells us which one was the kisser and which was the receiver of the kiss. To this extent, the syntax conveys meaning independent of the words slotted into the sentence form.

Unfortunately for a child learning to talk, some syntactic rules have only a small range of application, and still others are completely irregular. Most words, for example, signal pluralization (the existence of more than one) by adding /s/ or /es/ at the end; *book* means one volume, and *books* means many. But a few words use other methods to signal the plural. *Foot* means one, and *feet*, not "foots," means many; *child* means one, and *children* means many; and *deer* can mean either one animal or many of them.

Impact of syntax on language acquisition

Thus, in acquiring syntax, a young child confronts a mixed system of rules. Some apply widely and regularly, and others apply narrowly and exceptionally. Whatever skills the child brings to learning language, he must take these differences into account. Relying too much on the regularity of syntax will make him often sound ungrammatical, yet treating language rules too often as irregular will limit the child's ability to generalize and to generate truly new sentences. As shown below, most children require several years to balance these features of learning language — and some may never really achieve such a balance completely.

Beyond First Words: Duos and Telegraphic Speech

Before the age of two, the child begins linking two words together when she speaks; these utterances are sometimes called **duos** (meaning "twos"). Typically, morphemes of duos express relationships to each other that resemble the syntactic relationships in adult language. For example, a two-word utterance can express nonexistence ("Hat gone") or possession ("My hat"), just as adult utterances can. The difference lies, of course, in the subtlety and explicitness of the relationships expressed. Adult utterances are apt to convey several syntactic relationships in one sentence ("That blue hat of mine is gone now"); two-word utterances must state multiple relationships through multiple utterances ("Hat gone. My hat. Blue hat. Now gone. That hat . . . "). **Two-word sentences**

By nature, early speech also leaves out most small connecting words: articles (like *the* and *a*), prepositions (like *of* and *in*), and conjunctions (like *and* and *but*). These clarify relationships among morphemes and generally make complex grammar possible. Without them, syntactic relationships are still possible, but the child's speech sounds stilted. Early utterances are therefore also called **telegraphic speech,** presumably because they sound like a telegram ("Send money. No money? Send chocolates."). The telegraphic quality persists even after the child begins linking more than two words at a time, but it disappears by about age four or so, at least in simple conversations on familiar topics (R. Brown, 1973). **Function words omitted**

Individual Differences and Undergeneralizations Even though all children express syntactic relationships in their first utterances, they differ significantly in the particular relationships they express and in the rate at which relationships emerge. A number of universal "first grammars" have been suggested, but none has stood up to close scrutiny by psychologists and linguists (R. Brown, 1973). Unfortunately, there is little evidence that the proposed relationships actually reflect the child's own first methods of organizing morphemes; in other words, the child's grammar and the linguist's grammar may not coincide (Whitehurst, 1982).

To understand this problem, consider these two early duos: "my truck" and "red truck." In the child's mind, do these express two types of relations, the first of possession and the second of physical attribution? Or does the child regard them as two examples of one relationship, simply a general one of attribution? **Early grammars** Given the limited language of very young preschoolers, there is no way to be sure. First utterances are not numerous enough to allow linguists to group them reliably and thereby to infer the child's "true" grammar, and the children are still too young to comment usefully on their own utterances, as adults sometimes can do.

Some syntactic relationships apparently have a narrower meaning for some children than for adults. A wide range of such **undergeneralizations** occurs in early sentences (Nelson, 1981). A child's first sentences may draw on both nouns and verbs but not combine every available noun with every available verb. As *holophrases* (or one-word sentences), the child may be using *kitty, daddy,* and *sister* (all nouns) as well as *run, stand,* and *walk* (all verbs). But she may never use some of the nine sentences possible with these words; she may say, "Daddy stand," but never "Daddy walk." When the situation calls for it, she will instead use *daddy* and *walk* as single words. Eventually, of course, she does combine them; but throughout the preschool years, she continues to define grammatical categories more narrowly than adults do (J. DeVilliers, 1980).

Regularities and Overgeneralizations   After highly individual beginnings, certain aspects of syntax do develop in universal and predictable patterns. The present progressive form *-ing* occurs quite early in most children's language, the regular plural morphemes *-s* and *-es* somewhat later, and articles such as *the* and *a* still later (R. Brown, 1973).

At a slightly older age, most children begin using auxiliary verbs to form questions, but they do so without inverting word order, as adults normally do. At first, for example, a child will say, "Why you are cooking?" and only later "Why are you cooking?" This suggests that language acquisition involves more than just copying adult language; after all, adults rarely model incorrect forms. To a certain extent children's language seems to compromise between the new forms that children hear and old forms that they can already produce easily.

Sometimes, in fact, early syntax becomes too regular, and children make **overgeneralizations.** Around age three, for example, preschool children often make errors such as these:

- "I runned to the store."
- "Unpour this water, please."
- "All the childs came!"

In each case, the child used the wrong but more regular form, as opposed to the correct but irregular forms of an earlier age (R. Brown, 1973). Usually by early school age he shifts back again, although not necessarily because anyone teaches him or forces him to do so. Apparently his overgeneralizations represent efforts to try out new rules of syntax that he has finally noticed (Bowerman, 1982).

The Predisposition to Infer Grammar   As these examples suggest, young children seem to infer grammatical relationships rather than simply copy others' speech. Few parents try purposely to teach talking, and those who do usually discover that direct efforts tend to fail. Consider this example (Bellugi, 1970):

CHILD: My teacher holded the rabbits and we patted them.
MOTHER: Did you say your teacher held the baby rabbits?
CHILD: Yes.
MOTHER: What did you say she did?
CHILD: She holded the rabbits and we patted them.
MOTHER: Did you say she held them tightly?
CHILD: No, she holded them loosely.

In spite of her mother's apparently unsuccessful attempt to encourage adult grammar in this situation, the child will almost certainly switch from *holded* to *held* eventually. The child, not the adults around her, seems to control the timing of this change; she, not her mother, must solve the grammatical puzzles posed by language.

A classic study of early syntax showed the importance of the child's own inferences about grammatical rules. Instead of asking children about real words, the experimenter showed them pictures of imaginary creatures and actions that had nonsense words as names (Berko, 1958). With one picture, a child was told, "Here is a wug." Then he was shown two pictures and told, "Here are two of them. Here are two ——— ." Most children, even as young as age two and one-half, completed the sentences with the grammatically correct words, *wugs*. Because they could not possibly have heard the term before, they must have

A Talk with Audrey

Cognitive Development in the Preschool Years

Audrey was interviewed shortly after she returned from her day-care center. She asked me to come with her to the porch, where her toys were.

Interviewer: Audrey, you were saying that you like to eat chicken. What is chicken?

Audrey: Chicken is animal. And when it's dead it turns into food chicken.

Interviewer: When it's dead it turns into food?

Audrey: Yes.

Interviewer: And then you eat it up?

Audrey: Yes.

Interviewer: Where does the food go after you put it in your mouth?

Audrey: First we put it in the oven.

Interviewer: And then what?

Audrey: And then we eat it all up.

Interviewer: Audrey, you seem to be very big. Are you growing?

Audrey: Yes, I'm four. First, I was one, then I was three, and then four. And now I'm almost five.

Interviewer: And what happens when you get to be four? Do you get bigger?

Audrey: Yes. And I get five. You get 1, 2, 3, 4, 5, 6, 7, 8, 9, 10, 11, 12, 13, 14, 15, 16, 17, 18, 19, 20, 21, 22, 23, 24, 25, 26, 27, 28. We die when we get to be thirty.

Interviewer: We die when we get to be thirty? Why?

Audrey: 'Cause we're old. We're too much. We're too much numbers.

Interviewer: Audrey, do you know any stories you can tell me?

Audrey: No. I can't read stories. I'm going to sing "Somewhere over the Rainbow."

Interviewer: Okay.

Audrey (singing): Somewhere, over the rainbow, clouds are blue, and the land that I love, the one thing I love about . . . it's happy little blue bird fly beyond the rainbow, fly away . . . goodbye!

Interviewer: That was a lovely song.

Audrey: When am I going to come on the tape recorder?

Interviewer: You are on the tape recorder. You can see, when the little red light went on, it shows you are on the tape recorder.

Audrey: When is my voice going to come on it?

Interviewer: You want to hear your voice?

Audrey: Yes.

Interviewer: Okay, I'll turn it off and I'll let you hear yourself and then we can talk some more. Okay?

Audrey: Okay. When we turn it off we can hear my voice gonna come on the tape recorder.

Interviewer: Now, I'm going to play it back so you can hear your voice. . . . Now I have turned the recorder on again.

Audrey: I curled my hair today.

Interviewer: You did? Why did you do that?

Audrey: Because I wanted a haircut. I got hair in my eye.

Interviewer: Why are you holding your hair up now?

Audrey: So it can't get inside my ear.

Interviewer: Oh, when you put the earphones on to hear yourself on the tape recorder.

Audrey: So I can hear myself sing "Somewhere over the Rainbow."

Interviewer: Okay, I'm going to stop the tape recorder now. . . . Now the tape recorder is back on again.

Audrey: Do you want to see me do letters in Spanish?

Interviewer: You can do letters in Spanish?

Audrey: Yes. Uno, dos, tres, quatros, cinquo . . .

Interviewer: How did you learn to do that?

Audrey: I didn't. Sammy told me because Sammy can do that.

Interviewer: And Sammy is your friend.

Audrey: Yes.

Follow-up Questions

1. What specific comments of Audrey are good examples of the characteristics of preschool thinking discussed in this chapter?

2. In what ways are Audrey's comments examples of typical preschooler speech?

3. Why does Audrey seem so unselfconscious about being tape recorded? How would you interpret her behavior differently if she was equally unselfconscious as an adult?

applied a general rule for forming plurals, one that did not depend on copying any language experiences specifically but came from inferring the underlying structure of many experiences taken together. The rule most likely operated unconsciously because these children were very young indeed.

The Limits of Learning Rules   Such skill at acquiring syntactic rules, however, obscures a seemingly contradictory fact about the acquisition of syntax: much of it must be learned by rote. As we have pointed out, most children use irregular forms (like *foot/feet*) correctly before they shift to incorrect but more regular

Rote learning of language

A Multicultural View

Bilingualism as a First Language

*When children grow up bilingual, do they keep their two languages separate from the outset, or do they really acquire a single language system that they differentiate only gradually into two separate languages? Evidence for both possibilities exists, although the majority of linguists favor the idea of a single bilingual language that gradually differentiates (Grosjean, 1982). To help you make up your own mind, look briefly at the evidence.

In two ways, children raised bilingually seem to keep their two languages separate. First, bilingual preschoolers will rarely, if ever, confuse or mix the phonemes or sounds of their two languages. Thus, a three-year-old who speaks both French and English will say "J'ai du papier" (I have some paper) with a relatively perfect French accent; the *du,* for example, will sound something like an English /u/ pronounced with the lips nearly closed. This uniquely French sound, however, will never occur in the child's English words, such as *during* or *cure.*

Second, bilingual preschoolers almost always select words from just one language or the other, rather than from both, for any one sentence. A Spanish-English child will say, "It's raining," but not "Está raining," and "¿Cómo está usted?" but not "How are usted?" (Bergman, 1976). This bias in word selection suggests that bilingual preschoolers organize their languages separately.

But two other pieces of evidence suggest that bilingual children begin with a single language system and differentiate it gradually into two separate languages. First, the overall vocabulary, or **lexicon,** of bilingual preschoolers seems to begin with a single "dictionary" of words that intermingles the two languages and that contains few, if any, equivalent words in both languages. If a French-English three-year-old knows and uses the French word *rue,* she is unlikely to know and use its English equivalent, *street.* Conversely, if the child understands and uses the English word *water,* she will probably not understand or use its French equivalent, *eau.* Early in the preschool years, vocabularies from the two languages complement each other rather than duplicate each other (Imedadze and Uznadze, 1978). By the end of the preschool period, bilingual children learn translations of most common words, but the process of acquiring duplicate vocabularies continues for many years after — well into adulthood, in fact.

Second, bilingual preschoolers begin by applying a single set of syntactic rules to their utterances, derived primarily from whatever rules are common to both languages. The three-year-old French-English bilingual child begins forming questions by using rising intonation ("Daddy is coming home?") or by tagging a statement with the *eh?* ("Silly cat, eh?"). These methods are grammatically permissible in both languages. As the child develops, she eventually adds questioning methods that are unique to one language or the other, such as the inversion of auxiliary verb *is* in "Is Daddy coming home?" (Volterra & Teaschner, 1978).

*Bridges Do bilingual preschoolers begin with a single language system that gradually becomes two separate languages or do they keep their two languages separate from the start?

forms. The most reasonable explanation for the change is that they pick up the very first sentence forms simply by copying, word for word, the sentences that they hear spoken. Presumably they copy many regular forms by rote, too; but the very regularity of these forms hides the haphazard, unthinking way in which they are acquired.

Even though children eventually do rely on rule-governed syntax, they probably still learn a lot of language by rote. Many expressions in a language are **idiomatic,** which means that they bear no logical relation to normal meanings or syntax. The sentence "How do you do?" for example, is not usually a literal inquiry as to how a person performs a certain action; and the sentence "How goes it?" meaning "How is it going?" does not even follow the usual rules of grammar. Because words and phrases like these violate the rules of syntax and meaning, children must learn them one at a time.

Mechanisms of Language Acquisition

Exactly how, or by what means, do children learn to speak? For most children, several factors may be operating at once. In general, current evidence can best be summarized like this: language seems to grow by the interaction of an active, thinking child with certain key people and linguistic experiences. The preceding sections describe in part this active, thinking child; the sections below describe some possible key interaction experiences.

Reinforcement   One commonsense view, which was formerly held by some psychologists, is that children learn to speak through reinforcement. According to this idea, a child's parents reinforce vocal noises whenever they approximate a genuine word or utterance, and this reinforcement causes children to vocalize in more and more correct (or at any rate adultlike) ways (Mowrer, 1960; Skinner, 1957). In the course of babbling, an infant may happen to say "Ma-ma-ma-ma," to which his proud parent smiles and replies cheerfully, "How nice! You said 'Mama'!" The praise reinforces the behavior, so the infant says "Ma-ma-ma-ma" more often after that. After many such experiences, his parents begin to reinforce only closer approximations to mama, leading finally to a true version of this word.

Reinforcement of babbling

Among preschool children, the same process could occur if parents reinforced correct grammatical forms and ignored or criticized errors or relatively immature utterances. Parents might respond more positively to the sentence "I have three feet" than to the sentence "I have two foots." According to the principles of reinforcement (see Chapter 2), the child would tend not only to use the correct version more often but also to generalize the correct elements of this sentence to other, similar utterances.

Analysis of conversations between parents and children, however, shows convincingly that these kinds of reinforcements do not occur. Under normal circumstances, parents correct children's language for factual errors and ignore faulty grammar (J. DeVilliers & DeVilliers, 1977). They are more likely to criticize or correct "I have three feet" than "I have two foots." Furthermore, as we have pointed out, reinforcing infant babbling does not effectively shape early vocalizing in particular directions; it creates only more vocalizing overall (Dodd, 1972).

Reinforcement of truth value

Imitation and Practice   In some sense, children must obviously imitate their native language in order to acquire it. But the process of imitation is subtle and often indirect. Children do not imitate everything they hear, but most copy certain selected utterances — often immediately after hearing them (L. Bloom et al., 1974). Sometimes the utterances chosen for imitation involve familiar sentence forms that contain new, untried terms, and sometimes they contain familiar terms cast into new, untried forms. The imitated terms and forms return later in the child's spontaneous speech. At first, these utterances resemble the rote learning mentioned above, and they seem to help the child by emphasizing or calling attention to new morphemes and syntax (Nelson, 1985).

Importance of language models

The following four-year-old child had never before heard the form *-ish,* meaning "something similar to":

FATHER: We need to paint the fence soon. Maybe a kind of brownish-red.

CHILD (*pauses, listening*): Brownish-red. What's brownish-red?

FATHER: It's what you get when you mix brown and red. Brownish-red, or reddish-brown, or brownish-reddish.

CHILD (*smiles and pauses again*): Brownish-red. Brownish-red.

Imitation may also help children acquire language by initiating playful practice with new expressions. The child in essence plays around with the new forms he learns, and in doing so he consolidates his recently acquired knowledge (see Chapter 10 on play). Because quite a bit of language play remains unobserved by adults, its extent is hard to judge, but a lot obviously does go on (Garvey,

Language play

Children learn a great deal of language by imitating other, more experienced language models. Sometimes this learning happens intentionally, as with the mother and child above. Other times, as in the scene below, adults may not realize just how much a child learns through simple, everyday interactions.

1977). For example, the four-year-old mentioned above was talking to herself a few days later, just before falling asleep at night:

CHILD: You know what you get when you mix blue and red? Bluish-red. Bluish-reddish. Bluish-radish. Reddish, radish. You know what you get when you mix white and red? Whitish-red. Reddish-white. What do you get when you mix white and white? Whitish-white. Whitish-white?!

The earlier discussion of colors evidently set the stage for this monologue. At the least, the earlier, imitative encounter helped call the form *-ish* to her attention; and at the most, it precipitated practice of the form.

Innate Predisposition to Acquire Language: LAD

As we point out in Chapter 6, the ease and speed that children show in acquiring language have caused some linguists and psychologists to conclude that children have an innate predisposition, or built-in tendency, to learn language (Chomsky, 1976; Slobin, 1973). For convenience, the tendency is sometimes called the *language acquisition device,* or *LAD* for short. According to this viewpoint, LAD functions as a kind of inborn road map to language. It guides the child to choose appropriate syntactic categories as he tries to figure out the comparatively confusing examples of real speech that he ordinarily hears, and it helps him find his way through the mazelike structure of language with relatively few major errors, instead of having to explore and construct his own language map, as the Piagetian viewpoint implies.

Bridges Are children innately predisposed to acquire language?

Nature of LAD

Several pieces of evidence support this view. First, when exposed to appropriate models, all healthy infants acquire language without explicit training. Children learn languages almost universally, both in our own society and around the world. Contrary to a popular impression, the languages and dialects that children acquire are all about equally complex, at least in their syntax. Children from any one language community show surprisingly small individual differences in syntax by the time they reach age five or six.

Universality of language acquisition

Second, as described earlier in this chapter, certain specific features of syntax appear in the same sequence in a wide variety of children and even in a variety of languages. Prepositions referring to location (*in, on, between,* and so on), for instance, develop in the same sequence in several widely differing languages (J. Johnston & Slobin, 1979).

Common features of syntax

Third, children have trouble learning to speak if circumstances discourage them from learning normally during the first few years of their lives. Children isolated from language through parental neglect, for example, have learned some language later in life, but their language is usually limited in amount and complexity. In a less tragic example, identical twins often create a private language that they speak only with each other. In many cases their private language seems to delay normal language development, and occasionally it has caused serious language handicaps in later childhood (Savic, 1980).

Critical periods for language acquisition

Fourth, also as pointed earlier in this chapter, preschool children do not simply copy their parents' language directly; yet they seem to figure out and use many of its basic syntactical relationships remarkably well. For instance, most seem to know intuitively what a verb is, as shown by the way they use verbs more or less correctly almost as soon as they begin linking words into duos. Yet a concept such as "verb" is extremely abstract — far more so than other concepts mastered by three-year-olds.

Early grammars

The Limits of LAD Although this evidence does suggest that children have a built-in talent for acquiring language, it does not show that experience plays no role in the process at all. The evidence from twins and neglected children emphasizes just the opposite: that certain experiences with language may be crucial, especially early in life. Ordinarily, these experiences happen to practically every preschooler. They may consist of hearing others talk and of being invited to respond to others verbally. But the fact that they happen to everyone does not mean that children do not learn from them; it only means that what children learn is universal.

Experience that may create LAD

Furthermore, experiences affect the version of language that children acquire, even when they grow up supposedly in the same language community. As pointed out earlier, children vary in the vocabulary they learn, and they vary in the grammar they use: even by age three or four, children often do not define grammatical categories as abstractly as adults do or necessarily in the same way that other children do. Most preschoolers eventually do revise their grammatical categories to coincide with conventional adult grammar, thus obscuring their individuality. But as Chapter 12 shows, large differences persist in older children's styles of communicating, even after children have mastered the basic structure of language.

All things considered, the fairest conclusion we can draw is a moderate one: that children are both predisposed to acquire language and in need of particular experiences with it. Skill with language is neither given at birth nor divorced entirely from other cognitive development. A special talent for language may be

Perspectives

Signing and the Development of Language

Children with hearing impairments often do not develop verbal skills as well as other children, but they are quite capable of acquiring a language of gestures called **American Sign Language** (ASL). The language development of ASL children in fact provides much of the reason for considering ASL a true language, just as useful for communication as any verbal language, such as English.

To understand why this is so, consider the nature of ASL. Signing consists of subtle gestures of the fingers and hands made near the face. In general, each gesture functions like a morpheme. For example, holding the fingers together gently (which signers call a tapered O) can mean either *home* or *flower*, depending on whether it is placed near the cheek or under the nose. There are also sign-morphemes that affect the syntax of expressions — gestural equivalents of *-ing* and of *-ed*. Individual signs are linked together according to syntactic rules, just as in English. After some practice, signers can "speak" (or gesture) just as fast and effortlessly as people who use English can.

What happens to infants and young children with hearing impairments and who grow up learning ASL from their parents as their first language? Studies show that they experience the same steps in signing development as speaking children do in language development. At about the age when infants babble, signing children begin babbling with their hands, making gestures that strongly resemble genuine ASL signs but that signers recognize as gestural nonsense (Dale, 1976). As with verbal babbling, signing infants apparently engage in gestural babbles playfully when they are waking up in the morning or going to sleep at night.

When the signing infants become two- and three-year-olds, they experience a phase of one-word signing similar to the holophrases often observed among speaking children. And they experience two-word, telegraphic signing as well. As with speech, their signs at this point often omit important syntactic gestures and do not follow the usual conventions of word order (or in this case, signing order). Signing vocabulary increases rapidly during the early preschool period in amounts comparable to the increases experienced by speaking children. Even the kinds of words acquired parallel those acquired by speaking children (Bonvillian et al., 1983); signing preschoolers tend to learn signs for dynamic, moving objects first, just as other children do.

Sign language has the qualities of oral language, including grammar, subtlety, and expressiveness. This teacher and child are exchanging the sign for "love."

Still more reason for considering ASL a true language comes from observations of hearing preschoolers whose parents purposely used both English and ASL during the time when the children normally acquired language (Prinz & Prinz, 1979). During their preschool years, these children became thoroughly bilingual, using ASL and English interchangeably. Especially significant, however, were their patterns of language development, which essentially paralleled those shown by conventionally bilingual children. A clear example concerned vocabulary. As with verbal bilinguals, these children first acquired a single vocabulary that mixed or intermingled elements from both ASL and English but that included few direct translations. If a child understood and used the sign for "tree," she would not be likely to understand and use the spoken word *tree*. The children did eventually acquire translations, so that they finally possessed duplicate vocabularies. But acquiring duplicate terms took several years, just as it does with verbally bilingual children (Prinz & Prinz, 1979).

In addition to learning how language is structured, preschoolers begin acquiring skill with communication, or how language is used. By nature, competent communication requires practice at talking and listening with others.

given to all normal children, however, and many crucial experiences for developing that talent may just happen to occur rather frequently to infants as they grow up.

Parent-Child Interactions

Certain kinds of verbal interactions apparently help children to acquire language sooner and better. Parents are comparatively helpful when they speak in relatively short sentences to their preschool-age children and when they use relatively more concrete nouns than pronouns (Furrow et al., 1979). In this pair of comments, the first one helps a child to learn language more than the second does:

Bridges How can parent-child interactions encourage language development?

PARENT 1: Take your shoes off. Then put your shoes in the closet. Then come kiss Mama goodnight.
PARENT 2: After you take off your shoes and put them in the closet, come kiss me goodnight.

Short sentences, concrete terms

As we note in Chapter 6, this simplified style is one aspect of a version of language sometimes called *motherese*. Another aspect of this version of language is the use of a high-pitched voice. Motherese is spoken intuitively by adults with young children and even by older children with younger children (Snow & Ferguson, 1977).

One of the most helpful kinds of verbal interactions is **recasting** a child's utterances: repeating or reflecting back what the child says but in slightly altered form. For instance:

CHILD: More milk.
FATHER: You want more milk, do you?

Recasting helps because it highlights slight differences among ways of expressing an idea. In doing so, it may make the child more aware of how he expresses his idea—its form or organization — as well as call attention to the idea itself (Nelson, 1985).

Benefits of recasting

The techniques for stimulating language development have in common that they provide young preschoolers with a framework of language that simultaneously invites them to try new, unfamiliar language forms and simplify and clarify other aspects of language. Some psychologists call the framework **scaffolding** (Bruner, 1983): like real "scaffolds" used in building construction, parents' language scaffolds provide a temporary structure within which young children can build their own language structures. As such, it functions much like Vygotsky's zone of proximal development mentioned earlier: it changes and grows in response to the child's continuing development, always building a bit beyond the child's current independent abilities but never very far beyond.

These findings, and others like them, have been translated into curricula for education of young children and even for infants (Schweinhart & Kashel, 1986). Fortunately, the methods of interaction that help are often ones that parents and teachers do intuitively anyway; training for them therefore really consists of emphasizing and refining their use.

Language Variations

Not surprisingly, parents vary in how they talk to their children, and these differences may influence the version of language that children acquire as they grow up. It is unclear, however, how language variations affect other aspects of children's development, such as their thinking ability.

Bridges How do preschool girls and boys differ in their use of language?

Conversational styles

Nonverbal communications

Gender Differences in Language   Within any one community, girls learn nearly the same syntax as boys, but they acquire very different ways of using language. On the whole, the differences in language reflect society's gender stereotypes. For example, girls phrase requests indirectly more often than boys do; girls more often say, "Could you give that to me?" instead of "Give me that." And they more often expand on comments made by others rather than initiating their own. These differences appear especially in mixed-gender groups and are noticeable not only in adults but in children as soon as they are old enough to engage in conversation (Coates, 1986).

The sexes reinforce their differences in language by certain nonverbal gestures and mannerisms. Girls and women tend to maintain better eye contact than boys and men; they blink their eyelids at more irregular intervals and tend to nod their heads as they listen (Maltz & Borker, 1982). Boys and men use eye contact a good deal less in ordinary conversation, blink at regular intervals, and rarely nod their heads when listening. When these actions accompany the verbal differences, boys and girls (and men and women) run a distinct risk of misunderstanding each other. A boy talking to a girl may find the girl overly agreeable because she nods her head so much and never changes the subject, whereas a girl talking to a boy may find him self-centered because he seems not to acknowledge her comments when he listens and tends to change the subject.

Low-income children less verbal on tests

Bridges What is the significance of socioeconomic differences in tests of language development?

Socioeconomic Differences in Language   Most research finds low-income children less verbal than middle- or high-income children (Guthrie & Hall, 1983). What this means in practice is that low-income children perform less well in verbal test situations but that outside of these situations, their language differences are less clear-cut. These facts have created controversy about the importance of socioeconomic differences in language development.

Some psychologists point out that most tests of language skills favor middle-class versions of English, both in vocabulary and in style of *discourse* (or conversational patterns). This bias happens because of the content selected for individual test questions and because of the ways in which tests are normally conducted. A question on one of these tests might ask children to describe a dishwasher, yet low-income families rarely own this machine. Other questions might draw on experiences that usually occur only to middle-income children, such as trips on airplanes or visits to museums.

Other psychologists point out that normal methods of testing are inherently more threatening to low-income children. For one thing, the people who give such tests (teachers, graduate students) usually have more power and status. The greater inherent threat of test taking makes low-income children more cautious in their responses and hence less verbal (Miller-Jones, 1989). Middle-class children may worry about getting answers right, too, but not as much on the average.

Perhaps most important of all, middle-class families use styles of discourse that include many "test" questions or questions to which parents already and obviously know the answer. At the dinner table, parents may ask their pre-schooler, "What letter does your name begin with?" even though they already know the answer and even though their child knows that they know. Exchanges like these probably prepare young children for similar exchanges on genuine tests by making testing situations seem more natural and homelike.

In contrast, low-income children tend to lack prior experience with "test" question exchanges. Observations of their conversational and test behavior show that they can give relatively elaborate answers to true questions, such as "What did you do yesterday morning?" when the adult really does not know the answer (Steffenson & Guthrie, 1980). But they tend to fall silent when they suspect that the adult can already answer the question (for example, "What are the names of the days of the week?").

RELATIONSHIPS BETWEEN LANGUAGE AND THOUGHT

The variations observed in language suggest a crucial issue: how do language and thought relate? Is language just another sort of thought or a skill unto itself? The close connection between these two activities makes this question important but at the same time hard to answer. If you are talking, chances are that you are also thinking (except for occasional mindless blathering); and if you are thinking, you are probably either talking to others or verbalizing inwardly at least a little.

In spite of the potential confusion between these activities, language specialists and psychologists have attempted to explain their relationship (Rice, 1982). One explanation, often associated with Piaget, emphasizes the importance and priority of action in creating both language and thought. Another, often associated with the psychologists Jerome Bruner and Lev Vygotsky, proposes more equal roles for language and thought in which they develop independently but eventually become interdependent. Let us look briefly at each of these viewpoints.

Piaget: Action as the Basis for Both Language and Thought

Piaget and his supporters argue that action or activity promotes initial language development. Children, they argue, need to manipulate objects and to have a rich variety of concrete experiences (Piaget & Inhelder, 1971). This idea makes

Sensorimotor experiences precede language

considerable sense to anyone who works with preschool children; such children often learn the concepts of *heavier* and *lighter* more easily if they can have lots of actual experiences with hefting and observing objects of different weights. If young children are taught the definitions of these words without having such experiences, they often just learn the words by rote (Kamii & DeVries, 1977) — which is presumably an inferior way to learn them.

According to the Piagetian viewpoint, children's language can achieve no more sophistication or complexity than their general level of cognitive development (Inhelder, 1976; H. Sinclair, 1976). Cognitive ability consists of several interrelated symbolic skills, such as those described earlier in this chapter. All symbolic skills supposedly develop together, and their mutual dependence results in the general cognitive stages of development described by Piaget. But their mutual dependence also means that language cannot, in principle, become more complex than a child's other symbolic skills.

Language development reflects cognitive performance

Much evidence supports the idea that activity governs initial language acquisition. Two-year-olds tend to show more advanced language if they have achieved object permanence — the belief, described in Chapter 7, that objects exist even when they are not directly experienced (Smolak, 1982). Older children, too, show a close correlation between certain language habits and conservation tasks, like the water-glass task described earlier in this chapter. Children who are able to conserve use coordinated expressions relatively often; they say the glass is "shorter but wider" or "taller but thinner" (H. Sinclair, 1969). The nonconservers more often express such ideas in two separate statements: "This one is wider. That one is taller."

Piagetians point out that language has no priority in the normal timetable of development; for twelve to eighteen months, in fact, an infant obviously thinks without much help from language. And when language does appear, it develops in conjunction with other symbolic activities, most notably make-believe and dramatic play. Even children's dreams follow a timetable that parallels other symbolic activity (Foulkes, 1982); as a child gets older, it seems, dreams become less egocentric and tend to include more abstract themes or "thoughts."

Sometimes it seems as if preschoolers know more than they can say. This girl, for example, can show her mother exactly what her family likes to eat even though she may not be able to identify all of the foods by name.

Vygotsky: The Gradual Integration of Language and Thought

As plausible as these facts and arguments sound, they ignore important evidence that language can also guide other cognitive developments, including both early sensorimotor development and later symbolic thinking (Bruner et al., 1966; Berk, 1985). Three-year-old Paloma seems to talk to herself in order to improve her sensorimotor skill at making a sandcastle:

PALOMA: Now pour this *here*. Now little more. Oops! Too much. No spill. First I clean this up, then start again. Like this. (*pouring*)

Events such as this led Lev Vygotsky (1962) to propose that language and thought develop independently at first but gradually become integrated with each other sometime during childhood. In his view, early speech is learned without much understanding; toddlers imitate words and grammatical constructions but with only superficial comprehension of what they hear. At this point in development, toddlers' thinking occurs without much help from language; it resembles a sort of mental shorthand, which Vygotsky called **inner speech.**

Early language and thought are independent

As two- and three-year-old children acquire more verbal skill, they begin using speech to guide their actions. But this self-guiding speech does not show egocentrism, as Piaget argued, so much as it shows preschool children's need for help in solving problems — as Paloma perhaps does. When problem solving is not a priority, even very young children can sound very socially aware in their communications. Paloma had this conversation with her mother at about the same time that she built the sandcastle:

PALOMA: What's an eggplant?
MOTHER: A purple thing that people eat.
PALOMA: Does it have eggs on it?
MOTHER: No, but it's long like an egg.
PALOMA (*pausing*): When can I see one?
MOTHER: Tomorrow at the store. I'll show you.

In this conversation, Paloma's language and thought worked together closely, one guiding the other. Adults, too, often use verbal knowledge to guide further learning, even before they quite know what they are talking about; for example, scientific theories predict or state relationships that no person has ever actually experienced (or observed) before (Manicas & Secord, 1983). In this sense, the verbal content of such theories stimulates new thought and experiences about the world, and it does so precisely *because* it goes well beyond prior experiences.

Later language and thought are integrated

Whatever their actual relationship, language and thought remain only partly coordinated during the preschool years and especially during the early part of this period. This partial degree of coordination may actually account for some of preschoolers' most delightful qualities: often they can say exactly what they think, even though at other times their verbal comments carry *more* meaning than they realize.

COGNITION AND SOCIAL DEVELOPMENT

As this chapter shows, children make impressive gains in their cognitive skills during the preschool years. They begin using symbols widely, they acquire considerable language skill, and they sharpen their perceptual powers. They are not

Cognitive effects on social development

yet fully adult in any of these respects, of course, but by about the age of five, they have moved far beyond the cognitive limitations that helped to define them as infants.

Given the importance of these cognitive developments, it is not surprising that they affect young children's social development as well. Children's increasingly sophisticated thinking helps them to form increasingly astute concepts of morality or ethics as well as increasingly subtle concepts about friendship. Their growing language ability allows social interactions to become more complex and probably also more gratifying and meaningful. Their growing perceptual skills allow them to attend to what they experience more precisely. Such new sensitivity in turn helps children to respond more appropriately to their experiences, including social experiences in particular.

The next chapter describes these and other social gains. For convenience it places the cognitive developments described in this chapter somewhat in the background, but in real preschool children, social and cognitive developments depend on each other intimately.

SUMMARY OF MAJOR IDEAS

Thinking in Preschoolers

1. The preoperational stage of thinking, defined by Piaget, is characterized by increased symbolic thinking and by new knowledge of identities and of functional relationships.

2. Children's new reliance on symbolic thought helps them to recall experiences, to solve problems more effectively, and to communicate with others about their experiences.

3. In spite of advances in thinking, preschoolers also reveal egocentrism, or an inability to distinguish between their own viewpoint and those of others.

4. Egocentrism seems to result partly from perceptual dominance (or centration), which is a tendency to focus attention exclusively on a single obvious feature of a problem or situation.

5. In spite of frequent egocentrism, preschoolers can take the perspective of others in certain conditions and can also communicate relatively effectively with others in solving problems.

6. Two other limitations of preschoolers' thinking are animism (believing that everything is alive) and artificialism (believing that objects are all made in the same way, usually by human beings).

7. Preschool children can classify objects accurately as long as the system or criteria for classifying are relatively simple.

8. Preschoolers often cannot perform a class-inclusion task unless special efforts are made to clarify the nature of this task.

9. Preschoolers often cannot solve problems that require reversible thinking, such as the classic Piagetian tasks of conservation.

10. As with other classic Piagetian tasks, changes in the procedures often improve children's performances.

Perceptual Development in Preschool Children

11. During the preschool years, children come to rely increasingly on vision for sensing their environment.

12. Preschoolers show improvements in visual discrimination as well as in integration of visual perceptions among themselves and with motor skills.

13. Young children also show improvements in visual recall and recognition.

14. Auditory perception improves significantly during the preschool years, which smooths the way for language acquisition.

Language Acquisition in the Preschool Years

15. During the preschool years, children make major strides in acquiring the syntax, or grammar, of their native language.

16. Young children's first efforts to combine words often omit function words and ignore other rules of syntax common in adult speech.

17. Syntactic errors of preschool children include both undergeneralizations and overgeneralizations.

18. Even though preschoolers learn a great deal of language by the process of inference, they also learn language by rote.

19. Infants and preschoolers probably do not learn syntax by being actively reinforced for correct grammatical usage.

20. Children probably do acquire some syntax by imitation and practice of language models.

21. The ease of language acquisition has made some linguists argue that all children possess an innate language acquisition device, or LAD.

22. Parents probably assist children's language acquisition by recasting the children's own utterances and by providing a scaffolding that supports children's language efforts.

23. Language varies among children according to their gender and their socioeconomic class, and these differences have a variety of causes.

Relationships Between Language and Thought

24. Two major theories have been proposed for the relationship of language and thought.
25. According to Piaget, language develops only as rapidly and as far as other symbolic functions, such as dramatic play.
26. According to Vygotsky, language and thought begin as independent functions and gradually become integrated during the preschool years.
27. Piaget's viewpoint implies that language primarily reflects general cognitive development, whereas Vygotsky's implies that language and thought eventually come to assist each other's development equally.

KEY TERMS

make-believe *(308)*	visual integration *(321)*
symbol *(309)*	visual memory *(322)*
identity *(309)*	auditory acuity *(323)*
functional relationship *(309)*	communicative
symbolic thought *(309)*	competence *(323)*
egocentrism *(311)*	morpheme *(324)*
perceptual dominance *(311)*	generative *(324)*
centration *(311)*	duo *(325)*
animism *(313)*	telegraphic speech *(325)*
artificialism *(314)*	undergeneral-
classification *(314)*	ization *(325)*
class inclusion *(314)*	overgeneral-
decenter *(315)*	ization *(326)*
reversibility *(316)*	idiomatic *(328)*
conservation *(316)*	lexicon
zone of proximal	American Sign Language
development *(318)*	(ASL) *(332)*
visual discrimination *(321)*	recasting *(333)*
	scaffolding *(334)*
	inner speech *(337)*

WHAT DO YOU THINK?

1. As this chapter has shown, Piaget may have underestimated the cognitive skills of preschool children. How about the rest of society: do people generally underrate what preschoolers can do? Explain your opinion.
2. Given that nearly all preschoolers learn language without instruction, how do you account for the differences in verbal skill that seem to exist among older children and adults?
3. Do you ever think without talking, or talk without thinking? Describe these incidents, and why you believe that they show a separation of language and thought.
4. How might perceptual limitations affect preschoolers' abilities to engage in academic or school-like tasks? Describe some perceptual problems that four-year-olds might face on these tasks.

FOR FURTHER READING

Bissex, G. *Gnys at Wrk: A Child Learns to Read and Write.* Cambridge, MA: Harvard University Press, 1980.

Schickedanz, J. *More Than the ABCs: The Early Stages of Reading and Writing.* Washington, DC: National Association for the Education of Young Children, 1986.

The author of the first book describes how just one child, her own son, taught himself to read and write, beginning when he was about five years old. Her comments are thorough and insightful about the nature of reading and about how adults might foster reading and writing in the late preschool and early school years. The second book discusses the issues raised by Bissex in more general terms. Both books highlight the wide range of cognitive processes and motivations that usually surround early reading and writing.

Cohen, D. *Piaget: Critique and Reassessment.* New York: St. Martin's Press, 1983.

Carey, S. *Conceptual Change in Childhood.* Cambridge, MA: MIT Press, 1985.

Both of these books describe recent thinking about cognitive development in early childhood. They are good ways to get perspective on Piaget. The approach of Cohen's book is to critique Piaget in his classic form. Cohen uses post-Piagetian research studies to argue that cognitive development depends more on social experiences than Piaget originally thought. Carey argues that in spite of the limitations found in the classic Piagetian theory, moderately general cognitive stages occur nonetheless. They are just not as comprehensive as Piaget thought.

Garvey, C. *Children's Talk.* Cambridge, MA: Harvard University Press, 1984.

This book focuses on how children use language during normal conversations with each other. It is therefore *not* a book about syntax or the structure of language as such. Instead, it looks at how children learn to organize their comments so as to communicate as effectively as possible. Often they do so quite competently, but as the book shows, they also experience various problems in learning how to communicate.

Katz L., and Chard, S. *Engaging Children's Minds: The Project Approach.* Norwood, NJ: Ablex, 1989.

Here is a book that offers curriculum advice and research on child development at the same time. It focuses on cognitive activities of young children as these occur in early childhood classroom settings. The descriptions of activities are interspersed with justifications from developmental research, and the authors present both the descriptions and the justifications in a very readable style.

CHAPTER 10

The Preschool Years: Psychosocial Development

Focusing Questions

- What important developmental achievements occur during the preschool years?
- What distinguishes play from other activities, and why is it so important in preschoolers' development?
- How does children's play change during the preschool years?
- How do different styles of raising children influence young children?
- What are a preschooler's relationships with other children like?
- How does a young child learn the differences between boys and girls and how each should behave?

hen Melissa was two, she would crouch down on the floor with her rear end sticking out in imitation of the prominent haunches of Tigger, the family's cat. From time to time, she would make a noise sort of like a cat's meow. Keeping her head low, she would look around carefully for acknowledgement from her parents. Occasionally she would walk like a cat, although her walk looked more like a rabbit's hopping. Tigger herself was not impressed by all of this.

Melissa's skills as a performer and active awareness of her audience illustrate an important aspect of development during the preschool years: the development of psychological and social skills. During the preschool years, many activities and events that occupy a child's waking hours involve social interaction with other people. These include parents and other children within the family as well as friends and acquaintances in the neighborhood and community. The social skills and unique personality that a preschool child develops are largely a result of social interactions within and outside her family.

In this chapter we first describe what theorists have to say about social development during the preschool years. Then we look at evidence for these theories in three areas of social activity: play, relationships with others, and gender roles. As you will discover, each of these topics offers at least partial support for one or another of the developmental theories.

THEORIES OF EARLY SOCIAL DEVELOPMENT

Erik Erikson's psychosocial theory of development, and to a lesser extent Freud's psychosexual theory, have proven to be particularly helpful in understanding the changes that occur during the preschool years. As you recall from the chapters on infancy, most children have achieved both a basic sense of trust in others and a sense of autonomy by their third birthday. By now, a child is firmly convinced that he is a person on his own, separate and distinct from his parents. At the same time, he is still "deeply and exclusively *identified* with his parents, who most of the time appear to him to be powerful and even dangerous" (E. Erikson, 1968, p. 115).

According to the psychoanalytic view, this intense identification is largely a product of the Oedipal conflict. The resolution of this conflict, which Freud believed occurs during the phallic stage of psychosexual development (from age three to six), allows the preschool child to protect himself unconsciously from fears that his father will punish him for being sexually attracted to his mother and for the angry and competitive feelings he has toward his father. According to Freud, the superego and the sense of conscience and ego ideal that develop during this stage help a child to regulate his feelings and actions in socially acceptable ways.

The Freudian viewpoint

According to Erikson (1968), three important changes during the preschool years contribute to a child's developing sense of self; greater mobility, improved communication skills, and greatly expanded imagination. The child is now able to move about more freely and aggressively and to establish a wider range of goals for herself, by the age of three, she has mastered walking and running and takes them for granted. Her sense of language and communication skills are good enough for her to understand and ask questions about almost everything. And her ability to use language and to move around on her own lead to a dramatic expansion of her imagination; in fact, she is now able to imagine so many different roles that she cannot avoid sometimes frightening herself with the very things she has dreamed or thought up.

Erikson: improving skills

In Erikson's view, the child, faced with secret fantasies of very large and at times frightening proportions, must master the developmental crisis of **initiative versus guilt.** As we mentioned above, one of the most powerful of these fantasies is that of winning the competition with her same-sex parent for the parent of the opposite sex. Guilt and conscience, according to Erikson, grow out of a sense that such fantasies are wrong and punishable. They come to serve as an inner voice of right and wrong and serve to limit, sometimes rigidly and cruelly, the child's sense of initiative. Consequently, it is important for parents and society to support the child's sense of initiative and action in her fantasy play, physical activities, and social interactions and to appreciate the ways in which a preschooler is frequently her own worst critic.

Bridges How does a preschool child's developing ability to think symbolically affect the child's developing sense of self?

Harry Stack Sullivan (1953) proposed several additional concepts that are useful for understanding the developments during this period. He believed that preschoolers use **egocentric escape** to distance themselves from unpleasant and overwhelming experiences by acting as if they are unaffected by such experiences or by quickly forgetting them. For example, a child who has somehow become separated from his parents and been lost while at an amusement park may act as if he has been totally unaffected by the experience shortly after he is reunited with his parents, and he may not even remember the incident later on.

Sullivan: protective behaviors

Another development during this period takes the form of **dramatizations,** which are "as if" performances in which the child tries out the role of or plays at being someone else, typically her mother or father. As described by Sullivan, dramatizations allow a child to explore new psychological and social roles and to gain greater control over disturbing feelings and experiences. In acting as if she were an angry mother scolding her young daughter, for example, a four-year-old both learns about the mother's role and is able to become more comfortable with the feelings of fear, anger, and guilt that may be involved. Sullivan also proposed that a **malevolent transformation** may occur if a child's attempts to initiate contact and to obtain closeness with others are ridiculed and rejected. The feelings of anxiety and mistrust that result may lead to the development of a sense that the world is a harmful and evil place in which it is difficult to achieve closeness with others. If children successfully negotiate the psychological obstacles to their continuing development, however, they are ready to begin "social life" in more adult terms. One of the ways preschoolers do this is through play, which takes up a major part of their time.

PLAY IN EARLY CHILDHOOD

In our society and many others, play dominates the preschool years. Every child plays, it seems, and virtually all observers of young children agree that they have seen lots of examples of it. What are the play activities of a preschooler like, and what important contributions does play make to a child's development? Before we tackle these questions, we must first agree on what we mean by the term *play*.

The Nature of Play

Rewards of playing

One useful approach to defining play focuses on the attitudes and dispositions of children themselves (Rubin et al., 1984). First, children at play generally show *intrinsic motivation,* which means that they engage in the play because the activity is enjoyable and rewarding for its own sake rather than because it is useful in achieving something else. Think about ring-around-the-rosy or farmer-in-the-dell. It's hard to imagine a reason for playing these games other than the sheer satisfaction gained from the activity. As a result, to a large extent no one can command children to play. Although the mother who tells her children to go outside and play may succeed in getting them out of the house, the play part is up to them and really remains beyond her control.

Process-oriented activity

Second, children are generally more interested and involved in the *process* of doing things than in the *product* of what they do (B. Vandenberg, 1978; Schwartzman, 1978). At the local playground, for instance, children may care very little about the goal of using the slide, which is to get from top to bottom. But they are likely to care a lot about their style of sliding — whether they go head first or feet first or up the slide instead of down.

Different from reality

Third, play resembles real-life activities and differs from them in that it is not bound by reality. For example, a child who is playing at fighting looks different from one who is truly fighting (Aldis, 1975), and a child playing mommy will typically act differently from a child who is actually caring for a baby brother

In early childhood, the process of doing things often matters more than the outcome. Even taking a bath can seem like play.

		Family		
	Physical Development	How do different parenting styles during the preschool years affect children's development? (355–356)	**Peers**	
Genetics	What are the effects of preschoolers' physical growth on their parents and other care-givers? (300)		What qualities do preschoolers associate with friendship? (360–361)	**Social Context**
In what ways does genetics contribute to aggressiveness in preschool children? (367)				How can changes in preschool and day-care settings reduce sex-role stereotyping and sexism? (373)

THE PRESCHOOL YEARS: PSYCHOSOCIAL DEVELOPMENT

			How does make-believe play contribute to cognitive development during the preschool years? (349)	How do preschool boys and girls differ in their use of language? (334)
How do preschoolers' feelings relate to their capacity for empathy? (362)	How do preschoolers develop a sense of ethnic identity? (363)	How can overly aggressive children learn to control their aggressive behaviors? (370)		
Emotions				**Language**
	Self-concept and Identity		**Cognition**	
		Learning		

or sister. Nevertheless, the features that reveal that an activity is play rather than the real thing vary with the particular type of play and situation; a play fight may contain smiles and laughter, and a make-believe mother may be overly bossy. Whatever the signs, they communicate the message that "this behavior is *not* what it first may appear to be." Even so, it is not uncommon for a preschooler to become so caught up in a round of dramatic play that he forgets for a moment that it is not real and truly becomes frightened when his make-believe mother tells him he has been bad and must sit in the corner.

Fourth, play tends to be governed by *implicit rules* — that is, rules that can be discovered by observing the activity rather than rules that are formally stated and exist independently of the particular play activity. For example, although there is no rule book for playing house, it is implicitly understood that there can be only one mother and one father and that these actors must live up to certain expectations. If one player deviates too widely from the expected role, the other children are likely to correct her for it ("Hey, mommies don't suck on baby bottles; only babies do!")

Theories of Play

There are three main theoretical approaches to play: psychoanalytic, learning, and cognitive. Although each theory emphasizes a somewhat different aspect of play, all hold that play activities make a major contribution to the development of important social and emotional skills and understandings during the preschool years.

Psychoanalytic Theory   The psychoanalytic theories of both Freud and Erikson emphasize the social and emotional importance of play in early childhood. For one thing, play provides an opportunity for a child to *gain mastery over problems* by rearranging objects and social situations in ways that allow him to imagine that he is in control. Especially in the case of a painful and upsetting experience,

Ways of gaining control

a child may display **repetition compulsion,** again and again repeating the experience in symbolic play and thereby gaining greater control or resolution of it. For example, a young boy who felt abandoned by his hospitalized mother invented a game in which he tied a long string to a wooden doll and then repeatedly made the doll (his mother) leave by throwing her away, only to make her then come back by pulling the string (E. Erikson, 1963).

Play also allows a child to use fantasy *to gain satisfaction for wishes* and desires that are not possible to fulfill in reality because of limitations in the child's abilities and life situation. Another function of play is to provide an opportunity for **catharsis,** the release of upsetting feelings that cannot otherwise be expressed. Finally, play allows a child *to gain increased power* over the environment by rearranging it to suit her own needs and abilities; play also allows her to explore various tasks and activities that in reality may be beyond her current reach (Peller, 1954).

A major strength of the psychoanalytic approach to play is its focus on the importance of fantasy and inner life in children's play. On the other hand, it is vague about precisely how the changes result from play.

Learning adult skills

Learning Theory   Learning theorists view play as an opportunity for children to try out new behaviors and social roles safely. In their view, play is a major way in which children progressively learn adult social skills, either through successive reinforcement of behaviors that come closer and closer to correct adult behavior or through the processes of observational learning and imitation described in Chapter 2.

What, for example, might a toddler who is playing with wooden blocks be learning about the adult world? For one thing, building with blocks provides an opportunity to learn about the nature and design of physical structures and space and about how hard blocks are, how high they can be piled, and how many small ones equal a larger one. He might also learn about his own capabilities and limitations as a builder: about how high he can reach, how many blocks he can carry at once, and so forth.

Playing with blocks also exposes him to adult expectations and practices, such as when and where blocks can be used, picked up, and stored and how to share blocks, take turns, and cooperate with others. According to learning theory, a child learns both through observation of adults and other children being reinforced for their activities and through his own experience of being directly praised, encouraged, or otherwise reinforced for his own behaviors.

A major strength of the learning theory approach is that it describes the specific processes by which play influences development. A limitation is that it focuses almost exclusively upon the external, or extrinsic, functions and consequences of play rather than on its intrinsic qualities.

Cognitive Theory   Cognitive theorists have identified four major kinds of play, which they believe develop sequentially in parallel with the major stages of cognitive development (Piaget, 1962; Smilansky, 1968). According to their theories, *functional play* occurs during the sensorimotor period, *constructive play* and *dramatic play* during the preoperational period, and *games with rules* during the concrete operational period. The basic idea is that a child's play abilities depend upon her abilities to think and solve problems.

Because the cognitive theory of play is more systematic and specific than the other two theories and has generated a considerable body of literature, we discuss the cognitive approach to play in somewhat greater depth. Following that, we describe a systematic approach to thinking about the social levels of play (Parten, 1932).

Cognitive Levels of Play

Because most children do seem to develop certain styles of play in a standard sequence, the four cognitive levels of play are thought to reflect a developmental pattern or trend. (We should point out, however, that not every child engages in all four types of play or follows the developmental sequence described below.)

Functional Play   **Functional play** involves simple, repeated movements — sometimes with objects — and a focus on one's own body. The movements tend not to have a purpose other than movement itself. An infant exhibits functional play when she shakes a rattle joyfully or splashes the water in her bath just to see the effects. A preschool child shows functional play when he runs around the playground for no apparent reason other than the pleasure of running, when he digs in a sandbox with no visible purpose in mind, or when he pounds on some clay without forming anything. Functional play is important to a child because it teaches her about the physical world and the effects of her actions.

Because functional play by definition requires no symbolic activity, it makes up an especially large part of the play activity of older infants and toddlers — more than one-half, in fact (Sponseller & Jaworski, 1979). By the time a child reaches kindergarten or first grade, however, functional play has decreased to less than one-quarter of his total play (Hetherington et al., 1979). The shift happens partly because many symbolic activities incorporate some of the physical activity characteristic of functional play; a make-believe superhero story, for example, necessarily involves a good deal of moving around, while at the same time it requires symbolic skills such as role taking ("I'll be Batman!") and

Functional play decreases with age

This three-year-old on a swing is engaged in functional play, which focuses on simple, repeated body movements. Although this kind of play is especially prevalent among infants and toddlers, older children often engage in it, too.

Modeling with clay or playdough is a form of constructive play. It is probably the most common form of play in early childhood.

language. Functional play does not disappear in later childhood so much as it becomes combined with other playful ends.

Some purely functional play continues throughout life. Any new activity or object tends to recreate it. A child, or an adult, may ride a new bicycle just to get the feel of it; only later will riding the bicycle become a means to other ends, a part of some larger playful or recreational purpose.

Building things

Constructive Play   In contrast, **constructive play** involves manipulation of physical objects in order to build or construct something. It is not always clear where functional play ends and constructive play begins, especially in older infants and younger preschoolers. For example, a child who at first appears to be building a mountain out of sand may forget about her goal and end up just shoveling the sand for the fun of it. As a child becomes older, however, the constructive elements of play become quite clear. Not only does she build a mountain; she adds a road leading to it and perhaps a car or two that make the trip regularly.

Pretending to be someone or something else

Dramatic, or Make-Believe, Play   For several years after infancy, the most significant new form of play involves **dramatic,** or **make-believe, play.** Whether for an instant or for minutes at a time, a preschool child will "be" something else: a bird with arms as wings, a teacher with a stern face and a bossy manner, a monster with bared teeth. Sometimes objects are transformed as well: a block of wood becomes a telephone; a miniature toy car, a real car; or a doll, a live baby.

Such play occurs even among toddlers and probably begins as soon as a child can symbolize, or mentally represent, objects. Dramatic play grows in frequency and complexity during the preschool years, and eventually decreases again later in childhood (Rubin and Krasnor, 1980; Rubin et al., 1978).

Make-believe play is a good example of how new forms of experience are assimilated into existing schemes of cognitive understanding. In addition to allowing the child to practice and expand schemes that have already been acquired, such play contributes to the consolidation and expansion of cognitive skills during the preschool years (Piaget, 1962; Vygotsky, 1967).

The alternation between pretense and reality involved in make-believe play provides children with the opportunity to practice and more fully understand these distinctions. Through their play with nonrealistic toys and objects, children become more fully able to internally represent and manipulate objects in the form of symbols and fantasy rather than solely in terms of realistic representations (Rubin, Fein, & Vandenberg, 1983; Flavell, Green, and Flavell, 1986; Ungerer, Zelazo, Kearsley, & O'Leary, 1981).

In addition, a play activity such as building a make-believe house out of blocks gives practice in the motor skills of building as well as in rehearsing knowledge about typical arrangements and functions of rooms and furniture. At the same time, make-believe play may promote creativity by encouraging diverse uses for objects; a block of wood, the child learns, can represent a chair or a bed (Hutt, 1979). Dramatic play can also foster social skills by allowing young children to practice a variety of social roles: in play, a child can become a parent or a teacher, a hero or a monster (Saltz & Brodie, 1982).

Overall, make-believe play can help a child maintain optimal levels of arousal, in which he is neither too bored nor too excited (Fein, 1981b). As we mentioned earlier, when certain aspects of life become too taxing or anxiety provoking, the child can sometimes master such experiences through play and thereby make peace with them. Moving to a new house, for instance, may lead to make-believe reenactments of the move until the child feels more at ease with the experience. Make-believe can add excitement and interest to everyday activities; being Cinderella or Superman while getting ready for bed may make even brushing one's teeth more enjoyable.

Bridges How does make-believe play contribute to cognitive development during the preschool years?

Practicing motor and social skills

In dramatic play, children take on pretend roles, like the "doctor" and "patient" here. Realistic props, such as the stethoscope in this photograph, encourage dramatic play, but they are not always necessary.

Developing a conscious formality

Games with Rules   As children move into their school years (age five or six), play becomes increasingly dominated by **games with rules.** Compared to make-believe play, these are relatively formal activities, such as jump-rope or hide-and-seek. The rules governing them remain fixed during any one occasion of play, although they may generate heated debate and negotiation. In fact, on many occasions a group of children use all their playtime to focus on making, changing, and agreeing on the rules; at times this process seems more important than the game itself. Such play first appears in the late preschool years — especially when it is supervised or led by an older child or adult — and it reaches a peak late in elementary school (Eifermann, 1971; Rubin & Krasnor, 1980).

The rules for many such games apparently develop out of the more flexible, ad hoc rules of make-believe play. Instead of continuing to negotiate roles and behaviors as they go along, young children gradually learn to agree on them beforehand and learn to stand by their agreements throughout a play episode. Given their relatively conscious formality, games with rules can become traditions handed down from one sibling to another and from older playmates to younger ones (Opie & Opie, 1969). Hopscotch, for example, has been around in some form for decades.

The relative formality of games with rules can also help comparative new-comers to fit into play episodes more easily than when they join more improvised make-believe play, which tends to be unique to particular times and particular groups of children. Gaining access to an episode of make-believe play may therefore actually take relatively more social sensitivity (Corsaro, 1981). The very formality of games with rules, however, also separates participation in them from true social acceptance. Being allowed to play on a team may happen simply because the team needs one more player, not because the team likes the new-comer personally.

By early elementary school, most children can play games with rules. Not only do these games cultivate motor skills, but they also teach social skills, such as learning to take turns and knowing how to be a good loser.

Whereas older children engage in all the levels of play just discussed, to a significant degree the particular level of play they choose depends upon which other children are present, who they are, and where and under what circumstances the older children are playing.

Social Levels of Play

Play also varies according to how social it is — according to how much and in what ways children involve others in their play activities. Several decades ago, Mildred Parten studied social participation among preschool children (aged two to five) and proposed that children's play developed according to a series of six stages, or levels, of sociability (Parten, 1932). Although subsequent researchers have questioned whether her categories actually form a developmental sequence, her distinctions continue to be useful to people who are studying young children (Rubin et al., 1976, 1978). The six types of play identified by Parten are the following:

Parten's six levels

1. *Unoccupied play* This category describes a child who is wandering about, who is watching whatever is going on, and who does not become involved in any activity for more than a moment or two. She may pick up a ball, then walk over to a table and sit down, then quickly get up and wander over to watch what another person is doing.

2. *Solitary play* Here a child plays alone with toys or other objects and without any direct or indirect awareness of or involvement with other children, even if they are nearby. A preschooler may work a puzzle when he is alone at a table or while other children play with different toys; another may climb on the jungle gym when no one else is using it.

3. *Onlooker play* In this kind of play, a child watches others at play without actually entering into the activities herself. A two-year-old may simply watch two older children build with blocks without contributing to the building, and a five-year-old may watch classmates make paintings without making one himself. The difference between this and unoccupied behavior is that the child is clearly involved with what is happening and is usually within speaking distance of the actual participants.

4. *Parallel play* Parallel play involves two or more children playing with the same toys in much the same way, in close proximity, and with an awareness of each other's presence. They do not share their toys, talk, or interact except in very minimal ways, however. For example, two or three children may work at the sandtable in a preschool or day-care center; they may occasionally glance at each other and at each other's work, but they do not talk with one another or cooperate in the activity. If one child leaves, the others may notice, watch her go, or even quit the activity as a result.

5. *Associative play* Here children become more explicitly sociable. They engage in a common activity and talk with one another about it. But they do not assign tasks or roles to particular individuals in the group, nor are they very clear about exactly what they are trying to accomplish in the first place. For example, a group of preschoolers may play house together, but the roles and purposes of the episode never become clear: four children cook the meal, then two cooks lie down to be babies who need feeding, then three suddenly start cleaning the place up, and so on. Lots of friendly conversation and interchanges occur, but the activity lacks coordination.

6. *Cooperative play* In cooperative play, children consciously form into groups to accomplish some activity. Often the activity is dramatic, or make-believe, play; now, however, the children assign themselves roles and stick to them ("You be the mama, and I'll be the sister"). At other times the activity may

These children are involved in parallel play. They are probably aware of each other's presence, but they are using separate toys and are preoccupied primarily with their own activities.

be a game with rules, in Piaget's sense; tic-tac-toe, for example, is a favorite among kindergartners. Because each person in this sort of play makes a definite contribution to a common goal, cooperative play has a less hectic and competitive air than associative play does.

Often a preschooler's play includes several of the types Parten described. One recent study of free play among three-year-olds found that parallel play was frequently followed by associative or cooperative group play and that parallel play served as a transitional or warm-up strategy that enabled a child to move into play involving others (Bakeman & Brownlee, 1980). These findings suggest that the emergence of the ability to cooperate develops sequentially and that this sequence of play styles probably continues to help individuals successfully cooperate with others in new situations. The ability to cooperate with others in achieving common goals is an important aspect of successful social relationships throughout life.

Other Influences on Play

Setting   Although the cognitive and social levels of play are important, the composition of a particular child's play is also likely to be influenced by the range of play opportunities that her care-givers provide and by the types of play they encourage. For example, in a recent study of the effects of day-care quality on children's free play activities, researchers found that children in centers with qualified staffs, child-oriented programs, and appropriate facilities and equipment engaged in much less unoccupied and solitary play than did children in centers of lower quality. In addition, preschoolers in the better centers interacted more positively with adults (Vandell & Powers, 1983).

More social interaction in supportive settings

Siblings   The presence of siblings also influences play. A series of studies of two-year-olds revealed that their older siblings often (and with some success) tried to engage them in dramatic role playing well before they were two. In some of these families the children played together constantly, and many of the two-year-olds were able to collaborate in play at levels that were surprisingly sophisticated (J. Dunn, 1985).

Changes with Age   Social participation in various types of play also varies with age. Parallel play, which appears to be the most frequent type of preschool play activity, declines with age, as does solitary play. On the other hand, associative play and cooperative play, which involve greater social participation, increase with age (Parten, 1932). Even though play involving high degrees of social participation increases throughout childhood and adolescence and tends to be dominant throughout the rest of life, all forms continue to be important to various degrees. For example, the random, nondirected activity of a shy teenager at a party has much in common with the unoccupied play of a preschooler; devotees of jigsaw or crossword puzzles are clearly involved in forms of solitary play; television viewing and involvement in spectator sports are basically onlooker play activities; and aerobics, weight-lifting, and jogging sometimes have strong parallel play aspects.

What is important here is that although developmental shifts appear to be associated with increasing age and social competence, social play takes a variety of forms throughout childhood and later life. Of course, heavy reliance on onlooker, solitary, and parallel play in a young preschooler is more likely to be seen as age appropriate than does similar reliance on these less social forms among older children and adults. On a broader scale, the increasing reliance on spectator activities in our culture may reflect an increase in social isolation and alienation. Because of this, the development of social relationships, which we discuss in the next section, is more important for preschoolers than ever.

Forms of play vary throughout life

RELATIONSHIPS WITH OTHERS

As our discussion of play shows, young children spend a good deal of time relating to others. Most of the time, these contacts are positive: children share and cooperate, converse with and smile at each other, and in general show at least rudimentary evidence of empathy or mutual understanding. Such **prosocial behavior** sometimes leads to the development of genuine friendships. But social contacts can be negative, too. Conflict and aggression happen at least as often among young children as among older children and adults, and certain forms happen more often. The sections that follow describe both prosocial and aggressive social interactions during the preschool years.

Relationships with Parents

As we have noted already in this chapter, the preschool child's expanding powers to initiate verbal and physical activity and the explosive expansion of her powers of imagination lead to a crisis of initiative versus guilt. Successful resolution of this crisis requires parents to support a child's efforts to take on the world and at the same time to appreciate her need for restraints that respect her limitations and self-esteem. Preschoolers often test the limits that parents impose on their behavior and are often very uneven in their ability to understand and consistently conform to parental wishes.

Encouragements and limits

Patterns of Parental Authority   One of the most important aspects of a parent-child relationship is the parent's style of authority. Observations of families of

Styles of child-rearing behavior

preschoolers suggest that styles of child-rearing can be classified into three groups: authoritarian, permissive, and authoritative (Baumrind, 1967, 1973). According to Baumrind, each of these styles reflects a unique combination of four dimensions of child-rearing behavior: parental control (strictness of discipline), clarity of parent-child communication (parents' willingness to listen to their child's views and feelings and to give reasons for disciplinary actions), maturity demands (parental pressure and encouragement toward high achievement), and nurturance (warmth and concern for the child's feelings and well-being).

Authoritarian parents score high on control, low on clarity of communication, high on maturity demands, and low on nurturance. In these families, parents impose their wills by asserting their own power and authority. They tend to remain aloof or reserved from their children, except when they feel that their authority is needed or challenged.

Permissive parents are just the opposite. They score low on control, high on clarity of communication, low on maturity demands, and high on nurturance. Some of these parents tend to be **permissive-indulgent,** making relatively few demands on their children but clearly communicating their warmth and interest

Two types of permissive parents

Perspectives

Why Punishment Doesn't Work

Many parents rely on punishment as a means of disciplining their children or penalizing them for misbehavior. Punishment can take many forms: some parents physically punish their child. Other parents verbally punish their child –– for example, by threatening or yelling at him. Still others inflict various penalties, such as withholding a child's allowance, "grounding" her, or making her sit in a corner. Research consistently shows that punishing children may work in the short run but that it does not work in the long run. In the short run, it stops or suppresses unwanted behavior. Children will generally stop using curse words if they are scolded harshly, punished with a slap on the behind, or deprived of dessert. The dramatic success that often follows punishment can immediately reinforce an exasperated adult, and this success can tempt a parent to use the punishment repeatedly.

The catch comes later, however, often well after the punishing incident is over. In the long run, punishment is likely to cause several problems. One is that to be effective, punishment must be rather harsh (Radin, 1982). A mother's shaking her head in mild disapproval is unlikely to stop two children from fighting; for some, only loud words and physical restraint will work. But harsh punishment is destructive to a young child — a thorough spanking risks physical harm and abuse and can be a humiliating experience.

Even punishment that is not physical, such as very strong criticism, can have negative effects. In part this is because preschoolers are easily confused about the reasons for punishment and very sensitive to attacks on their feelings of competence and self-esteem: "Was I spanked because I was fighting? Or because I said nasty things? Or because I am a bad person?" This confusion may also have the unintended effects of inhibiting a child's sense of initiative and increasing his feelings of self-blame and guilt.

Another unintended result of punishment is that it often undermines the child's desire to conform to adult standards of behavior. This problem occurs whether the punishment is verbal or physical. A barrage of criticism may simply make a child ignore or "tune out" her parents because it is too painful to do otherwise, rather than stimulate her to think about her actions and their consequences (Parke, 1977). And the irrational nature of such punishment may lead a child to believe that more reasonable evaluations of her own actions are not really desired.

Punishment has two other important negative consequences. The first is that a parent who uses physical or verbal punishment in responding to a child is likely to discover the child imitating that way of relating to others at some future time, through the processes of modeling and observational learning (see Chapter 2). A good example of this is the parent who yells at and spanks a child to punish him for hitting and teasing his sister. The "do as I say, not as I do" philosophy generally backfires because an adult's actions often speak much louder than words, especially for preschool age children. A second undesirable consequence is the negative feelings that a punitive parent often has following the incident. At times these guilt feelings may make the parent behave more affectionately toward the child, thus confusing the child about his parent's true feelings. In addition, a child may fear and avoid a parent who has punished him, making it more difficult for both of them to experience the trust and intimacy their relationship needs.

If the goal of punishment is to eliminate unwanted or undesirable behavior, it probably rarely works. Rather, punishment serves to suppress the behavior for a given interval of time. Unless an alternative behavior is substituted,

and providing considerable care and nurturance. Others are **permissive-indifferent;** for these parents, permissiveness tends to reflect a "cop-out" or avoidance of their child-rearing responsibilities, sometimes with very detrimental results.

Authoritative parents score high on control, clarity of communication, maturity demands, *and* nurturance. Thus, they differ from both authoritarian and permissive parents in important ways. They do set rules and impose limits, as authoritarian parents do, but they do not justify these in terms of their own power. Instead, they rely on more democratic techniques. In most situations they foster family decisions and resolve differences between themselves and their children through fairly open discussion of each person's feelings, needs, and overall perspective. When their children misbehave, these parents are interested in understanding why and in explaining the reasons for the restrictions or punishments that may follow.

Not surprisingly, these three parenting styles have different consequences for children. Children who grow up with authoritarian parents tend to be relatively distrustful and unhappy with themselves; they also tend to achieve less well in school than other children. Children who grow up with permissive parents tend to lack self-reliance and self-control. Children of authoritative parents show

Bridges How do different parenting styles during the preschool years affect children's development?

however, the suppressed behavior is likely to recover spontaneously.

With these conclusions in mind, parents might use the following guidelines to help make punishment relatively effective in situations where it is used as a temporary means of suppressing certain behaviors — say, stopping a three-year-old from running into the street (O'Leary & O'Leary, 1977):

1. *Explain why you are punishing,* focusing on the specific undesirable behavior. Even if the child does not seem to be listening to the explanation, give it anyway.

2. *Give a positive alternative to the unwanted behavior.* For example, say, "Instead of running into the street to get your ball, you must come tell me and I will get it for you."

3. *Emphasize verbal rather than physical punishment.* Because punishment often comes at an emotional time for adults, they are in danger of running out of control. Physical punishment in this situation can be dangerous to the child and potentially abusive. For example, a parent can *tell* a child that she is feeling very angry and disappointed because of what the child has done, rather than *acting* out these feelings. Often, once things have calmed down, a parent can find constructive consequences for the child's unacceptable behavior that are neither physically nor psychologically harmful to the child or harmful to the parent-child relationship.

4. *Punish the beginning of unwanted behavior,* not the end. In this way the child will need to suppress less behavior and will need less punishment overall (Walters & Grusec, 1977). For example, if a child has been warned that she will get no dessert if she continues to disrupt dinner by

dropping food and utensils on the floor, a parent should immediately initiate the punishment ("You have had your warning and are still misbehaving. No dessert for you tonight.") as soon as the unwanted behavior occurs rather than waiting until it has reached an intolerable level. Parents avoid punishing at the beginning of unwanted behavior because they hope to avoid the upset that sometimes results when a punishment is eventually given. But the application of reasonable and appropriate punishment at the beginning of the unwanted behavior is much more likely to succeed in the longer run.

Although punishment may be a useful technique for stopping destructive or dangerous behavior in the short term, because of its undesirable side effects it should be used only when absolutely necessary. Parents can minimize their need to use punishment by carefully arranging their children's play environments and by teaching their children to understand rules and limits and to seek adult assistance when needed. They can emphasize *positive reinforcement* of desirable behaviors instead ("What a good boy you are for coming to get mommy to help get your ball and for not going into the street yourself!"). Also, many undesirable behaviors contain positive elements that deserve recognition and praise. A child who climbs dangerously high in a backyard tree, for example, may deserve criticism for her poor judgment and praise for her courage and her climbing ability.

All parents discipline their children sometimes. Their methods make a difference: calling attention to the consequences of misbehavior is more effective than spanking, at least in the long run.

Advantages of the authoritative style

the most desirable personal qualities, as judged by the standards of our society: they are the most self-reliant and self-controlled, yet also the friendliest and highest achieving. Interviews with families of young children found that parental use of reasoning was related to warmth toward their children; parental restrictiveness was related to power-assertion techniques, including physical punishment (W. Becker et al., 1962).

In addition, researchers have found that mothers who are more accepting, supportive, and loving; who are consistent in enforcing limits; and who are willing to listen to their children's views have sons with better self-esteem than mothers who are less warm and accepting, less consistent, and less willing to listen (Coopersmith, 1967). Similarly, discipline based on a combination of reasoning and a warm and caring relationship with the child appears to be related to positive moral development (M. Hoffman, 1970). Finally, the ability of parents to act as consultants in response to child-initiated requests for help appears to be related to the development of competence and self-esteem among preschoolers (White, 1975a, b).

One should interpret these findings with caution. Most ordinary parents do not fall neatly into one or another of these categories; they instead show mixtures of all three types of behaviors. At one time or another, even the best parents ignore their child's misbehavior and justify themselves on the basis of sheer power — perhaps when they, or their child, are too tired to explain for the fourth

Variations in parenting styles

time why it is time to go to bed.

Furthermore, parents, children, and their patterns of interacting tend to change over time. When their children grow older, for instance, authoritarian parents often ease up and shift to a more permissive or authoritative style. Changes in family situation, including the addition of more children, can also influence patterns of child-rearing. Because of the experience gained from rearing a first child, parents frequently are more comfortable and flexible in rearing subsequent children. In addition, older brothers and sisters often help parents in child-rearing, which in most cases lessens the stresses of parenting. Because additional children also increase the family's overall child-care and economic burdens, however, more relaxed parenting is not always the outcome. Other changes within a family — such as improvement or deterioration in work, income, neighborhood, and health — may also influence child-rearing. Families under stress tend to be more rigid, arbitrary, and authoritarian in rearing their children than families that are not. Furthermore, the "goodness-of-fit" between the child's temperamental style and the temperaments of her parents (and other family members) may influence child-rearing (Chess & Thomas, 1984).

The child-rearing and disciplinary techniques that a parent chooses may be influenced to some degree by the particular actions of the child. One study, which interviewed mothers of children aged four through eight years old about how they responded to different types of misbehavior, found that the disciplinary responses these parents chose appeared to be determined more by what the child did than by a general child-rearing style. Threats of punishment were widely used for most misdeeds, but reasoning and discussion were frequently used when the child's actions caused psychological harm to others (Grusec & Kuczynski, 1980).

Children's influence on parenting styles

Ultimately, it is the parents' responsibility to establish the sort of parent-child relationship that fosters the child's confidence and self-esteem and that sets the stage for his future social interactions. The authoritative parenting style seems to be most in tune with the goals just mentioned. Simply stated, for most children, the parent-child relationship establishes the central model for a child's relationship to himself and others. Authoritative parenting is probably successful in the long term because it models and promotes qualities that all children need. Although no parent displays these desirable qualities 100 percent of the time, given adequate motivation and support, the great majority of parents can more fully develop these qualities in their relationships with their children.

Relationships with Siblings

As we have noted in our discussion of play, brothers and sisters are major participants in the social activities of many preschoolers. Studies of children's behavior toward their siblings have shown that most young children are very interested in babies and that their repetitions, explanations, and "language practice" speech are very similar to those of adult care-givers (J. Dunn, 1985). Older siblings provide important role models for their preschool brothers and sisters, facilitating the learning of social skills and parental expectations. Further, observations of both friendly and aggressive interactions of siblings suggest that such interactions provide an important basis for the development of social understandings and the beginnings of children's grasp of the particular feelings, intentions, and needs of people other than themselves (J. Dunn, 1985).

For preschoolers, siblings serve as teachers and role models — as well as playmates sharing common pleasures and exciting activities.

The sophisticated understandings that young children have of their siblings may be due to several factors. First, brothers and sisters are very familiar with each other because they spend so much time together; second, they share very similar sources of excitement, pleasure, joy, and fear; third, the family setting in which brothers and sisters work, play, and fight is emotionally intense, involving feelings of conflict, jealousy, and affection. It is therefore very important for young children to understand what their siblings are feeling or intending to do (J. Dunn, 1985).

Given the social opportunities that siblings make available, one might guess that children growing up with brothers and sisters will develop social skills earlier and more rapidly and perhaps end up with better skills than children who have not had this opportunity. Nevertheless, although an older sister can be an excellent teacher and role model, her competence and need to outshine her younger brother might also discourage him from developing certain social skills as easily as he might if he were not in his older sister's shadow. Similarly, while experience with a younger sibling is likely to enhance social competence with younger children, being burdened with the care of a younger sister may limit an older child's opportunities to spend time with children his own age. Just how siblings will affect a particular child's social development is likely to depend upon the degree to which parents recognize and respond appropriately to the social needs of all of their children.

Perspectives

The Reactions of Firstborn Children to the Birth of a New Sibling

Although the birth of a younger brother or sister is generally a predictable and welcomed family event, it is also a source of stress, particularly for a firstborn brother or sister. In a series of studies conducted by Judy Dunn and her colleagues in Cambridge, England, interviews with mothers and direct observations of firstborn children following the birth of a new sibling revealed that more than 90 percent of the children showed increased "naughtiness," more than 50 percent demonstrated tearfulness and clinginess, and 50 percent of those who were already toilet trained regressed to pretraining patterns (J. Dunn 1983, 1985; J. Dunn & Kendrick, 1980).

Interestingly, although little aggression directed toward the newborn occurred, increased aggression was directed toward the mother. And in a number of cases, the same children who developed sleeping problems or increased naughtiness were also very affectionate toward the baby and interested in caring for, entertaining, and comforting him. Some children who showed increased problem behavior also showed increased independence and maturity following the birth, insisting on feeding themselves and going to the toilet alone.

How long do such disturbances persist? The Cambridge studies found that although most of the problems disappeared by the time the new baby was eight months old, many children showed an increase in fearful, worrying, and anxious behavior one year following the sibling's birth. Thirty-eight percent of the sample showed an increase in fears of such common everyday things as the vacuum cleaner, the dark, water in the bathtub, airplanes, and pets. Thirty-five percent of the sample increased in ritualistic behavior around bedtime, bathtime, or mealtime. Worrying behavior in three- and four-year-olds persisted for several years and was linked to difficult behavior when they were eight years old. In families in which the children reacted to the sibling's birth by withdrawing, the relationship that developed between the siblings during the next years was more likely to be hostile and full of conflict (J. Dunn, 1985; J. Dunn & Kendrick, 1980).

Which children were most vulnerable? For children less than five years old, the age of the child at the time of birth was less important than the child's particular personality. Children who previously were irritable, moody, or difficult to manage and who tended to be easily upset by change or frustration responded with the most disturbance to the birth of a sibling. A second factor that affected vulnerability was the child's relationship to her parents prior to the birth. For example, in families in which there had been high levels of conflict between mother and firstborn prior to the birth, the firstborns were reported to behave in particularly irritating and intrusive ways with the newborn. In families in which the child had a close relationship with the father before the birth, less conflict with the mother was reported following the birth.

A third important factor affecting vulnerability was associated with the mother's state of tiredness or depression following the baby's birth. In families in which the mother was extremely tired or depressed after the birth, the firstborns were more likely to become withdrawn (J. Dunn, 1985).

Are there things that parents can do to decrease the stress of a new baby for their firstborn children? One simple solution is to have only one child. Spacing the births of children further apart can also help in that the needs of older children are somewhat different and their ability to understand and cooperate somewhat greater. Nevertheless, although talking to a child in a way that is appropriate to his level of understanding may be helpful, it does not seem to prevent the strong and sometimes overwhelming emotional reactions that preschoolers experience. The Cambridge studies found that children were most likely to be upset during the time when the mother was occupied with bathing, caring for, cuddling, and feeding the newborn baby. It is important that parents be aware of the drastic decrease in time and attention available to the firstborn and that they find ways to maintain their firstborn child's routines and provide substitute sources of caring and attention.

One important way of decreasing the stress of a new baby for a firstborn child is to provide the mother with concrete help and with social and emotional support with her newborn so that she can be as available as possible to her firstborn. This can sometimes be achieved when the physical, social, and emotional responsibilities for primary parenting are shared by the father or another parenting partner. Finally, stress can be reduced by giving the firstborn child special attention so that she will know that her specialness has not been suddenly forgotten with the birth of the new baby. For example, friends and relatives can remember to bring a toy for the firstborn child and a special treat for the parents in addition to the more traditional gift for the new baby.

Friendships in Early Childhood

Preschool children are simultaneously pulled in two different directions. On the one hand, they seek the security and intimacy that comes from playing continually with a familiar friend; on the other hand, they want to participate in the variety of activities that are possible with many different children.

Although preschool friendships often involve shared activity and recognition of similarities, sometimes solidarity between two children involves exclusion of a third. In the following example, which takes place at a sink in a preschool classroom, Yolanda's alliance with Deanne involves exclusion of Shawn:

Importance of shared activity and similarities

YOLANDA: I have some gum and candy — not for Shawn.
SHAWN: Why not?
YOLANDA: 'Cause you won't help.
SHAWN: I'm rinsing.
DEANNE: These are hardly even clean. I have a whole bunch of suckers.
YOLANDA: Me, too. I'm not giving Shawn any gum.
SHAWN: Yes, you are.
YOLANDA: No, I ain't. I'm going to give Deanne gum 'cause —
DEANNE: 'Cause I don't fight with you?
YOLANDA: Yes.
DEANNE: I'll give Shawn a little teeny piece.
YOLANDA: Yes, give him a little teeny piece. . . . See, you're not helping.
SHAWN: I'm rinsing.
DEANNE: I already rinsed it twice.

The Evolution of Friendship   Even infants and toddlers show preferences for particular other children of their own age. Given a choice among several peers in a playroom, a one- or two-year-old is likely to smile at and approach his particular friend more often than a nonfriend (Furman, 1982); he will also be more skillful taking turns with a friend than with a nonfriend. If two friends are playfully making noises or movements, for example, they will wait longer for each other to finish and generally coordinate their activity better than two children who are not friends might (Vandell, 1980; Howes & Mueller, 1984). Although these early friendships are somewhat unstable and often change on a daily or weekly basis, they do suggest that young children begin discriminating among their peers at an early age. These preferences are an important step toward forming more lasting friendships later in childhood.

Early sensitivity to friends

By age four, friendships become more involved and durable. Certain pairs of children develop a liking for each other and purposely try to spend time together. Typically, the pairings develop in situations that encourage physical proximity, such as the children's neighborhood play group, day care, or preschool classroom. Typically, too, the friendships that develop emphasize shared activities more than shared feelings, thoughts, and dispositions (Chandler & Boyes, 1982). In part this is because preschoolers still lack the language skills needed to communicate effectively what they are thinking and feeling.

Emphasis on shared activities

But preschoolers do have enough symbolic skills to know — and to say — who their friends are. For example, if a child names Jose as a friend, then observations of the child and Jose show that the two really do have many more positive interactions than most pairs of children do and fewer negative ones (Masters & Furman, 1981). Home observations of children between the ages of three and six at play with best friends and new acquaintances indicate that self-declared friends are more willing to answer their friend's questions, to explain the reasons for their actions, and to discuss the reasons for disagreements that might arise (Gottman & Parkhurst, 1980). Interestingly, this is more true of three- and four-year-olds than of five- and six-year-olds, probably because younger children feel less able to manage disagreements and therefore attempt to avoid them.

Instability of early friendships

Such management problems and the concrete emphasis on overt, shared activities tend to make early friendships unstable. A preschool child will drop a friend relatively easily — but then make up to her later just as easily. Sometimes she will even exchange goods for friendship; one child will say to another, "If you give me a piece of candy, I'll be your best friend!"

By the end of the preschool period, stable friendships do emerge, but they are not necessarily as reciprocal or intimate as adult friendships are. A child may choose a friend because the friendship enhances his status among his peers. Having an especially popular friend may help a child feel more popular himself.

Friendship as a means to other ends

Or a child may choose a friend because the friend has a desired possession or skill — perhaps an especially attractive train set at home or the ability to protect herself from unwanted playmates. Because these relationships are somewhat more permanent than earlier ones, they are in a sense more mature or adultlike, but they still tend to focus mainly on fulfilling one-way or self-centered needs. Truly mutual and reciprocal relationships do not become common until the school years.

Bridges What qualities do preschoolers associate with friendship?

Conceptions of Friendship   During their preschool years, children also develop ideas about the nature of friendship; these parallel to a large degree the actual friendship behaviors they reveal. In the minds of younger preschoolers, a friend is someone who does certain things with you; she is someone (*anyone*, in fact) that you like to play with, share toys with, or talk with a lot. "A friend," as one preschooler put it, "lets you hold his doll or truck or something."

Disagreements and fights between preschool friends are upsetting to them. When friends fight, the fights generally have to do with objects and activities — whether to build a sandcastle, how to draw pictures, how to cook a pretend

During early childhood, friendships depend heavily on shared activities that children enjoy. Only later do more abstract qualities, such as intimacy and mutual loyalty, become important.

A Talk with Larry

Friendship and Play in Early Childhood

Larry, age four, was interviewed in his bedroom after he returned from his day-care center.

Interviewer: Tell me about your friends, Larry. Do you have a best friend?
Larry: No.
Interviewer: Who are some of the friends that you play with?
Larry: Kimmy, Judy. Nobody else.
Interviewer: And what do you do with your friends? What do you play?
Larry: Play dough. . . . You make it into things.
Interviewer: Why is someone your friend?
Larry: We play together. With baseball cards.
Interviewer: How?
Larry: We put doubles together.
Interviewer: What do you do with your doubles?
Larry: You pile them together.
Interviewer: What do you do during the day?
Larry: I like to play games and Mousetrap and Safely Home and Wheel of Fortune and go to that store across the street.

Interviewer: What do you do when you get up in the morning?
Larry: Get dressed. Sometimes I watch TV.
Interviewer: And then what do you do?
Larry: I eat breakfast. I have all kind of food. What you want. Bubble gum!
Interviewer: I mean for regular breakfast, not silly breakfast. What would you have?
Larry: Cereal.
Interviewer: And then what happens, after you have your breakfast?
Larry: I go to day care.
Interviewer: Tell me about day care. What is day care?
Larry: You play and there's a lot of toys and there's bikes and balls. A lot of bikes. And Big Wheels. Tricycles. A train. And drinks.
Interviewer: And drinks?
Larry: Right. And food. And there's a couch there. And there's a closet.
Interviewer: What about people. Who else is there?
Larry: Kimmy and Judy.
Interviewer: How many other kids are there at day care?
Larry: Ten people. And two new kids. Eric and Jason. And Aaron.
Interviewer: And are there grown-ups at day care, too?

Larry: Yes. Lots and lots and lots.
Interviewer: What do the grown-ups do at day care?
Larry: They tell us what to do.
Interviewer: What do they tell you?
Larry: Don't do bad things. Like hit or bite.
Interviewer: No hitting, no biting.
Larry: No throwing pillows, but you can make a hideout.
Interviewer: Do you make a hideout?
Larry: No. But you can if you want to. If you ask them if it's okay, you can make a hideout. And if they say no, we can't. And if they say yes, we can. And we play and go outside.

Follow-up Questions

1. In Larry's view, what is the basis of friendship? How does this fit with the discussion of preschool friendships in this chapter?

2. Which social and cognitive levels of play described in this chapter characterize Larry's play?

3. How typical are the types of aggression that Larry reports of children his age?

dinner. But, because the children usually are not yet able to think in terms of lasting feelings and dispositions, they do not usually hold grudges, and making up is relatively easy (Selman, 1981a).

As children near school age, however, more permanent, personal qualities enter into their conceptions (Furman, 1982). Now the crucial features of a friend are more often dispositional — that is, related to how the friend is likely to behave in the future. A friend is still very much "someone you like," but she is also someone whom you trust, whom you can depend upon, and who may like and admire you. To be friends in this sense, two children must know each other's likes and preferences better than before, and they must also be increasingly aware of thoughts and feelings that the friend may keep hidden and unstated. Nevertheless, each child is still likely to focus primarily on her own needs to the exclusion of her friend's. As one child said, "A friend is someone who does what you want"; and as another said, "A friend doesn't get you in trouble." Neither of these children happens to think that sometimes they should return these favors; later, during the school years, this is likely to occur to them.

Friendships based on disposition

Empathy and Prosocial Behavior

Empathy is a sensitive awareness of the thoughts and feelings of another person, and prosocial behavior refers to actions that benefit others. The development of both is related to good parent-child relationships and secure attachment during infancy and toddlerhood (see Chapter 7).

The Extent of Empathy and Helpfulness   In a variety of situations, preschool children will respond helpfully to another person's distress. For example, slides or films depicting people with various feelings elicit similar emotions in young children who watch them, as judged by the expressions on the children's faces (Eisenberg-Berg & Neal, 1979). In naturalistic situations as well, young children show an ample tendency to empathize. A study of children at a day-care center playground found that a crying child almost always (more than 90 percent of the time) generated concerned responses from the other children, almost all of whom were helpful (Sawin, 1979). About 50 percent of the children who were near the distressed child showed similar facial expressions, looking as though they might cry themselves. Almost 20 percent of the nearby children tried to console the child directly, and their actions did in fact usually reduce the crying. Other children sought out an adult on the playground. Still others threatened revenge on the child who caused the upset.

Not surprisingly, however, there are limits to how empathic and helpful young children can be. In part this is because of their limited sensitivity to the feelings of others, and in part because of their limited capacity to distance themselves from the emotion and protect themselves from the feelings it creates. In the playground just mentioned, not all the children responded in a truly helpful way; about 12 percent withdrew from the scene of the distress, and occasionally children were overtly aggressive or teasing toward the child who was upset. Nearby children were also much more likely to empathize with positive feelings than with unhappy ones. Looking happy in particular proved more contagious than looking sad, angry, or hurt. A second, and perhaps more important, limitation in the ability of young children to be empathic and helpful is that they do not yet have the cognitive maturity to see things from another person's perspective (see Chapter 9).

Developmental Changes   Helpfulness or prosocial behavior is well established by the time a child reaches the preschool years. An early, classic study found that all of the following helping behaviors occurred with significant frequency among four-year-olds (Murphy, 1937): assisting another child; comforting another child; protecting another child; warning another child of danger; giving things to another child; and inquiring of a child in trouble. Fifty years later, these and similar helping behaviors are still quite evident, not only among preschool children but even among children younger than two (Radke-Yarrow & Zahn-Waxler, 1984; Zahn-Waxler & Radke-Yarrow, 1982). For instance, when a toddler sees her brother cry, she may give him her bottle, or when a four-year-old at nursery school worries because his parents are late in picking him up, another child may put her arm around him and say, "It's okay — they'll be here soon."

Between ages two and six, children give increasingly complex reasons for helping and are more strongly influenced by nonaltruistic as well as altruistic motives and concerns (Yarrow & Waxler, 1978). An older child may justify her helpfulness in terms of gaining approval from peers in general, rather than in terms of her concern for the well-being of the particular child in distress. Or she may justify withholding help because of fear of disapproval from adults — if she has been instructed, perhaps, to let the day-care or nursery school teachers handle

Empathy with distressed children

Limits to empathy

Bridges   How do preschoolers' feelings relate to their capacity for empathy?

Bridges   In what way does cognitive development affect the development of empathy?

Reasons for helping change with age

A Multicultural View

The Development of Ethnic Awareness During the Preschool Years

In a society that is becoming increasingly diverse, ethnicity has emerged as an important influence on development, even during early childhood. A preschooler's **ethnic identity** refers to his sense of belonging to an ethnic group; the term also refers to the thoughts, perceptions, feelings, and behaviors that are part of ethnic group membership. Ethnic identity includes *ethnic awareness* (an understanding of one's own ethnic group), *ethnic self-identification* (the label used for one's own group), *ethnic attitudes* (feelings about one's own and other groups), and the patterns of *ethnic behaviors* that are specific to an ethnic group (Rotheram & Phinney, 1987).

*Developmental researchers Phyllis Katz and Francis Aboud have studied ethnic identity and have described the formation of ethnic identity at different ages. During children's first three or four years, they develop an elementary awareness of ethnic differences based on color and other observed physical and behavioral differences; by age four children are able to conceptually differentiate between groups. An awareness of group differences and of social comparisons based upon group characteristics now starts to emerge. So do the beginnings of racial attitudes and the knowledge that the characteristics associated with ethnic group differences are permanent and unchangeable. As a child approaches the early school years, she is better able to integrate strong social preferences, the reasons for them, and awareness of her group membership (Rotheram & Phinney, 1987; Aboud, 1987; Katz, 1976).

The development of ethnic identity is influenced by a child's perceptions of others, by the degree to which he feels and acts as a group member, and by how others see him. The views of others can be very important, especially when ethnicity is marked by distinctive physical characteristics such as skin color, facial features, and hair type. The degree to which a child possesses these physical characteristics can also influence the perceptions of others (and self). For example, although a dark-skinned black is likely to be considered black by most people who meet him, some people may consider him more or less "black" (or "white") than others.

A child's growing ability to accurately and consistently use an ethnic label based on perceptions and conceptions of herself as belonging to an ethnic group is called ethnic self-identification. Self-identification is typically assessed by showing children pictures or dolls representing various ethnic groups and asking them to select the one that is most like themselves. Correct self-identification requires that a child be able to recognize her group, perceive similarity between herself and others, know the label, and apply the label consistently over time regardless of other confusing or irrelevant cues. Studies of white, black, American Indian, and Chinese children reveal that accurate categorization and labeling of ethnic differences do not occur until approximately age seven and only after a sense of perceived similarity with one's own group has developed (Rotheram & Phinney, 1987).

Similarly, it is not until around age seven that a child will typically say that ethnicity is consistent and unchangeable — for example, that a white could not become an Indian and that he is still a white even though he is dressed in Indian clothing. This process continues through the early school years, and it is not until the age of nine or ten that ethnic attitudes crystallize and a child's awareness and curiosity about other ethnic groups increase (Aboud & Skerry, 1984: Aboud, 1987).

*Bridges How do preschoolers develop a sense of ethnic identity?

children in trouble. In fairness to older preschoolers, however, younger children may also have reasons like these and are simply not yet able to verbalize them clearly.

Most children of this age tend to be self-centered in their helping and are more likely to provide help when some self-benefit is apparent, although for some preschoolers and elementary school children their decision to help is also a genuine response to the perceived needs of others (N. Eisenberg et al., 1983).

Fostering Empathy, Altruism, and Prosocial Behavior Both verbal approval for altruistic behavior and an opportunity to discover the benefits of cooperation and helping in play situations have proven to be successful in increasing altruistic and prosocial behavior among preschoolers (Slaby & Crowley, 1977; Orlick, 1981). Preschool children are more willing to help if adults call attention to other children's distress. In one experiment, young children played a game in

Adult guidance fosters helping behavior

Important gains in children's capacity for empathy and emotional support occur during the preschool years.

which they won plastic tokens that could later be turned in for prizes (Howard & Barnett, 1981). Some children were told that certain other children who played the game would not be winning any tokens and that they could share their tokens with the less fortunate children later if they wished. In these conditions, a number of children voluntarily donated tokens after the experiment, and also reported feeling sad for their unfortunate peers. But they were particularly likely to do so if the experimenters had called attention not only to their peers' lack of winnings but also to the nonwinners' distressed feelings.

There is also growing evidence that differences in empathy and compassionate behavior in toddlers and preschool children are related to differences in parenting styles (Zahn-Waxler et al., 1979; Mussen & Eisenberg-Berg, 1977; Radke-Yarrow, Zahn-Waxler, & Chapan, 1983; Main & George, 1985). In a study of the reactions of children to other children's distress and the reactions of mothers when their own children were the cause of the distress, mothers of less compassionate toddlers tended to respond to the child's misbehavior in more authoritarian ways, using physical restraint, physical punishment, or unexplained commands to stop. Mothers of highly compassionate children were more likely to use affective explanations that focused on helping the child see the connections between his unacceptable actions and the upset and distress that they caused (Zahn-Waxler et al, 1979; Radke-Yarrow, Zahn-Waxler, & Chapan, 1983).

Parents serve as models

Does this sort of encouragement result in a permanent tendency to empathize? Authoritative answers to this question are scarce. It seems plausible that parents who emphasize the expression and discussion of feelings will have children who tend to be relatively empathic and helpful. A study of young adults confirmed this possibility: college students who showed especially empathic attitudes also reported having had parents who valued and fostered attention to feelings (Barnett et al., 1980). How accurate such self-reports are, however, remains open to question; to some extent, the empathic adults may have reconstructed memories of their childhoods to fit their current personalities, rather than the other way around.

Influence of adult encouragement

Some additional help in answering the question of how significant parental encouragement is comes from cross-cultural studies. One study, now a classic, compared child-rearing experiences in the United States and five other, non-Western cultures (B. Whiting & Whiting, 1975). The researchers found that in mainly rural societies where mothers worked in the fields and children assumed major child-care and household responsibilities, children had a greater opportunity to experience prosocial roles and to behave prosocially. Firstborn children, who had the most helping experience, tended to be more prosocial than lastborn or only children. Another study, which used a cooperative game to compare the performance of children from urban and rural cultures, found that children from small, closely knit urban communities were more cooperative than children from rural or big-city areas (Madsen, 1971). These findings suggest that exposure to empathic and prosocial role models and direct participation in community life rather than merely living in a rural or urban area are likely to increase empathy and prosocial behavior in children.

Conflict and Aggression

So far our discussion of social relationships has focused on the ability of preschoolers to get along reasonably well with one another, but of course preschoolers also get very angry and express their feelings in aggressive ways: grabbing each other's toys, pushing, hitting, scratching, and calling names. It is possible that research on friendship and altruistic behavior underestimates the role of conflict and aggression among preschoolers because the observations on which the research is based are often conducted in adult-supervised settings (Sutton-Smith, 1981; Sutton-Smith & Kelly-Byrne, 1984a, b).

The Nature of Aggression   No one agrees about how to define aggression. Some people define it strictly in terms of its consequences: as an action that results in harmful consequences to a person or object. Others point out that because harmful consequences can result from unintended or accidental actions, and actions that *are* intended to harm another sometimes fail to do so, harmful motivations or intentions are the key to defining an act as aggressive. Thus, **aggression** is an action that is intended to hurt another person or object and that in most circumstances succeeds in its objective. Quite frequently, aggressive behavior is associated with a child's frustration at not being able to solve a conflict; for example, one child may hit another because her attempts to get a turn with a favorite toy have all failed.

Aggressiveness differs from assertiveness. **Assertiveness** is the more general tendency to communicate clearly and effectively and thus fulfill one's needs, but not necessarily with the intention of or in a way that succeeds in hurting another person. Judgments about the extent to which a person is aware of his motivations and, more importantly, of the consequences of his actions are critical in deciding whether a hurtful incident is the result of aggressive behavior or the accidental by-product of assertiveness.

For instance, a preschooler may accidentally knock over another child's skyscraper, or she may knock it down on purpose; she may run over another child with her tricycle because she is intent on winning a race and does not see the other child standing there, or she may do it because she is angry at him. Frequently preschoolers (and at times their adult care-givers as well) find it difficult to distinguish between their own aggressive and assertive motivations; similarly, they become upset when hurtful acts occur, which makes it more difficult to figure out what has really happened. The context in which an action occurs can also be important; for example, a teacher's good-natured teasing may cause considerable anguish if it is aimed at his students, but the same teasing among fellow teachers after school may have little in the way of negative results.

Distinguishing between aggression and assertion

Generally, judgments about a child's aggressiveness are based on her motivations, on her level of knowledge of the effects of her actions, and on whether or not there have been destructive consequences. Knowledge of the child's previous patterns of response in similar situations is also helpful in making reliable judgments.

Changes in Aggression During Early Childhood   Young preschoolers show aggression more physically than older preschoolers do. As children get older, they shift to more verbal methods, and insults and demands replace pushing and grabbing — although aggression as a whole declines in frequency with age. These changes can be observed directly in nursery school classrooms (Hartup, 1974) and are also confirmed by parents' diaries about their children (Goodenough, 1931).

Having a practical goal

When a younger child behaves aggressively, she often has a more assertive, practical goal in mind, such as retrieving a toy from a child who has walked off with it. Grabbing the toy back is not necessarily aggressive and usually does not result in the other child's feeling wronged. The action ends when the little girl gets her toy back, rather than when the other child shows pain or humiliation. This type of assertive behavior is referred to as **instrumental aggression.**

Wanting to hurt

Sometimes, a child who feels that he has been hurt or mistreated may retaliate by trying to hurt the child who wronged him. Such behavior, which is aggressive in the sense of our earlier definition, is sometimes referred to as **hostile aggression** because harm is an important intent. A key change, then, among five- and six-year-olds is that aggression often involves a motivation to hurt the other person and his feelings.

Consistent with these changes are shifts in what stimulates or brings about aggression. Preschool children of all ages respond to assertiveness and instrumental aggression with about the same frequency. In the case of **blocking behaviors** — actions that interfere with a child's current activities or keep her from the toys she is using — preschool children of all ages will respond with hostile aggression around one-quarter of the time (Hartup, 1974). Personal insults, however, are another story. As preschool children get older, they insult each other more and respond to insults with increasing frequency — nearly four-fifths of the time by age five (Krasner & Rubin, 1983). And they respond in kind; insulting remarks and ridicule generate insults and ridicule in retaliation. In part this occurs because children perceive each other's intentions more accurately as they get older, and they are also more vulnerable to these kinds of attacks.

Insults increase with age

Influences on the Development of Aggression   When it is expressed in acceptable ways, aggression may be not only tolerable but even desirable. Assertive or instrumental aggressive actions allow a child to communicate and fulfill legitimate needs, as when the child takes back a toy that is rightfully his or stands up for his integrity against unfair insults. Quite often, however, hostile motivations complicate matters and create additional upset. This is particularly true for preschool children who are working hard to master the aggressive impulses associated with the Oedipal conflict and to assert their initiative successfully without experiencing undue guilt. The anger and rage that children sometimes experience can be quite upsetting to them as well as to their parents and others. For example, a mother who observes her four-year-old attack a playmate, perhaps biting him or pulling his hair, is likely to be upset for multiple reasons, including her child's unhappiness, the pain and upset of the other child, her feeling that biting is "dirty fighting," and concerns about how this all reflects upon her as a parent.

Several factors strongly influence the overall development of aggression. Important among them is the willingness of parents and others both to accept their children's "hostile-aggressive" impulses and actions and help them to discover nonhostile or "instrumentally aggressive" alternatives for resolving conflicts and asserting their needs.

Although human biology does not typically cause aggressive behavior directly, it can contribute to it indirectly. As we explain in Chapter 7, temperamental differences in children at birth may make aggressive behavior more likely during early childhood. Babies with especially "difficult" temperaments at six months of age were found to have more conflict with their mothers at age three than other babies did (Bates, 1979).

As six-month-olds, these difficult babies tended to have irregular levels of activity, including sudden bursts of arm waving and general restlessness. When they were three years old, their mothers used a very wide variety of methods to attempt to control them, including forbidding certain activities, threatening punishment, and using physical restraint. These children responded less cooperatively than did children who had had "easier" temperaments as infants. They were also more likely to get into trouble a second time, to ignore their parents' disciplinary efforts, and to respond in insulting and unpleasant ways. Thus, the ongoing interactions between these difficult children and their parents seemed likely to promote rather than reduce further aggression. (Of course, many active or difficult babies do not become aggressive three-year-olds, perhaps because the expression of temperament is to a significant degree a product of child–caregiver interactions [Bates, 1979]).

Physical looks may also make a difference. Preschool children seem just as able to judge physical attractiveness as adults are and are just as apt to attribute stereotyped behaviors to good and bad looks. Attractive children are thought to possess various positive traits such as friendliness, whereas unattractive children are thought to possess negative ones, including meanness and aggressiveness (Langlois & Stephan, 1981).

To some extent these stereotypes can actually be observed in young children (Langlois & Downs, 1980). Attractive and less attractive children, it seems, tend to be equally sociable or outgoing, but the less attractive ones hit their peers more often and generally exhibit more boisterous play. A probable explanation for these differences is a self-fulfilling prophecy: adults, peers, and the unattractive child herself learn to expect undesirable behavior from someone who is judged to be unattractive, and eventually the child learns to live up to those expectations.

Throughout the preschool years, boys exhibit more aggressive behavior than girls do (Maccoby & Jacklin, 1980). This difference holds true across a broad range of social classes, ethnic groups, and cultures. It is also true across a wide range of aggressive behaviors; contrary to popular belief, girls do not specialize in verbal aggression (such as name calling) or boys in physical aggression (such as pushing and hitting).

Overall levels of aggressive behavior and gender differences in aggressiveness depend on a number of circumstances. Preschool boys initiate aggressive actions a little more often than girls do, but they retaliate against aggression a lot more (Darvill & Chenye, 1981). When two children play together in nursery classrooms, they are more aggressive when the pairs include boys and particularly when they consist of two boys.

Child-rearing and educational philosophies and practices of parents and teachers also influence both overall levels of aggression and gender differences. Day-care centers that tolerate aggression and disobedience are likely to experience more of it than those that are less tolerant (Belsky & Steinberg, 1978). The same is probably true of families and informal play groups. And child-rearing environments that actively work to minimize sex-role stereotyping of young children are likely to minimize gender differences in aggression. If girls are encouraged to be as assertive as boys in their play and other social interactions and if their hostile aggressive actions are not unduly criticized, gender differences

Bridges In what ways does genetics contribute to aggressiveness in preschool children?

"Difficult" babies experience greater conflict

Aggressiveness of less attractive children

Gender differences

Influence of child-rearing practices

Early in the preschool years, aggression focuses on getting access to desirable toys and activities; physical and emotional harm are often unintentional by-products of these instrumental goals.

will probably be smaller than they are in situations in which girls are expected to be less assertive and aggressive (Hoffnung, 1983).

Parents' overall style or pattern of child-rearing is likely to influence both the desirable and undesirable behaviors of their children significantly. All of the following child-rearing characteristics have been found to contribute to aggressiveness in preschoolers, especially when they are part of an ongoing pattern (Baumrind, 1971; B. Martin, 1975):

1. Lack of acceptance of the child, dislike of the child, and criticism of the child for being the sort of person he currently is or is becoming

2. Excessive permissiveness, particularly if it involves indifference to the true needs of the child for reasonable but consistent limits and emotional support

3. Discipline that does not respect the child's ability and need to understand the reasons for the punishment and its meaning to the parent

4. Inconsistent discipline, which does not provide the child with a reasonable and predictable basis for learning to regulate her behavior

5. A "spare the rod and spoil the child" attitude, which often results in impulsive and overly harsh use of discipline

6. Unclear rules and expectations for the child, particularly regarding his interactions with other family members

As we pointed out earlier, peers can also contribute to aggression by acting in ways that provoke aggressive retaliation. Presumably a child surrounded by provocative peers will eventually acquire a similar style herself and in doing so

Provocation by peers

will stimulate further aggressive behavior in his peers. At the beginning of a nursery school year, for example, Karin may argue with Leila over who should use a favorite stuffed animal. Leila may bite Karin to get her own way; Karin may discover that unless she bites back, she will rarely get a turn with the animal. After several conflicts involving shoves and punches, Karin may begin biting too, even though she never intended to do so. Of course, Karin may instead become passive and withdraw to avoid being punched.

A series of aggressive exchanges among pairs of preschool children sometimes results in a **dominance hierarchy** — a pattern of status and authority that is influenced by who wins and who loses but that is also related to leadership and popularity within a group (Abramovitch & Strayer, 1978). These hierarchies are temporary and are generally maintained more by bluffing and threats than by overt acts of aggression. Although they do serve to reduce overt aggression in the short run, the climate they create can be destructive to the social development of both winners and losers; relationships based upon dominance and submission are not the best basis for the development of friendship and self-esteem.

Hierarchical relationships

Some preschool children find themselves involved in frequent conflicts anyway; they continually either lose battles and arguments or lose potential friends by depending too much on hostile, aggressive actions to get what they need. Why do some children have such troubles? Possibly because they lack skill in resolving conflicts peacefully; they may resort to violence too soon (Asher & Renshaw, 1981). Or their conception of social relationships may be poorly developed; they may think, for example, that a friend is simply someone who gives you what you want and that someone who does not is an enemy (Shantz & Shantz, 1985). Finally, a preschooler who is overly aggressive toward his peers may be upset and angry about other things, such as his family situation. Because he is unable to express his anger directly, he behaves aggressively at his day-care center.

As many concerned parents realize, television, films, and other media exert strong influences on children, and much of the influence centers on physical violence. According to a wide variety of well-documented studies, watching violence **disinhibits,** or releases, violent behavior in children who are already prone to be angry and aggressive. Most children, however, react by becoming desensitized to the pain and hurt that result from aggression.

Influence of media

Preschool children have a special problem in coping with violence in the media: their lack of skill in figuring out the motives of actors and the subtleties of plots. A completely villainous murder on television may look the same to a preschooler as one committed in self-defense or to protect innocent people (Collins et al., 1981). Adult supervision and help in understanding television programs therefore are especially important for very young children. Unfortunately, one of television's main attractions for some parents is that it makes adult supervision "unnecessary" by keeping children passively occupied.

Importance of adult supervision

Although aggressive responses to conflict are fairly common among preschoolers, physical differences, gender, child-rearing styles, peers, and the media may influence the frequency and type of aggressive behavior. Aggression is much less likely to cause problems when care-givers provide adequate guidance for preschool children and have realistic expectations of young children's ability to resolve conflicts and to regulate their aggressive impulses.

Responding to Aggressive Behavior   Children who cannot control their aggression experience considerable problems. Often they become aggressive at inappropriate times and in self-defeating ways, getting into fights with children and adults who are stronger than they are. Peers and parents alike find it difficult not to attribute malicious motives to children who seem out of control and who seem to be unresponsive to generally agreed upon standards of behavior (Kutner, 1989).

Bridges How can overly aggressive children learn to control their aggressive behaviors?

How can overly aggressive children and their parents be helped? Several principles have emerged from work with these children and their families (Kutner, 1989; Patterson, 1982; Patterson et al., 1989). Although individual differences in children certainly are a factor, the most successful approaches to children who cannot successfully control their aggression frequently involve working with the entire family. The first step is to carefully observe the child as she interacts with peers and adults so as to discover consistent patterns in what triggers the aggression and how each family member reinforces the patterns of problem behavior.

Careful observation

Structure, predictability, and consistency

Structure, predictability, and consistency of routine are important for all preschoolers, especially for children who have difficulty controlling their aggressive behavior. Aggressive outbursts are most likely to occur in unstructured and ambiguous situations in which a child perceives himself to be the object of harm or at risk. Overly aggressive children are prone to distort ambiguous information about harm. They may misinterpret neutral behavior such as the approach of another child as an aggressive act. This "cue distortion" appears to play a central role in these children's aggressive outbursts (Dodge, 1986).

Once the patterns are discovered, parents can learn to recognize the early signs and intervene either by changing the situation or by removing their preschooler before things escalate. Hitting a child for misbehaving is generally not successful because it models the very behaviors that are unwanted. Rather, the most successful methods are reinforcement of positive behaviors through warmth, affection, and parental approval and assertiveness training that helps the child meet her needs for attention in less self-destructive ways (Kutner, 1989; Patterson, 1982). In addition, parents can work to increase predictability and consistency in their children's everyday lives.

Emphasis on effective parent-child communication

For parents who lack communication and child-rearing skills, programs such as Parent Effectiveness Training (T. Gordon, 1975) help them to develop communication techniques that are consistent with the values and behaviors they feel are appropriate. This approach emphasizes clear and effective communication rather than positive and negative reinforcement or punishment. This training helps parents develop active listening and language skills that support the child's self-esteem and validates his experience. Alternative approaches to reducing unacceptable behavior are also taught. These include rearrangement of home environment and strategies for reducing win-lose conflicts.

Learning alternative responses

Another successful approach to modifying destructive family processes and problems with childhood aggression uses such social learning theory methods as coaching, modeling, and reinforcing alternative patterns of parent-child interaction. After carefully observing the parent-child interaction, the therapist describes and then demonstrates alternative ways of dealing with the child's hostile, aggressive, or disobedient behaviors. As parents gain more confidence in their competence, they become more effective parents, and as children learn to resolve conflicts in a better way, their problematic behavior decreases (Patterson, 1976, 1985). We now turn to another area of great importance during the preschool years, the development of gender.

GENDER DEVELOPMENT

Gender influences important aspects of social development in early childhood. As used here, the term **gender** refers to the behaviors and attitudes associated with being male or female. Most children experience it in at least three ways

(Shepherd-Look, 1982). First, they develop beliefs about **gender identity,** that is, which sex *they* are and will always be. Second, they develop **gender preferences,** attitudes about which sex they wish to be. Gender preference does not always coincide with gender identity. And third they acquire **gender constancy,** a belief that the sex of a person is biologically determined, permanent, and unchanging, no matter what else about them may change.

All three aspects of gender contribute to a child's general knowledge of society's expectations about sex roles. This particular knowledge is sometimes referred to as sex-role stereotypes. Even very young preschoolers have some awareness of these stereotypes and often act in ways that reflect them.

Developmental Trends During Early Childhood

Usually even two-year-olds can label themselves correctly as boys or girls; for that matter, they can correctly label other children and adults. At this age, however, a child may not believe in gender constancy, the idea that sex is biologically determined and permanent. A young preschool child may say that she can switch gender just by wanting to, or she may say that even though she is a girl now, she was a boy as an infant or may grow up to become a man as an adult. And a two-year-old may have only a hazy notion of what defines gender, believing, perhaps, that certain hairstyles, clothing, and toys make the crucial difference. Most children achieve gender constancy between ages seven and nine (Emmerich & Sheppard, 1982). Meanwhile, they undergo several significant developments.

Toys and Activities   Somewhere between ages two and three, children learn the conventional gender stereotypes associated with a variety of common objects and activities (Ruble & Ruble, 1980). They connect gender with many toys: they learn that trucks are "for boys" and that dolls are "for girls." They learn similar associations for most items of clothing ("Who wears a dress/pants?"), for many common tools ("Who uses a saw/eggbeater?"), and for common games ("Who plays hockey/hopscotch?"). By early school age they begin to connect certain family and occupational roles with the male or female gender: females stay home and take care of children and the house, and males go to work; nurses are female and pilots are male.

Gender stereotypes are learned early

In a variety of situations, children this young implement gender stereotypes by choosing toys and activities associated with their own sex (Lawson, 1989; Maccoby & Jacklin, 1974). To a significant extent, in fact, many children simply will not play with toys that they strongly associate with the other gender. Boys especially show a tendency to disown anything female in their lives; they may reject playing with dolls because it is "yucky girl stuff!" Girls seem somewhat less extreme in avoiding male interests and are more likely to play with trucks and blocks than boys are to play with dress-up clothes (Greenberg, 1984).

But even when boys and girls play with the same toy, they differ in their manner of play. Little girls sometimes make "dolls" out of the trucks they are given to play with, and boys make trucks or tanks out of grocery carts.

Personal Qualities   In contrast to toys and activities, preschool children develop gender stereotypes about personal qualities relatively slowly (Huston, 1983). Only by age five or so do children begin to know which sex is supposed to be aggressive, loud, and strong and which is supposed to be gentle, quiet, and weak. This kind of knowledge continues to develop throughout childhood and adolescence, but during the preschool years it has just begun.

This fact should not surprise us because an individual's understanding of personal qualities is based on abstractions from many experiences. The judgment

Difficulty in grasping concept of gender

that someone is a "loud" person, for example, is generally based on the observation that that person has behaved loudly on many occasions. Understanding such qualities requires cognitive skills that are beyond many preschool children. Even the concept of gender may require a level of abstract thinking that is difficult for a young child, so that it does not become a clear, stable idea for most children until the school years. Before this occurs, children apparently must sort through numerous ever-changing behaviors related to gender and somehow figure out which ones, if any, are essential to being a male (or female) and which ones are not.

Influences on Gender Development

Much theorizing holds parents responsible for the development of gender differences, either blaming or congratulating them, depending on the theorist's point of view. A close look suggests that parents do deserve some credit but perhaps not as much as is commonly thought. Other influences also matter.

Parents   When asked about their child-rearing philosophies, parents tend to express belief in gender equality, but their actions often differ from their statements (Fagot, 1982). Observations of parents playing with their preschool children show that parents support their children for sex-stereotyped activities more than for cross-sex activities; a boy gets praised more for playing with blocks, than for playing with dolls. Parents generally support physical activity in boys more than in girls, both by praising it and by participating in it. Possibly as a by-product of these differences, boys get punished more often and more physically than girls do. And as children approach school age, parents begin assigning household chores according to gender; boys more often have to take out the

Different treatment of boys and girls

trash, and girls more often have to fold the laundry (Huston, 1983). By the nature of things, many of these differences lead to greater freedom and independence for boys. Playing relatively actively leads to wider exploration and movement, whether around the house or around an entire neighborhood. Boys' larger territories remove them from adult surveillance more of the time and make peers relatively more important in their social lives.

Nevertheless, there are similarities in parents' treatment of the sexes. Observation shows that parents give similar amounts of warmth and affection to both boys and girls in the preschool period; they set similar limits on children's behavior, and they encourage similar levels of achievement (Maccoby & Jacklin, 1974).

How can we reconcile these two pictures of family influences on gender? One view is that in spite of considerable gender overlap, parents do indeed treat the sexes differently, although the difference becomes larger later in childhood, when parents may become more concerned about preparing children for adulthood (Block, 1978). Even the differences in treatment that do begin in early childhood may not have their full impact until well into middle childhood or even beyond. Learning gender stereotypes about jobs begins around kindergarten age; but this knowledge may not seem important to a child until he actually begins looking for work in adolescence. Before that time, the knowledge may not affect his behavior very much; he may willingly play at being a doctor (traditionally a male job) and at being a nurse (traditionally a female one).

Parents' influence also depends somewhat on which parent is involved. Usually the younger a child is, the more likely it is that she will be cared for by her mother, or by a female relative or friend. Women tend to express less stereotyped attitudes and practices about gender in dealing with their children than men do. From the child's perspective, the family may seem to expect less

Greater sex typing with age

sex typing when she is very young. As she gets older, her father may enter her life more and may bring with him more sharply defined sex-role expectations.

Perspectives

Sexism in Preschool and Day-Care Settings: Can It Be Reduced?

Do preschool and day-care teachers contribute to male-female or gender differences in young children? Several studies suggest that they do, especially through their moment-to-moment interactions with children.*

Consider how teachers label objects in preschool classrooms. One study purposely varied how teachers labeled new materials and activities (Serbin, 1979). Sometimes the teachers introduced activities in gender-linked ways, and sometimes they did not. In the gender-linked condition, they described a particular activity in gender-related terms, saying, for example, "This is a sewing card like mommies often use"; they related the activity to the child's own experiences with gender ("Can *you* remember when your mommy used one?"), and they chose a child of the "appropriate" sex to demonstrate the activity ("Sally, can you show us how to use the sewing card?"). Later, when the children had a chance to choose among several new activities, their choices were affected by the gender-linked introductions. Boys tended to choose male-typed activities and girls to choose female-typed ones, and there was almost no overlap between the sexes.

When teachers described the activities in gender-neutral ways, the effects were very different. For example, teachers described an activity in neutral terms ("This is a lacing card. Shoes have laces."). They related the activity to the children's personal experiences ("Who is wearing laces today?"), and they chose children of *both* sexes to demonstrate the activity ("Sally and Steven, can you show us how to use these lacing cards?"). Gender-neutral introductions like these prompted children of both sexes to try the activity.

Teachers also influence the sex composition of children's play groupings in nursery school. In one preschool program, teachers purposely reinforced children whenever they happened to form groups that included both sexes. If several boys and girls happened to be playing together with the blocks, the teachers made sure to comment on and praise their activity and to encourage further effort (Serbin et al., 1977). If only boys or only girls were playing with the blocks, however, the teachers refrained from any comment. In these conditions, the proportion of cross-sex groupings in the class jumped dramatically; within a two-week period, mixed groups rose from 25 percent of all groups to 75 percent. Equally dramatically, however, the proportion fell back to its original level almost immediately after the teachers stopped reinforcing cross-sex groupings and returned to praising any group activities, regardless of their sex composition. Apparently two weeks of reinforcement were not long enough to make a more lasting difference in these children's sex-role habits.

These findings suggest not only that teachers can build gender biases deliberately but also that they can do so accidentally, simply by tolerating any biases that they and the children already have. In making introductions, for example, teachers probably do gender-link many toys and activities, although often without dwelling on these connections. Many mommies do sew, but not many daddies do; avoiding mention of this fact may take less effort than simply stating it. But children deserve to know this bit of information about our culture. Likewise, groups composed of only one sex often do very good work and therefore deserve praise. Would it be fair to confine praise to groups that happen to include both sexes? The answer is not as simple as it first appears; it depends on how important gender equity is to children's development and on how hard educators are willing to work to find ways of achieving it that are compatible with the other important goals of preschool education.

On the other hand, Nancy Chodorow (1978), for example, argues that boys and girls undergo different, contrasting experiences of identity formation during their early years when women are their exclusive care-givers. Girls' identity and personality development are based on similarity and attachment to their mothers, who provide models for nurturing, care-giving, and closeness. Boys' identity are based on difference, separateness, and independence from these qualities, for to be a male in our society means possessing qualities that are incompatible with those traditionally associated with being a woman. Thus, Chodorow sees women's capacity to nurture, to raise children, and to develop close relationships and men's capacity to separate themselves from their feelings and to participate in the isolating and alienating world of work as rooted in these early experiences.

In some ways the task of identity formation for boys may be more difficult in that it requires a certain degree of rejection of essential qualities of their primary care-giver. At the same time, the higher degree of similarity and continuity of experience between daughter and mother may make it more difficult for girls to separate from their mothers and establish an independent and separate identity. After discussing the influence peers and the media have on gender differences, we return to the question of how we define gender difference and what its consequences are.

*Bridges How can changes in preschool and day-care settings reduce sex-role stereotyping and sexism?

Peers   In some ways, peers may shape gender differences more effectively than parents do. Early in the preschool years — even before age three — children respond differently to partners of the opposite sex than to ones of the same sex (Maccoby, 1990). In play situations, girls tend to withdraw more from a boy partner than from a girl, and boys heed prohibitions more often if they come from another boy than if they come from a girl. Even when preschoolers are not playing actively, they watch peers of the same sex more often than peers of the opposite sex.

Peer reinforcement of gender typing

Children of this age respond to a reinforcement more reliably if it comes from a child of their own sex. If a boy compliments another boy's block building, the second boy is much more likely to continue building than he is if a girl compliments it. And conversely, if a boy criticizes the building, the other boy is more likely to stop than if a girl criticizes the activity. Parallel patterns occur for girls, who tend to persist in whatever other girls compliment or praise and stop whatever they criticize or ignore. For both sexes, teachers' reinforcements have less influence than peers' reinforcements in determining children's persistence at activities (Fagot, 1982).

What makes these patterns important is that children tend to reinforce play activities appropriate for their own sex. Boys praise and support large-motor activity more than quiet art activities, and girls do the reverse. In the long run, therefore, children probably shape each other's play preferences along sex-typed lines. Children who deviate from conventional preferences find themselves largely ignored (Lamb & Roopnarine, 1979) — even after finally returning to conventional activities. So peer pressures to practice conventional gender roles are both strong and continual, and they occur even if teachers and other adults do not fully approve of them.

The Media   To some extent, peer expectations like these may result from the wider impact of the media. Television in particular shows heavy gender biases. Most programs, even the daytime soaps, are dominated by men (Lemon, 1977), as judged both by numbers of characters and by the importance assigned to them. In spite of recent efforts to broaden the portrayals of gender roles, the women who do appear on television are in strongly sex-typed roles: they are teachers, secretaries, nurses, or (most commonly) housewives. On television, women solve problems less often, need help more often, listen better and talk less than men, and otherwise behave in stereotypical ways (U.S. Commission on Civil Rights, 1977). The patterns also prevail for children's television despite efforts to present roles more equally (Shepherd-Look, 1982). One reason for this may be the large number of reruns of situation comedies and cartoons produced in the 1950s and 1960s, in which sex-role stereotyping was extremely common.

Media role models are strongly sex typed

Advertising on television shows similar biases but adds to them the style of presentation. Commercials aimed at boys and men tend to show more activity and to use rapid cuts and loud music. Those aimed at girls and women rely more on visual fades and dissolves and use gentle background music (Welch et al., 1979). Given the subtlety of these techniques, commercials may well influence children more strongly than the obvious, conscious biases of television shows themselves.

Androgyny

Androgyny may allow greater flexibility

Androgyny refers to a state of affairs in which sex roles are flexible, allowing all individuals, male and female, to behave in ways that freely integrate behaviors traditionally thought to belong exclusively to one sex or the other. In this view, both girls and boys can be assertive *and* yielding; independent *and* dependent;

instrumental (task oriented) *and* expressive (feeling oriented) (Kaplan & Bean, 1976).

In research using the Bem Sex-Role Inventory, Sandra Bem (1974, 1976) has found that both males and females used masculine *and* feminine characteristics to describe their own personalities. In a sample of more than two thousand undergraduates from both a university and a community college, approximately one-third of both populations could be classified as androgynous based on having masculinity and femininity scores that were approximately equal. One-third of the respondents were significantly sex typed as either masculine or feminine; fewer than one-tenth were classified as "sex reversed," based on the fact that they relied most heavily on characteristics of the opposite sex to describe their personalities.

More recently, Sandra Bem has suggested that androgynous individuals are more flexible and adaptable because they have not formed organized connections between gender and everyday activities — that is, they are less concerned about what activities are appropriate or inappropriate and are therefore more flexible in their responses to various situations (Bem, 1981). The very way in which we define the meaning of gender can also affect our understanding of what it means to be male or female. Most approaches tend to either exaggerate gender differences by finding differences that are really not there or minimize them by overlooking differences that actually do exist.

One positive consequence of focusing on male-female difference is an increased awareness and appreciation of feminine (and masculine) qualities. At the same time, the tendency to minimize such differences has helped to increase equal treatment under the law and access to equal opportunity (Hare-Mustin & Marecek, 1988).

What are the implications of androgyny? It has been suggested that the possibilities for the more flexible, integrated, and less stereotyped sex roles implied by androgyny will depend upon the sex stereotypes and child-rearing orientations of parents, families, schools, the media, and of the broader culture in which they exist (Block, 1973). For preschoolers, television programs with little sex stereotyping, such as "Sesame Street," are likely to help, as are increased awareness and efforts on the part of parents and day-care and preschool teachers to support and encourage more androgynous roles.

The ease with which this preschool girl includes in her play both the traditional male role of bus driver and the traditional female role of mother vividly illustrates the flexible qualities associated with androgyny.

THE END OF THE PRESCHOOL YEARS

Although the preschool period, considered as a whole, may not bring about physical changes as dramatic as those of infancy, the cognitive, social, and emotional changes that occur may be even more striking. By age five or six, a child has both worked and played with symbolic skills quite a lot, and sometimes he is beginning to do so according to prearranged rules. He can form friendships that last at least a little beyond the here and now and that both foster and draw upon genuine understanding of others. His new social skills do not eliminate hurting others; in fact they may allow him to hurt others in more sophisticated ways — by using personal qualities, for example, rather than just immediate activities. Increasing social sophistication may also allow the child to use less aggressive means of asserting his needs and dealing with conflict. All these new skills, both positive and negative, are guided significantly by the child's gender role — a concept to which the child himself makes important contributions during the preschool years.

But human development is far from over at this point. The child's social world broadens widely in the years ahead, most obviously through her entry into school and the development of important social relationships that are independent of her family. Major changes also occur in the child's cognitive abilities and in her physical growth and ability to use her body. The following chapters will explore these and other important features of the child's development as she progresses through middle childhood.

SUMMARY OF MAJOR IDEAS

1. Even the physical and cognitive activities of preschool children are highly social.

Theories of Early Social Development

2. Freud's theory emphasizes the importance of resolution of the Oedipal conflict during the phallic stage, whereas Erikson saw resolution of the psychosocial crisis of initiative versus guilt as the central task of the preschool years.
3. According to Sullivan, preschoolers use egocentric escape to avoid unpleasant or overwhelming situations and dramatizations to act out new relationships safely. If their anxiety and mistrust become too great, a "malevolent transformation" may occur.

Play in Early Childhood

4. Play is the major waking activity of preschoolers.
5. Play involves intrinsic motivation, process rather than product, pretense, and implicit and flexible rules.
6. Psychoanalytic theory emphasizes the mastery and wish-fulfillment functions of play, whereas learning theory stresses the acquisition of social skills through imitation and observation.
7. Cognitive theory emphasizes that play develops in a sequence that generally parallels the major stages of cognitive development.
8. Functional play involves simple, repeated movements or manipulation of the body or inanimate objects; in constructive play, a child manipulates objects in order to build or construct something.
9. Dramatic, or make-believe, play allows the child to practice motor skills and rehearse social roles, and play involving games with rules focuses more on the rules themselves.
10. Parten has identified six social levels of play: unoccupied, solitary, onlooker, parallel, associative, and cooperative play.
11. Unoccupied and solitary play are fairly unsocial. Onlooker and parallel play indicate increasing social awareness but minimal social interaction.
12. Associative play involves mutual interaction in a common activity, and in cooperative play children develop common goals.
13. The type of setting and the presence of siblings and other playmates facilitate the development of social play.
14. Although the preferred forms of social play change with age, all forms are observable throughout life.

Relationships with Others

15. Authoritarian parents exhibit a high degree of control and demands for maturity but low clarity of communication and a low degree of nurturance. Their children tend to be more distrustful, to be less happy with themselves, and to show lower school achievement than other children.
16. Permissive parents communicate clearly and are nurturant, but they exert little control and make few maturity demands. Their children tend to lack self-reliance and self-control.
17. Authoritative parents show high levels of control, strong demands for maturity, clarity of communication, and nurturance. Their children are likely to be better adjusted than children reared by authoritarian or permissive parents, showing greater self-reliance, self-control, and achievement.
18. Parents often use mixtures of more than one parenting style and may change in their preferred style as their children grow older.
19. Both siblings and friends also contribute to social development during the preschool years; ultimately, however, it is the parents' responsibility to establish the sort of parent-child interactions that foster positive social relationships.
20. Whereas early friendships are unstable and depend on specific shared activities, friendships among older preschoolers involve expectations about future behavior and popularity considerations.
21. Preschoolers' friendships become more durable and involve a greater degree of shared activity with age. As they near school age, the more permanent and personal qualities of a friend become increasingly important.
22. As children grow older, the support and judgments of parents and other adults contribute more and more to their feelings of empathy and prosocial activities.
23. Preschoolers commonly exhibit both hostile aggression and instrumental (nonhostile) aggression to assert their needs and resolve conflicts. As they grow older, verbal methods replace physical ones and overall aggression declines.
24. Biological differences, gender, family child-rearing tactics, peers, and the media influence the form and frequency of aggressive behavior.
25. Children who cannot control their aggression can be helped to do so using such methods as assertiveness training and social learning theory strategies. Parents can learn to spot the triggers of their children's aggression and respond effectively and confidently.

Gender Development

26. During early childhood, an understanding of gender-typed behaviors and of gender identity are acquired. A sense of gender constancy — the belief that being male or female is permanent — typically is not achieved until age eight or nine.

27. Because the development of stereotypes about personal qualities appears to depend on the ability to think abstractly, children do not gain a clear and stable concept of gender until the school years.

28. Influences on gender development include differential expectations and treatment of boys and girls by parents, peers, and the media.

29. A more flexible approach to sex roles enables children to adopt more androgynous behaviors and attitudes.

KEY TERMS

initiative versus guilt *(343)*	empathy *(362)*
egocentric escape *(343)*	aggression *(365)*
dramatization *(343)*	assertiveness *(365)*
malevolent transformation *(343)*	instrumental aggression *(366)*
repetition compulsion *(346)*	hostile aggression *(366)*
catharsis *(346)*	blocking behavior *(366)*
functional play *(347)*	dominance hierarchy *(369)*
constructive play *(348)*	disinhibit *(369)*
dramatic, or make-believe, play *(348)*	gender *(370)*
games with rules *(350)*	gender constancy *(371)*
prosocial behavior *(353)*	gender identity *(371)*
authoritarian *(354)*	gender preference *(371)*
permissive *(354)*	androgyny *(374)*
permissive-indulgent *(354)*	
permissive-indifferent *(355)*	
authoritative *(355)*	

WHAT DO YOU THINK?

1. Why is play so important to preschool children? If someone criticized a four-year-old for "just playing," what might you tell the critic?

2. In what ways is play during the preschool years similar to play during the college years? In what ways is it different?

3. Which style of parental authority best describes what you experienced as a child? What changes did you notice as you grew older?

4. What pattern of parenting do you plan to provide for your children? Why?

5. How would you help your child to be sensitive and helpful to others and be able to deal with conflict and aggression?

6. How should the problem of sex-role stereotyping in young children be handled? Why is it difficult for many parents and teachers to do anything about it?

FOR FURTHER READING

Adcock, D., and Segal M. *Making Friends: Ways of Encouraging Social Development in Young Children.* Englewood Cliffs, NJ: Prentice-Hall, 1983.

The authors of this book describe the development of friendships among preschool children in preschool and day-care settings. They provide many examples, illustrations, and useful suggestions for parents, teachers, and other care-giving adults.

Anthony, E. J., and Cohler, B. J. (eds.). *The Invulnerable Child.* New York: Guilford Press, 1987.

This collection of research articles describes young children's resilience in the face of destructive conditions and experiences of childhood.

Bernstein, A. *The Flight of the Stork.* New York: Dell, 1980.

Based on interviews with a large number of children aged three to twelve, this book describes and analyzes the development of children's knowledge about sex.

Dunn, J. *Sisters and Brothers.* Cambridge, MA: Harvard University Press, 1985.

Based largely on careful observations of families with two or more children, this book comprehensively explores the importance of siblings in the preschool and early school years. It does so in an interesting and easy-to-read style and includes many vivid descriptions of what actually happens between brothers and sisters.

Erikson, E. *Childhood and Society.* New York: W. W. Norton, 1950.

Of particular interest are Erikson's cross-cultural observations of childhood among the Sioux Indians, who were hunters, and among the Yuroks, who were fishers. Also interesting are his discussion of play and his presentation of the psychosocial theory of development.

Gordon, T. *P.E.T.: Parent Effectiveness Training.* New York: NAL Penguin, 1975.

This easy-to-read discussion of the P.E.T. theory and techniques uses many everyday life examples.

Parke, R. *Fathers.* Cambridge, MA: Harvard University Press, 1981.

This book offers interesting and informative coverage of father-child relationships and the special role of the father in child development.

PART FIVE

The Middle Years

Because growth slows after the preschool years, children in the middle years have more time and energy to develop skills of all sorts — from riding a skateboard to making friends. And all their years of language practice and symbolic play finally pay off: School-age children can often think rather logically, even if only about concrete matters. Partly because of these new competencies, and partly because of school life, peers take on more importance than ever before.

Maybe because children are now old enough to be aware of these changes, they often later remember the middle years as the best ones of their childhood. For most children, the world seems secure, their health is excellent, and their abilities improve visibly and steadily year by year.

Laura's Case

In many ways, the years from six to twelve were among the best of Laura's childhood. During this period, she developed many new skills and interests, and she felt mostly happy and secure at school. Laura came from a close-knit family. In addition to her older sister and her parents, there were many aunts and uncles and cousins. She was especially close to her father's parents and spoke to her grandparents practically every day. When she was six, her grandfather would tease her about how she was growing new teeth just when he was losing his.

At seven, Laura loved playing board games, especially checkers. She liked playing with her father, but only when he did not let her win. Laura sometimes got so annoyed when he played "easy" that she refused to finish a game. Finally he agreed to play "hard" against her and from then on always did — or so it seemed to Laura.

In third grade, Laura's best friend was Janet. They spent much time together, watching TV, coloring pictures, and talking about things such as the foods they liked or what their older sisters had done to them.

Her teachers often commented on her energy: she tried hard at anything active and enjoyed physical education a lot.

When she was ten, Laura's grandfather died unexpectedly. Laura was very affected by the event because she had always really enjoyed her times with her grandfather. She noticed, though, that her parents and grandmother seemed even sadder than she, and it upset her to see them cry. Privately, she wondered what she would feel if her own parents died — and who would take care of her then.

Student Progress Report

Name Laura Dunleavy   Grade: 1 2 3 4 ⑤ 6

Student's Teacher Mrs. Eleanor Leitner

ATTENDANCE DATA:
QUARTER AND NO. OF DAYS: 1 (43) 2 (40) 3 (38) 4 (50)   Total ( )

Absences	2	3	3	3
Late	5	3	0	2

ENGLISH LANGUAGE ARTS

Qrtr.	1st	2nd	3rd	4th	Final
Grade	A-	A	A-	A-	A-

Comment Good progress in composition skills. Laura often brings humor and originality to her treatment of topics. Work in spelling, grammar and vocabulary has been variable, but good overall. Very good work in literature. Very good L.A. skills.

MATHEMATICS

Qrtr.	1st	2nd	3rd	4th	Final
Grade	A-	B⁵/₈	B	B+	B+

Comment Tests and quizzes - very good. Daily assignments range 60's-80's. Strong problem solving skills.

SCIENCE

Qrtr.	1st	2nd	3rd	4th	Final
Grade	B	B	C	B+	B

Comment Laura continues to hold back during class discussions. She is usually prepared with homework and does well on tests.

SOCIAL STUDIES

Qrtr.	1st	2nd	3rd	4th	Final
Grade	A	B+	B-	A	A-

Comment Laura has done nicely on tests and her report. Her quizzes were very good, but she had several homework assignments missing.

PARENT'S SIGNATURE _____
PARENT'S COMMENTS: _____
Please return this form immediately except after final quarter.

In the weeks after her grandfather's death, Laura had trouble concentrating on her school work and her grades began to slip. Her parents and teacher were concerned, but they agreed that perhaps Laura just needed more time. Indeed, by the end of the year, she was doing just as well in school as she ever had done.

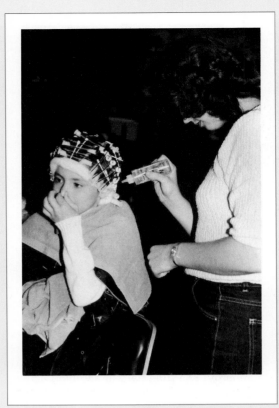

When Laura was eleven, she got a permanent — thanks to her big sister, Laura's perennial consultant in matters of style. Kathleen had begged her parents for months to let Laura get one, arguing that she was grown up enough to deserve it and that other girls Laura's age had permanents already.

At about that time, too, Laura's parents had a new baby. Laura started feeling ignored for a while, just as she had during the period after her grandfather's death. But she enjoyed the baby after it came home from the hospital. Sometimes she wished her grandfather could have seen it; she knew he would have enjoyed the baby a lot.

Gradually things began to stabilize around the house again. With a new baby around, Laura found herself helping her mother and father more than ever. Since her mother cut back on her working hours to care for the baby, Laura had more chances to talk with her; so instead of feeling ignored, as she had at first, she began feeling closer to her mother than ever before.

When Laura was twelve, it seemed as though she was always involved in some project. She helped her father paint the front steps — for a fee. She was planning to travel to Canada, she said, and suddenly became serious about saving up money.

By the summer between elementary school and junior high school, Laura and her baby brother, Jimmy, had become good friends. Her parents frequently recruited her as a baby sitter for Jimmy, and sometimes Jimmy even preferred being with Laura to being with his parents. Besides, baby sitting for Jimmy contributed to the travel fund to Canada.

Seven months after turning twelve, Laura started junior high school. Instead of being among the oldest at her school, now she was one of the youngest. To Laura, a lot of her schoolmates — especially in the older grades — seemed really grown up, and she wondered if she would ever look so adult! For now, Laura kept close to her friends from elementary school, but she looked forward to getting to know some of the other people in her classes. Overall, Laura was happy to be in a new school.

CHAPTER 11

The Middle Years: Physical Development

Focusing Questions

- What trends in height and weight occur among school-age children?
- How do differences in growth affect children's feelings about one another and about themselves?
- What improvements in motor skills do children usually experience during the school years, and how do these affect children's involvement in athletic activity?
- What kinds of illnesses, accidents, and physical conditions tend to occur among schoolchildren? How are they affected by their family and community circumstances?
- What is the relationship between physical growth and psychological development during this period?

Carmen and Mercedes were sisters. When Carmen was four and Mercedes was eight, they found an old pair of roller skates in a trash can behind their apartment building. The skates were too little for Mercedes, so Carmen got to keep them. Carmen could not believe her good fortune; their mother had always said they could not afford "extras," like skates.

But Carmen's pride was short-lived. To Carmen's dismay, their mother bought Mercedes a brand new pair of skates. "It's more practical," their mother tried to explain to Carmen, "because Mercedes won't grow out of them as fast as you will. And anyway she'll work at them, use them a lot." Carmen thought that *she* would use skates a lot, too. But time proved that her mother was right: Carmen used her skates only occasionally, but Mercedes was outside on hers almost every day. One time she even took lessons for a week when the city offered them as part of its summer recreation program. In these ways Mercedes eventually acquired quite a talent for roller-skating.

In general, as Mercedes' mother observed, children's physical growth slows down during the middle years (ages six to twelve) even more than it does during early childhood. And as with Jenny's skating talents, the results of growth begin to show more than ever before. Specific physical skills are easier to teach than they were because children now find them easier to learn. For a school-age child, instruction and practice in baseball make a more obvious difference to skill than they did when he was still a preschooler. This means that the child can now acquire physical and athletic skills that may give him a lifetime of satisfaction. But children *can* get hurt during physical activity, and athletic games can emphasize competition that is unrealistic or unpleasant.

Children are relatively healthy during the school years, but they do sometimes have accidents or get sick. A few children also develop problems that have ambiguous physical causes, and such children may show excessive motor activity even in quiet situations or difficulties in learning specific academic skills. Such problems may originate from subtle differences in how the nervous system operates in these children, although this is far from certain.

This chapter reviews these ideas in more detail. We begin by looking at normal trends and variations in overall growth during the middle years. Then we look at specific motor-skill and athletic development as well as the psychological effects of these on children. The chapter ends with a discussion of health in the school years, with special reference to children who are overly active and children who experience specific learning problems.

TRENDS AND VARIATIONS IN HEIGHT AND WEIGHT

Typical six-year-olds are about forty-six inches tall, but individual children vary two or three inches in each direction from this figure (Tanner, 1978a). This means that two first-graders can differ by as much as five or six inches and still be physically normal. During the next several years, children usually grow a bit more than two inches per year, so that by age ten, they are typically about fifty-four inches tall, and by age twelve, they are more like fifty-nine or sixty inches tall (see Figure 11.1).

During later childhood, variation around these averages becomes even more extreme than before. A small number of twelve-year-old girls may be sixty-six inches tall, for example — essentially adult in stature. And a small number of boys of this age may measure only about fifty-four inches, a full foot shorter. **Variations in height** Such extremes result partly from the growth spurt that most children experience at the beginning of adolescence. Because girls tend to undergo this spurt a year or two earlier than boys, they are especially likely to pull ahead of boys in size near the end of elementary school or at the beginning of junior high.

Similar patterns occur for weight. Six-year-olds average about forty-five pounds but may weigh as little as thirty-five or as much as fifty-five pounds (Tanner, 1978a). By age ten, children average about sixty-six pounds; by twelve, **Variations in weight** they are more than eighty pounds. As with height, variations in weight increase along with the averages. A perfectly normal twelve-year-old may weigh more than one hundred pounds or as little as seventy. Among the heavier children of this age — and especially among girls — are some who have achieved the weight of young adults.

But these trends and variations do not express the experience of growth as individual children know it over time. Any one child is blessed (or perhaps cursed) not only with particular dimensions at any one moment but also with unique patterns of growth rate during the months and years.

FIGURE 11.1
Growth in Height and Weight from Two to Eighteen Years

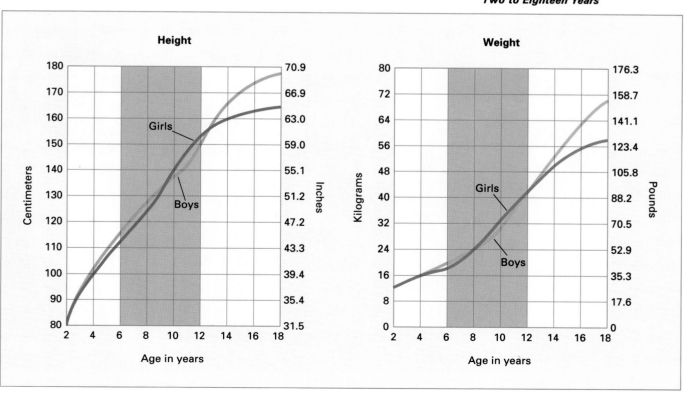

PROBLEMS RELATED TO GROWTH AND BODY BUILD

Stereotypes about body build

Growth gives children the potential to participate in many new activities. But it can also create problems for them, and the problems typically have both physical aspects and psychological ones (Tobin-Richards et al., 1984). Stereotypes about size and shape exist among school-age children as well as among adults. Wearing glasses may typecast some children as eggheads, and big ears may typecast others as clowns. The most important physical stereotypes, however, concern overall size and weight. Very small children may seem younger than they really are, and as a result their teachers and friends may treat them with less respect than they deserve. An overweight child may be regarded as unattractive, so friends and teachers may not respond as warmly to her as they otherwise would. Such reactions may happen unconsciously. And even though physical appearance may really stem largely from biological influences, children with the "wrong" looks may blame themselves.

Bridges How do variations in height and weight affect children's self-images during the middle years?

Height Variations Because of Puberty

As we have noted, toward the end of the elementary school years, girls tend to become significantly taller than boys of the same age. The difference results partly from girls' earlier puberty and partly from the timing of the growth spurt associated with puberty for each sex. For boys, a spurt in height tends to follow the other physical changes of adolescence, such as the growth of pubic hair and the deepening of the voice. For girls, a spurt in height usually happens before the growth of breasts and pubic hair.

Late in childhood, girls often grow taller and faster than boys of the same age. This disparity can create awkward moments for members of both sexes.

Inevitably, these changes create temporary embarrassments for at least some girls and boys. Late in childhood, most children become aware of social expec-

BRIDGES

		Family How can families help middle-years children who are seriously overweight? (390)		
Physical Development What are the physical effects of early athletics on middle-years children? (395)			**Peers** How does hyperactivity affect a child's peer relationships? (405)	
Genetics Is there a genetic predisposition toward hyperactivity? (406)				**Social Context** How does cultural context affect children's beliefs about the nature of illness? (402–403)

THE MIDDLE YEARS: PHYSICAL DEVELOPMENT

| What are the likely emotional effects on children of the death of a parent? (399)
Emotions | How do variations in height and weight affect children's self-images during the middle years? (388–389)
Self-concept and Identity | In what ways can overactive children learn how to concentrate better and respond more calmly? (407)
Learning | Is there a physical basis to the learning disabilities in processing language that some children experience? (433–434)
Language | How does cognitive development affect the ability of middle-years children to play team sports? (394)
Cognition |

tations or stereotypes about attractiveness, such as the idea that men "should" be taller than women. But this awareness dawns precisely when many boys and girls embody the opposite pattern. This discrepancy is undoubtedly felt more acutely by some individuals than by others; presumably it feels worse for children who seek the attentions of the opposite sex most strongly yet find that they are the "wrong" height. The exact amount by which a child violates height standards may matter little, except at the extremes. Very tall girls and very short boys probably have the most trouble forgetting about their unusual heights.

Emotional effects of height variations

On logical grounds, then, boys who mature early and girls who mature later should have the easiest time socially regarding their body builds and heights. Nevertheless, research suggests that this idea is only partly true (Livson & Peskin, 1981a, 1981b; Brooks-Gunn & Warren, 1989). The timing of puberty may have unique effects for each sex; "looks" matter more for girls than for boys. And the onset of adolescence has different effects in the short run from those in the long run.

Excess Weight and Obesity

At least one American child in ten suffers from **obesity,** meaning that he weighs more than 130 percent of the normal weight for his height and bone size (Walker & Shaw, 1988). This means that instead of weighing about sixty-five pounds when he is fifty-four inches tall, for example, he weighs more than eighty-five pounds. How does such a child feel about his size? In most cases, probably not very good. If he accepts social stereotypes about weight, he must regard himself as unattractive; but if he rejects those standards, he may find himself in subtle but chronic disagreement with his peers about what makes people good looking — not to mention disagreement about his own looks. No matter what attitude he adopts, obesity causes psychological problems (Winick, 1975).

Psychological impact of obesity

In the long run, it causes physical problems as well. Children who continue to be obese into adulthood run more risk of a variety of minor illnesses as well as of a few major ones such as heart attacks and diabetes (LeBow, 1986). Partly

Perspectives

Treating Obesity Successfully

A number of factors cause children to become seriously overweight or obese (that is, at least 30 percent over normal weight). Children and parents can control some of these but not others. Two factors beyond human control are *heredity* and *age*. Like it or not, thinness and fatness do run in families. Overweight children tend to have overweight parents, and underweight children tend to have underweight parents (LeBow, 1984). And most people inevitably put on fat more during some periods of life than others. Late childhood and early puberty form one of these periods; at this time, most children gain fat tissue out of proportion to increases in other tissues, such as muscle and bone. The change is especially noticeable in girls, who often look more shapely or sexually attractive as a result. Too much additional fat at this time, however, can create a definite weight problem for some children, male or female.

But not all influences on weight are beyond control. At least three depend on people's activities and choices and can therefore be the focus of effective efforts to lose weight (D. White, 1986):

1. *Amount and type of foods eaten* Children often get started toward obesity by eating foods that are overly rich in energy value. The chief culprits are foods full of sugar (cakes and pastries) and fat-filled foods (deep-fried chicken and potato chips). Although in theory a child can burn off these foods with enough exercise, in practice very few children (or adults) lead lives that are active enough to do so.

2. *Amount and type of exercise* If a child is relatively inactive, any excess energy provided by her daily food is gradually converted into fat. Relatively high levels of sustained activity raise the rate at which the body processes food and therefore prevent fat from forming. Exercise has this effect, however, only if it emphasizes the development of endurance rather than of strength. Walking a mile every day, for example, helps more than lifting weights, unless the weight-lifting sessions are organized to focus on persistence or endurance.

3. *Attitudes and habits about eating* Most of us attach important meanings to certain foods and eating times. A particular family may prefer children who are hearty eaters, which may unconsciously make children with small appetites feel antisocial. Another family may have an informal custom of serving a rich snack such as ice cream late in the evening, and turning the snack down may seem both unnecessary and unfriendly.

*By focusing on these three factors, children *can* control excess weight if they get proper support from family and friends (Pringle & Ramsey, 1982) as well as from a doctor or trained nutritionist. Such support can be given by following four steps. First, make sure that the child really needs to lose weight. Weighing only a little more than average poses no medical risk and may cause few social problems in the long run. Children certainly dislike being teased about their appearance, but if a child really has relatively small amounts of fat, the teasing may be caused by problems with social stereotypes and peer relations, and losing weight may prove to be a rather inefficient way of avoiding it.

Second, if the child does have a serious weight problem, start her on a diet under the care of a doctor or trained nutritionist. For most children, a diet should simply aim at stabilizing weight or at most at causing a loss of only about one pound a week. At all costs, avoid crash diets or other faddish "miracle" diets: these can jeopardize the child's health and almost never result in permanent weight loss. A truly effective diet for children should include *more* than three meals a day and should draw on all major groups of food. "Snacks" should count as small meals and should therefore consist of healthful, low-calorie ingredients.

Third, develop a program of exercise appropriate for the child. Doing so can sometimes prove challenging at first because overweight children tend to be less active than others. But with some thought and persistence, it can be done. A sustained exercise program should always begin slowly, so as to avoid overtaxing undeveloped muscles and help ensure feelings of success. In general, too, overweight children should avoid activities that inherently handicap them (such as jogging) or call attention to their appearance (such as ballet dancing). Wherever possible, they should try to incorporate more activity into their daily lives by walking to and from school, for example. A few activities, such as swimming, actually give overweight children a physical advantage because their extra fat tissue helps them stay afloat.

Fourth, seek support from the child's whole family as well as from teachers and other adults who may work with the child regularly. It helps to have these people express respect for the child's efforts — even if their own diets and exercise are not perfect! Because there are no shortcuts to controlling weight, a child is bound to get discouraged at times about keeping to a diet or exercise program. At these times, encouragement from others can make the difference between success and failure. For most children (and adults), controlling weight permanently usually depends on thousands of everyday decisions about eating and physical activity. The decisions may seem minor in the short run, but in the long run they add up to a major, and crucial, change in life-style.

*Bridges How can families help middle-years children who are seriously overweight?

Being overweight can interfere significantly with a child's social relationships. Sometimes overweight children are teased, both openly and behind their backs; and over time this may affect their own opinions of themselves.

as a result, they also tend to live shorter lives. Overweight people tend to be significantly less active than people of normal weight, even by the standards of our relatively sedentary society, and their lack of exercise can further aggravate their weight problem and the risks connected with it. For all these reasons, children who are obese deserve help, even if their problem cannot be cured easily.

Unfortunately, as anyone who has tried it knows, losing weight permanently is difficult to do. It is even more difficult for children than for adults, for both physical and psychological reasons. Unlike people who become overweight as adults, children may sometimes gain weight by growing more fat cells; and once these cells have formed, they prove very difficult to lose or destroy (Cahill & Rossini, 1978). With dieting and exercise, they can become smaller but not less numerous. Any return to overeating therefore creates pounds relatively easily: the ready-made fat cells simply fill up again. In contrast, adults who begin gaining weight later in life do not grow new fat cells but expand the volume or size of existing ones. Compared to childhood obesity, therefore, "middle-aged spread" is a relatively correctable problem — although still far from an easy one to cope with.

Obstacles to weight control

Losing weight can be difficult for a child for other reasons as well. Any dieting or exercise scheme must have the full support of the child's parents and siblings, because they usually have a substantial influence on meal preparations and on the child's daily life-style. Yet family members may find that support is difficult to sustain for the long periods of time that most weight-control programs require. The collective will power may just not be there, especially because overweight children tend to have siblings and parents who are overweight themselves.

In spite of such occasional weight problems, growth for most children is slow and predictable enough that they can afford to ignore it a lot of the time. For large parts of the middle years, children can therefore shift their attention away from how their bodies are and toward what their bodies can do. The development of new motor skills becomes possible during middle childhood in part because of this shift in focus.

MOTOR DEVELOPMENT IN THE MIDDLE YEARS

Fundamental motor skills continue to improve during the school years and gradually become specialized in response to each child's particular interests, physical aptitudes, life experiences, and the expectations of others. Unlike a preschooler, an older child no longer feels content simply to run, jump, and throw things; now he puts these skills to use in complex, active play. Sometimes this consists of informal, child-organized games such as hide-and-seek in which the child uses motor skills. At other times, as described below, active play involves formal sports such as gymnastics, swimming, or hockey.

Refinements of Fundamental Skills

Smaller improvements for strength and size

School-age children continue to refine fundamental motor skills, such as running, walking, and throwing. Their biggest improvements occur when engaging in activities — such as this three-legged race — that require coordination and timing at about the same rate and to the same degree.

During the elementary school years, all basic motor skills improve, but how much each does so depends on whether it relies primarily on strength and size or on coordination and timing. Skills relying on strength and size improve more or less in proportion to overall bodily growth: around 25 to 35 percent over the middle years as a whole. Running and jumping illustrate this difference clearly. As six-year-olds, children on the average can run faster than twelve feet per second, or about thirty-two yards in about eight seconds. By age ten, they can often run faster than fifteen feet per second, or about thirty yards in about five and one-half seconds (Roche & Malina, 1983). Likewise for jumping: as six-

A Talk with John

Growing Older

John was interviewed after school in his bedroom, which contained three fish tanks, plants, a cat, and a number of models and other construction projects that he had worked on.

Interviewer: John, how old are you now?

John: I was eleven in August.

Interviewer: What is it like to be eleven? Have you noticed yourself getting bigger?

John: I don't know. You do grow more.

Interviewer: How do you know?

John: I just have. My parents tell me, too. They say I've grown a lot.

Interviewer: Can you notice some things about your body compared with the way you were at nine or ten?

John: I don't know. I can reach things better. And I can run better, faster, and for a longer time if I go for a jog with my mom and dad.

Interviewer: What other things can you do better?

John: It's easier to play my guitar with bigger hands. It used to be harder to reach my fingers around the neck to make chords and now it's getting easier. It's still not that easy, though.

Interviewer: What about sports?

John: I like to play baseball, soccer, and basketball. Getting bigger and stronger helps there. You can hit the ball farther and throw better. In soccer being able to run and kick hard are important, and I can play much better than I did a couple of years ago. Of course, I also have more experience at playing.

Interviewer: What other things can you do that you couldn't do a couple of years ago?

John: I'm a better bike rider than I used to be. It's easier for me to ride. My legs are longer, and my seat is as high as it can go. Some of my clothing is also too small for me.

Interviewer: How is your size compared with other kids your age?

John: I think about the same size. Some kids are smaller and some are bigger . . . taller and heavier.

Interviewer: What does an eleven-year-old do to stay healthy and strong?

John: They don't want to get too fat.

Interviewer: Do you think about that?

John: Yes.

Interviewer: What would make you too fat?

John: Not getting any exercise and maybe eating too much candy and things like that. I don't think that will happen to me, but some kids are overweight and that's not healthy.

Interviewer: What other changes have you noticed in yourself?

John: My parents used to have to tell me to clean up my room, but I just keep it clean now. And I do my work and my parents don't have to tell me to do it.

Interviewer: Do you think differently about your work now? Does it feel different?

John: I still don't like it — I never have and I probably never will. I just do it before my parents tell me and then I'm done. And that way I don't get nagged.

Interviewer: Do people treat you differently now that you're older?

John: Yes. They treat me more like an adult than a little kid. Instead of just telling me to do something, now they sometimes talk about it. They discuss it with me. I also have more responsibilities. I have to take care of my sister when I get home from school and sometimes till five o'clock when my parents get home.

Interviewer: Any other changes?

John: I can go to my friend's house by myself. And I can stay home alone. And I can have my own room, too.

Follow-up Questions

1. What physical changes seem most important to John?

2. What effects have athletics had on John's development?

3. In what ways has John's physical development affected his psychosocial development?

---

year-olds, children can broad jump about three feet; by age ten, they can jump more than four and one-half feet. By age twelve, a child typically can do even better at both of these tasks. How much better depends, however, partly on when puberty begins for that particular child. An early growth spurt can create long legs and stronger muscles and therefore allow relatively large improvements in performance by the end of the elementary school years.

Much more dramatic improvements — 100 percent or more — happen with skills that depend mostly on coordination and timing. Basic ball skills (throwing and catching) show this pattern. A typical child can throw a ball only about fifteen feet at age six, but she can throw the same ball more than thirty feet at age ten or twelve. Similarly, most six-year-olds can catch an eight-inch rubber

Larger improvements for coordination and timing

Walking on a balance beam does not take special strength as much as coordination and agility. Improvements in this kind of skill are especially dramatic during the middle years.

ball most of the time if it is bounced to them from a distance of fifteen feet; many ten- or twelve-year-olds can catch a ball from two or three times this distance and sometimes even if it is not bounced (Cratty, 1986).

Such changes probably do not reflect increases in power or size so much as better use of existing muscles and better timing of reflexes. Although this idea may seem obvious for catching a ball, it also holds true for throwing. A preschool child barely senses at what instant or at which angle to release a ball during the act of throwing, and this fact often spoils his distance and accuracy. As he overcomes these timing problems, his throwing improves, even though he does not develop new muscles or longer bones.

Individual differences in motor development

As with other physical developments, children vary widely around these averages. Schoolteachers see this variation especially clearly whenever they plan group athletic activities. A baseball team from a class of eight-year-olds may contain children who can catch a baseball well and children who fail about one-half the time. It may also contain children who take twice as long to run the bases as some of their teammates do. And batting shows extreme differences. When good batters come up to bat, the outfielders become noticeably more alert and move twenty feet back. When a bad batter comes up, outfielders may come close in to home plate or even sit down and daydream. Obviously, such differences can prove embarrassing to less skilled players and are a challenge to teachers who are trying to foster every child's best development.

Influences of Early Athletics

Bridges How does cognitive development affect the ability of middle-years children to play team sports?

As we have noted, children in the school years develop the ability to play games with rules. Some of these are informal, as in afterschool hopscotch, and some are formal and adult-sponsored, as in Little League softball. In any case, traditional team sports now begin to have meaning for children because they can understand and abide by a game's rules. At the same time, children's improvements in coordination and timing make performance better in all kinds of sports, whether individual or group. Swimming, for instance, reveals the benefits of increasing coordination: some preschoolers can swim quite well, but usually only school-age children achieve adultlike coordination, speed, and grace in their strokes and breathing. The same can be said for other informal, individual activities, such as riding bicycles, roller-skating, and jumping rope.

What lasting physical and psychological effects do early athletics have on children? This question has not been studied as carefully for children as for adolescents and adults, but even so, a few tentative answers are possible. On balance, athletic activity probably helps children much more than it hurts them. But it does carry a few significant risks.

Physical Effects of Early Athletics   The most obvious risks are sports-related injuries: bruises of various kinds and severity, damage to muscles (sprains), and broken or dislocated bones (DiStefano, 1982). Do such injuries actually constitute a problem for child development? Pessimists point out that injuries happen to a substantial number of athletes, even in childhood. For example:

Bridges   What are the physical effects of early athletics on middle-years children?

Physical risks of sports

1. Child baseball pitchers (age eight and older) universally develop enlarged bones in their pitching arm (Bailey et al., 1978) and frequently develop pain in their pitching shoulder as well.
2. About two-thirds of child gymnasts report chronic stiffness in their lower back, and about 20 to 30 percent report recurrent back pain (Cratty, 1979).
3. Virtually all children who play football become injured sooner or later, even when they play touch football rather than the tackle version of the game (Cratty, 1979).

Such injuries usually receive medical attention, but the attention is almost always short term; once bones or muscles seem cured, they are promptly ignored, and the athlete is sent back to play. Given the special stresses of athletic activity, this relatively short-run approach may allow minor disabilities to develop. Children who play a lot of football throughout childhood, for example, may have vulnerable knees before they even begin more serious, competitive football playing in adolescence.

Optimists point out that most children who are injured during sports have relatively minor injuries and that the benefits of participation therefore considerably outweigh the risks. They cite the physical benefits of athletics. Children involved in regular athletics may be more in shape physically than other children; this means that their hearts and large muscles may function more efficiently (Bailey, 1982). As a result, they may feel more able to undertake ordinary daily activities with less effort. They also develop coordination and strength earlier.

Physical benefits of sports

Psychological Effects of Early Athletics   The immense popularity of early athletics probably stems at least in part from the psychological benefits attributed to participation; sports, it is hoped, develop achievement motivation, teamwork, and a tolerance for or even enjoyment of competition. How well do early athletics in fact realize these goals?

1. *Training in achievement motivation*   Most sports provide standards against which children can assess their performances. Goals can be scored, distances can be measured, and times can be clocked. Children's performances can then be compared with their own previous scores, with those of their peers, or with those of top-scoring individuals or teams.

Whether this information really encourages higher athletic achievement depends on how a child uses it. A young child—say, five or six years old — tends

In addition to their obvious physical benefits, early athletics can also encourage achievement motivation, discipline, and a sense of self-esteem. Critics worry, though, that some sport activities may also cause injuries and destructive competition.

Influences on motivation

to process the facts of her sports history poorly. She often ignores the significance of her wins and losses and of her long-term improvements and declines (J. Thomas et al., 1982). She therefore approaches each performance in much the same way. She may find each swim meet enjoyable in its own right, but she will not think much about bettering her previous performance or about correcting previous mistakes.

During the school years, however, comparing oneself to standards becomes a prominent concern (R. Smith & Smoll, 1982). Often this concern can motivate some children to better performance. But it can also undermine motivation if a child begins feeling that the standards are arbitrary, externally imposed, or too difficult to meet.

2. *Teamwork and competition* Many sports promote teamwork—meaning cooperation with a selected group of individuals. This goal is certainly a positive one, but research on children's teams suggests a problem: children practice teamwork better if their team tends to win than if it tends to lose. In other words, cooperation within a team is sometimes purchased at a cost to the losers.

Psychological effects of competition

What happens to the losers? Among schoolchildren, even the most gracious loser shows noticeable stress because of losing (Passer, 1982). Losers become less sociable, refuse to talk about the game, and miss game practices more often than winners do. Teams of losers also show a marked tendency to search for blame by scapegoating individual members or individual events during a sporting season (Gelfand & Hartmann, 1982). If one "big play" seemingly lost a crucial game of basketball, the players may dwell upon that event more than it deserves, and they may stew about one or two players who seemed most responsible for that play. Such blame is made worse if coaches and parents emphasize winning a lot; but all losing teams suffer from the problem to some extent. And team sports guarantee many losers.

For some children, the path away from being a loser consists of training harder to win. For substantial numbers of others, however, it consists of learning not to take sports too seriously — to treat them as "just a game." This often requires a child to adopt new interests or goals in life and perhaps a more sedentary life-style in the bargain. In surveys of athletic dropouts, most children and adolescents cite too much competition as their major reason for leaving organized sports, and about one-third to one-half do not pursue their sport even recreationally after they drop out (R. Grant, 1988).

Gender and Early Athletics   In North American society, girls seem especially likely to drop out of athletic activity late in their middle years. Apparently they do so for cultural reasons rather than physiological ones. Throughout childhood, they compare well to boys in strength, endurance, and motor skill, and late in childhood girls tend to be physically more mature than boys and presumably therefore potentially more rather than less athletic. But at about age twelve, they begin to test poorly: they run slower, jump less far, and lift less weight. Because physical training at this age can virtually eliminate these differences (Gill, 1986; Orlick, 1986), their poor performance must result from social expectations about gender. Instead of continuing to play ball as they reach puberty, some girls begin to emphasize nonathletic interests such as listening to rock music or playing a musical instrument. Some boys, of course, do the same. In the process, these children lose the benefits of physical activity. Fortunately, however, sex-role standards may be shifting, and as one indirect result, athletic activity has become more attractive for *both* sexes.

On the whole, girls and boys develop motor skills at about the same rate and to the same degree. Gender differences in participation seem to occur because of social expectations that boys should succeed in athletics.

HEALTH AND ILLNESS IN MIDDLE CHILDHOOD

In the middle years, children are usually rather healthy in the sense that they rarely experience serious illnesses or accidents with medical consequences. They also have colds and minor viral illnesses less often than preschool children and infants do. But illnesses and accidents still occur among this age group, which partly accounts for why medical professionals and parents sometimes disagree about whether or not schoolchildren are really healthy. From a doctor's perspective, schoolchildren do not need advanced medical services as much as most other age groups. From a parent's perspective, though, the illnesses that schoolchildren do get can still be very disruptive.

Death Rates Among Schoolchildren

One sign of good health of schoolchildren is their very low **mortality,** or the proportion who die at a given age. In recent years, only about three or four children in every ten thousand between the ages of six and thirteen die, compared to twice this number among preschoolers and four times this number among adolescents (U.S. Department of Commerce, 1988). The low rate for children is part of a long decline dating back several decades. In 1940, for example, more than ten school-age children out of every ten thousand died every year, and earlier in this century the figures were even higher (Preston, 1976).

The decline in mortality has changed the relative importance of different causes of death. Infectious diseases, such as pneumonia and chronic diarrhea, have become very infrequent among children from middle-income families in North America. As a result, accidents have become relatively more important as a cause of death among children. Almost one-half of all childhood deaths in recent years have occurred because of motor vehicle accidents (National Safety Council, 1987). A majority of these deaths were children who were *not* wearing seatbelts while riding with their parents or other relatives.

But school-age children do sometimes die from other kinds of accidents. For every two children who die in traffic accidents, a third dies from drowning and a fourth dies in a fire of some sort (see Table 11.1). But stating the figures in this way makes it sound as if accidents are evenly distributed throughout society, when in fact they are not. Some children face much more risk for certain accidents than others do, either because their environments contain more risks or because their parents and other adults responsible for them do not recognize the risks and therefore fail to teach the children proper safety precautions (Garling & Valsiner, 1985).

Accidents

For most school-age children, physical safety poses a serious health problem (Pringle & Ramsey, 1982). During these years, children begin playing in and exploring larger territories. They investigate the neighborhood around their home and school in particular, in spite of its unknown dangers. Because the improvised games (usually sports) children play at this age need more room than the play of preschoolers does, children in urban and some suburban areas often play in the street; they do their best to avoid traffic, but games such as baseball may require sudden sprints and allow no time to check for cars.

When not playing at formal and informal games, school-age children have a curiosity about the wider world that has increased since their preschool years.

As children get older, their everyday activities make them more likely to experience accidents — especially when their play takes them to unfamiliar and risky places.

Perspectives

What Children Know and Feel About Death

In modern society, death has become rare in childhood and common in old age. This seemingly natural state of affairs is actually quite unusual; throughout history and around the world, the majority of deaths have happened to infants and children. The modern reversal of this trend has had many benefits, of course, but it may also be leaving children unprepared to understand and cope with death when they do experience it at close hand. Instead of seeming natural, inevitable, and universal, death now seems to be a rare event, an unusual catastrophe happening to only a few people. In these circumstances, confusion about the nature and meaning of death may set in.

Studies confirm that children have only hazy understandings of death, even well into the middle years. Early in this period, around age six, they describe death with analogies that are often reversible (Wass & Corr, 1984): "Death is when you go to sleep," said one six-year-old. "It's like a flower wilting," said another. "Death is going on a trip," said a third. These analogies can be "undone": real sleep, for example, ends with waking up. In addition, many of the analogies refer not to universal events but to special ones; not everyone goes on trips. Perhaps for these reasons, young children do not seem to fear death as much as older children and adults do. They reveal concern and distress about the general idea of death, but unless they experience the death of a close relative (such as a parent) directly, their concerns tend to be comparatively limited (Swain, 1979).

Somewhere between the ages of eight and ten, most children realize that death is irreversible, permanent, and universal. "Dying is when you never, ever come back again," according to one child and "Your heart stops beating forever," said another. But they still focus on very concrete aspects of death and show relatively little understanding of its spiritual or psychological aspects (E. White et al., 1978). Many children of this age are easily persuaded that dead people can send and receive messages, as described in ghost stories. This fact may account for the increase in fear that children have about death later in childhood, when they sometimes ask their parents questions about death and occasionally have nightmares related to death and dying.

All of these developments happen more rapidly and vividly for children who do in fact lose a close relative, especially a parent, during early or middle childhood (Kane, 1977). These children face the same two challenges as adults who lose a close relative. First, they must *understand* the death as realistically as possible: it has indeed happened, cannot be ignored, and will never be undone. Unfortunately, younger children may have trouble understanding this reality because their general cognitive understanding is limited. Second, children must have chances to *mourn* the death or experience and work through the feelings that they still have about the person who died. For adults, mourning usually includes periodic rushes of sadness, pain, anguish, and guilt about how they treated the dead person (Kübler-Ross, 1983). Children may also experience these emotions. In the short run, however, the extent and mix of their feelings will depend on how emotionally attached they were to the deceased person and on their overall cognitive maturity. As one nine-year-old girl put it, "What bothered me most about my brother's death was that I did not seem to care about it as much as my parents did." The brother had died suddenly one year before, when he was five and she was eight. She did care about her brother and did mourn him. But she may not have understood the full importance of his death, either to her parents or to her own future development as a member of her family.

*In spite of limitations like this, most children react strongly to the death of the most important people in their lives, their parents. Research shows that the effects can be quite long-lasting. Even five or ten years after losing a parent, bereaved children tend to be more submissive and introverted and less aggressive than other children, including children who lose a parent through divorce (Berlinsky & Biller, 1982). The difference shows both in interviews of these children and in observations of their behavior with peers, and it happens to both sexes.

Losing a parent affects children most strongly, too, when they are younger. A parent's death tends to be harder for a six-year-old than for a ten-year-old, but it is even harder for a three-year-old. Age may matter partly because younger children experience the most confusion about the nature of their parent's death, so they tend more easily, and erroneously, to blame themselves for their parent's "leaving." At the same time, younger children probably need their parents more, both for affection and for practical care, so death deprives them more severely than it deprives older children. And the loss lasts longer for younger children; they have more years of growing to do before they can reach the relative independence of adulthood.

Poking around neighbors' backyards, they may find old equipment or machinery that looks too interesting *not* to investigate. Or they may find flammable or toxic substances, such as gasoline or paint thinner, that supposedly have been stored away safely. Construction sites are especially inviting: they contain old pieces of wood and partially completed nooks and crannies that make good hiding places. Unfortunately, these interesting spaces often lack structural strength; children can slip and fall in them, and pieces of steel or wood can land on their heads.

*Bridges What are the likely emotional effects on children of the death of a parent?

Increase in environmental dangers

TABLE 11.1   Selected Causes of Death in Childhood and Youth

Cause of Death	Frequency per 100,000 Children			
	Ages 5–14		Ages 15–24	
	Boys	Girls	Boys	Girls
All Causes	32	21	141	51
Accidents (all kinds)	17	8	76	22
Motor vehicle accidents	9	5	57	19
Drownings, fire, poisons	4	2	9	3
Other accidents	4	1	13	<1
Diseases (selected)				
Infections	<1	<1	1	1
Cancer (all kinds)	4	3	7	4
Heart diseases	1	1	3	2
Violence				
Homicides	1	1	18	6
Suicides	1	<1	21	4

Note: Compared to adolescents, schoolchildren are healthier, as reflected in lower mortalities. But even at this age, accidents are the chief cause of death, and boys begin a lifelong tendency to die more often than girls from accidents and violence.
Source: U.S. Department of Commerce (1988); and World Health Organization (1987).

Most of the time, accidents from such sources are relatively minor. But a significant number cause fractures, poisoning, or open wounds that require medical attention. Somewhere between 5 and 10 percent of all visits to doctors by schoolchildren, in fact, are for treatment of accidents such as these (Wright et al., 1988).

Illnesses

On the average, schoolchildren get sick only about one-half as often as preschoolers. From their parents' point of view, however, illnesses probably still seem rather frequent; nearly one-quarter of the parents in one survey reported that during the preceding two weeks their children had been "too sick to carry on as normal" (Roghmann & Pless, 1975), meaning that the children stayed home from school for at least one day. As parents often point out, a sick child has a substantial impact on the work and leisure schedules of the rest of the family, especially of parents.

Nature of acute illnesses

Acute Illness   Most common childhood diseases are **acute illnesses,** which means they have a definite beginning, middle, and end. Most childhood acute illnesses, such as colds, gastrointestinal flu, chicken pox, and measles, develop from **viruses,** which are complex protein molecules that come alive only when they infect a host tissue (such as a child's nose). In spite of popular belief, no drugs can combat viral infections. (This is not the case with bacteria that invade the body; they can be effectively fought off with antibiotic drugs.) Viral illnesses must instead run their course, and the child's natural immunities must work the real cure.

Perspectives

AIDS and Schoolchildren

Acquired immune deficiency syndrome (AIDS) is a viral illness that gradually destroys the body's ability to combat other diseases. In all officially recorded cases so far, the disease has proved fatal, although often not for several years. It increased dramatically in frequency during the 1980s. In 1987, more than ten thousand persons died of AIDS, and between 1 and 2 million are estimated to carry the virus — **human immunodeficiency virus (HIV)** — that eventually triggers the disease's actual symptoms (U.S. Department of Commerce, 1988).

So far only about 1 percent of the victims of AIDS have been schoolchildren, but worries about the disease have developed throughout society and have filtered into the elementary schools and homes of this age group. Without doubt, some fears come from prejudice against the populations in which AIDS first appeared in North America — namely, male homosexuals and heavy users of addictive drugs that are injected intravenously. (In some other parts of the world such as Africa, AIDS first appeared among heterosexuals.) Fears of catching the disease from casual contact at school have become widespread, even though medical evidence shows conclusively that AIDS is not spread in this way (Keough, 1988). Some parents have therefore demanded the immediate, complete removal from school of any child known to have contracted the disease.

These demands have raised difficult issues about civil rights and fairness in education. Should school leaders respect parents' wishes, even if the wishes are based on clearly mistaken notions about AIDS? Or should they keep a child with AIDS in school out of respect for the child's right to an education, even at the risk of alienating significant numbers of parents? In the short term, there are no easy answers to these questions.

But longer-term solutions may be possible. One of these is to offer education at school about sexuality in general and about AIDS in particular. Curricula about AIDS have already been written and published (Quackenbush & Sargent, 1986), and some school districts have begun using them. It is hoped that an AIDS curriculum can help to correct students' misinformation about the disease and therefore help them to avoid contracting AIDS and encourage them to respond sensibly when and if they learn of classmates with AIDS.

Another long-term solution lies with school staff, both teachers and administrators. Experience has shown that these individuals make a major difference in whether a community overreacts to news of a child with AIDS (DeArman, 1988). For teachers and principals, the key responses seem to be a calm attitude about such a child, accurate knowledge about AIDS, and active efforts to communicate its lack of contagiousness through casual contact. For high-level administrators, an additional key response lies with making policies related to AIDS before a crisis actually occurs rather than after (Helm, 1989). The most effective policies are constructed to apply to all infectious diseases, not solely to AIDS. These policies emphasize keeping children in regular classrooms wherever possible and attending to the differences among individual children and their specific ailments wherever possible.

Education in schools must be supplemented with education in society at large. The general education needs to make several points in particular:

1. AIDS is not a disease that is contracted only by homosexuals or IV drug users.
2. Quarantining or isolating people with AIDS (as used to be done with people suffering from leprosy or bubonic plague) is both unrealistic and ethically undesirable.
3. AIDS does not spread by casual contact, not even by sneezing in another person's face.
4. Uninfected persons can keep from getting AIDS by avoiding contact with others' blood for any purpose (sharing drugs, piercing ears, becoming "blood brothers"), by avoiding specific sexual practices, and by using latex condoms during all forms of sexual intercourse.

For such diseases, doctors usually prescribe simple bed rest. Sometimes they also prescribe medications, but these are not to cure the illness so much as to prevent complications. Many ear infections, for example, arise from viral infections, but doctors sometimes prescribe antibiotic drugs to prevent a more serious bacterial ear infection from developing.

Chronic Illness By the school years, about 5 to 10 percent of children develop **chronic illnesses,** or conditions that persist for many months without significant improvement. The most common chronic conditions occur in the lungs and affect breathing (Pless & Satterwhite, 1975). Some children develop **asthma,** or persistent congestion in their lungs; others develop chronic coughs or allergies. Still other chronic complaints concern specific sensory organs. About one child

Nature of lasting illnesses

A Multicultural View

Children's Conceptions of Illness in Different Cultures

Cultural patterns influence how children in different societies think of illness. Some societies (including our own) foster a *naturalistic* view of illness, meaning that children are led to think of illness as resulting from natural causes. Other societies tend to foster a *personalistic* view, meaning that children come to think of illness as caused by the intentions or attitudes of personal forces, either supernatural or human (Foster & Anderson, 1978).

*In a naturalistic system such as our own, children develop conceptions of illness through a series of cognitive steps of increasing complexity (Wilkinson, 1988). Young children (age four or five) tend to explain minor illness in terms of a single, obvious cause that is often related to outward symptoms. A cold is "coughing a lot"; being sick is "throwing up." As they get older, children take more causal factors into account, but the factors remain impersonal. For an eight-year-old, a cold is "coughing a lot, feeling tired, and having a stuffy nose at night," rather than just one of these at a time. Still later, by early adolescence, children may rely on simplified versions of human physiology to explain illness (Perrin & Gerrity, 1981). A twelve-year-old may describe a cold like this: "Little germs get into you from the air. They get into your blood, but after a while your blood kills them off again."

Even though these naturalistic explanations are not scientific, they have important effects on attitudes and beliefs about illness. For one thing, they encourage a belief that illness depends on having ever-more sophisticated, but impersonal knowledge about how illnesses function. For another thing, naturalistic explanations foster emotional independence among individuals. Other people can help you get well by providing medicines and physical comfort, but they do not "cause" the illness in the first place (Parmalee, 1986).

Compared to societies with naturalistic beliefs, those with personalistic beliefs about medicine encourage children to develop much different attitudes about the causes and cures for illness. Personalistic systems make no distinction between medical misfortunes and other misfortunes; the same persons, spirits, or gods cause *both* kinds and for largely similar (usually evil) motives (Ohnuki-Tierney, 1984). Children therefore learn to equate physical and psychological troubles. In rural China (a personalistic subculture), children can recognize the emotional dimension of many physical illnesses from an earlier age than is common in Western societies (Wang, 1983).

At the same time, personalistic beliefs about illness foster greater interdependence among family and community than is typical with naturalistic beliefs. In a personalistic system, the best person to cure illness is not a technical expert, as in naturalistic systems, but a social and spiritual expert: someone who understands the emotional dynamics not only among individuals but also between individuals and the various spirits or gods who might cause illness. These experts are called by various

*Bridges   How does cultural context affect children's beliefs about the nature of illness?

Effects of income level

in one hundred, for example, reports problems in hearing or seeing — or, technically speaking, parents report these problems to doctors.

Social Influences on Illness   The seriousness and frequency of illnesses vary a lot according to children's social and economic circumstances. Consider income differences among families. In general, parents from higher income families report that their school-age children get sick just about as often as parents from lower income families do. But the higher income parents also report keeping their children at home for *shorter* periods of time. In the highest 25 percent of families, children stay at home for an average of only one and one-half days per illness, whereas in the lowest 25 percent, they stay at home for nearly five days per illness (Roghmann & Pless, 1975).

What accounts for this difference? Low-income families probably lack money for doctors' visits and time for tending to sick children. To merit staying home from school, therefore, or to merit visiting a doctor, a child must have a relatively major illness, such as a seriously high fever or severe diarrhea. The result of these circumstances shows in the longer average stay at home when illness finally receives special attention.

Race and gender matter, too. Black families report fewer illnesses per child than do white families of similar income. And all families, black or white, report more illnesses for girls than for boys of the same age (Butler et al., 1984).

names, such as *shaman* or *witchdoctor*, depending on the society; put in Western terms, their role is a mixture of psychiatrist, religious leader, and expert in physical medicine.

In personalistic cultures, therefore, children come to regard illness as a social process as much as a physical or natural one. An anthropological study of rural Mexican-Americans found that children with illnesses were delayed in seeing a doctor in part because of the meaning that "being ill" held in the community (M. Clark, 1959). Among this group of Mexican-Americans, illness was not just a biological disorder in one individual that could be diagnosed and treated by a single expert (the doctor), perhaps in consultation with the child's parents. Instead, illness was a social crisis requiring adjustments by many people: it caused work loads and relationships to be redistributed within the community. As a result, an accurate judgment of whether the child was truly ill was imperative, more friends and relations were asked to assess the child's health status, and a group consensus emerged about the nature and severity of the child's sickness. Not surprisingly, these processes delayed taking the child to a (Western, naturalistic) doctor.

Although in this case such delays may seem contrary to the child's welfare, the personalistic approach also has strengths unavailable in naturalistic medicine. Personalistic beliefs about illness make maximum use of social support for the sick individual — a major factor in motivating an individual to get well. Naturalistic systems, while usually recognizing the value of such support, often do not provide it (Hahn & Gaines, 1985; Frankel & Lewis, 1989). Furthermore, naturalistic systems can neither prevent nor cure a vast array of physical sicknesses and injuries, and this fact is often noticed by both adults and children from personalistic cultures. In northern Siberia in the first half of this century, Western-style Soviet doctors made vast improvements in the health of the children of the Khanty people, a native tribe much like the Eskimos of North America (Balzer, 1983). After World War II, however, the Khanties began sending their children to the local Khanty shamans again. Why? Because, they said, Western-style medicine had not saved the lives of the earlier generation of Khanty children who had gone off to fight in the Soviet Army. For the Khanties, death in combat met the qualifications of a personalistic "illness" — a physical misfortune caused by evil intentions, either spiritual or human — which the Western-style Soviet doctors had proved incapable of curing.

School-age girls in fact appear to get sick almost as often as preschool children of both sexes; only boys decrease in frequency as they get older.

Note, however, that these trends result partly from families' beliefs about illness, as well as from real differences. Girls may not necessarily get sick more often than boys; instead, training in gender roles may lead them to talk about their ailments more and to request medical treatment more often (Roghmann, 1975). For similar reasons, parents may be more apt to consider girls physically delicate and therefore to keep them home for minor illnesses that they would not consider serious in boys. These facts may mean that girls exaggerate the extent of their illnesses, or that boys hide the extent of theirs, or both.

Beliefs about illness

Dental Health

Tooth decay presents the most widespread health problem of middle childhood in spite of recent advances in dental care that could drastically reduce the problem if they were implemented properly. When children enter school at about age six, they already average more than two dental caries (or cavities) per child. Throughout the school years, more than one-half of all children have one or more teeth that are decayed, filled, or missing; and one-third have two or more such teeth (Kovar & Meny, 1981; World Health Organization, 1987). Cavities

Tooth decay is less common than it was a few decades ago, but it is still the most widespread health problem among North American children. It is important for children to develop good habits of dental hygiene as early in life as possible.

result from improper diet and faulty habits in brushing and flossing teeth. Snacks containing a lot of sticky sugar, such as candy bars, are especially bad for teeth because the sugar creates a breeding ground for bacteria that lasts for many hours after the food has been eaten.

Cavities are a serious health risk

Because schoolchildren are beginning to acquire their permanent teeth, their cavities can pose a significant health problem in the long run. Left untreated, they can create enough discomfort ("toothache") to interfere with learning in school and social interactions. Left untreated still longer, cavities can result in serious infections of the gums and jaw as well as the loss of any infected teeth. Missing teeth mean that neighboring teeth lose their natural vertical alignment and become less effective as food processors.

For decades, the traditional treatment for cavities consisted of attaching metal fillings to the decaying tooth area and adding small amounts of chemicals called *fluorides* to the community water. In recent years, however, newer treatments have included coating teeth with fluorides and painting teeth with a clear acrylic plastic to create a barrier between the teeth and decay-causing bacteria. The newer techniques have reduced the need for fillings still further by preventing tooth decay before it begins (Besford, 1984).

Unfortunately, both access to and use of these preventive techniques is not distributed evenly across society. Low-income families are less likely to have access to dental services and less likely to have the money or the health insurance needed to pay for the services when they do exist.

To some extent, publicly supported programs compensate for these inequities. The local city, county, or region typically provides fluoridation out of tax dollars, which (it is hoped) come more from affluent than from lower income citizens. School health programs often screen children for dental caries and occasionally offer dental treatment for low-income families. But these efforts do not eliminate inequalities completely because poverty also makes it less likely that children will live in areas that provide fluoridation, attend schools that offer dental screening programs, or have the knowledge and parental support to practice good dental health habits (C. Anderson & Creswell, 1985).

Hyperactivity and Attention Deficit Hyperactivity Disorders

A small number of school-age children seem extremely active and have considerable trouble concentrating on any one activity for long (American Psychiatric Association, 1987). Their problem is called **hyperactivity,** or **attention deficit hyperactivity disorder (ADHD).** A second-grade teacher described one student with ADD like this:

> Joey was friendly when you greeted him; "Hi!" he would say brightly, and smile. But he would never settle down. First he dumped the class's main supply of pencils out on a table; he sort of lunged at one of the pencils, but before he began writing, he left the table, looking for something new. During a reading lesson, I asked Joey to read silently until I finished helping another child; but Joey found this hard to do. He glanced in my direction; tapped a neighboring child on the shoulder; giggled; and kept scanning the room for "more." A child happened to drop a book; Joey laughed at this harder than the others, and jumped up quickly to pick the book up. He was probably trying to help, but in doing so he knocked his own papers all over the floor. Instead of picking up the papers, he only picked up his pencil, and headed off to sharpen it. And the morning was still only half over!

In the long run, behavior like this both results from and contributes to emotional problems, to conflicts with teachers and other adults, and to poor relationships with peers. Such social problems eventually aggravate the child's troubles in concentrating. Joey, for example, may become wrought up over conflicts with teachers and self-conscious about what peers think of his behavior. He may become so upset, in fact, that he gets even more fidgety than before.

Bridges How does hyperactivity affect a child's peer relationships?

Reactions to Children with ADHD   Overly active children cause parents and teachers a lot of worry, and excessive activity is one of the most common reasons for referring children to psychiatrists and other health professionals (Rutter and Garmezy, 1983). How many children really have ADHD, however, depends somewhat on who is doing the estimating. Professional school psychologists usually estimate that around 5 to 10 percent of school-age children are seriously overactive; teachers give a somewhat higher figure. Parents give the highest figure of all; in one survey, fully one-half of all parents of preschool and school-age boys considered their child's activity level a major source of concern (Lord, 1982). All the estimates agree that the large majority of highly active children — about 85 percent — are boys. Whatever else these figures may show, they certainly reveal that adults find dealing with highly active children very difficult.

Excessive activity presents more problems in some situations than in others. During outdoor play, very active children hardly stand out at all and seem to make and be friends about as well as any other children. The structured atmosphere of most school classrooms poses more problems. During class, children with ADHD often get out of their seats, respond aggressively to teachers and peers, and run the risk of losing not only opportunities to learn but also the affection and respect of friends.

Note that *most* children show excessive activity *some* of the time. This fact may not make dealing with ADHD any easier, but it does make the disorder seem more understandable and manageable. Only a few children really exhibit extremely high activity consistently enough to deserve professional attention. Experts suggest four criteria for deciding when activity poses a truly serious problem (Ross & Ross, 1982):

1. The overactivity happens even when it is clearly inappropriate, such as when the child is riding in a car or sitting at a meal.
2. Seriously overactive children consistently fail to respond to pressures to inhibit their activity.
3. Seriously overactive children seem always to respond at the same fast speed, even when they are trying to respond more slowly, as in drawing a picture.
4. Seriously overactive children show other, related problems, such as high distractibility and problems with making friends.

Only children who meet all four criteria deserve the often misused label *hyperactive*; all others should probably just be called "very active" or "overactive."

Bridges Is there a genetic predisposition toward hyperactivity?

Causes of Hyperactivity and ADHD   No one can say why some children become extremely active or have trouble concentrating. But three possible explanations exist. The first of these is genetic. Some children may inherit stronger tendencies toward activity than other children do. And some children may inherit a disposition to shift attention frequently. Because infants show differences like these almost as soon as they can move and respond, it seems reasonable that children show similar differences.

Physical causes of ADHD

The second explanation is neurological. ADHD resembles the problems that result from damage to or disease of the brain or central nervous system; a noticeable number of such children become excessively active afterward (Shaffer et al., 1975). This fact suggests, but does not prove, that ADHD or hyperactivity may reflect unidentified brain differences or other physiological problems that could derive from events during the child's gestation or delivery. The trouble with this line of reasoning, however, is that doctors have no practical way to test it. Most of the time, behavior problems are the only evidence of possible physiological or neurological difficulties.

Social causes of ADHD

The third explanation concerns children's family and other social environments. Some parents or teachers may accidentally create hyperactive children by setting rules for behavior that are too precise or rigid (N. Lambert & Hartsough, 1984). In class, for example, forbidding children to wiggle in their seats actually makes many children more restless rather than less so. At home, watching television for too long can have the same effect. And on the way to school, very long bus rides, such as those experienced by children in many rural areas or large cities, can also create overactivity. When circumstances such as these operate for a long period of time on children with a naturally active temperament, they may help to create the extremes of ADHD, or hyperactivity.

Helping Children with ADHD and Their Families   Because no one is sure what makes some children overactive, no single strategy exists for treating or dealing with the condition (Hunt, 1988).

Effects of diet

Some experts have proposed feeding highly active children a diet that is completely free of artificial substances such as food colorings, preservatives, and flavorings. The best known of these is the Feingold diet, named after its originator (Feingold, 1974). Although many parents are convinced that such a diet has helped their children, scientific evaluations of dietary changes have not found much support for this strategy. Many children on the diet do quiet down eventually, but their improvement could just as easily come from the passage of time, which seems to "cure" many cases of ADHD. A strict diet may also work by encouraging parents to give more care and attention to their children, which may actually cause the cure. In any case, parents and professionals may sometimes mistakenly give credit to the diet when other factors are equally important.

Classical psychotherapy also does not work well, probably because active children do not sit still long enough for all the talking involved. But two variations on traditional therapy both show promise. With younger children, therapists can engage in **play therapy,** a technique in which child and therapist communicate through make-believe play, using dolls and other props. Together the adult and child might make up a story about "a child who could never stop running," constructing an ending to the story that helps the child finally to slow down. While play therapy continues with the child, more traditional, verbally oriented therapy with family members can help relatives to cope with the frustrations of living with such an active child.

Psychological techniques

With overactive children of all ages, **behavior modification** often helps. This approach identifies specific behaviors that need changing as well as straightforward techniques for eliminating or reducing them. In classrooms, one behavior modification technique consists of using high-status peers to model or demonstrate appropriate behaviors. The active child simply watches a classmate complete an assignment slowly instead of at lightning speed; then the child tries to copy the same slow style in doing the assignment himself. The teacher of course reinforces (usually with praise) the slower behavior when it occurs. She may also make reinforcement more likely by limiting the active child's choices to help prevent unwanted distractions. Instead of offering a choice of three activities, she might offer only two. As the child begins concentrating on activities better, the teacher can begin offering more options again (Ross & Ross, 1982).

Bridges In what ways can overactive children learn how to concentrate better and respond more calmly?

Many children with ADHD also improve significantly if teachers and parents provide them with a consistent, predictable environment. At home, this means meals, playtimes, and bedtimes should come at about the same time every day and happen in roughly the same way. At school, lessons should have a regular format that the child can expect. In either setting, rules of acceptable and unacceptable behavior should be clear, simple, and relatively unchanging. All of these strategies help ADHD by temporarily reducing the demands on the child's attention-directing capacities and by allowing these to develop gradually at the child's own pace.

Amid much controversy, doctors have sometimes prescribed medication. Ironically, the most effective medications for calming overactive children are the same drugs that stimulate normal adults. If not used properly, however, these drugs can have serious side effects — impairment of speech, eating problems, and decreased alertness — especially on young children (Sprague & Ullman, 1981).

Effects of drugs

EFFECTS OF GROWTH ON THINKING AND FEELING

This chapter has shown some ways in which physical growth can influence the other aspects of a child's development during the elementary school years. Growth may seem slower or less eventful than either before or after these years, but this is true only in a strictly physical sense. Psychologically, a child's growth makes new social opportunities possible, as in children's sports. When growth

Children's motor development and social growth are often closely intertwined.

problems such as childhood obesity do develop, they often cause serious psychological side effects during the school years. And some abnormal physical developments, such as brain damage, have effects that closely resemble purely psychological developments — so closely, in fact, that distinguishing between the physical and mental aspects may confuse our understanding of the child as much as help it. Real children consist of minds, bodies, and feelings combined; only textbooks separate these three. Keeping this idea in mind may help to clarify the next two chapters, which concern children's thinking and social relationships.

SUMMARY OF MAJOR IDEAS

Trends and Variations in Height and Weight

1. Although growth slows down during the middle years, children of any single age still show significant differences in height and weight.

Problems Related to Growth and Body Build

2. Differences in size and body build contribute to the stereotypes and impressions that children form about one another.

3. Toward the end of the elementary school years, girls tend to grow taller than boys, and this difference can create embarrassment for some children.

4. A few children weigh significantly more than average, and these children sometimes experience social rejection and risk medical problems if their condition persists.

Motor Development in the Middle Years

5. During the middle years, children refine a wide range of motor skills that first appeared during the preschool years.

6. Improvements are especially marked for skills that emphasize coordination and timing rather than strength and size.

7. Many children become involved in athletics, whether they are formal and organized or informal and spontaneous.

8. Certain popular sports carry definite physical risks, but these may be outweighed by the physical benefits of regular activity.

9. Athletics may encourage achievement motivation in children and (in some sports) teamwork as well.

10. Team sports encourage both cooperation and competition; the latter can have harmful social effects on some children.

11. Even though gender roles are now less distinct than they used to be, boys still tend to become involved in athletics more than girls do, especially toward the end of the school years.

Health and Illness in Middle Childhood

12. Overall, schoolchildren are among the healthiest people in society, as shown by their low mortality.

13. Because children now die much less often from infectious illnesses, accidental injuries (especially traffic accidents) have become comparatively more serious problems.

14. Compared to preschoolers, schoolchildren catch fewer minor acute illnesses, but a small percent do suffer from significant chronic medical problems.

15. Parents' income levels and beliefs about illness affect how much children actually stay at home as a result of getting sick.

16. The most widespread medical problem in childhood is tooth decay, which can lead to serious complications if left untreated.

17. Attention deficit hyperactivity disorder, or hyperactivity, affects a small percentage of school-age children.

18. Because parents and teachers find ADHD very difficult to deal with, they may be inclined to overestimate its prevalence.

19. ADHD may result from a combination of genetic, physical, and social causes.

20. Treatment of ADHD sometimes includes special drugs, special diet, play therapy for younger children, and behavior modification techniques.

KEY TERMS

obesity *(389)*
mortality *(398)*
acute illness *(400)*
virus *(400)*
AIDS *(401)*
HIV *(401)*
chronic illness *(401)*
asthma *(401)*

hyperactivity *(405)*
attention deficit hyperactivity disorder (ADHD) *(405)*
play therapy *(407)*
behavior modification *(407)*

WHAT DO YOU THINK?

1. How well do you like your particular height and weight? Do you remember when you began to feel this way about your build?

2. Are competitive athletics inevitably hard on some children? Explain what you think about this issue.

3. Some experts argue that excessively active children are not so much "disturbed" as "disturbing." What do you suppose they mean by this comment?

4. If you were a teacher, how would you feel about having a hyperactive child in your class? What about a child with learning disabilities? Explain your reasons for your feelings.

FOR FURTHER READING

Besford, J. *Good Mouthkeeping: How to Save Your Children's Teeth, and Your Own While You're at It.* New York: Oxford University Press, 1984.

As the title implies, this book is aimed at parents who are concerned about their children's dental health. It discusses many of the newer dental techniques (such as acrylic sealants), along with the old standbys (such as avoiding sticky candy). The book talks about *both* children and adults.

Buscaglia, L. (ed.). *The Disabled and Their Parents: A Counseling Challenge,* rev. ed. New York: Holt, Rinehart, and Winston, 1983.

This book discusses the impact of disabilities on individuals, their families, and counselors or others responsible for offering help. It conveys the personal points of view of these different people especially well, conveying the feel of living with a disability or of living close to someone with a disability.

Coles, G. *The Learning Mystique: A Critical Look at "Learning Disabilities."* New York: Pantheon, 1987.

In recent years, many educators — including the author of this book — have become critics of the concept of learning disabilities. They feel that the category has been applied too widely, that it stigmatizes children without really identifying their learning problems reliably. Partly as a result, many children are wrongly given special educational services and kept out of the mainstream of education. This book is a good introduction to that critical point of view.

Gill, D. *Psychological Dynamics of Sport.* Champaign, IL: Human Kinetics Publishers, 1986.

Grant, R. *The Psychology of Sport: Facing One's True Opponent.* Jefferson, NC: McFarland & Company, 1988.

Each of these books considers the psychological effects of athletic activity in childhood. The second one is especially critical of the effects of competition in amateur athletics. The first one is also concerned about this problem, but it focuses on other issues as well, such as techniques for overcoming excessive anxiety during competitions.

Turecki, S., and Tonner, L. *The Difficult Child.* New York: Bantam Books, 1985.

The authors have talked with parents and other adults who are responsible for excessively active children. They mix support and encouragement with advice for specific techniques, and their discussion distinguishes among settings (home versus school) and ages of children (infants, preschoolers, school age).

CHAPTER 12

The Middle Years: Cognitive Development

Focusing Questions

- What new cognitive skills do children acquire during the school years? What psychological and practical effects do these new skills have?

- What learning strategies do children acquire during the middle years, and how do these strategies affect their overall cognitive development?

- What unique cognitive styles do children begin to show during the school years?

- What learning disabilities do some school-age children demonstrate?

- How does bilingualism affect children's language development?

- What is general intelligence, how can it be measured, and what are the limitations of standardized tests of ability and achievement?

- What changes in moral reasoning do children undergo during the school years?

O ne day, two brothers, aged seven and nine, constructed a "science museum" in their living room. They systematically selected all the best chairs and blankets as building materials. Then they found all their stuffed animals and put them on display in this museum, grouping them both by color and by size. They finished the museum by hanging a sign on it: "ANIMAL MUSEUM. TIKETS $1." Not many people bought tickets, but this did not stop these boys from having a lively conversation about their project.

The activity drew on the kind of cognitive skills that school-age children have in more abundance than preschool children. It required the boys to make the building and to remember where to find particular stuffed animals. It took a rudimentary knowledge of reading and writing, so that they could make the sign. And it took the knowledge that museums store interesting objects in systematic ways and that they often cost money to visit.

This chapter describes the development of cognitive skills like these, as well as others that characterize school-age children. It begins by looking at Piaget's findings about thinking during children's middle years because, as always, his theory offers one of the most comprehensive overviews of cognitive development. Then we discuss how children organize and process information and pay special attention to the ways in which children use memory and learning strategies during the school years. After that, the chapter shifts focus to some practical implications of cognitive development. We look at how children differ in their thinking and learning styles, how these variations affect success in school, how children differ in their styles of speaking, and how language variations can affect children's educational and social success. We then discuss the nature of intelligence and why the measurement of intelligence has been not only one of psychology's major success stories but also one of its biggest sources of criticism over the years. Finally, the chapter includes a look at various theories about school-children's moral development.

CONCRETE OPERATIONAL SKILLS

During the middle years, children become skilled at **concrete operations,** which are mental activities focused on real, tangible objects and events. Concrete operations have three interrelated qualities: decentration, sensitivity to transformations, and reversibility (Piaget, 1965). None of these is reliably present among preschool children. **Decentration** means attending to more than one feature of a problem at a time. In estimating the number of pennies spread out on a table, for example, a school-age child will probably take into account not only how large the array is but also how far apart individual pennies seem to be. **Sensitivity to transformations** means noticing and remembering significant changes in objects. When judging whether the amount of liquid in a glass stays the same after it is poured into a new container, a school-age child concentrates on the actual process of change in appearance — the transformation — rather than on how the liquid looks either before or after pouring. **Reversibility** of thought means solving problems by mentally going back to the beginning of them. In judging the amount of liquid in a container, the child can imagine pouring the liquid back into its original glass without actually doing so.

Qualities of concrete operations

To understand these features of concrete operations, we should compare how preschool and concrete operational children solve the same problem. Consider how Ken and Murray each got started making a batch of muffins:

- Ken, age four, needed guidance from his day-care teacher in order to cook, but even so he kept coming dangerously close to ruining the recipe. The teacher set out the ingredients Ken needed: flour, sugar, salt, baking powder, and the like. Ken liked the look of the bag of flour (it was bright red), so he picked the bag up and happily began pouring flour into a large bowl. His teacher stopped him from overdoing it: "We only need two cups," she said. "But there is not as much in the bowl," said Ken, meaning that the bowl made the flour spread out and therefore look like less. "Okay," said Ken's teacher, "but we still need to measure two cups. How can we do that?" Ken took the measuring cup, filled it, and added one *more* cup of flour. Now there was far too much flour; apparently Ken did not think it was necessary to pour the first flour out of the bowl.

- Murray, age ten, worked much more independently than Ken, and when he made mistakes, they were less serious blunders. After setting out all the ingredients that he needed, Murray poured some flour into the bowl. "Oops," he said, "I forgot to measure it." So he poured the flour carefully back into the bag and checked the instructions in the recipe. Then he began again, first pouring exactly one cup into the measuring cup. "How am I going to get two cups into this small measuring cup?" he thought. He solved his problem by pouring the first cup of flour into the bowl and then carefully measuring out a second cup.

There are many reasons these two boys differed in their cooking performance, including variations in their prior experiences with cooking, measuring, and even reading. But part of the difference reflects the appearance of concrete operations in Murray. He was less distracted by immediate sensory cues, such as the color of the flour bag and the attractive feel of pouring out large amounts of flour. Murray was also more able to reverse his first mistake by returning the flour to its bag. And Murray seemed aware that the amount of flour did not depend on where the flour happened to be — that one cup of flour is one cup whether it is in the bowl or in the measuring cup.

In some ways, concrete operations amount to refinements of the skills that children form in the preoperational period. In terms of classification skills, by about age seven, children have improved their classifying or grouping ability substantially over what they could do as preschoolers. In particular they are less confused than they used to be by **class inclusion** — groupings in which one type of object is compared with some larger, more inclusive type of object. Boys and girls, for example, both belong to a larger category — children. School-age children not only realize this fact, but usually can handle the logical relations

Improved classification skills

among these three categories quite accurately. No matter what the particular mix of boys and girls in a classroom, they can usually answer correctly the teacher's question "Are there more boys in this class, or more children?" Preschool children, in contrast, often fail to answer this question correctly without further clarifying questions.

Conservation in the Middle Years

Some cognitive skills make their first real appearance during the middle years. Probably the best-known of these is **conservation,** which is a belief that certain properties of an object remain the same or constant in spite of changes in the object's appearance. An example of conservation of quantity is the one described in Chapter 9 involving two tall, narrow glasses with exactly the same amount of water in them. If you empty one glass into a wide, low tray, you create a substantial perceptual change in the water; it looks quite different from before and quite different from the water in the remaining tall glass. Will a child believe that the wide tray has the same amount of water as the tall glass does? If he does, then he conserves, meaning that he shows a belief in the water's underlying constancy in spite of a perceptual change.

Piaget found that after the age of about seven, most children did indeed conserve quantity in the water-glass experiment (1965). He found, in fact, that

In one of the most widely known Piagetian tasks, children evaluate whether the amount of liquid stays the same when poured into a beaker of a different shape. Most children over six believe that it does stay the same.

Genetics	Physical Development	Family	Peers	Social Context
How influential is genetics in determining intelligence? (98)	How might learning disabilities be related to difficulties in the way the brain processes information? (434)	How do parents' views affect children's learning of mathematics? (427)	How do peers influence moral judgment during the middle years? (446, 450)	How can social attitudes about a language affect the development of bilingualism? (439)

THE MIDDLE YEARS: COGNITIVE DEVELOPMENT

Emotions	Self-concept and Identity	Learning	Language	Cognition
How are emotions related to a child's learning disabilities? (435)	How is personality related to styles of thinking? (428–431)	How can children be helped to acquire learning strategies? (426–428)	What are the cognitive advantages to children of speaking two languages equally well? (437–438)	Do children remember better as they get older? (420–423)

by a year or two later, children conserve on a lot of other tasks as well, including the following (which are illustrated in Figure 12.1):

1. *Clay balls* Start with two identical clay balls. Flatten one so that it looks like a pancake. Ask, "Do these two balls weigh the same, or does one weigh more than the other?"   **Conservation of mass**

2. *Pennies and nickels* Lay out two matching rows of coins, one of pennies and the other of nickels. The rows should have the same number of coins in them, each penny should be set next to one of the nickels. Then bunch up the coins in one row but not those in the other. Ask, "Are there still as many pennies as nickels, or are there more of one than the other?"   **Conservation of number**

3. *Bent wires* Start with two identical wires or pipe cleaners. Then bend one of them in an arc or circle. Ask, "Is one wire just as long as the other, or is one of them longer?"   **Conservation of length**

4. *Overlapping pencils* Set two identical pencils parallel to each other. Then shift one pencil up or down by an inch or so. Ask, "Is one pencil just as long as the other, or is one of them longer?"

Each of these tasks requires a belief in some sort of conservation. The clay balls, like the water glasses, require conservation of mass; the bent wires and the pencils, conservation of distance or length; and the coins, conservation of number. Children in the middle years tend to conserve on all of them.

Typically, a child does not acquire all of these conservations at exactly the same time, a phenomenon that Piaget called **décalage,** which is a French term for "gap." Piaget believed that such gaps occur because children's thinking is still concrete. Perhaps, he argued, they do not grasp the general principles underlying conservation and therefore do not apply them to tasks that are logically similar. Critics have argued, however, that *décalage* may prove that concrete operational skills do not really form a coherent, universal stage in the sense proposed by Piaget (Flavell, 1985). This skepticism has led some psychologists to investigate whether skills such as conservation can be learned through explicit teaching.   **Gaps in times of acquisition**

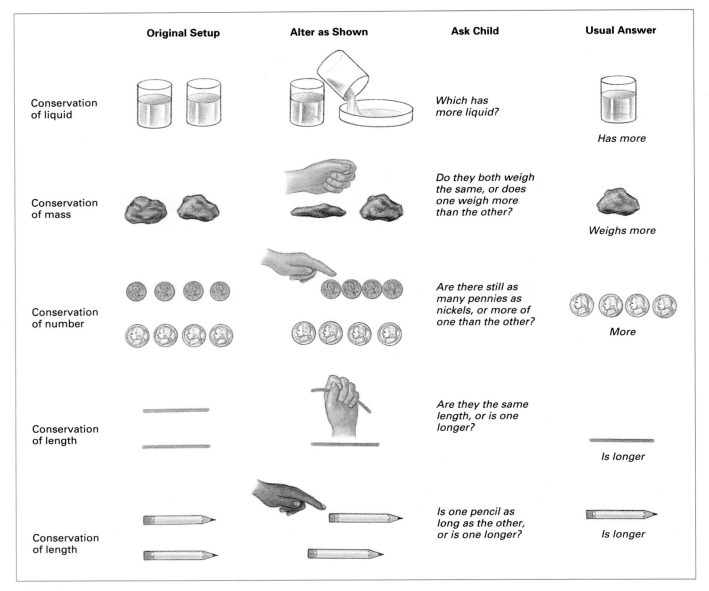

FIGURE 12.1
Conservation Experiments

Conservation Training

Everyone agrees that children do not begin life conserving but instead acquire this skill somehow. How do they do it? Piaget argued that biological maturation and countless experiences with physical objects that show conservation properties enable children to mentally construct conservation. These experiences are numerous and diverse; and although they can be taught explicitly, Piaget believed that they have fuller, more general influence on development if allowed to occur naturally.

But many psychologists have tried anyway. In general, they have had moderate but not complete success. One classic set of studies varied the usual water-glass experiment by putting a screen between the child and the glasses during the actual pouring of liquid (Bruner et al., 1966). In these conditions, children could rely only on their visual memories of the glasses and on their verbal

Conservation without viewing objects

reasoning abilities. As it turned out, the barrier caused many more children to conserve than had done so in Piaget's experiment. Apparently, therefore, some children found *not* seeing the glasses helpful, perhaps because it kept them from being distracted by the dramatic visual changes. With nothing to see, the children had to reason more carefully and relied less on their perceptions.

More recent studies have tried to help children avoid being distracted by coaching them to talk about what is happening ("Nothing is being added or taken away") or to compare the important dimensions closely ("Watch the height *and* the width") (Gelman, 1978; Gelman & Baillargeon, 1983). More often than not, these efforts do produce larger numbers of conserving children, especially among children who are uncertain how to respond. To this extent, conservation can be taught.

But trained children often do not stay loyal to conservation in the way that "natural" conservers tend to do; they are more likely to give up their belief at even a slight provocation. One study documented this tendency by using the clay-balls task described earlier (Robert & Charbonneau, 1978). Following Piaget's procedures closely, experimenters flattened one ball while keeping the other one round and then asked children to predict whether one would be heavier than the other or whether the two would still weigh the same. Then they actually weighed the balls on a balance scale. But here the experimenters changed the usual procedure. Without letting the children know, they removed some clay from one of the pieces before they weighed it. Of course this made it weigh less and therefore made it seem to violate the principle of conservation.

When recently trained conservers confronted this violation, most accepted it easily and reverted to their pretraining predictions. When "natural" conservers confronted it, however, about one-half persisted in their conservation beliefs. Some even suggested that a mistake had been made — that some clay had dropped on the floor accidentally, perhaps. All together, the results suggest that natural learning of conservation works better than training, but that neither works perfectly. In this experiment, even some "naturals" changed their beliefs when they confronted a violation of conservation. Conservation, it seems, may not be as inevitable and universal as Piaget led us to believe.

Limitations of trained conservation

Other Concrete Operational Skills

Piaget described many other forms of knowledge that appear during the middle years (Piaget, 1983). Among other things, school-age children can seriate, or arrange objects in sequence, better; they understand time more fully and accurately; and they can understand spatial relations better. Let us look briefly at each of these accomplishments.

Seriation   The term **seriation** refers to the ability to put items into a series or sequence. Given a dozen or so sticks of different lengths, an eight-year-old can usually arrange them easily in order of length. Four-year-olds often have trouble with this task; they may sequence a few of them correctly but not others. Or they may fudge their measurements, making one end of the sticks appear sequenced but allowing the other ends to extend at random.

Improved sequencing ability

A Sense of Time   School-age children understand the nature of time much better than younger children do. Eight-year-olds generally know that time refers to a single, constant flow of incidents marked off by calendars, clocks, and landmark events. This understanding helps them to realize that parents are indeed older than children, that "tomorrow" is usually sooner than "next week," and that a half-hour television show is shorter than a two-hour show.

Grasp of temporal relations

School-age children can often use their spatial relations skill to make accurate maps of familiar places, such as their own neighborhoods. But like some adults, they often have trouble using a map as a guide to unfamiliar territory.

New spatial abilities

Spatial Relations   Although preschool children usually can find their way around their own home, only concrete operational children can reliably navigate in complex and unfamiliar spaces, such as a neighborhood shopping mall. Even so, schoolchildren experience severe limitations to their spatial knowledge. For example, one study found that eight-year-olds could usually create a small-scale model of a set of rooms if they first had a chance to explore the full-scale rooms themselves (DeLoache & Kolstad, 1987). By the end of elementary school, furthermore, children can often create simple maps of places familiar to them, such as their classroom at school (A. Presson, 1987). But going the other way — from representations to the real thing — remains much more difficult throughout this period. After first seeing a small-scale model of an unfamiliar set of rooms, seven-year-olds have trouble finding their way through the real rooms; and even ten-year-olds have trouble with this task if they must work from a map (Hays & Siegel, 1981).

Piaget's Influence on Education

The cognitive theory of Piaget, described here and elsewhere in this book, has had an important influence on schools and education. Educators have evolved numerous programs that reflect Piagetian principles and findings or at least that try not to be inconsistent with them. Often these programs draw on other psychological approaches as well; but in one way or another, they all show Piaget's influence (Consortium for Longitudinal Studies, 1983). This influence is revealed in three areas: the overall style and sequencing of teaching, the content of particular curricula, and methods for assessing student progress.

Emphasis on active manipulation

Style and Sequencing of Teaching   Educators have borrowed Piaget's idea that true knowledge originates from active manipulation of materials. Children learn about weights, for instance, by actually weighing various objects on a scale rather than by reading about weights in a book or by hearing their teacher talk about such activities. A commitment to active learning in turn leads teachers and curriculum planners to put more tangible activities into educational programs wherever possible, as well as to sequence activities from the tangible to the abstract. Reading about bugs still has a place in learning about these creatures, but collecting (and handling) some real bugs should probably come first.

Curriculum Content   Piagetian theory has influenced particular curriculum content by providing many specific ideas about what cognitive competencies to expect from children of particular ages or levels of development. The conservation skills described in this chapter imply that elementary schoolchildren should be developing relative immunity to *how* problems are presented to them. Compared with preschoolers, older children should be less distracted by seemingly small changes in drawings in their books or by seemingly insignificant changes in how a teacher phrases assignments. In Piagetian terms, the children have become more decentered.

Likewise, acquisition of concrete operations should help school-age children in a number of other ways. For instance, many academic tasks require multiple classification, which preschoolers often cannot understand reliably. A written assignment may ask children to "list all the machines you can think of that begin with *c.*" This task requires classifying objects in two ways at once, first by whether or not something is in fact a machine and second by whether or not it begins with the letter *c.*

Use of multiple classification

Piaget's cognitive theory has helped many curriculum planners and teachers to select and evaluate academic tasks such as these. It does not, of course, lead to accurate selections for all children because not all children move through Piagetian stages at the same rate. Some preschoolers, it seems, can already conserve, and some school-age children still cannot (Lewis et al., 1986). But Piagetian ideas do give valuable guidance.

Piaget's theory has given elementary teachers a major justification for relying on active manipulation as a teaching strategy.

Assessment of Students' Progress   Throughout his work, Piaget has emphasized the importance of children's actual thought processes and of what these processes actually allow children to accomplish. This approach is shown graphically in Piaget's emphasis throughout his research on semistructured, informal interviews.

Focus on content of progress

Many educators feel that interviews offer a much better way of assessing students' progress than traditional classroom testing, which tends to promote comparisons among students and to obscure what they have actually learned (Elkind, 1987). The same criticism applies — perhaps even more strongly — to standardized achievement tests. Instead of helping teachers to know *what* their students have learned, the scores on such tests tend to focus on how much *better* one student performs than another. At best, such comparisons do not help teachers (or students) to diagnose students' learning needs; and at worst, they can hurt the self-esteem of students who do not rank highly when tested.

INFORMATION-PROCESSING SKILLS

During the middle years, children show important changes in how they organize and remember information. Their short-term memories are already well developed even at age five. In most other respects, their ways of processing information show significant limitations compared to adults; but the limitations diminish during this age period.

Memory Capacity

Bridges   Do children remember better as they get older?

According to popular wisdom, children remember better as they get older. Yet how true is this idea, really? In everyday life, children obviously do not perform as well as adults on some tasks, such as remembering to put away their clothes at the end of the day. But in other ways they do perform as well; they will remember their grandparents when they see them again after months or even years of absence.

Short-Term Memory   Some of these differences in memory may depend on which parts of the information-processing model the children happen to be using. Some tasks rely primarily on short-term memory (STM), which is a feature of thinking that holds information only for a short period — perhaps up to twenty seconds (see Chapter 2). On tasks that emphasize short-term memory, school-age children — and even preschoolers — perform just about as well as adults do. Experimenters demonstrated this trend by showing subjects a set of numbers briefly and then immediately asking them whether a particular number had been included in the set (Kail, 1988).

STM is constant across ages

In these conditions, individuals from age five through adulthood performed about equally well. Not surprisingly, the time people took to recognize a test digit did depend on how many digits were shown in the original set. Showing six digits made the task take longer than showing just three, no doubt because the person evaluated the test digit against a larger number of alternatives. What is striking, however, is how *little* performance depended on the age of the child or adult. Whether the subject was young or old, this particular problem took a certain amount of time and effort to solve.

This study assessed a variation of **recognition memory,** in which a person merely compares an external stimulus or cue with preexisting experiences or knowledge. Recognition memory is involved when children look at snapshots of a holiday celebration months in the past: their faces light up, and they may describe aspects of the celebration that they had apparently forgotten. In general, recognition memory develops early in life; even toddlers will respond to, or "recognize," a picture of a familiar face more than they will one of a stranger.

Long-term memory   Long-term memory (LTM) is the feature of thinking that holds information for very long periods — perhaps even indefinitely. Capacity for long-term memory develops more slowly than for short-term memory, probably because it relies more often on complex methods of storage and retrieval. This is the more difficult process of **recall memory,** in which we bring information back into awareness using relatively few external cues. In tasks of this type, schoolchildren generally perform better than preschoolers but not as well as adolescents or adults.

Memory with few cues

Consider how individuals — both children and adults — recall short stories that they have heard (Meyer & Rice, 1984). At about age six, children already show many similarities to adults at this task. Like adults, they recall important features of a story ("Goldilocks was not supposed to enter the bears' house") and ignore or forget trivial features ("Goldilocks was wearing brown shoes"). They also recall the essence of sentences rather than their exact wording.

But compared with adults, school-age children include fewer inferences based on the sentences they actually hear. If adults hear the two sentences "Red Riding Hood's grandmother was baking" and "Grandmother set the cookies out on the table," they automatically infer that (a) grandmother had an oven and that (b) she was the one who took the cookies out of the oven. Because of these inferences, adults are relatively likely to think they actually heard this information and to offer a sentence such as, "Grandmother finished her baking in the oven before she put the cookies out" (Calfee & Drum, 1986, p. 838 ff). Schoolchildren are significantly less likely to include such inferences, although they are more likely to do so than preschool children. As children get older, they seem to read between the lines more, at least in recalling stories. This tendency lends color and detail to their retellings as they get older, even though they sometimes risk misstating the "facts" of the story.

Recall of stories

Influences on Memory Development

As the example of recalling stories shows, LTM develops partly because other, related cognitive changes occur during childhood. One of these is an improvement in logical reasoning, such as described by Piaget. Another is an increase in specific knowledge or facts. Still another is an improvement in learning strategies used in solving problems — including problems that depend on long-term memory.

The Effects of Logical Reasoning on Memory   Reasoning skills affect children's memory, and because reasoning often improves with age, memories of specific experiences sometimes actually improve gradually rather than deteriorate. In one study that illustrates this fact, experimenters showed children a series of sticks of various lengths (see Figure 12.2); then they asked the children to reproduce the series from memory by drawing pictures of it (Piaget & Inhelder, 1973). Six or eight months later, they asked the children to draw the series from memory again.

On both occasions, not surprisingly, preschool children reproduced the series with considerably less accuracy than older, school-aged children did; the younger ones would simply draw a random group of sticks or perhaps correctly sequence only part of the series. The later drawings, however, showed a surprising result: nearly three-quarters of the children's drawings actually improved in

Possible spontaneous improvement of memory

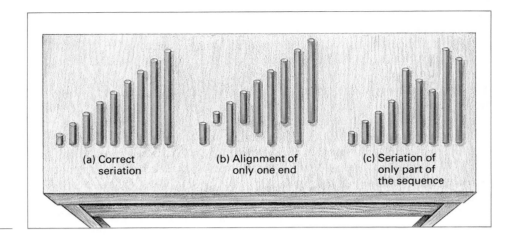

FIGURE 12.2
Seriation of Sticks

(a) Correct
seriation

(b) Alignment of
only one end

(c) Seriation of
only part of
the sequence

accuracy compared to the first time. Even though some of the change probably reflected improvements in motor skills, the drawings were too simple to depend on motor development entirely. Some improvement probably also reflected the children's increasing understanding of the underlying concept of seriation. Development of this concept apparently aided their later drawings, at least in part.

Other research suggests that children's ability to make inferences affects what they remember. Consider this task, which calls for recognition of sentences: ask children to listen to a set of sentences that express simple relationships, such as "Carlos is older than Bill," "Bill is older than Nicole,"and so on. Later, ask them to recognize whether certain sentences were in fact part of the original list. Some of the test sentences should indeed be identical to originals ("Bill is older than Nicole"); some should be logically true but worded differently ("Bill is younger than Carlos"); and some should be logically false but worded similarly ("Nicole is older than Carlos").

False recognition of sentences

On a task like this, people of all ages will falsely "recognize" some sentences that were not in the first list. Their mistakes, as it turns out, suggest how memory and reasoning may affect each other.

What determines which sentences they falsely recognize? The sophistication of their reasoning skills is responsible in part. Among young children (around age five), the similarity of wording seems to matter the most; in the examples above, a kindergartner is comparatively likely to think she heard, "Bill is older than Carlos." By the middle elementary school years, logical consistency matters more; a third- or fourth-grade child will think that he heard "Carlos is older than Nicole." Apparently his more developed reasoning skills color his memory. In reality he may have heard only the sentences "Carlos is older than Bill" and "Bill is older than Nicole." From these he reasons immediately that Carlos must be older than Nicole, but he apparently forgets that a sentence about Carlos and Nicole was not spoken (Bjorkland & Bjorkland, 1985).

Memory as active reorganization

Studies of both false recognition and spontaneous improvements in recall suggest that memory is active rather than passive. Memory it seems, is more than just a sort of mental filing cabinet for experiences. It also involves reorganizing those experiences using the best cognitive skills that children have at their command. For schoolchildren, these "best cognitive skills" may resemble those that Piaget described for the concrete operational period; but as we point out below, they may differ in some ways, too.

Familiarity and Richness of Knowledge   Common sense suggests that what a child already knows influences what she can learn and what she can remember. A child who knows a lot about cars will have an easier time learning the meaning of the term *vehicle* than a child who knows little about cars; and both will learn *vehicle* more easily than a child who has never seen a car in her life.

Familiarity matters not only during learning but during recall as well. One study showed this to be true by observing a young child who had expert knowledge about dinosaurs (Chi & Koeske, 1983; Chi & Ceci, 1987). The child could name and describe forty-six different dinosaurs, telling about their size, appearance, eating habits, and behavior. He could do so, however, only if given ample time (literally hours) and encouragement from adults. In a short, straightforward test of his recall, he named familiar dinosaurs far more often than he named less familiar ones. Being "familiar" in this case meant that the child had had more prior experience with reading about a particular species in books, playing with toy models of it, and viewing its skeleton in a museum (although *not,* presumably, more experience with seeing it on the hoof).

More often than not, older children show greater familiarity with or richness of knowledge about a variety of topics, simply because they have lived longer and therefore have accumulated more facts. But this is not always true; like the dinosaur expert, many young children have special areas of knowledge or experience that outstrip those of older people and that therefore promote unusually good memory. There are child experts in baseball and chess and among music lovers and performers.

Benefits of familiarity

Expertise tends to include a rich knowledge base in a specific area, as with these young experts in baseball lore. This extensive knowledge base fosters better organized, longer-lasting memory, which explains why these children can probably recall detailed information about the baseball players whose cards they are trading.

Metacognition and Learning Strategies

As children grow older, they pick up more knowledge about thinking itself — about how learning and memory operate in everyday situations and about how a person can improve her cognitive performance. Psychologists sometimes call this sort of knowledge **metacognition,** meaning "knowledge about cognition" (Flavell & Wellman, 1977; Flavell, 1985).

Compared with older children, young children are notably oblivious of factors that can affect their problem-solving performance. For example, ask two children of different ages which set of numbers will be harder to remember:

$$8 \quad 1 \quad 5 \qquad \text{or} \qquad 3 \quad 9 \quad 2 \quad 6 \quad 8 \quad 1 \quad 4 \quad 7$$

A preschool child is more likely to judge the two sets of digits as equally hard (or easy) to memorize. If he admits to any difference in difficulty, he is likely to be rather vague about how to cope with the special challenges. He may suggest that "thinking hard" will suffice to learn the more difficult set.

Knowledge about knowledge

By age ten or so, a child's approach to learning the two sets of digits will be quite different, or, at any rate, his statements about learning them will be different. By that age he will more likely say that the longer series is harder to memorize than the shorter one; that he might learn the longer series temporarily but fail to recall it later; and that learning the longer series would be easier if he used cognitive strategies such as writing the numbers down. All these ideas are metacognitive, and all are less likely to come from a very young child who evaluates the same task.

Types of Learning Strategies Such tasks are made easier by the use of broad **learning strategies,** or general methods or techniques that help in solving a variety of problems. Typically they draw not only on preexisting skills, such as the language skills developed during early childhood, but on brand-new ones, such as the conservation ability described by Piaget. Learning strategies give school-age children major advantages over younger children in solving certain sorts of problems, as explained below.

Focusing on small details

1. *Attention to detail* During the school years, children become much better at noticing details. For example, try showing children several similar pictures, only two of which are exactly the same. On the whole, younger children make relatively more errors in finding the identical pictures. Observing their eye movements carefully shows that they get sidetracked more often by the most noticeable aspects of the drawings. As a result, they sometimes forget to check all the details systematically, even when the details are crucial to solving the problem.

Repeating information

2. *Rehearsal* This term literally means "hearing again"; it refers to a purposeful repetition of information, either silently or out loud. Older children engage in rehearsal more often and with less prompting than younger children do (Ornstein & Naus, 1985). To see this difference, just ask children of different ages to remember a set of numbers (1, 2, 3, 5, 8, 13, . . .), and take note of how they do so. Older children are more likely to review the digits to themselves somehow, perhaps by whispering them, or looking at them, or pointing to each of them repeatedly. If younger children use any of these strategies at all, they are likely to apply them haphazardly.

Finding structure

3. *Organizing tactics* Older children more often notice the structure or organization of new information and exploit that structure more effectively. For example, older children are more likely to notice that each number in the list above is the sum of the two numbers preceding it, and they may simply use this relationship to remember the entire series.

As children gain educational experience, they acquire new strategies for learning, such as attending to important details and knowing how much attention to give to specific subtasks.

Strategies like these explain a lot of the advantage that older children have over younger ones in learning new material. Not only do older children know more strategies, but they use them more widely, spontaneously, and appropriately. The developmental difference is especially obvious when they are learning arbitrary information — the kind that takes deliberate effort to remember.

Note, however, that young children do not completely lack learning strategies; often they simply fail to use them (A. Brown et al., 1983). A three- or four-year-old will often point at and label the objects and words in a book, for example, but he will not do so consistently. And preschool children can be trained to use strategies such as rehearsal, even if they never do so as effectively as older children do. Simply reminding them to say each name on a list makes a big difference to later recall. So does recasting a problem in more familiar terms; preschoolers can learn a list of "things to buy at the store" much more effectively than if the very same list is presented as an arbitrary memory task (Istomina, 1975).

Preschoolers' use of learning strategies

Much of the difference between younger and older children, concerns how reliably and automatically they invoke learning strategies. Older children are less likely to need special coaching or specially designed problems in order to remember successfully. They can extract organization from material that is not already well organized, and they do so more often even when not explicitly asked for such behavior. In this sense, they make more able learners than younger children do.

Mechanisms for Acquiring Learning Strategies   Children acquire these strategies in at least three ways: trial and error, logical construction, and observational learning (Shatz, 1983; Brown et al., 1983). Each can be seen in children's own naturally occurring activities, and can also be assisted by parents and teachers.

1. *Trial and error* Sometimes children happen upon effective strategies more or less by accident, or trial and error. Often this process occurs in the midst of preexisting, more logical learning strategies. Some schoolchildren write many essays and follow all the advice of their teachers before they discover, by accident, the methods that work best for them. Even though their teachers advise

Accidental discovery of strategies

them to make an outline first, and even though they do so repeatedly, they may eventually discover that simply writing a first draft produces better results.

Inference and deduction

2. *Logical construction* A lot of so-called random learning of strategies may really reflect **logical construction** of knowledge instead. Logically constructed knowledge refers to one form of children's active efforts to understand the world — the sort of learning emphasized by Piaget's theory of development. Such thinking may especially help children to extend learning strategies to brand-new situations.

For example, children sometimes demonstrate knowledge of certain social relationships even though they rarely see people acting out the relationships. They can dramatize the behavior of firefighters even though they have not seen actual fires to observe the details of these people's conduct. Even what they see of fires in the media tends to lack the detail that children put into their reenactments. Instead, they seem to follow mental scripts or inferences constructed from knowledge of what fighting a fire *must* be like.

3. *Observational learning* These examples may also involve observational learning, as described in Chapter 2. In many situations, children watch others talking and acting and witness the consequences of these activities as well. Such observations provide models for children's learning strategies at other times and places, even far from the original demonstrations.

Modeling others

Siblings often learn by observation. A younger sister may watch her older sibling plead with their parents for an extra cookie. If the pleading proves successful, the younger child is likely to use the same method herself later; but if the pleading does not work, she is relatively unlikely to imitate this particular behavior.

Bridges   How can children be helped to acquire learning strategies?

Helping Children to Acquire Learning Strategies   The processes described above can all be assisted by adults and often are. Parents may purposely demonstrate effective ways of remembering the time of an appointment by writing it down as soon as they hear it and by pointing out the fact that they have done so to their child. Or teachers may help children to solve a problem in long division by encouraging them to whisper each step in the process to themselves as they do it.

When interventions like these are carried out systematically, they constitute various sorts of **strategy training,** or coaching in when and how to apply learning strategies to new and difficult problems. Studies of strategy training show that it improves learning substantially (Weinstein et al., 1988), although the amount of improvement depends on exactly how the training is done. The simplest forms — what might be called **blind training** — lead children to use particular learning strategies but do not give them any reasons for doing so or even explain that they are actually using strategies. More complex forms not only lead children to use strategies but also emphasize the advantages of using them. Sometimes, too, they may teach children ways to monitor the progress of their own learning. These more complex forms might be called **informed training** (Palincsar, 1986).

To understand the distinction between blind and informed training, imagine how teachers might help sixth-grade children to learn a lot of new biological terms. Suppose that the current biology unit requires students to learn the name. of a large number of animal species. Suppose, too, that the species are rather diverse; they include a number of birds, fish, and mammals. This task is one that usually reveals large differences among children. Some learn material like this much more easily and quickly than others do, so the task is a good one for teachers to help with.

Blind training methods

Blind training simply gets children to apply learning strategies to the task. Teachers might encourage children to say each species' name to themselves

A Multicultural View

Cultural Differences in Learning Mathematics

Research consistently shows that children from China and Japan learn mathematics sooner and more thoroughly than do children from North America. The advantage occurs not only in basic written computation (problems such as "How much is 34 × 26?"); it also occurs in a range of other mathematical skills, such as knowledge of concepts, graphing, estimating amounts, and mental calculations. The differences favoring Chinese and Japanese children occur as early as first grade, grow large by the end of the elementary school years, and persist throughout the high school years (Stigler & Perry, in press; Travers et al., 1985). Furthermore, international differences in mathematics achievement are wide and substantial: the highest few percent of American students perform mathematics only about as well as the lowest few percent of Chinese or Japanese students.

The best explanations for these differences center on cultural influences, especially on educational practices and attitudes about achievement. One obvious cultural difference is the priority given to mathematics: observations of Chinese and Japanese classrooms show that Asian teachers devote double or triple the amount of time to mathematics instruction each week as their American counterparts do (Stigler & Baranes, 1988). Most of this extra time involves the class as a whole group — the teacher gives verbal explanations of mathematical procedures and ideas and illustrates them using simple, concrete materials such as blocks and sticks of fixed, known sizes.

In American classrooms, by contrast, teachers spend more time with children individually or in small groups and simultaneously assign tasks or seat work to occupy the remainder of the class. These practices reflect Amer-

ican teachers' strong belief in individualizing instruction. But apparently these practices also encourage students to concentrate on getting paperwork done to the exclusion of interacting with the best-educated person in the classroom, the teacher (Lave et al., 1989).

*Differences in mathematics achievement may also stem from broader cultural beliefs about the sources of educational success. Surveys of parents in Japan, China, and the United States show that Japanese and Chinese parents tend to attribute success to students' effort and motivation and failure to lack of motivation or to unfortunate family problems (Stigler & Baranes, 1988). In the United States, parents tend to attribute success to ability and failure to lack of ability. They are also more likely to believe that a failing child has a physical impairment, such as minimal brain damage or some other condition that is strictly "in" the child. The differences in attitudes can be seen in parental responses to homework: apparently because Asian parents believe more strongly that effort pays off, they tend to involve themselves more thoroughly than American parents do in helping their children with homework (Chen & Stevenson, 1989).

All in all, international differences in mathematics learning challenge a widely held belief in North American society that mathematical knowledge is inherently more formal, difficult, and inaccessible than other kinds of knowledge and that success with it therefore depends on an innate, unchanging ability held by only a select number of individuals (Schoenfeld, 1985). This kind of belief may cause many American teachers to be less competent at teaching math than many other subjects and cause many American parents to give up relatively easily on supporting their child's efforts to learn mathematics.

whenever they see it in a book. Or teachers might covertly organize all their questions on the material: "First tell me all the birds you know," they might say, "and then tell me all the fish." Techniques like these do improve children's learning substantially, even when teachers make no real effort to justify the techniques. And they help *all* children, whether they are slow learners or fast ones. Ironically, however, such methods sometimes help faster learners more than slower ones, thereby increasing differences among children rather than decreasing them (Corno & Snow, 1986; Siegler, 1983).

Informed training goes beyond techniques like these and advises students about the value of using learning strategies as well as about techniques for checking on progress. In teaching the biology unit, teachers might suggest that "saying the name whenever you see it will help you remember it better." Or they might say, "Remembering the species in groups helps most people remember them better." In addition, teachers might give clues that help students to monitor their performance: "You might note that there are twenty-five species to remember altogether. And notice that there are the same number of birds and mammals,

*Bridges How do parents' views affect children's learning of mathematics?

Informed training methods

but fewer fish, to remember." Comments like these lead to even better learning than simple blind training does. Apparently they do so by motivating students and by helping them to take charge of their own learning (Stipek, 1988).

In any case, learning strategies do seem to help children to organize and process information, at least for problems similar to the ones for which they first learn the strategies. In and of themselves, however, learning strategies do not guarantee metacognition. In fact, children do not show metacognition in a wide variety of situations until adolescence or even adulthood, and it does not assist children's problem-solving performance reliably until then either (Flavell, 1985). Given the rather abstract quality of knowledge *about* thinking, we should not be too surprised at this. After all, a child cannot judge a math problem's difficulty or select strategies for solving it — metacognitive skills — before he has accumulated some basic experience with math problems, and accumulating that experience may simply take more time than most children have had by age ten or twelve.

STYLES OF THINKING

By the middle years, children have begun to develop definite **cognitive styles** — particular forms or ways of thinking. For example, some children habitually reflect about a problem before responding to it, whereas others respond fairly quickly; and some children separate a problem into many independent elements, whereas others tend to treat it as a single unit. Such differences are important to students of child development in two ways. First, they indirectly affect children's cognitive performance, and second, they may reflect differences in children's personalities. Here are examples of some major differences in cognitive styles, which are summarized in Table 12.1.

Bridges   How is personality related to styles of thinking?

Convergent and Divergent Thinking

Focused problem solving

One way in which schoolchildren differ is in their use of convergent and divergent thinking. **Convergent thinking** refers to focused, deductive reasoning that leads to a particular solution to a problem. Solving an arithmetic problem requires convergent thinking; so does working a jigsaw puzzle. A lot of school learning

TABLE 12.1 Cognitive Styles in School-Age Children

Style of Thinking	Characteristics
Convergent thinking	Focused, deductive thinking; seeks single right answer to problems
Divergent thinking	Produces a wide range of unusual associations; elaborates on ideas; seeks many possible answers to problems
Field dependence	Perceives visual displays as whole patterns; socially, a willingness to rely on others' opinions and modify one's own
Field independence	Perceives visual displays as many discrete parts; socially, a relative autonomy in responding to others' opinions
Reflectivity	Responds slowly to cognitive problems; a slow conceptual tempo
Impulsivity	Responds quickly to cognitive problems; a fast conceptual tempo

Because schoolwork focuses heavily on "right" answers, it tends to encourage convergent thinking. Does that style of thinking match this girl's talents and personality, or does some other cognitive style suit her better?

requires convergent thinking because there is often just one right answer, which students are supposed to figure out. The prevalence of convergent thinking in school in fact may partly explain why nearly all children can use this style of thinking at least some of the time. Over the years, they simply receive a lot of training in it.

But some children seem especially disposed to using convergent thinking widely. Such children seek out and prefer structured learning tasks, such as those offered by books of puzzles or by complex building toys. They may even engage in structured activities at the expense of freer, more open-ended recreation, such as hanging around with friends.

Divergent thinking refers to the production of a wide variety of ideas, regardless of how unusual or disconnected they may be. It closely resembles the notion of "creativity" but lacks its emphasis on quality; divergent thinking simply diverges, and in doing so it can end up as either bizarre or uniquely valuable. Divergent thinkers tend to produce ideas fluently and elaborately, and they tend to form associations among ideas relatively flexibly. Most of us use this style of thinking from time to time; it is illustrated by our answers to open-ended questions such as "How many uses can you think of for a brick?" (Guilford, 1967).

Wide-ranging thinking

Some children seem predisposed to think divergently. They are not necessarily better than average at focused, logical reasoning (Kogan, 1973, 1989). And they do not necessarily use their divergent thinking only in situations that explicitly encourage it. Throughout childhood and youth, some children produce ideas fluently even on timed tests of creativity, in spite of the stress that such tests can create. For them, divergent thinking is just as likely as in situations that are untimed, relaxed, and fun (Borland, 1988; Runco & Okuda, 1988).

On the whole, children who engage in a lot of make-believe play tend also to engage in divergent thinking, although it is often not clear which behavior is causing which. Both skills require departing from the conventional meanings or uses of objects. In make-believe play, a child must imagine and use an object as something new; he may transform a block of wood into a truck, for example. In divergent thinking, the child thinks about that same block of wood in some unusual way; he may name it as "something to make a truck with." Both play and divergent thinking foster associations between diverse ideas. The activities

Divergent thinking and play

differ, however, in that play calls for acting out an association and divergent thinking calls for stating it (Clark et al., 1989).

The connection between play and divergent thinking has provided a method for professionals to encourage divergent thinking in children. In one experiment, some children were given open-ended play materials (a variety of shapes and vehicles and toy animals); other children received more convergent or focused materials (puzzles that assembled into formboards). Children who received the more open-ended materials later proved to be more fluent at verbal tasks involving divergent thinking, such as thinking up alternate uses for a common object (Pepler & Ross, 1981). After their open-ended play, incidentally, these children also did better than before at focused, convergent tasks such as putting puzzles together.

Field Dependence and Field Independence

Noticing patterns vs. noticing parts

Field dependence and **field independence** refer to how people analyze the world. By definition, individuals who are field dependent see things in relatively large, connected patterns. Looking at a picture of a mountain, for example, such a person would primarily notice its overall shape and perhaps also the larger patches of color that make it up. Field independent individuals, on the other hand, tend to see things more as discrete, independent parts. Such a person might notice the individual trees on the mountainside or many individual rocks. Children as well as adults vary along this dimension, and most people show a mixture of the two viewpoints (Hardy et al., 1987).

Test for field dependence and field independence

Features of Field Dependence and Field Independence   One aspect of these styles refers to relatively simple behaviors about visual judgment. In one widely used test, an individual looks at a vertical rod surrounded by a tilted frame in a darkened room. The person has to judge whether the rod is truly vertical. In these conditions, the tilt in the frame tends to affect the judgments of highly field dependent people more than those of field independent people. The latter group in general is much more accurate in judging verticality.

Another test of field dependence and independence asks individuals to find familiar figures that are embedded in larger, more complex drawings (see Figure 12.3). People who are very field independent can do this task relatively successfully, whereas very field dependent people have more trouble with it. Both tasks — the embedded figures and the rod and frame — share an emphasis on visual analysis: for each, the person must identify or isolate parts of what she sees from the whole, and deal with them as independent units (Witkin & Goodenough, 1977; Hall et al., 1988).

FIGURE 12.3
Embedded Figures

The notions of field dependence and field independence have also been extended to personal relations (Kogan, 1989). Field independent individuals supposedly deal with others in relatively autonomous ways — by forming and relying on their own opinions and by expecting others to do the same. Field dependent people, on the other hand, rely on others more often by modifying their own opinions to be consistent with others' and by asking for help in solving problems. These differences imply only that the two styles are different, not that one is necessarily better than the other. After all, there are times when working alone or autonomously gets a job done best (reading a book) and other times when concern for others matters more (deciding what to give someone for a present).

Reflectivity and Impulsivity

Still another style of thinking varies along the dimension of **reflectivity** and **impulsivity (R-I** for short). These terms refer to cognitive tempo, or speed of thinking. At the reflective extreme, a person takes a relatively long time to respond to a problem — perhaps many seconds — and then finally does so rather carefully and accurately. At the impulsive extreme, a person responds almost instantly and often makes relatively more errors as a result. Psychologists often measure R-I in children by asking them to match a simple figure (say, a drawing of a face) to several other figures that resemble it. Only one resembles it exactly, and the child must discover this perfectly matching one (Messer, 1976). Highly reflective children are those who take a relatively long time at a task such as this, or who make fewer errors at it, or both.

Children with an impulsive cognitive style respond quickly on cognitive tasks, at the risk of making more errors. But this style does not necessarily carry over to noncognitive tasks.

This description makes the reflective style seem more desirable than the impulsive style. Naturalistic observations of reflective and impulsive children show a more complex picture, however. Highly impulsive children, by definition, respond quickly to simple cognitive tasks, but they do *not* tend to respond quickly during free play periods at school. On the contrary, their behavior often appears less aggressive than that of highly reflective children, and their teachers rate them as less defensive than their more reflective peers (Wapner & Conner, 1986). Reflectivity and impulsivity do not correlate very well with tempo of behavior; in the two situations, much depends on the cognitive demands encountered.

Up to about age ten, children generally become more reflective, in the sense used here. On the test of matching familiar figures, for example, children take longer to respond as the years go by and also make fewer errors (Welsh, 1987). After about age ten, however, they begin to respond more quickly again — but they continue to make few errors. Should this final shift be regarded as a return to more impulsivity or as a shift toward some higher level of competency? At present, developmental psychologists do not agree; but the question does raise the possibility that reflectivity and impulsivity are not stable personality traits, among either young children or older ones (Kogan, 1982; B. Jones & Duffy, 1982). Instead, a task like matching may simply pose a dilemma between thinking quickly and thinking accurately. How individuals solve that dilemma may depend a lot on the circumstances of the task, not necessarily on the individuals' age.

Changes in tempo with age

As differences in cognitive styles emerge — even if they do prove unstable — they begin accounting for much of the individuality among children, both in cognitive skills as such and in personalities. General stages of development, such as described by Piaget or Erikson, still occur and explain many important changes in the middle years. But development gradually becomes less channeled by stages and more dependent on the unique experiences of individuals. This new mixture of influences is also reflected in children's language development during the middle years. Some aspects of language retain the predictable, universal quality of the earlier steps in language acquisition, but others clearly result from events and circumstances that happen only to some children and not to others.

Cognitive individuality

Perspectives

Cognitive Effects of Television, Radio, and Books

Television has become a major competitor for the attention of children. In recent years, according to surveys, children have spent about as much time watching TV shows as they have spent in school (Re:act, 1984). Many parents worry about all this watching and for good reasons: some programs portray considerable violence, significant sexuality, and various other behaviors that are undesirable viewing for children.

In addition to these social concerns, parents and experts worry about the cognitive effects of television, compared with those of strictly verbal media such as radio and books. Do children really learn and retain information as well from a well-made television show as they do from radio or printed presentations of the same topic? Does television stimulate the imagination or stifle it? And does television encourage reflective thought or interfere with it? These are questions about cognitive development. Given the importance of television in children's lives, it is not surprising that psychologists have conducted research to find answers to all of them.

Television is indeed a powerful learning device, in large part because it does make use of people's sense of vision. In one study, school-age children watched a movie that had no dialogue, called *The Red Balloon*. Some children saw only the silent film of this story, but others heard a tape-recorded narration that had been carefully matched with the film, scene for scene (Pedzek & Stevens, 1985). Afterward, the children who had seen the silent film recalled the story better than those who had heard the soundtrack. The effect was strongest for the youngest children (age five) and weakest for the oldest (age twelve). A related experiment found that adults showed about equal immediate recall for *The Red Balloon,* whether they heard it or saw it, but over the long run, even adults remembered better when they had seen the silent film (Baggett, 1979). To this extent, vision seems to dominate human information processing throughout life.

Another frequent criticism of television is that it leaves nothing to the imagination and therefore stifles creativity. In some ways, research seems to confirm this popular impression. One group of researchers asked children to provide endings to incomplete stories, some of which were presented on videotapes and others through sound recordings (Greenfield et al., 1981). On the average, schoolchildren gave more imaginative endings to the soundtrack stories by introducing more novel elements into the stories. Another research group obtained comparable results when they asked children to draw pictures about stories that they had either seen on video or heard on recordings (Meringoff et al., 1981). Drawings based on audio stories incorporated more diverse elements, and children also introduced more novel elements that had not actually occurred in the stories at all.

Does television discourage reflective thinking? To some extent it does; but the effects may not matter much to most children's long-term cognitive development. The act of watching a program must interfere with reflection almost by the nature of the activity: television stories unfold in real time, leaving almost no chance for children to stop and think about what they are seeing. In this way, television viewing contrasts sharply with reading, in which print remains constantly available for backtracking and review.

Whether these facts permanently impair children's reflective tendencies, however, is another question. School-age children who watch extremely large amounts of television do seem less reflective, as measured by standardized tests of this cognitive style (Greenfield, 1984). But the amount of television these children view is large — much more than the twenty-seven hours or so per week that constitutes the national average in the United States. And there is no guarantee that television really causes this trend. Perhaps non-reflective children seek out television more simply because the medium, by presenting material at a fixed pace, makes fewer demands for reflection.

Compared with radio and printed materials, then, television seems especially good for some purposes but less good for others. It encourages better memory, at least if children make a special point of trying to remember what they are viewing. It may not really discourage imagination, as critics fear; but some evidence does suggest that it may not stimulate imaginative thinking as well as nonvisual presentations do. And its effects on reflective thinking remain unclear; large amounts of television viewing and less reflective children do go together, but we still do not really know why.

LEARNING DISABILITIES

During the middle years, about 5 percent of children develop **learning disabilities,** which are disorders in basic cognitive processes that interfere with understanding or using language, either written or spoken (Lerner, 1988). Usually a learning disability causes poor academic achievement, although low achievement is not in and of itself evidence for a learning disability. These disabilities have no obvious physical cause, as, for instance, blindness or hearing impairment do, and learning disabilities do not result from a general slowness of thinking, as with mental retardation.

Learning disabilities take so many forms that they are hard to classify. For convenience, educators often distinguish between developmental learning disabilities and academic learning disabilities. **Developmental learning disabilities** are deficits in underlying psychological processes, such as poor memory or ADHD, the attention deficit disorder discussed in Chapter 11. **Academic learning disabilities** are difficulties in learning specific academic subjects or tasks, such as reading, spelling, handwriting, or arithmetic. They are often the more visible of the two kinds of disabilities because, by definition, they involve poor performance in school.

One common form of academic disability is called *dyslexia* — literally, an inability to read. The diversity of symptoms among children with dyslexia is representative of the diversity among learning disabilities in general. For some children, dyslexia consists of "word blindness": they find that they can read letters singly (like *c* or *a* or *t*) but not in combinations that make words such as *cat*. In other forms of dyslexia, children can read words but fail to comprehend them. They can copy words accurately or take them from oral dictation, but they cannot explain what they have written afterward, no matter how simple the vocabulary. Sometimes children with dyslexia can read combinations of digits that make large numbers; they can read *123*, for example, as "one hundred and twenty-three," but not as "one, two, three," even when they try. Most children with dyslexia have these problems in combination. Yet they seem normal in every other respect; their everyday conversations seem perfectly intelligent, and their motor skills seem just as skillful as other children's.

Features of reading problems

Relationships Between Academic and Developmental Disabilities

As you might suppose, academic disabilities often result from developmental disabilities. But not necessarily: a child can do poorly in an academic subject even without having anything wrong psychologically. Poor math performance may come from a dislike of the subject or a fear of competing with a whiz-kid sibling, among other things — not necessarily from inability to handle figures.

And the converse is sometimes also true: some developmental disabilities can occur with only minimal impact on academic performance or on academic potential (McNellis, 1987). A child with somewhat poor visual perception (a developmental disability) may compensate for this problem in various ways, such as minimizing reading words by sight recognition and relying heavily on analyzing the context in which words occur. This strategy may not solve all of his reading problems (sometimes the context does not give enough clues), but it may alleviate his disability if it is not too severe.

Symptoms of learning disabilities are complex

Causes of Learning Disabilities

What causes some children to have learning disabilities? Their symptoms resemble what happens to individuals who suffer injuries to certain parts of their brains (Rutter & Garmezy, 1983). For this reason, some professionals have suggested that many learning disabilities, including dyslexia, may reflect undetected minimal brain damage that occurred during the birth process or even before birth. This hypothesis is extremely hard to prove, however. It also discourages some parents and professionals from helping children with learning disabilities on the grounds (probably mistaken) that organically based problems are beyond control.

A more helpful explanation for learning disabilities focuses on brain functions rather than on brain anatomy. In this view, disabilities may result from

Bridges   Is there a physical basis to the learning disabilities in processing language that some children experience?

Physical causes of learning disabilities

Bridges How might learning disabilities be related to difficulties in the way the brain processes information?

Causes related to cognitive processing

subtle differences in how the brain normally organizes and processes information (Ceci, 1987). To see what this idea means, consider what children must do to read an ordinary page of print. First they must perceive the letters and words as visual patterns. Then they must combine these patterns into larger strings that constitute phrases and sentences. Finally they must connect these strings with meanings to form ideas. While all of these steps are going on, they must also scan ahead to recognize the next visual patterns on the page. If any of these steps fails or occurs in the wrong sequence or at the wrong speed, a child may appear dyslexic (Siegler, 1983).

These mistakes in cognitive processing may indeed lie at the heart of many learning disabilities. Some children with dyslexia may find visual recognition especially difficult or time consuming. Several researchers have reached this conclusion by studying a phenomenon called **perceptual masking,** in which some letters are hard to read because of the presence of other letters nearby. To understand this problem, consider the letters below:

wek
qwekl
aqweklm
asqweklmn
dsaqweklmnp
gfdsaqweklmnpyb
cvghdsaqweklmnpybht

If you look at the *e* in the top line, you will probably still be able to see the letter *w* and *k* clearly, using your peripheral vision (the corner of your eye). If you look at the *e* in a line further down, you can still see the end letters relatively clearly, but the middle letters become almost impossible to pick out clearly. Trying to notice the middle letters does help in perceiving them, but when you make this effort, the end letters become hard to discern. Perceiving one set of features in this display masks others; hence the name *perceptual masking.* Without a lot of practice, few people — adults or children — can see very many letters at once.

Some children with dyslexia (although not all) show especially strong perceptual masking (Wilkinson, 1980). Compared to normal readers, they must stare at words for rather long periods, consciously shifting attention from one subset of letters to another in a way similar to the staring required to "see" the letters displayed on the preceding page. Once they figure out the letters in a word, however, they can connect meanings with them fairly quickly and accurately. For these children, verbal association may happen much faster than visual perception.

The gap in speed between perceiving and associating may account for many errors made by children with dyslexia. A ten-year-old may look at the word *conceal,* for example, and say something like "concol," or look at *alternate* and say "alfoonite." In making these mistakes, children may literally be reading what they see and guessing about the rest. Unfortunately, they may see fewer letters than normal readers usually discern. To put it differently, trying to see all letters clearly may simply take too much time and effort, and overall reading comprehension bogs down as a result.

Helping Children with Learning Disabilities

Because learning disabilities constitute a problem primarily in school settings, school professionals have taken increasing responsibility in recent years for helping children who develop these disabilities. Most commonly, help consists

Most learning-disabled students can be helped by instruction that focuses specifically on their particular learning problems.

of careful diagnosis of which steps of thinking cause a child's problem, followed by individual instructional plans to strengthen those particular steps. Children with problems in perceptual masking can be given exercises in which they purposely work to improve this skill. Often such special work can be done in a regular class during a normal school day, but at least some of it requires individual tutoring so that the professional can monitor and give precise assistance to the child's thinking as it actually occurs. Depending on the child's needs and the school's circumstances, regular classroom teachers, parents, or trained special educators can act as tutors.

Individual diagnosis and tutoring

Note that children with learning disabilities are usually old enough to have feelings and opinions about their problems. Eventually, in fact, the major part of some learning disabilities may become *self-consciousness* about not learning, in addition to any cognitive or perceptual problems as such. A child who cannot read well usually becomes painfully aware of this fact sooner or later and worries about what teachers, parents, and peers may think of her as a result. Adults can help this problem by being optimistic about the child's eventual capacity to learn academic skills and by encouraging tolerance of differences among classmates and other peers.

Bridges How are emotions related to a child's learning disabilities?

Social support

LANGUAGE DEVELOPMENT IN THE MIDDLE YEARS

Language continues to develop during middle childhood. Vocabulary keeps growing, of course; but even more importantly, word meanings become more subtle and complex and more like adults'. And contrary to the impressions that young school-age children sometimes give, they have not necessarily mastered syntax. They often become confused by a number of common sentence forms until well into the elementary school years — confused enough, in fact, to cause misunderstandings from time to time.

Word Meanings

Levels in defining words

Do children go through predictable levels or stages in giving meanings to words? According to one commonly held view, children first define words by associating concrete actions with them or by using them in appropriate sentences (Wood, 1981). Only later do they begin categorizing words, as a dictionary does. In defining the word *dog,* for instance, children might give the following responses:

- Level 1: "You pat it on the head." *(action)*
- Level 2: "A dog plays with you. A dog chases cats." *(appropriate sentences)*
- Level 3: "An animal with fur and four legs." *(dictionary classification)*

Research using word-association tests implies at least some universality to these levels of definition making. In word-association tests, a child is given a series of familiar words and asked to respond with the first word that comes into his head — with whatever occurs to him before he has time to mull over the stimulus word. The procedure assumes that response words reflect the network of meanings within the child's vocabulary, and it tries to reveal which words are connected with which others in the child's mind (R. Brown, 1973).

On this kind of test, young children tend to respond differently than older children do to a wide variety of words. The younger ones — around kindergarten age — more often respond with words that naturally occur in sentences with the stimulus words. A prompt of *cup,* leads to a response of *drink,* just as *sit* leads to *down,* because these pairings occur together in sentences. By about age eight, however, children respond more according to the syntactic class of the prompts, and their responses often share certain elements of meaning as well. Now *cup* may lead to *bowl,* and *sit* may lead to *rest* (P. DeVilliers & DeVilliers, 1978). These shifts in associations parallel the shifts in levels of definition making. At the earlier level, the child associates (or defines) words in context, and at the later level, he tends more to classify or categorize them.

In spite of this developmental trend, all three levels of definition are used at least some of the time throughout middle childhood (Nippold, 1988a). Even for older elementary-age children, many words are easier to demonstrate in a sentence (level 2) than to analyze in any formal or abstract way (level 3). How should the word *the* be defined? Or the word *I?* Furthermore, unfamiliar words are sometimes used unconsciously at first. An older child may correctly use the word *trepidation,* without realizing she has done so and without being able to give a definition for it at any level at all.

Evidently, vocabulary meanings can consist of more than vocabulary definitions, and word usages and word definitions may develop somewhat independently. A full sense of vocabulary development therefore depends on measuring how well children use words in context, in addition to how well they can define them out of context (Sternberg & Powell, 1983b).

Grammatical Usage

As we discussed in Chapter 9, most five-year-olds use a grammar that closely resembles that of adults, except that it often is more regular. A young child may say, "I runned to the store" instead of "I ran to the store." When he does, he applies a common adult rule of syntax more widely than adults do. At first glance, mistakes like these may seem like children's only noticeable deficits in grammar; and even they disappear during the school years.

More careful observations, however, often reveal a number of other grammatical limitations. Each of the following sentences can confuse most kindergartners and do not become completely clear until after about age ten (C. Scott, 1988).

1. *The baby is easy to see.* Older children and adults take this sentence to mean that the baby is clearly visible and that observers are looking at it. But children younger than age nine or ten seem to think that the sentence means that the baby can see well. How do we know? If we suggest blindfolding the baby, a younger child will say that the baby is no longer "easy to see" but has become "hard to see." Apparently the child models the syntax of this sentence on other adjective-infinitive expressions, such as "eager to see" and "willing to see." In these latter expressions, the baby (rather than observers) does indeed do the seeing.

   Confusing the subject with the observer

2. *I don't think it will rain tomorrow.* Instead of understanding this sentence as a statement of opinion, as adults and older children usually do, young children tend to take it as a statement of fact. For them, the sentence means about the same as, "I know that it will not rain tomorrow." This interpretation rids the sentence of its sense of uncertainty, which older children usually recognize reliably (Shatz, 1983).

   Confusing opinion and fact

3. *Even the rabbit is in the garage.* Many young children apparently confuse the words *even* and *only* in sentences like this one because the sentence often produces a comment that the rabbit is alone (Nippold, 1988b). In other words, the children take the sentence to mean *only* the rabbit is in the garage.

   Confusing words that emphasize

Because these sentences all involve rather simple vocabulary, children's confusions stem largely from their grammatical organization. Note, however, that some confusion may also come from their immature cognitive abilities. "The baby is easy to see" may reflect children's egocentrism, as described by Piaget; perhaps children assume that their own ability to see does not differ from anyone else's, including the baby's. For similar reasons, they cannot yet properly understand statements such as "I don't think . . ." because they still lack firm awareness of how often viewpoints can vary among individuals.

Bilingualism and Its Effects

Around the world, a majority of children are able to speak two languages and are therefore bilingual (Paulston, 1988). Bilingualism exists even in the supposedly monolingual society of the United States; somewhere between 25 and 35 million individuals (about 10–15 percent) regularly use another language in addition to English (Ruiz, 1988). Does this skill benefit their cognitive development? Research suggests that it does, but primarily when they acquire both languages equally well (Diaz, 1983). Language specialists call such children *balanced bilinguals.*

Bridges What are the cognitive advantages to children of knowing two languages equally well?

Cognitive Effects of Bilingualism   For one thing, balanced bilingual children show more **cognitive flexibility** — skill at detecting multiple meanings of words and alternative orientations of objects — than monolingual children do. Bilingual children can substitute arbitrary words for normally occurring words relatively easily without changing any other features of the sentence (R. Berman, 1987). If asked to substitute *spaghetti* for *I* in the sentence "I am cold," bilingual children more often produce the exact substitution "Spaghetti am cold" and resist the temptation to correct the grammar ("Spaghetti is cold"), thereby violating the instructions for the task. Presumably such a skill stems from bilinguals' special experience with the arbitrary, conventional nature of words and language.

Cognitive flexibility

Increased awareness of language

Partly, such flexibility shows **metalinguistic awareness** — the knowledge that language can be an object of thought. Metalinguistic awareness develops because bilingual experiences often challenge children to think consciously about what to say and how to say it (Savignon, 1983). A question such as, "What if a dog were called a cat?" therefore poses less conceptual problems because of bilingualism. So do follow-up questions such as, 'Would this 'cat' meow?" or "Would it purr?"

Knowing two languages may also affect cognitive style. Research suggests that bilinguals show more ability to analyze thought problems into constituent parts, a skill reminiscent of (although not identical with) the field independence discussed earlier in this chapter (Ben-Zeev, 1984). This analytic ability may develop more fully because bilingualism encourages consciousness of cognitive expression.

Field independence

Balanced vs. unbalanced bilinguals

But note that all of these cognitive advantages apply primarily to balanced bilingual children — the ones with equal skill in both languages. What of the unbalanced bilinguals — the ones with more skill in one language than in the other? Does knowledge of a second language help, even if it is poor knowledge? Evidence is scarce, but what there is suggests that unbalanced bilingualism has mixed effects on children's thinking skills (N. Miller, 1984). These effects seem to result from broad social attitudes surrounding the child's primary and secondary languages.

Bilingual children have cognitive advantages over monolinguals, but only as long as both languages are treated with respect by their teachers and by society.

Social Effects of Bilingualism   When children acquire two languages, one of them usually has more prestige than the other. In the United States, the "best"

or most important language almost always is English. Its prestige results not only from its widespread use but also from its association with success and power: all the important people in American society, it seems, speak English fluently. These circumstances cast a stigma or negative attitude on other languages.

The lower prestige of non-English languages has three important effects on bilingual people. First, they may sometimes feel unwilling to use their primary or "home" language in public, even when it is appropriate to do so. One study documented this tendency among bilingual Mexican-Americans by observing their conversations with white Americans (G. Barker, 1975). Even when the whites spoke perfect Spanish, and even when the Mexican-Americans knew that they did, the Mexican-Americans preferred to use English.

Second, social biases against a child's primary language can contribute to lack of confidence about linguistic skill in general. Studies of a number of bilingual groups in both Europe and the United States have found that bilinguals often underrate their language skills in both languages (Gal, 1979). Lack of confidence is felt most strongly when the bilingual is speaking to a monolingual, such as when a Polish-American child is talking to a teacher who speaks only English.

Third, and conversely, the lower prestige of one language can also stimulate loyalty among the group that speaks it. Observations of bilinguals in eastern Canada, suggest that even though many of them speak both French and English perfectly, they often refuse to use English in public places such as restaurants and department stores, even with English-speaking customers (Giles et al., 1977). This may help to give the lower status language (in this case, French) more prestige, at least in the minds of individuals who use that language. But its effect on the rest of society seems less clear.

Black English

In the United States, some black people use a dialect or version of English called **Black English,** one that differs from the middle-class dialect that linguists call **Standard English.** The two versions differ in three ways (Baugh, 1983). First, certain sounds occur differently: the sound /th/ becomes /d/, making the word *this* sound like *dis*. Second, certain grammatical forms are different. The verb *to be* is used to indicate a continuing situation or condition. The sentence "The coffee be cold" means approximately, "Every day, the coffee is always cold"; but the sentence "The coffee cold" means simply "The coffee is cold." Third, Black English contains many words and expressions that have very different meanings than in Standard English. The word *bad* can mean something undesirable ("I have a bad cold") but also something very good ("She look bad" usually means "She looks very good").

Studies of Black English find it just as complex as any other language, including Standard English, and just as capable of expressing the full range of human thought and emotion (Folb, 1980). Unfortunately, society's attitudes toward it remain rather negative (Labov, 1982), which has created dilemmas for teachers of students who do use Black English. Should they be allowed to speak this dialect in class, or even be encouraged to do so, because they know it best? Or should they always be expected to use Standard English in order to prepare them to function better in mainstream, white society? Educators typically recommend a compromise: teachers should respect Black English, understand its richness, and allow students to use it in class some of the time (Brooks, 1985). But they should also encourage students to practice Standard English because it is the dialect that will probably help them the most to become established in adult life.

Bridges How can social attitudes about a language affect the development of bilingualism?

Bridges What are some of the possible social effects of bilingualism?

Self-consciousness about primary language

Lack of confidence

In-group loyalty

Rich, complex language

DEFINING AND MEASURING INTELLIGENCE

Definitions of intelligence

Intelligence refers to adaptability, or, put differently, to a general ability to learn from experience. Usually intelligence also refers to the ability to reason abstractly, sometimes using language to do so; and it includes the ability to integrate old and new knowledge. Because these skills have proved especially helpful in school, assessing intelligence has become very important to those who plan educational programs, such as school administrators and school psychologists. Many tests of general ability or intelligence have therefore been developed, both for adults and for children.

Concepts of Intelligence

Partly as a result of devising and using ability tests, educators and psychologists have continually debated the precise nature of intelligence. Disagreement surrounds all of the following questions, among others.

Specific vs. general abilities

One Ability or Several?   Both common sense and research suggest that abilities come in many forms. But do these forms add up to one truly general "intelligence"? Some psychologists (and their tests) emphasize relatively specific skills; others emphasize one rather general ability, sometimes named *g* (Sternberg, 1988). Most tests (and their psychologists) acknowledge the presence of both general and specific factors, even though they differ in emphasis.

Conglomeration or Compound?   Granted that specific skills contribute to intelligence in some way, but how do they do it? Some psychologists argue that general ability consists of a loose conglomeration or grouping of diverse skills and that these do not necessarily relate to one another in a coherent, logical way (Gardner, 1983). This viewpoint also seems implicit in many ability tests that give only one general score of intelligence; questions on such a test are not grouped in any particular way and simply add up to general intelligence.

Relations among abilities

Others argue, however, that the specific elements of intelligence bear logical relationships to one another and that general intelligence cannot develop unless these elements exist and develop together. Probably the most widely known advocate of this idea is Piaget. In his view, specific cognitive skills, such as conservation, inevitably affect other specific skills, such as classification. Only together can these skills create the truly general ability of children — concrete operations.

Changes during development

Qualitative Development or Quantitative?   As children grow, what happens to their intelligence? Does it change in nature, as Piaget argued in his stage theory? Or does it simply become "more of everything"? Some ability tests imply the latter view by the way they are constructed. On these tests, children of all ages answer more or less the same questions, and the older, better developed children simply answer more of them correctly. But not all ability tests work this way; some purposely give different sorts of questions to children of different ages and score the results differently.

As these comments imply, ability tests have not only resulted from widespread concepts of intelligence but have also helped to create them. These tests have also affected the educational careers of numerous children during the twentieth century. For these reasons, among others, some psychologists point to intelligence testing as one of the major success stories of psychology. At the same time, others have expressed serious misgivings about and criticisms of such tests.

Perspectives

One Intelligence or Many?

If we assume that intelligence consists of just one unified factor, then different human talents should share common features — the ones that underlie basic intelligence. How much do they do so? To help answer this question, imagine children with each of the following talents.

1. *Language skill* A child with this talent can speak comfortably and fluently and can learn new words and expressions easily. She can also memorize verbal materials, such as poems, much more easily than other children can.

2. *Musical skill* This child not only plays one or more musical instruments but can also sing and notice subtle musical effects. Usually musical talent includes a good sense of timing or rhythm, too.

3. *Logical skill* A child with this skill can organize objects and concepts well. Using a microcomputer comes easily, for example; so do mathematics lessons at school.

4. *Spatial skill* This is a child who can literally find his way around. He knows the streets of the neighborhood better than most children his age do, or if he lives in the country, he can find his way across rather large stretches of terrain without getting lost.

5. *Kinesthetic or body skill* This child is sensitive to the internal sensations created by body movement. As a result, she finds dancing, gymnastics, and other activities requiring balance easy to learn.

6. *Interpersonal and intrapersonal skills* A child with interpersonal skill shows excellent understanding of others' feelings, thoughts, and motives. A child with intrapersonal skill has good understanding of his own. For children with either or both of these skills, handling social encounters comes relatively easily.

Described in this way, these talents do not look like they have much in common. In fact only two of them, language skill and logical skill, relate very closely to the content of most intelligence tests, even though the tests supposedly measure general ability (Wallaclh, 1985).

Some psychologists therefore urge that we give up the idea that one general intelligence exists and instead focus attention on the diversity of abilities possible among human beings. For a starting point in this change of focus, one psychologist, Howard Gardner, has proposed that each of the talents listed above may actually constitute a distinct form of intelligence (Gardner, 1983; Walters & Gardner, 1986). (Interpersonal and intrapersonal skills may really amount to two distinct forms of intelligence; but the research evidence makes Gardner unsure about this.)

These intelligences are separate, he argues, for several reasons. First, some of the six can be physically located within the brain. Certain language functions occur within particular, identifiable parts of the brain, as do kinesthetic or balance functions. Second, the intelligences sometimes occur in pure form; some retarded individuals play a musical instrument extremely well, even though they cannot talk well or reason abstractly. Third, the intelligences each have particular, core skills that clearly set them off from the others. Being musical requires a good sense of pitch, but this skill does not contribute to any of the other intelligences very much.

These comments may sound like criticisms of conventional intelligence testing. Strictly speaking, however, they really criticize the use of conventional tests beyond their intended purposes. As we point out in the text, such tests are designed to predict academic skills, and therefore they heavily emphasize verbal and logical activities. But school is not everything in life, in spite of its prominence in children's lives. Perhaps the fact that school attendance is compulsory has actually interfered with understanding intelligence because it may have made us all value verbal and mathematical skills more than we should.

Nature and Purposes of Standardized Tests

Tests of general ability or intelligence are one type of **standardized test.** All standardized tests (including intelligence tests) have several well-defined features. First, they always contain clearly stated questions that have relatively specific answers. The questions usually draw on logical reasoning and verbal skill, which are what schools typically require. Second, standardized tests always include clear, standard procedures for administration and scoring. Often they provide a script for the person giving the test, as well as specific printed advice about when and how to credit particular answers. Third, such tests present information about how large groups of comparable individuals perform in order to allow evaluation of the performance of particular groups or of individual children (Scarr, 1984a).

Features of standardized tests

Kinds of Standardized Tests   Standardized tests serve many purposes, but for convenience we can classify them into two major groups, achievement tests and aptitude or ability tests. **Achievement tests** measure skills or knowledge that individuals have already learned; they try to indicate current attainment in a particular realm of human behavior. Children often encounter such tests in the form of scholastic achievement tests: tests of reading achievement, for example, or of arithmetic achievement. By nature, such tests usually draw heavily on the typical curriculum content of the subject area being tested.

Achievement vs. aptitude tests

Aptitude tests measure ability or try to estimate future performance in some realm of behavior. A test of scholastic aptitude, for instance, tries to estimate a child's potential for success in school. Because of their goal, aptitude tests contain a broader range of questions than achievement tests do; a scholastic aptitude test would probably include questions from several major school subjects and draw on basic academic skills such as reading and mathematical reasoning.

In practice, aptitude and achievement tests are not as distinct as these definitions make them sound. Often achievement tests work very well as predictors of future performance; children's current skills in arithmetic, for instance, predict their future mathematical performance about as well as any aptitude tests can do (Anastasi, 1985). And aptitude tests can succeed at predicting future progress only by sampling skills and knowledge that children have already attained. Nonetheless, the distinction remains useful for those who develop and use tests. In general, measuring aptitude means looking to the future, and measuring achievement means assessing the past.

Comparing groups of children

Once norms have been calculated, standardized tests — and especially achievement tests — can serve two purposes. On one hand, they can help educators to know how well particular schools or classrooms are functioning in general. For example, all classrooms using a particular curriculum can be compared with classrooms using another curriculum, or all classrooms in one school can be compared with all classrooms in the city or even with a national cross-section.

Assessing individual children

On the other hand, standardized tests can sometimes aid individual children. The most common way involves screening students for special educational help. If teachers find a certain student learning the curriculum very slowly, they may ask a school psychologist to test her general scholastic ability in the hope of diagnosing or clarifying her learning problems. Although the results of such a test cannot stand alone, they often do contribute to the complex process of assessing the learning needs of a particular child.

As you may suspect, standardized tests do not serve either of these purposes perfectly. Reasons other than ability, such as a child's health or motivation to succeed, affect performance. So do physical disabilities, such as visual impairment. And more indirectly, cultural and language differences among children affect performance on standardized tests. These latter influences deserve special discussion because they operate systematically across all children throughout society.

Biases of Intelligence and General Ability Tests

In spite of trying to measure general qualities, tests of ability and intelligence contain various biases. For example, many intelligence tests rely heavily on language in all its forms — listening, speaking, and reading. Many also emphasize problems that have specific answers and that play down divergent or creative thinking. And although they do not focus on speed, intelligence tests tend to favor children who answer fairly rapidly and who do not take much time to mull over their solutions.

Because all of these features are also emphasized by schools, intelligence tests measure academic ability better than any other skill. Some psychologists in fact have suggested calling them measures of *academic intelligence* or of *school ability* in order to make this limitation clear (Anastasi, 1985).

Cultural Assumptions The biggest problem with intelligence tests, however, comes from their cultural assumptions, which have originated entirely from white, middle-class experiences in Western Europe and North America. The tests show their assumptions or biases in at least two ways. First, individual questions often demand knowledge that children can gain only by thorough immersion in white, middle-class society. One question might ask children to describe the purpose of a garden hose, thereby assuming previous contact with running water. Another question might ask children to define the word *drama* or *concerto*, thereby assuming the sort of education that provides this information (Flynn, 1987).

Even when tests avoid this sort of bias, they suffer from other, more subtle cultural assumptions. Many ethnic groups and cultures do not value conversations based on logic; speaking in abstractions may seem rude or at least boring (Heath, 1986). Children from these groups therefore cannot be expected to take tests that rely heavily on this sort of dialogue. In some cultural groups, too, contact with strange adults is extremely rare, so children from such groups may find sitting alone in a room with an unfamiliar test administrator rather perplexing or even frightening. For such children, any questions the administrator asks may seem much less important than figuring out this adult's real motives (Laboratory of Comparative Human Cognition, 1982).

This child's skill at quilt making would not be well assessed on most tests of general ability. But specialized tests of manual dexterity might give a valid indication of this kind of talent.

Common Misinterpretations of Intelligence Tests

Because of these problems, intelligence tests have sometimes been criticized strongly. Some school districts and states have even banned the less reliable group tests altogether. Individual intelligence tests have usually remained in use, however, because they are especially helpful in diagnosing children with special learning needs and because they are always administered by relatively well-trained psychologists.

A lot of criticism has stemmed from misinterpretations of the results of intelligence tests. In one way or another, all of the following mistakes have turned out to be all too easy to make.

1. *Equating test scores with true intelligence* As we have already pointed out, intelligence tests primarily measure academic talent. Yet life is full of many other kinds of talent, from cooking or playing the piano to always saying the tactful thing. The further removed these talents are from academics, the less well intelligence tests can measure them or predict them.

   Intelligence test scores vs. intelligence

2. *Confusing intellectual differences with intelligence* Most intelligence test scores reflect how much a child differs from other, comparable children. They usually do *not* report how much a child actually knows at any given point in time. Yet actual knowledge may matter more than differences in knowledge in many situations, such as when a child is trying to fix his bicycle or trying to find his way home along an unfamiliar street.

   Individual differences vs. actual skills

3. *Assuming too much precision* Because intelligence tests give numerical scores, adults are tempted to think that they are more precise than they really are. In reality, however, small differences in scores between children often reflect random variation rather than true differences in intelligence. Test manuals usually point out this fact, but unfortunately, the information sometimes does not reach parents, and even teachers or school psychologists may forget it.

   Overestimating precision

Implications for Teachers and Parents   Properly used, tests of intelligence and general ability can help parents and teachers to understand children. But the tests cannot substitute for the many other ways of gaining such understanding, such as through extended, informal observation in class or at home or just plain conversation. Most commonly, intelligence tests simply add to information already known or suspected about a particular child; they do not replace that information. Also, intelligence tests play a role with children who are academically at an extreme, whether extremely gifted or extremely slow. For the vast majority of children — the "middling" ones — the tests usually contribute little information that is really useful in planning their personal educational futures. For such children, teachers can usually learn more by devising or selecting achievement tests focused more precisely on the class's current curriculum. Parents can usually learn more by observing their children informally at home and by talking with teachers and other adults who know their children. This still leaves important work for ability tests, but the work has specific purposes and limitations.

MORAL DEVELOPMENT

During the school years, cognitive development also affects the social and emotional lives of children. One of the most important ways in which it does so is by influencing the development of morality. **Morality** refers to a sense of ethics, or of right and wrong. Questions of morality come up whenever one child can help or hurt another child. Because children nearly all have contact with their peers, questions of helping and hurting arise rather often: in deciding whether to share a lunch with a classmate, for example, or whether to take a sibling's favorite book without permission.

Features of moral development   As these examples suggest, morality has several aspects, and to varying degrees all require cognitive skills. First, children must learn to identify how various situations actually affect other children's welfare. For instance, what would be the consequences of "borrowing" a neighbor's bicycle without asking? Second, children must learn good moral judgment — how to select actions that truly help others and do not hurt them. Children must learn that forcing a candy bar on a friend who does not want it does not really constitute a good deed. And third, children must acquire skills for implementing moral judgments and actions. When someone cries because of an injury, a child may sympathize deeply yet not know how to respond. Should she say something, and if so, what? Or just offer a handkerchief?

Inconsistency of moral behavior   These complexities may help explain an important quality of moral development during childhood, namely, its lack of consistency. As has been documented now for decades, very few children do the "right thing" all the time or even a majority of the time (Hartshorne & May, 1928). At some time or other, virtually every child cheats at schoolwork, and virtually every child tattles or betrays a friend at least occasionally. These lapses may result from difficulties with some aspect of morality, ranging from lack of sensitivity to others' welfare, to poor judgment about appropriate actions, to lack of skill in implementing good intentions.

In an effort to make sense out of such complexities, theorists of cognitive development such as Piaget have focused on how children make moral judgments or form beliefs about right and wrong. They have given less attention to how children translate these judgments and beliefs into moral actions. Three major stage theories of moral development have come out of this effort, one originated by Piaget himself, a second developed by Lawrence Kohlberg, and a third conceived by Carol Gilligan.

Piagetian Stages of Moral Thinking

In observing children at play, Piaget noted differences in how younger and older children conceived of the rules for simple games such as marbles (Piaget, 1964). Younger children, aged about six to nine, tended to use what Piaget called **heteronomous morality,** or a "morality of constraint." In this way of thinking, children regarded the rules of a game as sacred and unchangeable, yet they were very lax about actually following the rules. Infractions were judged according to the amount of objective damage that a child did, regardless of whether the damage was accidental or purposeful. Knocking all the other children's marbles out of the playing circle was worse than knocking only one marble out, for example, whether or not the child had meant to do so. Yet children at this age would often commit precisely such a "sin" whenever they could get away with it in spite of judging it rather harshly.

> *The morality of constraint*

By the later years of elementary school (around ages nine to twelve), however, children shifted toward what Piaget called **autonomous morality,** or a "morality of cooperation." In this more mature philosophy, children began to take their peers' desires and intentions into account in evaluating their actions. Now, spoiling the entire circle of marbles might be judged less harshly if it happened accidentally, and moving just one marble illegally might be judged more harshly if the child moved it on purpose. At the same time, the children Piaget observed felt that they could change the rules if they wanted to through group discussion and decision; the rules were no longer fixed or sacred. Perhaps as a result, children at the later stage adhered to the rules more carefully because they felt more responsible for creating them. The very awesomeness of rules may have prevented younger children from taking responsibility for following them.

> *The morality of cooperation*

Piaget argued that children in the middle years shifted from heteronomous to autonomous morality because of repeated encounters in playing with peers. Inevitably, disagreements would arise, and the conflicts would stimulate children to take other viewpoints into account in playing games with rules. In the long run, according to Piaget, children therefore become more democratic — more willing to cooperate in changing rules, on the one hand, and more willing to follow the rules, on the other. Unfortunately, as plausible as this process sounds, very little research evidence actually supports it (Lickona, 1976). Children who must deal repeatedly with peers, that is, do not necessarily become more democratic over the long run. But Piaget was right about the sequencing of the two types of morality: heteronomous morality does appear more often in younger children, and autonomous morality does appear more in older ones (Karniol, 1978, 1980).

> *Influence of experience*

Kohlberg's Six Stages of Moral Judgment

Lawrence Kohlberg extended Piaget's ideas by proposing six stages of moral judgment rather than just two and by proposing that these span almost the entire first half of life (Kohlberg, 1976). The stages were derived from interviews conducted in much the same style as Piaget's classic interviews about cognitive development: children and adults of various ages responded individually to hypothetical or imaginary stories that contained moral dilemmas.

The six proposed stages are summarized in Table 12.2. In two ways, the stages form a progression. First, earlier stages represent more egocentric thinking than later stages do; and second, earlier stages by their nature require more specific or concrete thinking than later stages do. For instance, in Stage I (called "heteronomous morality," just as Piaget's concept is), a child makes no distinction between what he believes is right and what the world tells him is right; he simply accepts the perspective of the authorities as his own. By Stage 4 (social

> *Progression away from egocentric and concrete thinking*

TABLE 12.2 Kohlberg's Stages of Moral Judgment

Stage	Nature of Stage
Preconventional Level *(emphasis on avoiding punishments and getting rewards)*	
Stage 1 Heteronomous morality; ethics of punishment and obedience	Good is what follows externally imposed rules and rewards and is whatever avoids punishment
Stage 2 Instrumental purpose; ethics of market exchange	Good is whatever is agreeable to the individual and to anyone who gives or receives favors; no long-term loyalty
Conventional Level *(emphasis on social rules)*	
Stage 3 Interpersonal conformity; ethics of peer opinion	Good is whatever brings approval from friends as a peer group
Stage 4 Social system orientation: conformity to social system; ethics of law and order	Good is whatever conforms to existing laws, customs, and authorities
Postconventional Level *(emphasis on moral principles)*	
Stage 5 Social contract orientation; ethics of social contract and individual rights	Good is whatever conforms to existing procedures for settling disagreements in society; the actual outcome is neither good nor bad
Stage 6 Ethics of self-chosen universal principles	Good is whatever is consistent with personal, general moral principles

Moral stages in the middle years

Bridges How do peers influence moral judgment during the middle years?

system orientation), he realizes that individuals vary in their points of view, but he still takes for granted the existing overall conventions of society as a whole. He cannot yet imagine a society in which those conventions might be purposely modified. Only by Stages 5 and 6 (ethics) can he do so fully.

In the middle years, children most commonly show ethical reasoning at Stage 2, but a minority may begin showing Stage 3 or 4 reasoning toward the end of this period (Colby et al., 1983). In Stage 3 (interpersonal orientation), a child's chief concern is with the opinions of her peers: an action is right if her immediate circle of friends says that it is right. Often this way of thinking leads to helpful actions, such as taking turns and sharing toys or materials. But often it does not, as when a group of friends decides to let the air out of the tires of someone's car. In Stage 4 (social system orientation), children shift from concern with peers to concern with the opinions of their broader community or of society as a whole: now something is right if these wider groups approve. This broader source of moral judgment spares Stage 4 children from the occasional tyranny of friends' opinions; they will now no longer steal hub caps just because their friends urge them to do so. But they still cannot imagine the wider public holding unethical opinions or taking unjust actions; the notion of racial bigotry, for example, or of an unjust war, still seems like an impossibility. Such ideas become very real possibilities to some individuals in adolescence and beyond.

Evaluation of Cognitive Theories of Moral Development

Support for the six stages

Although research has tended to find Piaget's two-stage theory too simplistic, Kohlberg's six-stage theory has held up well when tested on a wide variety of children, adolescents, and adults (Colby et al., 1983). The stages of moral thinking (in Table 12.2) do seem to describe changes in moral judgment as children grow up, at least when children express their judgments about hypothetical dilemmas posed in stories.

Note, however, that Kohlberg's stages describe only the *form* of thinking, not its content. According to Kohlberg's theory, a child's specific moral opinions are relatively independent of his moral development. Three children may all believe that telling a fib is wrong. Yet the first child may hold this opinion out of fear of being caught lying (Stage 1); the second may want to agree with friends (Stage 3); and the third may feel a commitment to follow existing rules (Stage 4). In Kohlberg's theory, the form of ethics develops, but the content does not.

In spite of the theory's plausibility, a number of developmental psychologists have questioned important aspects of it. Can the form of ethical thinking really be separated from content as much as Kohlberg proposes? Perhaps not. Some studies have found that when children reason about familiar situations, they tend to mature (that is, higher stage) ethical responses (Damon, 1977). For instance, children have a better sense of fairness about playing four-square on the playground than about whether to steal a drug for a spouse who is dying (one of Kohlberg's fictional dilemmas). A similar bias for the familiar occurs among adults as well; women think in more mature or developed ways about ethical problems of special concern and familiarity to women, such as whether to procure an abortion (Gilligan, 1982). To some extent, therefore, what someone thinks about affects the ethics she applies.

Effects of familiarity on moral reasoning

These variations challenge Kohlberg's theory. According to some psychologists, the problem may arise because the theory does not fully distinguish between social convention and morality (Nucci, 1982; Turiel, 1978). **Social conventions** refer to the arbitrary customs and agreements about behavior that members of society use — such as table manners and forms of greeting. Morality, as we have already pointed out, refers to the more weighty matters of justice and right and wrong. By nature, social conventions inevitably generate widespread agreement throughout society, whereas morality does not necessarily do so. Yet Kohlberg's six-stage theory glosses over these differences by defining some of its stages in terms of social conventions and others in terms of morality. Stage 4 (social system orientation), for example, seems to refer to social conventions as well as to moral matters, but Stage 5 (social contract orientation) refers only to moral judgment.

Effects of knowledge of social conventions

For this youngster, stealing may be wrong only to the extent that her friends say it is. As with the rest of us, too, her actions may not always coincide with her moral beliefs.

Studies that have in fact distinguished between convention and morality have produced a less stagelike picture of moral development. In one such study (Nucci, 1978), children between the ages of six and seventeen were asked questions such as

- Is it wrong to steal? *(morality related)*
- Is it wrong to hit another person? *(morality related)*
- Is it wrong for a group to change the rules of a game? *(convention related)*
- Is it okay for a country to make the traffic lights blue and purple instead of red and green? *(convention related)*

At every age, most children felt that hitting and stealing were wrong but that changing the rules of a game or changing the color of traffic lights was acceptable. If morality had developed at all, then, this study suggested that it had already done so before the school years began. By the youngest age tested, six, children already clearly distinguished between moral behavior and conventional behavior.

Gilligan's Ethics of Care in Social Context

One especially important criticism of Kohlberg's six-stage theory has to do with possible gender bias. Do Kohlberg's stages apply equally well to both sexes? And does his theory undervalue ethical attitudes that may develop more fully in girls and women than in boys and men? The most well-known investigations of these questions have been pursued by Carol Gilligan and her associates (Gilligan, 1982, 1987; Gilligan & Wiggins, 1987).

Ethics of principles and justice

According to Gilligan, boys and girls tend to view moral problems differently. As they grow up, boys learn to think more often in terms of general ethical principles that they can apply to specific moral situations. They might learn that deceiving is always bad — in principle — and evaluate a specific instance of deception of a friend against this generalization. The principles that boys learn also tend to emphasize independence, autonomy, and the rights of others. This orientation biases boys to ignore or minimize others' possible needs: if a friend is at home sick with a cold, it may seem better to leave the friend alone until he gets better, rather than check on how well the friend is recovering.

Judgments must allow for circumstances

For their part, girls tend to develop a different sort of morality as they grow up. Instead of seeing moral judgment as a set of abstract principles to apply to specific situations, girls tend to see ethics as inseparable from the contexts in which judgments have to be made (see Table 12.3). A girl may therefore feel

TABLE 12.3   Stages of Moral Development According to Gilligan

Stage	Features
Stage 1 *Survival orientation*	Egocentric concern for self, lack of awareness of others' needs; "right" action is what promotes emotional or physical survival.
Stage 2 *Conventional care*	Lack of distinction between what others want and what is right; "right" action is whatever pleases others best.
Stage 3 *Integrated Care*	Coordination or integration of needs of self and of others; "right" action takes account of self as well as others.

Source: Gilligan (1982).

A Talk with Five Children

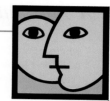

The Development of Moral Judgment

Both Gilligan's and Kohlberg's theories predict that children judge moral issues differently as they move from middle childhood to adolescence and adulthood. Some of those changes are visible in these excerpts of interviews with two school-age children (Ruth Ellen and John) and with three teenagers (Andrew, Lenny, and Beth). Each person was told the same ethical dilemma, which is reproduced here only in Ruth Ellen's case.

Ruth Ellen (age 8)

Interviewer: I'm going to tell you a story and ask you to think about it. It's about a man named George.

Ruth Ellen: All right. I like stories.

Interviewer: Something sad happened. His wife got sick. And she needed a special medicine or else she might die. George didn't have much money, even after he worked very hard to get all he could. He went to the only druggist who sold the medicine, but it was still much too expensive. He only had half the money he needed. So you know what George did?

Ruth Ellen: What?

Interviewer: He went one night and broke into the drug store and stole the medicine, so he could give it to his wife, and . . .

Ruth Ellen: That isn't a good way to get it.

Interviewer: Do you think George was right or wrong in doing it?

Ruth Ellen: Some ways right, some ways wrong. He's right to really think about his wife. The way he's wrong is to steal. He shouldn't of done it because he could get arrested. Then what would his wife do without him?

John (age 11)

Interviewer: Was George right or wrong to steal the drug?

John: It was wrong to steal it, but he needed it. It's wrong to steal things, but someone else is really sick and they may die if you don't get it.

Interviewer: Why is it wrong to steal?

John: Because other people have worked to make it and if you steal it, their work will go to waste because they won't make as much money as they would if it wasn't stolen.

Interviewer: And why would it be right to steal it?

John: Someone else was sick and might die.

Viewed from Kohlberg's perspective, Ruth Ellen and John express elements of both preconventional and conventional moral reasoning. Each child is concerned about rewards and punishments (going to jail, making money from the drug), as well as about social conventions (it is wrong to steal). From Gilligan's perspective, the two children both show a caring attitude about personal relationships (in this case, the husband-wife relationship), although stated at Gilligan's middle level, that of conventional caring for others. Note that the fact that Gilligan's stages happen more clearly among females does not prevent John from expressing a caring attitude as well.

Andrew (age 15)

Interviewer: Was George right or wrong to steal the drug?

Andrew: Well, he was both right and wrong. The stealing part is wrong because if everyone did that then there would be chaos and there would be, you know, no order. It just would really mess up our society. But the drug is really important for his wife and it sounds like the drug was probably overpriced and the people who were making the drug are probably being unfair about how they price it.

But you can't just totally go out of the system. By stealing, you're totally leaving the system. You have to get it through the system. And there's different ways to do that. He didn't do the right thing, but if it's worth it to him to pay the penalty — you know, of stealing — then maybe it was worth it to him.

Lenny (age 17)

Interviewer: Was George right or wrong to steal the drug?

Lenny: You know, from my political perspective, I say there should be a national health care system; drugs should be free. They should and there's no two ways about that. And I think if someone I loved was dying I would break the law to save them. I would consider that it's not really right, but it's what has to be done.

Andrew and Lenny's ideas show elements of Kohlberg's postconventional thinking. Although Andrew still implies concern with social conventions about stealing, he explains his concern primarily by the need for justice and order in society — one of the signs of postconventional thinking. Lenny goes further than Andrew: his reponse primarily defends a universal moral principle — a general human right to life and physical well-being. This principle guides his thinking enough that it leads him to advocate breaking the law.

Beth (age 15)

Beth: Was he right or wrong in stealing the drug? Well, I'm not sure if there's a right or wrong necessarily. I think that human life is much more important to me anyway than money is. And if human life has to be saved by something, this drug or *(continued)*

A Talk with Five Children (continued)

whatever, and there's no way to get it. I don't know. It's such a typical "story," that someone wouldn't give someone that, wouldn't let them save someone else. Was he right or was he wrong? I'd do the same thing probably, just to save my wife's life. I don't know; in a way if you say that that's justifiable and that's right, then you can say, well, stealing anything is right.

Beth's response reflects clearly the hesitation and mixed feelings that Gilligan observed widely in adolescent girls and that led Gilligan to formulate a

theory of moral development oriented to concrete care rather than to principles. Because Beth has trouble settling on a position based on principles, Kohlberg might classify her as conventional in her moral thinking and also as lower than Lenny and Andrew. Yet Gilligan's research suggested another interpretation for Beth's hesitation: instead of showing lack of principled moral thinking, Beth was showing awareness of the limitations of abstract principles in guiding moral judgment and awareness of how circumstances can affect decisions about right and wrong.

Follow-up Questions

1. Judging by the responses of these five individuals and of other persons you know, how different do you think moral development is for each gender?

2. Can you think of questions to ask these five people to clarify how well they really illustrate Kohlberg's and Gilligan's ideas?

3. Judging by these responses, do you think that Kohlberg and Gilligan really have opposing theories, or are they simply talking about different, complementary ethical developments?

Bridges How do peers influence moral judgment during the middle years?

Ethical hesitation can show moral sensitivity

that deception is usually bad but also feel that deception is ethical in certain circumstances, such as when a friend needs reassurance about the quality of a term paper that is actually mediocre but that took a lot of time and effort. Viewing ethics in context grows out of a general concern for the needs of others more than for their independence. A friend who is sick therefore deserves a visit or phone call; leaving the friend alone seems more like neglect than like respect for her autonomy.

These differences are only tendencies, not dramatic or sharply drawn sex differences. But they are enough, argues Gilligan, to make Kohlberg's theory underrate the moral development of girls and women. Concern with context and with others' needs causes girls to score closer to the middling, conventional levels of moral judgment, where peers' opinions matter the most. Asked if a child should inform authorities about a friend who is often shoplifting small items from a local department store, a girl is likely to give priority to one part of the problem in particular: that of balancing each person's views and needs in the situation. Doing this means wondering, among other things, whether informing will alienate peers not only from the shoplifter but also from the informer. On the other hand, it also means wondering whether keeping silent will risk losing the trust and respect of important adults, such as parents and teachers. And it means considering the amount of emotional pain that will befall the shoplifting friend, either at the hands of angry parents or at the hands of the police. Taking all of the considerations into account can make the final decision seem hesitant, tentative, and apparently lacking in principle, whichever way the decision goes.

Reviews of moral judgment have qualified Gilligan's ideas somewhat but have also lent them support. When faced with hypothetical dilemmas, females show just as much capacity as males to reason in terms of abstract ethical principles (Walker, 1984; Rest, 1983). When faced with real-life dilemmas, however, girls make different choices (L. Blum, 1987). Adolescent girls personally confronted with whether to engage in premarital intercourse, for example, more often show more concern than do boys for the context in which they make their decision and for the impact of their decision on the emotional needs of others. As with Kohlberg's justice-oriented stages, however, a needs-oriented ethics of care takes time to develop — years, in fact.

In addition to developing increasingly general ideas about justice, many young people orient their ethical ideas around issues of care and responsibility for others.

COGNITION AND SOCIAL DEVELOPMENT

Among the varieties of cognition discussed in this chapter, one idea predominates: cognition does not usually occur in isolation from social and emotional experiences. In order to use learning and memory strategies successfully, children must want to use them, must feel that using them is valued by others, and must enjoy the efforts they put into solving problems. Certain styles of thinking, such as divergent thinking, may depend heavily on social play, an activity that is certainly only partially cognitive. And language development involves more than acquiring a system of grammatical rules; it also involves some highly social communication.

Evidently, then, the social surroundings of children make a big difference to their development. The next chapter looks at these surroundings more closely. Instead of taking social and emotional development somewhat for granted, it highlights these areas while temporarily placing cognitive development in the background.

SUMMARY OF MAJOR IDEAS

Concrete Operational Skills

1. School-age children develop concrete operational thinking, or reasoning that focuses on real, tangible objects. Compared to preoperational thinking, it is more decentered, sensitive to transformations, and reversible.

2. A very important new skill is conservation, which is belief that an object's properties remain constant in spite of perceptual changes in the object.

3. Efforts to train children in conservation have had moderate success, although when applied in a variety of circumstances training does not persist as well as naturally developed conservation does.

4. Concrete operational children also acquire new skills in seriation, temporal relations, and spatial relations.

5. Considered as a whole, Piagetian ideas about cognitive development have influenced many educators' styles of teaching, the content of their curricula, and their methods of assessing students' progress.

Information-Processing Skills

6. Information-processing models divide thinking into several parts, such as short-term memory, recognition memory, long-term memory, and recall memory.

7. Short-term memory capacity does not change much during the school years, and in fact approximates adult capacity.

8. Long-term memory does improve with age, partly as a result of other cognitive developments.

9. Improvements in logical reasoning sometimes assist the development of long-term memory, as does increasing richness or familiarity of knowledge as schoolchildren grow older.

10. During the school years, children also begin being aware of how they think and begin using various learning strategies for improving their memory and reasoning.

11. Learning strategies are acquired in a variety of ways, and sometimes they can be taught to children purposely.

Styles of Thinking

12. In addition to increasing their cognitive capacities, school-age children acquire unique styles of thinking.

13. Children vary in their preference for convergent or divergent styles of thinking; in whether they are field dependent or field independent in analyzing the world; and in how reflective or impulsive they are in solving problems.

14. Field dependent children tend to perceive things in relatively large, connected patterns, whereas field independent children tend to perceive things as discrete parts. In some circumstances, field dependence and independence are associated with differences in social relations.

Learning Disabilities

15. About 5 percent of school-age children develop learning disabilities. Educators often divide these into developmental learning disabilities and academic learning disabilities.

16. Academic disabilities are often developmental in nature, but not always; conversely, developmental disabilities may have little or no impact on academic performance.

17. Although professionals are not sure what causes learning disabilities, they seem correlated with mistakes in cognitive processing.

Language Development in the Middle Years

18. Although school-age children are already quite skillful with language, they continue to develop new, more mature ways of defining words.

19. Schoolchildren continue to have difficulties with certain subtle features of syntax.

20. Bilingual children develop certain cognitive advantages over monolinguals, at least if their bilingualism is relatively balanced; these include cognitive flexibility and metalinguistic awareness.

21. Often, however, bilinguals must cope with prejudices against one of their languages and against the culture which that language represents.

22. Black English, a dialect of English that is as complex as any other language, is spoken by many blacks; educators recommend that teachers respect Black English while at the same time encouraging students to master the Standard English they will need to navigate the white world.

Defining and Measuring Intelligence

23. Intelligence is a general ability to learn from experience, although psychologists do not agree about many of the specific implications of this definition.

24. To measure both abilities and achievement, psychologists have developed standardized tests as well as norms and procedures for interpreting the scores on these tests.

25. Standardized tests often contain cultural biases, both in their content and in the method by which they are administered.

26. Standardized tests are sometimes misinterpreted in various ways: by equating scores with true intelligence, by confusing individual differences in scores with actual intelligence, and by overestimating tests' precision.

Moral Development

27. Moral development refers to the development of a sense of ethics, or right and wrong.

28. In ordinary circumstances, most children's moral behavior is rather inconsistent.

29. Piaget proposed two stages of moral development during the school years: an earlier stage of heteronomous morality and a later stage of autonomous morality.

30. Kohlberg proposed six stages of moral judgment: two at the preconventional level, two at the conventional level, and two at the postconventional level.

31. Research supports Kohlberg's six-stage model, but it also shows that moral reasoning depends partly on children's familiarity with particular moral issues, partly on the distinction between social convention and true morality, and partly on gender.

32. Gilligan's theory of moral judgment emphasizes a caring responsibility for others and attention to their circumstances.

KEY TERMS

concrete operation *(412)*
decentration *(413)*
sensitivity to
  transformation *(413)*
reversibility *(413)*
class inclusion *(413)*
conservation *(414)*
décalage (415)
seriation *(417)*
recognition memory *(420)*
recall memory *(421)*
metacognition *(424)*
learning strategy *(424)*
logical construction *(426)*
strategy training *(426)*
blind training *(426)*
informed training *(426)*

cognitive style *(428)*
convergent thinking *(428)*
divergent thinking *(429)*
field dependence *(430)*
field independence *(430)*
reflectivity *(431)*
impulsivity *(431)*
learning disability *(432)*
developmental learning
  disability *(433)*
academic learning
  disability *(433)*
perceptual masking *(434)*
bilingual *(437)*
cognitive flexibility *(437)*
metalinguistic
  awareness *(438)*

Black English *(439)*
Standard English *(439)*
intelligence *(440)*
standardized test *(441)*
achievement test *(442)*
aptitude test *(442)*

morality *(444)*
heteronomous
  morality *(445)*
autonomous morality *(445)*
social convention *(447)*
ethics of care *(448)*

WHAT DO YOU THINK?

1. Is concrete operational thinking "better" than preoperational thinking or just different? Explain your opinion and what it implies for training conservation and for educating children in general.

2. Do you believe that a computer makes a good model for human thinking? How does real human thinking differ from the operations of a computer?

3. Consider all the cognitive styles described in this chapter. Are they equally valuable to children, or are some more useful or advantageous to the individuals who possess them? Explain your opinion.

4. Think about a language that you wish you could speak. Why would you like to be able to use this language? In forming your opinion, what assumptions are you making about the culture or people who use the language?

5. Should standardized tests be used in schools? If so, what limitations should be placed on the kinds of tests used, on who gets to see the results, and on how the results are used?

6. In daily life, moral principles seem like a matter of personal opinion; yet Kohlberg's model of moral development seems to imply that we all develop toward some final common morality. How can these two impressions be reconciled?

FOR FURTHER READING

Gardner, Howard. *Frames of Mind: The Theory of Multiple Intelligences.* New York: Basic Books, 1983.

This book argues that human intelligence comes in several forms: linguistic, musical, logical, spatial, kinesthetic (or bodily balance), interpersonal, and intrapersonal. He presents interesting evidence for the distinctiveness of each kind of intelligence and then discusses the implications of these distinctions for education and society.

Gilligan, C. *In a Different Voice: Psychological Theory and Women's Development.* Cambridge, MA: Harvard University Press, 1982.

The author argues, among other things, that girls and women develop a uniquely female perspective on morality that is based on learning to care within a network of social relationships and on learning to include oneself in that network. She proposes that the major psychological stage theories, including Piaget's and Kohlberg's, do not take this feminine perspective into account; as a result, they may really only describe male development.

Greenfield, P. *Mind and Media: The Effects of Television, Video Games, and Computers.* Cambridge, MA: Harvard University Press, 1984.

This book explores the effects of visual media — especially television and video games — on children's cognitive development. It finds these media beneficial in many ways and more effective than printed books for certain purposes. The author favors a balanced use of visual and printed media, and she urges us to keep an open mind about visual media until we acquire more reliable information about their effects.

Neisser, U. (Ed.) *Memory Observed: — Remembering in Natural Contexts.* San Francisco: Freeman, 1982.

This book presents research and observational studies of memory as it occurs in everyday life. As a result of this focus, it makes fascinating reading. You can learn about memory for traffic accidents, about how individuals memorize very long poems and pieces of prose, and about how exceptional children and adults acquire photographic memories for objects and events. The book shows convincingly that memory is not necessarily a dry topic constructed by psychologists for artificial study.

Sternberg, Robert. *The Triarchic Mind: A New Theory of Human Intelligence.* New York: Penguin Books, 1988.

The author assesses several views about intelligence: the traditional psychometric one, the Piagetian theory as applied to general intelligence, and a version of information-processing theory. He expands on the information-processing view very persuasively, showing how it can explain many elements of thinking that originate during the middle years and that achieve full development in adulthood.

CHAPTER 13

The Middle Years: Psychosocial Development

Focusing Questions

- What particular challenges do children face in the middle years?
- What progress toward a sense of self do children make during this time?
- What forms does achievement motivation take?
- What special contributions do peers make to children's development?
- How does the changing nature of the family affect children, particularly when one change is the higher rate of divorce?
- What are some of the school's implicit and explicit influences on a middle-years child?
- How does a handicap influence the psychological and social development of a child?

N ickie is nine years old and in second grade. Between practicing soccer, baseball, or basketball and playing with his friends; playing videogames or watching TV with his older brother Alex; doing his homework; walking the dog; or carving a model racing car for his Cub Scout den with his father, he is always on the go. Until recently, if asked about his popularity or how he was doing at school or sports, Nickie would answer with a noncommittal, "OK" or "I don't know." Lately, however, he has begun to talk more about himself — who he is and how well he is (or is not) doing as a ballplayer, a friend, a student, a brother, and a son.

Middle childhood is a time when the developmental changes of infancy and the preschool years are rapidly consolidated and children ready themselves for adolescence and the movement to full adulthood. By the time they start school, most children have learned something about human nature and are beginning to pick up various practical skills. During the middle years, society fosters these developments further, by requiring children to attend school in order to learn socially valued skills such as reading and writing.

School also provides them with more contacts with other children of similar age and maturity, or **peers.** Peers offer certain benefits, such as freedom from the watchful eyes of parents and teachers. But they also demand loyalty and conformity. "Be nice to everyone except Rachel" was a rule in one circle of friends; "Do the assignment, but don't work too hard on it" was a rule in another. Middle-years children must learn to coordinate these expectations with those of parents, who sometimes disagree with peers.

To meet all of these demands simultaneously children must learn to regulate their behavior from within. Somehow they must find ways to control their expressions of aggression, impatience, grief, and other strong impulses and emotions. Doing so becomes easier as they develop concepts of themselves as individuals, knowledge of their own needs and values, and a sense of how these compare with the needs and values of other people.

PSYCHOSOCIAL CHALLENGES OF THE MIDDLE YEARS

This chapter discusses these developments as they occur during the years from approximately age six to about age twelve, considering in particular six major challenges to children's psychological lives: the challenge of knowing who you are, the challenge to achieve, the challenge of peers, the challenge of family relationships, the challenge of school, and (for some) the challenge of having a handicap.

The Challenge of Knowing Who You Are   Throughout the middle years, children evolve a deeper understanding of the kind of people they are and what makes them unique. These notions do not yet constitute a final, stable identity, such as that developed during adolescence and adulthood, but they do lay the groundwork for later development. During the middle years, a child can at least ask, "Am I a popular sort of person?" or "Am I athletic?" The answers may still be rather simplistic, but they are nonetheless beginning to take on meaning.

Growth of self-knowledge

The Challenge to Achieve   Some psychologists consider the major crisis of this age period to be the development of competence and of willingness to achieve to the best of one's ability. Of course, children do care about their competence even in infancy. But during the middle years, this motive is complicated by children's growing awareness of others' opinions about their efforts.

Awareness of standards of excellence

The older of two siblings showed this awareness one afternoon when talking with his sister about their paintings. Michael, age seven, said. "That's a nice painting, Elizabeth, but not as nice as usual." Elizabeth, age three, seemed unaware of possible insult; she simply smiled and continued to show her picture to Michael. Then she tried to be friendly by reciprocating: "That's a nice picture, too, Michael, but not as nice as yesterday's." Michael looked pained and replied, "It is *so* a good one!"

Both Elizabeth and Michael revealed some understanding of achievement in this interchange: they seem to know that paintings vary in quality and that painters need encouragement for their work. But Michael seemed more concerned about meeting certain standards of achievement. He worried about Elizabeth's implication that he might have fallen below these standards, and he also worried about whether Elizabeth had noticed this fact.

The Challenge of Peers   After discussing the motive to achieve, we look at the second major challenge of the middle years, namely, other children, or peers. As we point out, peers serve even more important purposes for schoolchildren than they do for preschoolers. The influence of peers is not always good, but peers do help each other a lot, and in any case, most children usually prefer peers to social isolation.

Relating to other children

The Challenge of Family Relationships   In spite of peers, family relationships have far from disappeared from the lives of schoolchildren. This chapter discusses several important aspects of family life, including recent changes in family roles and family membership, which have become much more varied than in the past. Who is supposed to do what within a family? What even constitutes a family in the first place? The chapter provides several answers currently given by parents and psychologists and examines in detail how changing family patterns affect school-age children.

Impact of family

The Challenge of School   During the middle years, school is second only to the family in its influence on children's social and emotional development. Observing and interacting with a large number of diverse children and adults other than their parents provide children with an opportunity to learn new social skills, values, and beliefs and to develop a fuller sense of identity. In this chapter we explore how school culture, the "hidden" curriculum, teacher influences, and the student's experience contribute to development during the middle years.

Impact of school

The Challenge of Having a Handicap   Some school-age children have special physical, emotional, or cognitive needs. These vary widely in nature and include

Adapting to special needs

such difficulties as a missing limb, a learning disability, and general retardation. To a large extent, children with these handicaps face the same challenge as other children: they need to achieve, get along with peers, and develop lasting, positive relationships with their families. But they also must learn how their differences affect what they can do in their lives and in their relationships with others.

THE SENSE OF SELF

Throughout infancy, childhood, and adolescence, a child develops a **sense of self,** which is experience and knowledge about his uniqueness as a human being. This sense evolves during the middle years, becoming more organized and generally more complex. In fact, even though a sense of self is often called a **self-concept,** it functions more like a theory than a single concept because it is a set of related ideas that the child continually tests and revises, based on his experiences, as he gets older (Wylie, 1974/1979).

At age six, for example, a girl named Mina loved playing with dolls and loved holding and caring for babies. She noticed that her parents and others commented on this, so nurturance became part of Mina's idea of herself; "I'm someone who likes babies," she sometimes thought. But later experience modified this idea. Toward the end of elementary school, Mina discovered that she often preferred playing softball to playing house. Somehow, at age ten or eleven, she had to incorporate this reality into her sense of self: "I'm a good ballplayer," she realized. By the start of adolescence, she still was not sure how to reconcile these two concepts of herself — her interest in child care and her interest in sports. Someday she might succeed in doing so, but at age twelve she was not yet able to.

Social influences

To a large extent, a child's notion of self grows out of social experiences with other selves — or put more plainly, out of contacts with other children and adults. Learning what it means to be female, for example, happens as girls meet other individuals who are also female. And learning what it means to be happy occurs as children see happiness expressed by other people. As personal and individual as a sense of self is, then, it reflects generalizations about others, and it cannot develop without considerable social contact (Lewis & Brooks-Gunn, 1979b).

The Development of Self in Childhood

Bridges How do middle-years children acquire a more stable sense of self?

How do children acquire a sense of self? The first step involves basic social labels or categories. By the end of the second year of life, most children can correctly label their gender ("I'm a boy" or "I'm a girl"), their age ("I'm two"), and their species ("I'm a person"). Labels such as these pave the way for later, more complete knowledge of self.

Belief in a stable identity

Self-constancy   At first, however, most such labels lack permanence. At age two or three, a boy may claim that he can become a girl under certain circumstances — "when I grow up," or "if I grew my hair long" (Marcus & Overton, 1978). Or a very young child may say that she can become a different individual "if I change my name" (Guardo & Bohan, 1971). **Self-constancy,** a belief that identity remains permanently fixed, does not become firm until the early school years, sometimes after age six. At this time a child becomes convinced that he will stay the same person indefinitely into the future, that he will remain human

Genetics	Physical Development	Family	Peers	Social Context
In what ways can genetic inheritance affect popularity during the middle years? (472)	How can differences in achievement motivation influence the development of physical skills? (463)	In what ways does the parent-child relationship change during the middle years? (477)	How do school-age boys and girls differ in patterns of friendships and play? (470)	Why is racial and ethnic awareness of special concern during middle childhood? (471)

THE MIDDLE YEARS: PSYCHOSOCIAL DEVELOPMENT

Emotions	Self-concept and Identity	Learning	Cognition	Language
What are the emotional effects of divorce on children during the middle years? (480–483)	How do middle-years children acquire a more stable sense of self? (458–460)	What role does school play in the identity development of middle-years children? (461–462)	How do peers help children's cognitive development? (466)	What are some of the possible social effects of bilingualism? (439)

in all circumstances, and that he will keep his gender forever. Beliefs such as these are what people mean by a sense of self.

At the same time that the child is developing a sense of personal constancy, her reasons for believing in constancy are shifting. Younger children, up to age five or six, tend to define themselves in terms of observable features and behaviors such as hairdos or how fast they can run (Rosenberg, 1979; Bannister & Agnew, 1971). These qualities have the advantage of being easily seen and comprehended, but as features of self-identity they have certain disadvantages. For one thing, they are often not really very stable; a child's running speed usually improves as the weeks and months go by. And observable features are often relative to particular people or situations; being big defines a child in one way among her nursery school peers but in another way among members of her family.

Basis for self-constancy

The First Beliefs in Psychological Traits   Other children, around age eight, form a more stable sense of self by including psychological traits as part of their self-descriptions. At first the traits are feelings and qualities that have no apparent reference to other human beings; "I am brave," says the child, or "I am cheerful." By implication these traits describe him as an entire personality and in all possible situations, with little recognition of people's usual variations in moods. At first, too, the child describes the traits in bold, global terms that ignore the possibility that opposing feelings or qualities can sometimes exist within the same person. The child may vacillate in describing his own qualities without realizing it. Sometimes he will say, "I am dumb," meaning *completely* dumb, and other times he will say, "I am smart," meaning *completely* smart (Harter, 1977). Neither statement suggests the recognition that both descriptions contain an element of truth.

Traits as general dispositions

How does a child eventually coordinate contradictions such as these? A first step is often to assign one trait to a particular person or situation and its opposite to another person or situation (Harter, 1982a). The belief that "I am cheerful" may become attached to the school playground and to the children who play there, whereas "I am grumpy" may attach itself to the classroom and to its usual

Resolving contradictions in traits

During the middle years, children develop preliminary notions of their personal qualities and psychological identity. What do you suppose this girl's sense of herself might be?

leader, the teacher. The child will then describe himself in the two situations in very different ways: on the playground, as cheerful, but in class, as grumpy. Both traits are permitted to exist, so to speak, but for the time being they lead isolated lives, at least in the child's mind.

By the end of the middle years, true integration of contradictory traits does occur. Around the age ten or twelve, children begin to recognize that they can feel more than one way about any particular situation or person — they can both like their teachers and hate them or enjoy school and dislike it, more or less at the same time (Selman, 1980). As they do so, they also begin using trait labels in less global ways and more to express qualities in particular situations. When an older child says, "I am smart," he no longer means, "I am always smart in every possible way and in every activity." Now he more likely means, "I am smart in a number of significant situations, but not in all."

These changes make possible a more stable sense of self. The situation-bound qualities expressed by older children do in fact usually describe them more accurately than the global traits and observable features that younger children rely on. But a middle-years child's consciousness of inner traits still lacks the subtlety found in adolescents and adults. A child may know that she is smart, but she may not know clearly how this quality differs from being intelligent, say, or creative, or wise.

Processes in Constructing a Self

Distinguishing self from others

Middle-years children construct their identities or self-theories by distinguishing their thoughts and feelings from those expressed by others. This idea is supported by studies of children's thinking and emotions. One group of researchers asked children of various ages how they would feel if their parents expressed certain emotions, such as sadness, anger, and happiness. Compared with school-age children, preschoolers more often said that they would feel the same emotion and be angry if their parents were angry, sad if they were sad, and so on (Harter & Barnes, 1983). Older children more often named complementary emotions rather than identical ones. If their parents felt angry, for example, they would feel fearful.

Another study showed how children gradually acquire a full understanding of the words *ashamed* and *proud* (Harter, 1982b). Among adults, these two feelings often depend on others' responses and opinions as well as on one's own; it can be hard to feel ashamed or proud unless someone is thinking about you and evaluating your behavior at least some of the time. As the study revealed, however, young children are only dimly aware of the importance of others in creating these emotions. When asked to define *ashamed* or *proud,* they simply said that *ashamed* was a bad feeling and *proud* was a good one; they did not mention how other people's opinions might help create these feelings.

By the early middle years (age six or seven), children began explicitly mentioning others in defining these two terms. For example, one seven-year-old's definition was, "My teacher was proud when I earned 100 percent on the test"; another's was, "My mother was ashamed when I lost my temper at the neighbor." Such attention to others implies awareness that others sometimes observe the child's self. Even more importantly, however, it suggests that school-age children distinguish between their own emotions and those of others — something they must do in order to develop a mature sense of self.

A child's emerging sense of self during the middle years is part of a broader process of personality development. In the following section we briefly discuss how two major developmental theorists — Sigmund Freud and Erik Erikson — view this process.

THE AGE OF INDUSTRY AND ACHIEVEMENT

When looked at as part of the entire life span, the years from six to twelve seem especially important to the achievement of competence. Children spend countless hours in school acquiring skills in reading, writing, and mathematics. And many of those hours also contribute to their learning the unofficial curriculum of school; how to get along with teachers and with other children. Outside of school, children often devote themselves to the long, slow mastery of particular skills. One child may spend years learning to play baseball, and another may devote just as much time to learning how to care for a zoo of pet hamsters, dogs, and birds.

Bridges What role does school play in the identity development of middle-years children?

Latency and the Crisis of Industry

Psychodynamic theories such as those proposed by Freud and Erikson explain such behavior in terms of the emotional relationships that precede it in early childhood. As we described in Chapter 10, preschool children feel envy, awe, and competitiveness about their parents. At first these feelings have a magical quality; children simply want to be like their parents. Inevitably, they are disappointed to learn that merely wanting such things does not make them come true.

Freud here emphasized the emotional hardship of preschoolers' disappointment and their consequent repression of their magical wishes toward their

Freud's theory of middle childhood

parents (Freud, 1983). A five-year-old, he argued, cannot continue indefinitely to wish for intimacy with his opposite-sex parent and for success in competition with his same-sex parent. These feelings (which Freud termed the Oedipus and Electra conflicts) disrupt life if they continue too long. So the child eventually represses the feelings, which means that he pushes them completely out of awareness. As it happens, this **repression** occurs at about the time that most children begin school — around age six or seven — and continues until adolescence. Because the child's earlier feelings have gone underground, Freud called this a period of **latency.** During this period, the schoolchild focuses on building competencies and skills as a **defense** — an unconscious, self-protective behavior — against his earlier romantic feelings about his parent. Developing talents, whether in sports, art, academics, or whatever, also helps to keep the child's mind off his earlier disappointment, which lingers on unconsciously.

Erikson agreed with Freud's account to this point, but he went beyond it to stress not only the defensive, negative functions of skill building but its positive functions as well (E. Erikson, 1963, 1968). According to Erikson, children respond to their romantic feelings toward their parents not only by repressing their feelings but also by trying consciously to become more like their parents and more like adults in general. Becoming competent helps children to reach this goal in two ways. First, it helps (by **identification)** them to see themselves as people capable of becoming genuine adults; and second, it helps them to gain this recognition from others.

Erikson: the crisis of industry versus inferiority

Erikson called this process the crisis of **industry versus inferiority,** meaning that children of this age concern themselves with their **industriousness,** or the capacity to do good work. Children who convince themselves and others of this capacity develop relatively confident, positive concepts of themselves. Those who do not tend to suffer from feelings of poor self-esteem and **inferiority,** which is a sense of inadequacy or general lack of competence. According to Erikson, most children end up with a mixture of self-confidence and fears of inferiority, but self-confidence predominates in most cases (we hope).

In addition, the crisis of industry gives healthy school-age children a more or less permanent motivation to achieve particular, definable standards of excellence. No longer are they happy just to draw pictures, for example; now they must draw *well.* With persistence and support, children often do reach higher standards of excellence in many activities than they did as preschoolers, and most of the time they are happy about doing so.

Partly because of the connection between industry and increasing competence, psychologists have devoted a lot of attention to the development of the achievement motivation in middle-years children. The next section of this chapter describes some of this work.

During the middle years, children focus considerable energy on acquiring specific skills. Tying a shoelace can be a major achievement.

Achievement Motivation

Achievement motivation refers to behavior that enhances competence or that enhances judgments of competence (Beck, 1978; Atkinson & Feather, 1966). It often refers to a desire or tendency to strive for some high but reasonable standard of excellence in a skill or area of knowledge. What matters is the approach to a task, not the importance of the task itself. An individual can reveal achievement motivation as either a student or a college professor, for example, and as either an amateur checkers player or a world-class chess grand master. As long as the individual strives toward a standard of excellence that is reasonable for her, she possesses achievement motivation. Usually, too, her motivation leads to increased competence compared with her previous level.

Differences in Achievement Motivation   Notice that the definition we have given implies two distinct kinds of achievement motivation: one that is focused on competence as such and another that is focused on the judgments that people make about competence (Dweck & Elliott, 1983; Dweck, 1986). The first of these leads children to concentrate on learning as such; they will practice jumping rope just to see if they can do it. The second kind of motivation orients children much more to performance; in this case, they will practice jumping rope so as to impress others at a later time. For convenience, let us call these two attitudes **learning orientation** and **performance orientation.** In a learning orientation, motivation is intrinsic; it comes from within the learner and the task. In a performance orientation, the learner's motivation is extrinsic; it comes not from the learner but from other individuals who may see and evaluate the learner. The person the learner is trying to please or satisfy is not the self but others.

Intrinsic and extrinsic motivation

The differences between these two orientations show in children who are learning to swim. To the extent that they adopt a learning orientation, they enjoy the actual activity — practicing new strokes, working up to faster speeds, and so on. They also feel relatively free to invite criticisms from coaches or fellow swimmers because these comments can often help them to improve.

Bridges   How can differences in achievement motivation influence the development of physical skills?

But for children who adopt a performance orientation, swimming is less enjoyable in itself and more a means of winning approval from others. The children are concerned more with receiving compliments from coaches and swimming friends or with performing well in competitive swimming meets. If others do happen to criticize aspects of their swimming, the comments are not welcome. Ironically, this fact may indirectly limit the children's ability to learn.

This description may make a learning motivation sound more desirable than a performance one, but keep in mind that most of us usually experience a mixture of the two throughout our lives. Like it or not, we all encounter situations in which judgments about achievement compete with achievement itself, such as taking an examination or serving a complicated dinner to friends.

Recent research has found another significant difference in achievement motivation. Some children display a more adaptive and self-confident "mastery-oriented" pattern of achievement behavior that is characterized by challenge seeking, persistence in the face of obstacles, and an ability to take failure in stride. Other children display a less confident "helpless" pattern, avoiding challenges, showing low persistence in the face of difficulty and greater confusion when failure does occur (Dweck, 1986). Studies of sex differences in achievement motivation suggest that the helpless pattern is more likely to be found in girls, particularly those who are bright, and that it is a learned response. But there is some evidence that learning situations designed to foster the "mastery" pattern can reduce patterns of learned helplessness (Licht & Dweck, 1984; 1986).

Mastery vs. helpless patterns

Achievement Motivation in the Middle Years   During the middle years, children become more performance oriented than they were at earlier ages. At the beginning of this period, children express considerable optimism about their abilities. Kindergartners tend to rank themselves at the top of their class in scholastic ability, even though they rank other children relatively accurately (Stipek & Hoffman, 1980). This implies a learning orientation; for young children, achievement is something that they do without either the involvement or the evaluations of others (Frieze et al., 1981).

Increases in performance orientation

During the next several years, however, children begin believing that whether they have ability depends partly on whether other people give them credit for having it (Ruhland & Feld, 1977). This belief lies at the core of the performance orientation. It does not replace a learning orientation; it takes a place alongside that orientation. Being "smart," for example, now partly means

A Multicultural View

Cultural Variations in How to Display Achievement

Over the years, certain ethnic groups have persistently achieved less well in school, on the average, than other ethnic groups have. Some experts have regarded this as the result of some sort of deficit in the low-achieving groups; families in these groups, they argue, lack the economic or intellectual resources to help their children succeed properly in school. This explanation became prominent during the 1960s, and it still guides many educational programs to improve the academic performance of these children (F. Erikson, 1986).

But whatever its merits, the deficit explanation suffers from a major problem: it ignores important cultural differences in how ethnic groups define the right or best ways for children to display their accomplishments. Normal school practices, it seems, have grown out of certain assumptions about how and when children like to learn and work. Unfortunately for some minority children, these sometimes contradict the expectations and practices of their ethnic cultures. Consider, for example, each of these common teaching practices:

1. *Spotlighting a child* During class discussion, teachers often ask one child to answer a particular question in front of the rest of the class. The other children are supposed to learn by watching this child display knowledge (or ignorance!); the named child is sup-

posed to feel proud of having been selected, at least if he gets the answer right.

2. *Rhetorical questioning* During a discussion, teachers often ask questions to which they already know the answers ("How many states are in the United States?"). Children are supposed to answer these questions even if they realize that the teacher already knows the answer. Rhetorical questioning in fact helps to establish "who's boss" in the class; children acknowledge the teacher's authority by answering rhetorical questions willingly.

3. *Working individually* On the whole, children are supposed to complete assignments alone. Assisting other children significantly without the explicit permission of the teacher is forbidden; it is cheating, rather than a laudable concern for others. Working individually tends to be considered the best expression of achievement, even if it means ignoring the learning needs of classmates some of the time.

But many ethnic groups (and individuals, for that matter) interpret these teaching practices in rather different ways. Spotlighting a child can seem overly brash and direct, rather too much like interrogating or putting pressure on the child for no good reason. Rhetorical ques-

---

that a child's teachers, parents, and friends *say* that she is smart and partly that she possesses certain skills in reading, mathematics, and the like regardless of what others say (Feld et al., 1979).

Achieving successfully becomes more complicated in the middle years. Consider swimming again. Late in infancy and during the preschool years, a child may be motivated to learn to swim simply if he is given chances to experiment in the water. In the middle years, however, he may ask himself what other people, especially parents and friends, will think about learning to swim; will they consider this skill a true achievement? Most people will value swimming to some extent, of course. But whether they do so quite a lot or only a little will depend partly on what values and standards they hold. Even very respectable progress in swimming may not look like much of an achievement if the child's family and friends hold very high athletic standards or if they do not value athletics much in the first place.

Nevertheless, in good conditions a performance orientation can help children by motivating them to acquire skills that prove especially valuable later in life. An obvious example is the academic basics, reading and arithmetic. Although some children pick up these skills on their own, many others require a bit of performance motivation in the form of periodic judgments such as grades on tests and teacher comments. With good teaching, such judgments do not prevent pupils from setting learning-oriented goals as well. If the academic basics are well taught, large numbers of schoolchildren later acquire other competencies that they might not have picked up spontaneously. After all, a wide range of life skills depend on prior literacy and skill with numbers (Donaldson, 1979).

Effects of performance orientation

tioning can seem either pointless or arrogant; why should an adult ask a child something if the adult already knows the answer to it? And the individualistic emphasis can seem a callous disregard of cooperation and concern for others. In this view, children not only should help each other to learn but should do so at every opportunity, not just when teachers allow it.

In departing from conventional practices, teachers of several Native American groups have sometimes stimulated higher levels of achievement than usual for such children (S. Phillips, 1982; Barnhardt, 1982; F. Erikson & Mohatt, 1982). Observational studies of these classrooms showed a paradox: the Native American children worked harder and talked more if their teachers did *not* demand participation directly and if the teachers encouraged the children to work in groups as much as possible, rather than individually.

Observational studies of Hawaiian children had much the same results. In these studies, teachers found that achievement improved if they allowed children to interrupt each other during discussions instead of requesting them to speak one at a time (Au & Mason, 1981). Overlapping speech seemed to be customary among Hawaiians; it signified not bad manners but lively interest in the current topic of conversation. But overlapping speech among Hawaiian children did make "classroom control" in the usual sense difficult to achieve. Often there were simply too many children talking at once for anyone to be sure where a particular discussion was heading or who was in charge of it. Overlapping speech discouraged the use of the conventional teaching techniques described above: the teachers could not call on one child at a time very conveniently, or ask rhetorical questions, or insist on a lot of individual displays of effort.

These findings raise a dilemma for educators: how much should they teach ethnic groups in their preferred cultural styles, and how much should they emphasize the more widespread but alien academic style of most classrooms? Opting for the first strategy may encourage higher achievement, at least in the short term. But it may also prevent children from learning how to function in the mainstream of public education. Opting for conventional academic methods may convey lack of respect for students and their culture, and in this way it may create poor relations between teacher and students and interfere with academic achievement. Therefore, the best strategy probably mixes both ethnic and mainstream classroom styles. Educators continue to debate what this mixture should consist of in the daily practice of teaching.

The shift toward a performance orientation makes children more similar to adults in their achievement motivation. The shift reflects another major social development of childhood — namely, the increasing importance of peers. As children grow older, they take others' opinions more and more seriously and often seek out those opinions on a variety of matters. Achievement motivation, it turns out, is just one peer-related concern among many.

PEER RELATIONSHIPS

Throughout childhood, some of the most important relationships involve peers. As early as age two, children enjoy playing with or next to each other, and by age three or four they often prefer the company of peers, even when adults are available. Time spent with peers increases steadily during the middle years. By late elementary school, children devote about one-half of their social interactions to peers (Ellis et al., 1981; R. Barker & Wright, 1955).

What Theorists Say About Peer Relationships

Piaget Many psychological theories emphasize the importance of peers in children's development, especially during the middle years. For example, Piaget

Bridges   How do peers help children's cognitive development?

Peers help overcome egocentrism

Peers stimulate cooperation and competition, promote emotional health

The first intimate friends

Limitations of peer relations

argued that peers help children to overcome their egocentrism — their tendency to assume that everyone views the world in the same way as they do (Piaget, 1963). In the course of playing together, children inevitably run into conflicts over toys and priorities, arguing over who should use a new set of felt pens or over what and where they should draw. In settling disagreements such as these, children gradually acquire understanding of others' points of view. They also come to understand and value the democratic process, at least in the down-to-earth form of minor haggling and compromise.

According to Piaget, parents and other authority figures cannot foster these cognitive developments because they cannot behave as true equals with children. Often adults give orders to children, and although they may give them pleasantly ("Please clean up your room before supper"), they expect compliance, not discussion or negotiation. And even when parents are not acting as managers, they cannot really function as equals with children. For one thing, they often do not have the same leisure interests or tastes; a father may like to play cards after dinner, but his son may prefer to ride bikes with his friends. For another thing, parents' skill levels often do not match those of their children; a mother and daughter may both enjoy cooking, but the child cannot really do it as well as her mother can. The mother can become "equal" with her child only by pretending to be less experienced than she really is.

Sullivan   The most well-developed theory about peers was proposed by Sullivan (1953). Like Piaget, Sullivan argued that relationships with peers have fundamentally different qualities from those with adults; in particular, peers stimulate skills in compromise, cooperation, and competition. But unlike Piaget, Sullivan emphasized the value of peers in promoting emotional health. Peers create a life for children outside their families, and in doing so, they help correct the emotional biases that families inevitably give their children — biases that Sullivan called emotional **warps.** An eight-year-old with shy, reserved parents, for instance, may learn from peers that not all people are shy and reserved, or a ten-year-old whose parents care little about competitive athletics may discover from peers that athletic competition matters quite a lot to some people.

According to Sullivan, this sort of learning occurs during the **juvenile period,** which begins around age five and continues until nine or ten. In this period, children show increasing interest in playmates of similar age and status. As they near the end of the elementary school years, they supposedly focus this interest on just a few select friends of the same sex, whom Sullivan called *chums.* These relationships provide children with models for later intimate relationships.

Support for Theories About Peer Relationships   Research into peer relationships supports Piaget's and Sullivan's ideas in broad outline but not in certain specifics. Conflict with peers does stimulate children's progress at solving cognitive problems, as Piaget proposed. Two seven-year-olds do learn from a discussion with each other about whether "the oldest people are always the tallest," but they learn only if they are already thinking at about the same level of maturity (N. Bell et al., 1985). Otherwise, such discussions easily turn into confrontation and browbeating, as the more advanced child forces the other to comply with her point of view.

Research also supports Sullivan's claim that playmates and peers matter a lot to schoolchildren. But children's relationships usually do not evolve into intimate chumships toward the end of this period. On the contrary, friendships and peer groups become more complex and diverse during preadolescence (Chapman & Chapman, 1980). Some relationships become closer and more important than others, of course, but few actually become intimate in the sense proposed by Sullivan; that is, very few friendships involve sharing children's most private or personal thoughts and feelings. Peer relationships do acquire special intensity just before adolescence and sometimes even rival family relationships in emotional impact at this time. This fact may account for some of parents' worries about their children "growing up too soon." An eleven-year-old may seem excessively concerned about attending parties, or a twelve-year-old may taste a can of beer without consulting the traditional authority, his parents.

Functions of Peers

All things considered, peers probably serve a variety of purposes, including some that duplicate the functions of parents. Like parents, peers can give a child a secure emotional base during anxiety-provoking experiences. Sometimes the mere presence of a friend increases a child's confidence in such situations; observing another child being examined by the dentist, for example, tends to calm the observing child when her turn comes (Melamed et al., 1975). Like parents, peers help to define ethical norms for a child. Peers also help to define friendship in particular, although contrary to widespread belief, standards of likability parallel those of adults more often than not (Hartup, 1983). And like parents, peers do a lot of teaching: they show a child how to paint or how to throw a ball. Sometimes schools take advantage of this process by arranging for children to tutor each other in academic skills (Allen, 1976).

In addition to these similarities, there are several features unique to peer relationships. They are by nature voluntary and involve comparative equals. These facts mean that a child must act in a way that explicitly supports the relationship — be friendly, that is — if he expects the relationship to survive. And he must do so with another individual whose social skills may not be much better or may sometimes even be a bit worse than his own. Children apparently understand these differences intuitively because they typically attribute an obedience orientation to relationships between adults and children but attribute play and recreation orientations to relationships among children (Youniss, 1980). In acting out a family scene with dolls, children tend to make adult dolls blame child dolls, or deprive child dolls of privileges, and they tend to make the child dolls demand something of or submissively obey the adult. When acting out a scene between two child dolls, however, children tend to make the dolls play together as equals, and bossiness disappears. (C. Edwards & Lewis, 1979).

Differences between parent and peer relationships

Influences on Peer Group Membership

As implied by the fact that peers are comparatively equal, children's peer groups are not simply random assortments of individuals but are influenced by many factors. Three of the most important of these are age, gender, and race or ethnic background of the children. Let us look briefly at each of these in turn.

Age Children do play mostly with others of approximately their own age. But contrary to a common impression, children spend considerable amounts of time with peers who are *not* their own age. One study found that schoolchildren spent anywhere from one-quarter to one-half of their time with companions who were more than two years older or younger (Ellis et al., 1981). School imposes an upper limit on these cross-age contacts, however, because classrooms usually group children according to age.

Groups with mixed ages have certain special qualities. Older children show more nurturant behavior, such as tying the shoelaces of a younger child or buttoning her sweater. And younger children show more dependence by asking for help with schoolwork or agreeing to older peers' preferences as to play activities. In spite of these qualities, however, mixed-aged groups tend to be less

Qualities of mixed-aged groups

"sociable" than single-age groups; they chat less or have friendly conversation less often. Furthermore, when group members differ in age, they are less aggressive than children in same-age groups; they get in fewer fights and have fewer arguments (B. Whiting & Whiting, 1975). All in all, same-age groups encourage the opposites of all these qualities: children give and receive less practical help, show more friendliness to each other, and get into conflicts more often.

Gender segregation

Gender   Although mixed-sex play does occur during the elementary school years, first-graders generally name children of their own gender as best friends. Observations of younger schoolchildren during free play show that they interact during cooperative play periods about four times as often with children of their own gender as with those of the opposite gender (Maccoby & Jacklin, 1987). This ratio actually increases as children approach adolescence; by third grade, most peer groups contain only one sex, and by fifth grade, virtually all do.

During the middle years, children tend to associate with peers of the same sex. Girls' friendships tend to be more intimate, whereas boys' friendships often reflect male stereotypes.

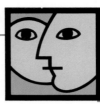

Boy-Girl Differences in Peer Groups and Play

Linda Maleska is a fourth grade teacher at a "follow-through" elementary school that serves students from Head Start preschool and kindergarten programs from all over the city, as well as children from the neighborhood in which the school is located. She was interviewed in her classroom toward the end of the school year.

Interviewer: How would you describe peer relations among fourth graders?

Linda: Often children's academic ability sets the tone and pace for their friendships. Children who do well academically tend to be friends with other kids who are bright.

Interviewer: What other factors seem to influence peer groups?

Linda: Boy-girl differences are very important. As much as I tried to encourage girls to play football or soccer and boys to do other things like four-square and jump-rope, it really does break down sexually as to how they play outside. Girls tend to play jump-rope and boys tend to play soccer on the field — that is almost automatic. Girls also tend to go to the swings and slide much more than the boys.

Interviewer: Why do you think this happens?

Linda: Girls are getting, at this age, more social, much less reliant on an adult for any kind of ideas or suggestions about what to do outside. They are much more self-reliant. Their play is also more directly social and interactive. Often I see girls walking slowly and talking. Or they'll make up clapping games. There are a lot of hand-clapping games. Even their jump-rope is more consistently interactive and coordinated — with turn taking and things like that — than the boys' play. . . . They like to use the swings

and to play . . . four-square. And that involves a lot of verbal interaction and social coordination.

Interviewer: Can you describe four-square?

Linda: There are four people standing in a 10-foot-by-10-foot square drawn in chalk and divided into four squares. And the person in the fourth square is in control of whatever the category will be. So, that person will say "colors." She will bounce the ball into any of the other players' squares and they will have to name a color and catch the ball, or they are out.

Interviewer: There's a rhythm to it?

Linda: You have to keep the rhythm and you can't name the same color twice (if color is the category), or animal, country, movie star, or whatever the category is. They get more complex as the year goes on. They almost always start the year with colors and by the end of the year it will be something much more specific, for example, Madonna's songs or rock stars. This group of girls also made up a real great hand-clapping game about music groups, and the way they thought it all through and the rules that were made up were fascinating.

Interviewer: What are the boys doing?

Linda: They are playing soccer and kickball, building forts, or surfboards, if they can. They may also be collecting things and investigating the environment. For example, at the beginning of the year we studied insects and their natural habitats in science. And once the boys got outside, they tried to find every single little bug they could, and they would come and show it.

Interviewer: It seems that fourth-grade boys are less interested in made-up games than girls.

Linda: Yes, that is true. Girls are much more likely to create their own games and rules, which involve social interaction. Boys tend to play games which emphasize physical

rather than social interaction and where they follow rules that are already made up for them.

Interviewer: How permanent are these peer group patterns?

Linda: They seem to be long-lasting. The group I described was made up of five girls who are very, very close. They're all good students and all white. They're into fads. They're into Madonna, the singer, and even come to school dressed up like her, although I think that is somewhat going by the wayside now. I've been trying to encourage them to interact with other people more because they are sort of the clique of the class.

Interviewer: Are there other things that teachers do to encourage greater interaction?

Linda: Yes. One of the things our school works to achieve is to have children interact in a way that does not break down along sex-role or racial lines. What I do in school is to try and compensate for that. I talk to them about it, very up-front, and I say that I think there should be more interaction between boys and girls and blacks and whites. So when we have social studies activities, the rule is that groups will be mixed. The children understand this and help make it work.

Follow-up Questions

1. How closely do the girl-boy differences described parallel those described in the chapter?

2. According to Linda, what are the main ways in which girls' play and boys' play differ?

3. Do you agree with Linda's approach to reducing cliques based on gender and race? What suggestions do you have?

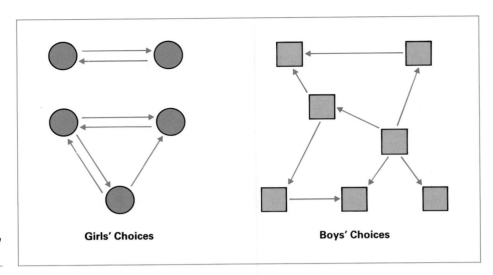

FIGURE 13.1
Typical Patterns of Peer Friendships in Girls and Boys

Girls' Choices   Boys' Choices

Bridges How do school-age boys and girls differ in patterns of friendships and play?

How do groups of boys differ from groups of girls? In general, boys' play parallels gender stereotypes about maleness: it is louder, more boisterous or active, and more competitive. It includes more rough-and-tumble play or mock fighting. Boys more often play in large groups of at least a half dozen children, and perhaps as a result, they more often play outdoors or in other large, expansive areas such as a gymnasium or a long hallway (DiPietro, 1981; Lever, 1976). Girls, in contrast, more often play in pairs or small groups, and they initiate interactions with members of the opposite sex more often than boys do (Foot et al., 1980).

Given these differences, it is not surprising that girls' long-term friendships tend more often toward exclusive intimacy. One study tested this idea by using a **sociometric questionnaire.** which is a written ballot that invited children to name their best friends (Hallinan, 1981; Eder & Hallinan, 1978). Tabulations of the friendship patterns show differences between the boys and the girls, as illustrated in Figure 13.1. Compared to the boys, the girls more often made mutually exclusive choices (**dyads,** or two-person relationships, as in Figure 13.1); and all-girl triads, in which a third girl's choice was not reciprocated, occurred more often, too. Boys more often formed patterns in which no choice was reciprocated. Several boys might pick each other as friends, as illustrated in Figure 13.1), even though not one was picked in return. Judging by these choices, therefore, boys spread their social attention widely, and girls tend to focus it on just a few individuals. Stated differently, boys' friendships tend to be extensive, and girls' tend to be intensive.

To a large extent, children acquire preferences for their own gender even before they begin school. Even toddlers tend to play longer and more happily with other toddlers of the same sex (Jacklin & Maccoby, 1978). Later, when children begin school, teachers do more than simply tolerate these preexisting gender preferences; they reinforce same sex groupings of children when they occur (Fagot, 1977, 1982). Teachers are especially likely to do so if the group is doing something that is traditionally gender specific. If several girls are playing with dolls, a teacher is more likely to compliment them than several boys, or even a mixed boy-girl group, who are doing so. To some extent, such experiences may help create conscious gender stereotypes in the minds of children.

Teachers reinforce same-sex groupings

Race and Ethnic Background Racial preference and prejudice are a fact of life in much of our society, and middle-years children are not immune from it (Asher, Singleton, & Taylor, 1982).

Racial and ethnic awareness are especially important during middle child-hood because children of this age are in the process of committing themselves to society and to the values and standards of the majority culture; they are also developing their own self-concepts.

Bridges Why is racial and ethnic awareness of special concern during middle childhood?

Preferences based on race and ethnicity can play a significant role in friend-ship choices and social activity during the middle childhood years. This is par-ticularly true when ethnic differences and social class differences are related, and they most frequently are (Asher, Singleton, & Taylor, 1982).

These preferences can also be a mask for **prejudice** — irrational, negative attitudes directed at members of another group. Prejudice can be based on a variety of characteristics, including race, ethnic or cultural background, religion, social class, and gender. Prejudiced individuals are predisposed to exclude or mistreat members of the targeted group, whom they view as inferior.

One study found racial preference suggested in who sat with whom at an elementary school cafeteria (Schofield & Sugar, 1977). The cafeteria served about two-hundred-fifty students, about one-half of whom were black and one-half of whom were white. With these numbers, about one hundred cross-race seatings — blacks and whites sitting next to or across from one another — would have occurred if race had made no difference to the students. In fact, only about one-quarter of this number actually occurred. In this situation, racial preference was clearly visible.

Racial preferences among peers

This kind of preference is also revealed when children name best friends, as in the sociometric procedure described earlier in this section. Children nom-inate people of their own race more often than people of another race, particu-larly if their own race is the majority one and the other race is a minority (in the United States, usually black or Hispanic). The trend begins in the preschool years and becomes stronger throughout the middle years and adolescence (Sin-gleton, & Asher, 1979; Asher, Singleton, & Taylor, 1982). The pattern may reflect not a general dislike, however, but only cautiousness about having a best friend of another race. When children instead nominate their "best playmate" or "best working partner," they choose someone of another race more frequently.

Note that even though children segregate themselves both by race and by gender, the two prejudices differ in nature and origin. Unlike the sexes, different races do not usually grow up in the same families, or often in the same neigh-borhoods. And more often than not, they do not expect to live in the same families or neighborhoods when they become adults.

Can racial and ethnocentric prejudice be reduced? Cooperative learning experiences that allow mixed groups of children to work as a team to achieve common academic goals have been highly successful in increasing cross-race acceptance and in increasing children's self-esteem (Slavin, 1986; D. Johnson, Johnson, & Maruyama, 1984).

In one such program, children were divided into four groups. In one group children worked in interracial teams on an interesting puzzle and all children were rewarded with praise. In another, they heard stories about an appealing black child. In the third group, children were reinforced for choosing pictures of black animals instead of white ones, and in the fourth group, children were taught the names of different black women whose faces were presented in slides. In the short run, all groups showed reduced prejudice, and six months later, those children who had learned to tell black faces apart and those who had heard stories about black children continued to be less prejudiced than the other two groups (P. Katz & Zalk, 1978). In another program based on this "jigsaw" technique, children from different racial and ethnic backgrounds were assigned to different parts of a single project. They quickly learned to work together to complete the task and developed more positive feelings about themselves and each other (E. Aronson & Bridgeman, 1979).

Interracial cooperation reduces prejudice

Popularity, Social Acceptance, and Rejection

Bridges   In what ways can genetic inheritance affect popularity during the middle years?

Early in the middle years, children begin to evaluate one another in various ways. By second and third grades, children already hold cultural stereotypes about body build; for example, they judge boys who are muscular more favorably than boys who are fat or thin (Staffieri, 1972). Easily noticed characteristics are quite important to acceptance in the early grades, when having the "right" kind of hair can help, as can having a name that sounds attractive. As children get older, they choose their friends increasingly on the basis of personal qualities such as honesty, kindness, humor, and creativity (Furman & Bierman, 1983; Reaves & Roberts, 1982). They still evaluate one another, however, and confer more popularity on some children than on others.

Social abilities of popular children

The Popular Child   Well-liked children are good at initiating and maintaining social interactions and at understanding social situations (Asher, Renshow, & Hymel, 1982). They recognize that group acceptance is not automatic but a slow process that takes work and patience. As one eight-year-old said, "You can't go up to kids who are playing and say, 'That's no good; let's do something different.' You have to do it their way for a while — and sometimes a long while."

Popular children are viewed by their peers as being confident, good-natured, and energetic (Hartup, 1983). Highly visible abilities and achievements help — especially in athletics, but also in academics or social activities. Nice clothing and special material possessions, such as an expensive fashion watch, also influence status with peers. Some of these assets (such as athletic ability) remain valuable to children as they move into adolescence, and others (such as the fashion watch) may not. But during childhood, such advantages create prestige for individual children within particular peer groups and also make membership in the "best" or highest status groups possible.

Social deficits of unpopular children

The Unpopular Child   Peers describe unpopular children as unpleasant, disruptive, selfish, and aggressive (Coie et al., 1982). Such children tend to be actively disliked and excluded from activities. All schoolchildren, it seems, struggle to control aggressive and selfish impulses in order to make themselves more likable. Unpopular children, by their nature, make this struggle more difficult. One child described the problem this way: "When Ginny doesn't get to play, she grabs things — like the checker pieces we were using today. Then the other kids feel like they have to grab things too, just to get them back. And then no one feels good anymore." In contrast, well-liked children are more likely to use indirect approaches to get what they want: "When Sonia sees you playing checkers, she just stands there, waiting for you to finish. She doesn't say anything until it's time for the next game."

Friends   During the early middle years, children base friendships on shared interests and activities, on exchanges of possessions, and on concrete supportive behaviors (Selman, 1981a). "A friend," according to one six-year-old, "is someone who plays what *you* want to play." And another says, "A friend lets you use his painting set." These comments emphasize the child's own needs rather than the friend's. But even when both parties are considered, friendships among younger school-age children tend to focus on practical behaviors rather than on psychological qualities:

TONY (age eight): Benjy, if you share your Galactica rocket with me, I'll be your friend.

BENJY (also age eight): Give me another piece of candy, will you? Then we'll see.

Unpopular children often behave aggressively or selfishly without realizing it. Ironically, since they tend to be excluded from groups, they find few chances to learn new ways of relating.

TONY: But I already gave you three pieces. It's time that I got to play with your rocket.

BENJY: It's really *my* rocket.

TONY: I *am* your friend, you know. So you should give me a turn.

BENJY: Not now. Maybe later. Where's the candy?

Exchanging favors and sharing activities continue to matter as children get older, but by the time they enter fifth and sixth grades, children place more emphasis on psychological qualities such as intimacy, trust, mutual support, and loyalty (Youniss & Volpe, 1978). Actually doing the same things or sharing the same objects becomes correspondingly less important.

Concepts of friendships

To some extent this change reflects children's increasing ability to coordinate social perspectives, which means that they can increasingly see themselves as others view them. Younger children realize that in many situations, two people see things differently, but they nonetheless have trouble coordinating their own perspective with that of a friend. As a result, they often alternate between trying to change their friend's viewpoint to fit their own and trying to make themselves feel the same way as their friend does.

By second or third grade, children become more able to live with differing perspectives within their friendships and feel less forced to choose between one or the other. By fifth or sixth grade, children can even adopt an independent or third-party perspective, comparing their own point of view with their friends' (Selman, 1980). As one eleven-year-old put it about a good friend, "He thinks that I don't study enough, and that he studies just about the right amount for

Perspectives

Shyness: What Are Its Causes and Can It Be Treated?

Approximately 40 percent of all adults report that they suffer from shyness. People who are shy suffer from high levels of anxiety and discomfort in social situations and a general lack of confidence when interacting with other people, including exaggerated concerns about how others view them and fears that they will be regarded as foolish, unattractive, unintelligent, or unworthy. Symptoms of shyness may include blushing; cold, clammy hands; dry mouth; excessive perspiration; trembling hands and legs; pounding heart; queasy stomach; a sinking feeling; or even a sudden need to go to the bathroom (Brody, 1989).

Shyness is a particularly painful experience for young and middle-years children who are struggling to achieve sufficient autonomy, initiative, competence, and self-esteem and to achieve these without being overcome by feelings of shame, doubt, guilt, loss of esteem, and inferiority.

Recent research has focused on both hereditary and environmental sources of shyness. Jerome Kagan and Nancy Snidman of Harvard University have studied children from birth through age seven and one-half and found that 10 to 15 percent of infants are born with a tendency to become shy and inhibited. Shy infants and toddlers appear to have nervous systems that are too easily aroused. When exposed to novel or unfamiliar situations, they display a pattern of very high motor arousal, high irritability, and high heart rate

as compared to infants with low levels of arousal (Kagan, 1989). As toddlers and during their early school years, three-fourths of these children retain their original temperamental pattern of high arousal and continue to be overly sensitive, anxious, uncomfortable, self-conscious, and inhibited in social situations. Many are also fearful of one or more relatively typical activities, such as speaking voluntarily in class, attending summer camp, remaining alone at home, taking out the trash at night, or going to bed alone in the evening (Kagan, 1989).

Kagan does not believe that all newborn infants who initially display a high degree of arousal will necessarily grow up to be shy and inhibited children. Rather, he suggests, the development of shy and inhibited behavior in the second year of life requires some form of environmental stress, such as marital quarrels, illness in the family, or the presence of a dominating older sibling. In fact, two-thirds of shy children had older siblings who tended to bully or belittle them, reducing their self-confidence (Kagan, 1989; Kagan, Reznick, & Snidman, 1988; Brody, 1989).

Philip Zimbardo, a Stanford University psychologist who has studied the problem of shyness for more than twenty years, also emphasizes the importance of experience in the development of shyness. According to Zimbardo, shyness frequently represents a learned pattern of reactions that

schoolwork. But you know what *I* think? I think that I'm just trying to keep schoolwork from bothering me too much, and that *he* works too hard. I wonder what the teachers think." Judging by statements such as this one, friendship at this stage appears to be an intimate collaboration of two people who are mutually committed to building the relationship, which has acquired an importance beyond the particular needs of either friend.

Conformity to Peers

Because peer groups involve social equals, they give children unique opportunities to develop their own beliefs without having parents or older siblings dominate or dismiss them. But in doing so, peer groups also present challenges. Acceptance and support by the group matter intensely to children, who are still learning what kind of people they are and are still acquiring the skills needed to deal with others. As a result, peer groups often influence their members very strongly indeed: they demand conformity to group expectations in return for continued acceptance and prestige.

Negative effects of peer pressure

Pressures to conform sometimes lead children to violate personal values or needs or those of parents and other adult authorities (Fine, 1982). One child might feel pressured into paying dues that she cannot afford, or into joining fights that she does not want to participate in, or into shunning children who do not belong to her own group. Another might feel pressured to wear clothes that his parents consider outrageous or to perform poorly at school. In return

grows out of social experiences in which the child was degraded or humiliated or in which the child lacked models from whom to learn needed social skills.

Observations of preschool and school-age children and interviews with children and their parents reveal that shyness appears to be related to several major areas: a child's self-image, birth order, parents' sensitivity to shyness, and children's experiences with parents and teachers (Zimbardo, 1977; Brody, 1989).

Shy children have negative self-images and feel less attractive, less intelligent, and less popular than their classmates who are not shy. Firstborn girls are more likely to be shy than later-born girls, a difference that appears to continue into adolescence, whereas firstborn boys are shyer through the preschool and very early school years but not by the time they enter early adolescence. The greater concern and anxiety that many inexperienced parents feel with their firstborn child may in part account for this. Other studies have found, however, that shy children tend to be later born and suggest that their shyness may result from being mistreated by older siblings (Brody, 1989).

Another cause of shyness appears to be parents who are overly sensitive to shyness in their children and may convey these concerns to their children. Shy children are also likely to have at least one shy parent in the family, suggesting that shy parents may serve as models (Zimbardo, 1977). Finally, teachers often do not recognize shyness in their students, in part because shy children are rarely seen as troublemakers and are easily overlooked, particularly if a preschool or kindergarten class is large. Because shy children find it hard to ask for or accept help and lack the confidence and social skills needed to engage the teacher on a personal level, teachers may find them less rewarding and at times feel rejected by them.

Whether they are at home, at school, or playing with their friends, children need to feel confidence in their environment and security in their relationships with others. Parents and teachers can be most helpful to the shy (and not-so-shy) child if they respond in a warm and sensitive way, have reasonable expectations of the child, and respect the child's self-esteem by not humiliating him or being unduly critical of his mistakes. A child's sense of self-esteem can be increased by helping her to build on her strengths and strong points and to avoid putting herself down. It is also important that parents and teachers provide opportunities for children to observe and imitate models who are socially confident and competent so that they, too, can acquire the social skills and confidence that they may lack (Brody, 1989).

for these behaviors and attitudes, the children remain in good standing with their peers.

Note, however, that peer groups can exert positive pressures as well. For example, they can encourage athletic achievement above and beyond what physical education teachers can produce in their students, and they can create commitments to fairness and reciprocity, at least within an immediate circle of peers. "When someone buys a candy bar at the drugstore, she shares it with the rest of us. Then we do the same thing the next time, if *we* get something nice." Whether the pressures are positive or negative, however, peer groups offer a key setting for acquiring social skills, for evaluating and managing personal relationships, and for handling competition and cooperation.

Positive effects of peer pressure

FAMILY RELATIONSHIPS

In spite of the growing importance of peers, families continue to influence children's development strongly during the middle years. Their influence differs in nature from peers', however, because of parents' much greater material power and psychological maturity. To some extent, the material and psychological gaps between parent and child dominate all families. At the same time, however, the circumstances and organization of particular families create variations in family relationships.

How Parents Influence Children

Even though children probably do influence their parents to some extent, most of the influence goes the other way, from parent to child, even in the middle years (Radin, 1982). Parents influence children in at least six different ways:

1. *Modeling of behaviors* Whether they intend to or not, parents often demonstrate or model a variety of behaviors that children later imitate. Some parents curse when they are angry; they should not be surprised if they hear the very same words from their children when their children get angry. But desirable behaviors are also modeled; if parents give lots of affectionate hugs when they feel happy, they may see pleasingly similar behavior developing in their children.

2. *Giving rewards and punishments* Parents influence their children by praising some of their behaviors and disapproving of others. A boy who is playing football with his friends may earn an approving comment from one of his parents, whereas a boy who is learning to draw may elicit indifference or even a look of disgust and a comment such as, "What are you doing *that* for?" (Maccoby, 1980). To some extent, children learn sex-appropriate behaviors in this way.

3. *Direct instruction* Sometimes parents simply tell their children how to act: "Don't pinch your brother"; "Come straight home from school without talking to any strangers." Much of the time, children seem to learn from such instruction (Radin, 1982).

4. *Stating rules* Again and again, parents state general rules such as, "In this family, everyone washes his or her own dishes." Children are supposed to deduce correct behavior by comparing the rule with the situation at hand ("Did I forget to wash my dishes this time?").

5. *Reasoning* In exasperated moments, parents may question their children's capacity to reason, but in fact parents often use reasoning to influence children anyway. For example, they may remind their children of gaps between their behavior and their values ("Is yelling at her a good way to make friends?"). Or they might define and label activities in ways calculated to influence behavior ("You did badly on the test because you didn't study hard enough, not because you're dumb.")

6. *Providing materials and settings* Parents can affect children's behavior by controlling materials and settings. They can buy certain things, such as a computer instead of new clothing, or they can offer situations, such as a place to do homework but not a place to keep pets. These influences make some behaviors more likely to occur than others.

Notice, however, that in spite of their importance, these six methods, are not really unique to parents. Peers also use them. How, then, do relationships with parents differ from those with peers? The answer lies not in the methods of influence but in how parents and children view their relationship.

The Separate Perspectives of Parent and Child

How parents view social relationships

In getting along together, children and parents approach their relationship in very different ways. For the most part, parents already know how social relationships work, whereas their child is trying to discover this for the first time. This gap makes misunderstandings almost certain (H. Sullivan, 1953). Because of their maturity, parents cannot help but regard social relationships as multifaceted and as unfolding over long periods of time. As a result, every action of their child, however simple, seems full of potential meanings. If the child resists going to school for two days in a row, parents are likely to wonder why. *Is she developing a permanent dislike of school? Is she socially clumsy and therefore unable to find friends? Did I say something wrong before breakfast this morning?* Like it or not, layers of meaning present themselves for parents' consideration.

Children bring much less understanding to their social relationships, and in fact look to their parents to gain more of that understanding. Unfortunately, developing social sensitivity and skill can prove very confusing. On one occasion, parents may say that getting angry is acceptable, but on another occasion, they may say that it is not. Many social skills do not seem to be open for discussion or modification; if a child interrupts his father when he is talking to a friend, the father is likely to insist that his son follow his rule of etiquette (namely, "Don't interrupt"). If the parent discusses this rule at all, he is likely to do so only to persuade the child to comply, not because he is really open to applying a different rule of etiquette.

How children view social relationships

From a child's viewpoint, therefore, getting along with parents — and with most other adults, for that matter — can seem like the old game of blind man's bluff, in which a blindfolded child searches clumsily for some person or object. In this case, the child searches for the "right" way to conduct her social relationships. If she blunders socially, she may simply have to keep hunting for better, more socially acceptable actions and pass up any hope of understanding her mistakes in the short run (Youniss, 1980). This happens because many social rules and conventions are based on subtleties that escape children's understanding. Parents may urge a child always to tell the truth, but the rule actually has many exceptions, such as when a person needs to be tactful. Or parents may repeat the rule "If you can't say something nice, don't say anything at all." But there are many exceptions to this one, too; sometimes people do need to tell someone that his behavior is very unacceptable.

The Quality of Parent-Child Relationships in the Middle Years

As middle-years children gradually learn more about their parents' attitudes and motivations and the reasons for family rules, they become more able to control their behavior. This change has a major impact on the quality of relations between school-age children and their parents (Galinsky, 1987). Parents find themselves monitoring the moment-to-moment behavior of their children less than in earlier years. They do not always have to watch carefully as their kids pour themselves a glass of milk, and they do not always have to remind them to use the toilet before they get in the car.

Bridges In what ways does the parent-child relationship change during the middle years?

Less close surveillance

Nevertheless, parents do continue to monitor children's efforts to take care of themselves but in more indirect ways (Maccoby, 1984). Instead of simply arranging for a child's friend to visit, parents increasingly use comments such as "If you want to have Lin over next week, you'd better call by tomorrow." And instead of helping their child to put on each item of clothing in the morning, they will more likely confine themselves to some simple reminder ("It's time to get dressed"), on the assumption that the child can take care of the details of dressing.

More distant monitoring

These changes contribute to one of the stereotypes of parenting during the middle years: that it just consists of fixing meals, providing taxi service, and enforcing a few rules. In reality, this stereotype does not take into account the activities that parents and children often still do together, ranging from shopping to watching television together to holiday celebrations. And it also does not take into account the emotional ties that underlie these activities. If children have

The empathic understanding and comfort displayed by this mother for her unhappy son and this father's willingness to help his daughter pursue her interests illustrate only two of the many different aspects of parent-child relationships during the middle years.

become securely attached during the preschool years, they and their parents often enjoy each other's company more than ever during the middle years.

Special feelings between parents and children

By this period, parents and children have accumulated a backlog or history of experiences together, and this shared history makes family relations increasingly unique and meaningful. One study documented this idea by analyzing letters that school-age children wrote to a local newspaper about "What Makes Mom Great." Many of the children said that they valued their mother's enduring presence in their lives (Weisz, 1980); "She is always there to listen," said one child. And they also valued the empathy or sensitivity that their mother provided: "She always seems to know how I feel." These comments imply that, the bonds between parents and children are normally very strong during the middle years.

The Changing Nature of Modern Families

More mothers working

Until recently, the popular stereotype of a typical family contained four people: a father who worked, a mother who cared full time for the family, and two children. In 1955, for example, 60 percent of families in North America fit this popular stereotype of the traditional family. By the mid-1980s, however, only 7

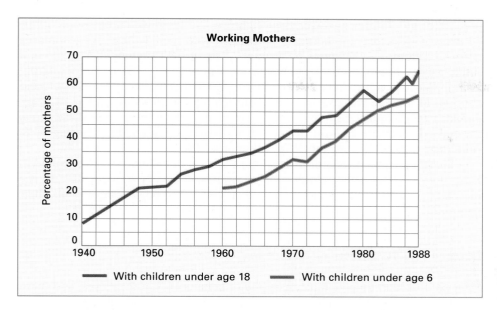

FIGURE 13.2
Working Mothers, 1940–1988

percent of North American families conformed to this model (Hodgkinson, 1985).

During this period, mothers began working outside the home in increasing numbers (U.S. Department of Labor, Aug. 1989). As of 1988, 65 percent of married women with children younger than eighteen were employed, more than double the 30 percent rate in 1960 (U.S. Department of Labor, Aug. 1989). In 1988, 56 percent of married mothers with children age five and younger were employed outside their homes, at least part-time, more than twice the rate of 22 percent in 1960. And when both single and married women with children are considered, more than 50 percent are employed outside of their homes (U.S. Department of Labor, 1986). Figure 13.2 summarizes this trend. If current increases continue, by the year 2000, an even larger majority of mothers of children younger than eighteen will work.

Divorce

Divorce has also become much more common (see Figure 13.3). Between 1960 and 1980, the U.S. divorce rate tripled. Recent figures show that about 50 percent of all marriages in the United States end in divorce. Approximately 23

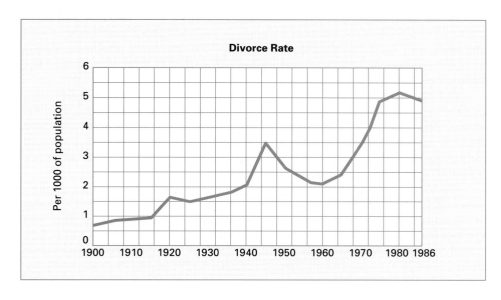

FIGURE 13.3
Percentage of U.S. Marriages Ending in Divorce, 1900–1986

Reconstituted families

percent of all children younger than eighteen live in single-parent households, 89 percent with their mothers and 11 percent with their fathers. It is estimated that children of divorce spend an average of six of their first eighteen years in a single-parent home (U.S. Department of Commerce, 1987a; Hetherington, 1979). Because approximately two-thirds of divorced parents remarry, most children of divorce will live in a *reconstituted family* consisting of parent, stepparent, siblings and stepsiblings, and in approximately 50 percent of these cases, the second marriage ends in divorce as well (Hetherington, Stanley-Hagen, & Anderson, 1989; Glick & Lin, 1987; Bumpass, 1984).

These changes have raised new questions about children's development. How does divorce affect children in the family? And how (if at all) do the increased demands of employment affect children's relationships with their parents?

Divorce and Its Effects on Children

Increased economic pressures

Most parents who divorce must make major adjustments in their lives, and these adjustments often affect their children deeply. First, many divorcing parents face sudden economic pressures. Some find themselves financially responsible for two households, that of their former spouse and children and that of a new spouse and children. Others (especially some mothers) find themselves responsible for only one household, but for the first time they have to take on new or additional employment to meet these responsibilities, and even so, their standard of living frequently declines, often severely. One study of divorced couples one year after a legal divorce found that men had experienced a 42 percent improvement in their standard of living following divorce while women had experienced a 73 percent loss (Weitzman, 1981). According to Hetherington (1989), 43 percent of divorced custodial mothers have annual incomes below the poverty line. For women who have physical custody of their children, reduction in economic resources is often accompanied by dependence upon welfare; changes in maternal employment; poorer quality in housing, neighborhoods, schools, and child care; and a necessary geographic mobility that often leads to loss of social networks and support for the child from familiar friends, neighbors, and teachers. Both noncustodial and custodial fathers typically maintain or improve their standard of living following divorce (Hetherington et al., 1989).

Isolation of parents

There are many psychological pressures as well. The parent who takes major physical custody of the children must learn to manage a household alone, which is a major physical and psychological burden. Some parents may feel deeply isolated from relatives or friends to whom they used to feel close. If relatives do live nearby, divorcing parents must often rely on them for the first time, simply to procure help with child care and household work. Yet these helpers may not approve of the divorce.

For most families, these pressures create considerable stress for at least two or three years following separation (Hetherington, Cox, & Cox, 1982; Hetherington, Stanley-Hagen, & Anderson, 1989). Even before actual separation and divorce, such families go through long periods of distress, tension, and discord. Nearly one-half of divorced parents, in fact, separate and reconcile at least once before they finally separate permanently (Kitson & Raschke, 1981).

Bridges What are the emotional effects of divorce on children during the middle years?

During all this time, children must endure several problems not of their own making. For one thing, they face problems of divided loyalty: loving, helping, or spending time with one parent often seems to alienate the other parent. In the months preceding a separation, this problem often arises because of inconsistent discipline. A mother may forbid her children to watch a certain television show, "because it is too violent," but her husband may permit or even encourage them to watch it "because it is just a show." Opposing expectations such as this

Divided loyalties for children

can persist for long periods because the parents communicate very little or because one parent may want to prove herself more likable or authoritative than the other parent. No matter which parent "wins" in this situation, the children lose; they necessarily must displease at least one parent.

Findings from Wallerstein's long-term follow-up study of sixteen girls and twenty-two boys who were between six and eight years old at the time of their parents' divorce suggest that even ten years later, they are burdened by fear of disappointment in love relationships, lowered expectations, and a sense of powerlessness. When compared with children who were older or younger at the time of a breakup, this group of children fared much more poorly on measures of their internal functioning (psychological integration, emotional stability, strength of defensive structure, and reality judgment) and on measures of their overall competence including school and social relationships. Yet these children's profound unhappiness about current relationships and concerns regarding future ones were often masked by their overall conformity to social expectations (Wallerstein, 1987).

But some critics have questioned the degree to which Wallerstein's findings, which are based upon naturalistic, case study techniques with a middle-class sample, are representative of the entire population of parents and children of divorce. These critics suggest that a more systematic analysis of her data might lead to a more careful evaluation of her findings; they also suggest comparison with studies using more quantitative approaches and families from a broader range of backgrounds (R. Weiss, 1989; Wallerstein, 1989; Hetherington & Furstenberg, 1989).

Marital breakups can also make children feel deeply lonely and isolated from their parents. Parents are preoccupied with their distress about the marriage; as a result, they may withdraw from their children emotionally or otherwise be unable to exercise their parental responsibilities effectively. Even when they are not withdrawn, they may have bitter and hurtful outbursts in front of the children. These scenes encourage children to be emotionally cautious and thus leave them lonelier than ever. Unfortunately, such behavior also provides undesirable models of how to handle social conflicts by demonstrating aggressive confrontation rather than compromise and respect for the people with whom you disagree (Emery, 1982; Wallerstein, 1986, 1987; Wallerstein & Blakeslee, 1989).

When a marriage breaks down, it can be especially hard on children. What is this girl thinking and feeling about her parents' argument?

Isolation of children from parents

Differing Effects on Boys and Girls   On the whole, boys and girls tend to respond differently to divorce. Boys often become more aggressive and willful during the period surrounding a separation and divorce. They often lose access to the parent with whom they identify most strongly — their father — because the majority of divorced children live with their mothers (Santrock & Warshak, 1979). Even in intact families, boys tend to be disciplined relatively more by both parents jointly; so during a divorce, boys tend to become victims of power struggles and inconsistencies in matters of discipline.

Special effects on boys

Girls' responses are less obvious than boys'. Some studies suggest that girls become *less* aggressive as a result of divorce, that they tend to worry more about schoolwork, and that they often take on more household responsibilities (Block et al., 1981). These changes could mean that they are **internalizing,** or holding inside, any stress they feel about their parents' divorce by trying to act more helpful and responsible than usual. Other research suggests that daughters of divorced parents develop a continuing preoccupation with their relationships with males; for example, such girls tend to become involved earlier — sometimes before the end of elementary school — in dating, and they engage in more sexual activities at earlier ages than other girls do, are more likely to get pregnant and are more likely to experience disruptions in heterosexual relations. (Wallerstein & Kelly, 1980; Wallerstein, 1987; Wallerstein & Blakeslee, 1989).

Special effects on girls

Perspectives

The Psychological Tasks Facing Children of Divorce

In her book *Second Chances,* Judith Wallerstein reviews what she and her colleagues have learned from their ten-year, in-depth study of divorce and its consequences in 60 divorcing families with 131 children, who were age three to eighteen at the time of separation. The families were first interviewed in 1971 at the time of the decision to separate and again at one year after separation. Fifty-eight of the families were seen again five years after separation, and 51 families and 98 children were interviewed again after ten years (Wallerstein, 1986, 1987; Wallerstein & Blakeslee, 1989; Wallerstein & Kelly, 1980).

According to Wallerstein, the typical child's experience of divorce is similar to the experience of a child who loses a parent through death or whose community is destroyed by a natural disaster. Such children have strong feelings of anger, vulnerability, sorrow, abandonment, and a fear of being unloved. Each divorce disrupts close family relationships and threatens the security of the family structure, and each results in an acute, time-limited crisis followed by an extended period of disequilibrium. Wallerstein believes that divorce has a long-term impact on family life and on a child's development that is much greater than previously imagined. Therefore, the child of divorce must master an additional set of challenges as well as the common tasks of childhood.

Wallerstein and her colleagues propose seven psycholog-

ical tasks that all children of divorce must master (Wallerstein, & Blakeslee, 1989).

*Task 1: Understanding the divorce This task occurs in two stages. The first involves accurately perceiving the immediate changes that divorce brings, and the second requires, especially for young children, differentiating fantasized fears of being abandoned or losing their parents from reality. The second stage occurs later when children have achieved the greater emotional distance and more mature understanding to evaluate their parents' actions and are able to draw useful lessons for their own lives.

Task 2: Strategic withdrawal Children and adolescents need to get on with their own lives as quickly as possible and get back physically and emotionally to the normal tasks of growing up. This poses a dual challenge to the child, who must actively and painfully remove himself emotionally from parental distress and conflict to safeguard his individual identity and separate life course.

Task 3: Dealing with loss In the years following divorce, children experience two profound losses: (a) the loss of the intact family together with the symbolic and real protection that it provided and (b) the loss of the presence of one parent, usually the father, from their daily lives. Dealing with loss may be the single most difficult task imposed by

---

Physical custody

Impact of custody

Who Has Primary Custody?   In these conditions, it is not surprising that relationships between parents and children deteriorate during and immediately after a divorce. The parent with physical custody of the children (usually the mother) finds herself dealing not only with her children but also with major new responsibilities for earning a living and making peace, at least in her mind, with the fact of divorce. The children may need more reassurance than usual, even though the mother feels less able to give it. These circumstances can create willfulness and aggression in some children and withdrawal or anxiety in others (Hetherington et al., 1989).

Parents without physical custody of the children (usually fathers) do not face these daily hassles, but they do report feeling rootless, dissatisfied, and unfairly cut off from their children. Seeing his children every other week or on school vacations may not really allow a father to know them intimately. In the long run, therefore, noncustodial parents may feel increasingly awkward in their interactions with their children and increasingly reliant on special events, such as going to Disneyland, for whatever contacts do occur. In the long run, too, noncustodial parents report feeling that their financial and emotional support for their children goes unappreciated. Perhaps for these reasons, fathers often actually increase the amount of time they spend with their children immediately after the divorce; yet they soon decrease such time well below what it was before the divorce (Furstenberg et al., 1982).

Involvement of noncustodial parents

The little research that exists on the role of noncustodial parents in the development of the child is not very consistent, but it does suggest that when conflict between the divorced parents is low, the continued involvement of a competent, supportive, and reasonably well-adjusted noncustodial father can

divorce. It requires children to overcome the profound sense of rejection, humiliation, unlovability, and powerlessness they feel with the departure of one parent. When the parent leaves, children of all ages blame themselves, thinking that "he left because I was not lovable or worthy" and believing that had they been more lovable, worthy, or different, the parent would have stayed.

Task 4: Dealing with anger Unlike death, divorce is always a voluntary decision for at least one of the partners in a marriage. The knowledge that their unhappiness has been caused by the very people they rely on for protection and care puts children in a terrible bind. Caught in a combination of anger and love, they feel both frightened and guilty. A major task for children is to resolve this anger, to recognize their parents as human beings capable of making mistakes, and to respect them for their real efforts and real courage.

Task 5: Working out guilt Young children often feel responsible for divorce, thinking that their misbehavior may have caused one parent to leave. They may also feel that any fantasies they had about driving a wedge between their parents have actually come true. Children of divorce need to separate from guilty "ties that bind" them too closely to a troubled parent and go with their own lives.

Task 6: Accepting the permanence of the divorce At first, children's strong need to deny the divorce can help them cope with the powerful realities they face. Denial functions as a screen that is alternately lowered and raised, helping children to confront the full reality of divorce little by little. Some children, however, refuse to accept the reality of divorce as a permanent state of affairs even five or ten years after it occurred. Unlike death, which cannot be reversed, divorce still appears to hold that possibility and stimulates fantasies that their parents can reconcile and once again be happy together. Some children do not overcome this fantasy of reconciliation until they have finally separated from their parents and left home.

Task 7: Taking a chance on love Achieving realistic hope regarding relationships may be the most important task both for the child and society. Here the young person must create and sustain a realistic vision of her own capacity to love and be loved, knowing that separation and divorce are always possible. Mastering this last task, which depends on successfully negotiating all of the others, leads to psychological freedom from the past and to a second chance.

positively affect the children's adjustment, especially for boys, and that it does not generally interfere with the development of close family relations in a new stepfamily. Continuing involvement of the noncustodial mother, however, is more likely to precipitate loyalty conflicts and upset between the children and their stepmothers (Hetherington et al., 1989).

Sometimes these problems can be alleviated by **joint custody** of children, in which the parents divide their child-rearing responsibilities relatively equally. The exact mechanics of the division vary with the circumstances of the family. The children may live with each parent during alternate weeks, parts of weeks, or even parts of the year. Or when the children are relatively old, one or more may live with one parent and the rest with the other parent (although perhaps this should really be called divided custody). Or children may reside in a house or apartment and the parents take turns living with them.

But none of these arrangements is ideal. Most of them assume that divorced parents still live close enough geographically to make frequent exchanges possible. Most also assume that the parents still trust each other enough after the divorce to support equal sharing of the children. And joint custody does not always please the children; often they must shuffle two schools and two sets of friends, even when they are only moving between different parts of the same city.

Blended Families   Most parents who get divorced remarry within a few years, creating what some call reconstituted or **blended families.** The new relationships in these families pose challenges for the children of both parents. The most common type of blended family occurs when a mother marries a man who does

*Bridges   What are the emotional effects of divorce on children during the middle years?

Methods for sharing custody

Relationships with stepparents

not have custody of his children by a previous marriage. In these situations, the stepfather and stepchildren must somehow acknowledge the previous attachments that they bring to the new family. Children must recognize and accept that their new stepfather has other children about whom he cares a great deal living somewhere else. And the new husband must recognize and accept that his stepchildren have another, "real" father somewhere and strong attachments to their mother.

Perhaps because of these complications, stepfathers initially tend toward extremes in their involvement with their stepchildren: either they remain aloof, or they get so involved as to seem restrictive to the children (Zill, 1983). Eventually, many stepfathers find an appropriate middle ground for involvement, especially if the mother helps them to do so, but it may take them as long as two years. Love and sensitivity do not occur automatically or immediately in blended families.

Younger children appear able to eventually form an attachment with a competent stepparent and to accept the stepparent in a parenting role, but young adolescents are especially vulnerable and unable to adapt to the transition of remarriage because of the developmental tasks that confront them at this age. Both stepmothers and stepfathers tend to take a much less active role in parenting than do custodial parents, and even after two years, disengagement is the most common parenting style for stepparents. Stepfathers who initially establish relations with their stepchildren by being warm and involved but do not assert parental authority may eventually be accepted by boys, but acceptance of the stepfather by the stepdaughter is more difficult to obtain and appears to be unrelated to his behavior toward her. Stepmothers are generally more emotionally involved and take a more active role in discipline than stepfathers do, but they do not easily gain acceptance from the stepchildren (Hetherington et al., 1989).

Relationships among stepsiblings

More difficult challenges arise when both parents bring children from previous marriages to live in the same household. The children must learn to get along not only with the parents but also with each other in spite of the prolonged distress of previous divorces. Parents in this sort of blended family report especially high rates of stress and daily conflict, at least during the first year or two of the new marriage (Hetherington, Cox, & Cox, 1982; Hetherington, Stanley-Hagen, & Anderson, 1989; Hobart, 1987; Santrock & Sitterle, 1987). This fact is not surprising given the complexities of the new relationships. The two families almost surely use somewhat different standards of discipline, for example, and they were probably inconsistent about these standards during the period surrounding their divorces. When the parents begin a new family together, then their children may at first feel betrayed by the presence of stepsiblings and the stepparent. At the same time, the new stepparents may find it hard not to treat their biological children differently from their stepchildren.

The Effects of Work on Families

Work affects family life profoundly, although not always in ways that are simple or straightforward. Jobs determine daily schedules, of course, which in turn affect how much time parents have for their children. Job schedules also influence which parent or child does particular household chores. At a more subtle level, work affects parents' self-esteem and thus their happiness as human beings and as parents. And jobs determine income and therefore affect many aspects of family life. All these effects are enlarged by the fact that an increasing number of families are headed by two working parents or by a single parent who works.

Importance of mother's choice

Effects of Maternal Employment   In spite of the once popular view that mothers should stay at home for the sake of their children, research suggests that maternal employment as such usually does children no developmental harm (L. Hoffman, 1984). What does matter is a woman's choice about employment. Mothers who choose to work or who choose not to work and who live in relatively supportive families apparently do no harm to their children by their employment situation. Mothers who feel forced either to work or not to work are less fortunate; they report more stressful relations with their children.

Maternal employment often does influence children's development in some ways, however. Most of these are positive or at least not negative. Families with working mothers, for example, divide housework and child care more evenly than do families without employed mothers (L. Hoffman, 1983). In two-job families, fathers wash dishes relatively more often, and they spend more time alone with their children (although mothers still do the large majority of housework and child care). In families with working mothers, children are often expected to help with household chores and with caring for younger brothers and sisters. It is not at all uncommon for a parent to instruct her ten-year-old to pick up several things from the neighborhood grocery store, set the table, and put the casserole in the oven.

Effects on daily life

The blend of housework and breadwinning seems to create less stereotyped attitudes in the children of working mothers about the proper roles of mothers and fathers (T. Gold & Andres, 1978a). Both sons and daughters witness nurturant behavior in their fathers and occupational competence in their mothers. As the children approach adolescence, they are especially likely to support women's employment generally (Scarr, 1984), and the daughters usually expect to work outside the home when they get older.

In considering these trends, keep in mind two facts. First, mothers who work outside the home usually differ from mothers who do not both in circumstances and in personality. Surveys show that working mothers tend to have fewer children than nonworking mothers do (L. Hoffman, 1984). Presumably this difference helps to reduce the amount of child care and housework in the working mothers' families. On the other hand, working mothers have more often experienced a marital breakup, and they often lack money as a result. These

Qualities and circumstances of working mothers

In families where mothers work, other family members often share household responsibilities.

circumstances explain not only why some mothers go to work in the first place but also why employment can prove difficult for many women and their families — their work as such may not be a problem, but the hard times that surround their need to work are.

Second, maternal employment is extremely common. As we have already pointed out, working mothers were a rarity a few decades ago but are in the majority today. This trend has resulted partly from changing sex roles and partly from a changing economy. Technological advances such as microwave ovens and home freezers make housework less time consuming than it used to be (Robinson, 1980). At the same time, general prosperity and its higher wages have made it relatively less economical to trade time at home for time at work; for example, it may be cheaper to buy bread for a family than to bake it on a regular basis.

Because of these conditions, employment has become an increasingly sensible choice for women, compared to full-time homemaking. Ironically, these same conditions may also create guilt in women who prefer *not* to work. Now, some women may feel they have to justify homemaking rather than employment to relatives and friends.

After-school supervision of children can be a problem for working parents, however. In cases in which after-school programs do not exist and siblings, friends, and other relatives are not available, older (and sometimes younger) elementary-school-age children are left at home by themselves. While many parents in this situation carefully work out after-school procedures, including strict limits on what a child may do and a check-up phone call from work to be sure that everything is okay, others leave their children to their own resources.

Latchkey children

It is estimated that more than 1 million children between the ages of five and fourteen regularly care for themselves when not in school (U.S. Bureau Department of Commerce, 1987b). Some of these "latchkey" children are at risk for both physical and psychological harm. Often such children live in neighborhoods that are not safe, and a growing number of children as young as seven, eight, and nine years old are being recruited by crack dealers (Kolata, 1989b).

Not all children who care for themselves after school are in danger, however. Recent research with fifth- through eighth-graders found that the type of latchkey arrangement was important, as was the way these children spent their time. Children whose after-school care was removed from an adult environment and whose parents did not know their whereabouts or call to check up on them were more likely to get into trouble than were children whose parents were aware of their plans and who returned to their home rather than hanging out with their peers after school (Steinberg, 1986).

Effects of Paternal Unemployment Whereas some segments of society regard maternal employment as worrisome, society in general regards paternal unemployment as a serious problem. Presumably this double standard occurs because of society's traditional emphasis on breadwinning for males (Bronfenbrenner & Crouter, 1982). Men, according to the popular impression, should be relatively hard hit by lack of work.

Father's reactions to unemployment

In this case, the popular impression contains a lot of truth. Studies of unemployed fathers find that they feel a great deal of stress and disruption, which seem likely to hurt their families (Cobb & Kasl, 1977). Unemployed fathers are depressed and anxious and report chronic lack of sleep. Such reactions are even more noticeable among fathers who have lost jobs than among fathers with steady work at near-poverty-level wages (Moen et al., 1981).

Stresses of unemployment

These stresses may explain the high frequency of violence in families with unemployed fathers. Wife beating is much more frequent among such families than among families generally. So is child abuse, although it is not necessarily committed by the father alone (Justice & Duncan, 1977). Presumably these problems develop because the fathers feel self-conscious, anxious, and ashamed about losing their status as the family breadwinner. At the same time, their wives and even their school-age children may worry about the family's economic future, so all members may get on one another's nerves.

Note, however, that the stress of unemployment is not unique to men. Because women often work out of economic necessity, their loss of employment sometimes proves just as devastating as that of many men. Sometimes, in fact, maternal unemployment can prove even more difficult, especially if a woman must suddenly care for children by herself after losing her job, without significant help from a spouse, relatives, or friends. The idea that men experience hard times because of unemployment is definitely true; but it does not mean that women have an easy time.

Although reliable statistics are not available, homelessness is a growing problem that has had a profound impact on the development of children. Frequent moves between shelters and substandard temporary housing deprive these children of the predictability and security that are so important to the formation of self-concept and to self-esteem during the middle years. These frequent moves also make it difficult or impossible for these children to develop a secure relationship with teachers, classmates, and neighborhood peers.

Other Sources of Social Support for Schoolchildren

So far, this chapter has emphasized two major sources of social experience for children: peers and parents. In reality, however, most children in their middle years establish other sources of social support as well. One study documented this fact by interviewing schoolchildren about people, places, and activities that they found satisfying and helpful in conducting their lives (Bryant, 1985). To help the children think of these, the interviewers took them on long walks around their neighborhoods. From time to time, the interviewers asked questions about what they saw ("Do you know who lives there?" or "Is this where you go to relax?").

The network of supports

This method revealed a tremendous number of social supports for children in their middle years, many of which are summarized in Table 13.1. Large numbers of children reported seeking out adults other than their parents —

TABLE 13.1   Sources of Support Reported by School-Age Children

Support	Average Number Mentioned in Interviews
Peers and siblings named among ten most important individuals	4.5
Adults (including parents) named among ten most important individuals	3.0
Grandparents and others of grandparents' generation named among ten most important individuals	1.3
Pets (including neighbors') considered as a special friend	1.7
Make-believe friends and make-believe identities	1.6
Hobbies that child attributes to self	2.3
Special places to go to be alone	2.1
Formally sponsored activities (public library, community pool, and church or temple)	4.5
Homes and informal meeting places where child feels free to visit	5.5

Source: Bryant (1985).

especially grandparents — to talk with and confide in. Family pets, and sometimes even the pets of neighbors, also served as confidants. Children reported using hobbies to unwind and feel better about themselves, although some of the hobbies were relatively nonsocial, such as collecting stamps or playing a musical instrument. Other children reported having special hideaways where they went to be alone for a while, which they said helped them to feel better. Many children sought out peers for activities when they needed an emotional lift or when they felt confused; but this was not the case on every occasion, and not all children did so.

Qualities of effective supports

In general, as children moved through the middle years, their sources of support became increasingly broad. This made them better able to manage particular stresses, whether inside or outside their families, when they arose. At all ages during the elementary school years, children seemed happiest when they reported the widest range of social supports and when that range emphasized informal supports rather than formal ones. For example, friends on the block to play games with offered more support than an adult-sponsored hockey league, and fooling around with a guitar offered more emotional release than regular formal music lessons. The most important trend, however, was the developmental one: the older children got, the more they lived in an expanding social world.

SCHOOL INFLUENCES

Next to the family, school is probably the single most important developmental influence during middle childhood. Each year children spend more than eleven hundred hours at school and often many additional hours in school-related activities. School is the main arena in which children resolve the crisis of industry versus inferiority. Interactions with teachers and peers provide children with important opportunities to develop cognitive and social skills, to gain knowledge about the world, and to develop peer relationships that are central to the development of self-concept during the middle years.

School Culture

Schools differ

Each school has its own culture, which includes the values, beliefs, traditions, and customary ways of thinking and behaving that make it unique and distinguish it from other schools and institutions. For example, one school may especially value its innovative academic programs and the high achievement levels of its students, another the degree of student involvement in school-sponsored activities, and a third the active involvement of parents in providing special resources. The greater the fit is between school culture and the values and expectations of the children (and families) that it serves, the more likely it is that the school's developmental impact will be positive. Students learn and feel better in classrooms in which the instructional approach, pattern and rhythm of verbal interaction and student participation, and strategies for motivating students are in tune with their family and cultural expectations (Tharp, 1989; Minuchin & Shapiro, 1983).

The Hidden Curriculum

Schools influence children through two curricula. The **explicit curriculum** helps children acquire the academic knowledge and skills thought to be necessary for successful participation in society. The **hidden curriculum** — the implicit norms, expectations, and rewards for certain ways of thinking and acting that are conveyed by school's social and authority relationships — teaches students the social roles and behaviors expected by society. The left side of the report card, which evaluates a child's academic performance, reflects the explicit curriculum, whereas the right side of the report card, which includes such areas as attendance, work habits, social skills, and conformity to other school norms, reflects the hidden curriculum. Critics argue that the hidden curriculum is a way of subtly preparing children to accept the hierarchical and authoritarian social relationships of society. Supporters point out that the hidden curriculum is no secret and that conformity to the dominant values of society is in fact a major purpose of schooling (Bowles & Gintis, 1976; Giroux & Penna, 1988).

Teacher Influences

With the exception of their parents, most elementary school children spend more time with their teacher than with any other adult. Teachers therefore play a very significant role in the lives of middle-years children. Observational studies of daily classroom life reveal that the elementary school teacher engages in as many as one thousand interpersonal exchanges with pupils each day (Cazden, 1988). Many of these interactions involve communicating academic material, regulating the verbal (and nonverbal) activity of students, evaluating student participation and providing feedback, dispensing supplies, and keeping track of time so things go as scheduled.

Although there is considerable variation in teachers' styles of classroom management, effective teachers are able to establish learning environments that are calm, predictable, and engaging and that provide smooth transitions from one activity to the next. Effective teachers are also able to stay "on top of" the classroom situation by being in tune with their students, both in their communication of academic content and in their responses to the constantly changing social and emotional needs of as many as thirty children.

Teacher beliefs and expectations regarding their students' potential can also affect their students' actual performance and overall school adjustment by changing students' behavior in the anticipated direction and thereby serving as a **self-fulfilling prophecy.** Early research by Robert Rosenthal and Lenore Jacobson found that when elementary school teachers were given information that falsely identified randomly selected students as potential academic "bloomers," these gains actually did occur for first- and second-graders but not for students in grades three through six (R. Rosenthal & Jacobson, 1968).

Teachers' expectations affect student performance

How do teachers form such expectations, and how are they transmitted to students? A general answer is that teachers treat students for whom they have high expectations differently than students for whom they do not. More specifically, teachers provide these students with more challenging materials, demand better performance, and are more likely to reward them for their good performance (Brophy, 1983; M. Harris & Rosenthal, 1985).

Teachers may also unintentionally communicate negative expectations of students, particularly if they do not fit the teacher's own expectations. In a classic study, Ray Rist intensively studied this process in a large, urban elementary school where on a daily basis he intensively observed a single classroom of black students from the first day of kindergarten through the last day of third grade.

Rist found that by the eighth day of kindergarten, the teacher had assigned students to permanent "slow learner," "average," and "fast learner" groups. Because she had no formal measures of academic ability or cognitive development to aid her evaluation, she did so primarily on the basis of students' economic status. Children who were assigned to the "slow learner" table turned out to be those who were poorly dressed and whose families were on welfare; students who were middle-class in their dress and behavior were seated together in the average or fast learner groups. A similar pattern of classroom organization was repeated by their first- and second-grade teachers, the only difference being that the teachers now based their decisions on children's test scores and readiness material from the prior year rather than on their subjective judgments. The end result of this "objective" placement was to reinforce the social class divisions initiated by the kindergarten teacher (Rist, 1973).

Rist and other investigators have found that these different groups within the same classroom receive different treatment. The fast learner group is much more likely to be given academic assignments and the slow learners busywork. In most grades, the teacher directs two to five times as much control-oriented and somewhat less supportive behavior toward the slow learner group than toward the fast learner group. Controlling behavior includes verbal and nonverbal reprimands and physical hitting, pushing, and restraint; supportive behavior includes verbal praise, smiles, and hugs (Dusek, 1985).

The Student's Experience

Delay, denial, distraction, disruption

What do students experience in the classroom? According to Philip Jackson (1968, 1986), delay, denial, interruption, and social distraction are among the most significant aspects of children's classroom experiences. Particularly in traditional, teacher-centered classrooms, students spend a great deal of time waiting for the teacher or other students, denying fulfillment of their needs until given permission to do so by the teacher, and contending with distractions and social disruption. Students must wait to ask a question, wait to get permission to leave their seats, wait to have a question answered, wait for the next assignment, or wait for their chance to use the stapler.

Waiting to be called on in class can sometimes seem to take forever. Unfortunately, in many classrooms, waiting to get the teacher's attention constitutes a major aspect of a student's experience.

Students experience denial of their desires when they are forced to refrain from answering a question until called upon, to wait to go to the bathroom until they can get the teacher's attention and permission, and so on. Other children, the teacher, the principal, the buzzers, and PA system are only some of the many sources of interruption and distraction during the course of a typical school day (Jackson, 1968). Note, however, that although these observations are cause for concern, many classrooms are consciously organized to minimize these difficulties and to provide a learning environment that is academically stimulating and supportive of children's developmental needs (Lightfoot, 1983).

Although the preceding discussion has by no means exhausted what is known about the impact of schools on middle-years children, what should be clear is that school experiences play a major role in influencing how children experience and interact with others, how they perceive and feel about themselves, and how they generally develop psychosocially.

PSYCHOSOCIAL CHALLENGES FACING CHILDREN WITH HANDICAPS

Children who have special needs or handicaps face many of the same challenges as any other children. They need to achieve in some area of activity; they need to feel accepted by other children; they need to get along comfortably with their families, especially with their parents. By meeting all of these challenges, they develop some understanding of who they are. In these ways, such children are exactly like other children.

But for children with special needs, solutions to these challenges are often complex and at times may require extra encouragement or support from others. The nature of the complexities depends partly on the nature of the handicap: a child with Down syndrome lives a very different life from a child who is missing **Effects of the handicap** a leg or an arm. Some handicaps by their very nature affect peer relations strongly; a child with a hearing impairment, for example, may have daily difficulties in speaking and hearing and may therefore have trouble keeping up with everyday conversations among her classmates. Other handicaps may be relatively invisible to the general public but have a strong impact on the child's family. For instance, a child's elementary school classmates may not know that he has leukemia because acute phases of this illness simply cause him to stay home. But parents and siblings feel the impact of this health problem profoundly in the form of frequent trips to the hospital, disrupted family schedules, and general worry about the child's health.

In spite of variations like these, children with special needs have something in common: they are substantially different from "normal" or usual children, whether the difference is physical, emotional, or cognitive. This section looks at how the fact of having a handicap affects the psychological and social development of these children during the school years.

The Challenge of Knowing Who You Are

Children with handicaps face the same task as other children in developing a unique sense of self, but their disabilities may complicate this task in special ways. Of course, by accentuating uniqueness and difference, a disability should facilitate the development of a self-concept because a child with a handicap **Early knowledge of human differences** learns in many social encounters that she cannot do everything that other children can do. Some children with disabilities therefore may learn sooner than "normal" children do to distinguish between their own thoughts and feelings and those of others (Buscaglia, 1983). Making this distinction is crucial to forming a self-concept.

But there are two problems with this idea. First, how quickly and how thoroughly children learn about the significance of their handicap depends on their cognitive and emotional capacities. By nature, some disabilities limit or delay the child's understanding or the significance of his disability; mental retardation is the most obvious example. Such children often take longer than usual to develop self-constancy.

Second, even when children experience no cognitive limitations, they must learn to accept their disability as only one part of themselves. Whether they like it or not, their sense of self must include their handicap. Yet they must also realize that as individuals, they consist of *more* than their handicap. Like everyone else, they can express happiness, have good ideas, and pursue special hobbies.

Because this dual realization is complex, children need time — perhaps even a lifetime — to develop it. Parents can help this process along by showing pride and pleasure in their children and by not giving undue attention to the disability (Rousso, 1984). For example, they can keep the disability in perspective by cultivating personal and family activities that purposely have nothing to do with the limitations of the child. This strategy is good advice for all parents, whether their children have handicaps or not.

Creating an identity beyond the handicap

The Challenge to Achieve

For children with disabilities, achievement may not be tied to conventional standards of success. Striving for conventional or "normal" standards of excellence can be frustrating and self-defeating. A child who learns academic material very slowly, for example, eventually discovers that no amount of extra study will put her at the top of her class or even anywhere near the top. A child with poor vision eventually discovers that he probably cannot become a star baseball player or even an average one.

These realities do not mean, however, that children with disabilities cannot achieve at all. On the contrary, many such children find activities in which their disabilities make relatively little difference to their performance (French, 1983); impaired vision may interfere with learning to draw, but it does not interfere with listening to and playing music. Some activities can be carried out in unconventional ways or with special physical aids that reduce the importance of a particular disability; poor motor control may make it difficult to write assignments in school, but special typewriter keyboards can often eliminate this problem altogether.

Selecting activities for achievement

Part of learning to achieve, then, consists of selecting appropriate realms of activity and helpful (if unconventional) ways of achieving. Parents and teachers can assist in this selection, and probably should, but in the end, children themselves must recognize how they can hope to achieve the most and then commit themselves more fully to those activities. The process really does not differ from the way in which we all arrange our lives: we all tend to find and emphasize activities in which we do especially well and in which our limitations interfere as little as possible.

Problems with pursuing conventional standards

But, these strategies do not solve all the achievement problems experienced by children with handicaps. Some "normal" standards of behavior and skill are hard to avoid. Society may not expect everyone to be a good athlete, but it does expect everyone to be able to walk gracefully for reasonable distances. Yet children with physical disabilities such as cerebral palsy may be incapable of meeting this everyday expectation; because of their condition, they walk clumsily and fitfully.

The special challenges facing children with handicaps are not only physical, but also cognitive, social, and emotional.

Situations such as these put children with handicaps in a bind. Striving to meet society's usual standards can be frustrating and self-defeating; yet ignoring those standards exposes these children to continual reactions of surprise and discomfort whenever they appear in public or meet new people. Sometime during the school years, children with disabilities gradually become aware of this dilemma and of the continual pain it promises to bring them.

Even when a child does achieve normal standards, the success often proves problematic (Buscaglia, 1983). Others may not view the success as a heroic triumph. "Look at how well she walks this year," they say, meaning something like, "She is approximating our standard of graceful walking better than ever." But the child herself, and anyone close to her, realizes that the achievement cost an extraordinary amount of effort, worry, and time. For this reason, when an achievement like walking well actually occurs, it sometimes feels more like a defeat than a victory. Children with handicaps cannot escape this sort of reaction, and they need constant encouragement to set their own standards of success rather than rely on those used by the rest of society.

The Challenge of Peers

Although children with disabilities want and need the acceptance and affection of other children, their disabilities often interfere with gaining acceptance (Gottlieb et al., 1978). The problem is more complicated than the rejection that "ugly ducklings," or children who have jug ears or an oversized nose sometimes

Limitations to peer relations

experience. Genuine handicaps can make other children anxious and defensive. Eventually children with handicaps begin to sense this fact and begin to expect less from their contacts with peers. Some handicaps, such as a speech problem or mild retardation, also limit a child's ability to interact skillfully. In the long run, these circumstances can combine to limit social life severely.

Studies of peer preferences have found that children often do not merely ignore but actively reject peers with handicaps (Hartup, 1983). The rejection applies to a variety of handicapping conditions, from learning disabilities and mild (or "educable") retardation to emotional disturbance. The extent of isolation and rejection depends a lot on the severity of the handicap; usually, the more severe it is, the more the child is rejected (Guralnick, 1981). Peers seem to dislike handicaps primarily because of the strange or unfamiliar behavior sometimes connected with them, not because children with handicaps often perform poorly at schoolwork.

Benefits of integrating special needs children

In an effort to reduce this isolation and rejection, many educators have worked in recent years toward integrating or **mainstreaming,** children with handicaps into regular classrooms (Turnbull & Turnbull, 1986). Obviously, such children often also require special, separate educational services along with their ordinary daily experiences in classrooms. For example, children with learning disabilities may need individual tutoring to help them keep up with their class. But with appropriate support and with encouragement and training for teachers, mainstreaming may help at least some children to feel more accepted by their peers.

The Challenge of Family Relationships

Disabilities of course affect children's relations with their parents and other family members (Gallagher & Gallagher, 1985). For one thing, parents often cannot influence and teach their children in the ways described earlier in this chapter. A child with a physical handicap may not learn easily from his parents' demonstrations how to tie shoelaces and how to button a shirt or blouse. He may still learn such simple behaviors, but his parents may have to modify their demonstrations to fit the child's capacities, and they may have to persist longer than usual.

Modified methods of influencing children

On the other hand, children with retardation or emotional disturbance may not learn easily from parents' direct teaching or statements of family rules. Simply telling such a child not to pull other children's hair may not get the message through very fast, and parents must expect to repeat themselves often before the child finally understands.

Practical demands on parents

Parents often experience a lot of stress as a result of having a child with a disability. Such children have special practical needs; they may have to be lifted, bathed, fed, and toileted. They may also require frequent trips to the doctor or hospital for physical therapy or medications. All of these needs can disrupt parents' and siblings' lives substantially, and meeting them sometimes costs money; not all insurance policies cover such needs adequately, and not all families can afford sufficient insurance coverage in any case.

Regardless of the kind of disability involved, families vary in how well they cope with these challenges. Among families with two parents, larger ones seem to fare better than smaller ones (T. Powell & Ogle, 1985). Possibly a larger number of siblings means more help for the parents, or possibly the siblings help to create an atmosphere of normality, or possibly parents with more children have accumulated extra skill in raising children and therefore feel less pressured by the special demands of a child with a handicap. Some mixture of these factors may operate; at present we do not really know.

One-parent families must cope with the pressures intrinsic to single parenthood in addition to the child's disability. Because most of these families are headed by women, they tend to have substantially less income than two-bread-winner families; yet they may need more money than usual to care for the child. Educational and therapeutic programs for the child with a disability may demand significant parental involvement, yet because single parents must work, they may have less time than others to attend meetings or get to special appointments.

Siblings react in various ways to a disability in the family. On one hand, many siblings report feeling emotionally neglected because parents give so much attention to the disabled child (Vadasy et al., 1984). On the other hand, they also report developing greater tolerance than usual for differences among people and more commitment to altruistic values and life goals as a result of having a sibling with a disability (Cleveland & Miller, 1977). As one girl put it, "My parents always expected me to do more things for my retarded brother, so I did them, and they seemed to appreciate my help." As long as parents do not overemphasize this helpfulness ethic, siblings apparently benefit from their experience and do not lose their own identities in the process.

Effects of disability of siblings

BEYOND CHILDHOOD

In a variety of ways, the middle years are the time when a child becomes a person in a more adult sense than ever before. This happens in part because the child has begun accumulating considerable experience with other people of roughly her own age and maturity and in part because of cognitive developments. Children begin setting goals and working toward them in more adult ways by taking into account others' opinions about their achievements as well as their own interest in learning.

As we have pointed out several times in this chapter, the developments of the middle years do not always result in happy feelings and experiences. With their newly developed maturity, children are able to hurt and snub some of their peers as well as to make new friends, and they are now able to worry about peer evaluations as well as to become commendably open-minded. Life has not gotten happier just because the child has gotten older; but it is not necessarily unhappier either.

Taken together, these experiences create a new, more mature sense of self within children of this age, one that has more inward or psychological properties than that of early childhood. In the years ahead — during adolescence — this psychological self becomes still more elaborate. Contrary to widespread belief, the adolescent years do not necessarily prove any more or less difficult than the middle years or early childhood, although some individuals, for special reasons, encounter special challenges.

SUMMARY OF MAJOR IDEAS

Psychosocial Challenges of the Middle Years

1. During the middle years, children face challenges concerning achievement, peer relationships, family relationships, and the development of identity or sense of self, school, and (for some) having a handicap.

The Sense of Self

2. During the middle years, children develop a sense of self, acquire a belief in self-constancy and in permanent psychological traits, and learn to distinguish their thoughts and feelings from those of others.

The Age of Industry and Achievement

3. According to some psychodynamic theorists, schoolchildren repress their earlier romantic attachments to their parents and focus instead on developing a sense of industry and achievement.

4. During the middle years, children shift their achievement orientation from an exclusive focus on learning or task mastery to one that is also concerned with others' responses to their achievements.

Peer Relationships

5. According to Piaget, peers help children to overcome egocentrism by challenging them to deal with differing perspectives.

6. According to Sullivan, peers help children to develop democratic ways of interacting and also offer the first opportunities to form close or intimate relationships with others.

7. In general, peers seem to serve unique functions by creating voluntary relationships of equality among children.

8. Groups of peers vary in membership and behavior according to the age mixture, gender, and race or ethnic group of their members.

9. Peer groups tend to segregate themselves by both gender and race.

10. Popular children possess a number of socially desirable qualities, such as social skill and confidence in themselves; unpopular children possess less desirable qualities, such as aggression, selfishness, and bossiness.

11. Early in the middle years, a friend is someone with whom a child shares activities and toys, but later in this period a friend becomes someone whom the child can count on and with whom she can share intimacies.

12. Peers do exert pressure to conform on individual children, and this pressure can have either good or bad effects.

Family Relationships

13. Compared with parents, children must engage in more hypothesizing and guesswork in order to understand family relationships.

14. In recent years, divorce has become more common in North American families, and it usually creates stress for all members of the family, although girls react differently to it than boys do.

15. Blended families, which result from remarriage, pose considerable challenges, although younger children form attachments with stepparents more easily than adolescents do.

16. Many mothers now work at least part time; their employment generally does not seem to have any negative effects on children; nevertheless, maternal employment does influence the division of household labor and children's attitudes about gender roles.

17. Dual-income families have created "latchkey children," some of whom are at psychological and physical risk but many of whom are not.

18. When fathers are unemployed, both they and their families experience significant stress.

19. Schoolchildren often find emotional support from adults other than parents, from friends, from pets, and from hobbies.

School Influences

20. Children are influenced by the school's culture; this influence is more likely to be positive if the school's culture and the child's familial culture are compatible.

21. The hidden curriculum — the school's implicit values, norms, and expectations — has a subtle but nevertheless powerful effect on students.

22. The environment a teacher creates and his expectations of his students shape their experience.

23. From the students' perspective, school is a place where they may encounter denial, interruption, delay, and distraction.

Psychosocial Challenges Facing Children with Handicaps

24. Children with handicaps can and should achieve, but they often must define achievement by more personal and less conventional standards than those used by others.

25. Children with handicaps experience awkward relations with peers, but intervention by parents and teachers can alleviate this problem.

26. Families with such children often must cope with unusual amounts of practical care, special financial burdens, and emotional stress.

27. Children with handicaps need an identity, just as other children do; their identity should recognize their disability but not be limited by it.

KEY TERMS

peers (457)
sense of self (458)
self-concept (458)
self-constancy (458)
repression (462)
latency (462)
defense (462)
industry versus
    inferiority (462)
industrious (462)
inferiority (462)
achievement
    motivation (463)
learning orientation (463)
performance
    orientation (463)

warp (466)
juvenile period (466)
sociometric
    questionnaire (470)
dyad (470)
prejudice (471)
internalizing (481)
joint custody (483)
blended family (483)
explicit curriculum (488)
hidden curriculum (489)
self-fulfilling prophecy (489)
mainstreaming (494)

WHAT DO YOU THINK?

1. What do you consider an appropriate balance between a learning and a performance orientation toward achievement? Explain whether you think this balance should apply to all children or should vary with individuals.

2. Do you feel that peer groups have the same structure as they used to? Are children still segregating themselves by gender and age as much they did in the past? Are they still segregating themselves as much by race? Explain.

3. Given that mothers' employment generally does no harm to children, why do you think many parents (and some segments of society) continue to worry about the impact of employment on child development?

4. Do children in the middle years really know who they are? Explain.

5. What are the most important things that children and adults can learn or do to assist children with handicaps?

FOR FURTHER READING

André, R. *Homemakers: The Forgotten Workers.* Chicago: University of Chicago Press, 1981.

This book examines homemaking as work: how the tasks of homemaking compare to the tasks of other, paid workers and what their approximate economic value may be to families. The author especially considers whether women who work outside the home essentially hold two jobs, one inside and the other outside the home She also describes and evaluates several strategies that couples and families have tried for distributing homemaking work more equitably.

Axline, V. *Dibs: In Search of Self.* New York: Ballantine, 1964.

This classic tells the true story of a boy with an emotional disturbance and how he eventually overcame his condition with the help of therapists and others. The story reveals several of the ways in which a disability — in this case, emotional disturbance — can interfere with the usual challenges of childhood, especially the challenges of identity development.

Dunn, J. *Brothers and Sisters.* Cambridge, MA: Harvard University Press, 1985.

The author describes how siblings' relationships evolve during childhood, especially during the middle years. She cites many vivid examples of brothers and sisters getting along — and failing to get along. The examples challenge many common assumptions about siblings, such as the impression that siblings show that they do not care about each other by fighting. On the contrary, siblings seem to understand each other better in some situations than their parents do.

Jackson, P. W. *The Practice of Teaching.* Chicago: University of Chicago Press, 1986.

Lightfoot, S. *The Good High School.* New York: Basic Books, 1983.

These two books describe the ups and downs of life in school, from both the teacher's and the student's perspectives. Jackson's book is based on a lifetime of teaching and observation; Lightfoot's is based on an anthropological study.

Klagsbrun, F. *Married People: Staying Together in the Age of Divorce.* New York: Bantam Books, 1985.

This book explores the reasons some marriages improve and flourish the longer they last, whereas others dissolve quickly, and still others persist under considerable tension. The author describes interviews with numerous couples and uses the couples' comments to suggest why some marriages survive better than others.

Saunders, A., and Remsberg, B. *The Stress-Proof Child.* New York: Signet Books, 1984.

This book is intended for the general public and describes how and why some children experience debilitating stress. In general, it suggests ways for parents to relieve stress in children. The advice is often quite concrete and ranges from giving children more hugs and phrasing comments in positive terms to encouraging a healthy diet.

Wallerstein, J., and Blakeslee, S. *Second Chances: Men, Women and Children a Decade After Divorce.* New York: Ticknor & Fields, 1989.

This rich, readable book describes the results of a long-term study of the lives of families who have undergone divorce. The use of case studies brings the experiences of the children and their parents to life for the reader.

PART SIX

Adolescence

The adolescent years present new and unique challenges for children. They must come to terms with their bodies as they suddenly grow taller and become sexually mature; they must establish more equal relationships with their parents; and they must come to grips with the need to leave home eventually and to become independent individuals.

How stressful these challenges prove, however, depends on a variety of circumstances. For some teens, the timing of puberty can make these years especially hard — or easy. For others, their newly forming ability to reason abstractly can make life seem suddenly confusing, at the same time that it also reveals exciting new possibilities for the future. For most young people, dating — or even just talking to — the opposite sex proves both intriguing and frustrating, as they slowly overcome childhood habits of relating only to members of their own sex. All in all, the changes of adolescence can be difficult, but on average, they are neither more nor less challenging than those faced during other periods of life.

Brian's Case

When Brian was ten, his parents divorced. At first he lived equal amounts of time with his mother and father, but when his mother became seriously involved with another man and the two of them decided to move to a distant city, Brian moved in permanently with his father. These were not easy adjustments to make for a twelve-year-old; but all things considered, Brian managed remarkably well. It helped that he was a self-reliant child, with many interests. Brian became especially close with Tigger, his cat. Tigger was a good companion when he was alone after school and helped Brian feel responsible and caring.

It also helped Brian's adjustment to his parents' divorce that he had a pretty good relationship with his father and that his father's job as an electrician enabled him to be home by five p.m. every work day. They both enjoyed special family rituals, such as chopping down their own Christmas tree each year.

Brian's grades took a serious slump right after the divorce, but by the time he moved in with his father, they had become much better. In the evenings, Brian took pride in completing his homework on his own without having to be reminded by his father. Brian hardly ever spoke about his mother, but sometimes he fantasized that his parents would get back together again.

Brian went away to summer camp when he was thirteen. The experience was unforgettable: he loved the out-of-doors and the feeling of being more on his own than ever before. He also discovered that he could make friends easily at camp — more easily, in fact, than back home.

Camp Sunnybrook

Dear Mom,

Got your letter and candy and swim fins. Thanks for the stuff. I was telling the guys in my bunk about your chocolate cookies—how about sending some next time?

There's a kid named Kenny in the next bunk. He's a real good ping pong player, but I beat him more than he beats me. His parents are also divorced, but he lives with his mom and visits his dad every other weekend. I still don't see why you needed to move so far away just because things were so bad between you and Dad. It's stupid. I know George works out there, but what's so great about him anyway? If you lived nearby, I could see you a lot more. Oh well, I guess you have your reasons.

Tomorrow we go on a hike to the spillway and then the reservoir. And there's a Baseball World Series—my bunk has a good chance of winning. The food is awful and the water stinks (even the horses have better water—it's true). So send FOOD and SODA soon. And especially those chocolate cookies.

Brian

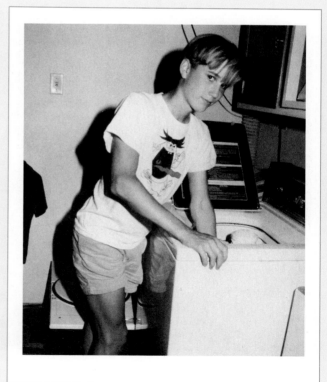

Getting housework done without Mom had been hard at first, but after a while Brian and his father figured out ways of dividing it up. Brian was in charge of doing the laundry and taking out the trash, his father did the vacuuming, and both shared the shopping.

501

When Brian was fifteen, it seemed that he was always hungry. He knew he was not supposed to eat junk food and soft drinks so much, but he felt that somehow *his* teeth and *his* health would not suffer. Anyway, it was fun going to fast food hangouts with his friends, and soon Brian and his friends were doing this every day.

At sixteen, Brian got his first skateboard. By now, he was spending more time than ever before with friends — many of whom his mother had never even met, since she now lived so far away. He had also started dating, but he still felt awkward around girls. He kept thinking that they noticed every thing he did wrong and every blemish on his face.

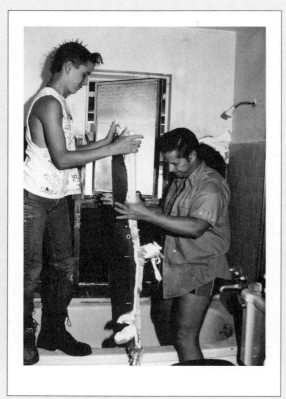

Most of the time Brian was on the go, but sometimes he helped his father do renovations around the house. He and his father often got into arguments now when they were together, over issues such as how Brian wore his hair or if he could use the car. Brian's father began seeing a woman steadily, and Brian began to spend many evenings away from home.

At seventeen, Brian had saved enough money to buy his own car. The car meant so much to him and opened up so many work and social opportunities that he often wondered what he would have done if he had never gotten one. That question sometimes even led him to wonder what society would be like if cars had never been invented!

June 12: I can't believe I'm done with school! This term's been a drag, but at least things worked out (sort of) between me and Dad's girlfriend. I kept worrying that Mom would ask me stuff about her and then argue with Dad about what I told her. Actually, Sue isn't all that bad -- although she still acts kind of like a "visitor."

July 4: Sue and I had a talk -- about how hard it's been for both of us. Funny that I never really thought about how she felt all this time. Just felt that she came between me and Dad. I still get mad at Dad for treating me like a kid sometimes. At least Sue doesn't do that, maybe because she's not really my parent.

August 7: Mom called and was really upset about my plans to travel out west. Maybe she's feeling guilty about not seeing me enough to talk about the trip sooner. Or something -- I don't know. It's harder to figure her out when we're apart so much. She seemed happier after I told her that me and my friends would definately stay at her house on the way out to the coast.

When Brian was eighteen, he went away to college where he met Karen. He liked living away from home. He still sometimes resented his parents' divorce, but increasingly, Brian regarded it as their problem, not his. He felt a bit uncertain about the future, but he liked the idea of being on his own and he was confident that he would be able to manage.

CHAPTER 14

Adolescence: Physical Development

Focusing Questions

■ What is meant by adolescence, and how did it come to be created as a period of development?

■ What changes in height and weight occur during adolescence?

■ What is puberty, and what are its important effects on physical development during adolescence?

■ How does the timing of puberty — early, average, or late — affect the psychological experience of adolescence for boys and girls?

■ What are the major health problems encountered by adolescents?

D avid is fourteen. Ever since the beginning of last summer, there have been some very noticeable changes in the way he looks and acts. He has grown nearly two inches in the last six months, and his mom jokes that his pants and sleeves will have to be reintroduced to his ankles and wrists before it is too late. But this rapid growth is no joking matter to David. Although he was well coordinated and athletic in junior high school, he is now awkward and klutzy, tripping over himself and bumping into things. His increased height, rather than being an advantage, seems to be limiting his ability to play baseball, his favorite sport.

David's voice is changing, too. Sometimes it sounds the way it always has; at other times it is deeper, like his father's; but often it seems to bounce around out of control, cracking and breaking as it fluctuates between the two. David has definite signs of a mustache on his upper lip and the fuzzy beginnings of a beard on his cheeks, and although David has become very shy and modest about his body lately, his dad has noticed that he has hair under his arms and around his pubic area.

David's personality has also changed. Usually a pretty easygoing and responsible person who is a pleasure to be around, he now seems very moody and self-centered. He blows up or sulks at unpredictable times and often fails to do what is expected of him around the house or at school.

David's sister, Miriam, is twelve. In the past year she, too, has been undergoing some striking physical changes. Not only has she gained three inches and thirteen pounds, but it is obvious to everyone that her body is rapidly changing. Her bust and hips have filled out, and she has considerable curves where just a year ago she had none at all. Miriam has begun to menstruate, and she, too, has grown hair under her arms and in her pubic area. Like David, she has become much shier and more uncomfortable about her body. Although she seems proud of becoming a woman, she easily blushes when someone mentions how grown-up she has become, and she worries that she is too fat.

Except for her increased shyness and embarrassment about the changes in her body, Miriam has not shown any striking changes in personality. She is much less willing to wrestle with her brother than she was just a few months ago, but she continues to be quietly responsible around the house and to do well at school. She lives up to her childhood reputation of being "emotionally steady as a rock."

As you have certainly guessed, both David and Debbie are undergoing many of the changes of adolescence. In this chapter and the two that follow, we explore the major physical, cognitive, social, and emotional developments that occur during adolescence. But first, let us take a brief look at the concept of adolescence itself.

THE CONCEPT OF ADOLESCENCE

Adolescence is defined as the stage of development that leads a person from childhood to adulthood. Marked by the major physical changes of puberty and important cognitive and social changes, it is generally considered to begin around age twelve and to end sometime around age twenty.

In every society, ceremonies and rituals such as confirmation, bar mitzvah, graduation, and marriage are used to signify important changes in a person's life stage status, and the transition to adulthood is perhaps the most important and widely recognized change that all people experience. In societies that still have relatively simple, agricultural economies and traditional cultural and social arrangements, this transition is fairly smooth and predictable and grows out of a long period of preparation. For example, when a teenage Australian aborigine goes on his year-long walkabout through the desert, with only a few simple weapons to protect him, his chances of returning safely are high because much of his childhood has been spent in learning skills that help him to meet this challenge. Similarly, a girl's initiation into womanhood in many tribal cultures is preceded by years of instruction in and imitation of the adult roles and activities she is now expected to perform.

In modern industrial societies such as ours, however, the roles and responsibilities that a person is to assume when he reaches sexual maturity are much less predictable, largely because technology and values are changing so rapidly. Our rites of passage tend to be more symbolic than real, and the transition from childhood to adulthood can be rather difficult and prolonged. For example, whereas a girl in a hunting and gathering society has a good idea of what her adult work will be — bearing and caring for children, gathering and preparing food, and so on — how can a girl in computer-age America know what kind of work she will do, what kind of family she will have, or even where she will live?

Rites of passage

Adolescence: From Idea to Social Fact

Although most of us take the idea of adolescence for granted, it is a relatively modern concept. Its invention, or discovery, in America was largely a response to the social changes that accompanied this country's industrial development in the nineteenth century (see Chapter 1 for a discussion of this development).

In fact, some researchers have proposed that adolescence was defined as a separate stage of development principally to prolong the years of childhood, so that the aims of the new urban-industrial society that rapidly developed after the Civil War could be fulfilled (Bakan, 1975). According to this view, the spread of railroads and the telegraph, accompanied by a general shift in population from the country to the industrial cities and the addition of a huge number of immigrants, threatened the American way of life. Because so much was changing so fast, people felt a growing fear that society would get out of control — that the country would be overrun by foreigners and that the dirty, unpleasant cities would breed crime and immorality. There were three major legal responses to this national "identity crisis" — compulsory education, child labor laws, and special legal procedures for juveniles — and together they played a major role in making adolescence a social reality (Bakan, 1975).

State-controlled education was believed to be so essential to ensure law, order, morality, and obedience in the workplace that school attendance was made compulsory for children between the ages of six and eighteen in most states. Children and adolescents had made up a significant part of the labor force until this point, but an increasing awareness of the harmful effects of factory work combined with the desire of adult laborers to protect their jobs from children

Bridges What social and economic changes influenced the development of the concept of adolescence in the United States?

Emergence of the idea of adolescence

willing to work at lower wages spurred the movement toward child labor laws. Laws restricting child labor came to define the end of adolescence.

As early as 1899, when the first Juvenile Court Act was passed by the Illinois state legislature, special legal procedures for juveniles were established as a way of dealing with the newly invented idea of "juvenile delinquency." Such developments served to solidify the social reality of adolescence further. Once this was accomplished, adolescence became an important focus of study for the newly emerging field of developmental psychology.

Adolescence as a psychological concept was popularized by psychologist G. Stanley Hall, one of the first developmentalists to study adolescence. He believed that each stage of a child's physical and biological growth and personality development was in a sense predetermined in that it repeated the same stages of development that occurred in the evolution of the human species. Thus, a child's selfish, self-centered, and aggressive nature was thought to reflect the more primitive stages of human history. Adolescence, according to Hall, represented a second birth, in which evolutionary instinct was replaced by social and cultural influences in the form of parents and other adults; they now replaced nature in protecting the child from unfavorable social conditions and in guiding her transformation into an altruistic, self-sacrificing, and moral human being. Hall believed that adolescence was a stressful period because of the repetition of evolutionary conflicts and a teenager's increased vulnerability to social pressures. Although there is virtually no support for Hall's theoretical explanations, his view of adolescence as a time of "storm and stress" (sometimes called *Sturm und Drang*) remains popular today.

Hall's theory

Theoretical Views of Adolescence

Since the "creation" of adolescence in the United States, there have been two somewhat conflicting views about its basic nature. One view concurs with Hall's — that adolescence is a time of "storm and stress," a time when major physical, intellectual, and emotional changes create tremendous upset and crisis within

There is no doubt that some teenagers experience periods of turmoil connected with growing up. But for most, adolescence is neither more nor less difficult than earlier periods of life.

Social Context

What social and economic changes influenced the development of the concept of adolescence in the United States? (507–508)

Physical Development

What effects does the timing of puberty have on the psychological development of adolescents? (521–526)

Peers

How important a factor is peer pressure in an adolescent's decision to use drugs? (533)

Genetics

In what ways does heredity account for variations in physical development during puberty? (514)

Family

How can parents help adolescents cope with the awkwardness of puberty? (519)

ADOLESCENCE: PHYSICAL DEVELOPMENT

In what ways do hormonal changes influence emotional development during puberty? (517)

Emotions

How is adolescent self-esteem affected by prevailing views of body image? (518–519)

Self-concept and Identity

How successful have been efforts to educate adolescents about the causes and prevention of AIDS? (530–531)

Learning

How does adolescents' understanding of the causes of illness influence their health care behaviors? (527)

Cognition

What effect do social expectations have on changes in adolescents' voices? (515)

Language

---

the individual and conflict between the individual and society. As you may recall, both Freud and Erikson believed that development, especially in adolescence, is full of conflict.

The other view, which has grown out of observation and research with adolescents, suggests that for the most part, adolescence contains no more conflict than any other period does. Most youngsters seem to adapt to the changes in themselves quite well and adjust to the changing demands and expectations of parents and society in a relatively smooth and peaceful way.

As with so many differences in point of view, there is truth to both these views of adolescence. For the minority of adolescents at the two extremes, the transition to adulthood can be either smooth and effortless or conflicted. But for the vast majority, it is much more likely to fluctuate, with long periods of relative calm and shorter periods of surprisingly intense upheaval.

We discuss these and other social aspects of adolescence in greater detail in the next two chapters. Here, however, we must look more closely at the physical changes of adolescence and at their effects on development.

GROWTH IN HEIGHT AND WEIGHT

Compared to childhood, the years of adolescence — roughly twelve to twenty — include less overall growth in height and weight but significantly greater irregularity and unevenness in the pattern and pace of growth. This is clearly illustrated by Figure 14.1. As it shows, the average height for both boys and girls at twelve years is about fifty-nine or sixty inches. By age eighteen, however, the average height for boys is sixty-nine inches, whereas the average for girls is only sixty-four.

Much of this rapid change in height and weight is due to a dramatic **growth spurt,** which is preceded and followed by years of comparatively little increase.

Unevenness of growth spurt

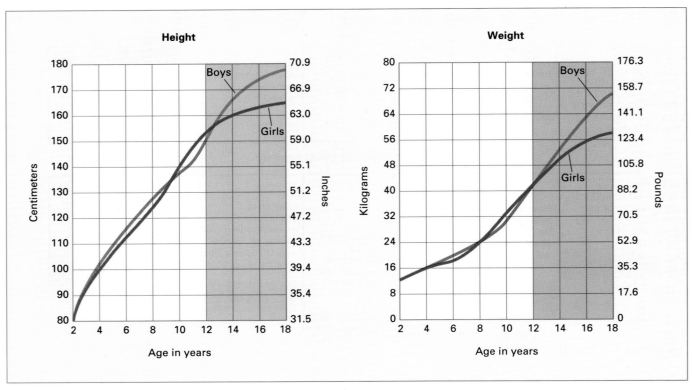

FIGURE 14.1
Growth in Height and Weight from Two to Eighteen Years

The change in height is particularly striking, as Figure 14.2 shows. The maximum rate of growth happens around age eleven or twelve for girls and about two years later for boys. In those years, many girls grow three inches in a single year, and many boys grow more than four inches (Marshall, 1978).

It is not the growth spurt that accounts for males' greater average height. Instead, the difference results because boys start their growth spurt two years later than girls and so have two more years of childhood growing than girls do. Thus, the average girl is around fifty-four or fifty-five inches tall when she begins her growth spurt, whereas the average boy is fifty-nine or sixty inches tall when he begins his. Because both boys and girls add around nine or ten inches during adolescence and grow relatively little afterward, women end up being shorter than men on average (Thissen et al., 1976).

Interestingly, growth patterns and height during childhood are better predictors of adult height than growth patterns and height during adolescence are. That is, a tall ten-year-old is more likely to become a tall adult than is a tall thirteen-year-old who was short as a ten-year-old (Faust, 1977).

Although weight also increases during adolescence (see Figure 14.1), it is more easily influenced than height by diet, exercise, and general life-style, and therefore changes in weight are less predictable. Girls begin puberty with slightly more total body fat than boys. During puberty, total body fat declines for boys from an average of 18 or 19 percent to 11 percent of body weight, whereas for girls it increases from about 21 percent to about 26 or 27 percent (D. Sinclair, 1978). The average weight gain during the growth spurt is about thirty-eight pounds for girls and forty-two pounds for boys, although there is considerable individual variation in how it is distributed.

Sex differences in weight and body fat

Of course, adolescents differ greatly in their rates and patterns of growth; the growth spurt in some may be barely noticeable and may have little impact on their day-to-day existence, whereas for others it may be very striking and may radically alter their lives and feelings. These differences are further complicated by the fact that different parts of the body, including hands, feet, legs, arms, and torsos, often grow at different rates.

David, the fourteen-year-old we described at the beginning of the chapter, is a good example. Although he is somewhat below average in height and weight for his age group, he currently wears a size twelve and one-half shoe — five shoe sizes larger than he wore two years ago. Although his family teases him about this, David secretly fears that he will always have very oversized feet because his arms, legs, and other assorted body parts have not yet caught up.

On the other hand, Miriam is concerned that she is too fat, that her chest is too big, and that her legs are too short for the rest of her body — or for boys to find attractive. Because Miriam's parents and friends, both male and female, think that she is very attractive and not fat at all, we might ask why Miriam has such different perceptions of herself. One answer might be **adolescent egocentrism,** the tendency of adolescents (both boys and girls) to find it difficult to perceive the world (and themselves) through anyone's eyes but their own. This is particularly true of their perceptions of how they look and of how others perceive them. An adolescent's view of her own irregularities and regularities, her personal ideals regarding how she should look, and current social ideals of attractiveness all contribute to a very complicated and confusing state of affairs. Many adults cannot remember their own adolescent confusion and thus cannot understand teenagers' dissatisfaction with themselves. As a result, the physical changes that accompany puberty are a common source of emotional upset for both teenagers and their parents.

Bridges How does adolescent egocentrism contribute to adolescents' concerns about their physical development?

FIGURE 14.2
Physical Development During Adolescence

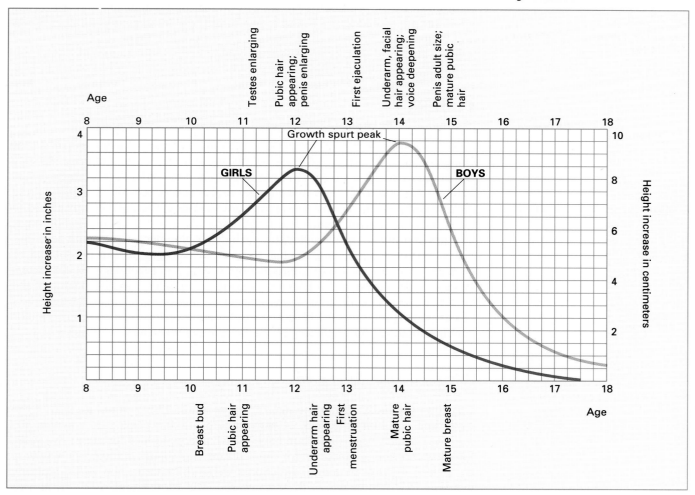

Much of the unevenness in growth that is typical of this period becomes better coordinated with time. But not everyone ends up with the height, weight, and other physical characteristics that match society's ideals or for that matter the individual's own.

The Secular Trend

Children's puberty at an earlier age than parents' puberty

During the past century children have gradually begun the physical changes of adolescence earlier and ended up taller and heavier than their parents, tendencies that are referred to as the **secular trend.** For example, the average age at which girls have their first menstrual period has dropped from between fifteen and seventeen a hundred years ago to between twelve and fourteen today, in both the United States and Western Europe. And although today's boys generally reach their full height between eighteen and twenty and girls between thirteen and fourteen, in 1880 the average male did not reach full height until between twenty-three and twenty-five and the average female between nineteen and twenty (Tanner, 1971).

How can the secular trend be explained? Improvements in health care, diet, and overall living conditions are thought to be the major reasons for these changes. Because the onset of puberty is related to body weight, improvements in diet have resulted in that weight being achieved at earlier ages than in previous generations. In addition, early childhood diseases that limit growth have been largely eliminated, and nutrition and medical care are greatly improved for children in developed countries. We can predict that a similar trend will occur wherever adequate nutrition and living conditions are available to all children and their families.

PUBERTY

Readiness for sexual reproduction

Rapid increases in height and weight are only one part of a larger pattern of changes, called **puberty,** that leads to full physical and sexual maturity. Puberty is marked by striking changes in both primary and secondary sex characteristics. **Primary sex characteristics** make sexual reproduction possible. For girls, these include complex changes in the vagina, uterus, fallopian tubes, and ovaries; the most obvious sign of these is the beginning of menstrual periods. For boys, changes in primary sex characteristics include development of the penis, scrotum, testes, prostate gland, and seminal vesicles, which lead to the production of enough sperm for successful reproduction. Changes in **secondary sex characteristics** include enlargement of breasts, growth of body hair, and deepening of the voice. Associated with these developments are important changes in the levels of hormones present in the bloodstream; these powerful chemicals play a major part in initiating and regulating all of the changes associated with puberty.

Primary Sexual Maturation

For boys, the most significant sign of sexual maturation is rapid growth of the penis and scrotum (the sack of skin underneath the penis that contains the testicles), which begins at around age twelve and continues for about five years for the penis and seven years for the scrotum — although individuals may vary by a year or two in either direction (Meredith, 1967). The penis typically increases in length by two or three times, so locker-room comparisons are almost inevitable as boys become increasingly aware of obvious changes in themselves and their friends. Although penis size has almost nothing to do with eventual success at overall sexual functioning (Marshall & Tanner, 1974), for adolescent boys it can sometimes seem all-important as a sign of their new status as men.

During adolescence, enough live sperm are produced in the testes to make reproduction a real possibility for the first time. Sometime around age twelve, boys are likely to experience their first ejaculation of **semen,** a sticky fluid produced by the prostate gland, which is located near the penis just inside the body cavity. Semen carries the sperm to the penis and provides it with a medium in which to live after ejaculation. Most boys have their first ejaculation during masturbation or as **nocturnal emissions,** or wet dreams, during sleep, or, less frequently, as waking emissions that occur spontaneously. Most males report experiencing nocturnal emissions about one or two years before puberty; the accompanying dreams are frequently but not always erotic in nature. The sexual changes just discussed and the unexpected erections and uncomfortable sexual fantasies and sensations that boys sometimes experience are common sources of embarrassment. Less frequently they are a source of more serious discomfort and conflict.

Production of sperm

For girls, the appearance of the first menstrual period, which is called **menarche,** signals sexual maturity. In most societies, menarche also symbolizes the shift from girlhood to womanhood (Logan, 1980). Nevertheless, menarche occurs rather late in a girl's sexual maturation and is preceded by a number of other changes, including enlargement of the breasts, appearance of pubic hair, and broadening of the hips and shoulders. Next, as the growth spurt peaks, the uterus, vagina, labia, and clitoris develop, as do the ovaries.

For most girls, menstruation involves a certain degree of inconvenience and discomfort but also feelings of happiness about the specialness of their reproductive capacity and womanhood. Adequate information about menstruation — including practical details about the purchase and use of sanitary napkins and tampons, about personal hygiene, and about birth control — is important. In addition, contact with women who have positive feelings about their monthly cycles will help to make menarche a positive experience and to allay fears and negative attitudes. As we shall see, the same informative and supportive climate is also helpful in dealing with the other physical changes of puberty.

Mixed feelings about menstruation

Maturation of Secondary Sex Characteristics

Breasts Girls first develop breast "buds," or slightly raised nipples, with the beginning of puberty. During the following several years, the nipples grow darker, the areolas around the nipples increase in size, and the breasts continue to grow until they reach their full size.

Breast development

Given the attention that our culture focuses on breasts, it is not surprising that breast development is a potential source of concern for many adolescent girls. Breasts that are too big, too small, or the "wrong" shape may cause embarrassment, and in rare cases girls experience outright harassment because of these physical developments.

Boys also have a small amount of breast development, and their areolas (the pigmented areas surrounding the nipples) become larger and darker much as girls' areolas do. A few boys may experience enough tissue growth to cause them some embarrassment, but these "breasts" usually return to typically male levels in a year or two.

Hair When their genital development is relatively advanced, boys and girls both acquire more body hair, although boys generally grow more of it than girls do. The first growth is simply a fine fuzz around the genitals; later this **pubic**

Pubic and axillary hair

Bridges   In what ways does heredity account for variations in physical development during puberty?

hair darkens and becomes coarser. At the same time underarm or **axillary hair** begins to appear; this eventually becomes dark and coarse as well.

Although there are considerable differences among individuals, in girls pubic hair and axillary hair begin to appear around age eleven and are fully grown by around age fourteen. In boys they begin around twelve and continue until about eighteen. At age fifteen or so, many boys begin growing facial hair, which usually appears first as just a suggestion of a mustache that begins on the outer corners of the lips and gradually grows in toward the nose. It should be noted, however, that there are inherited ethnic and individual differences in the amount of facial hair and body hair that develops for both boys and girls. For example, some boys have little or no facial hair at all, or growth that is limited to their upper lips or chins. Eventually boys may grow real whiskers on the chin and cheeks, as well as hair on the chest and back, although these later developments do not usually become obvious or significant until around age seventeen or older (Neyzi et al., 1975).

Social stereotypes to the contrary, girls typically grow facial and body hair as well. As with boys, a wide range of ethnic and individual differences exist. Differences in the lightness and darkness and coarseness and fineness of body hair influence how noticeable it is. Cultural attitudes and expectations influence women's feelings about axillary hair during puberty. For example, whereas many women in our culture spend considerable time and money to rid themselves of "unsightly" underarm, leg, and facial hair, women in a number of European countries feel that this hair is attractive and do not attempt to remove it.

For girls, breast development is one of the major occurrences of puberty, and getting a first bra can be an important event. Likewise, the growth of facial hair — and thus the need to shave — is a significant milestone for adolescent boys.

Voice   In both sexes the voice deepens near the end of puberty and becomes richer in overtones, so that it sounds less like a flute or whistle and more like a violin or clarinet. These changes make the adolescent's voice sound more truly adult and less childlike, but the fluctuations in voice qualities that some adoles-

cents experience can be a cause of considerable — although usually temporary — embarrassment.

Like many of the other changes of puberty, the deepening of the voice is not limited to one sex. Boys' voices do deepen somewhat more than girls', but social expectations encourage many girls to talk in voices that are higher than is comfortable, necessary, or natural for them (Sachs et al., 1973; Henley, 1977).

Bridges What effect do social expectations have on changes in adolescents' voices?

Hormonal Changes and Their Physical Consequences

As we have noted, at puberty boys and girls begin producing substantially more of several sex-related hormones. **Hormones** are chemicals produced by the endocrine glands and released or secreted directly into the bloodstream, by which they are carried to various organs of the body. Both the female sex glands, or **ovaries,** and the male sex glands, or **testes,** contain low levels of hormones that play a major role in sexual maturation. The pituitary gland, which is located at the base of the brain, can stimulate the testes or ovaries to produce more of the needed hormone. This overall process is in turn regulated by the hypothalamus, which is located in the upper brain stem.

Endocrine glands

Puberty increases the levels of all sex hormones in the blood of both sexes, but the pattern by which it does so differs for each sex. **Testosterone,** a particular type of androgen (also called male sex hormone), and **estrogen,** (also called female sex hormone) are two of the most important types of sex hormone. Even though both hormones are present in males and females, the high concentration of testosterone in boys stimulates the growth of the penis and related male reproductive organs, and the high concentration of estrogen in girls stimulates the growth of the ovaries and vagina. Androgens are thought to influence the strength of the sex drive in both genders.

Sex hormones

Hormones affect more than just sexual characteristics — for example, they are responsible for the typical differences between boys' and girls' overall body builds. In general, the sex that has shorter bones and more rounded curves — namely, female — also has higher estrogen levels; and the sex that has longer bones and larger muscles — namely, male — also has higher levels of testosterone (Villee, 1975; Cheek, 1974).

Testosterone stimulates muscle and bone growth in both sexes. Throughout childhood, boys and girls are about equally muscular. They have roughly the same number and sizes of muscle fibers, and they can exert about the same amount of strength with their muscles. Although individual children vary around the averages, as groups the two sexes differ very little (Malina, 1978a).

Puberty significantly changes this equality. During puberty, boys typically become more muscular looking than girls, even though girls, too, become more muscular as they grow. Boys experience close to a fourteenfold increase in the size of the largest muscle fibers between early childhood and adolescence, with most of the increase occurring during adolescence. Girls, in contrast, experience only a tenfold increase (Malina, 1978b; Brasel & Gruen, 1978).

Sex differences in muscle growth

Some of this difference may result from life experiences more specific to teenage boys than to girls. For example, teenage boys receive greater encouragement and opportunity to participate in sports and more responsibilities that involve work and other heavy muscular activity (Frisch, 1983; Warren, 1983). Differences in hormone levels may also be influenced by differences in behavior and life experiences. Sustained exercise, for example, tends to increase a person's level of testosterone (L. Rogers & Walsh, 1982).

Estrogen stimulates increased deposits of subcutaneous fat, that is, fat under the skin. It also stimulates the final maturation of bones, a process in which the growing areas within individual bones finally become hard and fixed in size.

Sex differences in amount of fat

Throughout childhood, boys and girls tend to possess almost identical amounts of fat (or adipose) tissue (F. Johnston et al., 1974). In the years just prior to the growth spurt, the body of a typical child might consist of about one-fifth fat; boys tend to have just a little less than this amount, and girls just a little more.

During adolescence, however, the two sexes begin to differ noticeably in their proportions of fat tissue. Boys tend to keep most of their deposits of fat and simply stretch them over an increasingly larger body. Because their muscles and bones tend to grow particularly rapidly during puberty, boys' fat tissue decreases as a proportion of their total body weight. The overall result? A relatively muscular, bony-looking person, at least compared to a typical girl (Chumlea et al., 1983).

Girls, on the other hand, develop significant new deposits of subcutaneous fat during adolescence while maintaining their previous ones from childhood. The new fat develops in all the locations that make girls look typically female: in their breasts, hips and buttocks, thighs, and upper arms (D. Sinclair, 1978). The new fat tissues combine with girls' smaller muscles and bones to make young females significantly more rounded than young males. By the end of adolescence, fat accounts for more than one-fourth of their body weight, but among males, it accounts for only about one-eighth.

Note, however, that this difference does not mean that girls tend to be overweight — only that their bodies are composed of different proportions of tissues and that these tissues are distributed differently. Adolescent boys and girls of the same height tend to weigh almost the same, yet in most cases the girls do not look fat, but simply female. Cultural standards of female beauty make some perfectly normal adolescent girls want to lose weight even though they do not need to or should not do so for their own health; this sort of weight "problem" is cultural and not physiological.

These relationships make it tempting to conclude that testosterone and estrogen "cause" physical sex differences in adolescence. To some extent, they may in fact do so, but the relationship is probably also more complicated. A large number of hormones act together at puberty, so that no one hormone can claim unique credit for "producing" physical sex differences. To some extent, too, hormone levels may also result from sex differences in behavior and life experiences. As already noted, for example, sustained exercise tends to result in a higher level of testosterone. So if one sex is consistently encouraged to exercise a lot and the other is not, cultural practices may account for some of the difference in hormone levels and body build — not the other way around.

The Extent of Physical Sex Differences

As the preceding information reveals, the sex differences that develop during puberty are matters of emphasis or degree. Except for eggs, sperm, and form of genitals, every physical structure and every characteristic exist in both sexes, sometimes in surprisingly similar amounts or levels. Both sexes grow new hair as a result of puberty, and both sexes develop substantially larger muscles and bones. The physical differences between males and females are triggered by the same set of hormones, which are produced in much the same ways in both.

Even differences in the timing of puberty are less significant than they first appear to be: the two-year gap between the sexes occurs mainly in the most visible of the physical changes of puberty, the growth spurt. As it happens, the spurt in growth is one of the first changes to happen to girls and one of the last to happen to boys. Changes that are less visible, such as the development of adult genitalia and shifts in hormonal balances, occur at almost the same average ages. On the whole, puberty begins and ends at nearly the same age for both sexes (Tanner, 1990).

From the biological standpoint, then, the sexes do not represent physical opposites so much as related but distinct patterns of similar physical elements and processes. The physical similarity between the sexes has not, of course, prevented society from constructing different roles and expectations for males and females. Indeed, society tends to focus a great deal of attention on gender differences and to exaggerate their significance.

More similarities than differences

Nor has the physical similarity between males and females kept individual adolescents from developing rigid standards for and preferences about their own physical development. Sometimes very slight physical differences either in amount of development or in its timing can have very significant psychological effects on a teenager. For example, the size of breasts or of the penis can be a source of pride or embarrassment, depending on personal expectations as well as the responses of others. So can being too tall, too short, too fat, or too thin or having physical characteristics that do not closely approximate cultural "ideals." The tyranny of fashion, emphasized by the media, plays a significant role in this, causing discomfort to boys and girls whose bodies do not fit the current ideals of physical attractiveness.

Perspectives

*Bridges In what ways do hormonal changes influence emotional development during puberty?

Hormonal Influences on Social and Emotional Development

As we have seen, puberty is a period of rapid physical development and dramatic increases in levels of hormones. Puberty also coincides with the major psychological changes of early adolescence. Recently there has been growing research interest in the role that increased hormone levels play in various aspects of adolescent social and emotional behavior.

*Rising hormone levels are thought to influence adolescent emotions in two ways. First, hormones may have an organizing and activating influence on emotions, facilitating negative emotions such as anger and inhibiting positive emotions such as happiness. Second, rapid increases in hormones may also influence emotions during adolescence by disrupting the preexisting hormonal balance (Inoff-Germain et al., 1988; Susman et al., 1987).

In one study of adolescents ages nine to fourteen years, hormone levels were found to be related to emotional dispositions and aggressive characteristics for boys but not for girls. Higher levels of androgens in boys were related to higher levels of disruptive or acting-out behavior problems, and higher levels of estrogen were related to lower levels of sadness and disruptive behavior. In another study, higher levels of estrogen and androgen were associated with higher degrees of aggressive behaviors for girls but not for boys (Susman et al., 1987; Inoff-Germain et al., 1988).

On the whole, however, few consistent relationships between levels of hormones and behaviors have been found. This is not surprising. Given what we already know about the complex causes of emotional and aggressive behaviors, it is unlikely that behaviors as complex as these can be understood simply in terms of biochemical influences (Peele, 1981). In addition, the presumption that hormones lead to certain behaviors rather than vice versa is unwarranted: it

ignores the very likely possibility that high-for-age hormone levels both influence and are themselves influenced by the adolescent behaviors under investigation. This last issue is addressed in a study conducted by Leonard Steinberg.

In a year-long study of the reciprocal relation between parent-child distance and pubertal maturation, Leonard Steinberg found that puberty led to increased adolescent autonomy, decreased parent-child closeness, increased mother-child conflict for both boys and girls, and increased father-child conflict for girls (Steinberg, 1988). But as Steinberg has noted, it is as yet unclear whether pubertal maturation causes or is caused by increased parent-child distance. Both psychoanalytic and social learning perspectives suggest that it is the adolescent that initiates the distancing from parents rather than the other way around. According to Freudian theory, puberty reactivates unresolved psychological conflicts, forcing the adolescent to seek more distance from her parents. Social learning theory suggests that during puberty, adolescent social relations reorient toward age mates and away from parents as sources of social rewards. In any case, the mechanism underlying the increase in parent-child distance is likely to involve a combination of unconscious psychological processes, conscious changes in adolescent self-conceptions and views of family relationships, and hormone-mediated changes in behavior or mood. The onset of puberty alone accounts for a very small percentage (approximately 5 percent) of the increased distance in adolescent-parent relations. It is likely that a variety of other factors, including family context, culture, and individual experience, play the leading roles in influencing the behaviors that are associated with puberty and early adolescence (Steinberg, 1987).

PSYCHOLOGICAL EFFECTS OF PHYSICAL GROWTH IN ADOLESCENCE

Given how rapid the physical changes of puberty are, it is not surprising that young people are often preoccupied and dissatisfied with the way they look. Dissatisfaction is most noticeable during the early adolescent years, when most teenagers are attending junior high school. During this time, every young adolescent must somehow continue to live with himself and manage relationships with others as well. He cannot ignore how tall he has grown within just a few months or how suddenly he has "developed." Even if he does try to ignore such changes, his peers will probably notice them and form their own opinions, either positive or negative, about them. At this age, adolescents find comparisons among their peers very important, for these comparisons provide an important basis for self-evaluation.

Body Image and Self-esteem

Bridges How is adolescent self-esteem affected by prevailing views of body image?

Almost all adolescents are concerned about their changing bodies and their attractiveness. Even the most attractive teenager worries about his hair, his nose, or a pimple on his chin. What determines just how much discomfort a particular adolescent feels about his own body?

Standards of attractiveness

For one thing, conventional standards of attractiveness have considerable influence. In our culture, people of all ages find certain body builds more attractive than others. One researcher documented these preferences by showing children and adolescents pictures of people with various builds and asking them for their opinions about the comparative attractiveness of the pictured people (Lerner, 1969). Some of the pictures showed people with muscular, or **mesomorphic,** builds; the second group showed rounder, more padded, **endomorphic** people; and the third group of pictures showed people with slender, **ectomorphic** builds. (See Figure 14.3.) Children and adolescents clearly considered the mesomorphic bodies to be the most attractive, especially if they were male. To some degree mesomorphic qualities were preferred even for females, although standards for females also allowed for bodies that were fuller, with more padding and curves. In general, too much or too little fat was judged to be less attractive, although not necessarily "ugly."

FIGURE 14.3
Three Body Types

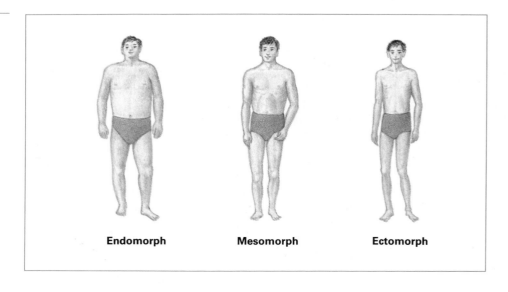

Endomorph   Mesomorph   Ectomorph

Adolescents evaluate themselves and their peers according to such stereotypes. Teenagers with mesomorphic body builds tend to be judged relatively more attractive than those with endomorphic and ectomorphic builds; they also tend to have more friends and to be rated relatively highly in status or prestige among their peers (Clausen, 1975). To a certain extent, positive judgments from others become a fact of life for many mesomorphic teenagers. Of course, such a fact of life does not guarantee happiness. In the right conditions, conventionally attractive youngsters may indeed develop greater self-esteem than others because of the appreciation they receive. In the wrong conditions, such appreciation can have negative effects. By receiving approval for something that is a matter of genetic chance, the person may come to believe that she is not appreciated for other important qualities and that she cannot influence the opinions of her friends by her conduct (Livson & Peskin, 1981a). Teenagers who are physically "unattractive" may compensate by developing other kinds of attractive qualities including being energetic and outgoing, having a good sense of humor, and being a good listener.

In any case, whether or not an adolescent considers himself truly attractive depends on more than what he thinks his peers think (Lerner et al., 1989). The impressions conveyed by parents and other close family members undoubtedly influence an adolescent's attitudes toward his body, no matter how conventionally attractive he is. Parents who value qualities other than physical attractiveness can help their teenager to cope better with the awkwardness of puberty (Schonfield, 1966). An adolescent's feeling of attractiveness also depends on how he feels about himself in general. If he suffers from low self-esteem — if he feels badly about himself as a human being regardless of his physical characteristics

Peers' and parents' influence

Bridges How can parents help adolescents cope with the awkwardness of puberty?

A Multicultural View

How Do Ethnic Differences in Physical Appearance Affect Social Development During Adolescence?

Physical appearance plays a very important role in adolescent development, especially during the junior and senior high school years when attitudes about physical differences can significantly affect social acceptance and popularity. How ethnic differences in physical appearance affect social development was one of the questions addressed by Jeannie Kang in her recent study of identity development in eighteen Korean-American female college students, ages eighteen to twenty-one, from a variety of regional backgrounds (Kang, 1990).

For the majority of the women, junior high was the hardest and most confusing time. They reported being very concerned with how they looked and with whether they could fit in, but they experienced little conscious awareness or understanding of conflicts regarding their ethnic identity during that period of their lives. Very few of the women remembered feeling socially successful or achieving acceptance as part of the "popular crowd" during their high school years. For many, it was not until they were sophomores or juniors in college that they felt more successful in gaining mainstream social acceptance and in more fully understanding and coming to terms with questions of bicultural identity.

Cultural context played an important role in how differences in physical appearance were experienced. For example, regional differences made an important impact on how their physical appearance affected their social

and emotional experiences. Girls who grew up as part of a small and isolated ethnic minority in all white, ethnically homogeneous communities in the Midwest were faced with the "blue-eyed, blond hair, cheerleader" type as the sole standard of beauty and popularity — a standard that they could never hope to achieve. Girls from these communities were more likely to feel ostracized and that they would never fit in. They were also more likely to have been less successful in their adjustment during their high school years than girls who grew up in more heterogeneous communities that provided alternative models of beauty and popularity and greater social acceptance of ethnic difference.

The majority of the women in the sample reported experiencing a period of withdrawal from the coed social scene during high school because their physical differences acted as barriers to social acceptance and popularity. During this period they rechanneled their energies into other activities, and success at academics, extracurricular activities, work, and friendships rather than group social life became their major sources of self-esteem. Nevertheless, a number reported that physical difference in appearance still had considerable importance because these differences fed the ethnic stereotype that Korean-Americans (and other Asian-Americans) are naturally successful at math, science, and music.

These women experienced considerable conflict

— he is more likely to worry about and feel negatively toward his body (Schonfield, 1971).

Perceptions about attractiveness are strongly influenced by the existing cultural stereotypes for feminine and masculine beauty. Role models such as fashion models and actors help create and gain widespread acceptance for these stereotypes. Although there may be more than one "ideal" type for men and women — which may reflect to some extent changing views of physical fitness and body building, for example — only a very small percentage of teenagers happen to have bodies that come even reasonably close.

One consequence is that successive generations of teenagers have attempted to modify their bodies to fit the prevailing stereotypes, sometimes with tragic results. For example, compulsive efforts to increase muscle mass may combine body building, unsafe dieting, and use of steroids and other drugs. Such a regimen poses serious health hazards to an increasing number of male and (more recently) female athletes. Steroids have been banned in most athletic programs because they have been shown to cause liver damage, testicular shrinking, increased cholesterol levels, and elevated blood pressure.

Influence of stereotypes

Obsessive concern about being slender has led many teenage girls to adopt diets that are seriously deficient in nutrition (Fowler, 1989). Anorexia nervosa and bulimia are eating disorders that involve distorted relationships between eating and body image; they appear to be connected, at least in part, to cultural stereotypes. We discuss them more fully later in the chapter.

between the cultural values, traditions, and expectations of their immigrant parents (who spoke little English) and those of mainstream American culture as represented by schools, peer groups, and the media. This conflict of cultures was extremely difficult for many of the girls, who could barely speak to their parents and relatives because of their own limited knowledge of Korean and who found it difficult to feel fully part of either culture. Even something as simple as getting a suntan — a major leisure time activity for many American adolescents — proved to be a source of cultural conflict. To be golden, beautiful, and tan is highly approved of in mainstream American culture; but most Korean-American parents forbid tanning because in Korea, being tan is associated with being uneducated and lower class. One of the most rebellious things a Korean girl can do is to get a really dark tan.

Most of the women reported that they did not really begin to come to terms with the meaning of these ethnic differences until their college years. Often, it was not until their second or third year of college that they were able to more actively explore personal issues of bicultural identity and acceptance (or lack of it) by both minority and mainstream cultures. This delay may in part be due to the fact that college was the first time many of these women found themselves with a sizable peer group of Korean-Americans among whom questions of identity and cultural difference could be explored.

The task of forging a coherent bicultural identity out of these two conflicting cultural experiences was a challenging one that potentially influenced every aspect of a Korean-American adolescent's experience. Even during the college years, physical difference remained a metaphor for the women's efforts to achieve a comfortable resolution of the dilemma of bicultural identity. (The derogatory terms *banana* and *twinkie* are occasionally used by Korean-Americans to refer to a person whom they feel has embraced a mainstream white American identity to the exclusion of her identity as a Korean.)

The above findings are generally consistent with Erik Erikson's view that identity achievement occurs in later adolescence and that the immigrant experience is significant (see Chapter 2 perspective for more on Erikson). They are also consistent with the findings of other researchers who report that college provides an extended moratorium period and that identity achievement status is often not reached until the later college years (Waterman, 1982; Meilman, 1979). Further research with larger and more diverse samples is needed to discover whether Korean-American males and Korean-American adolescents who do not attend college have similar experiences.

Adolescents who have atypical physical characteristics because of inherited or acquired abnormalities sometimes face more serious psychological problems regarding their bodies. For example, children who are badly scarred or whose movements are spasmodic must learn to cope with these added burdens. As suggested by the film *Mask,* which is about an adolescent whose face and head are grossly disfigured, strong, loving, and honest support from parents and friends can make it possible for a child with a handicap to feel good about herself and her body. Although physical appearance is certainly important, beauty and positive self-concept really are more than skin deep.

Atypical adolescents

Early- Versus Late-Maturing Adolescents

The timing of puberty can make a lasting difference to the psychological development of an adolescent, particularly if physical maturation is very early or very late. The effects of early and late maturation depend partly on the sex of the teenagers, and they tend to change over the long term.

Support for these ideas comes from several old but valuable longitudinal studies of adolescents in Oakland and Berkeley, California (Livson & Peskin, 1981b). These children were all born in the 1920s and 1930s and reached their teens during the 1940s. At that time, they were given a variety of psychological tests and were interviewed to learn more about their personalities. Records of

Bridges What effects does the timing of puberty have on the psychological development of adolescents?

these observations were preserved carefully, and the individuals were retested and interviewed at regular intervals throughout their lives to provide fairly direct comparisons with earlier observations. The results have indicated a number of ways in which the timing of puberty can affect individuals' psychological and social development.

Early-maturing boys have social advantages

For example, boys who mature early seem to experience certain advantages. As we have described, puberty tends to make all boys more muscular and mesomorphic in appearance. Those boys who acquire this appearance earlier than usual — by age twelve, say, instead of fourteen — gain favorable responses from peers, teachers, and other important people sooner and for longer than their age mates do. Some observers suggest that early-maturing boys seem to respond to these changes and the positive attitudes they elicit in very advantageous ways: they seem relatively more self-confident in their behavior and generally strike others as being more grown-up or mature (Livson & Peskin, 1981a). They are also more likely to be chosen as leaders in high school.

Nevertheless, a careful look suggests that there may also be some disadvantages in early maturation for boys. Although they are perceived as more mature, self-confident, and competent than others, they are also more somber, less creative, and less spontaneous, perhaps because of their need to live up to the expectations that accompany their adult, masculine body image.

Late-maturing boys are viewed less favorably

Late-maturing boys are a different story. These boys still resemble children, at least physically, as late as age sixteen. Teachers, parents, and other observers tend to judge them unfavorably, viewing them as being impulsive, immature, and lacking in self-confidence. In school, late-maturing boys tend to be regarded as socially inferior to earlier-maturing peers; they often regard themselves this way as well.

So, although early-maturing boys seem to have happier lives than late maturers do, the two groups may differ only in that one group receives more social approval. Long-term follow-ups of these youths strongly suggest that this explanation is correct. At age thirty-eight, for example, early-maturing boys who were still participants in these studies continued to be relatively responsible, sociable, and self-controlled; they also continued to be more rigid, moralistic, and conforming than their peers (Jones, 1965). Late-maturing boys interviewed at age thirty-eight appeared to have developed certain positive qualities not strongly evident during adolescence. Although they still conveyed the impression of being impulsive and inappropriately assertive, they also seemed more insightful and perceptive and more creative in solving problems. All in all, in the long run, a mixed picture emerges for both kinds of boys.

Bridges   Is there a connection between the timing of puberty and adolescents' cognitive development?

A mixed picture in the long term

Achieving puberty and sexual maturity may involve considerably more potential conflict for girls than for boys, in large part because of widely held stereotypes that associate puberty with increased willingness to engage in sexual activity. Although a youngster who has achieved puberty may have mature physical characteristics, there is no reason to assume that she is emotionally ready to make decisions about birth control or about sexual relationships; neither should it be assumed that she is developmentally ready to assume a greater degree of responsibility for adult work in or outside the home.

Early maturation can be stressful for girls

Keep in mind, too, that early maturation for a girl means that she enters puberty at around nine or ten, an age that most adults would definitely consider to be a child. Early maturation also puts a girl out of step with common standards for female beauty. Because of the hormonal changes of puberty, she becomes relatively tall, muscular, and sometimes heavyset for a ten-year-old; her later-developing age mates remain relatively slender and short. And because she also becomes more shapely and sexually mature, she may find herself in dating and sexual encounters for which she is not psychologically ready. Remember, a ten-year-old is still in the fifth grade.

A Talk with Jason

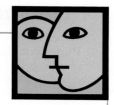

Physical Development at Age Fourteen

Jason agreed to be interviewed if I would give him a ride to soccer practice afterward. The interview was conducted in the kitchen of his home over an after-school snack.

Interviewer: What physical changes have you noticed in kids your age?

Jason: When we were in fifth grade, all the guys were taller than the girls or at least the same height. And then in sixth grade the girls shot up and all got much taller than us.

Interviewer: How did that feel?

Jason: We didn't grow in seventh grade. We had sex education so we started to understand it. So in sixth grade, seventh, and part of eighth grade, all the guys were much less developed than the girls and much less tall and less heavy and everything. And then the later part of eighth grade we all shot up.

Interviewer: I noticed. How tall are you now?

Jason: Five-eleven.

Interviewer: Almost as tall as me.

Jason: We all shot up. I'm as tall as my older brother.

Interviewer: Are there other differences besides height that you've noticed in kids your age?

Jason: Weight, for example, because some people were heavy before. The weight was not really part of them. It was excess. Now people have become heavier but more solid. I'm gaining weight, not a lot of weight. I've gained weight and it's in my bones, in my muscle, and in my skin and just a little bit of fat. I'm gaining it all over as opposed to gaining it in just fat. I'm gaining it in muscle.

I think that as you get older guys become less ashamed of their bodies and more likely to expose them. Not necessarily all the way, but just to take off your shirt. It's easier for them to do that because now they're bigger . . . now they feel that they can expose their chest and they don't have to be embarrassed about it.

Interviewer: Have you noticed differences in how rapidly people develop?

Jason: Different parts of people develop at different times. Some people stay shorter but get a full beard sooner. But they're not gonna shoot up as far. And some people shoot up and grow a beard at about the same time, but people in all four years of high school are getting interested in shaving and stuff like that. And usually it would seem ridiculous to an outsider to shave the little hair that you grow on your mustache, but it's a big thing to someone to have to shave or at this age it's important to look the best you can even if it's just a few hairs to get off.

Interviewer: How do kids your age deal with staying healthy?

Jason: They know what is healthy, but they don't necessarily follow what is always healthy.

Interviewer: Why do you think that is?

Jason: 'Cause, you know, there's the simple fact that junk food tastes good. And the other thing is that it is overemphasized that kids shouldn't eat that much junk food. I don't eat that much junk food. I eat a little bit, but I also eat really good food, too. I eat plenty of it to survive. So anything above that really doesn't matter.

Interviewer: Do you think that most kids basically eat a good diet and that junk food is on top of it?

Jason: A lot of girls don't need to eat as much, because they have stopped growing. But they still need to eat more than they do eat. They starve themselves to a certain extent when they are hungry because they think, "Oh, God, I have to lose weight!" I think it's just a fad just to be able to say it. It makes people feel better about themselves to say, "I'm fat, look at me, I'm fat," because they really want other people to say, "No, you're not." I think a lot of girls in the teenage years eat a crummy breakfast and then don't eat lunch and then go all day without eating. They eat at night. And then they go to sleep. Which is the wrong method. If you're only going to eat one meal a day, you should eat breakfast.

Interviewer: Why is that?

Jason: Because you need the nutrition more during the day when you are active. At night you don't really need that much.

Interviewer: Do you think that it's because girls are into being thin?

Jason: No, to some extent they're just not as hungry any more. And they don't know how to deal with that.

Interviewer: Guys your age are probably always hungry.

Jason: Right. I stuff myself and then fifteen minutes later I'm not full any more.

Interviewer: How do fourteen-year-olds handle drugs and drinking?

Jason: There is some pressure to do drugs and drink, but it comes from within. A lot of people are torn about it. And it's easy for them to blame it on peer pressure when it's really just people offering them some.

Interviewer: Has use of drugs and alcohol changed since junior high?

Jason: Oh, yeah. It increased 100 percent or more than that. Compared to junior high it's phenomenal. But compared to other high schools, at my school alcohol use is not as high, but drug use might be higher. I think that people have a certain knowledge and awareness about drugs and alcohol and that a lot of people try to balance off a little bit of drugs with a little bit of alcohol.

(continued)

A Talk with Jason (continued)

They realize that drugs like pot hurt your lungs and that alcohol hurts your liver. And if you do all alcohol you're going to hurt your liver a lot, and if you do all pot you're going to hurt your lungs a lot. If you do a little bit of each, it can heal itself over.

Follow-up Questions

1. How does Jason feel about the effects of physical maturation? How consistent are his views with those presented in the chapter?

2. How do hormonal changes influence the changes in height, weight, muscle, and body fat that Jason describes?

3. What nutritional problems might be related to the eating habits of Jason's peer group?

4. To what extent does Jason appreciate the importance of multiple causes of health and health problems? How typical of adolescents his age are his views about health?

The Oakland and Berkeley studies found that very-early-maturing girls seemed relatively awkward and ill at ease in social situations and that they seemed chronically under stress and preoccupied with their looks (Peskin, 1973). But, once physically precocious fifth-graders had successfully lived through the next several years, they were likely to have increased status and popularity and to be better able to cope with the challenges of adolescence than their peers. This may partly be a result of the skills they learned in dealing with adversity, or life may have become easier for these early maturers as their later-blooming peers caught up.

Late-maturing girls have social advantages

In contrast, girls who matured comparatively late — around age fourteen — experienced social advantages throughout adolescence. Teachers and other observers rated these late-maturing girls as more attractive and as better leaders, and they did in fact become school leaders relatively often.

Long-term changes

As with boys, however, the long-term effects differed from the immediate or short-term effects. When the Oakland and Berkeley girls were studied at age thirty, the anxiety-filled, early-maturing individuals seemed more poised and self-directed than the late-maturing girls did. The difference was especially visible in those women who had encountered difficult circumstances, such as divorce or serious illness, as adults.

Timing affects others' responses

Two explanations may account for how timing of puberty affects later development (Peterson & Taylor, 1980). First, peers and adults are likely to think of and treat a very early or late maturer in ways that deviate from attitudes expressed toward the individual's more average peers. The results may either be positive or negative, depending on the nature of this treatment. Among boys, very early maturation creates positive responses in others, although the longer run effects for the children themselves are not necessarily all positive. This may be partly because the muscular, mesomorphic physiques of many of these boys often enable them to excel early in athletics and to physically resemble culturally desirable stereotypes. On the negative side, boys who become overdependent upon these early advantages may experience a loss of self-esteem and self-worth when their normal and later-developing peers eventually catch up.

Deviation toward late maturity tends to create more negative responses, although here again the longer range effects may not be all negative. Boys who are very late developers may be perceived as being childish and socially immature, in part because their self-consciousness about their delayed physical development limits their opportunities to become involved in sports and social activities. On the other hand, their physical immaturity may to some degree protect them from the increasing pressures to become sexually and socially active — which are harder for their normal and early-developing peers to resist — and allow them greater freedom to develop their own unique identities.

Among girls, the effects are somewhat the opposite. Early maturation for a girl initially creates negative responses, but in the longer run, it often has positive results. As discussed earlier, the task of dealing with stereotyped and inappropriate sexual and social expectations is likely to be stressful for a physically mature fifth- or sixth-grader, although why this may be helpful in the longer run is still unclear. Later-maturing girls have an easier time during adolescence — perhaps for cultural reasons similar to those that benefit early-maturing boys — but it is not clear that they experience significant longer range benefits.

A second possible explanation is that the timing of puberty influences how much freedom and opportunity a child has to develop a strong sense of self and to prepare for the eventual challenges of adolescence. If puberty comes when society prefers it to come — early for boys and late for girls — the adolescent may have little reason to develop a strong inner sense of himself because he may be too busy living up to social expectations: that he be sexually active and involved in structured extracurricular activities, for example, rather than spend more time on informal activities and on his own. On the other hand, if puberty

Timing affects development of sense of self

Perspectives

Understanding Adolescent Development in Context

Paul Baltes (1987), a leading life-span developmental theorist, has suggested that we can think of any individual development as the result of interactions among three systems or contexts of developmental influence: age-graded influences, history-graded influences, and nonnormative influences.

1. *Age-graded influences* are what many people traditionally think of as having the major effect on development. They are those biological and environmental factors that (a) are generally correlated with chronological age and are therefore fairly predictable in the order and timing with which they occur and (b) that for the most part work similarly in all individuals. One age-graded influence is the biological maturation that all individuals experience (for example, the sequence of changes leading to walking in young children). Another influence is made up of the age-graded socialization events that occur in adolescence, such as sex-role socialization.

2. *History-graded influences* are those biological and environmental factors of historical importance to the evolution of a culture or group(s) of people. Long-term history-graded influences include ongoing advances in technology and modernization (for example, industrialization, urbanization, automation, education, and health care). Shorter term or period-specific historical influences include the Great Depression, the Vietnam War, and the AIDS epidemic (Baltes, 1987; Stewart & Healy, 1989).

3. *Nonnormative influences* are the biological and environmental circumstances and events that are unique to a given individual. Their occurrence, patterning, and sequencing are not clearly tied to or cannot be predicted from either age-graded or history-graded influences. The specific details of what your grandparents' situation was during the Great Depression, whether or not someone in your family fought in Vietnam, and whether someone you love has AIDS all shape your development in particular ways and can be considered nonnormative events.

To see how these three systems of developmental influence operate singly and together, consider the experience of puberty. The maturational changes associated with puberty are age graded in that all individuals experience the same predictable sequence of changes. These changes are history graded in the sense that each successive generation during the past hundred years has begun puberty earlier than the generation before did as a result of long-term changes related to nutrition and general health. Other history-graded influences such as famine and war, or cultural attitudes toward food and diet, can also impact the timing of puberty. Puberty can be shaped for a particular adolescent by such nonnormative influences as bulimia or anorexia nervosa.

Age-graded maturation and its impact on an individual's development, however, will also be affected by both history-graded and nonnormative influences. Consider the case of teenagers growing up one hundred years ago. Reaching puberty often meant marriage, parenthood, and the beginning of full participation in the world of adulthood, as compared with today, when for most teenagers marriage, children, and entry into the adult world are still one or two decades away. But for youngsters in both historical periods, the age-graded process of physical maturation and the history-graded expectations of adolescence are affected by nonnormative experiences unique to each individual. Thus, a teenager today may become a parent at a very young age because of his particular life circumstances and choices, whereas a teenager one hundred years ago might have delayed marriage and parenthood for equally specific reasons.

comes when society does not approve, the adolescent may feel much more pressed to understand himself. Indeed, he may feel forced to do a lot of reflecting in order to understand and overcome the feelings of anger and social inferiority that arise from failing to fulfill society's timetable for physical maturation. As with all developmental conflict, the experience of mastering the challenge may actually be beneficial rather than detrimental to future personality development.

Most adolescents, of course, mature at more or less the average age, rather than at the extremely early or late ones discussed here. Thus, the typical adolescent experiences a mixture of both pressure to conform to social standards and the need to reflect on her true identity.

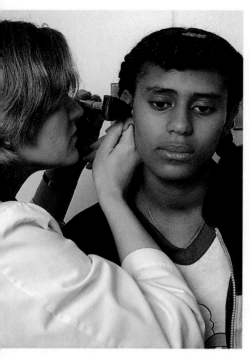

The health risks of today's society make it increasingly important for teenagers to take responsibility for their own health care.

HEALTH IN ADOLESCENCE

In some ways, adolescents are among the healthiest of all people. They are past most childhood diseases such as chicken pox, mumps, and measles, and they tend to have fewer colds and ear infections than young children or adults have (Fry, 1974). And compared with adults, they suffer fewer of the illnesses and physical damage that are associated with prolonged exposure to physical and emotional stress and with aging.

Nevertheless, adolescents actually experience *greater* health risks than either younger children or adults do. Compared with either age group, they are much more likely to be injured in motor vehicle accidents, to misuse alcohol and other drugs (Bachman et al., 1981), to find themselves unexpectedly pregnant, and to have poor eating and health care habits.

Continuity with Health in Childhood

The health and health care patterns of most individuals show considerable consistency and continuity from early childhood through adolescence (Starfield & Pless, 1980). This is true of common, recurring illnesses; of patterns of utilization of medical services; and of individuals' overall levels of health as judged by doctors and other health care professionals.

Recurrences of specific illnesses

Even though children tend to get sick less often as they grow into adolescence, individuals tend to show consistent patterns of illness over time. For example, a five-year-old who catches more colds than most children her age is likely to catch more colds than her age mates when she is fifteen, even though neither she nor her peers will be sick as often as they were when they were five years old. These trends are based on analyses of patients' medical records, and therefore represent doctors' opinions about the state of people's health.

What do we know about how adolescents use health care services? First, as you might expect, individuals differ in how often they visit the doctor, for what reasons, and in what circumstances. Second, individuals appear to remain relatively consistent in how often they make visits, no matter what their age. People who visit the doctor frequently as young children continue to do so as adolescents, whereas those who visit less frequently early in life tend to maintain this pattern later on (Densen et al., 1959; Starfield & Pless, 1980).

Use of medical services

Health care is extremely expensive and not available to all; many families are too poor to pay for care that adequately meets their needs. Thus, an individual's economic situation is apt to influence his use of medical resources. If poor families receive inferior medical care and are treated in humiliating ways, as is often the case, their children will probably develop negative attitudes toward doctors and hospitals. In contrast, children from families whose financial resources allow them more regular and positive contacts with the health care system are likely to have more positive attitudes and better health habits.

Regardless of their family situation, however, adolescents in general are less likely than other age groups to have consistently positive attitudes toward health care or to use health care resources in a consistent and appropriate manner. Why is this the case? For one thing, adolescents tend to believe that they are invulnerable; that is, they have an unrealistic sense that they are safe from illness and other physical harm (these are aspects of the personal fable discussed in the next chapter). For another, adolescents' struggles for independence and autonomy frequently include at least temporary rejection of their parents' positive attitudes and practices.

Concepts of Illness and Health in Adolescence

As we mentioned in Chapter 11, children's understanding of the relationship between their behavior and their health plays a key role in how much responsibility they can assume for their own health. It is not until adolescence that children are able to understand health in terms of multiple causes and cures and to realize that interrelationships among thoughts, feelings, and changes in physical health are significant.

Bridges How does adolescents' understanding of the causes of illness influence their health care behaviors?

In spite of this new capability, however, many adolescents (and adults) understand illness in terms of single events or causes rather than multiple ones. A teenager may say, "I caught a cold because I went out in the rain last night," when in reality she was tired to begin with and the friends she went out with were already sick. Only a minority of adolescents include psychological factors as a partial reason for getting sick or feeling ill. The teenager who went out in the rain may fail to mention that she has felt depressed and anxious lately and that these feelings have been interfering with her sleep and making her generally rundown. She may also fail to point out that her cold feels worse because of her poor spirits; if she felt better psychologically, the illness might be hardly worth mentioning.

Misunderstanding of multiple causes of illness

Such incomplete understandings of illness and its causes contribute to adolescents' seemingly irresponsible health habits. If a teenager happens to believe (wrongly) that he will catch a cold only if he does not wear enough warm clothes, presumably he should remain healthy if he bundles up. If he also believes (wrongly) that curing an illness is just as desirable as preventing it in the first place, he may not work particularly hard at preventing it. Breaking a leg while doing gymnastics may not seem like much of a risk as long as appropriate medical services can repair the leg; contracting an ear infection may not seem like much of a risk either as long as he believes that a doctor can always give him a drug to cure it.

Such beliefs reduce an individual's sense of personal responsibility for taking care of herself. From the point of view of young people, health, like schools and families, is managed by the adult world (C. Lewis & Lewis, 1983). This fact does not necessarily create hostility to health care, but it probably does encourage passivity or indifference to personal health.

But it need not do so. In certain circumstances, adolescents and even children can become very careful managers of their own health. Programs to encourage self-care have had significant success in elementary schools and high schools. In one program, students were given special passes to visit the school nurse whenever they needed to, and they were encouraged to use the passes freely (Lewis & Lewis, 1977). Contrary to the fears of the teachers, students rarely overused the passes or used them as excuses to get out of academic work.

Learning self-care skills

Instead, they nearly always used them for what the nurses judged to be genuine, health-related reasons. In the opinions of the nurses, in fact, the effectiveness of school health care improved because of the free-pass policy: students visited the nurses more often when they really were sick and less often when they were not. The former policy, in which teachers decided whether to refer students to the nurse, led to more visits when students were not really ill.

Causes of Death Among Adolescents

Although adolescents are less affected by the health problems that cause death in younger children and adults, the death rate during adolescence is one of the highest of all age groups. Motor vehicle accidents — a high proportion of which involve the use of alcohol and other drugs — kill more than fifteen thousand teenagers and young adults each year, more than all other accidents combined. More than six thousand teenagers and young adults die from homicide and other forms of intentional violence, and more than five thousand die from suicide and other self-inflicted causes (*Demographic Yearbook,* 1985). More information on teen suicide can be found in Chapter 16.

Greater risks for males

Note that males are significantly more at risk than females, in part because they have much riskier life-styles. Middle- and working-class males are likely to believe that risk taking and experimentation with cars and motorcycles, alcohol, and other drugs are signs of masculinity. Poor and minority males are at still greater risk for accidental death and homicide. The inner-city environments in which they generally live and the life-styles they lead are even more likely to involve the use and sale of drugs, participation in gangs, and exposure to various forms of physical violence, including the use of lethal weapons.

Among additional causes, war accounts for more deaths among adolescent males than any other. Cancer; cardiovascular, respiratory, and congenital disorders; kidney disorders; and infectious diseases kill both male and female teenagers (D. Smith, Bierman, & Robinson, 1978).

Automobiles give teenagers a great deal of independence. But they also have drawbacks: auto collisions are the leading cause of death in adolescence.

Adolescent Health Problems

Although adolescents are not prone to the infectious diseases of childhood, they often adopt habits that are damaging to their health. Poor diet, lack of sleep, use of drugs, and casual sexual relationships can all lead to a number of serious diseases.

Infectious Mononucleosis   Also known as "mono," infectious mononucleosis is caused by a virus and results in sore throat, irregular fever, swollen glands, extreme fatigue, and an enlarged spleen. It frequently occurs among adolescents whose resistance to illness has been lowered by lack of sleep and poor diet. Although mononucleosis generally lasts for two weeks or less and is easily treated with rest and good nutrition, it can cause injury to the spleen and lead to hepatitis.

Hepatitis   Hepatitis is an acute infection of the liver that most frequently occurs in adolescents and young adults and can cause permanent damage. One type of hepatitis is spread through poor sanitation. Another type is transmitted through blood transfusions or other injections, which means that drug users are at especially high risk. Hepatitis may also be transmitted sexually.

Sexually Transmitted Diseases   Sexually transmitted diseases have become a major problem among adolescents largely because of the increased acceptability of sexual activity throughout our culture. Use of the birth control pill has replaced condoms as the favored method for birth control among teenagers. Unfortunately, condoms provide significant protection against venereal diseases; the pill does not provide any. Inadequate health and sex education at home and in the schools must also be held accountable.

Syphilis and gonorrhea appear frequently among adolescents, who are often experimenting sexually without much experience, knowledge, or good judgment about sexual partners. Approximately 1.8 million cases of gonorrhea and 90,000 cases of syphilis are reported each year, with the greatest increase being among children between the ages of ten and fourteen (Centers for Disease Control, 1986). Current estimates indicate that one in five high school students will contract either syphilis or gonorrhea.

Syphilis is a highly contagious bacterial infection that is almost always **Syphilis** transmitted by direct sexual contact with an infected person. The first signs of infection usually appear two to six weeks after contact and include sores or lesions on various parts of the genitals and mucous membranes. Without treatment, other areas of the body are likely to become infected as well. Ultimately, syphilis can lead to slow chronic inflammation and destruction of the skin, mucous membranes, skeletal system, heart, and central nervous system. The disease can be prevented by avoiding sexual contact with carriers. Treatment with penicillin and other antibiotics is highly effective and should begin immediately after contact or in the early stages of the disease.

Gonorrhea is a bacteriological infection of the mucous membrane of the **Gonorrhea** urethra and genital tract, is highly contagious, and is almost always caused by sexual contact with an infected person. Symptoms occur from two to eight days after exposure and include discharge from the penis and pain during urination for males and discomfort when urinating, vaginal discharge, and abnormal periods for women. If untreated, it may cause pelvic inflammatory disease in women and sterility. Arthritis dermatitis, or meningitis can also result. Use of prophylactics during sex is an effective prevention, and penicillin or other antibiotics are an effective treatment.

Genital warts affect 1 million new cases each year. Caused by a viral **Genital warts** infection, they produce small, painless growths on the penis, urethra, or rectal area in men and similar growths on the genitals and anus of females. If not removed, such warts may increase women's chances of developing cervical cancer and if enlarged may obstruct the birth canal during pregnancy. As yet, no serious consequences have been reported for men.

Genital herpes

Recently there has also been an increase in the incidence of *genital herpes,* with approximately 500,000 new cases reported each year (Centers for Disease Control, 1986). Caused by a sexually transmitted virus, herpes causes chronic and painful inflammation and lesions on the genitals and in other areas of sexual contact; it is thought to pose some increased risk of cervical cancer in women. (Common cold sores, a different kind of herpes, are caused by a different virus.) There is as yet no known cure for genital herpes, but its symptoms can be controlled with an antiviral drug. In addition to the physical pain of herpes, for many adolescents, the stigma of having this highly infectious, sexually transmitted disease for the rest of their lives can be extremely upsetting. In fact, some high schools and universities have set up special counseling programs and support groups for youngsters who have contracted this illness.

Chlamydia

Chlamydia, a bacterial infection, is the most common sexually transmitted disease, with 4.6 million new cases reported in 1986 alone (Centers for Disease Control, 1986). The symptoms for males are pain during urination and discharge from the penis and in females vaginal discharge and abdominal discomfort, although in some cases there are no symptoms present. Chlamydia can be effectively treated with antibiotics, but if untreated it can cause pelvic inflammatory disease or eventual sterility in women.

AIDS

AIDS (acquired immune deficiency syndrome) is perhaps the best-known and most feared sexually transmitted disease in the 1980s and 1990s. To date, no one who has been definitively diagnosed as having AIDS has survived for more than a few years. In 1987, more than ten thousand persons died of AIDS, and between 1 and 2 million were estimated to carry the virus (human immunodeficiency virus, or HIV) that precedes the onset of the disease (Wolata, 1989).

Methods of transmission

First diagnosed in the United States in the early 1980s, the disease destroys the body's ability to maintain its normal immunity to diseases, and death is often caused by pneumonia or related complications. The disease is transmitted through introduction of body fluids from an infected person. The most common methods of transmission are sexual intercourse with an infected person, contact with the blood of an infected person (through sharing of needles, blood transfusion), and contact of a child with an infected mother during pregnancy, birth, and (possibly) breast feeding.

Because the AIDS virus cannot survive in air, water, or things people touch, it does not spread through casual, day-to-day contact. AIDS has *never* been transmitted by sharing food; shaking hands; hugging; using the same dishes and utensils; being spit, drooled, or cried on; or having any form of casual contact.

Experts are alarmed at the rate with which AIDS is spreading in teenagers (Kolata, 1989). Although the 705 reported cases of AIDS in adolescents ages thirteen to twenty-one years in 1988 was only 1 percent of all reported cases, the percentage is doubling each year. The number of adolescents infected with the HIV virus but not yet having AIDS is not yet known, but given the fact that young adults in their twenties currently represent 10 percent of all reported cases of AIDS and given the long incubation rate of the virus, it is likely that many of these cases were transmitted during the teenage years. For adolescent females, heterosexual contact accounted for 46 percent of the AIDS cases (J. Brooks-Gunn et al., 1988; Wolata, 1989).

Bridges How successful have been efforts to educate adolescents about the causes and prevention of AIDS?

Adolescents lack adequate knowledge about AIDS

Recent studies indicate that as of 1987, only a small proportion of teenagers had received formal instruction about AIDS in school. Although most know that sexual intercourse and sharing needles are the main routes to getting AIDS, many did not know that the use of condoms reduces risk of transmission and had the mistaken belief that AIDS could be contracted through casual contact (J. Brooks-Gunn & Furstenberg, 1989).

The growing danger of AIDS and other sexually transmitted diseases during adolescence has led to many new educational programs designed to reduce these risks.

Sexually active adolescents need to know ways that they can protect themselves against getting AIDS. They need to know that safe sex practices include massage, petting, masturbation, and kissing, providing that there is no chance of direct contact between the body fluids of the two partners. Kissing on the lips is also safe. Although no cases of AIDS have been traced to deep-tongue, "French" kissing, because small amounts of HIV have been found in saliva, people with open sores in their mouths or braces are better off not deep-tongue kissing. There is no such thing as "100 percent safe" sexual intercourse, but some sexual practices and behaviors are *safer* than others in that they very significantly reduce (but do not eliminate) the risk of AIDS. One such practice is to correctly use latex condoms with a water-based lubricant. A second way is to be monogamous — that is, to have sexual intercourse with only one person who has no history of intravenous drug use or sexual contact with high-risk individuals. A third way is to screen and limit the number of sexual partners one has (Hein & DiGeronimo, 1989).

Safe sex practices

Despite increased efforts to educate adolescents about the importance of using condoms to prevent AIDS, there is as yet little indication that adolescent contraceptive behavior has changed. For example, one recent study of more than thirteen hundred adolescents living in San Francisco reported that although 92 percent of the teenagers were aware that AIDS could be contracted by sexual intercourse, only 60 percent knew that using a condom might prevent transmission, and at least 30 percent thought that they could catch AIDS by shaking hands or touching someone with the disease (DiClemente et al., 1986). In another study of sexually active adolescents ages fourteen to nineteen, only 2 percent of the girls and 8 percent of the boys reported using condoms every time they had intercourse. Even though many said they believed that condoms were an effective way to prevent sexually transmitted diseases, the number of teens who intended to use condoms actually decreased during the year. Many of the teenagers wrongly believed that AIDS was strictly a disease of gay men and that because nobody their own age had AIDS, they were not at risk themselves (Bozzi, 1988).

Drug and Alcohol Abuse   High rates of experimenting with drugs and of drug abuse are typical of adolescence, although individuals' choices of drugs and patterns of use may change over time. According to 1985 estimates for younger adolescents (ages twelve to fifteen), smoking (45 percent) and drinking (56 percent) were the most common substances used. Nearly 30 percent had tried at least one illicit drug or controlled substance during their lives, with 24 percent using marijuana, 9 percent using inhalants, 6 percent using analgesics, 6 percent using stimulants, and 5 percent using cocaine.

Among high school students, as of 1985, 92 percent of seniors had used alcohol; 50.2 percent, marijuana; and 15.2 percent, cocaine at least once. Interestingly, 57 percent had tried an illicit drug, and more than 33 percent had tried an illicit drug other than marijuana (Johnston et al., 1987). This represents a decline in the use of marijuana, stimulants, and sedatives by high school students (as well as college students and young adults) since 1980 (Newcomb & Bentler, 1989). (See Figure 14.4.) Meanwhile, perceptions of risk associated with using cocaine have increased, as has disapproval of regular cocaine use (Berke, 1990; Newcomb & Bentler, 1989).

Although recent studies confirm a continuing decline in the use of most drugs, the number of students who used crack (a cocaine derivative) at least once has changed very little, decreasing from 6 percent in 1987 to 5 percent in 1988 and 4.7 percent in 1989 (Berke, 1990). Because these studies do not take into account high school dropouts, who make up an estimated 15 percent of the

Recent decrease in adolescents' use of most illegal drugs

Little or no reduction in crack use

FIGURE 14.4
Use of Selected Drugs Among High School Seniors, 1980 and 1985
Source: Data from Johnston et al., 1988.

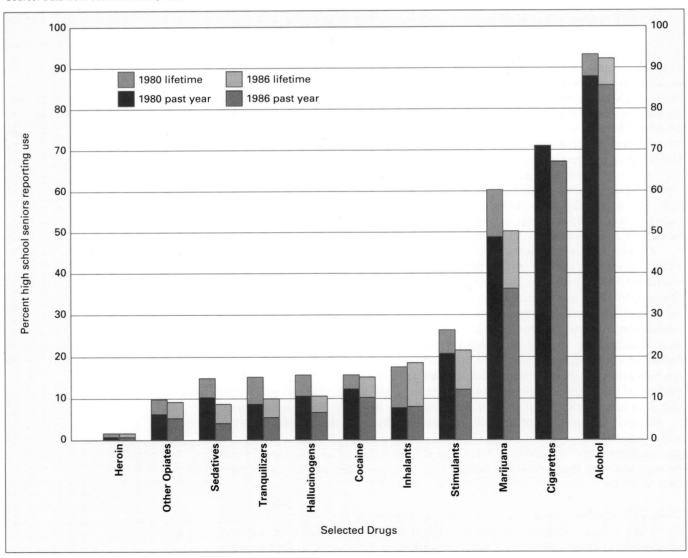

target group, it is likely that crack use may in fact be increasing among high school dropouts, particularly those who live in poor, inner-city neighborhoods where crack distribution and use appear to be widespread (Berke, 1989).

For several reasons, the effects of drug abuse on development are extremely destructive, particularly if the use is prolonged or chronic. For one thing, even short-term use of illegal drugs such as heroin, cocaine, crack, and Quaaludes exposes the user to considerable physical risk of injury or death due to overdose, contamination of the drug, or both. Second, even moderate use of certain drugs may have destructive physical and psychological effects in that they disrupt normal patterns of eating, sleeping, and physical activity and mask psychological problems that require solution. Third, a number of these drugs cause physical addiction and psychological dependence. Physical addiction involves a biological dependence upon the drug; withdrawal can be painful and sometimes life threatening. In most cases, tolerance to the drug increases with prolonged use, requiring higher doses to maintain the same level of effect and thus increasing the user's exposure to the drug's negative effects.

Destructive effects of drugs

Finally, even if a proper medicinal dose of the drug itself is not physically dangerous — as is true with heroin — the physical, social, and psychological risks involved in supporting a habit are enormous. Teenagers addicted to heroin are, with few exceptions, forced to sell drugs and steal to support their habit. They are at great risk for contracting hepatitis or AIDS from dirty and infected needles. They are exposed to situations that are both physically and psychologically violent. And the time and energy needed to support a habit often forces them to abandon normal social, emotional, and intellectual endeavors and threatens to halt their identity development prematurely.

Alcohol is the most widely advertised and heavily used drug in the United States today, and one of the most physically and psychologically damaging. Its association with serious automobile injuries (more than forty thousand each year) and fatalities among adolescents has led many states to prohibit its sale to teenagers.

Alcohol abuse

Other results of teenage alcoholism are staggering. Chronic alcohol abuse can lead to severe health problems, including destruction of the liver and damage to the central nervous system. It also seriously disrupts the drinker's ability to function effectively in school, at work, at home, and in other areas of social activity. Because alcohol is heavily advertised and socially valued as a sign of adulthood and independence, is readily available at low cost, and is a potent short-term reducer of anxiety, it continues to be very popular among adolescents.

The use of tobacco products has also been widely advertised as a sign of adulthood. Early adolescents are particularly susceptible to this "ready-made" symbol of maturity. Most adolescents are aware of the fact that smoking causes cancer and heart disease; overall smoking rates for teenagers dropped from 16 percent in 1974 to 12 percent in 1979. Smoking among females is increasing, however, at least in part because advertisers have targeted them as a highly lucrative market (U.S. Department of Health, Education and Welfare, 1980; McAlister et al., 1979).

Tobacco

Patterns of both drinking and smoking, which are closely associated, are strongly influenced by the life-styles of family members and peers. Minimal, moderate, and heavy levels of drinking, smoking, and use of drugs, including tranquilizers and other legal medications, among family members are strongly associated with very similar patterns of use among adolescents. The most consistent and strongest factor in adolescent drug use is peer pressure, which can strongly influence which drugs a teenager uses, in what circumstances, and how much and how often.

Family influence

Bridges How important a factor is peer pressure in an adolescent's decision to use drugs?

Other factors associated with drug use include poverty and low socioeconomic status, disturbed family situations, exposure to adult drug use, poor school adjustment, low self-esteem, nontraditional values regarding drug use, social deviance, stressful life events, and emotional problems. The greater the number

Drinking and cigarette-smoking make some teenagers feel more grown-up and more sociable and accepted by their friends. As a result, alcohol and cigarettes are used by more teenagers than any other drugs.

of risk factors, the higher is the likelihood of drug abuse (Newcomb & Bentler, 1989; Stein et al., 1987).

Because most initial experiences with cigarettes, alcohol, and illicit drugs occur during the middle school, some experts have suggested that prevention efforts must take place during the early teenage years. These efforts have focused on reducing exposure to drugs, altering the environment, and changing the attitudes and behaviors of the drug user (or potential user). In general, drug prevention programs have not proven very effective. The few that are promising are peer programs and prevention efforts aimed at building confidence and social competence and providing broadening experiences (Newcomb & Bentler, 1989).

In conclusion, we should note that at least in modern times, adolescence has always been a period of dramatic physical change and experimentation. As we see in Chapter 16, the potential conflicts and dangers of adolescence are largely determined by the values and opportunities that a society provides to its youth. If most adults in a society choose to rely on drugs in dealing with the problems of everyday life, it is almost certain that drug use will be an issue for adolescents in that society. Similarly, if people have limited access to adequate health care and health education, not to mention healthy living conditions and life-styles, it is likely that these limitations will be painfully obvious in the health and life-styles of adolescents.

Nutritional Problems   Adolescents have the highest prevalence of "unsatisfactory" nutritional status of all age groups. The average teenage girl requires approximately 2,200 calories per day, and the average boy needs about 2,800. The nutrient intake of boys comes closer to recommended daily allowance levels than girls because boys eat relatively greater amounts of food for their body weights than girls do; girls frequently diet.

Food habits of adolescents, which include increased tendency to skip meals (especially breakfast and lunch), snacking (especially on candies), consumption of fast foods, and dieting, place them at dietary risk. Surprisingly, iron-deficiency anemia, which is one of the most common nutritional disorders in this age group, is more frequently found in adolescent boys than girls (American Academy of Pediatrics, 1985).

Inadequate nutrition can interfere with a teenager's ability to concentrate at school and work and to actively engage in activities with peers. Poor nutritional habits established during adolescence can have more serious health consequences if continued on a long-term basis.

As with dependence on drugs, food dependence and the obesity that frequently results are problems that affect a significant portion of the teenage population; it is currently estimated that 15 percent of today's teenagers are significantly overweight (Maloney & Klykylo, 1983). Major causes of obesity include a biologically inherited tendency to be overweight, childhood diet and family attitudes and habits about food, and lack of exercise.

Obesity

Being obese is particularly difficult for an adolescent who is already struggling to develop a comfortable and realistic view of his changing body. Obesity can therefore have a significant impact on a teenager's sense of himself as a physically attractive person and on his overall identity development. In some cases it can severely limit social opportunities through both exclusion by peers and self-isolation.

Despite a growing appreciation of physical strength and fitness in women, a lean body is still the dominant cultural standard for feminine beauty. As a consequence, many adolescent girls try to lose weight in an effort to achieve a slenderness that may not be possible for them. Inadequate knowledge about dietary requirements and poor judgment lead to inadequate nutrition for many teenage girls.

An extreme form of this quest for thinness is **anorexia nervosa,** a physical and psychological disturbance in which the afflicted teenager starves herself, exercises compulsively, and develops an increasingly unrealistic view of her body. Ninety-five percent of anorexics are females. Many anorexics also suffer from **bulimia,** a disorder in which they eat huge amounts of food and then vomit so that they do not gain weight. The causes and treatment of these disorders are

Obsession with thinness

Whereas most teenagers suffer no shortage of calories, their diets often lack balance. This adolescent's meal consists entirely of refined sugar (in the drink and candy) and of fat and starch (in the potato chips).

Perspectives

Anorexia Nervosa: The Golden Cage

Anorexia nervosa is a complex emotional disorder characterized by an obsession with food and weight and the "relentless pursuit of excessive thinness" (Bruch, 1979). Its major symptoms include excessive weight loss (approximately 25 percent of body weight); amenorrhea, the cessation of menstruation; hyperactivity, perhaps including excessive exercise; social isolation; and feelings of insecurity, loneliness, inadequacy, and helplessness. Affecting 1 percent of all twelve- to twenty-five-year-old females in the United States, anorexia often involves a pattern of behavior combining a rigid diet with strenuous exercise to lose weight. When weight loss is maintained for a long period, a number of physical symptoms occur, including lack of energy, paleness of skin, brittle nails, constipation, difficulty urinating, numbness or tingling sensations in arms and legs, fine hairs appearing all over the body, thinning and loss of hair, and extreme sensitivity to cold (Gilbert & DeBlaise, 1984).

Based on observation of seventy anorexic patients, ten of them males, and psychotherapeutic treatment of about twenty of these cases, Hilde Bruch wrote about the causes, experience, and treatment of this illness (Bruch, 1979). She believes that anorexic youngsters experience severe disturbances in three areas of psychological functioning. The first is a disturbance in body image — the way they see themselves. Although an anorexic adolescent who is five foot six and weighs only eighty-seven pounds looks like a walking skeleton, when she views herself in the mirror she sees someone who is too fat and needs to continue dieting. The second disturbance involves misinterpretations of internal and external stimuli, especially with regard to the way anorexics experience hunger. Although they are literally starving, many strongly state that they enjoy the feeling of hunger; that it makes them feel good to have a flat, empty stomach; and that feeling hungry makes them feel thinner. The third area of disturbance involves a paralyzing sense of ineffectiveness and helplessness in their ability to change anything about their lives. Although self-starvation and physical exhaustion play a major role in these disturbances, they do not fully explain the development of the illness.

Most anorexics are girls from financially and socially successful upper-middle-class and upper-class families. A much smaller number come from upwardly mobile, success-oriented, lower-middle-class or lower-class families. The fathers of the girls in Bruch's study valued them highly for

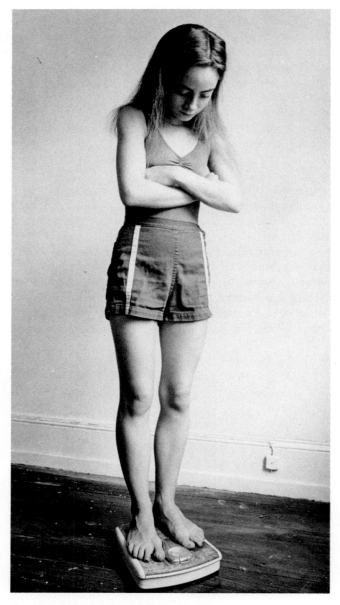

Anorexics, like this teenage girl, use dieting partly as a way of gaining control over their lives. No matter how thin they become, they are likely to view themselves as "too fat."

complex, and between 10 and 20 percent of those who do not receive professional treatment die of starvation and its complications.

What seems clear is that the most significant factor in adolescents' taking responsibility for their own health is whether they have a clear perception that they really *are* responsible for it. The achievement of a sense of responsibility for this and other aspects of one's life signals progress in the adolescent transition to young adulthood.

their intellectual and athletic achievements and paid little attention to their physical changes during puberty — although they did criticize them for becoming plump. Many of the children believed that they had to prove something to their parents and that it was their responsibility to make their parents feel good, successful, and superior. Curiously, however, they saw their parents' privileged life-style achievements as an excessive burden and obligation, feeling somehow condemned to be at least as special and successful as their parents were (Bruch, 1979).

For many of these girls during their childhood, their otherwise successful and well-functioning families somehow failed to help them develop an adequate sense of confidence and self-value, a clear sense of their body and its functions, or an adequate sense of identity, autonomy, and control. As children, the anorexics lacked a conviction of their own inner substance and value and were overly submissive and abnormally considerate, preoccupied with satisfying their parents' expectations of them and trying to outguess others in order to do what they expected. Even in their friendships, they rarely if ever were able to know or express what they wanted. Unsure of their own individuality, they tended to be chameleonlike, developing different interests and a different personality with each new friend (Bruch, 1979).

For many anorexics, their symptoms serve two important functions: as a means of forestalling and avoiding the physical, sexual, and psychosocial changes and challenges of puberty and adolescence, which they do not feel ready to face; and as a means of asserting control over their own bodies and daily activities and of resisting the intense pressure to conform to the parental expectations they experienced throughout their childhoods (Bruch, 1979, Romeo, 1984; Toner, Garfinkel & Garner, 1986).

Although anorexic adolescents are typically high academic achievers, their thinking, problem solving, and moral judgment are only at Piaget's concrete operational stage. Their thinking tends to be egocentric, rigid, and magical, and their capacity for formal operations, abstract thinking, and independent evaluation may be deficient or completely absent, especially when solving personal problems. When their illness becomes apparent, they find themselves out of step with their peers and socially isolated from friends, family, and schoolmates. They feel dominated and directed by some outside, mysterious force beyond their control and maintain their starvation diet and grueling physical activity

in the belief that it will somehow make them as "good" as they should be.

The serious health risks of prolonged malnutrition make early diagnosis and treatment very important. Also, electrolyte imbalance may result from the use of diet pills and from compulsive overeating followed by self-induced vomiting. Finally, prolonged isolation from the important social and emotional experiences of adolescence is unhealthy for the anorexic's psychological state.

Bruch suggests that successful treatment must involve a multiple focus. First, it must address the starvation problem in a way that appreciates the anorexic's need for control but makes clear that the resulting malnutrition and distortions in thinking must be addressed for fuller treatment to be possible. The treatment must also address the underlying family problems and abnormal interactions between family members that are invariably related to anorexia. Frequently parents tend to portray their family life as being more harmonious than it really is, and the perfection that the anorexic adolescent seeks to attain is a response to serious but unspoken inadequacies and unhappiness the parents feel. Lastly, individual therapy with the anorexic adolescent must focus on helping her to uncover her own abilities and resources for independent thinking, judging, and feeling. It must help her to achieve autonomy and self-directed identity by helping her to become aware of, express, and act upon her own impulses, feelings, and needs.

In some instances, behavior modification therapies have also proved to be a useful adjunct to family treatment approaches. Such programs typically employ a highly restricted environment in which the staff can carefully observe the person being treated and strictly reduce or eliminate rewards for behaviors leading to weight loss. Behavior modification can also be used to reinforce other activities thought to be constructive in learning more appropriate eating patterns (Bemis, 1978). Antidepressant medications have also proven to be helpful in reducing the depression and risk of suicide that are present in many cases (McDaniel, 1986).

FINALLY YOUNG ADULTS?

After all the bodily changes an adolescent experiences, he certainly looks like an adult. But as we have pointed out, he does not consistently *feel* like an adult yet. Especially early in adolescence, individuals are uncomfortable with their new physical features, which take up the foreground of teenagers' thinking, feeling, and acting. Young people are often self-conscious, meaning (among other things) that they are conscious of their bodies. The nature and strength of that self-consciousness depend in part on the nature, strength, and timing of puberty in all its facets.

It is not surprising, given the newness of their physical changes, that adolescents lack awareness of or concern for their health; so far in life, they have not had much reason to be aware or concerned. Soon, however, this changes. Just as their bodies develop during the teen years, so do their thoughts, feelings, and social relationships. These developments eventually help them to become truly adult in the physical sense as well as in others.

SUMMARY OF MAJOR IDEAS

The Concept of Adolescence

1. Adolescence, which begins around the age of twelve and lasts until about age twenty, is a developmental period of transition between childhood and adulthood.

2. Adolescence was "discovered" in the early part of this century as a way of prolonging childhood in a period of rapid social and economic change.

3. Child labor laws, compulsory education, and special laws to combat "juvenile delinquency" helped to solidify the idea of adolescence.

4. Some theories of adolescence emphasize the "storm and stress" of this period, whereas others find it no more conflict-ridden than earlier periods of development; for most youngsters it is mixed.

Growth in Height and Weight

5. While the amount of increase in height and weight are significant, the unevenness of the adolescent "growth spurt" is even more striking.

6. Increases in height can be predicted fairly accurately, but predicting weight increases is more difficult, in part because they are influenced by differences in living conditions and life-style.

7. During the last century, children have tended to begin to mature earlier and to grow taller and heavier than their parents.

Puberty

8. In addition to increases in height and weight, a larger pattern of changes occurs, which leads to full physical and sexual maturity, or puberty.

9. Primary sexual maturation among boys includes rapid growth of the penis and scrotum and the production of fertile semen.

10. Menarche, or the beginning of menstrual cycles, is a complex biological process that signals the beginning of sexual maturity for girls.

11. In many cultures, including our own, the onset of menarche can be stressful, in part because of the strong personal and cultural expectations that are associated with it.

12. Maturation of secondary sex characteristics includes enlargement and development of the breasts, the growth of body hair, deepening of the voice, and increased production of sex-related hormones.

13. Male and female hormones affect both sexes, although in differing degrees and with differing effects.

14. Although girls and boys are equally muscular prior to adolescence, during puberty boys experience significantly greater increases in muscle tissue than girls do.

15. Girls experience a somewhat greater increase in body fat than boys do.

16. Differences in how muscle and body fat are distributed rather than in their absolute amounts account for much of the differences in the physical appearances of male and female adolescents.

Psychological Effects of Physical Growth in Adolescence

17. Most adolescents are preoccupied with their physical appearance; a teenager's body image is influenced by conventional standards of attractiveness.

18. An adolescent's feelings of attractiveness depend upon the evaluation of peers, parents, and self and affect self-esteem.

19. For boys, the effects of early maturation are positive in the short run but somewhat negative in the long run; late maturation appears to have the reverse effects.

20. For girls, early maturation is more stressful in the short term but positive in the long run; late maturers tend to experience benefits during adolescence and no serious long-run negative effects.

Health in Adolescence

21. There is considerable continuity between childhood and adolescent patterns of illness and health care; both are influenced by individual and family attitudes and resources.

22. Adolescents are a high-risk group for injury and death due to risky life-styles and their "myth of invulnerability."

23. Growth in a child's ability to understand concepts of illness and health appears to follow stages of cognitive-development.

24. Major health problems during adolescence include sexually transmitted diseases, alcohol and drug abuse, and inadequate diet.

KEY TERMS

adolescence *(507)*	pubic hair *(513)*
growth spurt *(509)*	axillary hair *(514)*
adolescent	hormone *(515)*
egocentrism *(511)*	ovary *(515)*
secular trend *(512)*	testes *(515)*
puberty *(512)*	testosterone *(515)*
primary sex	estrogen *(515)*
characteristic *(512)*	mesomorphic *(518)*
secondary sex	endomorphic *(518)*
characteristic *(512)*	ectomorphic *(518)*
nocturnal emission *(513)*	anorexia nervosa *(535)*
menarche *(513)*	bulimia *(535)*

WHAT DO YOU THINK?

1. In what ways has the invention of adolescence as a developmental stage been helpful for teenagers and their families? In what ways has it been a problem?

2. What pattern (timing, rate) did your physical growth follow during adolescence?

3. What do you remember most about how you felt during puberty and how it influenced you socially?

4. In what ways is puberty easier for the opposite sex? In what ways might it be more difficult?

5. Why do you think adolescence is such a risky period for injury, death, and health-care problems? What recommendations might you make to a group of high school students and their parents?

6. What is your philosophy of sickness and health, and how did you come to think this way?

FOR FURTHER READING

Bell, R. *Changing Bodies, Changing Lives: A Book for Teens on Sex and Relationships.* New York: Random House, 1980.

This unusual book is based on interviews with hundreds of teenagers throughout the country, as well as parents, sex educators, and junior and senior high school teachers. Relying on direct quotes from the teenagers themselves for much of its material, the book provides thorough, practical, and readable information about the physical, sexual, and emotional changes of puberty and adolescence.

Boston Women's Health Book Collective. *The New Our Bodies, Ourselves.* New York: Simon & Shuster, 1984.

Written for a broad audience, this book covers a wide range of topics concerning women and their bodies.

Bruch, H. *The Golden Cage: The Enigma of Anorexia Nervosa.* New York: Vintage Books, 1979.

A very readable book about the causes, effects, and treatment of this life-threatening eating disorder, based upon seventy case studies from the author's own clinical practice.

Brumberg, J. J. *Fasting Girls: The Emergence of Anorexia Nervosa as a Modern Disease.* Cambridge, MA: Harvard University Press, 1988.

This book traces the history of anorexia from medieval through modern times with an emphasis on the relationship of the disorder to societal views of women.

Elkind, D. *All Grown Up and No Place to Go: Teenagers in Crisis.* Reading, MA: Addison-Wesley, 1984.

An intense and stimulating book about the pressures toward premature adulthood experienced by teenagers in a rapidly changing society. It is based on case studies, research, and clinical experiences of one of the best-known experts on adolescence.

Hein, K., and DiGeronimo, T. *AIDS: Trading Fears For Facts. A Guide For Teens.* Mount Vernon, NY: Consumers Union, 1989.

This up-to-date, well-researched guide for adolescents answers a wide range of questions about AIDS in clear and nontechnical language.

Salinger, J. D. *Catcher in the Rye.* New York: Bantam, 1977.

This is a humorous and touching novel about Holden Caulfield, a young man who encounters his share of excitement and upset during adolescence.

CHAPTER 15

Adolescence: Cognitive Development

■ To what extent, and in what situations, are adolescents capable of abstract reasoning?

■ How do adolescents show their improved information-processing skills in everyday activities?

■ What effects does cognitive development have on adolescents' knowledge and beliefs about ethics, political processes, and religion?

By about age thirteen, children have begun to think in ways that resemble adult thinking much more than before. Now they can consider possibilities and not just actualities; they can ask themselves, "What if the world were flat?" even though it is not really flat. And they can often use their time more efficiently than before; if a teacher assigns a book to read, a teenager is more likely than a younger child to know how to find its main ideas, focus his study on them, and skim the details relatively quickly. All in all, adolescents' cognitive talents tend to be more diverse than those of younger children, and they know when and how to apply those talents to particular problems.

This chapter looks at these new skills from two general viewpoints. The first of these is the *cognitive developmental viewpoint,* which is often associated with the work of Piaget. The second is the more recent approach of *information-processing theory,* which uses the workings of a computer as a model for human thinking. Because each of these theories is discussed elsewhere in this textbook, we focus attention here on their applicability to adolescence.

In real life, of course, thinking is always "about" something in particular; in recognition of that fact, this chapter ends with a section that discusses adolescents' ideas about themselves, about morality, about politics, and about religion. The two general theories about adolescent cognition help in understanding how adolescents (and others) make decisions about right and wrong, about the consequences of political actions, and about the nature of God. As it turns out, however, the theories do not deal with several aspects of such thinking. For one thing, they tend to ignore the emotions involved in daily thinking and problem solving. For another, they gloss over the difference between knowing and doing; they focus on a question such as, "Should I pay him back the money I owe?" rather than on the action "Here's the money." Because emotions and actions affect cognitive development significantly, we discuss them in some detail, even though they may not be strictly cognitive in nature — another demonstration that cognition, emotions, and behavior are often separated in textbooks but hardly ever in life.

THE COGNITIVE DEVELOPMENTAL VIEWPOINT

Jacob and Maria, both twelfth-graders, were discussing abortion.

> "What's the big deal about abortion, anyway?" said Jacob. "Why not just let anybody get one who wants one? It's a personal choice, like deciding which college to go to."

"You sound like you don't care about the people involved," said Maria. "How would you feel if *you* needed an abortion?"

"But I won't ever need one," said Jacob smugly. "Only girls get pregnant, you know."

"That's why you don't understand," said Maria. "What if it's *your* body that can grow babies, and everybody expects *you* to grow one at the right time — like when you get married. And everybody expects you *not* to grow one at the wrong time — like during high school. How do you deal with all those people — your parents and friends, and the baby's father too?"

Jacob looked thoughtful at this comment. Then he said, "You're getting bogged down in what other people think. Try to imagine what you yourself would want to do with your life if you found out that you were pregnant."

"I do that," said Maria, "and I also try to think about what the baby would want to do with *his* or *her* life if I allowed it to live."

This example reveals a number of new cognitive competencies acquired by adolescents and described in the cognitive developmental theory represented by Piaget (Inhelder & Piaget, 1958). Jacob and Maria reason about possibilities rather than about actual events; neither of them has ever experienced an abortion. And they use generalizations to draw specific conclusions (for Jacob, abortion is "a personal choice" and should always be treated as such). These are cognitive abilities that middle-years children usually lack.

General Features of Adolescent Thought

What are the practical effects of these new cognitive competencies? For one thing, attention to hypothetical ideas or "mere" possibilities broadens the horizons of adolescents' thinking substantially. For example, the question "What if there were a nuclear war?" is relatively more meaningful to an adolescent than to a child, even though both are equally inexperienced with actual nuclear war. So is the question "What if I had been born really poor, or fabulously rich?"

Compared to children, teenagers think more often about possibilities and about the future; they also daydream and fantasize more. What do you suppose this adolescent is thinking about?

Increased use of imagination

Adolescents can imagine what these situations might be like even though they have not experienced them in a concrete way. In general, thinking about the possible creates a new talent for speculating about important events and for guessing about daily experiences (Elkind, 1984). It also stimulates adolescents to daydream or fantasize about their actions and feelings. And it helps them to make more astute inferences about human motivations ("Perhaps she did that because . . .").

Tied to this ability is a greater capacity to plan ahead. Contrary to what frustrated parents sometimes claim, adolescents can set and plan goals for themselves, and they can do so much more competently than children can. Sometimes such goals are socially approved ones, such as making sure to take the best courses to get into a desirable college. Just as often, however, goals seem to lack redeeming value by conventional adult standards, as when an adolescent carefully plans and finances an expensive trip to a concert in a faraway city.

Thinking about thinking

Another way of stating these competencies is to say that during adolescence, young people develop an ability to think about thoughts and to do so in a logical way. Most of the time, such thinking serves some purpose, such as developing a better understanding of human nature or figuring out the best way to have fun. But sometimes thinking about thoughts has no concrete content at all. Many adolescents are quite capable of thinking simply about the form of statements or propositions, even when the statements lack content entirely:

- Some wugs are glibs.
- All glibs are bots.

From these two statements, some adolescents can decide — and even enjoy deciding! — whether or not any "wugs" are in fact "bots." (The answer, incidentally, is that some "wugs" are indeed "bots," although not necessarily all of them are "bots.")

Formal Operational Thinking

Because these cognitive skills attend to the logic or form of thinking, adolescent thought is sometimes referred to as **formal thought,** or **formal operational thought.** It differs from the style of thinking of middle-years children (concrete operational thought) in three important ways: in emphasizing the possible versus the real, in using scientific reason, and in skillfully combining ideas (Flavell, 1985).

Possibilities Versus Realities   Formal thought involves attention to possibilities, not just to actual realities. A parent discovered this feature when he tried to get his two children to make suggestions as to how to improve the humdrum weekly chicken dinner. "Fried is fine," said his nine-year-old. "I like it the way we always have it." But the fourteen-year-old insisted on a more complicated response: "Let me think about that," she said. Then later she remarked, "Can we make some brand-new sauce for it? Maybe one of the cookbooks has some ideas." Even though the older child had never eaten chicken cooked this way, she thought about trying it.

Scientific Reasoning   Formal thought also involves scientific reasoning — the same kind that psychologists use in designing many of their studies of human development. This quality reveals itself when adolescent students must solve some problem systematically. For example, how do youngsters in an art class figure out methods for mixing basic colors of paint to produce various inter-

Genetics	Physical Development	Social Context	Peers	Family
Is there a connection between the timing of puberty and adolescents' cognitive development? (522)	How does adolescent egocentrism contribute to adolescents' concerns about their physical development? (511)	How do social experiences and cognitive development combine to influence adolescents' perceptions about work? (547)	How does adolescent egocentrism affect teenagers' perceptions of their peer relationships? (558)	What role can parents play in reducing adolescent egocentrism? (559)

ADOLESCENCE: COGNITIVE DEVELOPMENT

Self-concept and Identity	Emotions	Learning	Language	Cognition
How do schools influence identity development in adolescents? (591)	How does cognitive development affect teenagers' ability to empathize with other people's feelings? (558)	Can formal operational thinking be taught? (552)	In what ways do perceptions of intelligence in different cultures depend on different types of language ability? (551)	What are the limits to formal operational thinking? (548)

mediate shades and other colors? Those capable of formal operations in effect design an experiment to test all the available combinations of colors. They form hypotheses or hunches about how certain colors affect each other when mixed; then they try out their hypotheses by mixing each basic color with every other basic color, being careful to try every possibility. By observing the results of this procedure carefully, they can draw logical conclusions about how to mix colors. This procedure in effect uses the scientific method.

In contrast, concrete operational children would rarely act so systematically. Like the formal operational thinkers, they would probably mix colors, but they would do so haphazardly, and they might not take note of the results of their experiences carefully. As a result, they might not learn to mix colors as rapidly as older, formal operational thinkers do. When confronted with this problem, of course, some younger children might draw on previous experience with art materials in order to solve it; but then their performance would reflect memory about how to mix colors rather than true scientific reasoning.

Systematic experimentation versus trial and error

Logical Combination of Ideas   The third feature of formal thought involves combining ideas logically. Compared to less cognitively mature children, formal thinkers can hold several ideas in mind at once and combine or integrate them in logical ways (Leahy & Hunt, 1983). When asked to explain why some students perform better in school than others, concrete operational thinkers are likely to latch on to one reason or another — "Some kids are smarter," or "Some kids work harder." In contrast, formal thinkers often give combinations of reasons, as this first-year university student did:

> Well, I think it depends. Sometimes it pays just to be smart. But it also helps to work hard — except when the teacher doesn't notice. Some kids do better, too, because they have taken courses before in the same area. Your first class in literature is likely to be harder than your fifth class in that subject.

As this example shows, the ability to combine ideas can sometimes make formal thinkers seem less definite about their opinions than younger children are.

Concrete Versus Formal Thought: Reasoning About Bending Rods

To understand the features of formal thought, consider how children at different stages of cognitive maturity approach a problem that Piaget designed (Inhelder & Piaget, 1958). A set of flexible rods is attached to the side of a basin of water. The rods differ in length, thickness, and material (metal or wood). In addition, a number of small weights are attached to the ends of the rods. A friendly experimenter — perhaps a teacher — asks the child to determine what factor or factors control how far the rods bend toward the water. Does the amount of bending depend on the rods' length, on their thickness, on what they are made of, or on the weight attached to them?

Imagine that you are a child asked to solve this problem. As a middle-years child, your attention would be captured primarily by the apparatus itself. You would enjoy varying anything that seemed to vary -— in this case, the length of the rods and the weights attached to them. You would also enjoy comparing one rod with another — wooden ones with metal ones and thick ones with thin ones. But your observations and comparisons would lack a system. You might vary more than one factor at a time (length *and* thickness) or forget to vary one of the factors at all. This haphazardness would be likely to prevent you from solving the problem fully, although you might nevertheless make a number of useful observations about the apparatus. The haphazard quality would also mark your efforts as concrete operational. At this age and stage, you are still tied closely to the real or concrete.

As a formal operational thinker, however, you would approach the problem much more systematically. First you would make some good guesses (or hypotheses) about the solution to the problem. You would take mental note of several factors that look like they might affect how far the rods bend: length, thickness, and weight, as well as whether the rods are made of wood or metal. Having noticed these possibilities, you would go on to the next step: devising and carrying out an informal experiment for testing each hypothesis in turn while holding all of the other factors constant. If you began by varying the weights on the rods, you would make sure that you used only rods of the same thickness, length, and material. Otherwise you could not be sure whether any variations in bending came from differences in weight or from differences in one of the other factors. Having checked for the effects of weight in this way, you could go on to test the effects of each of the other factors, keeping the other three factors constant in every case.

Such a formal operational approach contrasts sharply with the less systematic efforts of younger children. It guarantees that, given enough time, you will find a solution to the problem — if a solution actually exists. It also makes more cognitive demands: you must devise hypotheses, plan a way to test them, and draw reasonable conclusions from your observations. Using concrete operations, in contrast, simply requires careful observation of events as they unfold; in thinking concretely, the child in essence asks from moment to moment, "Is what I am looking at a solution?"

Cognitive Development Beyond Formal Thought

Piaget and other psychologists have identified formal, or abstract, thought as a major achievement of the adolescent years. But for most human beings, it may not be the final or highest cognitive achievement. One clue to this possibility comes from adolescents themselves: teenagers often overrate the importance of logical thinking, at least when they first achieve facility with it (Elkind, 1984). They may believe that all problems, including difficult ones such as achieving

Random comparison

Methodical manipulation

Adolescents overrate formal reasoning

Perspectives

How Cognitive Development Influences Perceptions About Work

As they get older, teenagers become more aware of the need to earn a living, and they become more knowledgeable about the opportunities and demands of particular occupations. The steps by which these changes occur depend partly on the social experiences of particular adolescents, but partly also on broader processes of cognitive development during this period. Older adolescents have had more time to learn about jobs and careers, particularly if they are male, white, and from reasonably well-off families (Raskin, 1985). But older adolescents have also had more time to develop sophisticated thinking skills, which they can use to understand jobs and careers about which they have no direct knowledge.

*Research about adolescents' perceptions of work confirm the importance of both social experience and cognitive development. One study did so by investigating changes in teenagers' concepts of employment and unemployment; it found that the two kinds of concepts seemed to have different sources (Santilli & Furth, 1987). In general, thinking related to employment changed primarily as a result of age. Younger teenagers (twelve-year-olds) confused the notions of "work" (labor) and "career" (lifelong vocation) much more than older teenagers (eighteen-year-olds) did. Younger teenagers also described job qualifications primarily in terms of stereotypical or formal qualifications ("A doctor needs a lot of education"); older teenagers often emphasized personal qualities as well ("A doctor needs a pleasant personality, too").

In contrast to these age-related changes, adolescents' concepts related to *un*employment depended heavily on an adolescent's level of cognitive development. Teenagers who reasoned in simpler, more concrete ways tended to attribute unemployment to personal qualities of individuals ("Some people are lazy"), whereas those who reasoned in more formal and mature ways tended to include societal trends among their explanations ("Maybe there's a recession and a lot of people are getting laid off"). Less cognitively developed individuals also showed less sensitivity to the psychological effects of unemployment ("Losing a job means you can't buy a car"); more developed individuals pointed out psychological effects more often ("You feel ashamed and worthless"). Note, however, that these differences are not age related; they actually occurred more often between individuals of the same age but who functioned at different levels of cognitive development.

One explanation of these findings is that social experience directly affects thinking about employment but not thinking about unemployment. The latter therefore develops primarily as a result of general reasoning skills. Parents, schools, and the media focus adolescents' attention overwhelmingly on the nature and desirability of jobs and careers, not on what a lack of job or career might be like. As teenagers get older, therefore, society helps them to develop their thinking about employment. But it leaves teen-

During adolescence, many teenagers develop increasingly detailed and accurate knowledge of the world of work — though their concepts of a "job" are still based on rather limited experience.

agers on their own to reason out what *un*employment means and what it might feel like.

Viewed broadly, these ideas suggest that adolescents' personal vocational goals may develop through steps or stages that are the combined result of social experience and cognitive development. As some vocational theories argue, young teenagers' career plans tend to rely on stereotypes and fantasy, and older teenagers' plans tend to be more realistic (Ginzberg, 1984; D. Super, 1984). A twelve-year-old may want to be a professional musician because "then I can play my favorite music and meet a lot of interesting people." An eighteen-year-old may have the same career goal because "I don't mind playing what other people hire me for, and I am good at staying awake at night [a major performing time]."

The differences in realism of these two goals probably reflects differences in both social experience and in cognitive development. Usually, a younger individual has less experience — or at least the experience has mostly occurred vicariously by watching, listening to, and reading about others in job roles. But younger individuals also have fewer thinking and reasoning strategies at their command to help fill in gaps in their work experience or to help them to interpret their observations of others who do already have jobs and careers.

*Bridges How do social experiences and cognitive development combine to influence adolescents' perceptions about work?

Bridges What are the limits to formal operational thinking?

world peace, can be solved by the proper application of rational principles and careful reasoning. Teenagers may fail to notice the limits of logic: that many problems by nature resist the application of general principles and may lend themselves instead to specific, case-by-case solutions.

Consider the case of Ana, a twelfth-grader who has recently begun sleeping with her boyfriend. Ana also gets along well with her parents, and she knows that they will worry and feel hurt if they learn of her sexual involvement. She also believes, in general, that friends and family should have no secrets. By continuing her sexual activities, she seems to be violating this principle. On the other hand, she (and her boyfriend) regard their intimacy as a private matter, and she worries that telling her parents would violate this privacy, which she also considers her right. Telling her parents might also create a lot of bad feelings among Ana, her boyfriend, and her parents. Her principles, in this case, do not seem to point her toward a good solution: no matter what she does, Ana feels that somebody will get hurt, or some ethical principle will be violated, or both.

Ana's situation suggests the importance of nonrational choices or judgments in solving real-life problems. Like Ana, many people may wish to be reasonable. They may wish, that is, to rely on formal logic and may even believe that they use it a lot. But in practice most people use formal logic consistently only when solving academic problems posed by teachers (Labouvie-Vief, 1982; Walberg, 1987). The rest of the time, formal reasoning either does not help or actually interferes with effective solutions to daily problems.

Even in approaching formal, academic problems — such as the "bending rods" problem posed in this chapter — most of us do not confine ourselves to logical procedures like those described by Piaget. More often, judgment and wisdom play a large role: instead of setting up a miniature scientific experiment, we recall any previous experiences with rods of different lengths and with problems of this particular type. If possible, we use these memories to "tell" us the solution, rather than going to all the trouble of "figuring out" a solution systematically. The more experience we accumulate, the better this informal approach works. So it should be no surprise that as we get older, we often use abstract reasoning *less* (Neimark, 1982b).

Learning to use abstract reasoning as a means, not an end

For older adolescents, the cognitive challenge consists of converting formal reasoning from a goal in itself, to a *tool* used for other, broader purposes (Gilligan & Murphy, 1979). Ana cannot reach a good decision about informing her parents, if she focuses on formal abstractions about truthfulness and privacy to the exclusion of more personal facts — which in this case include her knowledge of her boyfriend's and her parents' probable responses and feelings. Taking these circumstances into account leads to the "best" or most mature solution — but it may not lead to a solution that is fully logical in Piaget's sense.

Likewise, even the less emotional problem of the bending rods requires treating formal reasoning as a tool, rather than a goal in itself. The haphazard methods of an adult thinker really deserve to be called "mature" only if they supplement formal thinking, rather than replace it. Unlike a child, an adult must know when and how to return to the more laborious, systematic methods of abstract thinking described by Piaget. Adults must know, for example, whether they already know the answers to the bending-rods problem; if they do not have the answers, they must know how to do more than guess at them. Adults cannot confine themselves to haphazard methods when such methods do not work: if they do, their thinking will not differ from the concrete reasoning of schoolchildren.

Evaluation of the Cognitive Developmental Viewpoint

According to Piaget, formal operations begin developing early in adolescence and are fully formed by the end of the high school years. All teenagers supposedly

Many teenagers become able to solve problems scientifically. But like these high school students, they usually still rely on ample concrete experience to assist their thinking.

evolve wide-ranging thinking abilities that have a formal, abstract nature and that apply to many specific experiences and daily problems. In reality, however, the actual cognitive performance of adolescents fails to conform with this picture in several ways. A majority of adolescents (and even adults) use formal thinking inconsistently or even fail to use it at all (Byrnes, 1988; Fischer & Pipp, 1984). In explaining why a car is not working properly, for example, many adolescents and adults merely describe the car's symptoms: "It's got a bad noise in the brakes," or "It can't shift into third gear." Such comments are in effect concrete operational; even a young child could make them. They cast doubt on whether formal thinking really develops as universally as concrete operational thinking does.

Inconsistent use of formal thought

Another difficulty arises in determining when a person has truly attained formal operational thought. The answer depends to a large extent on the criteria or standards adopted to define attainment. The traditional Piagetian *méthode clinique*, or clinical method, adopts rather strict standards. This method involves questioning individuals about their beliefs in some detail and even cross-examining children with countersuggestions ("Another child said just the opposite from you; what do you think of that?"). As a result, children have to give relatively elaborate explanations of their responses. In the bending-rods problem, adolescents not only have to identify the true influences on the rods but also have to resist challenges to their answers ("Are you *sure* that the weight really matters?"). And they have to explain their reasons ("How do you know that the weight matters? Can you prove it to me?").

Variations in evaluative standards

Most adolescents and adults cannot meet all of these standards equally well and in fact might consider it artificial for someone to expect them to do so (Neimark, 1982a; Scribner, 1986). In real life, most problems are considered "solved" when much less demanding standards have been met — when a person gives either an explanation or an answer, for example, but not both. In real life, furthermore, hints and prompts are widespread and generally acceptable. Two people might try to figure out the bending-rods problem together, and in doing so they would freely offer each other ideas for solving it.

Most experimental studies of formal operational thinking have confirmed that cognitive peformance depends a lot on how it is observed or measured (Linn & Siegel, 1984). In a typical study, adolescents solve a Piagetian task, such as why a pendulum swings faster or slower. Is it affected by the length of the cord holding it, by the amount of weight on the end, or by the angle from which it starts? (The actual solution is length: shorter pendulums swing faster and longer ones swing slower, with the other variables having no effect.) The adolescents' responses are observed in various ways, such as by asking them to describe the general effect of each variable, or to construct an experiment that tests their ideas, or to interpret an experimental test.

In a study such as this, different ways of evaluating adolescents' knowledge do not correlate with one another very closely. A student who can meet one standard of success cannot necessarily meet the others (Linn & Siegel, 1984). In general, adolescents do best at constructing visual proofs of a solution and worst at constructing verbal proofs — although many exceptions also occur. In the pendulum experiment just described, comparatively more individuals can demonstrate the exclusive importance of length by actually displaying swinging pendulums of different lengths. Fewer individuals can explain verbally and coherently the ideas underlying the demonstratiion.

Note that most of the tasks that psychologists have used to assess formal thought, like the experiment described in Figure 15.1, have resembled lab experiments in a high school science course (Sternberg & Berg, 1987). As shown in the figure, all of the tasks isolate natural processes for observation and invite comment about these processes. Using a simple, nonsocial task helps psychologists to standardize the experiments and the interviews. The scientific nature of these tasks, however, may limit the number of skilled formal thinkers they reveal. Completing a formal operational task inevitably feels like performing for a high school science teacher, and as science teachers often point out, only a relatively small fraction of all students carry out this role consistently and well. Not surprisingly, then, many researchers have found that large numbers of adolescents show little or no evidence of formal operational thinking (Fischer et al., 1984). In some studies and some situations, in fact, a large majority of individuals "fail" such tasks, even as adults (Lave, 1988).

Studies like these are sometimes mistakenly taken as proof that Piagetian theory is wrong and that formal operations do not in fact constitute a universal stage of cognitive development. In fact, however, such studies may show only the importance of performance factors — influences having to do with human motivation or momentary variations in the situation. These, it seems, matter more than Piaget and his followers originally expected. The underlying compe-

Influence of experimental situation

FIGURE 15.1
Experiment Requiring Formal Operational Thought

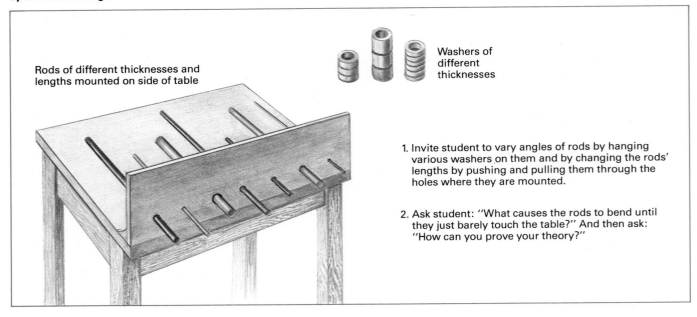

Rods of different thicknesses and lengths mounted on side of table

Washers of different thicknesses

1. Invite student to vary angles of rods by hanging various washers on them and by changing the rods' lengths by pushing and pulling them through the holes where they are mounted.

2. Ask student: "What causes the rods to bend until they just barely touch the table?" And then ask: "How can you prove your theory?"

A Multicultural View

Intelligence in Cross-cultural Perspective

Young people develop different kinds of intelligence, depending on the society in which they grow up. In North America, "intelligence" tends to refer to logical thinking ability combined with verbal skill for expressing ideas clearly and systematically (Gardner, 1983). Much of what we mean by intelligence is captured in Piaget's idea of formal operational thought — an ability to reason systematically about hypothetical problems. A young person in our society is intelligent who has learned to do this.

Yet research has found not only that a majority of adolescents never develop formal operational thinking but also that such thinking ability is rare in most nonindustrialized societies around the world (Mogdil et al., 1983; Dasen & Heron, 1981). The research is so clear-cut that Piaget himself felt compelled to modify his theory of cognitive development; instead of continuing to claim that formal operations are a universal cognitive stage, he argued that formal operations may be a relatively specialized skill dependent on particular cognitive experiences that are widespread only in our society (Piaget, 1972). The crucial experiences happen largely because of a cultural practice often taken for granted in North America — universal schooling.

*Schooling seems to develop three cognitive skills needed for formal operations (Laboratory of Comparative Human Cognition, 1986). One is sensitivity to subtle linguistic ambiguities, as contained in a statement such as, "They are bouncing balls," in which *they* can refer either to a type of ball or to the people doing the bouncing. Another is an ability and a motivation to deal with problems taken out of context, such as, "If all polar bears are white and many bears of all kinds are ferocious, then are some polar bears ferocious?" A third skill is a focus on organizing information mentally and on knowing how to retrieve it ("metacognition," discussed in Chapter 12), rather than on the content of knowledge itself (D. Olson, 1986).

These cognitive skills contribute to formal operational thinking and mark a person as "intelligent" in North American society (Sternberg, 1988). But they appear to be both less useful and less respected in other cultures and societies around the world. In the Piaroa society located in Borneo (north of Australia), individuals are regarded as "intelligent" if they learn as much as possible about the society's legends and lore and if they learn to communicate this knowledge colorfully and skillfully in verbal interactions and storytelling (Nicolaisen, 1988). Because the purpose of these stories is metaphorical, an intelligent person is one who can skillfully use the indirect analogies and the implied comparisons of metaphors. Explicit logical reasoning, such in Piagetian formal operations, has little importance in Piaroan society and in fact seems too blunt or direct for the solution of most daily problems.

In the rural Moslem villages of Tunisia, on the other hand, "intelligence" has separate meanings for the two sexes. These villages foster more rigid divisions of gender roles than in most North American communities (Abu Zahara, 1982; David, 1983). From birth until marriage, boys are given times specifically to play, whereas girls are expected to combine their relaxation times with productive activities, such as sewing while talking with friends. Boys are also encouraged to talk more than girls and to respond to adults' questions more directly and explicitly. And boys are allowed to explore the community more widely than girls are and are allowed or even encouraged to design and engage in mischievous activities with each other (such as practical jokes). They also receive more extensive education than girls, especially in memorizing and discussing the Koran, the sacred book of the Moslems.

Whatever the merits of this gender division judged by North American standards, it has distinct effects on Tunisian notions of intelligence (Platt, 1988). Because of their experiences, boys tend to develop relatively Western-style cognitive abilities. They learn to assert their views verbally, using clear forceful language; to focus their attention on problems set by peers or teachers; and to develop confidence in their ability to solve logical problems. Girls, for their part, learn *not* to use these skills: they learn self-restraint rather than verbal self-expression, and they learn to attend to others' thoughts and needs rather than to assert their own. For girls in rural Tunisia, being intelligent means having something closer to interpersonal sensitivity than to pure ability to reason. (Both sexes, incidentally, tend to adopt some of the opposite gender's qualities after marriage, in adulthood.)

Viewed cross-culturally, then, intelligence has different meanings in different settings. Different circumstances, it seems, produce different forms of human intelligence. Theories of cognitive development that originate in our culture, like Piaget's, must therefore be regarded partly as cultural products of North America: as descriptions of how thinking occurs in our particular society, not necessarily how it occurs around the world (LeVine, 1989). Furthermore, information from other societies, provides a useful reminder that development does not happen only inside the individual: it actually results from the interplay of the person and his social circumstances over a period of time (Rogoff & Morelli, 1989).

*Bridges In what ways do perceptions of intelligence in different cultures depend on different types of language ability?

tence — in this case, formal operational thought — may indeed exist more or less as Piaget proposed. Strong support for this idea comes from efforts to teach or train youngsters the skills of formal thought.

Such efforts have differed widely in pedagogical techniques, but all of them have either explained or demonstrated thinking that has the systematic, abstract quality characteristic of formal operations (Stone & Day, 1980). The techniques resemble the methods used for training children in conservation skills and other concrete operations described in Chapter 12; but unlike training for concrete operations, training for formal thought produces dramatic, sudden, and consistent results. The improvements depend very little on exactly how the training is conducted — on whether it consists mainly of telling or showing, for example, or whether it uses one phraseology for instructions or another. These facts suggest that such training actually just evokes preexisting capacities in adolescents and does not really teach these abilities for the first time. Apparently it sends a message to the learner, but not the message that the trainer intends; instead of showing *how* to think abstractly, the training shows that the learner *should* do so. This in turn implies that more adolescents can use formal thought than actually choose to do so when evaluated by Piaget's traditional and relatively strict tasks and standards.

Training in formal thinking

Bridges Can formal operational thinking be taught?

THE INFORMATION-PROCESSING VIEWPOINT

As explained in Chapter 2, information-processing theory describes development as if it worked like a computer. According to this view, a **sensory register** receives sensory information and holds it for a brief time — only seconds. If any of that information is processed, it is transferred to *short-term memory* (**STM**). It then may be further processed into a form where it can be stored indefinitely in *long-term memory* (**LTM**).

For adolescents, the most important part of this model concerns STM and LTM, both of which alter or process information in important ways. Suppose that a teenager hears the sentence "Cats like to purr." If she decides to respond to or remember this information permanently, she must relate it to corresponding information already in LTM: that cats also sleep a lot, that they also purr when they are hungry, that purring shows affection, and the like. This activation of prior knowledge orients her to the information and prepares her to respond to it.

Elements of information-processing

Actual responses to new information are organized by instructions contained in the LTM designated for this purpose and carried out in STM. In the information-processing model, these instructions operate much like computer programs: they consist of sequenced instructions for modifying, classifying, and transferring information bit by bit. Because of their "supervisory" purpose, the instructions are sometimes called **control processes**. In processing the sentence "Cats like to purr," a simple set of control processes might consist of the following instructions:

1. Save sentence ("Cats like to purr") in STM.
2. Recall all "cats" from LTM. Save in STM.
3. Consider the first of these "cats."
4. Did it ever purr?
5. If yes, then save this information in STM.
6. Consider the next "cat" from LTM.

Examples of control processes

7. Go to Instruction No. 4.

8. Continue until all "cats" have been considered in STM.

9. Add up the number of "yes" responses saved in STM.

10. Are the "yeses" more than one-half the number of "cats"?

11. If more than one-half, then speak these words: "That's true; cats do purr a lot."

12. If less than one-half, then speak these words: "I have not found that to be true in my experience."

Although this control process is less detailed than the ones usually proposed by information-processing psychologists, it conveys the spirit of the approach — namely, to analyze seemingly instantaneous thoughts into their components.

An Example of Information Processing: Studying for a Test

To see how the information-processing viewpoint helps to explain a more every-day example of problem solving, imagine how high school students might study for a midterm test in, say, history. Many aspects of their behavior illustrate facets of information-processing theory, although not always in precise form. Suppose that the test is multiple choice; that it covers a text that the students readjust before the test; and that they have taken one previous test, which was also multiple choice, from this history teacher. In these conditions, how are they likely to differ from elementary school children in preparing for the test?

Applying Expert Skills   First, adolescents have probably had more time to become experts in taking multiple-choice tests. They therefore already know, without even asking, the approximate form of the questions, as well as the instructions that the teacher will probably provide. They know these features so well, in fact, that they hardly think about them; instead they devote their short preparation time to more difficult matters. Younger children, in contrast, cannot afford to do this; for them, the format of the test itself might be part of the problem they are trying to solve. In information-processing terms, test taking requires use of STM, and because STM can handle test taking more automatically for older students, more memory capacity is available for analyzing the actual content of the test questions.

Selective Allocation of Attention   Second, adolescents have probably read enough textbooks to know that authors of such books usually organize material around headings, topic sentences, key terms, and summary paragraphs. They probably also know that the test questions will emphasize these points. So they read these sections of the assigned text carefully, skimming the intervening paragraphs and pages as rapidly as possible. In contrast, middle-years children are more likely to read all the material with equal attention and consequently to get bogged down in it. In information-processing terms, older children more often possess long-term memories about how to study, and this knowledge directs their attention more efficiently.

Developmental changes in information processing

Use of Domain-specific Knowledge   Older students have usually taken more courses in history and in subjects related to history, so they know more than younger children do. Older students use their richer prior knowledge to help remember the new material that they have to learn. Certain familiar historical themes might crop up in the text — ideas such as "Wars often begin in small, out-of-the-way places," or "Economic booms and busts come in cycles." Older students note that they have heard these ideas before, although not necessarily in these same words. Their memories help them to retain these main points better and to respond to test items about them more appropriately.

Information-Processing Features of Adolescent Thought

Information-processing theory tends not to emphasize qualitative changes or transformations between major stages or periods of life. Instead, it treats each major stage as a continuation or extension of processes begun earlier in childhood. We discuss some of these extensions in Chapter 12 in our description of childhood cognition. As we point out in that chapter, older children organize information more consistently and effectively than younger children do. Even though it seems obvious to say so, older children "know more" than younger children do.

Improved Capacity to Process Information   Typically, an adolescent can deal with, or process, more information than a child can. A first-grader may remember three or four random digits (3 9 5 1), but a teenager can usually remember six or seven. And when a first-grader asks an adult how to spell a word, he can hold just two or three letters in his mind at a time; the adult has to dole them out singly or in very small groups (LO . . . CO . . . MO . . . TI . . . VE). A teenager can more often receive much longer groupings of letters and still reconstruct the word accurately.

These differences may result from either of two sources. The first is what information-processing psychologists sometimes call **structural capacity,** a person's basic "mental power" or cognitive ability (Case, 1986). Differences in structural capacity are like the differences in physical strength between adolescents and children; because teenagers have bigger and more powerful muscles, they naturally can accomplish more physically. Likewise for performance on cognitive tasks: adolescents may remember more digits or letters, partly because their brains can handle more information at any one time.

The second source of differences between children and adolescents is sometimes called **functional capacity,** the ability to make efficient use of existing mental abilities (Prawat, 1989). Differences in functional capacity are more like the improvements in physical performance that come to a gymnast who is already perfectly conditioned: at a certain point in her training, her performance improves mainly because she learns to coordinate her movements more precisely, to rest her muscles when she does not really need them, and to take into account the unique features of the gymnasium in which she is performing. Similarly, functional capacity on cognitive tasks requires coordinating existing skills to best advantage — recalling random digits by using mental techniques or devices for remembering them, for instance.

When it comes to cognitive development, it is usually hard to discriminate between the relative influences of structural and functional capacity — between how much of an adolescent's improved thinking comes from more sheer ability to handle information and how much comes from greater efficiency in using existing talents (Siegler, 1983). Almost any cognitive task allows an individual the freedom to perform it more efficiently with practice, yet the person himself may not be aware that he is trying to do so. For example, many adolescents can write term papers much more easily than they could when they attended elementary school, but try as they may, they may not be able to explain *why* they can do so. Did their extra years of practice make them smarter than before? Or simply more efficient with skills that they have always had? Research on information processing suggests that cognitive development consists of a bit of both.

Growth in basic ability

More skill in using abilities

Perspectives

Encouraging Critical Thinking

Critical thinking is reflection or thought about complex issues, often for the purpose of choosing actions related to the issues (Nickerson, 1988). In spite of the term *critical*, it does not refer to thinking that is negative or full of complaints but to thinking that is thoughtful, that yields new insights, and that gives a basis for intelligent choice. Critical thinking is a broad, practical skill: it can help in figuring out why an unfamiliar appliance has broken down, in composing a term paper, in resolving a personal conflict with a friend, or in deciding what kind of career to pursue.

The examples above require critical thinking for three reasons. First, they lack cut-and-dried solutions and therefore call for persons to improvise specific steps toward a solution as they go along. Second, finding solutions works better if a person has a wide range of knowledge both about the problem itself and about the process of solving the problem. Repairing an unfamiliar appliance is easier if an individual knows something about how other, unrelated appliances work, as well as about how other appliances can be repaired. Third, the solutions call for certain beliefs and attitudes, such as a belief that thinking about a problem will in fact lead to a solution or that successful solutions will result from effort rather than from luck.

Educational psychologists have proposed various ways to classify the elements of critical thinking (Ennis, 1987). Most classifications include the following, although not always in precisely these terms:

1. *Basic operations of reasoning* To think critically, a person has to be able to classify, generalize, deduce conclusions, and perform other logical steps mentally.
2. *Domain-specific knowledge* To deal with a problem, a person has to know something about its topic or content. To evaluate a proposal for a new, fairer tax system, a person has to know something about the existing tax system. To resolve a personal conflict, a person has to know something about the person with whom he is having the conflict.
3. *Metacognitive knowledge* (knowledge about how human thinking works, including one's own) Effective critical thinking requires a person to monitor when she really understands an idea, to know when she needs new information, and to predict how easily she can gather and learn that information.
4. *Values, beliefs, and dispositions* Thinking critically means valuing fairness and objectivity. It means having confidence that thinking does in fact lead to solutions. And it means having a persistent and reflective disposition when thinking.

Educators have devised a number of programs intended to encourage the qualities needed for critical thinking (Chance, 1986; Kruse & Presseisen, 1987), many of which serve adolescents. The programs differ in their particulars: they last various lengths of time, emphasize different thinking skills, and draw on content from different areas of the standard school curricula. Some programs are integrated into the curricula, meaning that they replace a traditional course in some subject area; others are taught separately and draw content from several content areas at once. Experts on critical thinking have not yet agreed on the relative merits of these different approaches (Glaser, 1984).

But the experts do agree on several general principles that enhance the quality of programs that teach critical thinking:

1. First, teaching thinking is best done directly and explicitly. Critical thinking does not develop on its own by unconscious osmosis, so to speak (Nickerson, 1986). Watching the teacher or a classmate think critically does not guarantee that a student will become a better thinker. Neither does giving a student lots of practice in simple mental operations, such as basic addition or simple logical puzzles.
2. Second, good programs for teaching thinking offer lots of practice at solving actual problems. Just telling about the elements of critical thinking (as this text is doing!) does not turn students into skillful thinkers. To accommodate the need for practice, the most successful educational programs last at least a full academic year and sometimes also weave the thinking skills into other, related courses so as to extend the effects of the program still further.
3. Third, all successful programs try to create an environment explicitly conducive to critical thinking (Resnick, 1987). Typically, they expect teachers to model important critical thinking skills themselves, such as thinking out loud while they explain a solution to a problem. The programs also expect teachers to convey confidence in students' abilities to think, while providing constructive, explicit criticism of ideas, whether their own or the students'. For example, one technique is to invite individual students to act as teacher or constructive critic temporarily (Lochhead, 1985; Palincsar & Brown, 1984). To make time for these activities, most programs in critical thinking tend to minimize individual seat work, a time-consuming activity found in much traditional classroom instruction but one that gives students little on-the-spot feedback about the quality of their thinking process.

Whatever their differences, programs that teach critical thinking are good examples of the application of cognitive developmental theory to a practical, educational need of adolescents. Programs about critical thinking draw on the spirit, if not the literal research findings, of several strands of cognitive theory about the adolescent years. One strand is Piagetian, with its concern for how logic and reasoning develop; another is information-processing theory, with its focus on specific ways of organizing ideas and of coordinating new ideas with preexisting ones; and still another strand is research on cognitive styles, with its focus on the impact of reflection and analytic thinking when seeking solutions.

Expertise in Specific Domains of Knowledge   By adolescence, many individuals have become comparative experts in specific domains of knowledge or skill. These may or may not have much to do with school learning. One teenager excels in knowledge of mathematics, whereas another excels in knowledge of baseball, and still another excels in getting along with people.

Much of such expertise may depend not on generalized development of cognitive structures, as the Piagetians would claim, but on the long, slow acquisition of large amounts of specific knowledge. Studies of experts and novices among adults suggest this possibility. Experts in physics know many more concepts about physics than beginners do, but they do not necessarily know more about foreign policy, English grammar, or other areas of knowledge (Chi et al., 1989; Glaser, 1987). Experts also know more about problem solving in their particular field of expertise. A mathematician remembers countless formulas and equations, thanks to years of experience in memorizing them, and her memories naturally help her to solve new problems as they come up; she may realize that a new equation is similar to one she has worked with before and simply recall how she responded to the earlier one.

Remembering details

Ironically, then, expertise may often make creative problem solving unnecessary. Instead of using valuable energy in thinking through a solution, the expert can simply remember what to do; this fact, as much as any other, makes his performance seem fast and effortless. But because this advantage is confined to specific domains or types of problems, an expert's performance contradicts Piaget's assertion that powerful, abstract thought develops across many domains at once. Outside of his field, an expert must struggle for solutions just like the rest of us. Within his field, on the other hand, he may often only *look* as if he

A great deal of cognitive development consists of acquiring specific expertise rather than general knowledge.

is reasoning at a high level, when in reality much of his performance amounts to a simple recall — the kind we all engage in when we remember the letters of the alphabet or a phone number.

This conclusion does not mean, however, that experts work only by simple recall. On the contrary, their larger number of memories may free them to focus on more difficult aspects of a problem or on aspects that they have never encountered before. Students who are good writers tend to spend comparatively more time than others at planning an essay — making notes and outlines — and less time at actually putting words to paper (Applebee et al., 1981). To a large extent, the task of composing sentences takes care of itself for good writers, probably because they can draw on a rich memory of sentence constructions, terms, and phrases and therefore devote less attention to creating them.

Different allocation of attention

Evaluation of the Information-Processing Viewpoint

By focusing on the detailed features of problem solving, the information-processing viewpoint provides a valuable complement to the broader approach of cognitive developmental theory. By focusing on the fine details of thinking, information-processing theory has more to say about why individuals vary in their thinking performance from one occasion to the next. Some psychologists have also tried to identify developmental trends in information processing (Sternberg, 1984; Case, 1986). Their research has emphasized specific sequences within particular domains of thinking, rather than the more global stages of the cognitive developmental approach. In this way the information-processing viewpoint resembles research on adolescents' cognition about interpersonal and social knowledge, described next.

THE DEVELOPMENT OF SOCIAL COGNITION

No matter which approach they take, most developmental psychologists agree that the new cognitive skills of adolescents have important effects on their **social cognition** — their knowledge and beliefs about interpersonal and social matters. In this section we look at the most important forms of social cognition, beginning with a description of the special form of self-centeredness, or **adolescent egocentrism,** that affects teenagers' reactions to others and their beliefs about themselves. We consider what causes this form of egocentrism and how these causes affect three other important kinds of social cognition; moral beliefs, political attitudes, and religious orientation.

Egocentrism During Adolescence

When adolescents like Neira first begin reasoning abstractly, they often become overly impressed with this skill: it seems to them that anything can be solved "if only people would be reasonable" (that is, logical). This attitude can make teenagers idealistic and keep them from appreciating the practical limits of logic (Piaget, 1970). They may wonder why no one has ever "realized" that world war might be abolished simply by explaining to all the world powers the obvious dangers of war. Or they may wonder why their parents have not noticed the many "errors" they have made in raising children.

The development of formal thought also leads to a new kind of confusion between an adolescent's own thoughts and those of others. This confusion of viewpoints amounts to a form of egocentrism. Unlike the egocentrism of preschoolers, which is based on concrete problems, adolescent egocentrism concerns more abstract thoughts and problems. Consider what happened to Neira. When she was fourteen, she had to perform at a figure-skating recital. For weeks beforehand, she practiced daily to prepare; as the performance date drew near, she naturally began to worry about how well she would do. In fact, she became convinced that "everyone" was talking about her particular performance and wondering how good it would be. Her parents encouraged her not to worry and said that "people always like what you do on your skates." To Neira these comments just sounded as if her parents did not appreciate the unique importance of *her* performance. Even after the recital actually occurred, Neira fretted about others' reactions to it: Had they liked it? What were they saying about it?

Bridges How does adolescent egocentrism affect teenagers' perceptions of their peer relationships?

Preoccupation with reactions of others

The Imaginary Audience   Adolescent egocentrism like Neira's sometimes occurs and shows itself in teenagers' preoccupation with the reactions of others. Thirteen-year-olds often fail to differentiate between how they feel about themselves and how others feel about them (Elkind & Bowen, 1979). Instead, they act as if they are performing for an **imaginary audience,** one that is as concerned with their appearance and behavior as they are themselves.

Teenagers also reveal concern with an imaginary audience through **strategic interactions** with their peers — encounters that aim either to reveal or to conceal personal information indirectly (Elkind, 1980b, 1984). Telephoning often serves as a strategic interaction, especially for younger teenagers. Frequent phone calls help to sustain a belief in personal popularity with an imaginary audience, so a teenager may subtly encourage others to phone by casually promising to share special gossip or secrets "if you phone me tonight." An individual can also create the appearance of popularity by talking on the phone for very long periods of time, which means that potential callers get the "busy signal" — an implied message that the youngster is too popular to reach easily by telephone. This message can also be conveyed to the person on the line with an offhand comment such as, "Gotta go; I'm expecting some other calls."

The Personal Fable   As a result of their egocentrism, teenagers often believe in a **personal fable,** or the notion that their own lives embody a special story that is heroic and completely unique. For example, one high school student may be convinced that no love affair has ever reached the heights of romance of his involvement with a classmate; another may believe that she is destined for great fame and fortune by virtue of (what she considers to be) her unparalleled combination of charm and academic talent; still another may "know" that even though serious catastrophes happen to others, they will never happen to him — he will never get seriously ill, or have trouble finding a job, or die.

Overawareness of personal ideas and emotions

In experiencing these feelings and ideas, adolescents fail to realize how frequently other individuals feel them as well. Early in adolescence, they still have only limited **empathy,** or the ability to understand reliably the abstract thoughts and feelings of others and to compare these thoughts and feelings with their own. In fact, much of adolescence consists of developing these social skills. So does most of adulthood, for that matter; we never really finish learning how to understand others or ever really finish comparing our own experiences with those of others (Labouvie-Vief, 1982). But adolescence serves as the time when most people begin learning to consider other viewpoints in relation to their own and developing complex ideas about moral, political, and religious questions, among others, in response.

Bridges How does cognitive development during adolescence affect teenagers' ability to empathize with other people's feelings?

Note, however, that not all teenagers seem equally egocentric; and even those who do show this quality are only egocentric by comparison with adults, not by comparison with younger children. More recent investigations of adoles-

A Talk with Joan

Thinking in Adolescence

Joan is a slender, poised young woman of fifteen with a friendly but serious manner. She was interviewed on the back porch of her home after school.

Interviewer: How has your thinking and intellectual activity changed over the past several years?

Joan: For some kids it looks like they haven't changed very much, but for me they have. You read and think about different things — like *1984* — than you did before, and the discussions you have are a lot different . . . about bigger things.

Interviewer: Why does a book like that appeal to you now?

Joan: Well, you can understand it now. I mean, you can start thinking about all the different . . . the big questions. . . .

Interviewer: What would be an example?

Joan: Like . . . the type of government. Serious things. Now if I read a fairy tale it's fun, but I'm not so into it. It's not quite as interesting, while before that was exciting.

Interviewer: Have there been changes in the way you use your mind to figure out problems at school?

Joan: I don't think so. I mean, it's like I do more advanced math and stuff, but it doesn't seem to me that I couldn't have understood it before if someone had taught it to me. Of course, now you don't just deal with facts. You sort of write essays and things and read. You have to think about the connections. Which I'm not sure I couldn't have done before.

Interviewer: How has your thinking about problems changed?

Joan: It's hard to remember. I mean, I talked about problems before, but I suppose that I didn't think about so many realistic things. I remember thinking about "what if" after I read something or saw something, but it was generally about fantasy rather than something like world war or the nuclear threat. I think that I could have learned what I am learning now in sixth grade. When we get into more interesting things like in history and English, I end up talking about it out of school more. Like with my parents and with some friends. When it's not just facts. I mean, you never talk about math and French out of school, but you may talk about a book you read in history or something connected with other things.

Interviewer: Do you feel more like an intellectual equal with adults?

Joan: I don't ever remember feeling like I was not an equal. I always thought that if I didn't know it now, I'd learn it in a few months and then I would definitely be as smart or smarter.

Interviewer: Are all kids able to think the same way that you do?

Joan: Well, it sort of divides up more. I mean, before there were lots of different levels, and it was basically who could learn faster. And now it's like, some kids just never get that far and some kids, even if they don't get that far fast, are able to think about things. . . . So I think it does divide up more into two separate groups instead of many levels.

Interviewer: Have you thought about the reasons for this?

Joan: Well, sometimes I think it might be just like who spends time thinking about things. And sometimes I think the upper group are just extremely smart. I mean, I think a lot of it's how much energy you're putting into it and how much interest you have in thinking about it.

Interviewer: So the lower group may spend less time thinking . . .

Joan: Or at that time in their lives, they're not bothering to think so much about these things; they're worrying about other things. And some people look like they're thinking about things, and when you talk to them, . . . they're not really.

Interviewer: Do you get fooled the other way too?

Joan: Yes. And then you talk to them and they say something really smart that they thought of, and you say, "Hmmm!"

Follow-up Questions

1. What signs of adolescent egocentrism do you see in Joan?

2. Which of Piaget's stages of cognitive development best describes Joan's thinking? How typical do you think she is of children her age?

3. Joan mentions her increasing interest in what she calls the "big questions." What might this interest signify about her cognitive approach to moral and political issues?

---

cents' belief in an imaginary audience show that individuals are just as likely to increase their empathy or interpersonal sensitivity during this developmental period as to increase their self-centeredness (DeRosenroll, 1987). Accurate awareness of others' opinions about oneself apparently develops alongside, and sometimes even instead of, self-conscious preoccupation with others' opinions The relative balance between these two developments depends, among other things, on the quality of relationships between parents and the adolescent: better, more supportive relationships lead to more realism and less self-consciousness (Riley et al., 1984).

Bridges What role can parents play in reducing adolescent egocentrism?

The teenagers shown here illustrate two aspects of adolescent egocentrism: a preoccupation with the reactions of others and a belief that serious catastrophes may happen to others but never to them.

Bridges   How do advances in social cognition during adolescence affect teenagers' ability to make moral judgments?

Different forms of ethical development

Beliefs About Justice and Care

As adolescents gradually overcome egocentrism in their personal relationships, they develop their personal **ethics,** or sensitivity to and knowledge of what is right and wrong. Ethics develops in two ways: in the form of increasingly logical and abstract principles related to fairness and justice and in the form of increasingly sophisticated forms of caring about the welfare of friends, family, and self (Rest, 1983; Noddings, 1984). Each of these developments is modestly related to gender, with boys tending to emphasize ethical thinking about justice and girls emphasizing ethics of care. But the gender difference is not large; most individuals develop both kinds of ethical thinking to a significant extent (Gilligan & Wiggins, 1987).

Ethical Beliefs About Justice   When thinking about justice, teenagers begin making ethical judgments according to principles of some sort; compared to children, teenagers are less *opportunistic,* or inclined to judge according to immediate rewards or punishments that they experience personally. But for most young people, the principles remain rather conventional during these years (Colby et al., 1983). They base their evaluations of situations either on principles expressed by their immediate peers and relatives (Kohlberg's Stage 3) or on socially sanctioned rules and principles (Kohlberg's Stage 4). (See Chapter 12 for an overview of Kohlberg's six-stage theory of moral development.) If friends argue that premarital sex is permissible, many teenagers are likely to adopt this idea as their own — at least as a general principle. But if friends or family believes that premarital sex is morally wrong, teenagers may adopt this alternative belief as a principle. Note, however, that whether a teenager actually acts according to these principles is another matter, one that depends partly on the beliefs she also develops about caring for others (described below).

A few teenagers develop **postconventional moral judgment,** which means that for the first time, ethical reasoning goes beyond the judgments that society conventionally makes about right and wrong (Kohlberg, 1976). Adolescents' growing ability to use abstract formal thought makes this possible; unlike school-children, they can evaluate ethical ideas that *might* be right or wrong, given certain circumstances that can only be imagined.

Influence of abstract thought

Ethical Beliefs About Care   In addition to believing more consciously in principles of justice, adolescents develop ethical attitudes about caring for individuals — although these, too, remain somewhat conventional during the teenage years (Gilligan, 1982). Because most teenagers have developed significant sensitivity to others' needs and beliefs (Selman, 1988), they begin viewing actions as good if the actions respond to or take account of others' needs. Egocentrism remains, however, in that teenagers often fail to distinguish between actions that *please* others and actions that are right in a deeper, ethical sense. If parents will be pleased by a young person's enrolling in complex science and mathematics courses in high school, for example, doing so may seem "right" to the youngster, even if he has little interest or aptitude in those courses.

As with the ethics of justice, a few individuals move beyond the conventional pleasing of others toward **integrated care,** in which the young person realizes that pleasing everyone is not always possible but that it is important to balance everyone's needs — including her own (Noddings, 1984). Deciding whether or not to take a part-time job, for example, now becomes a matter of reconciling the impact of the job on important family, friends, and self. Some individuals may gain (the teenager herself may earn more money and make new friends), but others may lose (parents and prior friends may see less of her). The gains and losses must be balanced, not transformed completely into gains.

Interpersonally oriented ethics

Research on Ethical Development   Even though teengers may not always follow their own principles of justice, research suggests that such principles do represent true convictions and are not simply unthinking statements of conventional moral ideas. One study presented hypothetical moral dilemmas ("Should a man steal a drug to save his wife's life?") but also asked individuals to "fake" solutions that were not truly their own (Rest, 1983). In this condition, adolescents found it very hard to fake solutions higher than their normal stage of reasoning about justice but very easy to fake solutions lower than their normal stage.

Research has also found that another aspect of moral development — guilt — changes in both nature and focus as well. Compared with children, adolescents are more likely to feel guilty about taking no action ("sins of omission") as well as about actually doing something wrong ("sins of commission"). The shift occurs whether a teenager is evaluating a hypothetical story that portrays wrongdoing or is describing a situation in his own life (Hoffman, 1984). In deciding whether or not to steal a drug for a dying spouse, for example, teenagers are likely to view "doing nothing" as moral decision, whereas children are somewhat more likely to view this option as morally neutral or morally acceptable (Gilligan & Wiggins, 1987). Likewise, teenagers are more likely than children to see the problems with inaction in their own lives — that never bothering to invite a friend over to your home, for example, can sometimes hurt the friend as much as openly and actively criticizing her. These insights require formal thought: concern about something that might happen, not only about something that actually does.

Recognizing moral possibilities

Overall, then, beliefs about justice and care begin taking into account a broader array both of interpersonal circumstances and of general principles than was true during the school years. Teenagers more often refer to principles in evaluating actions, although they still do not always act on their principles. Often they also regard pleasing others as ethically good or right, even though they may still fail to see the impossibility of pleasing everyone perfectly. Like a lot of other cognitive developments, these changes result from adolescents' growing capacities to reason abstractly.

The Development of Political Ideas

Limits on more sophisticated thought

Political thinking develops in ways similar to ethical judgment — perhaps not surprisingly — because politics involves many ethical problems, and vice versa. As with moral development, adolescents show both progress and its limitations. Teenagers often do hold more sophisticated political ideas than children do; they handle political ideas and opinions more abstractly, and they see more relationships among them. They view the formation of laws and legal regulations more democratically, seeing these as something that applies equally to everybody in society rather than to isolated individuals or selected groups. In these ways, adolescent political thinking draws upon elements of formal operational thought and the more advanced forms of moral thinking described by Piaget and Kohlberg (see Chapter 12). At the same time, however, adolescents reveal serious gaps and inconsistencies in their political thinking. These suggest that political thinking is not acquired in an all-or-nothing, stagelike way but that it involves learning large amounts of specific political knowledge — an idea essential to the information processing viewpoint.

To understand these developments, consider a common political issue, poverty. What must be done to eliminate it? Can it in fact ever be really eliminated? The answers given by two children, one in the sixth grade and one in the twelfth, differ in significant ways that reflect the children's cognitive development. The answers also share some common limitations in spite of the six years of living and learning that separate the two individuals. First the sixth-grader:

INTERVIEWER: Do you know what I mean by poverty?
SIXTH-GRADER: No.
INTERVIEWER: That means poorness, not having any money. So . . . would it ever be possible to make it so that nobody was poor?
SIXTH-GRADER: I don't, well, if they got the person to really work hard that there might not be anyone that would, uh, be poor and that, but if there was someone that would just uh would uh be retired, he could just lay around the house because he's already put in his years of work and that.
INTERVIEWER: Do you think it would ever be that there wouldn't be any poor people?
SIXTH-GRADER: Maybe, in the future, if they could enforce the law that all lazy people should work.

The twelfth-grader answered in this way:

INTERVIEWER: Do you think it would ever be possible to eliminate poverty?
TWELFTH-GRADER: Yes, because this is the most highly advanced, richest country in the world. And the world knows because we're putting money over here, overseas there, or we're putting money over there. Money in Africa, putting a hell of a lot of money in Asia, the Southeast. I don't see why we should be putting money there while we still have poor here. I'd say we could put in a little money but why do we have to buy airplanes. (Gallatin, 1980, pp. 350–351)

Relationships among problems

Aside from obvious differences in content, how do these two responses differ in cognitive form? First, the adolescent seems to understand better that a political problem may concern many aspects of society at once. Unlike the younger child, he points out how poverty may be related to or aggravated by activities beyond the borders of his own particular country, the United States, by implying that poverty abroad may worsen poverty at home by stimulating foreign aid and thereby draining away dollars. In contrast, the younger child implies that poverty is simply the fault of the individuals who experience it (Leahy, 1990). If only they would work harder, they might escape their problem with little or no help from the rest of society and with little impact on society either.

The two children also have different views of how governments can help ordinary people. The sixth-grader implies that the most helpful thing government can do about poverty is to act like the police: the government, he says, should make poor people work harder ("enforce the law that all lazy people should work"). The twelfth-grader, on the other hand, suggests that government and citizens can genuinely cooperate with each other: in his view, the government should identify the people or groups who need money the most and give it to them. In his opinion, these are the domestic poor, not the foreign poor.

Although the twelfth-grader's ideas are more abstract and less personal than those of the sixth-grader, neither really expresses a true **ideology,** or coherent philosophy, about poverty. Admittedly, neither has a chance to do so in the short interviews quoted earlier; longer talks might allow them to show their political knowledge and sensitivities more completely. Probably not, however; studies show that most adolescents lack any sort of consistent, conscious system of beliefs about politics (Adams, 1985; Torney-Purta, 1984). Instead, they tend only to approximate consistency, frequently contradict themselves, and often base political ideas on values that are rather unconscious. The twelfth-grader in this example may freely contradict himself when the topic shifts to the problems of strategic planning for national defense, by deciding that foreign economic aid does serve a useful if indirect purpose by gaining allies abroad.

In a highly individualistic society like that of the United States, of course, lack of a coherent ideology may also represent a final or true maturity rather than a failure to attain one. Like most adolescents, very few adults really have

Lack of political ideology

Participation in political events both reflects and builds adolescents' involvement in society and is an indication of their more sophisticated political thinking. Chances are, though, that these two girls also find political activity gratifying socially — a good way to make and be friends.

explicit, complex political philosophies (Bellah et al., 1985), and many adults tend toward rather personalized beliefs on specific issues. The attitudes of the sixth-grader have been stated publicly in the U.S. Congress, as well as in many other adult forums. Furthermore, surveys of political knowledge generally suggest surprisingly sketchy knowledge of many basic political facts among both adolescents and adults. Many people do not know how many senators represent each American state in Congress (there are two), or how long members of Congress serve in either the House of Representatives (two years) or the Senate (six) (Jennings & Niemi, 1981). By supporting indifference to such knowledge, North American society may actually discourage full development of political thinking among its adolescents.

Religious Beliefs and Orientation

Increased sophistication in defining beliefs

During adolescence, cognitive development affects both specific religious beliefs and overall religious orientation. In general, specific beliefs become more sophisticated or complex than they were during childhood. The concept of religious denomination, for example, evolves from comparatively superficial notions to more accurate and abstract ones. In one study that used Piagetian-style interviews, middle-years children tended to identify denominations by easily observed behaviors (Elkind, 1979, pp. 264–265):

INTERVIEWER: What is a Catholic?
EIGHT-YEAR-OLD: He goes to Mass every Sunday.

or

INTERVIEWER: Can someone be a Catholic and a Protestant at the same time?
SEVEN-YEAR-OLD: No, because you couldn't go to two churches.

By early adolescence, however, the concept of religious denomination begins to depend significantly on the beliefs of adherents rather than on their outward behaviors. Teenagers in this study replied with relatively sophisticated concepts:

INTERVIEWER: What is a Jew?
TWELVE-YEAR-OLD: A person who believes in one God and doesn't believe in the New Testament.

or

INTERVIEWER: What is a Catholic?
TWELVE-YEAR-OLD: Someone who believes in the truths of the Roman Catholic Church.
INTERVIEWER: Can a dog or a cat be a Catholic?
TWELVE-YEAR-OLD: No, because it cannot think.

In these responses, abstract qualities have replaced the more concrete observations of the younger children. As with political ideas, however, these abstractions are not necessarily very profound, nor do they relate consistently to each other yet.

The development of faith

For those involved in religious education and development, children's acquisition of specific beliefs like these often matters less than their development of an overall view of the world, or of a **faith** — a coherent orientation to religious experiences that guides their responses to life. Faith is much more general than "mere" beliefs, and it usually involves feelings as well as thoughts (M. Parker, 1985). Because of its breadth, faith often touches on topics and problems that are not explicitly religious in content, such as the meaning of birth and death or the best ways of handling personal relationships (B. Cohen & Lukinsky, 1985).

In childhood, religious orientation amounts largely to loose groupings of concrete religious beliefs and images, often with relatively little coordination and with seemingly little relevance to daily experiences (J. Fowler, 1987). Consider this explanation of the nature of God by a ten-year-old:

INTERVIEWER: Can you tell me what God is?

MILLIE: God is a like a saint. He's good and he like — he like rules the world, but in a good way. And . . .

INTERVIEWER: How does he rule the world?

MILLIE: Well, he — not really rule the world, but um — let's see, he like — he lives on top of the world and he's always watching over everybody. At least he tries to. And he does what he thinks is right. He does what he thinks is right and tries to do the best and — he lives up in heaven and . . .

INTERVIEWER: What does God look like?

MILLIE: I imagine that he's an old man with a white beard and white hair wearing a long robe and that the clouds are his floor and he has a throne. And he has all these people and there's angels around him. (J. Fowler, 1981, pp. 138–140)

What is God?

Millie describes God in concrete terms that have little relevance to daily life. In contrast, a fifteen-year-old offers fewer visual images; for her, God is more of a universal presence that she feels permeates her life and helps her.

INTERVIEWER: What do you think God is?

LINDA: God is different to a lot of people . . . I just feel . . . he's there. There might not be any material proof but I *know*. I can bet my life on it. Really. I know because he *has* talked to me. . . . [Once when I had trouble with my friends,] I remembered that, you know, there was *God* and I just asked him to tell me something, tell me what I could do, because why can't I be good friends with everybody? Go places with her one time, and then with her and him, and you know, with everybody? (J. Fowler, 1981, pp. 155–156)

For this adolescent, God is not so much a person living in a specific place as an abstraction. He is a relationship that transcends specific situations and experiences, and that helps to give those specifics fuller meaning.

Religious orientation need not come out of an organized religion, of course, and for many adolescents and adults it does not. Many teenagers prefer to develop a personal faith without reference to other groups' or individuals' beliefs. Take this sixteen-year-old, who grew up attending an unusually liberal Protestant church and whose ideas resemble those of many people who never attend church at all:

INTERVIEWER: What means the most to you?

BRIAN: Just life. It fascinates me. I don't know what goes on before or after birth or death. And some things scare me. The unknown is really a factor in my life because I like to think about it a lot and the reason why everything got here. It really bothers me a lot because I don't know the answers and no one knows the answers, and I can't turn to anyone to get the answers — except to God, if there is a God. Maybe someday I'll get a vision from the Almighty! (*spoken sarcastically*) (J. Fowler, 1981, p. 159)

These ideas have much of the scope of Linda's comments. In spite of appearances, however, they may partially reflect social conformity rather than true, spontaneous conviction. Paradoxically, Brian may be conforming to an ideal of nonconformity or independent thinking. He implies this possibility elsewhere in the interview by stating that the worst thing that could happen to him would be to agree with conventional, majority opinions. But although Brian and Linda differ dramatically in the source of their religious orientation — Brian comes from a relatively secular, humanist social environment, whereas Linda comes from a more traditional Christian denomination — they are not entirely opposites. Compared to Millie, they share a quality of comprehensiveness; their specific beliefs range relatively widely over life's issues and fit together at least some of the time.

These developments may result from changes both in general cognitive structures and in knowledge and information-processing strategies. As predicted by Piaget for other realms of knowledge, Brian and Linda have developed the capacity to think abstractly, and as a result, they may have reconstructed their childhood beliefs and faith to use their new abilities. At the same time, they have had several years in which to acquire new knowledge about religion and about the meaning of life (Heller, 1986). Along with this knowledge may have come broad new strategies for dealing with and organizing this knowledge — strategies similar in scope to Piaget's formal operations but with more application to religious problems. In their own ways, they may therefore have become modest experts about faith, although not about the same kind of faith.

COGNITIVE AND SOCIAL DEVELOPMENT

As this chapter shows, cognition has significant influences on many areas of adolescent life that most of us would consider essentially social in nature. These influences can work in the other direction as well. A motivation to have many friends, for example, can foster the strong development of empathy, which is in part a cognitive skill. Similarly, deep involvement with a religion can promote relatively sophisticated knowledge and thinking about religious beliefs, at least as they exist in that particular religion.

In real life, then, cognitive and social development do not divide up neatly, as they are made to do in textbooks such as this one. Their blending will show up again in the next chapter, which discusses psychosocial development. As is evident there, most psychosocial developments assume the sorts of cognitive accomplishments discussed in this chapter. Some, such as identity development, do so rather explicitly, but all at least imply an awareness of the cognitive abilities described here.

SUMMARY OF MAJOR IDEAS

The Cognitive Developmental Viewpoint

1. During adolescence, teenagers become capable of formal thought, which is an ability to think about ideas.
2. Formal thought is characterized by an ability to think about possibilities, by scientific reasoning, and by an ability to combine ideas logically.
3. In general, formal thought fosters systematic solutions to many cognitive problems.
4. In daily life, however, adolescents (and adults) often do not use formal thinking, even when it might be appropriate to do so.
5. Some research suggests forms of thinking beyond formal operations.

The Information-Processing Viewpoint

6. During adolescence, information-processing skills continue to improve.
7. Teenagers acquire more expertise in particular areas of knowledge or skill, and they become more efficient at allocating their attention to tasks.
8. Both structural and functional capacities improve as a result of development, and both probably contribute to improved cognitive performance.
9. Information-processing theory helps the specific mechanisms of cognitive performance.

The Development of Social Cognition

10. In spite of their improved cognitive skills, adolescents still sometimes show egocentrism by believing in an "imaginary

audience," and by believing in a "personal fable" or biography of their lives.

11. Adolescents begin assessing ethical issues according to principles and interpersonal concerns, but their ethical thinking still tends to be guided by conventional attitudes and beliefs.

12. Teenagers also begin thinking about political processes in more sophisticated ways by seeing more relationships among political problems and by developing more of a sense of society as a community.

13. Even older teenagers, however, usually lack any sort of conscious political ideology or philosophy — just as many adults do.

14. By adolescence, teenagers have already acquired relatively accurate notions of religious denominations; by the end of adolescence, they often show abstract understandings of the concept of God.

KEY TERMS

formal thought *(544)*
formal operational
    thought *(544)*
structural capacity *(554)*
functional capacity *(554)*
critical thinking *(555)*
social cognition *(557)*
adolescent
    egocentrism *(557)*
imaginary audience *(558)*

strategic interaction *(558)*
personal fable *(558)*
empathy *(558)*
ethics *(560)*
postconventional moral
    judgment *(560)*
integrated care *(561)*
ideology *(563)*
faith *(564)*

WHAT DO YOU THINK?

1. All things considered, do you think that Piaget overrated the importance of formal operational thought in the development of adolescents? Explain.

2. Think of an activity or area of knowledge in which you consider yourself a relative expert. How much of your expertise seems to result from having an unusually large amount of knowledge or practice? How much seems to result from applying "merely" good knowledge in unusually skillful ways?

3. A teenager once said, "My parents get smarter every year." In what sense, if any, do you think this statement is true? What might cause a teenager to make the statement?

4. Why do you suppose that social cognition seem less definitely stagelike than the scientific thinking that Piaget described? Speculate about some of the possible reasons.

FOR FURTHER READING

Belenky, M., Clincy, B., Goldberger, N., and Tarule, J. *Women's Ways of Knowing: The Development of Self, Voice, and Mind.* New York: Basic Books, 1986.

These authors present phases or types of thinking and learning that they believe are unique — or at least relatively unique — to women as they develop from adolescents to adults. They base their ideas on extensive interviews with women of all ages and of all levels of economic privilege. This is a book about cognition, but it locates cognition in a social context related to gender.

Elkind, D. *All Grown Up and No Place to Go: Teenagers in Crisis.* Reading, MA: Addison-Wesley, 1984.

This is one of several books by Elkind intended to support new, helpful social policies for children — or in this case, teenagers. The policy recommendations are based on Elkind's general assessment of adolescents' developmental needs. Because of its practical orientation, the book does not confine itself to cognitive development but purposely discusses how cognitive, social, and physical changes interact to create teenagers' current needs.

Tipton, S. *Getting Saved, from the Sixties.* Berkeley: University of California Press, 1982.

Bellah, R., Madsen, R., Sullivan, W. Swidler, A. and Tipton, S. *Habits of the Heart: Individualism and Commitment in American Life.* Berkeley: University of California Press, 1985.

These two books explore how cultural assumptions and social conditions affect the thinking and beliefs of older adolescents and adults. The one by Tipton focuses on why some adolescents and young adults join alternative religious communities, such as a Zen commune or a fundamentalist Christian group that lives communally. The book by Bellah et al. argues that cultural beliefs in individualism make it hard, although not impossible, to think meaningfully about needs and beliefs held in common by the community. To support their ideas, both books contain many vivid interviews and descriptions of individual youths and adults.

CHAPTER 16

Adolescence: Psychosocial Development

Focusing Questions

■ What typical conflicts about identity do adolescents have, and what factors influence how they resolve them?

■ How do differences in parenting style affect parent-teenager relationships?

■ What changes in sexual activities and attitudes occur among adolescents?

■ To what extent do adolescents encounter special problems such as pregnancy, abuse, homelessness, delinquency, and suicide?

Separation and independence

A s we have discovered, a number of dramatic physical and cognitive changes occur during puberty and adolescence. Although there is a great deal of variation in how fast these changes happen, by the end of this period, adolescents look like adults and are physically and intellectually capable of most adult activities. But as important as these changes are, the most significant accomplishment for an adolescent is the achievement of a full-fledged, independent, psychological identity: one that is mature, adult, unique, and separate from parents, friends, and other important childhood figures. An identity provides the teenager with a fuller and more permanent sense of who she really is, what she really needs, what she believes in, and what she is and is not capable of doing. One high school senior put it this way:

> It's not just that I'm all grown up now — physically, I mean. It's that I have grown up inside, too. I feel different, more like a grownup than a child. Although there still are many things that I am unsure of, I finally have a much clearer sense of who I am and what is important to me and what I believe in. In a way, it feels like I am at the end of a long journey . . . and ready to start off on a new one.

In this chapter, we look at the process of identity development during adolescence, including the factors that influence identity and some of the possible outcomes. Then we explore several important aspects of the social world of the teenager, including relationships with parents and peers, the development of friendships, and the impact of school. We also look at adolescent sexuality and how it is influenced by current social trends and by personal beliefs. Last, we explore the special problems faced by adolescents today and some strategies for preventing them.

INDIVIDUATION AND IDENTITY DEVELOPMENT

The idea that each of us has our own **identity** — a relatively stable sense of our own individual uniqueness and a commitment to an integrated set of goals, values, and beliefs — does not surprise anyone, but despite our familiarity with this concept, identity is not easy to define. This is because each person's identity is a complicated affair involving many different qualities and dimensions, and it depends on subjective rather than objective experiences.

Four subphases of individuation

The process by which an adolescent develops a unique personal identity or sense of self, distinct and separate from all others, is called **individuation.** This process has four distinct but overlapping subphases: differentiation, practice and experimentation, rapprochement, and consolidation (Josselson, 1980).

For each of these adolescents, it is likely that their willingness to engage in activities that diverge from cultural expectations reflects a strong sense of individual identity and self-direction.

During the **differentiation** subphase, which occurs early in adolescence, the adolescent recognizes that he is psychologically different from his parents. This discovery often leads him to question and reject his parents' values and advice, even if the advice is reasonable. For instance, a thirteen-year-old who enjoys and is doing well at music lessons may refuse to continue them because they were his parents' idea, not his own. In addition, sometimes the realization that his parents are not as wise, powerful, and all-knowing as he earlier thought they were leads him to overreact and reject *all* their advice (Josselson, 1980). After attempting, on his parents' advice, to talk with his history teacher about a

Differentiation

Practice and experimentation

Rapprochement

Consolidation of self

classroom problem and failing miserably, the adolescent may go through a period where he refuses to listen to anything his parents have to say about school or, for that matter, social relationships in general.

In the **practice and experimentation** subphase, the fourteen- or fifteen-year-old feels that he knows it all and can do no wrong. He denies any need for caution or advice and actively challenges his parents whenever the opportunity presents itself. He also increases his commitment to friends, who provide him with the support and approval that he previously sought from adults. In a discussion of plans to go to a heavy metal rock concert, for example, he will completely dismiss his parents' concerns about the dangers involved in attending, asserting that his friends went to one last year and told him it was perfectly safe.

The **rapprochement** subphase occurs toward the middle of adolescence, when the teenager has achieved a fair degree of separateness from his parents. The pain and fear of being totally separate lead him to return to home base, and he conditionally and partially reaccepts his parents' authority. Often adolescents alternate between experimentation and rapprochement, at times challenging their parents and at other times being conciliatory and cooperative. Frequently, a teenager at this subphase will go to great lengths to accept responsibility around the house, yet will be indignant when his parents still insist on establishing a curfew and being informed about where he is going when he leaves the house in the evening.

The final subphase, which lasts until the end of adolescence, is the **consolidation of self**. During this phase, the adolescent develops a sense of personal identity, which continues to be the basis for understanding himself and others and for maintaining a sense of autonomy, independence, and individuality. Parents are often surprised at how much careful thought an eighteen- or nineteen-year-old has given to who he is and how strong a sense of personal direction he can have. For example, in a two-hour discussion with his mother that occurred quite by chance, Jorge, a high school senior, revealed that first and foremost, he thought of himself as an artist and worked very hard to develop a special way of seeing and translating what he saw into creative works; he also considered himself a person who was good at helping others. He said that he planned on first attending art school and becoming an artist but thought that he would eventually earn his living as a social worker or some other type of mental health professional.

The process of individuation continues through the teenage years and often into young adulthood. As we shall see shortly, it dovetails with Erikson's theory, which holds that the major task of adolescence is to resolve the crisis of identity successfully.

Theories of Identity Development

The Crisis of Identity Versus Role Confusion   Erik Erikson has contributed more than any other theorist to our understanding of identity development during adolescence. As you may recall from Chapter 2, Erikson believes that the psychosocial crisis of **identity versus role confusion** occurs during this stage of development. To resolve this crisis successfully and achieve a final identity, a person must integrate her many childhood **identifications**, or the conscious and unconscious ways in which she has come to experience herself as being like her parents and other important people in her life.

Teenagers both attempt to and succeed in integrating more knowledge about themselves than younger children do. A middle-years child may simply form disconnected, relatively separate impressions about himself; on one occasion he notices that he excels at hockey and on another that he excels at baseball or swimming. In adolescence, he mulls over the significance of all these impressions

Social Context

Are there significant social-class differences in parental values, child-rearing practices, and expectations for their teenage children? (582)

Physical Development

What are the physiological consequences of teenage pregnancy on the adolescent mother and her infant? (598)

Family

How great a gap is there typically between the values and attitudes of teenagers and those of their parents? (580–581)

Genetics

Is heredity thought to be a factor in the development of homosexuality? (595)

Peers

How do peer groups and friends contribute to teenagers' psychosocial development? (585, 589–590)

ADOLESCENCE: PSYCHOSOCIAL DEVELOPMENT

What is the relationship between adolescents' feelings of depression and suicide? (604–606)

Emotions

What stages do minority group adolescents go through in developing a sense of ethnic identity? (576–577)

Self-concept and Identity

What role does lack of knowledge about contraception play in adolescent pregnancy? (597)

Learning

How do advances in social cognition during adolescence affect teenagers' ability to make moral judgments? (560–561)

Cognition

What role does language play in adolescent cliques? (587)

Language

---

taken together. Do they mean that I am generally athletic? That I am popular? Or that I am just a conformist, just devoting myself to whatever others value — in this case, sports?

In forming an identity during adolescence, a youngster selectively accepts or rejects the many different aspects of herself that she acquired as a child, and society (or parts of society) must give her recognition and appreciation for her uniqueness. The ways in which a child's family, community, and society respond can be more or less in tune with her own feelings about herself. The identity that is achieved at the end of adolescence, according to Erikson, includes all significant identifications with individuals of the past, which are altered to form a unique and reasonably integrated whole.

During the final stage of her identity formation, the adolescent may experience more deeply than she ever did before or ever will again a confusion of roles. The adolescent personality is likely to be vulnerable, aloof, and lacking in commitment, as well as demanding and opinionated. Nevertheless, Erikson believes that these traits are all important elements of normal "I dare you" and "I dare myself" role experimentation. He also warns that conflicts about identity are normal and never completely resolved and that the risk taking and psychological instability of adolescence should not be too quickly interpreted as signs of serious problems (E. Erikson, 1975). Erikson also believes that in addition to fairly successful identity formation, a number of other possible identity outcomes exist along a scale of completion or resolution.

Identity conflicts are normal

Identity formation during adolescence is more complicated and demanding than in earlier childhood in purely practical terms as well. This is because it involves choices and decisions that must be made about such things as education, career, family, and personal beliefs — all of which are likely to have lifelong implications.

According to Erikson, just as the latency period that precedes puberty provides a temporary suspension or moratorium of psychosexual development, adolescence provides a **psychosocial moratorium,** during which the young adult can delay taking on adult commitments. Ideally, adolescence is when a person can be relatively free to experiment with different social roles in order to find a

A time for experimentation

Perspectives

Vanishing Markers of Adolescence

Developmental psychologist David Elkind has written extensively about the increasing pressures placed on teenagers in the United States to achieve adulthood prematurely and to forgo the special, protected period of time within which adolescents have previously constructed their personal identities. He believes that the absence of this moratorium period and the increasing stresses that the current generation of adolescents is experiencing are major contributors to the growing problems of substance abuse, pregnancy, suicide, and crime among teenagers (Elkind, 1984).

According to Elkind, the absence of a special place for teenagers in our society is evidenced by the progressive erosion of what he calls *markers* of their transition status. Markers are external signs indicating where people stand in their development.

> Markers can be as simple as the pencil lines on the kitchen wall that mark a child's progress in height from birthday to birthday, or as complex as a well-deserved promotion after years of hard work and dedication. Markers are signs of progress to others as well as to ourselves. . . . Confirmation, bar or bas mitzvah, graduation exercises, and the like provide a public acknowledgment that young people have attained new levels of maturity. (Elkind, 1984, p. 93)

Markers tell us about our past, present, and future and give us a sense of our own developmental progress. Giving up old markers that have been outgrown, such as the belief in Santa Claus or the need for training wheels, helps a youngster assess where she has been. Markers not yet attained serve as goals and guidelines for future development. For the college-bound high school student, attending college is a marker to be achieved; for the college senior, the immediate markers are likely to be graduation and getting a good job, while marriage, having children, and owning a house may serve as markers for the more distant future. In Elkind's words, "Markers protect teenagers against stress by helping them attain a clear self-definition, and they reduce stress by supplying rules, limits, taboos, and prohibitions that liberate teenagers from the need to make age-inappropriate decisions and choices" (p. 94).

Elkind discusses how the loss of five types of markers — clothing markers, activity markers, innocence markers, image markers, and authority markers — has influenced teenage development. In the last few decades, the clothing markers that distinguished teenagers from children and adults have disappeared. Thus, the bobby sox of the 1950s and the blue jeans and work shirts of the 1960s — both of which typified adolescents of these periods — have given way to a style of dress shared by individuals of all ages. In many ways, the clothing of today's teenagers is no longer distinguishable from that of younger children and adults. Because special teenage dress provided a firm, positive, secure, and automatic counterpoint to the anxiety and worry

place or niche that is clearly defined and yet seems to be uniquely made for him. He may devote this time to academic life, to trying different jobs, to travel, to social activism, or even to delinquency (a role that has been very attractive for some time), depending on prevailing social, cultural, and economic conditions as well as on his individual capacities and needs. Each society makes certain experiences available to its young people, who are also influenced by important historical changes and events such as the Great Depression and the Vietnam War. Children growing up during periods of war, poverty, and social upheaval are generally unlikely to experience the period of moratorium between childhood and adulthood. As a consequence, they may prematurely take on the work and family roles of adults and ultimately assume adult identities that are more limited than would have been the case had there been opportunities to explore alternative possibilities. On the other hand, an expansive economic and social climate such as that of the late 1950s and early 1960s provides adolescents with the opportunity to experiment and develop identities that are less restricted.

Setbacks in identity formation

Identity diffusion, or a failure to achieve a relatively integrated and stable identity, takes a number of different forms. The first is avoidance of intimacy and closeness with others. The second is a diffusion of time perspective in which there is a sense that one is out of step with others and that important opportunities may be lost forever. Time diffusion may also include feelings of depression and a sense of despair about whether the pain and confusion about identity will ever end and a comfortable sense of identity will finally be realized. The third form is a diffusion of industry, which is reflected either in an inability to con-

about height, weight, complexion, and facial features experienced during that period, its loss is significant.

Certain activities, such as organized team sports, were once the sole domain of adolescents and thus served as markers of their status. But now Little League baseball and Pee Wee hockey and soccer make these same activities and their trappings — uniforms, formal league schedules, and so forth — available to middle-years and even preschool children. The increasing degree of adult involvement and control in these activities has led to a decrease in the players' spontaneity and independence and to an overall decline in participation in high school athletics.

Elkind suggests that contemporary society no longer believes in childhood innocence or values it as a characteristic, and thus innocence markers have vanished as well. Young children are readily exposed through television, films, and advertising to all aspects of human life, including sexuality, aggression, and misery. Whereas such exposure is not likely in itself to destroy children's innocence, it does frighten them to see adults so out of control. More importantly, by making such information available to children whether they understand it or not, we destroy its value as a marker for those who are ready for it — in this case, older teenagers.

Image markers, the unique ways in which teenagers as a group are portrayed, have also disappeared. Teenagers were once pictured as flighty, impulsive, rash, overambitious, and in need of the restraint, common sense, and good judgment associated with adulthood. Television and films have now reversed these roles and created a new teenage image — the adultified child. This adultified child is portrayed as being sensitive, intelligent, knowledgeable, mature, and worldly; he frequently assumes leadership and parental responsibility in solving family problems. Although a view of teenagers that sees them as being less competent and mature than they actually are is problematic, so, too, is a view that pressures them prematurely to act as adults, thereby depriving them of appropriate image markers.

The final type of marker that has been undermined is the authority marker. The authority of parents and teachers, which is based primarily on superior competence, wisdom, and experience, has been weakened by increasing pressures on families and schools and decreasing economic and social support for the adults who rear and educate children. Media images reinforce a picture of children and teenagers who assume authoritative adult roles that have been abdicated by parents and teachers who are unable to fulfill their traditional roles of leadership and authority.

centrate on required or suggested tasks such as school or work or in a self-destructive preoccupation with some one-sided activity such as reading.

The fourth form of identity diffusion is the choice of a **negative identity,** which involves rejection and disparagement of the roles offered by one's family or community as proper and desirable and an acceptance of socially undesirable roles, such as that of the delinquent. Erikson suggests that widespread negative adult attitudes toward teenagers serve to convince many troubled teenagers who are struggling with negative identities that the role of delinquent is best (E. Erikson & Erikson, 1957). Problems of identity confusion are more likely to occur and are more difficult to resolve in families that are experiencing serious problems such as alcoholism and other drug abuse, physical and sexual abuse, marital conflict, and parental separation and divorce.

Various historical, cultural, and personal events and experiences may affect how one's identity is resolved. For example, many people who grew up during the Great Depression developed identities that were preoccupied with work, economic survival, and self-sacrifice, whereas some people who grew up in the 1960s, when traditional social roles were being rejected, developed identities based on alternative roles.

The Relationship Between Identity and Intimacy For Erikson, successful resolution during adolescence of the crisis of identity versus identity confusion prepares the individual to move on to confront the central crisis of early adulthood: intimacy versus isolation. A fairly clear and coherent sense of identity is **Identity resolution as basis for intimacy**

A Multicultural View

The Development of Ethnic Identity in Minority Group Adolescents

Belonging to a minority group plays an important role in the formation of identity during adolescence. To assess the stages that are involved in ethnic identity development, Jean Phinney conducted in-depth interviews with ninety-one Asian-American, black, Hispanic, and white, American-born tenth-grade students from integrated urban high schools representing both lower and middle-class backgrounds (Phinney, 1989).

The interviews assessed the students' exploration of ethnicity, commitment to an ethnic identity, and attitudes about ethnicity. Exploration was assessed with questions such as, "Do you ever talk with your parents or other adults about your ethnic background or what it means to be. . . ?" and "Have you ever thought about whether your ethnic background will make a difference in your life as an adult?" Commitment to ethnic identity was assessed with questions such as, "Some people find these questions about their background pretty confusing and are not sure what they really think about it, but others are pretty clear about their culture and what it means to them. Which is true of you?" Attitudes about ethnicity were assessed by questions such as, "Are there things you especially like or enjoy about your own cultural background or things you consider to be strengths of your culture?"

*Subjects were reliably assigned to one of three following stages of ethnic identity development; these stages were derived from previous theory and research (Meil-man, 1978; Waterman, 1982; Archer, 1982; Phinney & Tarver, 1988; Jones, 1989).

1. *Diffusion/foreclosure:* Little or no exploration or understanding of one's ethnicity or of the issues involved sometimes joined with a strong but unexamined attitude about one's ethnicity that has been learned from one's family
2. *Moratorium:* Evidence of exploration, accompanied by some degree of confusion about the meaning of one's own ethnicity
3. *Achievement:* Evidence of exploration and of a clear, secure understanding and acceptance of one's own identity

Phinney found no significant differences based on ethnic group or sex in the percentages of youngsters at each stage of ethnic identity development. Regardless of the specific ethnic group or sex, these youngsters faced a similar need to deal with the fact that they belonged to a minority ethnic group in a predominantly white society. In contrast, the white students did not show any evidence of these stages and were frequently unaware of their own ethnicity apart from being American. Phinney notes that these results may imply an ethnocentric view that is out of touch with the increasingly pluralistic nature of our

*Bridges   What stages do minority group adolescents go through in developing a sense of ethnic identity?

needed to tolerate the loss of self that intense relationships often threaten and the loneliness and isolation that the end of such relationships brings. It is not unusual for teenage couples to break up suddenly and then unexpectedly reconcile; this behavior may in part reflect a level of identity resolution that is not yet adequate to the task of sustained intimacy. Thus, the development of identity provides the necessary basis for intimacy.

In addition, achievement of a clearer sense of identity is an important basis for developing and maintaining intimacy in friendships and love relationships as a young adult and for making a good choice of a life partner. It is much more difficult to successfully work out conflicting needs and expectations with someone who does not have a clear picture of who she is and what she needs or to meet someone else's needs if you are unclear about who you are and what you need.

A somewhat different view of the relationship between identity and intimacy was proposed by Harry Stack Sullivan in his interpersonal theory of development (H. Sullivan, 1953). According to Sullivan, the achievement of intimacy is the central task of adolescence. Intimacy develops first through same-sex friendships, or "chumships," during early adolescence and then through heterosexual relationships in the middle stages of adolescence.

Identity Status   Guided by Erikson's ideas, researchers have been able to study identity development during adolescence. James Marcia, for instance, interviewed eighteen- to twenty-two-year-old students about their occupational choice and

society. It is estimated that by the mid-1990s, minority youths will make up more than 30 percent of the fifteen- to twenty-five-year-olds in this country.

Approximately 55 percent of the tenth-graders studied were in the initial stage of ethnic identity, which is characterized by the absence of exploration of ethnicity as an identity issue. Evidence of both ethnic identity diffusion and foreclosure was found, although there was little evidence of negative attitudes toward their own ethnic group for foreclosed individuals. The following responses are representative for students at this stage: "Why do I need to learn about who was the first Black woman to do this or that? I'm just not too interested" (black female). "I don't go looking for my culture. I just go by what my parents say and do, and what they tell me to do, the way they are" (Mexican-American male) (p. 44).

Approximately one-fourth of the youngsters studied showed evidence of the second, or moratorium, stage of ethnic identity search. The following responses illustrate the experiences of youngsters at this stage: An Asian-American male said that "there are a lot of non-Japanese people around me and it gets pretty confusing to try and decide who I am." A Mexican-American female said, "I want to know what we do and how our culture is different from others. Going to festivals and cultural events helps me to learn more about my own culture and about myself" (p. 44).

Finally, about one-fourth of the youngsters in the study appeared to be in the third, or achievement, stage of ethnic identity, as evidenced by their understanding and acceptance of themselves as minority group members. A black female put it this way: "I used to want to be White, because I wanted long flowing hair. And I wanted to be real light. I used to think being light was prettier, but now I think there are pretty dark-skinned girls and pretty light-skinned girls. I don't want to be White now. I'm happy being Black" (p. 44).

Only one-fifth of all of the subjects, including some from each stage, had negative attitudes toward their own group as indicated by a desire to change their ethnicity if they could. These are mainly Asian-American students, which is surprising given the generally positive view of Asians in American society. Phinney reports that the interview responses of these students reveal the lack of a social movement stressing ethnic pride as has been available to blacks and Mexican-Americans. Phinney also suggests that the attitudes of Asian students tended more toward assimilation than toward ethnic pride and pluralism.

religious and political beliefs and values (Marcia, 1967, 1980). He classified them into four categories of **identity status** based on two judgments: (a) whether or not they had gone through an "identity crisis" as described by Erikson and (b) the degree to which they were now committed to an occupational choice and to a set of religious and political values and beliefs. The four categories are:

Four states of identity development

1. *Identity achievement* Individuals in this group had experienced a crisis and were now committed to an occupation and to a religious and political ideology. Both their occupational choices and religious and political beliefs were based on serious consideration of alternatives and were relatively independent of those of their parents.

2. *Identity diffusion* These students may or may not have experienced a crisis but showed little commitment to or concern about occupational choice and religious and political beliefs.

3. *Moratorium* Individuals in this category were presently *in* crisis, actively struggling to make commitments and preoccupied with achieving successful compromises among their parents' wishes, the demands of society, and their own capabilities.

4. *Foreclosure* These students had not had a crisis but expressed commitment. Interestingly, it was difficult to tell where their parents' goals for them ended and where their own goals began. Their college experiences served only to confirm their childhood beliefs, which they held to rather rigidly.

Identity achievement increases with age

In general, adolescents seem to progress in status toward identity achievement. Researchers using Marcia's categories have found that for both males and females, identity achievement is rarest among early adolescents and most likely among older high school students, college students, and young adults. Although identity achievement significantly increases and identity diffusion and foreclosure significantly decrease during the high school and college years, identity diffusion and identity foreclosure remain the most common identity statuses during junior and senior high school. Only about one-third of college juniors and seniors and one-quarter of adults are found to have reached identity achievement status (Meilman, 1979; Archer, 1988). Frequency of identity status appeared to differ with the specific content area involved. Identity achievement was most likely to occur in the areas of vocational choice and religious beliefs and moratorium in the vocational choice area, whereas foreclosure was most likely in the area of sex-role preferences and identity diffusion in the area of political philosophies (Meilman, 1979; Pomerantz, 1979; Waterman, 1982; Archer, 1982).

Few male-female differences

Few differences between males and females have been found on measures of identity. Both genders are equally represented among the four identity statuses and seem to develop in similar ways. Although early studies suggested that the identity statuses might have different psychological meanings and consequences for males and females, more recent research indicates that the meanings and implications of the statuses appear to be quite similar for both males and females (Gilligan, 1987; Archer & Waterman, 1988).

SOCIAL RELATIONSHIPS DURING ADOLESCENCE

The search for identity affects all of an adolescent's relationships. Ties with parents must make room for increasing interest in peers and a new commitment to the life among comparative equals that peers provide. A young teenager's efforts to become more physically and emotionally separate from his parents and closer to his friends may be stressful, but more often than not, the problems and conflicts of this period are relatively minor. Full-blown upheavals happen to only a minority of families of adolescents in spite of popular stereotypes to the contrary (Rutter et al., 1976).

Relationships with Parents

A generation gap?

It is a widely held belief in our culture that leaving home, at least in a psychological sense, is an important part of the process of becoming a self-reliant individual and achieving an identity. Much of this process occurs during adolescence, and the differences in experiences and understandings between parents and their leave-taking children account for what is sometimes referred to as the **generation gap.** Leaving home is a powerful metaphor for finishing the developmental tasks of adolescence and symbolizes the end of childhood (Coleman, 1980). Many of the conflicts between adolescents and their parents over chores, curfews, school, and social activities reflect mutual ambivalence about the imminent separation. For example, consider an eighteen-year-old about to leave for college. Her blatant disregard of household responsibilities and violations of clearly agreed-upon rules leads her father to angrily say, "As long as you are living in my house, you had better abide by the rules; otherwise, you can move out tomorrow." In a sense both teenager and parent probably desire and dread

Although leaving home is often accompanied by mixed feelings, the overall quality of adolescent-parent relationships often improves after teenagers have left.

the separation; their fights reflect their struggles to resolve their conflicting feelings.

Interestingly, the overall quality of adolescent-parent relationships may improve after teenagers have left home. For example, in one study, two hundred adolescent males starting college and their parents were asked to describe their relationships with one another at two points in time: at the end of the men's senior year in high school, when they were all still living at home, and during the first months of their freshman year. One-half of the students were commuters who continued to live at home, and one-half lived in a dormitory or apartment. Those students who no longer lived at home showed greater affection toward their parents, improved communication, and a greater sense of independence (R. Sullivan & Sullivan, 1980).

The identity confusions that teenagers experience may restimulate similar unresolved feelings in their parents. For many parents, adolescent changes create or magnify conflicts in their own lives. As one parent put it, "Sometimes I'm not sure which is more upsetting to me, my teenage daughter's pain and confusion about who she is or similar feelings which are stirred up from my own difficult adolescence."

Parental empathy and envy

Parents may be threatened by their teenager's experimentation with sex or may be jealous of him, particularly if he has economic privileges, social opportunities, and freedom from responsibility that they themselves did not have in adolescence. And even if they are well established in their careers, family life, and personal identity, middle-aged parents often feel caught between the conflicting demands and needs of their adolescent children, their own aging parents, and their own lives (Rapoport et al., 1980).

Their children's seemingly unlimited opportunities for career and happiness sometimes confront parents with the limitations of their own work and emotional lives. Thus, their dissatisfaction and upset can make them difficult people for adolescents to live with. As one twenty-year-old girl who was about to leave for an exciting summer job in another country put it:

Mom has been absolutely impossible for this last month, and Dad hasn't been much better. They can be so rigid and unreasonable, and even the smallest thing can set them off. Sometimes I think that Mom thinks that *she* is the one who is actually going and that Dad criticizes whatever I do because he is afraid that I will be more successful than he. I get angry and tell him to find someone else to help solve his midlife crisis. Sometimes raising middle-aged parents can be an absolute drag!

On the positive side, however, we should note that although teenagers and their parents at times feel overwhelmed by the challenges of adolescence, on the whole it is the exciting and rewarding culmination of a long process of developmental change in the parent-child relationship. In fact, the majority of adolescents and parents continue to share important values and to get along rather well together (Csikszentmihalyi & Larson, 1984).

Bridges How great a gap is there typically between the values and attitudes of teenagers and those of their parents?

Parents and children share similar attitudes about important issues and decisions: about ideas of right and wrong, for example, or what makes a marriage good, or what the long-run value of education is (Coleman, 1980). Where they differ is more in the emphasis or strength of those attitudes. One teenager and his parent may agree that premarital intercourse is not by nature wrong but may disagree about the specific conditions under which it is all right. A second teenager and her parent may argue about the comparative importance of a career in medicine versus one in law, but both will agree that getting some sort of education is important.

Agreement on basic values

Adolescents and parents most often disagree about matters affecting the teenager's current social life and behavior, such as styles of dress, hair length, choices of friends, social activities, participation in household chores and family activities, and choice of music. For preferences such as these, teenagers agree more with their peers than with their parents. Yet no one — not even the teenager himself — considers such personal preferences as important as more basic attitudes or values because the latter usually guide many life choices over long periods. When asked how much they value various people's opinions, adolescents consistently rated their parents' advice more highly than their friends' advice (Curtis, 1975).

How large a gap is there between generations? It depends on the age of the adolescent and who is making the evaluation. It is likely that early adolescents

Most parents and teenagers have plenty of disagreements and conflicts, but they tend to share long-run interests, goals, attitudes, and values.

who are in the differentiation and practicing subphases of identity formation will report greater differences with their parents than older adolescents in the rapprochement and consolidation subphases. Overall, adolescents tend to overestimate and parents to underestimate both the extent of parental influence and the size of the generation gap (Bengston & Troll, 1978; Lerner & Shea, 1982). When asked what attitudes they think the other generation holds about global issues such as disarmament, the real differences that emerge are smaller than what teenagers guess and larger than what parents guess they are (Lerner & Knapp, 1975).

Parenting Styles   Four aspects of parent-adolescent relationships appear to be involved in the adolescent's development of identity: (a) parental interest and involvement, (b) the emotional intensity of family interaction, (c) the degree and nature of family conduct, and (d) the nature of parental authority. The most successful adolescent experiences seem to occur in families in which interest, involvement, and intensity of interaction are at moderate levels — families in which teenagers are able to express their own viewpoints freely, even if those viewpoints conflict with those of their parents, and in which they can actively participate in family decision making (Douvan & Adelson, 1966).

In a study involving more than seven thousand adolescents, researchers found that teenagers felt most positively about two parental styles, **democratic parenting** and **equalitarian parenting.** Democratic parents generally encouraged their children to participate in discussions and consulted them about decisions but reserved the right to make the final decisions; equalitarian parents tried to give adolescents equal say in decisions. Teenagers gave their lowest ratings to parents who were **autocratic** and did not consult with their children in making family decisions (Elder, 1980). These results are consistent with other research, discussed in Chapter 10, which has found that parents who use democratic styles of child-rearing (as contrasted with authoritative, authoritarian, and permissive child-rearing styles) provide children with both the opportunity to gain experience in decision making and an adequate degree of adult guidance and control (Baumrind, 1989).

Benefits of democratic style

There is some indication, however, that a fine line exists between sensitive, respectful involvement and intrusive overinvolvement that does not adequately respect adolescents' need for separateness and independence. Here is what Allen, who is almost sixteen, has to say:

> I really appreciate that my parents are interested in what I am doing and what I am feeling — in whether I am happy or unhappy — but sometimes it's just too much. Like, I don't always know just how I am feeling, or maybe I don't feel like talking to them about things. It sometimes makes me guilty to keep things from them, but I think that I have a right to. I sometimes get angry that they can't respect me as being a separate person from them.

In summary, it is not surprising that parents and children get along best in families who make and carry out decisions consistently and jointly, who perceive those decisions as being fair and reasonable rather than arbitrary, and who respect the developmental needs and sensitivities of all family members — both parents and children.

The quality of the relationship between a teenager and her parents may strongly influence the course of her identity development. To the extent that parents encourage her to see herself as a unique, worthwhile, competent, and independent person who is capable of entering the adult world — and also give her the opportunity to explore and integrate the different and sometimes conflicting aspects of her identity — their contribution will be highly positive. To the extent that circumstances and the parents' own personal limitations prevent them from doing this, the teenager will have a more difficult time achieving an integrated and resilient adult identity. For example, if parents are upset with their daughter's "punk" life-style and sexual experimentation because of their own conflicts in these areas and if they therefore belittle her, it may pressure her to foreclose her identity prematurely.

Social-Class Differences   As we note earlier in the chapter, adolescents are significantly influenced by the type of family in which they grow up. One useful way of describing families is by social class, which is determined by parents' level of education, income, and type of work, as well as by their life-style and cultural values. A major series of studies of families in the United States, Great Britain, and Italy revealed some important social-class differences that affected adolescents' development (Kohn, 1969).

In general, differences between the values, child-rearing practices, and expectations of middle-class parents and working- and lower class parents closely paralleled differences in the nature of their day-to-day work experiences. For example, parents who worked as professionals (doctors, lawyers), who were upper level executives, or who owned their own businesses generally experienced a high degree of autonomy and independence in deciding how they spent their time at work. Although they often worked quite hard and earned high salaries, much of their sense of satisfaction came from intrinsic sources that they controlled, rather than from extrinsic sources that were controlled by others. Their values and expectations for their children were consistent with these experiences. Adolescents in middle-class families were encouraged to be independent and to regulate or control their own behavior, rather than to rely upon the rewards or punishments of others to determine how they would act. The parents' child-rearing styles tended to be democratic or authoritative rather than authoritarian.

Although lower-middle-class adolescents shared such influences, they were oriented more toward jobs than careers. A study that compared the work expectations of students at an elite, a midrange, and a working-class university revealed that working-class students were much less likely to aspire to professional careers and anticipated having lower levels of leadership and control over their day-to-day work than did children of middle- and upper-middle-class families. In addition, differences in student perceptions of the degree to which their schoolwork was internally motivated (intrinsically controlled) or extrinsically motivated (behaviorally controlled through grades and other tangible rewards) paralleled the social-class makeup of the colleges (Hoffnung & Sack, 1981).

Compared with middle-class families, working-class parents were much more authoritarian in their child-rearing patterns and until their children were ready to leave home were less likely to support their children's attempts to be independent and to participate in family decision making (Kohn, 1969). Both their work experience and their family life were more likely to emphasize conformity to extrinsic expectations. For instance, the amount of punishment that a working-class teenager received for unacceptable behavior was apt to be based on the amount of damage he did rather than on his motivation; the opposite was more likely to be true in middle-class families.

Divorce, Remarriage, and Single Parenthood   It is common knowledge that divorce rates have increased dramatically during the past twenty-five years and that almost one-half of marriages will end in divorce. It is estimated that one-third of all eighteen-year-olds in 1990 will have lived with a divorced parent, and of the children born in the 1980s, almost one-half will spend an average of six years in a one-parent household (Glick, 1979; Glick & Lin, 1986).

The impact of separation and divorce on adolescent development is influenced by a variety of factors, including when the divorce occurs, the nature and length of the family conflicts that lead up to and follow the divorce, the quality of the child's relationship with both the absent parent (usually the father) and the parent who has primary physical custody, and the economic circumstances

---

Bridges   Are there significant social-class differences in parental values, child-rearing practices, and expectations for their teenage children?

Middle-class families: careers

Middle-class families: intrinsic motivation

Lower-middle-class families: jobs

Working-class families: extrinsic motivation

A Talk with Don

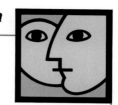

Social Relationships Among Adolescents

Don took time out between homework and football practice to be interviewed. He is athletically built and of average height.

Interviewer: In general, what do kids your age look for in friends?

Don: Right now, a friend to me can be anybody. I don't care if they have a drinking problem. That's up to them, although I wouldn't like a person to drink too much. I have a lot of friends who are college freshmen already, I have friends who are my own age, and I have friends who are sophomores and juniors in high school.

Interviewer: What are relationships like with parents for kids your age?

Don: I think they give you a lot more freedom when you're a freshman or sophomore and come down on you when you're a junior or senior. They tell you that once you get your license, you can drive me around and you can do this or that once you start dating; they won't be as strict. But it tends to be somewhat the opposite. Like I didn't get my license until I was almost eighteen years old.

Interviewer: How come?

Don: My father, who I am living with right now, my only parent, kind of uses a two-way street. He tends to say, "Don't bring up the past when you're trying to prove your point," but when he's trying to prove his point, he always brings up the past. He'll say something like, "You're almost grown, but while you're living under my roof, you'll play by my rules." So you're in a no-win situation. It's plain and simple.

Interviewer: How did this affect your getting a license?

Don: My father would not let me go for my license test until he thought that I drove at a level that he was proud of. He said, "I don't want you to be like all those other kids who can barely drive." I wouldn't say I'm a pro or specialist, but I was at a higher level and my skills were more refined when I got my license. That's how my father wanted it to be, and I'm happy now because of it. And I say, "Hey, well, he was right." I can drive better. I can drive on the highway and in the city and take control of certain situations when another person might freeze.

Interviewer: What other hassles do older teenagers have with their parents?

Don: Being a senior now I find that I never really know what my parent is going to say. I mean, I'll come in and he'll say, "Ah, it's one-thirty," and you start to say, "The movie didn't get out until this time, we had a flat tire, we ran out of gas . . ." and he goes, "It's okay, just be in a little bit earlier next time." And you go upstairs and you sit there and go, "Huh?" And then another time, you come in and he says, "It's two-thirty — where have you been?" and you're saying, "We were just all over Freddie's house, we rented a couple of movies and we watched them on the VCR, and after that we sat and talked about our teachers. Nothing really big; it was a boring night." And he says, "It's two-thirty, you should have been in here a long time ago," and this time he really gets on me. So you say, "I really don't understand this." And it gets a lot trickier, too. They start saying things like, "You're going to be in college next year. You should work on this because when you go to college, your roommate won't want you to have a messy room."

Interviewer: Are your parents worried about your leaving?

Don: Maybe not worried too much but worried to a point of thinking, "Have I taught him the right way, or have I taught him enough to make his own way?"

Follow-up Questions

1. Which parenting style best characterizes the relationship between Don and his father?

2. What indications do you see of a generation gap between Don and his father?

3. Which of Josselson's four subphases of individuation are reflected in Don's description of his social relationships?

of the family after the divorce. Separation from the father early in life seems to have a greater effect on both girls and boys than later separation does (Levitin, 1979; Wallerstein, 1984, 1987; Wallerstein & Corbin, 1989; Hetherington et al., 1982).

As we have pointed out, adjusting to divorce is a long-term process that in some ways resembles mourning the death of a loved one. Divorce and its aftermath are particularly hard for teenagers, who are so sensitive about being "normal" and are so insecure about their identities. Follow-up studies of divorcing families reveal that even ten years afterward, many adolescent children still struggle to resolve their anger and self-blame and to accept the permanence of the divorce. Barbara, a seventeen-year-old whose parents separated when she was ten, reported that "my mom and I are real close now. I stopped being angry at her when I was fifteen, when I suddenly realized that all of the kids who lived in tract houses with picket fences were not any happier than I was. It took me a long, long time to stop blaming her for not being in one of those houses." (Wallerstein, 1983, p. 239).

Divorce's effect on intimacy

It can also be difficult for an adolescent in a divorced family to achieve realistic hopes about his own love relationships. Jay, who is fourteen, said, "Dad left because Mom bored him. I do that all the time." And Pamela, also fourteen, said, "I'm afraid to use the word *love*. I tell my boyfriend that I love him, but I can't really think about it without fear" (Wallerstein, 1983, p. 241). Perhaps the most important factor in an adolescent's adjustment to divorce is his *parents'* ability to resolve their own angry feelings and to allow their child to do the same.

The quality of postdivorce relationships with divorced parents and current families appeared to be a major factor in influencing how successfully these adolescents were in negotiating the tasks of later adolescence and young adulthood (Wallerstein, 1987; Wallerstein & Blakeslee, 1989). But, the conclusion that divorce directly causes these effects is probably unwarranted, at least not until we have research that compares children of divorce with children from families with parents who have equally troubled marriages but who do not divorce.

Although a single-parent family is the most likely outcome of divorce, there are several other possibilities: the single parent may remarry, bringing a stepparent into the family; or she may not remarry but may bring an informal stepparent into the family. In some cases, divorced parents continue to share parenting with or without sharing legal custody. Whatever the arrangement, the family's economic situation and the social and emotional resources and support available to its members are key factors (Blechman, 1982).

Single parents lack social support

For single parents, support is often hard to find, and sometimes hard to accept when it is offered. Said one single parent, "Help from my old married friends was a mixed blessing — they cared for me and their help was invaluable. Yet my dependence on them kept me tied in with part of my life that I was moving away from" (Boston Women's Health Book Collective, 1978, p. 146).

Stepparents may seem intrusive

On the other hand, the addition of a stepparent can be particularly difficult for an adolescent because of the extensive family history that the new spouse has not shared, the lack of commonly accepted roles for stepparents and stepchildren, and the teenager's intense need to be independent of adult control and authority. Both teenagers and their parents may also find it difficult to switch to a new set of rules and expectations (Lutz, 1983). Sometimes children adjust by enlarging their view of the family to make room for three parents — mother, father, and stepfather. For example, when Jerry, who is fifteen, was asked how often he saw his father, he asked, "Which dad do you mean?" But at other times, acceptance of a stepfather can be a problem (Parke, 1981, p. 97). Phillip, a sixteen-year-old whose parents separated almost four years ago, describes it this way:

> At first I was very upset about my mom and dad breaking up. Like, I knew that they weren't getting along for quite a while, but I never thought that they would really split up. It's all right now and I get to see my dad pretty regularly. But the biggest problem is my mom's new husband. He thinks that he's my father or stepfather or something, and tries to boss me around. No way! Things were better when it was just me and my mom.

As we have already briefly noted, although relationships with their parents are very important, adolescent identity is shaped by other social influences as well. One of the most important are a teenager's friendships with peers.

Friendship

Friends matter a lot during adolescence. Friends offer easier and more immediate acceptance than do most adults, who often are trying to "improve" many of a teenager's behaviors and skills, and so friends ease the uncertainty and insecurity of the adolescent years. They offer reassurance, understanding and advice, and a person to talk with when necessary.

Sam is thirteen. Here is how he describes what a best friend is:

> A best friend to me is someone you can have fun with and you can also be serious with about personal things, about girls or what you're going to do with your life or whatever. My best friend, Jeff, and I can talk about things. His parents are divorced too, and he understands when I feel bummed out about the fights between my mom and dad. A best friend is someone who's not going to make fun of you just because you do something stupid or put you down if you make a mistake. If you're afraid of something or someone, they'll give you confidence. (R. Bell, 1980, p. 62)

An unquestioning appreciation of friends helps adolescents to become more independent of parents and other symbols of authority and to resist the seemingly arbitrary demands of family living. Friends also promote independence simply by providing knowledge of a world beyond the family. Teenagers learn through their friends that not every young person is required to be home by the same hour every night, that some parents expect their children to do more household chores than other parents do, and that other families hold different religious or political views.

Qualities of Adolescent Friendships   Studies of adolescent peer relations reveal a trend toward greater **mutuality** in friendship through increased loyalty and intimacy over the teen years (Douvan & Adelson, 1966; Douvan & Gold, 1966).

Bridges How do peer groups and friends contribute to teenagers' psychosocial development?

Sharing interests with friends is important to teenagers, as it is to children. At the same time, though, less tangible qualities such as loyalty, mutual respect, and intimacy become increasingly important in friends — especially among older adolescents.

Researchers conducting one large-scale study asked children and adolescents to define friendship; to describe how two people initiate, maintain, and end a friendship; and to explain how people become close or best friends. Adolescents indicated that mutual understanding and intimacy were most important, whereas children emphasized shared activities.

Appreciating others' uniqueness

Mutual understanding involves an appreciation of how different people can interact in ways that are mutually beneficial. Unlike younger children's cooperation, adolescent mutuality depends on the understanding that other people share some of one's own abilities, interests, and inner experiences and on an appreciation of each person's uniqueness. In fact, a characteristic of early adolescence is a fascination with the particular interests, life histories, and personalities of one's friends. Teenagers want to understand friends as unique individuals and to be understood by them in the same way. The ability of adolescents to recognize the advantages of *complementary relationships* — that is, relationships in which two people with different strengths and abilities cooperate for mutual benefit — makes possible friendships involving greater commitment, permanence, and loyalty (Youniss, 1980; Damon, 1983).

Mutual emotional sharing

The other main dimension of friendship for teenagers is **intimacy** — feelings of closeness. Intimacy comprises three aspects: self-revelation, confidence, and exclusivity, which teenagers describe in the following ways:

> A friend is a person you can talk to, you know, show your feelings and she'll talk to you. You can talk more freely to a friend. Someone you can tell your problems to and she'll tell you her problems. They are open. . . . A friend is a person you can really tell your feelings to. . . . You can be yourself with them.

> Friends can keep secrets together. They can trust that you won't tell anybody. You won't expect them to tell anybody else. You know she won't tell anybody anything. If you tell somebody something, they won't use it to get revenge on you when you get into a fight. You talk about things you wouldn't tell other people. (Youniss, 1980, p. 181)

Now that we have described the importance of mutuality and intimacy in adolescent friendships and how these features differ from friendships in childhood, let us take a brief look at differences between male and female friendships.

Girls show greater intimacy

Male-Female Differences   Intimacy as reflected in a friend's willingness to disclose things about herself and to be empathetic to another person's feelings is a key aspect of friendship. In a study of changes in intimacy among fifth-, seventh-, ninth-, and eleventh-graders, researchers found that friendships formed by boys had lower levels of intimacy than those of girls (Sharabany et al., 1981). Girls appeared to be better able to express feelings and to be more comfortable with giving emotional support than boys were.

Girls also developed more intimacy with the opposite sex than boys did. Although fifth-grade boys and girls showed little intimacy with the opposite sex, seventh- and ninth-grade girls reported much more intimacy with boys than boys did with girls. Toward the end of the eleventh grade, however, differences in reported intimacy between same-sex and opposite-sex friends decreased.

How might these differences in intimacy be explained? Perhaps the most likely explanation is that they are products of traditional sex-role stereotyping, which defines and values intimacy much more as a feminine quality than as a masculine one. Adolescent girls tend to have one or two close friends, whereas adolescent boys tend to have many friends with whom they are less intimate. It is also likely that adolescent males equate intense intimacy exclusively with heterosexual friendships, whereas females at this age are more comfortable in being close with both male and female friends. These and related issues are explored more fully later in this chapter.

Peer Groups

For most adolescents, social relationships extend beyond family and individual friends to include **peer groups,** or age mates who know each other, sometimes quite well. Adolescent peer groups share many of the characteristics of those in middle childhood (see Chapter 13 for further discussion of middle childhood): they involve social equals who are of roughly the same age, maturity, and background and who enjoy spending time together pursuing shared activities and goals. Peer groups, however, play an even greater role in the everyday life of adolescents than the peer groups of younger children do, and they are much less likely to be all male or all female.

For a teenager, peers are a central source of information about himself and others. They provide him with critical information about who he is, how he should act, what he is like, and so forth. They serve as a basis for making comparisons between his own actions, attitudes, and feelings and those of others.

One major study used participant observation, interviews, questionnaires, and journals to learn about the social interactions of 303 boys and girls ages thirteen to twenty-one. The participants were studied at beaches, social clubs, parties, on street corners, and inside their homes and were asked about their friendships and other peer relationships (Dunphy, 1963). The researchers discovered two types of peer groups. The first, the **clique,** was a closely knit group of two or more people who were intimately involved in a number of shared purposes and activities and who excluded those who were not. The second, the **crowd,** was a larger, less cohesive group of between fifteen and thirty people. Adolescent crowds were generally informal associations of two to four cliques.

Membership in a clique allows a teenager to have a few select friends whom she knows well and who share important interests and activities, whereas membership in a crowd provides contact with a much broader group of peers on a more casual and informal basis. The small size and the intimacy of a clique make it like a family in which the adolescent can feel comfortable and secure; the major clique activity seems to be talking, and cliques generally meet during the school week. Crowds usually gather at parties and other organized social functions, which typically take place on weekends.

How Do Peer Groups Develop?   As adolescents grow older, their cliques and crowds change in important ways. Early in this period, teenagers usually form same-sex cliques that have little to do with each other. Clique members are still very much like schoolchildren; family activities compete heavily with peers for recreational time, and children's general inexperience outside their families tends to prevent the development of true crowds.

With time, however, boys' and girls' cliques initiate contact with each other through activities such as meeting at a shopping mall and watching a video cassette together. These activities still offer the comparative safety of numbers; no one really has to interact intensely with a member of the opposite sex if she does not want to (although complete avoidance is no longer possible either). The first heterosexual contacts tend to be initiated by the leaders of associated cliques, and when (and if) these contacts become frequent enough, they help create a new, heterosexual clique. This change in turn helps to bring about a general shift toward heterosexual memberships in all cliques. Dual-sex cliques and crowds, however, contain the seeds of their own destruction in the sense that serious dating results in involvements that eventually reduce the importance of the clique or crowd to the participants.

Parents, teachers, and adolescents all encourage membership in peer groups (Newman, 1982). For example, parents usually discover that children in their teens have less time than ever before for family activities and are thus less subject

A basis for self-evaluation

Roles of cliques and crowds

Bridges What role does language play in adolescent cliques?

Gradual inclusion of the opposite sex

Influences favoring peer group membership

Peer group cliques such as the one pictured here help young teenagers to achieve a degree of intimacy and security and to share important interests, activities, and experiences with a few close friends.

to influence than ever before. Parents may try to make up for this by encouraging certain friendships and discouraging others. Whether or not they succeed, their efforts become a force to be reckoned with in the social life of an adolescent.

Teachers and other authorities tend to reinforce most peer groups that develop in their schools. They usually tolerate existing cliques and crowds, thereby implying approval of them; in addition, they sometimes actively encourage particular groupings of students by choosing members of one crowd to monitor the halls or members of another to organize a school dance. School authorities also rely on the leaders of cliques to help enforce school rules; when vandalism occurs, for instance, leaders are sometimes called in to identify the culprits or to help restore order.

And teenagers themselves encourage membership in peer groups. They do so partly for the reason we have already mentioned: to give themselves a socially secure base for developing a sense of personal identity and for becoming more independent of parents and other adult authorities. The support and protection of peer groups also provide a relatively safe environment in which to test out ideas and behaviors that individuals might not be secure enough to try alone, such as signing up for a drama class, dressing in a certain way, or trying drugs.

Breaking into a group can sometimes be difficult, given some adolescents' possessiveness about their relationships. Because joining a new clique or crowd is usually harder than staying in one, peer groups tend to maintain themselves, at least for a while.

Popularity and Social Acceptance   Peer groups are central to adolescent experience and provide the adolescent with a basis for evaluation of who he is and how well he is doing. Clearly, then, peer groups are extremely hard to live without. Being popular is very important to teenagers, and popularity is often linked with a particular clique or crowd. But personal qualities are also important.

Bases of popularity

In general, both boys and girls who are popular are perceived as liking other people; they are tolerant, flexible, and sympathetic and help others by making them feel accepted and involved and by planning and initiating interesting and enjoyable group activities. Popular teenagers are also described as being lively, cheerful, and good-natured and as having a good sense of humor; they possess initiative, enthusiasm, drive, and good ideas (Conger, 1977).

Teenagers who are not admired and who are most likely to be neglected or rejected outright in many ways have the opposite characteristics of those who are popular. Adolescents who are ill at ease and lacking in self-confidence and who respond to uncomfortable situations by acting timid, nervous, or withdrawn are more likely to be neglected and socially isolated by peers. In contrast, teens who handle their discomfort in an aggressive, conceited, or demanding way are apt to be actively disliked and rejected (Conger, 1977). Finally, physical attractiveness, socially visible talents, and achievements in athletics, the performing arts, and (in some environments) intellectual activity are positively related to popularity.

Conformity   Adolescents do pressure each other to conform, although probably not as much as the popular stereotype decrees. In one classic study of conformity, adolescent boys were shown simple sets of lines that differed in length in various ways (Constanzo, 1970; Asch, 1956). Each boy was asked to judge the comparative length of one particular line. He was also told how three other boys had judged the length, but he was not told that the other boys were actually fictitious. The judgments of the "other boys" were rigged so as to contradict obvious differences in the lengths of the lines. This put the real boy under pressure in making his judgments: should he go by the evidence of his own eyes, or should he conform to the obviously wrong judgments of the group? In these conditions, between one-third and one-half of all boys conformed to the imaginary group judgments. The proportion of conformers was highest among those around age twelve or thirteen and somewhat lower at older and younger ages.

Conformity experiments

Whether this finding really represents a high degree of conformity, however, depends on how we interpret it. Fifty percent conformity may sound like a lot, but in fairness to the adolescents, note that many adults conform in situations like this one. The same study found that about one-third of college-age students, around twenty years old, conformed in the same situation. To this extent, the young adolescents were not unique. Furthermore, note that the "peer groups" in this experiment were actually total strangers to the children who served as subjects. This could encourage more conformity than would be found among friends because the subjects may have been trying to be courteous and not to ruin the experiment.

Real peer groups, be they cliques or crowds, have a history of relationships that evolve over time, and the overall vitality of the group depends to some extent on its tolerance of differences in these relationships. For example, one person in a clique may slowly become its social center because she has good social skills and a great sense of humor. An articulate person may become the group's spokesperson to other cliques and in this sense become its most visible member. Still another teenager may become the group's "keeper of transportation" by virtue of owning a car or having ready access to his parents' wheels. The group derives vigor from such differences and cannot afford to demand complete conformity if it wishes to survive. At the same time, group survival is endangered by total diversity among its members; if friends feel completely free to go their own way, they may end up spending little time together and may not develop many common interests or much loyalty to one another. To avoid disintegrating, therefore, the group does need some discipline and conformity, although only in moderation.

Role variety lessens conformity

As we have seen, peer groups contribute in important ways to adolescents' overall social development and particularly to their achievement of identity. Groups are a central source of information for the adolescent about herself and

Bridges How do peer groups and friends contribute to teenagers' psychosocial development?

It is probably no coincidence that all these teenagers wear similar clothing. Adolescent peer groups do encourage conformity, although they also allow for a certain amount of diversity and role distinctions among their members.

others. Through both observation and direct interaction with peers, a teenager acquires essential social and leadership skills and an increased ability to evaluate herself and others accurately.

Groups allow experimentation

Most importantly, adolescent groups provide a support base outside of the family from which the teenager can more freely try on and experiment with the different identity roles that will ultimately contribute to her adult personality: good girl, bad girl, jock, greaser, punk, grind, clown, banger, druggie, lover, and so forth. Groups can also exert powerful pressures to conform. Especially when the family fails to serve as a constructive corrective, such pressures may contribute to a prolonged period of identity diffusion or to premature identity foreclosure — for example, as a gang member, drug addict, or teenage parent.

In the following section we briefly explore how school — a situation in which groups are very much in evidence — influences adolescent identity development.

The Influence of School

School plays a central role in the development of adolescents in the United States, who spend most of their days attending school, engaging in extracurricular activities, and doing homework. In addition to laws that require them to attend school until they are sixteen, social expectations, parental pressures, and vocational requirements help to keep most adolescents in high school through graduation and, increasingly, in post–high school education of some kind.

Schools influence identity development through the academic demands of formal curricula and through exposure to teachers who emphasize academic achievement, motivation to learn, skill mastery, self-improvement, and attitudes toward responsibility, leadership, and authority. For example, one study of junior high school boys found that strong patterns of identification with their fathers, teachers, school values, and peer groups appeared to be related to academic achievement. High achievers perceived the school as helping them to develop their talents, whereas average and low achievers saw the school as preparing them for a vocation (Ringness, 1967).

Bridges How do schools influence identity development in adolescents?

School peer groups also contribute to socialization by rewarding such attributes as athletic ability, courage, leadership, popularity, and physical attractiveness. Conflicts between the demands of peer groups and those of the curriculum are frequently related to underachievement (Braham, 1965).

An adolescent is most likely to do well in school if he feels that he can meet his teachers' expectations, that his studies are relevant to his long-range objectives, and that required skills fit in with his life-style, his emerging sense of identity, and his feelings of self-esteem. Congruence between school values and values of peers, family, and community help to foster social and academic success at school (Muuss, 1975).

Nationally, junior and senior high schools have failed to achieve such a scenario. School attendance drops significantly for teenagers who are sixteen and older. The number of ungraduated sixteen- and seventeen-year-olds in school is about 80 percent for males and females. Dropout rates for poor, black, or Hispanic teenagers are significantly higher (Conger & Peterson, 1984).

The dropout population

A study of why capable students dropped out of high school found that lower class adolescents were more likely to do so because they did not conform as readily to the school's expectations and teachers' demands and were less likely to be academically successful. They were also less successful in meeting the demands of peer groups regarding clothing, participation in extracurricular activities, and the like. They received little encouragement and support from their families, and they dropped out of school as a means of avoiding frustration and deprivation from lack of conformity to the school's and peer group's definition of success (Elliot et al., 1966).

Negative contributions to socialization

School dropouts exhibit lower self-esteem and greater alienation than do students who complete high school. Dropping out is correlated with various forms of deviant behavior, including delinquency, drug and alcohol addiction, and teenage pregnancy, all of which are more often than not related to unsuccessful identity resolutions. School failure among adolescents is related to family problems, poverty, and minority status, and failure to complete high school further compounds such problems (Fitzsimmons et al., 1969).

SEXUALITY DURING ADOLESCENCE

Not surprisingly, developmental changes in sexuality during adolescence are closely tied to the achievement of physical maturity during puberty. The popular idea that adolescence is a very sexual period of life is in fact correct, but people tend to focus on sexual intercourse and the risks of pregnancy rather than consider the broader pattern of interrelated changes that are involved.

During adolescence, the expression of sexual urges interacts closely with two other needs: the need for security, or freedom from anxiety, and the need for intimacy, or close, collaborative relationships with others. Teenagers are intensely and passionately engaged in establishing intimate relationships that are independent of their families, developing social skills, experimenting with new social roles, and establishing a unique personal identity. Sexual maturity is a central aspect of acting and feeling like a mature adult person, and of being recognized as one (Sullivan, 1953; Erikson, 1982).

Adolescent egocentrism

During this period the quality of adolescent love continues to be largely egocentric and self-centered, although the capacity to appreciate the feelings and perspectives of peers and adults even when they differ from one's own increases in older adolescents. This shift can often be uneven. For example, a teenager who is usually considerate and appreciative of the needs of other family members may on occasion "regress" and act as if her feelings and needs are the only important ones. Because teenagers are often uncomfortable with their own egocentrism, a parent who responds with moral indignation and anger is likely to be met with defensiveness and indignation in return. Relationships with family and friends that are characterized by mutual respect and understanding are likely to foster the development of altruism during adolescence.

Over the course of adolescence, teenagers move from the indirect, relatively nonthreatening sexuality of childhood to the more intense, complex, and socially "loaded" sexual feelings and activities of adulthood. Both teenagers and their parents devote a considerable amount of time and emotional energy to these issues, which we examine in this section.

Masturbation

Decrease in guilt

Survey research has indicated that approximately 70 percent of boys and 45 percent of girls said that they had masturbated by ages fifteen, and about 65 percent of boys and 50 percent of girls age sixteen to nineteen reported that they had masturbated once a week or more. Sexually experienced adolescents tended to masturbate more than those who were less experienced. Boys tended to give up masturbation when they were involved in an ongoing sexual relationship, whereas girls tended to masturbate more often (Hass, 1979; Coles & Stokes, 1985). Although exact percentages vary depending on the particular survey; the number has increased over the past several decades (Dreyer, 1982). Feelings of discomfort and guilt resulting from cultural and religious beliefs about masturbation have decreased in recent years, but many teenagers still find the subject embarrassing. When boys and girls ages thirteen to nineteen who had masturbated in the past month were asked how often they felt guilty, anxious, or concerned about it, 49 percent replied, "Sometimes" or "Often." In contrast, only 33 percent of those who had experienced premarital intercourse admitted to these same feelings (Sorensen, 1973).

It is likely that the increasing stress on developing safe sexual practices because of the AIDS epidemic will lead to increased acceptance of and decreased guilt regarding masturbation as a form of sexual satisfaction.

Sexual Fantasies

Sexual fantasies about real or imaginary situations often accompany masturbation, although adolescents of all ages report having sexual fantasies throughout their waking hours. Both sexes report that they most commonly imagine or fantasize "petting or having intercourse with someone [they] are fond of or in love with" (Miller & Simon, 1980). In one study, more than 80 percent of all college students reported this sort of theme (Komarovsky, 1976). For their second most common fantasy, however, males reported imagining anonymous sex ("petting or having intercourse with someone you don't know"), whereas women reported imagining intimate but not explicitly sexual activity ("doing nonsexual things with someone you are fond of or in love with").

Heterosexuality

Sexual Experience At every age, boys have, or at least report, more sexual experience than girls do, and, not surprisingly, older adolescents report more experience than younger ones do. By the end of high school, depending upon the particular research study, about 20 to 25 percent of young people have experienced full intercourse at least once (Elkind & Weiner, 1978). During the last thirty years, there has been a significant increase in sexual activity among adolescents, particularly among females. In the late 1960s, only 29 percent of college-age females reported having premarital intercourse as compared with 65 percent of college males; by 1980, roughly 63 percent of college females reported premarital intercourse at least once, compared with 77 percent of college males (I. Robinson & Jedlicka, 1982). (See Figure 16.1.)

Striking increase in sexual activity among females since 1960

Sexual Attitudes The "sexual revolution" of the 1960s and 1970s resulted in greater acceptance of premarital intercourse, masturbation, homosexuality, and

FIGURE 16.1
Sexual Activity Among Older Adolescents, 1965–1980
Source: Data from I. Robinson & Jedlicka, 1982.

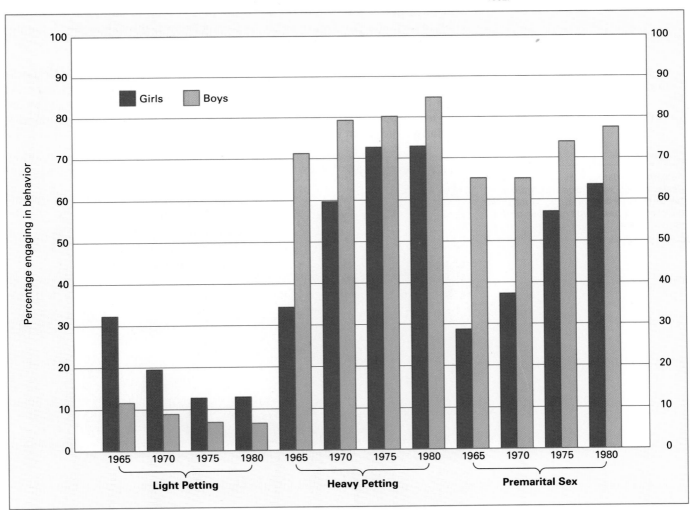

Current status of the double standard is unclear

lesbianism and a decline in the double standard that holds that sexual activity outside of marriage is less acceptable for females than for males. In the 1980s, however, teenagers appeared to have more cautious attitudes concerning sexual activity. Some studies have found that the double standard seems to have made a comeback, with both boys and girls viewing males as being responsible for initiating and pursuing sexual activity and females as being responsible for setting the limits on "how far to go." Other reports, however, have found that the double standard has declined and that both male and female adolescents reject sexual relationships that exploit women (Dreyer, 1982; Morrison, 1985; Darling et al., 1984).

Although sexual activity may now be fairly similar for boys and girls, differences in attitudes and expectations continue to exist. On the whole, girls still tend to be more conservative than boys in their sexual attitudes, values, and actions. Boys tend to be more sexually active and to have more sexual encounters. Girls are more likely to emphasize intimacy and love as a necessary part of sexual activity and are less likely to experience sex merely as a physically pleasurable activity. A recent study of thirty-six hundred Canadian high school students found that although there was fairly high agreement between males and females about holding hands and kissing on the first date and a fair degree of agreement regarding necking, males were much more likely to think it was all right to pet on the first date and to have intercourse on either the first date or after a few dates (Bibby & Posterski, 1985).

Girls and boys also differ in their emotional reactions to their first experience with intercourse. Girls most frequently report feeling afraid, guilty, worried, embarrassed, and curious; boys report feeling excited, thrilled, satisfied, happy, and joyful (Sorenson, 1973).

Dating   In the United States, dating is the major way in which adolescents begin their sexual activity. Dating serves a wide variety of purposes for teenagers. It can be a form of recreation involving both entertainment and sexual stimulation; it can be a way to gain status by increasing a teenager's reputation and popularity; and it can be a means of asserting independence and separating from

Dating is a central aspect of teenage life

Reasons for dating vary widely, from a desire to "be seen" and thus gain status or to have a good time, to intrinsic interest in a particular member of the opposite sex.

one's family. Teenagers also date to learn social skills and thus increase their interpersonal competence and to experiment with sexual activity. Courtship, or searching for a husband or wife, is another reason to date (Damon & Hart, 1982).

During the past ninety years there has been a trend for dating to begin earlier, thus increasing the time span over which teenage dating takes place. Currently many adolescent girls begin dating at age twelve and boys at age thirteen. By the time adolescents are high school seniors, almost one-half of the boys and more than one-half of the girls report dating at least once a week, with approximately one-third dating two or three times per week. Only a little more than one-tenth of male and female seniors report never having dated (Johnston et al., 1983).

Date Rape   "Date rape" or acquaintance rape refers to situations in which a person, usually a female, is forced to have sex with a person she is dating. It is a growing problem that affects adolescents of all ages and young adults (Elkind, 1989; Rivers & Regoli, 1987). Research indicates that the individuals involved generally know each other fairly well. In a recent study, more than six hundred college men and women were asked about their most recent dates and worst experience with sexual aggression, which was defined as any time a woman was forced to engage in sexual acts ranging from kissing to petting to sexual intercourse. More than three-quarters of the women reported being treated in a sexually aggressive way and more than one-half of the men reported acting in a sexually aggressive manner on a date, either in high school or college. Almost 15 percent of the women and 7 percent of the men said they had intercourse against the woman's will. Date rape and sexual aggression were most likely to occur between two partners who knew each other, with students reporting that they had known the partner for almost a year before the incident. Sexual aggression was most likely when a man initiated the date, provided transportation, and paid for the date. If both people got drunk or found themselves in the man's dorm room or apartment, forced sex was also more likely (Meuhlenhard & Linton, 1987).

Trends toward earlier dating

Sexual aggression on dates a widespread experience

Homosexuality

Largely due to the political and educational efforts of the women's liberation and gay rights movements, public acceptance of homosexuality has increased significantly during the past several decades. This acceptance acknowledges the right of individuals to freely practice their own sexual orientations and life-styles and to be protected from discrimination. Approximately two-thirds of adolescents interviewed approve in principle of same-sex contacts (Hass, 1979; Dreyer, 1982). In this context, a "contact" is defined as petting: touching and fondling the genitals and kissing in its various forms. Approximately 15 percent of boys and 10 percent of girls report having one sexual experience with a member of the same sex, and between 2 and 3 percent have participated in an ongoing same-sex relationship (Dreyer, 1982).

Although early same-sex play and adolescent experiences with same-sex partners typically precede "coming out" — publicly acknowledging one's homosexuality — as yet there is no agreement on the specific pattern of factors that lead to the development of homosexuality. Experiences within the family have long been considered an important contributor, but a growing number of researchers are exploring the possibility that a biological predisposition may play a central role (Offir, 1982).

Achieving a secure sexual identity is a challenging task for most adolescents. It is considerably more difficult for many gay adolescents, who may be rejected

Growing acceptance of freedom to choose

Bridges Is heredity thought to be a factor in the development of homosexuality?

by their parents, peer groups, schools, churches, and other community institutions — the very groups that adolescents depend on for support during this period of development. A seventeen-year-old girl reports; "When I told my folks that I was a lesbian, they totally freaked out. It was so against their religion, their life style and friends, that they just couldn't deal with it. I'm not living at home anymore and I hardly ever talk with them" (R. Bell, 1980, p. 115).

Although adolescent acceptance of homosexuality in others has increased during recent years, the AIDS epidemic appears to have increased irrational fears about gays, or "homophobia," among adolescents, with some teenagers reporting that they avoid gays because of fear of AIDS. A number of factors are probably involved. For one, gays have been severely stigmatized during the course of the AIDS epidemic, and adolescents are at least as prone as others to this tendency. For another, the fact that most teens still lack an accurate understanding about how AIDS is actually transmitted provides fertile ground for the development of irrational fears of casual contact with homosexuals, who have, in fact, been a high-risk group for contracting AIDS through noncasual means (for example, through exchange of body fluids). Information and support for gay teens is available from hotlines, high school and college health and counseling services, and community organizations such as the Hetrick-Martin Institute in New York, which is established to serve gay adolescents, and the National Federation of Parents and Friends of Gays (Brooks-Gunn & Furstenberg, 1987, 1988; Hein & DiGeronimo, 1989; Robinson, Skeen, & Walters, 1987).

Sex and Everyday Life

Although sex plays an important role in adolescents' feelings, fantasies, and social relationships, it does not necessarily dominate their lives. Even a single sexual experience involving intercourse is the rare exception for most junior high

Sometime during adolescence, teenagers begin to experiment with sexual activities. But teenagers may worry so much about when, how, and with whom to be sexual that they do not really get much pleasure from early sexual attempts.

school students, and although sexual activity increases during high school, most adolescents have intercourse on a rather sporadic, unpredictable basis, if at all. Masturbation and various forms of petting appear to be the mainstay of adolescent sexual activity.

Whatever their level of experience, all adolescents must somehow navigate among the various emotions, meanings, and expectations that their parents, their peers, the media, and they attach to sexuality. As we note at the beginning of this section, changes in sexuality during adolescence are tied not only to the achievement of physical maturity and the development of new social skills and social roles; they are aspects of the most important development: the emergence of a person's identity as a man or woman. Sometimes that identity is complicated by sexual issues; it can also be affected by social problems specific to teenagers, as we see in the next section.

SPECIAL PROBLEMS OF ADOLESCENCE

In Chapter 14 we discuss the special physical and health risks faced by adolescents as a group. Their lack of experience, their egocentrism, and their need to experiment with new and sometimes risky social roles in order to establish a unique identity also place them at high risk for developing certain psychosocial problems. In the following section we discuss four such special problems of adolescence: pregnancy and parenthood, physical and sexual abuse, depression and suicide, and juvenile delinquency.

Adolescent Pregnancy and Parenthood

Teenage pregnancy continues to be a major problem, despite widespread and long-standing concern. Each year more than 1 million American teenagers become pregnant. It is estimated that 19 percent of white females and 41 percent of black females become pregnant by age eighteen and that close to 66 percent of all white and 97 percent of all black teen first-time mothers were unmarried when they became pregnant (Hofferth & Hayes, 1987).

Prevalence

Poor Contraceptive Practices The great majority of teenage pregnancies are the result of inadequate or no contraception. Approximately one-half of all teenagers do not use contraceptives the first time they have sex, and many, particularly younger adolescents, delay for a year or more after first intercourse before using contraception (Hofferth & Hayes, 1987). A recent review of the research on adolescent contraceptive behavior found that many teenagers were startlingly uninformed about the basics of reproduction and believed that they were "immune" to pregnancy, or at least at very low risk. Even though birth control pills are popular, they are not reliable during the first month of use. Only foam and condoms or a diaphragm and contraceptive jelly are really effective for first intercourse. But adolescents do not like to use these contraceptives because they imply a readiness for or premeditation of sex, they are expensive or unavailable when needed, they are messy, and they reduce pleasure and increase levels of anxiety because of inexperience in their use. Irregular use of contraception is common and is correlated with economic disadvantage, poor communication with parents, lack of knowledge about parental contraceptive experience, experience of friends who become parents, low educational achievements and aspirations, high levels of anxiety, low self-esteem, and feelings of fatalism, powerlessness, and alienation (Brooks-Gunn & Furstenberg, 1988).

Bridges What role does lack of knowledge about contraception play in adolescent pregnancy?

Little knowledge about contraception

Irregular contraceptive use

Choosing Between Abortion and Parenthood   Approximately 44 percent of all teenage pregnancies end in abortion (more than four hundred thousand in 1984), and teenagers receive more than 25 percent of all abortions performed in the United States, which has one of the highest pregnancy and abortion rates for teens of any developed country. A higher proportion of pregnancies end in abortion for younger teens than older teens and for white teenagers than for black and Hispanic teenagers, who are twice as likely to give birth. Nevertheless, abortion has become a common way of managing unintended pregnancies for all teens (Hayes, 1987). Confronting an unintended pregnancy, deciding what to do, and, where chosen, having an abortion are all sources of upset for a teenager. Nevertheless, the degree, nature, and impact of abortion on a teenager depend to a large extent upon such factors as her motivations and attitudes concerning the pregnancy and abortion; the attitudes and support available from parents, other adults, peers, and her sexual partner; and her overall personal adjustment and life circumstances.

Attitudes toward pregnancy

Changing attitudes toward pregnancy have also contributed to the increase in teenage pregnancies. During the past twenty years or so, adolescent girls have grown less concerned about becoming pregnant. A growing percentage choose to keep their baby, and they seem to feel an increasing sense of responsibility for pregnancy: a study of pregnant girls revealed that in 1979, 81 percent felt responsible for their pregnancies, whereas only 26 percent felt responsible in 1963. Girls are also less worried than they used to be about how their pregnancies will affect their friendships and marriage plans (Patten, 1981).

Although most teenage mothers report that they did not plan to become pregnant and would not choose to do so if confronted with that choice, the 56 percent who decide to carry their children to term become increasingly committed to having the child during the course of the pregnancy. A teenager's reactions to unplanned pregnancy are influenced by a variety of factors, including her feelings about school, relationship with the baby's father, perceived family support for keeping the child, how many of her peers have become parents, and sense of self-esteem. Teens who decide to have an abortion tend to be good students with higher educational aspirations, are from higher socioeconomic backgrounds and less religious families, have mothers and peers who have more positive attitudes toward abortion, and are less likely to have friends and relatives who are teenage single parents. Most teen mothers do not give up their babies for adoption.

Consequences of Teenage Parenthood   One of the most helpful ways of understanding teenage pregnancy is in terms of its role in resolving the psychosocial crisis of identity during adolescence. Many teenage mothers may see having a baby as a way of prematurely crystallizing their identity, because motherhood and marriage promise to establish them in a secure adult role and to help them escape role confusion. Some boys and girls tend to believe that teenage parenthood and marriage also promise an intense, intimate, and lasting relationship with another human being, a relationship that they may have been deprived of and that figures heavily in a teenager's search for identity.

As we shall soon see, it is generally the exception rather than the rule that such fantasies are actually realized. The consequences of teenage parenthood and the identity foreclosure that it frequently entails are generally negative, not only for the teenage mother and father and their infant but for their parents, friends, teachers, and health care providers as well. For one thing, teenage mothers are more likely than older women to experience complications such as anemia and toxemia during pregnancy, as well as a prolonged labor. Their babies are more likely to be premature, to have low birth weight, and to have neurological defects. Their infants are also more likely to die during the first year.

Bridges   What are the physiological consequences of teenage pregnancy on the adolescent mother and her infant?

A young woman's life can be quite negatively affected by early child-bearing. Compared with women of similar socioeconomic background and academic aptitude who do not have children at such a young age, teenage mothers are more likely to drop out of high school. They are less likely to find stable, paid jobs; to enter stable marriages; or to achieve equal job status or income in their lifetimes. Recent longitudinal research suggests, however, that the long-term effects of early parenthood may not be as severe as was earlier thought. For example, although a high proportion of teen mothers come to rely on public assistance, the majority of teenage mothers who used public assistance in their late teens to cope with the economic strains of early parenthood eventually began working when their youngest children reached school age (Furstenberg et al., 1989). Teenage fathers appear to be less negatively affected, which is not surprising given that they do not generally assume responsibility for raising their children (Furstenberg et al., 1989).

Negative effects of early child-bearing

The children of teen mothers are also more likely to suffer developmentally. They are disadvantaged in cognitive development and in preschool and elementary school functioning and are more likely to have learning and social adjustment problems as adolescents when compared with children born to older mothers. They are also more likely to become teen parents themselves. These consequences are due in part to the fact that teenage mothers are more likely to be poor and less educated, and their children are more likely to grow up in disadvantaged neighborhoods with poor schools and high rates of family instability. Teen mothers, because they are still children themselves and focused on their own developmental needs, may also be less well emotionally equipped to be competent parents (Furstenberg et al., 1989).

Children of teenage mothers

Many of the problems of teenage parents appear to be closely tied to the social, economic, and emotional burdens of premature parenthood, as well as single parenthood, which is most often the outcome. We should keep in mind that even for the majority of adult single mothers, surviving economically and emotionally while singlehandedly raising a young child is a very difficult struggle. Thus, although many adolescent mothers are strongly committed to their children, they tend to be limited by their circumstances. Teenage fathers often have

A teenage mother's fantasies about motherhood are often dashed once her baby is born and she realizes how much time and energy mothering requires. In addition, teenage parents face a multitude of problems created by the social, economic, and emotional burdens of early parenthood.

positive attitudes toward their children but generally they lack the material and emotional resources needed to carry out the considerable responsibilities of parenthood.

Prevention and Support Programs   Prevention of teen pregnancy requires a delay of early sexual activity as well as improved use of contraceptives among teenagers who are sexually active. Prevention programs have taken four approaches: (a) educating teens about sexuality and contraception; (b) changing attitudes about early sexual involvement; (c) providing contraceptive and family planning services; (d) increasing self-esteem of girls so they have higher aspirations regarding education and career. Currently, contraception and family planning services appear to have the highest chance of success. The increased awareness of contraception because of the AIDS epidemic may have a positive effect on the prevention of teen pregnancy.

Most services to provide medical, educational, financial, and parent support have been only moderately successful. Of these, prenatal care programs have been most successful because teens who obtain adequate prenatal services are more likely to have healthy babies than those who are not. School-based medical clinics that provide easy access to contraception and an openness to teenagers and their problems have been very effective.

Some programs that have been developed to help the children of teen mothers have been directed at improving the children's cognitive and social functioning and the parenting skills of their mothers. Other programs have been designed to benefit the children indirectly by enhancing the mother's development through education and job training. These approaches have had only moderate success, largely because of lack of adequate funding rather than because of the inadequacy of the programs. Teenage pregnancy remains a significant and growing problem.

Abuse of Adolescents

Although public attention has recently focused on abuse of young children, violent encounters between adults and adolescents are quite common. Reliable figures are difficult to obtain, but national surveys of family violence indicate that approximately 66 percent of children ages ten to fourteen and 34 percent of those ages fifteen to seventeen have been hit by their parents. Surveys also indicate that 12 percent of adolescent girls have been beaten and 9 percent raped (Libbey & Bybee, 1979).

Extent of abuse

Abuse tends to be highest for children between three and four and adolescents between fifteen and seventeen. It is more likely to go unnoticed in the case of adolescents because their injuries tend to be less severe than those of younger children. This is particularly the case in communities where physical punishment such as hitting, slapping, and whipping with a belt is thought to be acceptable and in the twenty states where child abuse laws specify that only "serious injuries" must be reported (Libbey & Bybee, 1979). When a teenager has broken a rule or law and is perceived by others as intentionally contributing to the situation and therefore deserving of punishment, some people find it difficult to distinguish between discipline and abuse. And of course a teenager sometimes treats his parent in a physically abusive way.

Explanations for abuse

Three sets of explanations have been offered for abuse of adolescents. (See Chapter 10 for a discussion of the causes, treatment, and prevention of child abuse.) The first suggests that the developmental tasks of adolescence, particularly conflicts regarding separation and control, interact with the normal stresses of middle age and with socioeconomic difficulties to create a situation in which a parent "goes too far." The second proposes that parents who are immature, isolated, and irrational in their behavior respond abusively to their adolescent children who display these same characteristics. The third emphasizes the importance of poverty, job loss, and social isolation as stressful conditions that increase the likelihood of abusive behavior (Libbey & Bybee, 1979). No one explanation appears to be sufficient to explain abuse, and all three probably highlight factors that contribute in varying degrees to the likelihood of abuse. Note that young teenage parents exhibit more physical aggression toward their babies and that the offspring of adolescents experience higher rates of child abuse than offspring of older parents (Lawrence et al., 1981).

Because a parent or stepparent is generally responsible for abuse, teenagers often find it hard to know whom to turn to for help. Particularly in the case of sexual abuse, the nonabusing parent may find the reality so difficult to accept that she denies that it has happened, leaving her child with a sense of betrayal and abandonment.

Sexual abuse

Estimates of the incidence of sexual abuse vary depending upon who was surveyed, how the survey was conducted, and how abuse is defined. In one retrospective study of college students, 19.2 percent of the women and 8.6 percent of the men reported some type of sexual exploitation or abuse before age seventeen (Finkelhor, 1979). Because the victim's fears of further harm, of not being believed, and of the stigma that will result are often warranted, there is widespread underreporting of sexual abuse of children and adolescents (Kempe & Kempe, 1984).

Sexual abuse is more likely to occur under circumstances that encourage adults to have sexual feelings toward children, that reduce or overcome both internal and external factors that inhibit abuse, and that lower a child's resistance to the abusive actions (Finkelhor, 1984). For example, a lack of physical and personal privacy in a family and the encouragement of nudity and physical contact that are not clearly affectionate rather than sexual may contribute to sexual abuse. Portrayal in the media of adolescents and younger children in adult situations and roles and in sexual relationships with adults may also be a contributing factor in that it suggests that such roles and behaviors are acceptable.

Ways to decrease sexual abuse

How can sexual abuse of adolescents and children be prevented? Increasing public awareness of how frequently abuse actually occurs, of both the direct and more subtle forms that it often takes, and of the family situations and patterns of interacting that increase the risk of abuse could help to reduce its incidence. Greater awareness on the part of teachers, clergy, doctors, and other professionals of their legal responsibility to report abuse, stricter sanctions for failure to report abuse, and greater protection and support for the victims are also needed. Teenagers who report abuse must be taken seriously and not dismissed, even in the face of denial and countercharges that they are lying or that they are responsible for what happened. Of additional help would be more shelters, halfway houses, and foster homes to provide abused teenagers with a temporary or even permanent place to stay and more programs to help their families resolve the destructive patterns that have allowed the abuse to occur.

Recently, a model has been proposed to help conceptualize and evaluate the degree of trauma that results from sexual abuse. It involves four trauma-causing dynamics: traumagenic sexualization, betrayal, powerlessness, and stigmatization (Finkelhor & Browne, 1985). *Traumagenic sexualization* refers to the destructive ways in which a child's sexual feelings and attitudes are shaped in a developmentally inappropriate and interpersonally destructive way as a result of abuse. *Betrayal* refers to the process by which children discover that someone upon whom they were vitally dependent has caused them harm. *Powerlessness* refers to the process that undermines a child's ability to protect himself and assert his needs. Lastly, *stigmatization* refers to the negative connotations — including badness, shame, and guilt — that are communicated to the child and become part of his self-image and sexual identity.

This model can help to guide treatment of the adolescent victims of abuse, their families, and the abuser (who is more often than not a family member). In addition, steps should be taken to prevent a recurrence, which generally means that contact between the abuser and victim (and perhaps potential victims) must be eliminated or controlled in a way that reasonably assures all concerned parties that abuse will not happen again.

Schools can take an active role in identifying and reporting abusive situations and in helping adolescents to take active roles in learning to avoid potentially abusive situations and in seeking help from peers and professionals. The victim must overcome both the shame, guilt, and stigma involved in admitting to others that she has been abused and the fear that she will not be believed. Ultimately, communitywide changes in how people think and feel about physical and sexual violence, particularly with regard to children and adolescents, must be achieved through new laws, through education, and through economic policies that place a high value on protecting and fostering the growth and development of children and their families.

Homeless and Runaway Adolescents

It is estimated that there are approximately 1.5 million runaways and 500,000 homeless youths living on their own in the United States in a given year (Shane, 1989). Runaways are youngsters who leave home over parental objections. There are five major categories of homeless youngsters: (a) *castaways, pushouts, or throwaways*, whose parents have put them out of their homes; (b) those who have been *abandoned*; (c) those who have left by *mutual consent* with their care-giver(s); (d) those have been legally *removed by protective agencies* from their homes; and (e) those who have no home because of family *emergency*. Two additional subgroups of homeless youths — *missing/abducted* and *conditions unknown* — include many "street kids" who essentially live on the street (Hersch, 1988). A recent study of 536 clients of youth services agencies in New Jersey during a six-month period revealed that 29 percent of the sample were runaways, 60 percent were homeless, and 11 percent were missing or unaccounted for (Shane, 1989).

Troubled families

Although homeless and runaway youths come from all socioeconomic levels, racial and ethnic groups, and types of family, they are more likely to come from female-headed, single-parent, or stepfamilies with many children, and from families with multiple problems, particularly those with high levels of conflict or alcohol abuse. In addition, a variety of other problems appear to be related. These include economic adversity, substance abuse, overcrowding, impending or actual divorce or separation, remarriage, relocation, and the death of a resident relative. These children are likely to have experienced abuse (verbal, physical, emotional, or sexual), neglect, and rejection, often starting at an early age (Shane, 1989; Bassuk & Rubin, 1987).

Programs and services

Solutions to the problems of teenage homelessness and runaways include policies and programs that focus on helping their families to function more adequately in general and to successfully meet the demanding tasks of raising children, especially during the adolescent years. There is also a need for policies that allow older adolescents to become legally and financially emancipated from their dysfunctional families by making health and mental health services, education, job training, and other social benefits *directly* available to teenagers, as is the case in countries such as the Netherlands (Shane, 1989).

More immediately, improved shelters, halfway houses, and outreach programs such as Covenant House (New York City's largest shelter for homeless and runaway children) are needed (Hersch, 1988). Covenant House sends out a nightly van to offer services to "street kids" and has a "nine-line" (1-800-999-

Homeless teenagers such as these who are squatting in this empty house are part of a growing population of youngsters whose future development is at serious risk.

9999) for counseling, shelter, and other referral information. The National Network of Runaway and Youth Services runs two similar hotlines, 1-800-HIT HOME and 1-800-621-4000.

Juvenile Delinquency

Juvenile delinquency refers to antisocial and lawbreaking activities that are reported to authorities and to antisocial behavior that does not get reported. Minority and lower class teenagers are much more likely to be labeled as delinquents than are suburban, middle-class youngsters, who often commit the very same acts but do not get caught or are not reported (Empey, 1975). A large-scale interview study of almost fourteen hundred male and female teenagers found that 80 percent or more had committed delinquent acts, including drinking, theft, truancy, destruction of property, assault, gang fighting, carrying a concealed weapon, and using false identification (Haney & Gold, 1973; J. Williams & Gold, 1972).

As discussed earlier, experimentation with socially deviant roles and countercultural values and activities is a normal part of adolescent development in our society. In many ways delinquency is a distortion and exaggeration of that experimentation. The particular limitations of the teenager, her family, and her general life circumstances interact with the particular moratorium opportunities that are culturally available to prematurely solidify and make permanent roles and activities that might under other conditions be passing experiments.

Reviews of the research on delinquency reveal that family situation, friendships, and personality are associated with a teenager's delinquency. More specific factors associated with delinquency include: a poor parent-child relationship

Factors associated with delinquency

characterized by hostility, lack of affection, and underinvolvement; overly harsh and authoritarian methods of discipline; a high degree of family conflict and disorganization; and the presence of a parent with a personality disturbance and a delinquent history of her own (Sarafino & Armstrong, 1986).

Many delinquents belong to gangs, which are similar to crowds in that they include cliques but are different in that they are more highly structured and focus most of their energies on antisocial activities (Sarafino & Armstrong, 1986). Gangs provide the kind of acceptance and social support that members do not get from their families or at school. Delinquents have consistently been found to be more impulsive, more resentful of authority, less self-confident, lower in self-esteem, less happy, and less popular than nondelinquents (Sarafino & Armstrong, 1986). The gang peer group protects each member from his failures and from maturity demands from parents, teachers, and more main-stream teenagers that he is unwilling or unable to fulfill. Long-term participation in the antisocial activities and roles that are typical of gangs creates a risk of identity foreclosure and the establishment of an identity pattern that lacks positive identifications with many of the important values and goals of society that contribute to adult happiness.

Society and delinquency

The problem of juvenile delinquency is difficult to solve because its underlying source may be a basic disturbance in the relationship of society to its adolescent members. As Erikson has pointed out, successful resolution of the identity crisis of adolescence requires adequate opportunities and support for the sometimes deviant and antisocial role experimentations of that period. It also requires not only that society promise teenagers the possibility of productive lives but also that it keep that promise by providing educational, vocational, and career opportunities and support.

Nevertheless, adolescents who are in danger of being confirmed in their delinquent roles can be helped by programs that work to prevent such identity foreclosure by making available the necessary support and opportunities that will allow successful experimentation with other roles and identities. Community houses, YMCA's, police athletic leagues, summer camps, crisis drop-in centers and telephone hotlines as well as outpatient and residential treatment programs that help more disturbed teenagers and their families can help teenagers already in trouble.

Teenage Suicide

As we note in Chapter 14, suicide is the third leading cause of death among adolescents. Teenage suicide rates have continued to increase during the past three decades. In 1960, there were 8.2 male and 2.2 female suicides per 100,000 individuals between the ages of fifteen and twenty-four in the United States. By 1980, the rate had climbed to 20.2 male suicides and 4.3 female suicides per 100,000, representing a 146 percent increase for males and a 95 percent increase for females (Klagsbrun, 1981). Even though more suicide attempts are made by girls, boys succeed three times as often, in part because they use more effective methods, such as knives, guns, or other lethal weapons (Holden, 1986).

Background for suicide

Studies of the backgrounds of teenagers who attempt suicide suggest that they often experience serious family difficulties, personal turmoil, and intense loneliness and isolation and that suicide attempts are almost always cries for help (Shaffer, 1974).

Bridges What is the relationship between adolescents' feelings of depression and suicide?

Symptoms of depression usually precede a suicide attempt. These symptoms may include feelings of despair, worthlessness, and hopelessness; loss of interest and motivation in usual activities; decreased ability to concentrate and to think clearly; suicidal thoughts; loss of appetite and weight; and difficulty in sleeping. Approximately 10 percent of teenagers admitted to psychiatric hospitals and clinics receive a primary diagnosis of depression, although it is likely that some symptoms of depression are present in many other cases (Albert & Beck, 1975; D. Murray, 1973).

Being taken seriously by others, particularly when feeling upset or depressed, is a central issue in adolescents' search for recognition and identity. And yet a teenager's concerns and upsets can be too easily overlooked or dismissed by parents whose own guilt or unhappiness makes it difficult to acknowledge their children's feelings. According to Beth, who is sixteen,

> Problems that teenagers have are real. They aren't phony or unimportant. Your first crush, the first time you fall in love, deciding whether to go to college, looking for a job — hey, that's real stuff and parents should take it seriously. I know some parents say, "Oh, that's nothing. At least you don't have to worry about putting food on the table." But when you're going through a problem, I don't care who you are, it's real to you. It hurts you, and if parents make us feel like our problems aren't worth anything, then we grow up thinking our feelings don't matter. It's like *you* don't matter. (R. Bell, 1980, p. 134)

Perspectives

Teenage Suicide Prevention

Because teenagers as a group have one of the highest suicide rates, many cities have instituted educational programs, twenty-four-hour suicide hotlines, crisis intervention, and counseling services for teenagers who are threatening suicide. The following information taken from Bell is typical of that provided by suicide prevention programs (R. Bell, 1980, p. 141).

Warning Signs

1. A big change in eating or sleeping habits
2. Suddenly not caring for prized possessions — giving away favorite records, a pet, clothing
3. A loss of interest in friends
4. A long and deep depression over a breakup or the death of a beloved person
5. A great change in school grades
6. Feeling hopeless or full of self-hate
7. Feeling constantly restless or hyperactive
8. Actually making a suicide attempt

Danger Signs

1. They say they intend to hurt themselves.
2. They have a plan for how to do it.
3. They have in their possession pills or a weapon of some kind.
4. There is evidence they have already hurt themselves.
5. The person is dazed or unconscious.

In an Emergency, Contact Any of the Following:

1. Your local police
2. An adult you trust
3. An ambulance service in your town
4. The emergency room of a local hospital

DO NOT LEAVE THE PERSON ALONE!

Myths and Facts about Suicide

In [this] column are a number of myths about suicide and the facts that correct them:

Myth: People who talk about suicide don't kill themselves.
Fact: Eight out of ten people who commit suicide tell someone that they're thinking about hurting themselves before they actually do it.

Myth: Only certain types of people commit suicide.
Fact: All types of people commit suicide — male and female, young and old, rich and poor, country people and city people. It happens in every racial, ethnic, and religious group.

Myth: Suicide among kids is decreasing.
Fact: The suicide rate for young people has [increased by 137% between 1960 and 1980].

Myth: When a person talks about suicide, change the subject to get his or her mind off it.
Fact: Take them seriously. Listen carefully to what they are saying. Give them a chance to express their feelings. Let them know you are concerned. And help them get help.

Myth: Most people who kill themselves really want to die.
Fact: Most people who kill themselves are confused about whether they want to die. Suicide is often intended as a cry for help. (R. Bell, 1980, p. 142)

Although there is no way to guarantee that the signs and danger signals of suicide will be apparent or that the response will successfully prevent suicide from occurring, the above information and suggestions are likely to be helpful.

Most teenagers who are not depressed experience moments of unhappiness, and most who are depressed do not attempt suicide. Nonetheless, signs of unhappiness and depression should not be dismissed, particularly if they persist. And because a large percentage of those who attempt suicide have threatened or attempted it before, such threats should be taken very seriously.

THE EMERGING ADULT

We have now come to the end of our discussion of adolescence. We have seen how relationships with parents, friendships, and activities with groups of peers contribute to the development of identity during this stage. We have also discussed the important contribution of sexuality and sexual experiences to identity formation and explored several of the special problems that can interfere with identity achievement.

Just as the growth spurt and physical changes of puberty and the development of formal cognitive thinking at the beginning of adolescence were a culmination of the long series of maturational and cognitive changes that began with conception and birth, the achievement of identity culminates the psychosocial developments that preceded it.

Although adolescence marks both the end of childhood and the last developmental stage covered in this book, it by no means marks the end of development. As we noted at the beginning of this section, adolescence is a period of

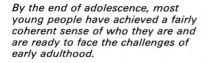

By the end of adolescence, most young people have achieved a fairly coherent sense of who they are and are ready to face the challenges of early adulthood.

transition to adulthood, and many other important developmental changes are yet to come.

The social changes of adolescence make a good place to end this book because they show vividly one of its major themes: that individuals change dramatically as they grow up. As we have seen, in a matter of months, an infant who smiles at everyone becomes devoted to particular adults and siblings; and in just a few years more, persons well outside the family compete seriously with these attachments. The other domains of development show equally dramatic changes. In just a few years, a child grows physically from diapers to climbing trees and riding a bicycle; in just a few years more, he starts looking (almost) like an adult. Cognitive changes are equally sweeping: individuals change from infants who think by looking and touching to children who can reason out concrete problems to teenagers who can imagine possibilities they have never personally experienced.

Yet no matter how dramatic they are, developmental changes remain whole, continuous, and human. For convenience, this book has divided human change into topics and discussed the topics one at a time. But real children and youths do not come divided. As this book has tried to show, children and adolescents not only grow, think, and feel; they also do all of these things at once, in a pattern that makes each person truly unique.

SUMMARY OF MAJOR IDEAS

Individuation and Identity Development

1. A key task of adolescence is successful resolution of the psychosocial crisis of identity versus role confusion.

2. The process of individuation, or becoming a separate and independent person, appears to follow a fairly predictable pattern: differentiation, practice and experimentation, rapprochement, and consolidation of self.

3. Identity formation involves selectively keeping and integrating certain aspects of one's earlier childhood identity while discarding others.

4. Successful resolution of the identity conflicts that are typical of adolescence depends in part on having adequate opportunities to experiment with different identities and roles.

5. Erikson calls the period of experimentation and uncertainty that precedes the achievement of a firm adult identity the psychosocial moratorium.

6. Marcia has identified four identity statuses among older adolescents: identity achievement, identity diffusion, moratorium, and foreclosure.

Social Relationships During Adolescence

7. Struggles over separation and the growing independence of teenagers create the generation gap.

8. The middle-aged parents of adolescents face their own developmental crises, which are caused in part by the conflicting demands they experience.

9. Teenagers appear to feel most positive about democratic and equalitarian parenting styles and more negative about parents who are autocratic.

10. Social-class differences influence the educational and career expectations that parents have for their adolescent children and that adolescents have for themselves.

11. In recent years, an increasing number of adolescents have encountered the stresses of growing up in a family that has experienced divorce, remarriage, or single parenthood.

12. During adolescence, friendships become increasingly stable, intimate, and mutual.

13. Male friendships appear to involve lower levels of intimacy than friendships between females.

14. Both small, cohesive cliques and larger, less intimate crowds appear to be important in peer group participation.

15. Teenagers participate in peer groups to please parents and teachers, to gain peer acceptance and popularity, and to conform.

16. Many of the social experiences of adolescence take place in school.

17. The quality of both a school's curriculum and its social relationships within and outside the classroom affect students' academic performance, personal development, and likelihood of their dropping out.

Sexuality During Adolescence

18. Adolescents' sexual needs are closely tied to their need to establish a secure identity and to achieve both intimacy and independence.

19. Masturbation and sexual fantasies play a significant part in adolescent sexual development.

20. In the last thirty years, more young people have engaged in sexual intercourse, particularly girls; nevertheless, girls and boys differ in their attitudes toward sexual experiences.

21. In the United States, dating is the major way in which adolescents begin their sexual activity; unfortunately, considerable sexual aggression occurs during dating.

22. Acceptance of homosexuality has increased, but fear of AIDS gives rise to homophobia among teenagers.

Special Problems of Adolescence

23. Pregnancy and parenthood continue to be a major problem faced by a growing number of adolescents.

24. Other problems that are common during adolescence are physical and sexual abuse, homeless and runaway youths, juvenile delinquency, and suicide.

KEY TERMS

identity *(570)*
individuation *(570)*
differentiation *(571)*
practice and
    experimentation *(572)*
rapprochement *(572)*
consolidation of self *(572)*
identity versus role
    confusion *(572)*
identification *(572)*
psychosocial
    moratorium *(573)*
identity diffusion *(574)*

negative identity *(575)*
identity status *(576)*
generation gap *(578)*
democratic parenting *(581)*
equalitarian parenting *(581)*
autocratic parenting *(581)*
mutuality *(585)*
intimacy *(586)*
peer group *(587)*
clique *(587)*
crowd *(587)*
juvenile delinquency *(603)*

WHAT DO YOU THINK?

1. To what degree are you aware of having experienced the developmental crisis of identity versus identity confusion proposed by Erikson? Which of Marcia's identity styles best describes you at the present time?

2. In what ways have the parental role conflicts of midlife influenced relationships in your own family?

3. What are your opinions about the positive and negative effects of divorce, remarriage, and single parenthood on a teenager's development?

4. In what ways do your own experiences confirm this chapter's description of the development of friendship and peer groups, and in what ways do they differ?

5. As someone who has experienced adolescent changes in sexuality, what questions would you ask the authors about the information they have presented and the conclusions they have drawn?

6. Why do you think that so little progress has been made in the past twenty-five years in solving the problems of adolescent pregnancy and parenthood, abuse, depression and suicide, and delinquency?

FOR FURTHER READING

Adelson, J. (ed.). *Handbook of Adolescent Psychology.* New York: Wiley, 1980.

This excellent collection of original articles reviews recent theory and research on various aspects of adolescent development — a high-level reference source.

Bell, R., et al. *Changing Bodies, Changing Lives.* New York: Vintage, 1988.

This book provides accurate and up-to-date information on a variety of issues affecting the lives of teenagers including sexuality, relationships with friends and parents, and typical adolescent problems.

Coles, R., and Stokes, G. *Sex and the American Teenager.* New York: Harper & Row, 1985.

This thoughtful book examines contemporary teenage sexuality and teenagers' feelings, attitudes, and behaviors.

Freidenberg, E. *Coming of Age in America: Growth and Acquiescence.* New York: Vintage, 1965.

This is a classic, thought-provoking book about the conflicts and confusions in our high schools and in our mass culture and how they influence and are influenced by the lives of adolescents.

Grinder, R. *Studies in Adolescence: A Book of Readings in Adolescent Development.* New York: Macmillan, 1975.

This collection of readings includes more than forty interesting articles from various books and professional journals. Among the topics covered are the history of the concept of adolescence, schooling, socialization, youth culture, and drugs, deviance, and delinquency. It is an excellent resource.

Potok, C. *The Chosen.* Greenwich, CN.: Fawcett, 1967.

The Chosen is a best-selling novel set in New York City in the late 1940s. It tells the story of the struggles of two teenagers from very different Jewish immigrant families to develop a friendship and to establish their identities.

Rutter, M. *Changing Growth in a Changing Society: Patterns of Adolescent Development and Disorder.* Cambridge, MA.: Harvard University Press, 1980.

This book presents clear, well-documented coverage of the problems and disorders of adolescents with an emphasis on the important contributions of social factors.

Steinberg, L. D. *Understanding Families with Young Adolescents.* Carrboro, NC: Center for Early Adolescence, 1980.

This book reviews the parallel processes of maturation of adolescents and maturation of parents and provides useful suggestions for how parents and families can effectively deal with adolescent change.

GLOSSARY

accommodation According to Piaget, the process of modifying existing ideas or action-skills to fit new experiences.

achievement motivation Behavior that enhances competence or that enhances judgments of competence.

acquired immune deficiency syndrome (AIDS) A viral illness that gradually destroys the body's ability to combat other diseases.

adaptation Piaget's term for the process by which development occurs; concepts are deepened or broadened by assimilation and stretched or modified by accommodation.

adolescence The stage of development between childhood and adulthood, around ages twelve to twenty.

adolescent egocentrism The tendency of adolescents to perceive the world (and themselves) from their own perspective. See also *egocentrism.*

aggression A bold, assertive action that is intended to hurt another person or to procure an object.

allele One of several alternate forms of a gene.

American Sign Language A system of gestures used in place of oral language by the hearing-impaired.

amniocentesis A prenatal diagnostic method in which a sample of amniotic fluid is withdrawn and tested to detect chromosomal abnormalities.

amniotic sac A tough, spongy bag filled with salty fluid that surrounds the embryo, protects it from sudden jolts, and helps to maintain a fairly stable temperature.

anal stage According to Freud, the second stage in psychosexual development, in which the physical center of pleasure shifts to the anus and to activities related to elimination; occurs during toddlerhood.

androgyny A tendency to integrate both masculine and feminine behaviors into the personality.

animism A belief that nonliving objects are alive and human.

anorexia nervosa A physical and psychological disturbance causing a person to refuse to eat sufficient food and to develop an increasingly unrealistic view of his or her body; most anorexics are teenage girls.

AnotB error Tendency of infants to look for a hidden object in the first place it disappears (at "A"), rather than where they have seen it most recently (at "B").

anxious-avoidant attachment An insecure bond between infant and care-giver, in which the child rarely cries when separated from the care-giver and tends to avoid or ignore the care-giver when reunited.

anxious-resistant attachment An insecure bond between infant and care-giver, in which the child shows signs of anxiety preceding separation, is intensely upset by separation, and seeks close contact when reunited while at the same time resisting the care-giver's efforts to comfort.

Apgar score A rating of newborns' health immediately following birth, based on heart rate, strength of breathing, muscle tone, color, and reflex responsiveness.

approach behaviors Infant behaviors that establish and maintain physical closeness with caregivers, such as smiling, clinging, non-nutritional sucking, and following.

aptitude test Measurement of ability that estimates future performance in some realm of behavior.

artificial insemination Alternative method to normal conception, in which sperm is inserted with a syringe into a woman's vagina, either on or near the cervix.

artificialism A belief that all objects, whether living or not, are made in the same way, usually by human beings.

assimilation According to Piaget, a method by which a child responds to new experiences by using existing concepts to interpret new ideas and experiences.

associative play A form of social play in which children play together or with the same materials, but each from a separate frame of reference or with separate goals.

attachment An intimate and enduring emotional relationship between two people, such as infant and parent, characterized by reciprocal affection and a periodic desire to maintain physical closeness.

attention deficit disorder See *hyperactivity.*

auditory cortex Area of the brain, located near the left side of the cerebral cortex, where the sounds of speech produce their primary response.

authoritarian parenting A style of child rearing characterized by a high degree of control and demands on children's maturity and a low degree of clarity of communication and nurturance.

authoritative parenting A style of child rearing characterized by a high degree of control, clarity of communication, maturity demands, and nurturance.

autocratic parenting A style of child rearing in which parents do not consult with children in making decisions.

autonomous morality According to Piaget, a "morality of cooperation" used by children aged nine to twelve. Children begin to take their peers' intentions into account when evaluating their actions.

autonomy The ability to govern and regulate one's own thoughts, feelings, and actions freely and responsibly.

autonomy versus shame and doubt According to Erikson, the psychosocial crisis of children aged one to three involving the struggle to control their own thoughts, feelings, and actions; the second of Erikson's developmental stages.

babbling The combination, repetition, and elaboration of verbal sounds; a normal step in language acquisition.

baby biography A detailed diary recording a child's development, popular in the nineteenth century; one basis of modern observational studies of children.

basic trust versus mistrust According to Erikson, the psychosocial crisis of children from birth to twelve months, involving the infant's development of a sense of trust in his or her care-givers; the first of Erikson's developmental stages.

battered-child syndrome A clinical condition in young children who have received serious physical abuse, generally from a parent or foster parent.

behavior genetics The scientific study of the relationship between genotype and phenotype, especially with regard to intelligence, personality, and mental health.

behaviorism A learning theory that focuses on changes in specific observable behaviors and their causes.

behavior modification A body of techniques based on behaviorism for changing or eliminating specific behaviors.

bilingualism The ability to speak two languages.

Black English A dialect or version of English spoken by many black people in the United States.

blastocyst The tiny sphere formed from the original cells of the zygote, after dividing and redividing several times. About one week after conception, the blastocyst adheres to the wall of the uterus and becomes the embryo.

blended family A family created from a combination of stepchildren, stepparents, and stepsiblings.

blind administration In psychological research, the strategy of intentionally concealing the purposes of an experiment from the subjects of the experimental treatment, from the administrators of the treatment, or both.

body image An individual's concept and evaluation of his or her own physical build.

brain stem Relatively primitive, or "lower," area of the brain. Along with the midbrain, this area regulates relatively automatic functions such as breathing, digestion, and consciousness.

Brazelton Neonatal Behavior Assessment Scale A detailed assessment of newborns' neurological development and responsiveness; usually given a few days after birth.

breech presentation The position or orientation, of a fetus in which the feet and rump are pointing downward and emerge first during labor and delivery.

Broca's area Area of the brain located on the left side of the cerebral cortex, vital to the production of language. See also *Wernicke's area.*

bulimia A disorder in which a person, usually a teenage girl, eats huge amounts of food and then vomits it up to avoid gaining weight.

caesarean section A childbirth procedure in which the baby is removed surgically from the mother's abdomen.

canalization The tendency of many developmental processes to unfold in highly predictable ways under a wide range of conditions.

case study A research study of a single individual or small group of individuals considered as a unit.

catch-up growth Process by which children recover from slow growth by growing faster than usual until they reach the normal size for their age.

central nervous system The brain and nerve cells of the spinal cord.

centration Perceptual dominance; the tendency (common among preschoolers) to focus on only one aspect of an object or situation and to ignore other relevant aspects.

cephalic presentation The position, or orientation, of the fetus in which the head is pointing downward; the most common and most medically desirable orientation during labor and delivery.

cephalocaudal development The tendency for organs, reflexes, and skills to develop sooner at the top (or head) of the body, and later in areas farther down the body.

cerebral cortex "Higher" part of the brain. With the cerebrum, it controls vision, hearing, and touch, as well as motor actions such as lifting the arm.

cerebrum See *cerebral cortex.*

child abuse Violent mistreatment or neglect of children. See also *battered-child syndrome.*

chorionic villus sampling (CVS) A medical procedure for detecting genetic abnormalities before birth in which a small bit of tissue surrounding the embryo is removed and examined microscopically.

chromosome Threadlike, rod-shaped structure containing genetic information transmitted from parents to their children; each human sperm or egg cell contains twenty-three and these determine a person's inherited characteristics.

circular reaction Piaget's term for an action often repeated, apparently because it is self-reinforcing.

classical conditioning According to Pavlov, learning in which a neutral stimulus gains the power to bring about a certain response by repeated association with another stimulus that already elicits that same response.

classification Putting objects in groups or categories according to some sort of standards or criteria.

class inclusion The ability to compare a subset of objects with some larger, more inclusive set of objects to which it belongs.

cognition All processes by which humans acquire knowledge; methods for thinking or gaining knowledge about the world.

cognitive domain The area of human development concerned with cognition; concerns all psychological processes by which individuals learn and think about their environment.

cognitive flexibility Skills at detecting multiple meanings of words, alternative orientations of objects, and alternative strategies for solving problems.

cohort A group of individuals born at about the same time and who therefore share certain developmental experiences.

communicative competence How one adjusts one's utterances to the needs and expectations of different situations and speakers.

conception The moment at which the male's sperm cell penetrates the female's egg cell (ovum), forming a zygote.

concrete operational period According to Piaget, the period (from about age seven to age eleven) when children can see logical relationships among concepts or schemes but are still unable to think abstractly.

conditioned response According to Pavlov, a learned behavior that is elicited by a conditioned stimulus through association with an unconditioned stimulus.

conditioned stimulus According to Pavlov, a neutral sight, sound, or other stimulus that has acquired the power to elicit a certain response.

conservation A belief that certain properties (such as quantity) remain constant in spite of changes in perceived features such as dimensions, position, and shape.

consolidation of self The final subphase of individuation in which the adolescent develops a sense of personal identity.

constructive play A type of play that involves manipulation of physical objects in order to build or construct something.

context In developmental research, the circumstances surrounding a child's experience and development.

control group In an experimental research study, the group of subjects who experience conditions similar or identical to the experimental group, but without experiencing the experimental treatment.

control processes In information-processing theory, the cognitive activities that direct attention and guide responses.

conventional stages of moral development According to Kohlberg, the third and fourth stages of moral development; characterized by an emphasis on accepted social rules and standards.

convergent thinking Focused, deductive reasoning that leads to a particular solution to a problem.

cooperative play A form of social play in which children carry out roles or informally delegate tasks to each other.

critical period Any period during which one is particularly susceptible to an event or influence, either negative or positive.

cross-sectional study Study that compares individuals of different ages at the same point in time.

décalage "Gap"; Piaget's term for the differences in when a child acquires the skills of a particular cognitive stage.

decentration Attending to more than one feature or dimension of a problem or situation at a time.

defense mechanism According to Freud, an unconscious way of reducing anxiety by distorting or repressing reality.

deferred imitation Piaget's term for the ability of preoperational children (ages two to seven) to imitate behavior at a significantly later time than when they first witness it.

democratic parenting A style of parenting in which parents generally encourage their children to participate in discussions and decisions, but reserve the right to make final decisions.

deoxyribonucleic acid (DNA) Molecule containing hereditary information; has a chemical structure of two chains of polynucleotides arranged in a double helix or spiral.

dependent variable A factor that is measured in an experiment and that *depends* on, or is controlled by, one or more independent variables. See also *independent variable*.

deprivation dwarfism A condition in a few preschool children not to grow to normal height and weight, induced by severe stress in the family; also called failure-to-thrive syndrome.

depth perception A sense of how far away objects are or appear to be.

development Long-term changes in a person's growth, feelings, patterns of thinking, social relationships, and motor skills.

developmental psychology The scientific study of how thoughts, feelings, personality, social relationships, and body and motor skills evolve as an individual grows older.

developmental quotient (DQ) A measure of an infant's performance on activities that assess how quickly the infant is developing motor skills, compared to other infants of the same age.

developmental stages Stages that mark the process of change of an individual, all sharing certain features: (1) all intact organisms follow the same sequence of stages in their development, (2) each stage is qualitatively different from all other stages, (3) stages represent a logical progression in development.

dichotic listening A task in which an individual is fed information or sounds to each ear separately; demonstrates hemispheric lateralization.

differentiation The subphase of individuation in which one recognizes that one is psychologically different from one's parents.

disequilibrium In Piaget's theory, the cognitive state, usually temporary, in which new information cannot be integrated or reconciled with pre-existing information or experiences.

divergent thinking The production of a wide variety of ideas even though they are associated in unusual or indirect ways.

dizygotic twins Twins that develop from two different fertilized ova; fraternal twins.

dominance hierarchy The pattern of status and influence within a group, such as a classroom or a clique of peers.

dominant gene In any paired set of genes, the gene with greater influence in determining physical characteristics that are physically visible or manifest.

dominant trait A trait that tends to dominate or be expressed in the phenotype even when present in just one of a pair of matched chromosomes. See also *recessive trait*.

Down syndrome A genetic abnormality in which an individual has an extra twenty-first chromosome; accompanied by some degree of mental retardation and characteristic physical features.

dramatic play Cognitive level of play involving pretense; begins as soon as a child can symbolize or mentally represent objects. Also called *make-believe play*.

dramatization "As if" performance in which a child tries out the role of or plays at being someone else, such as parents or teachers.

duo A two-word utterance.

dyad A two-person relationship, such as between parent and infant, or a mutual friendship between two pairs.

dyslexia A common learning disability involving significant difficulties in reading.

eclampsia A disease related to hypertension that can occur toward the end of pregnancy; involves a build-up of fetal waste materials in the mother's bloodstream.

ecological view The view that developmental changes and problems such as child abuse result not from any single cause but from multiple and overlapping levels of influence that include an individual's history, family situation, work and neighborhood experiences, and prevailing cultural values.

ecosystem The somewhat broader influences outside of the family that directly contribute to the quality of life.

ectoderm The upper layer of the blastocyst, which later develops into the epidermis, nails, teeth, hair, and sensory organs and nervous system.

ectomorph A person with a slender build. See also *endomorph*.

ego According to Freud, the rational, realistic part of the personality, which coordinates impulses from the id with demands imposed by the superego and by society.

ego integrity versus despair According to Erikson, the final psychosocial crisis, reached during late adulthood and old age. In this stage, one looks back on one's life with dignity, optimism, and wisdom while faced with the despair resulting from the negative aspects of old age.

egocentric escape The concept that people distance themselves from unpleasant and overwhelming experiences by acting as if they are unaffected by them or by quickly forgetting them.

egocentrism The inability to distinguish between one's own point of view and that of another person; behavior and thoughts centered only on one's own body, needs, and opinions. See also *adolescent egocentrism*.

ejaculation The sudden discharge or ejection of semen; can happen during intercourse, masturbation, or (less frequently) sleep.

Electra conflict In psychoanalytic theory, a girl's desire for her father and disappointment at realizing that she cannot obtain him.

embryo The fully implanted blastocyst; refers specifically to the developing human from the second to eighth week after conception.

embryonic disc A structure along one side of the blastocyst out of which the baby will eventually develop.

embryonic stage Stage in prenatal development that lasts from week 2 through week 8.

empathy A sensitive awareness of the thoughts and feelings of another person.

endocrine glands Glands that produce growth hormones.

endoderm The lower layer of the blastocyst, which becomes the digestive system, liver, pancreas, salivary glands, and respiratory system.

endomorph A person with a round, padded build. See also *ectomorph*.

equalitarian parenting A style of parenting in which parents try to give their children an equal say in decisions.

equilibration According to Piaget, a stage of cognitive equilibrium in which an individual's thinking becomes increasingly stable, general, and in harmony with the environment.

estrogen A sex hormone, sometimes called the female sex hormone, since its high concentration in girls stimulates the growth of the ovaries and vagina during puberty.

ethnic identity A sense of belonging to a particular cultural group, as well as the thoughts, feelings, and behaviors associated with belonging to that group.

experimental group In an experimental research study, the group of subjects who experience the experimental treatment while in other respects experiencing conditions similar or identical to the control group.

experimental study Study in which circumstances are arranged so that just one or two factors or influences vary at a time.

expressive language Language that a child can actually use appropriately in conversation.

extinction According to Skinner, the disappearance of response resulting from the removal of the reinforcer that was maintaining it.

factor In the psychometric tradition, a group of cognitive skills that tend to occur together and that therefore form a superordinate ability or more general type of intelligence.

failure-to-thrive syndrome A condition in which an infant seems seriously delayed in physical growth and is noticeably apathetic in behavior; tangible evidence of neglect; also called *deprivation dwarfism*.

fetal alcohol syndrome A congenital condition exhibited by babies born to mothers who consumed too much alcohol during pregnancy. They do not arouse easily and tend to behave sluggishly in general; they also have distinctive facial characteristics.

fetal stage Stage in prenatal development that lasts from the eighth week of pregnancy until birth.

fetus An embryo that has developed its first bone cells, after about eight weeks of gestation.

field dependence The ability to see things in relatively large, connected patterns, such as overall shape and large patches of color.

field independence The ability to view things as discrete, independent parts-such as noticing individual trees in a forest, or particular colors of flowers in a garden.

fine motor coordination The ability to carry out smoothly small movements that involve precise timing but not strength.

fine motor skills Voluntary movements of the body that involve the small muscles located throughout the body.

first stage of labor In childbirth, the stage that begins with relatively mild and irregular contractions of the uterus. As contractions grow stronger, the cervix dilates enough for the baby's head to begin fitting through. May take from eight to twenty-four hours for a first-time mother.

fluid intelligence In psychometrics, quickness at handling abstract symbols, such as problems in logical reasoning.

fontanelle A "soft spot" on an infant's skull; actually a gap in bones covered with tough membrane that grows over with bone by eighteen months.

formal operational period According to Piaget, the period characterized by hypothetical, logical, abstract, and scientific thinking. This stage is generally not reached until adolescence, if at all.

fragile X syndrome A genetic abnormality afflicting males only in which the X-chromosome is damaged or fragmented.

functional play Cognitive level of play that involves simple, repeated movements and a focus on one's own body.

functional relationships Variations in an environment that normally occur together.

games with rules Cognitive level of play involving relatively formal activities with fixed rules.

gamete Reproductive cell (sperm or ovum).

gender The thoughts, feelings, and behaviors associated with being male or female.

gender constancy A belief that a person's sex is biologically determined, permanent, and unchanging, no matter what else about that person may change.

gender identity One's beliefs about what sex one is.

gender preference Attitudes about the sex one prefers to be.

gene Molecular structure, carried on chromosomes, containing genetic information. A gene is the basic unit of heredity.

generation gap Differences in experiences and attitudes between parents and their children.

generative rules Syntactic rules that allow speakers to generate new sentences almost infinitely by applying them to new morphemes.

generativity versus stagnation The seventh of Erikson's psychosocial crises, reached in middle adulthood. One must balance the feeling that one's life is personally satisfying and socially meaningful with feelings of purposelessness.

genetic counseling Assessment of and consultation with a couple about their genetic background and risks for bearing a genetically abnormal child.

genital stage According to Freud, the final stage of psychosexual development. As adolescents undergo the major physical changes associated with puberty, their libidinal energy resurfaces.

genotype The set of genetic traits inherited by an individual. See also *phenotype*.

germinal stage Stage in prenatal development that occurs during the first two weeks of pregnancy; characterized by rapid cell division. Also called the period of the ovum.

glia Brain cells that emit a sheathing that encases neurons and their fibers; helps to transmit impulses more quickly and reliably.

gross motor skills Voluntary movements of the body that involve the large muscles of the arms, legs, and torso.

growth spurt Rapid change in height and weight preceded and followed by years of comparatively little increase, which occurs during puberty.

habituation The tendency to attend to novel stimuli and to ignore familiar ones.

hemispheric lateralization A tendency for the left and right halves of the brain to perform separate functions.

hemophilia A disease in which the blood will not clot properly and therefore characterized by excessive bleeding; example of a sex-linked recessive trait.

heteronomous morality According to Piaget, a "morality of constraint" used in play by children ages six to nine. Children regard the rules of the game as sacred and unchangeable, yet are lax about following them.

heterozygous Describes a genotype consisting of distinct forms of chromosomes for the same gene.

hidden curriculum The unstated or implicit norms, expectations, and behaviors that schools foster in students.

holophrases One-word utterances, or "whole phrases," that express a complete thought; early communication typical of eighteen-month-olds.

homozygous A genetic condition in which an individual inherits two identical genes at a particular location on a particular chromosome.

hormones Chemicals produced by the endocrine glands and secreted directly into the bloodstream.

hostile aggression Aggressive behavior in which harm is an important intent.

Huntington's chorea A genetic abnormality in which the nervous system gradually deteriorates but which does not begin to manifest itself until about age thirty-five.

hybrid vigor The tendency of genetically dissimilar individuals to produce comparatively larger and more vigorous offspring.

hyperactivity Attention deficit disorder (ADD); excessive levels of activity and the inability to concentrate for normal periods of time.

hypothesis A precise prediction based on a scientific theory; often capable of being tested in a scientific research study.

id According to Freud, the part of an individual's personality that contains basic, unprocessed sexual energy. The id motivates behavior by demanding reduction of the tension that builds up around a person's physical and emotional needs.

identification According to Freud, the process by which an individual wants to become like a model, usually a parent or another attachment figure.

identity (1) Piagetian term for the constancy of an object. (2) A unique and relatively stable set of personal characteristics.

identity diffusion A failure to achieve a relatively integrated and stable identity.

identity status Marcia's four categories of identity development: identity achievement, identity diffusion, moratorium, and foreclosure.

identity versus identity confusion The fifth of Erikson's psychosocial crises in which one must integrate one's many childhood skills and beliefs, and gain recognition for them from society.

imaginary audience A characteristic of young adolescents in which they act as if they are performing for an audience and believe that others are as concerned with their appearance and behavior as they themselves are.

implantation The attachment of the blastocyst to the wall of the uterus.

imprinting Tendency in some species of animals for newborn young to follow the first moving object they see.

impulsivity A style of thinking characterized by rapid tempo and relative inattention to errors. See also *reflectivity*.

inclusive fitness The tendency of genotypes to persist, which encourages the survival of an entire genetic lineage, regardless of the effects on particular individuals.

independent variable A factor that an experimenter manipulates (varies) to determine its influence on the population being studied. See also dependent variable.

individuation The process by which an adolescent develops a unique and separate personal identity; consists of four subphases: differentiation, practice and experimentation, rapprochement, and consolidation.

induced labor Artificial contractions that result from the injection of the hormone oxytocin.

industry versus inferiority Erikson's fourth crisis during which children concern themselves with their capacity to do good work and thereby develop confident, positive self-concepts or else be faced with feelings of inferiority.

information-processing theory Explanations of cognition that focus on the precise, detailed features or steps of mental activities. These theories often use computers as a model for human thinking.

informed consent An agreement to participate in a research study based on understanding the nature of the research, protection of human rights, and freedom to decline to participate at any time.

initiative versus guilt Erikson's third crisis, during which a child's increasing ability to initiate verbal and physical activity and expanding imaginative powers lead to fantasies of large and sometimes frightening proportions.

in loco parentis In developmental research, the principle that investigators should act in the best interests of the child at all times.

inner speech Toddlers' "mental shorthand"; thinking that occurs without much help from language.

insecure attachment A relationship between parent and child marked by the child's overdependence on the parents, or else by the child's indifference to them. See also *anxious-resistant attachment* and *anxious-avoidant attachment*.

instrumental aggression Assertive behavior with a goal in mind; the action ends when the goal is achieved and sometimes may unintentionally hurt others.

integrity vs. despair The eighth crisis of development in Erikson's theory, in which older adults assess the value of their life's work and fight the tendency to lose hope about life in general.

intelligence A general ability to learn from experience; also refers to ability to reason abstractly.

internalization (1) According to Freud, the process of taking into one's own personality many of the important qualities of the same-sex parent; operates as the child struggles to resolve oedipal conflict. (2) The process of holding in feelings.

interview Face-to-face, directed conversations used in research studies for gathering in-depth information.

intimacy Feelings of closeness comprised of self-revelation, confidence, and exclusivity.

intimacy versus isolation The sixth of Erikson's psychosocial crises, in which young adults must be able to develop intimate relationships with others while dealing with the fear of loss of identity that such intimacy entails.

intrinsic motivation Interest in an activity because it is enjoyable and rewarding for its own sake rather than because it is useful in achieving something else.

intuitive phase According to Piaget, the second phase of the preoperational period (ages four to seven). Children begin to cease confusing their own thoughts with those of other people and also stop thinking that objects and events are constructed primarily for their own benefit.

in vitro fertilization Alternative method to normal conception in which one or more ova are removed from the mother surgically and mixed in a petri dish with sperm from the father. The zygote is then reinserted surgically into the mother's womb.

joint custody Arrangement in which divorced parents share legal child-rearing responsibility for their children.

Klinefelter's syndrome A genetic abnormality in which a person has at least one extra sex chromosome, usually an X. Such a person is phenotypically male but tends to have small testes and to remain sterile throughout life.

kwashiorkor A condition resulting from protein-calorie deficiency in children. Symptoms are an enlarged abdomen, a tendency to lose hair, and lesions that don't heal.

labor The physical activity involved in giving birth, including periodic contractions of the uterus, delivery of the baby, and expulsion of the placenta. See also specific stages of labor.

language acquisition devise (LAD) The inborn skills through which infants may acquire language.

lanugo Fine, downy hair on the fetus and neonate; especially visible on preterm infants.

latency According to Freud, the stage of development between the phallic and genital stages. Sexual feelings and activities are on hold as the child struggles to resolve the oedipal conflict.

lateralized behaviors Actions that individuals prefer to perform with one side of their body more than the other.

learning Changes that result from relatively specific experiences or events. Learning contributes to development but usually encompasses shorter periods of time and more specific experiences.

learning disabilities Difficulties in learning specific academic skills such as reading and arithmetic.

learning orientation Achievement motivation that comes from the learner and the task.

learning strategies General methods or techniques that help to solve a variety of problems.

learning theory A theory that focuses on explaining changes in specific behavior or thinking, and that identifies specific, observable causes of behavior or thinking.

libido According to Freud, all of the ways in which human beings seek to increase pleasure and avoid discomfort by fulfilling their physical and emotional needs.

localization The ability to identify where a sensation (sight, sound, or touch) is coming from.

logical construction Refers to children's active efforts to understand the world; includes a mixture of assimilation and accommodation.

longitudinal study A study of the same subjects over a relatively long period, often months or years.

long-term memory (LTM) Type of memory that saves information permanently.

low birth weight A birth weight of less than 2,500 grams (about 5½ pounds).

macrosystem The social and economic values and conditions that influence a child's development.

mainstreaming Integrating children with handicaps into regular classrooms to as great a degree as is possible.

make-believe play See *dramatic play.*

malnutrition Chronically insufficient food or nutrients. Deficiencies can occur in protein, calories, and/or specific vitamins and minerals.

malevolent transformation The development of a sense that the world is a harmful and evil place in which it is difficult to achieve closeness with others; may occur if a child's attempts to initiate social contacts with others are undermined.

marasmus A disease that affects infants who have suffered from prolonged periods of protein and calorie deficiency. They may have delays in motor development and perform lower than healthy infants on intelligence tests.

maturation Physical growth and other developmental changes that occur primarily as a result of growing older.

meiosis   A complex process by which gametes form involving duplication and division of reproductive cells and their chromosomes.

menarche   The first menstrual period.

mesoderm   The middle layer of the blastocyst, which becomes the dermis, muscles, skeleton, and circulatory and excretory systems.

mesomorph   A person with a muscular build.

metacognition   Knowledge and thinking about cognition, about how learning and memory operate in everyday situations, and about how a person can improve cognitive performance.

metalinguistic awareness   The ability to attend to language as an object of thought rather than attending only to the content or ideas of a language.

microsystem   The everyday life situations, especially within the family, that influence a child's development.

midbrain   Area of the brain that, with the brain stem, regulates relatively automatic functions such as breathing, digestion, and consciousness.

mitosis   The creation of new cells through duplication of chromosomes and division of cells.

modeling   An approximate copy or imitation of another's behavior.

monozygotic twins   Twins that result from a single fertilized ovum that divided into two zygotes; identical twins.

moral judgment   Understandings of the actions that promote human welfare in a variety of situations.

Moro reflex   The reflexive startle response of newborns. Healthy infants will fling their arms out suddenly and sometimes shake all over or cry in response to sudden loud noise or sudden loss of support.

morphemes   The smallest meaningful units of language; includes words as well as a number of prefixes and suffixes that carry meaning.

motherese   The simplified language characteristically used by mothers and others to talk with babies and toddlers; tends to emphasize key words and rely on repetitions and questions.

motor cortex   Area of the brain located just forward of the top of the head where simple voluntary movements produce their largest neural activity.

motor skills   Physical skills using the body or limbs, such as walking and drawing.

myelin   The sheathing, emitted by glia, that encases neurons and their fibers.

naturalistic research   A study in which the researcher purposely observes behavior as it normally occurs in its natural setting.

nature   (1) The essence or basic character of a person or thing. (2) The inborn qualities of a person.

negative identity   A form of identity diffusion involving rejection of the roles preferred by one's family or community in favor of socially undesirable roles.

negative reinforcer   According to Skinner, a stimulus that increases the frequency or rate of an operant or learned behavior by reducing a person's pain or discomfort.

neonate   A newborn infant.

neurons   Nerve cell bodies and their extensions or fibers.

nocturnal emissions   Ejaculation of semen during sleep.

non-REM sleep   A relatively quiet, deep period of sleep. See also *REM sleep.*

norms   Behaviors typical at certain ages and of certain groups; standards of normal development.

nurture   Environmental influences and experiences that affect a person's development.

obesity   The state of being extremely overweight, specifically more than 130 percent of normal weight for height and bone size; affects one American child in ten.

object constancy   The perception that an object remains the same in size or shape in spite of continual changes in the sensations it sends to the eye.

object permanence   According to Piaget, the belief that people and things continue to exist even when one cannot experience them directly; emerges around age two.

observational learning   The tendency of a child to imitate or model behavior and attitudes of parents and other nurturant individuals.

oedipal conflict   In Freudian theory, a child's desire for the opposite-sex parent and disappointment that follows the realization that the same-sex parent will

always win the sexual competition for this parent; emerges in the phallic stage.

onlooker play   A precursor to more truly social forms of play, in which one child observes another child playing.

ontogenic level   With regard to child abuse, the unique background and personal history of parents which may contribute to the abuse.

operant conditioning   According to Skinner, a process of learning in which a person or animal increases the frequency of a behavior in response to repeated reinforcement of that behavior.

oral stage   Freud's term for the psychosexual stage of development in which the id is dominant and the infant seeks physical and emotional pleasure through the mouth; lasts from birth to one year.

ovaries   The female reproductive glands, which produce ova (egg cells).

overgeneralizations   Utterances in which a child shifts from using correct but irregular forms to using wrong but more regular forms; represents efforts to try out newly noticed rules of syntax.

ovulation   The release of a fully matured egg from the ovary.

ovum   Reproductive cell, or gamete, of the female; the egg cell.

parallel play   An early form of social play, in which children play near each other but with separate materials and without significant interaction.

parent-infant synchrony   Patterns of closely coordinated social and emotional interaction between parent and infant.

partial reinforcement   In behavioral theory, rewards that happen only on some occasions and not on others.

peer group   A group of age-mates who know and interact with one another.

penis envy   According to Freud, a four- or five year-old girl's desire for a penis and resultant jealousy of boys.

perception   The neural activity of combining sensations into meaningful patterns.

perceptual dominance   See *centration.*

perceptual masking   A phenomenon in which some letters are hard to read because of the presence of other letters nearby.

performance orientation   Achievement motivation stimulated by other individuals who may see and evaluate the learner, rather than by the intrinsic nature of the task itself.

permissive parenting   Style of child rearing characterized by a high degree of clarity of communication and nurturance and a low degree of demands on children's maturity and control.

permissive-indifferent parenting   A type of parenting in which parents' permissiveness reflects an avoidance of child-rearing responsibilities, sometimes with detrimental results.

permissive-indulgent parenting   A type of parenting in which parents make relatively few demands on their children but clearly communicate their warmth and interest and provide considerable care and nurturance.

personal fable   Adolescents' belief that their own lives embody a special story that is heroic and completely unique.

personality   A person's unique pattern of physical, emotional, social, and intellectual characteristics.

phallic stage   According to Freud, the stage of psychosexual development (around age four or five) in which a child shifts libidinal interest to the genitals.

phenotype   The set of traits an individual actually displays during development; reflects the evolving product of genotype and experience. See also *genotype*.

phenylketonuria (PKU)   A disorder that severely diminishes an individual's ability to utilize a particular amino acid-phenylalanine-which is found in milk and milk products and which is essential to normal nutrition and growth.

phoneme   A sound, which combines with other sounds to form words.

phonology   The individual vocal sounds of a language.

physical domain   The area of human development concerned primarily with physical changes, such as growth, motor skill development, and basic aspects of perception.

placenta   An organ that delivers oxygen and nutrients from the mother to the fetus and carries away the fetus's waste products, which the mother will excrete.

play therapy   A therapeutic technique in which child and therapist communicate through make-believe play, using dolls and other props.

pleasure principle   According to Freud,

the motivation of the id; focuses on the immediate satisfaction of physical and emotional needs.

polygenic   Transmitted or influenced by more than one gene simultaneously.

polygenic traits   Traits resulting from the combined influence of many genes.

population   In experimental research, the group being studied.

positive reinforcer   Skinner's term for a stimulus that increases the frequency of a response by rewarding the person for making it.

postconventional stages of moral development   According to Kohlberg, the fifth and sixth stages of moral development characterized by universal moral principles.

preconceptual phase   According to Piaget, the first stage of the preoperational period (ages two to four), in which children begin to use symbolic thinking widely, though without the organized properties characteristic of later thought.

preconventional stages of moral development   According to Kohlberg, the first two stages of moral development, which emphasize avoiding punishments, getting rewards, and exchanging favors.

premature baby   A baby born prior to the thirty-seventh week of pregnancy; also called *preterm baby*.

preoperational period   According to Piaget, the second stage of development (around age two to seven), during which there is a major shift from the action-oriented schemes of the sensorimotor period to schemes based on symbolic representation, such as language and dramatic play.

prepared childbirth   A method of childbirth in which parents have rehearsed or simulated the actual sensations of labor and delivery well before the actual delivery date.

preterm baby   See *premature baby*.

primary circular reaction   According to Piaget, a behavior that is repeated and that focuses on the baby's own body and movements; occurs during the second stage of infant cognition (usually at about one to four months of age).

primary sex characteristics   Characteristics that make sexual reproduction possible-for girls, the vagina, uterus, fallopian tubes, and ovaries; for boys, the penis, scrotum, testes, prostate gland, and seminal vesicles.

primitive reflex   An inborn behavioral response of newborn infants that serves no obvious physical purpose; contrasted to survival reflex.

prosocial behavior   Positive social contacts: actions that benefit others.

proximodistal development   Growth that exhibits a near-to-far pattern of development, that is, from the center of the body outward.

psychoanalytic theory   A group of theories of psychology concerned primarily with the dynamics of emotions and of unconscious drives and motivations. Freud's and Erikson's theories are prominent examples.

psychosocial domain   The area of human development concerned primarily with personality, social knowledge and skills, and emotions.

psychosocial moratorium   According to Erikson, the latency period that precedes puberty and provides a temporary suspension of psychosexual development.

puberty   The period of early adolescence characterized by the development of full physical and sexual maturity.

pubic hair   Hair that grows around the genital area as a result of puberty.

punishment   According to Skinner, any stimulus that temporarily suppresses the response that it follows.

qualitative study   A research project that observes or records features, aspects, or qualities of behavior without primarily attaching numerical values or quantities to them.

quantitative study   A research project that measures behavior, meaning that it attaches numerical values or quantities to observations.

quasi-experimental research   Studies that combine elements of both experimental and naturalistic studies.

quickening   A mother's sensations of the fetus's simple and reflexive actions in the womb; usually felt by the fourth or fifth month of pregnancy.

random sample   In research studies, a group of subjects from a population chosen so that each member of the population has an equal chance of being selected.

reactive attachment disorder   Psychosocial dwarfism; a slowing of growth due to family stress.

reality principle According to Freud, the motivation of the ego; the tendency to express physical and emotional needs in socially acceptable ways, delaying immediate gratification.

recall memory Retrieval of information by using relatively few external cues.

receptive language Language that is understood or comprehended when used by others.

recessive gene In any paired set of genes, the gene that influences or determines physical characteristics only when no dominant gene is present.

recessive trait A genetic trait that is expressed in the phenotype only when carried by both chromosomes of a matched pair in the genotype. See also *dominant trait*.

recognition memory Retrieval of information by comparing an external stimulus or cue with preexisting experiences or knowledge.

reflectivity A cognitive style characterized by slow tempo and careful avoidance of errors. See also *impulsivity*.

reflex An involuntary, automatic response to a stimulus. The very first movements or motions of an infant are reflexes.

regression In Freudian theory, a defense mechanism in which a person returns to earlier and less mature ways of handling conflicts.

reinforcer According to Skinner, any stimulus that increases the likelihood that a behavior will be repeated in similar circumstances.

REM sleep A relatively active period of sleep, named after the rapid eye movements that usually accompany it. See also *non-REM sleep*.

repetition compulsion The repetition of an experience-usually a painful one-in symbolic play, which helps the child to resolve feelings about it.

repression According to Freud, a defense mechanism in which a person forces thoughts and feelings out of consciousness by forgetting a significant experience.

respiratory distress syndrome (RSD) Irregular breathing, a leading cause of death among preterm infants. One cause is a lack of surfactin, a substance that prevents the lungs from sticking together.

reversibility Piaget's term for the ability to undo a problem mentally and go back to its beginning.

Rh disease A genetic condition in which the mother's blood develops antibodies that attack the red corpuscles of a fetus's blood.

Rh factor A substance in the mother's blood which in certain forms causes antibodies to develop, and which attack the red corpuscles of the fetus's blood, weakening or killing the fetus before it is born.

Rhogam blood Rh negative blood that contains antibodies. Rh negative mothers are inoculated with rhogam blood to prevent them from developing further antibodies that might jeopardize future pregnancies.

risk factor With regard to pregnancy, an environmental or biological condition that increases the chances that a baby will have medical problems after it is born.

rooting A reflexive searching behavior that orients an infant to the mother's breast or a bottle.

rubella German measles; a virus that can cause blindness, deafness, damage to the central nervous system, and other handicaps in a child if the mother contracts it during early pregnancy.

scheme According to Piaget, a behavior or thought that represents a group of ideas and events in a child's experience.

scientific method General procedures of study involving (1) formulating research questions, (2) stating questions as a hypothesis, (3) testing the hypothesis, and (4) interpreting and publicizing the results.

second stage of labor The period of labor that starts with "crowning"-the first moment that the baby's head can be seen-and ends with the baby's birth. Usually lasts between one and one and one half hours.

secondary circular reaction According to Piaget, the third stage of infant cognition that occurs at the age of four to eight months; repeated behaviors that are motivated by external objects and events.

secondary sex characteristics Sex characteristics other than the sex organs themselves, such as extra layers of fat and pubic hair.

secretary IgA One of the proteins of human milk that binds to viruses and bacteria in the infant's intestine; acts as an intestinal "paint," preventing gastrointestinal disorders.

secular trend (1) In general, any long-term historical trend. (2) In human development, the tendency of each new generation in industrialized countries to grow larger and heavier and to experience puberty earlier than their parents.

secure attachment A healthy bond between infant and care-giver. The child is happy when the caregiver is present, somewhat upset during the caregiver's absence, and easily comforted upon the care-giver's return.

self-concept A sense of self or idea about oneself.

self-constancy The belief that identity remains permanently fixed; established sometime after age six.

self-esteem An individual's feeling that he or she is an important, competent, powerful, and worthwhile person who is valued and appreciated.

semantics The purposes and meanings of a language.

semen A sticky fluid produced by the prostate gland; carries sperm to the penis and provides it with a medium in which to live after ejaculation.

sensorimotor intelligence According to Piaget, thinking that occurs by way of sensory perceptions and motor actions; characteristic of infants.

sensorimotor period Paiget's term for the period from birth to age two, when thinking is limited to sensing and manipulating.

sensory register In information-processing theory, the part of memory that holds information or sensations initially, without transformation or processing.

separation anxiety A child's discomfort at being separated from his or her caregiver.

separation-individuation According to Margaret Mahler, the process by which a child achieves increasingly greater autonomy and independence from the caregiver and develops a distinct and separate identity; occurs about halfway through the infant's first year and continues through the second.

seriation The ability to put objects or quantities into a logical series or sequence.

sex-linked recessive traits Recessive traits resulting from genes on the X chromosome. Because women must inherit two of the recessive genes in order to have the trait, they experience these much less than men do.

sex-role stereotypes   General knowledge of a society's expectations about sex roles.

sexual dimorphism   The physical differences between males and females.

shape constancy   The perception that an object remains the same even though its shape seems to change when it is viewed from different angles.

short-term memory (STM)   "Momentary awareness"; type of memory that retains information for a very short time-no more than a few seconds.

sickle-cell anemia   A genetically transmitted condition in which a person's red blood cells intermittently acquire a curved, sickle shape. The condition can sometimes clog circulation in the small blood vessels.

signaling behaviors   Infant behaviors that establish and maintain physical closeness with caregivers, such as crying, smiling, and babbling.

size constancy   The tendency to perceive an object as the same size even though its distance, and therefore the visual sensation of it, varies.

sleep apnea   Temporary stoppage of breathing during sleep.

small-for-date infant   An infant who develops more slowly than normal during pregnancy; could be born full-term or preterm.

social cognition   Knowledge and beliefs about interpersonal and social matters.

social conventions   Arbitrary customs and agreements about behavior that members of a society use.

social learning theory   The theory that learning results from observing and imitating others.

social transmission   According to Piaget, the process by which people are influenced by, and to some extent adopt, the information and ideas of their culture and society.

sociobiology   The study of the biological and genetic basis of social behavior, including human social behavior.

sociometric questionnaire   A technique for identifying friendship patterns in a social group, such as a classroom, by asking individuals to write down their social preferences.

solitary play   Play that occurs alone, either by choice or by accident.

spermatozoa   Male gametes, or reproductive cells; produced in the testicles. (Also known as *sperm.*)

stage theory   A theory that proposes steps of development that occur in a fixed sequence, and that often form a logical hierarchy with one another.

Standard English   The dialect or version of English spoken by the majority of middle-class adults in the United States.

stimulus   Any event that causes a physical or mental response, such as a sight, sound, taste, or smell; in some usages, mental activity itself can also serve as a stimulus to physical or mental responses.

"strange situation"   A widely used method for studying attachment; confronts the infant with a series of controlled separations and reunions with a parent and stranger.

stranger anxiety   An infant's wariness and avoidance of unfamiliar people and places.

strategic interaction   Social encounters intended to reveal or conceal information indirectly.

sublimation   Freud's term for a defense mechanism in which sexual and aggressive energies are channeled into socially acceptable outlets, such as school, sports, hobbies, and friendships.

sucking reflex   One of the neonate's first and most powerful reflexes, triggered by any object intruding into the mouth.

sudden infant death syndrome (SIDS)   "Crib death" syndrome in which apparently healthy infants stop breathing unaccountably and die in their sleep; most frequently strikes infants between the ages of two and four months.

superego   According to Freud, the portion of one's personality that acts like an all-knowing, internalized parent and enforces morality and social conventions; the conscience.

survey   A research study that samples specific knowledge or opinions of large numbers of individuals.

survival reflex   An inborn behavioral response of newborn infants that serves a clear physical purpose (for example, breathing).

symbiotic mother-child relationship   According to Margaret Mahler, a characteristic of the infant's first year in which the mother psychologically experiences the child as an extension of herself rather than as an independent person, and vice versa.

symbolic thought   Cognition that makes one object or action stand for another.

symbol   A word, object, or behavior that stands for something else.

syntax   The organizational rules of words and phrases in a language; its grammar.

tactile perception   The ability to recognize an object or discriminate among objects by touching them.

Tay-Sachs disease   A genetically transmitted disorder of the nervous system that occurs mainly among infants of Jewish people of Eastern European descent.

telegraphic speech   Early utterances that leave out most articles, prepositions, and conjunctions.

temperament   Characteristic patterns or styles of physical and emotional activity and responsiveness.

teratogen   Any substance ingested by a pregnant woman that can harm the developing embryo or fetus.

tertiary circular reaction   According to Piaget, repeated variations of action schemes, organized by trial and error; the fifth stage in infant cognition, occurring between twelve and eighteen months of age.

testes   Male sex glands, responsible for producing sperm, or male gametes.

testosterone   Sex hormone sometimes called the male sex hormone since its high concentration in boys stimulates the growth of the penis and related male reproductive organs.

third stage of labor   Final stage, in which the afterbirth (placenta and umbilical cord) is expelled; normally lasts only a few minutes.

Tourette's syndrome   A genetic condition in which a person develops recurrent involuntary movements or makes involuntary sounds.

toxoplasmosis   A disease caused by a parasite present in uncooked meat and the feces of infected cats; can lead to fetal brain damage, blindness, and death.

transition   Follows the first stage of labor; the cervix nears full dilation, contractions become rapid and irregular and the baby's head begins to move into the birth canal.

transverse presentation   A birth in which the baby emerges with shoulders first.

trimester   One of the three-month stages in the nine months of pregnancy.

trophoblast   The outer layer of blastocyst cells; produces villi, which attach to the placenta.

ultrasound   A prenatal diagnostic method that allows medical personnel and others to view the fetus by projecting high-frequency sound waves through the mother's womb.

umbilical cord   Three large blood vessels that connect the embryo to the placenta, one to provide nutrients and two to remove waste products.

unconditioned response   According to Pavlov, an involuntary response that is elicited by an unconditioned stimulus; a reflex.

unconditioned stimulus   Pavlov's term for a stimulus that elicits an involuntary reaction.

undergeneralizations   Early utterances in which children tend to define grammatical categories more narrowly than adults do.

unoccupied play   A precursor to true play, in which a child's activities seem to have no clear purpose or goals.

validity   The degree to which research findings measure or observe what is intended.

vernix   A white, waxy substance on the skin of neonates, especially those born preterm.

villi   Threads produced by the outer layer of blastocyst cells that enable it to attach to the uterine wall.

visual cliff   Classic laboratory setup of a ledge covered by a sheet of glass, used to test the acquisition of depth perception. Young babies crawling on the glass discriminate between the two sides of the "cliff."

visual cortex   Area of the brain located near the back of the head in the cerebral cortex, where visual images produce the strongest activity.

visual discrimination   The ability to distinguish or discern differences in what is seen.

visual integration   The ability to coordinate particular sights with each other, as well as with appropriate physical actions.

visual memory   The ability to recall or recognize simple sights.

Wernicke's area   Part of the auditory cortex where the sounds of speech produce their primary response.

working memory (WM)   Memory that is concerned with information currently being processed.

zone of proximal development   According to Vygotsky, the level of difficulty at which problems are too hard for children to solve alone but not too hard when given support from adults or more competent peers.

zygote   The single new cell formed when a sperm cell attaches itself to the surface of an ovum (egg).

REFERENCES

Aboud, F. E. (1987). The development of ethnic self-identification and attitudes. In J. S. Phinney and M. J. Rotheram (Eds.), *Children's ethnic socialization: Pluralism and development.* Newbury Park, Calif.: Sage.

Aboud, F. E., and Skerry, S. A. (1984). The development of ethnic attitudes: A critical review. *Journal of Cross-Cultural Psychology, 15,* 3–34.

Abramovitch, R., and Strayer, F. (1978). Preschool social organization: Agonistic, spacing and attentional behaviors. In P. Pliner, T. Kramer, and T. Alloway (Eds.), *Recent advances in the study of communication and affect* (vol. 6). New York: Plenum Press.

Abu Zahara, N. (1982). *Sidi Ameur: A Tunisian village.* London: Ithaca Press.

Acredolo, L. (1979). Laboratory versus home: The effect of environment on the 9-month-old infant's choice of spatial reference system. *Developmental Psychology, 15,* 666–667.

Acredolo, L., and Evans, D. (1980). Developmental changes in the effects of landmarks on infant spatial behavior. *Developmental Psychology, 16,* 312–318.

Acredolo, L., and Hake, J. (1983). Infant perception. In B. Wolman, G. Stricker, S. Ellman, P. Keith-Spiegel, and D. Palermo (Eds.), *Handbook of developmental psychology.* Englewood Cliffs, N.J.: Prentice-Hall.

Adams, G. (1985). Identity and political socialization. In A. Waterman (Ed.), *Identity in adolescence: Processes and contents.* San Francisco: Jossey-Bass.

Ainsworth, M. (1973). The development of infant mother attachment. In B. M. Caldwell and H. N. Ricciuti (Eds.), *Review of child development research* (vol. 3). Chicago: University of Chicago Press.

Ainsworth, M. (1975). *Infancy in Uganda.* Baltimore, Md.: Johns Hopkins University Press.

Ainsworth, M. (1979). Infant-mother attachment. *American Psychologist, 34,* 932–937.

Ainsworth, M., Blehar, M., Waters, E., and Wall, S. (1978). *Strange-situation behavior of one-year-olds. Its relation to mother-infant interaction in the first year and to qualitative differences in the infant-mother attachment relationship.* Hillsdale, N.J.: Erlbaum.

Albert, N., and Beck, A. (1975) Incidence of depression in early adolescence: A preliminary study. *Journal of Youth and Adolescence, 4,* 301–308.

Aldis, O. (1975). *Play fighting.* New York: Academic Press.

Allen, V. (1976). *Children as teachers. Theory and research on tutoring.* New York: Academic Press.

Ambrus, C., Ambrus, J., and Horvath, E. (1978). Phenylalanine depletion for the management of phenylketonuria: Use of enzyme reactors with immobilized enzymes. *Science, 201,* 837–839.

American Academy of Pediatrics. (1985). *Pediatric Nutrition Handbook* (2nd ed.). Elk Grove Village, Ill.: Author.

American Psychological Association (1981). Ethical principles of psychologists. *American Psychologist, 36,* 633–638.

American Psychological Association. (1985). *Violence on television.* Washington, D.C.: APA Board of Ethical and Social Responsibility for Television.

American Psychiatric Association. (1987). *Diagnostic and statistical manual of mental disorders* (3rd ed., rev.). Washington, D.C.: Author.

Ames, L., Gillespie, C., Haines, J., and Ilg, F. (1979). *The Gesell Institute's child from one to six.* New York: Harper and Row.

Anastasi, A. (1985). Psychological testing: Basic concepts and common misconceptions. In A. Rogers and C. J. Scheirer (ed.), *The G. Stanley Hall lecture series* (vol. 5). Washington, D.C.: American Psychological Association.

Anderson, C. W., Nagle, R. J., Roberts, W. A., and Smith, J. W. (1981). Attachment to substitute caregivers as a function of center quality and caregiver involvement. *Child Development, 52,* 53–61.

Anderson, L. (1989a). Classroom instruction. In M. Reynolds (ed.), *Knowledge base for the beginning teacher.* New York: Oxford University Press.

Anderson, L. (1989b). Learners and learning. In M. Reynolds (Ed.) *Knowledge base for the beginning teacher.* New York: Oxford University Press.

Anders, T., and Chalemian, R. (1974). The effect of circumcision on sleep-wake states in human neonates. *Psychosomatic Medicine, 36,* 174–179.

Annett, M. (1985). *Left, right, hand, and brain: The right-shift theory.* Hillsdale, N.J.: Erlbaum.

Antenatal diagnosis (1979). *Report of a conference sponsored by the National Institute of Child Health and Human Development.* Bethesda, Md.: NIH.

Anthony, E. J., and Cohler, B. J. (Eds.). (1987). *The invulnerable child.* New York: Guildford Press.

Apgar, V. (1953). A proposal for a new method of evaluation in the newborn infant. *Current Research in Anesthesia and Analgesia, 32,* 260.

Apgar, V., and Beck, J. (1973). *Is my baby all right?* New York: Trident.

Applebee, A., Lehr, F., and Auten, A. (1981). Learning to write in the secondary school. *English Journal 70,* 78–82.

Archer, S. L. (1982). The lower age boundaries of identity development. *Child Development, 53,* 1551–1556.

Archer, S. L., and Waterman, A. S. (1988). Psychological individualism: Gender differences or gender identity? *Human Development, 31,* 65–81.

Arehart-Treichel, J. (1981). Down's syndrome: The father's role. *Science News, 116 (22),* 381–382.

Arend, R., Gove, F., and Sroufe, L. (1979). Continuity of individual adaptation from infancy to kindergarten: A predictive study of ego-resiliency and curiosity in preschoolers. *Child Development, 50,* 950–959.

Ariès, P. (1962). *Centuries of childhood: A social history of family life.* (R. Baldick, trans.). New York: Vintage.

Aronson, E., and Bridgeman, D. (1979). Jigsaw groups and the desegregated classroom: In pursuit of common goals. *Personality and Social Psychology Bulletin, 5,* 438–446.

Asch, S. E. (1956). Studies of independence and conformity: A minority of one against a unanimous majority. *Psychological Monographs, 70,* 1–70.

Asher, S., Renshaw, P., and Hymel, S. (1982). Peer relations and the development of social skills. In S. Moore and C. Cooper (Eds.), *The young child-Reviews of research* (vol. 3). Washington, D.C.: National Association for the Education of Young Children.

Asher, S., Singleton, L., and Taylor, A. (1982). *Acceptance versus friendship: A longitudinal study of racial integration.* Paper presented at the meeting of the American Educational Research Association, New York.

Aslin, R., Pisoni, D., and Jusczyk, P. (1983). Auditory development and speech perception in infancy. In P. Mussen (Ed.), *Handbook of child psychology* (vol. 2). New York: Wiley.

Atkinson, J., and Feather, N. (Eds.). (1966). *A theory of achievement motivation.* New York: Wiley.

Au, K., and Mason, J. (1981). Social organizational factors in learning to read: The balance of rights hypothesis. *Reading Research Quarterly, 17,* 115–152.

Bachman, J., Johnson, L., and O'Malley, P. (1981). Smoking, drinking and drug use among American high school students: Correlates and trends, 1975–79. *American Journal of Public Health, 71,* 59–69.

Baggett, P. (1979). Structurally equivalent stories in movie and text and the effect of the medium on recall. *Journal of Verbal Learning and Verbal Behavior, 18,* 333–356.

Bailey, D. (1982). Sport and the child: Physiological considerations. In R. Magill, M. Ash, and F. Smoll (Eds.), *Children in sport.* Champaign, Ill.: Human Kinetics Publishers.

Bailey, D., Malina, R., and Rasmussen, R. (1978). The influence of exercise, physical activity, and athletic performance on the dynamics of human growth. In F. Faulkner and J. Tanner (Eds.), *Human growth* (vol. 2). New York: Plenum Press.

Bakan, D. (1975). Adolescence in America: From idea to social fact. In R. E. Grinder (Ed.), *Studies in adolescence* (3rd ed.). New York: Macmillan.

Bakeman, R., and Brownlee, J. (1980). The strategic use of parallel play: A sequential analysis. *Child Development, 51,* 873–878.

Baltes, P. (1987). Theoretical propositions of life-span developmental psychology: On the dynamics of growth and decline. *Developmental Psychology, 23,* 611–626.

Balzer, M. (1983). Doctors or deceivers? The Siberian Khanty shaman and Soviet medicine. In L. Romanucci-Ross, D. Moerman, and L. Tancredi (Eds.),. *Anthropology of Medicine.* New York: Praeger.

Bandura, A. (1977). *Social learning theory.* Englewood Cliffs, N.J.: Prentice-Hall.

Bandura, A. (1986). *Social foundations of thought and action: A social-cognitive theory.* Englewood Cliffs, N.J.: Prentice-Hall.

Banks, M. (1983). Infant visual perception. In P. Mussen (Ed.), *Handbook of child psychology* (vol. 2). New York: Wiley.

Bannister, D., and Agnew, J. (1971). The child's construing of self In J. Cole (Ed.), *Nebraska symposium on motivation.* Lincoln: University of Nebraska Press.

Bard, B., and Sachs, J. (1977). *Language acquisition patterns in two normal children of deaf parents.* Paper presented to the second annual Boston University Conference on Language Acquisition.

Barker, G. (1975). Social functions of language in a Mexican-American community. In E. Hernandez Chavez, A. Cohen, and A. Beltramo (Eds.), *El lenguaje do los Chicanos.* Arlington, Va.: Center for Applied Linguistics.

Barker, R., and Wright, H. (1955). *Midwest and its children.* New York: Harper and Row.

Barnard, K. (1981). A program of temporally patterned movement and sound stimulation for premature infants. In V. Smeriglio (Ed.), *Newborns and parents.* Hillsdale, N.J.: Erlbaum.

Barnes, A., Colton, T., Gundersen, J., Noller, K., Tilley, B., Strama, T., Townsend, D., Hatab, P., and O'Brien, P. (1980). Letter. *New England Journal of Medicine, 303* (5), 281.

Barnett, M., Howard, J., King, L., and Dino, G. (1980). Antecedents of empathy: Retrospective accounts of early socialization. *Personality and Social Psychology Bulletin, 6,* 361–365.

Barnhardt, C. (Ed.) (1982). *Cross-cultural issues in Alaskan education* (vol. 2). Fairbanks: University of Alaska Center for Cross-Cultural Studies.

Barrett, D., Radke-Yarrow, M., and Klein, R. (1982). Chronic malnutrition and child behavior: Effects of early caloric supplementation on social and emotional functioning at school age. *Developmental Psychology, 18,* 541–556.

Bassuk, E., and Rubin, L. (987). Homeless children: A neglected population. *American Journal of Orthopsychiatry, 51,* 258–264.

Bartol. B. (1986, July 28). Cocaine babies: Hooked at birth. *Newsweek,* pp. 56–57.

Bates, J. (1979). A naturalistic study of sex differences in children's aggression. *Merrill-Palmer Quarterly, 25,* 193–203.

Baugh, J. (1983). *Black street speech: Its history, structure and survival.* Austin: University of Texas Press.

Baumrind, D. (1967). Child care practices anteceding three patterns of preschool behavior, *Genetic Psychology Monographs, 75,* 43–88.

Baumrind, D. (1971). Current patterns of parental authority. *Developmental Psychology, 4,* 1–103.

Baumrind, D. (1973). The development of instrumental competence through socialization. In A. Pick (Ed.), *Minnesota symposium on child psychology* (vol. 7). Minneapolis: University of Minnesota Press.

Baumrind, D. (1989). Raising competent children. In W. Damon (Ed.), *Child development today and tomorrow.* San Francisco: Jossey-Bass.

Bayley, N. (1969). *Bayley scales of infant development.* New York: Psychological Corporation.

Beard, R. (1969). *An outline of Piaget's developmental psychology.* London: Routledge & Kegan Paul.

Beck, R., (1978). *Motivation: Theories and principles.* Englewood Cliffs, N.J.: Prentice-Hall.

Becker, W., Peterson, D., Lurie, A., Schoemaker, D., and Helimer, K. (1962). Relations of factors derived from parent interviews to ratings of behavior problems of five-year-olds. *Child Development, 33,* 509–535.

Beeson, P., and McDermott, W. (Eds.). (1971). *Cecil-Loeb textbook of medicine* (13th ed.). Philadelphia: Saunders.

Belenky, M., Clinchy, B., Goldberger, N., and Tarule, J. (1986). *Women's ways of knowing.* New York: Basic Books.

Bell, N., Grossen, M., and Perret-Clermont, A.-N. (1985). Sociocognitive conflict and intellectual growth. In M. Berkowitz (Ed.). *Peer conflict and psychological growth.* New Directions for Child Development, No. 29. San Francisco: Jossey-Bass.

Bell, R. (1980). *Changing bodies, changing lives: A book for teens on sex and relationships.* New York: Random House.

Bell, R. *et al.* (1988). *Changing bodies, changing lives.* New York: Vintage.

Bellah, R., Madsen, R., Sullivan, W., Swidler, A., and Tipton, S. (1985). *Habits of the heart: Individualism and commitment in American life.* Berkeley: University of California Press.

Bellugi, V. (1970). Learning the language. *Psychology Today, 4,* 32–35 ff.

Belmont, J. (1989) Cognitive strategies and strategic learning: The socio-instructional approach. *American Psychologist, 44,* 142–148.

Belsky, J. (1980). Child maltreatment: An ecological integration. *American Psychologist, 35,* 320–335.

Belsky, J. (1988). The "effects" of infant day care reconsidered. *Early Childhood Research Quarterly, 3,* 235–272.

Belsky, J., Gilstrap, B., and Rovine, M. (1984a). Stability and change in mother-infant and father-infant interaction in a family setting: One-to-three-to-nine months. *Child Development, 55,* 706–717.

Belsky, J., Gilstrap, B., and Rovine, M. (1984b). The Pennsylvania Infant and Family Development Project, I: Stability and change in mother-infant and father-infant interaction in a family setting. *Child Development, 59,* 692–705.

Belsky, J., Lerner, R., and Spanier, G. (1984). *The child in the family.* Reading, Mass.: Addison-Wesley.

Belsky, J., and Rovine, M. (1988). Nonmaternal care in the first year of life and the security of infant-parent attachment. *Child Development, 59,* 157–176.

Belsky, J., and Steinberg, L. (1978). The effects of day care: A critical review. *Child Development, 49,* 920–949.

Bem, S. (1974). The measurement of psychological androgyny. *Journal of Consulting and Clinical Psychology, 42,* 155–162.

Bem, S. (1976). Probing the promise of androgyny. In A. Kaplan and J. Bean (Eds.), *Beyond sex-role stereotypes: Readings toward a psychology of androgyny.* Boston: Little, Brown.

Bem, S. L. (1977). On the utility of alternative procedures for assessing psychological androgyny. *Journal of Consulting and Clinical Psychology, 45,* 196–205.

Bem, S. (1981). Gender scheme theory: A cognitive account of sex typing. *Psychological Review, 88,* 354–364.

Bemis, K. (1978). Current approaches to the treatment and etiology of anorexia nervosa. *Psychological Bulletin, 85,* 593–617.

Bench, J. (1978). The auditory response. In V. Stave (Ed.) *Perinatal psychology.* New York: Plenum Press.

Bench, J., Collyer, V., Langford, C., and Toms, R. (1976). A comparison between the neonatal sound-evoked staftle response and the head-drop (Moro) reflex. *Developmental Medicine and Child Neurology, 14,* 308–317.

Bengston, V., and Troll, L. (1978). Youth and their parents: Feedback and intergenerational influence in socialization. In R. Lerner and G. Spanier (Eds.), *Child influences on marital and family interaction.* New York: Academic Press.

Bensen, D. F., and Zaidel, E. (Eds.). (1985).

The dual brain: Hemispheric specialization in humans. New York: Guildford Press.

Ben-Zeev, S. (1984). Bilingualism and cognitive development. In N. Miller (Ed.). *Bilingualism and language disability: Assessment and remediation.* San Diego, Calif.: College-Hill Press.

Berg, K., and Berg, K. (1979). Psychophysiological development in infancy: Stat, sensory function, and attention. In J. Osofsky (Ed.) *Handbook of infant development.* New York: Wiley.

Bergman, C. (1976). Interference vs. independent development in infant bilingualism. In G. Kellar, R. Teschnes, and S. Viera (Eds.), *Bilingualism in the bicentennial and beyond.* New York: Bilingual Press.

Berk, L. (1985). Why children talk to themselves. *Young Children, 40,* 46–52.

Berke, R. L. (1990, February 14). Survey shows use of drugs by students fell last year. *New York Times,* p. A-16.

Berko, J. (1958). The child's learning of English morphology. *Word, 14,* 150–177.

Berlinsky, E., and Biller, H. (1982). *Parental death and psychological development.* Lexington, Mass.: Lexington Books.

Berman, P. (1980). Are women more responsive than men to the young? A review of developmental and situational variables. *Psychological Bulletin, 88,* 668–695.

Berman, R. (1987). Cognitive components of language development. In C. Pfaff (Ed.), *First and second language acquisition processes.* Cambridge, Mass.: Newbury House.

Bernstein-Ratner, N. (1987). The phonology of parent-child speech. In K. Nelson and A. van Kleech (Eds.), *Children's language* (vol. 6). Hillsdale, N. J.: Erlbaum.

Besford, J. (1984). *Good mouthkeeping: How to save your child's teeth.* New York: Oxford University Press.

Bibbo, M., Gill, W., and Azizi, F. (1977). Follow-up study of male and female offspring of DES-exposed mothers. *Obstetrics and Gynecology, 49,* 1.

Bibby, R. W., and Posterski, D. C. (1985). The emerging generation: An inside look at Canada's teenagers. Toronto: Irwin.

Bijou, S. W., and Baer, D.M. (1965). *Child development* (vol. 2). *Universal stage of infancy.* New York: Appleton Century Crofts.

Birch, L. (1976). Age trends in children's time-sharing performance. *Journal of Experimental Child Psychology, 22,* 331–345.

Bittman, S. J., and Zalk, S. R. (1978). *Expectant fathers.* New York: Hawthorne Books.

Bjorkland, D., and Bjorkland, B. (1985). Organization versus item effects of an elaborate knowledge base on children's memory. *Developmental Psychology, 21,* 1120–1131.

Blechman, E. (1982). Are children with one parent at psychological risk? A methodological review. *Journal of Marriage and the Family, 44,* 179–195.

Blendon, R. (1986). The problems of cost, access, and distribution of medical care. *Daedalus, 115,* 119–135.

Blendon, R., Aiken, L., Freemen, H., Kirkman-Liff, B., and Murphy, J. (1986).

Uncompensated care by hospitals or public insurance for the poor: Does it make a difference? *New England Journal of Medicine, 314,* 1160–1163.

Block, J. (1973). Conceptions of sex role: Some cross-cultural and longitudinal perspectives. *American Psychologist, 28,* 516–526.

Block, J. (1978). Another look at sex differentiation in the socialization behaviors of mothers and fathers. *Merrill-Palmer Quarterly, 22,* 285–308.

Block, J. H., Block, J., and Morrison, A. (1981). Parental agreement-disagreement on child-rearing orientations and gender-related personality correlates in children. *Child Development, 52,* 965–974.

Bloom, L., Hood, L., and Lightbown, P. (1974). Imitation in language development: If when and why. *Cognitive Psychology, 6,* 380–428.

Blum, L. (1987). Particularity and responsiveness. In J. Kagan and S. Lamb (Eds.), *Emergence of morality in young children.* Chicago: University of Chicago Press.

Boismier, J. (1977). Visual stimulation and the wake-sleep behavior in human neonates. *Developmental Psychology, 10,* 219–227.

Borland, J. (1988). Cognitive controls, cognitive styles, and divergent production in gifted preadolescents. *Journal for the Education of the Gifted, 11,* 57–82.

Bornstein, M. (1985). Habituation of attention as a measure of visual information processing in human infants: Summary, systemization, and synthesis. In G. Gottlieb and N. Krasnegor (Eds.), *Development of audition and vision during the first year of postnatal life: A methodological overview.* Norwood, N.J.: Ablex

Bornstein, M., and Tamis-Lemonda, C. (1989). Maternal responsiveness and cognitive development in children. In M. Bornstein (Ed.), *Maternal responsiveness: Characteristics and consequences.* San Francisco: Jossey-Bass.

Boston Women's Health Book Collective (1978). *Ourselves and Our Children.* New York: Random House.

Bouchard, T. (1981, August). *The Minnesota study of twins reared apart.* Paper presented at the annual meeting of the American Psychological Association, Los Angeles, Calif.

Bouchard, T. J. (1984). Twins reared together and apart: What they tell us about human diversity. In S. W. Fox (Ed.), *Individuality and determinism.* New York: Plenum Press.

Bouchard, T., and McGue, M. (1981). Familial studies of intelligence: A review. *Science, 212,* 1055–1059.

Bower, T. G. R. (1981). *Development in infancy* (2nd ed.). San Francisco: Freeman.

Bower, T. G. R. (1977). *The perceptual world of the infant.* Cambridge, Mass.: Harvard University Press.

Bower, T. G. R. (1981), *Development in infancy* (2nd ed.). San Francisco: Freeman.

Bower, T. G. R. (1989). *The rational infant.* New York: Freeman.

Bower, T. G. R., and Paterson, J. (1973). The separation of place, movement, and object in the world of the infant. *Journal of Experimental Child Psychology, 15,* 161–168.

Bowerman, M. (1982). Starting to talk worse: Clues to language acquisition from children's late speech errors. In S. Strauss and R. Stavey (Eds.), *U-shaped behavioral growth.* New York: Academic Press.

Bowles, S., and Gintis, H. (1976). *Schooling in capitalist America.* New York: Basic Books.

Bozzi, V. (1988). Teens and condoms: An uncomfortable fit. *Psychology Today, 22,* 14.

Braham, M. (1965). Peer group deterrents to intellectual development during adolescence. *Educational Theory, 15,* 251–258.

Brasel, J., and Gruen, R. (1978). Cellular growth: Brain, liver, muscle and lung. In F. Falkner and J. Tanner (Eds.), *Human growth* (vol. 2). New York: Plenum Press.

Brazelton, T. B. (1973). *The Infant Neonatal Assessment Scale.* Philadelphia: Lippincott.

Brazelton, T. B. (1977). *The goals and structure of face-to face interaction between infants and fathers.* Paper presented at the biennial meeting of the Society for Research in Child Development, New Orleans.

Brazelton, T. B. (1979). Behavioral competence of the newborn infant. *Seminars in Perinatology, 3,* 35–44.

Brazelton, T. (1983). *Infants and mothers: Differences in development* (rev. ed.). New York: Delacorte.

Bredekemp, S. (1986). *Developmentally appropriate practice in early childhood programs serving children from birth through age 8.* Washington, D.C.: National Association for the Education of Young Children.

Bremner, J., and Bryant, P. (1977). Place versus response as the basis of spatial errors made by young infants. *Journal of Experimental Child Psychology, 23,* 162–17 1.

Brennan, J. (1985). *Patterns of human heredity.* Englewood Cliffs, N.J.: Prentice-Hall.

Breslau, N., Klein, N., and Allen, L. (1988). Very low birth weight: Behavioral sequelae at nine years of age. *Journal of the American Academy of Child and Adolescent Psychiatry, 27,* 605–612.

Bretherton, I. (1985). Attachment theory: Retrospect and prospect. In 1. Bretherton and E. Waters (Eds.), *Growing points of attachment theory and research. Monographs of the Society for Research on Child Development, 50* (1–2, Serial No. 200).

Bretherton, I., McNew, S., and Beeghly-Smith, M. (1981). Early person knowledge as expressed in gestural and verbal communications. In M. Lamb and L. Sherrod (Eds.), *Infant social cognition.* Hillsdale, N.J.: Erlbaum.

Bricker, D., Carlson, L., and Schwartz, R. (1981). A discussion of early intervention for infants with Down's syndrome. *Pediatrics, 67,* 45–46.

Bridges, K. (1933). A study of social development in early infancy. *Child Development, 4,* 36–49.

Brierley, J. (1976). *The growing brain.* London: NFER Publishers.

Brierly, J. (1987). *Give me a child until he is seven: Brain studies and early childhood education.* London: Falmer Press.

Briggs, G. C., Freeman, R. K., and Yaffe,

S. J. (1986). *Drugs in pregnancy and lactation.* (2nd ed.). Baltimore: Williams and Wilkins.

Brody, J. (1982). *Jane Brody's New York Times guide to personal health.* New York: Avon.

Brody, J. E. (1985, November 16). Personal health. *New York Times*, p. B-19.

Bronfenbrenner, U. (1970). *Two worlds of childhood: U.S. and U.S.S.R.* New York: Russell Sage.

Bronfenbrenner, U. (1979a). Contexts of child rearing: Problems and prospects. *American Psychologist, 34,* 844–850.

Bronfenbrenner, U. (1979b). *The ecology of human development.* Cambridge, Mass.: Harvard University Press.

Bronfenbrenner, U., and Crouter, A. (1982). Work and family through time and space. In S. Kamerman and C. Hayes (Eds.), *Families that work: Children in a changing world.* Washington, D.C.: National Academy Press.

Bronfenbrenner, U., Kessel, F., Kessen, W., and White, S. Toward a critical social history of developmental psychology: A propaedeutic discussion. *American Psychologist, 41,* 1218–1230.

Bronson, W. C. (1975). Developments in behavior with age mates during the second year of life. In M. Lewis and L. A. Rosenblum (Eds.), *The origins of behavior: Friendship and peer relations.* New York: Wiley.

Brookover, W., Beady, C., Flood, P., Schweitzer, J., and Wisenbaker, J. (1979). *School social systems and student achievement: Schools can make a difference.* New York: Praeger.

Brooks, C. (Ed.) (1985). *Tapping potential: English and language arts for the black learner.* Urbana, Ill.: National Council of Teachers of English.

Brooks-Gunn, J., Boyer, C., and Hein K. (1988). Preventing HIV infection and AIDS in children and adolescents: Behavioral research and intervention strategies. *American Psychologist, 43,* 958–964.

Brooks-Gunn, J., and Furstenberg, F. (1989). Adolescent sexual behavior. *American Psychologist, 44,* 249–257.

Brooks-Gunn, J., and Warren, M. P. (1985). The effects of delayed menarche in different contexts: Dance and nondance students. *Journal of Youth and Adolescence, 14,* 285–299.

Brooks-Gunn, J., and Warren, M. P. (1988). The psychological significance of secondary sexual characteristics in nine- to eleven-year-old girls. *Child Development, 59,* 1060–1069.

Brooks-Gunn, J., and Warren, M. (1989, April). *How important are pubertal and social events for different problem behaviors and contexts?* Paper presented at the annual meeting of the Society for Research on Child Development, Kansas City, Missouri.

Brophy, J. (1983). Research on the self-fulfilling prophecy and teacher expectations. *Journal of Educational Psychology, 75,* 631–666.

Brophy, J. (1986). Teacher influences on student achievement. *American Psychologist, 41,* 1069–1077.

Brophy, J., and Good, T. (1974). *Teacher-student relationships: Causes and consequences.* New York: Holt, Rinehart and Winston.

Brown, A., Bransford, J., Ferrara, R., and Campione, J. (1983). Learning, remembering, and understanding. In P. Mussen (Ed.) *Handbook of child psychology* (vol. 3). New York: Wiley.

Brown, C. (1984). *The many facets of touch.* Skillman, N.J.: Johnson and Johnson.

Brown, L., and Allen, D. (1988). Hunger in America. *Annual Review of Public Health, 9,* 503–526.

Brown, R. (1973). *A first language: The early stages.* Cambridge, Mass.: Harvard University Press.

Brown, W. T., Friedman, E., and Jenkins, E. C. (1982). Association of fragile X syndrome with autism. *Lancet, 1,* 100.

Browne, J. C. M., and Dixon, G. (1978). *Antenatal care.* Edinburgh: Churchill Livingstone.

Bruch, H. (1979). *The golden cage: The enigma of anorexia nervosa.* New York: Vintage.

Bruner, J. (1983). *Child's talk: Learning to use language.* New York: Norton.

Bruner, J., Oliver, R., and Greenfield, P. (1966). *Studies in cognitive growth.* New York: Wiley.

Bryant, B. (1985). The neighborhood walk: Sources of support in middle childhood. *Monographs of the Society for Research on Child Development, 50* (3, #210).

Buckley, K., and Kulb, N. (Eds.). (1983). *Handbook of maternal-newborn nursing.* New York: Wiley.

Buehler, J. W., Kaunitz, A. M., Hogue, C. J. R., Hughes, J. M., Smith, J. C., and Rochat, R. W. (1986). Maternal mortality in women aged 35 years or older: United States. *Journal of the American Medical Association, 255,* 53–57.

Bumpass, L. L. (1984). Children and marital disruption: A replication and update. *Demography, 21,* 71–82.

Bumpass, M., and Martin, (1989). *Demography, 26,* 37–51.

Burgess, R., and Conger, R. (1978). Family interaction in abusive, neglectful, and normal families. *Child Development, 49,* 1163–1173.

Buscaglia, L. (Ed.). (1983). *The disabled and their parents* (rev. ed.). New York: Holt, Rinehart, and Winston.

Bushnell, E. (1981). The ontogeny of intermodal relations: Vision and touch in infancy. In R. Walk and H. Pick (Eds.), *Intersensory perception and sensory integration.* New York: Plenum Press.

Buss, A. H., and Plomin, R. (1984). *Temperament: Early developing personality traits.* Hillsdale, N.J.: Erlbaum.

Butler, J., Starfield, B., and Stenmark, S. (1984). Child health policy. In H. Stevenson and A. Siegel (Eds.), *Child development research and social policy.* Chicago: University of Chicago Press.

Butler, J., Vudetti, P., McManus, P., Stenmark, S., and Newacheek, P. (1984). Health care expenditures for children with chronic disabilities. In N. Hobbs, H. Ireys, and J. Perrin (Eds.), *Public policies affecting chronically ill children and their families.* San Francisco: Jossey-Bass.

Butnarescu, G. F., and Tillotson, D. M. (1983). *Maternity nursing.* New York: Wiley Medical.

Butterworth, G. (1977). Object disappearance and error in Piaget's Stage 4 task. *Journal of Experimental Child Psychology 23,* 391–401.

Bybee, R. (1979). Violence toward youth: A new perspective. *The Journal of Social Issues, 35,* 1–14.

Brynes, J. (1988). Formal operations: A systematic reformulation. *Developmental Review, 8,* 66–87.

Cahill, G., and Rossini, A. (1978). Obesity. In G. Faulkner and J. Tanner (Eds.), *Human growth* (vol. 2). New York: Plenum Press.

Cairns., R.B. (1979). *Social development: The origins and plasticity of interchanges.* New York: Freeman.

Calfee, R., and Drum, P. (1986). Research on teaching reading. In M. Wittrock (Ed.), *Handbook of research on teaching* (3rd ed.). New York: Macmillan.

Campos, J., Hiatt, S., Ramsay, D., Henderson, C., and Svejda, M. (1978). The emergence of fear on the visual cliff. In M. Lewis and L. Rosenblum (Eds.), *The origins of affect.* New York: Plenum Press.

Campos, J., and Stenberg, C. (1981). Perception, appraisal, and emotion: The onset of social referencing. In M. Lamband, L. Sherrod (Eds.), *Infant social cognition.* Hillsdale, N.J.: Erlbaum.

Caron, A., Caron, R., and Carlson, V. (1979). Infant perception of the invariant shape of objects varying in slant. *Child Development, 50,* 7 16–721.

Caron, R., Caron, A., Carlson, V., and Cobb, L. (1979). Perception of shape-at-a-slant in the young infant. *Bulletin of the Psychonomic Society, 1,* 229–243.

Carpenter, N. J., Leichtman, L. G., and Say, B. (1982). Fragile X-linked mental retardation. *American Journal of Diseases of Children, 136,* 392–398.

Carey, S. (1985). *Conceptual change in childhood.* Cambridge, Mass.: MIT Press.

Case, R. (1986). The new stage theories in intellectual development: Why we need them; what they assert. In M. Perlmutter (Ed.), *Perspectives in intellectual development: Minnesota symposia on child psychology* (vol. 19). Hillsdale, N.J.: Erlbaum.

Cataldo, C. (1982, January-February). Very early education for infants and toddlers. *Childhood Education,* 149–164.

Cater, J. (1980). Correlates of low birth weight. *Child: Care, Health, and Development, 6,* 267–277.

Cazden, C. (1988). *Classroom discourse.* Portsmouth, N.H.: Heinemann.

Ceci, S. (Ed.) (1987). *Handbook of cognitive, social and neuropsychological aspects of learning disabilities.* Hillsdale, N.J.: Erlbaum.

Centers for Disease Control. (1986). *Statistical information.* Atlanta: Author.

Champion, P. (1987). An investigation of the sensorimotor development of Down's syndrome infants involved in an ecologically based early intervention program: A longitudinal study. *British Journal of Mental Subnormality*, *33*, 88–99.

Chance, P. (1986). *Thinking in the classroom*. New York: Teachers' College Press.

Chandler, M., and Boyes, M. (1982). Social-cognitive development. In B. Wolman (Ed.), *Handbook of developmental psychology*. Englewood Cliffs, N.J.: Prentice-Hall.

Chang, H., and Trehub, S. (1977). Infants' perception of temporal grouping in auditor patterns. *Child Development, 48*, 1666–1670.

Chapman, A., and Chapman, M. (1980). *Harry Stack Sullivan's concepts of personality development and psychiatric illness*. New York: Brunner/Mazel.

Chavez, C., Ostrea, E., Stryker, J., and Smialek, Z. (1979). Sudden infant death syndrome among infants of drug-dependent mothers. *Journal of Pediatrics, 95*, 407–409.

Cheek, D. (1974). Body composition, hormones, nutrition and growth. In M. Grumbach, G. Grave, and F. Mayer (Eds.), *Control of the onset of puberty*. New York: Wiley.

Chen, C., and Stevenson, H. (1989). Homework: A cross-cultural examination. *Child Development, 60*, 551–561.

Cherry, R. R., and Eaton, E. L. (1977). Physical and cognitive development in children of low-income mothers working in the child's early years. *Child Development, 48*, 158–166.

Chess, S., and Thomas, A. (1984). *Origins and evolution of behavior disorders*. New York: Brunner/Mazel.

Chi, M., and Ceci, S. (1987). Content knowledge: Its role, representation, and restructuring in memory. In H. Reese (Ed.), *Advances in child development and behavior* (vol. 20). New York: Academic Press.

Chi, M., Glaser, R., and Farr, M. (1989). *The nature of expertise*. Hillsdale, N.J.: Erlbaum.

Chi, M., and Koeske, R. (1983). Network representations of knowledge base: Exploring a child's knowledge and memory performance of dinosaurs. *Developmental Psychology, 19*, 29–39.

Chodorow, N. (1978). *The reproduction of mothering*. Berkeley: University of California Press.

Chomsky, N. (1976). *Reflections on language*. New York: Pantheon.

Chu, A. (1988). Health and safety concerns in infant care. In A. Godwin and L. Schrag (Eds.), *Setting up for infant care: Guidelines for centers and family day care homes*. Washington, D.C.: National Association for the Education of Young Children.

Chugani, H., and Phelps, M. (1986) Maturational changes in cerebral function in infants determined by FDG positron emission tomography. *Science, 231*, 840–843.

Chumlea, W., Knittle, J., Roche, A., Siervogel, R., and Webb, P. (1983). Size and number of adipocytes and measures of body fat in boys and girls 10 to 18 years of age. *American Journal of Clinical Nutrition*.

Claridge, G., and Margan, G. (1983). Genetics of human nervous system functioning. In J. Fuller and E. Simmel (Eds.), *Behavior genetics*. Hillsdale, N.J.: Erlbaum.

Clark, J., and Phillips, S. (1985). A develop-mental sequence of the standing long jump. In J. Clark and J. Humphrey (Eds.), *Motor development: Current selected research* (vol. 1). Princeton, N.J.: Princeton Book Company.

Clark, M. (1959). *Health in the Mexican-American culture: A community study*. Berkeley: University of California Press.

Clark, P., Griffing, P., and Johnson, L. (1989, April). *Pretend play and other aspects of creativity as expression of the divergent cognitive style in young children*. Paper presented at the biennial meeting of the Society for Research in Child Development, Kansas City, Missouri.

Clark, R. (1977). What is the use of imitation? *Child Language, 3*, 341–358.

Clarke-Stewart, A. (1973). Interactions between mothers and their young children: Characteristics and consequences. *Monographs of the Society for Research on Child Development, 38*.

Clarke-Stewart, K. A. (1987). The social ecology of early childhood. In N. Eisenberg (Ed.), *Contemporary topics in developmental psychology*. New York: Wiley-Interscience.

Clarke-Stewart, K. A. (1989). Day care: Maligned or malignant. *American Psychologist, 44*, 266–273.

Clarren, S., and Smith, D. (1978). The fetal alcohol syndrome. *New England Journal of Medicine, 298*, 1063–1067.

Clausen, J. (1975). The social meaning of differential physical and sexual maturation. In S. Dragastin and G. Elder (Eds.), *Adolescence and the life cycle*. New York: Halsted.

Clifton, R., Morrongiello, B., Kulig, J., and Dowd, J. (1981a). Developmental changes in auditory localization in infancy. In R. Aslin, J. Alberts, and M. Petersen (Eds.), *Development of perception: Psychobiological perspectives* (vol. 1). New York: Academic Press.

Clifton, R., Morrongiello, B., Kulig, J., and Dowd, J. (1981b). Newborns' orientation toward sound: Possible implications for cortical development. *Child Development, 53*, 833–838.

Coates, J. (1986). *Women, men and language*. New York: Longman.

Cobb, S., and Kasl, S. (1977). *Termination: The consequences of job loss*. Department of Health, Education and Welfare Publication No. 77–224. Washington, D.C.: U.S. Government Printing Office.

Cochrane, S., and Mehra, K. (1983). Socioeconomic determinants of infant and child mortality in developing countries. In D. Wagner (Ed.), *Child development and international development: Research-policy interfaces*. San Francisco: Jossey-Bass.

Cogan, R. (1980). Effects of childbirth preparation. *Clinical Obstetrics and Gynecology, 23*, 1–14.

Cohen, B., and Lukinsky, J. (1985). Religious institutions as educators. In M. Fantini and R. Sinclair (Eds.), *Education in school and non-school settings*. 84th Yearbook of the National Society for the Study of Education, Pan 1. Chicago: University of Chicago Press.

Cohen, D. (1983). *Piaget: Critique and reassessment*. New York: St. Martin's Press.

Cohen, J., and Parmalee, A. (1983). Prediction of five year Stanford Binet scores in preterm infants. *Child Development, 54*, 1242–1253.

Cohen, L., DeLoache, J., and Strauss, M. (1979). Infant visual perception. In J. Osofsky (Ed.), *Handbook of infant development*. New York: Wiley.

Cohen, L., and Strauss, M. (1979). Concept acquisition in the human infant. *Developmental Psychology, 50*, 410–424.

Cohn, J. F., and Tronick, E. Z. (1987). Mother-infant face-to-face interaction: The sequence of dyadic states at 3, 6 and 9 months. *Developmental Psychology, 23*, 68–77.

Coie, J., Dodge, K., and Coppotelli, H. (1982). Dimensions and types of social status: A cross-age perspective. *Developmental Psychology, 18*, 557–570.

Colby, A., Kohlberg, L., Gibbs, J., and Lieberman, M. (1983). A longitudinal study of moral judgment. *Monographs of the Society for Research on Child Development, 48* (200).

Coleman, J. (1980). Friendship and the peer group in adolescence. In J. Adelson (Ed.), *Handbook of adolescent psychology*. New York: Wiley.

Coles, R., and Stokes, G. (1985). *Sex and the American teenagers*. New York: Harper and Row.

Collins, W., Sobol, B., and Westby, S. (1981). Effects of adult commentary on children's comprehension and inferences about a televised aggressive portrayal. *Child Development, 52*, 158–163.

Comer, J., and Poussaint, A. (1975). *Black child care*. New York: Simon & Schuster.

Condon-Paolini, D., Johnston, F., Cravioto, J., DeLicardie, E., and Scholl, T. (1977). Morbidity and growth of infants and young children in a rural Mexican village. *American Journal of Public Health, 67*, 651–656.

Conger, J. (1977). *Adolescence and youth: Psychological development in a changing world* (2nd ed.). New York: Harper and Row.

Conger, J. J., and Peterson, A. C. (1984). *Adolescence and youth: Psychological development in a changing world* (3rd ed.). New York: Harper and Row.

Consortium for Longitudinal Studies. (1983). *As the twig is bent*. Hillsdale, N.J.: Erlbaum.

Constanzo, P. (1970). Conformity development as a function of self-blame. *Journal of Personality and Social Psychology, 14*, 366–374.

Coopersmith, S. (1967). *The antecedents of self esteem*. San Francisco: Freeman.

Corballis, M. (1988). *Human laterality*. New York: Academic Press.

Corea, G. (1986). *The mother machine*. New York: Harper and Row.

Coren, S., Porac, C., and Duncan, P. (1981). Lateral preference behaviors in preschool children and young adults. *Child Development, 52*, 443–450.

Cornell, E., and Gottfried, A. (1976). Intervention with premature human infants. *Child Development, 47*, 32–39.

Corno, L., and Snow, R. (1986). Adapting teaching to individual differences. In M. Wittrock (Ed.), *Handbook of research on teaching* (3rd ed.). New York: Macmillan.

Corsaro, W. (1981). Friendship in the nursery school: Social organization in a peer environment. In S. Asher and J. Gottman (Eds.), *The development of children's friendships.* Cambridge, England: Cambridge University Press.

Cratty, B. (1979). *Perceptual and motor development in infants and preschool children* (2nd ed.). Englewood Cliffs, N.J.: Prentice Hall.

Cratty, B. (1986). *Perceptual and motor development of infants and pre-school children* (4th ed.). Englewood Cliffs, N.J.: Prentice-Hall.

Cravioto, J., and Delicardie, E. (1982). Nutrition, mental development, and learning. In D. Falkner and J. Tanner (Eds.), *Physical growth.* New York: Wiley.

Crawley, S. B., and Spiker, D. (1983). Mother-child interactions involving two-year-olds with Down's syndrome: A look at individual differences. *Child Development, 54,* 1312–1323.

Crnic, K., Ragozin, A., Greenberg, M., Robinson, N., and Basham, R. (1983). Social interaction and developmental competence of preterm and full-term infants in the first year of life. *Child Development, 54,* 1199–1210.

Crockenberg, S. (1981). Infant irritability, mother responsiveness, and social support influences on the security of infant-mother attachment. *Child Development, 52,* 857–865.

Crockenberg, S. B., and McCluskey, K. (1986) Change in maternal behavior during the baby's first year of life. *Child Development, 57,* 746–753

Crook, C. (1978). Taste perception in the newborn infant. *Infant Behavior and Development, 1,* 52–69.

Csikszentmihalyi, M., and Larson, R. (1984). *Being adolescent: Conflict and growth during the teenage years.* New York: Basic Books.

Csikszentmihalyi, M., Larson, R., and Prescott, S. (1977). The ecology of adolescent activity and experience. *Journal of Youth and Adolescence, 6,* 281–294.

Cummings, J. (1985). Hemispheric assymetries in visual-perceptual and visual-spatial function. In D. F. Bensen and E. Zaidel (Eds.), *The dual brain: Hemispheric specialization in humans.* New York: Guilford Press.

Curtis, R. (1975). Adolescent orientations toward parents and peers: Variations by sex, age, and socioeconomic status. *Adolescence, 10,* 483–494.

Curtiss, S. (1977). *Genie: A psycholinguistic study of a modern-day "wild child."* New York: Academic Press.

Curtiss, S. (1985). The development of human cerebral lateralization. In D. F. Bensen and E. Zaidel (Eds.), *The dual brain: Hemispheric specialization in humans.* New York: Guilford Press.

Dale, P. (1976). *Language development.* New York: Holt, Rinehart, and Winston.

Damon, W. (1977). *The social world of the child.* San Francisco: Jossey-Bass.

Damon, W. (1983). *Social and personality development: Infancy through adolescence.* New York: Norton.

Damon, W., and Hart, D. (1982). The development of self-understanding from infancy through adolescence. *Child Development, 53,* 831–857.

Darling, C. A., Kallen, D. J., and Van Dusen, J. E. (1984). Sex in transition 1900–1984. *Journal of Youth and Adolescence, 13,* 385–399.

Darvill, D., and Cheyne, J. (1981). *Sequential analysis of responses to aggression.* Paper presented at the meeting of the Society for Research on Child Development, Boston.

Davis-Floyd, R. E. (1986). Birth as an American rite of passage. In K. L. Michaelson (Ed.), *Childbirth in America: Anthropological perspectives.* South Hadley, Mass.: Bergin & Garvey.

Darwin, C. (1877). A biographical sketch of an infant. *Mind, 2,* 286–294.

Dasen, P., and Heron, A. (1981). Cross-cultural tests of Piaget's theory. In H. Triandis and A. Heron (Eds.), *Handbook of cross-cultural psychology* (vol. 4). Boston: Allyn and Bacon.

David, S. (1983). *Patience and power: Women's lives in a Moroccan village.* Cambridge, Mass.: Schenkman.

DeArman, J. (1988). Quick decisive action heads off AIDS crisis. *American School Board Journal, 175,* 40.

Deaux, K. (1985). Sex and gender. *Annual Review in Psychology, 36,* 49–81.

DeLoache, J., and Kolstad, V. (1987, April). *Young children's understanding of representational functions of a scale model.* Paper presented at the biennial meeting of the Society for Research in Child Development, Baltimore, Md.

Demijian, A. (1978). Dentition. In F. Falkner and J. Tamer (Eds.), *Human Growth* (vol. 2). New York: Plenum Press.

Demographic yearbook. (1985). New York: United Nations.

Denny, F., and Clyde, W. (1983). Acute respiratory tract infections: An overview. *Pediatric Research, 17,* 1026–1029.

Densen, P., Shapiro, S., and Einhorn, M. (1959). High and low utilizers of service in a medical care plan. *Milbank Memorial Fund Quarterly, 37,* 217–250.

DeRosenroll, D. (1987). Early adolescent egocentrism: A review of six articles. *Adolescence, 22,* 791–802.

Despande, R. (1979). *Cheap and healthy homes for the middle classes in India.* Poona, India: United Book Corporation.

DeVilliers, J. (1980). The process of rule learning in child speech. In K. Nelson (Ed.) *Children's language* (vol. 2). New York: Gardner Press.

DeVilliers, J., and DeVilliers, P. (1977). *Early language.* Cambridge, Mass.: Harvard University Press.

DeVilliers, P., and DeVilliers, J. (1978). *Language development.* Cambridge, Mass.: Harvard University Press.

Diaz, R. (1983). Thought and two languages: The impact of bilingualism on cognitive development. In E. Gordon (Ed.), *Review of research in education* (vol. 10). Washington, D.C.: American Educational Research Association.

DiClemente, R., Zorn, J., and Temoshok, L. (1986). Adolescents and AIDS: A survey of knowledge, attitudes and beliefs about AIDS in San Francisco. *American Journal of Public Health, 76,* 1143–1145.

DiPietro, J. (1981). Rough-and-tumble play: A function of gender. *Developmental Psychology, 17,* 50–58.

DiSimoni, F. (1975). Perceptual and perceptual-motor characteristics of Phonemic development. *Child Development, 46,* 243–246.

DiStefano, V. (1982). Athletic injuries. In R. Magill, M. Ash, and F. Smoll (Eds.), *Children in sport.* Champaign, Ill.: Human Kinetics Publishers.

Ditzion, J. S., and Wolf, P. W. (1978). Beginning parenthood. In Boston Women's Book Collective (Ed.), *Ourselves and our children.* New York: Random House.

Dodd, B. (1972). Effects of social and vocal stimulation of infant babbling. *Developmental Psychology, 7,* 80–83.

Dodge, K. A. (1986). A social information processing model of social competence in children. In M. Perlmutter (Ed.), *Minnesota symposia on child psychology* (vol. 18). Hillsdale, N.J.: Erlbaum.

Donaldson, M. (1979). The mismatch between school and children's minds. *Human Nature, 2,* 60–67.

Dorian, N. (1988). The Celtic languages in the British Isles. In C. Paulson (Ed.), *International handbook of bilingualism and bilingual education.* New York: Greenwood Press.

Douvan, E., and Adelson, J. (1966). *The adolescent experience.* New York: Wiley.

Douvan, E., and Gold, H. (1966). Modal patterns in American adolescence. In M. L. Hoffman and L. W. Hoffman (Eds.), *Review of developmental research* (vol. 2). New York: Russell Sage.

Dowd, J., and Tronick, E. Z. (1986). Temporal coordination of arm movements in early infancy: Do infants move in synchrony with adult speech? *Child Development, 57,* 762–776.

Doyle, J. A. (1985). *Sex and gender: The human experience.* Dubuque, Iowa: William C. Brown.

Dreyer, P. H. (1982). Sexuality during adolescence. In B. B. Wolman (Ed.), *Handbook of developmental psychology.* Englewood Cliffs, N.J.: Prentice-Hall.

Drotar, D. (1985a). *Failure to thrive: Implications for research and practice.* New York: Plenum Press.

Drotar, D. (Ed.). (1985b). *New directions in failure to thrive.* New York: Plenum Press.

Drotar, D., Woychik, J., Mantz-Clumpner, C., Bricknell, C., Negray, J., Wallace, M., and Malone, C. (1985). The family context of failure to thrive. In D. Drotar (Ed.), *Failure to thrive: Implications for research and practice.* New York: Plenum Press.

Dubois, S., Hill, D., and Beaton, G. (1979). An examination of factors believed to be associated with infantile obesity. *American Journal of Clinical Nutrition, 32,* 1997–2004.

Dunn, J. (1983). Sibling relationships in early childhood. *Child Development, 54,* 787–811.

Dunn, J. (1985). *Sisters and brothers.* Cambridge, Mass.: Harvard University Press.

Dunn, L., and Dunn, L. (1981). *Peabody picture vocabulary test* (rev. ed.). Circle Pines, Minn.: American Guidance Services.

Dunn, J., and Kendrick, C. (1980). The arrival of a sibling: Changes in patterns of interaction between mothers and first-born child. *Journal of Child Psychology and Psychiatry, 21,* 119–132.

Dunphy, D. C. (1963). The social structure of urban adolescent peer groups. *Sociometry, 26,* 230–246.

DuRandt, R. (1985). Ball-catching proficiency among 4-, 6- and 8-year old girls. In J. Clark and J. Humphrey (Eds.), *Motor development: Current selected research* (vol. 1). Princeton, N.J.: Princeton Book Company.

Dusek, J. (Ed.). (1985). *Teacher expectancies.* Hillsdale, N.J.: Erlbaum.

Dweck, C. (1986). Motivational processes affecting learning. *American Psychologist, 41,* 1040–1048.

Dweck, C., and Elliott, E. (1983). Achievement motivation. In P. Mussen (Ed.), *Handbook of child psychology* (vol. 4). New York: Wiley.

Easterbrooks, M. A. (1989). Quality of attachment to mother and to father: Effects of perinatal risk status. *Child Development, 60,* 825–830.

Easterbrooks, M. A., and Goldberg, W. A. (1985). Effects of early maternal employment on toddlers, mothers and fathers. *Developmental Psychology, 4,* 774–783.

Eaves, L., and Eysenck, H. J. (1976). A genotype-environment model for psychoticism. *Advances in Behavioral Research Therapy, 1,* 5–26.

Edelstein, W. (1983). Cultural constraints on development and the vicissitudes of progress. in F. Kessel and A. Siegel (Eds.), *The child and other cultural inventions.* New York: Prager.

Eder, D., and Hallinan, M. (1978). Sex differences in children's friendships. *American Sociological Review, 43,* 237–250.

Edwards, C., and Lewis, M. (1979). Young children's concepts of social relations. In M. Lewis and L. Rosenblum (Eds.), *The child and its family: Genesis of behavior* (vol. 2). New York: Plenum Press.

Edwards, L., Alton, I., Barrada, M., and Hakanson, E. (1979). Pregnancy in the underweight woman: Course, outcome, and growth patterns of the infant. *American Journal of Obstetrics and Gynecology, 135,* 297–302.

Eichorn, D. (1979). Physical development: Current foci of research. In J. Osofsky (Ed.), *Handbook of infant development.* New York: Wiley.

Eifermann, R. (1971). Social play in childhood. In R. Heffon and B. Sutton-Smith (Eds.), *Child's play.* New York: Wiley.

Eimas, P., and Miller, J. (1980). Discrimination of information for manner of articulation. *Infant Behavior and Development, 3,* 367–375.

Eimas, P., and Miller, J. (1981). Organization in the perception of segmental and suprasegmental information by infants. *Infant Behavior and Development, 4,* 395–399.

Eisenberg, N., Lennon, R., and Roth, K. (1983). Prosocial development: A longitudinal study. *Developmental Psychology, 19,* 846–855.

Eisenberg, R. (1976). *Auditory competence in early life: The roots of communicative behavior.* Baltimore: University Park Press.

Eisenberg-Berg, N., and Neal, C. (1979). Children's moral reasoning about their own spontaneous prosocial behavior. *Developmental Psychology, 15,* 228–229.

Elder, G., Jr. (1980). Adolescence in historical perspective. In J. Adelson (Ed.), *Handbook of adolescent psychology.* New York: Wiley.

Elias, M. F., Nicolson, N. A., Bora, C., and Johnston, J. (1986). Sleep-wake patterns of breast fed infants in the first 2 years of life. *Pediatrics, 77,* 322–329.

Elkind, D. (1979). The study of spontaneous religion in the child. In D. Elkind, *The child and society.* New York: Oxford University Press.

Elkind, D. (1984). *All grown up and no place to go. Teenager in crisis.* Reading, Mass.: Addison-Wesley.

Elkind, D. (1987). *Miseducation: Preschoolers at risk.* New York: Knopf.

Elkind, D. (1989, April). Preventing date rape. *Parents' Magazine,* 198.

Elkind, D., and Bowen, R. (1979). Imaginary audience behavior in children and adolescence. *Developmental Psychology, 15,* 38–44.

Elkind, D., and Weiner, I. (1978). *Development of the child.* New York: Wiley.

Elliot, D., Voss, H., and Aubarcy, W. (1966). Capable dropouts and the social milieu of the high school. *Journal of Educational Research, 60,* 180–186.

Ellis, S., Rogoff, B., and Cromer, C. (1981). Age segregation in children's social interactions. *Developmental Psychology, 17,* 399–407.

Elms, A. (1981). Skinner's dark year and Walden Two. *American Psychologist, 36,* 470–479.

Emde, R., Gaensbauer, T., and Harmon, R. (1976). Emotional expression in infancy: A biobehavioral study. *Psychological Issues Monograph Series, 10,* 37.

Emde, R., and Robinson, J. (1979). The first two months: Recent research in developmental psychobiology and the changing view of the newborn. In J. Noshpiz and J. Call (Eds.), *Basic handbook of child psychiatry.* New York: Basic Books.

Emery, R. (1982). Interparental conflict and the children of discord and divorce. *Psychological Bulletin, 92,* 310–330.

Emery, R. E. (1989). Family violence. *American Psychologist, 44,* 321–328.

Emmerich, W., and Sheppard, K. (1982). Development of sex-differentiated preferences during late childhood and adolescence. *Developmental Psychology, 18,* 406–417.

Empey, L. (1975). Delinquency theory and recent research. In R. E. Grinder (Ed.), *Studies in adolescence.* New York: Macmillan.

Ennis, R. (1987). A taxonomy of critical thinking dispositions and abilities. In J. Baron and R. Sternberg (Eds.), *Teaching thinking skills.* New York: Freeman.

Erikson, E. (1963). *Childhood and society* (2nd ed.). New York: Norton.

Erikson, E. (1969). *Gandhi's truth.* New York: Norton.

Erikson, E. (1968). *Identity: Youth and crisis.* New York: Norton.

Erikson, E. (1975). 'Identity Crisis' in autobiographic perspective. In E. Erikson, *Life history and the historical moment.* New York: Norton.

Erikson, E., and Erikson, K. (1957). The confirmation of the delinquent. *Chicago Review, 10,* 15–23.

Erikson, F. (1986). Qualitative methods in research on teaching. In M. Wittrock (Ed.), *Handbook of research on teaching* (3rd ed.). New York: Macmillan.

Erikson, F., and Mohatt, G. (1982). The cultural organization of participation structures in two classrooms of Indian students. In G. Spindler (Ed.), *Doing the ethnography of schooling.* New York: Holt, Rinehart, and Winston.

Evans, D., Newcombe, R., and Campbell, H. (1979). Maternal smoking habits and congenital malformations: A population study. *British Medical Journal, 2,* 171–173.

Eveleth, P. (1979). Population differences in growth: Environmental and genetic factors. In F. Falkner and J. Tanner (Eds.), *Human growth* (vol. 2). New York: Plenum Press.

Fagan, J. (1973). Infants' delayed recognition memory and forgetting. *Journal of Experimental Child Psychology, 16,* 425–450.

Fagot, B. (1977). Consequences of moderate cross-gender behavior in preschool children. *Child Development, 48,* 902–907.

Fagot, B. (1982). Adults as socializing agents. In T. Field, A. Huston, H. Quay, L. Troll, and G. Finley (Eds.), *Review of human development.* New York: Wiley.

Fagot, B., and Kronsberg, S. (1982). Sex differences: Biological and social factors influencing the behavior of young boys and girls. In S. Moore and C. Cooper (Eds.), *The young child: Reviews of research* (vol. 3). Washington, D.C.: National Association for the Education of Young Children.

Falek, A. (1975). Ethical issues in human behavior genetics. In K. W. Schaie, V. E. Anderson, G. McClearn, and J. Money (Eds.), *Developmental human behavior genetics.* Lexington, Mass.: Heath.

Fantz, R. (1963). Pattern vision in newborn infants. *Science, 140,* 296–297.

Farnham-Diggory, S., and Gregg, L. (1975). Color, form and function as dimensions of natural classification, *Child Development, 46,* 101–114.

Faust, M. (1977). Somatic development in adolescent girls. *Monographs of the Society for Research on Child Development,* No. 169.

Feinbloom, R. I., and Forman, B. Y. (1987). *Pregnancy, birth and the early months: A complete guide.* Reading, Mass.: Addison-Wesley.

Fein, G. (1981). Pretend play: An integrative view. *Child Development, 52,* 1095–1118.

Feingold, B. (1974). *Why your child is hyperactive*. New York: Random House.

Feiring, C., Fox, N. A., Jaskir, J., and Lewis, M. (1987). The relation between social support, infant risk status, and mother-infant interactions. *Developmental Psychology, 23,* 400–405.

Feld, S., Ruhland, D., and Gold, M. (1979). Developmental changes in achievement motivation. *Merrill-Palmer Quarterly, 25,* 43–60.

Field, T. (1978). Interaction behaviors of primary versus secondary caretaker fathers. *Developmental Psychology, 14,* 183–185.

Field, T. (1979). Visual and cardiac responses to animate and inanimate faces by young term and preterm infants. *Child Development, 83,* 353–375.

Field, T. (1980). Interactions of high risk infants: Quantitative and qualitative differences. In D. Sawin, R. Hawkins, L. Walker, and J. Penticuff (Eds.), *Exceptional infants. Vol. 4: Psychosocial risks in infant environmental transactions.* New York: Brunner/Mazel.

Field, T., Muir, D., Pilon, R., Sinclair, M., and Dodwell, P. (1980). Infants' orientation to lateral sounds from birth to three months. *Child Development, 50,* 295–298.

Field, T., and Roopnarine, J. (1982). Infant-peer interactions. In T. Field (Ed.), *Review of human development.* New York: Wiley.

Fine, G. (1982). Friends, impression management, and preadolescent behavior. In S. Asher and J. Gottman (Eds.), *The development of children's friendships.* New York: Cambridge University Press.

Finkelhor, D. (1979). *Sexually victimized children.* New York: Free Press.

Finkelhor, D. (1984). *Child sexual abuse: New theory and practice.* New York: Free Press.

Finkelhor, D., and Browne, A. (1985). The traumatic impact of child sexual abuse: A conceptualization. *American Journal of Orthopsychiatry, 55,* 530–541.

Fischer, K., Hand, H., and Russell, S. (1984). The development of abstractions in adolescence and adulthood. In M. Commons, F. Richards, and C. Armon (Eds.), *Beyond formal operations: Late adolescent and adult cognitive development.* New York: Praeger.

Fischer, K., and Pipp, S. (1984). The process of stage transition: A neo-Piagetian view. In R. Sternberg (Ed.), *Mechanisms of cognitive development.* San Francisco: Freeman.

Flavell, J. (1985). *Cognitive development* (2nd ed.). Englewood Cliffs, N. J.: Prentice-Hall.

Flavell, J., Green, F., and Flavell, E. (1986). Development of knowledge about the appearance-reality distinction. With commentaries by M. Watson and J. Campione. *Monographs of the Society for Research on Child Development, 51* (1, Serial No. 212).

Flavell, J., and Wellman, H. (1977). Metamemory. In R. Kail and J. Hagen (Eds.), *Perspectives on the development of memory and cognition.* Hillsdale, N.J.: Erlbaum.

Flavell, J. (1987). *Cognitive development* (2nd ed.). Englewood Cliffs, N.J.: Prentice Hall.

Flora, J., and Thoresen, C. (1988). Reducing the risk of AIDS in adolescents. *American Psychologist, 43,* 965–970.

Flynn, J. (1987). Massive IQ gains in 14 nations: What IQ tests really measure. *Psychological Bulletin, 101,* 171–191.

Folb, E. (1980). *Running down some lines: The language and culture of black teenagers.* Cambridge, Mass: Harvard University Press.

Food Research and Action Center. (1987). *Miles to go: Barriers to federal food programs.* Washington, D.C.: Author

Foot, H., Chapman, J., and Smith, J. (Eds.). (1980). *Friendship and social relations in children.* New York: Wiley.

Forrest-Pressley, D.; Mackinnon, G.; and Waller, T. (1985) *Metacognition, cognition and human performance.* Orlando, Fla.: Academic Press.

Fortney, V. (1983). The kinematics and kinetics of the running pattern of two-, four- and six-year-old children. *Research Quarterly for Exercise and Sport, 54,* 126–135.

Foster, G., and Anderson, B. (1978). *Medical anthropology.* New York: Wiley.

Foulkes, D. (1982). *Children's dreams: Longitudinal studies.* New York: Wiley.

Fowler, B. (1989). Relationship of body-image perception and weight status to recent change in weight status of the adolescent female. *Adolescence, 24,* 557–568.

Fowler, F. (1988). *Survey research methods.* Newbury Park, Calif.: Sage.

Fowler, J. (1981). *Stages of faith: The psychology of human development and the quest for meaning.* San Francisco: Harper and Row.

Fowler, J. (1987). *Faith development and pastoral care.* Philadelphia: Fortress.

Fox, N., Steinbrecher, M., Pessel, D., Inglis, J., Medvid, L., and Angel, E. (1978). Maternal ethanol ingestion and the occurrence of human fetal breathing movements. *American Journal of Obstetrics and Gynecology, 132,* 354–358.

Franciosi, R. (1983). Perspectives on sudden infant death syndrome. In J. Schowalter (Ed.), *The child and death.* New York: Columbia University Press.

Frankel, S., and Lewis, G. (1989). *Continuing trial of treatment: Medical pluralism in Papua New Guinea.* Boston: Dordrecht.

Frankenburg, W., and Dodds, J. (1967). The Denver Developmental Screening Test. *Journal of Pediatrics, 71,* 181–191.

Freedman, D. (1976). Infancy, biology, and culture. In L. P. Lipsitt (Ed.), *Developmental psychobiology: The significance of infancy.* New York: Wiley.

Freedman, D. (1979). Ethnic differences in babies. *Human nature, 2,* 36–43.

Freeman, N. (1980). *Strategies of representation in young children.* London: Academic Press.

French, M. (1983). Stepping stones. In L. Buscaglia (Ed.), *The disabled and their parents* (rev. ed.). New York: Holt, Rinehart, and Winston.

Freud, S. (1938). The transformations of puberty. In A. A. Brill (ed. and trans.), *The basic writings of Sigmund Freud.* New York: Random House.

Freud, S. (1965). *New introductory lectures in psychoanalysis.* New York: Norton.

Freud, S. (1983). *A general introduction to psychoanalysis* (rev. ed.). New York: Washington Square Press.

Friedrich-Cofer, L., and Huston, A. (1986). Television violence and aggression. *Psychological Bulletin, 100,* 373–378.

Frieze, I., Francis, W., and Hanusa, B. (1981). Defining success in classroom settings. In J. Levine and M. Wang (Eds.), *Teacher and student perceptions.* Hillsdale, N.J.: Erlbaum.

Frisancho, A., Cole, P., and Klayman, J. (1977). Greater contribution to secular trend among offspring of short parents. *Human Biology, 49,* 51–60.

Frisch, R. (1983). Fatness, puberty, and fertility: The effects of nutrition and athletic training on menarche and ovulation. In J. Brooks-Gunn and A. Peterson, (Eds.), *Puberty in girls: Biological and psychological perspectives.* New York: Plenum Press.

Frostig, M., Lefever, W., and Whittlesey, J. (1966). *Administration and scoring of the developmental test of visual perception.* Palo Alto, Calif.: Consulting Psychologists Press.

Fry, J. (1974). *Common diseases: Their nature, incidence, and care.* Philadelphia: Lippincott.

Fucigna, C., and Wolf, D. (1981). *The earliest two-dimensional symbols: The onset of graphic representation.* Unpublished manuscript.

Furman, W. (1982). Children's friendships. In T. Field (Ed.), *Review of human development.* New York: Wiley.

Furman, W., and Bierman, K. (1983). Developmental changes in young children's conceptions of friendship. *Child Development, 54,* 549–556.

Furrow, D., Nelson, K., and Benedict, H. (1979). Mothers' speech to children and syntactic development. *Journal of Child Language, 6,* 423–442.

Furstenberg, F. F., Brooks-Gunn, J., and Chase-Lansdale, L. (1989). Teenaged pregnancy and childbearing. *American Psychologist, 44,* 313–320.

Furstenberg, F., Spanier, G., and Rothschild, N. (1982). Patterns of parenting in the transition from divorce to remarriage. In P. Berman and E. Ramey (Eds.), *Women: A developmental perspective.* Washington, D.C.: National Institutes of Health.

Furth, H. (1973). *Deafness and learning.* Boston: Little, Brown.

Gal, S. (1979). *Language shift.* New York: Academic Press.

Galinsky, E. (1987). *The six stages of parenthood.* Reading, Mass.: Addison-Wesley.

Gallagher, J., and Gallagher, R. (1985). Family adaptation to a handicapped child and assorted professionals. In A. Turnbull and H. Turnbull (Eds.), *Parents speak out: Then and now.* Columbus, Ohio: Merrill.

Gallatin, J. (1980). Political thinking in adolescence. In J. Adelson (Ed.), *Handbook of adolescent development.* New York: Wiley.

Gamble, T., and Zigler, E. (1986). Effects of infant day care: Another look at the evidence. *American Journal of Orthopsychiatry, 56,* 26–41.

Garbarino, J., and Sherman, D. (1980). High-risk neighborhoods and high-risk families: The human ecology of child maltreatment. *Child Development, 51,* 188–198.

Gardner, H. (1980). *Artful scribbles: The significance of children's drawings.* New York: Basic Books.

Gardner, L. (1972). Deprivation dwarfism. *Scientific American, 227,* 76–82.

Garling, T., and Valsiner, J. *Children within environments: Toward a psychology of accident prevention.* New York: Plenum Press.

Garmezy, N. (1985). Stress-resistant children: the search for protective factors. In *Recent research in developmental psychopathology, book supplement no. 4 to Journal of Child Psychology & Psychiatry.* Oxford: Pergamon Press.

Garvey, C. (1977). *Play.* Cambridge, Mass.: Harvard University Press.

Garvey, C. (1984). *Children's talk.* Cambridge, Mass.: Harvard University Press.

Gazzaniga, M. (1988) *Mind matters: How the mind and brain interact to create our conscious lives.* Boston: Houghton Mifflin.

Gelfand, D., and Hartmann, D. (1982). Some detrimental effects of competitive sports on children's behavior. In R. Magill, M. Ash, and F. Smoll (Eds.), *Children in sport.* Champaign, Ill.: Human Kinetics Publishers.

Gelles, R. (1978). Violence toward children in the United States. *American Journal of Orthopsychiatry, 48,* 580–592.

Gelles, R. J. (1982). Problems in defining and labeling child abuse. In R. H. Starr (Ed.), *Child abuse prediction: Policy implications.* Cambridge, Mass.: Ballinger.

Gelman, R. (1978). Cognitive development. *Annual Review of Psychology, 29,* 297–332.

Gelman, R., and Baillargeon, R. (1983). A review of some Piagetian concepts. In P. Mussen (Ed.), *Handbook of child psychology, Vol. 3, Cognitive Development.* New York: Wiley.

Gelman, R., and Shatz, M. (1977). Appropriate speech adjustments: The operation of conversational constraints on talk to two-year-olds. In M. Lewis and L. Rosenblum (Eds.), *Interaction, conversation, and the development of language.* New York: Wiley.

Genesee, F. (1988). The Canadian second language immersion program. In C. Paulston (Ed.), *International handbook of bilingualism and bilingual education.* New York: Greenwood Press.

Genishi, C., and Dyson A. (1984). *Language assessment in the early years.* Norwood, N.J.: Ablex.

George, C., and Main, M. (1979). Social interactions of young abused children: Approach, avoidance, and aggression. *Child Development, 50,* 306–318.

Geschwind, P. (1985). *Selected papers on language, and the brain.* New York: Reidel.

Gesell, A. (1926). *The mental growth of the preschool child* (2nd ed.). New York: Macmillan.

Gesell, A. (1943). *Infant and child in the culture of today.* New York: Harper.

Gesell, A., and Thompson, H. (1929). Learning and growth in identical infant twins. *Genetic Psychology Monographs, 6,* 1–125.

Gibson, D., and Harris, A. (1988). Aggregated early intervention effects for Down's syndrome persons: Patterning and longevity of benefits. *Journal of Mental Deficiency Research, 32,* 11–17.

Gibson, E. (1969). *Principles of perceptual learning and development.* New York: Appleton-Century-Crofts.

Gibson, E., and Walk, R. (1960). The visual cliff. *Scientific American, 202,* 64–71.

Gibson, J., and Yonas, P. (1968). A new theory of scribbling and drawing in children. In H. Levin, E. Gibson, and J. Gibson (Eds.), *The analysis of reading skill.* Washington, D.C.: U.S. Office of Education.

Gilbert, E., and DeBlassie, R. (1984). Anorexia nervosa: Adolescent starvation by choice. *Adolescence, 19,* 839–846.

Giles, H., Bourhis, R., and Taylor, D. (1977). Towards a theory of language in ethnic group relations. In H. Giles (Ed.), *Language, ethnicity, and intergroup relations.* New York: Academic Press.

Gill, D. (1986). *Psychological dynamics of sport.* Champaign, Ill.: Human Kinetics Publishers.

Gilligan, C. (1982). *In a different voice: Psychological theory and women's development.* Cambridge, Mass.: Harvard University Press.

Gilligan, C. (1987). Adolescent development reconsidered. In C. Irwin (Ed.), *Adolescent social behavior and health.* San Francisco: Jossey-Bass.

Gilligan, C., and Murphy, J. (1979). Development from adolescence to adulthood: The philosopher and the dilemma of the fact. *New Directions for Child Development, 5,* 85–99.

Gilligan, C., and Wiggins, G. (1987). Origins of morality in early childhood relationships. In J. Kagan and S. Lamb (Eds.), *The emergence of morality in young children.* Chicago: University of Chicago Press.

Ginzberg, E. (1984). Career development. In D. Brown, L. Brooks, and Associates (Eds.), *Career choice and development.* San Francisco: Jossey-Bass.

Giroux, H. A., and Penna, A. N. (1988). Social education in the classroom: The dynamics of the hidden curriculum. In H. A. Giroux (Ed.), *Teachers as intellectuals: Toward a critical pedagogy of learning.* Granby, Mass.: Bergin & Garvey.

Glaser, R. (1984). The role of knowledge. *American Psychologist, 39,* 93–104.

Glaser, R. (1987). Thoughts on expertise. In C. Schooler and K. W. Schaie (Eds.), *Cognitive functioning and social structure over the life course.* Norwood, N.J.: Ablex.

Glick, P. (1979). Children of divorced parents in demographic perspective. *Journal of Social Issues, 35* (4), 170–182.

Glick, P. C., and Lin, S. (1986). Recent changes in divorce and remarriage. *Journal of Marriage and the Family, 48,* 737–747.

Glick, P. C., and Lin, S. (1987). Remarriage after divorce: Recent changes and demographic variations. *Sociological Perspectives, 30,* 162–179.

Godwin, A., and Schrag, L. (Eds.),. (1988). *Setting up for infant care: Guidelines for centers and family day care homes.* Washington, D.C.: National Association for the Education of Young Children.

Gold, D., and Andres, D. (1978a). Developmental comparisons between ten-year-old children with employed and non-employed mothers. *Child Development, 48,* 75–84.

Gold, D., and Andres, D. (1978b). Relations between maternal employment and development of nursery school children. *Canadian Journal of Behavioural Science, 10,* 116–129.

Gold, M. (1985). The baby makers. *Science, 85,* 26–38.

Goldberg, S., and DeVitto, B. A. (1983). *Born too soon: Preterm birth and early development.* San Francisco: W.H. Freeman.

Goldberg, S., Perrotta, M., Minde, K., and Corter, C. (1986). Maternal behavior and attachment in low-birth-weight twins and singletons. *Child Development, 57,* 34–46.

Goldberg, W. A., and Easterbrooks, M. A. (1988). Maternal employment when children are toddlers and kindergarteners. In A. E. Gottfried and A. W. Gottfried (Eds.), *Maternal employment and children's development: Longitudinal research.* New York: Plenum Press.

Goldman, A., and Goldblum, R. (1982). Anti-infective properties of human milk. *Pediatric Update, 2,* 359–363.

Goldsmith, H. H., Buss, A. H., Plomin, R., Rothbart, M. K., Thomas, A., Chess, S., Hinde, R., and McCall, R. B. (1987). Roundtable; What is temperament? Four approaches. *Child Development, 58,* 505–527.

Goldsmith, H. H., Buss, A. H., Plomin, R. R., Klevjord, M., Thomas, A., Chess, S., Hinde, R. A., and McCall, R. B. (1987). Roundtable: What is temperament? Four approaches. *Child Development, 58,* 505–529.

Golinkoff, R. (Ed.). (1983). *The transition from preverbal to verbal communication.* Hillsdale, N.J.: Erlbaum.

Golomb, C. (1981). Representation and reality: The origins and determinants of young children's drawings. *Review of Research in Visual Arts Education, 14,* 36–48.

Gonzalez-Mena, J. (1986). Toddlers: What to expect. *Young Children, 42,* 47–51.

Good, T., and Weinstein, R. (1986). Schools make a difference: Evidence, criticisms and new directions. *American Psychologist, 41,* 1090–1097.

Goode, W. (1975). *World revolution and family patterns.* New York: Free Press.

Goodenough, F. (1931). *Anger in young children.* Minneapolis: University of Minnesota Press.

Goodlad, J. (1984). *A place called school: Prospects for the future.* New York: McGraw-Hill.

Goodnow, J. (1977). *Children's drawing.* Cambridge, Mass.: Harvard University Press.

Gordon, T. (1975). *P.E.T. parent effectiveness training.* New York: NAL Penguin.

Gottesman, I. I. (1963). Heritability of personality: A demonstration. *Psychological Monographs, 77* (Whole No. 572).

Gottesman, I. (1978). Schizophrenia and genetics. In L. Wynne (Ed.), *The nature of schizophrenia*. New York: Wiley.

Gottfried, A., Wallace-Lande, P., Sherman-Brown, S., King, J., and Coen, C. (1981). Physical and social environment of newborn infants in special care units, *Science, 214*, 673–675.

Gottlieb, J., Semmel, M., and Veldman, D. (1978). Correlates of social status among mainstreamed mentally retarded children. *Journal of Educational Psychology, 70*, 396–405.

Gottman, J., and Parkhurst, J. (1980). A developmental theory of friendship and acquaintanceship. In A. Collins (Ed.), *Minnesota symposia on child psychology* (vol. 13). Hillsdale, N.J.: Erlbaum.

Grant, J. (1982). *The state of the world's children*. New York: Oxford University Press.

Grant, R. (1988). *The psychology of sport: Facing one's true opponent*. Jefferson, N. C.: McFarland & Company.

Greenberg, S. (1984). Early education for educational equity. In S. Klein (Ed.), *Handbook of educational equity*. Baltimore: Johns Hopkins University Press.

Greene, L., and Johnston, F. (1980). *Social and biological predictors of nutritional status, physical growth, and neurological development*. New York: Academic Press.

Greenfield, P. (1982). The role of perceived variability in the transition to language. *Journal of Child Language, 9*, 1–12.

Greenfield, P. (1984). *Mind and media: The effects of television, video games and computers*. Cambridge, Mass.: Harvard University Press.

Greenfield, P., Geber, B., Beagles-Roos, J., Farrar, D., and Gat, I. (1981). Television and radio experimentally compared: Effects of the medium on imagination and transmission of content. Paper presented at the biennial meeting of the *Society for Research in Child Development*, April, 1981. Boston, Mass.

Greeno, J. (1989). A perspective on thinking. *American Psychologist, 44*, 134–141.

Greenspan, S., and Greenspan, N. T. (1985). *First feelings: Milestones in the emotional development of your baby and child*. New York: Penguin.

Greulich, W. (1976). Some secular changes in the growth of American-born and native-born Japanese children. *American Journal of Physical Anthropology, 45*, 55–558.

Griffiths, P. (1985). The communicative functions of children's single-word speech. In M. Barrett (Ed.), *Children's single-word speech*. New York: Wiley.

Grimes, D., and Gross, G. (1981). Pregnancy outcomes in black women aged 35 and older. *Obstetrics and Gynecology, 58*, 614–620.

Grosjean, F. (1982). *Living with two languages*. Cambridge, Mass.: Harvard University Press.

Grossman, K., Grossman, K., Spangler, G., Suess, G., and Unzner, L. (1985). Maternal sensitivity and newborns' orientation responses as related to quality of attachment in northern Germany. In I. Bretherton and E. Waters (Eds.), Growing points of attachment theory

and research. *Monographs of the Society for Research on Child Development, 50*, 209.

Grotevant, H. (1989). Child development within the family context. In W. Damon (Ed.), *Child development today and tomorrow*. San Francisco: Jossey-Bass.

Grubb, W. N. (1989). Young children face the state: Issues and options for early childhood programs. *American Journal of Education, 94*, 358–397.

Grusec, J., and Kuczynski, L. (1980). Direction of effect in socialization: A comparison of the parent's versus the child's behavior as determinants of disciplinary technique. *Developmental Psychology, 16*, 1–9.

Guardo, C., and Bohan, J. (1971). Development of a sense of self-identity in children. *Child Development, 42*, 1909–1921.

Guilford, J. (1967). *The nature of human intelligence*. New York: McGraw-Hill.

Guilleminault, C. (1988). Sleep-related respiratory function and dysfunction in postneonatal infantile apnea. In J. Culbertson, H. Krous, and R. D. Bendell (Eds.), *Sudden infant death syndrome: Medical aspects and psychological management*. Baltimore: Johns Hopkins University Press.

Guralnik, M. (1981). The efficacy of integrating handicapped children in early education settings: Research implications. *Journal of Early Childhood Special Education, 1*, 57–81.

Guthrie, L., and Hall, W. (1983). Continuity/discontinuity in the function and use of language. In E. Gordon (Ed.), *Review of research in education* (vol. 10). Washington, D.C.: American Educational Research Association.

Guttmacher, A., and Kaiser, I. (1984). *Pregnancy, birth, and family planning*. New York: Signet.

Hagen, M., and Jones, R. (1978). Cultural effects on pictorial perception: How many words is one picture really worth? In R. Walk and H. Pick (Eds.), *Perception and experience*. New York: Plenum Press.

Hahn, R., and Gaines, A. (1885). *Physicians and western medicine: Anthropological approaches*. Boston: Dordrecht.

Haith, M. (1980). Visual competence in early infancy. In R. Held, H. Liebowitz, and H. Teube (Eds.), *Handbook of sensory physiology* (vol. 8). Berlin: Springer-Verlag.

Hall, C., Gregory, G., Billinger, E., and Fisher, T. (1988). Field independence and simultaneous processing in preschool children. *Perceptual and Motor Skills, 66*, 891–897.

Hall, M. (1989). Reading comprehension. *American Psychologist, 44*, 157–162.

Hallinan, M. (1981). Recent advances in sociometry. In S. Asher and J. Gottman (Eds.), *The development of children's friendships*. New York: Cambridge University Press.

Hamill, P., Drizd, T., Johnson, C., Reed, R., Roche, A., and Moore, W. (1979). Physical growth: National Center for Health Statistics percentiles. *Clinical Nutrition, 32*, 607–629.

Hamilton, P. M. (1984). *Basic maternity nursing* (5th ed.). St. Louis: Mosby.

Haney, B., and Gold, M. (1973). The juvenile delinquent nobody knows. *Psychology Today*, September, pp. 49–55.

Hanshaw, J. B., Dudgeon, J. A., and Marshall, W. C. (1985). *Viral diseases of the fetus and newborn* (2nd ed.). Philadelphia: Saunders.

Hardy, R., Eliot, J., and Burlingame, K. (1987). Stability over age and sex of children's responses to Embedded Figures Test. *Perceptual and Motor Skills, 64*, 399–406.

Hareven, T. (1986). Historical changes in the family and the life course: Implications for child development. In A. Smuts and H. Hagen (Eds.), *History and research in child development. Monographs of the Society for Research on Child Development, 50* (4–5, Serial No. 211.)

Hare-Muslin, R. T., and Mareck, J. (1988). The meaning of difference: Gender theory, postmodernism, and psychology. *American Psychologist, 43*, 455–464.

Harkness, S., and Super, C. (1987). The uses of cross-cultural research in child development. *Annals of Child Development, 4*, 209–244.

Harley, R., and Lawrence, G. A. (1984). *Visual impairment in the schools*. (2nd ed.). Springfield, Ill.: Charles Thomas.

Harlow, H. (1959). Love in infant monkeys. *Scientific American, 200*, 68–74.

Harlow, H., and Harlow, M. (1962). Social deprivation in monkeys. *Scientific American, 207*, 136–144.

Harp, C. D., (Ed.). (1987). *Risking the future: Adolescent sexuality, pregnancy and childbearing* (vol. 1). Washington, D.C.: National Academy Press.

Harper's Index. (1986). *Harper's, 272* (1629), 13 ff.

Harris, M., and Rosenthal, R. (1985). Mediation of interpersonal expectancy effects: 31 meta-analysis. *Psychological Bulletin, 97*, 363–386.

Harris, P. (1983). Infant cognition. In Paul Mussen (Ed.), *Handbook of child psychology* (vol. 4). New York: Wiley.

Harris, P. (1987). The development of search. In P. Salapatek and L. Cohen (Eds.), *Handbook of infant perception* (vol. 2). New York: Academic Press.

Harter, S. (1977). A cognitive-developmental approach to children's expression of conflicting feelings and a technique to facilitate such expression in play therapy. *Journal of Consulting and Clinical Psychology, 45*, 417–432.

Harter, S. (1982a). Children's understanding of multiple emotions: A cognitive-developmental approach. In W. Overton (Ed.), *The relationship between social and cognitive development*. Hillsdale, N.J.: Erlbaum.

Harter, S. (1982b). A cognitive-developmental approach to children's use of affect and trait labels. In F. Serafica (Ed.), *Social cognition and social relations in context*. New York: Guilford.

Harter, S., and Barnes, R. (1983). *Children's understanding of parental emotions: A developmental study*. Unpublished paper, 1981. Cited in S. Harter, Developmental perspectives on the self-system. in P. Mussen (Ed.), *Handbook of child psychology* (vol. 4). New York: Wiley.

Hartshorne, H., and May, M. (1928). *Studies in deceit*. New York: Macmillan.

Hartup, W. (1974). Aggression in childhood: Developmental perspectives. *American Psychologist 29*, 336–341.

Hartup, W. (1983). Peer relations. In P. Mussen (Ed.), *Handbook of child psychology*, (vol. 4). New York: Wiley.

Hartup, W. (1983). Social relationships and their developmental significance. *American Psychologist, 44*, 120–126.

Hasenstab, M. S., and Horner, J. (1987). *Comprehensive intervention with hearing-impaired infants and preschool children.* Rockville, Md.: Aspen.

Hass, A. (1979). *Teenage sexuality: A survey of teenage sexual behavior.* New York: Macmillan.

Hausknecht, R., and Heilman, J. (1978). *Having a Caesarean baby.* New York: Dutton.

Hayes, C. (1987). *Risking the future: Adolescent sexuality, pregnancy and childbearing.* Washington, D.C.: National Academy Press.

Hays, J., and Siegel, A. (1981). *Wayfinding and spatial representation: A test of a developmental model of cognitive mapping of large-scale environments.* Paper presented to the Society for Research on Child Development, April 1981. Boston.

Heath, S. (1986). Sociocultural contexts of language development. In Bilingual Education Office (Ed.), *Beyond language: Social and cultural factors in schooling language minority students.* Sacramento: California State Department of Education.

Hein, K. D., and DiGeronimo, T. F. (1989). *AIDS: Trading fears for facts. A guide for teens.* Mount Vernon, N.Y.: Consumers Union.

Helders, P., Cats, B., Van der Net, J., and Debast, S. (1988). The effects of tactile stimulation/range-finding program on the development of very low birth weight infants during initial hospitalization. *Child: Care, Health and Development, 14*, 341–354.

Heller, D. (1986). *The children's God.* Chicago: University of Chicago Press.

Helm, V. (1989). Keep these guidelines in mind when developing AIDS policy. *American School Board Journal, 176*, 25–27.

Henker, B., and Whalen, C. (1989). Hyperactivity and attention deficits. *American Psychologist, 44*, 209–215.

Henley, N. (1977). *Body politics: Power, sex, and nonverbal communication.* Englewood Cliffs, N.J.: Prentice-Hall.

Herek, G., and Glunt, E. (1988). An epidemic of stigma: Public reactions to AIDS. *American Psychologist, 43*, 886–891.

Hernandez, D. (1988). Demographic trends and the living arrangements of children. In E. M. Hetherington and J. D. Arasteh (Eds.), *Impact of divorce, single-parenting and stepparenting on children.* Hillsdale, N. J.: Erlbaum.

Hersch, P. (1988). Coming of age on city streets. *Psychology Today, 22*, 30–32, 34–37.

Hetherington, E. M. (1979). Divorce: A child's perspective. *American Psychologist, 34*, 851–858.

Hetherington, E. M. (1984). Stress and coping in children and families. In A. Doyle, D. Gold, and D. S. Moskowitz (Eds.), Children and families under stress. *New Directions for Child Development, 24*, 7–34.

Hetherington, E. M. (1989). Divorce: A child's perspective. *American Psychologist, 44*, 303–312.

Hetherington, E. M., and J. D. Arasteh (Eds.), *Impact of divorce, single-parenting and stepparenting on children.* Hillsdale, N.J.: Erlbaum.

Hetherington, E. M., Cox, M., and Cox, R. (1979). Play and social interaction in children following divorce. *Journal of Social Issues, 35*, 26–49.

Hetherington, E. M., Cox, M., and Cox, R. (1982). Effects of divorce on parents and children. In M. Lamb (Ed.), *Nontraditional families: Parenting and child development.* Hillsdale, N.J.: Erlbaum.

Hetherington, E.M., Cox, M., and Cox. R. (1985). Long-term effects of divorce and remarriage on the adjustment of children. *Journal of the American Academy of Psychiatry, 24*, 518–530.

Hetherington, E. M., and Furstenberg, F. (1989). Follow-up. Letter to the editor. *Readings: A Journal of Reviews and Commentary in Mental Health.* 22–23.

Hetherington, E. M., Stanley-Hagen, M., and Anderson, E. (1989). Marital transitions: A child's perspective. *American Psychologist, 44*, 303–312.

Hinde, R. A. (1983) Ethology and child development. In M. M. Haith and J. J. Campos (Eds.), *Handbook of child psychology* (vol. 2). *Infancy and developmental psychobiology.* New York: Wiley.

Hinde, R., and Stevenson-Hinde, J. (Eds.). (1973). *Constraints on learning.* New York: Academic Press.

Hirschman, R., Melamed, L., and Oliver, C. (1982). The psychophysiology of infancy. In B. Wolman (Ed.), *Handbook of developmental psychology.* Englewood Cliffs, N.J.: Prentice-Hall.

Hiscock, M., and Kinsbourne, M. (1980). Asymmetries of selective listening and attention switching in children. *Developmental Psychology, 16*, 70–82.

Hobart, C. (1987). Parent-child relations in remarried families. *Journal of Family Issues, 8*, 259–277.

Hodapp, R., and Mueller, E. (1982). Early social development. In B. Wolman (Ed.), *Handbook of developmental psychology.* New York: Wiley.

Hodgkinson, H. L. (1985). *All one system: Demographics of education, kindergarten through graduate school.* Washington, D.C.: Institute of Educational Leadership.

Hofer, M. (1987). Early social relationships: A psychobiologist's view. *Child Development, 58*, 633–647.

Hofferth, S., and Hayes, C. (Eds.). (1987). *Risking the future: Adolescent sexuality, pregnancy and childbearing (vol. 2). Working papers and statistical reports.* Washington, D.C.: National Academy Press.

Hofferth, S., Kahn, J., and Baldwin, W. (1987). Premarital sexual activity among U. S. teenage women over the past three decades. *Family Planning Perspectives, 19*, 46–53.

Hoffman, L. (1983). Increased fathering: Effects on the mother. In M. Lamb and A. Sagi (Eds.), *Fatherhood and family policy.* Hillsdale, N.J.: Erlbaum.

Hoffman, L. W. (1984a). Maternal employment and the young child. In M. Perlmutter (Ed.) *The Minnesota symposium on child psychology* (vol. 17). Hillsdale, N.J.: Erlbaum.

Hoffman, L. (1984b). Work, family, and the socialization of the child. In R. Parke (Ed.), *Review of child development research* (vol. 7). Chicago: University of Chicago Press.

Hoffman, L. W. (1989). Effects of maternal employment in the two-parent family. *American Psychologist, 44*, 283–292.

Hoffman, L., and Hoffman, M. (1973). The value of children to parents. In J. T. Fawcett (Ed.), *Psychological perspectives on population.* New York: Basic Books.

Hoffman, M. (1970). Moral development. In P. H. Mussen (Ed.), *Carmichael's manual of child psychology* (vol. 2, 3rd ed.). New York: Wiley.

Hoffman, M. (1984). Interaction of affect and cognition on empathy. In C. Izard, J. Kagan and R. Zajonc (Eds.), *Emotions, cognition and behavior.* Cambridge: Cambridge University Press.

Hoffman, N. (1986). Feminist scholarship and women's studies. *Harvard Education Review, 56*, 511–519.

Hoffnung, R. (1983). *Parent run day care cooperatives and the development of community child rearing networks.* Paper presented to the American Orthopsychiatric Association, Boston.

Hoffnung, R., and Sack, A. (1981). *Does higher education reduce or reproduce social class differences? The impact of Yale University, University of Connecticut, and University of New Haven on student attitudes and expectations regarding future work.* Paper presented at the annual meeting of the Eastern Psychological Association, New York.

Holden, C. (1986). Youth suicide: New research focuses on growing social problem. *Science, 233*, 839–841.

Hollaway, S. (1988). Concepts of ability and effort in Japan and the U.S. *Review of Educational Research, 58*, 327–346.

Holwerda-Kuipers, J. (1987). The cognitive development of low birth weight children. *Journal of Child Psychology and Psychiatry, 28*, 321–328.

Honig, A. (1985). High quality infant/toddler care: Issues and dilemmas. *Young Children, 41*, 40–46.

Honzik, M. P. (1957). Developmental studies of parent-child resemblance in intelligence. *Child Development, 28*, 215–228.

Howard, J., and Barnett, M. (1981). Arousal of empathy and subsequent generosity in young children. *Journal of Genetic Psychology, 138*, 307–308.

Howes, C. (1983). Caregiver behavior in center and family day care. *Journal of Applied Developmental Psychology, 4*, 99–107.

Howes, C., and Mueller, E. (1984). Early peer friendships: Their significance for development. In W. Spiel (Ed.), *The psychology of the twentieth Century.* Zurich: Kindler.

Howes, C., and Stewart, P. (1987). Child's play with adults, toys, and peers: An examination of family and child-care influences. *Developmental Psychology, 23,* 423–430.

Huesmann, L., and Eron, L. (Eds.) *Television and the aggressive child: A cross-national comparison.* Hillsdale, N.J.: Erlbaum.

Hunt, R. (1988). Attention deficit disorder and hyperactivity. In C. Kestenbaum and D. Williams (Eds.), *Handbook of clinical assessment of children and adolescents.* New York: New York University Press.

Hurley, L. (1977). Nutritional deficiencies and excesses. In J. Wilson and F. Fraser (Eds.), *Handbook of teratology* (vol. 1). New York: Plenum Press.

Hurley, L. (1980), *Developmental nutrition.* Englewood Cliffs, N.J.: Prentice-Hall.

Huston, A. (1983). Sex-typing. In P. Mussen (Ed.), *Handbook of Child Psychology* (vol. 4). New York: Wiley.

Huston, A., Watkins, B., and Kunkel, D. (1989). Public policy and children's television. *American Psychologist, 44,* 424–433.

Hutt, C. (1979). Exploration and play. In B. Sutton-Smith (Ed.), *Play and Learning.* New York: Gardner.

Hyde, J. (1981). How large are cognitive gender differences? *American Psychologist, 36,* 892–901.

Imedadze, N., and Uznadze, D. (1978). On the psychological nature of child speech formation under conditions of exposure to two languages. In E. Hatch (Ed.), *Second language acquisition.* Rowley, Mass.: Newbury House.

Inhelder, B. (1976) The sensorimotor origins of knowledge. In B. Inhelder and H. Chipman (Eds.), *Piaget and his school.* New York: Springer-Verlag.

Inhelder, B., and Piaget, J. (1958). *The growth of logical thinking from birth to adolescence.* New York: Basic Books.

Inoff-Germain, G., Arnold, G., Nottelmann, E. Susman, E., Cutler, G., Jr., and Chrousos, G. (1988). Relations between hormone levels and observational measures of aggressive behavior of young adolescents in family interactions. *Developmental Psychology, 24,* 129–139.

Istomina, Z. (1975). The development of voluntary memory in preschool-age children. *Soviet Psychology, 13,* 5–64.

Itard, J. (1806/1962). *The wild boy of Aveyron.* New York: Appleton-Century-Crofts.

Izard, C. E. (1982). *Measuring emotions in infants and children.* New York: Cambridge University Press.

Jacklin, C., and Maccoby, E. (1978). Social behavior at 33 months in same-sex and mixed-sex dyads. *Child Development, 49,* 557–569.

Jackson, A. (1989). Educating young adolescents: Why we must restructure grade schools. *American Psychologist, 44,* 831–836.

Jackson, P. (1968). *Life in classrooms.* New York: Holt, 1968.

Jackson, P. (1986). *The practice of teaching.* Chicago: University of Chicago Press.

Jennings, M., and Niemi, R. (1981). *Generations and politics.* Princeton, N.J.: Princeton University Press.

Jester, R. E., and Guinagh, B. (1983). The Gordon parent education infant and toddler program. In Consortium for Longitudinal Studies, *As the twig is bent.* Hillsdale, N.J.:Erlbaum.

Johnson, D. W., Johnson, R. T., and Maruyama, G. (1984). Goal interdependence and interpersonal attraction in heterogeneous classrooms: A meta-analysis. In N. Miller and M. B. Brewer (Eds.), *Groups in contact: The psychology of desegregation.* New York: Academic Press.

Johnson, L., Driscoll, S., Hertig, A., Cole, P., and Nickerson, R. (1979). Vaginal adenosis in stillborns and neonates exposed to DES and steroidal estrogens and progestins. *Obstetrics and Gynecology, 53,* 671–679.

Johnson, L., Townsend, R., and Wilson, M. (1975). Habituation during sleeping and waking. *Psychophysiology, 3,* 8–17.

Johnston, L. D., Bachman, J. G., and O'Malley, P. M. (1983). *Monitoring the future: Questionnaire responses from the nation's high school seniors.* Ann Arbor, Mich.: Institute for Social Research.

Johnston, L. D., Bachman, J. G., and O'Malley, P. M. (1987). *Drug use among American high school students, college and other young adults: National trends through 1986.* Rockville, Md.: National Institute on Drug Abuse.

Johnston, L., O'Malley, P., and Bachman, J. (1988). *Drug use among American high school students, college students and other young adults: National trends through 1987.* Rockville, Md.: National Institute on Drug Abuse.

Johnston, F. (1979). Somatic growth of the infant and preschool child. In F. Falkner and J. Tanner (Eds.), *Human growth* (vol. 2). New York: Plenum Press.

Johnston, F., Hamill, P., and Lemshow, S. (1974). *Skinfold thickness of youths 12–17 Years.* U.S. Public Health Service Publication no. 132. Washington, D.C.: U.S. Government Printing Office.

Johnston, J., and Slobin, D. (1979). The development of locative expressions in English, Italian, Serbo-Croatian, and Turkish. *Journal of Child Language, 6,* 529–545.

Jones, B., and Duffy, J. (1982). An analysis of performance by preschool children on the KRISP and on a length discrimination task. *Acta Psychologica, 52,* 197–211.

Jones, C. (1985). *Sharing birth: A father's guide to giving support during labor.* New York: Quill.

Jones, M. C. (1965). Psychological correlates of somatic development. *Child Development, 36,* 899–911.

Jones, R. L., (Ed.). (1989). *Black adolescents.* Berkeley, Calif.: Cobb & Henry.

Josselson, R. (1980). Ego development in adolescence. In J. Adelson (Ed.), *Handbook of adolescent psychology.* New York: Wiley.

Justice, B., and Duncan, D. (1977). Child abuse as a work-related problem. *Journal of Behavior Technology, Methods and Therapy, 23,* 53–55.

Kagan, J. (1973). Meaning and memory in two cultures. *Child Development, 44,* 221–223.

Kagan, J. (1979). Structure and process in the human infant: The otogeny of mental representation. In M. Bornstein and W. Kessen (Eds.), *Psychological development from infancy: Image to intention.* Hillsdale, N.J.: Erlbaum.

Kagan, J. (1981). *The second year.* Cambridge, Mass.: Harvard University Press.

Kagan, J. (1984). *The nature of the child.* New York: Basic Books.

Kagan, J. (1989). Temperamental contributions to social behavior. *American Psychologist, 44,* 668–674.

Kagan, J., and Moss, H. A., (1962). *Birth to maturity: A study in psychological development.* New York: Wiley.

Kagan, J., Reznick, J. S., and Snidman, N. (1986). Temperamental inhibition in early childhood. In R. Plomin and J. Dunn (Eds.), *The study of temperament: Changes, continuities, and challenges.* Hillsdale, N.J.: Erlbaum.

Kagan, J., Reznick, J. S., and Snidman, N. (1988). Biological bases of childhood shyness. *Science, 240,* 167–171.

Kail, R. (1988). Developmental functions for speeds of cognitive processes. *Journal of Experimental Child Psychology, 45,* 339–364.

Kaitz, M., Meschulach-Sarfaty, O., Auerbach, J., and Eidelman, A. (1988). A re-examination of newborns' ability to imitate facial expressions. *Developmental Psychology, 24,* 3–7.

Kakar, S. (1982). *The inner world: A psychoanalytic study of childhood and society in India.* Delhi: Oxford University Press.

Kalter, N. (1987). Long-term effects of divorce on children: A developmental vulnerability model. *American Journal of Orthopsychiatry, 57,* 587–600.

Kang, J. (1990). *Identity development in Korean-American college women.* Unpublished manuscript, Yale University.

Kamii, C., and DeVries, R. (1977). Piaget for early education. In M. Day and R. Parker (Eds.), *The preschool in action.* (2nd ed.). Boston: Allyn and Bacon.

Kane, B. (1977). Children's concepts of death. *Journal of Genetic Psychology, 24,* 315–320.

Kaplan, A., and Bean, J. (Eds.). (1976). *Beyond sex-role stereotypes: Readings toward a psychology of androgyny.* Boston: Little, Brown.

Karniol, R. (1978). Children's use of intention cues in evaluating behavior. *Psychological Bulletin, 85,* 76–86.

Karniol, R. (1980). A conceptual analysis of imminent justice responses in children. *Child Development, 51,* 118–130.

Katz, L. (1984). Ethical issues in working with young children. In L. Katz (Ed.), *More talks with teachers.* Urbana, Ill.: ERIC Clearinghouse.

Katz, P. A. (1976). The acquisition of racial attitudes in children. In P. Katz (Ed.), *Towards the elimination of racism.* New York: Pergamon Press.

Katz, P., and Zalk, S. (1978). Modification of children's racial attitudes. *Developmental Psychology, 14,* 447–461.

Kaye, K. (1976). Infants' effects upon their mothers' teaching strategies. In J. Glidewell (Ed.), *The social context of learning and development*. New York: Gardner.

Kegeles, S. M., Adler, N. E., and Irwin, C. E. (1988). Sexually active adolescents and condoms: Changes over one year in knowledge, attitudes and use. *American Journal of Public Health, 78,* 450–461.

Kellogg, R. (1969). *Analyzing children's art.* Palo Alto, Calif: National Press Books.

Kelly, D., and Shannon D. (1988). The medical management of cardiorespiratory monitoring in infantile apnea. In J. Culbertson, H. Krous, and R. D. Bendell (Eds.), *Sudden infant death syndrome: Medical aspects and psychological management.* Baltimore: Johns Hopkins University Press.,

Kelly, J., and Wallerstein, J. (1976). The effects of parental divorce: Experiences of the child in early latency. *American Journal of Orthopsychiatry, 46,* 20–32.

Kempe, C. H., Silverman, E., Steele, B., Droegemueller, W., and Silver, H. (1962). The battered-child syndrome. *Journal of the American Medical Association, 181,* 17.

Kempe, R., and Kempe, C. H. (1984). *The common secret: Sexual abuse of children and adolescents.* New York: Freeman.

Kennell, J., Voos, D., and Klaus, M. (1979). Parent-infant bonding. In J. Osofsky (Ed.), *Handbook of infant development.* New York: Wiley.

Keogh, K. (1988). *Dealing with AIDS: Breaking the chain of infection.* Arlington, Va.: American Association of School Administrators.

Kessel, S. (1988). The American context: The health care system in the United States. In U.S. Department of Health and Human Services, *Proceedings of the International Collaborative Effort on Perinatal and Infant Mortality* (vol. 1). Hyattsville, Md.: U.S. Department of Health and Human Services.

Kessen, W. (1983). The child and other cultural inventions. In F. Kessel and A. Siegel (Eds.), *The child and other cultural inventions.* New York: Praeger.

Khalakdina, M. (1979). *Early child care in India.* London: Gordon and Breach.

Kiernan, K., Colley, J., Douglas, J., and Reid, D. (1976). Chronic cough in young adults in relation to smoking habits, childhood environment, and chest illness. *Respiration, 33,* 236–244.

Kisilevsky, B., and Muir, D. (1984). Neonatal habituation and dishabituation to tactile stimulation during sleep. *Developmental Psychology, 20,* 367–373.

Kitchen, W., Ford, G., Rickards, A., Lissenden, J., and Ryan, M. (1987). Children of birth weight <1000 grams: Changing outcome between ages 2 and 5 years. *Journal of Pediatrics, 110,* 283–288.

Kitchen, W., Rickards, A., Ryan, M., Ford, G., Lissenden, J., and Boyle, L. (1986). Improved outcome to two years of very-low-birth weight infants: Fact or artifact? *Developmental Medicine and Child Neurology, 28,* 579–588.

Kitson, G., and Raschke, H. (1981). Divorce research: What we know; what we need to know. *Journal of Divorce, 4,* 1–37.

Kitzinger, S. (1980). *The complete book of pregnancy and childbirth.* New York: Knopf.

Kitzinger, S. (1985). Birth over thirty. New York: Penguin.

Klagsbrun, F. (1981). *Too young to die: Youth and suicide.* New York: Pocket Books.

Klaus, M., and Kennell, J. (1976). *Maternal-infant bonding.* St. Louis: Mosby.

Klein, S. (Ed.). (1985). *Handbook for achieving sex equity through education.* Baltimore: Johns Hopkins University Press.

Kleinman, M. (1983). *The acquisition of motor skill.* Princeton, N.J.: Princeton Book Company.

Klienman, J. (1988). Perinatal and infant mortality: Recent trends in the United States. In U.S. Department of Health and Human Services *Proceedings of the International Collaborative Effort on Perinatal and Infant Mortality* (vol. 1). Hyattsville, Md.: U.S. Department of Health and Human Services.

Klinnert, M. D., Emde, R. N., Butterfield, P., and Campos, J. J. (1986). Social referencing: The infant's use of emotional signals from a friendly adult with mother present. *Developmental Psychology, 22,* 427–432.

Kliot, D., and Silverstein, L. (1980). The Leboyer approach: A new concern for psychological aspects of childbirth experience. In B. Blum (Ed.), *Psychological aspects of pregnancy, birthing, and bonding.* New York: Human Sciences Press.

Knittle, J., Tiommer, K., Ginsberg-Fellner, F., Brown, R., and Katz, D. (1979). The growth of adipose tissue in children and adolescents. *Journal of Clinical Investigation, 63,* 239–246.

Kogan, N. (1973). Creativity and cognitive style: A lifespan perspective. In P. Baltes and K. Schaie (Eds.), *Life span developmental psychology: Personality and socialization.* New York: Academic Press.

Kogan, N. (1982). Cognitive styles in older adults. In T. Field (Ed.), *Review of human development.* New York: Wiley.

Kogan, N. (1989). *A 15-year longitudinal analysis of the correlates of field dependence-independence.* Paper presented at the biennial meeting of the Society for Research in Child Development, Kansas City, Missouri.

Kohlberg, L. (1964). Development of moral character and moral ideology. In M. L. Hoffman and L. W. Hoffman (Eds.), *Review of child development research* (vol. 1). New York: Russell Sage.

Kohlberg, L. (1966). A cognitive-developmental view of sex-role development. In E. Maccoby (Ed.), *The development of sex differences.* Stanford, Calif.: Stanford University Press.

Kohlberg, L. (1976). Moral stages and moralization: The cognitive-developmental approach. In T. Lickona (Ed.), *Moral development and behavior.* New York: Holt, Rinehart, and Winston.

Kolata, G. (1989a, July 1). Gender gap in standard tests is narrowing, experts find. *New York Times,* pp. A-1, 8.

Kolata, G. (1989b, August 11). In cities, poor families are dying of crack. *New York Times,* pp. A-1, 13.

Kolata, G. (1989c, October 8). AIDS is spreading in teen-agers, a new trend alarming to experts. *New York Times,* pp. A-1, 30.

Komarovsky, M. (1976). *Dilemmas of masculinity: A study of college youth.* New York: Norton.

Konner, M. (1989). Where should baby sleep? *New York Times Magazine,* pp. 39–40.

Kopp, C., and Parmalee, A. (1979). Prenatal and perinatal influences on infant behavior. In J. Osofsky (Ed.), *Handbook of infant development.* New York: Wiley.

Korner, A. (1981). Intervention with preterm infants: Rationale, aims, and means. In V. Smeriglio (Ed.), *Newborns and parents.* Hillsdale, N.J.: Erlbaum.

Korner, A. F. (1974). The effect of the infant's state, level of arousal, sex and ontogenic stage on the caregiver. In M. Lewis and L. A. Rosenblum (Eds.), *The effect of the infant on its caregiver.* New York: Wiley.

Kotelchuck, M. (1976). The infant's relationship to the father: Experimental evidence. In M. E. Lamb (Ed.), *The role of the father in child development.* New York: Wiley.

Kovar, M., and Meny, D. (1981). A statistical profile. In the Report of the Select Panel for the Promotion of Child Health, *Better health for our children* (vol. 3). Washington, D.C.: U.S. Government Printing Office.

Krasnor, L., and Rubin, K. (1983). Preschool social problem solving: Attempts and outcomes in naturalistic interaction. *Child Development, 54,* 1545–1558.

Krech, D., Rosenzweig, M., and Bennett, E. (1966). Environmental impoverishment, social isolation, and changes in brain chemistry and anatomy. *Physiology and Behavior, 1,* 99–104.

Kruse, J., and Presseisen, B. (1987). *A catalog of programs for teaching thinking.* Philadelphia: Research for Better Schools.

Kubler-Ross, E. (1983). *On children and death.* New York: Macmillan.

Kuhl, P. (1976). Speech perception by the chinchilla. *Journal of the Acoustical Society of America, 60,* #S81.

Kunkel, D. (1982). Children and host-selling television commercials. *Communications Research, 15,* 71–92.

Kutner, L. (1989, March 16). Parent and child: Responding to aggressive behavior. *New York Times,* p. C-1.

Laboratory of Comparative Human Cognition. (1982). Culture and intelligence. In R. Sternberg (Ed.), *Handbook of human intelligence.* New York: Cambridge University Press.

Laboratory of Comparative Human Cognition. (1986). Contributions of cross-cultural research to educational practice. *American Psychologist, 41,* 1049–1058.

Labouvie-Vief, G. (1982). Discontinuities in development from childhood to adulthood: A cognitive-developmental view. In T. Field (Ed.), *Review of human development.* New York: Wiley.

Labov, W. (1982). *Social stratification of English in New York City.* Washington, D. C.: Center for Applied Linguistics.

Lacey, B., and Lacey, J. (1978). Two-way communication between the heart and the brain. *American Psychologist, 33,* 99–113.

La Leche League International. (1988). *The womanly art of breastfeeding* (4th ed.). New York: Plume Books.

Lamb, M. (1977a). The development of mother-infant and father-infant attachments in the second year of life. *Developmental Psychology, 13,* 637–648.

Lamb, M. (1977b). Father-infant and mother-infant interactions in the first year of life. *Child development, 48,* 167–181.

Lamb, M., and Hwang, C. (1982). Maternal attachment and mother-neonate bonding: A critical review. In M. Lamb and A. Brown (Eds.), *Advances in developmental psychology* (vol. 2). Hillsdale, N.J.: Erlbaum.

Lamb, M., and Roopnarine, J. (1979). Peer influences on sex-role development in preschoolers. *Child Development, 50,* 1219–1222.

Lambert, N., and Hartsough, C. (1984). Contribution of predispositional factors to the diagnosis of hyperactivity. *American Journal of Orthopsychiatry, 54,* 97–109.

Lane, H. (1976). *The wild boy of Aveyron.* Cambridge, Mass.: Harvard University Press.

Langer, E. (1985). Playing the middle against both ends: The usefulness of adult cognitive activity as a model for cognitive activity in childhood and old age. In S. Yussen (Ed.), *The growth of reflection in children.* Orlando, Fla.: Academic Press.

Langer, W. (1972). Checks on population growth: 1750–1850. *Scientific American, 226,* 93–100.

Langlois, J., and Stephan, C. (1981). Beauty and the beast: The role of physical attractiveness in the development of peer relations and social behavior. In S. Brehm, S. Kassin, and F. Gibbons (Eds.), *Violence and the mass media.* New York: Harper and Row.

Lasch, C. (1975–1976). The family and history. *New York Review of Books.* November–January.

Laslett, P. (1975). *The world we have lost.* New York: Scribner's.

Laslett, P., and Wall, R. (Eds.). (1975). *Household and family in past time.* Cambridge, England: Cambridge University Press.

Lassen, N., Ingvar, D., and Skinhoj, E. (1978). Brain function and blood flow. *Scientific American, 227,* 62–71.

Laurendeau, M., and Pinard, A. (1972). *Casual thinking in the child.* New York: International Universities Press.

Lave, J. (1988). *Cognition in practice: Mind, mathematics and culture in everyday life.* Cambridge: Cambridge University Press.

Lave, J., Smith, S., and Butler, M. (1989). Problem solving as an everyday practice. In R. Charles and E. Silver (Eds.), *Setting a research agenda: Teaching and evaluation of problem solving.* Hillsdale, N.J.: Erlbaum.

Lawrence, R., McAnarney, E., Aten, M., Ike, H., Baldwin, C., and Baldwin, A. (1981). Aggressive behaviors in young mothers: Marks of future morbidity? *Pediatric Research, 15,* 443.

Lawson, C. (1989, June 15). Toys: Boys fight wars, girls still apply makeup. *New York Times,* p. C-1.

Lazar, I., and Darlington, R. (1982). Lasting effects of early education: A report from the Consortium for Longitudinal studies. *Monographs of the Society for Research on Child Development, 147* (2–3, Serial No. 195).

Leach, P. (1987). *Babyhood.* (2nd ed.). New York: Knopf.

Leahy, R. (1990). Development of concepts of economic and social inequality. In V. McLoyd and C. Flanagan (Eds.), *Economic stress: Effects on family life and child development.* San Francisco: Jossey-Bass.

Leahy, R., and Hunt, T. (1983). A cognitive-developmental approach to the development of conceptions of intelligence. In R. Leahy (Ed.), *The child's conception of social inequality.* New York: Academic Press.

Leavitt, L., Brown, J., Morse, P., and Graham, F. (1976). Cardiac orienting and auditory discrimination in six week-old infants. *Developmental Psychology, 12,* 514–523.

Lebel, R. (1978). Ethical issues arising in the genetic counseling relationship. In D. Bergsma (Ed.), *Birth defects.* Washington, D.C.: March of Dimes.

LeBow, M. (1984). *Childhood obesity.* New York: Springer.

LeBow, M. (1986). Child obesity: Dangers. *Canadian Psychology, 27,* 275–285.

Leboyer, F. (1975). *Birth without violence.* New York: Knopf.

Lecours, A. (1975). Myleogenetic correlates of the development of speech and language. In E. H. Lenneberg and E. Lenneberg (Eds.), *Foundations of language development.* New York: Academic Press.

Leifer, M. (1977). Psychological changes accompanying pregnancy and motherhood. *Genetic Psychology Monographs, 95,* 68.

Lemon, J. (1977). Women and blacks on prime-time television. *Journal of Communication, 27,* 70–79.

Lenneberg, E. (1967). *Biological foundations of language.* New York: Wiley.

Lerner, J. (1988). *Learning disabilities* (5th ed.). Boston: Houghton Mifflin.

Lerner, R., Jovanovic, J., and Lerner, J. (1989). Objective and subjective attractiveness and early adolescent adjustment. *Journal of Adolescence, 12,* 225–229.

Lerner, R., and Knapp, J. (1975). Actual and perceived intrafamilial attitudes of late adolescents and their parents. *Journal of Youth and Adolescence, 4,* 17–36.

Lerner, R., and Shea, J. (1982). Social behavior in adolescence. In B. Wolman (Ed.), *Handbook of developmental psychology.* Englewood Cliffs, N.J.: Prentice-Hall.

Lerner, R. M. (1985). Adolescent maturational changes and psychosocial development: A dynamic interactional perspective. *Journal of Youth and Adolescence, 14,* 355–369.

Lever, J. (1976). Sex differences in the games children play. *Social Problems, 23,* 479–487.

LeVine, R. (1988). Human parental care: Universal goals, cultural strategies, individual behavior. In R. LeVine, P. Miller, and M. West (Eds.), *Parental behavior in diverse societies.* San Francisco: Jossey-Bass.

LeVine, R. (1989a). Cultural environments in child development. In W. Damon (Ed.), *Child development today and tomorrow.* San Francisco: Jossey-Bass.

LeVine, R. (1989b). Cultural environments in cultural perspective. In W. Damon (Ed.), *Child development today and tomorrow.* San Francisco: Jossey-Bass.

Levinson, D. (1986). A conception of adult development. *American Psychologist, 41,* 3–13.

Levitin, T. (1979). Children of divorce. *Journal of Social Issues, 35,* 1–25.

Lewin, T. (1988, March 20). Fewer teen mothers, but more are unmarried. *New York Times,* p. E–6.

Lewis, C., and Lewis, M. (1983). Improving the health of children: Must the children be involved? *Annual Review of Public Health, 4,* 259–283.

Lewis, M., and Brooks-Gunn, J. (1979a). *Social cognition and the acquisition of self.* New York: Plenum Press.

Lewis, M., and Brooks-Gunn, J. (1979b). Toward a theory of social cognition: The development of the self. In I. Uzgiris (Ed.), *Social interaction and communication during infancy.* San Francisco: Jossey-Bass.

Lewis, M., Feiring, C., and McGuffog, C. (1986). Profiles of young gifted and normal children. *Topics in Early Childhood and Special Education, 6,* 9–23.

Libbey, P., and Bybee, R. (1979). The physical abuse of adolescents. *The Journal of Social Issues, 35,* 101–116.

Licht, B., and Dweck, C. (1984). Determinants of academic achievement: The interaction of children's achievement orientations with skill area. *Developmental Psychology, 20,* 628–632.

Lickona, T. (1976). Research on Piaget's theory of moral development. In T. Lickona (Ed.), *Moral development and behavior.* New York: Holt, Rinehart, and Winston.

Lightfoot, S. (1983). *The good high school.* New York: Basic Books.

Lindzey, G., and Thiessen, D. (Eds.), (1970). *Contributions to behavior genetic analysis: The mouse as a prototype.* New York: Appleton.

Linn, M., and Siegel, H. (1984). Postformal reasoning: A philosophical model. In M. Commons, F. Richards and C. Armon (Eds.), *Beyond formal Operations: Late adolescent and adult cognitive development.* New York: Praeger.

Lipsitt, L. (1982). Infant learning. In T. Field (Ed.), *Review of human development.* New York: Wiley.

Lipsitt, L., and Kaye, H. (1964). Conditioned sucking in the newborn. *Psychonomic Science, 1,* 29–30.

Lipsitt, L., and Levy, N. (1959). Electrotactual threshold in the neonate. *Child Development, 30,* 547–554.

Livson, N., and Peskin, H. (1981a). Perspectives on adolescence from longitudinal research. In J. Adelson (Ed.), *Handbook of adolescent psychology.* New York: Wiley.

Livson, N., and Peskin, H. (1981b). Psychological health at 40: Predictions from adolescent personality. In D. Eichorn, J. Clausen, N. Haan, M. Honzik, and P. Mussen (Eds.), *Present and past in middle life.* New York: Academic Press.

Locke, J. (1693/1699). *Some thoughts concerning education.* London: Churchill.

Lochhead, J. (1985). Teaching analytical reasoning skills through pair problem solving. In J. Segal, S. Chipman, and R. Glaser (Eds.), *Thinking and learning skills: Relating instruction to research* (vol. 1). Hillsdale, N.J.: Erlbaum.

Logan, D. D. (1980). The menarche experience in twenty-three foreign countries. *Adolescence, 58,* 247–257.

Lohman, G., and Roche, A. (1988). *Anthropometric standards reference manual.* Champaign, Ill.: Human Kinetics Press.

Londerville, S., and Main, M. (1981). Security of attachment, compliance and maternal training methods in the second year of life. *Developmental Psychology, 17,* 289–299.

Lord, C. (1982). Psychopathology in early development. In S. Moore and C. Cooper (Eds.), *The young child: Reviews of research* (vol. 3). Washington, D.C.: National Association for the Education of Young Children.

Lord, L. J., Scherschel, P. M., Thornton, J., Moore, L. J., and Quick, B. E. (1987, October 5). Desperately seeking baby. *U. S. News & World Report,* pp. 58–64.

Lorenz, K. (1952). *King Solomon's ring.* New York: Thomas Y. Crowell.

Lorenz, K. (1960). *On aggression.* New York: Harcourt, Brace, and World.

Lorenz, K. (Ed.). (1970). *Studies in animal and human behavior* (vol. 1). Cambridge, Mass.: Harvard University Press.

Lozoff, B. (1989). Nutrition and behavior. *American Psychologist, 44,* 231–236.

Lozoff, B., Wolf, A. W., and Davis, N. S. (1984). Cosleeping in urban families with young children in the United States. *Pediatrics, 74,* 171–182.

Lutz, P. (1983). The stepfamily: An adolescent perspective. *Family Relations, 32,* 367–376.

Lynch, G., and Gall, C. (1979). Organization and reorganization in the central nervous system. In F. Falkner and J. Tanner (Eds.), *Human Growth.* New York: Plenum Press.

McAlister, A., Perry, C., and Maccoby, N. (1979). Adolescent smoking: Onset and prevention. *Pediatrics, 4,* 650–658.

McAuliffe, K., and McAuliffe, S. (1983, November 6). Keeping up with the genetic revolution. *The New York Times Magazine,* pp. 41–44, 93–97.

McCabe, M. P. (1985). Toward a theory of adolescent dating. *Adolescence, 19,* 150–170.

McCall, R. (1981). Nature-nurture and the two realms of development: A proposed integration with respect to mental development. *Child Development, 52,* 1–12.

McCall, R., and Kagan, J. (1967). Stimulus schema discrepancy and attention in the infant. *Journal of Experimental Child Psychology, 5,* 381–390.

McCall, R., and Kennedy, C. (1980). Attention to babyishness in babies. *Journal of Experimental Child Psychology, 29,* 189–201.

McCall, R., Parke, R., and Kavanaugh, R. (1977). Imitation of live and televised models by children one to three years of age. *Monographs of the Society for Research on Child Development, 42,* 173.

Maccoby, E. (1980). *Social development, psychological growth, and parent-child relations.* New York: Harcourt Brace Jovanovich.

Maccoby, E. (1984). Socialization and developmental change. *Child Development, 55,* 317–328.

Maccoby, E., and Jacklin, C. (1974). *The psychology of sex differences.* Stanford, Calif: Stanford University Press.

Maccoby, E., and Jacklin, C. (1980). Sex differences in aggression: A rejoinder and reprise. *Child Development, 48,* 964–980.

Maccoby, E., and Jacklin, C. (1987). Gender segregation in childhood. In H. Reese (Ed.), *Advances in child development and behavior,* (vol. 20.). New York: Academic Press.

McDaniel, K. D. (1986). Pharmacological treatment of psychiatric and neuro-developmental disorders in children and adolescents (Parts 1, 2, & 3). *Clinical Pediatrics, 25,* 65–71, 198–224.

MacFarlane, A. (1977). *The psychology of childbirth.* Cambridge, Mass.: Harvard University Press.

McGarrigle, J., and Donaldson, M. (1974). Conservation accidents. *Cognition, 3,* 341–350.

McGarrigle, J., Grieve, R., and Hughes, M. (1978). Interpreting inclusion. *Journal of Experimental Child Psychology, 26,* 528–550.

MacGregor, S. N., Keith, L. G., Chasnoff, I. J., Rosner, M. A., Chisum, G. M. Shaw, P., and Minogue, J. P. (1987). Cocaine use during pregnancy: Adverse perinatal outcome. *American Journal of Obstetrics and Gynecology, 1,* 66–90.

McKay, H., Sinisterra, L., McKay, A., Gomez, H., and Lioreda, P. (1978). Improving cognitive ability in chronically deprived children. *Science, 200,* 270–278.

McKenzie, B., and Day, R. (1987). Perceptual development in infancy: Reflections on some central issues. In B. McKenzie and R. Day (Eds.), *Perceptual development in early infancy.* Hillsdale, N.J.: Erlbaum.

McKenzie, C. (1983). Risk factors in perinatology. In C. McKenzie and K. Vestal (Eds.), *High-risk perinatal nursing.* Philadelphia: Saunders.

McKie, R. (1988). *The genetic jigsaw: The story of the new genetics.* New York: Oxford University Press.

McKinney, J., Fitzgerald, H., and Strommen, E. (1982). *Developmental Psychology: The Adolescent and young adult.* Homewood, Ill.: Dorsey Press.

McNellis, K. (1987). In search of the attentional deficit. In S. Ceci (Ed.), *Handbook of cognitive, social and neuropsychological aspects of learning.* Hillsdale, N.J.: Erlbaum.

Madsen, M. (1971). Developmental and cross-cultural differences in the cooperative and competitive behavior of young children. *Journal of Cross-Cultural Psychology, 2,* 365–371.

Mahler, M. (1974). Symbiosis and individuation. *Psychoanalytic Study of the Child, 29,* 89–106.

Mahler, M., Pine, F., and Bergman, A. (1975). *The psychological birth of the human infant: Symbiosis and individuation.* New York: Basic Books.

Main, M., and George, C. (1985). Responses of abused and disadvantaged toddlers to distress in agemates: A study in the day care setting. *Developmental Psychology, 21,* 407–412.

Main, M., Kaplan, N., and Cassidy, J. (1985). Security in infancy, childhood, and adulthood: A move to the level of representation. In 1. Bretherton and E. Waters (Eds.), Growing points of attachment theory and research. *Monographs of the Society for Research on Child Development, 50* (209).

Malina, R. (1982). Motor development in the early years. In S. Moore and C. Cooper (Eds.), *The young child: Reviews of research* (vol. 3). Washington, D.C.: National Association for the Education of Young Children.

Mall, J. (1985, March 17). A study of U. S. teen pregnancy rate. *Los Angeles Times,* part 7, p. 27.

Maloney, M. J., and Klykylo, W. M. (1983). An overview of anorexia nervosa, bulimia and obesity in children and adolescents. *Journal of the American Academy of Child Psychiatry, 22,* 99–107.

Malson, L. (1972). *Wolf Children.* London: NLB Publishers.

Maltz, D., and Borker, R. (1982). A cultural approach to male-female miscommunication. In J. Gumperz (Ed.), *Language and social identity.* New York: Cambridge University Press.

Mandelbaum, D. (1970). *Society in India.* Cambridge, Mass.: Harvard University Press.

Mandell, F. (1988). The family and sudden infant death syndrome. In J. Culbertson, H. Krous, and R. D. Bendell (Eds.), *Sudden infant death syndrome: Medical aspects and psychological management.* Baltimore: Johns Hopkins University Press.

Manicas, P., and Secord, P. (1983). Implications for psychology of the new philosophy of science. *American Psychologist, 38,* 399–413.

Mannle, S., and Tomasello, M. (1987). Fathers, siblings and the bridge hypothesis. In K. Nelson and A. van Kleeck (Eds.), *Children's language* (vol. 6). Hillsdale, N.J.: Erlbaum.

Marcia, J. (1967). Ego identity status: Relationship to change in self-esteem, 'general maladjustment,' and authoritarianism. *Journal of Personality, 35,* 119–133.

Marcia, J. (1980). Identity in adolescence. In J. Adelson (Ed.), *Handbook of adolescent psychology.* New York: Wiley.

Marcus, D., and Overton, W. (1978). The development of cognitive gender constancy and sex role preferences. *Child Development, 49,* 434–444.

Marion, R. W., Wilznia, A. A., Hutcheon, R. G., and Rubinstein, A. (1986). Human T-cell lymphotropic virus type III (HTLV-III) embryopathy. *American Journal of Diseases of Children, 140,* 638–640.

Marks, L., Hammeal, R., and Bornstein, M. (1987). Perceiving similarity and comprehending metaphor. With commentary by L. Smith. *Monographs of the Society for Research on Child Development, 52* (1, No. 215).

Marshall, W. (1978). Puberty. In F. Falkner and J. Tanner (Eds.), *Human growth* (vol. 2). New York: Plenum Press.

Marshall, W., and Swan, A. (1971). Seasonal variation in growth rates of normal and blind children. *Human Biology, 43,* 502–516.

Marshall, W., and Tanner, J. (1974). Puberty. In J. Davis and J. Dobbing (Eds.), *Scientific foundations of pediatrics.* London: Heinemann Publishers.

Martin, B. (1975). Parent-child relations. In F. Horowitz (Ed.), *Review of child development research* (vol. 4). Chicago: University of Chicago Press.

Martinez, G., and Nalezienski, J. (1981). 1980 update: The recent trend in breastfeeding. *Pediatrics, 67,* 260.

Marx, F., and Silegson, M. (1988). *The public school early childhood survey: Early childhood study: The state survey.* New York: Bank Street College of Education.

Masters, J., and Furman, W. (1981). Popularity, individual friendship selection, and specific peer interactions among children. *Developmental Psychology, 17,* 344–350.

Matas, L., Arend, R., and Sroufe, L. (1978). Continuity and adaptation in the second year: The relationship between quality of attachment and later competence. *Child Development, 49,* 547–556.

Mather, K., and Jinks, J. (1977). *Introduction to biometrical genetics.* London: Chapman and Hall.

Matthews, K. A., and Rodin, J. (1989). Women's changing work roles: Impact on health, family, and public policy. *American Psychologist, 44,* 1389–1393.

Mazar, B., Piper, M., and Ramsay, M. (1988). Developmental outcome in very low-birth-weight infants 6 to 36 months old. *Journal of Developmental and Behavioral Pediatrics, 9,* 293–297.

Maziade, M., Boudreault, M., Copte, R., and Thivierge, J. (1986). Influence of gentle birth delivery procedures and other perinatal circumstances on infant temperament: Developmental and social implications. *Journal of Pediatrics, 108,* 134–136.

Meichenbaum, D. (1977). *Cognitive behavior modification.* New York: Plenum Press.

Meichenbaum, D., and Goodman, J. (1971). Training impulsive children to talk to themselves. *Journal of Abnormal Psychology, 77,* 115–126.

Meilman, P. (1979). Cross-sectional age changes in ego identity status during adolescence. *Developmental Psychology, 15,* 230–231.

Melamed, B., Hawes, R., Heiby, E., and Glick, J. (1975). Use of filmed modeling to reduce uncooperative behavior of children during dental treatment. *Journal of Dental Research, 54,* 797–801.

Meltzoff, A. (1988). Infant imitation after a one-week delay: Long-term memory for novel acts and multiple stimuli. *Developmental Psychology, 24,* 470–476.

Menning, B. (1980). The emotional needs of infertile couples. *Fertility Sterility, 34* (4), 313 ff.

Merck Laboratories. (1985). *The Merck manual of diagnosis and therapy* (10th ed.). Rahway, N.J.: Merck, Sharp, and Dohme.

Meredith, H. (1967). A synopsis of pubertal changes in youth. *Journal of School Health, 37,* 171–176.

Meredith, H. (1981). Body size and form among ethnic groups of infants, children, youth, and adults. In R. Munroe, R. Munroe, and B. Whiting (Eds.), *Handbook of cross-cultural human development.* New York: Garland STPM Press.

Meringoff, L., Vibbert, M., Kelly, H., and Char, C. (1981). *How shall you take your story: With or without pictures?* Paper presented at the biennial meeting of the Society for Research on Child Development, April 1981. Boston.

Messer, S. (1976). Reflection-impulsivity: A review. *Psychological Bulletin, 83,* 1026–1053.

Meyer, B., and Rice, E. (1984). The structure of text. In P. Pearson (Ed.), *Handbook of reading research.* New York: McGraw-Hill.

Michaels, R., and Mellin, G. (1960). Prospective experience with maternal rubella and the associated congenital malformations. *Pediatrics, 26,* 200–209.

Miesels, S. (1984). Prediction, prevention, and developmental screening in the EPSDT Program. In H. Stevenson and A. Siegel (Eds.), *Child development and social policy.* Chicago: University of Chicago Press.

Mikaye, K., Chen, S., and Campos, J. (1985). Infant temperament, mother's mode of interaction, and attachment in Japan. In I. Bretherton and E. Waters (Eds.), Growing points of attachment theory and research. *Monographs of the Society for Research on Child Development, 50* (209).

Miller, J. B. (1976). *Toward a new psychology of women.* Boston: Beacon Press.

Miller, L., and Bizzell, R. (1983). Long-term effects of four preschool programs, Sixth, seventh and eighth grades. *Child Development, 54,* 727–741.

Miller, N. (1984). Language problems and bilingual children. In N. Miller (Ed.), *Bilingualism and language disability: Assessment and remediation.* San Diego: College-Hill Press.

Miller, P. (1988). *Theories of child development* (2nd ed.). New York: Freeman.

Miller, P., and Simon, W. (1980). The development of sexuality in adolescence. In J. Adelson (Ed.), *Handbook of adolescent psychology.* New York: Wiley.

Miller-Jones, D. (1989). Culture and testing. *American Psychologist, 44,* 360–366.

Minkoff, H., Deepak, N., Menez, R., and Fikrig, S. (1987). Pregnancies resulting in infants with acquired immunodeficiency syndrome of AIDS-related complex: Follow-up of mothers, children, and subsequently born siblings. *Obstetrics and Gynecology, 69,* 288–291.

Minuchin, P., and Shapiro, E. (1983), The school as a context for social development. In E. M. Hetherington (Ed.), *Handbook of child psychology: Vol. 4: Socialization, personality and social development.* (4th ed.). New York: Wiley.

Mischel, W. (1984). Convergences, challenges, and the search for consistency. *American Psychologist, 39,* 351–364.

Mitchell, A. (1988). *The public school early childhood survey* (vols. 1–2). New York: Bank Street College of Education.

Mitchell, A., and Modigliani, K. (1989). Young children in public schools? *Young Children, 44,* 56–61.

Mitchell, A., Seligson, M., and Marx, F. (1989). *Early childhood programs and the public schools: Between promise and practice.* Dover, Mass.: Auburn House.

Mitchell, J. (1974). *Psychoanalysis and feminism.* New York: Pantheon.

Mittwoch, U. (1973). *Genetics and sex differentiation.* New York: Academic Press.

Miura, I., and Okamoto, Y. (1989). Comparisons of U.S. and Japanese first-graders' cognitive representation of number and understanding of place value. *Journal of Educational Psychology, 81,* 109–114.

Modgil, S., Modgil, C., and Brown, G. (1983). *Jean Piaget: An interdisciplinary critique.* London: Routledge & Kegan Paul.

Moen, P., Kain, E., and Elder, G. (1981). *Economic conditions and family life.* Washington, D.C.: National Academy of Sciences, Committee on Child Development and Public Policy.

Molfese, D., Molfese, V., and Carrell, P. (1982). Early language development. In B. Wolman (Ed.), *Handbook of developmental psychology.* New York: Wiley.

Money, J. (1975). Counseling in genetics and applied behavior genetics. In K. W. Schaie, V. E. Anderson, G. McClearn, and J. Money (Eds.), *Developmental human behavior genetics.* Lexington, Mass.: Heath.

Money, J. (1987). Sin, sickness, or status? Homosexual gender identity and psychoneuroendocrinology. *American Psychologist, 42,* 384–399.

Monkus, E., and Bancalari, E. (1981). Neonatal outcome. In K. G. Scott, T. Field, and E. G. Robertson (Eds.), *Teenage parents and their offspring.* New York: Grune and Stratton.

Montessori, M. (1964). *The Montessori method.* New York: Schocken Books.

Moores, D. (1987). *Educating the deaf: Psychology, principles and practices.* Boston: Houghton Mifflin.

Morrison, D. M. (1985). Adolescent contraceptive behavior: A review. *Psychological Bulletin, 98,* 538–568.

Morrongiello, B., Clifton, R., and Kulig, J. (1982). Newborn cardiac and behavioral orienting responses to sound under varying precedence-effect conditions. *Infant Behavior and Development, 5,* 249–260.

Morse, J. M., and Park, C. (1988). Differences in cultural expectations of the perceived painfulness of childbirth. In K. L. Michaelson (Ed.), *Childbirth in America: Anthropological perspectives.* South Hadley, Mass.: Bergin & Garvey.

Morse, P., and Snowdon, C. (1975). An investigation of categorical speech discrimination by rhesus monkeys. *Perception and Psychophysics, 17,* 9–16.

Mowrer, A. H. (1960). *Learning theory and the symbolic process.* New York: Wiley.

Muehlenhard, C., and Linton, M. (1987). Date rape. *Journal of Counseling Psychology, 34,* 186–196.

Mueller, E., and Vandell, D. (1978). Infant-infant interaction. In J. Osofsky (Ed.), *Handbook of infancy.* New York: Wiley.

Muir, B. (1983). *Essentials of genetics for nurses.* New York: Wiley.

Muir, D., and Field, J. (1979). Newborn infants' orientation to sound. *Child Development, 50,* 431–436.

Munroe, R., Munroe, R., and Whiting, J. (1981). Male sex-role resolutions. *In Handbook of cross-cultural human development.* New York: Garland.

Murphy, L. (1937). *Social behavior and child personality.* New York: Columbia University Press.

Murray, D. (1973). Suicidal and depressive feelings among college students. *Psychological Reports, 33,* 175–181.

Mussen, P., and Eisenberg-Berg, N. (1977). *Roots of caring, sharing and helping: The development of prosocial behavior in children.* San Francisco: Freeman.

Mussen, P., and Jones, M. (1957). Self-conceptions, motivations, and interpersonal attitudes of late and early-maturing boys. *Child Development, 28,* 243–256.

Muuss, R., (Ed.). (1975). *Adolescent behavior and society: A book of readings* (2nd ed.). New York: Random House.

Naeye, R. (1979). Causes of fetal and neonatal monality by race in a selected U.S. population. *American Journal of Public Health, 69,* 857.

Naeye, R., Blanc, W., and Paul, C. (1973). Effects of maternal nutrition on the human fetus. *Pediatrics, 52,* 494.

National Academy of Sciences/National Research Council (1980). Food and Nutrition Board. *Toward healthful diets.* Washington, D.C.

National Governors' Association. (1986, August). *Time for results: The governors' report 1991 report on education.* Washington, D.C.: National Governors' Association Center for Policy Research and Analysis.

National Safety Council. (1987). *Accident facts: 1987.* Chicago: Author.

Neimark, E. (1982a). Adolescent thought: Transition to formal operations. In B. Wolman (Ed.), *Handbook of developmental psychology.* Englewood Cliffs, N.J.: Prentice-Hall.

Neimark, E. (1982b). Cognitive development in adulthood: Using what you've got. In T. Field (Ed.), *Review of human development.* New York: Wiley.

Nelms, B., and Mullins, R. (1982). *Growth and development: Primary health care approach.* Englewood Cliffs, N.J.: Prentice-Hall.

Nelson, K. (1981). Individual differences in language development. *Developmental Psychology, 17,* 170–187.

Nelson, K. (1985). *Making sense: Acquisition of shared meaning.* New York: Academic Press.

Nelson, K., and Lucariello, J. (1985). The development of meaning in first words. In M. Barrett (Ed.), *Children's single-word speech.* New York: Wiley.

Nelson, N. M., Murray, W. E., Saroj, S., Bennet, K. J., Milner, R., and Sackett, D. L. (1980). A randomized clinical trial of the Leboyer approach to childbirth. *New England Journal of Medicine, 303,* 655–660.

Newcomb, M., and Bentler, P. (1989). Substance use and abuse among children and teenagers. *American Psychologist, 44,* 242–248

Newell, A., and Simon, H. (1972). *Human problem solving.* Englewood Cliffs, N.J.: Prentice-Hall.

Newman, P. (1982). The peer group. In B. Wolman (Ed.), *Handbook of developmental psychology.* Englewood Cliffs, N.J.: Prentice-Hall.

Neyzi, O., Alp, H., and Orhon, A. (1975). Sexual maturation in Turkish boys and girls. *Annals of Human Biology, 2,* 249–251.

Nichols, R. C. (1978). Twin studies of ability, personality, and interests. *Homo, 29,* 158–173.

Nickerson, R. (1986). Reasoning. In R. Dillon and R. Sternberg (Eds.), *Psychology and curriculum design.* New York: Academic Press.

Nickerson, R. (1988). On improving through instruction. In E. Rothkopf (Ed.), *Review of research in education* (vol. 15). Washington, D.C.: American Educational Research Association.

Nippold, M. (1988a). The literate lexicon. In M. Nippold (Ed.), *Later language development: Ages 9 through 19.* Boston: Little, Brown.

Nippold, M. (1988b). Verbal ambiguity. In M. Nippold (Ed.), *Later language development: Ages 9 through 19.* Boston: Little, Brown.

Nocolaisen, I. (1988). Concepts and learning among the Punan Bah of Sarawak, In G. Jahoda and I. Lewis (Eds.), *Acquiring culture: Cross-cultural studies in child development.* London: Croom Helm.

Noddings, N. (1984). *Caring.* Berkeley: University of California Press.

Norbeck, J. S., and Tilden, V. P. (1983). Life stress, social support and emotional disequilibrium in complications of pregnancy: A prospective multivariate study. *Journal of Health and Social Behavior, 24,* 30–46.

Norton, A. J., and Glick, P. C. (1986). One parent families: A social and economic profile. *Family Relations, 35,* 9–18.

Nucci, L. (1982). Conceptual development in the moral and conventional domains. *Review Educational Research, 52,* 92–122.

Nussbaum, R. L., and Ledbetter, D. H. (1986). Fragile X syndrome: A unique mutation in man. *Annual Review of Genetics, 20,* 109–145.

Nyhan, W. (1976). *The heredity factor.* New York: Grosset and Dunlap.

O'Brien, M., and Huston, A. C. (1985). Development of sex-typed play behavior in toddlers. *Developmental Psychology, 21,* 866–871.

Offir, C. W. (1982). *Human sexuality.* New York: Harcourt Brace Jovanovich.

Ogbu, J., and Matute-Bianchi, M. (1986). Understanding sociocultural factors: Knowledge, identity and school adjustment. In Bilingual Education Office (Ed.), *Beyond language: Social and cultural factors in schooling language minority students.* Sacramento, Calif.: California State Department of Education.

Ohnuki-Tierney, E. (1984). *Illness and culture in contemporary Japan.* New York: Cambridge University Press.

O'Leary, K., and O'Leary, S. (Eds.). (1977). *Classroom management: The successful use of behavior modification* (2nd ed.). New York: Pergamon Press.

Olson, D. (1986). Intelligence and literacy: Relationships between intelligence and the technologies of representation and communication. In R. Sternberg and R. Wagner (Eds.), *Practical Intelligence.* New York: Cambridge University Press.

Olson, D., and Torrance, N. (1983). Literacy and cognitive development: A conceptual transformation in the early school years. In S. Meadows (Ed.), *Developing thinking: Approaches to children's cognitive development.* London: Methuen.

Olson, G., and Sherman, T. (1983). Attention, learning, and memory in infants. In P. Mussen (Ed.), *Handbook of Child psychology* (vol. 2). New York: Wiley.

Opie, I., and Opie, P. (1969). *Children's games in streets and playgrounds.* London: Clarendon Press.

Orlick, T. D. (1981). Positive socialization via cooperative games. *Developmental Psychology, 17,* 426–429.

Orlick, T. (1986). *Psyching for sport: Mental training for athletes.* Champaign, Ill.: Leisure Press.

Ornstein, P., and Naus, M. (1985). Effects of knowledge base on children's memory strategies. In H. Reese (Ed.) *Advances in child development and behavior* (vol. 19). New York: Academic Press.

Osborn, J. (1988). The AIDS epidemic: Six years. In L. Breslow, J. Fielding, and L. Lave (Eds.), *Annual Review of Public Health* (vol. 9). Palo Alto, Calif.: Annual Reviews.

Otten, A. L. (1984, August 7). Medical efforts to help childless couples post host of difficult issues. *Wall Street Journal,* pp. 1, 14.

Palincsar, A. (1986). Metacognitive strategy instruction. *Exceptional Children, 53,* 118–124.

Palincsar, A., and Brown, A. (1984). Advances in cognitive instruction of handicapped children. In M. Wang, H. Walberg and M. Reynolds (Eds.), *Handbook of Special Education.* New York: Pergamon Press.

Palmer, R., Ouellette, M., Warner, L., and Leichtman, S. (1974). Congenital malformations in offspring of a chronic alcoholic mother. *Pediatrics 53,* 490–494.

Parke, R. (1977). Some effects of punishment on children's behavior-revisited. In P. Cantor (Ed.), *Understanding a child's world.* New York: McGraw-Hill.

Parke, R. D. (1981). *Fathers.* Cambridge, Mass.: Harvard University Press.

Parke, R., and O'Leary, S. (1976). Father-mother-infant interaction in the newborn period: Some feelings, some observations, and some unresolved issues. In K. Riegel and J. Meacham (Eds.), *The developing individual in a changing world. Vol 2. Social and environmental issues.* The Hague: Mouton.

Parke, R., and Sawin, D. (1976). The father's role in infancy: A re-evaluation. *The Family Coordinator, 25,* 365–371.

Parker, M. (1985). Identity and the development of religious thinking. In A. Waterman (Ed.), *Identity in adolescence: Processes and contents.* San Francisco: Jossey-Bass.

Parmalee, A. (1986). Children's illnesses: Their beneficial effects on behavioral development, *Child Development, 57,* 1–10.

Parmalee, A., and Sigman, M. (1983). Perinatal brain development and behavior. In P. Mussen (Ed.), *Handbook of child psychology* (vol. 2). New York: Wiley.

Parmalee, A., and Stern, E. (1972). The development of states in infants. In C. Clemente, D. Purpura, and F. Mayer (Eds.), *Sleep and the maturing nervous system.* New York: Academic Press.

Parten, M. (1932). Social play among preschool children. *Journal of Abnormal and Social Psychology, 27,* 243–269.

Passer, M. (1982). Psychological stress in youth sports. In R. Magill, M. Ash, and F. Smoll (Eds.), *Children in sport.* Champaign, Ill.: Human Kinetics Publishers.

Patten, M. (1981). Self-concept and self-esteem: Factors in adolescent pregnancy. *Adolescence, 16,* 765–778.

Patterson, G. R. (1976). The aggressive child: Victim and architect of a coercive system. In L. Hammerlyck, E. Marsh, and L. Handy (Eds.), *Behavior modification and families.* New York: Brunner/Mazel.

Patterson, G. R. (1982). *Coercive family processes.* Eugene, Ore.: Castilia Press.

Patterson, G. R. (1985). *A social learning approach to family intervention: Vol. 1: Families with aggressive children.* Eugene, Ore.: Castilia Press.

Patterson, G. R., DeBaryshe, B. D., and Ramsey, E. (1989). A developmental perspective on antisocial behavior. *American Psychologist, 44,* 329–340.

Pauls, D. L., and Leckman, J. F. (1986). The inheritance of Gilles de la Tourette's syndrome and associated behaviors: Evidence for autosomal dominant transmission. *New England Journal of Medicine, 315,* 993–997.

Paulston, C. (Ed.). (1988). *International handbook of bilingualism and bilingual education.* New York: Greenwood Press.

Payne, V. G., and Isaacs, L. (1987). *Human motor development: A lifespan approach.* Mountain View, Calif.: Mayfield.

Pederson, D., Evans, B. Chance, G., Bento, S., and Fox, A. M. (1988). Predictors of one-year developmental status in low birth weight infants. *Journal of Developmental and Behavioral Pediatrics, 9,* 287–292.

Pederson, N. L., McClearn, G. E., Plomin, R., and Friberg, L. (1985. Separated fraternal twins: Resemblance for cognitive abilities. *Behavior Genetics, 15,* 407–419.

Pedzek, K., and Stevens, E. (1985). Children's memory for auditory and visual information on television. *Developmental Psychology, 21,* 400–415.

Peele, S. (1981). Reductionism in the psychology of the eighties: Can biochemistry eliminate addiction, mental illness, and pain? *American Psychologist, 36,* 807–818.

Peller, L. (1954). Libidinal phases, ego development, and play. *Psychoanalytic Study of the Child, 9,* 178–198.

Pepler, D., and Ross, H. (1981). The effects of play on convergent and divergent problem solving. *Child Development, 52,* 1202–1210.

Perrin, E., and Gerrity, P. (1981). There's a demon in your belly: Children's understanding of illness. *Pediatrics, 67,* 841–849.

Perry, W. (1970). *Forms of intellectual and ethical development in the college years.* New York: Holt, Rinehart and Winston.

Perry, W. (1981). Cognitive and ethical growth: The making of meaning. In A. Chickering (Ed.), *The modern American college.* San Francisco: Jossey-Bass.

Peskin, H. (1973). Influence of the developmental schedule of puberty on learning and ego functioning. *Journal of Youth and Adolescence, 2,* 273–290.

Petersen, A., and Taylor, B. (1980). The biological approach to adolescence: Biological change and psychological adaptation. In J. Adelson (Ed.), *Handbook of adolescent psychology.* New York: Wiley.

Peterson, D. (1988) The epidemiology of sudden infant death syndrome. In J. Culbertson, H. Krous, and R. D. Bendell (Eds.), *Sudden infant death syndrome: Medical aspects and psychological management.* Baltimore: Johns Hopkins University Press.

Peterson, G. H., Mehl, L. E., and Leiderman, P. T. (1979). The role of some birth related variables in father attachment. *American Journal of Orthopsychiatry, 49,* 330–339.

Phillips, D., McCartney, K., and Scarr, S. (1987). Child-care quality and children's social development. *Developmental Psychology, 23,* 537–543.

Phillips, J. (1969). *The origins of intellect: Piaget's theory.* San Francisco: Freeman.

Phillips, S. (1982). *The invisible culture: Communication in classroom and community.* New York: Longmans.

Phinney, J. S. (1989). Stages of ethnic identity development in minority group adolescents. *Journal of Early Adolescence, 9,* 34–49.

Phinney, J. S., and Tarver, S. (1988). Ethnic identity search and commitment in Black and White eighth graders. *Journal of Early Adolescence, 8,* 265–277.

Phnuke-Tierney, E. (1984). *Illness and culture in contemporary Japan.* New York: Cambridge University Press.

Physician's Task Force on Hunger in America. (1985). *Hunger in America: The growing epidemic.* Middletown, Conn.: Wesleyan University Press.

Piaget, J. (1959). *The language and thought of the child* (M. Gabain, trans.). London: Routledge & Kegan Paul.

Piaget, J. (1962). *Play dreams, and imitation in childhood.* New York: Norton.

Piaget, J. (1963). *The origins of intelligence in children.* New York: Nonon.

Piaget, J. (1964). *The moral judgment of the child.* New York: Free Press.

Piaget, J. (1965). *The child's conception of the world.* Totowa, N.J.: Littlefield, Adams.

Piaget, J. (1970). Piaget's theory. In P. Mussen (Ed.), *Carmichael's manual of child psychology* (3rd ed. vol. 1). New York: Wiley.

Piaget, J. (1972). Intellectual evolution from adolescence to adulthood. *Human Development, 15,* 1–12.

Piaget, J. (1982). Intellectual evolution from adolescence to adulthood. *Human Development, 15,* 1–12.

Piaget, J. (1983). Piaget's theory. In P. Mussen (Ed.), *Handbook of child psychology* (vol. 1). New York: Wiley.

Piaget, J., and Inhelder, B. (1967). *The child's conception of space.* New York: Norton.

Piaget, J., and Inhelder, B. (1969). *The psychology of the child.* New York: Basic Books.

Piaget, J., and Inhelder, B. (1971). *Science of education and the psychology of the child.* New York: Viking.

Piaget, J., and Inhelder, B. (1973). *Memory and intelligence.* New York: Basic Books.

Piaget, J., Sinclair, H., and Bang, V. (1968). *Knowledge and the psychology of identity.* Paris: Presses Universitaires de France.

Piaget, J., and Szeminska, A. (1952). *The child's conception of number* (C. Gattegno and F. M. Hodgson, trans.). New York: Humanities Press.

Pissanos, B., Moore, J., and Reeve, T. (1983). Age, sex, and body composition as predictors of children's performance on basic motor abilities and health-related fitness items. *Perceptual and Motor Skills, 56,* 71–77.

Pittman, R. K., Green, R. C., Jenike, M. A., and Mesulam, M. M. (1987). Clinical comparison of Tourette's disorder and obsessive-compulsive disorder. *American Journal of Psychiatry, 144,* 1166–1171.

Platt, K. (1988). Cognitive development and sex roles in the Kerkennah Islands of Tunisia. In G. Jahoda and I. Lewis (Eds.), *Acquiring culture: Cross-cultural studies in child development.* London: Croom Helm.

Pless, B., and Haggerty, R. (1985). Child health: Research in action. in R. Rapoport (Ed.), *Children, youth, and families: The action research relationship.* London: Cambridge University Press.

Pless, I., and Satterwhite, B. (1975). Chronic Illness. In R. Haggerty, K. Roghmann, and I. Pless (Eds.), *Child health and the community.* New York: Wiley.

Plomin, R. (1986). *Development, genetics and psychology.* Hillsdale, N.J.: Erlbaum.

Plomin, R. (1989). Environment and genes: Determinants of behavior. *American Psychologist, 44,* 105–111.

Plomin, R., and Rowe, D. (1979). Genetic and environmental etiology of social behavior in infancy. *Developmental Psychology, 15,* 62–72.

Pollitt, E. (1987). Effects of iron deficiency on mental development. In F. Johnston (Ed.), *Nutritional anthropology.* New York: Alan R. Liss.

Pollitt, E., Eichier, A., and Chan, C. (1975). Psychosocial development and behavior of mothers of failure-to-thrive children. *American Journal of Orthopsychiatry, 45,* 527–537.

Pollitt, E., Garza, C., and Leibel, R. (1984). Nutrition and public policy. In H. Stevenson and A. Siegel (Eds.), *Child development research and social policy.* Chicago: University of Chicago Press,

Pomerantz, S. (1979). Sex differences in the relative importance of self-esteem, physical self-satisfaction, and identity in predicting adolescent satisfaction. *Journal of Youth and Adolescence, 8,* 51–61.

Poskitt, E., and Cole, T. (1977). Do fat babies stay fat? *British Medical Journal, 1,* 7–9.

Powell, D. (1986). Parent education and support programs. *Young Children, 41,* (3), 47–52.

Powell, T., and Ogle, P. (1985). *Brothers and sisters — A special part of exceptional families.* Baltimore: Brookes.

Prawat, R. (1989). Promoting access to knowledge, strategy and disposition in students: A research synthesis. *Review of Educational Research, 59,* 1–41.

Presson, A. (1987, April). *Primary and secondary frames of reference in map use.* Paper presented at the biennial meeting of the Society for Research in Child Development, Baltimore.

Preston, S. (1976). *Mortality patterns in national populations.* New York: Academic Press.

Pringle, S., and Ramsey, B. (1982). *Promoting the health of children.* St. Louis: Mosby.

Prinz, P., and Prinz, E. (1979). Simultaneous acquisition of ASL and spoken English. *Sign Language Studies, 25,* 283–296.

Prior, M., Kyrios, M., and Oberklaid, F. (1987). Temperament in Australian, American, Chinese, and Greek infants: Some issues and directions for future research. *Journal of Cross-Cultural Psychology, 17,* 455–474.

Pueschel, S. M., and Goldstein, A. (1983). Genetic counseling. In J. L. Matson and J. A. Mulick (Eds.), *Handbook of mental retardation.* Oxford: Pergamon Press.

Purkey, S., and Smith, M. (1983). Effective schools: A review. *Elementary School Journal, 83,* 427–452.

Quackenbush, M., and Sargent, P. (1986). *Teaching AIDS: A resource guide on acquired immunity deficiency syndrome.* Santa Cruz, Calif.: Network Publications.

Quigley, M., Sheehan, K., Wilkes, M., and Yen, S. (1979). Effects of maternal smoking on circulating catecholamine levels and fetal heart rates. *American Journal of Obstetrics and Gynecology, 133,* 68 5–690.

Rader, N., Bausano, M., and Richards, J. (1981). On the nature of the visual-cliff avoidance response. *Child Development, 51,* 61–68.

Radin, N. (1982). The unique contribution of parents to early childrearing: The preschool years. In S. Moore and C. Cooper (Eds.), *The young child: Reviews of research* (vol. 3). Washington, D.C.: National Association for the Education of Young Children.

Radke-Yarrow, M., Zahn-Waxler, C., and Chapman, M. (1983). Children's prosocial dispositions and behavior. In P. H. Mussen (Ed.), *Handbook of child psychology: Vol. 4: Socialization personality and social development* (4th ed.). New York: Wiley.

Radke-Yarrow, M., and Zahn-Waxler, C. (1987). Roots, motives, and patterns in children's prosocial behavior. In J. Reykowski, J. Karylowski, D. Bar-Tal, and E. Staub (Eds.), *Origins and maintenance of prosocial behaviors.* New York: Plenum Press.

Rapoport, R., Rapoport, R., and Strelitz, A. (1980). *Father, mothers, and society: Perspectives on parenting.* New York: Vintage.

Raskin, P. (1985). Identity and vocational development. In A. Waterman (Ed.), *Identity in adolescence: Processes and contents.* San Francisco: Jossey-Bass.

Re:act (1984). Viewing goes up. *Action for Children's Television Magazine, 13,* 4.

Reaves, J., and Roberts, A. (1983). The effect of type of information on children's attraction to peers. *Child Development, 54,* 1024–1031.

Rebelsky, F., and Hanks, C. (1971). Fathers' vocal interactions with infants in the first three months of life. *Child Development, 42,* 63–68.

Resnick, L. (1987). *Education and learning to think.* Washington, D.C.: National Academy Press.

Resnick, L. (1989). Developing mathematical knowledge. *American Psychologist, 44,* 162–169.

Rest, J. (1983). Morality. In P. Mussen (Ed.), *Handbook of child psychology* (vol. 3). New York: Wiley.

Rice, M. (1982). Child language: What children know and how. In T. Field (Ed.), *Review of human development.* New York: Wiley.

Richman, A., LeVine, R., New, R., Howrigan, G., Welles-Nystrom, B., and LeVine, S. (1988). Maternal behavior to infants in five cultures. In R. LeVine, P. Miller and M. West (Eds.),. *Parental behavior in diverse societies.* San Francisco: Jossey-Bass.

Riese, M. L. (1987) Temperament stability between the neonatal period and 24 months. *Developmental Psychology, 23,* 216–222.

Rieser, J., Yonas, A., and Wikner, K. (1976). Radial localization of odors by human neonates. *Child Development, 47,* 856–859.

Riley, R., Adams, G., and Nielson, E. (1984). Adolescent egocentrism: Associations among imaginary audience, cognitive development and parental support and rejection. *Journal of Youth and Adolescence, 13,* 401–417.

Ringness, T. (1967). Indentification patterns, motivation, and school achievement of bright junior high school boys. *Journal of Educational Psychology, 58,* 93–102.

Rist, R. (1973). *The urban school: A factory for failure.* Cambridge, Mass.: MIT Press.

Rivers, G., and Regoli, R. (1987). Sexual victimization experiences of sorority women. *Sociology and Social Research: An International Journal, 72,* 39.

Robert, M., and Charbonneau, C. (1978). Extinction of liquid conservation by modeling: Three indicators of its artificiality. *Child Development, 49,* 19–200.

Roberton, M., and Halverson, L. (1984). *Developing children: Their changing movement.* Philadelphia: Lea and Febiger.

Robinson, B., and Barrett, R. (1985). Teenage fathers. *Psychology Today, 19,* pp. 67–70.

Robinson, B., Skeen, P., and Walters, L. (1987, April). The AIDS epidemic hits home. *Psychology Today, 21,* pp. 48–52.

Robinson, E. (1988). Teenage pregnancy from the father's perspective. *American Journal of Orthopsychiatry, 58,* 46–51.

Robinson, I. E., and Jedlicka, D. (1982). Change in sexual attitudes and behavior of college students from 1965 to 1980: A research note. *Journal of Marriage and the Family, 40,* 237–240.

Robinson, J. (1980). Housework technology and household work. In S. Bern (Ed.), *Women and household labor.* Beverly Hills: Sage.

Roche, A. (Ed.). (1979). Similar trends in human growth, maturation, and development. *Monographs of Society for Research on Child Development, 44* (3–4, Serial No. 179).

Roche, A., and Malina, R. (1983). *Manual of physical status and performance in childhood* (vols. 1–2). New York: Plenum.

Rodin, J. (1977). Bidirectional influences in emotionality, stimulus responsivity, and metabolic events in obesity. In J. Maser and M. Seligman (Eds.), *Psychopathology: Experimental models.* San Francisco: Freeman.

Roff, M. F. (1974). Childhood antecedents of adult neurosis, severe bad conduct, and psychological health. In D. F. Ricks, A. Thomas and M. Roff (Eds.), *Life history research in psychopathology* (vol. 3). Minneapolis: University Press.

Rogers, L., and Walsh, J. (1982). Shortcomings of the psychomedical research of John Money and co-workers into sex differences in behavior: *Sex Roles, 8,* 269–281.

Roghmann, K. (1975). The use of medications: A neglected aspect of health and illness behavior. In R. Haggerty, K. Roghmann, and I. Pless (Eds.), *Child health and the community.* New York: Wiley.

Roghmann, K., and Pless, I. (1975). Acute illness. In R. Haggerty, K. Roghmann, and I. Pless (Eds.), *Child health and the community.* New York: Wiley.

Rogoff, B., and Morelli, G. (1989). Perspectives on children's development from cultural psychology. *American Psychologist, 44,* 343–348.

Roopnarine, J., and Field, T. (1982). Peer-directed behaviors of infants and toddlers during nursery school play. In T. Field (Ed.), *Review of human development.* New York: Wiley.

Root, A. L. (1983). Respiratory crises. In K. Vestal and C. McKenzie (Eds.), *High-risk perinatal nursing.* Philadelphia: Saunders.

Rose, S., and Blank, M. (1974). The potency of context in children's cognition. *Child Development, 45,* 499–502.

Rosenberg, M. (1979). *Conceiving the self.* New York: Basic Books.

Rosenberg, M. S. (1989). New directions for research on the psychological maltreatment of children. *American Psychologist, 42,* 166–171.

Rosenberg, M. S., and Repucci, N. D. (1985). Primary prevention of child abuse. *Journal of Consulting and Clinical Psychology, 53,* 576–585.

Rosenfeld, A. A., Wenegrat, A. O., Haavik, D. K. Wenegrat, B. G., and Smith, C. R. (1982). Sleeping patterns in upper-middle-class families when the child awakens ill or frightened. *Archives of Genetic Psychology, 39,* 943–947.

Rosenthal, R. and Jacobson, L. (1968). *Pygmalion in the classroom: Teacher expectations and pupils' intellectual development.* New York: Holt, Rinehart, and Winston.

Rosett, H., Weiner, L., Zuckerman, B., McKinlay, S., and Edelin, K. (1980). Reduction of alcohol consumption during pregnancy with benefits to the newborn. *Alcoholism: Clinical and Experimental Research, 4,* 178–184.

Ross, D., and Ross, S. (1982). *Hyperactivity: Current issues, research, and theory* (2nd ed.). New York: Wiley.

Roth, P. (1987). Temporal characteristics of maternal verbal styles. In K. Nelson and A. van Kleek (Eds.), *Children's language* (vol. 6). Hillsdale, N.J.: Erlbaum.

Rotheram, M. J., and Phinney, J. S. (1987). Definitions and perspectives in the study of children's ethnic socialization. In J. S. Phinney and M. J. Rotheram (Eds.), *Children's ethnic socialization: Pluralism and development.* Newbury Park, Calif.: Sage.

Rousseau, J. (1763/1911). *Emile, or on education.* London: Dent.

Rousso, H. (1984). Fostering healthy self-esteem. *The Exceptional Parent, 8,* 9–14.

Rowland, D., Lyons, B., and Edwards, J. (1988). Medicaid: Health care for the poor in the Reagan era. *Annual Review of Public Health, 9,* 427–450.

Rubenstein, J., and Howes, C. (1976). The effects of peers on toddler interaction with mother and toys. *Child Development, 47,* 597–605.

Rubenstein, J. L., and Howes, C. (1979). Caregiving and infant behavior in day care and in homes. *Developmental Psychology, 15,* 1–24.

Rubenstein, J. L., and Howes, C. (1983). Social-emotional development of toddlers in day care: The role of peers and of individual differences. *Advances in Early Education and Child Care, 3,* 13–45.

Rubenstein, J. L., Howes, C., and Boyle, P. (1981). A two year follow-up of infants in community based infant day care. *Journal of Child Psychology and Psychiatry, 22,* 209–218.

Rubin, K., and Krasnor, L. (1980). Changes in the play behaviors of preschoolers: A short-term longitudinal investigation. *Canadian Journal of Behavioral Science, 12,* 278–282.

Rubin, K. H., Fein, G. G., and Vandenberg, B. (1983). Play. In E. M. Hetherington (Ed.), *Handbook of Child Psychology: Vol. 4: Socialization, personality and social development* (4th ed.). New York: Wiley.

Rubin, K., Maioni, T., and Hornung, M. (1976). Free play behaviors in middle and lower class preschools: Parten and Piaget revisited. *Child Development, 47,* 414–419.

Rubin, K., Watson, K., and Jambor, T. (1978).
Free play behaviors in preschool and kindergarten children. *Child Development, 49,* 534–536.

Ruble, D., and Ruble, T. (1980). Sex stereotypes. In A. G. Miller (Ed.), *In the eye of the beholder: Contemporary issues in stereotyping.* New York: Holt, Rinehart, and Winston.

Ruiz, R. (1988). Bilingualism and bilingual education in the United States. In C. Paulston (Ed.)., *International handbook of bilingualism and bilingual education.* New York: Greenwood Press.

Ruff, H. (1980). Infant recognition of the invariant form of objects. *Child Development, 49,* 293–306.

Ruhland, D., and Feld, S. (1977). The development of achievement motivation in black and white children. *Child Development, 48.* 1362–1368.

Runco, M., and Okuda, S. (1988). Problem discovery, divergent thinking and the creative process. *Journal of Youth and Adolescence, 17,* 211–220.

Ruopp, R., and Travers, J. (1982). Janus faces day care: Perspectives on quality and cost. In E. F. Zigler and E. W. Gordon (Eds.), *Day care scientific and social policy issues.* Boston: Auburn House.

Russo, D., and Kedesdy, J. (Eds.). (1988). *Behavioral medicine with the developmentally disabled.* New York: Plenum Press.

Rutter, M. (1983). School effects on pupil progress: Research findings and policy implications. *Child Development, 54,* 1–29.

Rutter, M. (1985). Resilience in the face of adversity: Protective factors and resistance to psychiatric disorder. *British Journal of Psychiatry, 147,* 568–611.

Rutter, M., and Garmezy, N. (1983). Developmental psychopathology. In P. Mussen (Ed.), *Handbook of Child Psychology* (vol. 4). New York: Wiley.

Rutter, M., Graham, P., Chadwick, O., and Yule, W. (1976). Adolescent turmoil: Fact or fiction? *Journal of Child Psychology and Psychiatry, 17,* 35–36.

Sachs, J. (1985). Prelinguistic development. In J. Gleason (Ed.), *The development of language.* Columbus, Ohio: Merrill.

Sachs, J., Liebeman, P., and Erickson, D. (1973). Anatomical and cultural determinants of male and female speech. In R. Shay and R. Fasold (Eds.), *Language attitudes.* Washington, D.C.: Georgetown University Press.

Saitz, E., and Brodie, J. (1982). Pretend-play training in childhood: A review and critique. In D. Pepler and K. Rubin (Ed.), *The play of children: Current theory and research.* Basel, Switzerland: Karger.

Sameroff, A. (1979). *The organization and stability of newborn behavior.* Chicago: University of Chicago Press.

Sameroff, A., and Cavanaugh, P. (1979). Learning in infancy: A developmental perspective. In J. Osofsky (Ed.), *Handbook of infant development.* New York: Wiley.

Sameroff, A. J., and Chandler, M. J. (1975). Reproductive risk and the continuum of caretaking causality. In F. D. Horowitz, M. Hetherington, S. Scarr-Salapatek, and G. Siegel (Eds.), *Review of Child Development Research* (vol. 4). Chicago: University of Chicago Press.

Santilli, N., and Furth, H. (1987). Adolescent work perception: A developmental approach. In J. Lewko (Ed.), *How children and adolescents view the world of work.* San Francisco: Jossey-Bass.

Santrock, J., and Sitterle, K. (1987). Parent-child relationships in stepmother families. In K. Pasley and M. Ihinger-Tallman (Eds.), *Remarriage and stepparenting: Current research and theory.* New York: Guilford Press.

Santrock, J., and Warshak, R. (1979). Father custody and social development in boys and girls. *Journal of Social Issues, 35,* 112–125.

Sarafino, E., and Armstrong, J. (1986). *Child and adolescent development.* New York: West.

Savic, S. (1980). *How twins learn to talk.* London: Academic Press.

Savignon, S. (1983). *Communicative competence: Texts and contexts in second language learning.* Reading, Mass.: Addison-Wesley.

Sawin, D. (1979). *Assessing empathy in children: A search for an elusive construct.* Paper presented at the meeting of the Society for Research on Child Development, San Francisco.

Saxe, G., Gearhart, and Guberman, S. (1984). The social organization of early number development. In B. Rogoff and J. Wertsch (Eds.), *Children's learning in the "zone of proximal development."* San Francisco: Jossey-Bass.

Scarr, S. (1984a). Intelligence: What the introductory psychology student might want to know. In A. Rogers and C. J. Scheirer (Eds.), *The G. Stanley Hall lecture series* (vol. 4). Washington, D.C.: American Psychological Association.

Scarr, S. (1984b). *Mother care, other care.* New York: Basic Books.

Scarr, S. (1985). Constructing psychology: Making facts and fables for our times. *American Psychologist, 40,* 499–512.

Scarr, S., and McCartney, K. (1983). How people make their own environments: A theory of genotype-environment effects. *Child Development, 54,* 424–435.

Scarr, S., Phillips, S., and McCartney, K. (1989). Working mothers and their families. *American Psychologist, 44,* 1402–1409.

Scarr, S., and Salapatek, P. (1970). Patterns of fear development during infancy. *Merrill-Palmer Quarterly, 16,* 53–90.

Scarr-Salapatek, S. (1976). An evolutionary perspective on infant intelligence: Species patterns and individual variations. In M. Lewis (Ed.), *Origins of intelligence.* New York: Plenum Press.

Schachter, F. F., and Stone, R. K. (1985). Difficult sibling, easy sibling: Temperament and the within-family environment. *Child Development, 56,* 1335–1344.

Schaffer, H., and Emerson, P. (1964). Patterns of response to physical contact in early human development. *Journal of Child Psychology and Psychiatry, 5,* 1–13.

Schmidt, R. (1988). *Motor control and learning.* Champaign, Ill.: Human Kinetics.

Schoenfeld, A. (1985). *Mathematical problem solving.* Orlando, Fla.: Academic Press.

Schofield, J. (1981). Complementary and conflicting identities: Images and interactions in an interracial school. In S. Asher and J. Gottman (Eds.), *The development of children's friendships.* New York: Cambridge University Press.

Schofield, J., and Sugar, H. (1977). Peer interaction patterns in an integrated middle school. *Sociometry, 40,* 130–138.

Schooler, C., and Schaie, K. W. (Eds.). (1987). *Cognitive functioning and social structure over the life course.* Norwood, N.J.: Ablex.

Schowalter, J., Patterson, P., Talimer, M., Kutscher, A., Gullo, S., and Peretz, D. (Eds.). (1983). *The child and death.* New York: Columbia University Press.

Schulman-Galambos, C., and Galambos, R. (1979). Brain stem evoked response audiometry in newborn hearing screening. *Archives of Otolaryngology, 105,* 86–90.

Schwartz, J., Strickland, R., and Krolick, G. (1974). Infant day care: Behavioral effect at preschool age. *Developmental Psychology, 10,* 502–506.

Schwartz, P. (1988). The cardiac theory and sudden infant death syndrome. In J. Culbertson, H. Krous, and R. D. Bendell (Eds.), *Sudden infant death syndrome: Medical aspects and psychological management.* Baltimore: Johns Hopkins University Press.

Schwartz, P., Southall, D., and Valdes-Dapena, M. (Eds.),. (1988). *Sudden infant death syndrome: Cardiac and respiratory mechanisms and interventions.* New York: New York Academy of Sciences.

Schwartz, R., and Leonard, L. (1982). Do children pick and choose? An examination of phonological selection and avoidance. *Journal of Child Language, 9,* 319–336.

Schwartzman, H. B. (1978). *Transformations: The anthropology of children's play.* New York: Plenum Press.

Schweder, R., Mahapatra, M., and Miller, J. (1987). Culture and moral development. In J. Kagan and S. Lamb (Eds.), *The emergence of morality in young children.* Chicago: University of Chicago Press.

Schweinhart, L., and Koshel, J. (1986). *Policy options for preschool programs.* High/Scope Early Childhood Policy Papers, No. 5. Ypsilanti, Mich.: High/Scope Educational Research Foundations.

Scott, C. (1988). Spoken and written syntax. In M. Nippold (Ed.), *Later language development: Ages 9 through 19.* Boston: Little, Brown.

Scribner, S. (1986). Thinking in action: Some characteristics of practical thought. In R. Sternberg and R. Wagner (Eds.), *Practical intelligence: Nature and origins of competence in the everyday world.* Cambridge: Cambridge University Press.

Searle, L. V. (1949). The organization of hereditary maze-brightness and maze-dullness. *Genetic Psychology Monographs, 39,* 279–325.

Seefeldt, C. (Ed.). (1987). *The early childhood curriculum: A review of current research.* New York: Teachers College Press.

Seefeldt, C. (Ed.). (1990). *Continuing issues in early childhood education.* New York: Teachers College Press.

Selman, R. (1980). *The growth of interpersonal understanding.* New York: Academic Press.

Selman, R. (1981). The child as friendship philosopher. In S. Asher and J. Gottman (Eds.), *The development of children's friendships.* New York: Cambridge University Press.

Selman, R. (1988). Fostering intimacy and autonomy. In W. Damon (Ed.), *Child development today and tomorrow.* San Francisco: Jossey-Bass.

Selman, R. (1989). Fostering intimacy and autonomy. In W. Damon (Ed.), *Child development today and tomorrow.* San Francisco: Jossey-Bass.

Serbin, L. A., Conner, J. M., and Citron C. C. (1981). Sex-differentiated free play behavior: Effects of teacher modeling, location and gender. *Developmental Psychology, 17,* 640–646.

Serbin, L., Tonick, I., and Sternglanz, S. (1977). Shaping cooperative cross-sex play. *Child Development, 48,* 924–929.

Shaffer, D. (1974). Suicide in childhood and adolescence. *Journal of Child Psychiatry, 15,* 275–291.

Shaffer, D., Chadwick, O., and Rutter, M. (1975). Psychiatric outcome of localized head injury in children. In R. Poner and D. Fitz-Simons (Eds.), *Outcome of severe damage to the central nervous system.* Amsterdam: Excerpta Medica.

Shaftesbury, Earl of (A. A. Cooper). (1868). *Speeches of the Earl of Shaftesbury.* London: Chapman and Hall.

Shane, P. (1989). Changing patterns among homeless and runaway teens. *American Journal of Orthopsychiatry, 59,* 208–214.

Shantz, C., and Shantz, D. (1985). Conflict between children: Social-cognitive and sociometric correlates. In M. Berkowitz (Ed.), *Peer conflict and psychological growth: New Directions for Child Development, No. 29.* San Francisco: Jossey-Bass.

Sharabany, R., Gershoni, R., and Hoffman, J. (1981). Girlfriend, boyfriend: Age and sex differences in intimate friendship. *Developmental Psychology, 17,* 800–809.

Sharma, V. (1981). *Indian urban families: Child-rearing practices and child growth.* Delhi: National Council of Educational Research and Training.

Shattuck, R. (1980). *The forbidden experiment: The story of the wild boy of Aveyron.* New York: Washington Square Press.

Shatz, M. (1983). Communication. In P. Mussen (Ed.), *Handbook of child psychology,* (vol. 4). New York: Wiley.

Shepherd-Look, D. (1982). Sex differentiation and the development of sex roles. In B. Wolman (Ed.), *Handbook of developmental psychology.* Englewood Cliffs, N.J.: Prentice-Hall.

Sherman, G. (1965). Soviet Youth: Myth and reality. In E. H. Erikson (Ed.), *The challenge of youth.* Garden City, N.Y.: Anchor Books.

Shiono, P. H., Klebanoff, M. A., and Rhoads, G. G. (1986). Smoking and drinking during pregnancy: Their effects on preterm birth. *Journal of the American Medical Association, 225,* 82–84.

Sidell, R. (1972). *Women and child care in China.* New York: Hill and Wang.

Sieber, J. (1982). Ethical dilemmas in social research. In J. Sieber (Ed.), *The ethics of social research* (vol. 1). New York: Springer-Verlag.

Siegler, R. (1983a). Information processing approaches to cognitive development. In P. Mussen (Ed.), *Manual of child psychology* (4th ed., vol. 1). New York: Wiley.

Siegler, R. (1983b). Information processing approaches to cognitive development. In P. Mussen (Ed.), *Handbook of child psychology* (vol. 3). New York: Wiley.

Silber, S. J. (1980). *How to get pregnant.* New York: Wamer.

Simmel, E. C., and Bagwell, M. (1983). Genetics of exploratory behavior and activity. In J. Fuller and E. Simmel (Eds.), *Behavior genetics.* Hillsdale, N.J.: Erlbaum.

Sinclair, D. (1978). *Human growth after birth.* New York: Oxford University Press.

Sinclair, H. (1969). Developmental psycholinguistics. In D. Elkind and J. Flavell (Eds.), *Studies in cognitive development.* New York: Oxford University Press.

Sinclair, H. (1976). Epistemology and the study of language. In B. Inhelder and H. Chipman (Eds.), *Piaget and his school.* New York: Springer-Verlag.

Singleton, L., and Asher, S. (1979). Racial integration and children's peer preferences: An investigation of developmental and cohort differences. *Child Development, 50,* 936–941.

Skinner, B. F. (1957). *Verbal behavior.* New York: Appleton-Century-Crofts.

Skinner, B. F. (1967). Autobiography. In E. Boring and G. Lindzey (Eds.), *A history of psychology in autobiography* (vol. 3). New York: Appleton-Century-Crofts.

Skinner, B. F. (1976). *Particulars of my life.* New York: Knopf.

Skodak, M., and Skeels, H. M. (1949). A final follow-up study of one hundred adopted children. *Journal of Genetic Psychology, 75,* 85–125.

Slaby, R. G., and Crowley, C. G. (1977). Modification of cooperation and aggression through teacher attention to children's speech. *Journal of Experimental Child Psychology, 23,* 442–458.

Slade, A. (1987). Quality of attachment and early symbolic play. *Developmental Psychology, 23,* 78–85.

Slater, A., Morrison, C., and Rose, D. (1985). Movement perception and identity constancy in the newborn baby. *British Journal of Developmental Psychology, 3,* 211–220.

Slaughter, D. (1983). Early intervention and its effects on maternal and child development, *Monographs of the Society for Research on Child Development 48,* 202.

Slavin, R. E. (1986). Cooperative learning: Engineering social psychology in the classroom. In R. S. Feldman (Ed.), *The social psychology of education: Current research and theory.* Cambridge: Cambridge University Press.

Slobin, D. (1973). Cognitive prerequisites for

the development of grammar. In C. Ferguson and D. Slobin (Eds.), *Studies of child language development*. New York: Holt, Rinehart, and Winston.

Smilansky, S. (1968). *The effects of sociodramatic play on disadvantaged preschool children*. New York: Wiley.

Smith, A. N., and Spence, C. M. (1981). National day care study: Optimizing the day care environment. *American Journal of Orthopsychiatry, 50*, 718–721.

Smith, D. W., Bierman, E. L., and Robinson, N. M. (Eds.), (1978). *The biologic ages of man: From conception through old age*. Philadelphia: Saunders.

Smith, E. A., and Udry, J. R. (1985). Coital and non-coital sexual behavior of white and black adolescents. *American Journal of Public Health, 75*, 1200–1203.

Smith, R., and Smoll, F. (1982). Psychological stress: A conceptual model and some intervention strategies in youth sports. In R. Magill, M. Ash, and F. Smoll (Eds.), *Children in sport*. Champaign, Ill.: Human Kinetics Publishers.

Smolak, L. (1982). Cognitive precursors of receptive vs. expressive language. *Journal of Child Language, 9*, 13–22.

Snow, C., and Ferguson, C. (Eds.), (1977). *Talking to children*. Cambridge: Cambridge University Press.

Snow, C., Perlmann, R., and Nathan, D. (1987). Why routines are different: Toward a multiple-factors model of the relation between input and language acquisition. In K. Nelson and A. van Kleeck (Eds.), *Children's language* (vol. 6). Hillsdale, N.J.: Erlbaum.

Somerville, J. (1984). *The rise and fall of childhood*. Beverly Hills: Sage.

Sorensen, R. (1973a). *Adolescent sexuality in contemporary America: Personal values and sexual behavior ages 13–19*. New York: Abrams.

Sorenson, R. C. (1973b). *Adolescent sexuality in contemporary America*. New York: World.

Spelke, E. (1983). Constraints on the development of intermodal perception in infancy. In L. Liben (Ed.), *Piaget and the foundations of knowledge*. Hillsdale, N.J.: Erlbaum.

Spelke, E. (1987). The development of intermodal perception. in P. Salapatek and L. Cohen (Eds.), *Handbook of infant perception* (vol. 2). New York: Academic Press.

Spence, J. T., Helmreich, R., and Sapp, J. (1975). Ratings of self and peers on sex role attributes and their relation to self-esteem and conceptions of masculinity and feminity. *Journal of Personality and Social Psychology, 32*, 29–39.

Spock, B. (1976). *Baby and child care* (rev. ed.). New York: Bantam.

Spock, B., and Rothenberg, M. (1985). *Baby and child care*. New York: Pocket Books.

Sponseller, D., and Jaworski, A. (1979). *Social and cognitive complexity in young children's play*. Paper presented at the annual meeting of the American Educational Research Association, San Francisco.

Sprague, R., and Ullman, R. (1981). Psychoactive drugs and child management. In J. Kaufman and D. Hallahan (Eds.), *Handbook of special education*. Englewood Cliffs, N.J.: Prentice-Hall.

Springer, S., and Deutsch, G. (1989). *Left brain, right brain* (3rd ed.). New York: Freeman.

Sprunger, L. W., Boyce, W. T., and Gaines, J. A. (1985). Family-infant congruence: Routines and rythmicity in family adaptions to a young infant. *Child Development, 56*, 564–572.

Sroufe, L. A. (1979). The coherence of individual development: Early care, attachment, and subsequent developmental issues. *American Psychologist, 34*, 834–841.

Sroufe, L. A., Fox, N., and Pancake, V. (1983). Attachment and dependency in developmental perspective. *Child Development, 54*, 1615–1627.

Sroufe, L. A., and Waters, E. (1976). The onogenesis of smiling and laughter: A perspective on the organization of development in infancy. *Psychological Review, 83*, 173–189.

Sroufe, L. A., and Wunsch, J. (1972). The development of laughter in the first year of life. *Child Development, 43*, 1326–1344.

Staffieri, J. (1972). A study of social stereotypes of body image in children. *Journal of Personality and Social Psychology, 7*, 101–104.

Starfield, B., and Pless, I. (1980) Physical health. In O. Brim and J. Kagan (Eds.), *Constancy and change in human development*. New York: Erlbaum.

Stark, E. (1986, October). Young, innocent and pregnant. *Psychology Today, 20*, pp. 28–35.

Starr, R. (1979). Child abuse. *American Psychologist, 34*, 872–878.

Staurovsky, L. (1983). Reproductive related health care problems of women. In G. Butnarescu and D. Tillotson (Eds.), *Maternity nursing*. New York: Wiley.

Steffenson, M., and Guthrie, L. (1980). *Effect of situation on the verbalization of black inner-city children* (Report No. 180). Urbana, Ill.: University of Illinois, Center for the Study of Reading.

Stein, A. (1983). Pregnancy in gravidas over age 35 years. *Journal of Nurse-Midwifery, 28*, 17–20.

Stein, J. Newcomb, M., and Bentler, P. (1987). An 8-year study of multiple influences on drug use and drug use consequences. *Journal of Personality and Social Psychology, 53*, 1094–1105.

Stein, Z., Susser, M., Saenger, G., and Marolia, F. (1975). *Famine and human development*. New York: Oxford University Press.

Steinberg, L. (1986). Latchkey children and susceptibility to peer pressure: An ecological analysis. *Developmental Psychology, 22*, 433–439.

Steinberg, L. (1987). Impact of puberty on family relations: Effects of pubertal status and pubertal timing. *Developmental Psychology, 23*, 451–460.

Steinberg, L. (1988). Reciprocal relation between parent-child distance and pubertal maturation. *Developmental Psychology, 24*, 122–128.

Steinberg, L. D. (1980). *Understanding families with young adolescents*. Carrboro, N.C.: Center for Early Adolescence.

Steinberg, R., and Powell, J. (1983a). Comprehending verbal comprehension. *American Psychologist, 38*, 878–893.

Steininger, M., Newell, J.D., and Garcia, L. (1984). *Ethical issues in psychology*. Homewood, Ill.: Dorsey Press.

Steinmetz, S. (1977). The use of force for resolving family conflict: The training ground for abuse. *Family Coordinator, 26*, 19–26.

Stern, D. (1977). *The first relationship: Infant and mother*. Cambridge, Mass.: Harvard University Press.

Stern, D. N. (1985a). *The first relationship: Infant and mother*. (4th ed.). Cambridge, Mass.: Harvard University Press.

Stern, D. N. (1985b). *The interpersonal world of the infant: A view from psychoanalysis and developmental psychology*. New York: Basic Books.

Sternberg, R. (1988). *The triarchic mind: A new theory of human intelligence*. New York: Penguin.

Sternberg, R., and Berg, C. (1987). What are theories of adult intellectual development theories of? In C. Schooler and K. W. Schaie (Eds.), *Cognitive functioning and social structure over the life course*. Norwood, N.J.: Ablex.

Sternberg, R., and Powell, J. (1983a). The development of intelligence. In P. Mussen (Ed.), *Handbook of child psychology*, (3rd. ed., vol. 3). New York: Wiley.

Sternberg, R., and Powell, J. (1983b). Comprehending verbal comprehension. *American Psychologist, 38*, 878–893.

Stevenson, H., Lee, S., and Stigler, J. (1986) Mathematics achievement in Chinese, Japanese, and American children. *Science, 231*, 593–699.

Stewart, A. J., and Healy, J. M., Jr. (1989). Linking individual development and social changes. *American Psychologist, 44*, 30–42.

Stewart, R. B., Mobley, L. A., Van Tuyl, S. S., and Salvador, M. A. (1987). The firstborn's adjustment to the birth of a sibling: A longitudinal assessment. *Child Development, 58*, 341–355.

Stigler, J., and Baranes, R. (1988). Culture and mathematics learning. In E. Rothkopf (Ed.), *Review of research in education* (vol. 15). Washington, D. C.: American Educational Research Association.

Stigler, J., and Perry, M. (in press). Mathematics learning in Japanese, Chinese and American classrooms. In G. Saxe and M. Gearhart (Eds.), *Children's mathematics*. San Francisco: Jossey-Bass.

Stini, W. (1972). Malnutrition, body size and proportion. *Ecology of Food and Nutrition, 1*, 121 ff.

Stipek, D. (1988). *Motivation to learn: From theory to practice*. Englewood Cliffs, N.J.: Prentice Hall.

Stipek, D., and Hoffman, J. (1980). Children's achievement related expectancies as a function of academic performance histories and sex. *Journal of Educational Psychology, 72*, 861–865.

Stone, C., and Day, M. (1980). Competence

and performance models and the characterization of formal operational skills. *Human Development, 23,* 323–353.

Strauss, M. E., Lessen-Firestone, J. K., Starr, R. H., and Ostrea, E. M. (1975). Behavior of narcotics-addicted newborns. *Child Development, 46,* 887–893.

Strauss, M., Starr, R., Ostrea, E., Chavez, C., and Stryker, J. (1976). Behavioral concomitants of prenatal addiction to narcotics. *Journal of Pediatrics. 89,* 842–846.

Streissguth, A., Herman, C., and Smith, D. (1978). Intelligence, behavior, and dysmorphogenesis in the fetal alcohol syndrome: A report on 20 patients. *Journal of Pediatrics 92,* 363–367.

Streissguth, A. P., Martin, D. C., Barr, H. M., Kirchner, G. L., and Darby, B. L. (1984). Intrauterine alcohol and nicotine exposure: Attention and reaction time in four-year-old children. *Developmental Psychology, 20,* 533–541.

Sugarman, S. (1983). *Children's early thought: Developments in classification.* New York: Cambridge University Press.

Sullivan, H. (1953). *The interpersonal theory of psychiatry.* New York: Norton.

Sullivan, K., and Sullivan, A. (1980). Adolescent-parent separation. *Developmental Psychology, 16,* 93–99.

Suomi, S. J., and Harlow, H. (1978). Production and alleviation of depressive behaviors in monkeys. In J. Maser and M. Seliman (Eds.), *Psychopathology: Experimental models.* San Francisco: Freeman.

Super, C. (1981). Behavioral development in infancy. In R. Munroe, R. Munroe, and B. Whiting (Eds.), *Handbook of cross-cultural human development.* New York: Garland STPM Press.

Super, C. (1982). Unpacking African infant precocity. In N. Warren (Ed.), *Studies in cross-cultural psychology* (vol. 3). London: Academic Press.

Super, D. (1984). Career and life development. In D. Brown, L. Brooks and Associates (Eds.), *Career choice and development.* San Francisco: Jossey-Bass.

Susman, E., Inoff-Germain, G., Nottelmann, E., Loriaux, D. L., Cutler, G., Jr., and Chrousos, G. (1987). Hormones, emotional dispositions, and aggressive attributes in young adolescents. *Child Development, 58,* 1114–1134.

Susman, E. J., Nottelmann, E. D., Inoff-Germain, G. E., Dorn, L. D., Cutler, G. B., Jr., Loriaux, D. L., and Chrousos, G. P. (1985). The relation of relative hormonal levels and physical development and social-emotional behavior in young adolescents. *Journal of Youth and Adolescence, 14,* 245–263.

Sutton-Smith, B. (1981). *A history of children's play.* Philadelphia: University of Pennsylvania Press.

Sutton-Smith, B. (1986). *Toys as Culture.* New York: Gardner Press.

Sutton-Smith, B., and Kelly-Byrne, D. (1984a). The idealization of play. In D. Smith (Ed.), *Play in animals and humans.* London: Van Nostrand.

Sutton-Smith, B., and Kelly-Byrne, D. (1984b). *The masks of play.* West Point, N.Y.: Leisure Press.

Suzuki, D., and Knudtson, P. (1989). *Genethics: The clash between the new genetics and human values.* Cambridge, Mass.: Harvard University Press.

Swain, H. (1979). Childhood views of death. *Death Education, 2,* 341–358.

Tanner, J. (1973). Trend towards earlier menarche in London, Oslo, Copenhagen, the Netherlands and Hungary. *Nature, 243,* 95–96.

Tanner, J. (1978a). *Education and physical growth* (2nd ed.). London: Hodder and Stoughton.

Tanner, J. (1978b). *Fetus into man. Physical growth from conception to maturity.* Cambridge, Mass.: Harvard University Press.

Tanner, J. (1990). *Fetus into man: Physical growth from conception to maturity* (Rev. ed.). Cambridge, Mass.: Harvard University Press.

Task Force on Pediatric AIDS. (1989). Pediatric AIDS and human immunodeficiency virus infection: Psychological issues. *American Psychologist, 44,* 258–264.

Taub, H., Goldstein, K., and Caputo, D. (1977). Indices of neonatal prematurity as discriminators of development in middle childhood. *Child Development, 48,* 797–805.

Teitelbaum, M. (Ed.) (1976). *Sex differences: Social and biological perspective.* Garden City, N.Y.: Doubleday.

Thevenin, T. (1987). *The family bed.* Wayne, N.J.: Avery.

Thissen, D., Bock, R., Wainer, H., and Roche, A. (1976). Individual growth in stature: A comparison of four growth studies in the USA. *Annals of Human Biology, 3,* 529–542.

Thomas, A., and Chess, S. (1977). *Temperament and development.* New York: Brunner/Mazel.

Thomas, A., and Chess, S. (1981). The role of temperament in the contributions of individuals to their development. In R. Lerner and N. Busch-Rossnagle (Eds.), *Individuals as producers of their development: A life-span perspective.* New York: Academic Press.

Thomas, J., Gallagher, J., and Thomas, K. (1982). Developmental memory, factors in children's perception of sport. In R. Magill, M. Ash, and F. Smoll (Eds.), *Children in sport.* Champaign, Ill.: Human Kinetics Publishers.

Thompson, R. A., Lamb, M. E., and Estes, D. (1982). Stability of infant-mother attachment and its relationship to changing life circumstances in an unselected middle-class sample. *Child Development, 53,* 144–148.

Thorp, R. G. (1989). Psychocultural variables and constraints: Effects on teaching and learning in the schools. *American Psychologist, 44,* 349–359.

Tinsley, B. R., and Parke, R. D. (1984). Grandparents as support and socializing agents. In M. Lewis (Ed.), *Beyond the dyad.* New York: Plenum Press.

Tobach, E., and Rosoff, B. (Eds.), (1978). *Genes and gender.* New York: Gordian Press.

Tobin-Richards, M. Boxer, A., Kavrell, S., and Peterson, A. (1984). Puberty and its psycho-logical and social significance. In R. Lerner and N. Galambos (Eds.),. *Experiencing adolescents: A sourcebook for parents, teachers and teens.* New York: Garland.

Toner, B. B., Garfinkel, P. E., and Garner, D. M. (1966). Long-term follow-up of anorexia nervosa. *Psychosomatic Medicine, 48,* 520–529.

Torney-Purta, J. (1984). Political socialization and policy: The United States in a cross-national context. In H. Stevenson and A. Siegel (Eds.), *Child development research and social policy.* Chicago: University of Chicago Press.

Travers, K., Crosswhite, F., Dossey, J., Swafford, J., McKnight, C., and Cooney, T. (1985). *Second international mathematics study summary report for the United States.* Champaign, Ill.: Stipes.

Tronick, E. Z. (1989). Emotions and emotional communication in infants. *American Psychologist, 44,* 112–119.

Tryon, R. C. (1940). Individual differences. In F. A. Moss (Ed.), *Comparative psychology.* Englewood Cliffs, N.J.: Prentice-Hall.

Turiel, E. (1978). Distinct conceptual and developmental domains: Social-convention and morality. In C. Keasey (Ed.), *Nebraska symposium on motivation* (vol. 25). Lincoln: University of Nebraska Press.

Turnbull, A., and Turnbull, H. (1986). *Families, professionals, and exceptionality: A special partnership.* Columbus, Ohio: Merrill.

Ungerer, J. A. Zelazo, P. R., Kearsley, R. B., and O'Leary, K. (1981). Developmental changes in the representation of objects in symbolic play from 19–34 months of age. *Child Development, 52,* 186–195.

U.S. Bureau of the Census. (1987a). *Current population reports* (Series P–20). Washington, D.C.: U.S. Government Printing Office.

U.S. Bureau of the Census, (1987b). *Statistical Abstract of the United States: 1987.* Washington, D.C.: U.S. Government Printing Office.

U.S. Bureau of the Census. (1987c). *Who's minding the kids? Current population reports* (Series P–70). Washington, D.C.: U.S. Government Printing Office.

U.S. Commission on Civil Rights (1977). *Window dressing on the set: Women and minorities in television.* Washington, D.C.: Government Printing Office.

U.S. Conference of Mayors. (1984). *The urban poor and the economic recovery.* Washington, D.C.: Author.

U.S. Department of Agriculture, Food and Nutrition Service. (1987). *Annual historical review of foods and nutrition services programs.* Washington, D.C.: Author.

U.S. Department of Commerce. (1988). *Statistical abstract of the United States.* Washington, D.C.: U.S. Government Printing Office.

U.S. Department of Health, Education and Welfare (1980). (Publication No. PHS 80–1232). Hyattsville, Md.

U.S. Department of Labor, Bureau of Labor Statistics. (1981). *Marital and family characteristics of labor force.* Washington, D.C.: Author.

U.S. Department of Labor, Bureau of Labor

Statistics. (1986, February). *Monthly labor review*. Washington, D.C.: U.S. Government Printing Office.

U.S. Department of Labor, Bureau of Labor Statistics. (1987a, August). (Press release No. 87–345). Washington, D.C.: Author.

U.S. Department of Labor, Bureau of Labor Statistics. (1987b, August 12). *News*. Washington, D.C.: U.S. Government Printing Office.

Uzgiris, I., and Hunt, J. (1975). *Assessment in infancy*. Chicago: University of Illinois Press.

Vandell, D. (1980). Sociability with peers and mothers in the first year. *Developmental Psychology, 16,* 355–361.

Vandell, D., and Powers, C. (1983). Day care quality and children's free play activities. *American Journal of Orthopsychiatry, 53,* 493–500.

Vandenberg, B. (1978). Play and development from an ethological perspective. *American Psychologist, 33,* 724–738.

VanOefflen, M., and Vos, P. (1984). The young child's processing of dot patterns. *International Journal of Behavioral Development, 7,* 53–66.

Van Wieringen, J. (1979). Secular growth changes. In F. Falkner and J. Tanner (Eds.), *Human growth* (vol. 2). New York: Plenum Press.

Vaughn, B. E., Bradley, C. F., Joffe, L. S., Seifer, R., and Barglow, P. (1987). Maternal characteristics measured prenatally are predictive of ratings of temperamental "difficulty" on the Carey Infant Temperament Questionnaire. *Developmental Psychology, 23,* 152–161.

Vaughn, B., Gove, F., and Egeland, B. (1980). The relationship between out-of-home care and the quality of infant-mother attachment in an economically disadvantaged population. *Child Development, 51,* 1203–1204.

Vaughn, D., Asbury, T., and Cook, R. (1986). *General opthalmology* (11th ed.). Los Altos, Calif.: Lange Medical Publications.

Vermeersch, J. (1981). The physiological basis of nutritional needs. In B. Worthington-Roberts, J. Vermeersch, and S. R. Williams (Eds.), *Nutrition in pregnancy and lactation*. St. Louis: Mosby.

Volterra, V., and Teaschner, R. (1978). The acquisition and development of language by bilingual children. *Journal of Child Language, 5,* 311–326.

VonHofsten, C., and Fazel-Zandy, S. (1984). Development of visually guided hand orientation in reaching. *Journal of Experimental Child Psychology, 38,* 208–219.

Vygotsky, L. (1962). *Thought and language*. Cambridge, Mass.: M.I.T. Press.

Vygotsky, L. (1967). Play and its role in the mental development of the child. *Soviet Psychology 12,* 62–76.

Vygotsky, L. (1978). *Mind in society: The development of higher psychological processes*. Cambridge, Mass.: Harvard University Press.

Waddington, C. H. (1966). *Principles of development and differentiation*. New York: Macmillan.

Wadsworth, M. (1986). Serious illness in childhood and its association with later-life achievement. In R. Wilkinson (Ed.), *Class and health: Research and longitudinal data*. London: Tavistock.

Wagner, M. (1988). Having a baby in Europe: Lessons for North America. In U.S. Department of Health and Human Services, *Proceedings of the international collaborative effort on perinatal and infant mortality* (vol. 1). Hyattsville, Md.: U.S. Department of Health and Human Services.

Walberg, H. (1987). Learning and life-course accomplishments. In C. Schooler and K. W. Schaie (Eds.), *Cognitive functioning and social structure over the life course*. Norwood, N.J.: Ablex.

Walker, C., and Shaw, W. (1988). Assessment of eating and elimination disorders. In P. Karoly (Ed.). *Handbook of child health assessment: Biosocial perspectives*. New York: Wiley.

Walker, L. (1984). Sex differences in the development of moral reasoning: A critical review. *Child Development, 53,* 1330–1336.

Walker, L. J., de Vries, B., and Trevethan, S. D. (1987). Moral stages and moral orientations in real-life and hypothetical dilemmas. *Child Development, 53,* 842–858.

Wallach, M. (1985). Creativity testing and giftedness. In F. Horowitz and M. O'Brien (Eds.), *The gifted and talented: Developmental perspectives*. Washington, D.C.: American Psychological Association.

Wallerstein, J. (1983). Children of divorce: The psychological tasks of the child. *American Journal of Orthopsychiatry, 53,* 230–243.

Wallerstein, J. (1984). Children of divorce: Preliminary report of a ten-year follow-up of young children. *American Journal of Orthopsychiatry, 54,* 444–458.

Wallerstein, J. (1986). Women after divorce: Preliminary report from a ten-year follow-up. *American Journal of Orthopsychiatry, 56,* 65–77.

Wallerstein, J. (1987). Children of divorce: A ten-year follow-up study of early latency-age children. *American Journal of Orthopsychiatry, 57,* 199–211.

Wallerstein, J. (1989). Follow-up. Letter to the editor. *Readings: A Journal of Reviews and Commentary in Mental Health, 4,* 21–22.

Wallerstein, J., and Blakeslee, S. (1989). *Second chances: Men, women and children a decade after divorce*. New York: Ticknor & Fields.

Wallerstein, J. S., and Corbin, S. B. (1989). Daughters of divorce: Report from a ten-year follow-up. *American Journal of Orthopsychiatry,* 593–604.

Wallerstein, J. S., Corbin, S. B., and Lewis, J. M. (1988). Children of divorce: A ten-year study. In E. M. Hetherington and J. Arasteh (Eds.), *Impact of divorce, single-parenting and stepparenting on children*. Hillsdale, N.J.: Erlbaum.

Wallerstein, J. S., and Kelly, J. (1980). *Surviving the breakup: How children actually cope with divorce*. New York: Basic Books.

Walters, G., and Grusec, J. (1977). *Punishment*. San Francisco: Freeman.

Walters, J., and Gardner, H. (1986). The theory of multiple intelligences: Issues and answers. In R. Sternberg (Ed.), *Practical intelligence*. Cambridge: Cambridge University Press.

Wang, J. (1983). Psychosomatic illness in the Chinese cultural context. In L. Romanucci-Ross, D. Moerman, and L. Tancredi (Eds.), *Anthropology of medicine: From culture to method*. New York: Praeger.

Wapner, J., and Conner, K. (1986). The role of defensiveness in cognitive impulsivity. *Child Development, 57,* 1370–1374.

Wartella, E., and Hunter, L. (1983). Children and the formats of television advertising. In M. Meyer (Ed.), *Children and the formal features of television*. Munich: K. G. Saur.

Wass, H., and Corr, C. (1984). *Helping children cope with death. Guidelines and resources*. Washington, D.C.: Hemisphere.

Waterman, A. (1982). Identity development from adolescence to adulthood: An extension of theory and a review of research. *Developmental Psychology, 18,* 341–358.

Waters, E. (1978). The stability of individual differences in infant-mother attachment. *Child Development, 49,* 483–494.

Waters, E., Vaughn, B., and Egeland, B. (1980). Individual differences in infant-mother attachment relationships at age one: Antecedents in neonatal behavior in an urban, economically disadvantaged sample. *Child Development, 51,* 208–216.

Watson-Gego, K., and Gego, D. (1986). Calling-out and repeating routines in Kwara'ae children's language socialization. In B. Schieffelin and E. Ochs (Eds.), *Language socialization across cultures* (Part 1). New York: Cambridge University Press.

Weatherall, D. J. (1985). *The new genetics and clinical practice*. New York: Oxford University Press.

Weikart, D. (1986). What do we know so far? *High/Scope ReSource*, Winter. Ypsilanti, Mich.: High/Scope Educational Research Foundation.

Weinberger, N., Gold, P., and Sternberg, D. (1984). Epenephrine enables Pavlovian fear conditioning under anesthesia. *Science, 223,* 605–607.

Weinraub, M., Jaeger, E. and Hoffman, L. W. (1988). Predicting infant outcomes in families of employed and non-employed mothers. *Early Childhood Research Quarterly, 3,* 361–387.

Weinstein, C. Goetz, E. and Alexander, P. (1988). *Learning and study strategies*. Orlando, Fla.: Academic Press.

Weisner, T. S. and Gallimore, R. (1977). My brother's keeper: Child and sibling caretaking. *Current Anthropology, 18,* 169–190.

Weiss, R. (1989). Follow-up. Letter to the editor. *Readings: A Journal of Commentary in Mental Health, 4,* 19–20.

Weiss, R. D. and Mirin, S. M. (1987). *Cocaine*. Washington, D.C.: American Psychiatric Press.

Weisz, J. (1980). Autonomy, control, and other reasons why "Mom is the greatest": A content analysis of children's Mother's Day letters. *Child Development, 51,* 801–807.

Weitzman, L. (1981). The economics of divorce: Social and economic consequences of property, alimony and child support awards. *UCLA Law Review, 28,* 1251.

Welsh, M. (1987). Verbal mediation underlying inductive reasoning: Cognitive tempo differences. *Cognitive Development, 2,* 37–57.

Welch, M., Huston-Stein, A., Wricht, J., and Plehal, R. (1979). Subtle sex-role cues in children's commercials *Journal of Communication, 29,* 202–209.

Werler, M. M., Prober, B. R., and Holmes, L. B. (1985). Smoking and pregnancy. *Teratology, 32,* 473–481.

Wertsch, J. (1985). *Vygotsky and the social formation of mind.* Cambridge, Mass.: Harvard University Press.

Wertsch, J. (1989). A sociocultural approach to mind. In W. Damon (Ed.). *Child development today and tomorrow.* San Francisco: Jossey-Bass.

White, B. (1959). Motivation reconsidered: The concept of competence. *Psychological Review, 66,* 297–333.

White, B. (1975a). Critical influences in the origins of competence. *Merrill-Palmer Quarterly, 21,* 243–266.

White, B. (1975b). *The first three years of life.* New York: Avon.

White, B. (1985). *The first three years of life* (rev. ed.). Englewood Cliffs, N.J.: Prentice-Hall.

White, B., Kaban, B., and Attanucci, J. (1979). *The origins of human competence.* Lexington, Mass.: Lexington Books.

White, D. (1986). Treatment of mild, moderate, and severe obesity in children. *Canadian Psychology, 23,* 262–274.

White, E., Elsom, B., and Prawat, R. (1978). Children's conceptions of death. *Child Development, 49,* 307–310.

Whitehurst, G. (1982). Language development. In B. Wolman (Ed.), *Handbook of developmental psychology.* New York: Wiley.

Whiting, B. (1978). The dependency hand-up and experiments in alternative life-styles. In Scutler and M. Yinger (Eds.), *Major social issues. A multidisciplinary view.* New York: Free Press.

Whiting, B.,and Edwards, C. (1988). *Children of different worlds: The formation of social behavior.* Cambridge, Mass.: Harvard University Press.

Whiting, B., and Whiting, J. (1975). *Children of six cultures: A Psychocultural analysis.* Cambridge, Mass.: Harvard University Press.

Whiting, J. W.,and Child, I. L. (1953). *Child training and personality.* New Haven, Conn.: Yale University Press.

Whiting, J. W. M. (1981). Environmental constraints on infant care practices. In R. Munroe, R. H. Monroe and B. B. Whiting (Eds.),. *Handbook of cross-cultural development.* New York: Garland Press.

Whitley, B. E., Jr. (1983). Sex-role orientation and self-esteem: A critical meta-analytic review. *Journal of Personality and Social Psychology, 44,* 765–778.

Wilkinson, D. (1980). *Information processing in reading.* New York: Wiley.

Wilkinson, S. (1988). *The child's world of illness.* Cambridge: Cambridge University Press.

Williams, H. (1983). *Perceptual and motor development.* Englewood Cliffs, N.J.: Prentice-Hall.

Williams, H., Temple, I., and Bateman, J. (1979). A test battery to assess intrasensory and intersensory development of young children. *Perceptual and Motor Skills, 48,* 643–659.

Williams, J. R., and Gold, M. (1972). From delinquent behavior to official delinquency. *Social Problems, 20,* 209–229.

Wilson, M. N., and Tolson, T. F. J. (1986). A social interaction analysis of two- and three-generational black families. *Journal of Black Psychology, 12,* 43–60.

Wilson, R. (1972). Twins: Early mental development. *Science, 175,* 915–917.

Winick, M. (Ed.). (1975). *Childhood obesity.* New York: Wiley.

Winner, E. (1982). *Invented worlds. The psychology of the arts.* Cambridge, Mass.: Harvard University Press.

Witkin, H., and Goodenough, D. (1977). Field dependence and interpersonal behavior. *Psychological Bulletin, 84,* 661–689.

Wolff, P. (1966). The causes, controls, and organization of behavior in the neonate, *Psychological Issues, 5,* 1–105.

Wood, B. (1981). *Children and communication: Verbal and nonverbal language development* (2nd ed.). Englewood Cliffs, N.J.: Prentice-Hall.

World Health Organization. (1987). *World health statistics annual: 1987.* Geneva: Author.

Wright, L., Flagler, S., and Friedman, A. (1988). Assessment for accident prevention. In P. Karoly (Ed.), *Handbook of child health assessment: Biosocial perspectives.* New York: Wiley.

Wylie, L. (1965). Youth in France and the United States. In E. H. Erikson (Ed.), *The challenge of youth.* Garden City, N.Y.: Anchor Books.

Wylie, R. (1974/1979). *The self-concept* (vols. 1 and 2). Lincoln: University of Nebraska Press.

Yarrow, L. (1979). Emotional development. *American Psychologist, 34,* 951–957.

Yarrow, M., and Waxler, C. (1978). The emergence and functions of prosocial behavior in young children. In M. Smart and R. Smart (Eds.), *Infants, development and relationships.* New York: Macmillan.

Yeterian, E. and Pandya, N. (1988). Architectonic features of the primate brain: Implications for information processing and behavior. In H. Markowitsch (Ed.), *Information processing by the brain.* Toronto: Hans Huber.

Yogman, M., Dixon, S., Tronick, E., Als, H. and Brazelton, T. B. (1977). *The goals and structure of face-to-face interaction between infants and fathers.* Paper presented at the biennial meeting of the Society for Research in Child Development, New Orleans.

Yogman, M., Dixon, S., Tronick, E., Als, H., and Yonas, A. (1979). Studies of spatial perception in infants. In A. D. Pick (Ed.), *Perception and its development.* Hillsdale, N.J.: Erlbaum.

Yonas, A., and Petersen, L. (1979). *Responsiveness of newborns to optical information for collision.* Paper presented at the biennial meeting of the Society for Research in Child Development, San Francisco.

Youniss, J. (1980). *Parents and peers in social development: A Sullivan-Piaget perspective.* Chicago: University of Chicago Press.

Youniss, J., and Volpe, J. (1978). A relationship analysis of children's friendships. In W. Damon (Ed.), *Social cognition.* New Directions for Child Development, No. 1. San Francisco: Jossey-Bass.

Zahn-Waxler, C., and Radke-Yarrow, M. (1982). The development of altruism. In N. Eisenberg-Berg (Ed.), *The development of prosocial behavior.* New York: Academic Press.

Zahn-Waxler, C., Radke-Yarrow, M., and King, R. A. (1979). Child rearing and children's prosocial initiations toward victims of distress. *Child Development, 50,* 319–330.

Zelazo, P., Zelazo, N., and Kalb, S. (1972). "Walking" in the newborn. *Science, 176,* 314–315.

Zelson, C. (1973). The infant of the addicted mother. *New England Journal of Medicine, 288,* 1393–1395.

Zigler, E. (1987). Formal schooling for four-year-olds? No. *American Psychologist, 42,* 254–260.

Zigler, E., and Finn-Stevenson, S. (1987). *Children's development and social issues.* New York: Heath.

Zill, N. (1983). *Healthy, happy, and insecure.* New York: Doubleday.

Zimbardo, P. (1977). *Shyness.* Reading, Mass.: Addison-Wesley.

ACKNOWLEDGMENTS

FRONT MATTER PHOTO CREDITS

Frontispiece: © 1987 Bruce Plotkin/The Image Works

Contents: **Part 1**: © 1988 Jeffry W. Myers/Stock Boston; **Part 2**: © Lennart Nilsson, *Behold Man*, Little, Brown & Co.; **Part 3**: © Alan Carey/The Image Works; **Part 4**: © Erika Stone; **Part 5**: © Betts Anderson/Unicorn Stock Photos; **Part 6**: © Mary Messenger

PART AND CHAPTER OPENER PHOTO CREDITS

Part 1: © Jerry Howard/Stock Boston; **Chapter 1**: © 1988 Jeffry W. Myers/Stock Boston; **Chapter 2**: © Ellis Herwig/Stock Boston; **Part 2**: © 1987 James P. Dwyer/Stock Boston; **Chapter 3**: © Aaron Haupt/David R. Frazier Photolibrary; **Chapter 4**: Lennart Nilsson, *Behold Man*, Little, Brown & Co.; **Part 3**: © Carol Palmer; **Chapter 5**: © Larry Kolvoord/TexaStock; **Chapter 6**: © Elizabeth Crews; **Chapter 7**: © Elizabeth Crews; **Part 4**: © Julie Houck/Stock Boston; **Chapter 8**: © Stephen Frisch/Stock Boston; **Chapter 9**: © Kindra Clineff; **Chapter 10**: © David R. Frazier Photolibrary; **Part 5**: © Bob Daemmrich/Stock Boston; **Chapter 11**: © Carol Palmer; **Chapter 12**: © David R. Frazier Photolibrary; **Chapter 13**: © Willie Hill, Jr./The Image Works; **Part 6**: © D. H. Hessell/Stock Boston; **Chapter 14**: © Jean-Claude Lejeune; **Chapter 15**: © Susan Lapides; **Chapter 16**: © David R. Frazier Photolibrary

CASE-STUDY PHOTO ESSAY CREDITS

David's Case: All photographs (except page 145, *top left*) by Alan Carey/The Image Works; page 145, *top left*, Mark Antman/The Image Works; **Jennifer's Case**: All photographs by Erika Stone; **Laura's Case**: All photographs by Betts Anderson/Unicorn Stock Photos; **Brian's Case**: All photographs by Mary Messenger

CHAPTER PHOTO CREDITS

Chapter 1: **P. 6**: *top*, © Elizabeth Crews; *bottom*, © Jean-Claude Lejeune; **p. 9**: © Elizabeth Crews; **p. 11**: *left*, *Family Portrait* (1830–1840), Jacob Maentel, courtesy, Henry Francis du Pont Winterthur Museum; *right*, *Children Playing on Beach* (1884), Mary Cassatt, National Gallery of Art, Washington, Ailsa Mellon Bruce Collection; **p. 13**: © David R. Austen/Stock Boston; **p. 17**: *top*, Julie O'Neil; *bottom*, Rafael Macia/Photo Researchers; **p. 20**: *left*, Gabor Demjen/Stock Boston; *right*, © Carol Lee/The Picture Cube; **p. 22**: © 1988 Susan Lapides; **p. 26**: both photos © Judy Gelles/Stock Boston.

Chapter 2: **P. 37**: © Kevin Syms/David R. Frazier Photolibrary; **p. 39**: National Library of Medicine; **p. 41**: Dennis Mansell; **p. 45**: Historical Pictures Service, Chicago; **p. 48**: © 1989 Aldo Mastrocola/Lightwave; **p. 52**: Steven M. Stone/The Picture Cube; **p. 53**: Barbara Rios/Photo Researchers; **p. 56**: Historical Pictures Service, Chicago; **p. 61**: both photos by Jerry Howard/Positive Images; **p. 65**: © 1988 Susan Lapides; **p. 68**: © Carol Palmer.

Chapter 3: **P. 80**: © 1988 Erika Stone; **p. 82**: © Richard Hutchings/Photo Researchers; **p. 86**: Meri Houtchens-Kitchens/The Picture Cube; **p. 92**: *left*, © 1989 Kindra Clineff/The Picture Cube; *right*, © Mark M. Walker/The Picture Cube; **p. 95**: © Sarah Putnam/The Picture Cube; **p. 97**: Michael Weisbrot; **p. 99**: © 1990 Jerry Howard/Positive Images; **p. 101**: Ira Kirschenbaum/Stock Boston.

Chapter 4: **P. 110**: © Petit Format/Nestle/Science Source/Photo Researchers; **p. 113**: Lennart Nilsson, *A Child Is Born*, Dell Publishing Company; **p. 114**: *top*, © Petit Format/Nestle/Science Source/Photo Researchers; *bottom*, Lennart Nilsson, *A Child Is Born*, Dell Publishing Company; **p. 121**: courtesy of James W. Hanson, M.D.; **p. 123**: © Richard Hutchings/Photo Researchers; **p. 126**: Nancy Durrell McKenna/Photo Researchers; **p. 127**: © Elizabeth Crews/Stock Boston; **p. 128**: © Elizabeth Crews; **p. 132**: both photos © SIU/Peter Arnold, Inc.; **p. 139**: © SIU/Peter Arnold, Inc.

Chapter 5: **P. 151**: © John Sherlock/Positive Images; **p. 156**: © Spencer Grant/The Picture Cube; **p. 158**: © Nancy Durrell McKenna/Photo Researchers; **p. 164**: © 1988 Kathy Sloane/Photo Researchers; **p. 166**: © Elizabeth Crews; **p. 167**: © Elizabeth Crews/Stock Boston; **p. 168**: © Elizabeth Crews; **p. 170**: © 1986 Erika Stone; **p. 174**: Lionel Delevingne/Stock Boston; **p. 177**: Janice Fullman/The Picture Cube; **p. 178**: © Lorraine Rorke/The Image Works.

Chapter 6: **P. 190**: Jason Laure/Woodfin Camp & Associates; **p. 193**: © Elizabeth Crews; **p. 195**: William Vandivert/courtesy Scientific American; **p. 198**: © Elizabeth Crews; **p. 201**: Suzanne Szasz/Photo Researchers; **p. 213**: © 1985 Peter Menzel/Stock Boston; **p. 218**: © Marianne Gontarz/The Picture Cube; **p. 220**: © 1988 Ann Purcell/Photo Researchers; **p. 222**: © 1988 Charles Gupton/Stock Boston.

Chapter 7: **P. 230**: © Larry Kolvoord/TexaStock; **p. 233**: © 1987 Erika Stone; **p. 234**: © Carol Palmer; **p. 238**: *left*, © 1988 Bill Bachman/Photo Researchers; *right*, George N. Peet/The Picture Cube; **p. 243**: © Elizabeth Crews; **p. 248**: © 1990 Erika Stone; **p. 249**: © Carol Palmer; **p. 251**: © 1986 Bill Bachman/Photo Researchers; **p. 253**: © Erika Stone; **p. 259**: Frank Siteman/The Picture Cube.

Chapter 8: **P. 276**: Dennis Mansell; **p. 283**: © Joel Dexter/Lightwave; **p. 285**: © Bob Daemmrich/Stock Boston; **p. 287**: © Carol Palmer/The Picture Cube; **p. 290**: © Robert Kalman/The Image Works; **p. 292**: © Larry Kolvoord/TexaStock; **p. 293**: © Jerry Howard/Positive Images; **p. 295**: © 1986 Erika Stone; **p. 298**: © Nancy Sheehan/The Picture Cube; **p. 301**: Susan Woog Wagner/Photo Researchers; **p. 303**: © David R. Frazier Photolibrary.

Chapter 9: **P. 310**: © Carol Palmer; **p. 315**: © Jerry Howard/Positive Images; **p. 318**: © 1990 Erika Stone; **p. 320**: © Martin Miller/Positive Images; **p. 322**: © 1987 Susan Lapides; **p. 330**: *top*, © Vandivier/TexaStock; *bottom*, © Jeffrey Mark Dunn/Stock Boston; **p. 332**: © 1985 Erika Stone; **p. 333**: © David M. Grossman/Photo Researchers; **p. 336** © 1989 Susan Lapides.

Chapter 10: **P. 344**: © Carol Palmer/The Picture Cube; **p. 347**: © Elizabeth Crews; **p. 348**: © Carol Palmer; **p. 349**: © Jean-Claude Lejeune; **p. 350**: © Barbara Rios/Photo Researchers; **p. 352**: © Elizabeth Crews; **p. 356**: Jim Cronk/Photographic Illustrations; **p. 357**: © 1989 Susan Lapides; **p. 360**: © Peter Southwick/Stock Boston; **p. 364**: Fredrik D. Bodin/Stock Boston; **p. 368**: © Carol Palmer/The Picture Cube; **p. 375**: © Elizabeth Crews.

Chapter 11: **P. 388**: Julie O'Neil/The Picture Cube; **p. 391**: Leonard Speier; **p. 392**: © Jean-Claude Lejeune; **p. 394**: © Bob Daemmrich/Stock Boston; **p. 396**: *top,* © Gale Zucker/Stock Boston; *bottom,* © Smiley/TexaStock; **p. 397**: © Kolvoord/TexaStock; **p. 398**: © Bob Daemmrich/The Image Works; **p. 404**: Lawrence Migdale/Stock Boston; **p. 408**: © Paul Conklin.

Chapter 12: **P. 414**: Sam Falk/NYT Pictures; **p. 418**: © Andrew Brilliant; **p. 419**: © Andrew Brilliant; **p. 423**: © Bob Daemmrich/Stock Boston; **p. 425**: © Paul Conklin; **p. 429**: © Stephen Frisch/Stock Boston; **p. 431**: © Elizabeth Crews; **p. 435**: © 1987 Alan Carey/The Image Works; **p. 438**: © Paul Conklin; **p. 443**: © Bob Daemmrich/Stock Boston; **p. 447**: © Gale Zucker/Stock Boston; **p. 451**: © Richard S. Orton.

Chapter 13: **P. 460**: © Jean-Claude Lejeune/Stock Boston; **p. 462**: © Elizabeth Crews/Stock Boston; **p. 468**: *top,* © Elizabeth Crews; *bottom,* © Bob Daemmrich/The Image Works; **p. 473**: © Elizabeth Crews; **p. 478**: *left,* © Bob Daemmrich/Stock Boston; *right,* © Bob Daemmrich/Stock Boston; **p. 481**: © Erika Stone; **p. 485**: © Andrew Brilliant; **p. 490**: © Richard S. Orton; **p. 493**: © 1985 Erika Stone.

Chapter 14: **P. 508**: © Richard Hutchings/Photo Researchers, Inc.; **p. 514**: *left,* David Witbeck/The Picture Cube; *right,* © 1987 Peter Menzel/Stock Boston; **p. 519**: © Susan Lapides; **p. 526**: © Stephen Frisch/Stock Boston; **p. 528**: © 1988 Susan Lapides; **p. 531**: Chas Chancellare/Picture Group; **p. 534**: © Mark M. Walker/The Picture Cube; **p. 535**: © Carol Palmer; **p. 536**: Susan Rosenberg/Photo Researchers.

Chapter 15: **P. 543**: © 1989 Erika Stone; **p. 547**: © Kindra Clineff; **p. 549**: © Paul Conklin; **p. 556**: © Kolvoord/TexaStock; **p. 560**: *left,* © Bob Daemmrich/Stock Boston; *right,* © Smiley/TexaStock; **p. 563**: David Walberg.

Chapter 16: **P. 571**: *top,* James Holland; *bottom,* © Paul Conklin; **p. 579**: © 1989 David Lissy/The Picture Cube; **p. 580**: © Elizabeth Crews; **p. 585**: © James Carroll; **p. 588**: © Paul Conklin; **p. 590**: © Jean-Claude Lejeune; **p. 594**: © 1989 Susan Lapides; **p. 596**: © Susan Lapides; **p. 599**: John Harding; **p. 603**: © 1988 David H. Wells/The Image Works; **p. 606**: © 1988 Susan Lapides.

TEXT, TABLE, AND LINE ART CREDITS

Pp. 46–47: Excerpts from *Life History and the Historical Moment* by Erik H. Erikson, by permission of W.W. Norton & Company, Inc. Copyright © 1975 by Rikan Enterprises, Ltd.
P. 169: Table 5.4 adapted from W. Frankenburg and J. Dodds, "The Denver Developmental Screening Test," *Journal of Pediatrics, 71* (1967), 181, by permission of the C. V. Mosby Company.
P. 430: Figure 12.3 reproduced from David Elkind, "Ambiguous Pictures for the Study of Perceptual Development and Learning," *Child Development, 35* (1964), 1391–1396, by permission of The Society for Research in Child Development. © The Society for Research in Child Development, Inc.
P. 479: Figure 13.2 based on data from the U.S. Bureau of the Census, 1978, and the U.S. Department of Labor, Bureau of Labor Statistics, Washington, D.C., USDL 88–431.
P. 479: Figure 13.3 based on data from the U.S. Department of Commerce, U.S. Bureau of the Census, *Statistical Abstract of the United States,* (Washington, D.C.: U.S. Government Printing Office, 1990) and the U.S. National Center for Health Statistics, *Vital Statistics of the United States* (Washington, D.C.: U.S. Government Printing Office, 1990).
P. 605: Excerpts from *Changing Bodies, Changing Lives,* by Ruth Bell et al. Copyright © 1980 by Ruth Bell. Reprinted by permission of Random House, Inc.

SUBJECT INDEX

Ability, *see* Competence
Abnormalities (disorders), *see* Genetic abnormalities; Handicaps; Illnesses
Abortion
  in adolescence, 598
  spontaneous, 118
Abruptio placenta, 137
Abstract thinking, in Piaget's theory, 61–62
Abuse, *see* Child abuse; Drugs
Academic learning disabilities, 433
Accidents
  in adolescence, 528
  in middle years, 398–400, 400(tab)
Accommodation, in Piaget's theory, 58, 198, 199
  language acquisition and, 214–215
  sensorimotor intelligence and, 198, 199
Achievement, in handicapped children, 492–493
Achievement motivation, 462–463
  early athletics and, 395–396
  in middle years, 463–465
Achievement tests, 442
Acquired immune deficiency syndrome, *see* AIDS
Activity, in developmental theories, 38
Acute illnesses, 400–401
Adaptation, in Piaget's theory, 58
ADHD, *see* Attention deficit hyperactivity disorder
Adolescence, 66
  concept of, 10, 507–509
  as young adulthood, 537–538
  see also Cognitive development in adolescence; Physical development in adolescence; Psychosocial development in adolescence
Adolescent egocentrism, 511, 557–559, 592
Adoption design, heredity-environment relationship studied with, 97–102
Adulthood, in Erikson's theory, 45(tab), 48
Afterbirth, 132
Age-graded influences, on adolescent development, 525
Aggression
  hormone levels in adolescence and, 517
  in preschoolers, 365–370
  sexual, 595
AIDS (acquired immune deficiency syndrome)
  in adolescence, 525, 530–531, 533, 596, 600
  masturbation and, 592
  prenatal development and, 119
  preschool children and, 285
  schoolchildren and, 401
Albinism, 93
Alcohol

in adolescence, 531–534, 532(fig)
  prenatal development and, 121–122
Alleles, 81–82
Altruism, *see* Prosocial behavior
America
  mathematics learning in, 427
  temperament of infants in, 100, 100(tab)
American Sign Language (ASL), 332
Amniocentesis, 90–91, 91(tab)
Amniotic sac, 111, 113
Anal-explosive personality, 41
Anal-retentive personality, 41
Anal stage, of psychosexual development, 40–41, 40(tab), 240
Androgens, 517
Androgyny, 374–375
Anesthetics, during childbirth, 135, 136(tab)
Anger, divorce of parents and, 483
Anglo-Saxon infants, motor stimulation in, 175
Anhidrotic ectoderma dysplasia, 84(tab)
Animal breeding studies, heredity-environment relationship and, 96–97
Animism, in preschool years, 313–314
Anorexia nervosa, in adolescence, 520, 535–537
AnotB error, 202, 203, 207–208
Anthropomorphism, 96
Anxious-avoidant attachment (Type A) infants, 245, 246, 247, 249
Anxious-resistant attachment (Type C) infants, 245, 246
Apgar Scale, 152–153, 152(tab)
Apnea, 160
  preterm infants and, 172
Appearance, *see* Attractiveness
Approach behaviors, 242
Aptitude tests, 442
Arousal
  infant heart rate measuring, 189–190
  in infants, 159–160, 159(tab)
Artificial insemination, 116
Artificialism, in preschool years, 314
Assertiveness, aggression differing from, 365–366
Assimilation, in Piaget's theory, 57–58
  sensorimotor intelligence and, 198–199
Associative play, 351, 353
Asthma, 401
Athletics, in middle years, 394–397
Attachment formation, 242–249
  anxious-avoidant attachment, 245–246, 249
  anxious-resistant attachment, 245–246
  autonomy and, 250–252
  breast feeding and, 178
  competence and, 255, 260–261
  cultural differences in, 246

day care and, 248–249
  father and, 247
  in low birth-weight infants, 173
  mother and, 247–248
  phases of, 243–244
  reactive attachment disorder and, 278
  secure attachment pattern, 244–245, 246, 247, 249
  self-awareness and, 252–255
  self-esteem and, 255
  "strange situation" assessing, 244–245, 248
  see also Bonding
Attention deficit hyperactivity disorder (ADHD), 433
  in middle years, 405–407
Attractiveness
  in adolescence, 518
  aggressiveness and, 367
Auditory acuity
  in infancy, 161–162
  in preschool years, 284, 323
Auditory cortex, 280, 281(fig)
Auditory perception
  in infancy, 196–197
  in preschool years, 323
Australia, temperaments of infants in, 100, 100(tab)
Authoritarian parents, 354, 355, 356, 364
Authoritative parents, 354, 355–356, 357, 364
Autocratic parents, 581
Autonomous morality, 445
Autonomy
  emergence of, 250–252
  in Erikson's theory, 45(tab), 46, 240–241
  psychological development in infancy and, 228–229
Axillary hair, 514

Babbling, in infancy, 216–217, 242, 329
Babinski reflex, 114, 165(tab)
Baby biographies, 12
Baby M, 117
Balanced bilinguals, 437, 438
Balanced translocation type, of Down syndrome, 85
Behavioral learning theory, 38, 49–55, 67(tab), 210–213
  classical conditioning (Pavlov), 38, 50, 51(fig), 67(tab), 210–211
  cognitive behavioral approaches, 54
  imitation, 212–213
  operant conditioning (Skinner), 38, 50–54, 55, 67(tab), 211–212
  strengths and weaknesses of, 54
  time-out technique and, 55
Behavior genetics, 94. *See also* Heredity-environment relationship

Reader Response Form

We would like to find out what your reactions are to *Child and Adolescent Development,* Second Edition. Your evaluation of the book will help us respond to the interests and needs of the readers of future editions. Please complete the questionnaire below and mail it to College Marketing, Houghton Mifflin Company, One Beacon Street, Boston, MA 02108.

1. We would like to know how you rate our textbook in each of the following areas:

	Excellent	Good	Adequate	Poor
a. Selection of topics	_____	_____	_____	_____
b. Writing style/readability	_____	_____	_____	_____
c. Explanation of concepts	_____	_____	_____	_____
d. Bridges	_____	_____	_____	_____
e. Multicultural Views and Perspectives	_____	_____	_____	_____
f. Interviews	_____	_____	_____	_____
g. Case-study photo essays	_____	_____	_____	_____
h. Study aids (e.g., marginal glosses, focusing questions, end-of-chapter summaries and key terms lists, glossary)	_____	_____	_____	_____
i. Attractiveness of design	_____	_____	_____	_____
j. Illustrations	_____	_____	_____	_____

2. Please cite specific examples that illustrate any of the above ratings.

_____

_____

_____

3. Describe the strongest feature(s) of the book.

_____

_____

_____

4. Describe the weakest feature(s) of the book.

_____

_____

_____

5. What other topics should be included in this text?

_____

_____

_____

6. What recommendations can you make for improving this book?

_____

_____

_____

7. We would appreciate any other comments or reactions you are willing to share with us:

_____

_____

_____